CARBURETTOR Manual

Charles White and Christopher Rogers

Carburettors covered:

Ford types: Motorcraft 1V and Variable Venturi (VV)

Pierburg types: 1B1, 1B3, 2B5, 2B6, 2B7, 2BE, 2E2 and 2E3

Pierburg (Solex) types: PDSI and PIC-7

Solex types: BIS, EEIT, PBISA, SEIA, Z1, Z10 and Z11

Weber types: DARA, DFT, DFTH, DFTM, DGAV, DIR, DMTE, DMTL, DRT, DRTC, IBSH, ICEV, ICH, ICT, TL, TLA, TLDE, TLDR, TLDM, TLF, TLM and TLP

A book in the **Haynes Service and Repair Manual Series**

© Haynes Publishing 2004

All rights reserved. No part of this book may be reproduced or transmitted in any form or by any means, electronic or mechanical, including photocopying, recording or by any information storage or retrieval system, without permission in writing from the copyright holder.

ISBN **1 84425 177 2**

British Library Cataloguing in Publication Data
A catalogue record for this book is available from the British Library.

Printed in the USA

Haynes Publishing
Sparkford, Yeovil, Somerset BA22 7JJ, England

Haynes North America, Inc
861 Lawrence drive, Newbury Park, California 91320, USA

Editions Haynes
4, Rue de l'Abreuvoir, 92415 COURBEVOIE CEDEX, France

Haynes Publishing Nordiska AB
Box 1504, 751 45 Uppsala, Svergie

(4177-400)

Contents

INTRODUCTORY PAGES
About this Manual	Page	0•4
Acknowledgements	Page	0•4

PART A: INTRODUCTION TO THE CARBURETTOR
Basic theory	Page	A•1
Carburettor functions	Page	A•2
Vacuum	Page	A•3
Simple carburettor	Page	A•3
Fixed venturi carburettor	Page	A•3
Twin venturi carburettor	Page	A•8
Constant depression or variable venturi carburettors	Page	A•10
Twin carburettors	Page	A•10
Modern carburettor design	Page	A•10
Gas analysis	Page	A•13

PART B: WORKING ON THE CARBURETTOR
A place to work	Page	B•1
Tool selection and care	Page	B•1
Fasteners	Page	B•2
Gasket sealing surfaces	Page	B•2
Hose replacement	Page	B•2
Automotive chemicals	Page	B•2
Carburettor identification	Page	B•2
Carburettor removal and refitting	Page	B•4
Carburettor servicing	Page	B•6
Carburettor adjustments	Page	B•9

PART C: CARBURETTOR APPLICATION
Vehicle listing	Page	C•1

PART D: FAULT DIAGNOSIS
Introduction to Fault diagnosis	Page	D•1
General carburettor faults	Page	D•1

PART E: FORD CARBURETTOR
Chapter 1: Motorcraft IV carburettor	Page	E1•1
Chapter 2: Variable Venturi (VV) carburettor	Page	E2•1

PART F: PIERBURG CARBURETTOR
Chapter 1: 1B1 carburettor	Page	F1•1
Chapter 2: 1B3 carburettor	Page	F2•1
Chapter 3: 2B5, 2B6 and 2B7 carburettors	Page	F3•1
Chapter 4: 2BE carburettor	Page	F4•1
Chapter 5: 2E2 carburettor	Page	F5•1
Chapter 6: 2E3 carburettor	Page	F6•1
Chapter 7: (Pierburg-Solex)	Page	F7•1

PART G: SOLEX CARBURETTOR
Chapter 1: BIS carburettor	Page	G1•1
Chapter 2: EEIT carburettor	Page	G2•1
Chapter 3: PBISA carburettor	Page	G3•1
Chapter 4: SEIA carburettor	Page	G4•1
Chapter 5: Z1 (CISAC) carburettor	Page	G5•1
Chapter 6: Z10 carburettor	Page	G6•1
Chapter 7: Z11 carburettor	Page	G7•1

PART H: WEBER CARBURETTOR
Chapter 1: DARA carburettor	Page	H1•1
Chapter 2: DFT carburettor	Page	H2•1
Chapter 3: DFTH carburettor	Page	H3•1
Chapter 4: DFTM carburettor	Page	H4•1
Chapter 5: DGAV carburettor	Page	H5•1
Chapter 6: DIR carburettor	Page	H6•1
Chapter 7: DMTE carburettor	Page	H7•1
Chapter 8: DMTL carburettor	Page	H8•1
Chapter 9: DRT carburettor	Page	H9•1
Chapter 10: DRTC carburettor	Page	H10•1
Chapter 11: IBSH carburettor	Page	H11•1
Chapter 12: ICEV carburettor	Page	H12•1
Chapter 13: ICH carburettor	Page	H13•1
Chapter 14: ICT carburettor	Page	H14•1
Chapter 15: TL carburettor	Page	H15•1
Chapter 16: TLA carburettor	Page	H16•1
Chapter 17: TLDE carburettor	Page	H17•1
Chapter 18: TLDR carburettor	Page	H18•1
Chapter 19: TLDM carburettor	Page	H19•1
Chapter 20: TLF carburettor	Page	H20•1
Chapter 21: TLM carburettor	Page	H21•1
Chapter 22: TLP carburettor	Page	H22•1

REFERENCE
Emission regulations	Page	REF•1
Abbreviations	Page	REF•1
Conversion factors	Page	REF•2
Safety first!	Page	REF•3
Glossary of technical terms	Page	REF•4

Introduction

About this manual

The aim of this manual is to provide sufficient information to enable the professional mechanic or the home engineer to service, adjust and diagnose faults on a carburettor. Due to the very nature of carburation and its dependence on the correct operation of many other engine functions, it is not possible to cover everything as widely as perhaps one would like. Some descriptions are necessarily brief and the problem is not what to include but what must be left out!

The manual deals purely with servicing and adjustments. It does not deal with complete overhauls, although information for that task can often be gleaned from a study of the text.

Advice on fitting a carburettor to a non-standard application is not the purpose of this manual. Altering the standard calibration is also beyond the terms of reference. The technical data will enable you to make adjustments and to check the jet calibration against the manufacturer's original specifications.

The manual has drawings and descriptions to show the function of the various components so that their layout can be understood. Then the tasks are described and photographed in a clear step-by-step sequence.

Acknowledgements

We would like to thank all those people who have helped us in the production of this manual. In particular, we are indebted to all the carburettor manufacturers and specialists who provided us with many of the carburettors and much of the technical data and information used in the compilation of this manual.

Furthermore, we acknowledge and give special thanks to N. E. Motors, Pierburg Gmbh, Weber Carburatori, and various car manufacturers for their assistance in the production of this manual.

This manual is not a direct reproduction of the carburettor or vehicle manufacturers' data, and its publication should not be taken as implying any technical approval by the carburettor or vehicle manufacturers or importers.

We take great pride in the accuracy of the information given in this manual, but manufacturers make alterations and design changes during the production run of a particular carburettor or vehicle of which they do not inform us. No liability can be accepted by the publishers for loss, damage or injury caused by any errors in, or omissions from, the information given.

Illegal Copying

It is the policy of Haynes Publishing to actively protect its Copyrights and Trade Marks. Legal action will be taken against anyone who unlawfully copies the cover or contents of this Manual. This includes all forms of unauthorised copying including digital, mechanical, and electronic in any form. Authorisation from Haynes Publishing will only be provided expressly and in writing. Illegal copying will also be reported to the appropriate statutory authorities.

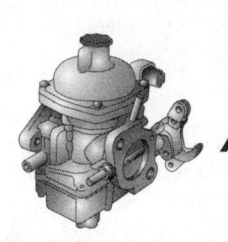

Part A
An introduction to the carburettor

Contents

Basic theory 1	Modern carburettor design 9
Carburettor functions 2	Simple carburettor 4
Constant depression or variable venturi carburettors 7	Twin carburettors 8
Fixed venturi carburettor 5	Twin venturi carburettor 6
Gas analysis 10	Vacuum 3

1 Basic theory

1 The purpose of the fuel system is to supply correct amounts of air and fuel, to mix them regardless of speed and load and to regulate the resultant air/fuel mixture according to the demand of the engine and requirements of the driver.

2 The fuel system for an internal combustion engine comprises a fuel tank, fuel filter(s), fuel pump, carburettor, air filter, throttle valve and inlet manifold *(see illustration)*. Each must work efficiently and in harmony. A weakness or failure in any one of these components will cause poor operation of the system as a whole.

3 The physical rule which affects all carburettors is the movement of air. Consider the fact that air masses move from areas of high pressure to low pressure. Imagine a petrol engine as being a powerful suction engine. When the piston descends, it creates an area of low pressure, or vacuum, in the combustion chamber and inlet manifold. Air will flow through the carburettor from atmospheric (high) pressure to the area of low pressure created by the fall of the piston. A carburettor, therefore, works on the principle of differential pressure.

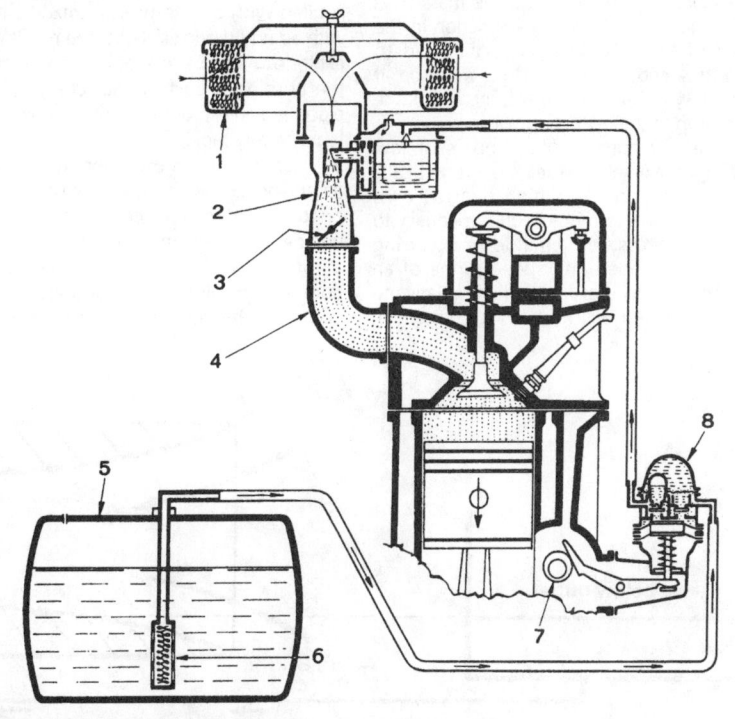

Typical engine air and fuel system

1 Air filter
2 Carburettor
3 Throttle valve
4 Inlet manifold
5 Fuel tank
6 Fuel filter
7 Camshaft
8 Mechanical fuel pump

A•1

Chapter A

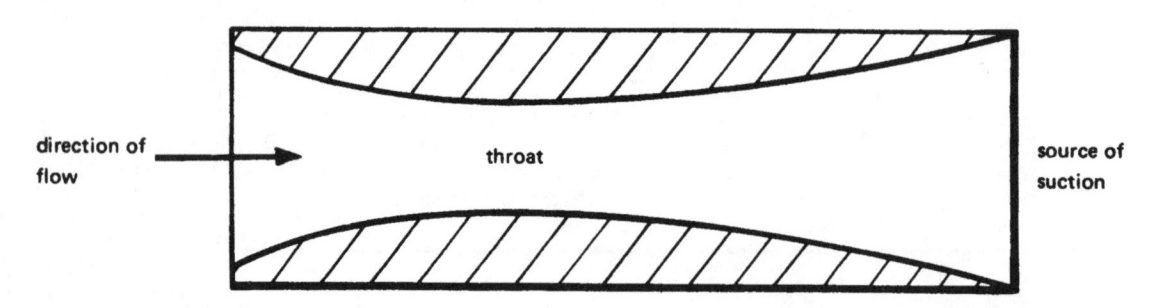

The venturi principle

4 If a restriction is placed in the carburettor throat, the airflow will speed up while flowing through the restriction and there will be a drop in pressure. This restriction is known as a *venturi (see illustration)*.
5 The term venturi (rather than choke) is best used to describe a restriction in the carburettor throat and this convention is observed throughout this manual. *Choke* is the term used to describe a cold-starting device. *Carburettor barrel* is used to describe a single tube from the air intake, through the venturi to the throttle plate. A carburettor can therefore be referred to as a single venturi or single barrel, or a twin venturi or twin barrel, etc.
6 In physics, the principle of air flowing through a venturi is known as Bernoulli's Principle, which considers the case of fluid moving through a tube *(see illustration)*. Providing the mass flow of fluid remains constant, any restriction in the diameter of the tube will cause the fluid to increase its speed and its pressure will drop. If the mass flow through the tube is increased, the pressure drop at the restriction will increase.
7 Air is readily compressible and is of low density. Conversely, fuel is practically incompressible and has a high density. As a consequence, air and fuel respond unequally to differential pressure changes occurring throughout the operating speed range of an engine. This means that fuel will lag, relative to air movement and will also resist changes in flow direction as the throttle valve is opened and closed.
8 Air is a mixture of 80% nitrogen and 20% oxygen. The compounds which make up petrol are called hydrocarbons and are a mixture of about 15% hydrogen and 85% carbon.
9 The potential energy from petrol is considerably greater than dynamite and three times greater than TNT. This energy will only be liberated when petrol is completely mixed with air in the correct proportion. Petrol, therefore, needs to be combined with oxygen (air) in order to burn.
10 If a container is filled with petrol and set alight, the surface of the fuel will merely burn and the heat energy will be used up very slowly. This is because only the surface of the petrol is exposed to air. Alternatively, if a small container is filled with a little petrol, mixed thoroughly with air and then set alight, the result will be an explosion. All of the fuel is exposed to air and the burning is so fast that combustion takes place and an explosion occurs. An explosion is in reality a very rapid burning process.
11 Containing this explosion in the cylinder of an engine causes an expansion of gases and the piston is thereby forced down to drive the engine. For the combustion process to liberate all of the fuel energy, air and petrol must be completely blended together. The more complete this process, the greater will be the power obtained from the engine. An instrument known as a carburettor is used for this purpose in automotive applications.

2 Carburettor functions

Main functions

1 The carburettor has two main functions, the first being to atomise the fuel and then blend it thoroughly with air so that vaporisation occurs in the inlet manifold and combustion chamber. The second function of the carburettor is to satisfy the varying requirements of the engine by mixing fuel and air together in correctly-metered proportions to ensure efficient combustion. The optimum (or stoichiometric) mixture strength is expressed as a ratio of approximately 14.7 parts of air to 1 part of fuel, by weight.
2 The ratio of air to petrol (or the degree of richness of air/fuel mixture) needed by the engine is variable. The engine must have a higher percentage of fuel (a richer mixture) for starting from cold, for acceleration and for high-speed running. A less rich (leaner) mixture is required for intermediate or cruising speeds

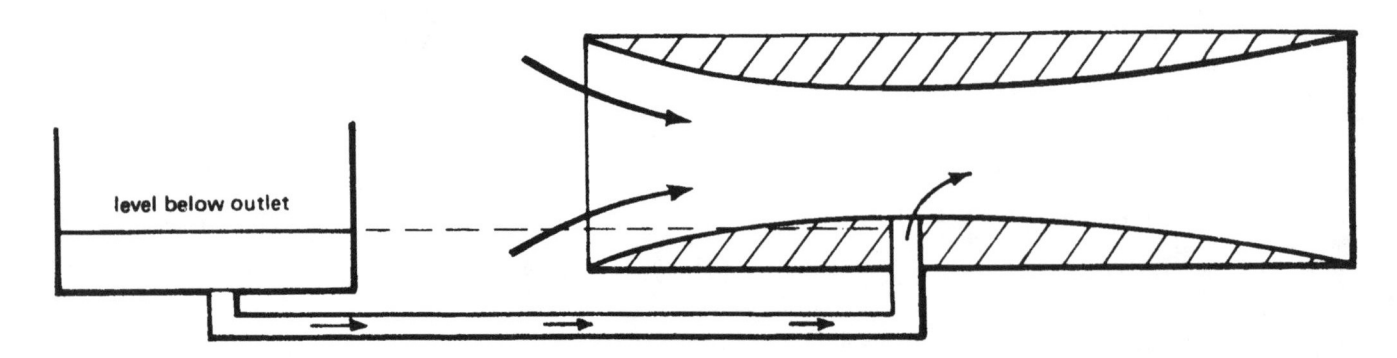

The principle of fuel flow through a venturi
Large arrows indicate airflow, small arrows indicate fuel flow

An introduction to the carburettor

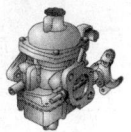

with part-throttle and a warm engine. Each operating condition of the engine has its own specific fuel requirement and the carburettor is designed with different systems or fuel circuits to supply these varying needs. A carburettor for any given engine type is calibrated (after an extensive range of tests) to provide correct fuelling for all production engines of that type in service.

3 In point of fact, an engine will operate (albeit inefficiently) on ratios from as rich as 8:1 to as lean as 22:1. Too rich a mixture will result in poor economy and increased emissions, while too lean a mixture will cause a loss of power and poor performance. The closer that the ratio is to 14.7:1, the more efficiently will the engine run.

4 Because of concern for the environment leading to additional government legislation, the modern engine is required to emit fewer polluting gases. This demands much tighter control over the air/fuel ratio and has led to a tendency to provide leaner mixtures than is desirable for maximum power.

Fuel atomisation

5 Fuel atomisation is the process of breaking the droplets of petrol down to their smallest possible size. Good fuel atomisation is important for reduced exhaust emissions and can be achieved in two ways. One method is to draw air into a stream of petrol. This will cause turbulence and break the solid stream into smaller particles. Another method is to position a nozzle at the point of greatest air velocity, thereby causing the petrol to be buffeted into a fine spray as it enters the airstream.

6 The carburettor is responsible for atomisation and not vaporisation of the fuel. Vaporisation occurs in the inlet manifold and cylinder of the engine. It is important that the intake manifold is properly heated, both to facilitate vaporisation and to reduce condensation of fuel onto the manifold walls. Heating is often accomplished by water circulation through passages in the manifold, or sometimes through the throttle body or carburettor body itself.

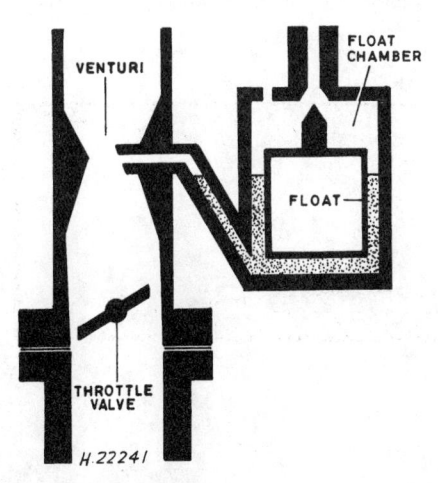

A simple carburettor

7 The venturi size in a fixed venturi carburettor is a compromise of performance against carburettor efficiency. At high engine speeds, the venturi must be large enough to satisfy the engine's demand for a high volume of air to give maximum power. This volume of air will achieve a velocity of approximately 120 m/sec to give good atomisation. At low engine speeds, the much-reduced air volume will cause a reduction in velocity to approximately 12 m/sec. This sluggish velocity will result in much less efficient atomisation. Use of a small venturi would speed up the air velocity but would strangle performance at higher engine speeds. The methods used to overcome this fundamental problem will be examined later.

8 Mixture strength is influenced by changes in ambient weather conditions. Variations in temperature, relative humidity and barometric pressure will all slightly affect the air/fuel ratio (AFR) and the efficiency of the carburettor.

3 Vacuum

1 Vacuum is a negative pressure, or a pressure less than atmospheric. A vacuum is formed in the inlet manifold of a petrol engine because the pistons are continually trying to draw air into each cylinder at a greater speed than the partially-open throttle plate will allow. The amount of vacuum will depend on engine speed and throttle opening. Vacuum in the manifold will be lowest with engine on full-load (wide-open throttle) and highest when the throttle is closed (idle condition, or when descending a hill).

2 Any fault that affects the amount of vacuum created by the engine will also affect the total amount of air drawn into each cylinder. This, in turn, will affect the power and economy developed by the engine. Good carburation depends primarily on good vacuum.

3 Before looking at the specific operation of a carburettor, it would be useful to look at the workings of a simple carburettor. The shortcomings of such a design will become apparent and the methods used to overcome the flaws can then be examined.

4 Simple carburettor

1 A simple carburettor comprises a tube, one end being open to atmosphere. The other end will contain a throttle valve and be connected to the induction manifold of an engine. The internal cross-section of the tube is reduced in diameter by a curved restriction to form a venturi. A float chamber (fuel reservoir) is connected to the narrowest point of the venturi by a channel with an outlet into the venturi. The fuel level in the float chamber will be maintained by a float and valve so that the level is just below the outlet into the venturi (see illustration). A metering jet could be placed in the channel to the venturi.

2 As the engine turns and the piston descends, it creates an area of low pressure in the combustion chamber and inlet manifold. Air will flow through the carburettor from atmospheric (high) pressure to the area of low pressure created by the fall of the piston. Air in the float chamber will also be at atmospheric pressure and therefore higher than the low pressure that exists in the venturi. Pressure of air in the float chamber will push the fuel through the channel so that it enters the airstream in the venturi. Control of the airflow and therefore engine speed, is by virtue of the throttle valve position.

3 As the air velocity changes, so too does the degree of pressure drop in the venturi. Low air velocity will cause a slight pressure drop, whereas high air velocity will cause a substantial pressure drop.

4 This simple carburettor would be suitable only for an application that demanded a constant speed at all times. A metering jet could be fitted in the fuel outlet channel that would give the optimum AFR at a certain engine speed. However, unless the engine was rotated to running speed by a starter motor, the depression (pressure drop) in the venturi would be too low to draw sufficient fuel for starting. Also, starting would be difficult because there is no facility to enrich the mixture during cold running.

5 When the engine is accelerated, the fuel would lag relative to air movement, causing a hesitation for a moment until equilibrium is restored. As the engine speed is raised and pressure drops, a disproportionate amount of fuel would be discharged from the jet. Eventually the AFR would become so rich that the engine could not run.

6 On the other hand, if engine speed was decreased, depression would also decrease but in a proportion greater than the reduced airflow. This would result in a weak mixture and eventually vacuum would be insufficient to draw fuel from the orifice. At this point, the engine would again cease running.

7 Plainly, an increase in airflow will result in a disproportionate increase in fuel flow and a decrease in airflow will result in a disproportionate decrease in fuel flow.

8 Clearly, the simple carburettor would be of little use for most automotive applications. An examination of the basic carburettor systems deployed to overcome these problems can now be made.

5 Fixed venturi carburettor

1 When air passes through a fixed venturi, the pressure differential acting on the fuel jets will vary with engine demand. Thus, compensating air and fuel jets are required to produce the correct fuel flow, with a compromise on the size of venturi to satisfy performance at the extremes of the engine operating range.

A•3

Chapter A

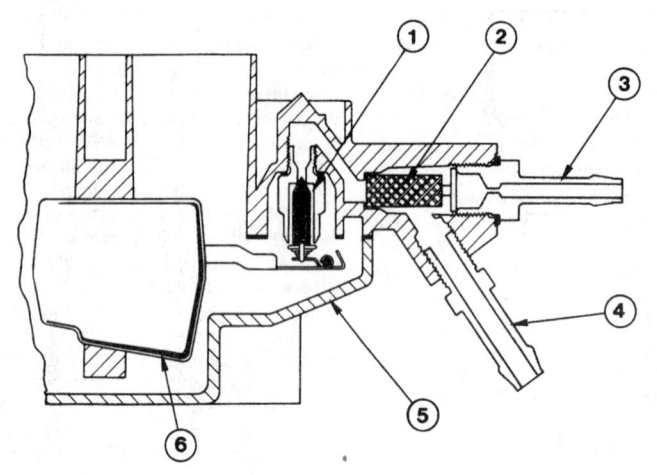

Typical fuel inlet and float system
1 Needle valve
2 Fuel filter
3 Fuel return connector
4 Inlet connector
5 Carburettor main body
6 Float

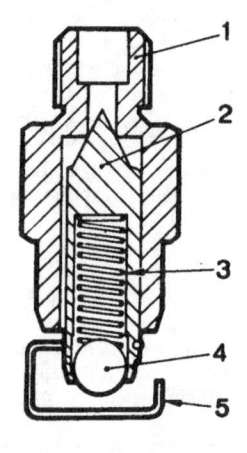

Needle valve and seat
1 Seat
2 Needle valve
3 Damper spring
4 Anti-vibration ball
5 Hairpin or plastic hook

2 The six systems normally used in this type of carburettor are:
a) Float system.
b) Idle and progression.
c) Accelerator pump.
d) Main metering system.
e) Power system.
f) Cold starting device.

3 Different carburettor manufacturers use slightly differing methods to overcome the problems brought to light by the simple carburettor. However, all six circuits will be present in one form or another in all fixed venturi carburettors. Described below are the most commonly-used systems. Where a different method is used, this will be depicted in the Section covering that particular carburettor.

Float system

4 Fuel flow into the carburettor is controlled by a needle valve and float. As the fuel level drops, the float riding on top of the fuel also drops. The needle valve is in contact with a hinge attached to the float and will open to allow fuel to enter the float chamber. As the fuel level rises, the float hinge closes the needle valve. During engine operation, the needle valve is constantly opening and closing to maintain a fairly constant level of fuel in the float chamber. Many modern needle valves are spring-loaded, the spring action absorbing chatter and preventing flooding caused by excess engine vibration *(see illustrations)*.

5 The float level controls the point at which fuel is discharged from the main nozzle and is a very important function of carburettor operation. A low float level will delay discharge, while a high float level will cause an early discharge.

6 The float chamber must be vented, because adding fuel creates pressure and removing fuel creates vacuum. The float chamber vent passage could lead externally to atmosphere, or into the venturi or clean air side of the air filter (where pressure is lower).

7 Imagine that the air cleaner is choked and obstructive to the passage of air. A partial vacuum is formed in the venturi and this adds to the total venturi vacuum. Where the float chamber is vented to atmosphere, atmospheric pressure will be the force pressing upon the fuel in the float chamber to push it through the fuel nozzle. Carburettor flooding would therefore result. By venting the float chamber into the venturi, the partial vacuum produced by a blocked air filter will also be applied to the float chamber and the effect will be equalised. However, the reduction in airflow will tend to enrich the AFR.

8 Petrol vapour from the float chamber can pass through the internal vent into the venturi, thereby causing unwanted enrichment of the air/fuel mixture. This is most likely to affect the engine during periods of hot weather. Starting the engine when hot may be difficult and hesitations may occur during low-speed driving and idling. This problem is overcome in certain carburettors with a dual venting arrangement. The carburettor is vented to atmosphere at idle and slow running speeds, but at higher speeds, a lever (usually attached to the throttle linkage) switches the vent to an internal outlet in the upper reaches of the venturi, on the clean air side of the air filter.

Idle and progression

Idle and slow running

9 Fuel will only be discharged from the main nozzle when the air velocity is high enough to form a low pressure area at the nozzle. Under low-speed running and idle conditions, the air velocity is too low for this condition to be met. A fuel circuit to supply fuel for idling is provided by drilling a channel from the float chamber (or main fuel well) to a point just below the throttle plate *(see illustration)*.

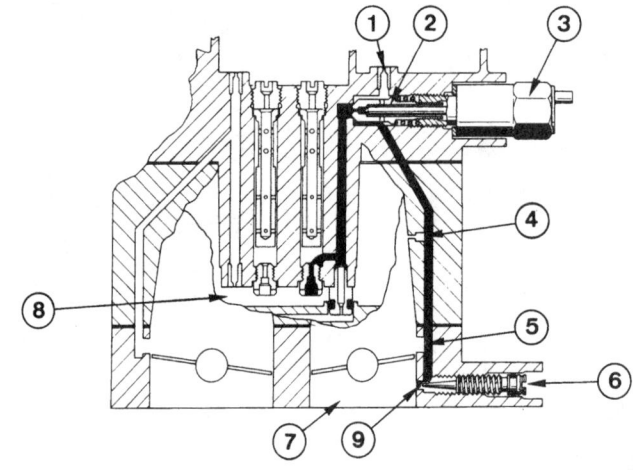

Typical primary idle system
1 Primary idle air bleed
2 Primary idle jet
3 Idle cut-off valve
4 Anti-syphon hole (some carburettors)
5 Progression slot or drillings
6 Idle mixture screw
7 Primary barrel
8 Main fuel well
9 Idle discharge orifice

A•4

An introduction to the carburettor

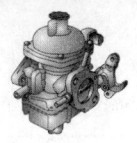

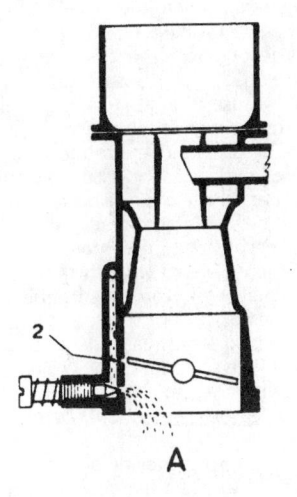

A   Idle stage

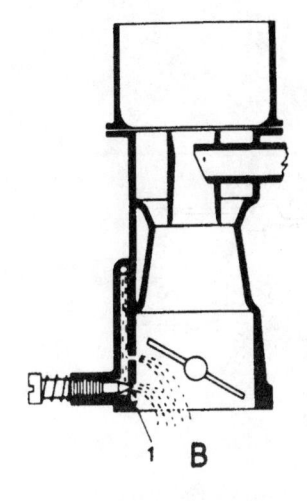

B   Progression stage

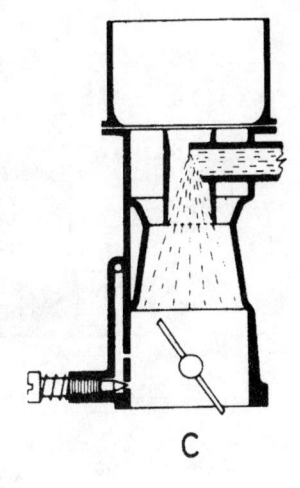

C   Main circuit stage

Various stages of progression

1   Mixture screw   2   Progression drilling

10 When the throttle plate is slightly open, a small gap exists between the plate and the carburettor body. Air will increase in velocity as it passes through the gap and a low pressure area will form at the idle outlet. Furthermore, vacuum formed in the inlet manifold by the almost-closed throttle plate will increase the depression at the idle orifice.

11 Atmospheric pressure in the float chamber will push fuel into the primary idle well through a metered idle jet. Here it is mixed with a small amount of air from a calibrated air bleed. Pre-mixing air and fuel in this way vastly improves atomisation of the idle mixture. The emulsion formed is drawn through a channel to the throttle body, where it is discharged from the idle orifice under the primary throttle plate. A tapered mixture screw is used to vary the outlet and this ensures fine control of the idle mixture.

Progression

12 As the throttle is opened from the idle position and the gap between the plate and the inner barrel wall increases, the depression at the idle discharge orifice is reduced. Less fuel is drawn from the idle outlet and the mixture is weakened. The progression circuit provides extra fuel to compensate for this weakness until the main circuit chimes in *(see illustration)*.

13 Several small drillings (or a single slot) are uncovered by the opening throttle and become subject to manifold vacuum. Fuel (sourced from the idle circuit) will be discharged from these progression drillings, to prevent hesitation on transition from idle to the main circuit. Furthermore, under idle conditions with a closed throttle, air will be drawn into the progression drillings to further emulsify the idle mixture.

14 There is an overlap period during which fuel is provided by both main and idle systems. Eventually, the throttle will open so wide that depression on progression and the idle orifice will cease altogether. Therefore, the idle circuit only influences mixture strength up to 1500 to 2000 rpm. Idle adjustment will only affect mixture strength for idle and cruise conditions with a small throttle opening.

15 During wide-open throttle conditions with a high airflow, a certain amount of air back-bleed may occur into the main fuel circuit through the idle and progression outlets. This will tend to weaken the mixture. One carburettor manufacturer may allow for this in his overall strategy, while another may include an anti-syphon hole to prevent such an occurrence.

Accelerator pump

16 When the throttle is opened quickly during acceleration, the relative velocity of fuel will tend to lag behind the velocity of air. This leads to a weakening of the AFR and will cause a hesitation or flat spot. The normal method of overcoming this problem is to use an accelerator pump to inject a metered quantity of fuel into the airstream. An accelerator pump could be operated by plunger or by a diaphragm. The diaphragm type is either mechanically operated (by a lever or rod attached to the throttle linkage) or by manifold vacuum. The most common type utilises a mechanically-operated diaphragm and is described below *(see illustration)*. The function of all other types is basically similar, the main difference being the method of operation.

17 Under acceleration, a lever attached to the

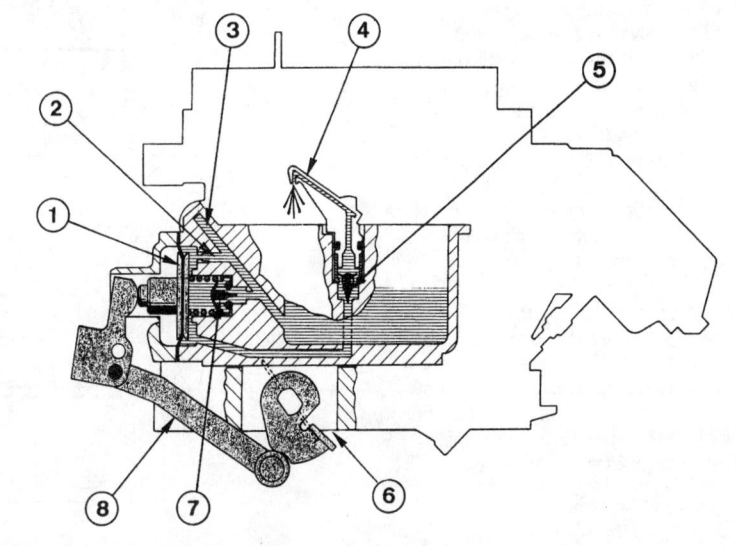

Typical accelerator pump system

1 Spring-loaded diaphragm	3 Fuel supply drilling	6 Primary barrel
2 Back-bleed	4 Pump injector	7 Valve assembly (inlet)
	5 Valve assembly (outlet)	8 Pump actuating lever

A•5

Chapter A

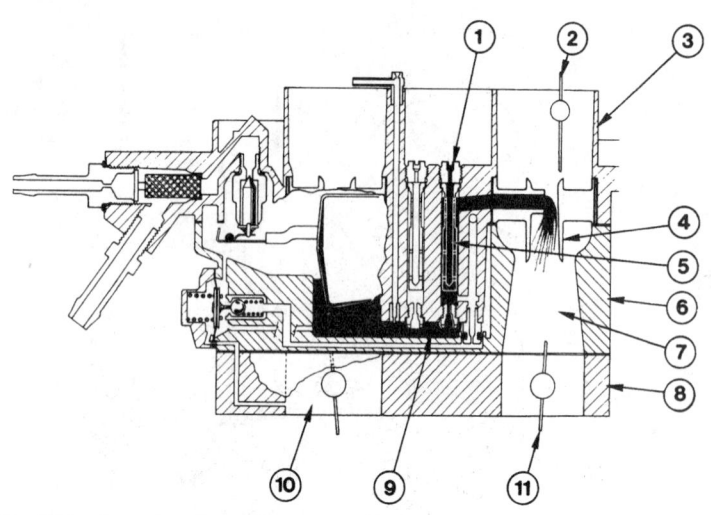

Typical primary main system

1. Air correction jet
2. Choke flap
3. Upper body assembly
4. Auxiliary venturi
5. Emulsion tube
6. Main body
7. Primary barrel
8. Throttle body
9. Primary main well
10. Secondary barrel
11. Throttle plate

primary throttle linkage bears against the pump diaphragm and compresses it. Fuel from the reservoir in the pump housing is pushed through the pump outlet channels, past the pump outlet valve, and is injected from the pump nozzle into the venturi. The inlet valve remains closed, to prevent fuel from being returned to the float chamber. Usually the action is arranged to provide one long stroke which will further aid powerful acceleration.

18 As the throttle action is reversed, a spring will return the diaphragm to its starting position. Depression will then draw fuel from the float chamber into the pump reservoir, past an inlet valve. The outlet valve remains closed to prevent fuel from returning via the outlet channel. The inlet and outlet valves are usually simple ball bearings positioned in the appropriate channel. However, later carburettors are beginning to use rubber diaphragm types which are sometimes called Vernay Valves.

19 During high-speed engine operation, the strong vacuum formed at the pump injector nozzle could draw fuel from the pump reservoir into the venturi. A vacuum break hole in the pump nozzle prevents this occurrence by reducing vacuum in the outlet channel.

20 Under certain conditions, the fuel in the pump reservoir may become overheated and boil or turn to vapour. This is prevented by use of a pump back-bleed hole, which allows vapour to bleed back into the float chamber. Vacuum would then draw fresh, cooler fuel into the pump reservoir to maintain the level.

Main circuit

21 As the throttle is further opened, the vacuum draw on the idle and progression drillings diminishes and the main circuit provides all further fuel requirements *(see illustration)*.

22 The amount of fuel discharged into the airstream is controlled by a calibrated main jet. Fuel passes from the float chamber through the main jet and into the base of a vertical well. This hollow tube is known as the emulsion tube well. Fuel will rise in the well and settle at the same height as the float level - this is slightly lower than the outlet to the main discharge nozzle. Into the well is fitted a calibrated emulsion tube, which has a number of calibrated cross holes and which dips down into the fuel. A calibrated air correction jet caps the top of the well.

23 Once the engine is running appreciably above idle speed, the pressure drop in the venturi will cause the fuel in the well to discharge from the main nozzle. Air is drawn through the air corrector jet into the well. Here it passes through the cross holes in the emulsion tube and mixes with the outgoing fuel. As the depression drops still further, the level of fuel in the well will drop. This exposes more cross holes in the emulsion tube, to weaken the mixture. Thus the problem of high-speed enrichment caused by increased depression is overcome. Correct calibration of the main and air corrector jets, together with selection of the position, size and quantity of the emulsion tube holes are essential for proper operation of the main circuit.

24 Many carburettors provide a secondary or auxiliary venturi to boost the depression in the main venturi. Fuel and air mixing is improved and better distribution results.

Power enrichment and economy circuit

25 During light-load conditions with a partially-open throttle, a leaner mixture is required for good economy and emissions. The jet calibration of the main system is usually calculated with this aim in mind. Extra fuel is therefore required for powerful acceleration and wide-open throttle operation at high speeds. This is accomplished by a power circuit (usually vacuum-operated), which enriches the mixture at high speed and leans it off during cruising *(see illustration)*.

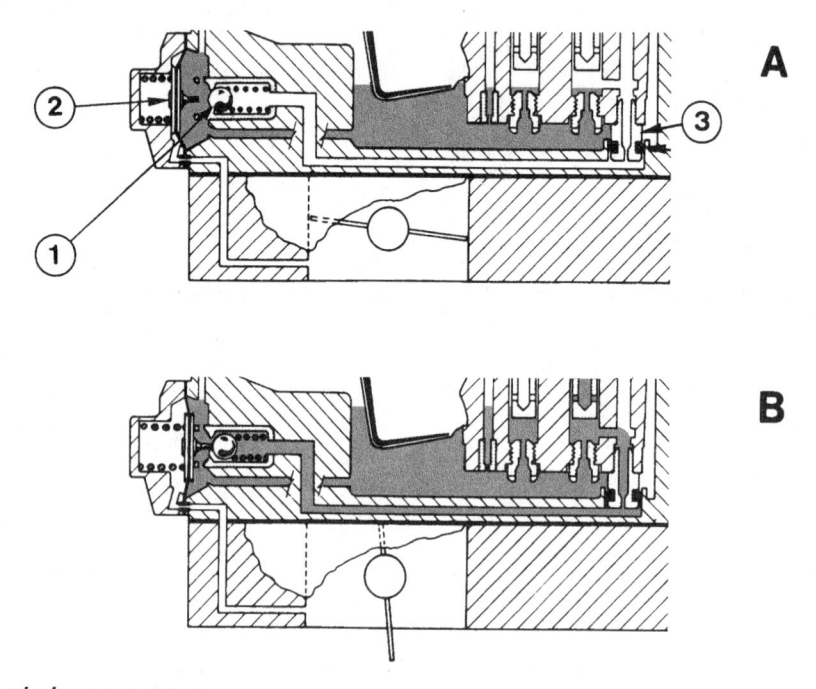

Typical power system

A Low power demand
B High power demand
1 Spring-loaded ball
2 Spring-loaded diaphragm
3 Power jet

An introduction to the carburettor

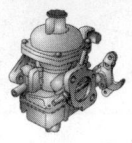

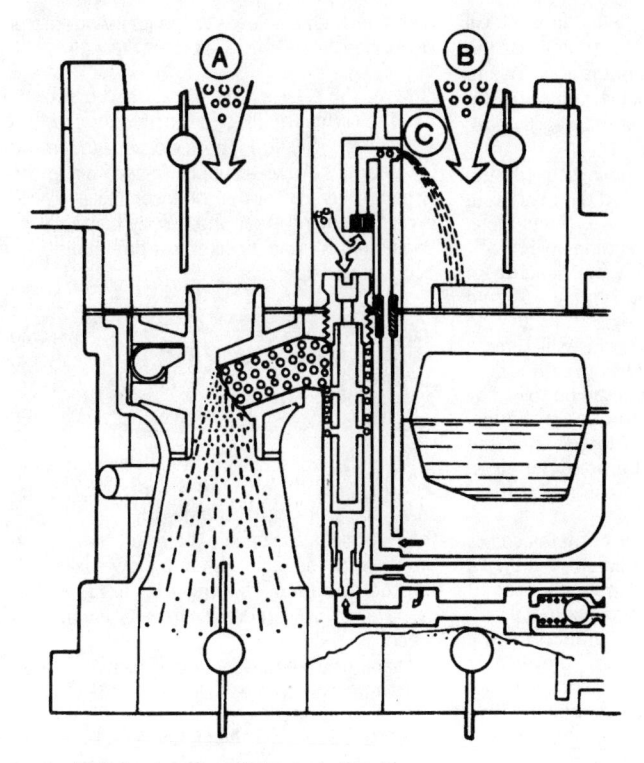

Typical high-speed enrichment circuit

A Primary barrel
B Secondary barrel
C High-speed discharge orifice

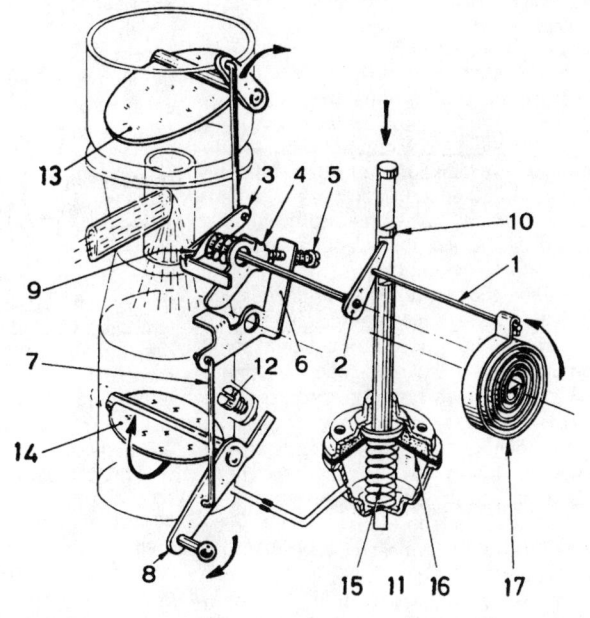

Typical automatic choke

1, 2 & 3 Bi-metal operating mechanism
4 Fast idle cam
5 Fast idle adjusting screw
6 & 7 Fast idle/throttle linkage
8 Throttle lever
9 Spring
10 Pull-down rod
12 Idle speed adjusting screw
13 Choke flap
14 Throttle valve
15 Spring
16 Pull-down diaphragm
17 Bi-metal spring

26 Most circuits operate in a similar fashion to the one described below.

27 Fuel flows from the float chamber into the power valve chamber through a fuel channel. An air passage is taken from under the throttle plate to the cover of the power diaphragm chamber. At idle and during light throttle operation, manifold vacuum in the passage draws the diaphragm back against spring pressure. The diaphragm pintle is withdrawn from the brass outlet valve and the spring-loaded ball is seated to close off the channel. Under acceleration and wide-open throttle operation, the vacuum in the manifold is depleted. The diaphragm returns under spring pressure and the power diaphragm pintle pushes the ball to open the outlet valve. Fuel then flows through the valve and a calibrated jet to supplement the fuel in the primary main well. The fuel level rises in the well and the fuel mixture is enriched.

High-speed enrichment

28 At full-load and high engine speeds, even more fuel is required. The velocity of air creates a depression sufficient to raise fuel from the float chamber into a channel. The fuel then passes through a calibrated bushing to the upper section of the air intake. Here it is mixed with a small amount of air from a calibrated air bleed and the emulsified mixture is then discharged into the airstream from the full-load enrichment tube or orifice. In twin venturi carburettors, the discharge is normally into the secondary venturi *(see illustration)*.

Cold starting device

29 Carburation during cold starting and the warm-up period is grossly inefficient. A low cranking speed with consequent low airflow will give poor atomisation. Also, no heat is present in the inlet manifold or cylinder head to assist in fuel vaporisation. Much of the fuel condenses on the cold inlet manifold walls and the mixture must be greatly enriched to allow the engine to run properly until it reaches running temperature. A form of choke or other enrichment device is used, which can be manually or automatically operated. An increase of friction in a cold engine demands a higher idle speed - this speed is known as a *fast idle*.

30 A common method of enrichment is to use a strangler choke flap to completely block the air intake at the top of the carburettor. The pressure drop in the venturi is so great that a large amount of fuel is discharged from the main and idle outlets.

Manual choke

31 The manually-operated choke is worked by a dash-mounted cable. When the cable is pulled, it operates a lever that pulls the choke flap closed across the air intake. In turn, a linkage rod opens the throttle into the fast idle position. Once the engine has started, the depression partially opens the choke flap against the action of a spring or diaphragm. A stop ensures that the choke is only opened a small amount. During engine warm-up, the cable should be progressively pushed home until the choke flap is fully open.

Automatic choke

32 Most so-called automatic chokes are actually of the semi-automatic variety. A semi-automatic choke requires priming by the vehicle operator. For starting the engine from cold, the choke flap and fast idle are set by depressing the accelerator pedal once or twice. In a fully-automatic environment, no action is required other than operating the ignition switch.

33 Operation of a typical automatic choke using a strangler choke flap is very similar to the basic manual choke described above, the main difference being the use of a heat-sensitive bi-metal spring or coil to control the choke operating phase *(see illustration)*. The spring is constructed of two strips of metal (such as brass and steel) which expand at different rates. These strips of metal are laid on top of each other and wound into a coil spring.

34 One end of the choke flap spindle projects into the choke housing and culminates in a short lever which slots into the turned-over end of the bi-metal spring. When cold, the spring will curl up and pull the choke flap into the

Chapter A

closed position. Heating the bi-metal coil causes it to uncurl and the choke flap is slowly opened.
35 Once the engine has fired, the choke flap must open slightly to weaken the mixture and avoid flooding. During initial idle and light-throttle operation, this is achieved by using manifold vacuum to actuate a pull-down diaphragm. A linkage attached to the diaphragm will then act upon the choke flap. Once the bi-metal has warmed sufficiently to partially open the flap, the pull-down operation becomes largely irrelevant.
36 On some engines, a single pull-down stage causes either a weak mixture (too large a gap) or too rich a mixture (too small a gap) at some period during early choke operation. Utilising a two stage pull-down system overcomes these problems. The first pull-down stage ensures maximum richness for a few seconds after a cold start and then a rapid opening of the choke flap to the second stage to reduce over-richness. The second stage pull-down may be actuated by a vacuum reservoir, thermal time valve (TTV) or a thermal valve.
37 Fast idle is achieved with the aid of a stepped or snail cam attached to the choke spindle. When the choke flap is pulled into the closed position, the cam indexes around, placing its highest step against an adjustable screw connected to the throttle lever mechanism and butting against the cam. The throttle plate is held further open than normal and the adjustable screw can be used to vary the throttle position (and therefore the fast idle speed). As the bi-metal coil is heated and the choke flap opens, the screw will rest on successively less-stepped (or less-curved) parts of the cam. Idle speed is thus progressively reduced, until ultimately the cam is released and the idle speed returns to normal.

38 Heating of the coil may be by an electrical supply or by coolant from the engine cooling system. Because many carburettors are joined to the inlet manifold via a flexible mounting, an earth lead is used to complete an earth path from the carburettor to the engine.
39 Where an electrical supply is used, the choke will open fairly quickly and this may cause engine hesitation during warm-up. The bi-metal coil may cool quickly after engine switch-off, closing the choke completely and leading to poor starting with a hot engine. Should the engine be inadvertently left with the ignition switched on, the choke will remain fully open, causing poor starting with a cold engine. This particular problem can be solved by routing the voltage supply through a thermal switch. The switch remains closed when the engine is cold and opens at a pre-determined coolant temperature to cut off the voltage supply.
40 Where a coolant-heated bi-metal coil is used, the problems are reversed and the choke will remain almost closed until the coolant becomes hot enough to heat the bi-metal coil. This may initially cause rich operation for the first few minutes after a cold start. To overcome these shortcomings, some applications may use a combination of these (and other) methods to operate the automatic choke.
41 Depending on carburettor models, the flap closes off either both primary and secondary air intakes or just the primary air intake.

Wide-open kick

42 If the throttle is fully opened shortly after a cold start, the pull-down vacuum will collapse, causing the choke flap to close. This may cause flooding. To prevent this, a wide-open kick mechanism is employed. When the throttle is fully opened, a cam on the throttle lever will rotate the choke lever to partially open the choke flap.

Air filter

43 The air filter fulfils two functions. It provides a silencing of induction noise and, more importantly, allows a supply of clean air to the engine. Dust and dirt in the incoming air cause excessive engine wear and quickly contaminate engine oil. A clean air filter is a pre-requisite to good engine operation.

6 Twin venturi carburettor

1 All multiple installations (which includes twin venturi carburettors and twin carburettors) share one slight disadvantage, which is a higher than normal stall speed, where fuel will not be drawn from the main system on low-speed full-throttle operation. The single (or fixed) venturi carburettor will generally have a lower stall speed.
2 There are three distinct types of twin venturi carburettor, detailed as follows:

Progressive twin venturi carburettor

3 The modern engine often has a spread of power from 600 rpm to over 6000 rpm. There is therefore a basic difficulty in choosing a single venturi diameter that will be small enough to give good idling characteristics, yet large enough to allow full power at maximum rpm. By choosing a carburettor with a twin venturi and a progressive linkage, the best of both worlds can be obtained *(see illustration)*. The

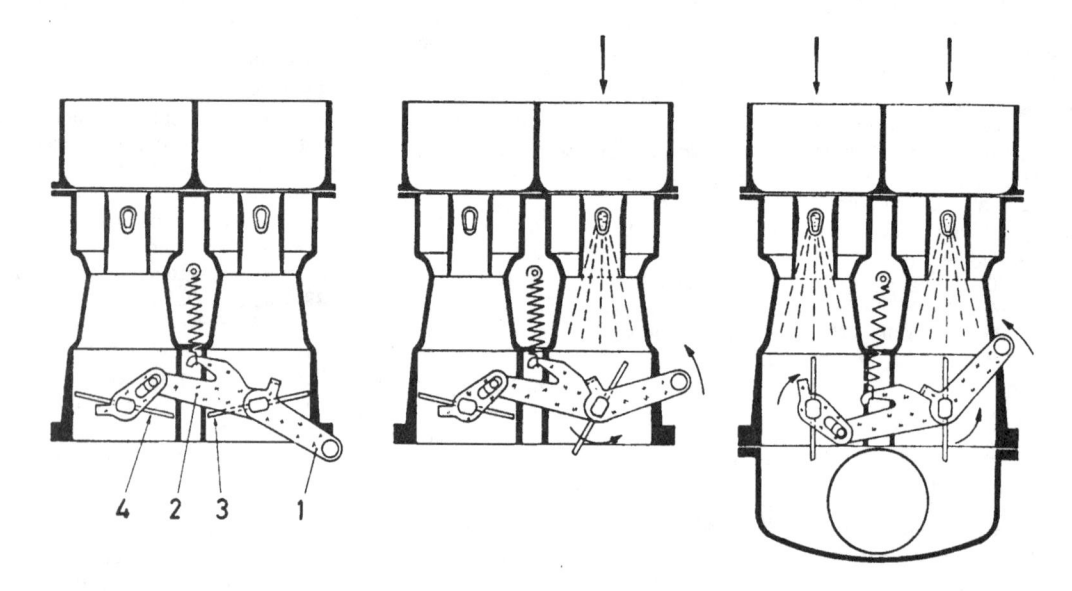

Typical progressive twin venturi carburettor

1 Primary throttle lever
2 Intermediate lever
3 Primary throttle valve
4 Secondary throttle valve

An introduction to the carburettor

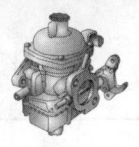

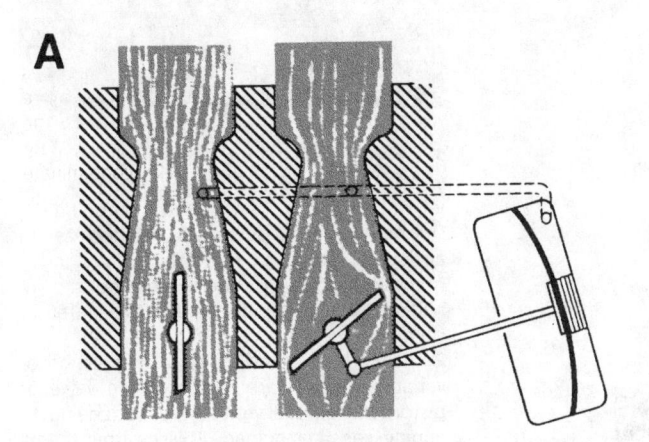

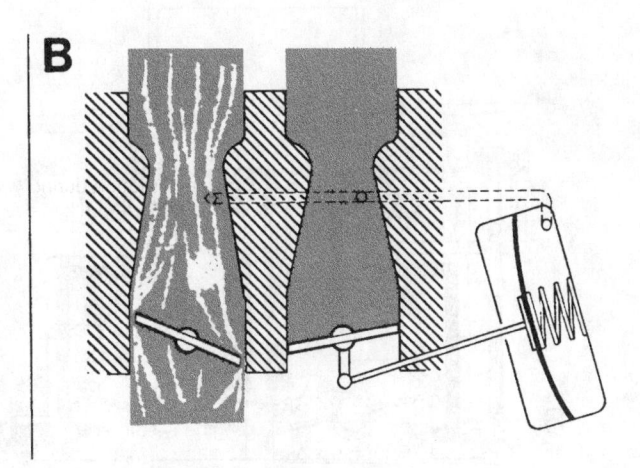

Vacuum-controlled twin venturi carburettor operation
A High air speed in primary venturi, secondary throttle plate open
B Low air speed in primary venturi, secondary throttle plate closed

primary venturi (which is smaller than the secondary) is used for low-speed running with a small throttle opening. Thus, all the advantages of a small-bore carburettor with good air velocity are available at low engine speeds. The secondary throttle begins to open at the half- to two-thirds-open position of the primary throttle. When both venturis are fully open at maximum engine rpm, the engine receives the benefit of full airflow to give full power.

4 The main problem of the progressive twin venturi carburettor occurs at low rpm. If full-throttle is used at low engine speeds, then both venturis will open together. The rush of air into the manifold will cause a low-speed stumble and slow initial acceleration. On some carburettors, an attempt is made to overcome this by allowing the accelerator pump injector to discharge into both venturis simultaneously, instead of into one venturi as normal. However, injection into the secondary venturi will also occur when only the primary venturi is drawing air and this is a waste of petrol. It was for this reason that the vacuum-controlled twin venturi carburettor came into being.

Vacuum-controlled twin venturi carburettor

5 The primary venturi in this type of carburettor operates in a similar fashion to the primary venturi in a progressive twin venturi carburettor.
6 A port is located in both the primary and the secondary venturi. Airways run from these ports into a common passage leading to the diaphragm that operates the secondary throttle plate *(see illustration)*.
7 During normal operation at low speeds, the engine uses only the primary venturi. As the throttle is opened further, the velocity of air will increase through the primary venturi until a point is reached when the velocity is high enough to reduce the pressure and form a strong vacuum pull. This is relayed to the diaphragm, which operates the linkage to open the secondary throttle plate. Vacuum created in the secondary venturi will also be relayed via the port to the diaphragm and will further control the rate of secondary opening. Only when the air velocity through the primary venturi is sufficient, will the secondary plate begin to open. Full-throttle at low speeds will thus not cause secondary plate operation with this system.

8 The primary linkage is also arranged to prevent the secondary plate from opening when the air speed may be high but the engine is cruising on a light throttle. Secondary action will not take place until the primary throttle is about two-thirds-open. Vacuum created during the cruise period will bleed off through the secondary port. As air velocity in the primary venturi increases, the stronger vacuum created will overcome the bleed through the secondary port. At lower engine speeds or loads, the vacuum level will fall and the secondary throttle plate will close, irrespective of the primary throttle position.

9 It should be noted that the pressure drop caused by air speed in the carburettor is totally different to the vacuum present in the intake manifold.

10 In some applications, a control is used to prevent secondary action until the engine reaches full operating temperature. This may take various forms and will be described for the relevant carburettor.

11 Many vehicle manufacturers prefer the use of a vacuum-controlled secondary throttle, which generally gives better performance and economy in roadgoing cars.

12 A separate jet may be used in progressive and vacuum-controlled twin venturi systems to prevent hesitation as the secondary throttle plate commences opening. This is in reality a progression jet, although it is often referred to as the secondary idle jet. The secondary progression circuit functions in a similar fashion to the primary idle circuit. An emulsified mixture is discharged into the secondary venturi via a progression drilling or slot at the initial opening of the secondary throttle plate *(see illustrations)*. Once the secondary throttle plate has opened,

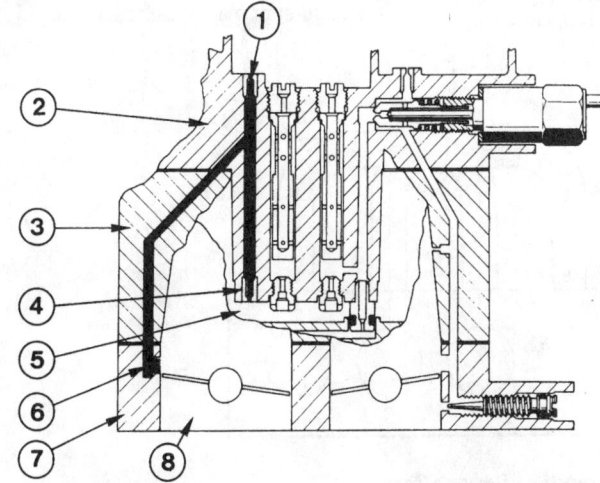

Typical secondary progression circuit

1 Secondary idle air bleed
2 Upper body
3 Main body
4 Secondary progression jet
5 Main fuel well
6 Secondary progression slot
7 Throttle body
8 Secondary barrel

A•9

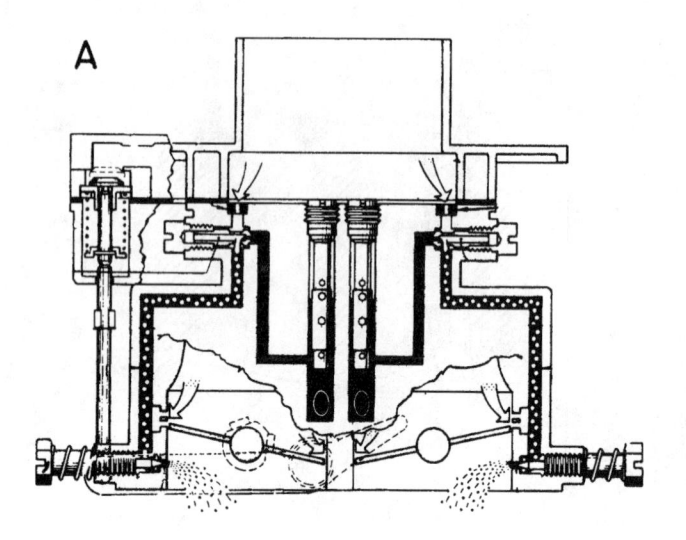

Chapter A

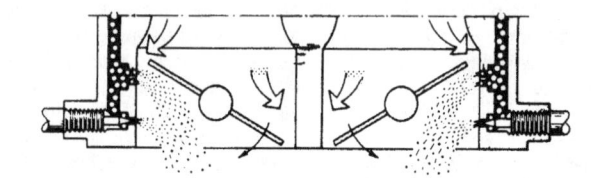

Twin venturi carburettor at idle (A) and progression (B)

the action of the secondary main circuit is similar to that of the primary circuit.

Synchronised twin venturi carburettor

13 The throttles on this type of carburettor (one for each venturi or barrel) are geared to open simultaneously. This carburettor is often used in V-type engines, so that one barrel can be used to feed half of the cylinders and the other barrel to feed the remaining half. However, in a six-cylinder V engine, each carburettor barrel would not feed one bank of the V. Rather, the left barrel would feed the first and third cylinders on the left and the middle cylinder on the right side. The right barrel would feed the first and third cylinders on the right and the middle cylinder on the left side. This type of carburettor may have a primary and secondary venturi in a similar manner to the progressive or vacuum-controlled twin venturi carburettor. If so, the carburettor may be called a quad.

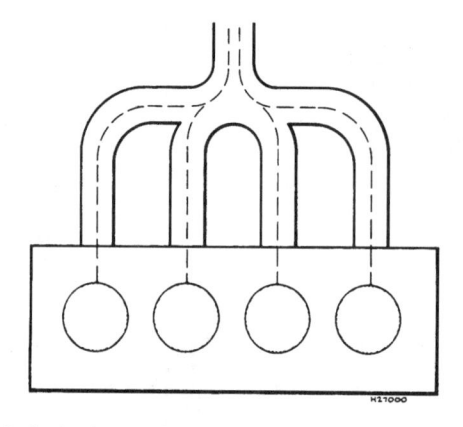

Single carburettor air/fuel mixture flow pattern

7 Constant depression or variable venturi carburettors

1 When air is drawn through a fixed venturi, its velocity and therefore depression over the fuel jet will vary with the demand of the engine. During low-speed operation, the decrease in airflow causes poor fuel atomisation and a number of compensating bleeds and jets are necessary to compensate for the different conditions.

2 On the other hand, constant depression or variable venturi carburettors use a valve or piston to vary the venturi area according to engine speed and load. This ensures that a constant depression exists over the main jet at all speeds and loads. Air velocity remains constant and airflow will always be according to engine requirements. Fuel flow is regulated by a single jet and a tapered metering needle is used to allow more fuel at higher engine speeds.

3 A number of constant depression types of carburettor have no separate idle circuit. Due to emission constraints, an idle circuit is now considered desirable for most variations of these carburettor types.

4 Constant depression carburettors are generally more tolerant of engine faults than fixed venturi types.

8 Twin carburettors

1 Consider the flow pattern of the air and fuel mixture in a normal four-cylinder, single carburettor engine which has a firing order of 1-3-4-2. When the piston for cylinder No. 1 descends, the mixture must negotiate two 90° turns in the inlet manifold during its journey from the carburettor. As the next piston descends, the mixture must immediately reverse its flow for the journey to cylinder No. 3. Next, the mixture is discharged to cylinder No. 4, with a final reverse to cylinder No. 2. The complete cycle will then repeat itself as the engine is continuously operated *(see illustration)*.

2 Negotiating these turns (and the reversal of airflow) brings forward other problems. As the airflow changes direction, the fuel part of the atomised mixture will tend to separate and go straight on, where it will settle on the inlet manifold walls.

3 If the single carburettor is replaced with two carburettors and a twin manifold, the installation becomes much more efficient *(see illustration)*. The pattern of flow is less disrupted and the 90° turns have now become smooth curves. Each carburettor has only two cylinders to service. The improved intake efficiency will lead to a small increase in engine power or fuel

An introduction to the carburettor

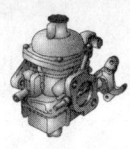

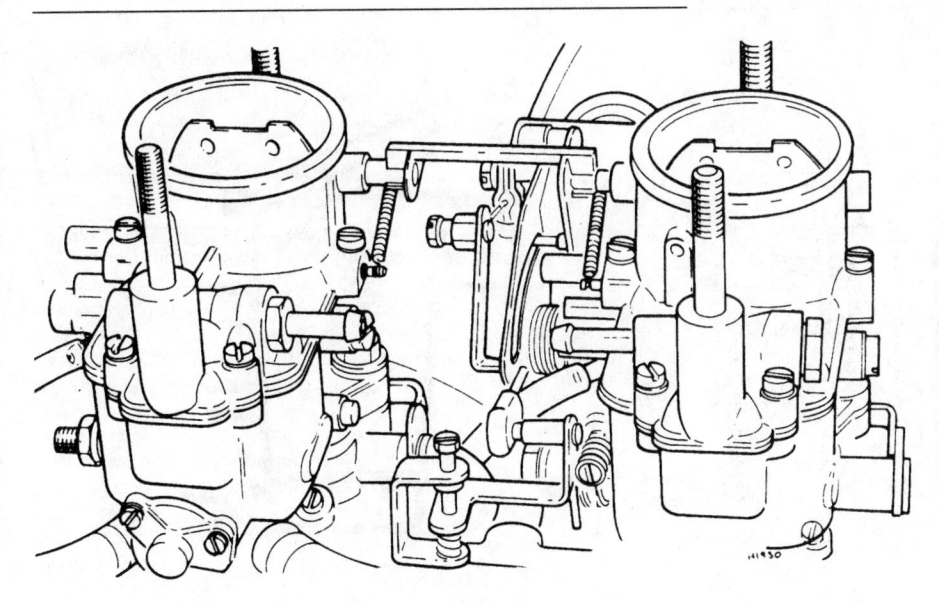

Typical twin carburettor installation

economy, depending on how the engine is driven.

4 Maximum engine power is not usually affected by fitting twin carburettors alone. If the venturi size of each one of the twin carburettors is the same size as the single carburettor, the same volume of mixture will be drawn into the cylinder in both cases. Only one cylinder will require mixture at any one time, regardless of carburettor layout. Fitting carburettors with a larger venturi will also fail to increase engine power, unless the carburettor was already too small for that engine. This is because the volumetric efficiency of a particular engine will limit the maximum volume that can be drawn into any one particular cylinder. Once that maximum is reached, fitting carburettors with a larger venturi will reduce air velocity, resulting in a reduction in efficiency and poor atomisation. Increasing airflow into the cylinder would be the only sensible reason for fitting a larger carburettor.

5 A number of installations (usually on high performance engines) use one venturi per cylinder. Efficiency and power output are excellent, although the set-up is very sensitive and difficult to tune. Cost is another constraint that places this type of installation in a different area to mass-produced vehicle applications.

6 Multiple carburettors are tending to be used less in modern times. Cost considerations and the basic issue of poor atomisation at low speed are some of the reasons.

9 Modern carburettor design

1 Many problems are raised by the need to control emission levels. Some of the methods employed in an attempt to overcome these problems are described in this Section.

2 Modern carburettor design is a compromise between power, economy and reduced emissions. The difficulties in mixing air and fuel at very lean ratios are such that, even in the best-designed carburettor, the result is not always perfect. Smoothness of running and power are often sacrificed to comply with an emission specification, or for maximum economy. Another difficulty is the variation of production tolerances for any given engine. The calibration of a carburettor will be suitable for most engines of the type to which it is fitted. However, where the calibration is marginally weak for that type, a small proportion of engines may lose power and tend to hesitate under acceleration. To improve running under difficult conditions, a mixture of the following systems are incorporated into the carburettor/fuel supply system (not all systems are fitted to all carburettors).

Heated air warm-up system

3 The heated air system provides a faster engine warm-up, with improved fuel consumption and reduced exhaust emissions. Instances of carburettor icing are also considerably reduced.

4 Manifold vacuum is piped via a small hose to the temperature sensor in the air filter casing. Another hose is connected to a vacuum motor or damper which controls a flap or door in the air filter nozzle. Alternatively, some systems use a thermostat which is directly connected to the flap. In both types of system, the flap opens or closes according to air temperature (see illustration).

5 On most systems, when the under-bonnet air temperature is below a certain level, vacuum pulls the door open to allow heated air from around the exhaust system to enter the carburettor intake (see illustration). As the under-bonnet air temperature rises, the sensor gradually closes and the vacuum door shuts off the exhaust-heated air, thus allowing unheated air to feed the carburettor.

6 During periods of cold-engine acceleration, the supply of warm air may be inadequate for

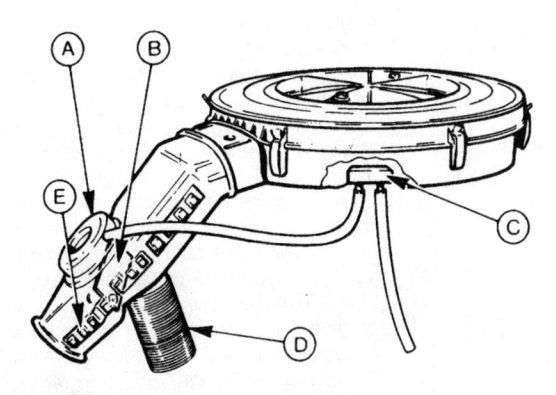

Typical heated air warm-up system

A Vacuum diaphragm assembly
B Flap valve
C Heat sensor
D Hot air intake
E Cool air intake

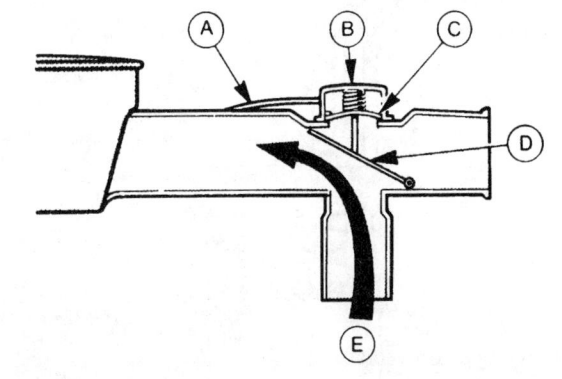

Heated air warm-up system at high vacuum (flap valve open)

A Vacuum hose
B Diaphragm unit
C Diaphragm
D Flap valve
E Hot airflow

A•11

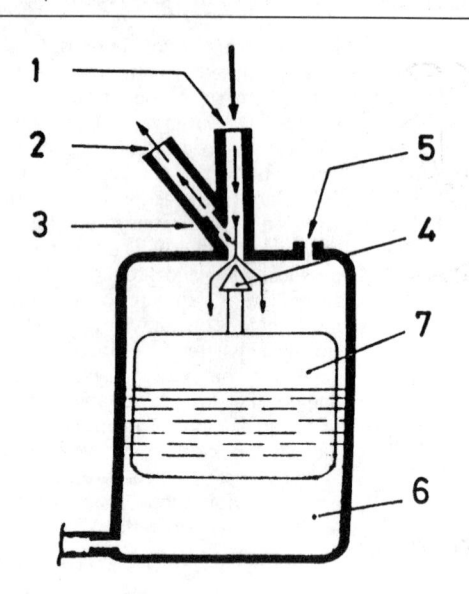

Chapter A

Typical fuel return system
1 Fuel supply from pump
2 Fuel return to tank
3 Restrictor
4 Needle valve
5 Float chamber vent
6 Float chamber
7 Float

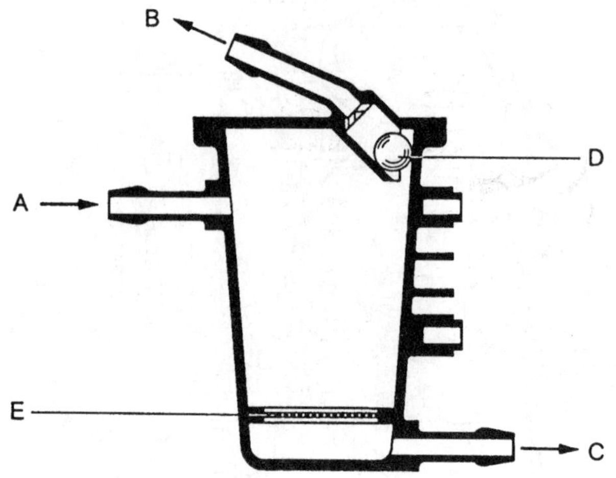

Typical vapour separator
A From fuel pump
B Return pipe
C To carburettor
D Ball valve
E Filter

acceptable engine performance. In this instance, the damper should be fully open to provide enough cold air for the engine's demands. The drop in intake manifold vacuum on sudden acceleration causes the vacuum motor return spring to open the damper. However, some later systems deploy a vacuum sustain device to maintain a supply of heated air during sudden acceleration.

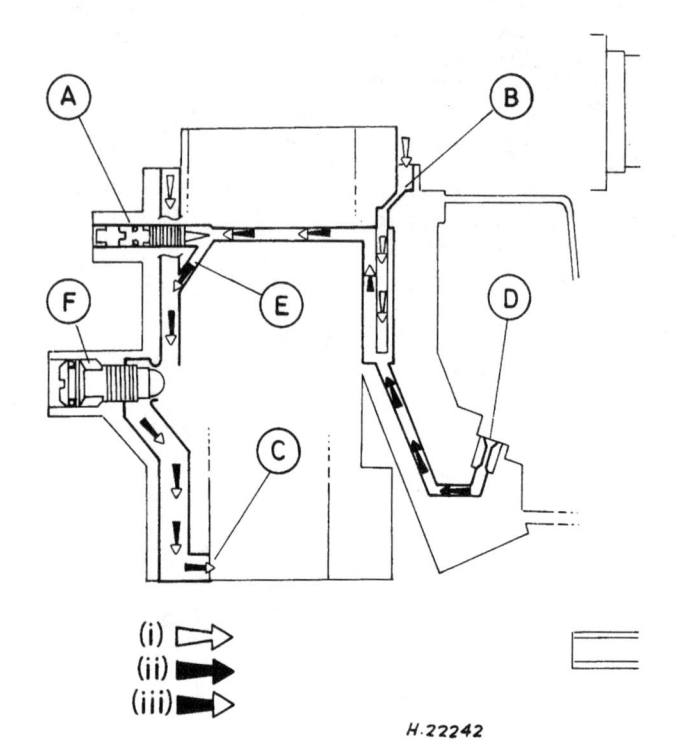

Fuel return

7 A calibrated fuel return system may be provided to prevent a build-up of pressure at the needle valve after engine shut-down. Also, the continuous circulation of fuel ensures that relatively cool fuel is supplied to the carburettor. The return operates through a restrictor, so that the majority of fuel enters the carburettor through the inlet connector (see illustration).

Vapour separator

8 A vapour separator (or trap) may be used to prevent poor starting when the engine is hot. Gas bubbles and excess vapours are separated and conducted back to the fuel tank via a fuel return pipe. The vapour separator also relieves heat-induced rises in fuel pressure, thus returning the excess fuel to the tank (see illustration).

Idle bypass circuit

9 The idle bypass circuit provides a means of more accurately controlling idle emissions than that in a carburettor with conventional idle mixture circuits (see illustration). The throttle plate is locked in a set position, so that only a proportion of the mixture required for idle will pass it. A supplementary air passage is drilled from under the throttle valve and through the carburettor body to atmosphere. A fuel channel links the idle fuel circuit with the bypass passage and it is regulated by an adjustable screw. Manifold vacuum will draw air through the passage, the volume of air being controlled by an air regulating screw. The majority of air required for idle passes through the bypass passage. Fuel and air are mixed in the passage and the mixture is discharged into a gallery under the throttle plate where it is drawn into the engine. About 20% of the mixture required for idle is controlled through the idle bypass circuit.

Typical idle bypass circuit
A Bypass mixture screw
B Air bleed
C Fuel discharge channel
D Bypass fuel jet in float chamber
E Air/fuel entry point
F Bypass air speed regulating screw
i Air supply
ii Fuel supply
iii Air/fuel mixture

An introduction to the carburettor

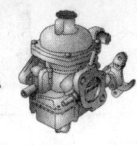

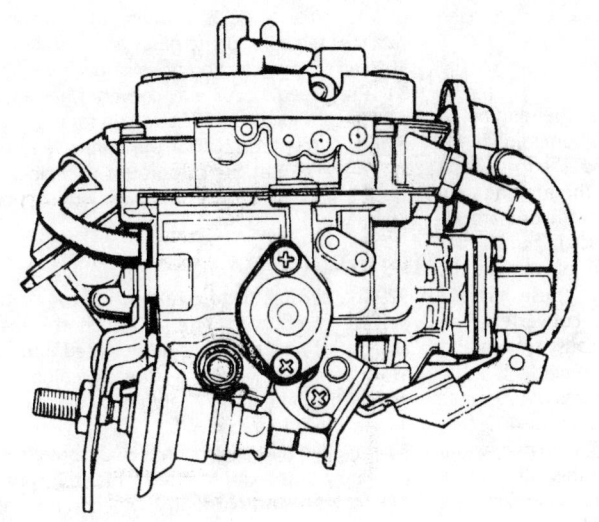

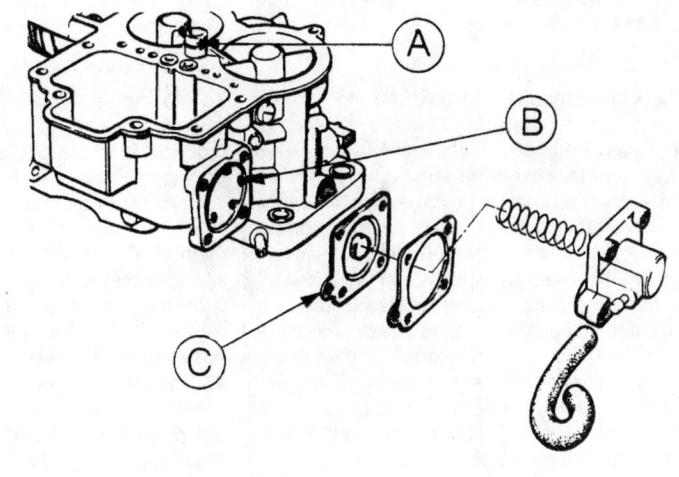

Throttle damper assembly

Typical anti-stall device
A Pump injector   B Fuel inlet   C Diaphragm

Anti-run-on (idle cut-off) valve

10 Because of emission controls, the modern carburettor is designed to provide a very lean mixture. In turn, this requires a high idle speed and the combination of high idle and a lean mixture increases the risk of engine run-on (sometimes referred to as dieseling) when the engine is switched off.

11 A device to reduce run-on is often referred to as an anti-run-on valve. It may take several forms but commonly uses an ignition-switched solenoid to accomplish its function.

12 The device most commonly used is an idle cut-off valve incorporated into the carburettor. A plunger attached to the solenoid will operate to seal the idle fuel channel or idle jet when the engine is switched off. This effectively cuts the idle fuel supply.

13 Some manufacturers may use a solenoid-operated device to open the inlet manifold to atmosphere. The resulting vacuum leak stops the engine dead.

14 Another solenoid-controlled device that is sometimes used shuts the throttle completely on engine switch-off.

Deceleration

15 A manifold vacuum that is higher than idle vacuum is suddenly introduced when the throttle is snapped shut. This can remove droplets of fuel clinging to the manifold walls and this extra fuel will often pass through the engine unburnt, resulting in excess hydrocarbon emissions. Also, in engines with an emissions carburettor or automatic gearbox, a momentary weakening of the mixture can cause the engine to hesitate or even stall. Measures have been introduced to reduce emissions during deceleration, they are as follows:

Deceleration valve

16 On sudden throttle closure, the build-up of vacuum causes a pre-set valve to open against a spring. This prevents any further increase in vacuum. The spring will shut the valve when normal idle vacuum conditions are resumed. The decel or over-run valve is often mounted in the throttle plate, or adjacent to the throttle spindle. In the latter case, a high vacuum may cause a diaphragm to open a bypass to the throttle plate to achieve the same end.

Throttle dashpot

17 The throttle dashpot allows the throttle plate to close slowly, introducing normal idle vacuum in a controlled manner (see illustration).

Hot idle temperature compensator (HITC)

18 When under-bonnet temperatures become very high, such as during long periods of idling in congested traffic on a hot day, there is a tendency for fuel vapours to collect in the intake manifold. These vapours are caused by heat expansion of the fuel in the carburettor float chamber. Fuel viscosity also increases. The result is a rich fuel mixture, which prompts stalling and rough idle.

19 The HITC is a thermostatically-operated device. It makes use of a flat bi-metal spring to open a vent into the air filter casing, PCV hose or the carburettor base. The compensator remains closed under normal operating temperatures. However, once the under-bonnet temperature reaches an specified high level the valve will open. Additional air will then bleed into the manifold to dilute the rich fuel mixture. When the operating temperature returns to normal, the valve will seat itself and the air-bleed will be shut off.

Anti-stall device

20 With lean mixtures, there is a possibility of the engine stalling during the warm-up phase. When automatic transmission is fitted, the possibility is even greater. The anti-stall device is usually a vacuum-operated accelerator pump which injects a metered quantity of fuel into the venturi through the accelerator pump injector (see illustration). When the engine speed drops (as the engine is about to stall) manifold vacuum collapses. This causes the pump to discharge and the richer mixture effectively prevents the stall. It is sometimes operated through a thermal switch, so that operation only occurs during engine warm-up. The device is disabled when the engine is hot by virtue of the thermal switch operating to cut off the device. This anti-stall device is sometimes referred to as a Low Vacuum Enrichment (LOVE) valve.

Coolant-heated thermal switch

21 A thermal switch supplies voltage to components such as the automatic choke, inlet manifold heater and/or throttle body heater when the engine coolant is cold. As the engine coolant rises above a pre-determined temperature, the thermal switch opens and the voltage supply is cut. One thermal switch may supply several components, or each component may function through its own thermal switch. The switch is usually placed in a coolant hose or located in the coolant passage of the inlet manifold (see illustration). However, depending on application, the automatic choke and

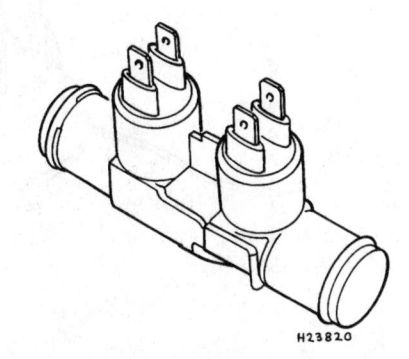

Coolant-heated thermal switch - double connector type

A•13

Chapter A

throttle body heater may not always function through a thermal switch.

Inlet manifold heater

22 Carburation during cold starting and the warm-up period is grossly inefficient. Much of the fuel condenses on the cold inlet manifold walls and the mixture must be greatly enriched to allow the engine to run properly until it reaches running temperature. Another problem is the lack of heat present in the inlet manifold or cylinder head to assist in fuel vaporisation. When an electrical heater is fitted to the inlet manifold, it quickly generates a large amount of heat and improves atomisation of the air/fuel mixture during the warm-up period. A thermal switch is usually wired to the supply voltage so that the heater is switched off at a pre-determined temperature.

23 The inlet manifold heater is sometimes called a hedgehog because of its distinctive shape *(see illustration)*. It functions on the positive temperature coefficient (PTC) principle. As the temperature rises, the heater resistance also rises.

24 The voltage supply to the inlet manifold heater is usually made through a relay. When the thermal switch is closed, the relay earth connection is made and the relay is triggered. As the engine coolant temperature rises, the thermal switch opens, the earth to the relay is cut and the relay opens to cut off the voltage supply to the manifold heater.

Throttle body heater

25 A throttle body heater may be used to prevent carburettor icing. This may take the form of a coolant-heated channel or an electrical heater. When an electrical heater is used, it quickly warms the carburettor throttle body to about 45°C. Like the inlet manifold heater, it functions on the positive temperature coefficient (PTC) principle. As the temperature rises, the heater resistance also rises *(see illustration)*.

Catalytic converter

26 No matter how efficient the engine, a certain amount of noxious emissions are produced from the exhaust pipe. The three main pollutants that are health-threatening are carbon monoxide (CO), unburnt hydrocarbons (HC) and oxides of nitrogen (NOx). An effective method of meeting anti-pollution regulations and reducing the emissions of these gases is with the aid of a catalytic converter. The converter is fitted into the exhaust system and acts as an additional combustion unit.

27 The catalytic converter consists of a ceramic element with a honeycomb of about 400 cells to the square inch. The element is coated with a rough-surfaced washcoat and this is fired in a kiln to give a total surface area of approximately one to two football pitches (depending upon the size of the converter). A very thin layer of precious metals such as platinum, palladium or rhodium is applied to the washcoat.

28 A minimum temperature of 300°C is required for the catalyst to start to work. As the temperature in the exhaust exceeds 300°C and the carbon monoxide and hydrocarbons come into contact with the precious metals, oxidation occurs. The carbon monoxide becomes carbon dioxide and the hydrocarbons are burned to form more carbon dioxide and water. As the oxides of nitrogen contact rhodium, the oxygen is stripped and harmless nitrogen is produced.

29 The type of converter fitted to a carburettor-controlled engine could be a 2-way or 3-way converter. The 2-way converter catalyses carbon monoxide and hydrocarbons in open loop mode. The 3-way converter catalyses carbon monoxide, hydrocarbons and oxides of nitrogen, in either open loop mode or under closed loop control.

30 An open loop 2- or 3-way converter could be fitted to a vehicle as an aftermarket option. It catalyses the appropriate gases and has about a 50% effect on reduction of emissions.

31 The closed loop 3-way converter has about a 90% conversion rate. The reason for the much higher percentage is that the controlled loop keeps the AFR at the carburettor very close to 14.7:1 and the converter thus works more efficiently.

Lambda

32 The air/fuel mixture ratio (AFR) for almost perfect combustion and at which the least amount of noxious gases are released into the atmosphere, is known as the stoichiometric point. This ratio is 14.7:1 air/fuel by weight and it is also called Lambda = 1.

33 An electronic control unit (ECU) controls the air supply of the carburettor so that the correct AFR is obtained according to speed and load. During the engine operating cycle, varying amounts of fuel and air are drawn into each cylinder. Once combustion is completed, the exhaust fumes will be expelled into the exhaust system. By measuring the amount of oxygen (air) that is left in the exhaust after combustion, it can immediately be seen how near combustion is to Lambda = 1. The oxygen (or Lambda) sensor measures a deficit or surplus of air to combustion (weak or rich mixture) and sends this signal back to the ECU, which instantaneously adjusts the air supply. By controlling the engine electronically so that the air/fuel ratio is always at the stoichiometric point, almost perfect combustion will always be achieved. This gives the catalytic converter less work to do and it will last longer. An engine so controlled is said to be under closed loop control.

Tamperproofing

34 Modern carburettors are fitted with some form of tamperproofing. The purpose is to

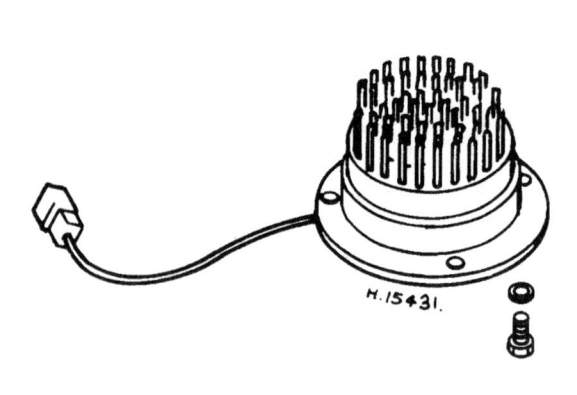

Typical inlet manifold heater

Throttle body heater
1 Heater element 2 Electrical connector

An introduction to the carburettor

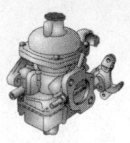

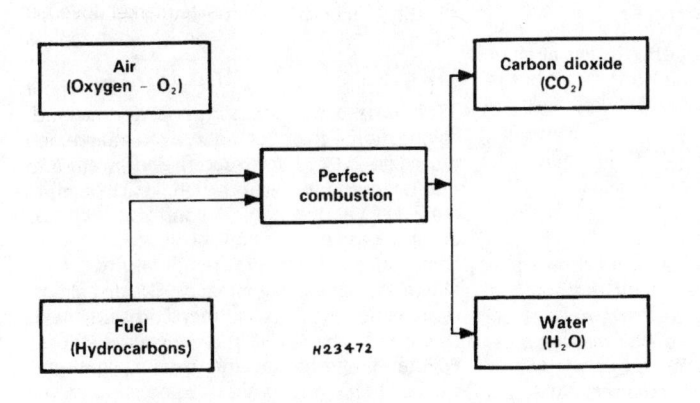

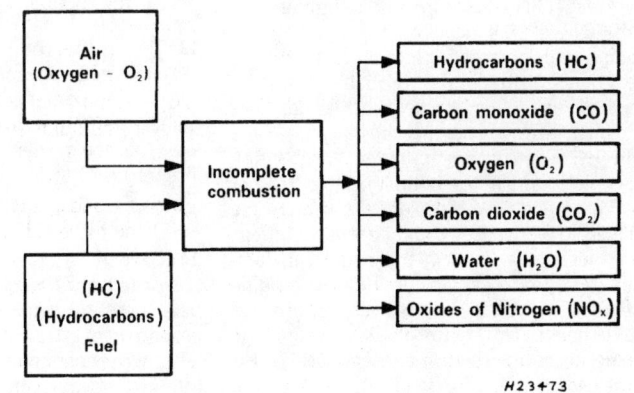

Combustion process in an "ideal" engine

Combustion process in a typical petrol engine

prevent unauthorised tampering with adjustment screws so that control over emissions is kept within certain specifications. The idle mixture control screw is either sealed or is rendered inoperative without use of a special tool. In carburettors with air bypass outlets, the throttle plate angle (stop) screw is often sealed. Other carburettor controls, such as the fast idle adjustment screw, may also be sealed.

10 Gas analysis

Combustion

1 Air is a mixture of approximately 80% nitrogen and 20% oxygen. The compounds which make up petrol are called hydrocarbons and are a mixture of about 15% hydrogen and 85% carbon.
2 If all the petrol was completely burnt during the combustion process, the oxygen (O_2) would combine with carbon to form carbon dioxide (CO_2) and with the hydrogen to form water (H_2O).
3 The ideal engine would thus breathe in a perfect mixture of fuel and air, and exhaust carbon dioxide and water *(see illustration)*.
4 Unfortunately, the ideal engine is non-existent and, for a number of reasons, incomplete combustion occurs in all engines to a greater or lesser degree *(see illustration)*. The engine will exhaust varying quantities of unburnt hydrocarbons (HC), carbon monoxide (CO), carbon dioxide (CO_2), oxides of nitrogen (NOx), water (H_2O) and oxygen (O_2). The carbon dioxide, oxygen and water are harmless but the unburnt hydrocarbons, carbon monoxide and oxides of nitrogen are pollutants of the atmosphere. An engine that is less efficient will exhaust a greater volume of the more harmful pollutants.

Stoichiometric ratio

5 The optimum (or stoichiometric) mixture strength at which fuel burns most efficiently is expressed as an AFR of approximately 14.7 parts of air to 1 part of fuel, by weight. This is the point where HC and CO are at their lowest levels and CO_2 is at its highest level.

Carbon monoxide (CO)

6 Carbon monoxide is poisonous and is formed during partial burning of the fuel due to a lack of oxygen. The amount of CO produced is inversely proportional to the AFR (the less fuel, the lower the CO level) *(see illustration)*.
7 A high proportion of CO in the exhaust would indicate too little oxygen, causing a rich fuel mixture.
8 A very low proportion of CO in the exhaust would indicate too much oxygen or air in the AFR. It could also indicate a mechanical or ignition fault. Where poor combustion, or even none at all, exists in a cylinder, the CO level from that cylinder will be reduced. The total CO level in the exhaust will also be reduced.
9 In conclusion, if there is no combustion then there can be no CO. The exhaust CO level is used as an indicator of mixture strength but this can only be accurate when the engine is mechanically sound and the ignition system fault-free.

Hydrocarbons (HC)

10 The level of HC in the exhaust signifies the general efficiency of the engine and how well the AFR is maintained.
11 Petrol is composed of almost-pure hydrocarbons. In exhaust gas analysis, HC is the amount of fuel remaining after combustion. A high level of hydrocarbons would be due to unburnt or partly-burnt fuel.

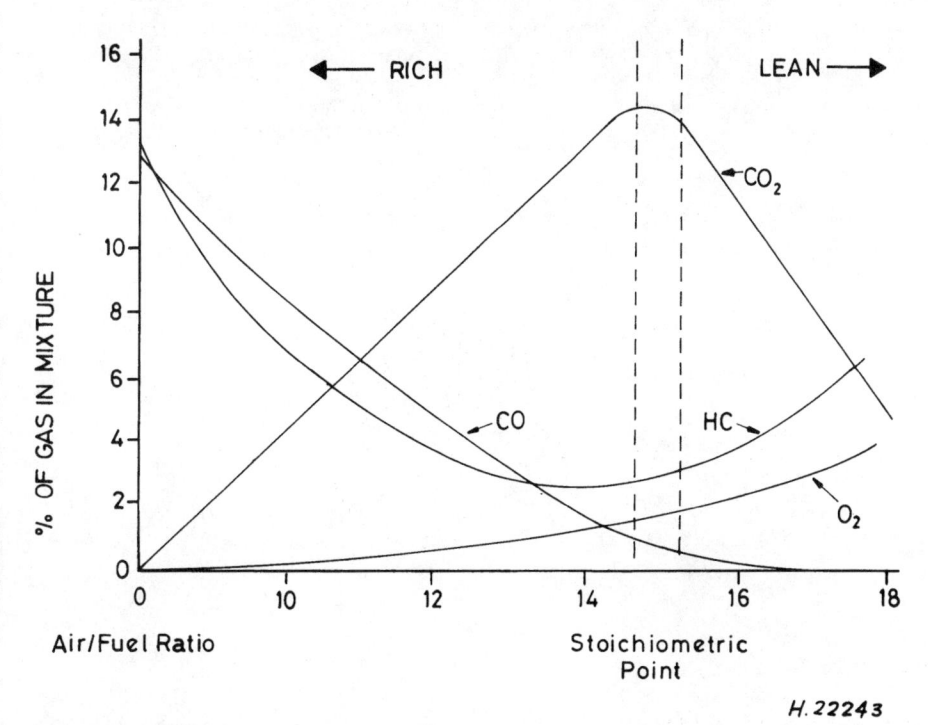

Effect of AFR on exhaust gas composition

12 A high HC level normally accompanies a high CO level (AFR incorrect). In fact, a high HC reading with normal CO levels would indicate that the CO reading is probably fictitious. However, an ignition problem such as defective plugs, HT leads or incorrect timing can cause a high HC level. If one cylinder is not firing properly (or at all), the air/fuel mixture will not be burned and will go straight out through the exhaust. Other causes could be a vacuum leak or a mechanical fault in the engine. In fact, anything that causes inefficient engine operation will release excess hydrocarbons into the exhaust. No matter how efficient the engine, there will always be a small level of HC in the exhaust.

Carbon dioxide (CO_2)

13 This is the product of an efficient engine. CO_2 is directly proportional to the AFR but is inversely proportional to CO. The less fuel, the higher the CO_2. When HC and CO levels are low, the percentage of CO_2 in the exhaust is likely to be 13 to 15%.

Oxygen (O_2)

14 Oxygen should be almost completely consumed during combustion if the AFR has been properly maintained. However, a small proportion of oxygen (0.5 to 2%) will always be left after proper combustion. Too much or too little would indicate an incorrect AFR, an ignition or mechanical problem, or an exhaust leak.

Oxides of nitrogen (NOx)

15 NOx is a poisonous gas formed in the combustion chamber at a temperature exceeding 2500°C. It is exacerbated by an AFR that is close to, or weaker than, stoichiometric (14.7:1). Various engine controls, such as exhaust gas recirculation, are used to lower combustion chamber temperatures and minimise NOx emissions. Exhaust gas recirculation (EGR) is the recycling of a small amount of exhaust gas into the inlet manifold. Pollutants present in the exhaust gas are oxidised to harmless gases by being re-burnt.

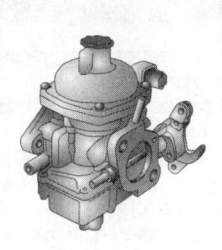

Part B
Working on the carburettor

Contents

Automotive chemicals 6
A place to work 1
Carburettor adjustments 10
Carburettor identification 7
Carburettor removal and refitting 8
Carburettor servicing 9
Fasteners 3
Gasket sealing surfaces 4
Hose replacement 5
Tool selection and care 2

1 A place to work

1 Some form of suitable working area is essential whenever a vehicle component is to be serviced. Any dismantling of a component should be done on a clean, flat workbench or table at a comfortable working height. When servicing carburettors, special care must be taken to ensure that the work surface remains clean at all times and the most satisfactory way to ensure this is to have a number of sheets of clean paper upon which to work, replacing each one as it becomes contaminated.
2 The working area must be well lit to ensure that all areas of the component being serviced are readily visible. Carburettors in particular have many small component parts which can be easily misplaced. A strong light will also be required for inspecting component parts, a desk lamp is ideal.
3 Gather together a selection of clean containers in which to place component parts as they are removed. Also gather together a supply of clean, lint-free rags.
4 A clean dry storage space is also required for tools, as well as for any lubricants, seals, cleaning fluids and so on.

2 Tool selection and care

General selection

1 A selection of good quality tools is a fundamental requirement for anyone contemplating maintenance of a carburettor. For the person who does not possess any tools, their purchase will prove expensive, offsetting some of the savings made by doing-it-yourself. However, provided that the tools purchased meet the relevant national safety standards and are of good quality, they will last for many years and prove an extremely worthwhile investment.
2 The experienced do-it-yourselfer will have a tool kit good enough for most carburettor maintenance procedures. To help the average person to decide which tools are needed to carry out the various tasks detailed in this manual, we have compiled the following list:
3 When buying tools, we recommend the purchase of combination spanners (ring one end, open-ended the other). Although more expensive than the open-ended type, they do give the advantages of both types of spanner. Also included in this list is a set of sockets. Although these are expensive, they will be found invaluable as they are so versatile, particularly if various drives are included in the set. If you cannot afford a socket set, even

B•1

Chapter B

bought piecemeal, then inexpensive tubular box spanners are a useful alternative.

Set of metric combination spanners
Set of metric combination sockets (or box spanners)
Reversible ratchet drive (for use with sockets)
Extension piece, 250 mm (for use with sockets)
Screwdrivers:
 Flat blade - narrow (electrician's) type
 Flat blade - approx. 100 mm long x 6 mm dia.
 Cross blade - approx. 100 mm long x 6 mm dia.
Pliers:
 Standard
 Long-nosed
 Side cutters
 Circlip
Hammers:
 Ball pein
 Soft-faced
Set of Allen keys
Set of feeler blades
Set of twist drills
Steel rule or straight-edge
Micrometer and/or vernier calipers
Scriber
Scraper
Hacksaw (junior)
Fine emery paper
Wire brush (small, fine)
Carburettor cleaning agent
Container (for cleaning carburettor)

4 For practically all tools, a tool factor is the best source, since he will have a very comprehensive range compared with the average garage or accessory shop. Having said that, accessory shops often offer excellent quality tools at discount prices, so it pays to shop around.

5 Remember, you do not have to buy the most expensive items on the shelf but it is always advisable to steer clear of the very cheap tools. There are plenty of good tools around at reasonable prices but always aim to purchase items which meet the relevant national safety standards. If in doubt, ask the proprietor or manager of the shop for advice before making a purchase.

Carburettor special tools

6 The following is a list of special tools that will make carburettor work easier. The tools listed are not absolutely essential and much of the work can be attempted without them. The list is not exhaustive:

Vacuum pump
Vacuum gauge
Temperature gauge
Jet keys
Gas analyser with CO (and optionally HC) testing facilities
Float level gauges
Multimeter (suitable for ECU testing)
Test light
Twin carburettor synchronising tool (synchrometer)
Throttle angle setting tool
Venturi extractor (Weber)

7 Suppliers of many of these special tools are: Webcon UK Ltd., Sunbury, Middlesex; Uro Automotive Ltd., Birmingham; Sykes-Pickavant Ltd., Lytham St. Annes, Lancs.

8 Carburettor importers have a network of carburettor dealers and carburettor specialists nationwide. A greater expertise in dealing with carburettor faults, and a wider range of spare parts, is likely to be found from a carburettor specialist than from the manufacturer of the vehicle to which a particular carburettor may be fitted.

Tool care

9 Having purchased tools, it is necessary to keep them in a clean and serviceable condition. After use, always wipe off any dirt, grease and metal particles using a clean, dry cloth, before putting the tools away. Never leave them lying around after they have been used. A simple tool rack for items such as screwdrivers and pliers is a good idea. Store all spanners and sockets in a box or toolroll. Any measuring instruments, gauges, meters, etc., must be carefully stored where they cannot be damaged or become rusty.

10 Take a little care when tools are used. Hammer heads inevitably become marked and screwdrivers lose the keen edge on their blades from time to time. A little timely attention with emery cloth or a file will soon restore items like this to a good serviceable finish.

3 Fasteners

1 Seized nuts, bolts and screws can be a common occurrence where corrosion has set in on a carburettor. The use of penetrating oil or releasing fluid will often overcome seizure if the offending item is soaked for a while before attempting to release it. The use of an impact driver may also provide a means of releasing such stubborn fasteners, when used in conjunction with the appropriate screwdriver bit or socket, but be careful as carburettor casings are fragile.

2 Studs can be removed by locking two nuts together on the threaded part and then using a spanner on the lower nut to unscrew the stud. Studs or bolts which have broken off below the surface of the component into which they are threaded can sometimes be removed using a proprietary stud extractor.

3 Always ensure that a blind tapped hole is completely free from oil, grease, water or any other fluid before installing a bolt or stud. Failure to do this can cause the housing to crack due to the hydraulic action of the bolt or stud as it is screwed in.

4 When tightening a castellated nut to accept a split pin, tighten the nut to the specified torque, where applicable, and then tighten further to the next split pin hole. Never slacken the nut to align the split pin hole, unless stated in the repair procedure.

5 When checking or retightening a nut or bolt to a specified torque setting, slacken the nut or bolt by a quarter of a turn and then retighten to the specified setting.

6 Any fastener which will rotate against a component or housing in the course of tightening should always have a washer between it and the relevant component or housing. Spring or split washers should always be renewed, as should locktabs.

7 Self-locking nuts tend to lose their effectiveness after long periods of use and in such cases, should be renewed as a matter of course.

8 Split pins must always be replaced with new ones of the correct size for the hole in which they fit.

9 When thread-locking compound is found on the threads of a fastener which is to be re-used, it should be cleaned off with a wire brush and solvent, and fresh compound applied on reassembly.

4 Gasket sealing surfaces

1 When separating a carburettor at its mating faces, never insert a screwdriver or similar implement into the joint between the faces in order to prise them apart. This can cause severe damage to the soft alloy from which the carburettor casing is made. Separation is usually achieved by carefully tapping along the joint with a soft-faced hammer in order to break the seal. However, note that this method may not be suitable where dowels are used for component location.

2 Where a gasket is used between mating faces, ensure that it is renewed on reassembly and fit it dry unless otherwise stated in the repair procedure. Ensure that the mating faces are clean and dry, with all traces of old gasket removed. When cleaning a joint face, use a tool which is not likely to score or damage the face and remove any burrs or nicks with an oilstone or fine file.

5 Hose replacement

1 Before disconnecting any air or fuel hose fitted to the carburettor, note the fitted position and mark each hose for correct connection during reassembly.

2 Remember that petrol is highly flammable. Never smoke or have any kind of naked flame around when disconnecting a hose. Always disconnect the battery earth terminal. A spark caused by an electrical short-circuit, by two metal surfaces contacting each other, by careless use of tools, or even by static electricity built up in your body under certain conditions, can ignite petrol vapour.

3 It is recommended that a fire extinguisher of a type suitable for fuel fires is kept handy when disconnecting any fuel hose.

4 If a hose is secured with a crimp-type clip, then the crimp must be cut away and a new hose clip used on reassembly. To cut the crimp, use a pair of side cutters.

5 Particular care should be taken when disconnecting a fuel hose, to ensure that petrol

Working on the carburettor

does not pour out onto a hot component. Always disconnect a fuel hose slowly and hold a cloth or suitable container under the joint to catch any fuel spillage.

6 Remember that an air hose may well contain fuel vapour so treat it as you would a fuel hose with regard to fire precautions.

7 When reconnecting any hose, ensure that all connections are securely made and new securing clips fitted where necessary.

6 Automotive chemicals

1 When disposing of fuel or used cleaning solvents, etc, give due consideration to any detrimental environmental effects. Do not, for instance, pour any of the above liquids down drains into the general sewage system, or onto the ground to soak away. Many local council refuse tips provide a facility for waste oil disposal, as do some garages. If none of these facilities are available, consult your local Environmental Health Department, or the National Rivers Authority, for further advice.

7 Carburettor identification

1 Before any work is carried out on a carburettor, it should first be identified. This sounds rather obvious but there are many engineers who have attempted to adjust a carburettor to the wrong specifications, or went to obtain spares for a Weber when a Solex was fitted.

2 The calibration of the carburettor is often altered as engine specification changes. Other carburettor modifications occur in the course of production and certain engines may be fitted with an alternative carburettor from a different manufacturer. It is important, therefore, that the correct type and specification of carburettor is identified at the outset.

Pierburg identification markings on carburettor body

Pierburg and Solex

3 On Pierburg and German Solex carburettors, the name will be stamped upon the upper and main bodies. The manufacturer identification code may be stamped on a metallic tag attached to the cover by an upper body fixing screw, or on a corner of the carburettor main body *(see illustrations)*.

4 On French Solex carburettors, the Solex identification code is stamped on a metallic tag attached to the cover by an upper body fixing screw *(see illustration)*. The tag will quote the Solex part number, vehicle manufacturer part number and identify the carburettor type. Later carburettors may have the following information stamped upon the carburettor body:

12788	Solex part number
34 PBISA 5	Carburettor type
PEU A 110	Vehicle manufacturer part number

5 Unfortunately, metal tags frequently become lost. In most cases, the Solex or Pierburg identity stamp will be sufficient to identify the carburettor but if not, carry out the following procedures:

a) Measure the carburettor throttle plate size *(see illustration)*. The throttle plate size is frequently used to describe the carburettor model. For example, 28/30 2E2 is a twin venturi carburettor with a primary throttle plate size of 28 mm and a secondary throttle plate size of 30 mm. A marking 32 DIS

Pierburg identification tag

Solex (French) identification tag

would describe a single venturi carburettor with a throttle plate size of 32 mm
b) Look for the manufacturer's name stamped upon the carburettor body
c) Compare the shape of the carburettor with any illustrations in the relevant Chapter of this manual
d) Locate and note the date code stamped upon the carburettor body
e) Examine the jets, record their sizes, and compare these figures with the Specifications in the relevant Chapter of this manual. The jet orifice is calibrated in mm. For example, a jet stamped with 230 will have an orifice diameter of 2.3 mm. A set of jet keys can be used to measure the diameter of a particular jet *(see illustration)*.

Measuring the throttle plate diameter

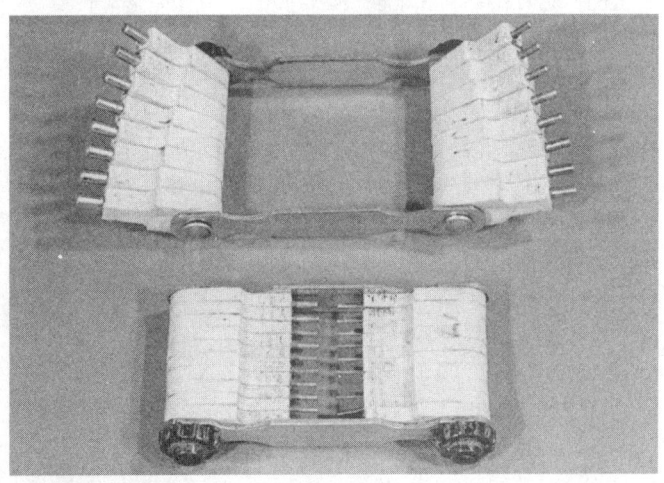

Jet measuring keys

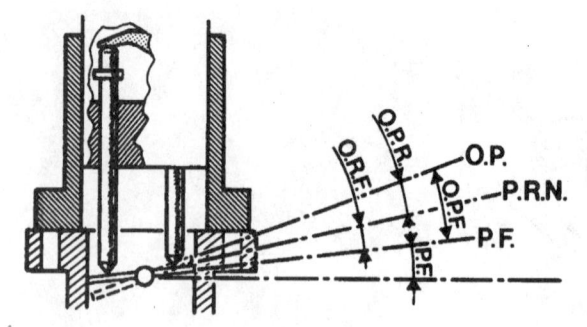

Chapter B

Solex (French) throttle angles

OP	Fast idle position
OPF	Just open to fast idle position
OPR	Idle to fast idle position
ORF	Just open to idle position
PF	Parked throttle position (just open)
PRN	Basic idle position

Date code - Pierburg

6 On Pierburg carburettors, the date code is in the form - year (end digit), followed by the day (number). If, for example, the date code is 6 147, the end digit 6 signifies 1986, and 147 is day number 147 into 1986 (counting from January 1st). Take this information to a Pierburg agent who will be able to identify the exact type from a book of technical sheets.

Date code - French Solex

7 On French Solex carburettors, the date code is in the form - day, month (letter code), year (end digit), carburettor identification code and additional code. If, for example, the code is 12 M 5 02 1, the date of manufacture of this carburettor was 12th November 1985. The month code is denoted by an alphabetical letter, as shown in the following list:

- A January
- B February
- C March
- D April
- E May
- F June
- G July
- H August
- K September
- L October
- M November
- N December

8 The Solex identification code for this carburettor is 13202. This is denoted by the code 02 in this date code and it is specific to this carburettor. No other French Solex carburettor has a suffix code of 02. A Solex application list is required to decode the suffix code and this is available from a French Solex carburettor dealer. The additional code 1 can be disregarded and plays no part in interpretation of the identification codes.

Component identification

9 Solex and Pierburg use a letter-code convention for naming most of the main carburettor components, particularly the jets. These are as follows:

- a   Air correction jet
- g   Idle jet
- Gg Main jet
- i   Accelerator pump jet
- K   Venturi
- P   Needle valve
- s   Emulsion tube

10 A similar convention is used to denote the various stages of choke pull-down:

- a   Choke pull-down (1st stage)
- a1   Choke pull-down (2nd stage)
- a2   Choke pull-down (3rd stage)

11 These letter codes appear in the Specifications for each carburettor type and may also be used in some of the illustration captions.

12 The Specifications for French Solex carburettors include references to the throttle positions. The positions are throttle angles for use with a Solex throttle setting tool and are included where the information is available *(see illustration)*.

Weber

13 Weber carburettors have the model type stamped upon the base flange or on the float chamber body *(see illustrations)*. Often the vehicle manufacturers will tag the carburettor with their own identification marking. This is usually a metal identity tag stamped with the model number or part number.

14 Where the identity tag has become lost, the Weber identity stamp will usually be sufficient to identify the carburettor but if not, carry out the following procedures:

a) Measure the carburettor throttle plate size. The throttle plate size is frequently used to describe the carburettor model. For example, 30/32 DMTE is a twin venturi carburettor with a primary throttle plate size of 30 mm and a secondary throttle plate size of 32 mm. Similarly, 32 ICEV would describe a single venturi carburettor with a throttle plate size of 32 mm

b) Look for the manufacturer's name stamped upon the carburettor body

c) Compare the shape of the carburettor with any illustrations in the relevant Chapter of this manual

d) Examine the jets, record their sizes, and compare these figures with the Specifications in the relevant Chapter of this manual. The jet orifice is calibrated in mm. For example, a jet stamped with 230 will have an orifice diameter of 2.3 mm. A set of jet keys can be used to measure the diameter of a particular jet.

Ford

Weber and Pierburg

15 Ford place their own identification markings on both Weber and Pierburg carburettors. Identification is stamped onto Pierburg carburettors whereas Weber carburettors are tagged *(see illustrations)*.

Weber identification markings on carburettor base flange

Weber identification markings on carburettor float chamber

Ford and Pierburg identification markings

Ford identification tag on Weber carburettor

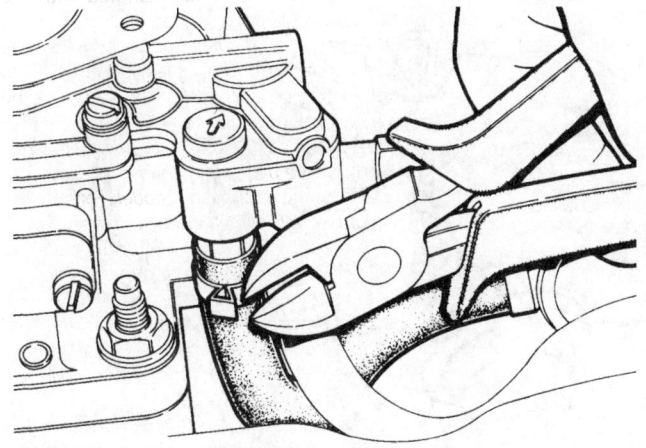

Working on the carburettor

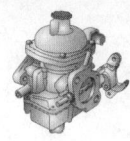

Cutting a crimped type hose clip

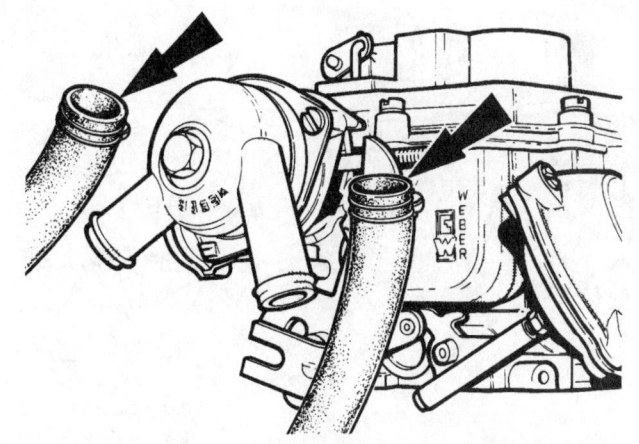

Choke coolant hoses positioned with ends facing upwards

Motorcraft IV
16 The carburettor identification code is stamped on the float chamber body. A manufacturer's date code is stamped on the next line.

Variable Venturi
17 The carburettor identification code is stamped on the float chamber body and a manufacturer's date code stamped on the next line. The choke mounting flange is also stamped with an identification code letter.

All carburettor types
18 Small modifications to the carburettor fitted to a particular vehicle may result in a slight change to the model number. The carburettor listed for a particular vehicle may be one of a number of carburettors fitted within the same lineage. Often these carburettors can be treated as being one and the same, and the calibration will alter very little from one variation to another.

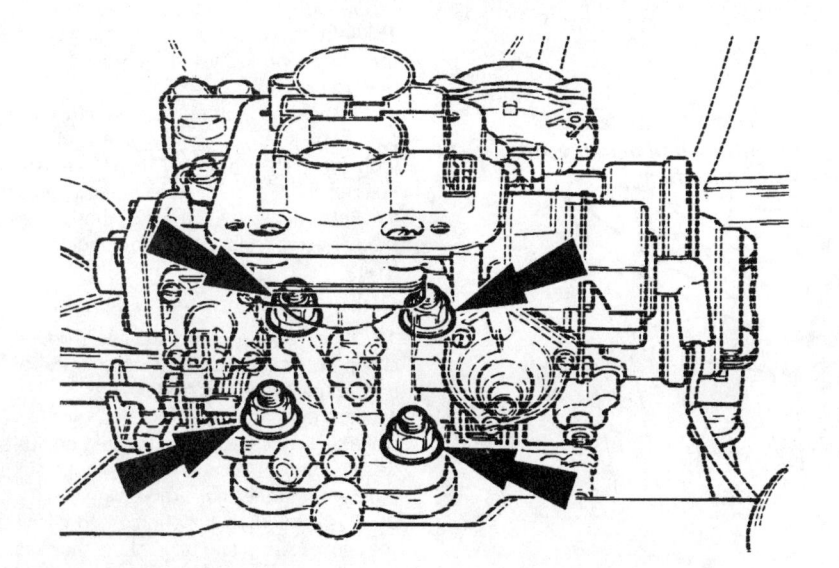

Carburettor retaining nuts

8 Carburettor removal and refitting

Removal
1 Remove the air filter assembly and any connecting vacuum and breather hoses. Note the location of all hoses.
2 Remove the distributor vacuum hose and disconnect the electrical connection to the idle cut-off valve (where fitted).
3 Detach the throttle cable by removing the clip (where fitted) from the carburettor linkage.
4 Disconnect the fuel line and fuel return line (where fitted). Note and mark the hoses for correct connection during reassembly. If a hose is crimped, the crimp must be cut away and a new hose clip used on reassembly *(see illustration)*.

Carburettors with automatic choke
5 Remove the fixing screws that secure the bi-metal coil housing to the choke assembly housing. Note the position of the alignment marks and remove the coil housing complete with heating hoses from the carburettor body. Lay this assembly to one side.
6 Where the bi-metal coil housing is coolant-heated and is to be removed with the carburettor, de-pressurise the cooling system by removing and refitting the radiator cap. Disconnect the two choke coolant hoses and tie them up out of the way, ends facing upwards so that coolant loss is minimised *(see illustration)*.
7 Where the coil is electrically heated, disconnect the electrical supply cable.

Carburettors with manual choke
8 Disconnect the choke cable from the choke lever.

All carburettors
9 Remove the carburettor fixing nuts and washers. In some instances, the fixing nuts may be under the inlet manifold *(see illustration)*.
10 Remove the carburettor from the engine and drain any petrol into a suitable container whilst observing the necessary fire precautions.
11 Insert a rag into the manifold opening to prevent the ingress of foreign matter.

Refitting
12 Clean the carburettor and manifold flange faces of old gasket material. Do not use a gasket jointing compound on the carburettor or manifold flange when refitting the carburettor to the engine. If jointing compound gains entry to the myriad passages and channels that run through the body, the carburettor may easily be ruined and a new one will have to be fitted.
13 Place the carburettor on the manifold with a new base gasket and secure it using the fixing nuts and washers. Do not over-tighten the nuts. The recommended torque setting from most manufacturers is 10 Nm.

Carburettors with automatic choke
14 Where applicable, refit the internal heat

Chapter B

Refitting internal heat shield

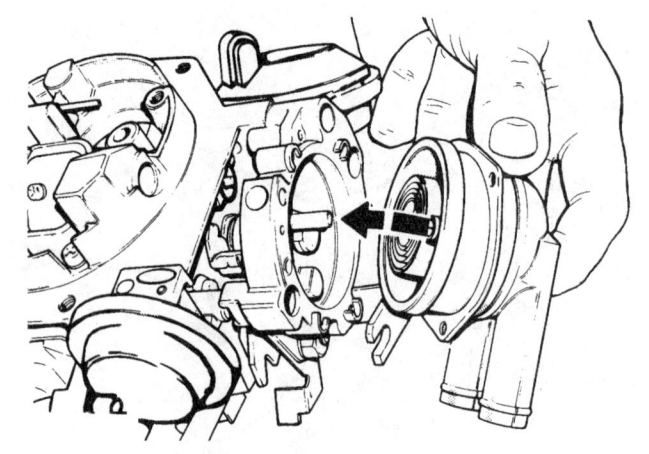

Aligning bi-metal-to-choke lever arm

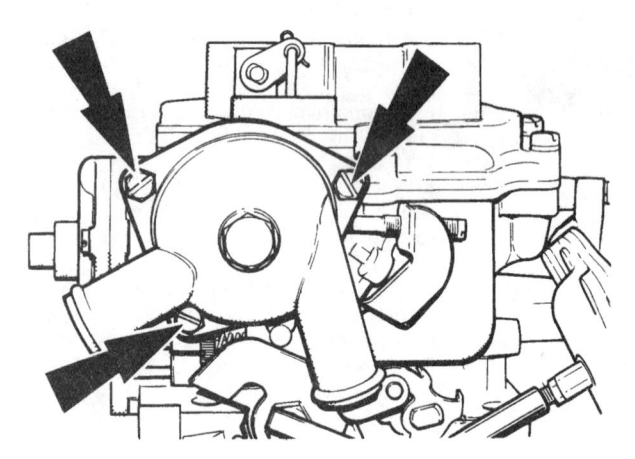

Choke housing securing screws

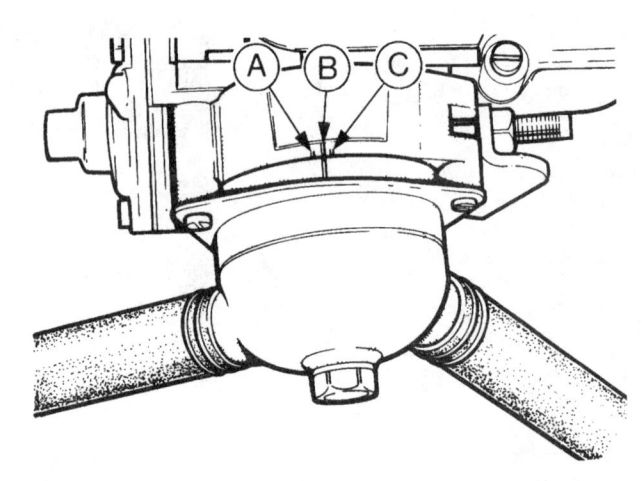

Choke housing alignment marks
A Rich position   B Index mark   C Lean position

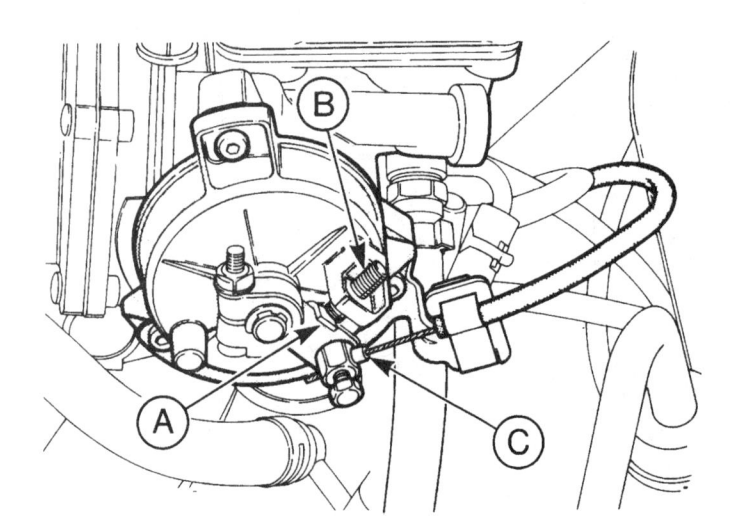

Manual choke assembly
A Choke lever   B Full-choke stop   C Cable in fully-on position

shield and ensure that it is correctly located *(see illustration)*.

15 Refit the bi-metal coil housing, ensuring that the spring locates in the slot of the choke lever *(see illustration)*.

16 Secure the housing loosely with the three screws. Align the cut mark on the bi-metal cover with the correct mark on the choke assembly housing and tighten the screws *(see illustrations)*.

17 Reconnect the coolant hoses (where disconnected) and top up the engine coolant level.

Carburettors with manual choke

18 Slide the inner choke cable through the clamp on the operating lever up to the ferrule and secure it *(see illustration)*.

19 Pull the choke control knob (on the dash panel) fully out and hold in this fully on position. Secure the outer cable to the choke support bracket using the choke cable clip.

20 Push the knob fully home and check that the choke lever is fully off. Pull the choke control knob fully out and check that the lever is fully on.

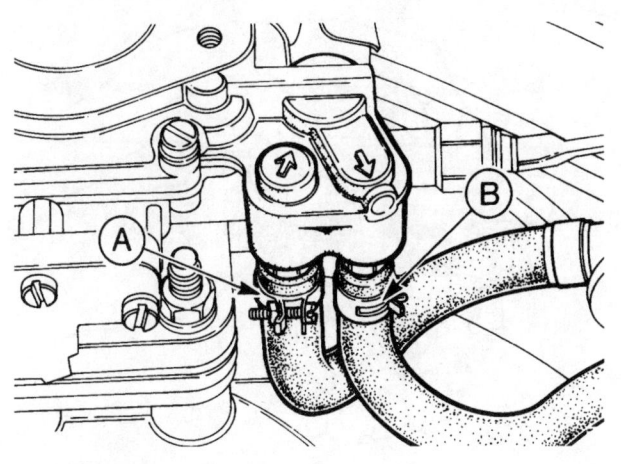

Working on the carburettor

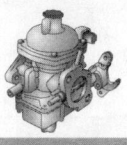

Fuel supply and return pipes
A Fuel supply with screw-and-nut clip
B Fuel return pipe

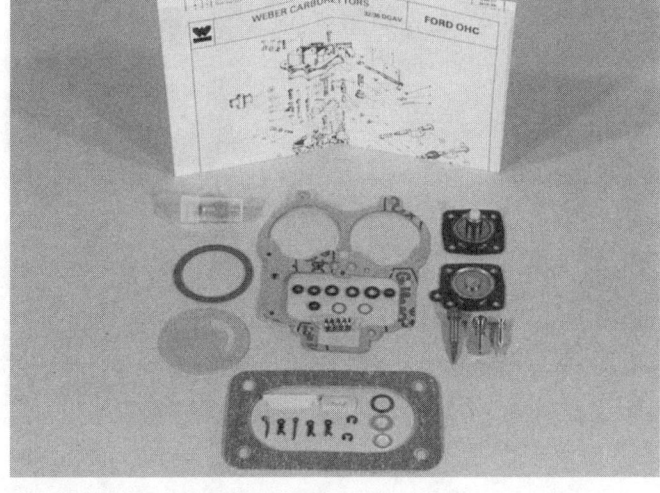

A typical carburettor service kit

All carburettors

21 Reconnect the fuel line and fuel return line (where fitted) to the correct connections and use new hose clips to secure *(see illustration)*.
22 Reconnect the throttle cable and clip and adjust the idle speed adjustment screw so that the throttle is slightly open.
23 Reconnect the idle cut-off valve (where fitted) and the vacuum connection to the distributor.
24 Loosely fit the air filter assembly and any connecting vacuum and breather hoses.
25 If the mixture control screw has been removed, gently screw it fully in until it just seats. From this position, unscrew it three full turns. This will provide an approximate setting to allow the engine to run.
26 Start the engine. It may be a little slow to fire until fuel is pumped into the float chamber. Note whether the choke works satisfactorily, both coming on and going off correctly. However, note that the choke will not work properly until the carburettor idle mixture has been correctly adjusted.
27 Run the engine at idle speed and bring it to normal operating temperature.
28 Adjust the idle speed and mixture.
29 Make other adjustments as necessary to complete. If an automatic choke is fitted, allow the engine to cool completely then restart the engine from cold and check for correct choke operation.
30 Tighten the air filter assembly fixings and check that all connecting hoses are in position.

9 Carburettor servicing

General

1 The text for each carburettor type covered in this manual describes a general carburettor service and not a complete overhaul. There is a limit on how far a service can go on modern carburettors. Many parts are not serviceable or are available only as an assembly.
2 Once the carburettor is removed from the engine, the initial inspection is designed to spot serious faults that would require a new carburettor. Where possible, it is best to make this diagnosis at an early stage so that time is not wasted in servicing the old unit.
3 Before any dismantling (and this includes upper body removal) a set of gaskets or a service kit should be obtained *(see illustration)*. Broken gaskets often result from cover removal because some manufacturers glue the gasket to one or both flanges. An engine will run badly if old and fractured gaskets are re-used.
4 A description of a general carburettor service follows. A number of the procedures will vary according to application. Some of the operations are described here in more detail than in the specific text in the following Chapters. This section should therefore be read in conjunction with the specific Chapter for a particular carburettor type.
5 Carefully lay out the dismantled component parts in the order of removal. Such a logical method is a great aid to reassembly.
6 It is assumed that the carburettor is removed for this service. However, many of the operations can be tackled with the carburettor in place. Where this is undertaken, soak the fuel out of the float chamber using a clean tissue or soft cloth, after removing the upper body assembly.
7 Note the sizes and locations of all jets and emulsion tubes during dismantling, to ensure correct installation into their original positions during assembly.
8 Be very careful when removing any cover as it may house a spring under tension.

Dismantling and inspection

9 Invert the carburettor and check the position of the mixture control screw tip or tips in the outlet channel (only where the tip exits into the throttle bore). If the screw has been forced home, it may have broken and be blocking the idle outlet. Try unscrewing the mixture screw. The tip should move easily in and out of its idle orifice. Renew the carburettor if the mixture screw is broken or if the tip is seized in the idle outlet *(see illustration)*.
10 Use a straight-edge to check for a distorted base flange *(see illustration)*. A warped flange is the result of over-tightening the carburettor mounting bolts or of excess heat. If the flange is not too badly warped, machining may be possible or it could be rubbed on a piece of plate glass with the aid of valve grinding paste. Although this may effect a cure it is very time-

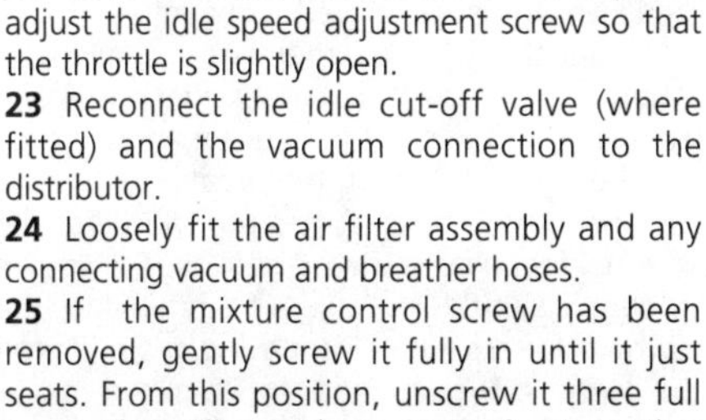

Inspect idle orifice for a seized mixture screw

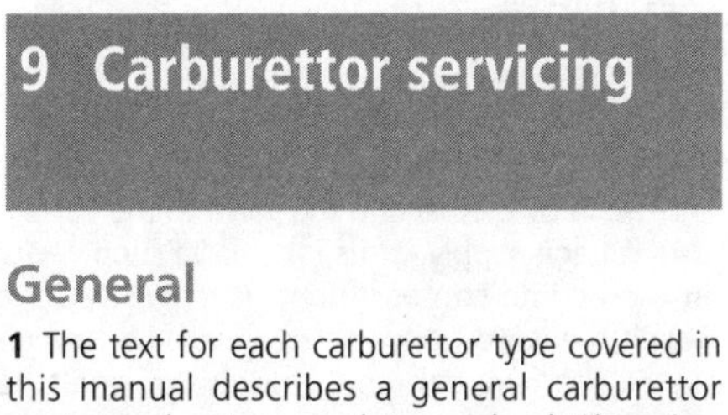

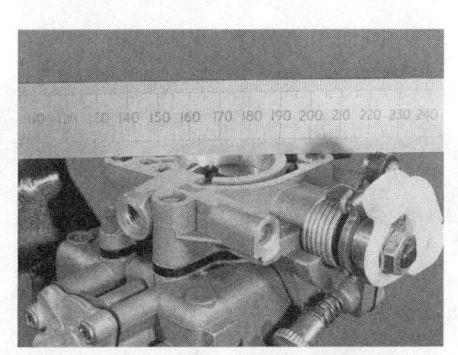

Checking base flange for distortion

B•7

Chapter B

Testing idle cut-off valve

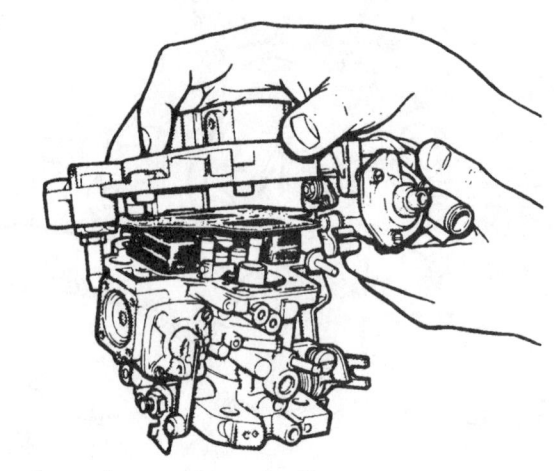

Removing carburettor upper body

consuming. The alternative is to renew the carburettor. Warping of the base flange is unfortunately commonplace and leads to air leaks and poor carburettor operation.

11 Inspect the throttle spindle(s) and plate(s) for movement, excess wear and stickiness. Excess wear is more likely in the softer aluminium throttle shaft bores than in the steel spindle commonly used. A worn body will cause an uneven idle, variation in idle speed, a sticky throttle action and a varying CO level. Where the body is worn, bushes can sometimes be fitted by a specialist carburettor shop. Otherwise, renew the carburettor or (where possible) the throttle body assembly.

12 The forming of a carbon ring where the throttle plate meets the body can cause a rich idle, sticky throttle movement and flat spots. This may afflict either primary or secondary operation in a twin venturi carburettor. What happens is that the throttle plate is now fixed in a higher position. As a result, the progression drillings will no longer draw air to emulsify the idle mixture but will start to discharge fuel at idle.

13 Inspect the carburettor and choke bodies for missing or loose blanking plugs. Look for splits and irreparable damage to the casing. Minor damage can sometimes be repaired with a plastic metal solution. Also check for broken springs, worn throttle and choke linkages and worn fixing screws. Renew all worn components.

14 Inspect the choke spindle, mechanism and linkage for stickiness and wear. Plastic linkages in particular are very prone to breaking.

15 Clean the carburettor body with a good carburettor cleaner and a stiff brush.

16 Remove the idle cut-off valve assembly and clean with carburettor cleaner. Test the plunger operation by connecting the valve to the battery or a voltage supply (or use the valve supply wire in the engine compartment) *(see illustration)*. Touch the valve body to earth with the ignition on. Repeat several times and ensure that the plunger tip advances and retracts cleanly. Renew the valve if the action is faulty or if cleaning does not improve its operation.

17 Remove the screws and detach the carburettor upper body *(see illustration)*. If the top is tight, a gentle tap with a plastic hammer is usually sufficient to free it. On most carburettors the float chamber gasket must be removed with the upper body.

18 Use a straight-edge to check for distorted flanges on all facing surfaces *(see illustration)*. Alternatively, remove the float chamber gasket and place the two faces together. Slight warping will be taken up by the gasket but excessive distortion will be obvious and will necessitate a new carburettor *(see illustration)*. Warping of the facing surfaces is commonplace and leads to poor carburettor operation.

19 Inspect the float chamber for a chalk-coloured flaky substance *(see illustration)*. This is caused by reaction between water and the alloy of the carburettor. If the float chamber is seriously contaminated, it is probable that the internal fuel channels are also clogged. Serious thought should be given to renewing the carburettor because clearing the channels can be very difficult, not to mention time-consuming.

20 Remove the upper body gasket, float, float pin and needle valve assembly *(see illustration)*.

21 Check that the anti-vibration ball (where fitted) is free in the valve end.

22 Check the needle valve tip for wear and ridges. Wear is more likely with the brass needle valve tip than when a viton one is used. Use a viton-tipped replacement when possible.

23 The float should be checked for damage

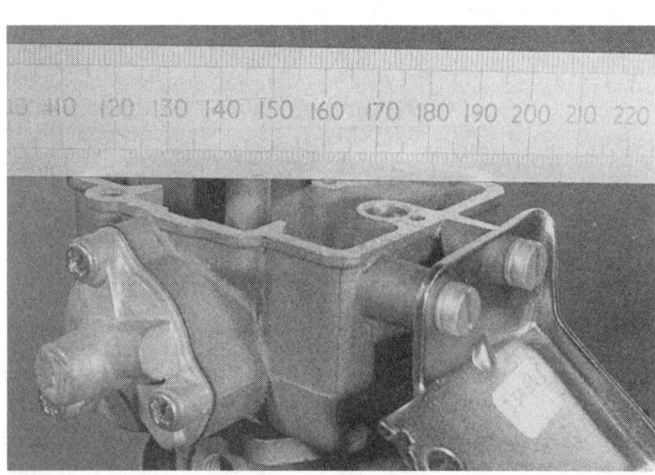

Checking main body upper flange for distortion

Distortion of upper and main body facing surfaces (arrowed)

Working on the carburettor

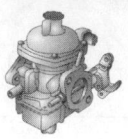

Example of corroded float chamber

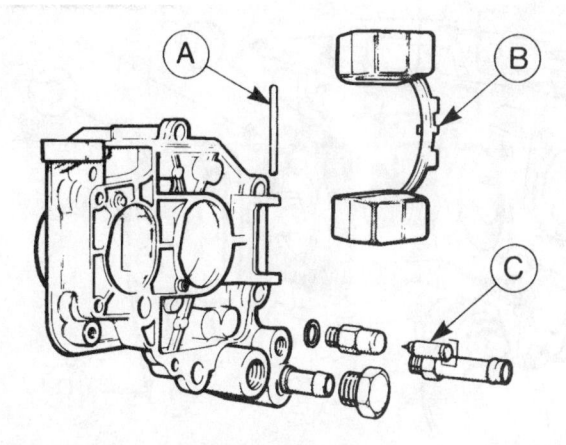

Upper body and float components
A Float retaining pin   B Float   C Needle valve

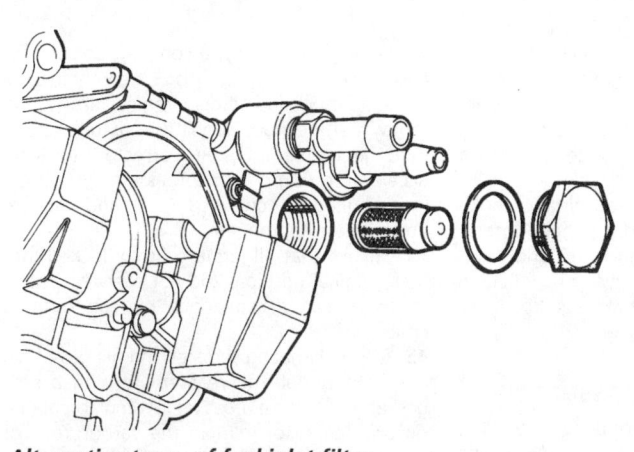

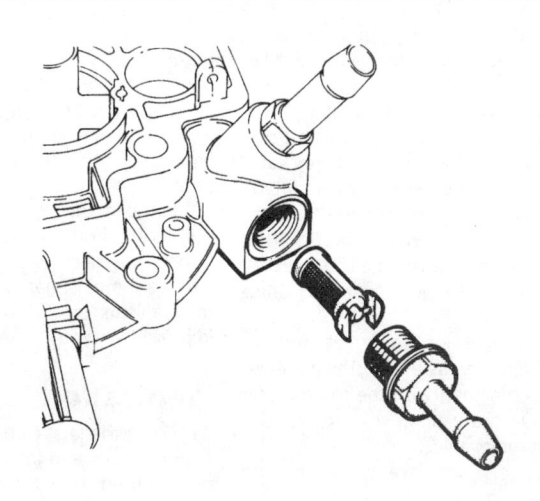

Alternative types of fuel inlet filter

Accelerator pump injector assembly with vernay valve

and for ingress of petrol. Shaking the float will indicate the presence of petrol. Alternatively, submerge the float in water and watch for bubbles. Renew a defective float. Do not attempt to repair a float by soldering as this will result in an increase in weight which could impair float operation.

24 Renew the float pin if it shows signs of wear.

25 Remove the inlet fuel filter and inspect it. Clean the filter chamber of debris and dirt *(see illustration)*.

26 Unscrew the mixture screw and inspect the tip for damage and ridges.

27 Usually, the accelerator pump injector is a push fit in the main carburettor body *(see illustration)*. Carefully prise it from its location and test it by shaking it. No noise from the outlet ball would indicate that the valve is seized.

28 Early Weber carburettors utilised an injector and pump discharge valve. Unscrew the pump discharge valve from the body and remove the valve and the pump injector. Shake the discharge valve. No noise from the outlet ball would indicate that the valve is seized. Check that the lead pellet that seals the valve is present. Pump action will be impaired if the pellet is loose or missing

29 The pump inlet ball in most Weber carburettors is placed in a channel and the position is plugged. Gently shake the carburettor body. No noise from the ball would indicate that the valve is seized. A new carburettor is the only cure.

B•9

Chapter B

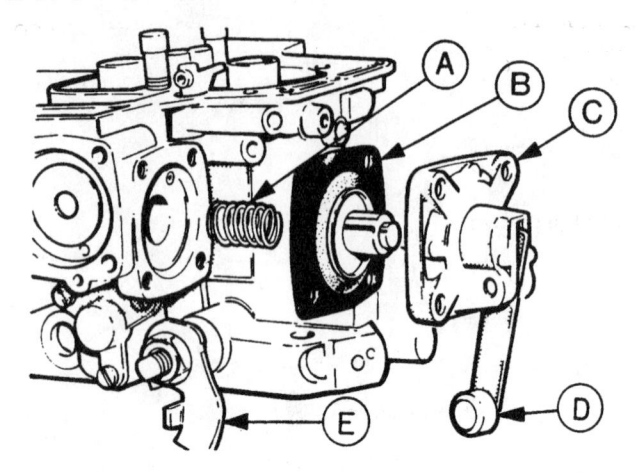

Accelerator pump assembly

A Pump return spring
B Accelerator pump diaphragm
C Accelerator pump housing
D Roller
E Cam

Power valve assembly

A Diaphragm
B Diaphragm return spring
C Cover
D Power valve brass outlet
E Vacuum passage

30 Check the accelerator pump cam and roller for wear *(see illustration)*.

31 Detach the covers to the accelerator pump, anti-stall device, power valve *(see illustration)*, choke pull-down and all other diaphragm-controlled devices, where these items are fitted.

32 Check all diaphragms for fatigue, damage and porosity. Where porosity occurs, the diaphragm may appear undamaged but fuel will pass through the diaphragm material to cause rich running.

33 Remove the idle jet, main jet and air corrector/emulsion tube assembly. The emulsion tube is usually combined with the air corrector jet and placed into a well. In some cases, this assembly is not removable.

34 Check all jets for ovality, wear and blockages.

35 Check that the channel from the float chamber into the emulsion tube well is clear.

36 Check the jet calibration against the Specifications. It is possible that the wrong size jets may have been fitted during the last overhaul.

37 Where fitted, the outlet ball in the brass power valve assembly should seal the outlet. Depress and release the ball with a small screwdriver and it should move smoothly in and out. Renew the power valve if defective. In some carburettors, the brass outlet for the power valve is cast into the body and is not removable. If defective, a new carburettor is the only cure.

38 Remove the screws and separate the carburettor main body and throttle body assemblies (where these are separate assemblies). The throttle body can be renewed separately if the spindles or throttle bores are worn.

39 On Weber carburettors, remove the primary and secondary auxiliary venturis from the upper body where necessary. Weber provide an extractor tool for removing these items if required *(see illustration)*. Check that the primary and secondary auxiliary venturis are not loose in the main body, since loose venturis are a source of uneven running. If a venturi is loose, knurl the mating flanges with a file to ensure a tight fit.

40 Remove the manual or automatic choke pull-down housing assembly (where fitted). Inspect the mechanism for stickiness and wear. Use a maintenance spray on sticking mechanisms and if the stickiness does not improve, renew the assembly.

Preparation for reassembly

41 Clean the jets, carburettor body assemblies, float chamber and internal channels. An air line may be used to clear the internal channels once the carburettor is dismantled.

> **Warning:** *If high-pressure air is directed into the channels and passages of a carburettor with the diaphragms still in place, diaphragm damage may result. Take care also that loose components are not blasted away with the upper body removed. Spraying carburettor cleaner into all of the channels and passages in the carburettor body will often clear them of gum and dirt.*

42 Carefully inspect and clear all the tiny air bleeds and outlets in the upper body. Trace the path of each internal channel and passage, then squirt carburettor cleaner into one end of the channel and check that it comes out of the outlet.

43 During reassembly, a complete set of new gaskets should be fitted. Also renew the needle valve, float pin and all diaphragms. Inspect and renew (where necessary) the mixture screw, main jets, idle jets, air corrector jets and accelerator pump injector assembly. Renew worn linkages, screws, springs and vacuum hoses where appropriate.

44 Ensure that all jets are firmly locked into their original positions (do not over-tighten). A loose jet can cause a rich or lean running condition.

45 Clean all mating surfaces and flanges of old gasket material and reassemble with a new gasket. Do not use a gasket jointing compound on any flange or joint in the carburettor, or when refitting the carburettor to the engine. If jointing compound gains entry to the myriad passages and channels that run through the body, the carburettor may easily be ruined and a new one will have to be fitted.

46 Ensure that all housings are positioned with their air and fuel routes correctly aligned.

Reassembly

47 Place the choke pull-down housing onto the carburettor body, with a new gasket or seal (where fitted).

Weber auxiliary venturi extractor tool

Working on the carburettor

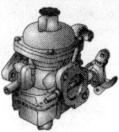

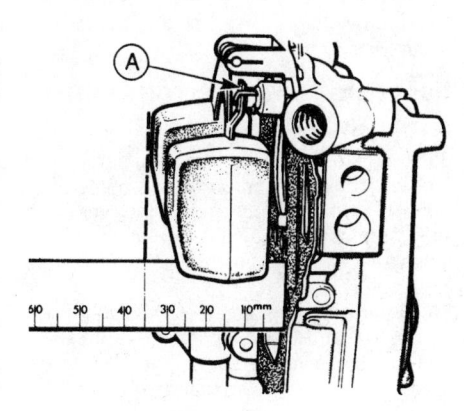

Checking the float level
A Adjusting tag

48 Check that the secondary throttle plate is fully closed. The adjustment screw should not normally be used to alter the throttle plate position. However, if necessary, it can be adjusted so that the plate is open just sufficiently to prevent its seizure in the throttle body. Where a throttle setting gauge is available, use it to set the throttle angle.

49 Similarly, in carburettors with a bypass idle system and a locked primary throttle plate angle, the adjustment screw should not normally be used to alter the throttle plate position. However, if necessary, it can be adjusted so that the plate is open just sufficient to prevent seizure in the throttle body. Where a throttle setting gauge is available, use it to set the throttle angle. Otherwise, a method of setting the throttle angle with the engine running is detailed in the appropriate carburettor Chapter.

50 Refit all diaphragm and cover assemblies and secure with the screws. Ensure that all springs are correctly located.

51 Screw all jets into their original locations (do not transpose jets).

52 Refit the idle cut-off valve (where fitted).

53 Refit the accelerator pump injector and pump inlet valve.

54 Refit the idle mixture and bypass control screws. Turn each screw in gently until it just seats, then unscrew three full turns. This will provide an approximate setting to allow the engine to be started. Note that the threads in the carburettor body are very fine and care should be taken that the mixture screw is not entered cross-threaded. Damage to the threads will result in a new carburettor body being required.

55 Clean or renew the fuel filter then refit the inlet tube.

56 Renew the float chamber gasket and locate in position on the upper body.

57 Renew the needle valve assembly, using a new sealing washer. Ensure that it is firmly locked into position (do not over-tighten).

58 Refit the float and secure with the float pin.

59 Adjust the float level. Bend the float tag and not the arm when making adjustments *(see illustration)*. In some instances, the float level is not adjustable. Where this is the case, the float should be weighed. A correct float weight normally results in a correct level.

60 Refit the upper body to the main body and secure with the fixing screws. Tighten the screws progressively and evenly to avoid distortion of body or cover. Ensure that the carburettor earth strap (where fitted), is properly secured.

61 Reconnect the choke pull-down hose (where fitted).

62 Reconnect the choke linkage and ensure that the choke flap and choke linkage move smoothly and progressively.

63 Adjust the choke fast idle and choke pull-down, then make other adjustments as necessary.

64 Refit the carburettor to the engine.

65 Always adjust the idle speed and mixture after any work has been carried out on the carburettor, preferably with the aid of a CO meter.

10 Carburettor adjustments

Adjustment preconditions

1 Correct setting of the idle speed and mixture is particularly important for reasons of economy and emission control. These adjustments should be the final adjustments in any engine tuning operation. To ensure maximum accuracy, the following points should be observed before the idle speed and mixture are set.

2 Warm the engine thoroughly before adjustment. About ten minutes at fast idle if starting from cold is usually sufficient, although a ten-minute drive would be better. Note that if other tuning tasks have been carried out, or the ambient temperature is very high, the engine may become overheated. This will cause the fuel to flow more readily and the CO reading may become fictitiously high. If the CO is set under these conditions, it will be incorrect. Once the engine has cooled and is restarted (and the fuel temperature has returned to normal), the CO will become too lean.

3 As a further guide, the oil temperature should be as specified by the manufacturer (usually 80 to 90°C), to avoid the problems outlined above.

4 Isolate the electric fan if there is a danger of it operating during idle adjustment and switch off all other electrical loads.

5 Refer to the Special Conditions heading in the Specifications for the particular carburettor being worked on. Where the idle speed is to be set with the engine cooling fan in operation, run the engine until the fan operates. Disconnect the connector plug to the fan sensor and temporarily bridge the plug terminals with a piece of wire *(see illustration)*. Switch on the headlights (or other specified electrical load) where this is required.

6 Connect a tachometer and CO meter to the vehicle. Use an exhaust gas analyser capable of measuring HC emissions, if available.

7 When adjustment is made with a new, tight engine, readjustment will be required once the engine is fully run-in.

8 Ensure that the valve clearances are correctly adjusted.

9 The engine must be free from mechanical or ignition faults.

10 Spark plugs of the correct type and heat range must be fitted and the gaps correctly set.

11 The dwell angle and ignition timing must be correctly set for the grade of petrol in use.

12 The air filter must be in place and all vacuum and breather hoses connected (unless otherwise noted). For convenience, the air filter assembly may be unbolted and loosely placed upon the carburettor while adjustments are made. Visually inspect the air filter body and element for cleanliness.

13 The exhaust system must be free from leaks. An exhaust leak will draw oxygen into the system which will dilute the CO in the exhaust pipe, and produce a false (lean) reading.

14 The air intake system must be free from vacuum leaks.

15 The choke flap must be fully open (no choke).

16 The throttle linkage and cable must be correctly adjusted and free from binding.

17 The crankcase breather system must be operating correctly. Check all breather pipes for cleanliness and ensure that all calibrated orifices in the inlet manifold or breather pipe are clear and unplugged. Note that blocked breather systems are the single most common reason for incorrectly-adjusted carburettors.

18 When all adjustments are complete, disconnect the breather hose from the air filter. If the CO level decreases by more than 1 to 1.5%, change the sump oil. If the CO level still decreases after an oil change, suspect worn or sticking piston rings.

19 In some instances, the breather hose should be disconnected from the air filter, and the opening in the air filter plugged during adjustment. Reconnect the breather hose after adjustment is completed. If the CO level increases by more than 1 to 1.5% on

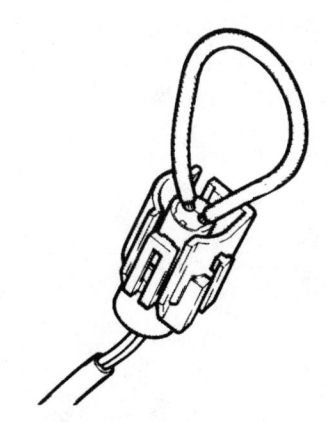

Temporary wiring connected to cooling fan sensor multi-plug

Chapter B

reconnecting the hose, change the sump oil. If the CO level still increases after an oil change, suspect worn or sticking piston rings.

20 In all instances, if no CO change is noted when connecting or disconnecting the breather hose, check for a clogged PCV valve or metering orifice.

Removing tamperproof caps or plugs

21 When removing a tamperproof cap, use a pair of pliers to squeeze the cap. This action will compress the outside of the cap and it can then be levered off.

22 When removing a tamperproof plug, use a sharp point to puncture the plug then lever it off.

Idle speed and mixture (CO)

23 Refer to the specific carburettor Chapter for the adjustment method for the particular carburettor being worked on.

24 If the CO is stable but the engine cannot be made to idle smoothly (even when adjusted slightly rich), then suspect a mechanical fault such as tight valve clearances (where applicable), an intake vacuum leak, compression problem, or an ignition misfire. The HC level is also likely to be higher than normal.

Alternative method of adjustment

Note: It may not be possible to set the carburettor in this way once emission laws are finalised.

25 If engine blow-by is excessive due to worn pistons and rings, then it may only be possible to obtain a satisfactory idle when the mixture is set slightly richer than specified.

26 Remove the PCV valve or breather pipe so that it sucks fresh air. The CO reading should drop by a maximum of 1 to 1.5%. No drop would indicate a clogged PCV valve. If the drop is more than 1.5%, then either the sump oil is fuel-contaminated and must be changed, or the pistons/rings are badly worn. In this case, it may be necessary to set the CO with the breather disconnected.

27 The final idle CO with the breather reconnected will read rich and the engine may idle a little lumpily but the only real cure is an engine overhaul.

Idle mixture adjustment (without a gas analyser)

28 Run the engine at 3000 rpm for 30 seconds to clear the manifold of fuel vapours, then allow the engine to idle.

29 Use the idle speed adjustment screw to set the correct idle speed at the upper limit of the tolerance given in the Specifications.

30 Remove the tamperproof plug and adjust the idle mixture control screw until the highest engine speed is recorded. On all Weber, Pierburg and Solex carburettors covered by this manual (with the exception of the Pierburg 2E2), turning the screw clockwise (inwards) will weaken the idle mixture and turning the screw anti-clockwise (outwards) will enrich the idle mixture.

31 Repeat paragraphs 29 and 30 until the highest steady idle speed is reached (using the correct idle speed as a starting point).

32 Clear the manifold every 30 seconds during the setting operation by running the engine at 3000 rpm for 30 seconds.

33 Screw in the idle mixture control screw until the engine speed is reduced by 25 rpm.

34 Fit a new tamperproof plug to the mixture control screw.

Fast idle (without removing carburettor)

35 The recommended method of setting the fast idle for most carburettors is made after removing the carburettor. However, the following method may give acceptable results when it is inconvenient to remove the carburettor.

36 Observe the adjustment preconditions given above. It is particularly important that the dwell and ignition timing are correct and that the idle speed and mixture are accurately set.

Carburettors with automatic choke

37 Place the fast idle adjustment screw against the second-highest step of the fast idle cam.

38 Start the engine without moving the throttle and record the fast idle speed. A value between 1500 and 2000 rpm will give acceptable results on most engines.

39 Adjust as necessary by turning the adjustment screw in the appropriate direction.

Carburettors with manual choke

40 Use the manual choke control to fully close the flap.

41 Start the engine and open the choke flap as far as possible.

42 Adjust as necessary by turning the adjustment screw in the appropriate direction.

Throttle angle

43 The basic throttle angle and fast idle throttle angle may also be set by means of a throttle angle gauge. For the throttle angles, refer to the Specifications in the appropriate Chapter.

Working on the carburettor

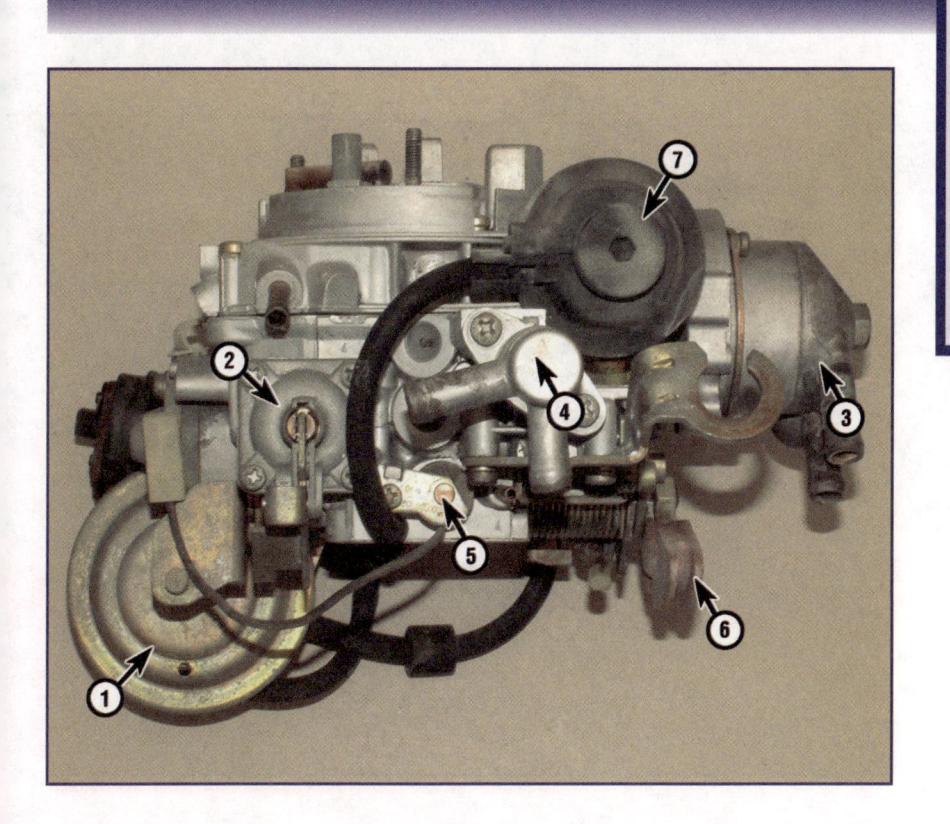

Pierburg 2E2

1. Throttle plate actuator
2. Accelerator pump diaphragm assembly
3. Bi-metal housing assembly
4. Waxstat assembly
5. Throttle body heater
6. Accelerator cable quadrant
7. Choke pull-down diaphragm
8. Secondary throttle diaphragm assembly
9. Fast idle adjustment screw
10. Idle speed regulating valve

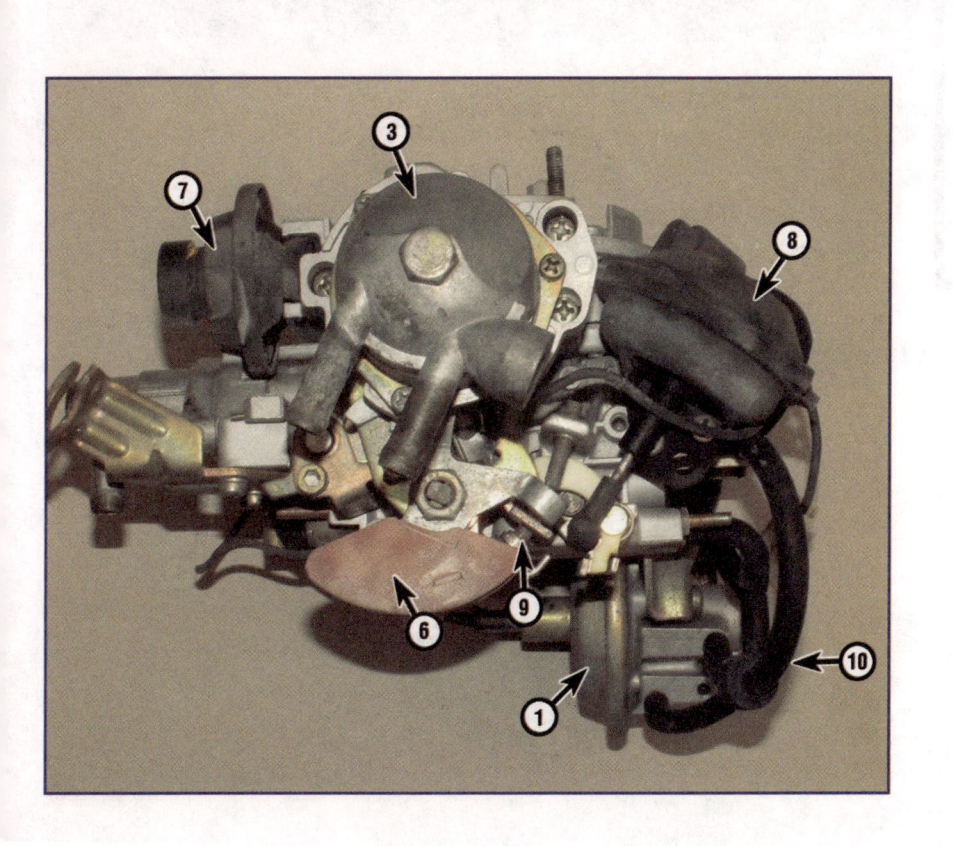

Chapter B

Pierburg 2E2 (viewed from above)

2. Accelerator pump diaphragm assembly
3. Bi-metal housing assembly
4. Waxstat assembly
7. Choke pull-down diaphragm
8. Secondary throttle diaphragm assembly
11. Idle (mixture) air control screw
12. Thermal time valve
13. Part load enrichment valve assembly
14. Accelerator pump jet
15. Choke butterfly valve

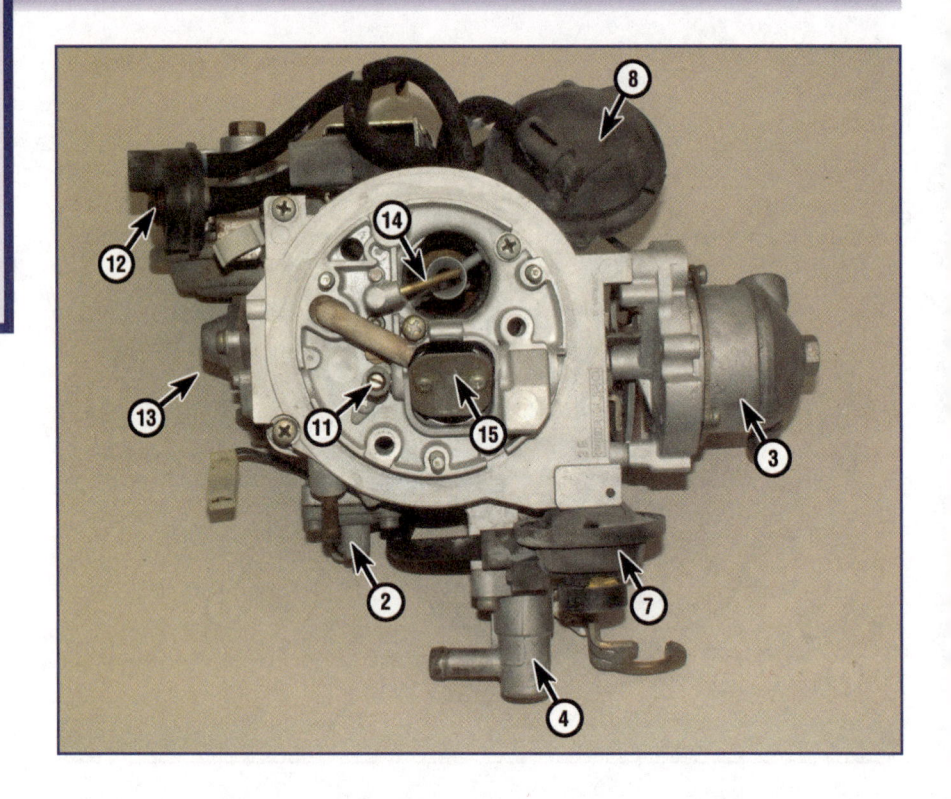

Pierburg 2B5 (viewed from above)

1. Secondary throttle valve assembly
4. Float chamber vent valve
6. Choke pull-down diaphragm
7. Bi-metal housing assembly
9. Accelerator cable quadrant
10. Accelerator pump jet
11. Choke butterfly valve

B•14

Working on the carburettor

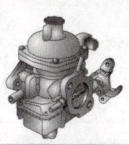

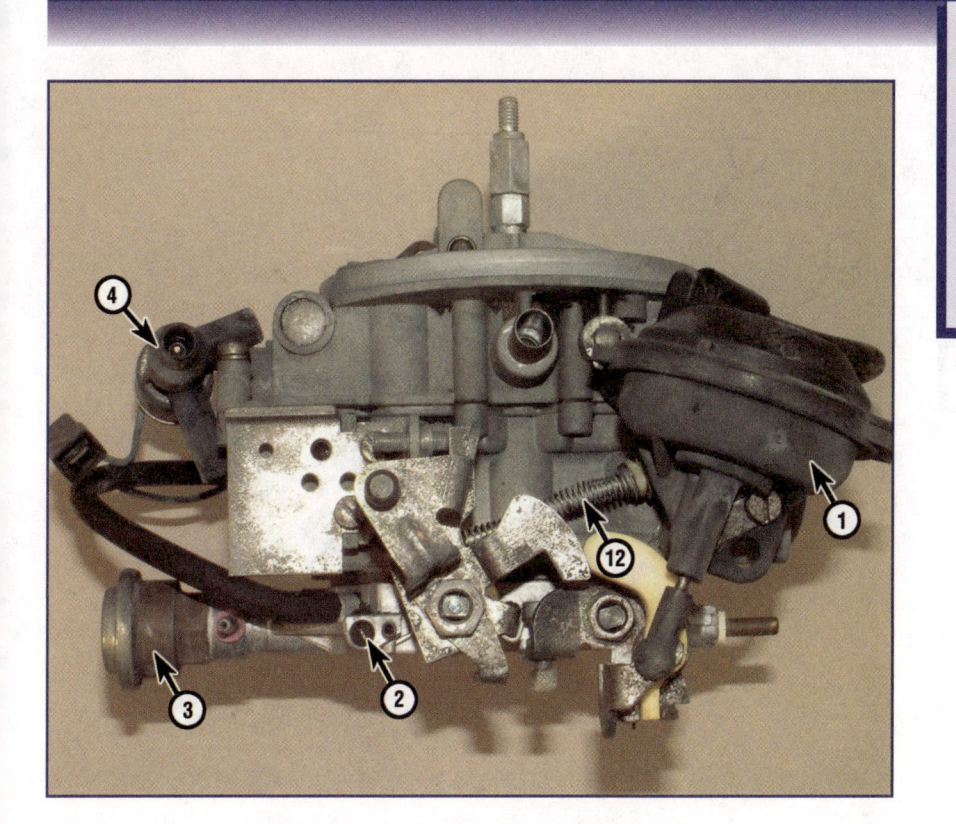

Pierburg 2B5

1. Secondary throttle valve assembly
2. Idle mixture screw
3. Idle cut-off valve
4. Float chamber vent valve
5. Idle bypass screw
6. Choke pull-down diaphragm
7. Bi-metal housing assembly
8. Air filter mounting stud
12. Accelerator pump linkage

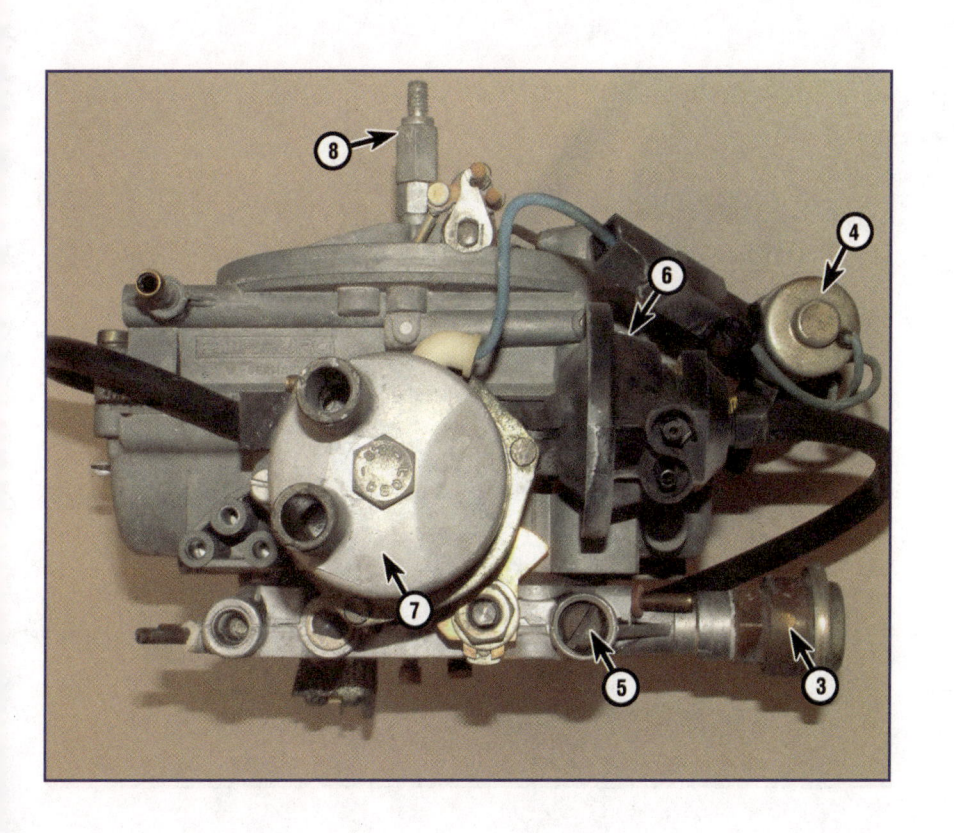

Chapter B

Weber 32 DARA

1. Choke coolant housing
2. Choke diaphragm
3. Secondary throttle valve adjustment screw
4. Heating flange
5. Accelerator cable quadrant
6. Idle mixture control screw
7. Coolant bleed screw
8. Accelerator pump assembly
9. Idle cut-off solenoid valve
10. Fuel inlet port
11. Idle speed adjustment screw

Working on the carburettor

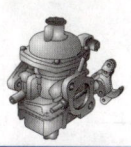

Weber 32 DARA (viewed from above)

1 Choke coolant housing
2 Choke diaphragm
5 Accelerator cable quadrant
9 Idle cut-off solenoid valve
10 Fuel inlet port
12 Choke butterfly valves

Solex Z1 (viewed from above)

1 Choke housing
2 Choke coolant housing
3 Accelerator pump diaphragm assembly
4 Choke butterfly valve
5 Choke pull-down diaphragm assembly
6 Float chamber vent valve assembly
7 Fuel inlet port
8 Idle cut-off solenoid

Chapter B

Solex Z1

1. Choke housing
2. Choke coolant housing
3. Accelerator pump diaphragm assembly
5. Choke pull-down diaphragm assembly
8. Idle cut-off solenoid
9. Idle mixture adjustment screw
10. Accelerator cable quadrant
11. Idle speed adjustment screw

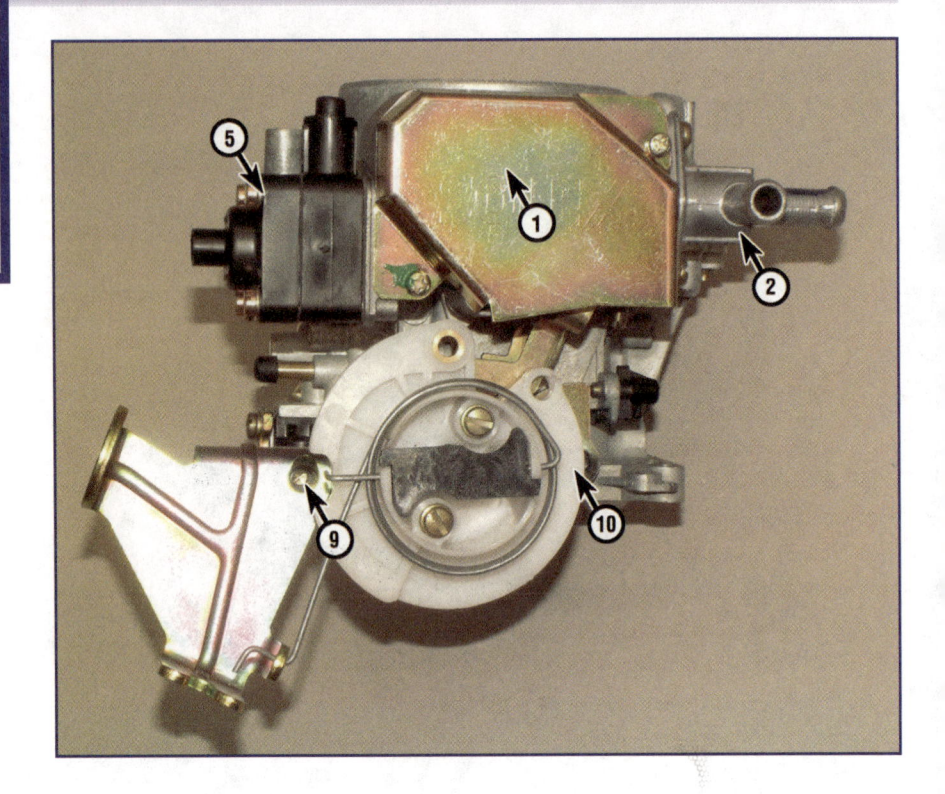

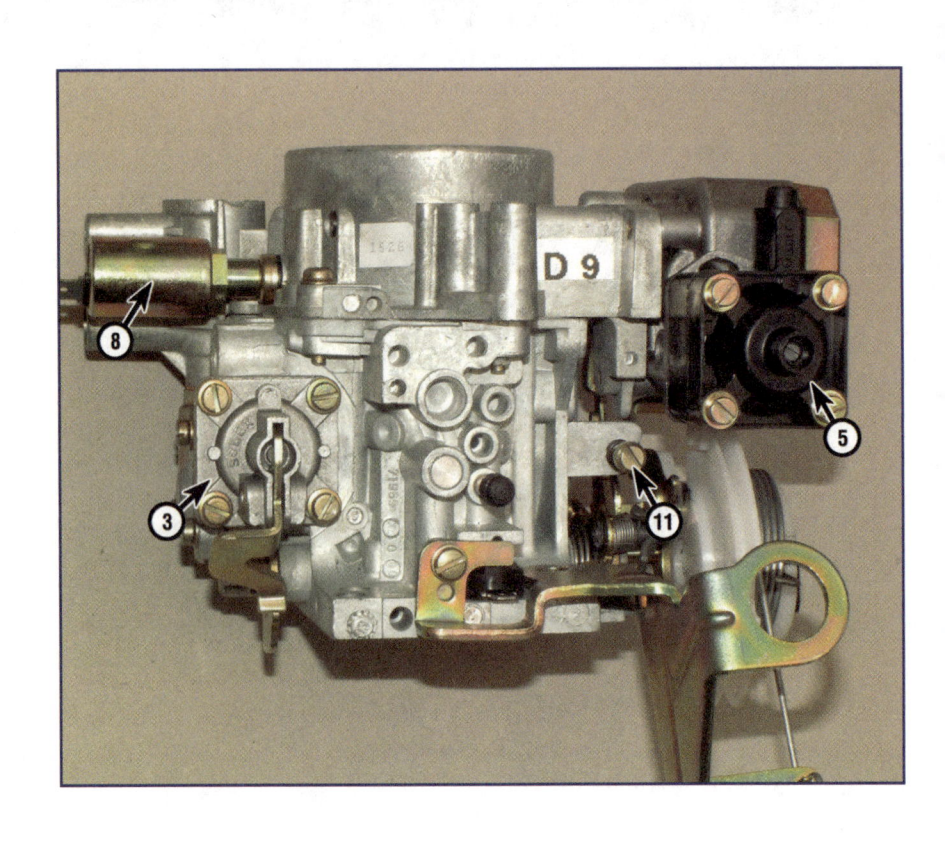

Working on the carburettor

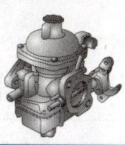

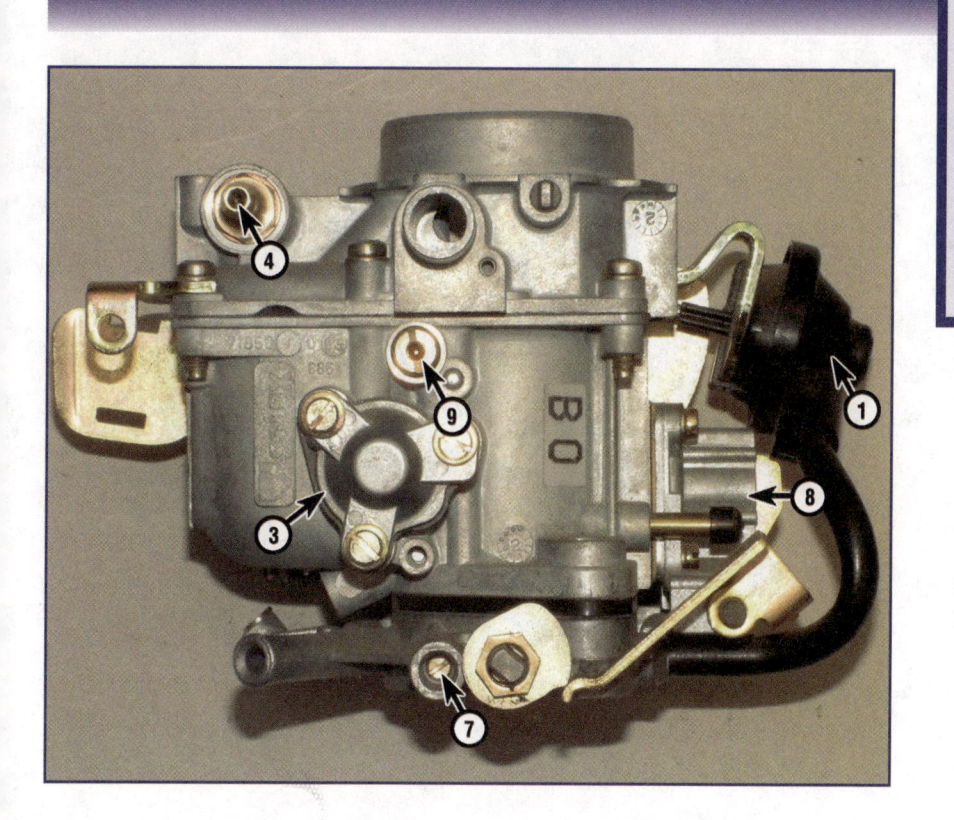

Solex 32 BIS

1 Choke pull-down diaphragm assembly
3 Power valve diaphragm assembly
4 Fuel inlet port
5 Vent valve
7 Idle mixture adjustment screw
8 Accelerator pump assembly
9 Idle jet
10 Idle speed adjustment screw
11 Throttle spindle

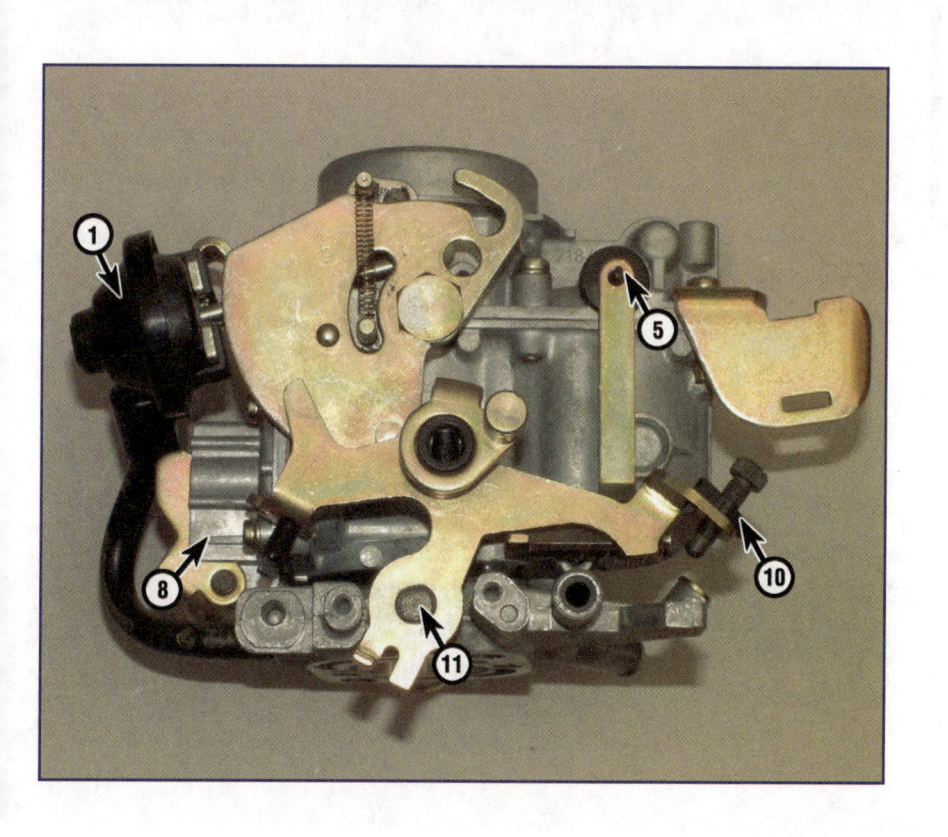

Chapter B

Solex 32 BIS (viewed from above)

1. Choke pull-down diaphragm assembly
2. Choke butterfly valve
3. Power valve diaphragm assembly
4. Fuel inlet port
5. Vent valve
6. Accelerator pump jet

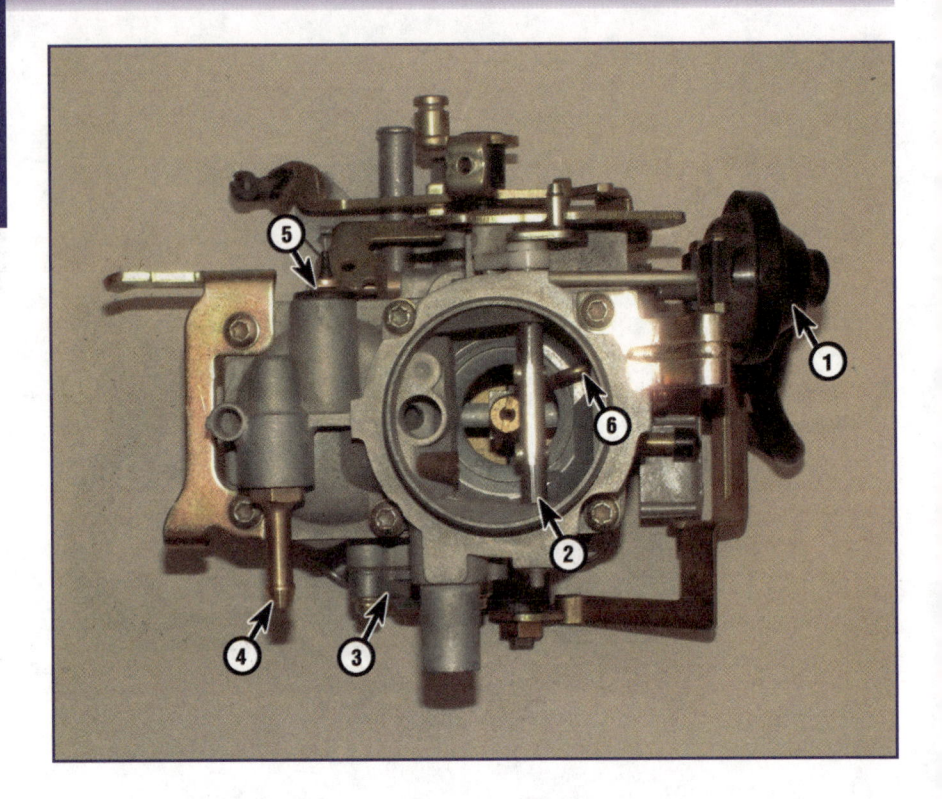

Weber 32TL (viewed from above)

1. Choke pull-down diaphragm
5. Fuel inlet port
7. Throttle stop screw
8. Accelerator pump diaphragm assembly
11. Choke butterfly valve

Working on the carburettor

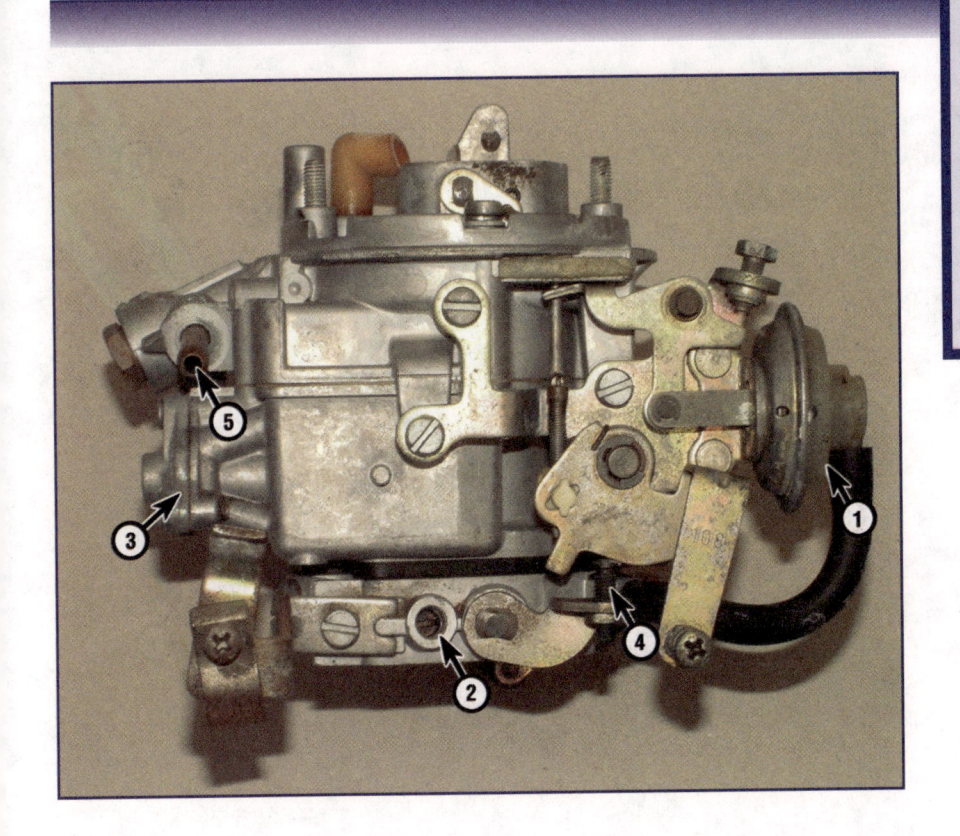

Weber 32TL

1. Choke pull-down diaphragm
2. Idle mixture adjustment screw
3. Power valve diaphragm
4. Fast idle speed adjustment
5. Fuel inlet port
6. Idle bypass air regulation screw
7. Throttle stop screw
8. Accelerator pump diaphragm assembly
9. Throttle spindle
10. Fuel inlet filter

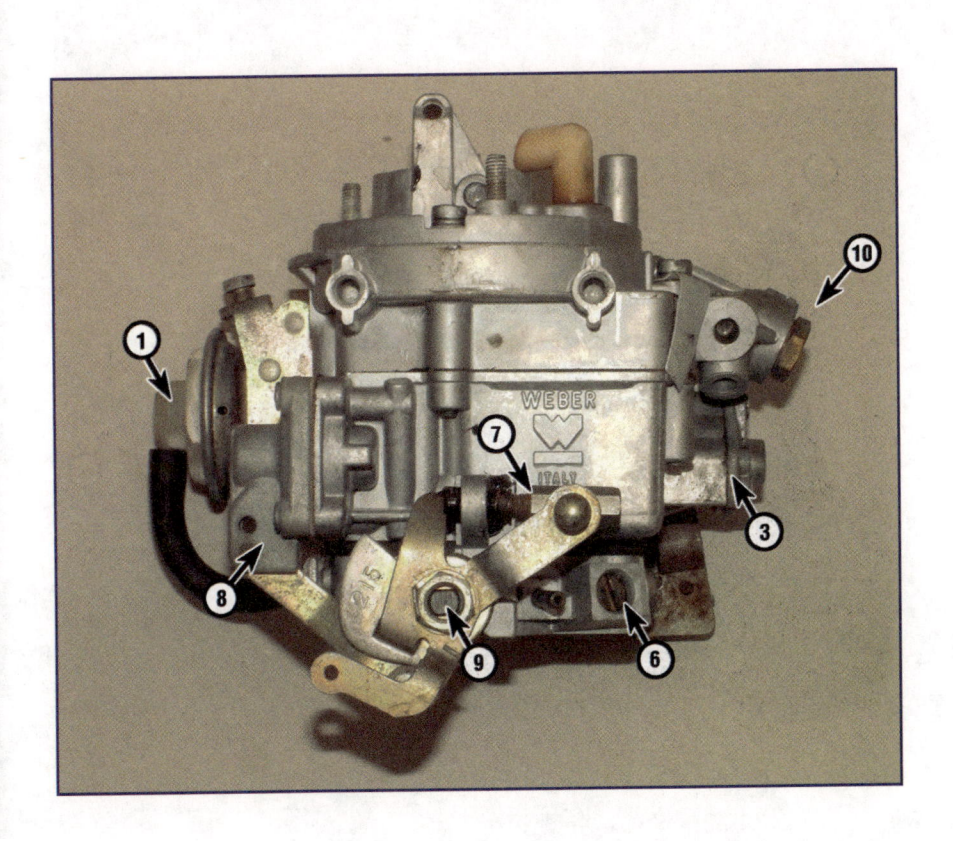

Chapter B

Pierburg 1B1

1. Throttle damper
2. Bypass idle speed adjustment screw
3. Choke pull-down diaphragm assembly
4. Accelerator cable quadrant
5. Delay valve
6. Choke inner cable clamp
7. Idle mixture adjustment screw
8. Idle cut-off valve solenoid
9. Part-load enrichment assembly

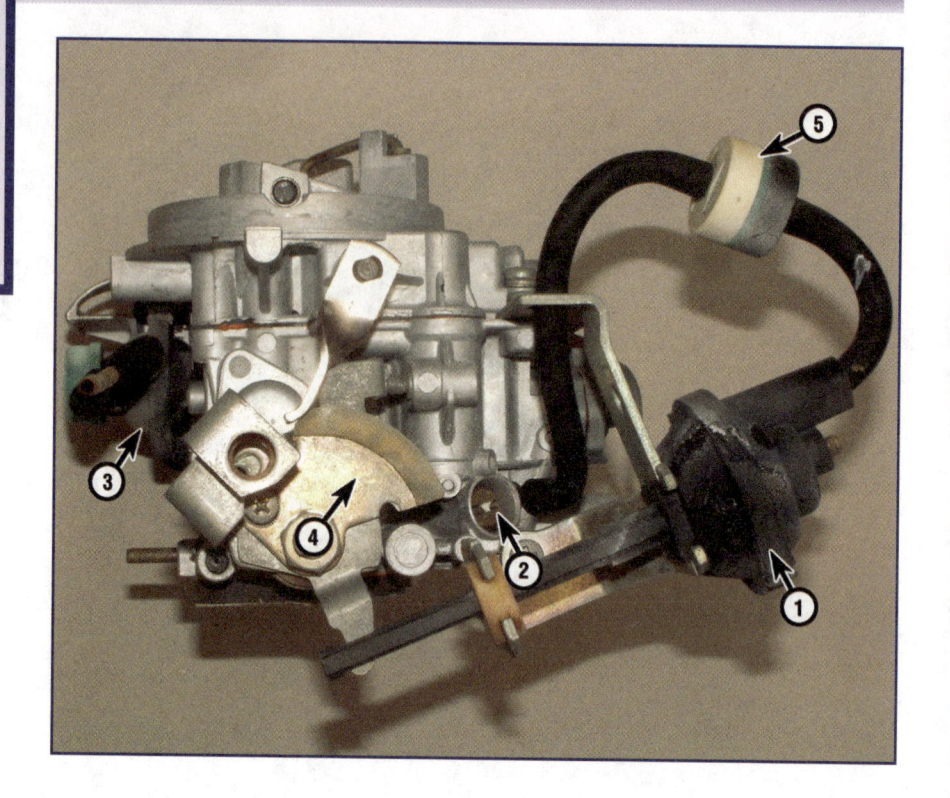

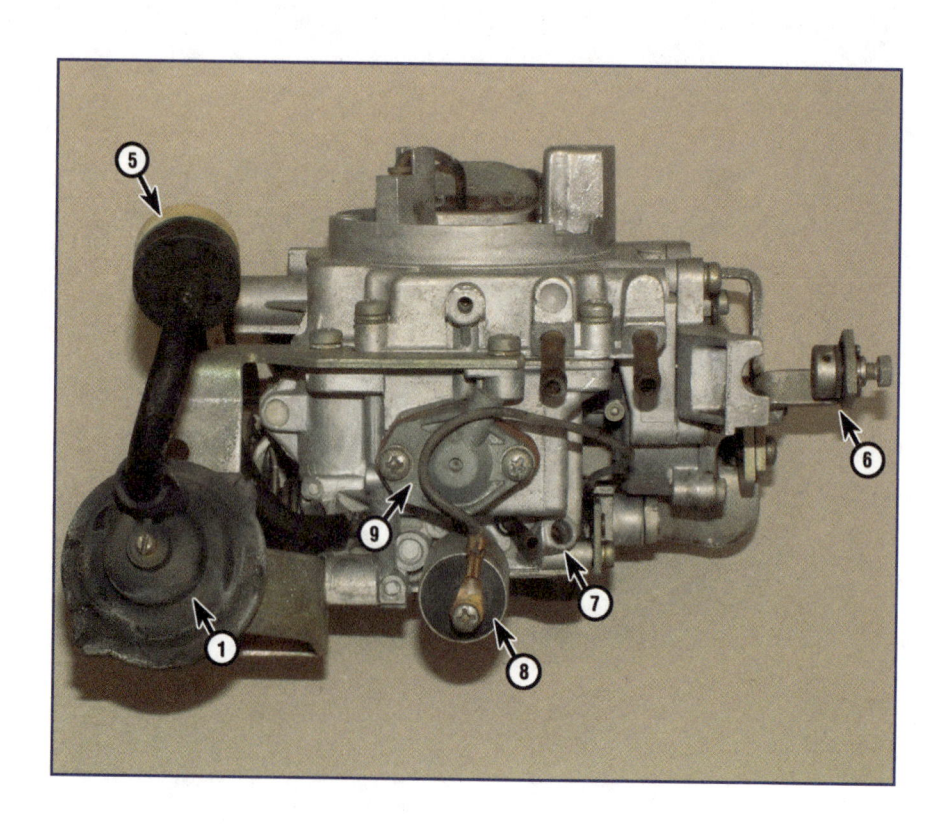

Working on the carburettor

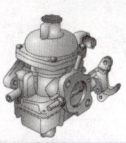

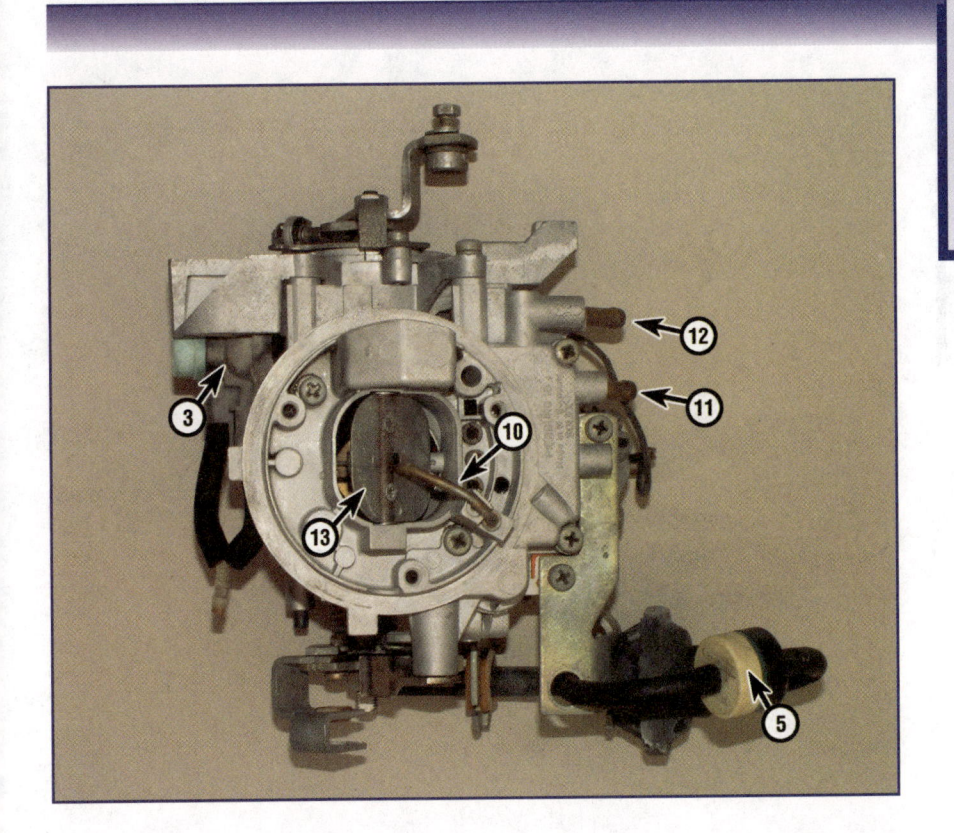

Pierburg 1B1 (viewed from above)

3 Choke pull-down diaphragm assembly
5 Delay valve
10 Accelerator jet
11 Fuel inlet port
12 Fuel return port
13 Choke butterfly valve

Weber TLDM (viewed from above)

1 Secondary throttle diaphragm
4 Choke coolant housing
5 Fast idle speed adjustment screw
7 Accelerator pump diaphragm assembly
9 Throttle 'kicker' assembly
10 Idle cut-off valve
11 Fuel inlet port
12 Choke butterfly valve
13 Accelerator pump jet
14 Air correction jets

B•23

Chapter B

Weber TLDM

1. Secondary throttle diaphragm
2. Idle speed adjustment screw
3. Choke pull-down diaphragm housing
4. Choke coolant housing
5. Fast idle speed adjustment screw
6. Idle mixture adjustment screw
7. Accelerator pump diaphragm assembly
8. Power valve housing
9. Throttle 'kicker' assembly
10. Idle cut-off valve

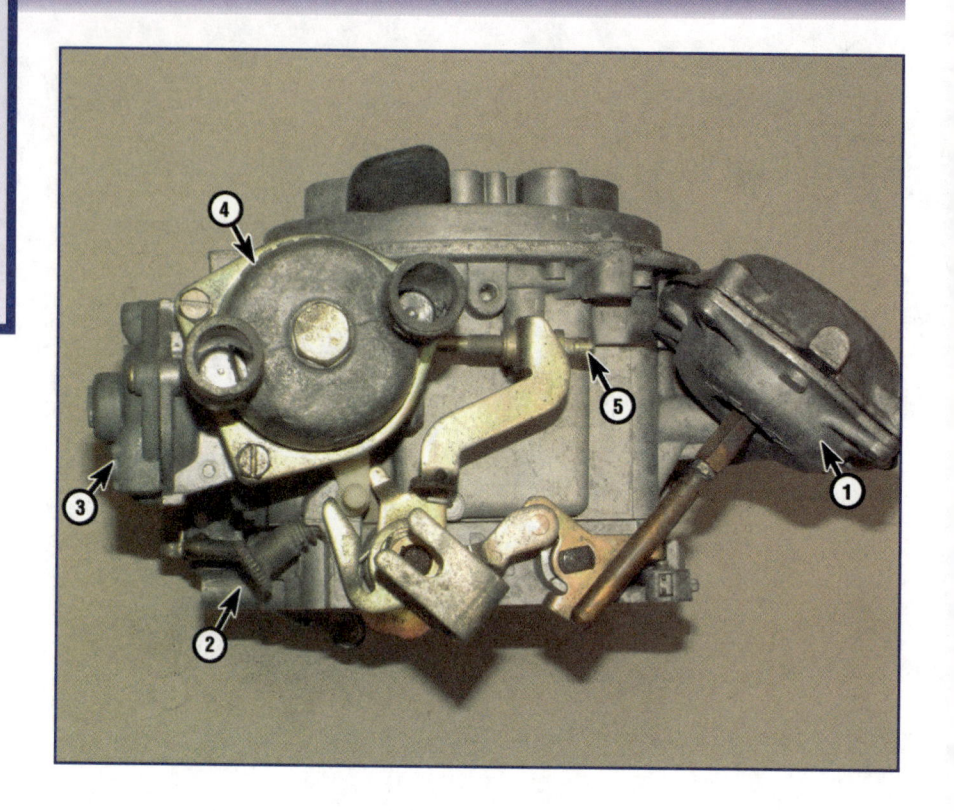

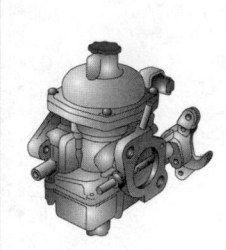

Part C
Carburettor application

Use the following list to identify the manufacturer and model of the carburettor fitted to your vehicle then refer to the information in Parts E, F, G or H (as applicable) for detailed information on each carburettor type. The numbers after the carburettor manufacturer's name refer only to the throttle bore diameter(s) (as applicable), the carburettor type being identified by the last group of letters/numbers - eg. Pierburg 36 1B1 is a Pierburg 1B1 carburettor with a single 36 mm throttle bore, whereas a Pierburg 28/30 2E2 is a Pierburg 2E2 carburettor with a primary throttle bore of 28 mm and a secondary throttle bore of 30 mm.

Vehicle	Year	Carburettor	Page
Alfa Romeo			
Alfasud 1.3 & 1.5	79 to 91	Weber 32 DIR	H9•1
Audi			
80 1.3	81 to 82	Pierburg 36 1B1	F1•1
80 1.6 S, CL	79 to 83	Pierburg 36 1B3	F2•1
80 1.6 CL	83 to 86	Pierburg 28/30 2E2	F5•1
80 1.6 GL, GLS	81 to 83	Pierburg 34/34 2B5	F3•1
80 GL & Coupe 1.8	83 to 86	Pierburg 28/30 2E2	F5•1
80 Coupe	81 to 82	Pierburg 36 1B3	F2•1
80 & Coupe 1.9	81 to 83	Pierburg 34/34 2B5	F3•1
100 1.6	80 to 82	Pierburg 34/34 2B5	F3•1
100 & Avant 1.8	83 to 86	Pierburg 36 1B3	F2•1
100 & Avant 1.8	83 to 87	Pierburg 28/30 2E2	F5•1
100 2.1	81 to 82	Pierburg 34/34 2B5	F3•1
Bedford			
CF 1.8 & 2.3	69 to 84	Weber 34 ICT	H14•1
CF2 2.0	84 to 87	Weber 34 ICT	H14•1
BMW			
316	83 to 88	Pierburg 34/34 2BE	F4•1
518	83 to 85	Pierburg 34/34 2BE	F4•1

Vehicle	Year	Carburettor	Page
Citroën			
AX 10	87 to 91	Weber 32 IBSH	H11•1
AX 10 & 1.0	87 to 92	Solex 32 PBISA	G3•1
AX 11 & 1.1	87 to 92	Solex 32 PBISA	G3•1
AX 14	87 to 88	Weber 34 TLP	H22•1
AX 14 & 1.4	88 to 92	Solex 34 PBISA	G3•1
BX 14	88 to 92	Solex 34 PBISA	G3•1
BX 16	83 to 84	Weber 32/34 DRTC	H10•1
BX 16	83 to 91	Solex 32/34 Z1 (CISAC)	G5•1
BX 16	84 to 88	Weber 32/34 DRTC	H10•1
BX 16 RE	87 to 89	Weber 36 TLP	H22•1
BX 19	86 to 90	Weber 32/34 DRTC	H10•1
BX 19	84 to 92	Solex 34/34 Z1 (CISAC)	G5•1
LNA 11E, 11RE	82 to 86	Solex 32 PBISA	G3•1
Visa 1.0	85 to 87	Solex 32 PBISA	G3•1
Visa 1.1	81 to 87	Solex 32 PBISA	G3•1
Visa Super X 1.2	81 to 82	Solex 32 PBISA	G3•1
Visa 14 TRS	84 to 86	Solex 34 PBISA	G3•1
Visa GT	83 to 86	Weber 35 IBSH	H11•1
XM 2.0 (carburettor)	89 to 92	Solex 34/34 Z1 (CISAC)	G5•1
C15E 1.4 Super Van	86 to 88	Solex 32 PBISA	G3•1
C15E 1.4 Super Van	88 to 92	Solex 34 PBISA	G3•1
C25E 1.8	87 to 88	Solex 34 PBISA	G3•1
C25E 1.8	89 to 91	Solex 34 PBISA	G3•1
C25E 2.0	87 to 92	Solex 34 PBISA	G3•1

Chapter C

Vehicle	Year	Carburettor	Page	Vehicle	Year	Carburettor	Page
Fiat				Escort & Orion 1.4	90 to 91	Weber 28/30 TLDM	H19•1
127 & Fiorino 1050	81 to 88	Weber 32 ICEV	H12•1	Escort 1.6	80 to 86	Ford VV	E2•1
Panda 45 (903)	81 to 86	Weber 32 ICEV	H12•1	Escort 1.6 Auto	80 to 86	Ford VV	E2•1
Panda 45 (903)	89 to 91	Weber 32 ICEV	H13•1	Escort & Orion 1.6	86 to 90	Weber 28/32 TLDM	H19•1
Panda 750	86 to 91	Weber 32 TLF	H20•1	Escort & Orion 1.6 auto	86 to 90	Weber 28/32 TLDM	H19•1
Panda 1000	86 to 91	Weber 32 TLF	H20•1	Escort XR3	80 to 82	Weber 32/34 DFT	H2•1
Panda 1000 4x4	86 to 91	Weber 32 TLF	H20•1	Escort & Orion 1.6	90 to 91	Weber 28/32 TLDM	H19•1
Regata 70	86 to 90	Weber 30/32 DMTE	H7•1	Escort & Orion 1.6 auto	90 to 91	Weber 28/32 TLDM	H19•1
Regata 70ES	84 to 86	Weber 30/32 DMTE	H7•1	Escort & Orion 1.6 Cat.	90 to 91	Weber 26/28 TLDM	H19•1
Regata 75	85 to 88	Weber 32/34 TLDE	H17•1	Cortina 1300 (OHV)	80 to 83	Ford VV	E2•1
Regata 85	85 to 88	Weber 32/34 TLDE	H17•1	Cortina 1300 (OHC)	79 to 82	Ford VV	E2•1
Strada 60	83 to 85	Weber 32 ICEV	H12•1	Cortina 1600	80 to 83	Ford VV	E2•1
Strada 60	85 to 88	Weber 30/32 DMTE	H7•1	Cortina 1600 auto	80 to 83	Ford VV	E2•1
Strada 60 ES & City Matic	83 to 85	Weber 30 DMTE	H7•1	Cortina 1600 (2V)	81 to 83	Weber 32/36 DGAV	H5•1
Strada 65	79 to 83	Weber 32 ICEV	H12•1	Cortina 2000	81 to 83	Weber 32/36 DGAV	H5•1
Strada 70 & City Matic	85 to 88	Weber 30/32 DMTE	H7•1	Cortina 2000 auto	81 to 83	Weber 32/36 DGAV	H5•1
Strada 85	85 to 88	Weber 32/34 TLDE	H17•1	Cortina 2300	79 to 81	Solex 35 EEIT	G2•1
Tempra 1.4 & Selecta	90 to 91	Weber 32/34 TLDE	H17•1	Cortina 2300 auto	79 to 81	Solex 35 EEIT	G2•1
Tempra 1.6 & Selecta	90 to 91	Weber 32/34 TLDE	H17•1	Cortina 2300	81 to 82	Solex 35 EEIT	G2•1
Tipo 1.4 & Selecta	88 to 91	Weber 32/34 TLDE	H17•1	Cortina 2300 auto	81 to 82	Solex 35 EEIT	G2•1
Tipo 1.6	88 to 91	Weber 32/34 TLDE	H17•1	Sierra 1300	82 to 86	Ford VV	E2•1
Uno 45 (903)	83 to 91	Weber 32 ICEV	H12•1	Sierra 1600	82 to 86	Ford VV	E2•1
Uno 45 (999)	85 to 91	Weber 32 TLF	H20•1	Sierra 1600 auto	82 to 86	Ford VV	E2•1
Uno 55 (1116)	83 to 85	Weber 32 ICEV	H12•1	Sierra 1600 Economy	82 to 84	Ford VV	E2•1
Uno 60	85 to 88	Weber 30/32 DMTE	H7•1	Sierra 1600 E-max	83	Weber 28/30 DFTH	H3•1
Uno 60 (1108)	90 to 91	Weber 32 TLF	H20•1	Sierra & Sapphire 1600	84 to 88	Weber 28/30 DFTH	H3•1
Uno 70 (1300)	85 to 90	Weber 30/32 DMTE	H7•1	Sierra & Sapphire 1600	88 to 91	Weber 28/30 DFTH	H3•1
Citivan	88 to 91	Weber 30/32 DMTE	H7•1	Sierra & Sapphire 1600	87 to 91	Weber 28/30 DFTH	H3•1
Ducato 1.8	82 to 88	Solex 34 PBISA	G3•1	Sierra 1800	84 to 87	Pierburg 2E3	F6•1
Ducato 2.0 (not Catalyst)	82 to 92	Solex 34 PBISA	G3•1	Sierra 1800 auto	84 to 87	Pierburg 2E3	F6•1
Fiorino	88 to 91	Weber 30/32 DMTE	H7•1	Sierra & Sapphire 1800	87 to 88	Pierburg 2E3	F6•1
Ford				Sierra & Sapphire 1800 auto	87 to 88	Pierburg 2E3	F6•1
Fiesta 950 LC	78 to 83	Ford (Motorcraft) 1V	E1•1	Sierra & Sapphire 1800	88 to 91	Pierburg 2E3	F6•1
Fiesta 950 HC	78 to 83	Ford (Motorcraft) 1V	E1•1	Sierra & Sapphire 1800 auto	88 to 91	Pierburg 2E3	F6•1
Fiesta 950	78 to 83	Weber 32 ICH	H13•1	Sierra 2000	82 to 85	Weber 32/36 DGAV	H5•1
Fiesta 950	83 to 86	Ford (Motorcraft) 1V	E1•1	Sierra 2000 auto	82 to 85	Weber 32/36 DGAV	H5•1
Fiesta 950	86 to 89	Weber 32 TLM	H21•1	Sierra & Sapphire 2000	85 to 89	Weber 30/34 DFTH (ISC)	H3•1
Fiesta 1.0 L & van	89 to 91	Weber 32 TLM	H21•1	Sierra & Sapphire 2000 auto	85 to 89	Weber 30/34 DFTH (ISC)	H3•1
Fiesta 1100	78 to 83	Ford (Motorcraft) 1V	E1•1	Sierra & Sapphire 2000	89 to 91	Weber 28/32 TLDM	H19•1
Fiesta 1100	83 to 84	Ford VV	E2•1	Sierra & Sapphire 2000 Cat.	89 to 91	Weber 28/32 TLDM	H19•1
Fiesta 1100	84 to 89	Ford VV	E2•1	Sierra 2300	82 to 84	Solex 35 EEIT	G2•1
Fiesta 1.1 & Van 15/04	89 to 91	Weber 26/28 TLDM	H19•1	Sierra 2300 auto	82 to 84	Solex 35 EEIT	G2•1
Fiesta 1.1 & Van 15/05	89 to 91	Weber 26/28 TLDM	H19•1	Capri 1300 (OHV)	79 to 82	Ford VV	E2•1
Fiesta 1300	78 to 82	Weber 32 DFT	H2•1	Capri 1300 (OHC)	79 to 82	Ford VV	E2•1
Fiesta 1300	83 to 86	Ford VV	E2•1	Capri 1600	79 to 88	Ford VV	E2•1
Fiesta 1400	86 to 89	Weber 28/30 DFTM	H4•1	Capri 1600 auto	79 to 88	Ford VV	E2•1
Fiesta 1.4	89 to 91	Weber 28/30 DFTM	H7•1	Capri 1600 S/GT	81	Weber 32/36 DGAV	H5•1
Fiesta 1.4 auto	89 to 91	Weber 28/30 DFTM	H7•1	Capri 2000	79 to 88	Weber 32/36 DGAV	H5•1
Fiesta 1.4	89 to 91	Weber 28/30 TLDM	H19•1	Capri 2000 auto	79 to 88	Weber 32/36 DGAV	H5•1
Fiesta XR2	81 to 83	Weber 32/34 DFT	H2•1	Granada & Scorpio 1.8	84 to 87	Pierburg 2E3	F6•1
Fiesta XR2	83 to 86	Weber 32/34 DFT	H2•1	Granada 2000	78 to 82	Weber 32/36 DGAV	H5•1
Fiesta XR2	86 to 89	Weber 28/32 TLDM	H19•1	Granada 2000 auto	78 to 82	Weber 32/36 DGAV	H5•1
Fiesta 1.6S	89 to 91	Weber 28/32 TLDM	H19•1	Granada 2000	82 to 85	Weber 32/36 DGAV	H5•1
Escort 1.1	80 to 83	Ford VV	E2•1	Granada 2000 auto	82 to 85	Weber 32/36 DGAV	H5•1
Escort 1.1	84 to 87	Ford VV	E2•1	Granada 2000	85 to 89	Weber 30/34 DFTH (ISC)	H3•1
Escort 1.1	89 to 90	Weber 26/28 TLDM	H19•1	Granada 2000 auto	85 to 89	Weber 30/34 DFTH (ISC)	H3•1
Escort 1.1	90 to 91	Weber 26/28 TLDM	H19•1	Granada 2000	89 to 90	Weber 28/32 TLDM	H19•1
Escort & Orion 1.3	80 to 84	Ford VV	E2•1	Granada 2000 auto	89 to 90	Weber 28/32 TLDM	H19•1
Escort & Orion 1.3	84 to 86	Ford VV	E2•1	Granada 2000 Catalyst	89 to 90	Weber 28/32 TLDM	H19•1
Escort & Orion 1.3	86 to 88	Ford VV	E2•1	Granada 2300	78 to 79	Solex 35 EEIT	G2•1
Escort & Orion 1.3	88 to 90	Weber 26/28 TLDM	H19•1	Granada 2300 auto	78 to 79	Solex 35 EEIT	G2•1
Escort & Orion 1.3	90 to 91	Weber 26/28 TLDM	H19•1	Granada 2300	80 to 81	Solex 35 EEIT	G2•1
Escort & Orion 1.3 Cat.	90 to 91	Weber 26/28 TLDM	H19•1				
Escort & Orion 1.4	86 to 90	Weber 28/30 DFTM	H4•1				

Carburettor application

Vehicle	Year	Carburettor	Page
Granada 2300 auto	80 to 81	Solex 35 EEIT	G2•1
Granada 2300	82 to 85	Solex 35 EEIT	G2•1
Granada 2300 auto	82 to 85	Solex 35 EEIT	G2•1
Granada 2800	78 to 79	Solex 38 EEIT	G2•1
Granada 2800 auto	78 to 79	Solex 38 EEIT	G2•1
Granada 2800	80 to 81	Solex 38 EEIT	G2•1
Granada 2800 auto	80 to 81	Solex 38 EEIT	G2•1
Granada 2800	82 to 85	Solex 38 EEIT	G2•1
Granada 2800 auto	82 to 85	Solex 38 EEIT	G2•1
P100-L	82 to 87	Ford VV	E2•1
P100	88 to 91	Ford VV	E2•1
Transit 1.6	78 to 83	Ford (Motorcraft) 1V	E1•1
Transit 1.6	83 to 85	Ford VV	E2•1
Transit 1.6	85 to 91	Ford VV	E2•1
Transit 2.0	78 to 83	Ford (Motorcraft) 1V	E1•1
Transit 2.0 auto	78 to 83	Ford (Motorcraft) 1V	E1•1
Transit 2.0 economy	78 to 83	Ford (Motorcraft) 1V	E1•1
Transit 2.0	83 to 85	Ford VV	E2•1
Transit 2.0 auto	83 to 85	Ford VV	E2•1
Transit 2.0	85 to 91	Ford VV	E2•1

Lancia

Vehicle	Year	Carburettor	Page
Y10 Fire	85 to 91	Weber 32 TLF	H20•1
Y10 Touring	85 to 88	Weber 32 ICEV	H12•1

Land Rover

Vehicle	Year	Carburettor	Page
90 & 110	83 to 90	Weber 32/34 DMTL	H8•1

Mercedes-Benz

Vehicle	Year	Carburettor	Page
210/310/410	82 to 92	Pierburg 36 1B1	F1•1
210/310/410	82 to 92	Pierburg 36 1B3	F2•1

Opel

See Vauxhall/Opel

Peugeot

Vehicle	Year	Carburettor	Page
104 1.0	79 to 83	Solex 32 PBISA	G3•1
104 1.1	82 to 83	Solex 32 PBISA	G3•1
104 1.2	79 to 83	Solex 32 PBISA	G3•1
205 1.0	83 to 92	Solex 32 PBISA	G3•1
205 1.0	88 to 91	Weber 32 IBSH	H11•1
205 1.1 & Van	83 to 92	Solex 32 PBISA	G3•1
205 1.4 GR	83 to 87	Solex 34 PBISA	G3•1
205 1.4 GR	87 to 88	Weber 34 TLP	H22•1
205 1.4 XR, GR, CJ	88 to 92	Solex 34 PBISA	G3•1
205 GT, XS, XT, Lacoste	83 to 87	Weber 35 IBSH	H11•1
305 & Van 1.3	78 to 86	Solex 34 PBISA	G3•1
305 & Van 1.5	78 to 83	Solex 35 PBISA	G3•1
305 & Van 1.5	83 to 88	Solex 34 PBISA	G3•1
305 GL	83 to 86	Solex 34 PBISA	G3•1
305 GT	83 to 88	Solex 32/34 Z1 (CISAC)	G5•1
305 GT	83 to 88	Weber 32/34 DRTC	H10•1
305 Automatic	83 to 88	Solex 32/34 Z1 (CISAC)	G5•1
305 1.9	84 to 88	Solex 32/34 Z1 (CISAC)	G7•1
305 & Van 1.6	85 to 91	Weber 36 TLP	H22•1
309 1.1	86 to 89	Weber 32 IBSH	H11•1
309 1.1	89 to 92	Solex 32 PBISA	G3•1
309 1.3	86 to 91	Weber 32 IBSH	H11•1
309 1.4	89 to 92	Solex 34 PBISA	G3•1
309 1.6	86 to 89	Weber 36 TLP	H22•1
309 1.6	88 to 92	Solex 34/34 Z1 (CISAC)	G5•1
405 1.4	88 to 92	Solex 34 PBISA	G3•1
405 1.6	88 to 92	Solex 34/34 Z1 (CISAC)	G3•1
405 1.9	88 to 92	Solex 34/34 Z1 (CISAC)	G3•1
505 2.0	85 to 92	Solex 34/34 Z1 (CISAC)	G3•1
605 2.0	90 to 92	Solex 34/34 Z1 (CISAC)	G3•1

Renault

Vehicle	Year	Carburettor	Page
5 & Extra 1.1	85 to 92	Solex 32 BIS	G1•1
5 & Extra 1.4	85 to 91	Solex 32 BIS	G1•1
5 Auto 1.4	81 to 85	Weber 32 DIR	H6•1
5 1.4	85 to 90	Weber 32 DRT	H9•1
5 1.7	87 to 90	Solex 28/34 Z10 (CISAC)	G6•1
5 Gordini Turbo	82 to 84	Weber 32 DIR	H6•1
9 1.1	82 to 86	Solex 32 BIS	G1•1
9 1.4	82 to 85	Solex 32 BIS	G1•1
9 1.4	85 to 89	Weber 32 DRT	H9•1
9 Auto 1.4	85 to 89	Weber 32 DRT	H9•1
9 1.7	84 to 86	Weber 32 DRT	H9•1
9 1.7	86 to 89	Solex 28/34 Z10 (CISAC)	G6•1
11 1.1	82 to 86	Solex 32 BIS	G1•1
11 1.4	82 to 85	Solex 32 BIS	G1•1
11 1.4	85 to 89	Weber 32 DRT	H9•1
11 Auto 1.4	85 to 89	Weber 32 DRT	H9•1
11 1.7	84 to 86	Weber 32 DRT	H9•1
11 1.7	86 to 89	Solex 28/34 Z10 (CISAC)	G6•1
14 1.2	77 to 82	Solex 32 PBISA	G3•1
18 1.4	78 to 84	Solex 32 SEIA	G4•1
18 1.6	83 to 86	Weber 32 DIR	H6•1
18 1.6	83 to 86	Weber 32 DARA	H1•1
18 2.0	82 to 86	Weber 32 DARA	H1•1
18 2.0 Auto	84 to 86	Weber 32 DARA	H1•1
18 Turbo	80 to 85	Solex 32 DIS	G3•1
19 & Chamade 1.2	90 to 91	Solex 32 BIS	G1•1
19 & Chamade 1.4	89 to 91	Weber 32/34 TLDR	H18•1
20 2.0	81 to 84	Weber 32 DARA	H1•1
20 2.2	80 to 84	Weber 32/36 DARA	H1•1
21 & Savanna 1.7	86 to 88	Solex 28/34 Z10 (CISAC)	G6•1
21 & Savanna 1.7	86 to 92	Solex 28/34 Z10 (CISAC)	G6•1
25 2.0 &GTS	84 to 91	Weber 28/36 DARA	H1•1
Espace	85 to 88	Weber 32 DARA	H1•1
Espace	88 to 91	Weber 28/36 DARA	H1•1
Fuego 1.4	80 to 84	Solex 32 SEIA	G4•1
Fuego 1.6	82 to 86	Weber 32 DARA	H1•1
Fuego 2.0	80 to 84	Weber 32 DARA	H1•1
Trafic P1000, P1200 rwd	81 to 86	Solex 35 SEIA	G4•1
Trafic P1400 rwd	84 to 92	Solex 35 SEIA	G4•1
Trafic T1000 fwd	86 to 89	Solex 35 SEIA	G4•1
Trafic T1000, T1200 fwd	81 to 86	Solex 35 SEIA	G4•1
Trafic T1100 fwd	89 to 92	Solex 35 SEIA	G4•1
Trafic T1300	86 to 89	Solex 35 SEIA	G4•1
Trafic T1400	89 to 92	Solex 35 SEIA	G4•1
Master P35 rwd	81 to 91	Solex 35 SEIA	G4•1
Master T35 fwd	81 to 92	Solex 35 SEIA	G4•1

Seat

Vehicle	Year	Carburettor	Page
Ibiza 900	87 to 91	Weber 32 ICEV	H12•1
Ibiza 1.2	85 to 92	Pierburg 36 1B3	F2•1
Marbella 850 & 900	88 to 91	Weber 32 ICEV	H12•1
Malaga 1.2	85 to 92	Pierburg 36 1B3	F2•1
Terra 900	88 to 91	Weber 32 ICEV	H12•1

Talbot/Chrysler

Vehicle	Year	Carburettor	Page
Horizon 1.1	78 to 86	Weber 32 IBSH	H11•1
Samba 1.0	83 to 86	Solex 32 PBISA	G3•1
Samba 1.1	82 to 86	Solex 32 PBISA	G3•1
Samba 1.4	83 to 86	Weber 35 IBSH	H11•1
Express, Sportsman 1.8	82 to 91	Solex 34 PBISA	G3•1
Express, Triaxle 2.0	82 to 92	Solex 34 PBISA	G3•1
Dodge Simca 1100 Van	78 to 84	Weber 32 IBSH	H11•1

Chapter C

Vehicle	Year	Carburettor	Page
Vauxhall/Opel			
Ascona C	81 to 88	Pierburg 36 1B1	F1•1
Astra 1.2	80 to 84	Pierburg (Solex) 35 PDSI	F7•1
Astra 1.2	84 to 91	Weber 32 TL	H15•1
Astra 1.3N	84 to 89	Pierburg (Solex) 35 PDSI	F7•1
Astra 1.3S	84 to 89	Pierburg 28/30 2E3	F6•1
Astra 1.4	89 to 91	Pierburg 28/30 2E3	F6•1
Astra 1.6	89 to 91	Pierburg 28/30 2E3	F6•1
Belmont 1.3	84 to 89	Pierburg 28/30 2E3	F6•1
Belmont 1.4	89 to 91	Pierburg 28/30 2E3	F6•1
Belmont 1.6	89 to 91	Pierburg 28/30 2E3	F6•1
Cavalier 1.3	85 to 88	Pierburg 28/30 2E3	F6•1
Cavalier 1.4	89 to 92	Pierburg 28/30 2E3	F6•1
Cavalier 1.6	88 to 92	Pierburg 28/30 2E3	F6•1
Cavalier 1.8	89 to 92	Pierburg 28/30 2E3	F6•1
Carlton 1.8	87 to 90	Pierburg 28/30 2E3	F6•1
Corsa 1.0	83 to 91	Weber 32 TL	H15•1
Corsa 1.2	87 to 91	Weber 32 TL	H15•1
Corsa 1.2	90 to 92	Pierburg 32 1B1	F1•1
Corsa 1.4	89 to 92	Pierburg 28/30 2E3	F6•1
Kadett 1.2	80 to 84	Pierburg (Solex) 35 PDSI	F7•1
Kadett 1.2	83 to 84	Weber 32 TL	H15•1
Kadett 1.3	79 to 87	Pierburg (Solex) 35 PDSI	F7•1
Kadett 1.4	89 to 91	Pierburg 28/30 2E3	F6•1
Kadett 1.6	89 to 91	Pierburg 28/30 2E3	F6•1
Nova 1.0	83 to 91	Weber 32 TL	H15•1
Nova 1.2	83 to 90	Pierburg 32 1B1	F1•1
Nova 1.2	85 to 91	Weber 32 TL	H15•1
Nova 1.2	90 to 92	Pierburg 32 1B1	F1•1
Nova 1.3	82 to 87	Pierburg 36 1B1	F1•1
Nova 1.3	85 to 89	Pierburg 28/30 2E3	F6•1
Nova 1.4	89 to 92	Pierburg 28/30 2E3	F6•1
Rekord E	82 to 86	Pierburg 36 1B1	F1•1
Vectra 1.4	89 to 92	Pierburg 28/30 2E3	F6•1
Vectra 1.6	88 to 92	Pierburg 28/30 2E3	F6•1
Vectra 1.8	89 to 92	Pierburg 28/30 2E3	F6•1
Volkswagen			
Caddy 1.6	83 to 92	Pierburg 28/30 2E2	F5•1
Golf 1.05	84 to 85	Pierburg (Solex) 31 PIC-7	F8•1
Golf 1.05	85 to 91	Pierburg 32 1B3	F2•1
Golf 1.05	85 to 91	Weber 32 TLA	H16•1
Golf & Van 1.1	81 to 83	Pierburg (Solex) 31 PIC-7	F8•1
Golf 1.1 Formel-E	81 to 83	Pierburg (Solex) 31 PIC-7	F8•1
Golf & Van 1.3	83 to 91	Pierburg 28/30 2E3	F6•1
Golf 1.5	81 to 84	Pierburg 36 1B3	F2•1
Golf 1.6	83 to 92	Pierburg 28/30 2E2	F5•1
Golf 1.6 Cat.	86 to 92	Pierburg 28/30 2E2	F5•1
Golf Cabrio 1.8	83 to 91	Pierburg 28/30 2E2	F5•1
Golf & Synchro 1.8	84 to 92	Pierburg 28/30 2E2	F5•1
Golf 1.8 Cat.	86 to 92	Pierburg 28/30 2E2	F5•1
Jetta 1.05	85 to 91	Weber 32 TLA	H16•1
Jetta 1.1 Formel-E	81 to 83	Pierburg (Solex) 31 PIC-7	F8•1
Jetta 1.3	83 to 91	Pierburg 28/30 2E3	F6•1
Jetta 1.5	81 to 84	Pierburg 36 1B3	F2•1
Jetta 1.6	79 to 83	Pierburg 34/34 2B5	F3•1
Jetta 1.6	83 to 92	Pierburg 28/30 2E2	F5•1
Jetta 1.6 Cat.	86 to 92	Pierburg 28/30 2E2	F5•1
Jetta & Synchro 1.8	84 to 92	Pierburg 28/30 2E2	F5•1
Jetta 1.8 Cat.	86 to 92	Pierburg 28/30 2E2	F5•1
LT 2.0	80 to 82	Pierburg 36 1B1	F1•1
LT 2.4	83 to Oct 86	Pierburg 34/34 2B6	F3•1
LT 2.4	Oct 86 to 92	Pierburg 28/30 2E3	F6•1
Passat 1.3	81 to 83	Pierburg 36 1B1	F1•1
Passat 1.6	81 to 82	Pierburg 34/34 2B5	F3•1
Passat 1.6	81 to 83	Pierburg 36 1B3	F2•1
Passat 1.6	83 to 88	Pierburg 28/30 2E2	F5•1
Passat 1.8	83 to 88	Pierburg 28/30 2E2	F5•1
Passat 1.9	81 to 83	Pierburg 34/34 2B5	F3•1
Polo 1.05	81 to 85	Pierburg (Solex) 31 PIC-7	F8•1
Polo & Van 1.05	85 to 90	Weber 32 TLA	H16•1
Polo & Van 1.05	85 to 90	Pierburg 32 1B3	F2•1
Polo & Van 1.05 Cat.	89 to 90	Pierburg 32 1B3	F2•1
Polo 1.1	81 to 84	Pierburg (Solex) 31 PIC-7	F8•1
Polo 1.1 Formel-E	82 to 84	Pierburg (Solex) 31 PIC-7	F8•1
Polo 1.3	83 to 90	Pierburg 24/28 2E3	F6•1
Santana 1.6	81 to 82	Pierburg 34/34 2B5	F3•1
Santana 1.9	81 to 83	Pierburg 34/34 2B5	F3•1
Scirocco 1.5	81 to 84	Pierburg 36 1B3	F2•1
Scirocco 1.6	79 to 83	Pierburg 34/34 2B5	F3•1
Scirocco 1.6	83 to 92	Pierburg 28/30 2E2	F5•1
Scirocco 1.8	83 to 92	Pierburg 28/30 2E2	F5•1
Transporter/Caravelle 1.9	82 to 87	Pierburg 28/30 2E3	F6•1
Volvo			
240 2.3	87 to 90	Solex 34/34 Z11 (CISAC)	G7•1
340, 343 & 345 1.4	82 to 87	Solex 32 SEIA	G4•1
340	84 to 91	Weber 32 DIR	H6•1
340 1.7	86 to 91	Solex 28/34 Z10 (CISAC)	G6•1
343 & 345	80 to 83	Weber 32 DIR	H6•1
360 2.0	85 to 89	Solex 34/34 Z11 (CISAC)	G7•1
440, 460 1.7	89 to 91	Solex 28/34 Z10 (CISAC)	G6•1
740 2.0	87 to 88	Solex 34/34 Z11 (CISAC)	G7•1
740 2.3	84 to 86	Pierburg 34/34 2B5	F3•1
740 2.3	87 to 90	Pierburg 34/34 2B7	F3•1
Yugo			
45 (903)	83 to 86	Weber 32 ICEV	H12•1

Part D
Fault diagnosis

Contents

Accelerator pump 7	Hesitancy or lack of smoothness 8
Automatic choke 11	Idle faults 6
Carburettor icing 16	Idle repeatability 5
Cold starting and warm-up problems 9	Inlet manifold heater 12
Coolant-heated thermal switch testing 10	Introduction 1
Coolant-heated thermal valve testing 14	Poor hot starting 18
Cooling system faults 17	Pull-down reservoir and hoses (leakage test) 15
Gas analysis 4	Quick check of carburettor functions 3
General carburettor faults 2	Throttle body heater 13

1 Introduction

1 All carburettor service publications advise those contemplating carburettor work to first consider the effect of ignition or mechanical faults. In this respect this manual is no different. One often disregards other factors before going straight to the carburettor. Unless it is absolutely certain that the fault is fuel-related, that is, petrol pouring from the float chamber or black smoke from the exhaust, then always consider other possibilities first.
2 A flat spot or loss of power is more likely to be caused by defective spark plugs, faulty high tension leads or incorrect timing than a carburettor fault. After all, the carburettor will only respond to a pressure differential and changes in amplitude from the engine. Poor idle is more about engine condition than carburettor adjustment. If an initial investigation reveals no fault in the engine or ignition, then turn your attention to the carburettor.
3 The gas analysis checks in this Chapter should establish which circuit the fault lies in and whether it is a weak or rich mixture problem. Only then should the carburettor be dismantled.
4 It is one thing to discourage unnecessary carburettor dismantling, but regular carburettor servicing is definitely worthwhile. Over the miles, a carburettor is worked very hard and faults develop that can affect starting, economy and general running. A general carburettor service at intervals of 50 000 miles, or when the engine is overhauled/renewed, will rejuvenate the instrument to something like new condition.
5 As the carburettor ages, the mixture tends to become rich. Where air and fuel routes pass from the lower body to the upper body, a fractured upper body gasket can have a disastrous effect. Vacuum-controlled devices will cease to operate and fuel may leak or even pass into an air passage. A faulty diaphragm can often affect other circuits. A faulty power diaphragm will cause that circuit to be inoperative and give rich running at all times.

Vacuum diagnosis

6 The vacuum pump and gauge are two useful tools for testing vacuum controlled components (see illustration). The pump can be used to introduce vacuum to a component and verify its satisfactory operation. In some tests, the component is required to maintain vacuum for a period of time (usually at least ten seconds).
7 The vacuum gauge can be used to verify that a vacuum source is available and not blocked, for instance at the connectors for the secondary throttle diaphragm and choke pull-down.

Testing a carburettor vacuum source with a vacuum gauge

2 General carburettor faults

1 Unless there is an obvious carburettor fault, the engine mechanical condition should first be established and all relevant adjustments checked (ignition timing, valve clearances, spark plug gaps, etc).
2 Make a careful visual inspection of the carburettor. Many faults such as broken or missing linkages or fuel leaks can be quickly diagnosed by eyesight.
3 Look for split vacuum hoses, loose manifold bolts, carburettor fixing nuts and upper body fixing screws. Where the carburettor is flexibly mounted, check the rubber mounting for splits and cracks.
4 Check the air filter condition. A clogged filter causes rich running.
5 Check and clean the in-line fuel filter, including the one in the carburettor (if appropriate). Renew the filter if in any doubt about its condition.
6 With all the above inspections carried out, attempt to identify the fault by consulting the following list:

Chapter D

Poor idle and/or stalling

Too lean
- [ ] Idle mixture too lean.
- [ ] Broken volume screw - tip snapped off in body.
- [ ] Defective idle cut-off valve - stuck in closed position.
- [ ] Worn carburettor body or throttle spindle.
- [ ] Throttle sticking due to worn throttle spindle.
- [ ] Vacuum leak through defective carburettor base, manifold gasket or hose.
- [ ] Loose or missing fuel and air passage plugs.
- [ ] Poor idle jet seat.
- [ ] Blocked idle jet or idle channel.
- [ ] Defective or badly-adjusted throttle damper.
- [ ] Defective upper body gasket.

Too rich
- [ ] Choke stuck in the on position.
- [ ] Carbon ring around throttle plate.
- [ ] Blocked idle air bleed or air corrector.
- [ ] Incorrectly set secondary throttle plate.
- [ ] Loose idle jet or idle solenoid.
- [ ] Plugged PCV system.
- [ ] Loose needle valve.
- [ ] Secondary throttle plate slightly open.
- [ ] Leaking float.
- [ ] Defective upper body gasket.

Idle speed too fast
- [ ] Worn throttle spindle or carburettor body spindle bores (on reverting to idle from speed, the rpm will not always return to the same figure).
- [ ] Choke stuck in on position.
- [ ] Idle bypass screw incorrectly adjusted.
- [ ] Choke fast idle adjustment screw in wrong position.
- [ ] Sticking or badly-adjusted throttle linkage or cable.
- [ ] Secondary throttle slightly open.

Poor cold starting
- [ ] Mechanical or ignition fault.
- [ ] Choke fault.
- [ ] Lack of fuel.
- [ ] Defective fuel pump.
- [ ] Stuck needle valve.
- [ ] Driver failing to set semi-automatic choke correctly.

Poor hot starting
- [ ] Leaking float or needle valve.
- [ ] Worn float pin.
- [ ] Blocked float vent.
- [ ] Wrong float height.
- [ ] Carburettor flooding due to first four items above.
- [ ] Too rich or too lean idle mixture.
- [ ] Any of the faults under Poor Cold Starting.

Poor choke operation
- [ ] Too rich or too lean basic idle mixture.
- [ ] Maladjusted or defective choke pull-down assembly.
- [ ] Maladjusted or defective bi-metal unit (try adjusting to a weaker or richer setting).
- [ ] Missing blanking plugs on choke or carburettor body.
- [ ] Stuck coolant thermostat (check by feeling heater hoses).
- [ ] Lack of fast idle.
- [ ] Sticky linkage resulting in semi-automatic choke failing to set correctly.

No choke operation
- [ ] Choke stuck in off position.
- [ ] Maladjusted or defective bi-metal coil (try adjusting to richer setting).
- [ ] Bi-metal coil detached - check that tang of bi-metal coil is engaged in slot of choke assembly lever.

Heavy fuel consumption
- [ ] Any of the faults under Poor Hot Starting.
- [ ] Engine out of tune.
- [ ] External fuel leaks.
- [ ] Internal fuel leaks.
- [ ] High idle speed.
- [ ] Make fuel consumption tests.
- [ ] Check driver habits and operating conditions.
- [ ] Check the driver's own fuel consumption figures.

Intermittent problems
- [ ] Travelling particles in idle channels.
- [ ] Loose particle in a fuel channel or in the float chamber occasionally being sucked into a jet.

Backfiring or spitting (through carburettor intake)
- [ ] Inlet manifold vacuum leak.
- [ ] Burnt out inlet valve.
- [ ] Incorrect ignition timing (retarded).
- [ ] Stuck needle valve or other fuel blockage.
- [ ] Weak mixture.

Hesitation or lack of power
- [ ] Too lean or too rich idle fuel mixture.
- [ ] Defective idle cut-off valve.
- [ ] Choked or partially choked jet or internal fuel channel.
- [ ] Loose air corrector or main jet.
- [ ] Choked air filter.
- [ ] Defective fuel pump or choked fuel filter.
- [ ] Choked high-speed enrichment tube.
- [ ] Restrictor in the fuel return too large (not enough fuel enters the carburettor).
- [ ] Kickdown mechanism (automatic transmission models) out of adjustment.
- [ ] Blocked secondary idle jet (will cause hesitation on progression as the secondary throttle valve opens).
- [ ] Sticking primary or secondary throttle valve.
- [ ] If the engine will only operate on the secondary venturi of a progressive twin carburettor (full-throttle only), it is likely that the primary main jet is blocked.

Defective accelerator pump
- [ ] Defective, stiff, or porous diaphragm.
- [ ] Blockage in pump channels or nozzle.
- [ ] Missing pump ball and/or weight.
- [ ] Defective inlet/outlet valve.

Very lean mixture at speed
- [ ] If the idle mixture is correct and there are no apparent faults in the carburettor, the overall mixture may be too weak. Confirm with a CO check at 3000 rpm - the mixture should not be less then 50% of the idle CO. A check on spark plug condition after a period of high-speed running on the road will also aid diagnosis.

Failure of throttle to open fully
- [ ] Push the accelerator down fully and check for a wide-open throttle. Also check, on a twin venturi carburettor, that both throttles open fully.

Fault diagnosis

3 Quick check of carburettor functions

1 Check the following, with reference to the appropriate Chapter if necessary:

a) *Air filter heated air warm-up system.*

b) *Inlet manifold heater (hedgehog), throttle body heater and all thermal switches and valves.*

c) *Idle cut-off valve - switch the ignition on. Disconnect and then reconnect the electrical wire to the valve. There should be an audible click as the valve functions.*

d) *Accelerator pump - blip the throttle. A strong stream of petrol should be squirted from the pump injector.*

e) *Part-load enrichment (power) valve.*

f) *Secondary choke diaphragm - check for leakage.*

g) *Choke bi-metal, choke pull-down (check adjustment and for vacuum leaks) and fast idle.*

h) *Choke flap - check for smooth opening.*

i) *All diaphragms - check for petrol leaks and renew if necessary.*

j) *Throttle shaft or throttle shaft bores - check for wear.*

k) *Secondary throttle levers - check for excess wear.*

4 Gas analysis

1 Check the CO level and (where possible) the HC level at idle. If the CO level is outside the specified tolerance, attempt adjustment. Note whether the resulting level is in specification, too rich, or too weak.
2 Check the CO and HC levels at 2000 rpm. At this engine speed, the CO is likely to be up to 50% less than the reading at idle. Note whether the results are acceptable, too rich, or too weak.
3 Check the CO and HC levels at 3000 rpm. At this engine speed, the CO is likely to be slightly less than the reading at 2000 rpm. Note whether the results are acceptable, too rich, or too weak.
4 Snap open the throttle from 1000 rpm. Note if the engine hesitates and watch the accelerator pump injector. Note whether the CO goes lean (no enrichment) or rich (correct response).
5 Check the idle repeatability.
6 The results of this gas analysis should establish the areas or circuits of the carburettor to investigate and whether it is a weak or rich mixture problem.

5 Idle repeatability

1 Run the engine at idle speed and at normal operating temperature.
2 Set the idle speed and CO level to within the manufacturer's specifications, then note the exact values obtained.
3 If an HC meter is available, note the HC level.
4 Blip the throttle and check that the CO level and idle speed quickly return to stabilize within ± 0.25% and ± 10 rpm of the values previously noted. Repeat this several times. If the readings do not fall within even twice the allowable tolerance, or the CO reading tends to drift, then refer to paragraph 6.
5 If an HC meter is available, the return figure should be within ± 20 ppm of the value previously noted.
6 Readings outside these values indicate the following:
a) *Throttle linkage or cable badly adjusted or sticking.*
b) *Tight valve clearances or a vacuum leak.*
c) *Throttle shaft worn or sticking, or worn shaft bores in the carburettor body.*
d) *Excessive engine blow-by.*
e) *Carburettor service required.*
7 Jiggle the throttle shaft to check for excess movement.

6 Idle faults

1 Because the idle circuit is often sourced from the main fuel circuit, it is possible for a main jet fault to affect idle stability. Also, stalling or intermittent faults can be the result of dirt or a calcium-like substance causing partial narrowing of the internal channels that run between the jets. The calcium is formed by reaction between water and the carburettor alloy. Water is formed by the condensation present in a fuel tank. Condensation can be reduced by keeping the fuel tank level high, or by the use of an upper cylinder lubricant. This lubricant allows the water to pass more easily through the carburettor channels without reaction taking place.
2 One of the most common problems to affect a carburettor is a blocked idle jet. This is when a small piece of grit blocks the tiny jet orifice and causes the engine to stall or idle roughly. The CO reading will also be very low.
3 Another problem is that of a blocked idle fuel channel or worn idle seat. It is by no means unknown for a piece of dirt to travel about the idle duct. On occasions, it will block the idle orifice, causing intermittent stalling. Blocked channels can theoretically be cleared by drilling out the lead plugs and clearing the channels with air or a strong solvent. A new lead plug can then be punched back into place. In practice, this is a very difficult operation, best left to a specialist carburettor shop.
4 A fairly rare complaint is for the secondary throttle to be slightly open at idle. This will often cause a very rich idle, as discharge occurs at the secondary progression drillings or slot. It could occur due to a carbon ring holding open the throttle plate or through maladjustment of the secondary throttle stop screw. The screw should be adjusted so that the plate is open just enough to prevent it seizing in the throttle bore.

7 Accelerator pump

1 A defective accelerator pump is a common reason for hesitancy, particularly at low speed. To test it, blip the throttle. A strong stream of petrol should be squirted from the pump injector. If not, then make the following checks.
2 Test the bleed-back system through the outlet valve. If bleed-back occurs, the pump action will be poor. After removing the accelerator pump injector, attach the hose of a vacuum pump to the injector body (opposite end to injector nozzle) *(see illustration)*. Operate the pump until 300 mmHg (400 mbar) is registered. Renew the injector assembly if the vacuum is not maintained for at least 10 seconds.
3 Shake the injector assembly. No noise from the outlet ball would indicate that the valve is seized.
4 In many carburettors, the inlet valve is placed in the float chamber. Remove the valve and shake it. No noise from the inlet ball would indicate that the valve is seized.
5 Inspect the diaphragm for damage and fatigue. Renew the diaphragm if petrol drips from the pump housing.

8 Hesitancy or lack of smoothness

1 Thoroughly check the ignition system and spark plugs.
2 Check the ignition timing at idle and ensure that the mechanical and vacuum advance is functioning correctly.

Testing accelerator pump outlet valve with a vacuum pump

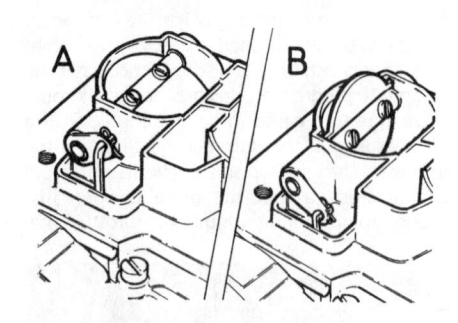

Chapter D

Choke flap operation

A *Choke flap closed - engine cold*
B *Choke flap open - engine hot*

3 Check the operation of the accelerator pump.
4 Check for vacuum leaks.
5 Adjust the carburettor to the rich side of the specification.
6 Carry out the gas analysis checks, paying particular attention to the CO level at 2000 and 3000 rpm.
7 If the results obtained from the gas analysis were too rich or too lean, service the carburettor and check for blocked jets.
8 If the fuel mixture is still too lean after a carburettor service, consider fitting a slightly larger idle jet or primary main jet.

9 Cold starting and warm-up problems

1 Check the operation of the air filter hot air warm-up system. Ensure that all vacuum hoses are connected and that the heat riser pipe from exhaust to air filter is in place. Check that the flap is open to hot air at an under-bonnet temperature below (typically) 15°C and that the cold air flap gradually opens at temperatures above this figure. The flap to hot air should be fully closed at temperatures over 25°C on most systems. If the operation is faulty, check the action of the hot air thermostat which is usually mounted in the air filter.
2 Allow the engine to cool, then remove the air filter and place to one side with vacuum hoses connected.
3 Where the choke control is semi-automatic, prime the system and set the choke flap by slowly depressing the accelerator pedal to the floor once or twice.
4 The choke flap should block the carburettor air intake. If not, check that the bi-metal coil is connected to the choke mechanism. The bi-metal coil can be adjusted so that the flap will block the air intake. However, if the index marks no longer align, the bi-metal coil may be defective. In this case, the choke flap may still be partially closed once the engine reaches normal running temperature. The cure is to renew the bi-metal coil assembly.
5 Start the engine.
6 Check that the fast idle speed is within limits.
7 Check that the choke pull-down operates satisfactorily and is correctly adjusted.
8 As the engine warms, the choke flap should gradually become open and the fast idle speed should decrease *(see illustration)*. It may be necessary to blip the throttle occasionally to simulate driving conditions and release the fast idle cam.
9 If the choke flap operation is unsatisfactory, look for a sticking, worn or broken linkage. Also check the electrical or coolant supply, as appropriate. Where the engine dies immediately after starting, or becomes very lumpy, try altering the choke flap angle with your finger. If the engine now runs better, check the pull-down adjustment *(see illustration)*. If the adjustment is within the specifications, try altering the adjustment to give less or more pull-down as appropriate. Some engines, particularly as they grow older, will benefit from either a weaker or (more likely) richer initial mixture.

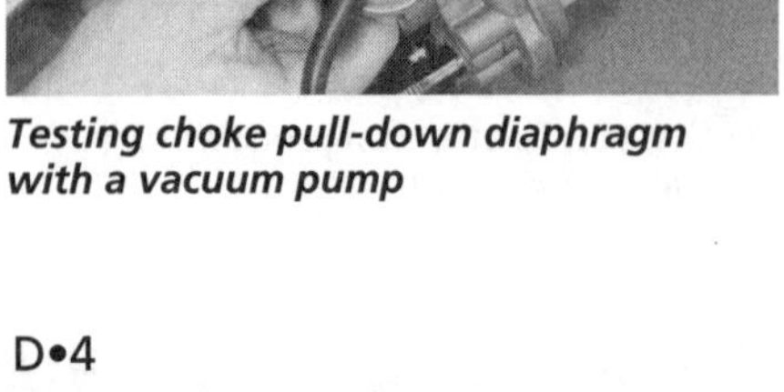

10 Coolant-heated thermal switch testing

1 The thermal switch supplies voltage to components such as the automatic choke, inlet manifold heater and/or throttle body heater when the engine coolant is cold. As the engine coolant rises above a pre-determined temperature, the thermal switch opens and the voltage supply is cut. One thermal switch may supply several components or each component may function through its own thermal switch. The switch is usually placed in a coolant hose or located in the coolant passage of the inlet manifold. In some applications, the automatic choke and throttle body heater do not function through a thermal switch.
2 Because of the many different wiring methods, always refer to the vehicle wiring diagram. The voltage supply to the inlet manifold heater is usually made through a relay. When the thermal switch is closed, the relay earth connection is made and the relay is triggered. As the engine coolant rises, the thermal switch opens, the earth to the relay is cut and the relay opens to cut the supply to the manifold heater.
3 The inlet manifold heater is sometimes called a hedgehog because of its distinctive shape. Both manifold and throttle body heaters functions on the positive temperature coefficient (PTC) principle. As the temperature rises, the heater resistance also rises.
4 A quick test of these manifold/carburettor body heating components is to switch on the ignition when the engine is cold and feel the manifold/body area. The heated areas should warm up very quickly. Be very careful, as the heat generated could cause a skin burn. When the engine is hot, these areas should not feel over-hot.
5 Starting with the engine cold, turn the ignition on.
6 Connect a voltmeter between the supply side of the thermal switch and an earth through a fixing screw of the carburettor *(see illustration)*. If battery voltage is not obtained, check the earth strap from the carburettor body to engine, then check the supply back to the ignition switch if necessary.
7 Connect a voltmeter between the output side of the thermal switch and earth. If battery voltage is not obtained, renew the switch.
8 Now connect the voltmeter between the thermal switch-controlled component terminal (at the component) and earth. If battery voltage is not obtained, check the wiring between the component and thermal switch.
9 Run the engine and allow it to warm up.
10 Connect the voltmeter between the output side of the thermal switch and earth. As the coolant temperature rises above a pre-determined temperature, the voltmeter should drop to zero. If not, renew the thermal switch. If the opening temperature is unknown, check that the switch is open at normal engine operating temperature.
11 The thermal switch can also be tested with an ohmmeter. When the switch is closed, the resistance should be infinity. When open, the resistance should be zero ohms.
12 If the supply voltage is correct but the component does not function properly, check that the carburettor earth is satisfactory.

11 Automatic choke

1 Disconnect the electrical connector to the automatic choke.
2 Connect a test lamp between the battery positive terminal and the connector terminal

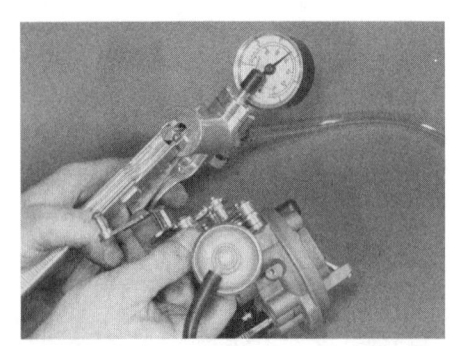

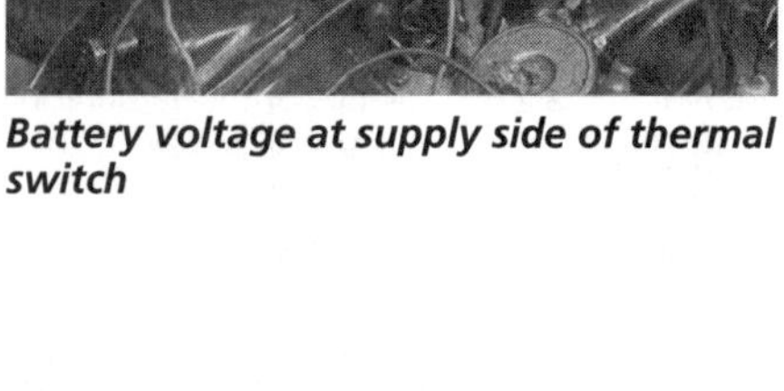

Testing choke pull-down diaphragm with a vacuum pump

Battery voltage at supply side of thermal switch

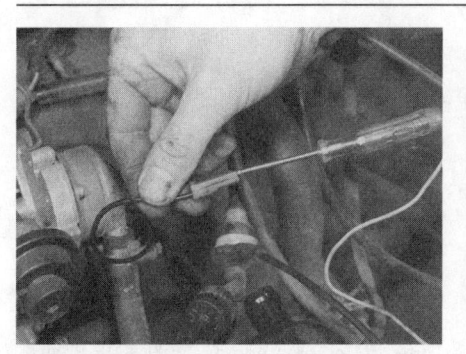

Fault diagnosis

Using a test lamp to test the automatic choke

Using an ohmmeter to check resistance of the inlet manifold heater

Using a test lamp to test the throttle body heater

leading to the choke *(see illustration)*. If the lamp does not light, renew the choke heating assembly.

12 Inlet manifold heater

1 Connect an ohmmeter between the connector terminal leading to the manifold heater and earth *(see illustration)*. The resistance registered should be 0.25 to 0.5 ohms.

13 Throttle body heater

1 Disconnect the electrical connector to the heater.
2 Connect a test lamp between the battery positive terminal and the connector terminal leading to the heater *(see illustration)*. If the lamp does not light, renew the heater. Take care when reassembling the type of heater that requires dismantling. An incorrectly-assembled heating resistance may result in a short circuit to earth.

14 Coolant-heated thermal valve testing

1 The thermal valve allows vacuum to be provided or depleted, depending on temperature, to components such as the choke pull-down or secondary throttle. Two different versions can be used, according to application, Type 1 or Type 2.
2 When the engine coolant is cold, the Type 1 valve is open to atmosphere and vacuum is reduced. As the engine coolant rises above a pre-determined temperature, the valve closes and full vacuum is restored. The valve is usually placed in a coolant hose or located in the coolant passage of the inlet manifold or automatic choke.
3 When the engine coolant is cold, the Type 2 valve is closed so that vacuum cannot reach the component. As the engine coolant rises above a pre-determined temperature, the valve opens and full vacuum is restored. The valve is usually located in the coolant passage of the automatic choke.
4 Remove the vacuum hoses and plug them.
5 Connect a vacuum pump to a connector on the thermal valve.

Type 1 valve

6 With the valve cold (open), operate the pump to register little or no vacuum reading.
7 Heat the valve or run the engine. As the temperature rises above a pre-determined temperature, the valve should close. Operate the pump to register a high vacuum reading upon the gauge. If the closing temperature is unknown, check that the valve functions correctly when the engine is cold and at the normal operating temperature.
8 Renew the valve if it does not behave as above.

Type 2 valve

9 With the valve cold (closed), operate the pump to register a high vacuum reading upon the gauge.
10 Heat the valve or run the engine. As the temperature rises above a pre-determined temperature, the valve should open. Operate the pump to register little or no vacuum reading. If the opening temperature is unknown, check that the valve functions correctly when the engine is cold and at the normal operating temperature.
11 Renew the thermal valve if it does not behave as above.
12 Note that a slight leakage is built into the valve and it will therefore slowly lose the vacuum reading when the valve is closed.

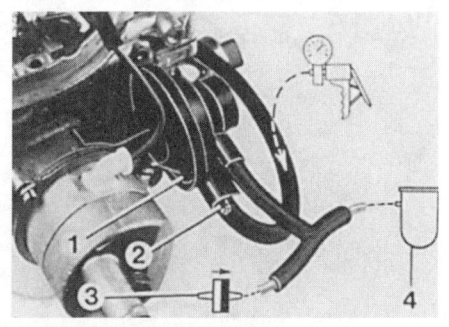

15 Pull-down reservoir and hoses (leakage test)

1 Remove the vacuum hose from the white side of the non-return valve. Plug this side of the valve.
2 Attach a vacuum pump to the vacuum supply side of the choke pull-down connector.
3 Operate the pump until 225 mmHg (300 mbar) is obtained. If the diaphragm does not fully operate, or if vacuum is not maintained for at least 10 seconds, check the pull-down, vacuum reservoir, non-return valve and hoses for leaks.
4 Test the non-return valve by connecting the pump and attempting to pull vacuum through each side in turn. Vacuum may only flow through the valve in the direction of the arrow *(see illustration)*.

Testing vacuum pull-down, reservoir and hoses
1 Pull-down unit
2 Vacuum supply connector
3 Non-return valve
4 Vacuum reservoir

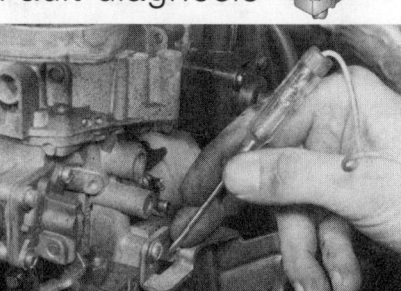

16 Carburettor icing

1 Icing occurs during periods of low ambient temperature and high humidity (cold and damp weather conditions) due to evaporation of fuel in the venturi. This causes a refrigerating effect which will lower the temperature in the area of the throttle butterfly to below freezing point. The ambient temperature does not, in fact, have to be particularly low for this to be a problem. If conditions are right, the cold fuel and moisture may be just as likely to give trouble at an air temperature ten degrees above freezing.
2 What happens is that the droplets of moisture present in the air passing through the carburettor venturi freeze and begin to form an ice coating in the throttle plate area.

D•5

Chapter D

3 Problems that occur as a result of icing are usually of two distinct types:

4 Problem 1 is that an ice formation will build up on the throttle plate, reducing the size of the venturi. This will restrict airflow and upset the AFR. Extreme richness caused by too much fuel and too little air will occur and the engine will gradually lose all power. Excessive black exhaust smoke may result and eventually the engine will over-choke and stop.

5 Problem 2 is that ice obstructs the idle and progression fuel channels. This results in frequent stalling during the warm-up period. Power, however, will probably not be affected.

6 It can sometimes take twenty or more miles before a problem occurs. If conditions are right, problems can occur even after fifty or sixty miles. In such instances, the problem can be very annoying and difficult to diagnose.

7 A temporary cure would be to park the vehicle and wait for a few minutes for the ice deposits to melt by conducted heat from the engine. Often, once the ice is melted and the engine is restarted, icing will not reoccur on that journey. The provision of heated air is used by most manufacturers to overcome the icing problem. A complete check of the hot air system is desirable when a problem is encountered.

8 Where a problem occurs, check the heated air system, inlet manifold heater and throttle body heater for satisfactory operation. Also try changing to a different brand of petrol. Modern fuels are more volatile than previous types and this results in a higher percentage of vaporisation at the discharge outlets (including main, idle and progression) which can aggravate the condition.

17 Cooling system faults

1 With the engine warm, feel the hoses leading to the automatic choke (if fitted). Both hoses should be hot and at the same temperature. Coolness would indicate a fault in the cooling system, resulting in poor or non-existent choke operation.

2 Any fault in the cooling system will affect engine temperature and therefore carburation.

18 Poor hot starting

1 Poor starting from hot can be caused by either an ignition or fuel fault. Even when the carburettor is correctly tuned and there are no faults in the ignition or fuel system, starting from hot may still be difficult.

2 The problem is due in part to the reduction of lead levels in petrol. Additives, such as iso-butane, which are used to replace lead are more volatile and harder to ignite when the engine is hot, particularly so when a high degree of emission control is used. Some engines seem more affected than others.

3 An internal float chamber vent can be a problem during idling and at low speeds during hot weather. Petrol vapour from the chamber can escape through the vent into the venturi to enrich the air/fuel mixture. An engine with an internal vent can take up to five seconds to start when hot and this is considered normal.

4 Modern, high-performance, hot-running engines with a low bonnet line, small sump and a high degree of emission control have shown a dramatic rise in under-bonnet temperatures.

5 On engine shutdown, the cooling effect of coolant circulating in the block stops, as does the cooling effect of fuel flowing through the carburettor. Within a few minutes, the engine compartment becomes like an oven and the carburettor, float chamber and fuel lines are subjected to both convected and conducted heat. The fuel in the float chamber will expand or even boil and the level will rise, causing flooding. Sometimes, fuel will drip from the accelerator pump injector nozzle and this could set off a syphoning effect to drain the float chamber into the inlet manifold.

6 The fuel in the fuel lines between the fuel pump and carburettor will expand. Because the heated fuel cannot return to the fuel pump through the closed non-return outlet valve, pressure will continue building until, in an extreme case, it may push the carburettor needle valve open and the engine will flood. Provision of a fuel return prevents a pressure build-up and also recirculates the fuel so that it is kept relatively cool.

7 On engine shutdown, the under-bonnet temperature will rise for a considerable time. This can, in some engines, cause the fuel to overheat and turn to vapour. After the engine starts, it may run hesitantly for a short while and then behave normally after fresh cool fuel arrives from the fuel tank.

8 The cures for a hot starting problem can sometimes be a little tricky and are as follows:

   a) Check that the ignition is not faulty. An overheated electronic ignition pick-up is a common reason for poor hot starting.
   b) Ensure that the idle fuel mixture is correctly set.
   c) Check that the automatic choke does not remain on when hot and service the carburettor with new gaskets, diaphragms and needle valve.
   d) Lowering the float level may sometimes help.
   e) Check and service the cooling system.
   f) Try re-routing fuel lines well away from the engine heat and/or wrap with a heat-insulating material.
   g) Fit a fuel return or vapour trap. This relieves the pressure on the needle valve and prevents flooding from overheated fuel lines.
   h) Make and fit a carburettor heat shield or fit a thicker insulator block where possible.
   i) A final measure could be to fit an electric fuel pump, preferably near the fuel tank (where it is cooler). Electric pumps are more efficient at pushing then pulling.

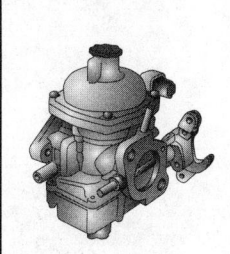

Part E Chapter 1
Ford Motorcraft 1V carburettor

Contents

Fault diagnosis 5
General servicing 3
Identification 2
Principles of operation 1
Service adjustments 4

Specifications

Model	Fiesta 950 LC	Fiesta 950 LC	Fiesta 950 HC	Fiesta 950 HC
Year	1978 to 1983	1978 to 1983	1978 to 1983	1978 to 1983
Engine code	TKA (OHV)	TKA (OHV)	TLA (OHV)	TLA (OHV)
Capacity (cm³)/no. of cyls	957/4	957/4	957/4	957/4
Oil temperature (°C)	80	80	80	80
Transmission	Manual	Manual	Manual	Manual
Carb. ident. (Ford)	77BF 9510 KBA/KGA	79BF 9510 KFA	77BF 9510 KAA/KHA	79BF 9510 KFA
Idle speed (rpm)	800 ± 50	800 ± 50	800 ± 50	800 ± 50
Fast idle speed (rpm)	1400 ± 100	1400 ± 100	1400 ± 100	1400 ± 100
CO @ idle (% vol.)	1.5 ± 0.5	1.5 ± 0.5	1.5 ± 0.5	1.5 ± 0.5
Venturi diameter	23	23	23	23
Main jet	112	115	110	115
Accel. pump stroke (mm)	2.0 ± 0.13	2.0 ± 0.13	2.0 ± 0.13	2.0 ± 0.13
Float level (mm)	29 ± 0.75	29 ± 0.75	29 ± 0.75	29 ± 0.75
Choke pull-down (mm)	3.5 ± 0.25	3.5 ± 0.25	3.5 ± 0.25	3.5 ± 0.25

Model	Fiesta 950	Fiesta 1100	Transit 1.6	Transit 2.0
Year	1983 to 1986	1978 to 1983	1978 to 1983	1978 to 1983
Engine code	TKB (OHV)	GLA (OHV)	LAT	NAT
Capacity (cm³)/no. of cyls	957/4	1117/4	1593/4	1993/4
Oil temperature (°C)	80	80	80	80
Transmission	Manual	Manual	Manual	Manual
Carb. ident. (Ford)	84BF 9510 KHA	77BF 9510 KEA/KJA	78HF 9510 KEA	78HF 9510 KFA
Idle speed (rpm)	800 ± 50	800 ± 50	800 ± 25	800 ± 25
Fast idle speed (rpm)	1400 ± 100	1500 ± 100	2000 ± 100	1000
CO @ idle (% vol.)	1.25 ± 0.5	1.25 ± 0.5	1.0 ± 0.2	1.0 ± 0.2
Venturi diameter	23	24	27	27
Main jet	107	122	137	135
Accel. pump stroke (mm)	2.0 ± 0.13	2.0 ± 0.13	2.8 ± 0.13	2.8 ± 0.13
Float level (mm)	29 ± 0.75	31 ± 0.75	29 ± 0.75	29 ± 0.75
Choke pull-down (mm)	3.5 ± 0.25	3.0 ± 0.25	3.0 ± 0.25	4.5 ± 0.25
Bi-metal housing mark	-	-	on index	-

Chapter E1

Model	Transit 2.0	Transit 2.0	Transit 2.0
Year	1978 to 1983	1978 to 1983	1978 to 1983
Engine code	NAT	NAT	NAV
Capacity (cm³)/no. of cyls	1993/4	1993/4	1993/4
Oil temperature (°C)	80	80	80
Transmission	Manual	Manual	Automatic
Carb. ident. (Ford)	78HF 9510 KGA	78HF 9510 KJA	78HF 9510 KHA
Idle speed (rpm)	800 ± 25	800 ± 25	800 ± 25
Fast idle speed (rpm)	2000 ± 100	1000	2000 ± 100
CO @ idle (% vol.)	1.0 ± 0.2	1.0 ± 0.2	1.0 ± 0.2
Venturi diameter	27	27	27
Main jet	135	115	127
Accel. pump stroke (mm)	2.8 ± 0.13	2.0 ± 0.13	2.8 ± 0.13
Float level (mm)	29 ± 0.75	29 ± 0.75	29 ± 0.75
Choke pull-down (mm)	3.8	3.0 ± 0.25	3.8 ± 0.25
De-choke (mm)	5.3	-	5.3 ± 0.50
Bi-metal housing mark	on index	on index	on index

Ford Motorcraft 1V carburettor

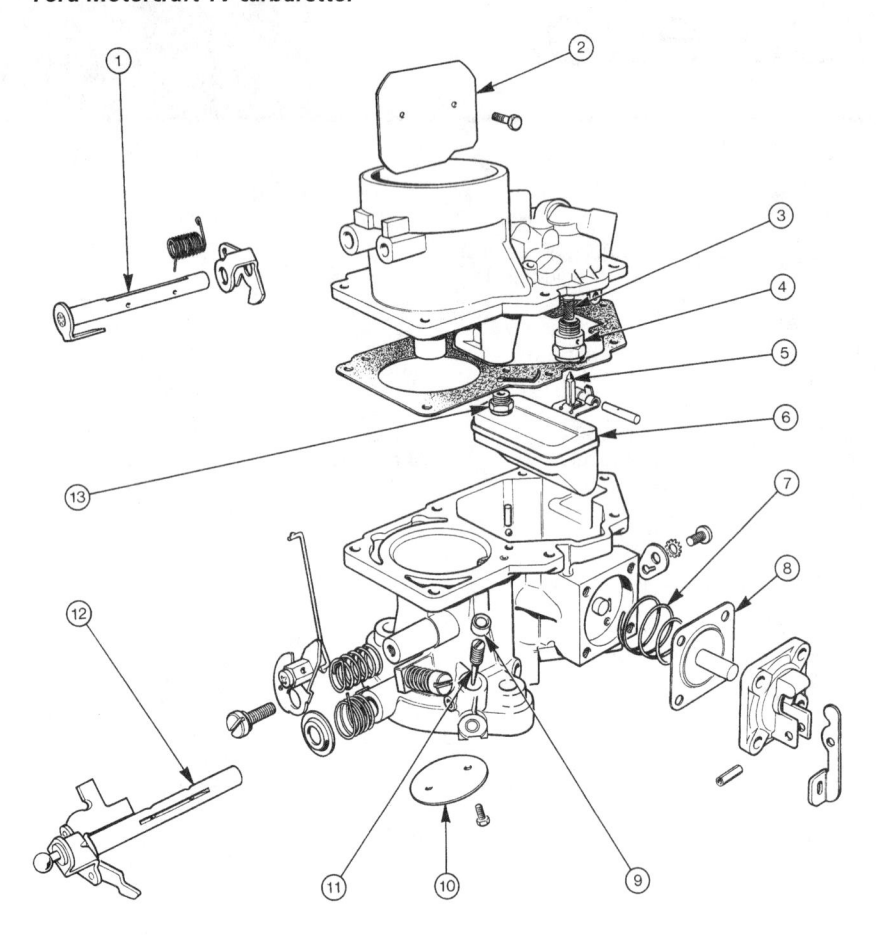

1 Choke spindle
2 Choke flap
3 Fuel inlet filter
4 Needle valve seat
5 Needle valve
6 Float
7 Accelerator pump return spring
8 Accelerator pump diaphragm
9 Tamperproof plug
10 Throttle plate
11 Mixture screw
12 Throttle spindle
13 Main jet

1 Principles of operation

Introduction

1 The following technical description of the Ford Motorcraft 1V carburettor should be read in conjunction with the more detailed description of carburettor principles in Part A.
2 This carburettor is a downdraught single venturi instrument *(see illustration)*. The choke control can be semi-automatic or manual in operation. All calibrated air and fuel jets, other than the main jet, are bushings pressed into the body of the carburettor. These bushings are not renewable.

Fuel control

3 Fuel flows into the carburettor through a fine mesh filter. The fuel level in the float chamber is controlled by a needle valve and brass float assembly. An anti-vibration ball is incorporated into the needle valve design. The float chamber is normally vented to atmosphere.

Sonic bypass idle system

4 The idle system is similar to the sonic system used in the Ford VV carburettor *(see illustration)*.

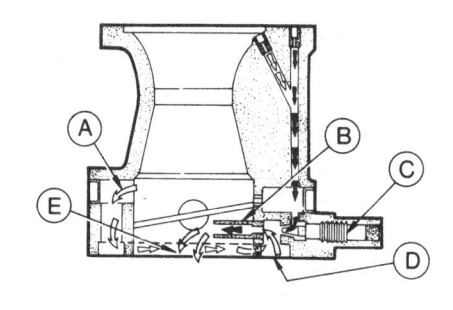

Sonic bypass idle system

A Air supply
B Discharge tube
C Idle mixture screw
D Air/fuel mixing chamber
E Air channel chamber

Ford Motorcraft 1V carburettor

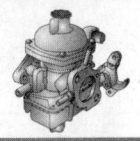

5 Air supply for the sonic idle system is sourced from a drilling in the main venturi. The majority of air required for idle is drawn from the venturi into the idle bypass gallery. The remaining quantity of air will pass the throttle plate, which is varied to allow the engine to idle.

6 Fuel drawn from the top of the main well passes through a metered idle bushing and is emulsified with air from a calibrated air bleed bushing. This air/fuel mixture passes down a channel into the idle mixing chamber where it is atomised with the air drawn into the bypass idle gallery. The idle mixture is drawn into the engine through a sonic discharge tube regulated by an adjustable mixture control screw.

7 A high pressure difference exists across the discharge tube and the air is accelerated to a very high speed. The shock waves formed are used to atomise the air/fuel mixture which is fed to the engine under the throttle plate. The result is a finely atomised and stable idle mixture that meets low emission requirements. Fuel for progression is drawn from two drillings which are uncovered by the opening throttle as the engine is accelerated.

8 Idle speed is set by an adjustable screw. Idle mixture is regulated by a tapered adjustable mixture screw. This is tamper proofed at production level in accordance with the emission regulations.

Idle cut-off valve

9 Some variations utilise an idle cut-off valve to prevent run-on after engine shutdown. A 7-volt solenoid plunger is used to block the idle channel when the ignition is switched off (see illustration).

Accelerator pump

10 The accelerator pump is controlled by a diaphragm and is mechanically operated by a rod attached to the throttle linkage. The outlet valve consists of a ball and weight placed into the outlet channel. Pump discharge into the venturi is made via an injection bushing pressed into the upper air intake.

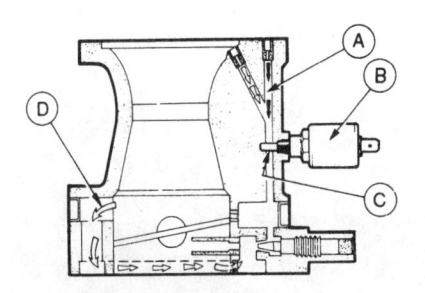

Idle mixture cut-off valve

A Idle fuel and air channels
B Idle cut-off valve
C Plunger blocking idle channel
D Air intake to bypass idle system

Main circuit

11 The amount of fuel discharged into the air stream is controlled by a calibrated main jet. Fuel is drawn through the main jet into the base of a vertical well which dips down into the fuel in the float chamber. An emulsion tube is placed in the well. The fuel is mixed with air drawn in through a calibrated air correction bushing and the holes in the emulsion tube. The resulting emulsified mixture is discharged into the airstream from the main nozzle.

Power enrichment and economy circuit

12 A piston opens and closes a channel to supplement the fuel in the main well. An air passage is taken from under the throttle plate to a chamber over the piston. At idle and during light-throttle operation, manifold vacuum in the passage causes the piston to rise and seat a valve to close off the channel. Under acceleration and wide-open throttle operation, the vacuum in the manifold collapses. The piston returns under spring pressure and the power valve opens the supplementary channel. Fuel then flows through the channel to supplement the fuel in the main well. The fuel level in the well rises and the mixture is enriched *(see illustration)*.

Cold start system

13 Most variations of this carburettor use a manual choke which is operated by a dash-mounted cable. Some variants use a semi-automatic mechanism that is controlled by a bi-metal spring and engine coolant.

Automatic choke operation

14 When cold, the spring will curl up and pull a strangler-type choke flap into the closed position. Heating the bi-metal coil causes it to uncurl and the choke flap is slowly opened. A cam bears against the throttle stop to place it into a fast idle position.

15 The choke pull-down system utilises a vacuum piston connected by levers to the choke spindle. The piston is operated from a constant vacuum source beneath the throttle plate. Once the engine has started, the piston is pulled downwards with a force strong enough to pull open the choke flap by a small amount. This will prevent over-rich operation and flooding.

Manual choke operation

16 The manual choke is operated by a dash-mounted cable. When the cable is pulled, it operates a lever that pulls the choke flap closed across the air intake. A linkage rod opens the throttle to give the necessary fast idle. Once the engine has started, the depression partially opens the choke flap against the action of a spring. A stop ensures that the choke is only opened a small amount. During engine warm-up, the cable should be progressively pushed home until the choke flap is fully open.

2 Identification

1 The carburettor identification code is stamped on the float chamber body. A manufacturer's date code is stamped on the next line.

2 In the Ford emission carburettor with the sonic bypass idle system, seven screws are used to secure the upper body cover. Pre-emission carburettors (prior to May 1976) use only six screws to fix the cover.

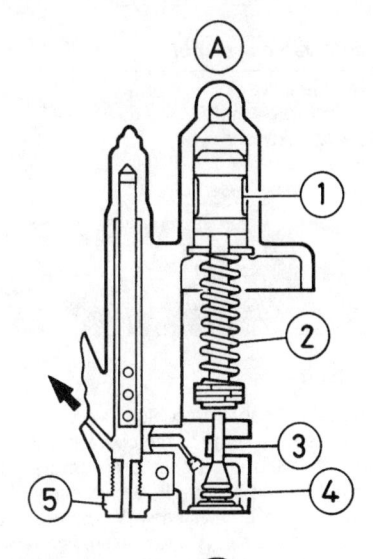

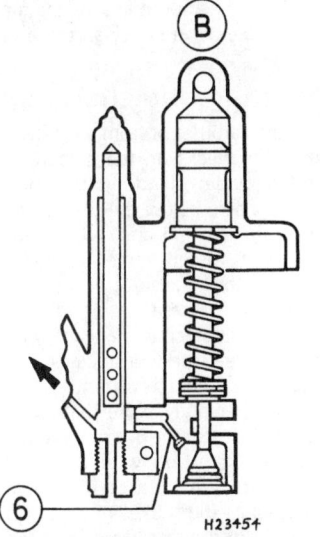

Power valve operation - closed (A) and open (B)

1 Piston
2 Spring
3 Power valve
4 Light spring
5 Main jet
6 Enrichment channel

Chapter E1

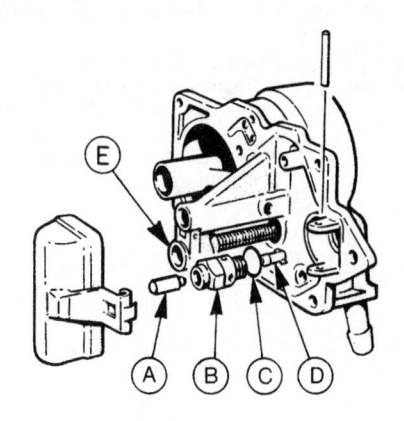

Needle valve assembly

A Needle valve
B Valve seat
C Sealing washer
D Inlet filter
E Power valve assembly

Accelerator pump outlet ball and weight location

3 General servicing

Introduction

1 Read this Chapter in conjunction with Part B, which describes some of the operations in more detail. It is assumed that the carburettor is removed for this service. However, many of the operations can be tackled with the carburettor in place. Where this is undertaken, first remove the upper body assembly and soak the fuel out of the float chamber using clean tissue or soft cloth.

Dismantling and checking

2 Remove the carburettor from the engine.
3 Make visual checks on the carburettor for wear and damage. In addition, inspect the mixture outlet hole below the throttle valve. If the hole is starred and cracked, the mixture screw has been forced home at some stage. Renewal of the carburettor is strongly recommended in this case.
4 Remove the float chamber vent tube and check that it is clear and unrestricted.
5 Remove the seven screws and detach the carburettor upper body. Note that on models with a manual choke, the choke cable securing clamp will be removed with one of these screws. Rotate the fast idle assembly downwards when the choke linkage rod can be disengaged from the fast idle cam. Disengage and remove the choke rod from the choke spindle assembly. Renew the choke rod if the retaining lugs have worn away (as commonly happens).
6 Use a straight-edge to check for distorted flanges on all facing surfaces.
7 Inspect the float chamber for corrosion.
8 Remove the upper body gasket, float, float pin and needle valve assembly (see illustration).

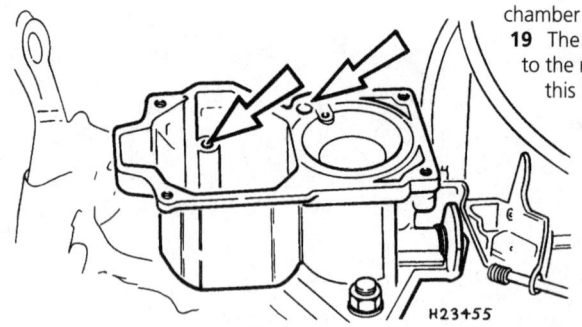

Removal of the needle valve seat requires a thin socket or box spanner.
9 Check that the anti-vibration ball is free in the valve end.
10 Check the needle valve tip for wear and ridges. This is more likely with the brass needle valve tip than when a viton one is used. Use a viton-tipped replacement when possible.
11 The float should be checked for damage and ingress of petrol. Shaking the float will indicate the presence of fuel.
12 Renew the float pin if it shows signs of wear.
13 The fuel filter pushed into the end of the needle valve seat is prone to fluff build-up and this can be serious enough to cause a lack of power.
14 Unscrew the mixture screw and inspect the tip for damage and ridges.
15 Invert the carburettor body, with a hand cupped over the float chamber to catch the accelerator pump outlet ball and weight (see illustration).
16 Remove the four screws and detach the accelerator pump cover, diaphragm and spring. Check the diaphragm for fatigue and damage and renew it if petrol drips from the pump housing.
17 Remove the main jet and check the emulsion well for a blockage. Check all bushings and channels for ovality, wear and blockages.
18 Inspect the power valve mechanism for stickiness and check that the blanking plug is not loose in the base of the valve. The plug may fall out, and be found on the float chamber floor.
19 The channel from the power valve to the main well is a brass bushing and this bushing sometimes works loose and blocks the main well. Fuel flow is then usually reduced which results in a severe power loss. After removal of the main jet, the bushing can sometimes be seen lying in the main well. It may be necessary to detach the power valve assembly casting from the main well casting in order to place the bushing back into position. This can be accomplished by pushing out a small pin that secures the housings together (see illustrations). After separation, the channel is exposed and the bushing can be put back into place.
20 If an automatic choke is fitted, remove the two choke assembly housing securing screws and inspect the mechanism for stickiness and wear.
21 If a manual choke is fitted, inspect the choke spindle, mechanism and levers for stickiness and wear.

Preparation for reassembly

22 Clean the carburettor body, clear all internal channels and mop out any sediment from the float chamber. An air line may be used to clear the internal channels once the carburettor is fully dismantled. Spraying carburettor cleaner into all the bushings and orifices originating in the air intake and venturi will often clear the passages and channels of gum and dirt. This carburettor is particularly prone to blocking of the air bleed passages (see illustration).
23 Note that if an air line is used to direct air into the accelerator pump passages with the diaphragm still in place, diaphragm damage may result. Take care that the pump outlet ball and weight are not blasted away with the upper body removed.
24 During reassembly, a complete set of new gaskets should be fitted. Also renew the needle valve, float pin and accelerator pump diaphragm. The mixture screw and main jet should not need renewal unless obviously worn. Renew worn linkages and springs where necessary.

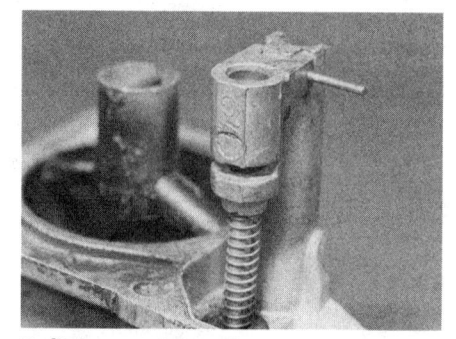

Refitting retaining pin

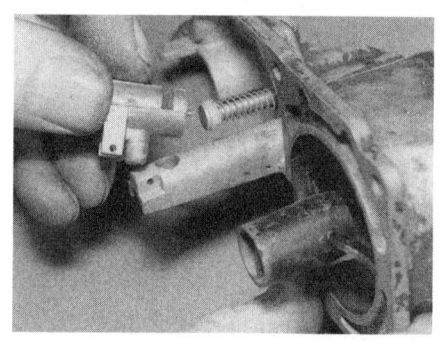

Refitting power valve assembly

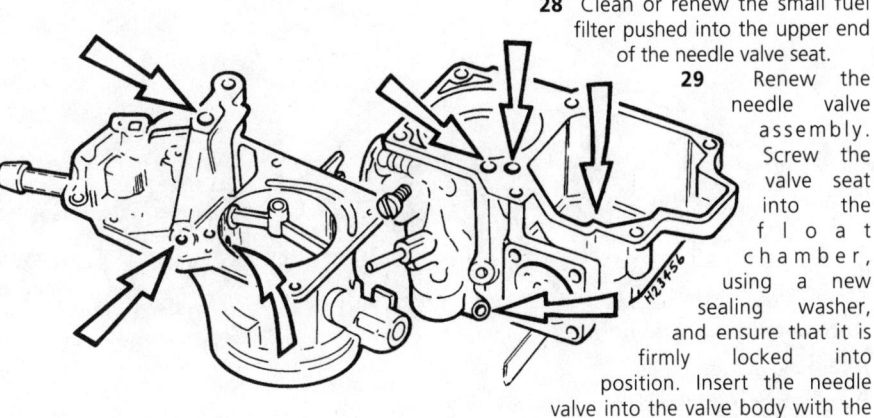

Ford Motorcraft 1V carburettor

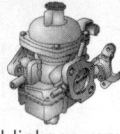

Air and fuel passage location

25 Clean all mating surfaces and flanges of old gasket material and reassemble with a new upper gasket. Ensure that housing covers are assembled with their air and fuel routes correctly aligned.

Reassembly

26 Refit the main jet, ensuring that it is firmly locked into position.
27 Refit the pump spring, diaphragm and cover assembly, securing with the four screws.

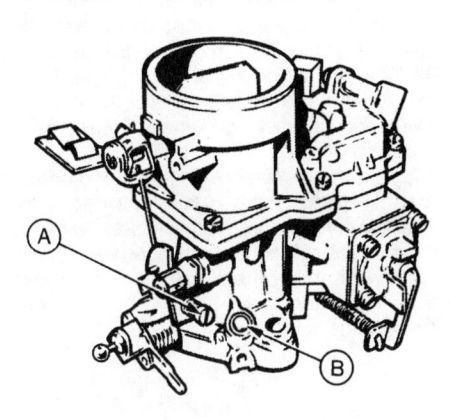

Idle adjustment screws

A *Idle speed screw*
B *Idle mixture (CO) screw*

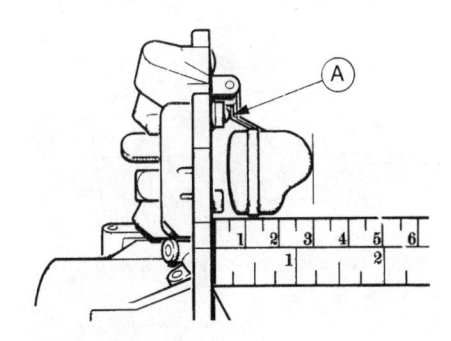

Float level adjustment

A *Adjusting tag*

28 Clean or renew the small fuel filter pushed into the upper end of the needle valve seat.
29 Renew the needle valve assembly. Screw the valve seat into the float chamber, using a new sealing washer, and ensure that it is firmly locked into position. Insert the needle valve into the valve body with the ball facing outwards, then refit the float and pin.
30 Adjust the float level.
31 Drop the small ball into the accelerator pump outlet channel and place the weight on top of the ball.
32 Refit the idle mixture screw. Carefully turn the screw in until it just seats, then unscrew it three full turns. This will provide a basic setting to allow the engine to be started.
33 Renew the float chamber gasket and place into position on the main body.
34 Slot the upper piece of the choke rod (straight section) into the lever attached to the choke spindle (top). Rotate the fast idle assembly downwards until the choke linkage rod can be engaged into the fast idle cam as the carburettor upper body is fitted. Rotate the fast idle assembly upwards and secure the top cover with the fixing screws. Where a manual choke is fitted, secure the choke cable securing clamp with one of these screws so that it faces the choke assembly.
35 Refit the idle cut-off valve assembly (where fitted).
36 If an automatic choke is fitted, place the choke assembly housing onto the carburettor body with a new gasket and secure with the two fixing screws.
37 On carburettors with a manual choke,

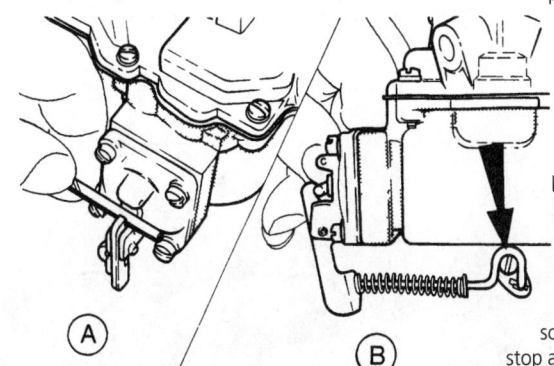

Accelerator pump adjustment

A *Checking pump stroke*
B *Adjustment point (arrowed)*

ensure that the choke flap and linkage move smoothly and progressively.
38 Refit the carburettor to the engine.
39 Refit the float chamber vent tube.
40 Always adjust the carburettor idle speed and mixture after any work has been carried out on the carburettor, preferably with the aid of a CO meter.
41 Adjust the choke.

4 Service adjustments

Adjustment preconditions

1 Refer to Part B for general advice on preconditions to correct adjustment of this carburettor.

Idle speed and mixture (CO)

2 Run the engine at 3000 rpm for 30 seconds to clear the manifold of fuel vapours, then allow the engine to idle.
3 Use the idle speed screw to set the specified idle speed *(see illustration)*.
4 Check the CO level against the Specifications. If incorrect, remove the tamperproof plug over the mixture screw and adjust to the correct level. Turning the screw clockwise (inwards) will reduce the CO level. Turning the screw anti-clockwise (outwards) will increase the CO level.
5 Repeat paragraphs 3 and 4 until both adjustments are correct. Clear the manifold every 30 seconds during the setting operation by running the engine at 3000 rpm for 30 seconds.
6 Increase the speed to 2000 rpm and note the CO reading. The cruise reading should be less than half the idle CO reading.
7 Fit a new tamperproof plug to the mixture adjusting screw.
8 The manufacturer states that variations of 0.5% CO and 40 rpm during idle are acceptable.

Float level

9 Hold the upper body in a vertical position, with the float tag gently touching the ball of the fully-closed needle valve.
10 Measure the distance between the upper body (gasket removed) and the base of the float.
11 Adjust as necessary by bending the float tag *(see illustration)*.

Accelerator pump stroke

12 Unscrew the idle speed screw until it is clear of the throttle stop and the throttle plate is fully closed.
13 Push in the pump diaphragm to its stop and use the shank of a twist drill to measure the clearance between the pump lever and diaphragm.
14 Adjust as necessary by bending the U-section on the pump control rod *(see illustration)*.

E1•5

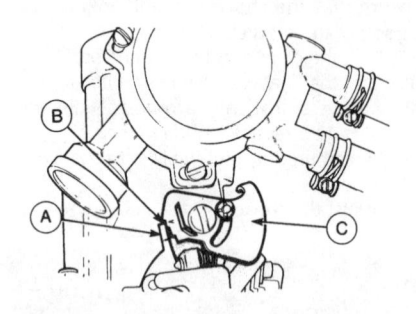

Chapter E1

Automatic choke set in fast idle position

A *Adjusting tag*
B *Fast idle position*
C *Fast idle cam*

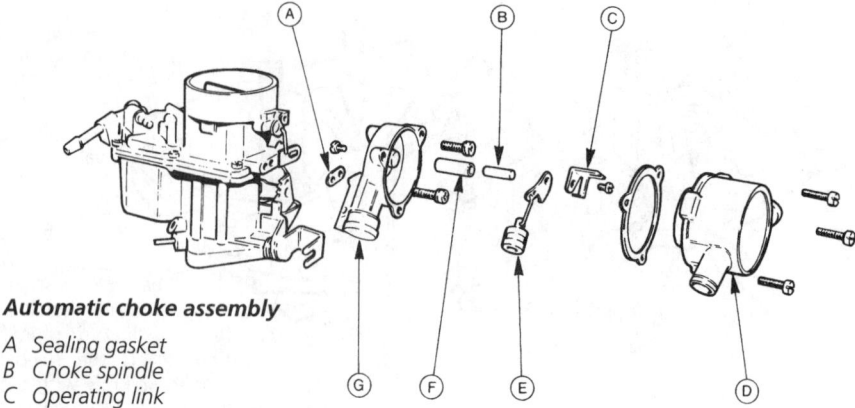

Automatic choke

Fast idle

15 Warm the engine to normal running temperature before adjustment.
16 Open the throttle and place the fast idle cam in its fast idle position against the throttle stop. The V mark on the cam will be aligned with the top of the throttle lever *(see illustration)*. Release the throttle and the cam should remain in position.
17 Start the engine without moving the throttle. Record the fast idle speed and compare with the specified value.
18 Adjust as necessary by bending the tag on the throttle lever.

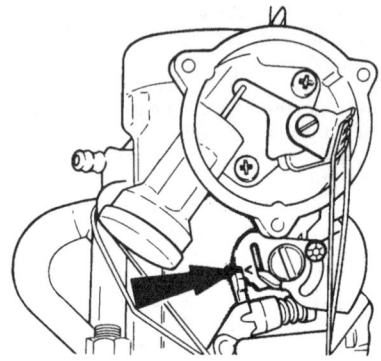

Automatic choke assembly

A *Sealing gasket*
B *Choke spindle*
C *Operating link*
D *Outer housing (and bi-metal spring)*
E *Vacuum piston assembly*
F *Spindle sleeve*
G *Main choke housing*

V mark and de-choke mechanism

19 Remove the three screws and detach the bi-metal coil housing from the carburettor. Remove the choke gasket *(see illustration)*.
20 Place an elastic band around the choke operating lever so that it exerts a downward pressure.
21 Open the throttle, allow the choke flap to close fully, then release the throttle.
22 Use the shank of a 5.0 mm twist drill to measure the gap between the lower part of the choke flap and the air intake.
23 Slightly open the throttle and the fast idle cam should drop into position. The V mark on the cam should now be aligned with the top of the throttle lever *(see illustration)*.
24 Adjust as necessary by bending the choke control rod *(see illustration)*.
25 Fully open the throttle with the choke flap in the closed position. Just before full-throttle, the choke flap will de-choke.
26 Use the shank of a 5.3 mm twist drill to measure the gap between the lower part of the choke flap and the air intake.
27 Adjust as necessary by bending the de-choke lever on the fast idle cam *(see illustration)*.
28 Remove the elastic band.

Choke vacuum pull-down

29 Open the throttle and place the fast idle cam in its highest cam position against the throttle stop. The V mark on the cam will not be aligned with the top of the throttle lever.
30 Start the engine without moving the throttle and position a preload tool (Ford special tool) on the choke lever. Ensure that the tool is floating.
31 Use the shank of a twist drill to measure the gap between the lower part of the choke flap and the air intake *(see illustration)*. Refer to Specifications for the appropriate drill size.
32 Stop the engine and adjust as necessary by bending the choke pull-down lever.
33 Renew the choke gasket and ensure that it is correctly located.
34 Refit the bi-metal coil housing and ensure that the spring locates in the slot of the choke lever *(see illustration)*. Secure loosely with the three screws. Align the cut mark on the bi-metal cover with the correct mark on the choke assembly housing and tighten the three screws *(see illustration)*.

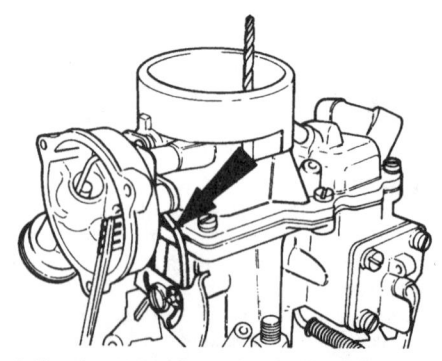

V mark on cam aligned with throttle lever (arrowed)

Adjusting V mark setting by bending control rod (arrowed)

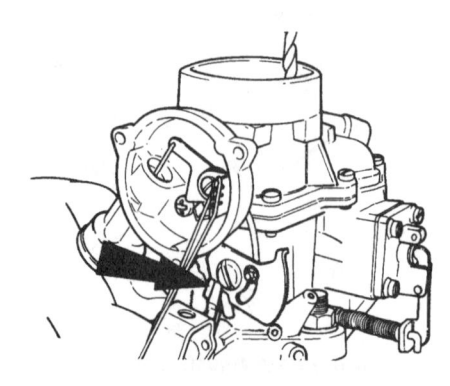

De-choke adjustment (adjusting tag arrowed)

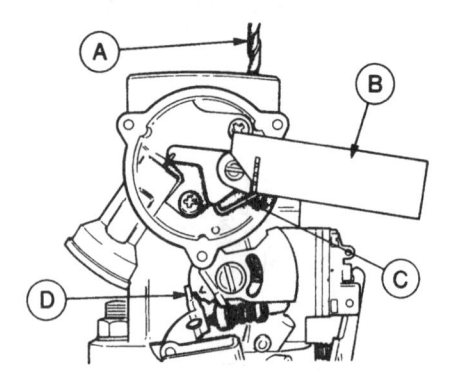

Choke vacuum pull-down adjustment

A *Twist drill*
B *Automatic choke preload tool (Ford special tool)*
C *Pull-down adjustment lever*
D *Throttle set on highest cam*

Ford Motorcraft 1V carburettor

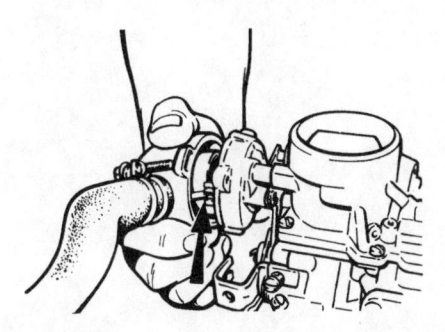

Engaging spring in middle slot of choke lever

Manual choke

Fast idle

35 Warm the engine to normal running temperature before adjustment.
36 Hold the choke flap fully open whilst rotating the choke control mechanism towards the closed position. After about a third of the total movement, the mechanism will stop.
37 Start the engine, record the fast idle rpm, and compare with the specified value.
38 Adjust as necessary by bending the tag *(see illustration)*.

Choke pull-down

39 Fully close the choke flap by rotating the choke cam onto its stop.
40 Open the choke flap against spring tension up to its stop.
41 Use the shank of a twist drill to measure the gap between the lower part of the choke flap and the air intake *(see illustration)*. Refer to Specifications for the appropriate drill size.
42 Bend the tag to adjust the gap, if necessary.

5 Fault diagnosis

Refer to Part D for general faults affecting all carburettors. The following faults are specific to the Ford Motorcraft 1V carburettor:

Poor idle and/or stalling

☐ Choked or dirty idle fuel passages or idle bushing

Over-rich air/fuel mixture

☐ Faulty float chamber gasket allowing excess air into the power valve circuit. This will put the power valve piston out of action

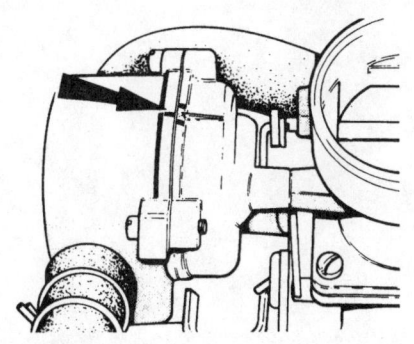

Automatic choke alignment marks (arrowed)

☐ Seized power valve piston
☐ Loose or missing power valve blanking plug
☐ Choked or dirty air bushings

Lack of power

☐ Choked needle valve fuel filter
☐ Fuel blockage caused by misplaced power valve bushing

Poor starting

☐ Fuel draining from float chamber via leaking accelerator pump diaphragm

Carburettor set for fast idle check
A Adjusting tag
B Choke flap held open

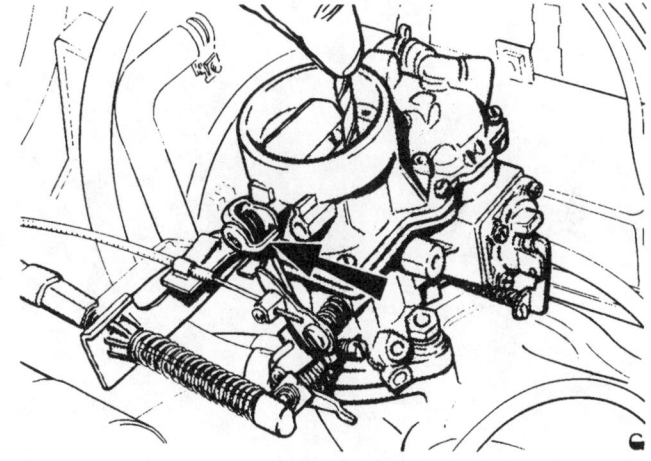

Choke mechanism held in closed position to check choke flap pull-down
Adjusting tag arrowed

Notes

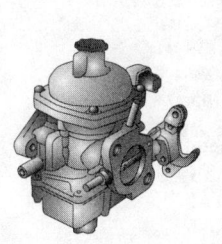

Part E Chapter 2
Ford Variable Venturi (VV) carburettor

E2

Contents

Component testing 5
Fault diagnosis 6
General servicing 3
Identification 2
Principles of operation 1
Service adjustments 4

Specifications

Model	Fiesta 1100	Fiesta 1100	Fiesta 1300	Escort 1.1
Year	1983 to 1984	1984 to 1989	1983 to 1986	1980 to 1984
Engine code	GSF (OHV)	GSF (OHV)	JPC (CVH)	GLB (OHV)
Capacity (cm³)/no. of cyls	1117/4	1117/4	1296/4	1117/4
Oil temperature (°C)	80	80	80	80
Transmission	Manual	Manual	Manual	Manual
Carb. ident. (Ford)	79BF 9510 KCB	84BF 9510 KFB/KFC	84SF 9510 KEA	81SF 9510 KMA
	81SF 9510 KMA	84BF 9510 KJA	-	-
	84BF 9510 KGA	85BF 9510 KAA	-	-
Idle speed (rpm)	800 ± 50	800 ± 50	800 ± 50	800 ± 50
CO @ idle (% vol.)	1.5 ± 0.5 (fan on)	1.5 ± 0.5 (fan on)	1.5 ± 0.5	1.5 ± 0.5 (fan on)
Jet needle	FCH (back off 2.5 turns)	-	-	FCH
Choke gauging (mm)	3.0	-	-	3.0
Choke pull-down (mm)	3.3 (clockwise)	-	-	3.3 (clockwise)

Model	Escort 1.1	Escort & Orion 1.3	Escort & Orion 1.3	Escort & Orion 1.3
Year	1984 to 1987	1980 to 1984	1984 to 1986	1986 to 1988
Engine code	GSG (OHV)	JPA (CVH)	JPA (CVH)	JLA (OHV)
Capacity (cm³)/no. of cyls	1117/4	1296/4	1296/4	1297/4
Oil temperature (°C)	80	80	80	80
Transmission	Manual	Manual	Manual	Manual
Carb. ident. (Ford)	84BF 9510 KFB/KFC	81SF 9510 KCA	84SF 9510 KAA/KEA	86BF 9510 KAA/KCA
	KDA/KFA/KJA	84SF 9510 KWA	84SF 9510 KJA	86BF 9510 KEA
	85BF 9510 KAA	-	-	-
Idle speed (rpm)	800 ± 50	800 ± 50	800 ± 50	800 ± 50
CO @ idle (% vol.)	1.5 ± 0.5 (fan on)	1.5 ± 0.5	1.5 ± 0.5	1.5 ± 0.5
Jet needle	FCH	FDK	-	-
Choke gauging (mm)	-	3.4	-	-
Choke pull-down (mm)	-	3.8 (anti-clockwise)	-	-

Model	Escort 1.6	Escort 1.6	Cortina 1300	Cortina 1300
Year	1980 to 1986	1980 to 1986	1980 to 1983	1979 to 1982
Engine code	LPA (CVH)	LPA (CVH)	J2R (OHV)	JCR (OHC)
Capacity (cm³)/no. of cyls	1597/4	1597/4	1297/4	1294/4
Oil temperature (°C)	80	80	80	80
Transmission	Manual	Automatic	Manual	Manual
Carb. ident. (Ford)	81SF 9510 KFA/KFB	82SF 9510 KAA	791F 9510 KAA	79HF 9510 KAB
	81SF 9510 KHA/KHB	83SF 9510 KDA	-	-
	83SF 9510 KCB	85SF 9510 KBA	-	-
Idle speed (rpm)	800 ± 50	850 ± 50	800 ± 25	800 ± 50
CO @ idle (% vol.)	1.5 ± 0.5	1.5 ± 0.5	1.75 ± 0.5	1.5 ± 0.5
Jet needle	FCX	FCX	FBT	FAG
Choke gauging (mm)	3.4	3.4	3.4	3.1
Choke pull-down (mm)	3.3 (clockwise)	3.3 (clockwise)	4.5 (clockwise)	4.7 (clockwise)

Chapter E2

Model	Cortina 1600	Cortina 1600 Auto	Sierra 1300	Sierra 1600
Year	1980 to 1983	1980 to 1983	1982 to 1986	1982 to 1986
Engine code	LCR (OHC)	LCR (OHC)	JCT (OHC)	LCT (OHC)
Capacity (cm³)/no. of cyls	1593/4	1593/4	1294/4	1593/4
Oil temperature (°C)	80	80	80	80
Transmission	Manual	Automatic	Manual	Manual
Carb. ident. (Ford)	79HF 9510 KCB	79HF 9510 KDB	83HF 9510 KBA/KBC	83HF 9510 KCA/KCB
Idle speed (rpm)	800 ± 50	800 ± 50	800 ± 50	800 ± 50
CO @ idle (% vol.)	1.5 ± 0.5	1.5 ± 0.5	1.5 ± 0.5	1.5 ± 0.5
Jet needle	FAJ	FAJ	FBT	FAJ
Choke gauging (mm)	3.4	3.4	3.3	3.3
Choke pull-down (mm)	3.7 (anti-clockwise)	3.7 (anti-clockwise)	4.0 (clockwise)	4.3 (anti-clockwise)

Model	Sierra 1600	Sierra 1600 Economy	Capri 1300	Capri 1300
Year	1982 to 1986	1982 to 1984	1979 to 1982	1979 to 1982
Engine code	LCT (OHC)	LCS (OHC)	J2N (OHV)	JCR (OHC)
Capacity (cm³)/no. of cyls	1593/4	1593/4	1297/4	1294/4
Oil temperature (°C)	80	80	80	80
Transmission	Automatic	Manual	Manual	Manual
Carb. ident. (Ford)	83HF 9510 KDA/KDB	83HF 9510 KAA	791F 9510 KAA	79HF 9510 KAB
Idle speed (rpm)	800 ± 50	800 ± 50	800 ± 25	800 ± 50
CO @ idle (% vol.)	1.5 ± 0.5	1.5 ± 0.5	1.75 ± 0.5	1.5 ± 0.5
Jet needle	FAJ	FAJ	FBT	FAG
Choke gauging (mm)	3.3	3.3	3.4	3.3
Choke pull-down (mm)	4.3 (anti-clockwise)	4.3 (anti-clockwise)	4.5 (clockwise)	4.5 (clockwise)

Model	Capri 1600	Capri 1600	P100-L	P100
Year	1979 to 1988	1979 to 1988	1982 to 1987	1988 to 1991
Engine code	LCN (OHC)	LCN (OHC)	LCT (OHC)	NAE (OHC)
Capacity (cm³)/no. of cyls	1593/4	1593/4	1593/4	1993/4
Oil temperature (°C)	80	80	80	80
Transmission	Manual	Automatic	Manual	Manual
Carb. ident. (Ford)	79HF 9510 KCB	79HF 9510 KDB	-	86HF 9510 KDA
Idle speed (rpm)	800 ± 50	800 ± 50	800 ± 25	800 ± 50
CO @ idle (% vol.)	1.5 ± 0.5	1.5 ± 0.5	1.5 ± 0.5	1.0 ± 0.5
Jet needle	FAJ	FAJ	-	-
Choke gauging (mm)	3.4	3.4	-	-
Choke pull-down (mm)	3.7 (anti-clockwise)	3.7 (anti-clockwise)	-	-

Model	Transit 1.6	Transit 1.6	Transit 2.0	Transit 2.0
Year	1983 to 1985	1985 to 1991	1983 to 1985	1983 to 1985
Engine code	LAT (OHC)	LA (OHC) 47kw	NAT (OHC)	NAV (OHC)
Capacity (cm³)/no. of cyls	1593/4	1593/4	1993/4	1993/4
Oil temperature (°C)	80	80	80	80
Transmission	Manual	Manual	Manual	Automatic
Carb. ident. (Ford)	79HF 9510 KHC	86HF 9510 KHA	79HF 9510 KNA	79HF 9510 KKC
Idle speed (rpm)	800 ± 50	800 ± 50	800 ± 50	800 ± 50
CO @ idle (% vol.)	1.0 ± 0.5	1.0 ± 0.5	1.0 ± 0.5	1.0 ± 0.5
Choke gauging (mm)	3.4	3.4	3.4	3.4
Choke pull-down (mm)	4.0	4.0	4.0	4.0

Model	Transit 2.0
Year	1985 to 1991
Engine code	NA (OHC) 57kw
Capacity (cm³)/no. of cyls	1993/4
Oil temperature (°C)	80
Transmission	Manual
Carb. ident. (Ford)	86HF 9510 KJA
Idle speed (rpm)	800 ± 50
CO @ idle (% vol.)	1.0 ± 0.5
Choke gauging (mm)	3.4
Choke pull-down (mm)	4.0

Ford Variable Venturi (VV) carburettor

Ford Variable Venturi carburettor

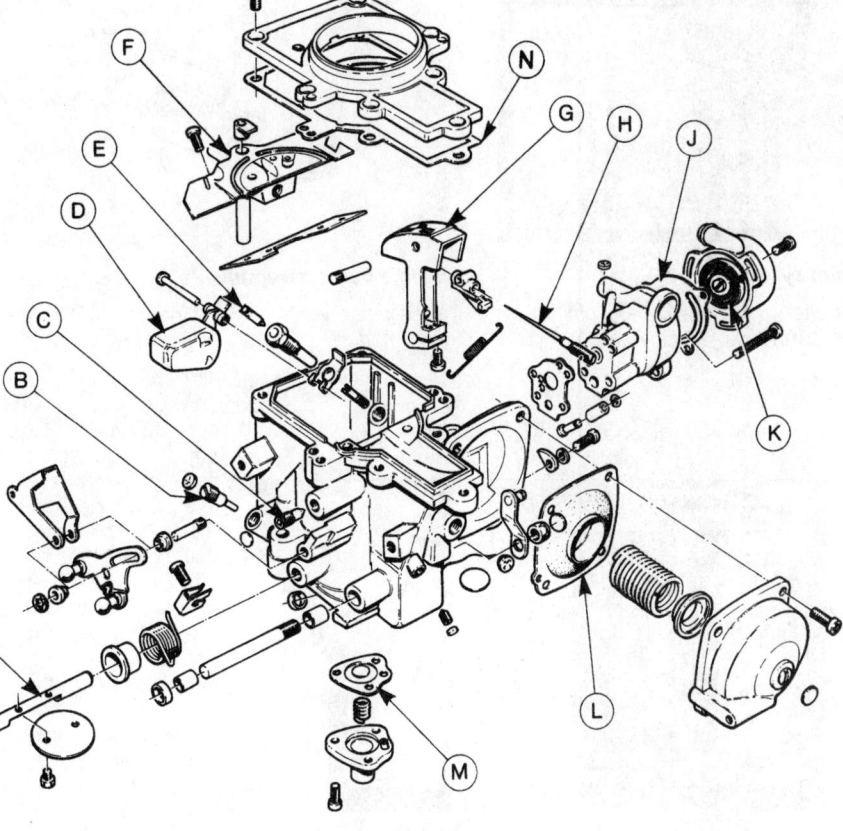

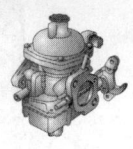

1 Principles of operation

Fuel atomisation

1 Fuel atomisation is the process of breaking the droplets of petrol down to their smallest possible size. Good fuel atomisation is important for reduced engine exhaust emissions and it is achieved when the air velocity through a carburettor venturi is high (approximately 120 m/sec).

2 The venturi size in a conventional fixed venturi carburettor is a compromise of performance against carburettor efficiency. At high engine speeds, the venturi must be large enough to satisfy the engine's demand for a high volume of air to give maximum power. This volume will achieve the required velocity of 120 m/sec to give good atomisation. At low engine speeds, the much-reduced volume will also reduce the velocity to approximately 12 m/sec, resulting in inefficient atomisation. Use of a small venturi would speed up the air velocity but strangle performance at higher engine speeds.

Air control

3 The Ford VV carburettor *(see illustration)* uses a variable venturi so that air volume may be varied according to the engine's demand. Air velocity will remain high no matter what the engine speed or load. At low speeds, the venturi is small, but air velocity is high (approximately 90 m/sec) *(see illustration)*. As the throttle is opened and speed increases, the venturi will open so that high air velocity is always matched with the correct volume of air. This has the further advantage of supplying only the amount of air that a particular engine requires.

4 Due to production tolerances, engines of a similar type and swept volume may require less air at maximum throttle opening than others. The VV will automatically adjust the venturi to give the exact volume of air required. Other than when at maximum throttle (and full load) and at idle, the VV improves atomisation over the fixed venturi type. A leaner air/fuel mixture is thus allowed, engine power output is increased, emissions are reduced and fuel consumption is improved.

5 The variable venturi is controlled by an air valve assembly which is directly coupled to a control diaphragm. At rest and at idle, the control diaphragm is held in its closed position by a strong spring and the air valve almost closes the venturi *(see illustration)*. A vacuum passage runs from the venturi into the control diaphragm housing. As the throttle is opened and airflow in the venturi increases, the pressure will drop to create a vacuum *(see illustration)*.

A Throttle spindle
B Mixture screw
C Air bypass adjuster
D Float
E Needle valve
F Metering block
G Air valve
H Metering rod
J Choke assembly
K Bi-metal coil
L Control diaphragm
M Accelerator pump diaphragm
N Float chamber gasket

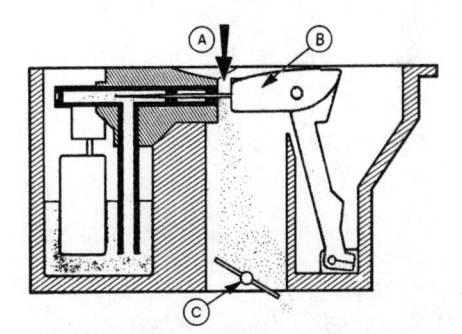

Carburettor at low engine speed/load

A Air intake
B Air valve (almost closed)
C Throttle plate

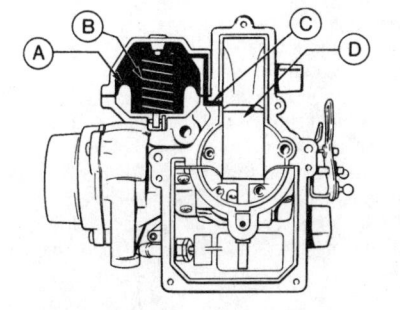

Carburettor control vacuum - low

A Control diaphragm in rest position
B Diaphragm spring
C Vacuum passage
D Air valve almost closed

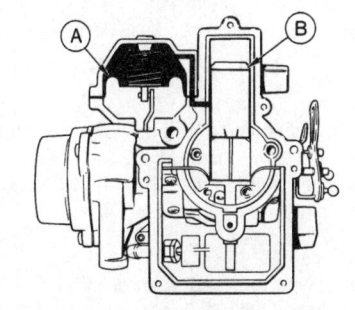

Carburettor control vacuum - high

A Control diaphragm pulled back
B Air valve open

E2•3

Chapter E2

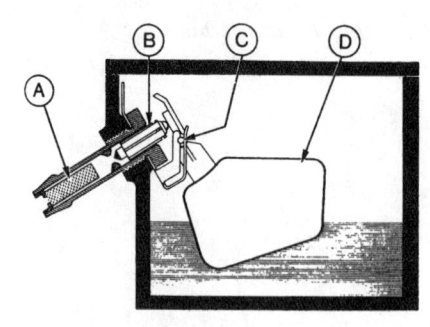

Fuel inlet system

A Inlet filter
B Needle valve
C Float pin
D Float

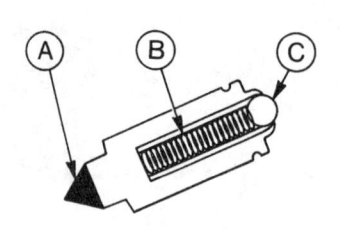

Needle valve assembly

A Lead end viton-coated
B Spring
C Ball

Main fuel system

1 Float chamber
2 Float
3 Fuel pick-up tube
4 Vent
5 Main and secondary jets
6 Main fuel outlet
7 Metering needle
8 Air valve
9 Venturi
10 Throttle plate

6 This vacuum, known as the control vacuum, will act upon the control diaphragm and move the air valve against spring pressure. In turn, this will move the venturi to its proper position for any given airflow. As the throttle is closed and airflow reduces, the venturi will decrease in size to further balance volume of air against high velocity.

7 The control vacuum alters according to throttle position and engine load. A high air velocity is always maintained, consistent with the correct volume of air to satisfy the engine's demand.

Fuel control

8 Fuel flows into the carburettor through a fine mesh filter and the fuel level in the float chamber is controlled by a needle valve and plastic float assembly (see illustration). The leading end of the needle valve is viton-coated to give better fuel sealing. A spring (built into the valve) and ball arrangement is used to dampen vibrations that may cause needle chattering (see illustration).

9 The float level is not adjustable because the main jet is located well above the fuel level. This means that the level has little effect upon main jet operation. Ventilation of the float chamber is achieved by an internal passage which runs from the float chamber to the carburettor throat, just above the air valve. All float chamber vapours are thus contained in the venturi throat area (see illustration).

10 The main jet is located directly opposite the air valve. Maximum vacuum (according to airflow) is exerted at this point and fuel is drawn from the float chamber, via a pick-up tube, into the main jet assembly. A tapered metering needle is attached to the air valve body and locates into the jet assemblies. This needle almost blocks the main and secondary jets at idle and low engine loads. As engine load increases and the air valve moves in response to an increased air requirement, the needle is withdrawn from the jets to maintain the AFR and allow more fuel to be drawn into the engine. The needle is very accurately machined so that the correct amount of fuel is delivered at all speeds and loads. A different needle profile is required for each engine type and it is important that the correct needle is used.

Idle system

11 The idle system is similar to the sonic system used in later versions of the Ford Motorcraft IV carburettor. 30% of fuel required for idle is provided by the main system and the remaining 70% provided by the idle system (see illustration).

12 Air is drawn through the venturi where it splits into two streams. One stream passes the slightly-open throttle plate and the other is drawn into the idle bypass gallery.

13 Fuel, sourced from the main pick-up tube, is drawn through a metered idle jet where it is mixed with air from a small air bleed. This air/fuel mixture passes down through a channel into the idle mixing chamber where it is atomised with air drawn into the bypass idle gallery. The idle mixture is drawn into the engine through a sonic discharge tube, regulated by an adjustable mixture control screw. A very high pressure difference exists across the discharge tube and the air is accelerated to a very high speed of approximately 365 m/sec. Shock waves are then formed to atomise the air/fuel mixture which is then fed to the engine under the throttle plate. The result is a finely-atomised and stable idle mixture that meets low emission requirements.

14 Idle speed is set by an adjustable screw. Idle mixture is regulated by a tapered adjustable volume screw which is tamper-proofed at production level in accordance with emission regulations.

15 Because fuel from the main jet system is provided at idle, the VV carburettor does not require a separate progression system and transition from idle to higher speeds is much smoother than with a fixed type venturi.

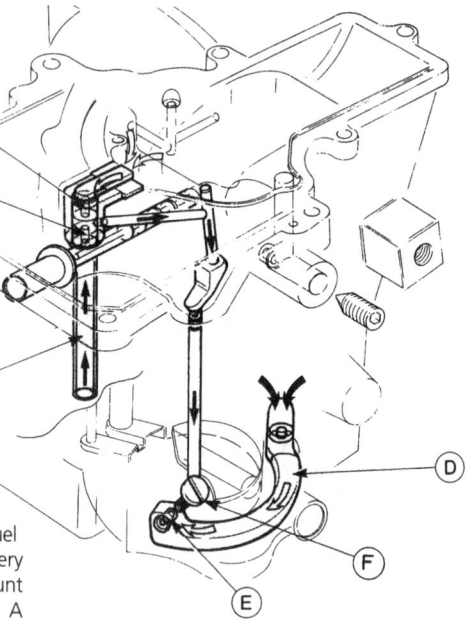

Idle system

A Fuel pick-up tube
B Idle jet
C Idle air jet
D Idle bypass gallery
E Idle mixing chamber
F Idle mixture screw

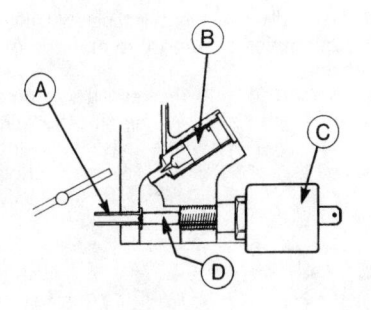

Ford Variable Venturi (VV) carburettor

Idle cut-off valve

A Sonic discharge tube
B Idle mixture control screw
C Idle cut-off valve
D Solenoid plunger

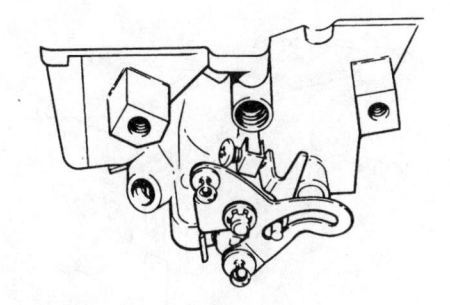

Progressive throttle system

Idle cut-off valve

16 An idle cut-off valve is used on most VV carburettors (see illustration). It functions in the conventional manner, using a 12-volt solenoid plunger to block the idle sonic discharge channel when the ignition is switched off. The plunger is viton-tipped to ensure a good seal in the idle channel.

Throttle operation

17 The throttle bore of the VV carburettor is designed to meet the air requirements of the largest engine likely to be used. The same bore is used for smaller engines which may achieve maximum air requirements on 75% of throttle opening. This could lead to poor running on small throttle openings due to a very sensitive initial throttle movement but this problem is overcome by use of a progressive throttle linkage (see illustration). A cam-and-roller mechanism is used so that a large throttle pedal movement will give only a small throttle plate opening. Throttle plate movement becomes more rapid as full pedal travel is reached.

Accelerator pump

18 During acceleration, the relative velocity of fuel will tend to lag behind the velocity of air, leading to a time lag that could weaken the AFR and cause a hesitation or flat spot. The VV carburettor employs two systems to overcome this problem (see illustration). A restrictor is located in the air passage which links the control diaphragm to the control vacuum area. During acceleration, the control diaphragm and air valve will react slowly. A brief increase in airflow in the venturi will cause an increase in vacuum at the main jet and result in a momentary increase in fuel discharge. This will compensate for all but heavy acceleration, when even more fuel is needed.

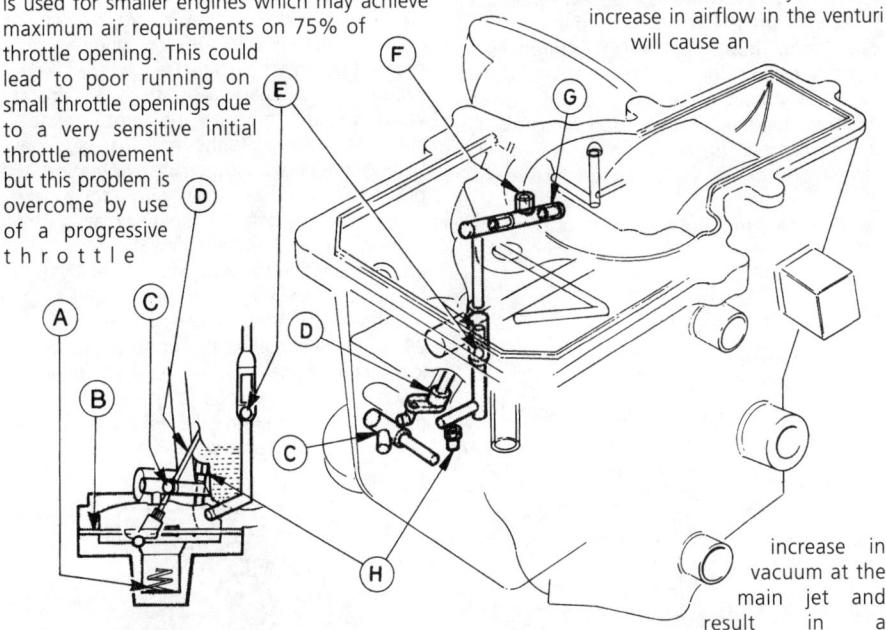

19 The accelerator pump supplies the extra fuel required and is vacuum-operated. A constant vacuum signal is supplied to the pump diaphragm. During operation with a closed or steady throttle opening, this vacuum signal will pull the diaphragm down against a spring. Fuel is then drawn from the float chamber into the pump reservoir past an inlet valve (see illustration). The outlet valve (a ball and weight) remains closed to prevent fuel from returning via the outlet channel.

20 Under acceleration, the vacuum signal drops and the diaphragm is pushed back by the spring to its rest position. Fuel from the reservoir in the pump housing is pushed through the pump outlet channels, past the pump outlet valve and is injected from the pump injector into the venturi. The inlet (ball) valve remains closed to prevent fuel from being returned to the float chamber (see illustration).

21 During high speed engine operation, the strong vacuum formed at the pump injector could draw fuel from the pump reservoir into the venturi. A vacuum break hole in the pump injector nozzle prevents this occurrence by reducing vacuum in the outlet passage.

22 Under certain conditions, the fuel in the pump reservoir may become overheated and boil or turn to vapour. This is prevented by the use of a pump back-bleed hole which allows vapour to bleed back into the float chamber. Vacuum would then draw fresh, cooler fuel into the pump reservoir to maintain the level.

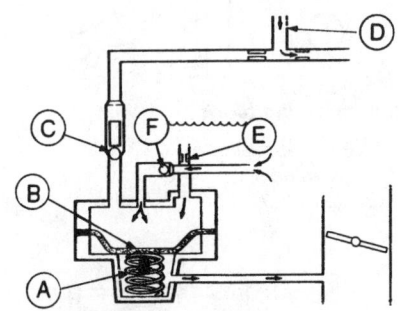

Accelerator pump inlet system

A Diaphragm spring
B Diaphragm
C Pump outlet valve
D Vacuum break hole
E Back-bleed hole
F Fuel inlet valve

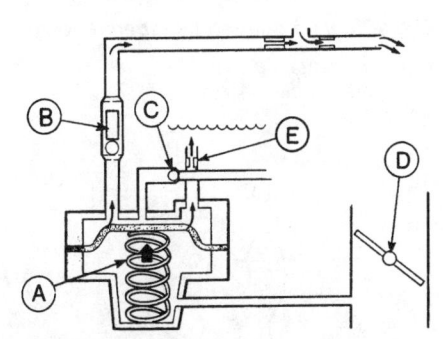

Accelerator pump component location

A Diaphragm spring
B Diaphragm
C Fuel inlet valve
D Vacuum passage
E Pump outlet valve (ball valve and weight)
F Vacuum break hole
G Pump outlet injector
H Back-bleed hole

Accelerator pump outlet system

A Diaphragm spring
B Pump non-return valve
C Fuel inlet valve
D Throttle plate
E Back-bleed hole

E2•5

Chapter E2

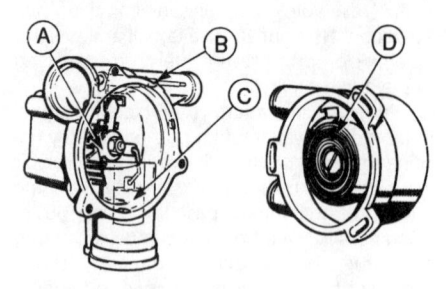

Choke assembly

A Bi-metal spring/mechanism actuating lever
B Choke needle valve
C Choke pull-down piston
D Bi-metal spring

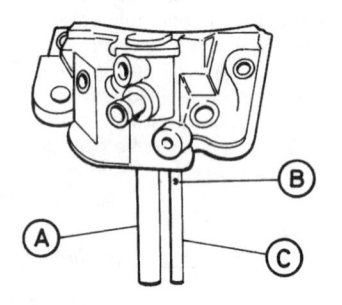

Main metering block

A Main pick-up tube
B Air bleed hole
C Choke pick-up tube

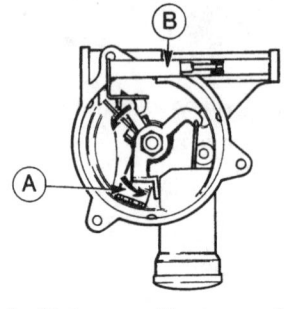

Choke fuel jet opened by tapered needle

A Choke actuating lever
B Tapered choke needle

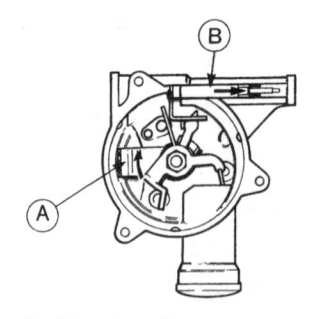

Choke fuel jet closed by tapered needle

A Choke actuating lever
B Needle valve closed

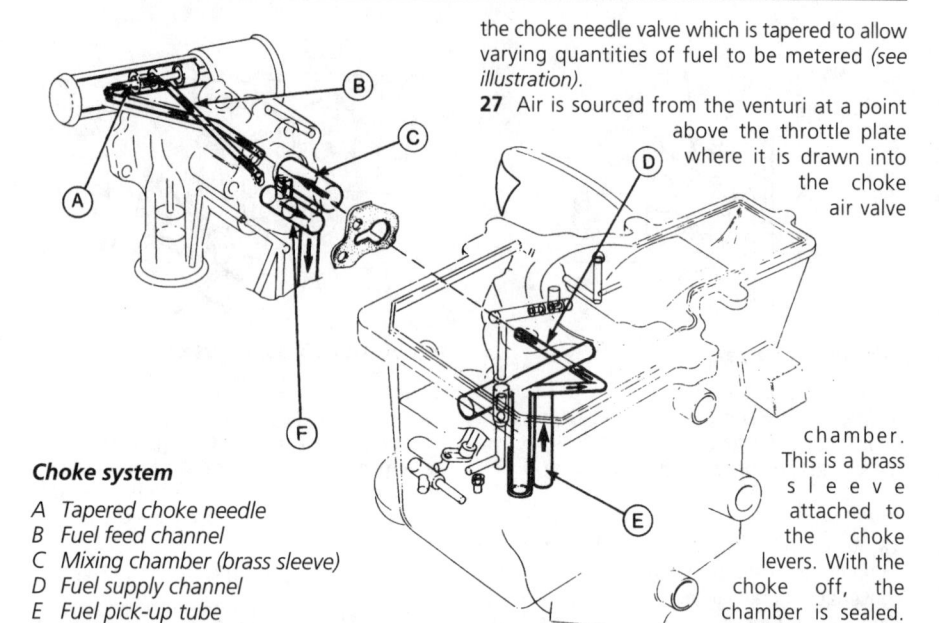

Choke system

A Tapered choke needle
B Fuel feed channel
C Mixing chamber (brass sleeve)
D Fuel supply channel
E Fuel pick-up tube
F Choke mixture discharge outlet

Choke operation

23 All versions of the VV carburettor use a similar type of choke (see illustration). This may be fully automatic or manual in operation.
24 The choke is similar to a miniature carburettor, with its own variable fuel and air supplies.
25 In early carburettors, fuel was originally sourced from the main pick-up tube in the carburettor body. In later carburettors, a separate pick-up for the choke was introduced. An air bleed hole in the upper part of this pick-up allows the mixture to be partly emulsified in the main metering block, to improve overall atomisation of the choke air/fuel mixture (see illustration).
26 Fuel is drawn through internal channels into the choke needle valve which is tapered to allow varying quantities of fuel to be metered (see illustration).
27 Air is sourced from the venturi at a point above the throttle plate where it is drawn into the choke air valve chamber. This is a brass sleeve attached to the choke levers. With the choke off, the chamber is sealed. When the choke operates, the sleeve rotates to allow the air to exit into a chamber where it is mixed with fuel. The resulting air/fuel mixture is returned to the main carburettor body and is introduced to the engine below the throttle plate. This supply augments the normal fuel systems and provides the necessary enrichment for cold engine operation (see illustrations).
28 To reduce emission levels and improve fuel economy during warm-up, the engine uses a choke pull-down system (see illustration). A vacuum piston, operated from a constant vacuum source beneath the throttle plate, is connected by levers to the central choke spindle. During idle and steady throttle operation, the piston is pulled downwards with a force strong enough to overcome the choke operating spring tension. This will partially shut the needle valve and air supply to lean off the AFR. Under acceleration, the vacuum will be reduced and the piston will rise to restore rich operation.
29 An engine starting from cold will produce a low vacuum signal and so full enrichment occurs. Once the engine has started, vacuum is produced that will lean off the initial rich mixture by operating the vacuum pull-down mechanism.

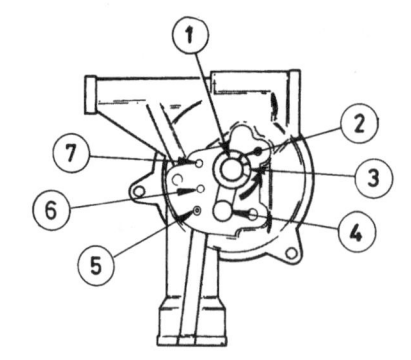

Choke housing seen from flange side

1 Mixing chamber (brass sleeve)
2 Air inlet from venturi
3 Choke mixture outlet
4 Choke mixture discharge to inlet manifold
5 Vacuum supply to choke pull-down
6 Fuel feed channel from choke fuel jet to mixing chamber
7 Fuel supply channel to choke

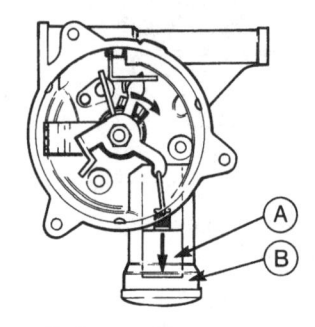

Choke pull-down system

A Piston pulled down by high vacuum
B High vacuum

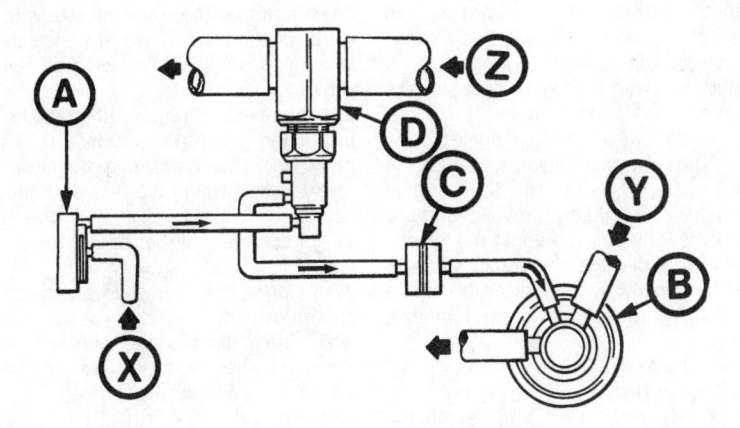

Ford Variable Venturi (VV) carburettor

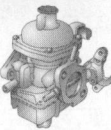

Carburettor Speed Control System (CSCS)

- A Thermal Vacuum Switch (TVS)
- B Carburettor Speed Control Valve (CSCV)
- C Vacuum Delay Valve (VDV)
- D Ported Vacuum Switch (PVS)
- X Manifold vacuum
- Y From air filter
- Z Engine coolant

30 An adjustable linkage, connecting both the fuel needle valve and the air supply, ensures that the correct mixture may be maintained. When the choke is off, the air and fuel supplies to the choke are also cut off.

31 Where an automatic choke is used, a water-heated bi-metal coil spring is used to control the air and fuel supplies. A hook on this spring couples it to the choke levers.

32 The coil contracts when the engine is cold and moves the linkage so that the tapered needle is pulled out of the jet. Fuel then flows through the choke channels to the mixing chamber where it is mixed with air drawn from the venturi. As the engine warms up, the coolant becomes heated and the spring expands to restore the tapered needle into the jet, shutting off the fuel flow.

33 The manual choke functions in the same manner as the automatic choke but a cable is used to operate the mechanism manually. This type of choke uses a conventional coil spring, not a bi-metal type.

34 The choke design is such that it is unnecessary to press down the accelerator pedal during cold starting. Only if flooding occurs should the pedal be pressed to the floor. This will open the throttle wide and a snail cam attached to the throttle shaft will actuate a small rod to half-open the air valve and ventilate the engine.

35 Because the accelerator pump is operated by manifold depression, it will discharge when the engine is switched off. Coupled with the internal venting system, this can often cause a slightly longer hot-start cranking period. Ford suggest that a hot cranking time of anything up to five seconds is acceptable. The accelerator pedal should be held half-open during this operation.

Carburettor speed control system (CSCS)

36 The CSCS was introduced to overcome over-rich running during choke operation *(see illustration)*. The AFR is weakened by the supply of additional air under the throttle plate, according to ambient air and coolant temperatures.

37 A Carburettor Speed Control Valve (CSCV) is fitted on some models and is located in a hose that connects the air filter to the inlet manifold *(see illustration)*. Control of the CSCV is by manifold vacuum, through a small-bore hose taken from the inlet manifold and via a Thermal Vacuum Switch (TVS), Ported Vacuum Switch (PVS) and Vacuum Delay Valve (VDV).

38 During hot engine operation, the TVS and PVS are closed and the CSCV is partially open to draw clean air from the air filter through the breathing system. When the coolant temperature is below 35°C, the PVS will open and allow manifold vacuum to act upon the CSCV. In turn, manifold vacuum will draw clean air through the now completely-open CSCV valve to weaken the AFR. As the coolant temperature rises above 35°C, the PVS will close, the vacuum signal will cease and the CSCV will close to its former partially-open condition to shut off the additional air supply. Similarly, the TVS opens below an ambient air temperature of 10°C and closes as the air temperature rises above this level. In order for the system to function, the air and coolant temperatures must be below their respective control levels.

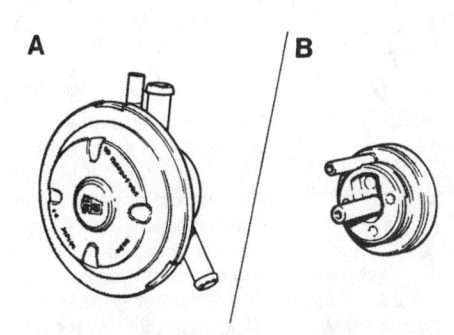

Carburettor Speed Control Valve (A) and Thermal Vacuum Switch (B)

39 The VDV delays operation of the CSCV until the engine is running and also dampens the constantly-varying vacuum signal as the throttle is opened and closed.

2 Identification

1 The carburettor identification code is stamped on the float chamber body and a manufacturer's date code is stamped on the next line. The choke mounting flange is also stamped with an identification code letter.

2 The VV carburettor has been subject to a great number of modifications during its life. There are too many to list separately but all important modifications are mentioned at the appropriate point in the text.

3 General servicing

Introduction

1 Read this Chapter in conjunction with Part B, which describes some of the operations in more detail. It is assumed that the carburettor is removed for this service. In addition to the information given in Part B, note the following:

a) After detaching the throttle cable from the carburettor linkage, remove the bolt which holds the cable to the side of the carburettor.
b) On carburettors with manual choke, disconnect the choke cable from the choke housing.
c) When removing the carburettor fixing nuts and washers, it may be necessary on some models to unscrew and partially withdraw the idle speed setting screw so that the bottom fixing nut can be removed.
d) Where a manual choke is fitted, remove the three screws and detach the coil housing from the main choke assembly.

Dismantling and checking

2 Invert the carburettor and check the position of the mixture adjusting screw tip in the outlet channel. If the screw has been forced home, it may have broken and be blocking the idle outlet.

3 Attempt to unscrew the mixture screw. The tip should move easily in and out of its idle orifice. Renew the carburettor if the mixture screw is broken and/or seized in the idle outlet.

4 Unless necessary, it is not always wise to remove the mixture screw which tends to fit extremely tightly and damage can result to the body and screw thread. If the mixture screw is loose in the body, renew the screw or the carburettor.

5 Inspect the air valve retaining screws in the

Chapter E2

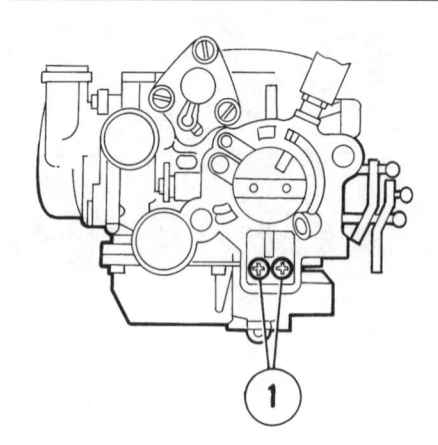

Air valve screws (1)

base of the carburettor *(see illustration)*. Renew the carburettor if the screws are sheared.

6 Inspect the throttle spindle area for movement, excess wear and stickiness. Excess wear is more likely in the softer aluminium throttle shaft bores of the carburettor body than in the steel spindle. A worn carburettor body will cause an uneven idle, variation in idle speed and a varying CO level.

7 Inspect the throttle progression roller for wear. If not spotted in time, the nylon roller and spindle can become sawn through by interaction with the progression plate. Renew the roller and retaining circlip. A curved or straight type of plate may be fitted. Later type carburettors and service repair kits include an improved and larger nylon roller and modified progression plate.

8 Inspect the carburettor and choke bodies for missing or loose blanking plugs.

9 Use a straight edge to check for a distorted base flange. The VV carburettor does not seem to suffer from this fault as readily as many other types of carburettors.

10 Clean the carburettor body with a good carburettor cleaner and a stiff brush.

11 Remove the idle cut-off valve and clean it with carburettor cleaner. If the plunger sticks or fails, it can mask other idle faults.

12 Test the idle cut-off plunger operation by connecting the valve to a 12-volt supply (or use the valve supply wire in the engine compartment) and holding the valve body to earth with the ignition on. Repeat this several times and ensure that the plunger tip advances and retracts cleanly. Renew the valve if the action is faulty or if cleaning does not improve its operation.

13 Remove the seven screws and detach the carburettor upper body.

14 Remove the four screws and detach the main metering block from the carburettor body *(see illustration)*. Slide open the air valve. Carefully raise the metering block until the needle is clear of the discharge tube, then remove the block from the carburettor body.

15 Invert the carburettor, with a hand cupped over the float chamber to catch the accelerator pump outlet ball and weight.

16 Remove the float, float pin, bracket and needle valve assembly and inspect for wear and damage.

17 Ensure that the anti-vibration ball is free in the valve end.

18 Early type needle valves tended to stick, causing bad starting from cold. This was cured by a hairpin clip that connects the needle valve and float arm. As the fuel level drops, after a period of non-use, the float weight will pull the needle valve apart and so prevent sticking. In turn, the float is prevented from dropping too far by the retaining clip.

19 The float seems rarely to give problems. However, it should be checked for damage and ingress of petrol.

20 Renew the float pin if it shows signs of wear.

21 Remove the inlet fuel filter (behind the needle valve seat) and inspect it. Clean the filter chamber of debris and dirt.

22 Remove the three screws and detach the accelerator pump cover. Catch the spring, plate, diaphragm and coloured spacer (where fitted). The diaphragm rarely splits, but can become stiff with age. It often becomes porous and this can cause very rich and erratic running at all engine speeds. It is best renewed at every carburettor service.

23 Carefully inspect the main metering needle for wear and damage. Renewal every 35 000 to 40 000 miles will improve economy and performance.

24 Check that the correct needle is fitted. The identification code is stamped upon the needle shank and is visible after removal from the air valve.

25 The needle is removed by tapping out the inspection plug from inside the carburettor body. Unclip the bias spring, then insert a small screwdriver through the hole and unscrew the needle.

26 Check the main jet orifice for ovality and wear.

27 Remove the four screws and detach the control diaphragm cover. Prise away the cover, which often sticks to the diaphragm, and catch the cup washer and spring *(see illustration)*.

28 Check the control diaphragm for splits and swelling and renew it if at all doubtful. The early (black) diaphragms often failed and they have generally been superseded in service with the much stronger blue types. The blue types, however, tend to be sucked in around the small vacuum drilling, which can cause fraying about the diaphragm aperture and affect its operation. Renew where necessary, using a good quality replacement. The diaphragm is held onto the air valve assembly by a small C-clip, which can be prised off with a small screwdriver.

29 Remove the three screws and detach the choke assembly housing. These screws sometimes become loose in service, resulting in vacuum leaks between body and housing and poor running in both hot and cold conditions. Sometimes, the left outer fixing screw is mistakenly inserted in the vacuum passage, causing poor choke operation.

30 Inspect the choke mechanism for stickiness and wear. Excessive wear in the choke body can cause faulty choke operation and a failure to set

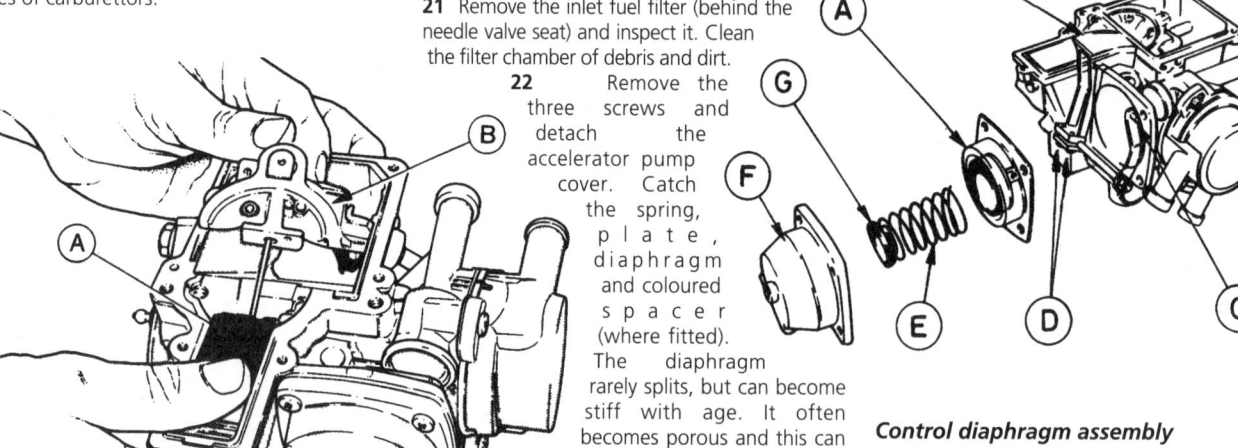

Metering block removal

A Air valve held fully open
B Metering block body

Control diaphragm assembly

A Control diaphragm
B Air valve
C Diaphragm C-clip
D Air valve screws
E Diaphragm spring
F Diaphragm housing
G Spring cup washer

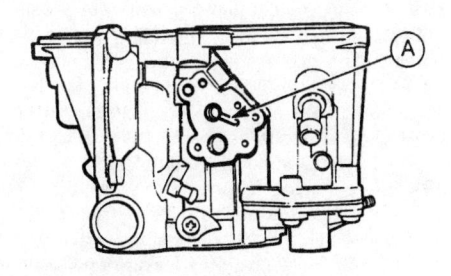

Ford Variable Venturi (VV) carburettor

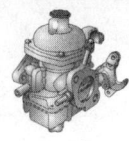

Choke assembly mating face identification

Type with cast channel (A) requires the thin gasket

when cold. The wear prevents the bi-metal spring from rotating the choke lever enough to activate the choke. Check for sideways movement of the choke spindle. Too much movement means a worn casing. The vacuum piston washer can become displaced and cause a vacuum leak through the choke.

Preparation for reassembly

31 Clean the carburettor body, float chamber, metering block and internal channels. An air line may be used to clear the internal channels once the carburettor is fully dismantled, but note that if an air line is used to direct air into the accelerator pump or air valve channels with the diaphragms in place, diaphragm damage may result. Take care that the pump outlet ball and weight are not blasted away with the metering block removed.
32 During reassembly, a complete set of new gaskets should be fitted. Also renew the needle valve, float pin and all diaphragms. Renew worn linkages, springs and other parts where necessary.
33 Clean all mating surfaces and flanges of old jointing material and reassemble with new gaskets. Ensure that housings are assembled with their air and fuel routes correctly aligned.
34 Note that the correct tightening torque for the carburettor screws is 2.0 Nm (1.5 lbf ft).

Reassembly

35 Place the choke assembly housing onto the carburettor body with a new gasket. The main body facing surface with a cast channel requires a thin gasket *(see illustration)*. Where there is no channel, a thick gasket is used. Secure with the three fixing screws. Be careful not to misplace the left outer fixing screw into the vacuum passage. Refer to Section 4 for details on adjustment of choke gauging and choke pull-down.
36 Refit the control diaphragm and secure with the circlip. Locate the spring and cup washer, then refit the main vacuum diaphragm cover while holding the air valve fully open. Ensure that the hole in the diaphragm aligns with the vacuum drilling in both the housing and cover. Secure evenly with the four fixing screws. Check for full air valve movement. Block the vacuum diaphragm hole in the venturi and check that the diaphragm and air valve slowly return to the rest position.
37 Invert the carburettor and refit the accelerator pump spacer, diaphragm (gasket face towards the cover), metal plate, spring and cover assembly and secure with the three screws *(see illustration)*. The Ford service kit includes a modified pump cover and various size coloured spacers to limit the pump stroke, according to engine type and size. The correct spacers are:

  Black   1.3 CVH engine
  Blue   1.6 OHC engine
  Red   All other engines

38 Renew the small fuel filter in the fuel inlet pipe.
39 Renew the needle valve assembly *(see illustration)*. Screw the valve body into the float chamber so that it correctly locates the retaining clip for the float pin. Insert the needle valve into the valve body, with the viton tip facing inwards.
40 Refit the float and pin, ensuring that the spring clip is correctly connected to the float and to the float needle. The float level is non-adjustable.
41 Drop the small ball into the accelerator pump outlet channel and place the weight on top of the ball.
42 Fit the metering block to the carburettor body, using a new gasket. Be careful not to bend or scratch the metering needle if it is already in position. Adjust the metering block so that the alignment flanges are flush with the top face of the carburettor body and secure with the four fixing screws in this position *(see illustration)*.
43 If the metering needle was removed, insert it through the hole in the casing and screw it several turns into the air valve. Use a pair of thin nose pliers to reconnect the bias spring. Open the air valve and place a 0.03 mm feeler gauge blade between the valve and metering block body *(see illustration)*. Close the air valve and trap the feeler blade. Maintain a slight upwards pressure on the blade while gently screwing in the needle. As the needle bottoms in the jet, the feeler gauge will be released. Now screw the needle out one complete turn (most carburettors). This datum position will enable the engine to run well enough for adjustment proper to begin. Refer to Specifications at the start of this Chapter for those carburettors that require a different number of turns and refer to Section 4 for details on needle adjustment.

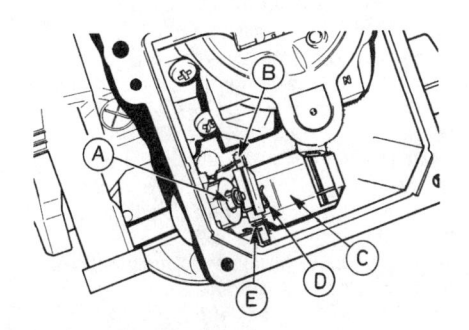

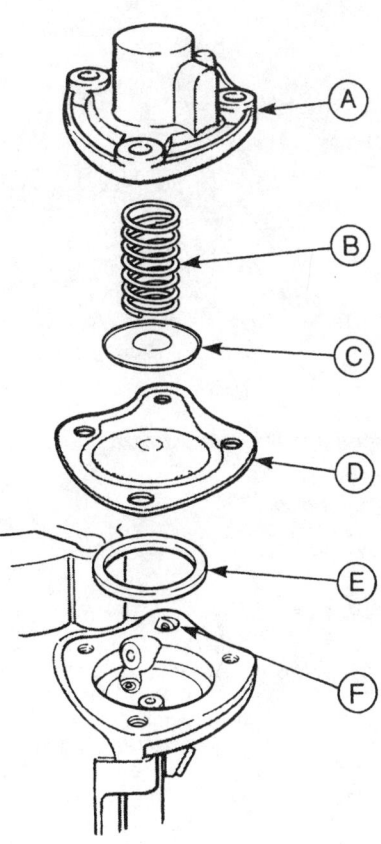

Accelerator pump assembly

A Pump cover
B Spring
C Metal plate
D Diaphragm
E Coloured spacer (see text)
F Vacuum passage

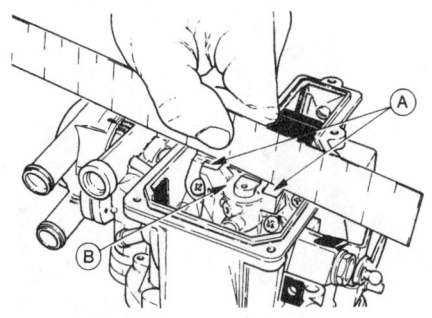

Needle valve installation

A Needle valve
B Float pivot pin
C Float
D Valve clip
E Spacing washer

Metering block alignment

A Alignment flanges
B Metering block body

E2•9

Chapter E2

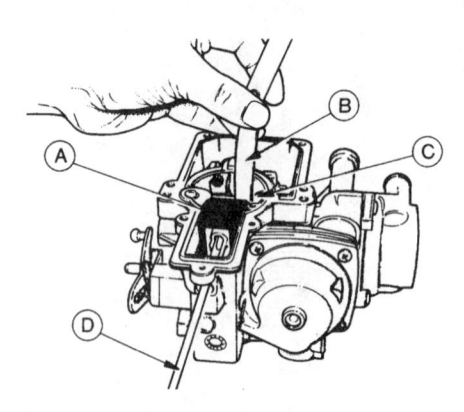

Metering needle adjustment

A Air valve
B Feeler blade
C Metering block
D Screwdriver

44 Use a new tamperproof plug to seal the hole in the carburettor casing.
45 Renew the float chamber gasket. A poorly-fitting or swollen gasket will cause vacuum leaks. Unlike some carburettors, the VV type will not run with the float chamber cover removed. Refit the upper body and screws. Tighten the screws progressively and evenly to avoid distortion of the main or upper body assemblies.
46 Screw the idle cut-off valve into the carburettor body.

Refitting to engine

47 Read the following information in conjunction with Part B:
 a) Tighten the carburettor to manifold nuts to a torque of 21 Nm (15 lbf ft).
 b) When running the engine at idle speed and at normal operating temperature, temporarily plug the choke vent hole in the venturi. If the engine note changes, then the choke is ON, which indicates a fault of some description. This should be diagnosed and corrected before carrying out final adjustment of the metering needle, idle speed and mixture.

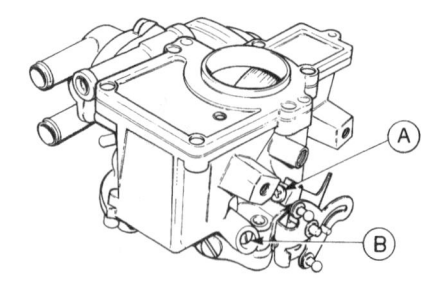

Idle adjustment screw location

A Idle speed screw
B Idle mixture (CO) screw

4 Service adjustments

Adjustment preconditions

1 Refer to Part B for general advice on preconditions to correct adjustment of this carburettor.

Idle speed and mixture (CO)

2 Start the engine and run it to its normal operating temperature.
3 Where the idle speed is set with the fan running (see Specifications), run the engine until the cooling fan operates. Disconnect the connector plug to the fan sensor and temporarily bridge the plug terminals with a piece of wire.
4 Connect a tachometer and CO meter, then run the engine at 3000 rpm for 30 seconds to clear the manifold of fuel vapours.
5 Allow the engine to idle, then use the idle speed screw to set the specified idle speed *(see illustration)*.
6 Check the CO level. If it is not as specified, remove the tamperproof plug and adjust to the correct level. Turning the screw clockwise (inwards) will reduce the CO level. Turning the screw anti-clockwise (outwards) will increase the CO level.
7 Repeat paragraphs 5 and 6 until both adjustments are correct.
8 Clear the manifold every 30 seconds during the setting operation by running the engine at 3000 rpm for 30 seconds.
9 Check for carburettor idle repeatability (Part D).
10 Fit a new tamperproof plug to the mixture adjusting screw after adjustment is completed.
11 Remove the temporary bridge wire and reconnect the temperature sensor plug (if disconnected).

Metering needle

12 Normally, adjustment of the main metering needle will only be required after needle renewal. If an over-lean or over-rich mixture is diagnosed by gas analysis, a full carburettor service should be completed before proceeding further. If, after servicing, the mixture at above 3000 rpm is not between 0.5 and 1.0%, needle adjustment may be attempted.
13 Remove the top cover and tap out the inspection plug from inside the carburettor body. Insert a small screwdriver through the hole to adjust the needle.
14 Use a rubber grommet to temporarily seal the hole in the carburettor casing.
15 Start the engine and run to normal operating temperature, then connect a CO meter and tachometer.
16 Use the idle speed screw to raise the engine speed to 2000 rpm.
17 Disconnect the electrical supply lead to the idle cut-off valve so that the idle system is shut down. This ensures that the CO reading corresponds only to the main system. If the idle mixture was included with the main mixture at 2000 rpm, then a false CO reading would be obtained and incorrect adjustment of the needle would follow.
18 Re-adjust the engine speed to 2000 rpm. If the CO level is not between 0.5 and 1.0%, needle adjustment may be attempted.
19 Reduce the engine speed then switch off the engine. Engine shutdown at 2000 rpm is not recommended but remember that the engine will not idle with the idle cut-off valve disconnected.
20 Remove the temporary seal and adjust the needle 1/4 turn. Screw in the needle to reduce the CO level and *vice versa*.
21 Repeat paragraphs 16 to 20 until the correct CO level is obtained.
22 Use a new tamperproof plug to seal the hole in the carburettor casing. Reconnect the idle cut-off valve and re-adjust the idle speed and idle CO level.
23 Renew the metering needle if difficulty is experienced in setting the CO at 2000 rpm.

Choke adjustments

24 Choke adjustments are not always successful and, in any case, adjustment data is not available for manual variants and some automatics. Choke faults are usually best cured by a new choke assembly unit. For those who wish to attempt adjustment, the methods of adjusting choke gauging and pull-down follow:

Choke gauging

25 This adjustment controls the correct relationship between the choke air and fuel supplies in order to maintain the correct mixture during choke use. Both choke gauging and pull-down adjustments may be made with the choke either on or off the carburettor.
26 Remove the bi-metal coil housing.
27 Remove the tamperproof plug from the alignment hole in the choke assembly housing.
28 Look into the hole and push the actuating lever clockwise so that the hole in the housing aligns with the guide hole in the choke spindle.
29 Insert the shank of a twist drill into the alignment hole and through the guide hole (see Specifications for the required drill diameter) *(see illustration)*.

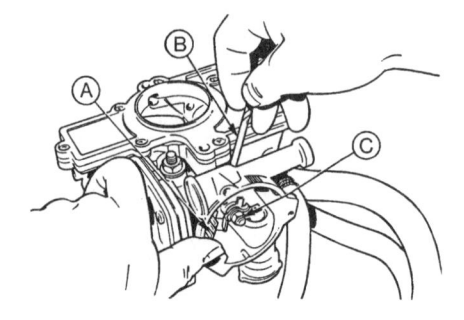

Choke gauging adjustment

A Operating lever held fully clockwise
B Twist drill held fully in position
C Nut securing linkage to central shaft

Ford Variable Venturi (VV) carburettor

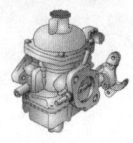

30 Slacken the choke spindle nut, then turn the actuating lever fully clockwise and tighten the nut. Remove the twist drill.
31 Adjust the vacuum pull-down lever.

Choke vacuum pull-down and fast idle

32 Check that the choke gauging is correct, as described above.
33 Position a small rod or twist drill in the location shown (see illustration), where it will stop linkage movement and prevent damage.
34 Bend back the pull-down lever with the aid of a small pair of pliers. This is necessary so that the vacuum piston has complete freedom of movement during adjustment. Remove the twist drill.
35 Look into the hole and push the actuating lever clockwise so that the hole in the housing aligns with the guide hole in the choke spindle.
36 Insert the shank of a twist drill into the alignment hole and through the guide hole (see Specifications for the required drill diameter - note that this may be a different size to the drill used for the choke gauging).
37 Press down the vacuum piston while maintaining clockwise or anti-clockwise pressure (see Specifications) against the bi-metal lever (A) (see illustration). There should be a small clearance between the pull-down lever (C) and the bi-metal lever (A).
38 Bend the pull-down lever (C) until it just touches the bi-metal lever (A).
39 Remove the twist drill and fit a new tamperproof plug into the alignment hole.
40 Renew the choke gasket and ensure that it is correctly located.
41 Refit the bi-metal coil housing and ensure that the spring locates in the middle slot of the choke lever. Secure loosely with three screws. Fitting the lower screw first will aid installation.
42 A new choke housing is supplied with untapped screw holes. However, the existing screws are thread-forming and can be used to cut new threads. Align the cut mark on the bi-metal cover with the centre mark on the choke assembly housing. Do not use the raised cast line mark. Tighten the three fixing screws (see illustration).

Air bypass screw

43 This adjustment is normally only necessary if the idle speed is too high and will not reduce after adjusting the idle speed screw.
44 Remove the tamperproof plug.
45 Use an Allen key to adjust the bypass screw. Turning the screw clockwise reduces idle speed, anti-clockwise increases it.
46 Renew the tamperproof plug on completion.

Throttle damper (where fitted)

47 To remove the throttle damper, slacken the locknut and simply unscrew the damper from its securing bracket.
48 To refit the damper, hold open the throttle and fully screw the damper into the bracket.
49 Start the engine and run to normal operating temperature.

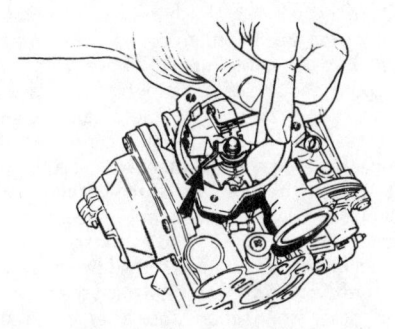

Choke vacuum pull-down and fast idle initial setting

Choke pull-down lever (arrowed) bent back to ensure that correct fast idle position can be achieved

50 Disconnect the connector plug to the fan sensor and temporarily bridge the plug terminals with a piece of wire.
51 Start the engine and use the idle speed screw to increase the engine speed to 3200 ± 50 rpm.
52 Once the engine speed has stabilised, switch off the engine.
53 Rotate the secondary throttle lever clockwise so that all backlash is eliminated between primary and secondary throttle levers. Place a finger upon the primary lever so that it does not move.
54 Insert a feeler gauge (0.1 to 0.3 mm thickness) between the damper and the secondary throttle lever, then unscrew the damper until it just touches the feeler gauge. Tighten the locknut and remove the feeler gauge (see illustration).
55 Restart the engine and reset the idle speed screw to give the correct idle speed.

5 Component testing

Air valve

1 Open the air valve and allow it to close. The

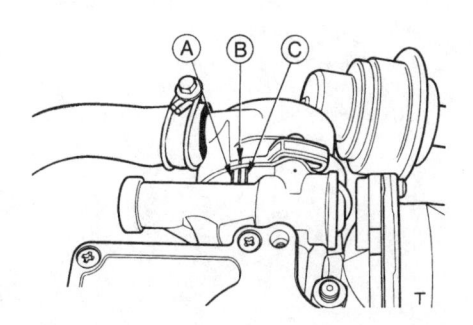

Choke housing alignment marks

A Lean setting
B Index mark
C Rich setting

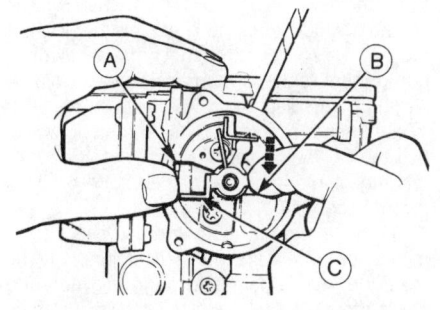

Choke vacuum pull-down and fast idle adjustment correct

A Bi-metal lever held fully clockwise
B Vacuum piston pushed fully downwards
C Pull-down lever just touching bi-metal lever

action should be smooth, without any trace of stickiness.
2 If the action is poor, clean the venturi area. If sticking persists, remove the float cover and re-check. If the sticking condition has now disappeared, check the metering block adjustment (see Section 3) and refit the float cover. Tighten the screws evenly and continually check for sticking. If the sticking cannot be cured, renew the carburettor.
3 Open the air valve and hold open for five seconds to evacuate the diaphragm chamber of air. Block the vacuum diaphragm hole in the venturi. Release the valve. It should move quickly over the first half of its travel and then slowly return to the rest position. If the action is poor, inspect the diaphragm. Check that the vent and vacuum passages are clear.

Choke unit

4 Run the engine at idle speed and at normal operating temperature. Temporarily plug the choke vent hole in the venturi. If the engine note changes, the choke is still operating and this indicates faulty choke operation. This could be due to a fault in the cooling system, a faulty bi-metal assembly, a sticking or incorrectly adjusted choke mechanism, or a displaced pull-down washer.

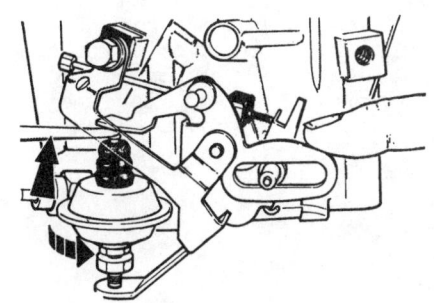

Throttle damper adjustment

Set damper clearance using a feeler gauge

Chapter E2

5 Set the CO level and rpm at idle, then run the engine at 3000 rpm and check the CO level. If much greater than 1%, check the accelerator pump diaphragm for damage and porosity. A leaking pump diaphragm will cause an over-rich mixture under almost all running conditions.

6 If the CO level is very lean, check for loose or missing blanking plugs in the choke or main carburettor body.

7 Remove the upper body top and check for a missing or loose metering needle tube plug. The metering needle passes through the metering block into a brass tube and this tube is sealed by a plug.

8 Firmly grip the choke body and try to rotate it. Any movement indicates loose choke assembly fixing screws, resulting in very poor engine operation.

9 It is possible to assemble the choke spindle 180° out, resulting in total lack of choke operation.

10 Feel the choke coolant hoses (where applicable). Coolness indicates a faulty cooling system and will result in poor or non-existent choke operation.

Carburettor speed control system (CSCS)

11 A vacuum pump and temperature gauge will be required to test the operation of the CSCV, PVS, TVS and VDV.

12 Inspect all of the system hoses and renew any that are damaged.

13 Remove the hoses and check for internal blockages.

14 Attach a vacuum gauge to the manifold vacuum control connection. If normal manifold vacuum of 425 to 525 mm Hg (567 to 700 mbar) is not recorded, check the connection for a blockage. It is common for this connection (and the hoses and emission filter) to become gradually blocked with blow-by fumes from the crankcase breather system.

15 To test the CSCV, attach the vacuum pump to the small vacuum control connection and pull 300 mm Hg (400 mbar). At all temperatures, the vacuum should pull open the CSCV valve so that air can be drawn through the two large connections.

16 To test the PVS, attach the vacuum pump to one of the small vacuum connections and pull 300 mm Hg (400 mbar). Above 35°C, the vacuum should hold. Below 35°C, vacuum should be drawn easily through the switch and the vacuum figure will only be reached if a finger is placed over the other connection.

17 To test the TVS, attach the vacuum pump to one of the small vacuum connections and pull 300 mm Hg (400 mbar). Above 10°C, the vacuum should hold. Below 10°C, vacuum should be drawn easily through the switch and the vacuum figure will only be reached if a finger is placed over the other connection.

18 To test the VDV, attach the vacuum pump to one of the small vacuum connections and pull 300 mm Hg (400 mbar). At all temperatures, the vacuum should slowly deplete to zero over a few seconds. Attach the pump to the other connection and attempt to pull vacuum. The vacuum should be drawn easily through the valve and 300 mm Hg (400 mbar) will only be reached if a finger is placed over the first connection. When reconnecting the valve, it should be placed so that the former (sustain) connection faces away from the CSCV.

6 Fault diagnosis

Refer to Part D for general faults affecting all carburettors. The following faults are specific to the Ford VV carburettor:

Poor idle and/or stalling

- [ ] Broken volume screw - tip snapped off in body
- [ ] Defective idle cut-off valve - stuck in closed position
- [ ] Choke stuck in on position
- [ ] Vacuum leaks through choke - check for:
  Loose choke housing
  Displaced vacuum washer
  Missing blanking plugs
  Worn carburettor body in throttle area
  Displaced float cover gasket
  Defective carburettor base-to-manifold gasket

Idle speed too high

- [ ] Worn carburettor body in throttle area (on reverting to idle from speed, engine speed will not always return to the same figure)
- [ ] Choke stuck in on position
- [ ] Idle bypass screw requires adjustment

Hesitation or lack of power

- [ ] Split control diaphragm
- [ ] Defective accelerator pump - check for:
  Defective, stiff or porous diaphragm
  Blockage in pump channels or injector nozzle
  Missing pump ball and/or weight
- [ ] Idle mixture too lean
- [ ] Defective idle cut-off valve
- [ ] Worn throttle progression roller
- [ ] Missing metering rod adjustment plug
- [ ] Displaced float cover gasket
- [ ] Sticking air valve
- [ ] Very lean mixture at speed:
  If the idle mixture is correct and there are no apparent faults in the VV, then the overall mixture may be too weak. Confirm with a CO check at 3000 rpm - the mixture should not be less than 0.3% CO

Poor choke operation

- [ ] Missing blanking plugs on choke or carburettor body
- [ ] Displaced vacuum pull-down washer in choke assembly housing
- [ ] Loose choke assembly housing
- [ ] Misplaced screw - fitted into the vacuum passage instead of the choke assembly securing hole

No choke operation

- [ ] Choke stuck in off position (worn choke body)
- [ ] Maladjusted or defective bi-metal coil (try adjusting to richer setting)
- [ ] Bi-metal coil detached:
  Remove the coil cover screws and carefully pull the housing away from the choke assembly by 3 mm. Check that the tang of the bi-metal coil is engaged in the centre slot of the choke assembly lever
- [ ] Choke spindle assembled 180° out
- [ ] Defective choke assembly unit

Poor hot starting

- [ ] Choke fault
- [ ] Ignition or mechanical fault
- [ ] Because the accelerator pump is operated by manifold depression, it will discharge when the engine is switched off. Coupled with the internal venting system, this can often cause a slightly longer hot-start cranking period. Ford suggest that a hot cranking time of anything up to 5 seconds is acceptable. The accelerator pedal should be held half-open during this operation

Heavy fuel consumption

- [ ] Defective accelerator pump diaphragm
- [ ] Defective control diaphragm
- [ ] Choke fault

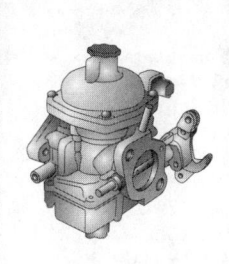

Part F Chapter 1
Pierburg 1B1 carburettor

Contents

Component testing	5	Identification	2
Fault diagnosis	6	Principles of operation	1
General servicing	3	Service adjustments	4

Specifications

Manufacturer	Audi	Mercedes-Benz	Opel	Opel
Model	80 1.3	210/310/410	Ascona C	Ascona C
Year	1981 to 1982	1982 to 1992	1981 to 1988	1981 to 1988
Engine code	EP (40kW)	M102 OHV	16N (55kW)	16N (55kW)
Capacity (cm³)/no. of cyls	1297/4	2299/4	1598/4	1598/4
Oil temperature (°C)	80	80	80	80
Transmission	-	MT	MT	AT
Carb. identification	036 129 016 C	001 070 93 04 (to 84) 002 070 24 04 (85 on)	90 107 500	90 107 501
Idle speed (rpm)	950 ± 50	800 ± 50	925 ± 25	925 ± 25
Fast idle speed (rpm)	4500 ± 200	2900 ± 150	4200 ± 200	4200 ± 200
CO @ idle (% vol.)	1.0 ± 0.5	1.0 ± 0.5	1.25 ± 0.25	1.25 ± 0.25
Venturi diameter (K)	25	28	26	26
Idle jet (g)	52.5	55	47.5	47.5
Main jet (Gg)	115	130	127.5	127.5
Air correction jet (a)	95	140	57.5	57.5
Accelerator pump jet (i)	30	40	40	40
Float level (mm)	27 ± 1.0	27 ± 1.0	27 ± 1.0	27 ± 1.0
Needle valve (mm) (P)	1.5	2.0	1.5	1.5
Float weight (grams)	7.2 ± 0.5	7.2 ± 0.5	7.2 ± 0.5	7.2 ± 0.5
Basic throttle position (mm)	0.3 ± 0.03	0.41	0.05 ± 0.02	0.05 ± 0.02
Choke fast idle gap (mm)	0.8 ± 0.05	0.85	0.82 ± 0.1	0.82 ± 0.1
Choke pull-down (mm)	3.2 ± 0.15	3.3	4.4 ± 0.1	4.4 ± 0.1

Chapter F1

Manufacturer	Opel	Opel	Vauxhall	Vauxhall
Model	Rekord E	Rekord E	Nova 1.2	Nova 1.2 (15/04)
Year	1982 to 1985	1985 to 1986	1983 to 1990	1990 to 1992
Engine code	18N (55kW)	18N (55kW)	12ST SOHC (40kW)	12NV SOHC (38kW)
Capacity (cm^3)/no. of cyls	1796/4	1796/4	1196/4	1196/4
Oil temperature (°C)	80	80	80	80
Carb. identification	9 276 942	90 107 524	9 276 983	9 276 983
Idle speed (rpm)	825 ± 25	825 ± 25	925 ± 25	925 ± 25
Fast idle speed (rpm)	4200 ± 200	4200 ± 200	3800 ± 200	3800 ± 200
CO @ idle (% vol.)	1.25 ± 0.25	1.25 ± 0.25	1.25 ± 0.25	1.25 ± 0.25
Venturi diameter (K)	26	26	23	23
Idle jet (g)	47.5	47.5	47.5	47.5
Main jet (Gg)	122.5	127.5	105	105
Air correction jet (a)	57.5	57.5	57.5	57.5
Accelerator pump jet (i)	40	40	30	30
Float level (mm)	27 ± 1.0	28.5 ± 1.0	27	27
Needle valve (mm) (P)	1.5	1.5	1.5	1.5
Float weight (grams)	7.2 ± 0.5	7.2 ± 0.5	7.2 ± 0.5	7.2 ± 0.5
Basic throttle position (mm)	0.55 ± 0.02	0.05 ± 0.02	-	-
Choke fast idle gap (mm)	0.8 ± 0.1	0.8 ± 0.1	0.65 ± 0.05	0.65 ± 0.05
Choke pull-down (mm)	4.4 ± 0.2	4.4 ± 0.1	3.2	3.2

Manufacturer	Vauxhall	Vauxhall	Volkswagen	Volkswagen
Model	Nova 1.3	Nova 1.3	Passat 1.3	LT Van 2.0
Year	1982 to 1983	1983 to 1987	1981 to 1983	1980 to 1982
Engine code	13SB SOHC (51kW)	13SB SOHC (51kW)	FY (40kW)	CH (55kW)
Capacity (cm^3)/no. of cyls	1297/4	1297/4	1272/4	1984/4
Oil temperature (°C)	80	80	80	80
Carb. identification	9 276 966	9 276 984	036 129 016 D	060 129 016
Idle speed (rpm)	925 ± 25	925 ± 25	950 ± 50	925 ± 25
Fast idle speed (rpm)	3700 ± 200	3700 ± 200	4500 ± 200	4000 ± 200
CO @ idle (% vol.)	0.75 ± 0.25	0.75 ± 0.25	1.00 ± 0.5	0.75 ± 0.25
Venturi diameter (K)	25	25	25	28
Idle jet (g)	47.5	47.5	52.5	55
Main jet (Gg)	120	117.5	115	135
Air correction jet (a)	75	57.5	95	140
Accelerator pump jet (i)	30	30	30	40
Float level (mm)	27 ± 1.0	27 ± 1.0	27 ± 1.0	27 ± 1.0
Needle valve (mm) (P)	1.5	1.5	1.5	2.0
Float weight (grams)	7.2 ± 0.5	7.2 ± 0.5	7.2 ± 0.5	7.2 ± 0.5
Basic throttle position (mm)	-	-	0.3 ± 0.03	0.3 ± 0.03
Choke fast idle gap (mm)	0.65 ± 0.05	0.65 ± 0.05	0.8 ± 0.05	1.2 ± 0.05
Choke pull-down (mm)	4.4 ± 0.2	4.4 ± 0.2	3.0 ± 0.15	4.1 ± 0.15

1 Principles of operation

Introduction

1 The following technical description of the Pierburg 1B1 carburettor should be read in conjunction with the more detailed description of carburettor principles in Part A.

Construction

2 The Pierburg 1B1 carburettor is a downdraught single venturi instrument with a manual choke control *(see illustration opposite)*. Major body components are cast in light alloy for weight-saving purposes. The jet systems are arranged so as to be unaffected by the centrifugal or braking forces imposed during engine operation, for both transversely- or longitudinally-mounted engine applications. The throttle shafts are made of steel, while the throttle valves, all jets and the emulsion tube are manufactured from brass. The internal fuel channels and air passages are drilled and sealed with lead plugs where necessary.

3 Most carburettor versions operate in conjunction with an electrical heater fitted to the inlet manifold. The purpose of the heater is to improve atomisation of the air/fuel mixture during the warm-up period. A thermal switch is usually wired to the supply voltage, so that the heater is switched off at a pre-determined

Pierburg 1B1 carburettor

Pierburg 1B1 carburettor

1A Upper body
1B Upper body (alternative)
2 Fuel inlet filter
3 Float pin
4 Float
5 Needle valve
7 Accelerator pump injector
8 Main jet
9 Idle jet
10 Bypass idle jet
13 Main body
18 Fast idle adjustment screw
19 Idle mixture control screw
21 Tamperproof cap
22 Bypass idle speed screw
24 Float chamber gasket
25 Accelerator pump assembly
26 Part-load enrichment assembly
29 Idle cut-off valve (where fitted)
34 Choke pull-down diaphragm
35 Choke flap
36 Throttle body heater
37 Earth strap
38 Throttle damper
39 Delay valve

temperature. Some versions also use a throttle body heater to prevent carburettor icing. Both heaters function on the positive temperature coefficient (PTC) principle. As the temperature rises, the heater resistance also rises.

Fuel control

4 Fuel flows into the carburettor through an inlet connection. The fuel level in the float chamber is controlled by a spring-loaded needle valve and plastic float assembly *(see illustration overleaf)*. The float level is considered critical and is set very accurately during production. The float chamber is vented internally to the clean-air side of the air filter. A calibrated fuel return system is provided to ensure that relatively cool fuel is supplied to the carburettor.

Idle, slow running and progression

5 Fuel is drawn from the primary main well into the base of a vertical well which dips down into the fuel. A combined idle jet, emulsion tube and air corrector is placed in the well. Fuel is mixed with air drawn in through the calibrated air corrector and the holes in the tube to form an emulsion. The resulting mixture is drawn through a channel into a chamber where it is mixed with the bypass emulsion. The total idle mixture is then discharged from the main idle orifice under the primary throttle plate. A tapered mixture screw is used to

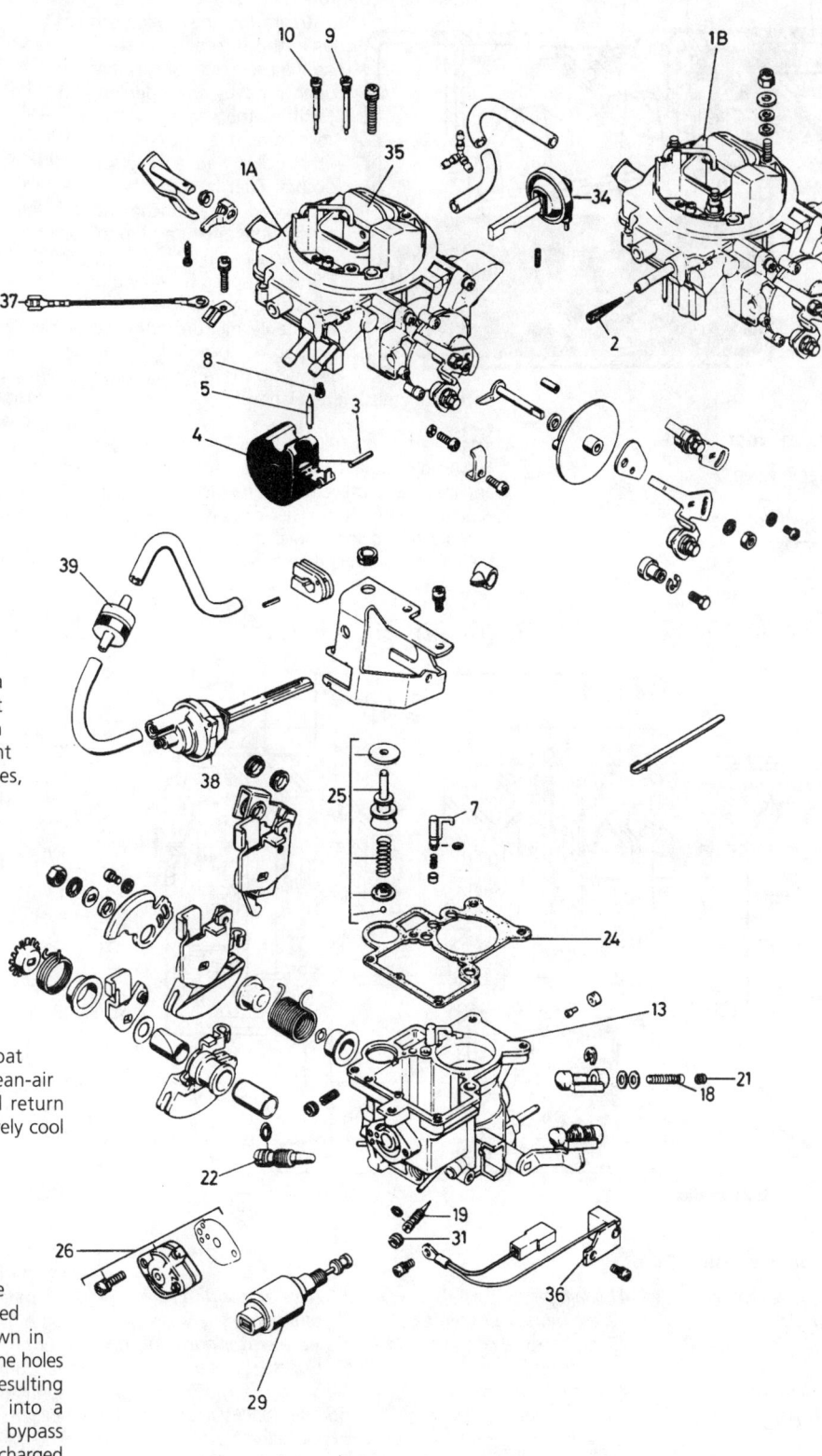

F1•3

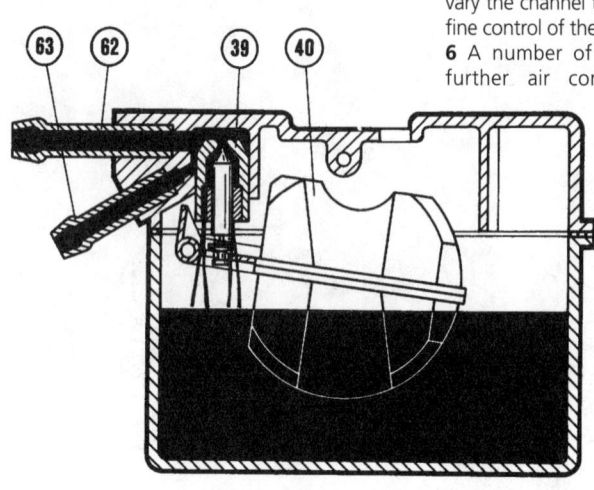

Chapter F1

vary the channel to the chamber and this ensures fine control of the idle mixture *(see illustration)*.

6 A number of progression holes provide a further air contribution to the emulsion (upstream of the chamber) while the throttle is closed. As the progression holes are uncovered by the opening throttle, the vacuum draw overcomes the air bleed into the holes and a reversal occurs. Fuel is now drawn out to add extra enrichment to the idle mixture during initial acceleration.

7 The idle speed is set by the adjustable bypass screw. The adjustable mixture screw is tamper proofed at production level, in accordance with emission regulations.

Idle cut-off valve

8 An idle cut-off valve is used on some applications to prevent run-on when the engine is shut down. It utilises a 12-volt solenoid plunger to block the idle mixture outlet when the ignition is switched off.

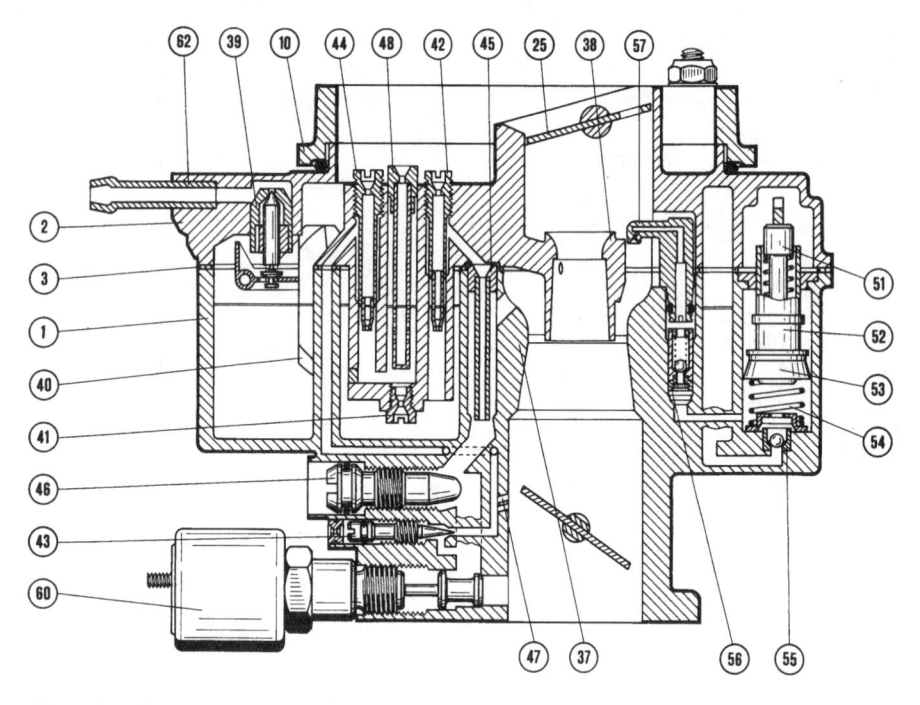

Idle bypass circuit

9 The idle bypass circuit provides a means of more accurately controlling idle emissions than a conventional idle mixture circuit. The throttle plate is locked in a specified position and sealed with a tamperproof cap. Eighty percent of the fuel required for idle is provided by the normal idle circuit. The remainder of the idle mixture is controlled through the idle bypass circuit.

10 Fuel, sourced from the float chamber, is drawn into the bypass well. Air is supplied through the bypass air corrector and the emulsion is drawn through the bypass passage where additional air from the main venturi is introduced. The resulting mixture is drawn past the regulating screw into a chamber, where it is mixed with the idle emulsion. The total idle mixture is then discharged from the main idle orifice under the primary throttle plate. The emulsion is controlled by a regulating screw which is also used to adjust the idle speed.

Accelerator pump

11 The accelerator pump is controlled by a piston and is mechanically operated by a lever and cam linked to the throttle pedal. Under acceleration, a lever, actuated by the throttle linkage, bears against the pump piston and compresses it. Fuel from the pump chamber is pushed through the pump outlet channels, past the pump outlet valve and injected from the pump nozzle into the venturi. The inlet valve remains closed to prevent fuel from being returned to the float chamber.

12 As the throttle action is reversed, a spring returns the piston to its starting position. Depression then draws fresh fuel from the float chamber into the pump chamber.

Main circuit

13 The amount of fuel discharged into the airstream is controlled by a calibrated main jet. Fuel is drawn through the jet into the base of a vertical well which dips down into the fuel in the float chamber. A combined emulsion tube and air correction jet is placed in the well. The fuel is mixed with air, drawn in through the calibrated air correction jet and the holes in the emulsion tubes, to form an air/fuel emulsion. The resulting mixture is discharged from the main nozzle through an auxiliary venturi into the main airstream.

Part-load enrichment (power valve)

14 Fuel flows from the float chamber into the enrichment chamber through a fuel channel. An air passage is taken from under the throttle plate to the cover of the chamber. At idle, and during light throttle operation, manifold vacuum draws the diaphragm back against spring pressure to close off the enrichment valve and the fuel outlet channel. Under acceleration and wide-open throttle operation, the vacuum in the manifold is depleted. The diaphragm returns under spring pressure and the valve opens the fuel channel. This allows fuel to flow

Fuel control system

39 Float needle valve
40 Float
62 Fuel supply inlet
63 Fuel return

Idle and main systems

1 Main body assembly
2 Upper body assembly
3 Gasket
10 Intermediate piece
25 Choke flap
37 Venturi
38 Auxiliary venturi
39 Float needle valve
40 Float

41 Main jet
42 Idle bypass air corrector
43 Idle mixture control screw
44 Idle jet air corrector
45 Idle bypass emulsion well
46 Bypass idle speed screw
47 Progression holes
48 Main air corrector

51 Accelerator pump plunger
52 Accelerator pump piston
53 Cup seal
54 Spring
55 Inlet (ball) valve
56 Outlet valve
57 Injection nozzle
60 Idle cut-off valve
62 Fuel supply inlet

Pierburg 1B1 carburettor

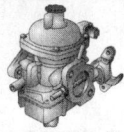

Partial and full-load enrichment

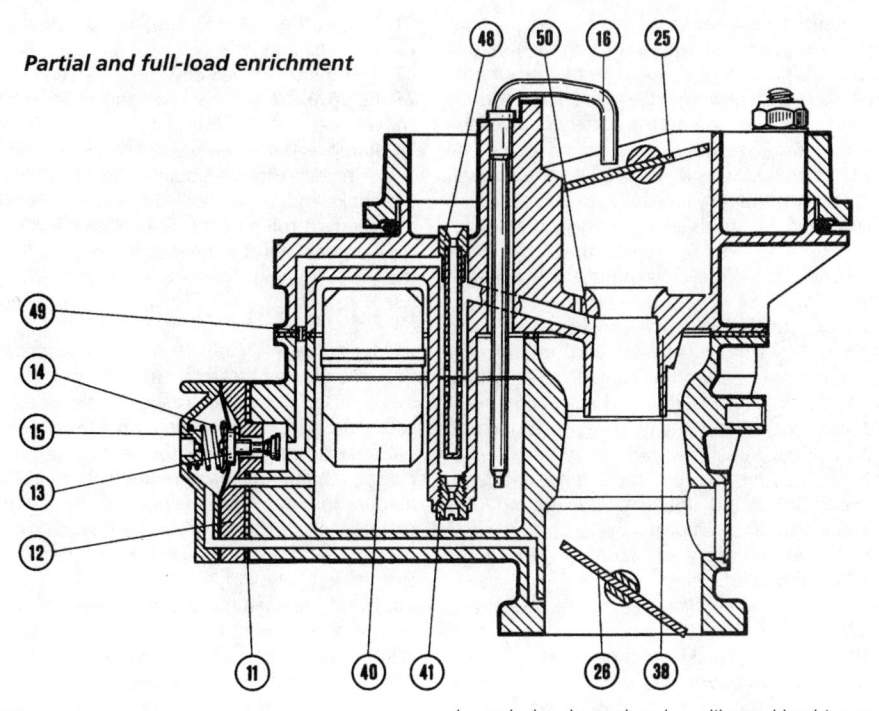

11 Gasket
12 Intermediate piece
13 Part-load enrichment valve
14 Spring
15 Diaphragm cover
16 Full-load enrichment nozzle
25 Choke flap
26 Throttle valve
38 Auxiliary venturi
40 Float
41 Main jet
48 Main air corrector
49 Part-load enrichment jet
50 Main fuel nozzle

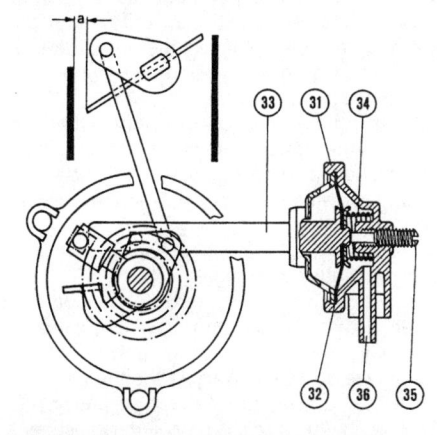

through the channel and a calibrated bushing to supplement the fuel in the upper part of the main well. The fuel level rises in the well and the fuel mixture is enriched *(see illustration)*.

Full-load enrichment

15 At full-load and high engine speeds, the velocity of air creates a depression sufficient to raise fuel from the float chamber into a channel. The fuel then passes through a calibrated bushing to the upper section of the air intake, where it is discharged into the airstream from the full-load enrichment nozzle.

Cold start system

16 The cold start system is basically a manually-controlled thermo-choke *(see illustration)*. The choke flap is controlled by a bi-metal spring that takes position according to the ambient temperature.

17 The manual choke is operated by a dash-mounted cable control. When the cable is pulled, it operates a lever that releases the choke mechanism. The choke flap is controlled by a bi-metal spring and will take position across the air intake depending on ambient temperature. Fast idle is achieved with the aid of a curved cam attached to the choke operating lever. An adjustable screw, attached to the throttle lever and butting against the cam, is used to vary the fast idle speed.

Choke pull-down

18 Once the engine has fired, the choke flap must open slightly to weaken the mixture and avoid flooding during idle and light-throttle operation. This is achieved by using manifold vacuum to actuate a pull-down diaphragm. A linkage attached to the diaphragm will then pull upon the flap.

19 The pull-down hose is connected to a delay reservoir. When the engine fires, vacuum applied to the pull-down diaphragm is low and the choke flap will only be partially opened. As the engine continues to run, the vacuum increases and acts upon the delay reservoir, causing the pull-down to operate fully so that over-rich running is avoided. This method of operation ensures maximum richness for the few seconds after a cold start, followed by a rapid opening of the choke flap to reduce over-richness.

20 As the engine warms up, the choke control should be progressively pushed home until the choke flap is fully open. However, if the control is not pushed home, any increase in ambient temperature at the choke body will cause the bi-metal to open the choke flap.

Throttle damper

21 The throttle damper (where fitted) slows down the rate of throttle closing to aid emissions during over-run. Two alternative versions may be fitted. One version is controlled by a delay valve in the vacuum hose.

Throttle governor

22 When the engine is stopped, the throttle governor pushrod *(see illustration)* will extend to partially open the throttle, ready for the next hot or cold start. If the choke is employed, the governor will hold the throttle open to a wider position than the highest position of the fast idle cam. Once the engine has fired, vacuum will operate the governor diaphragm and the plunger will withdraw. The throttle opening will now depend on the position of the throttle stop screw (engine hot), or fast idle cam (engine cold).

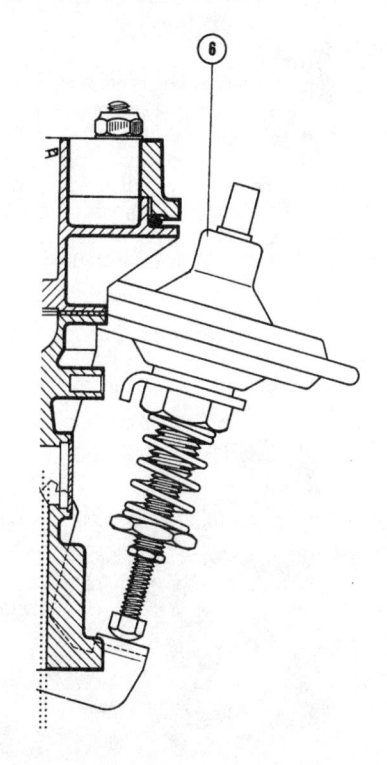

Choke operation - cold start, engine running

31 Pull-down assembly
32 Diaphragm
33 Diaphragm rod
34 Spring
35 Adjustment screw
36 Vacuum connection
a First stage pull-down

Throttle governor (6)

Chapter F1

Lever (1) on inside of choke cover must be left of lever (2)

2 Identification

1 Pierburg 1B is stamped upon the carburettor upper and main bodies. The manufacturer identification code may be stamped on a metallic tag attached to the cover by an upper body fixing screw or on a corner of the carburettor main body.
2 Where the tag is missing, refer to Part B for other means of identifying the carburettor.
3 Early versions of this carburettor may be stamped with the trade name Solex.

3 General servicing

Introduction

1 Read this Chapter in conjunction with Part B, which describes some of the operations in more detail. It is assumed that the carburettor is removed for this service. However, many of the operations can be tackled with the carburettor in place. Where this is undertaken, first remove the upper body assembly, and soak the fuel out of the float chamber using a clean tissue or soft cloth.

Dismantling and checking

2 Remove the carburettor from the engine (see Part B).
3 Check the carburettor visually for damage and wear.

Alignment of choke cover

4 Remove the idle cut-off valve assembly, after slackening the nut with a 17 mm open-ended spanner. Clean the valve with carburettor cleaner and test the plunger operation by connecting the valve to the battery or a voltage supply (or use the valve supply wire in the engine compartment). Touch the valve body to earth with the ignition on. Repeat this several times and ensure that the plunger tip advances and retracts cleanly. Renew the valve if the action is faulty or if cleaning does not improve its operation.
5 Disconnect the choke vacuum hose, then remove the four screws and detach the carburettor upper body. The earth strap (where fitted) should also be removed at this time.
6 Inspect the float chamber for corrosion and calcium build-up.
7 Tap out the float pin and remove the float, needle valve and float chamber gasket. The needle valve seat is not removable.
8 Check that the anti-vibration ball is free in the needle valve end.
9 Check the needle valve tip for wear and ridges.
10 The float should be checked for damage and ingress of petrol.
11 Renew the float pin if it shows signs of wear.
12 Use a straight-edge to check for distorted flanges on all facing surfaces.
13 Unscrew the mixture and bypass screws and inspect the tips for damage or ridges.
14 The pump injector is a push fit in the body. Carefully prise it from its location. On the early type of injector, the spring and outlet ball are held by a retaining ring in the main body (these components are not removable). If a later type of injector is fitted, test it by shaking it. No noise from the outlet ball would indicate that the valve is seized.
15 Remove the accelerator pump seal, piston and spring. Check the piston assembly for fatigue and damage. Inspect the choke operating lever for wear and smooth operation.
16 Unscrew the primary idle jet and bypass jet assemblies, noting their locations for correct installation during assembly. Note that the primary idle and bypass jets can be removed from the carburettor without removing the upper body.
17 Check the jet calibration (see Specifications). It is possible that the idle jets may have been transposed (or the wrong size fitted) during the last overhaul.
18 Unscrew the main jet. It is not possible to remove the air corrector or emulsion tube. Check that the channel from the main jet into the main emulsion tube well is clear.
19 Remove the two screws and detach the power valve housing cover, spring and diaphragm assembly. Check the diaphragm for damage and fatigue. Check the action of the power valve and the condition of the small seal. Check that the channel (through both bodies) into the emulsion tube well is clear.
20 Do not disturb the adjustment of the throttle angle, unless absolutely necessary.

21 Inspect the choke flap, spindle and linkage for stickiness and wear.
22 Test the choke pull-down unit, (Section 4).
23 Remove the three screws and remove the choke cover from the housing.
24 Remove the three screws that secure the choke housing to the upper body. Disconnect the choke rod and detach the housing. Punch out the two roll pins (or one roll pin and star clip), and detach the pull-down assembly from the choke housing.

Preparation for reassembly

25 Clean the jets, carburettor body assemblies, float chamber and internal channels. An air line may be used to clear internal channels once the carburettor is fully dismantled. Note that if high-pressure air is directed into the channels and passages with the diaphragms still in place, diaphragm damage may result. Spraying carburettor cleaner into all the channels and passages in the carburettor body will often clear them of gum and dirt.
26 During reassembly, a complete set of new gaskets should be fitted. Also renew the needle valve, float pivot pin and all diaphragms.
27 Inspect and renew (where necessary) the mixture screw, main jet, idle and bypass jets, and the accelerator pump injector. Renew worn linkages, springs, vacuum hoses and other parts where necessary.
28 Ensure that all jets are firmly locked into their original positions (but do not over-tighten). A loose jet can cause a rich (or even lean) running condition. Clean all mating surfaces and flanges of old gasket material and reassemble with a new gasket. Ensure that housings are positioned with their air and fuel routes correctly aligned.

Reassembly

29 Slide the choke diaphragm assembly into position and secure with new roll pins (or roll pin and star clip). Reconnect the choke link rod, then refit the choke housing and secure with the three screws.
30 Refit the choke cover, ensuring that the lever on the inside of the cover is to the left of the choke flap operating lever *(see illustration)*. Align the marks *(see illustration)* and secure with the three screws.
31 Ensure that the choke flap and linkage move smoothly and progressively.
32 Where the primary throttle position has been disturbed and a throttle setting gauge is available, use it to set the throttle angle. Otherwise, temporarily adjust the throttle plate so that it is open just enough to prevent its seizure in the throttle body. An adjustment method with the engine running is detailed in Section 4.
33 Refit the power diaphragm, spring and cover assembly, and secure with the two screws.
34 Refit the main jet into its original position.
35 Refit the primary and bypass idle jets into the upper body. Do not transpose the jets.
36 Refit the accelerator pump spring, piston and seal into the main body.

Pierburg 1B1 carburettor

Idle adjustment screw location

1 Bypass idle speed screw
2 Idle mixture control screw

37 Align the pump injector and tap it into position after renewing the small seal on the injector body.
38 Refit the idle mixture screw after renewing the seal. Turn the screw in gently until it just seats. From this position, unscrew it three full turns. This will provide a basic setting to allow the engine to be started.
39 Refit the bypass regulating screw after renewing the seal. Obtain a basic setting in the same way as for the mixture screw above.
40 Insert the needle valve into the seat with the ball facing outward. Refit the float and pivot pin. Ensure that the top of the needle valve engages into the slot on the float.
41 Check the float level, see Section 4. Refit the float gasket to the upper body.
42 Refit the upper body to the main body and secure with the four screws. Ensure that the carburettor earth strap (where fitted) is secured with an upper body fixing screw. Refit all vacuum hoses in their original positions.
43 Refit the idle cut-off valve and lock it firmly into position.
44 Adjust the choke with reference to Section 4.
45 Refit the carburettor to the engine (see Part B).
46 Always adjust the carburettor idle speed and mixture after any work has been carried out on the carburettor - preferably with the aid of a CO meter.

4 Service adjustments

Adjustment preconditions

1 Refer to Part B for general advice on the preconditions for correct adjustment of this carburettor.

VW/Audi/Mercedes

2 Disconnect the engine breather hose from the air filter. Plug the opening in the air filter.
3 Reconnect the breather hose when all adjustments are completed. If the CO level increases more than 1 to 1.5%, change the sump oil. If the CO level still increases after an oil change, suspect worn or sticking piston rings.

Vauxhall/Opel

4 The breather hose may remain connected during adjustment. However, after adjustment, disconnect the breather hose and note the CO reading. If the CO level decreases more than 1 to 1.5%, change the sump oil. If the CO level still decreases after an oil change, suspect worn or sticking piston rings.

All models

5 In all instances, if no CO change at all is noted on connecting/disconnecting the breather hose, suspect a clogged crankcase ventilation (PCV) system.

Bypass idle adjustment

6 Run the engine at 3000 rpm for 30 seconds to clear the manifold of fuel vapours, then allow the engine to idle.
7 Use the idle bypass regulating screw to set the specified idle speed (see illustration).
8 Check the CO level. Remove the tamperproof plug and adjust the idle mixture screw if necessary to obtain the correct level. Turning the screw clockwise (inwards) will reduce the CO level. Turning the screw anti-clockwise (outwards) will increase the CO level.
9 Repeat paragraphs 7 and 8 until both adjustments are correct. Adjusting the idle bypass screw will also affect the CO level.
10 Fit a new tamperproof plug to the idle mixture screw on completion.

Basic throttle position

11 If the idle speed and CO cannot be set correctly, it is possible that the basic throttle position is incorrect.
12 One method of setting is to remove the carburettor and use a Pierburg throttle setting gauge to accurately set the throttle position (see illustration). Another method is to use a very low-reading vacuum gauge connected to the

Float level checking

1 Float lever
2 Needle valve pin
3 Needle valve

Setting basic throttle position using a Pierburg gauge

1 Throttle stop screw
2 Pierburg setting gauge

vacuum advance connector. The correct angle is set when the gauge registers 8 ± 4 mmHg (10 ± 5 mbars).
13 An alternative method of throttle plate setting follows. Note that this is not the manufacturer's recommended method but will nevertheless result in an accurate and stable idle speed and CO level:

a) Allow the engine to idle.
b) Screw in the bypass regulating screw until it is fully seated. The idle speed should drop to approximately two-thirds of the idle speed figure. For example, if the idle speed is specified as 950 rpm, the speed should drop to between 600 and 650 rpm.
c) Adjust the throttle stop screw until 600 to 650 rpm is obtained.
d) Unscrew the bypass screw until 950 rpm is once again attained.
e) Reset the CO to the correct level.
f) If the CO needs a large adjustment at this stage, repeat paragraphs a) to e). Once the proper level of CO is reached at the specified idle speed, the carburettor is properly adjusted.

14 The rpm figures used in the above example are based on a hypothetical idle speed of 950 rpm. Substitute the correct figures for the carburettor being adjusted (see Specifications).

Float level

15 It is not possible to adjust the plastic float. It is possible, however, to check the float level.
16 Hold the carburettor upper body at an angle of 45°, with the float tag gently touching the ball of the fully-closed needle valve. Note that the ball of the needle valve must not be depressed (see illustration).

Chapter F1

Accelerator pump adjustment

1 Pump cam
2 Clamping screw

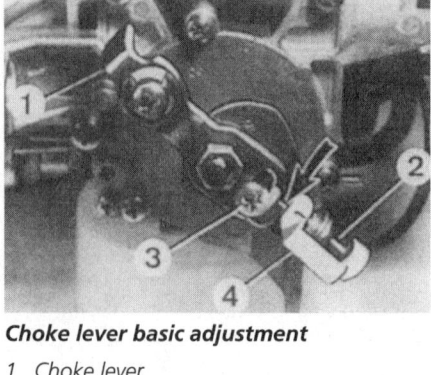

17 Measure the distance between the upper body (without its gasket) and the top of the float. Refer to Specifications for the correct float level.
18 If the level is incorrect, check the needle valve seat for correct position. Remove the float and check the float weight (see Specifications). If the seat and float weight are satisfactory, renew the float if the level is incorrect.

Accelerator pump

19 On the Pierburg 1B1 carburettor, it is possible to adjust the volume of fuel injected by the accelerator pump.
20 Loosen the clamping screw (2) *(see illustration)*.
21 Move the cam (1) in direction (+) to increase the fuel volume, or in direction (–) to decrease volume.
22 Tighten the clamping screw on completion.

Fast idle adjustment - carburettor removed

1 Choke lever
2 Fast idle adjustment screw

Choke lever basic adjustment

1 Choke lever
2 Fast idle adjustment screw
3 Clamping screw
4 Fast idle assembly

Choke adjustments

Fast idle adjustment (carburettor removed)

23 Invert the carburettor.
24 Fully close the choke flap using the choke control lever. The lever must be against the choke stop.
25 The centre of the fast idle adjustment screw (2) *(see illustration)* must face the marking on the cam, as shown by the arrow.
26 Adjust as necessary by loosening screw (3) and moving the cam in the appropriate direction. Tighten the screw on completion.
27 Set the choke flap as in paragraph 24. The fast idle screw will butt against the fast idle cam and force open the throttle plate to leave a small clearance.
28 Use the shank of a twist drill to measure

Choke pull-down adjustment

1 Vacuum pump
2 Pull-down
3 Adjustment screw

the clearance between the wall of the throttle bore and the throttle plate. Refer to Specifications for the required drill size. Measure from the side opposite the progression holes *(see illustration)*.
29 Remove the tamperproof plug and adjust as necessary by turning the fast idle adjustment screw in the appropriate direction.
30 Fit a new tamperproof plug on completion.
31 Check the fast idle speed against the specified figure once the carburettor has been refitted to the engine.

Fast idle adjustment (engine running)

32 Run the engine to normal operating temperature, then switch off.
33 Check the position of the cam as described in paragraphs 24 to 26.
34 Fully close the choke flap using the choke control lever. The lever must be against the choke stop.
35 Start the engine and open the choke flap. Refer to Specifications for the fast idle speed.
36 Adjust as necessary by turning the adjustment screw in the appropriate direction.

Choke pull-down

37 Refer to Part D for a method of testing the vacuum reservoir (where fitted).
38 Remove the vacuum hose from the carburettor base to the inlet connection (supply side) of the pull-down unit, then attach a vacuum pump to the connection. Remove the second hose from the outlet side and leave the connection unplugged *(see illustration)*.
39 Operate the pump and the pull-down should move to the first stage.
40 Maintaining the vacuum, plug the pull-down outlet connection and operate the pump until 225 mmHg (300 mbars) is obtained. The pull-down should now move to the second stage and maintain vacuum for at least 10 seconds. If the diaphragm does not operate as described, renew the pull-down unit. If the pull-down unit is a single-stage type, follow the procedure for testing the second stage of the two-stage unit above.
41 Fully close the choke flap using the choke control lever. The lever must be against the choke stop.
42 Loosen the three starter cover fixing screws and rotate the cover anti-clockwise until the choke flap is closed. Tighten the fixing screws.
43 Maintain the vacuum obtained in paragraph 40. At the same time, use the shank of a twist drill to measure the clearance between the lower section of the choke flap and the air intake. Refer to Specifications for the required drill size.
44 Adjust as necessary by turning the pull-down adjusting screw in the appropriate direction *(see illustration)*.
45 Loosen the three starter cover fixing screws and rotate the cover clockwise until the markings are aligned. Tighten the fixing screws on completion.

Pierburg 1B1 carburettor

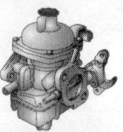

Choke pull-down adjustment - alternative type

3 Adjustment screw

Throttle damper adjustment

1 Lever in idle position
2 Locknut
3 Damper

Throttle damper adjustment - type with delay valve

1 Diaphragm rod
2 Adjustment screw
3 Throttle lever
4 Delay lever

Throttle damper

Type without delay valve

46 Warm the engine to normal running temperature, then ensure that the idle speed and mixture are correctly adjusted.
47 Loosen the damper locknut *(see illustration)*.
48 Wind the damper up until a gap of 0.05 mm exists between the dashpot rod and the throttle lever.
49 Wind the damper downwards by 2.5 turns, and tighten the locknut in this position.

Type with delay valve

50 Warm the engine to normal running temperature, then ensure that the idle speed and mixture are correctly adjusted.
51 Allow the engine to idle.
52 Push the diaphragm rod fully home in the direction of the arrow *(see illustration)*.
53 Maintaining the pressure on the rod, adjust screw (2) to obtain 1400 ± 50 rpm.
54 Open the throttle and raise the engine speed to approximately 3000 rpm. The diaphragm rod should become withdrawn.
55 Close the throttle. The diaphragm rod should slowly extend and return the idle speed to normal.
56 Stop the engine and connect a vacuum pump to the suction side of the delay valve.
57 Operate the pump to build a vacuum. The diaphragm rod should be withdrawn until the pump is no longer operated and should then slowly return to its fully-extended position.

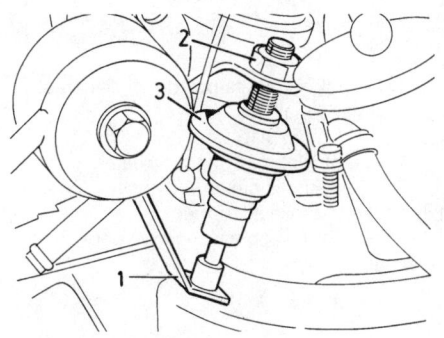

Throttle governor

58 Run the engine to normal operating temperature and allow it to idle.
59 Disconnect and plug the vacuum hose to the governor *(see illustration)*.
60 Loosen nut (4) and adjust rod (5) to obtain 1800 ± 50 rpm. Tighten nut (4) on completion.
61 Unplug and reconnect the vacuum hose to the governor.
62 Check the clearance at B. This should be a minimum of 0.5 mm while the engine is idling.
63 If the clearance at B is smaller than 0.5 mm, disconnect and plug the vacuum hose to the governor. Turn nut (6) to increase dimension C, which should be a minimum of 21.5 mm in the relaxed position.
64 Repeat paragraphs 60 to 63 until the correct governor speed is obtained, with a clearance at B of less than 0.5 mm.

Full-load enrichment nozzle

65 Close the choke flap and measure the clearance between the enrichment nozzle and the flap *(see illustration)*. Gap 'a' must be 1.0 ± 0.3 mm. Carefully bend the nozzle as necessary.

5 Component testing

1 Refer to Part D for general tests on the thermal switch, manifold heater and throttle body heater.

Thermal switch

2 Below 40°C ± 10°C, a voltmeter should indicate battery voltage (switch open).

Throttle governor adjustment

1 Throttle governor
2 Vacuum hose
3 Diaphragm rod
4 Locknut
5 Adjustment screw
6 Adjustment nut
For B and C, refer to text

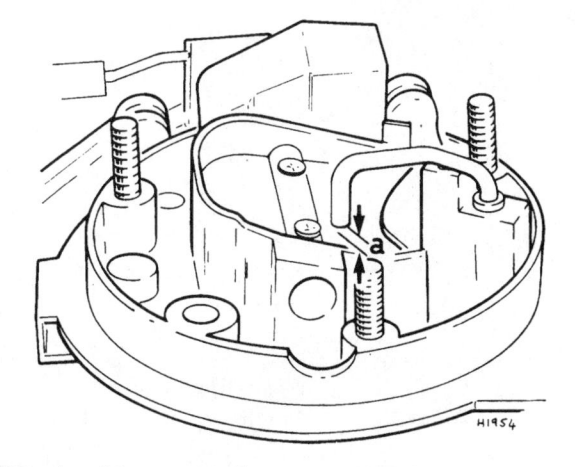

Full-load enrichment nozzle

a Clearance = 1.0 ± 0.3 mm

F1•9

Chapter F1

3 Above that temperature, the voltmeter should indicate zero volts (switch closed).
4 Renew the thermal switch if it does not function in accordance with the above.

6 Fault diagnosis

Refer to Part D for diagnosis of general carburettor faults. The following faults are specific to the 1B1 carburettor:

Poor choke operation/poor cold running

- [ ] Over-choking due to pull-down diaphragm or reservoir failure.
- [ ] Sticking choke flap.
- [ ] Failure of inlet manifold pre-heater.
- [ ] Failure of choke bi-metal.
- [ ] Incorrect choke adjustment.
- [ ] Choke earth strap missing or in poor condition.

Heavy fuel consumption/idle CO level high

- [ ] Leaking power valve diaphragm.

Hesitation

- [ ] Defective or sticking accelerator pump piston.
- [ ] Worn accelerator pump lever or shaft.
- [ ] Plugged accelerator pump injector.

Poor hot starting

- [ ] Vapour bubble formation in float chamber.
- [ ] Sticking needle valve.

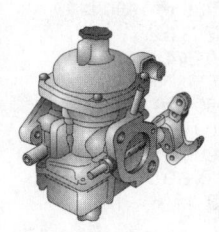

Part F Chapter 2
Pierburg 1B3 carburettor

F2

Contents

Component testing	5	Identification	2
Fault diagnosis	6	Principles of operation	1
General servicing	3	Service adjustments	4

Specifications

Manufacturer	Audi	Audi	Audi	Audi
Model	80 1.6 S, CL	80 1.6S, CL	80 Coupe	80 Coupe
Year	1979 to 1983	1979 to 1983	1981 to 1982	1981 to 1982
Engine code	WV, YN (55kW) SOHC	WV, YN (55kW) SOHC	DD (55kW)	DD (55kW)
Capacity (cm³)/no. of cyls	1588/4	1588/4	1781/4	1781/4
Oil temperature (°C)	80	80	80	80
Transmission	MT	AT	MT	AT
Carb. identification	049 129 017 N	049 129 017 M	026 129 015 B	026 129 015 C
Idle speed (rpm)	950 ± 50	950 ± 50	750 ± 50	750 ± 50
Fast idle speed (rpm)	3700 ± 200	3900 ± 200	3600 ± 200	3600 ± 200
CO @ idle (% vol.)	1.0 ± 0.5	1.0 ± 0.5	1.0 ± 0.5	1.0 ± 0.5
Venturi diameter (K)	26	26	24	24
Idle jet (g)	50	50	47.5	47.5
Main jet (Gg)	122.5	125	112.5	110
Air correction jet (a)	100	100	90	90
Accelerator pump jet (i)	40	50	40	45
Float level (mm)	27 ± 1.0	27 ± 1.0	27 ± 1.0	27 ± 1.0
Needle valve (mm) (P)	1.75	1.75	1.75	1.75
Float weight (grams)	7.2 ± 0.5	7.2 ± 0.5	7.2 ± 0.5	7.2 ± 0.5
Basic throttle position (mm)	0.3 ± 0.03	0.3 ± 0.03	0.3 ± 0.03	0.3 ± 0.03
Choke fast idle gap (mm)	0.7 ± 0.15	0.83 ± 0.15	0.77 ± 0.15	0.94 ± 0.15
Choke pull-down (mm) (a)	-	-	2.1 ± 0.15	2.05 ± 0.15
Choke pull-down (mm) (a1)	2.7 ± 0.5	2.9 ± 0.5	2.8 ± 0.15	2.85 ± 0.15

Manufacturer	Audi	Audi	Mercedes-Benz	Seat
Model	100 & Avant 1.8	100 & Avant 1.8	210/310/410	Ibiza 1.2
Year	1983 to 1986	1983 to 1986	1982 to 1992	1985 to 1986
Engine code	DR (55kW)	DR (55kW)	M102 OHV	O21A1000
Capacity (cm³)/no. of cyls	1781/4	1781/4	2299/4	1193/4
Oil temperature (°C)	80	80	80	100
Transmission	MT	AT	AT	-
Carb. identification	026 129 015 B	026 129 015 C	001 070 94 04 (to 84) 002 070 25 04 (85 on)	7.17627.39
Idle speed (rpm)	750 ± 50	750 ± 50	800 ± 50	925
Fast idle speed (rpm)	3600 ± 200	3600 ± 200	2900 ± 150	2600
CO @ idle (% vol.)	1.0 ± 0.5	1.0 ± 0.5	1.0 ± 0.5	2.0
Venturi diameter (K)	24	24	28	25
Idle jet (g)	47.5	47.5	55	47.5
Main jet (Gg)	112.5	110	130	120
Air correction jet (a)	90	90	140	57.5
Accelerator pump jet (i)	40	45	40	30
Float level (mm)	27 ± 1.0	27 ± 1.0	27 ± 1.0	28.5
Needle valve (mm) (P)	1.75	1.75	2.0	1.5
Float weight (grams)	7.2 ± 0.5	7.2 ± 0.5	7.2 ± 0.5	7.2 ± 0.5
Basic throttle position (mm)	0.3 ± 0.03	0.3 ± 0.03	0.41 ± 0.02	-
Choke fast idle gap (mm)	0.77	0.94	0.85 ± 0.05	-
Choke pull-down (mm) (a1)	2.45 ± 0.35	2.45 ± 0.4	3.3 ± 0.15	2.7

Chapter F2

Manufacturer	Seat	Seat	Seat	Volkswagen
Model	Ibiza 1.2	Malaga 1.2	Malaga 1.2	Polo & Van 1.05
Year	1987 to 1992	1985 to 1986	1987 to 1992	1985 to 1990
Engine code	O21A1000	O21A1000	O21A1000	HZ (33kW)
Capacity (cm³)/no. of cyls	1193/4	1193/4	1193/4	1043/4
Oil temperature (°C)	100	100	100	80
Carb. identification	-	7.17627.39	-	030 129 O16 A
Idle speed (rpm)	925	925	925	800 ± 50
Fast idle speed (rpm)	2600	2600	2600	2000 ± 100
CO @ idle (% vol.)	2.0	2.0	2.0	2.0 ± 0.5
Venturi diameter (K)	25	25	25	23
Idle jet (g)	47.5	47.5	47.5	50
Main jet (Gg)	120	120	120	105
Air correction jet (a)	57.5	57.5	57.5	57.
Accelerator pump jet (i)	30	30	30	40
Float level (mm)	28.5	28.5 ± 1.0	28.5 ± 1.0	28.5 ± 1.0
Needle valve (mm) (P)	1.5	1.5	1.5	1.5
Float weight (grams)	7.2 ± 0.5	7.2 ± 0.5	7.2 ± 0.5	7.2 ± 0.5
Basic throttle position (mm)	-	-	-	0.1 ± 0.05
Choke fast idle gap (mm)	-	-	-	0.75 ± 0.05
Choke pull-down (mm) (a)	-	-	-	1.8 ± 0.15
Choke pull-down (mm) (a1)	2.7	2.3 ± 0.15	2.3 ± 0.15	3.0 ± 1.0

Manufacturer	Volkswagen	Volkswagen	Volkswagen	Volkswagen
Model	Polo & Van 1.05 Cat.	Golf 1.05	Golf 1.05	Golf/Jetta/ Scirocco 1.5
Year	June 1989 to 1990	1985 to June 1989	June 1989 to 1991	1981 to 1984
Engine code	HZ (33kW)	HZ (37kW)	HZ (37kW)	JB (51kW)
Capacity (cm³)/no. of cyls	1043/4	1043/4	1043/4	1457/4
Oil temperature (°C)	80	80	80	80
Transmission	-	-	-	MT
Carb. identification	030 129 O16 L	030 129 016A	030 129 016L	055 129 025 J
Idle speed (rpm)	800 ± 50	800 ± 50	800 ± 50	800 ± 50
Fast idle speed (rpm)	2000 ± 100	2000 ± 100	2000 ± 100	3900 ± 200
CO @ idle (% vol.)	0 to 2.5	2.0 ± 0.5	2.0 ± 0.5	1.0 ± 0.5
Venturi diameter (K)	23	23	23	26
Idle jet (g)	50	50	50	50
Main jet (Gg)	102.5	105	102.5	122.5
Air correction jet (a)	100	57.5	100	100
Accelerator pump jet (i)	40	30	40	55
Float level (mm)	28.5 ± 1.0	28.5 ± 1.0	28.5 ± 1.0	27 ± 1.0
Needle valve (mm) (P)	1.5	1.5	1.5	1.75
Float weight (grams)	7.2 ± 0.5	7.2 ± 0.5	7.2 ± 0.5	7.2 ± 0.5
Basic throttle position (mm)	-	0.1 ± 0.05	-	0.3 ± 0.03
Choke fast idle gap (mm)	-	0.75 ± 0.05	-	0.7 ± 0.15
Choke pull-down (mm) (a)	-	1.8 ± 0.15	-	2.1 ± 0.15
Choke pull-down (mm) (a1)	2.5 ± 0.2	3.0 ± 1.0	2.5 ± 0.2	3.5 ± 0.15

Manufacturer	Volkswagen	Volkswagen	Volkswagen
Model	Golf/Jetta/Scirocco 1.5	Passat 1.6	Passat 1.6
Year	1981 to 1984	1981 to 1983	1981 to 1983
Engine code	JB (51kW)	WV (55kW)	WV (55kW)
Capacity (cm³)/no. of cyls	1457/4	1588/4	1588/4
Oil temperature (°C)	80	80	80
Transmission	AT	MT	AT
Carb. identification	055 129 025 K	049 129 017 N	049 129 017 M
Idle speed (rpm)	800 ± 50	950 ± 50	950 ± 50
Fast idle speed (rpm)	3700 ± 200	3700 ± 200	3900 ± 200
CO @ idle (% vol.)	1.0 ± 0.5	1.0 ± 0.5	1.0 ± 0.5
Venturi diameter (K)	26	26	26
Idle jet (g)	50	50	50
Main jet (Gg)	120	122.5	125
Air correction jet (a)	100	100	100
Accelerator pump jet (i)	50	40	50
Float level (mm)	27 ± 1.0	27 ± 1.0	27 ± 1.0
Needle valve (mm) (P)	1.75	1.75	1.75
Float weight (grams)	7.2 ± 0.5	7.2 ± 0.5	7.2 ± 0.5
Basic throttle position (mm)	0.3 ± 0.03	0.3 ± 0.03	0.3 ± 0.03
Choke fast idle gap (mm)	0.78 ± 0.15	0.7 ± 0.15	0.83 ± 0.15
Choke pull-down (mm) (a)	2.3 ± 0.15	-	-
Choke pull-down (mm) (a1)	3.4 ± 0.15	2.9 ± 0.7	2.9 ± 0.5

Pierburg 1B3 carburettor

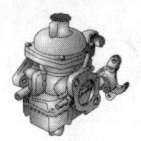

1 Principles of operation

Introduction
1 The following technical description of the Pierburg 1B3 carburettor should be read in conjunction with the more detailed description of carburettor principles in Part A.

Construction
2 The Pierburg 1B3 carburettor is a downdraught single venturi instrument with a semi-automatic choke control *(see illustration)*. Major body components are cast in light alloy for weight-saving purposes. The jet systems are arranged so as to be unaffected by the centrifugal or braking forces imposed during engine operation, for both transversely or longitudinally-mounted engine applications. The throttle shafts are made of steel, while the throttle valves, all jets and the emulsion tube are manufactured from brass. The internal fuel channels and air passages are drilled and sealed with lead plugs where necessary.

3 Most versions of the 1B3 carburettor operate in conjunction with an electrical heater fitted to the inlet manifold. The purpose of the heater is to improve atomisation of the air/fuel mixture during the warm-up period. A thermal switch is usually wired to the supply voltage so that the heater is switched off at a pre-determined temperature. Some versions also use a throttle body heater to prevent carburettor icing. Both heaters function on the positive temperature coefficient (PTC) principle. As the temperature rises, the heater resistance also rises.

Fuel control
4 Fuel flows into the carburettor through an inlet connection. The fuel level in the float chamber is controlled by a spring-loaded needle valve and plastic float assembly *(see illustration overleaf)*. The float level is considered critical and is set very accurately during production. The float chamber is vented internally into the upper air intake which is on the clean-air side of the air filter. Some variations use a vapour trap to prevent excess fuel vapours and poor starting when the engine is hot. A calibrated fuel return system is provided to ensure that relatively cool fuel is supplied to the carburettor.

Idle, slow running and progression
5 Fuel is drawn from the primary main well into the base of a vertical well which dips down into the fuel. A combined idle jet, emulsion tube and air corrector is placed in the well. The fuel is mixed with air drawn in through the calibrated air corrector and the holes in the tube to form an emulsion. The resulting mixture is drawn

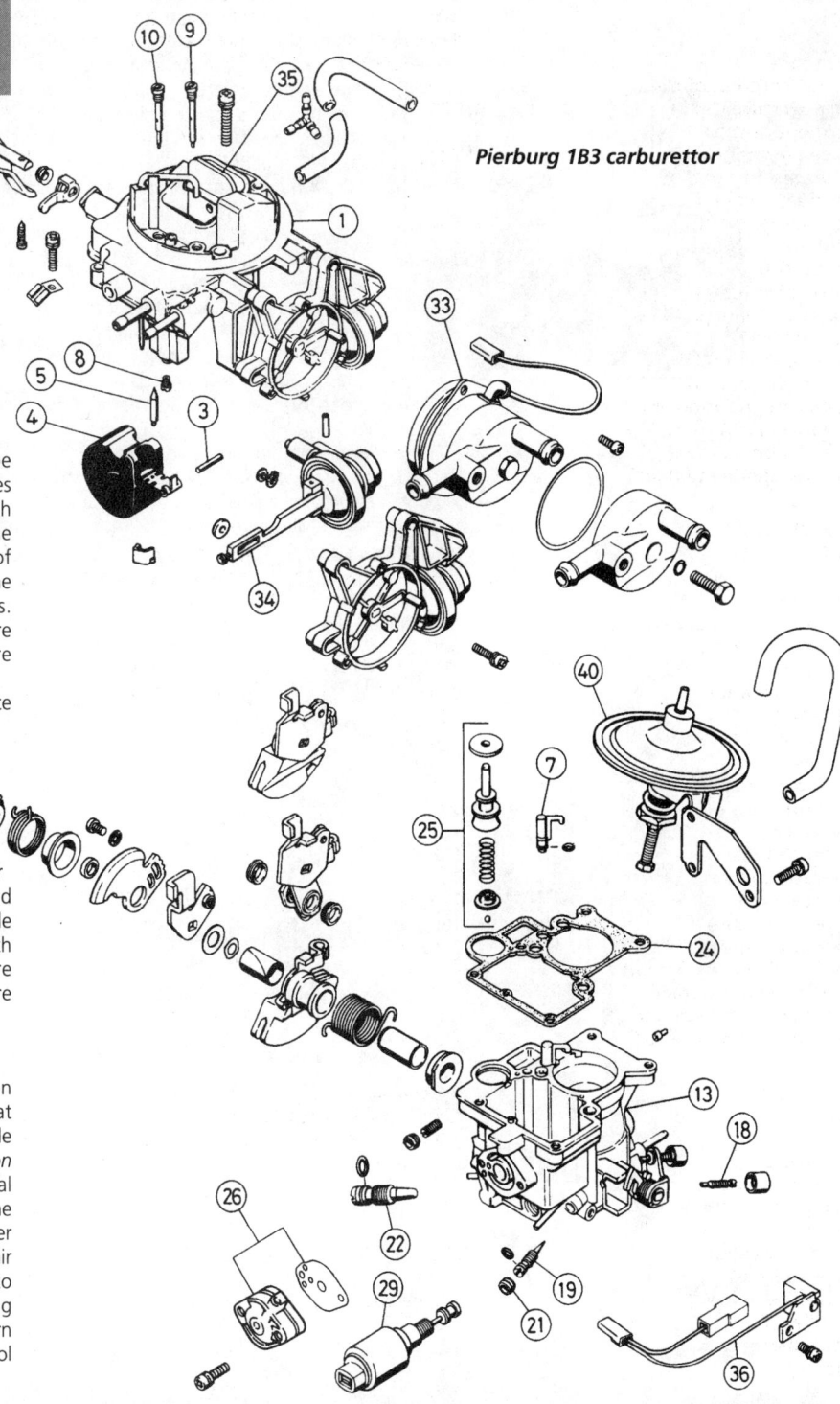

Pierburg 1B3 carburettor

1 Upper body
3 Float pin
4 Float
5 Needle valve
7 Pump injector
8 Main jet
9 Idle jet
10 Bypass idle jet
13 Main body
18 Fast idle adjustment screw
19 Idle mixture control screw
21 Tamperproof cap
22 Bypass idle speed screw
24 Float chamber gasket
25 Accelerator pump assembly
26 Part-load enrichment valve assembly
29 Idle cut-off valve (where fitted)
33 Choke bi-metal assembly
34 Choke pull-down diaphragm
35 Choke flap
36 Throttle body heater
40 Throttle governor

Chapter F2

Fuel control system

39 Float needle valve
40 Float
62 Fuel supply inlet
63 Fuel return

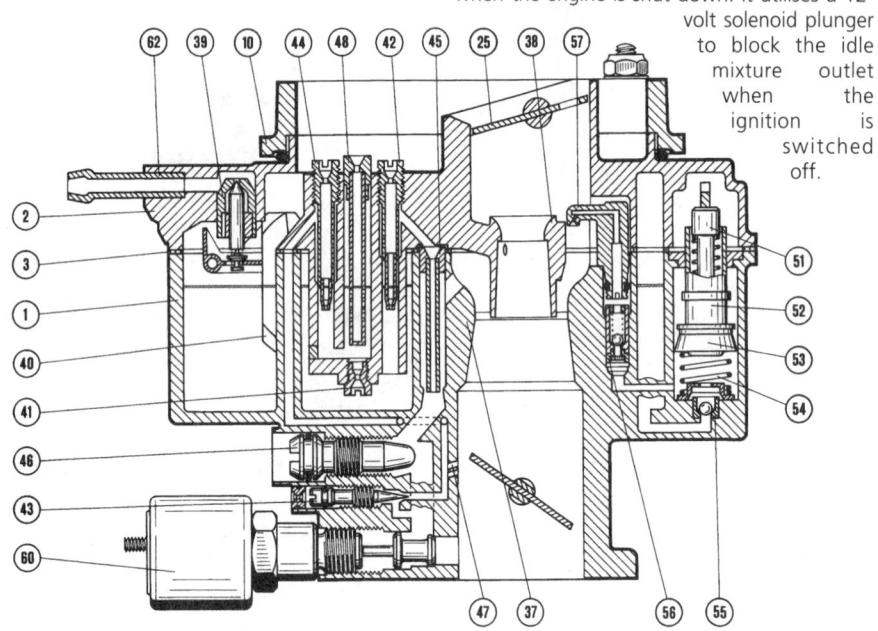

Idle and main systems

1 Main body assembly
2 Upper body assembly
3 Gasket
10 Intermediate piece
25 Choke flap
37 Venturi
38 Auxiliary venturi
39 Float needle valve
40 Float
41 Main jet
42 Idle bypass air corrector
43 Idle mixture control screw
44 Idle jet air corrector
45 Idle bypass emulsion well
46 Bypass idle speed screw
47 Progression holes
48 Main air corrector
51 Accelerator pump plunger
52 Accelerator pump piston
53 Cup seal
54 Spring
55 Inlet (ball) valve
56 Outlet valve
57 Injection nozzle
60 Idle cut-off valve
62 Fuel supply inlet

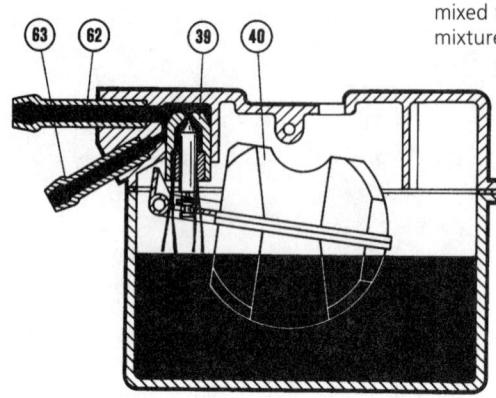

through a channel into a chamber where it is mixed with the bypass emulsion. The total idle mixture is then discharged from the main idle orifice under the primary throttle plate. A tapered mixture screw is used to vary the channel to the chamber and this ensures fine control of the idle mixture *(see illustration)*.

6 A number of progression holes provide a further air contribution to the emulsion (upstream of the chamber) while the throttle is closed. As the progression holes are uncovered by the opening throttle, the vacuum draw overcomes the air bleed into the holes and a reversal occurs. Fuel is now drawn out to add extra enrichment to the idle mixture during initial acceleration.

7 The idle speed is set by the adjustable bypass screw. The adjustable mixture screw is tamper proofed at production level, in accordance with emission regulations.

Idle cut-off valve

8 An idle cut-off valve is used to prevent run-on when the engine is shut down. It utilises a 12-volt solenoid plunger to block the idle mixture outlet when the ignition is switched off.

Idle bypass circuit

9 The idle bypass circuit provides a means of more accurately controlling idle emissions than with a conventional idle mixture circuit. The throttle plate is locked in a specified position and sealed with a tamperproof cap. Eighty percent of the fuel required for idle is provided by the normal idle circuit. The remainder of the idle mixture is controlled through the idle bypass circuit.

10 Fuel, sourced from the float chamber, is drawn into the bypass well. Air is supplied through a bypass air corrector and the emulsion is drawn through the bypass passage where additional air from the main venturi is introduced. The resulting mixture is drawn past the regulating screw into a chamber where it is mixed with the idle emulsion. The total idle mixture is then discharged from the main idle orifice under the primary throttle plate. The emulsion is controlled by a regulating screw which is also used to adjust the idle speed.

Idle speed boost valve

11 On the 1B3 carburettor fitted to a number of VW engines (engine code letter HZ), the idle speed is regulated by an adjustable air valve. As a load is placed upon the engine and the speed falls below 700 rpm, the air valve admits extra air via a two-way boost valve and the idle speed is increased.

Accelerator pump

12 The accelerator pump is controlled by a piston and is mechanically operated by a lever and cam linked to the throttle pedal. Under acceleration, a lever, actuated by the throttle linkage, bears against the pump piston and compresses it. Fuel from the pump chamber is pushed through the pump outlet channels, past the pump outlet valve and is injected from the pump nozzle into the venturi. The inlet valve remains closed to prevent fuel from being returned to the float chamber.

13 As the throttle action is reversed, a spring returns the piston to its starting position. Depression then draws fresh fuel from the float chamber into the pump chamber.

Main circuit

14 The amount of fuel discharged into the airstream is controlled by a calibrated main jet. Fuel is drawn through the jet, into the base of a vertical well which dips down into the fuel in the float chamber. A combined emulsion tube and air correction jet is placed in the well. Fuel is mixed with air, drawn in through the calibrated air correction jet and the holes in the emulsion tubes, to form an air/fuel emulsion. The resulting mixture is discharged from the main nozzle through an auxiliary venturi into the main airstream.

Part-load enrichment (power valve)

15 Fuel flows from the float chamber into the enrichment chamber through a fuel channel. An air passage is taken from under the throttle

Pierburg 1B3 carburettor

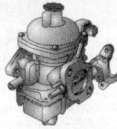

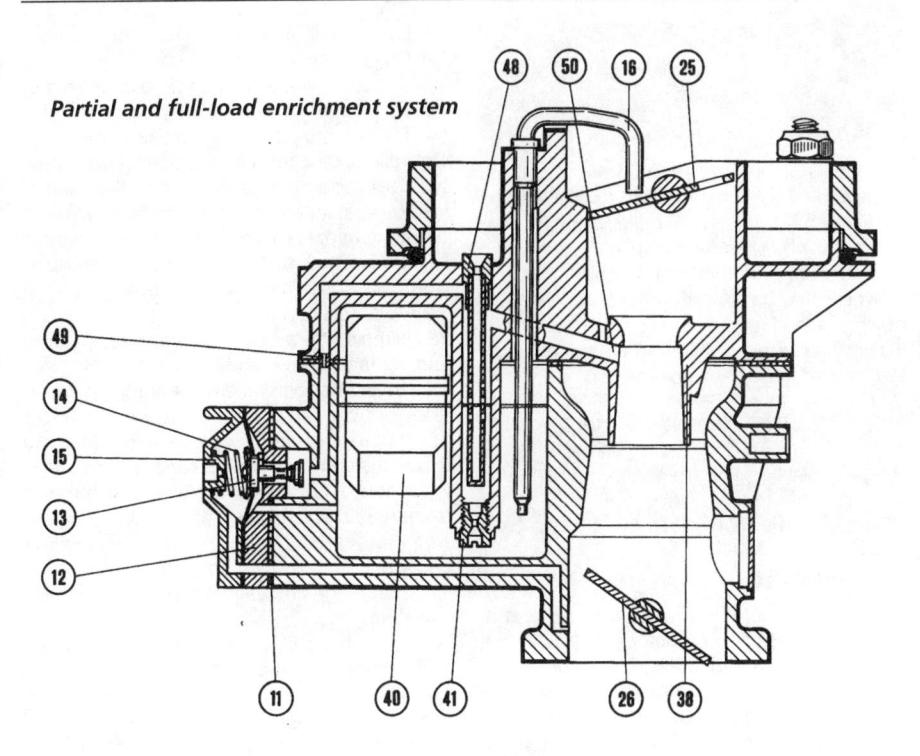

Partial and full-load enrichment system

11 Gasket
12 Intermediate piece
13 Part-load enrichment valve
14 Spring
15 Diaphragm cover
16 Full-load enrichment nozzle
25 Choke flap
26 Throttle valve
38 Auxiliary venturi
40 Float
41 Main jet
48 Main air corrector
49 Part-load enrichment jet
50 Main fuel nozzle

plate to the cover of the chamber. At idle and during light-throttle operation, manifold vacuum draws the diaphragm back against spring pressure to close off the enrichment valve and the fuel outlet channel. Under acceleration and wide-open throttle operation, the vacuum in the manifold is depleted. The diaphragm returns under spring pressure and the valve opens the fuel channel. This allows fuel to flow through the channel and a calibrated bushing to supplement the fuel in the upper part of the main well. The fuel level rises in the well and the fuel mixture is enriched *(see illustration)*.

Full-load enrichment

16 At full-load and high engine speeds, the velocity of air creates a depression sufficient to raise fuel from the float chamber into a channel. The fuel then passes through a calibrated bushing to the upper section of the air intake where it is discharged into the airstream from the full-load enrichment nozzle.

Cold start system

17 The choke system is semi-automatic in operation and actuates a flap in the air intake *(see illustration)*. The system is primed by depressing the accelerator pedal once or twice.
18 The choke strangler flap is controlled by a combined electrically- and coolant-heated bi-metal coil spring. The electrical supply to the choke is made through a coolant-heated thermal switch. The electrical supply initially heats the choke coil after the first start from cold. As the coolant passing through the choke coil's water housing becomes warm, it adds to the heating of the choke spring. When the coolant reaches a pre-set temperature, the thermal switch cuts out the electrical supply and the coolant flow remains the only source of choke heating. The choke flap will thus remain open while the coolant (and engine) remains warm.
19 Fast idle is achieved with the aid of a stepped cam attached to the choke spindle. An adjustable screw, connected to the throttle lever mechanism and butting against the cam, can be used to vary the fast idle speed. This screw is fitted with a tamperproof cap. As the bi-metal coil is heated and the flap opens, the screw will rest on successively less stepped parts of the cam. Idle speed is thus progressively reduced until ultimately the cam is released and the idle speed returns to normal.

Choke pull-down

20 The choke flap is eccentrically mounted, so that during cranking it is partially opened to prevent an over-rich fuel mixture. Once the engine has fired, the choke flap must open slightly to weaken the mixture and avoid flooding during idle and light-throttle operation. This is achieved by using manifold vacuum to actuate a pull-down diaphragm. A linkage attached to the diaphragm will then pull upon the flap. The type of pull-down system fitted either makes a single movement to actuate the diaphragm or operates in two stages. The two pull-down stages ensure maximum richness for the few seconds after a cold start and then a rapid opening of the choke flap to reduce over-richness.

Dechoke (wide-open kick)

21 If the throttle is opened fully when the engine is cold, the pull-down vacuum will deplete and the choke flap will tend to close. This may cause flooding and, to prevent this, a wide-open kick mechanism is employed. When the throttle is opened fully, a cam on the throttle lever will turn the choke lever anti-clockwise to partially open the flap.

Throttle damper

22 The throttle damper (where fitted) slows down the rate of throttle closing to aid emissions on the engine over-run.

Throttle governor

23 Fitted to some applications, the throttle

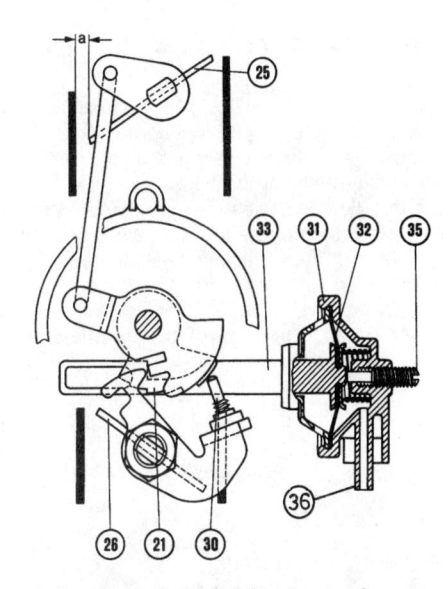

Choke operation - cold start, engine running

21 Stepped cam
25 Choke flap
26 Throttle valve
30 Fast idle adjustment screw
31 Pull-down assembly
32 Diaphragm
33 Diaphragm rod
35 Adjustment screw
36 Vacuum connection
a First stage pull-down

Chapter F2

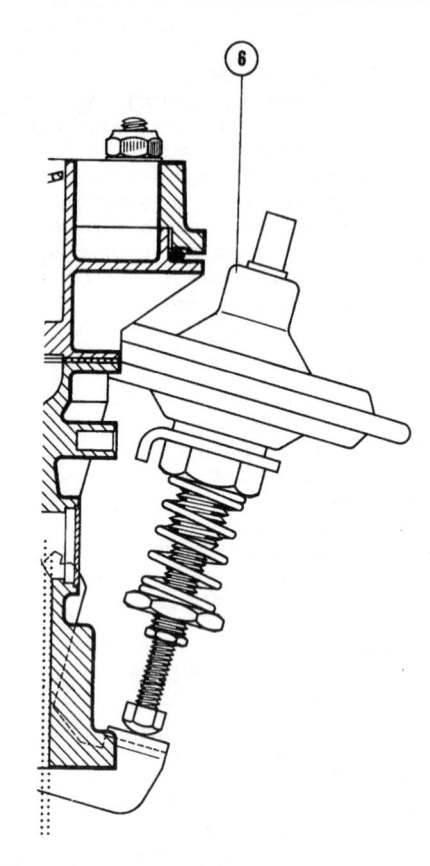

Throttle governor (6)

governor pushrod *(see illustration)* will extend to partially open the throttle when the engine is stopped, ready for the next hot or cold start. If the choke is employed, the governor will hold the throttle open to a wider position than the highest position of the fast idle cam. Once the engine has fired, vacuum will operate the governor diaphragm and the plunger will withdraw. The throttle opening will now depend on the position of the throttle stop screw (engine hot) or fast idle cam (engine cold).

Pull-down assembly

8 Roll pin
9 Star clip
10 Pull-down rod

2 Identification

1 Pierburg 1B is stamped upon the upper and main bodies. The manufacturer identification code may be stamped on a metallic tag attached to the cover by an upper body fixing screw or on a corner of the carburettor main body.
2 Where the tag is missing, refer to Part B for other means of identifying the carburettor.
3 Early versions of this carburettor may be stamped with the trade name Solex.

3 General servicing

Introduction

1 Read this Chapter in conjunction with Part B, which describes some of the operations in more detail. It is assumed that the carburettor is removed for this service. However, many of the operations can be tackled with the carburettor in place. Where this is undertaken, first remove the upper body assembly and soak the fuel out of the float chamber using a clean tissue or soft cloth.

Dismantling and checking

2 Remove the carburettor from the engine (see Part B).
3 Check the carburettor visually for damage and wear.
4 Remove the idle cut-off valve assembly, after slackening the nut with a 17 mm open-ended spanner. Clean the valve with carburettor cleaner and test the plunger operation by connecting the valve to the battery or other voltage supply (or use the valve supply wire in the engine compartment). Touch the valve body to earth with the ignition on. Repeat this several times and ensure that the plunger tip advances and retracts cleanly. Renew the valve if the action is faulty or if cleaning does not improve its operation.
5 Disconnect the choke vacuum hose then remove the four screws and detach the carburettor upper body. The electrical earth strap (where fitted) which is retained by one of the screws, will also be removed at this time.
6 Inspect the float chamber for corrosion and calcium build-up.
7 Tap out the float pin and remove the float, needle valve and float chamber gasket. The needle valve seat is not removable.
8 Check that the anti-vibration ball is free in the needle valve end.
9 Check the needle valve tip for wear and ridges.
10 The float should be checked for damage and ingress of petrol.
11 Renew the float pin if it shows signs of wear.
12 Use a straight-edge to check for distorted flanges on all facing surfaces.
13 Unscrew the mixture and bypass screws and inspect the tips for damage or ridges.
14 The pump injector is a push fit in the body. Carefully prise it from its location. On the early type of injector, the spring and outlet ball are held by a retaining ring in the main body. These components are not removable. If a later type of injector is fitted, test it by shaking it. No noise from the outlet ball would indicate that the valve is seized.
15 Remove the accelerator pump seal, piston and spring. Check the piston assembly for fatigue and damage. Check the pump operating lever for wear and smooth operation.
16 Unscrew the primary idle jet and bypass idle assemblies, noting their locations for correct installation during assembly. Note that the primary idle and bypass jets can be removed from the carburettor without removing the upper body.
17 Check the jet calibration against those specified. It is possible that the idle jets may have been transposed (or the wrong size fitted) during the last overhaul.
18 Unscrew the main jet. It is not possible to remove the air corrector or emulsion tube. Check that the channel from the main jet into the main emulsion tube well is clear.
19 Remove the two screws and detach the power valve housing cover, spring and diaphragm assembly. Check the diaphragm for damage and fatigue. Check the action of the power valve and the condition of the small seal. Check that the channel (through both bodies) into the emulsion tube well is clear.
20 Do not disturb the adjustment of the throttle angle unless absolutely necessary.
21 Inspect the choke flap, spindle and linkage for stickiness and wear.
22 Test the choke pull-down unit as described in Section 4.
23 Remove the three screws and circlip, then detach the choke housing from the upper body. Punch out the roll pin, remove the star clip and detach the pull-down assembly from the choke housing *(see illustration)*.

Preparation for reassembly

24 Clean the jets, carburettor body assemblies, float chamber and internal channels. An air line may be used to clear the internal channels once the carburettor is fully dismantled. Note that if high-pressure air is directed into the channels and passages with the diaphragms still in place, diaphragm damage may result. Spraying carburettor cleaner into all the channels and passages in the carburettor body will often clear them of gum and dirt.
25 During reassembly, a complete set of new gaskets should be fitted. Also renew the needle valve, float pivot pin and all diaphragms.
26 Inspect and renew (where necessary) the mixture screw, main jet, idle and bypass jets, and the accelerator pump injector. Renew worn linkages, springs, vacuum hoses and other parts where necessary.

Pierburg 1B3 carburettor

27 Ensure that all jets are firmly locked into their original positions (but do not over-tighten). A loose jet can cause a rich (or even lean) running condition. Clean all mating surfaces and flanges of old gasket material and reassemble with a new gasket. Ensure that housings are positioned with their air and fuel routes correctly aligned.

Reassembly

28 Slide the choke diaphragm assembly into position and secure with a new roll pin and star clip. Reconnect the choke link rod and secure with the circlip. Refit the choke housing and secure with the three screws.
29 Ensure that the choke flap and linkage move smoothly and progressively.
30 Where the primary throttle position has been disturbed and a throttle setting gauge is available, use it to set the throttle angle. Otherwise, temporarily adjust the throttle plate so that it is open just enough to prevent its seizure in the throttle body. An adjustment method with the engine running is detailed in Section 4.
31 Refit the power diaphragm, spring and cover assembly and secure with the two screws.
32 Refit the main jet into its original position.
33 Refit the primary and bypass idle jets into the upper body (do not transpose the jets).
34 Refit the accelerator pump spring, piston and seal into the main body.
35 Align the pump injector and tap it into position after renewing the small seal on the injector body.
36 Refit the idle mixture screw after renewing the seal. Turn the screw in gently until it just seats. From this position, unscrew it three full turns. This will provide a basic setting to allow the engine to be started.
37 Refit the bypass regulating screw after renewing the seal. Obtain a basic setting in the same way as for the mixture screw above.
38 Insert the needle valve into the seat with the ball facing outwards. Refit the float and pivot pin. Ensure that the top of the needle valve engages into the slot on the float.
39 Check the float level, see Section 4. Refit the float gasket to the main body.
40 Refit the upper body to the main body and secure with the four screws. Ensure that the carburettor earth strap (where fitted) is secured with an upper body fixing screw. Reconnect the choke vacuum hose.
41 Refit the idle cut-off valve and lock it firmly into position.
42 Adjust the choke with reference to Section 4.
43 Refit the carburettor to the engine.
44 Always adjust the carburettor idle speed and mixture after any work has been carried out on the carburettor, preferably with the aid of a CO meter.

4 Service adjustments

Adjustment preconditions

1 Refer to Part B for general advice on the preconditions for correct adjustment of this carburettor.
2 Disconnect the engine breather hose from the air filter and plug the opening in the air filter.
3 Reconnect the breather hose after all adjustments are completed. If the CO level increases by more than 1 to 1.5%, change the sump oil. If the CO level still increases after an oil change, suspect worn or sticking piston rings.
4 If no CO change is noted on connecting/disconnecting the breather hose, suspect a clogged crankcase ventilation (PCV) system.

Bypass idle adjustment

5 Run the engine at 3000 rpm for 30 seconds to clear the manifold of fuel vapours, then allow the engine to idle.
6 Use the idle bypass regulating screw to set the specified idle speed *(see illustration)*.
7 Check the CO level and if necessary, remove the tamperproof plug and adjust the idle mixture screw to obtain the correct level. Turning the screw clockwise (inwards) will reduce the CO level and turning the screw anti-clockwise (outwards) will increase the CO level.
8 Repeat paragraphs 6 and 7 until both adjustments are correct. Adjusting the idle bypass screw will also affect the CO level.
9 Fit a new tamperproof plug to the mixture control screw on completion.

Basic throttle position

10 If the idle speed and CO cannot be set correctly, it is possible that the basic throttle position is incorrect.
11 One method of setting is to remove the carburettor and use a Pierburg throttle setting gauge to accurately set the throttle position *(see illustration)*. Another method is to use a very low-reading vacuum gauge connected to the vacuum advance connector. The correct angle is set when the gauge registers 8 ± 4 mmHg (10 ± 5 mbars).
12 An alternative method of setting the throttle plate follows. Note that this is not the manufacturer's recommended method but will nevertheless result in an accurate and stable idle speed and CO level:
 a) Allow the engine to idle.
 b) Screw in the bypass regulating screw until it is fully seated. The idle speed should drop to approximately two-thirds of the idle speed figure. For example, if the idle speed is specified as 950 rpm, the speed should drop to between 600 and 650 rpm.
 c) Adjust the throttle stop screw until 600 to 650 rpm is obtained.
 d) Unscrew the bypass screw until 950 rpm is once again attained.
 e) Reset the CO to the correct level.
 f) If the CO needs a large adjustment at this stage, repeat paragraphs a) to e). Once the proper level of CO is reached at the specified idle speed, the carburettor is properly adjusted.

13 The rpm figures used in the above example are based on a hypothetical idle speed of 950 rpm. Substitute the correct figures for the carburettor being adjusted (see Specifications).

Float level

14 It is not possible to adjust the plastic float. It is possible, however, to check the float level.
15 Hold the carburettor upper body at an angle of 45° with the float tag gently touching the ball of the fully-closed needle valve. Note that the ball of the needle valve must not be depressed *(see illustration)*.
16 Measure the distance between the upper body (without its gasket) and the top of the float. Refer to Specifications for the correct float level.

Idle adjustment screw location
1 Bypass idle speed screw
2 Idle mixture control screw

Setting basic throttle position using a Pierburg gauge
1 Throttle stop screw
2 Pierburg setting gauge

Chapter F2

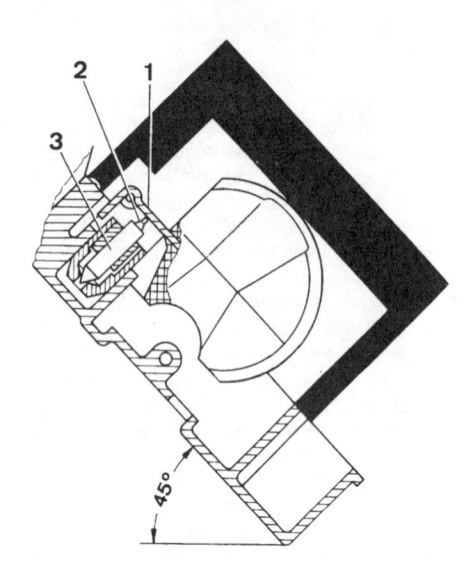

Float level checking

1 Float lever
2 Needle valve pin
3 Needle valve

17 If the level is incorrect, check the needle valve seat for correct position. Remove the float and check the float weight (see Specifications). If the seat and weight are satisfactory, renew the float if the level is incorrect.

Accelerator pump

18 On the Pierburg 1B3 carburettor, it is possible to adjust the volume of fuel injected by the accelerator pump.
19 Loosen the clamping screw (2) *(see illustration)*.
20 Move the cam (1) in direction (+) to increase volume, or in direction (-) to decrease volume.
21 Tighten the clamping screw on completion.

Choke adjustments

Fast idle adjustment (carburettor removed)

22 Invert the carburettor.
23 Partially open the throttle and fully close the choke flap. Release the throttle and the flap.

Fast idle adjustment - carburettor removed

21 Stepped cam
28 Fast idle adjustment screw

The fast idle adjustment screw should remain against the highest step of the fast idle cam, forcing open the throttle plate to leave a small clearance *(see illustration)*.
24 Use the shank of a twist drill to measure the clearance between the wall of the throttle bore and the throttle plate. Refer to Specifications for the required drill size. Measure from the side opposite the progression holes.
25 Remove the tamperproof plug and adjust as necessary by turning the fast idle adjustment screw in the appropriate direction.
26 Fit a new tamperproof plug on completion.
27 Check the fast idle speed against the specified figure once the carburettor has been refitted to the engine.

Fast idle adjustment (engine running)

28 Warm the engine to normal operating temperature and ensure that the idle speed and CO level are correctly adjusted. Switch off the engine.
29 Remove the air filter assembly and place it clear of the carburettor. All vacuum hoses must remain connected.
30 Partially open the throttle and fully close the choke flap. Release the throttle and the flap. The fast idle adjustment screw should remain against the highest step of the fast idle cam.
31 Start the engine without moving the throttle and record the fast idle speed (refer to Specifications for the correct figure).
32 Adjust as necessary by turning the fast idle screw in the appropriate direction.
33 Refit the air filter, ensuring that the vacuum hoses remain connected (unless continuing with the following pull-down tests).

Choke pull-down

34 Remove the three screws and detach the bi-metal coil housing from the carburettor.
35 Refer to Part D for a method of testing the vacuum reservoir (where fitted).
36 Remove the vacuum hose from the carburettor base to the inlet connection (supply side) of the pull-down unit and attach a vacuum pump to the connection. Remove the second hose from the outlet side and leave the connection unplugged *(see illustration)*.
37 Operate the pump and the pull-down should move to the first stage.
38 Maintaining the vacuum, plug the pull-down outlet connection and operate the pump until 225 mmHg (300 mbars) is obtained. The pull-down should now move to the second stage and hold vacuum for at least 10 seconds. If the diaphragm does not operate as described, renew the pull-down unit. If the pull-down unit is a single-stage type, follow the procedure for testing the second stage of the two-stage unit above.
39 Position the fast idle screw on the highest step of the fast idle cam.
40 Where a single-stage pull-down unit is fitted, remove the vacuum hose and plug the pull-down outlet connection. Move the pull-down operating rod up to its stop by operating the vacuum pump. Lightly close the choke flap and use the shank of a twist drill to measure the

Accelerator pump adjustment

1 Pump cam
2 Clamping screw

'a1' gap between the lower section of the choke flap and the air intake - see illustration below. Refer to Specifications for the required drill size. Adjust as necessary by turning the pull-down adjusting screw 'a1' *(see illustration opposite)* in the appropriate direction.
41 Where a two-stage pull-down unit is fitted, detach the hose from the pull-down unit to the vacuum reservoir. Do not plug this hose. Operate the vacuum pump and the choke flap should open to the first stage setting 'a'. Lightly close the choke flap and use the shank of a

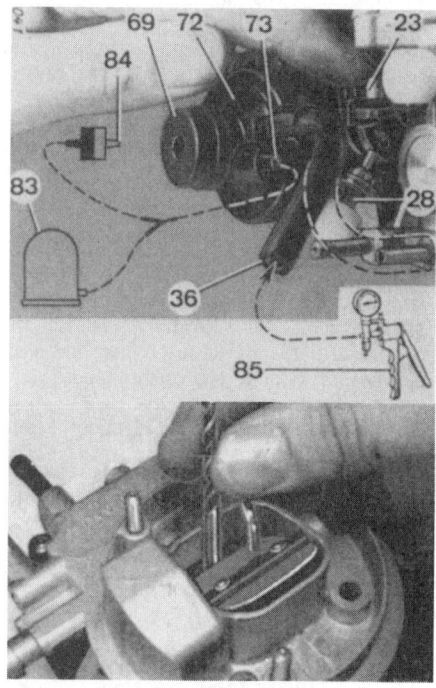

Choke pull-down adjustment

23 Stepped cam
28 Fast idle adjustment screw
36 Vacuum connection (inlet)
69 Adjustment screw 'a'
72 Pull-down unit
73 Vacuum connection (outlet)
83 Vacuum reservoir
84 Non-return valve
85 Vacuum pump

Pierburg 1B3 carburettor

Choke pull-down adjustment

68 Adjustment screw 'a1'

twist drill to measure the a gap between the lower section of the choke flap and the air intake. Refer to Specifications for the required drill size. Adjust as necessary by turning the screw 'a' (item 69 in the illustration at the bottom of the opposite page) in the appropriate direction. Plug the pull-down outlet connection and fully operate the vacuum pump. The choke flap should open to the second stage setting. Lightly close the choke flap and use the shank of a twist drill to measure the 'a1' gap between the lower section of the choke flap and the air intake. Refer to Specifications for the required drill size. Adjust as necessary by turning the adjusting screw 'a1' *(see illustration above)* in the appropriate direction.

42 Note that where a vacuum pump is not available, a small screwdriver can also be used to push fully on the a1 adjusting screw. In this instance, the screw should be pushed until a resistance is felt. The clearance obtained is the first stage gap. Continue pushing until the screw cannot be pushed any further. The clearance now obtained is the second stage gap.

43 Reconnect the vacuum hoses.

44 Refit the bi-metal coil housing, ensuring that the spring locates in the slot of the choke lever. Secure loosely with the three screws.

45 Align the cut mark on the bi-metal cover

Choke alignment marks

with the correct mark on the choke assembly housing, then tighten the three screws *(see illustration)*.

46 Refit the air filter assembly, ensuring that the vacuum hoses remain connected.

Throttle damper

47 Warm the engine to normal running temperature and ensure that the idle speed and mixture are correctly adjusted.

48 Loosen the damper locknut *(see illustration)*.

49 Wind the damper up until a gap of 0.05 mm exists between the dashpot rod and the throttle lever.

50 Wind the damper downward for 2.5 turns and tighten the locknut in this position.

Throttle governor

51 Run the engine to normal operating temperature and allow it to idle.

52 Disconnect and plug the vacuum hose to the governor *(see illustration)*.

53 Loosen nut (4) and adjust rod (5) to obtain 1800 ± 50 rpm. Tighten nut (4) on completion.

54 Unplug and reconnect the vacuum hose to the governor.

55 Check the clearance at B. This should be a minimum of 0.5 mm while the engine is idling.

56 If the clearance at B is smaller than 0.5 mm, disconnect and plug the vacuum hose to the governor. Turn nut (6) to increase dimension C, which should be a minimum of 21.5 mm in the relaxed position.

57 Repeat paragraphs 53 to 56 until the correct governor speed is obtained, with a clearance at B of less than 0.5 mm.

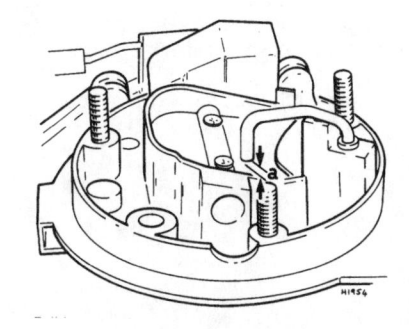

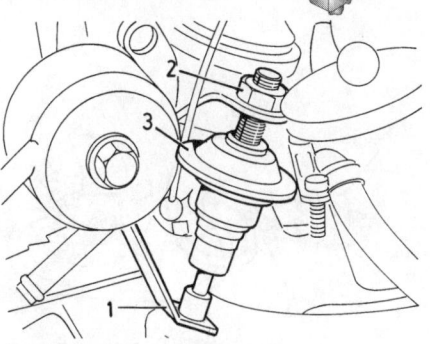

Throttle damper adjustment

1 Lever in idle position
2 Locknut
3 Damper

Full-load enrichment nozzle

58 Close the choke flap and measure the clearance between the enrichment nozzle and the flap *(see illustration)*. Gap 'a' must measure 1.0 ± 0.3 mm. Carefully bend the nozzle as necessary.

5 Component testing

Idle speed boost valve

1 The basic operation of the valve can be checked as follows:

2 Remove the air filter assembly and place it clear of the carburettor. Disconnect and plug the vacuum hose *(see illustration)*.

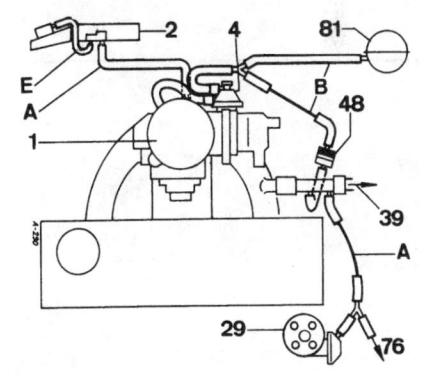

Typical vacuum hose connections - VW/Audi

1 Carburettor
2 Air filter
4 Pull-down
29 Ignition distributor
39 To brake servo
48 Non-return valve
76 To fuel consumption indicator
81 Vacuum reservoir
A Black hose
B Light green hose
E Natural colour hose

Throttle governor adjustment

1 Throttle governor
2 Vacuum hose
3 Diaphragm rod
4 Locknut
5 Adjustment screw
6 Adjustment nut
For B and C, refer to text

Full-load enrichment nozzle

a Clearance = 1.0 ± 0.3 mm

F2•9

Chapter F2

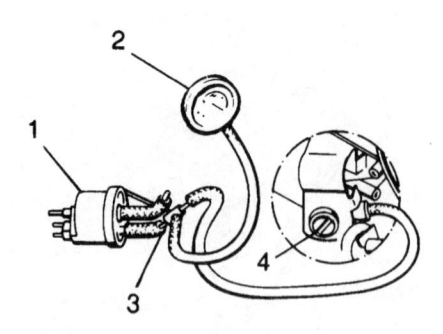

Checking idle speed boost valve with a vacuum gauge

1 Two-way boost valve
2 Vacuum gauge
3 T-piece
4 Idle speed air valve

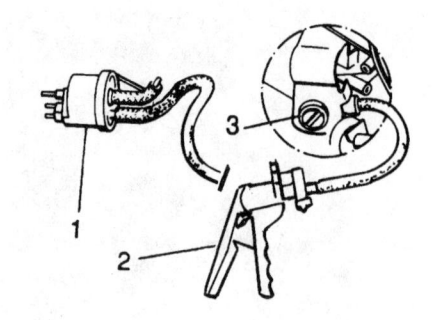

Applying vacuum to idle speed air valve

1 Two-way boost valve
2 Vacuum pump
3 Idle speed air valve

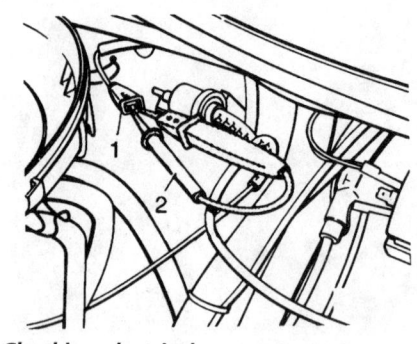

Checking electrical connector to 2-way boost valve

1 Electrical connector
2 Test lamp

3 Use a T-piece to connect a vacuum gauge between the two-way valve and the idle speed air valve *(see illustration)*.
4 Allow the engine to idle. The vacuum indication on the gauge should be zero.
5 Slowly close the choke flap so that the idle speed falls below 700 rpm.
6 Below 700 rpm, the idle speed will increase and vacuum should be indicated upon the gauge.
7 If vacuum is not indicated, or the idle speed does not increase, proceed with testing as follows:
8 Allow the engine to idle.
9 Remove and plug the vacuum hose to the idle speed air valve.
10 Attach a vacuum pump to the valve and operate the pump to obtain 300 to 500 mmHg (400 to 700 mbars) *(see illustration)*.
11 If the idle speed does not increase, renew the idle speed air valve.
12 Pull the electrical connector from the two-way boost valve.
13 Allow the engine to idle.
14 Connect a test lamp to the detached connector plug *(see illustration)*.
15 Slowly close the choke flap so that the idle speed falls below 700 rpm. The test lamp should light.
16 Raise the engine speed to over 1100 rpm. The test lamp should go out.
17 If the lamp lights as specified and the vacuum hoses are intact, renew the two-way valve if its operation is still unsatisfactory.
18 If the lamp does not light as specified, an electrical supply fault is indicated. The tracing of such faults is regrettably beyond the scope of this manual.

Thermal switch

19 Refer to Part D for general tests on the thermal switch, automatic choke electrical heater and the inlet manifold and throttle body heaters.
20 Below 40°C ± 10°C, a voltmeter should indicate battery voltage (switch open).
21 Above that temperature, the voltmeter should indicate zero volts (switch closed).
22 Renew the thermal switch if it fails to function in accordance with the above.

6 Fault diagnosis

Refer to Part D for diagnosis of general carburettor faults. The following faults are specific to the 1B3 carburettor:

Poor choke operation/poor cold running

- [ ] Over-choking due to pull-down diaphragm or reservoir failure.
- [ ] Sticking choke flap or mechanism.
- [ ] Failure of inlet manifold pre-heater or thermal switch.
- [ ] Failure of choke bi-metal spring.
- [ ] Incorrect choke fast idle or pull-down adjustment.
- [ ] Choke earth strap missing or in poor condition.

Heavy fuel consumption/idle CO level high

- [ ] Leaking power valve diaphragm.

Hesitation

- [ ] Defective or sticking accelerator pump piston.
- [ ] Worn accelerator pump lever or shaft.
- [ ] Plugged accelerator pump injector.

Poor hot starting

- [ ] Vapour bubble formation in float chamber.
- [ ] Sticking needle valve.

F2•10

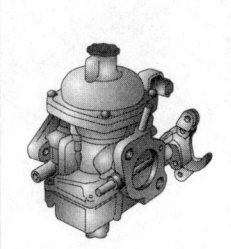

Part F Chapter 3
Pierburg 2B5, 2B6 & 2B7 carburettors

Contents

Component testing 5
Fault diagnosis 6
General servicing 3
Identification 2
Principles of operation 1
Service adjustments 4

Specifications

Manufacturer	Audi	Audi	Audi
Model	80 1.6 GL, GLS	80 1.6 GL, GLS	80 & Coupe 1.9
Year	1981 to 1983	1981 to 1983	1981 to 1983
Engine code	YP (63kW) SOHC	YP (63kW) SOHC	WN (85kW) SOHC
Capacity (cm³)/no. of cyls	1588/4	1588/4	1921/5
Oil temperature (°C)	80	80	80
Transmission	MT	AT	MT
Carb. identification	049 129 017 H	049 129 017	035 129 015 G
Idle speed (rpm)	950 ± 50	950 ± 50	800 ± 50
Fast idle speed (rpm)	3400 ± 50	3600 ± 50	3600 ± 100
CO @ idle (% vol.)	1.0 ± 0.5	1.0 ± 0.5	1.0 ± 0.5
Stage (venturi)	1 2	1 2	1 2
Venturi diameter (K)	24 28	24 28	24 28
Idle jet (g)	52.5 40	52.5 40	42.5 40
Main jet (Gg)	117.5 125	117.5 125	115 122.5
Air correction jet (a)	135 92.5	135 92.5	135 115
Float level (mm)	28 30	28 30	28 30
Needle valve (mm) (P)	2.0 2.0	2.0 2.0	2.0 2.0
Basic throttle position (mm)	0.05 ± 0.02 0.05 ± 0.02	0.05 ± 0.02 0.05 ± 0.02	0.05 ± 0.03 0.1 ± 0.03
Accelerator pump jet (i)	40	40	40
Float weight (grams)	5.85 ± 0.1	5.85 ± 0.1	5.85 ± 0.1
Choke fast idle gap (mm)	2.8 ± 0.15	3.15 ± 0.15	4.0 ± 0.15
Choke pull-down (mm) (a)	1.8 ± 0.15	1.8 ± 0.15	1.8 ± 0.15
Choke pull-down (mm) (a1)	3.9 ± 0.15	3.7 ± 0.15	3.6 ± 0.15
De-choke (mm)	5.0 ± 0.5	5.0 ± 0.5	4.5 ± 0.5

Manufacturer	Audi	Audi	Audi
Model	80 & Coupe 1.9	100 1.6	100 1.6
Year	1981 to 1983	1980 to 1982	1980 to 1982
Engine code	WN (85kW) SOHC	YV (63kW)	YV (63kW)
Capacity (cm³)/no. of cyls	1921/5	1588/5	1588/5
Oil temperature (°C)	80	80	80
Transmission	AT	MT	AT
Carb. identification	035 129 015 H	049 129 017 B	049 129 017
Idle speed (rpm)	800 ± 50	950 ± 50	950 ± 50
Fast idle speed (rpm)	3700 ± 50	3400 ± 100	3600 ± 50
CO @ idle (% vol.)	1.0 ± 0.5	1.0 ± 0.5	1.0 ± 0.5

Chapter F3

Manufacturer	Audi (continued)		Audi (continued)		Audi (continued)	
Model	80 & Coupe 1.9		100 1.6		100 1.6	
Year	1981 to 1983		1980 to 1982		1980 to 1982	
Stage (venturi)	1	2	1	2	1	2
Venturi diameter (K)	24	28	24	28	24	28
Idle jet (g)	42.5	40	42.5		42.5	
Main jet (Gg)	115	122.5	117.5	125	117.5	125
Air correction jet (a)	135	115	135	92.5	135	92.5
Float level (mm)	28	30	28	30	28	30
Needle valve (mm) (P)	2.0	2.0	2.0	2.0	2.0	2.0
Basic throttle position (mm)	0.05 ± 0.03	0.1 ± 0.03	0.05 ± 0.03	0.05 ± 0.03	0.05 ± 0.03	0.1 ± 0.03
Accelerator pump jet (i)	40		40		40	
Float weight (grams)	5.85 ± 0.1		5.85 ± 0.1		5.85 ± 0.1	
Choke fast idle gap (mm)	4.35 ± 0.15		2.85 ± 0.15		3.15 ± 0.15	
Choke pull-down (mm) (a)	1.8 ± 0.15		1.8 ± 0.15		1.8 ± 0.15	
Choke pull-down (mm) (a1)	3.4 ± 0.15		3.9 ± 0.15		3.7 ± 0.15	
De-choke (mm)	4.5 ± 0.5		5.0 ± 0.5		5 ± 0.5	

Manufacturer	Audi		Audi		Volkswagen	
Model	100 2.1		100 2.1		Jetta/Scirroco 1.6	
Year	1981 to 1982		1981 to 1982		1979 to 1983	
Engine code	WB (85kW) SOHC		WB (85kW) SOHC		FR (63kW)	
Capacity (cm³)/no. of cyls	2144/5		2144/5		1588/4	
Oil temperature (°C)	80		80		80	
Transmission	MT		AT		MT	
Carb. identification	035 129 016 B		035 129 016 A		055 129 024 T	
Idle speed (rpm)	800 ± 50		800 ± 50		950 ± 50 (With DIS: 800 ± 50)	
Fast idle speed (rpm)	3600 ± 100		3700 ± 50		3400 ± 50	
CO @ idle (% vol.)	1.0 ± 0.5		1.0 ± 0.5		1.0 ± 0.5	
Stage (venturi)	1	2	1	2	1	2
Venturi diameter (K)	24	28	24	28	24	28
Idle jet (g)	42.5	40	42.5	40	52.5	40
Main jet (Gg)	117.5	125	117.5	125	117.5	125
Air correction jet (a)	135	115	135	115	135	92.5
Float level (mm)	28	30	28	30	28	30
Needle valve (mm) (P)	2.0	2.0	2.0	2.0	2.0	2.0
Basic throttle position (mm)	0.05 ± 0.03	0.1 ± 0.03	0.05 ± 0.03	0.1 ± 0.03	0.05 ± 0.03	0.05 ± 0.03
Accelerator pump jet (i)	40		40		40	
Float weight (grams)	5.85 ± 0.1		5.85 ± 0.1		5.85 ± 0.1	
Choke fast idle gap (mm)	4.25 ± 0.15		4.35 ± 0.15		2.85 ± 0.15	
Choke pull-down (mm) (a)	1.8 ± 0.15		1.8 ± 0.15		1.8 ± 0.15	
Choke pull-down (mm) (a1)	3.9 ± 0.15		3.7 ± 0.15		3.9 ± 0.15	
De-choke (mm)	4.5 ± 0.5		4.5 ± 0.5		5.0 ± 0.5	

Manufacturer	Volkswagen		Volkswagen		Volkswagen	
Model	Jetta/Scirroco 1.6		Passat/Santana 1.6		Passat/Santana 1.6	
Year	1979 to 1983		1981 to 1982		1981 to 1982	
Engine code	FR (63kW)		YP (63kW)		YP (63kW)	
Capacity (cm³)/no. of cyls	1588/4		1588/4		1588/4	
Oil temperature (°C)	80		80		80	
Transmission	AT		MT		AT	
Carb. identification	055 129 025 F		049 129 017 A		049 129 017	
Idle speed (rpm)	950 ± 50 (With DIS: 800 ± 50)		950 ± 50		950 ± 50	
Fast idle speed (rpm)	3600 ± 50		3400 ± 50		3600 ± 50	
CO @ idle (% vol.)	1.0 ± 0.5		1.0 ± 0.5		1.0 ± 0.5	
Stage (venturi)	1	2	1	2	1	2
Venturi diameter (K)	24	28	24	28	24	28
Idle jet (g)	52.5	40	52.5	40	52.5	40
Main jet (Gg)	117.5	125	117.5	125	117.5	125
Air correction jet (a)	135	92.5	135	92.5	135	92.5
Float level (mm)	28	30	28	30	28	30
Needle valve (mm) (P)	2.0	2.0	2.0	2.0	2.0	2.0
Basic throttle position (mm)	0.05 ± 0.03	0.05 ± 0.03	0.05 ± 0.03	0.05 ± 0.03	0.05 ± 0.03	0.05 ± 0.03
Accelerator pump jet (i)	40		40		40	
Float weight (grams)	5.85 ± 0.1		5.85 ± 0.1		5.85 ± 0.1	
Choke fast idle gap (mm)	3.1 ± 0.15		2.85 ± 0.15		3.15 ± 0.15	
Choke pull-down (mm) (a)	1.8 ± 0.15		1.8 ± 0.15		1.8 ± 0.15	
Choke pull-down (mm) (a1)	3.7 ± 0.15		3.9 ± 0.15		3.7 ± 0.15	
De-choke (mm)	5.0 ± 0.5		5.0 ± 0.5		5.0 ± 0.5	

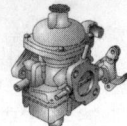

Pierburg 2B5, 2B6 & 2B7 carburettors

Manufacturer	Volkswagen		Volkswagen		Volkswagen	
Model	Passat/Santana 1.9		Passat/Santana 1.9		LT 2.4	
Year	1981 to 1983		1981 to 1983		1983 to Oct 1986	
Engine code	WN (85kW)		WN (85kW)		DL (66kW)	
Capacity (cm³)/no. of cyls	1921/5		1921/5		2383/6	
Oil temperature (°C)	80		80		80	
Transmission	MT		AT		-	
Carb. identification	035 129 015 G		035 129 015 H		073 129 015	
Idle speed (rpm)	800 ± 50		800 ± 50		800 ± 50	
Fast idle speed (rpm)	3600 ± 100		3700 ± 50		1800 ± 50	
CO @ idle (% vol.)	1.0 ± 0.5		1.0 ± 0.5		1.0 ± 0.5	
Stage (venturi)	1	2	1	2	1	2
Venturi diameter (K)	24	28	24	28	24	28
Idle jet (g)	42.5	40	42.5	40	60	35
Main jet (Gg)	115	122.5	115	122.5	115	112.5
Air correction jet (a)	135	115	135	115	110	100
Float level (mm)	28	30	28	30	28	30
Needle valve (mm) (P)	2.0	2.0	2.0	2.0	2.0	2.0
Basic throttle position (mm)	0.05 ± 0.03	0.1 ± 0.03	0.05 ± 0.03	0.1 ± 0.03	0.05 ± 0.03	
Accelerator pump jet (i)	40		40		40	
Float weight (grams)	5.85 ± 0.1		5.85 ± 0.1		5.85 ± 0.1	
Choke fast idle gap (mm)	4.00 ± 0.15		4.35 ± 0.15		3.7 ± 0.1	
Choke pull-down (mm) (a)	1.8 ± 0.15		1.8 ± 0.15		-	
Choke pull-down (mm) (a1)	3.6 ± 0.15		3.4 ± 0.15		3.0 ± 0.15	
De-choke (mm)	4.5 ± 0.5		4.5 ± 0.5		-	

Manufacturer	Volvo		Volvo		Volvo	
Model	740 2.3		740 2.3		740 2.3	
Year	1984 to 1986		1984 to 1986		1987 to 1990	
Engine code	B230K		B230K		B230K	
Capacity (cm³)/no. of cyls	2316/4		2316/4		2316/4	
Oil temperature (°C)	Hot		Hot		Hot	
Transmission	MT		AT		MT	
Carb. identification	1 317 036		1 317 036		1 357 108	
Idle speed (rpm)	800		900		800	
Fast idle speed (rpm)	3100 ± 100		3100 ± 100		-	
CO @ idle (% vol.)	1.25 ± 0.75		1.25 ± 0.75		1.0 ± 0.5	
Stage (venturi)	1	2	1	2	1	2
Venturi diameter (K)	24	28	24	28	-	
Idle jet (g)	47.5		47.5		45	47.5
Main jet (Gg)	112.5	137.5	112.5	137.5	115	142.5
Air correction jet (a)	140	65	140	65	140	140
Float level (mm)	28	30	28	30	28 ± 1.0	30 ± 1.0
Needle valve (mm) (P)	2.0	2.0	2.0	2.0	-	-
Basic throttle position (mm)	0.15 ± 0.03	0.15 ± 0.03	0.15 ± 0.03	0.15 ± 0.03	-	
Accelerator pump jet (i)	40		40		-	
Float weight (grams)	5.85 ± 0.1		5.85 ± 0.1		5.85 ± 0.1	
Choke fast idle gap (mm)	3.85 ± 0.12		3.85 ± 0.12		4.0	
Choke pull-down (mm) (a)	1.4 ± 0.15		1.4 ± 0.15		1.4 ± 0.1	
Choke pull-down (mm) (a1)	3.7 ± 0.15		3.7 ± 0.15		3.7 ± 0.1	
Choke pull-down (mm) (a2)	-		-		6.0 ± 0.1	
De-choke (mm)	5.7		5.7		-	

Manufacturer	Volvo		Volvo		Volvo	
Model	740 2.3		740 2.3 Catalyst		740 2.3 Catalyst	
Year	1987 to 1990		1987 to 1990		1987 to 1990	
Engine code	B230K		B230K		B230K	
Capacity (cm³)/no. of cyls	2316/4		2316/4		2316/4	
Oil temperature (°C)	Hot		Hot		Hot	
Transmission	AT		MT		AT	
Carb. identification	1 357 108		-		-	
Idle speed (rpm)	900		800		900	
CO @ idle (% vol.)	1.0 ± 0.5		1.0 ± 0.5		1.0 ± 0.5	
Stage (venturi)	1	2	1	2	1	2
Idle jet (g)	45	47.5	45	47.5	45	47.5
Main jet (Gg)	115	142.5	115	142.5	115	142.5
Air correction jet (a)	140	140	140	140	140	140
Float level (mm)	28 ± 1.0	30 ± 1.0	28 ± 1.0	30 ± 1.0	28 ± 1.0	30 ± 1.0
Float weight (grams)	5.85 ± 0.1		5.85 ± 0.1		5.85 ± 0.1	
Choke fast idle gap (mm)	4.0		4.0		4.0	
Choke pull-down (mm) (a)	1.4 ± 0.1		1.4 ± 0.1		1.4 ± 0.1	
Choke pull-down (mm) (a1)	3.7 ± 0.1		3.7 ± 0.1		3.7 ± 0.1	
Choke pull-down (mm) (a2)	6.0 ± 0.1		6.0 ± 0.1		6.0 ± 0.1	

Chapter F3

1 Principles of operation

Pierburg 2B series carburettor

Introduction

1 The following technical description of the Pierburg 34/34 2B series carburettor should be read in conjunction with the more detailed description of carburettor principles in Part A.

Construction

2 The Pierburg 2B series carburettor is a downdraught progressive twin venturi instrument with a vacuum-controlled secondary throttle *(see illustration)*. The throttle shafts are made of steel, while the throttle valves, all jets and the emulsion tube are manufactured from brass. Internal fuel channels and air passages are drilled and sealed with lead plugs where necessary.

3 The carburettor is constructed in three main bodies. These are the upper body, main body and throttle body (which contains the throttle assembly). An insulating block placed between the main carburettor body and the throttle body, prevents excess heat transference to the main body.

4 Most versions of the 2B series carburettor operate in conjunction with an

1 Upper body
2 Float pins
3 Float - primary
4 Float - secondary
5 Needle valves
6 Idle jet - primary
7 Idle jet - secondary
8 Idle bypass jet
9 Idle cut-off valve (electrically-operated type)
11 Bypass idle speed screw
12 Idle mixture control screw
13 Accelerator pump piston assembly
14 Pump injector
15 Auxiliary venturi - primary
16 Auxiliary venturi - secondary
17 Main jet - primary
18 Main jet - secondary
19 Fuel jet - secondary progression
20 Air corrector jet - secondary progression
21 Tamperproof cap
22 Float chamber gasket
23 Main body
24 Insulating block
25 Diaphragm assembly - secondary throttle
26 Vacuum hose - secondary throttle
27 Choke housing
28 Bi-metal housing assembly
29 Choke flap
30 Choke pull-down diaphragm
31 Choke pull-down hose
33 'a1' adjustment screw cover
34 Accelerator pump linkage
35 Accelerator pump lever

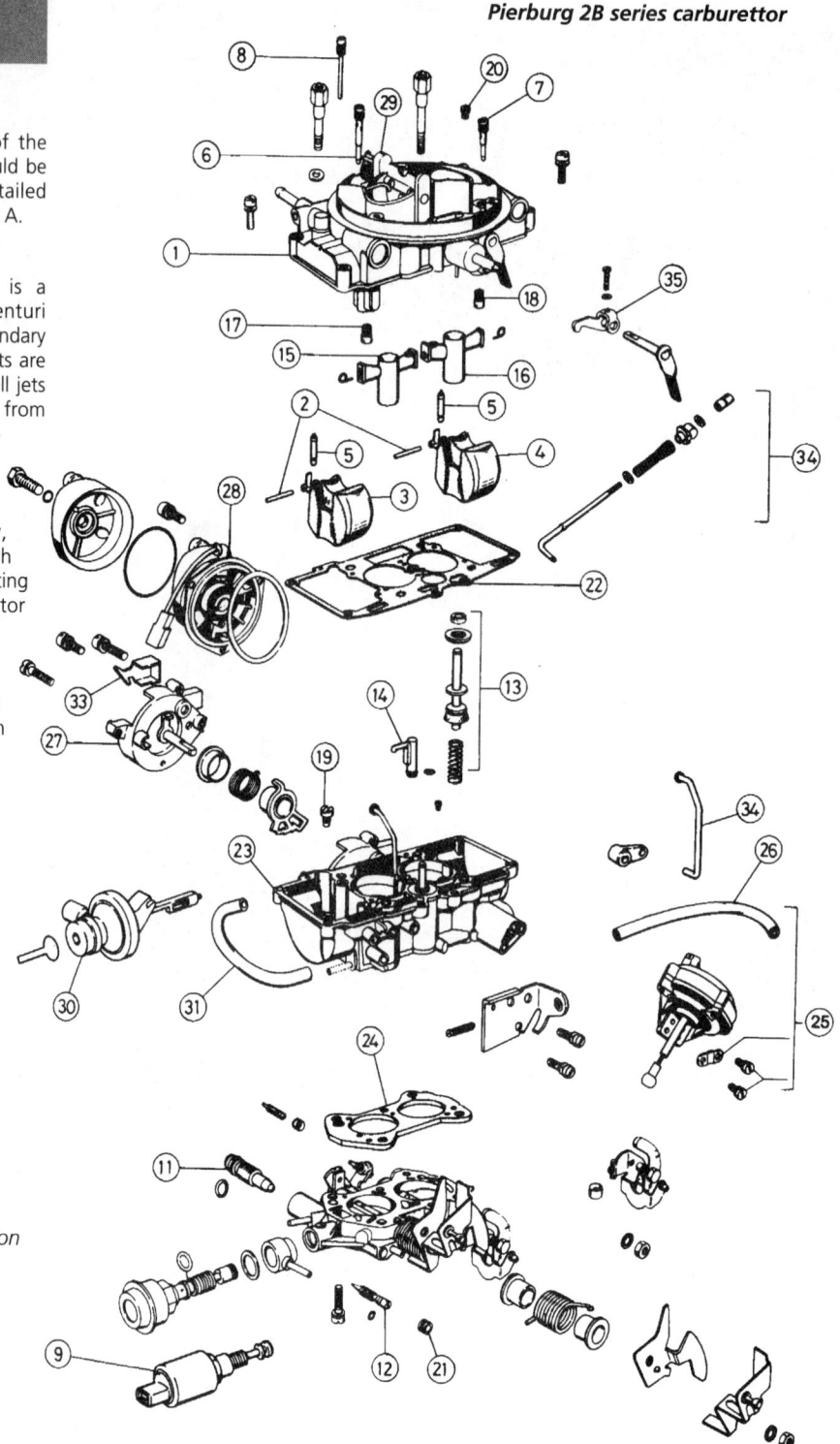

Pierburg 2B5, 2B6 & 2B7 carburettors

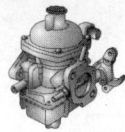

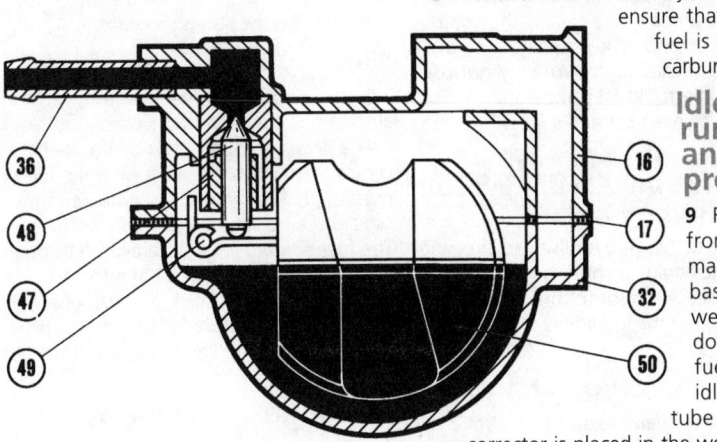

Fuel supply and float arrangement

- 16 Carburettor upper body
- 17 Gasket
- 32 Float chamber
- 36 Fuel supply inlet
- 47 Float needle valve insert
- 48 Float needle
- 49 Float pivot pin
- 50 Float

electrical heater fitted to the inlet manifold. The purpose of the heater is to improve atomisation of the air/fuel mixture and to prevent carburettor icing during warm-up. A thermal switch is normally wired to the supply voltage so that the heater is switched off at a pre-determined temperature.

5 Versions of the 2B series carburettor are the 2B5, 2B6 and 2B7. The choke system is semi-automatic in operation and acts on the primary venturi alone. The major differences between the versions concern the operation of the cold start system. The choke strangler flap is controlled by a bi-metal coil that is heated by an electrical supply (all versions) and also by the engine coolant (2B5 and 2B7 only). Choke pull-down operation in the 2B5 and 2B6 is controlled by a two-stage system and in the 2B7 by a three-stage system. Variations within each version will be noted in the relevant section.

Fuel control

6 The 2B carburettor utilises a twin float system with separate chambers for the primary and secondary fuel systems. Fuel flows into the carburettor through an inlet connection and a single fuel channel supplies fuel to both chambers. Each chamber has its own spring-loaded needle valve and plastic float and maintains its own fuel level *(see illustration)*. The float levels are considered critical and are set very accurately during production.

7 The float chamber is vented internally into the upper air intake which is on the clean-air side of the air filter. In 2B5 and 2B7 Volvo applications, the venting is switched by an electrical valve so that venting to atmosphere occurs with the engine stopped or at idle.

8 A calibrated fuel return system is provided to ensure that relatively cool fuel is supplied to the carburettor.

Idle, slow running and progression

9 Fuel is drawn from the primary main well into the base of a vertical well which dips down into the fuel. A combined idle jet, emulsion tube and air corrector is placed in the well. Fuel is mixed with air drawn in through the calibrated air corrector and the holes in the tube to form an emulsion. The resulting mixture is drawn through a channel into a chamber, where it is mixed with the bypass emulsion. The idle mixture is then discharged from the idle orifice under the primary throttle plate. A tapered mixture screw is used to vary the channel to the chamber and this ensures fine control of the idle mixture *(see illustration)*.

10 A number of progression holes provide a further air contribution to the emulsion (upstream of the chamber) while the throttle is closed. As the progression holes are uncovered by the opening throttle, the vacuum draw overcomes the air bleed into the holes and a reversal occurs. Fuel is now drawn out to add extra enrichment to the idle mixture during initial acceleration.

11 The adjustable mixture screw is tamper-proofed at production level, in accordance with emission regulations.

Idle bypass circuit

12 The idle bypass circuit provides a means of more accurately controlling idle emissions than a conventional idle mixture circuit. The throttle plate is locked in a specified position and sealed with a tamperproof cap. A high percentage of the fuel required for idle is provided by the normal idle circuit. The remainder of the idle mixture is controlled through the idle bypass circuit and the additional (secondary) idle system.

Idle and progression circuits

- 1 Combined idle fuel and air corrector jet - primary idle
- 3 Combined idle fuel and air corrector jet for idle bypass circuit
- 4 Bypass idle emulsion
- 10 Air bleed drilling - secondary progression
- 11 Emulsion tube - secondary progression
- 12 Air corrector jet - secondary progression
- 14 Air corrector jet with emulsion tube - secondary venturi
- 15 Combined idle fuel and air corrector jet - secondary idle
- 19 Main jet - secondary venturi
- 20 Fuel jet - secondary progression
- 22 Idle mixture orifice - secondary idle
- 23 Progression holes - secondary venturi
- 24 Throttle valve - secondary venturi
- 25 Throttle valve - primary venturi
- 27 Idle mixture orifice - primary idle
- 28 Electrical idle cut-off valve (where fitted)
- 29 Idle mixture control screw
- 30 Bypass idle speed screw
- 31 Main jet - primary venturi

F3•5

Chapter F3

13 Fuel, sourced from the primary main well, is drawn into the base of a vertical well which dips down into the fuel. A combined bypass (auxiliary) idle jet, emulsion tube and air corrector is placed in the well. The fuel is mixed with air, drawn in through the calibrated air corrector and the holes in the tube, to form an emulsion. The emulsion is drawn through the bypass passage and a further emulsion tube where additional air from the main venturi is introduced. The resulting mixture is drawn past the regulating screw into a chamber where it is mixed with the idle emulsion. The idle mixture is then discharged from the main idle orifice under the primary throttle plate. The emulsion is controlled by a regulating screw which is also used to adjust the idle speed.

Additional (secondary) idle mixture

14 An additional idle mixture is discharged from an outlet under the secondary throttle plate. Fuel is drawn from the secondary main well into the base of a vertical well which dips down into the fuel. A combined idle jet, emulsion tube and air corrector is placed in the well. The fuel is mixed with air, drawn in through the calibrated air corrector and the holes in the tube, to form an emulsion. The resulting mixture is drawn through a channel where it is discharged from the idle outlet under the secondary throttle plate.

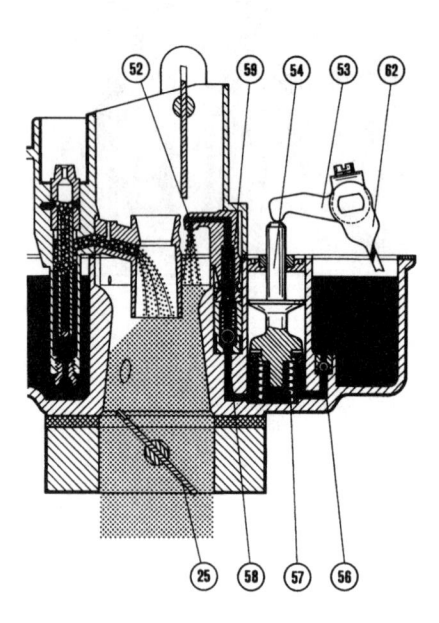

Accelerator pump circuit

25 Throttle valve - primary venturi
52 Pump injector
53 Accelerator pump lever
54 Pump assembly
56 Inlet (ball) valve
57 Spring
58 Outlet (ball) valve
59 Float
62 Accelerator pump operating lever

15 The total mixture required during idle is thus supplied by the primary idle circuit, the bypass system and the secondary idle circuit. Note that some variations (including Volvo) may not use the secondary idle facility. In this instance, the channel will be blanked off and a jet will not be fitted.

Idle cut-off valve (2B5 & 2B6 - VW/Audi versions)

16 An idle cut-off valve is utilised to prevent run-on when the engine is shut down. A 12-volt solenoid plunger is used to block the idle mixture outlet when the ignition is switched off.

Fuel cut-off system (2B5 & 2B7 - Volvo versions)

17 An idle cut-off valve is used as above to prevent run-on when the engine is shut down. In addition, the device is also activated during engine deceleration from high engine speeds with a closed throttle (overrun) so that the fuel supply to the engine is cut off. This results in a fuel saving and improved emissions. Once engine speed falls below 1550 rpm or the throttle is opened, the device re-activates and normal idle flow is restored.

18 The cut-off valve plunger is vacuum-operated and electrically controlled by a switchover valve. A switch on the accelerator pedal and a speed signal from the ignition circuit provide the information required to energise the switchover valve.

19 A vacuum hose is taken from the carburettor base to the idle cut-off valve via the switchover valve. When the engine is at idle, the switchover valve is energised to close the vacuum channel. The cut-off plunger is not actuated and will remain at its rest position. During deceleration with a closed throttle, the switchover valve is de-activated and will therefore close. The vacuum channel to the idle cut-off valve opens and the plunger is actuated to cut off the primary idle mixture. Once engine speed falls below 1550 rpm or the throttle is opened, voltage is restored to the switchover valve, the vacuum passage is closed, the cut-off valve opens and normal idle flow is restored.

20 Similarly, once the ignition is switched off, the switchover valve is de-energised and the plunger activates to close off the idle mixture, thereby preventing run-on.

Accelerator pump

21 The accelerator pump is controlled by a piston and is mechanically operated by a rod and lever linked to the throttle pedal. Under acceleration, a lever, actuated by the throttle linkage, bears against the pump piston and compresses it. Fuel from the pump chamber is pushed through the pump outlet channel, past the pump outlet valve and is injected from the pump nozzle into the primary venturi. The inlet valve remains closed to prevent fuel from being returned to the float chamber *(see illustration)*.

22 As the throttle action is reversed, a spring returns the piston to its starting position. Depression then draws fresh fuel from the float chamber into the pump chamber.

Main circuit

23 The amount of fuel discharged into the airstream is controlled by a calibrated main jet. Fuel is drawn through the jet, into the base of a vertical well which dips down into the fuel in the primary float chamber. A combined emulsion tube and air correction jet is placed in the well. The fuel is mixed with air, drawn in through the calibrated air correction jet and the holes in the emulsion tubes, to form an air/fuel emulsion. The resulting mixture is discharged from the main nozzle through an auxiliary venturi into the main airstream.

Part-load enrichment

24 An air passage is taken from under the throttle plate to the part-load enrichment chamber. At idle and during light-throttle operation, manifold vacuum in the passage pulls a plunger away from the part-load enrichment valve. The valve closes to shut off a fuel outlet channel. During acceleration and wide-open throttle operation, vacuum in the manifold is depleted. The plunger returns under spring pressure and pushes on the valve to open the channel. Fuel then flows from the primary float chamber through a calibrated bush in the channel to supplement the fuel in the upper section of the primary main well. The fuel level rises in the well and the fuel mixture is enriched.

Secondary action

25 A port is located in both primary and secondary venturis. Airways run from these ports into a common passage. A vacuum hose is connected to the passage and to the diaphragm that controls the secondary throttle plate.

26 During normal operation at low speeds, only the primary venturi is employed. When the air velocity through the primary venturi reaches a certain level, depression acts upon the port to operate the secondary diaphragm and the secondary throttle. Vacuum created in the secondary venturi will further control the rate of secondary opening.

27 The primary linkage is arranged to prevent the secondary plate from opening when air speed may be high but the engine is cruising on a light throttle. Secondary action will not take place until the primary throttle is about two-thirds-open.

28 On some variants, a thermal valve is connected to the vacuum supply hose so that the secondary throttle plate is inoperative during the engine warm-up period. The switch remains open when the engine is cold and closes at a pre-determined temperature.

29 A progression jet is used to prevent hesitation as the secondary throttle plate starts to open. Fuel is drawn from the secondary float chamber, through the secondary progression jet, into the base of a vertical well which dips down into the fuel. An emulsion tube is placed in the well, capped by an air bleed jet. A

Pierburg 2B5, 2B6 & 2B7 carburettors

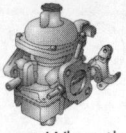

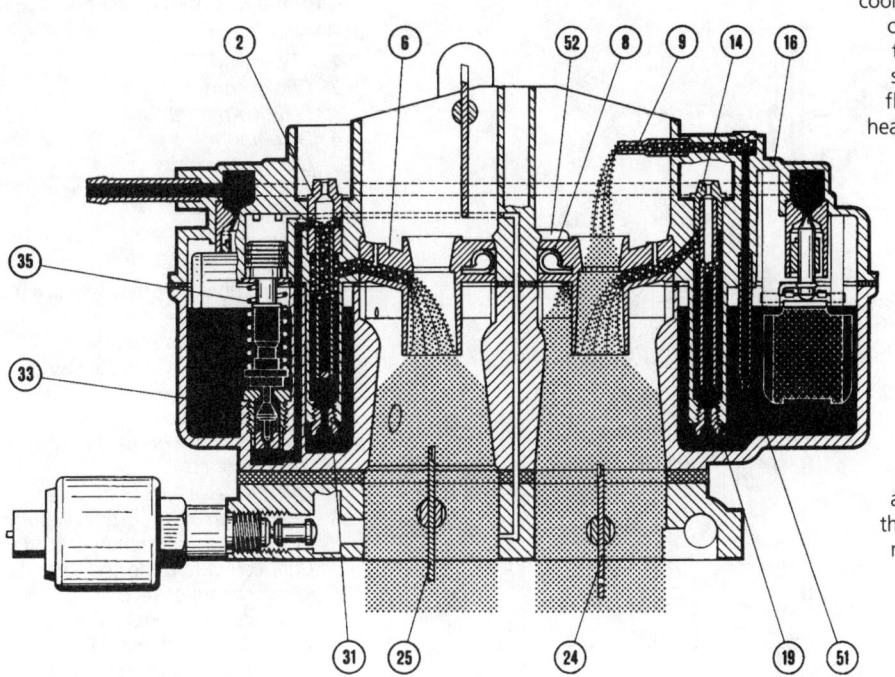

Full-load enrichment circuits

2 Air corrector jet with emulsion tube - primary venturi
6 Main fuel nozzle - primary venturi
8 Main fuel nozzle - secondary venturi
9 Nozzle for full-load enrichment - secondary venturi
14 Air corrector jet with emulsion tube - secondary venturi
16 Carburettor upper body
19 Main jet - secondary venturi
24 Throttle valve - secondary venturi
25 Throttle valve - primary venturi
31 Main jet - primary venturi
33 Part-load enrichment valve
35 Enrichment valve piston
51 Calibrated tube for full-load enrichment - secondary venturi
52 Pump injector

calibrated air corrector jet adds a further air supply. The fuel is mixed with air drawn in through the air bleed, the air corrector and the holes in the tube, to form an emulsion. The resulting mixture is drawn through a channel where it is discharged into the secondary venturi, via a number of progression holes, at the initial opening of the secondary throttle plate.

30 Once the secondary throttle is fully open, discharge ceases at both the progression holes and the secondary idle outlet.

Full-load enrichment

31 At full-load and high engine speeds, the velocity of air creates a depression sufficient to raise fuel from the float chamber into a channel. The fuel then passes through a calibrated bushing to the upper section of the air intake. Here it is mixed with a small amount of air from a calibrated air bleed and is discharged into the airstream from the full-load enrichment nozzle. Full-load depression also draws fuel from the accelerator pump injector (see illustration).

32 The full-load enrichment outlet may be in the upper air intake of the primary barrel, secondary barrel, or both barrels, depending on application.

Cold start system

33 The choke system used by the 2B series carburettor is semi-automatic in operation and actuates a flap in the primary air intake. The system is primed by depressing the accelerator pedal once or twice.

34 Fast idle is achieved with the aid of a stepped cam attached to the choke spindle. An adjustable screw, connected to the throttle lever mechanism and butting against the cam, can be used to vary the fast idle speed. This screw is fitted with a tamperproof cap. As the bi-metal coil is heated and the flap opens, the screw will rest on successively less-stepped parts of the cam. The idle speed is thus progressively reduced until, ultimately, the cam is released and the idle speed returns to normal.

2B5 and 2B7 carburettors

35 The choke strangler flap on these versions is controlled by a combined electrically and coolant-heated bi-metal coil. On VW/Audi engines (but not Volvo), the electrical supply to the choke is made through a coolant-heated thermal switch. The electrical supply initially heats the choke coil after the first start from cold. As the coolant passing through the bi-metal water housing becomes warm, it adds to the heating action applied to the choke spring. The choke flap will thus remain open while the coolant (and engine) remain warm. When the coolant reaches a pre-set temperature, the thermal switch cuts out the electrical supply (VW/Audi only) and the coolant flow remains the only source of choke heating.

2B6 carburettor

36 The choke strangler flap is totally controlled by an electrically-heated bi-metal coil.

Choke pull-down

37 The choke flap is eccentrically mounted so that during cranking it is partially opened to prevent an over-rich fuel mixture. Once the engine has fired, the choke flap must open slightly to weaken the mixture and avoid flooding during idle and light-throttle operation. This is achieved by using manifold vacuum to actuate a pull-down diaphragm. A linkage attached to the diaphragm will then pull upon the flap. Depending on the application, the pull-down operation can utilise a single, double or triple-stage movement.

2B5 carburettor

38 The 2B5 carburettor utilises a two-stage pull-down movement to actuate the diaphragm. The pull-down hose is connected to a delay reservoir. When the engine fires, vacuum applied to the pull-down diaphragm is low and the choke flap is partially opened to gap pull-down 'a'. As the engine continues to run, vacuum increases and acts upon the delay reservoir. An additional vacuum supply, piped through a non-return valve, assists the emptying of the delay reservoir. The pull-down then fully operates, opening the choke flap to gap 'a1'. The two pull-down stages ensure maximum richness for the few seconds after a cold start and then a rapid opening of the choke flap to reduce over-richness.

2B6 carburettor

39 The 2B6 carburettor utilises a single-stage pull-down movement to actuate the pull-down diaphragm. Once the engine has fired, the choke flap will be pulled open to setting 'a1' in a single movement.

2B7 carburettor

40 The 2B7 carburettor utilises a three-stage pull-down movement to actuate the diaphragm. When the engine fires, vacuum is applied to the pull-down connector A (see illustration) and the choke flap is partially opened to gap 'a'. As the engine continues to run, a second vacuum signal acts upon the delay reservoir. This is connected to pull-down 'B' and slowly opens the choke flap to gap 'a1'. When the throttle is opened, a vacuum signal on the upstream side of the throttle plate is introduced to pull-down 'C' and the choke flap is opened to gap 'a2'. The three pull-down stages ensure that the mixture is correct during the initial period of choke operation.

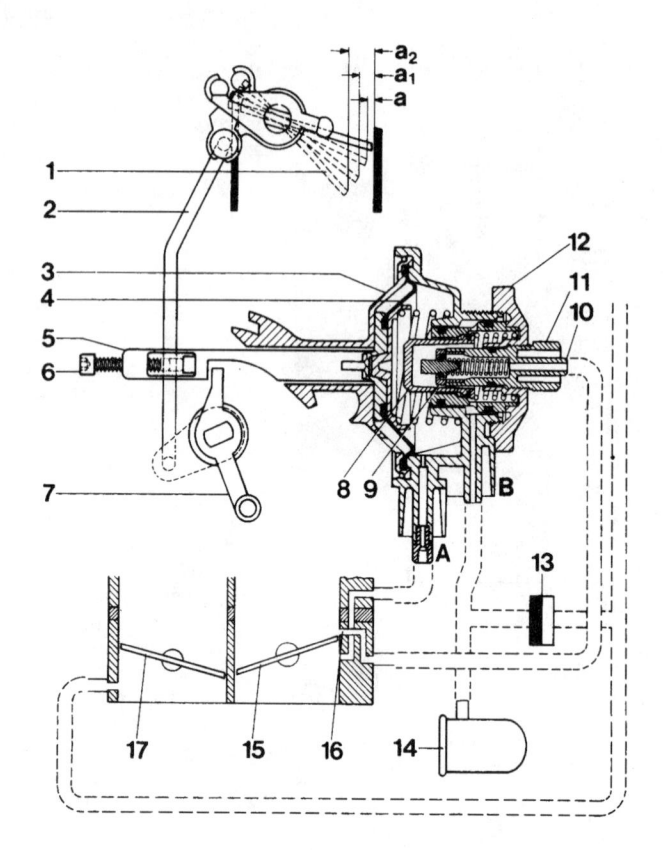

Chapter F3

Choke pull-down operation - 3-stage type

1 Choke flap
2 Choke connecting rod
3 Pull-down assembly
4 Diaphragm
5 Diaphragm rod
6 Pull-down adjustment screw 'a2'
7 Choke lever
8 Valve
9 Valve
10 Connection to ported vacuum (upstream of throttle valve)
11 Pull-down adjustment screw 'a1'
12 Pull-down adjustment screw 'a'
13 Non-return valve
14 Vacuum reservoir
15 Throttle valve - primary venturi
16 Drilling for (10)
17 Throttle valve - secondary venturi
A Connection to unported vacuum (downstream of primary throttle valve)
B Connection to unported vacuum (downstream of secondary throttle valve) and vacuum reservoir
a First stage pull-down gap
a1 Second stage pull-down gap
a2 Third stage pull-down gap

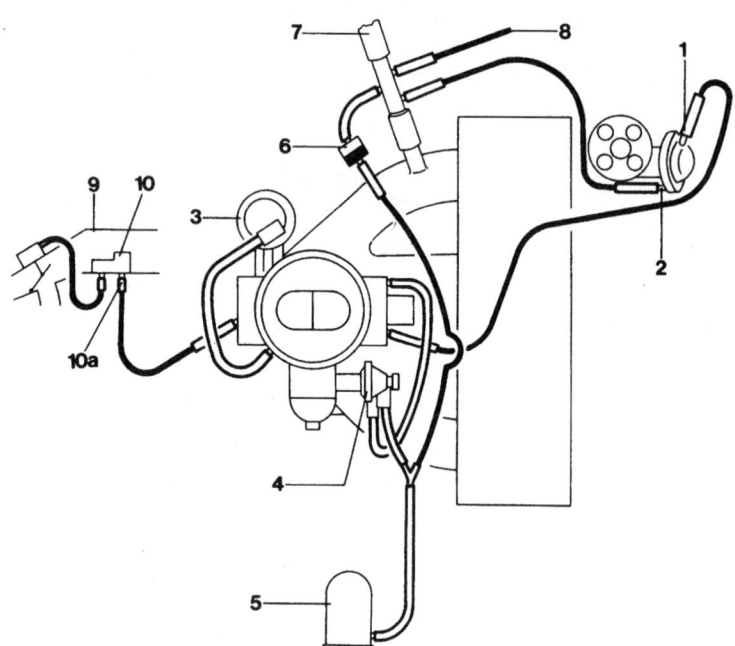

Dechoke

41 If the throttle is opened fully when the engine is cold, the pull-down vacuum will deplete and the choke flap tend to close. This may cause flooding and to prevent this, a wide-open kick mechanism is employed. When the throttle is opened fully, a cam on the throttle lever will turn the choke lever anti-clockwise to partially open the flap *(see illustrations)*.

2 Identification

1 Pierburg 2B is stamped upon the carburettor upper and main bodies. The manufacturer's identification code may be stamped on a metallic tag attached to the cover by an upper body fixing screw or on a corner of the carburettor upper body.
2 Where the tag is missing, refer to Part B for other means of identifying the carburettor.
3 Early versions of this carburettor may be stamped with the trade name Solex or Zenith.

3 General servicing

Introduction

1 Read this Chapter in conjunction with Part B, which describes some of the operations in more detail. It is assumed that the carburettor is

Typical vacuum connection chart - 2B5 carburettor (VW/Audi)

1 Vacuum advance capsule (distributor)
2 Vacuum retard capsule (distributor)
3 Secondary throttle diaphragm
4 Pull-down diaphragm
5 Vacuum reservoir
6 Non-return valve
7 Vacuum source on inlet manifold
8 Connection to econometer instrument on facia panel
9 Air filter
10 Thermal valve
10a Connection to vacuum source on carburettor

Pierburg 2B5, 2B6 & 2B7 carburettors

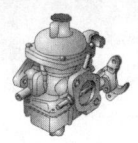

removed for this service. However, many of the operations can be tackled with the carburettor in place. Where this is undertaken, first remove the upper body assembly and soak the fuel out of the float chamber using a clean tissue or soft cloth.

Dismantling and checking

2 Remove the carburettor from the engine (see Part B).
3 Check the carburettor visually for damage and wear.
4 Remove the idle cut-off valve assembly and clean it with carburettor cleaner. Test the plunger operation by connecting the valve to the battery or other voltage supply (or use the valve supply wire in the engine compartment). Touch the valve body to earth with the ignition on. Repeat this several times, ensuring that the plunger tip advances and retracts cleanly. Renew the valve if the action is faulty or if cleaning does not improve its operation. If a vacuum-operated idle cut-off valve is fitted, refer to Section 5 for the correct test procedure.
5 Carefully prise the upper choke link rod from the plastic retainer on the choke spindle. Twist out and remove the lower part of the link rod from its position on the choke housing assembly. Disengage the accelerator pump linkage from the throttle, then remove the four screws and central bolt and detach the carburettor upper body. The electrical earth strap (where fitted), which is retained by a fixing screw, will also be removed at this time (see illustration).
6 A float chamber vent valve will be detached with an upper body screw in 2B5 and 2B7 versions fitted to Volvo engines.
7 Inspect the float chamber for corrosion and calcium build-up.
8 Remove the float chamber gasket.
9 Use a straight-edge to check for distorted flanges on all facing surfaces.
10 Tap out each float pin and remove the float and needle valve from both primary and secondary float chambers. The needle valve seats are not removable.
11 Check that the anti-vibration ball is free in the needle valve end.
12 Check the needle valve tip for wear and ridges.

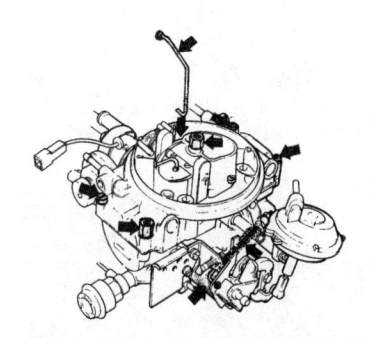

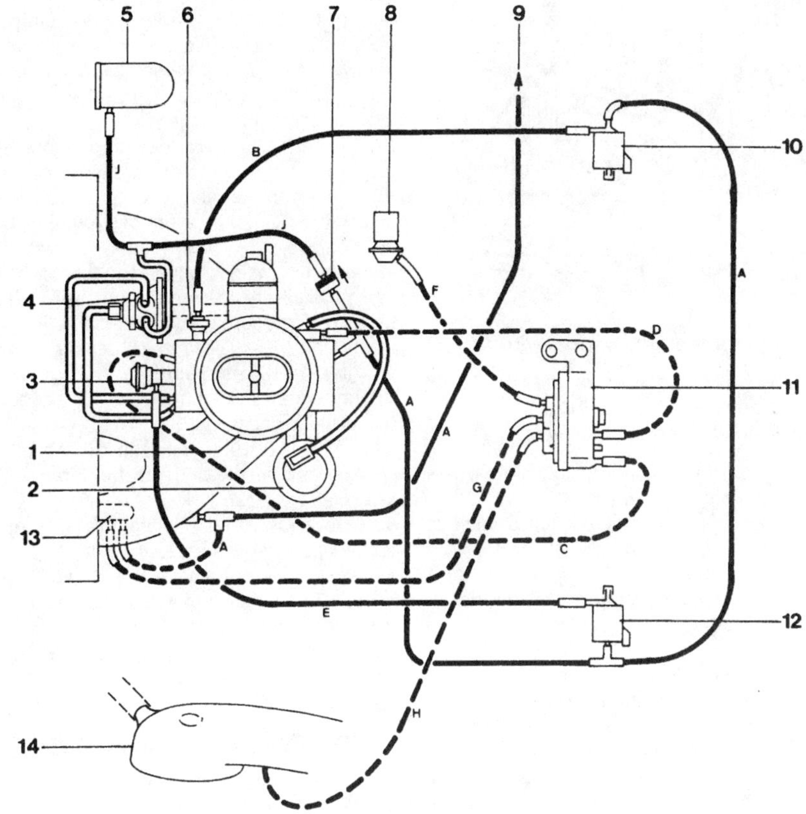

Typical vacuum connection chart - 2B7 carburettor (Volvo)

1 Carburettor
2 Secondary throttle diaphragm
3 Vacuum-operated idle cut-off valve
4 Pull-down diaphragm
5 Vacuum reservoir
6 Vacuum-operated valve*
7 Non-return valve
8 Exhaust gas recirculation valve**
9 Connection to ignition control unit
10 Electric switchover valve*
11 Pressure amplifier
12 Electric switchover valve
13 Thermal valve
14 Air filter trunking
* Only fitted to vehicles with air conditioning
** Only fitted to vehicles with emission control

Colour code

A White
B Brown
C Red
D Green
E Lilac
F Yellow
G Grey
H Blue
J Orange

13 The float should be checked for damage and ingress of petrol.
14 Renew the float pin if it shows signs of wear.
15 Unscrew the idle mixture and bypass screws and inspect the tips for damage or ridges.
16 The pump injector is a push fit in the body. Carefully prise it from its location and test it by shaking. No noise from the outlet ball would indicate that the valve is seized.
17 Remove the accelerator pump seal, bearing, piston and spring. Check the piston assembly for fatigue and damage. Inspect the pump operating lever for wear and check for smooth operation.
18 Unscrew the primary idle jet and bypass idle assemblies (see illustration).

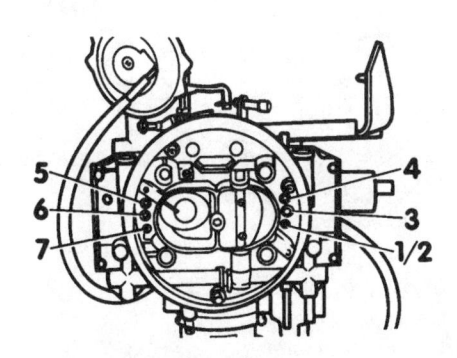

Location of upper jets in upper body

1/2 Bypass fuel/air jet - primary venturi
3 Main emulsion tube/air corrector - primary venturi (not removable)
4 Idle fuel/air jet - primary venturi
5 Idle fuel/air jet - secondary venturi
6 Main emulsion tube/air corrector - secondary venturi (not removable)
7 Air corrector jet - secondary progression

Removing/refitting carburettor upper body

Locate accelerator pump linkage, choke link rod and screws (arrowed)

F3•9

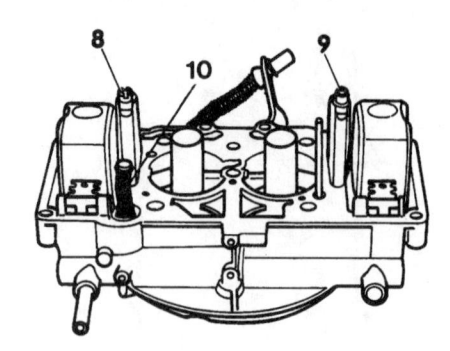

Chapter F3

Location of lower jets in upper body

8 Main jet - primary venturi
9 Main jet - secondary venturi
10 Part-load enrichment plunger

19 Unscrew the secondary idle jet (where fitted) and progression air jet.
20 Remove both main jets. It is not possible to remove the main air corrector jets or emulsion tubes *(see illustration)*.
21 Remove the secondary progression fuel jet from the secondary float chamber *(see illustration)*.
22 Check that the channels from the float chamber into the emulsion tube wells are clear.
23 Note all jet sizes and their locations for correct installation during assembly.
24 Check jet calibration against that specified. It is possible that the jets may have been transposed (or the wrong size fitted) during the last overhaul. Note that all of the above jets, other than the two main jets and the secondary progression fuel jet, can be removed from the carburettor without removing the upper body.
25 Check the action of the enrichment valve plunger.
26 Unscrew the enrichment valve from the primary float chamber and check the action of the actuating pin. Attach a vacuum pump to the valve body. Operate the pump until 200 mmHg (265 mbars) is registered. Renew the valve if the vacuum is not maintained for at least 10 seconds. Check that the channel into the emulsion tube well is clear.
27 Remove the secondary throttle vacuum hose. Attach a vacuum pump to the vacuum connector.

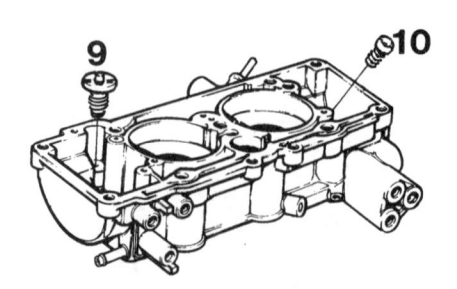

28 Fully operate the throttle lever to open the primary throttle and operate the vacuum pump until the secondary diaphragm is actuated. Renew the diaphragm assembly if it does not operate fully or if vacuum is not maintained for at least 10 seconds.
29 Disconnect the secondary throttle operating rod by twisting the rod out of its socket on the throttle lever. Remove the two screws and detach the diaphragm assembly from the body.
30 Remove the screw and separate the carburettor main body and throttle body assemblies. Note the position of the insulation block for reference when reassembling. The throttle body can be renewed separately if the spindles or throttle bores are worn. Use a straight-edge to check for distorted flanges on the facing surfaces.
31 Do not disturb the adjustment of the primary and secondary throttle angle, unless absolutely necessary.
32 Check the choke flap, spindle and linkage for stickiness and wear *(see illustration)*.
33 Disconnect the choke pull-down vacuum hoses. Test the choke pull-down unit as described in Section 4.
34 Remove the 'a1' adjustment screw cover and prise off the diaphragm assembly from the upper body.

Preparation for reassembly

35 Inspect all vacuum hoses for damage and deterioration, and renew where necessary.
36 Clean the jets, carburettor body assemblies, float chambers and internal channels. An air line may be used to clear the internal channels once the carburettor is fully dismantled. Note that if high-pressure air is directed into the channels and passages with the diaphragms still in place, diaphragm damage may result. Spraying carburettor cleaner into all the channels and passages in the carburettor body will often clear them of gum and dirt.
37 During reassembly, a complete set of new gaskets should be fitted. Also renew the needle valves, float pivot pins and the accelerator pump piston assembly. Inspect and renew (where necessary) the mixture screw, the jets and the accelerator pump injector. Renew worn linkages, springs, vacuum hoses, diaphragm assemblies and other parts where necessary.

38 Ensure that all jets are firmly locked into their original positions (but do not over-tighten). A loose jet can cause a rich (or even lean) running condition. Clean all mating surfaces and flanges of old gasket material and reassemble with new gaskets. Ensure that housings are positioned with their air and fuel routes correctly aligned.

Reassembly

39 Slide the choke diaphragm assembly into position on the housing.
40 Assemble the main and throttle bodies with a new gasket block and secure with the screw. Pay particular attention that the bodies are positioned with their air and fuel routes correctly aligned.
41 Where the primary throttle position has been disturbed and a throttle setting gauge is available, use it to set the throttle angle. Otherwise, temporarily adjust the throttle plate so that it is open just enough to prevent its seizure in the throttle body. An adjustment method with the engine running is detailed in Section 4.
42 Refit the secondary throttle diaphragm assembly and secure with the fixing screws. Reconnect the operating rod and the vacuum hose.
43 Check that the secondary throttle plate is fully closed. The adjustment screw should not normally be used to alter the throttle plate position. However, if necessary, it can be adjusted so that the plate is open just enough to prevent its seizure in the throttle body.
44 Refit the enrichment valve into the primary float chamber.
45 Refit the two main jets and the primary idle, bypass idle, secondary idle (where fitted), secondary progression air and fuel jets into their original positions (do not transpose the jets).
46 Refit the accelerator pump spring and piston assembly, then push the bearing into position flush with the facing surface (ridge facing outwards). Refit the seal and check that the pump operates smoothly.
47 Tap the pump injector into position after renewing the small seal on the injector body.
48 Refit the idle mixture and idle bypass screws after renewing the small seal on the respective bodies. Turn each screw in gently until it just seats. From this position, unscrew it three full turns. This will provide a basic setting to allow the engine to be started.
49 Insert the needle valve into the seat with the ball facing outwards. Refit the float and pivot pin.
50 Check the float level with reference to Section 4. Refit the float gasket to the main body.
51 Refit the upper body to the main body and secure with the four screws and central bolt. Pull the choke actuating lever upwards so that the lower end of the link rod may be twisted and pushed into position. Carefully snap the top end of the rod into the plastic retainer. Engage the accelerator pump linkage into the throttle lever.

Location of jets in main body

9 Part-load enrichment valve
10 Fuel jet - secondary progression

Choke linkage

A Plastic link can be removed or refitted with a small screwdriver

Pierburg 2B5, 2B6 & 2B7 carburettors

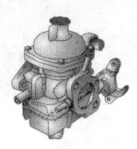

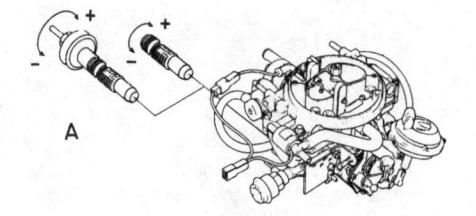

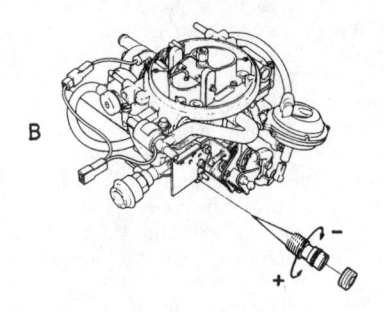

Idle adjustment screw location

A *Idle bypass screw*
B *Idle mixture screw*

52 Ensure that the choke earth strap and the vent valve (where fitted) are secured with an upper body fixing screw.
53 Refit the idle cut-off valve.
54 Check that the full-load enrichment nozzle is 0.5 ± 0.75 mm above the primary choke flap. Gently bend the nozzle if necessary to achieve this.
55 Ensure that the choke flap and linkage move smoothly and progressively. Reconnect the choke vacuum hoses.
56 Adjust the choke (see Section 4). Refit the plastic 'a1' adjustment screw cover.
57 Refit the carburettor to the engine.
58 Always adjust the carburettor idle speed and mixture after any work has been carried out on the carburettor, preferably with the aid of a CO meter.

4 Service adjustments

Adjustment preconditions

1 Refer to Part B for general advice on the preconditions for correct adjustment of this carburettor.
2 Disconnect the engine breather hose from the air filter and plug the opening in the air filter.
3 Reconnect the breather hose after all adjustments are completed. If the CO level increases more than 1 to 1.5%, change the sump oil. If the CO level increases after an oil change, suspect worn or sticking piston rings. If no CO change is noted on connecting /disconnecting the breather hose, suspect a clogged crankcase breather (PCV) system.

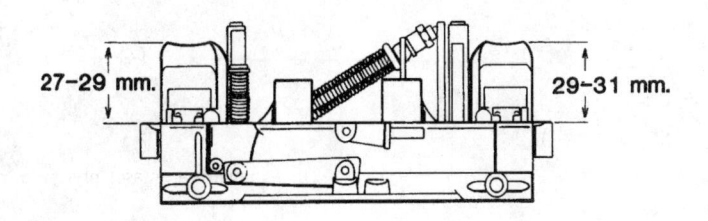

Float level checking

Bypass idle adjustment

4 Run the engine at 3000 rpm for 30 seconds to clear the manifold of fuel vapours, then allow the engine to idle.
5 Use the idle bypass regulating screw to set the specified idle speed *(see illustration)*.
6 Check the CO level. If incorrect, remove the tamperproof plug and adjust the idle mixture screw to obtain the correct level. Turning the screw clockwise (inwards) will reduce the CO level. Turning the screw anti-clockwise (outwards) will increase the CO level.
7 Repeat paragraphs 5 and 6 until both adjustments are correct. Adjusting the idle bypass screw will also affect the CO level.
8 Fit a new tamperproof plug to the mixture control screw on completion.

Basic throttle position

9 If the idle speed and CO cannot be set correctly, it is possible that the basic throttle position is incorrect. One method of setting is to remove the carburettor and use a Pierburg throttle setting gauge to accurately set the throttle position. Another method is to attach a very low-reading vacuum gauge to the vacuum advance connector. The correct angle is set when the gauge registers 8 ± 4 mmHg (10 ± 5 mbars).
10 An alternative method that can be used to set the throttle plate follows. Please note that this is not the manufacturer's recommended method but will nevertheless result in an accurate and stable idle speed and CO level:
a) Allow the engine to idle.
b) Screw in the bypass regulating screw until it is fully seated. The idle speed should drop to approximately two-thirds of the idle speed figure. For example, if the idle speed is specified as 950 rpm, the speed should drop to between 600 and 650 rpm.
c) Adjust the throttle stop screw until 600 to 650 rpm is obtained.
d) Unscrew the bypass screw until 950 rpm is once again attained.
e) Reset the CO to the correct level.
f) If the CO needs a large adjustment at this stage, repeat paragraphs a) to e). Once the proper level of CO is reached at the specified idle speed, the carburettor is properly adjusted.
11 The rpm figures used in the above example are based on an idle speed of 950 rpm.

Substitute the correct figures for the carburettor being adjusted (see Specifications).

Float level

12 It is not possible to adjust the plastic float. It is possible, however, to check the level.
13 Invert the upper body so that the float faces upwards. The float needle pin must not be depressed.
14 Measure the distance between the upper body (without its gasket) and the top of the float *(see illustration)*.
15 If the float level is incorrect, check the needle valve seat for correct position. Remove the float and check the float weight (see Specifications). If the seat and weight are satisfactory, renew the float if the level is still incorrect.

Accelerator pump

16 On the Pierburg 2B series carburettor, it is possible to adjust the volume of fuel injected by the accelerator pump.
17 Turn the adjusting nut in direction (+) to increase volume, or in direction (-) to decrease volume *(see illustration)*.

Automatic choke

Fast idle adjustment (carburettor removed - Volvo only)

18 Position the fast idle adjustment screw against the sixth step of the fast idle cam.

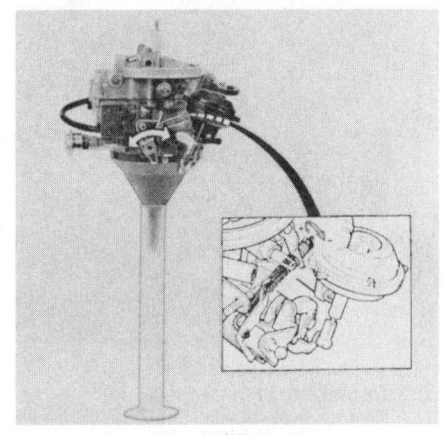

Accelerator pump adjustment

F3•11

Chapter F3

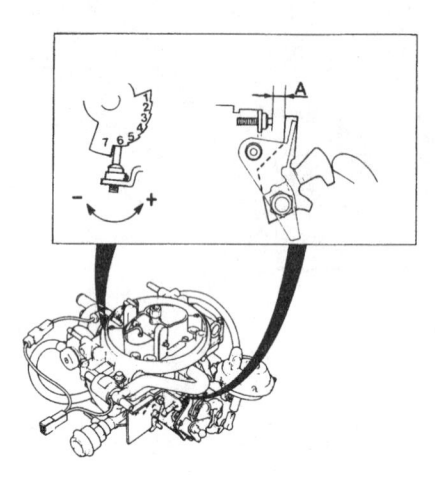

Fast idle adjustment - Volvo only

A Clearance (refer to Specifications)

19 Use the shank of a twist drill to measure clearance 'A' (see illustration). Refer to Specifications for the required drill size.
20 Remove the tamperproof plug and adjust as necessary by turning the fast idle screw in the appropriate direction.

Fast idle adjustment (engine running)

21 Warm the engine to normal running temperature and check that the idle speed and mixture are correctly adjusted. Switch the engine off.
22 Remove the air filter assembly (air inlet trunking on Volvos) and place it clear of the carburettor. Where fitted, all the vacuum hoses must remain connected.
23 Place the fast idle adjustment screw against the highest step of the fast idle cam.
24 Start the engine without moving the throttle and record the fast idle speed.
25 Remove the tamperproof plug and adjust as necessary by turning the fast idle screw in the appropriate direction.
26 Unless continuing with the following pull-down tests, refit the air filter assembly, ensuring that the vacuum hoses remain connected.

Closure of choke flap

1 Move choke control lever fully in direction of arrow
2 Fast idle adjustment screw
3 Stepped cam
4 Pull-down adjustment screw
5 Adjust clearance by bending this lever
A Clearance = 0.75 ± 0.25 mm

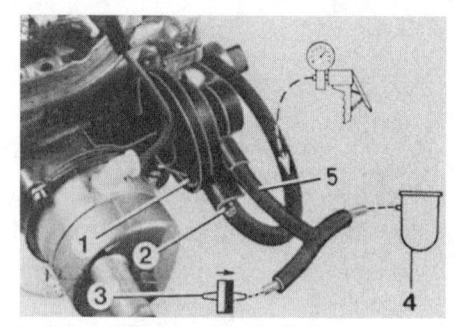

Testing choke vacuum pull-down

1 Pull-down unit
2 Vacuum pump connection - be careful not to lose reducing jet
3 Non-return valve
4 Vacuum reservoir
5 Remove hose from outlet connection

Choke pull-down

27 Remove the three screws and detach the bi-metal coil housing from the carburettor. Remove the 'a1' adjustment screw cover.
28 Refer to Part D for a method of testing the vacuum reservoir (where fitted).
29 Remove the vacuum hose from the carburettor base to the inlet connection (supply side) of the pull-down unit and attach a vacuum pump to the connection (see illustration). Remove the second hose from the outlet side and leave the connection unplugged. Be careful not to lose the reducing jet (Volvo applications) and also check that this jet is not blocked.
30 Operate the pump and the pull-down should move to the first stage.
31 Maintaining the vacuum, plug the pull-down outlet connection and operate the pump until 225 mmHg (300 mbars) is obtained. The pull-down should now move to the second stage and hold vacuum for at least 10 seconds. If the diaphragm does not operate as described, renew the pull-down unit. If the pull-down is a single-stage type, follow the procedure for testing the second stage of the two-stage unit above.
32 Position the fast idle screw on the highest step of the fast idle cam.
33 Fully close the choke flap and measure the clearance between the tag on the choke operating lever and the pull-down rod (see illustration). The dimension 'A' should be 0.75 ± 0.25 mm.
34 Adjust as necessary by bending the tag on the choke operating lever.

Single-stage pull-down unit

35 Where a single-stage pull-down unit is fitted, remove the outlet vacuum hose and plug the pull-down connection. Move the pull-down operating rod up to its stop by operating the vacuum pump. Lightly close the choke flap and use the shank of a twist drill to measure the 'a1' gap between the lower section of the choke flap and the air intake. Refer to Specifications for the required drill size. Adjust as necessary by turning the pull-down adjusting screw in the appropriate direction (see illustration).

Two-stage pull-down unit

36 Where a two-stage pull-down unit is fitted, detach the pull-down to vacuum reservoir hose from the connection on the pull-down. Do not plug the connection. Operate the vacuum pump and the choke flap should open to the first stage setting. Lightly close the choke flap and use the shank of a twist drill to measure the 'a' clearance (A) between the lower section of the choke flap and the air intake. Refer to Specifications for the required drill size.
37 Adjust as necessary by turning the first stage pull-down adjusting screw (see illustration below left) in the appropriate direction. Note that the a clearance should only be checked after the pull-down unit has been renewed or if the setting has been disturbed. Plug the pull-down outlet connection. Fully operate the vacuum pump and the choke flap should open to the second stage setting. Lightly close the choke flap and use the shank of a twist drill to measure the 'a1' clearance between the lower section of the choke flap and the air intake. Refer to Specifications for the required drill size.
38 Adjust as necessary by turning the second stage pull-down adjusting screw (see illustration below) in the appropriate direction. Where a vacuum pump is not available, a small screwdriver can also be used to fully push on the 'a1' adjusting screw. In this instance, the screw should be pushed until a resistance is felt. The clearance obtained is the first stage setting. Continue pushing until the screw cannot be pushed any further. The clearance now obtained is the second stage setting.

Three-stage pull-down unit

39 Where a three-stage pull-down unit is fitted, remove the vacuum hose from the carburettor base to the connection 'A' of the

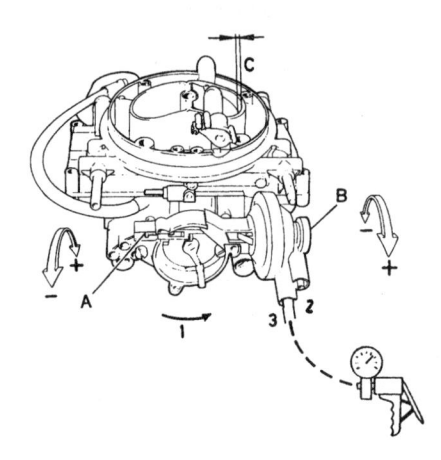

Choke pull-down adjustment - 2-stage type

1 Close choke flap by moving choke control lever fully in direction of arrow
2 Outlet connection and reducing jet
3 Inlet connection
A Second stage adjustment screw 'a1'
B First stage adjustment screw 'a'
C Clearance

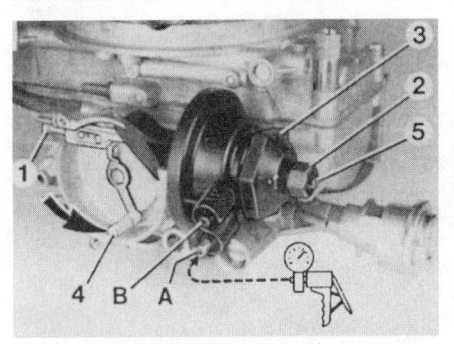

Pierburg 2B5, 2B6 & 2B7 carburettors

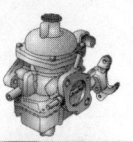

Choke pull-down adjustment - 3-stage type

1 Third stage adjustment screw 'a2'
2 Second stage adjustment screw 'a1'
3 First stage adjustment screw 'a'
4 Close choke flap by moving choke control lever fully in direction of arrow
5 Vacuum connection
A Vacuum connection
B Vacuum and reservoir connection

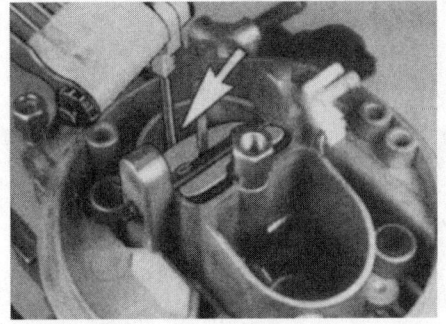

Measuring clearance for pull-down with a measuring rod

Choke alignment marks

pull-down unit *(see illustration)*. Attach a vacuum pump to the connection. Detach the hoses from connections 'B' and '5'. Do not plug the connections.

40 Operate the vacuum pump and the choke flap should open to the first stage setting. Lightly close the choke flap and use the shank of a twist drill (or a measuring rod) to measure the a clearance between the lower section of the choke flap and the air intake *(see illustration)*. Refer to the specifications for the required drill size.

41 Adjust as necessary by turning the first stage pull-down adjusting screw (3) in the appropriate direction *(see illustration above)*. Plug the pull-down connection 'B' and fully operate the vacuum pump. The choke flap should open to the second stage setting. Lightly close the choke flap and use the shank of a twist drill to measure the 'a1' clearance between the lower section of the choke flap and the air intake. Refer to Specifications for the required drill size.

42 Adjust as necessary by turning the second stage pull-down adjusting screw (2) in the appropriate direction *(see illustration above)*. Plug the pull-down connections 'B' and '5'. Fully operate the vacuum pump and the choke flap should open to the third stage setting. Lightly close the choke flap and use the shank of a twist drill to measure the 'a2' clearance between the lower section of the choke flap and the air intake. Refer to Specifications for the required drill size. Adjust as necessary by turning the third stage pull-down adjusting screw '1' in the appropriate direction.

All types

43 Reconnect all the vacuum hoses and refit the plastic 'a1' adjustment screw cover.
44 Refit the bi-metal coil housing and ensure that the spring locates in the slot of the choke lever. Secure loosely with the three screws.
45 Align the cut mark on the bi-metal cover with the correct mark on the choke assembly

housing and tighten the three screws *(see illustration)*.

De-choke adjustment

46 Fully close the choke flap and hold it in this position with the aid of a rubber band arranged between the choke operating rod and the carburettor body.
47 Fully operate the throttle and the choke flap should be forced open to leave a small clearance.
48 Use the shank of a twist drill to measure the gap between the lower section of the choke flap and the air intake. Refer to Specifications for the required drill size.
49 Adjust as necessary by loosening the primary throttle spindle nut and moving the cam lever in the appropriate direction *(see illustration)*.

5 Component testing

Coolant-heated thermal switches

1 Refer to Part D for general tests on the thermal switch, automatic choke and manifold heater.

Thermal switch for manifold heater

2 Below 50°C, a voltmeter should indicate battery voltage (switch open).

De-choke adjustment

1 Close choke flap by moving choke control lever fully in direction of arrow
2 Throttle spindle nut
3 Move cam lever in appropriate direction

3 Above that temperature, the voltmeter should indicate zero volts (switch closed).
4 If the switch does not function in accordance with the above, renew the switch.

Thermal switch for automatic choke (VW/Audi)

5 Below 30°C, a voltmeter should indicate battery voltage (switch open).
6 Above that temperature, the voltmeter should indicate zero volts (switch closed).
7 If the switch does not operate in accordance with the above, renew the switch.

Coolant-heated thermal valve

8 Refer to Part D for general tests on the thermal valve fitted to the secondary throttle vacuum hose (some VW/Audi variants).
9 Below 45°C, high vacuum should register (valve closed).
10 Above 68°C, no vacuum should register (valve open).
11 If the valve does not function in accordance with the above, renew the valve.

Vacuum-operated fuel cut-off system

12 Warm the engine to normal running temperature.
13 Use a T-piece to attach a vacuum gauge to the idle cut-off valve *(see illustrations)*.
14 Start the engine and raise the speed to over 3000 rpm. The gauge needle should indicate no vacuum.
15 Close the throttle sharply, decelerating the engine. The gauge should immediately register a vacuum reading.

Testing vacuum-operated idle cut-off valve

Chapter F3

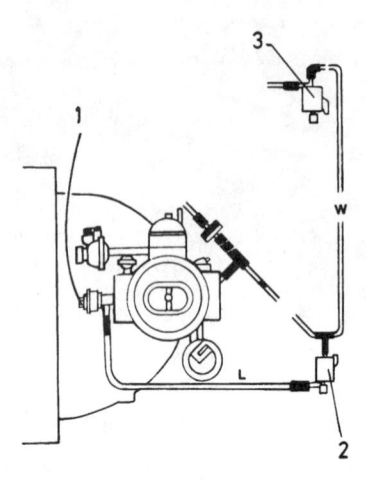

Vacuum-operated fuel cut-off valve system

1 Vacuum-operated cut-off valve
2 Switchover valve
3 Switchover valve (additional valve for vehicles with air conditioning)

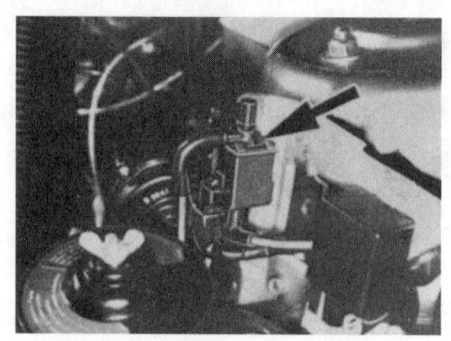

Location of switchover valve

Fuel cut-off system wiring

A Idle condition: switchover valve closed
B Deceleration/engine shut-down condition: switchover valve open

1 Switchover valve
2 Ignition control unit
3 Accelerator pedal switch

Colour code
BL   Blue
OR   Orange
R   Red
SB   Black

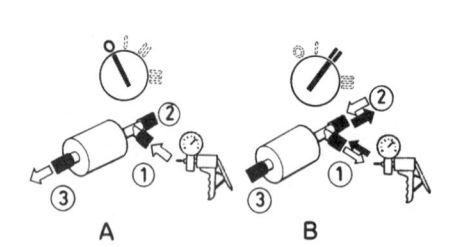

Testing vent valve operation

1, 2 & 3 Vacuum connections - see text
A Ignition off
B Ignition on

Float chamber vent valve

1 Float chamber vent valve
2 Hose connection to air filter trunking
3 Hose connection to carburettor

Idle cut-off valve (carburettor installed)

19 Disconnect the vacuum hose, attach a vacuum pump to the valve connector and allow the engine to idle.
20 Operate the pump and the engine should stall.
21 If the engine does not stall, check the valve for tightness. Also check or renew the seal after dismantling the valve.

Idle cut-off valve (carburettor removed)

22 Check that the valve is tight in the carburettor body.
23 Attach a vacuum pump to the connector and operate the pump until the valve is actuated. If the valve does not operate fully, or if vacuum is not maintained for at least 10 seconds, renew the seal and again check the valve for tightness. Note that the valve must be tested whilst connected to the carburettor body.
24 Renew the valve assembly if it will not maintain vacuum after servicing.

Switchover valve

25 Disconnect the vacuum hose from the switchover valve (output side) and attach a vacuum gauge (use a T-piece if appropriate) *(see illustrations)*.
26 Start the engine and raise the speed to over 3000 rpm. The gauge needle should indicate no vacuum.
27 Close the throttle sharply, decelerating the engine. The gauge should immediately register a vacuum reading.
28 As normal idle speed is approached, the gauge needle should drop sharply to register zero vacuum once more.
29 Allow the engine to idle, then switch off the ignition or remove the electrical connection to the valve. The gauge should register a vacuum reading until the engine stops rotating.
30 If the valve does not operate as specified, check for a voltage supply to the switch. Also check the wiring to the accelerator pedal switch and the ignition system control unit. If the wiring is satisfactory, the control unit is suspect.

Float chamber vent valve

31 Remove the vacuum hose from the float chamber and attach a vacuum pump to connection (1) *(see illustrations)*.
32 With the ignition off, plug connection '2'. Operate the pump. No vacuum should be registered until connection '3' is plugged.
33 With the ignition on, plug connection '3'. Operate the pump. No vacuum should be registered until connection '2' is plugged.
34 If the valve does not operate as specified, check for a voltage supply and for a good earth connection on the carburettor.
35 Renew the valve if the electrical supply and earth are satisfactory.

16 As normal idle speed is approached, the gauge needle should drop sharply to register zero once more.
17 Allow the engine to idle then switch off the ignition. The gauge should register a vacuum reading until the engine stops rotating.
18 If the system does not behave as outlined above, carry out the following checks.

Pierburg 2B5, 2B6 & 2B7 carburettors

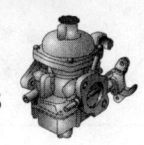

6 Fault diagnosis

Refer to Part D for diagnosis of general carburettor faults. The following faults are specific to 2B carburettors.

Poor choke operation/poor cold running
- [ ] Over-choking due to pull-down diaphragm failure, relaxing of bi-metal or poor choke adjustment.
- [ ] Sticking choke flap.
- [ ] Broken choke flap lever.
- [ ] Failure of inlet manifold pre-heater.
- [ ] Primary full-load enrichment nozzle in too high a position.

Heavy fuel consumption
- [ ] Primary full-load enrichment nozzle in too low a position.

Hesitation
- [ ] Worn secondary throttle shaft. Check for wear on lever and rocker.

Uneven running
- [ ] Air leak due to defective rubber mounting flange.

Lack of power
- [ ] Failure of secondary throttle plate diaphragm.
- [ ] Failure of coolant-heated thermal valve to secondary diaphragm.
- [ ] Loose secondary needle valve seat, allowing float to drop and fuel starvation in secondary fuel system.

F3•15

Notes

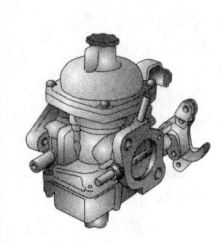

Part F Chapter 4
Pierburg 34/34 2BE carburettor

Contents

Component testing 5
Fault diagnosis 6
General servicing 3
Identification 2
Principles of operation 1
Service adjustments 4

Specifications

Manufacturer	BMW		BMW	
Model	316 (E30)		518 (E28)	
Year	1983 to 1988		1983 to 1985	
Engine code	M10/B18		M10/B18	
Capacity (cm³)/no. of cyls	1766/4		1766/4	
Oil temperature (°C)	80		80	
Carb. identification	1 287 342		1 287 342	
Idle speed (rpm)	850 ± 50		800 ± 50	
CO @ idle (% vol.)	0.75 ± 0.25		1.0 max	
Stage (venturi)	**1**	**2**	**1**	**2**
Venturi diameter (K)	24	28	24	28
Main jet (Gg)	120	110	120	110
Air correction jet (a)	140	70	140	70
Needle valve (mm) (P)	2.0	2.0	2.0	2.0
Float level (mm)	28 ± 0.75	30 ± 0.75	28 ± 0.75	30 ± 0.75
Idle jet (g)	47.5		47.5	
Float weight (grams)	5.85 ± 0.2		5.85 ± 0.2	
Basic throttle position (mm)	0.05 ± 0.02		0.05 ± 0.02	

Chapter F4

1 Principles of operation

Introduction

1 The following technical description of the Pierburg 34/34 2BE carburettor should be read in conjunction with the more detailed description of carburettor principles in Part A.

Construction

2 The Pierburg 2BE carburettor is a down-draught progressive twin venturi instrument with a vacuum-controlled secondary throttle (see illustration). The throttle shafts are made of steel, while the throttle valves, all jets and the emulsion tube are manufactured from brass. The internal fuel channels and air passages are drilled and sealed with lead plugs where necessary. The choke system is automatic in operation and acts on the primary venturi alone.

3 The carburettor is constructed in three main bodies. These are the upper body, main body and throttle body (which contains the throttle assembly). An insulating block, placed between the main carburettor body and the throttle body, prevents excess heat transference to the main body.

4 Essentially, the air supply during starting, warm-up, acceleration, part-load, deceleration and engine cut-off is controlled by an Electronic Control Unit (ECU), according to information supplied by the various engine sensors. The system is sometimes referred to as the ECOTRONIC system (see illustrations).

Fuel control

5 The 2BE carburettor utilises a twin float system with separate chambers for primary and secondary fuel systems (see illustration overleaf). Fuel flows into the carburettor through a fine mesh filter and a single fuel channel supplies fuel to both chambers. Each chamber has its own spring-loaded needle valve and plastic float and maintains its own fuel level. The float levels are considered critical and are set very accurately during production.

6 The float chamber is vented internally into the upper air intake which is on the clean-air side of the air filter.

Pierburg 2BE carburettor

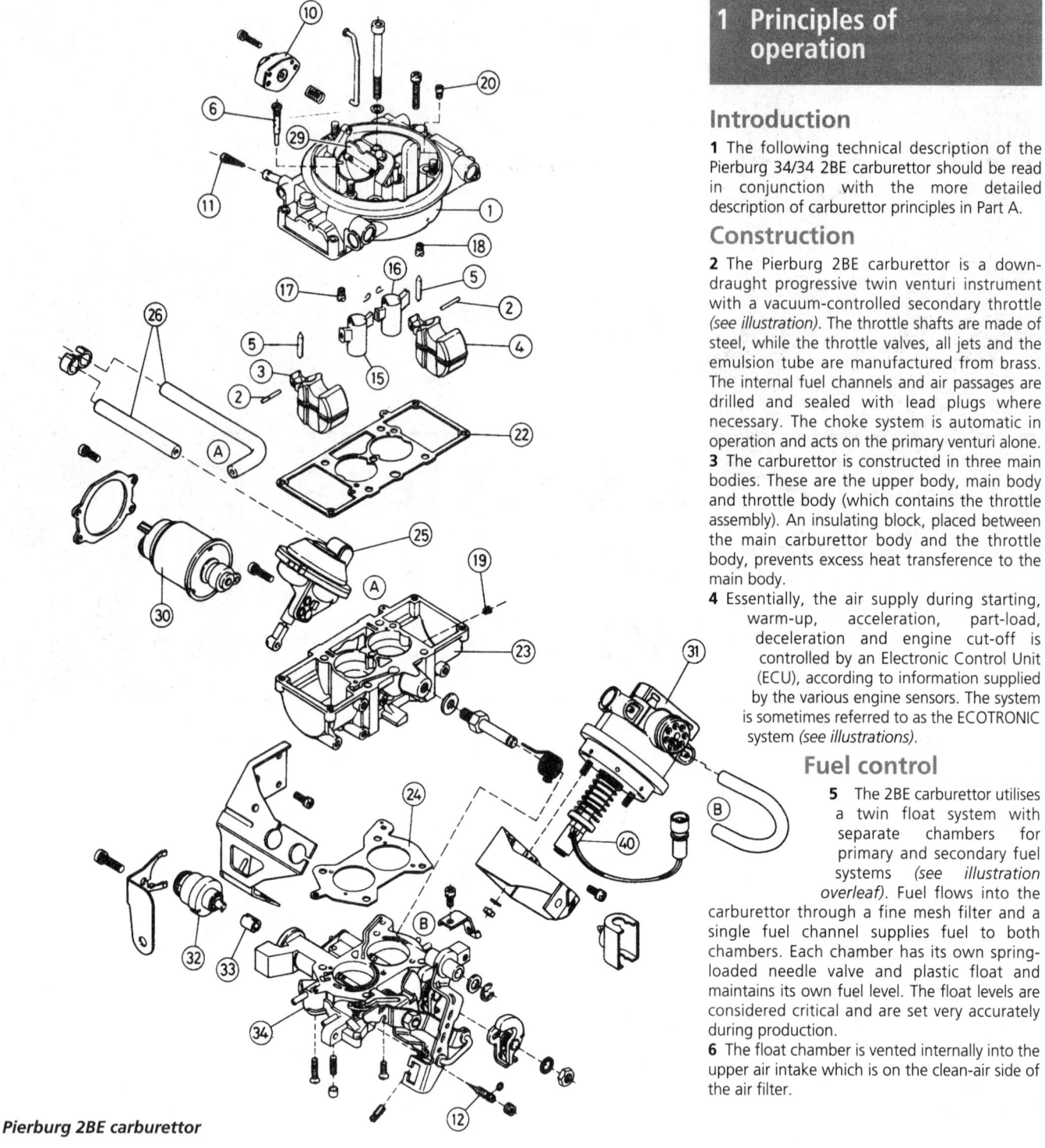

1 Upper body
2 Float pin
3 Float - primary
4 Float - secondary
5 Needle valve
6 Idle jet - primary
10 Secondary fuel cut-off diaphragm
11 Fuel filter
12 Idle mixture control screw
15 Auxiliary venturi - primary
16 Auxiliary venturi - secondary
17 Main jet - primary
18 Main jet - secondary
19 Fuel jet - secondary progression
20 Air corrector jet - secondary progression
22 Float chamber gasket
23 Main body
24 Insulating block
25 Diaphragm assembly - secondary throttle
26 Vacuum hose - secondary throttle
29 Choke flap
30 Choke flap actuator
31 Throttle plate actuator
32 Throttle potentiometer
33 Plastic coupling piece
34 Throttle body
40 Plunger

Pierburg 34/34 2BE carburettor

Secondary fuel cut-off

7 The fuel supply to the secondary float chamber is made via a fuel cut-off valve (see illustration overleaf). Fuel flows through the inlet channel, past the primary system into the chamber. An air passage is taken from under the throttle plate to the cover of the secondary fuel cut-off valve chamber. At idle and during light-throttle operation, manifold vacuum draws the diaphragm back against spring pressure to close off the valve and therefore the fuel channel to the secondary float chamber. Under acceleration and wide-open throttle operation, the vacuum in the manifold is depleted. The diaphragm returns under spring pressure and the valve opens the fuel channel. This allows fuel to flow through the valve to reach the secondary float chamber.

Idle, slow running and progression

8 Fuel is drawn from the primary main well into the base of a vertical well which dips down into the fuel. A combined idle jet and emulsion tube is placed in the well. The idle air supply is controlled by a tapered needle positioned in the air corrector inlet. The fuel is mixed with air, drawn in from the metered air corrector and the holes in the emulsion tube, to form an emulsion. The resulting mixture is drawn through a channel to the throttle body where it is discharged from the idle orifice under the primary throttle plate. A tapered mixture screw is used to vary the outlet and this ensures fine control of the idle mixture (see illustration on page F4•5).

9 A number of progression holes provide a further air contribution to the emulsion while the throttle is closed. As the progression holes are uncovered by the opening throttle, the vacuum draw overcomes the air bleed into the holes and a reversal occurs. Fuel is now drawn out to add extra enrichment to the idle mixture during initial acceleration. The adjustable mixture screw is tamper proofed at production level, in accordance with emission regulations.

Location of components in engine compartment

1 Carburettor
2 Ignition distributor
3 ECU under driver's side facia panel or glovebox
4 Ignition switch valve (vacuum advance)
5 Temperature sensor in manifold
6 Ignition switch unit
7 Deceleration air valve
8 Thermal valve

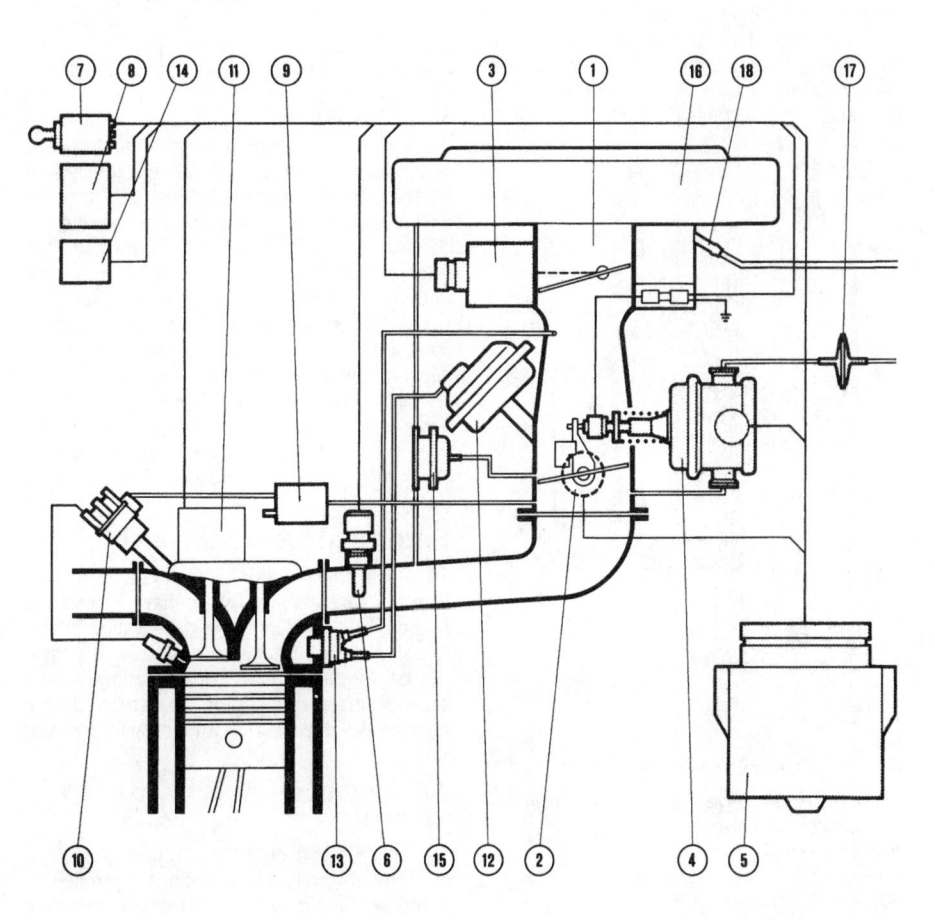

Schematic diagram of 2BE carburettor sensors and actuators

1 Carburettor
2 Throttle potentiometer
3 Choke flap actuator
4 Throttle plate actuator
5 Electronic Control Unit (ECU)
6 Temperature sensor
7 Throttle switch
8 System control relay
9 Ignition thermal switch valve
10 Ignition distributor
11 Engine rpm sensor
12 Secondary throttle diaphragm assembly
13 Thermal valve
14 Econometer
15 Deceleration air valve
16 Air filter
17 Filter
18 Fuel inlet connection

Chapter F4

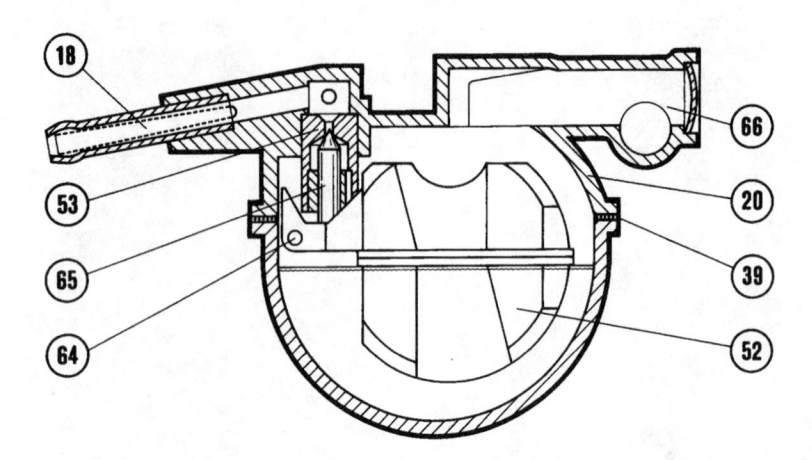

Fuel supply and float arrangement

18 Fuel supply inlet
20 Carburettor upper body
39 Gasket
52 Float
53 Float needle valve insert
64 Float pivot pin
65 Float needle valve
66 Float system fuel channel

Idle speed control

10 The engine speed at idle is maintained at a constant speed, irrespective of engine load or temperature. The ECU monitors the idle speed and compares it to a nominal value. As idle conditions alter or a temperature or load change occurs, the ECU uses a throttle plate actuator to maintain the correct idle position.

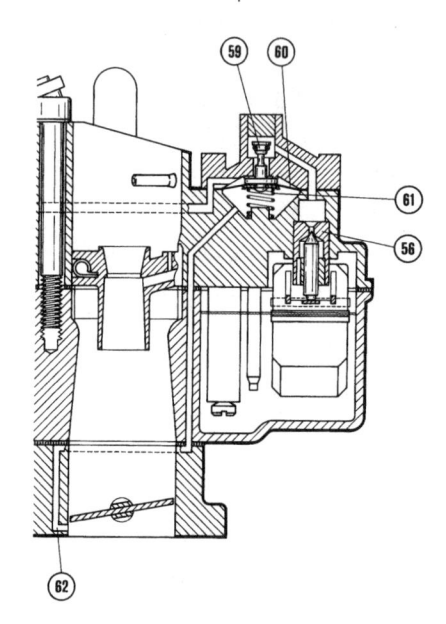

Secondary venturi fuel cut-off

56 Float needle valve - secondary venturi
59 Fuel cut-off valve
60 Diaphragm
61 Spring
62 Vacuum drilling

11 Idle speed adjustment is not possible, although an electrical facility exists to raise the idle speed by 100 rpm. During production, a throttle plate bypass screw is set in a specified position. This screw is then sealed. The seal should not be broken and the screw should not be tampered with.

Throttle position potentiometer

12 As the throttle is opened and closed, the resistance of the throttle potentiometer (pot) increases and decreases. In conjunction with the throttle switch, a variable voltage signal is returned to the ECU so that the throttle position and rate of throttle opening may be calculated.

Deceleration

13 During deceleration from engine speeds over 1400 rpm, the throttle plate is totally shut by the actuator to cut off the fuel. Damping occurs during the closing operation so that the throttle does not abruptly snap shut. As the engine speed falls below 1400 rpm, the actuator re-opens the throttle to regain the normal idle speed. When the throttle is totally shut, a drilling in the throttle bore is exposed to vacuum under the throttle plate. Vacuum from the drilling is relayed to a depression valve. The valve is actuated to open a passage from the inlet manifold to the air filter casing. Pressure in the manifold is thus relieved during deceleration.

Engine shut-down

14 Once the ignition is switched off, the throttle plate actuator will behave in a similar fashion as it did during the deceleration phase. The throttle will totally close to prevent engine run-on as the engine stops rotating. A few seconds after the engine has stopped, the actuator will open the throttle ready for the next start.

Acceleration and part-load enrichment

15 Unlike a conventional carburettor system, enrichment during acceleration is controlled by a momentary movement of the choke flap towards the closed position. Duration of the movement is controlled by the ECU, in accordance with information by the sensors on engine speed, temperature, throttle position and rate of throttle opening.

16 The flap is positioned by an actuator so that the correct mixture for all part-load conditions is maintained. In addition, the flap mechanism is connected to the idle needle valve. As the flap moves to the closed position, the needle is inserted into the idle air corrector and the idle and progression mixture is enriched.

Choke flap actuator

17 This device controls the mixture during the part-load, acceleration and warm-up phases by controlling the position of the choke flap. It is mechanically connected to the flap and electrically connected to the ECU.

Main circuit

18 The amount of fuel discharged into the airstream is controlled by a calibrated main jet. Fuel is drawn through the jet into the base of a vertical well which dips down into the fuel in the primary float chamber. A combined emulsion tube and air correction jet is placed in the well. The fuel is mixed with air, drawn in through the calibrated air correction jet and the holes in the emulsion tubes, to form an air/fuel emulsion. The resulting mixture is discharged from the main nozzle through an auxiliary venturi into the main airstream.

Secondary action

19 A port is located in both primary and secondary venturis. Airways run from these ports into a common passage. A vacuum hose is connected to the passage and to the diaphragm that controls the secondary throttle plate.

20 During normal operation at low speeds, only the primary venturi is employed. When the air velocity through the primary venturi reaches a certain level, depression acts upon the port to operate the secondary diaphragm and the secondary throttle. Vacuum created in the secondary venturi will further control the rate of secondary opening.

21 The primary linkage is arranged to prevent the secondary plate from opening when air speed may be high but the engine is cruising on a light throttle. Secondary action will not occur until the primary throttle is about two-thirds-open.

22 A thermal switch is connected to the vacuum supply hose so that the secondary throttle plate is inoperative during the engine warm-up period. The switch remains closed when the engine is cold and opens at a pre-determined temperature.

23 A progression jet is used to prevent hesitation as the secondary throttle plate starts to open. Fuel is drawn from the secondary float chamber, through the secondary progression jet, into the base of a vertical well which dips down into the fuel. An emulsion tube is placed in the well, capped by an air bleed drilling. A

Pierburg 34/34 2BE carburettor

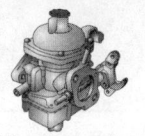

further supply of air is introduced from a calibrated air corrector jet. The fuel is mixed with air (drawn in through the air bleed, air corrector and the holes in the tube) to form an emulsion. The resulting mixture is drawn through a channel where it is discharged into the secondary venturi, via a number of progression holes, at the initial opening of the secondary throttle plate.

Full-load enrichment

24 At full-load and high engine speeds, the velocity of air creates a depression sufficient to raise fuel from the float chamber into a channel. The fuel then passes through a calibrated bushing to the upper section of the air intake. Here it is mixed with a small amount of air from a calibrated air bleed and discharged into the airstream from the full-load enrichment nozzle. A full-load enrichment nozzle is used in the upper air intakes of both primary and secondary barrels *(see illustration overleaf)*.

Cold start system

25 The choke system is fully automatic in operation and actuates a flap in the primary air intake, according to manifold temperature and engine fuel requirements. The throttle position for both hot and cold starting is also automatically determined. Priming the system, by depressing the accelerator pedal, is therefore unnecessary.

26 The throttle plate is placed in the starting position by the throttle actuator shortly after the engine is shut down. Once the ignition is switched on, the choke flap is positioned according to temperature. A linkage attached to the idle needle valve ensures that the needle partially blocks the idle air corrector so the idle mixture is also enriched.

27 Once the engine fires, the throttle position and choke flap are positioned according to manifold temperature. As the engine warms up, the throttle actuator will reduce the throttle angle. Once the engine reaches operating temperature the throttle is placed in the hot idle position. Similarly, the choke flap will open during warm-up. However, since part-load

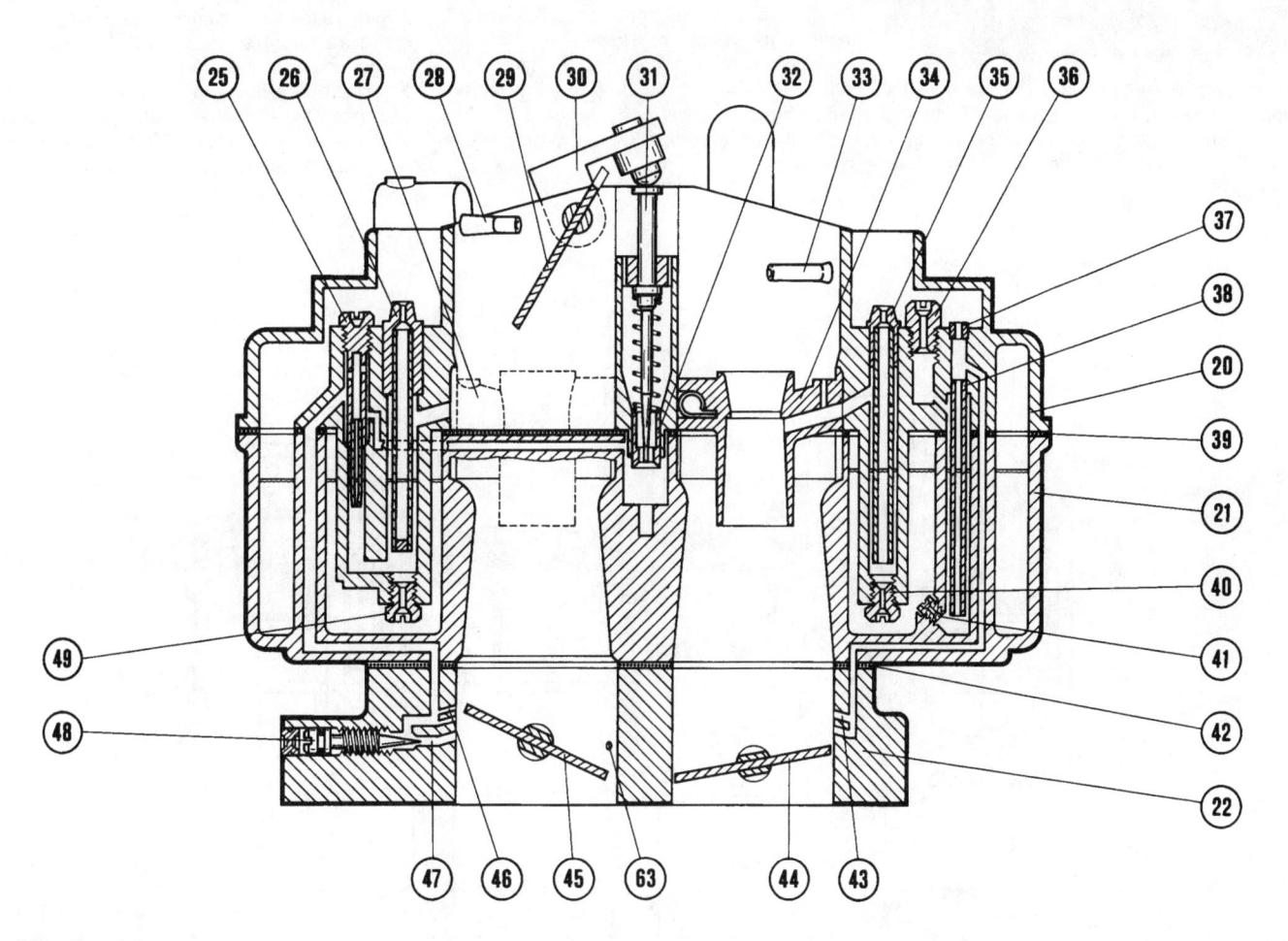

Idle and main systems

20 Carburettor upper body
21 Main body assembly
22 Throttle body assembly
25 Combined idle fuel and emulsion tube - primary idle
26 Air corrector jet with emulsion tube - primary venturi
27 Auxiliary venturi - primary venturi
28 Nozzle for full-load enrichment - primary venturi
29 Choke flap
30 Choke flap actuating lever
31 Idle air corrector needle
32 Idle air corrector jet
33 Nozzle for full-load enrichment - secondary venturi
34 Auxiliary venturi - secondary venturi
35 Air corrector jet with emulsion tube - secondary venturi
36 Air corrector jet - secondary progression
37 Air bleed drilling - secondary progression
38 Emulsion tube - secondary progression
39 Gasket
40 Main jet - secondary venturi
41 Fuel jet - secondary progression
42 Insulation block
43 Progression holes - secondary venturi
44 Throttle valve - secondary venturi
45 Throttle valve - primary venturi
46 Progression holes - primary venturi
47 Idle mixture outlet
48 Idle mixture control screw
49 Main jet - primary venturi
63 Vacuum drilling for deceleration valve

Chapter F4

enrichment depends on the flap position, even when the engine is warm, the flap will always be positioned so that the engine receives the correct air/fuel mixture.

Temperature sensor

28 The temperature sensor is a varying potentiometer and functions on the negative temperature coefficient (NTC) principle. As the temperature rises, the sensor resistance falls. A variable voltage signal is returned to the ECU so that the inlet manifold temperature may be calculated.

2 Identification

1 Pierburg 2B is stamped on the carburettor upper and main bodies. The manufacturer's identification code may be stamped on a metallic tag attached to the cover by an upper body fixing screw or on a corner of the carburettor upper body.
2 Where the tag is missing, refer to Part B for other means of identifying the carburettor.
3 Early versions of this carburettor may be stamped with the trade name Zenith.

3 General servicing

Introduction

1 Read this Chapter in conjunction with Part B, which describes some of the operations in more detail. It is assumed that the carburettor is removed for this service. However, many of the operations can be tackled with the carburettor in place. Where this is undertaken, first remove the carburettor upper body and soak the fuel out of the float chamber using a clean tissue or soft cloth.

Dismantling and checking

2 Remove the carburettor from the engine (see Part B).
3 Check the carburettor visually for damage and wear.
4 Inspect the choke flap, spindle and linkage for stickiness and wear.
5 Carefully prise the upper choke link rod from the plastic retainer on the choke spindle. Twist out and remove the lower part of the link rod from its position on the choke housing assembly. Disengage a spring (noting its position), then remove the four screws and central hexagon-head bolt and detach the carburettor upper body.
6 Inspect the float chamber for corrosion and calcium build-up.
7 Remove the float chamber gasket.
8 Use a straight-edge to check for distorted flanges on all facing surfaces.
9 Tap out each float pin and remove the float and needle valve from both primary and secondary float chambers. The needle valve seats are not removable.

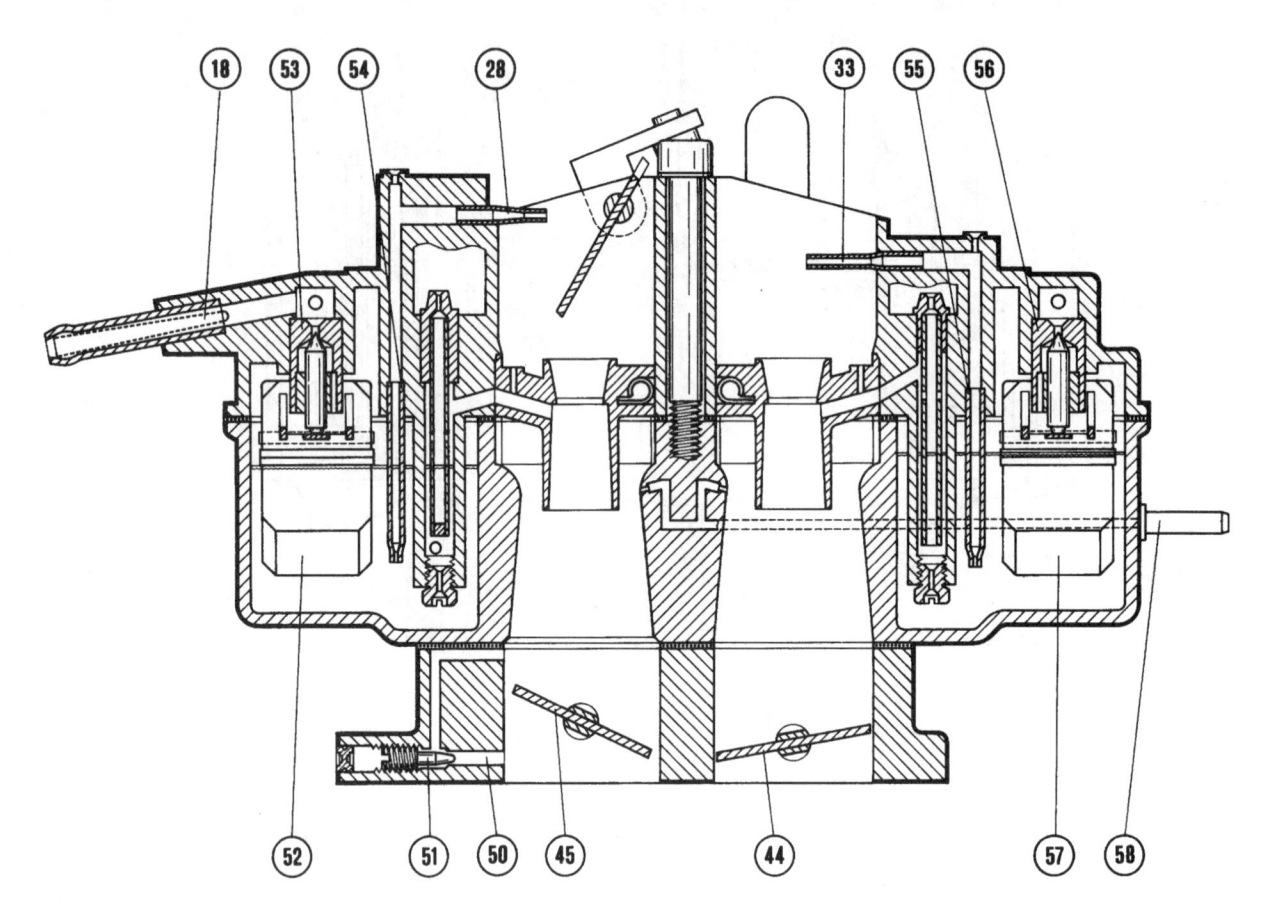

Full-load and float systems

18 Fuel supply inlet
28 Nozzle for full-load enrichment - primary venturi
33 Nozzle for full-load enrichment - secondary venturi
44 Throttle valve - secondary venturi
45 Throttle valve - primary venturi
50 Air bypass
51 Bypass idle speed screw
52 Float - primary venturi
53 Float needle valve insert - primary venturi
54 Calibrated tube for full-load enrichment - primary venturi
55 Calibrated tube for full-load enrichment - secondary venturi
56 Float needle valve insert - secondary venturi
57 Float - secondary venturi
58 Connection to secondary throttle vacuum diaphragm

Pierburg 34/34 2BE carburettor

10 Check that the anti-vibration ball is free in the needle valve end.
11 Check the needle valve tips for wear and ridges.
12 The float should be checked for damage and ingress of petrol.
13 Renew the float pin if it shows signs of wear.
14 Remove the fuel filter from its position in the fuel inlet connection. Screwing an M3 screw into the filter opening may assist in its withdrawal. Clean the filter and renew it if necessary.
15 Remove the two screws and detach the secondary fuel supply housing cover, diaphragm and spring assembly. Check the diaphragm for damage and fatigue.
16 Unscrew the mixture screw and inspect the tip for damage or ridges.
17 Unscrew the primary idle jet assembly.
18 Unscrew the secondary progression air jet.
19 Remove both main jets. It is not possible to remove the main air corrector jets or emulsion tubes.
20 Remove the secondary progression fuel jet from the secondary float chamber.
21 Check that the channels from the float chamber into the emulsion tube wells are clear.
22 Note all the jet sizes and their locations for correct installation during reassembly.
23 Check the jet calibration against Specifications. It is possible that the jets may have been transposed (or the wrong size fitted) during the last overhaul. The idle jet and the progression air jet can be removed from the carburettor without removing the upper body.
24 Remove the secondary throttle vacuum hose and attach a vacuum pump to the vacuum connector *(see illustration)*.
25 Fully operate the throttle lever to open the primary throttle and operate the vacuum pump until the secondary diaphragm is actuated. Renew the diaphragm assembly if it does not operate fully or if vacuum is not maintained for at least 10 seconds.
26 Disconnect the secondary throttle operating rod by twisting the rod out of its socket on the throttle lever. Remove the two screws and detach the diaphragm assembly from the body.
27 Remove the four screws and detach the throttle cable mounting bracket.
28 Disconnect the vacuum hose, then remove the three nuts and withdraw the throttle plate actuator assembly *(see illustration)*.
29 Remove the two screws and detach the throttle plate actuator mounting bracket. Note that the primary throttle will need to be opened and the plastic secondary throttle actuating lever lifted so that the front screw can be released.
30 Check the condition of the plastic secondary throttle operating lever. When worn, this will be deeply grooved.
31 Remove the three screws and separate the carburettor main body and throttle body assemblies. Note the position of the insulation block for reference when reassembling. The throttle body can be renewed separately if the spindles or throttle bores are worn. Use a straight-edge to check for distorted flanges on the facing surfaces.
32 Do not disturb the adjustment of the secondary throttle angle unless absolutely necessary. The primary angle is not adjustable.

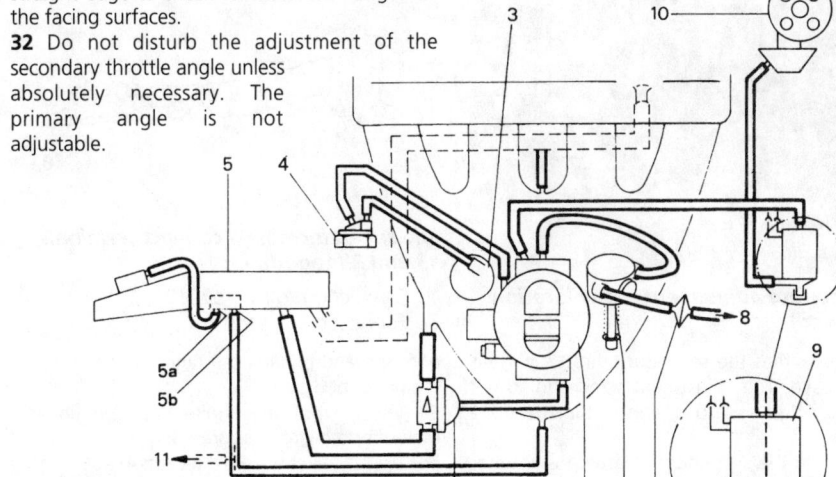

Preparation for reassembly

33 Inspect all vacuum hoses for condition and splits and renew where necessary.
34 Clean the jets, carburettor body assemblies, float chambers and internal channels. An air line may be used to clear the internal channels once the carburettor is fully dismantled. Note that if high-pressure air is directed into the channels and passages with the diaphragms still in place, diaphragm damage may result. Spraying carburettor cleaner into all the channels and passages in the carburettor body will often clear them of gum and dirt.
35 Carefully inspect and clear all the tiny air bleeds and outlets in the upper body. Trace the path of the internal channels and passages, squirt carburettor cleaner into the inlets and check that it issues from the outlets. Any blockages will interfere with proper carburettor operation.
36 During reassembly, a complete set of new gaskets should be fitted. Also renew the needle valves and float pivot pins. Inspect and renew (where necessary) the mixture screw and the jets. Renew worn linkages, springs, vacuum hoses and other parts where necessary.
37 Ensure that all jets are firmly locked into their original positions (but do not over-tighten). A loose jet can cause a rich (or even lean) running condition.
38 Clean all mating surfaces and flanges of old gasket material and reassemble with new gaskets. Ensure that housings are positioned with their air and fuel routes correctly aligned.

Reassembly

39 Assemble the main and throttle bodies with a new gasket block and secure with the three screws. Pay particular attention that the bodies are positioned with their air and fuel routes correctly aligned.
40 Refit the throttle plate actuator mounting bracket and secure with the two screws.

Vacuum connection chart

1 Carburettor
2 Throttle plate actuator
3 Diaphragm assembly - secondary throttle
4 Coolant-heated thermal valve
5 Air filter
5a Brass tube
5b Plastic tube
6 Deceleration air valve
7 Filter
8 Glovebox connection
9 Ignition switch valve (vacuum advance)
10 Ignition distributor
11 BMW 518 models only - temperature sensor in driver's compartment

41 Open the primary throttle lever, refit the throttle plate actuator assembly and secure with the three nuts.
42 Refit the throttle cable mounting bracket and secure with the four screws.
43 Refit the secondary throttle diaphragm assembly and secure with the two fixing screws. Reconnect the operating rod and the vacuum hose.

Detach throttle plate actuator

1 Three securing nuts
2 Throttle stop screw

Chapter F4

Idle mixture adjustment screw location (arrowed)

44 Check that the secondary throttle plate is fully closed. The adjustment screw should not normally be used to alter the throttle plate position.
45 Where the secondary throttle position has been disturbed and a throttle setting gauge is available, use it to set the throttle angle. Otherwise, temporarily adjust the throttle plate so that it is open just enough to prevent its seizure in the throttle body.
46 Check the secondary throttle clearances Y and Z. Refer to Section 4 for the correct procedure.
47 Refit the two main jets and the primary idle and secondary progression air and fuel jets into their original positions (do not transpose the jets).
48 Refit the idle mixture screw after renewing the small seal on the body. Turn the screw in gently until it just seats. From this position, unscrew it three full turns. This will provide a basic setting to allow the engine to be started.
49 Refit the secondary fuel supply spring, diaphragm and cover assembly, securing it with the two screws.
50 Place the fuel filter in the fuel inlet tube.
51 Insert the needle valve into the seat with the ball facing outwards. Refit the float and pivot pin.
52 Check each float level (see Section 4). Refit the float gasket to the lower body.
53 Refit the upper body to the main body and secure with the four screws and central hexagon-head bolt. Pull the choke actuating lever upwards so that the lower end of the link rod may be twisted and pushed into position. Carefully snap the top end of the rod into the plastic retainer. Preload the spring by rotating

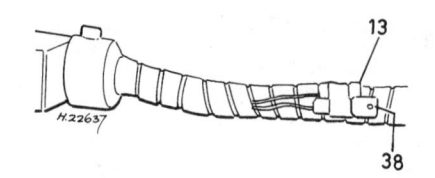

Float level checking

Idle speed increase - connect terminals 13 and 38 together

13 Connection to ECU pin 13
38 Connection to earth

one turn and engage the tang into position on the upper body.
54 Ensure that the choke flap and linkage move smoothly and progressively.
55 Adjust the choke (see Section 4).
56 Refit the carburettor to the engine.
57 Always adjust the carburettor idle mixture after any work has been carried out on the carburettor, preferably with the aid of a CO meter.

4 Service adjustments

Adjustment pre-conditions

1 Refer to Part B for general advice on the pre-conditions for correct adjustment of this carburettor.
2 Disconnect the engine breather hose from the air filter and plug the opening in the air filter.
3 Reconnect the breather hose after all adjustments are completed. If the CO level increases more than 1 to 1.5%, change the sump oil. If the CO level increases after an oil change, suspect worn or sticking piston rings. If no CO change is noted on connecting/disconnecting the breather hose, suspect a clogged crankcase breather (PCV) system.

Idle mixture (CO)

4 Run the engine at 3000 rpm for 30 seconds to clear the manifold of fuel vapours, then allow the engine to idle.
5 Check the CO level. If not as specified, remove the tamperproof plug and adjust the idle mixture screw to obtain the correct level. Turning the screw clockwise (inwards) will reduce the CO level. Turning the screw anti-clockwise (outwards) will increase the CO level *(see illustration)*.
6 Fit a new tamperproof plug to the mixture control screw on completion.

Idle speed

7 Under normal circumstances, the idle speed is controlled by the ECU and set by the throttle actuator position. It is therefore not adjustable. However, an electrical facility exists to raise the idle speed by 100 rpm. This facility may only be available on early versions of the system.
8 Connect together the two loose terminals of a plug on the wiring harness as shown *(see illustration)*. This effectively connects ECU terminal 13 to earth and should raise the idle speed as stated.

Float level

9 It is not possible to adjust the plastic float. It is possible, however, to check the level.
10 Invert the upper body so that the float faces upwards. The float needle pin must not be depressed.
11 Measure the distance between the upper body (without its gasket) and the top of the float (see Specifications) *(see illustration)*.
12 If the float level is incorrect, check the needle valve seat for correct position. Remove the float and check the float weight (see Specifications). If the float seat and weight are satisfactory, renew the float if the level is still incorrect.

Secondary throttle clearances

13 Place the throttle actuator in the deceleration position (refer to Section 5).
14 Measure the clearances 'Y' and 'Z' at their narrowest point *(see illustration)*.
15 Adjust as necessary by bending the fork '1'.

5 Component testing

Quick check of cold start and system operation

Engine cold

1 Check that the throttle is in the cold start position and that the choke flap is partially open.

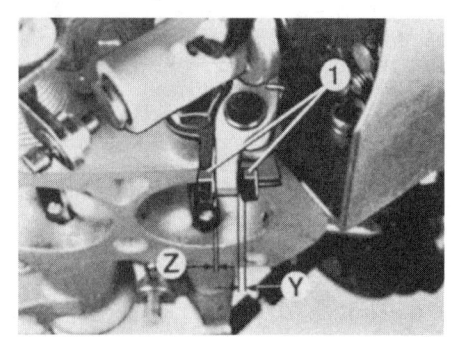

Secondary throttle clearances

1 Adjustment fork
Y = 1.3 to 1.7 mm
Z = 0.1 to 0.5 mm

27–29 mm.   29–31 mm.

F4•8

Pierburg 34/34 2BE carburettor

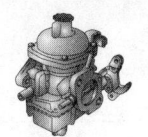

2 Switch on the ignition. The choke flap should assume its cold start position according to temperature.

3 Start the engine and allow it to warm-up. The choke flap and throttle actuator should assume positions that allow for a fast idle and for the engine to run satisfactorily.

Engine hot

4 Test the deceleration valve.

5 Blip the throttle. The choke flap should move towards the closed position then return.

6 Switch off the ignition. The throttle actuator should fully retract as the engine cuts and then fully extend to the cold start position.

7 Restart the engine. The throttle actuator should retract slightly and assume the hot idle position.

8 Check the idle CO level.

9 If all operations are satisfactory, the system is functioning correctly. Otherwise, make the following electrical tests and checks as necessary.

Component resistance tests - general

10 During resistance tests with an ohmmeter, always ensure that the ignition is off and that the circuit being tested is isolated from a voltage supply. To avoid damage to sensitive components, resistance tests should not be made at the ECU pins but only at the ECU multi-plug.

11 In the following resistance tests, the following general test procedure should be followed:

12 Remove the electrical plug to the component being tested.

13 Check the connection for corrosion and ensure that the pins make good contact.

14 Connect an ohmmeter across the specified terminals of the plug connection leading to the component *(see illustration)*.

15 If the relevant test results cannot be obtained, renew the component.

16 Reconnect the electrical plug to the component being tested.

17 Ensure that the ignition switch is off.

18 Remove the multi-plug from the ECU.

19 Connect an ohmmeter across the multi-plug terminals that lead to the component (the relevant ECU terminals are listed in the following component tests).

20 If a component is within specification when tested at the plug terminals, yet out of specification when tested at the ECU, use an ohmmeter to check for wiring continuity between the component and ECU. Note that resistances which are slightly out of specification do not always signify a fault. Open-circuits, short-circuits, or very high or low resistances are more indicative of a fault condition.

Idle switch
See Table 1 and illustrations.

Temperature sensor
See Table 2 and illustrations.

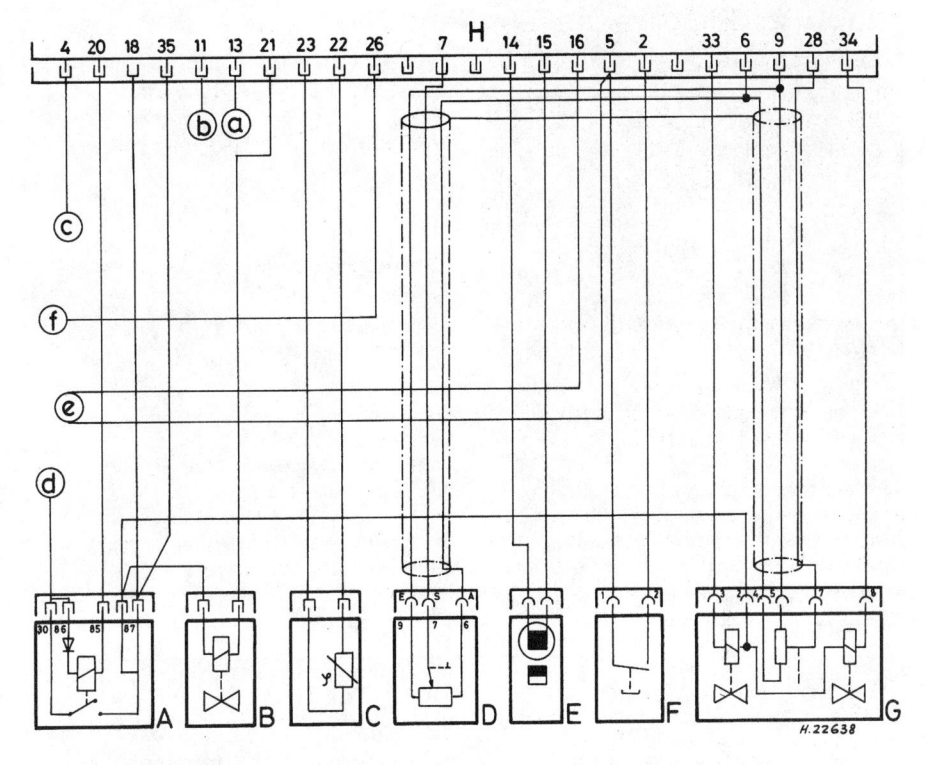

System wiring diagram

- 1 to 35 ECU pins
- A Carburettor system relay
- B Ignition control relay
- C Temperature sensor in inlet manifold
- D Throttle potentiometer
- E Choke flap actuator
- F Idle switch
- G Throttle plate actuator
- H ECU
- a Idle speed booster (when connected to earth)
- b Fuel economy control
- c Ignition switch voltage supply (terminal 15)
- d Constant nominal battery supply (live at all times)
- e Earth connection
- f Ignition control unit (terminal TD)

Table 1: Idle switch test

Condition	Test result (ohms)	ECU multi-plug terminals
Switch open (throttle lever in rest position)	Infinity	2 & 5
Switch closed (throttle lever open)	0 to 15	2 & 5

Checking idle switch resistance
1 Idle switch plug
2 Idle switch
3 Throttle lever

Idle switch connector plug, showing ECU pin numbers

Chapter F4

Table 2: Temperature sensor test

Condition	Test result (ohms)	ECU multi-plug terminals
Manifold temperature 20°C	2000 to 3000	22 & 23
Manifold temperature 80°C	280 to 360	22 & 23

Remove electrical plug (arrowed) and measure temperature sensor resistance across terminals

Temperature sensor connector plug, showing ECU pin numbers

Table 3: Throttle plate potentiometer test

Condition	Pot terminals	Test result (ohms)	ECU multi-plug terminals
Throttle closed	A & E	1400 to 2600	6 & 9
Minimum	A & S	Less than 250	6 & 7
Maximum	A & S	1300 to 2500	6 & 7

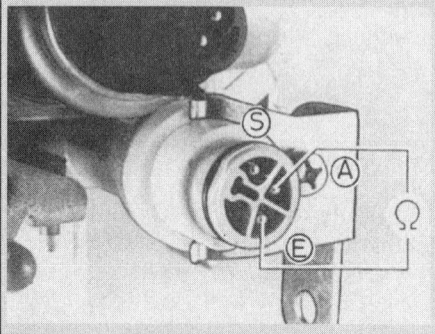

Measuring throttle potentiometer resistance

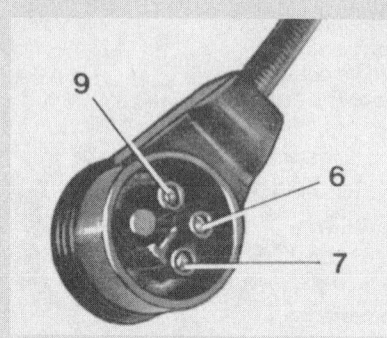

Throttle potentiometer connector plug, showing ECU pin numbers

Measuring choke plate actuator resistance

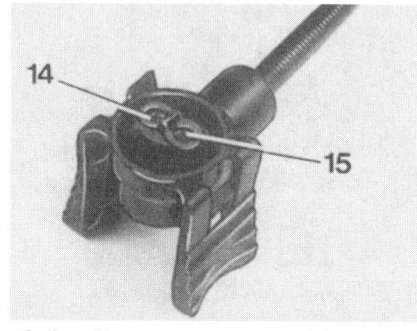

Choke plate actuator connector plug, showing ECU pin numbers

Refitting throttle potentiometer
1 Plastic coupling
2 Locking slots must be engaged

Throttle plate potentiometer

See Table 3 and illustrations.
21 Place the throttle actuator in deceleration mode (totally withdrawn).
22 Measure the resistance with the throttle closed. The resistance should correspond to the minimum figure. Slowly open the throttle. The resistance should gradually increase until it corresponds to the maximum figure.
23 Attempt to rock the throttle pot. The reading should not waver. If necessary, bend the fixing bracket so that the pot is held more firmly.

Potentiometer renewal

24 Remove the one screw and withdraw the potentiometer. Detach the fixing bracket from the pot body.
25 Remove the plastic coupling piece and inspect the locating slots for damage.
26 Refit the coupling and potentiometer. Ensure that the pot and coupling are correctly located. Attach the fixing bracket, locate the tang in position on the pot body and secure with the one screw *(see illustration)*.
27 Recheck the resistances as described previously.

Choke plate actuator

See illustrations below left.

ECU multi-plug terminals	Test result
14 & 15	0.9 to 1.7 ohms
14 & Earth	Infinity
15 & Earth	Infinity

28 Check the free movement of the choke flap actuator and linkage *(see illustration)*. Push the choke flap towards the closed position. The choke flap and linkage should move easily and freely and should spring back to the open position once released. If not, check the choke flap, spindle, idle needle and choke actuator lever. If the actuator movement is tight, renew the actuator. Operation of the choke plate actuator can be tested using Pierburg tool 4.07360.07 *(see illustration)*.

Actuator renewal

29 Remove the four screws, detach the fixing bracket and withdraw the actuator from the link rod.
30 Push the new actuator into the housing and

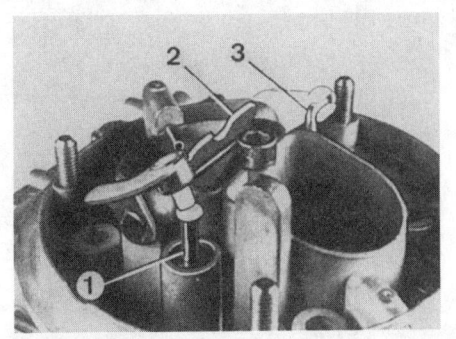

Pierburg 34/34 2BE carburettor

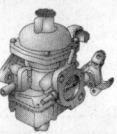

Choke flap mechanism
1 Idle air correction needle
2 Choke flap
3 Link rod

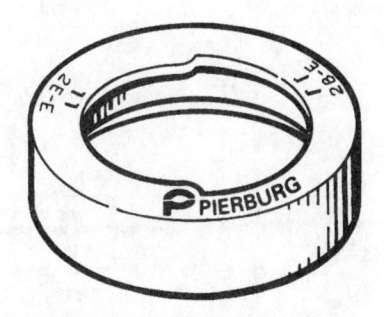

Pierburg test tool 4.07360.07

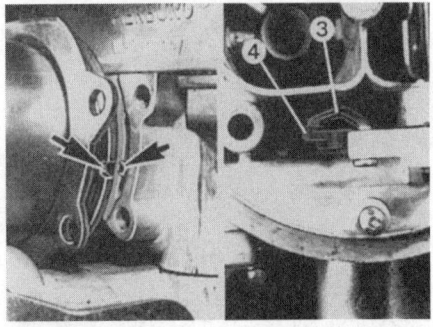

Choke flap actuator position during fitting
3 Link rod
4 Actuator lever

Arrows indicate correct actuator locking pin and cut-out positions

reconnect the link rod. Ensure that the cut-out on the actuator locates into the pin on the carburettor body and the actuator lever is correctly positioned *(see illustration)*. Refit the fixing bracket and secure with the four screws.

Throttle plate actuator

31 Ensure that a voltage supply is not connected to terminals 4, 5 and 7 during the following tests. Connect an ohmmeter across terminals 4 and 7 of the actuator connection *(see illustration)*. The ohmmeter should register a resistance in the range 900 to 1500 ohms. Note the reading.
32 Connect a vacuum pump to the evacuating valve.
33 Connect a battery voltage supply (with a 5 amp fuse) to terminal 2.
34 Complete the circuit by connecting an earth to terminal 3. The actuator motor will click.
35 Operate the vacuum pump until the resistance reading reduces to between 500 and 700 ohms and note the reading. The actuator plunger will activate and partially withdraw.
36 Disconnect, in turn, the earth and voltage supply from terminals 3 and 2 and the vacuum pump.
37 The resistance reading registered in paragraph 35 should not increase by more than 200 ohms in one minute.
38 Reconnect the fused battery voltage supply to terminal 2.
39 Complete the circuit by connecting an earth to terminal 8. The actuator plunger should fully extend downwards within one second.
40 If the plunger does not extend, clean or renew the ventilating filter and the filter in the vent hose. If the filters are satisfactory, renew the actuator assembly.
41 Repeat paragraphs 31 to 34. Slowly operate the vacuum pump until the plunger is completely withdrawn (deceleration position). The resistance should progressively fall to register a reading that is less than 500 ohms.

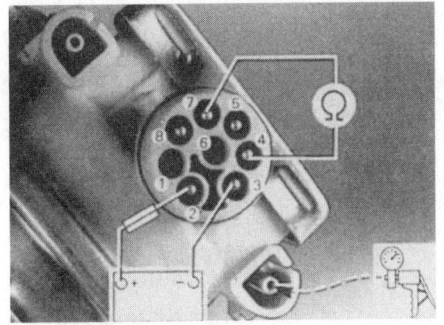

42 Remove the earth, voltage supply and vacuum pump.
43 Carry out the resistance tests, shown in table 4, at the terminals of the throttle plate actuator *(see illustration)*.
44 Renew the throttle actuator if it fails any test.

Ventilating filter cleaning

45 Screw an M4 screw into the thread on the actuator housing as shown *(see illustration)* then withdraw the cover.
46 Remove the filter. Clean the filter and its housing.
47 Refit the filter, ensuring that the wide edge is inserted first.

Non-return valve renewal

48 Screw an M4 screw into the thread on the actuator housing as shown *(see illustration)* then withdraw the cover.
49 Remove the non-return valve assembly.
50 Refit the assembly in the correct order.

Testing throttle plate actuator

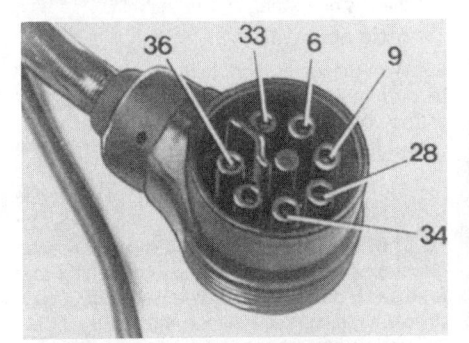

Throttle actuator connector plug, showing ECU and source pin numbers
36 Connection to carburettor control relay

Table 4: Throttle plate actuator test

Test	Terminals	Test result	Terminals
Evacuating valve	2 & 3	35 to 80 ohms	-
Ventilating valve	2 & 8	35 to 80 ohms	-
Potentiometer total	4 & 5	1400 to 2600 ohms	6 & 9

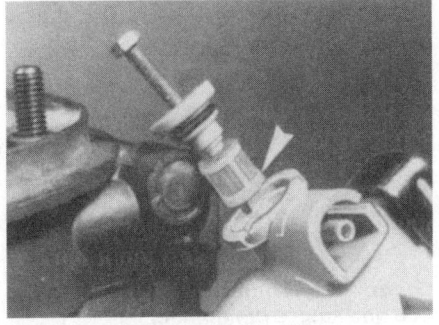

Renewing the ventilating filter

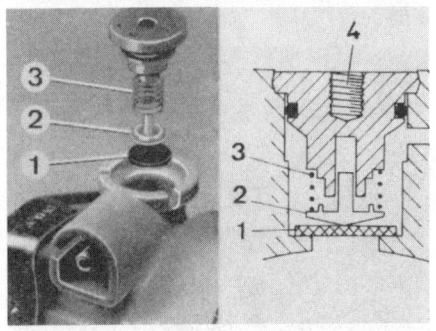

Renewing the non-return valve
1 Valve plate
2 Guide
3 Valve spring
4 M4 screw thread

F4•11

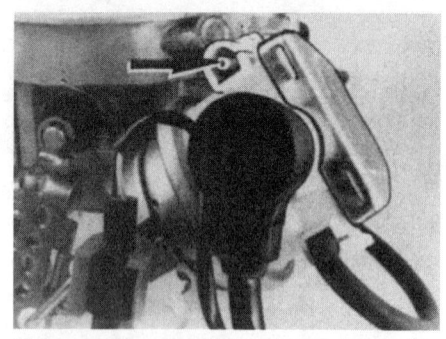

Chapter F4

Plug vent (arrowed) to place actuator in deceleration position

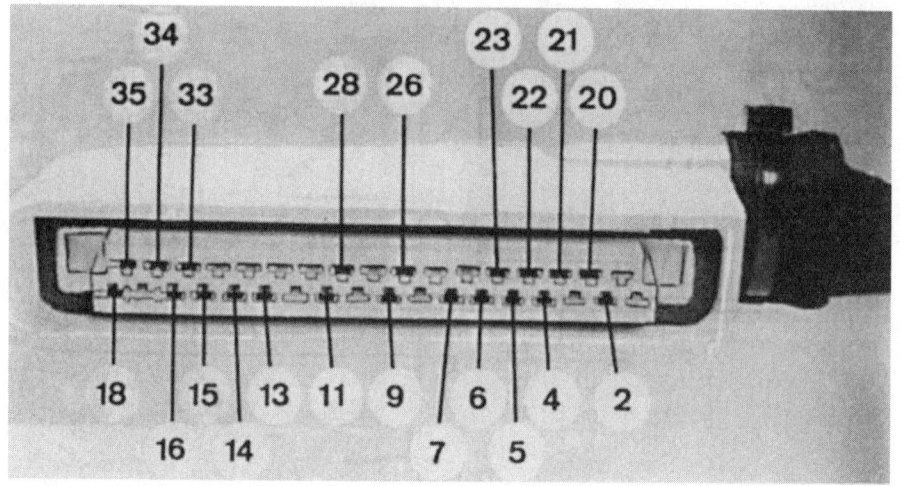

ECU multi-plug pin positions

Placing throttle plate actuator in deceleration position

51 If the carburettor is removed, a method of placing the throttle actuator in the deceleration position is described under throttle plate actuator testing (paragraph 41).

52 If the carburettor is installed, plug the actuator vent shown *(see illustration)* and allow the engine to idle. Switch off the ignition and the actuator should remain in the deceleration position.

Component voltage tests - general

53 Switch the ignition on for all voltage tests. Avoid component damage by switching the ignition off when making or breaking electrical connections (particularly at the ECU multi-plug) *(see illustration)*.

Using a variable potentiometer to simulate engine at running temperature

At 330 ohms resistance, voltage obtained is 0.6 volts

Location of carburettor control relay on nearside front wing

54 When carrying out the following voltage tests, connect the voltmeter negative probe to a good earth. Touch the terminal under test with the positive probe.

Temperature sensor

55 Probe the voltage supply terminal. At a manifold temperature of 20°C, the voltage obtained should be 2.0 to 2.5 volts.

56 Run the engine. As the engine warms up, the voltage should fall. This indicates correct operation of the temperature sensor.

57 At a manifold temperature of 80°C, the voltage obtained should be 0.6 to 0.8 volts.

58 Probe the earth terminal (engine running). A maximum of 0.5 volts should be obtained.

59 A variable potentiometer can be connected to the terminal connection in place of the temperature sensor *(see illustration)*. Various resistances (and therefore temperatures) can then be simulated and the ECU response evaluated by movement of the choke flap.

60 With the engine running, disconnect the sensor plug. An open-circuit (very high resistance) signal will be returned to the ECU, which will simulate very cold running. The choke flap should close.

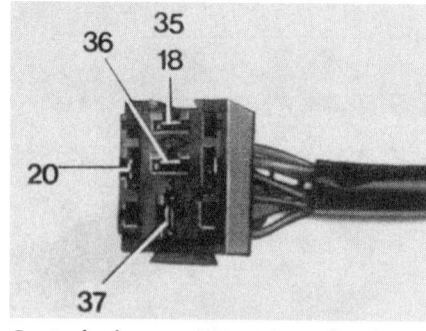

Control relay connector plug, showing ECU and source pin numbers

36 Connection to throttle actuator and ignition control relay
37 Connection to live battery voltage

61 Still with the engine running, disconnect the sensor plug and use a jumper wire to connect the two terminals together. A very low resistance signal will be returned to the ECU, which will simulate very hot running. The choke flap should open.

Carburettor control relay

62 A single relay is used to control the power supply to the 2BE carburettor and its ECU. This relay is located on the nearside front wing *(see illustration)*.

63 If the carburettor electrical controls have ceased functioning, check for the following voltages at the relay terminals:

Terminal	Test result
30	A constant nominal battery voltage
86	A constant nominal battery voltage
85	A maximum of 0.5 volts should be obtained at the earth connection (made through terminal 20 at the ECU) *(see illustration)*
87	Ignition on - battery voltage. These two terminals supply voltage to ECU terminals 18 and 35, and terminal 2 of the throttle actuator

64 The terminal numbers are marked upon the relay. If all relay input voltages are satisfactory but there is no output, renew the relay.

Throttle actuator

65 With the ignition on, battery voltage should be present at terminal 2. If there is no voltage, or the voltage is low, check the control relay output from terminal 87 of the relay.

Carburettor ECU

66 The ECU may be located behind the glovebox on the passenger's side or behind the facia panel on the driver's side *(see illustration)*. Unscrew the four screws and remove the ECU. Pull back the retainer and detach the multi-plug. A voltmeter or ohmmeter can now be used to measure voltages or resistances at the pins on the multi-plug. Be careful not to bend the pins

Pierburg 34/34 2BE carburettor

One possible ECU location - under driver's side facia panel

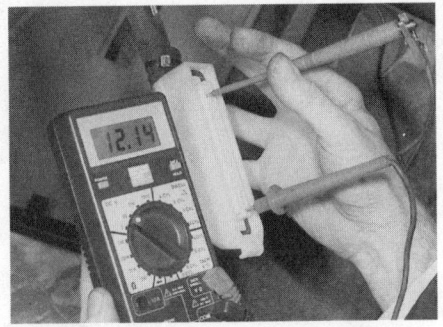

Testing carburettor ECU
Upper probe - terminal 20 to earth
Lower probe - in pin for terminal 18
Control relay output voltage can be measured at ECU terminals 18 & 35

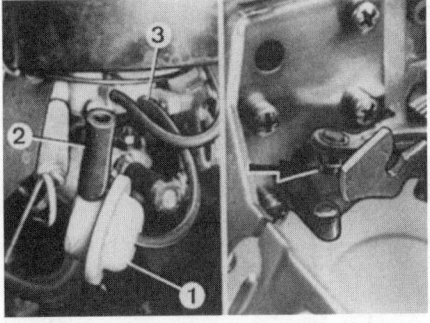

Testing deceleration air valve
1 Deceleration air valve
2 Hose to air filter
3 Vacuum connection to carburettor
Arrow shows throttle stop screw in deceleration position

on the multi-plug when probing for voltages or resistances *(see illustration)*.

Terminal	Test result
18 & 35	Ignition on - battery voltage (see note, paragraph 67). If voltage is low or zero, check relay output from terminal 87
4	Ignition on - battery voltage. If voltage is low or zero, check the supply back to the ignition switch
5 & 20	Earth connections - connect voltmeter (+) connection to each terminal and crank or run the engine. Less than 0.5 volts should register on the meter.

67 Note that ECU terminals 18 & 35 receive the voltage output from terminal 87 of the control relay. Voltage will only be obtained at these terminals when the relay is activated. Activate the relay by using a jumper lead to connect ECU terminal 20 to earth.

Deceleration air valve

68 Disconnect the hose from the air filter to the deceleration valve *(see illustration)*.
69 Raise the engine speed to over 3000 rpm and place your thumb over the disconnected hose end.
70 Release the throttle. The throttle actuator will fully withdraw into the deceleration position and a vacuum draw should be felt on your thumb.
71 As the engine speed falls below 1400 rpm, the throttle actuator will extend and the vacuum draw will disappear.
72 If no vacuum draw is felt but the throttle actuator performs correctly, check the vacuum pipe from the carburettor to the deceleration valve. A vacuum signal should be obtained on this hose when the throttle actuator is totally withdrawn. If a vacuum signal is now available, renew the deceleration valve. If not, check the carburettor connection for a blockage.
73 If the throttle actuator is not withdrawing, carry out the throttle actuator tests above.

Coolant-heated thermal valve

74 Refer to Part D for general tests on the thermal valve fitted to the secondary throttle.
75 Below 20°C, high vacuum should be registered on a vacuum gauge (valve closed). Note that a slight leakage is built into the valve. A vacuum reading will therefore be maintained for only a short period of time when the valve is cold *(see illustration)*.
76 Above that temperature, a zero-vacuum reading should be obtained (valve open).
77 If the valve does not function in accordance with the above, renew it.

6 Fault diagnosis

Refer to Part D for diagnosis of general carburettor faults. The following faults are specific to the 2BE carburettor.

Poor cold running
- [ ] Sticking choke flap.
- [ ] Broken choke flap lever.
- [ ] Failure of inlet manifold pre-heater.
- [ ] Defective throttle actuator.

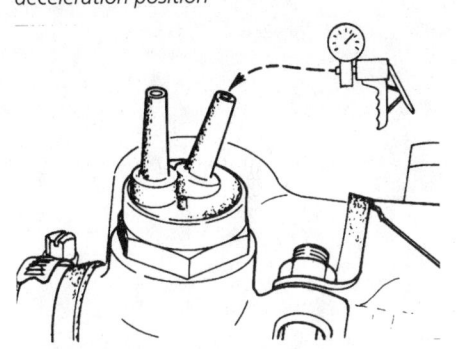

Use a vacuum pump to pull vacuum through thermal valve

Heavy fuel consumption
- [ ] Broken idle air corrector needle spring.
- [ ] Worn idle air corrector.

Hesitation
- [ ] Worn secondary throttle shaft.
- [ ] Check for wear on plastic lever and rocker.

Uneven running
- [ ] Loose throttle potentiometer - check mounting plate for tightness.
- [ ] Sticking choke flap.
- [ ] Broken choke flap lever.

Lack of power
- [ ] Failure of secondary throttle plate diaphragm.
- [ ] Failure of secondary diaphragm coolant-heated thermal switch.
- [ ] Loose secondary needle valve seat, allowing float to drop, causing fuel starvation in secondary fuel system.
- [ ] Defective secondary fuel cut-off valve assembly.

Notes

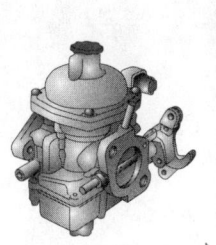

Part F Chapter 5
Pierburg 28/30 2E2 carburettor

F5

Contents

Component testing 5
Fault diagnosis 6
General servicing 3
Identification 2
Principles of operation 1
Service adjustments 4

Specifications

Manufacturer	Audi	Audi	Audi
Model	80 1.6 CL	80 1.6 CL	80 GL & Coupe 1.8
Year	1983 to 1986	1983 to 1986	1983 to 1986
Engine code	DT (55kW) SOHC	DT (55kW) SOHC	DS/NE (66kW) SOHC
Capacity (cm³)/no. of cyls	1595/4	1595/4	1781/4
Oil temperature (°C)	80	80	80
Transmission	MT	AT	MT
Carb. identification	026 129 015 T	026 129 016 F	026 129 015
Idle speed (rpm)	750 ± 50	750 ± 50	750 ± 50
Fast idle speed (rpm)	3000 ± 200	3000 ± 200	3000 ± 200
CO @ idle (% vol.)	1.0 ± 0.5	1.0 ± 0.5	1.0 ± 0.5
Stage (venturi)	1 2	1 2	1 2
Venturi diameter (K)	22 26	22 26	22 26
Main jet (Gg)	107.5 127.5	107.5 127.5	105 120
Air correction jet (a)	80 105	80 105	100 100
Basic throttle position (mm)	0.5 0.08 ± 0.02	0.6 0.08 ± 0.02	0.5 0.08 ± 0.02
Idle jet (g)	42.5	42.5	40
Accelerator pump jet (i)	35	50	35
Float level (mm)	27.5 ± 1.0	27.5 ± 1.0	27.5 ± 1.0
Needle valve (mm) (P)	2.5	2.5	2.5
Float weight (grams)	8.3 ± 0.3	8.3 ± 0.3	8.3 ± 0.3
Choke pull-down (mm) (a)	2.6 ± 0.2	2.9 ± 0.2	2.6 ± 0.2
Choke pull-down (mm) ('a1')	5.0 ± 0.15	6.0 ± 0.15	4.9 ± 0.15
De-choke (mm)	5.0 ± 0.5	5.0 ± 0.5	5.0 ± 0.5

Chapter F5

Manufacturer	Audi	Audi	Volkswagen
Model	80 GL & Coupe 1.8	100 & Avant 1.8	Golf/Jetta/Scirocco 1.6
Year	1983 to 1986	1983 to 1987	1983 to 1992
Engine code	DS/NE (66kW) SOHC	DS (66kW) SOHC	EW/EZ (55kW)
Capacity (cm^3)/no. of cyls	1781/4	1781/4	1595/4
Oil temperature (°C)	80	80	80
Transmission	AT	-	MT
Carb. identification	026 129 015 A	026 129 016 A	027 129 015 G
Idle speed (rpm)	750 ± 50	750 ± 50	750 ± 50
Fast idle speed (rpm)	3000 ± 200	3000 ± 200	3000 ± 200
CO @ idle (% vol.)	1.0 ± 0.5	1.0 ± 0.5	1.0 ± 0.5
Stage (venturi)	1 2	1 2	1 2
Venturi diameter (K)	22 26	22 26	22 26
Main jet (Gg)	105 120	105 120	110 127.5
Air correction jet (a)	105 100	100 100	90 105
Basic throttle position (mm)	0.6 0.08 ± 0.02	0.5 0.08 ± 0.02	0.5 0.08 ± 0.02
Accelerator pump jet (i)	50	35 50	50
Idle jet (g)	42.5	40	42.5
Float level (mm)	27.5 ± 1.0	27.5 ± 1.0	27.5 ± 1.0
Needle valve (mm) (P)	2.5	2.5	2.5
Float weight (grams)	8.3 ± 0.3	8.3 ± 0.3	8.3 ± 0.3
Choke pull-down (mm) (a)	2.7 ± 0.2	2.6 ± 0.2	2.8 ± 0.2
Choke pull-down (mm) ('a1')	5.1 ± 0.15	4.9 ± 0.15	5.6 ± 0.15
De-choke (mm)	4.5 ± 0.5	5.0 ± 0.5	5.0 ± 0.5

Manufacturer	Volkswagen	Volkswagen	Volkswagen
Model	Golf/Jetta 1.6	Scirocco 1.6	Caddy 1.6
Year	1983 to 1992	1983 to 1992	1983 to 1992
Engine code	EW/EZ (55kW)	EW (55kW)	EW (55kW)
Capacity (cm^3)/no. of cyls	1595/4	1595/4	1595/4
Oil temperature (°C)	80	80	80
Transmission	AT	AT	-
Carb. identification	027 129 016 G	026 129 016 F	027 129 015 G
Idle speed (rpm)	750 ± 50	750 ± 50	950 ± 50
Fast idle speed (rpm)	3000 ± 200	3000 ± 200	3000 ± 200
CO @ idle (% vol.)	1.0 ± 0.5	1.0 ± 0.5	1.0 ± 0.5
Stage (venturi)	1 2	1 2	1 2
Venturi diameter (K)	22 26	22 26	22 26
Main jet (Gg)	110 127.5	107.5 127.5	110 127.5
Air correction jet (a)	105 105	80 105	90 105
Basic throttle position (mm)	0.6 0.08 ± 0.02	0.6 0.08 ± 0.02	0.5 0.08 ± 0.02
Float level (mm)	27.5 ± 1.0	27.5 ± 1.0	27.5 ± 1.0
Idle jet (g)	42.5	42.5	42.5
Accelerator pump jet (i)	50	50	50
Needle valve (mm) (P)	2.5	2.5	2.5
Float weight (grams)	8.3 ± 0.3	8.3 ± 0.3	8.3 ± 0.3
Choke pull-down (mm) (a)	2.9 ± 0.2	2.9 ± 0.2	2.8 ± 0.2
Choke pull-down (mm) ('a1')	6.0 ± 0.15	6.0 ± 0.15	5.6 ± 0.15
De-choke (mm)	5.0 ± 0.5	5.0 ± 0.5	5.0 ± 0.5

Pierburg 28/30 2E2 carburettor

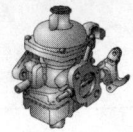

Manufacturer	Volkswagen	Volkswagen	Volkswagen
Model	Golf/Jetta 1.6 Cat.	Golf/Jetta 1.6 Cat.	Golf Cabrio/Scirocco 1.8
Year	1986 to 1992	1986 to 1992	1983 to 1992
Engine code	RF (53kW)	RF (53kW)	EXZ (66kW)
Capacity (cm³)/no. of cyls	1595/4	1595/4	1781/4
Oil temperature (°C)	80	80	80
Transmission	MT	AT	MT
Carb. identification	027 129 016 H	027 129 016 P	027 129 015
Idle speed (rpm)	750 ± 50	750 ± 50	750 ± 50
Fast idle speed (rpm)	3000 ± 200	3000 ± 200	3000 ± 200
CO @ idle (% vol.)	0.5 to 1.0	0.5 to 1.0	1.0 ± 0.5
Stage (venturi)	1 2	1 2	1 2
Venturi diameter (K)	22 26	22 26	22 26
Main jet (Gg)	102.5 127.5	102.5 127.5	105 120
Air correction jet (a)	100 105	100 105	105 100
Basic throttle position (mm)	0.5 0.08 ± 0.02	0.6 0.08 ± 0.02	0.5 0.08 ± 0.02
Idle jet (g)	42.5	42.5	42.5
Accelerator pump jet (i)	50	50	35
Float level (mm)	27.5 ± 1.0	27.5 ± 1.0	27.5 ± 1.0
Needle valve (mm) (P)	2.5	2.5	2.5
Float weight (grams)	8.3 ± 0.3	8.3 ± 0.3	8.3 ± 0.3
Choke pull-down (mm) (a)	2.5 ± 0.2	2.9 ± 0.2	2.5 ± 0.2
Choke pull-down (mm) ('a1')	5.0 ± 0.15	4.8 ± 0.15	4.9 ± 0.15
De-choke (mm)	5.0 ± 0.5	5.0 ± 0.5	5.0 ± 0.5

Manufacturer	Volkswagen	Volkswagen	Volkswagen
Model	Golf/Jetta/Synchro 1.8	Golf/Jetta/Synchro 1.8	Scirocco 1.8
Year	1984 to 1992	1984 to 1992	1986 to 1992
Engine code	GU (66kW)	GU (66kW)	EXZ (66kW)
Capacity (cm³)/no. of cyls	1781/4	1781/4	1781/4
Oil temperature (°C)	80	80	80
Transmission	MT	AT	AT
Carb. identification	027 129 015	027 129 015 Q	027 129 015 A
Idle speed (rpm)	950 ± 50 (to 85) 750 ± 50 (85 on)	950 ± 50	950 ± 50
Fast idle speed (rpm)	3000 ± 200	3000 ± 200	3000 ± 200
CO @ idle (% vol.)	1.0 ± 0.5	1.0 ± 0.5	1.5 ± 0.5
Stage (venturi)	1 2	1 2	1 2
Venturi diameter (K)	22 26	22 26	22 26
Main jet (Gg)	105 120	105 120	105 122
Air correction jet (a)	105 100	105 100	105 100
Basic throttle position (mm)	0.5 0.08 ± 0.02	0.6 0.08 ± 0.02	0.6 0.08 ± 0.02

Model	Golf/Jetta/Synchro 1.8	Golf/Jetta/Synchro 1.8	Scirocco 1.8
Year	1984 to 1992	1984 to 1992	1986 to 1992
Engine code	GU (66kW)	GU (66kW)	EXZ (66kW)
Idle jet (g)	42.5	42.5	42.5
Accelerator pump jet (i)	35	35	50
Float level (mm)	27.5 ± 1.0	27.5 ± 1.0	27.5 ± 1.0
Needle valve (mm) (P)	2.5	2.5	2.5
Float weight (grams)	8.3 ± 0.3	8.3 ± 0.3	8.3 ± 0.3
Choke pull-down (mm) (a)	2.5 ± 0.2	2.3 ± 0.2	2.7 ± 0.2
Choke pull-down (mm) ('a1')	4.9 ± 0.15	4.7 ± 0.15	5.1 ± 0.15
De-choke (mm)	5.0 ± 0.5	4.5 ± 0.5	4.5 ± 0.5

Chapter F5

Manufacturer	Volkswagen		Volkswagen		Volkswagen	
Model	Golf/Jetta 1.8 Cat.		Golf/Jetta 1.8 Cat.		Passat 1.6	
Year	1986 to 1992		1986 to 1992		1983 to 1988	
Engine code	RH (62kW)		RH (62kW)		DT (55kW)	
Capacity (cm³)/no. of cyls	1781/4		1781/4		1595/4	
Oil temperature (°C)	80		80		80	
Transmission	MT		AT		MT	
Carb. identification	027 129 016 Q		027 129 016 R		026 129 015 T	
Idle speed (rpm)	750 ± 75		750 ± 75		750 ± 50	
Fast idle speed (rpm)	3000 ± 200		3000 ± 200		3000 ± 50	
CO @ idle (% vol.)	1.0 ± 0.5		1.0 ± 0.5		1.0 ± 0.5	
Stage (venturi)	1	2	1	2	1	2
Venturi diameter (K)	22	26	22	26	22	26
Main jet (Gg)	102.5	125	102.5	125	107.5	127.5
Air correction jet (a)	105	100	105	100	80	105
Basic throttle position (mm)	0.5	0.08 ± 0.02	0.5	0.08 ± 0.02	0.5	0.08 ± 0.02
Idle jet (g)	42.5		42.5		42.5	
Accelerator pump jet (i)	30		30		35	
Float level (mm)	27.5 ± 1.0		27.5 ± 1.0		27.5 ± 0.5	
Needle valve (mm) (P)	2.5		2.5		2.5	
Float weight (grams)	8.3 ± 0.3		8.3 ± 0.3		8.3 ± 0.3	
Choke pull-down (mm) (a)	2.1 ± 0.2		2.1 ± 0.2		2.6 ± 0.2	
Choke pull-down (mm) ('a1')	4.4 ± 0.15		4.4 ± 0.15		5.0 ± 0.15	
De-choke (mm)	4.0 ± 0.5		4.0 ± 0.5		5.0 ± 0.5	

Manufacturer	Volkswagen		Volkswagen		Volkswagen	
Model	Passat 1.6		Passat 1.8		Passat 1.8	
Year	1983 to 1988		1983 to 1988		1983 to 1988	
Engine code	DT (55kW)		DS (66kW)		DS (66kW)	
Capacity (cm³)/no. of cyls	1595/4		1781/4		1781/4	
Oil temperature (°C)	80		80		80	
Transmission	AT		MT		AT	
Carb. identification	026 129 016 F		026 129 015		026 129 015 A	
Idle speed (rpm)	750 ± 50		750 ± 50		750 ± 50	
Fast idle speed (rpm)	3000 ± 50		3000 ± 50		3000 ± 50	
CO @ idle (% vol.)	1.0 ± 0.5		1.0 ± 0.5		1.0 ± 0.5	
Stage (venturi)	1	2	1	2	1	2
Venturi diameter (K)	22	26	22	26	22	26
Main jet (Gg)	107.5	127.5	105	120	105	120
Air correction jet (a)	80	105	100	100	105	100
Basic throttle position (mm)	0.6	0.08 ± 0.02	0.5	0.8 ± 0.02	0.6	0.8 ± 0.02
Idle jet (g)	42.5		40		42.5	
Accelerator pump jet (i)	35		35		35	
Float level (mm)	27.5 ± 0.5		27.5 ± 1.0		27.5 ± 1.0	
Needle valve (mm) (P)	2.5		2.5		2.5	
Float weight (grams)	8.3 ± 0.3		8.3 ± 0.3		8.3 ± 0.3	
Choke pull-down (mm) (a)	2.9 ± 0.2		2.6 ± 0.2		2.7 ± 0.2	
Choke pull-down (mm) (a1)	6.0 ± 0.15		4.9 ± 0.15		5.1 ± 0.15	
De-choke (mm)	5.0 ± 0.5		5.0 ± 0.5		4.5 ± 0.5	

1 Principles of operation

Introduction

1 The following technical description of the Pierburg 28/30 2E2 carburettor should be read in conjunction with the more detailed description of carburettor principles in Part A.

Construction

2 The Pierburg 2E2 carburettor is a down-draught progressive twin venturi instrument with a vacuum-controlled secondary throttle (see illustration). The throttle shafts are made of steel, while the throttle plates, all jets and the emulsion tube are manufactured from brass. The internal fuel channels and air passages are drilled and sealed with lead plugs, where necessary. The choke system is fully automatic in operation (acting on the primary venturi) and also controls the idle speed. The choke strangler flap is controlled by a bi-metal coil that is heated by both an electrical supply and the engine coolant. Major body components are cast in light alloy.

3 Most versions of the 2E2 carburettor operate in conjunction with an electrical heater fitted to the inlet manifold. The purpose of the heater is to improve atomisation of the air/fuel mixture during the warm-up period. A thermal switch is usually wired to the supply voltage so that the heater is switched off at a pre-determined temperature. Some versions also use a throttle body heater to prevent carburettor icing. Both heaters function on the positive temperature coefficient (PTC) principle. As the temperature rises, the heater resistance also rises.

Fuel control

4 Fuel flows into the carburettor through a fine mesh filter located in the fuel inlet connection. The fuel level in the float chamber is controlled

Pierburg 28/30 2E2 carburettor

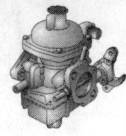

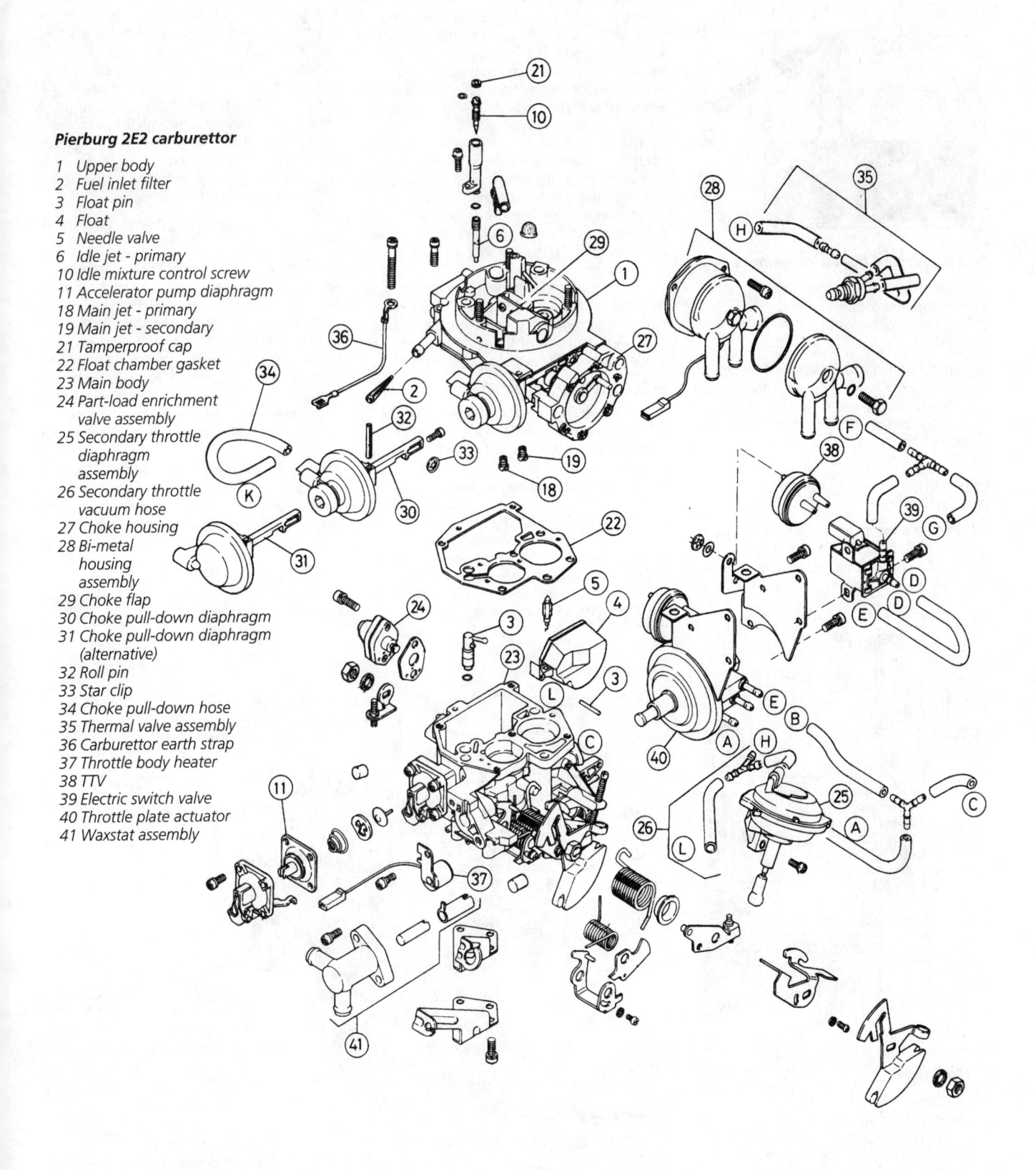

Pierburg 2E2 carburettor

1. Upper body
2. Fuel inlet filter
3. Float pin
4. Float
5. Needle valve
6. Idle jet - primary
10. Idle mixture control screw
11. Accelerator pump diaphragm
18. Main jet - primary
19. Main jet - secondary
21. Tamperproof cap
22. Float chamber gasket
23. Main body
24. Part-load enrichment valve assembly
25. Secondary throttle diaphragm assembly
26. Secondary throttle vacuum hose
27. Choke housing
28. Bi-metal housing assembly
29. Choke flap
30. Choke pull-down diaphragm
31. Choke pull-down diaphragm (alternative)
32. Roll pin
33. Star clip
34. Choke pull-down hose
35. Thermal valve assembly
36. Carburettor earth strap
37. Throttle body heater
38. TTV
39. Electric switch valve
40. Throttle plate actuator
41. Waxstat assembly

F5•5

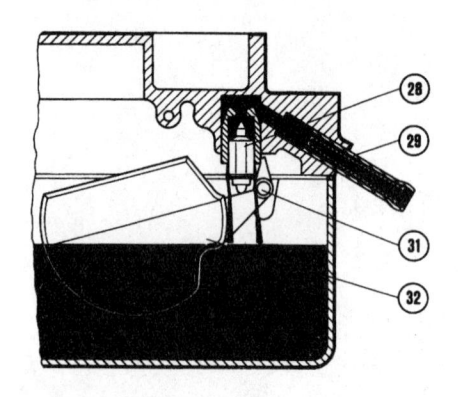

Chapter F5

mixed with air, drawn in through the calibrated air corrector and the holes in the tube, to form an emulsion. The resulting mixture is drawn through a channel to be discharged from the idle orifice under the primary throttle plate. A tapered air control screw, positioned in the air supply passage to the idle jet, is used to vary the emulsion and this ensures fine control of the idle mixture *(see illustration)*.

6 A progression slot provides a further air contribution to the emulsion while the throttle is closed. As the progression slot is uncovered by the opening throttle, the vacuum draw overcomes the air bleed into the slot and a reversal occurs. Fuel is now drawn out to add extra enrichment to the idle mixture during initial acceleration.

7 The idle speed is controlled by a throttle plate actuator and can be adjusted (within certain limits) by a regulating valve on the actuator body. A description of the operating principles of the throttle plate actuator is given below.

Accelerator pump

8 The accelerator pump is controlled by a diaphragm and is mechanically operated by a lever and cam attached to the primary throttle linkage. The outlet valve consists of a ball incorporated into the pump outlet injector. The inlet valve consists of an inlet seal located in a channel from the float chamber. Excess fuel is returned to the float chamber through an additional channel and calibrated bush. The pump is designed to operate only when the throttle is less than half-open and it discharges into the primary venturi *(see illustration)*.

Main circuit

9 The amount of fuel discharged into the airstream is controlled by a calibrated main jet. Fuel is drawn through the jet, into the base of a vertical well which dips down into the fuel in the float chamber. A combined emulsion tube and air correction jet is placed in the well. The fuel is mixed with air, drawn in through the calibrated air correction jet and the holes in the emulsion tubes, to form an air/fuel emulsion. The resulting mixture is discharged from the main nozzle, through an auxiliary venturi, into the main airstream.

Part-load enrichment (power valve)

10 Fuel flows from the float chamber into the enrichment chamber through a fuel channel. An air passage is taken from under the throttle plate to the cover of the chamber. At idle, and during light-throttle operation, manifold vacuum draws the diaphragm back against spring pressure to close off the enrichment valve and the fuel outlet channel. Under acceleration and wide-open throttle operation, the vacuum in the manifold is depleted. The diaphragm returns under spring pressure and the valve opens the fuel channel. This allows fuel to flow through the channel and a calibrated bushing to supplement the fuel in the upper part of the main well. The fuel level rises in the well and the fuel mixture is enriched.

Secondary action

11 A port is located in both primary and secondary venturis. Airways run from these

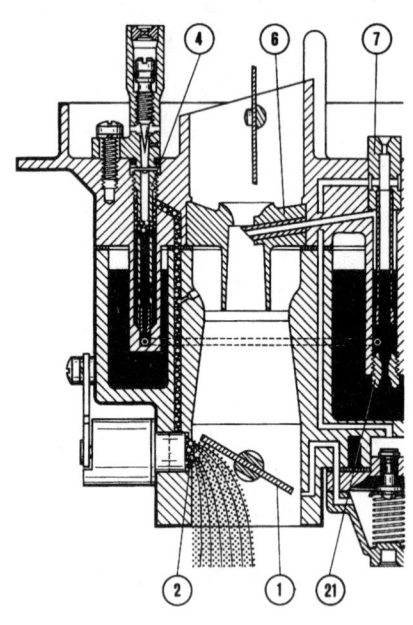

Fuel supply and float arrangement

28 Float needle valve
29 Fuel supply inlet
31 Float pivot pin
32 Float

by a spring-loaded needle valve and plastic float assembly *(see illustration)*. The float level is considered critical and is set very accurately during production. The float chamber is vented internally into the upper air intake which is on the clean-air side of the air filter.

Idle, slow running and progression

5 Fuel is drawn from the primary main well into the base of a vertical well which dips down into the fuel. A combined idle jet, emulsion tube and air corrector is placed in the well. The fuel is

Idle circuit

1 Throttle plate
2 Idle mixture orifice
4 Combined idle fuel and air corrector jet
6 Main fuel nozzle - primary venturi
7 Air corrector jet - primary venturi
21 Main jet - primary venturi

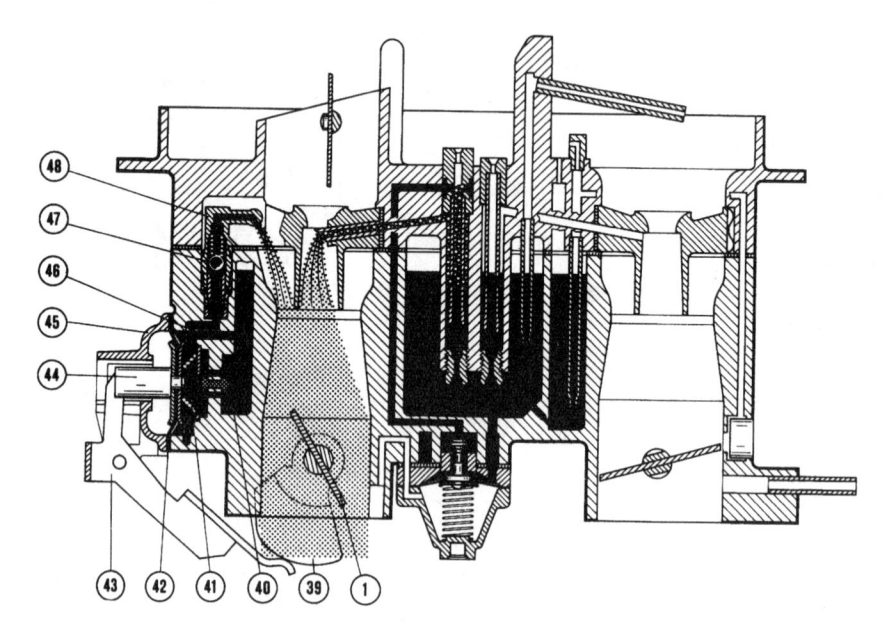

Accelerator pump circuit

1 Throttle plate - primary venturi
39 Accelerator pump cam
40 Suction valve
41 Spring
42 Diaphragm
43 Accelerator pump lever
44 Plunger
45 Pump cover
46 Return jet
47 Outlet (ball) valve
48 Pump injector

Pierburg 28/30 2E2 carburettor

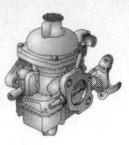

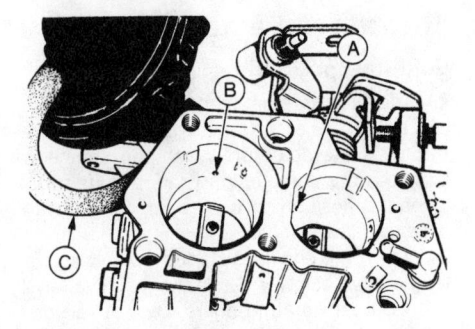

Venturi vacuum sources

A Primary venturi port
B Secondary venturi port
C Vacuum supply pipe

ports into a common passage. A vacuum hose is connected to the passage and to the diaphragm that controls the secondary throttle plate (see illustration).

12 During normal operation at low speeds, the primary venturi alone is employed. When the air velocity through the primary venturi reaches a certain level, depression acts upon the port to operate the secondary diaphragm and the secondary throttle. Vacuum created in the secondary venturi will further control the rate of secondary opening.

13 The primary linkage is arranged to prevent the secondary plate from opening when air speed may be high but the engine is cruising on a light throttle. Secondary action will not take place until the primary throttle is about half-open.

14 On some variants, a thermal valve is connected to the vacuum supply hose so that the secondary throttle plate is inoperative during the engine warm-up period. The switch remains open when the engine is cold and closes at a pre-determined temperature.

15 Once the secondary throttle plate has opened, the action of the secondary main circuit is similar to that of the primary circuit.

16 A progression jet is used to prevent hesitation as the secondary throttle plate starts to open. Fuel is drawn from the float chamber into the base of a vertical tube which dips down into the fuel. The fuel is mixed with air drawn in through a calibrated air jet to form an emulsion. The emulsified mixture is discharged into the secondary venturi, via a progression slot, at the initial opening of the secondary throttle plate. However, unlike the primary progression circuit, the secondary progression supplements the secondary main fuel system during full-load operation.

Full-load enrichment

17 At full-load and high engine speeds, the velocity of air creates a depression sufficient to raise fuel from the float chamber into the base of a vertical tube. The fuel then passes through a calibrated bushing to the upper section of the secondary air intake where it is discharged into

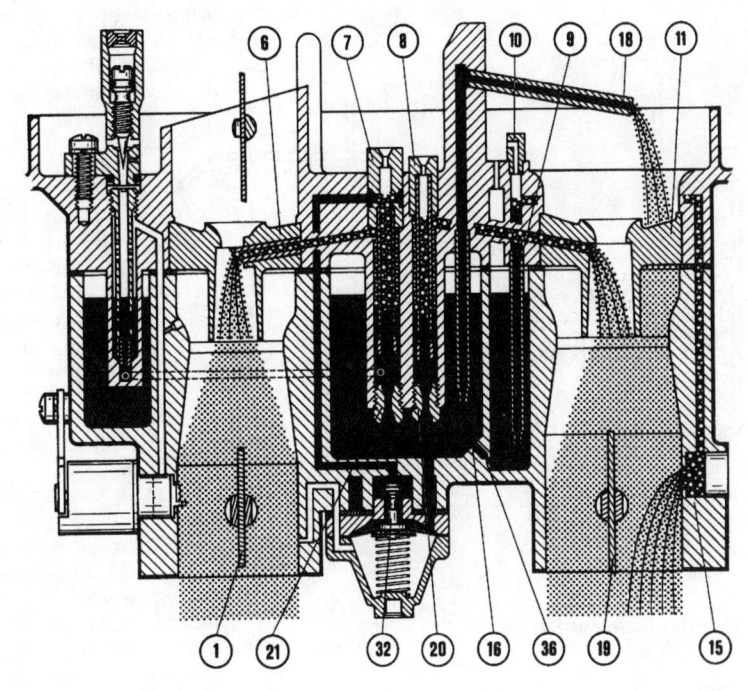

Full-load enrichment circuit

1 Throttle plate - primary venturi
6 Main fuel nozzle - primary venturi
7 Air corrector jet with emulsion tube - primary venturi
8 Air corrector jet with emulsion tube - secondary venturi
9 Progression tube for progression fuel - secondary venturi
10 Air bleed for progression fuel - secondary venturi
11 Main fuel nozzle - secondary venturi
15 Progression slot - secondary venturi
16 Calibrated tube for full-load enrichment - secondary venturi
18 Nozzle for full-load enrichment - secondary venturi
19 Throttle plate - secondary venturi
20 Main jet - secondary venturi
21 Main jet - primary venturi
32 Part-load enrichment valve
36 Fuel drilling

the airstream from the full-load enrichment nozzle (see illustration).

Cold start system

18 The choke system is fully automatic in operation and actuates a flap in the primary air intake, according to coolant temperature. The throttle position for both hot and cold starting is

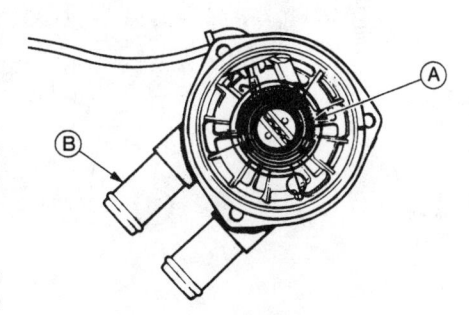

Bi-metal coil heating sources

A Electric heating coil
B Coolant water housing

also automatically determined. Priming the system by depressing the accelerator pedal is therefore unnecessary.

Choke flap and pull-down operation

19 The choke strangler flap is controlled by a combined coolant and electrically-heated bi-metal coil (see illustration). The electrical supply to the choke is made through a coolant-heated thermal switch and initially heats the choke coil after the first start from cold. As the coolant passing through the bi-metal water housing warms up, it adds to the heating of the choke spring. When the coolant reaches a preset temperature, the thermal switch cuts out the electrical supply and the coolant flow remains the only source of choke heating. The choke flap will thus remain open while the coolant (and engine) remain warm.

Choke pull-down

20 The choke flap is eccentrically mounted so that it is partially open during cranking to prevent an over-rich fuel mixture. Once the engine has fired, the choke flap must open slightly, to weaken the mixture and avoid flooding during idle and light-throttle operation.

F5•7

Chapter F5

This is achieved by using manifold vacuum to actuate a pull-down diaphragm *(see illustration)*. A linkage attached to the diaphragm will then pull upon the flap. A two-stage pull-down system is used. When the engine fires, the vacuum applied to the pull-down diaphragm is low and the choke flap will be partially moved to pull-down gap 'a' *(see illustration)*.

21 As the engine continues to run, vacuum increases and acts upon an air reservoir. Additionally, a second vacuum signal is relayed via a non-return valve, to further aid the emptying of the reservoir and complete the pull-down of the choke flap to the second stage, gap 'a1'. The two pull-down stages ensure maximum richness for the few seconds after a cold start and then a rapid opening of the choke flap to reduce over-richness.

Dechoke (wide-open kick)

22 If the throttle is opened fully when the engine is cold, the pull-down vacuum will deplete and the choke flap will tend to close, causing flooding. This is prevented by employing a wide-open kick mechanism. When the throttle is fully opened, a cam on the throttle lever will turn the choke lever anti-clockwise to partially open the flap.

Throttle plate actuator
Cold start position

23 The initial throttle opening position for the cold start is one of the functions provided by the throttle plate actuator. When the engine is stopped, the actuator pushrod is in its fully-extended position to push open the throttle plate *(see illustration)*.

24 When the engine is started from cold at a temperature below 4°C, the thermal time valve (TTV) is open to atmosphere. Lack of vacuum allows the throttle actuator to remain unaffected and the pushrod opens the throttle plate to its fully-extended position. An electrical supply (present once the ignition is switched on) is used to heat the TTV. As the valve temperature rises, the TTV air passage gradually closes. It is fully closed at 15°C. The closing of the TTV enables vacuum to act on the throttle actuator and the pushrod is gradually withdrawn to reduce the fast idle speed.

25 Fast idle during the warm-up period is achieved with the aid of a coolant-heated waxstat *(see illustration)*. When the coolant is cold, the waxstat pushrod is withdrawn and a spring and series of levers combine to push open the throttle plate. As the coolant is heated, the waxstat pushrod extends to close the throttle plate to its normal idle position.

Hot idle position

26 An electric switchover valve is used to govern the vacuum at the throttle actuator so that the actuator pushrod position can be regulated. The switchover valve is controlled by a relay that is energised by an engine speed signal from the ignition. The voltage supply is switched on and off, depending on whether the signal is above or below 1200 rpm.

Typical vacuum hose connections (VW/Audi)

1. Carburettor
2. Throttle plate actuator
3. TTV
4. Electric switch valve
5. Diaphragm assembly - secondary throttle
6. Pull-down diaphragm
7. Vacuum reservoir
8. Non-return valve
10. Ignition distributor
11. Econometer
12. Brake servo
13. Air filter
14. Thermal valve
15. Heated air diaphragm
16. Heated air vacuum connection

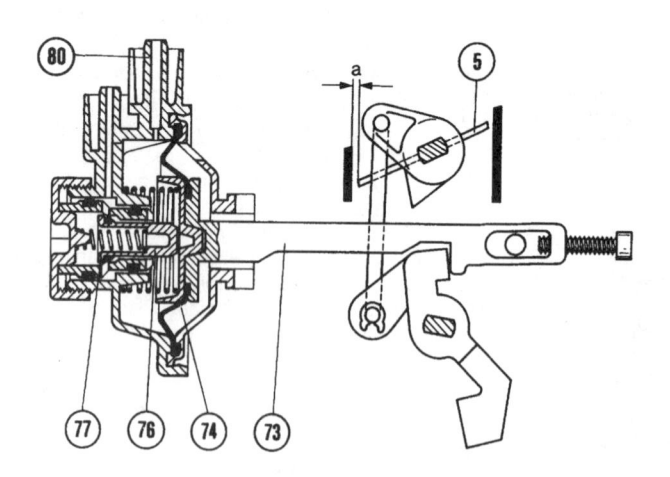

Choke pull-down operation

5 Choke flap
73 Diaphragm rod
74 Diaphragm
76 Valve
77 Spring
78 Adjustment screw for pull-down gap 'a'
79 Connector for vacuum supply
80 Connector to vacuum reservoir (outlet)
81 Adjustment screw for pull-down gap 'a1'
a First stage pull-down gap
a1 Second stage pull-down gap

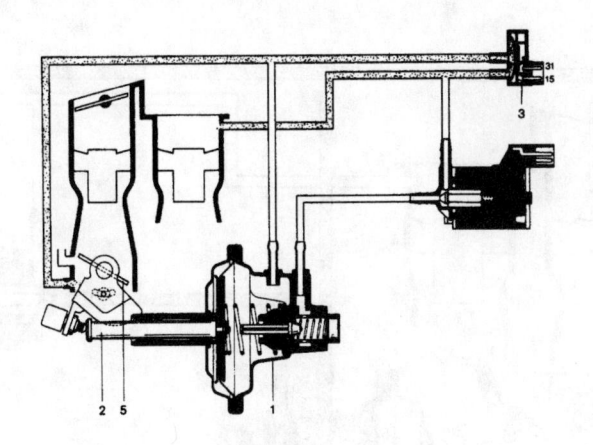

Pierburg 28/30 2E2 carburettor

Cold start conditions

1. Throttle plate actuator
2. Pushrod
3. TTV - terminal 15: supply voltage/ terminal 31: earth
4. Electric switchover valve
5. Throttle plate
6. Pin
7. Intermediate lever (actuated by waxstat and used to open throttle plate)
8. Waxstat
9. Spring

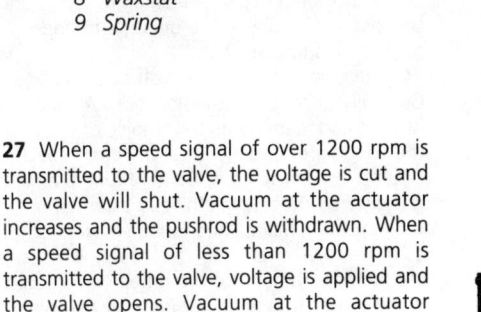

27 When a speed signal of over 1200 rpm is transmitted to the valve, the voltage is cut and the valve will shut. Vacuum at the actuator increases and the pushrod is withdrawn. When a speed signal of less than 1200 rpm is transmitted to the valve, voltage is applied and the valve opens. Vacuum at the actuator collapses and the pushrod extends to place the throttle plate in the hot idle position *(see illustration)*.

Deceleration (overrun) fuel cut-off

28 When a speed signal of over 1200 rpm is transmitted to the valve during deceleration, the voltage supply is cut and the valve will shut. Vacuum at the actuator increases and the pushrod is withdrawn, closing the throttle plate to stop the fuel supply. Note that during the warm-up phase, the throttle will be held open by the position of the waxstat. As the decelerating engine falls below 1200 rpm, voltage is applied and the valve opens. Vacuum at the actuator collapses, the pushrod extends to place the throttle plate in the hot idle position and the fuel supply is restored *(see illustration overleaf)*.

Engine shut-down (anti-run-on)

29 Once the ignition is switched off, the switchover valve voltage supply is cut and the valve will close. Vacuum will be present for a moment in the still-rotating engine and the actuator pushrod will withdraw to completely shut the throttle plate. Engine run-on is thus avoided. When the engine stops, the vacuum at the actuator collapses and the pushrod is extended to the start position.

2 Identification

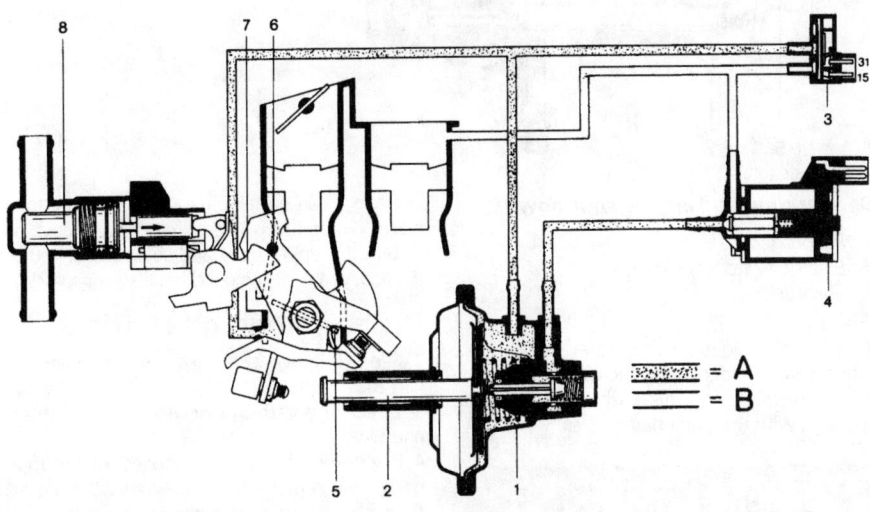

Warm-up period
For key, refer to the illustration at the top of the page

A Vacuum signal
B Open passage

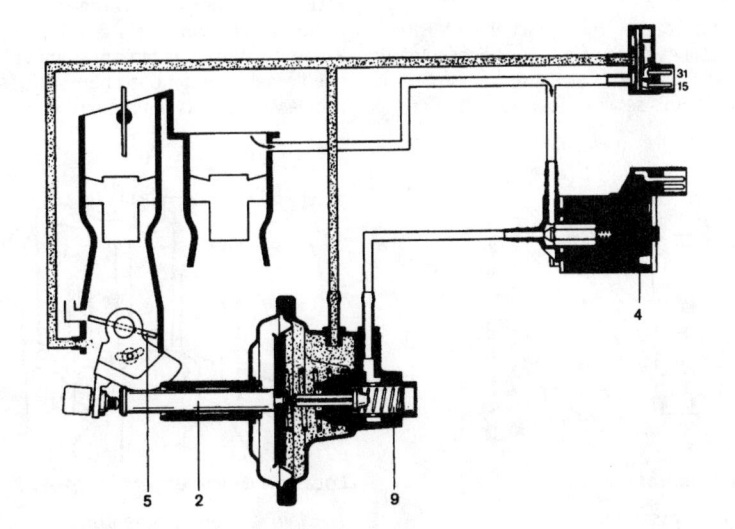

Hot idle position
For key, refer to the illustration at the top of the page

1 Pierburg 2E is stamped on the carburettor upper and main bodies. The manufacturer's identification code may be stamped on a metallic tag attached to the cover by an upper body fixing screw or on a corner of the carburettor upper body.

F5•9

Chapter F5

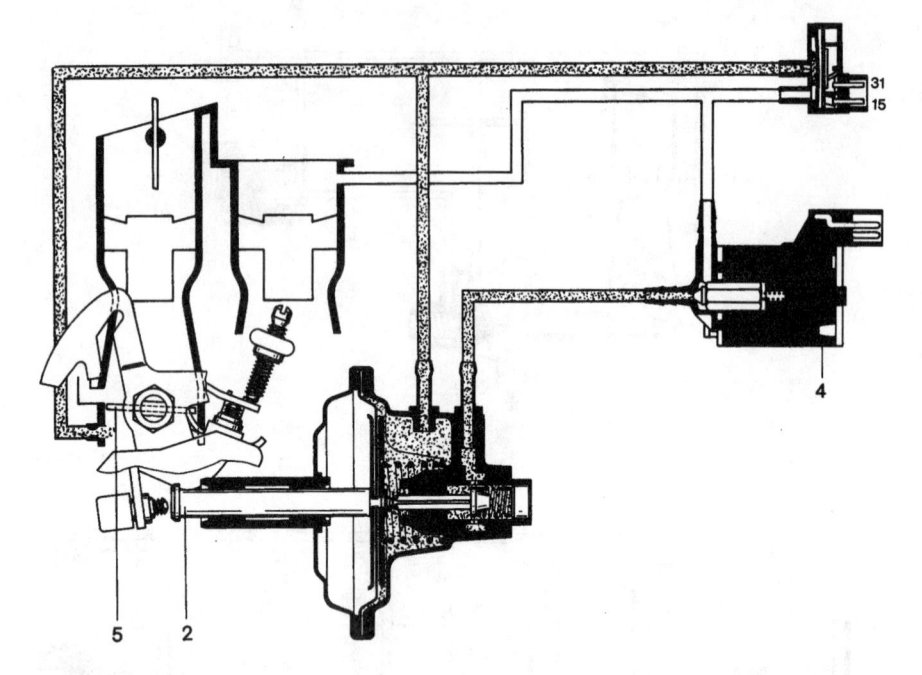

Deceleration and engine shut-down

2 Pushrod
4 Electric switchover valve
5 Throttle plate

2 Where the tag is missing, refer to Part B for other means of identifying the carburettor.
3 Early versions of this carburettor may be stamped with the trade name Solex.

3 General servicing

Introduction

1 Read this Chapter in conjunction with Part B, which describes some of the operations in more detail. It is assumed that the carburettor is removed for this service. However, many of the operations can be tackled with the carburettor in place. Where this is undertaken, first remove the carburettor upper body and soak the fuel out of the float chamber using a clean tissue or soft cloth.

Dismantling and checking

2 Remove the carburettor from the engine (see Part B).
3 Check the carburettor visually for damage and wear.
4 Disconnect the vacuum hoses to the upper body then remove the five screws and detach the carburettor upper body. The electrical earth strap (where fitted) is retained by a fixing screw and will also be removed at this time.
5 Inspect the float chamber for corrosion and calcium build-up.
6 Use a straight-edge to check for distorted flanges on all facing surfaces.
7 Tap out the float pin and remove the float, needle valve and float chamber gasket. The needle valve seat is not removable.

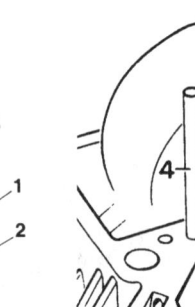

Idle air assembly

A Standard assembly
B Modified assembly
1 Air holes (A type) or air slot (B type)
2 Seal

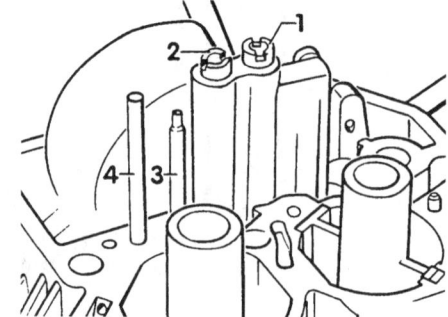

Location of lower jets in upper body

1 Main jet - primary venturi
2 Main jet - secondary venturi
3 Full-load enrichment tube
4 Secondary progression tube

8 Check that the anti-vibration ball is free in the needle valve end.
9 Check the needle valve tip for wear and ridges.
10 The float should be checked for damage and ingress of petrol.
11 Renew the float pin if it shows signs of wear.
12 Remove the fuel filter from its position in the fuel inlet connection. Screwing an M3 screw into the filter opening may assist in its withdrawal. Clean the filter and renew it if necessary.
13 Remove the four screws and detach the accelerator pump cover, diaphragm, spring and seal assembly. Check the diaphragm and seal for fatigue and damage.
14 The pump injector is a push fit in the body. Carefully prise it from its location. Attach the hose of a vacuum pump to the injector body (on the opposite end to the injector nozzle). Operate the pump until 300 mmHg (400 mbars) is registered. Renew the injector assembly if the vacuum is not maintained for 30 seconds.
15 Unscrew the idle air assembly (see illustration). The air holes can become blocked, causing a rich, lumpy idle. Remove the idle air screw and inspect the tip for damage and ridges. Note that a modified idle air adjustment assembly is available from Pierburg agents, to reduce instances of rich idle running. The assembly with holes is replaced by one with a slot, the slot being less prone to blockage.
16 Remove the primary idle jet assembly and both main jets (see illustration). It is not possible to remove any of the other jets or emulsion tubes. The primary idle jet and adjustment assembly can be removed from the carburettor without removing the upper body.
17 Check that the channels from the float chamber into the emulsion tube wells are clear.
18 Note the jet sizes and their locations, for correct installation during reassembly.
19 Check the jet calibration against the Specifications. It is possible that the jets may have been transposed (or the wrong size fitted) during the last overhaul.
20 Remove the two screws and detach the power valve housing cover, spring and diaphragm assembly. Check the diaphragm for damage and fatigue. Check the action of the power valve and the condition of the small seal. Also check that the channel into the emulsion tube well is clear.
21 Inspect all vacuum hoses for condition and splits, renewing where necessary.
22 Note the location and routing of the choke and idle vacuum hoses and disconnect them where necessary. The vacuum hose routes are coded with coloured rings. Take care that the rings do not become lost.
23 Remove and check the condition of the secondary throttle vacuum hose. Attach a vacuum pump to the vacuum connector and operate the pump until the secondary diaphragm is actuated (see illustration). Renew the diaphragm assembly if it does not operate fully or if vacuum is not maintained for at least 10 seconds.

Pierburg 28/30 2E2 carburettor

Use a vacuum pump to test secondary throttle diaphragm

24 Disconnect the secondary throttle operating rod by twisting the rod out of its socket on the throttle lever. Remove the two (or three) screws and detach the diaphragm assembly from the body.
25 Do not disturb the adjustment of the primary or secondary throttle angle, unless absolutely necessary.
26 Remove the two screws and detach the waxstat assembly.
27 Conduct the following test at a temperature of 20°C. Apply a force of 30N (3kgf/6.8 lbf) to the waxstat and measure the dimension 'A' shown *(see illustration)*. If the measured value is not 2 mm ± 1 mm, renew the waxstat.
28 Inspect the choke flap, spindle and linkage for stickiness and wear.

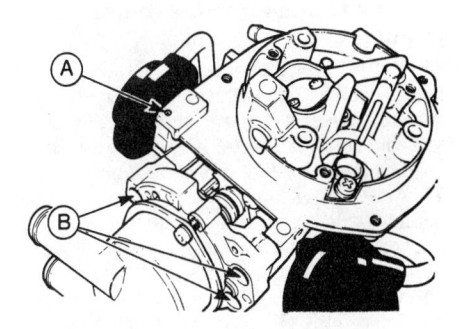

Choke diaphragm assembly and lever housing

A *Diaphragm assembly securing roll pin*
B *Choke lever housing securing screws*

Star clip (arrowed) retaining diaphragm arm

29 Test the choke pull-down unit as described in Section 4.
30 Punch out the roll pin that secures the choke diaphragm assembly to the upper body. Remove the three screws that secure the choke housing to the upper body. Allow the housing to drop out of the way. It is unnecessary to disconnect the choke linkage. Remove the star fixing clip and detach the pull-down diaphragm assembly *(see illustrations)*.

Preparation for reassembly

31 Clean the jets, carburettor body assemblies, float chamber and internal channels. An air line may be used to clear the internal channels once the carburettor is fully dismantled. Note that if high-pressure air is directed into the channels and passages with the diaphragms still in place, diaphragm damage may result. Spraying carburettor cleaner into all the channels and passages in the carburettor body will often clear them of gum and dirt.
32 During reassembly, a complete set of new gaskets should be fitted. Also renew the needle valve, the float pivot pin and all diaphragms. Inspect and renew (where necessary) the idle air control assembly, main jets, idle jet, pump injector and waxstat. Renew worn linkages, springs, vacuum hoses and other parts where necessary.
33 Ensure that all the jets are firmly locked into their original positions (but do not over-tighten). A loose jet can cause a rich (or even lean) running condition.
34 Clean all mating surfaces and flanges of old gasket material and reassemble with new gaskets. Ensure that housings are positioned with their air and fuel routes correctly aligned.

Reassembly

35 Slide the choke diaphragm assembly into position and secure with a new star clip and roll pin. Refit the choke housing and secure with the three screws.
36 Refit the waxstat assembly and secure with the two screws.
37 Ensure that the choke flap and linkage move smoothly and progressively.
38 Refit the secondary throttle diaphragm assembly and secure with the fixing screws. Reconnect the throttle operating rod and the vacuum hose.
39 Check that the secondary throttle plate is fully closed. The adjustment screw should not normally be used to alter the throttle plate position. However, if necessary, it can be adjusted so that the plate is open just enough to prevent its seizure in the throttle body. Where a throttle setting gauge is available, use it to set the throttle angle.
40 The primary throttle plate was fixed in position during manufacture and the throttle stop screw sheared off. Adjustment should therefore not be attempted.
41 Refit the power diaphragm, spring and cover assembly, then secure with the two screws.

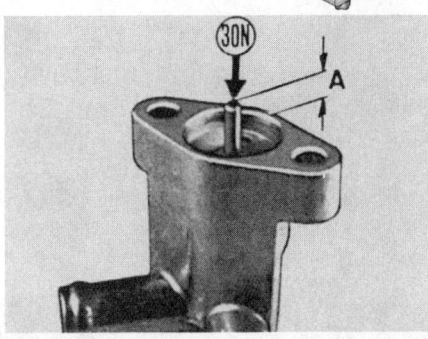

Apply 30N force to waxstat and measure dimension 'A'

A = 2 mm ± 1 mm

42 Refit the two main jets into their original positions (do not transpose the jets).
43 Refit the primary idle jet into the upper body. Fit the idle air screw into the adjustment housing, after renewing the small seal. Turn the screw in gently until it just seats. From this position, unscrew it three full turns. This will provide a basic setting to allow the engine to be started. Locate the assembly above the idle jet and secure with the screw.
44 Align the accelerator pump injector *(see illustration)* and tap it into position after renewing the small seal on the injector body.
45 Refit the pump seal, spring, diaphragm and cover assembly, then secure with the four screws.
46 Place the fuel filter in the fuel inlet tube.
47 Insert the needle valve into the seat with the ball facing outwards. Refit the float and pivot pin. Ensure that the top of the needle valve engages in the slot on the float.
48 Check the float level (see Section 4). Refit the float gasket to the upper body.
49 Refit the upper body to the main body and secure with the five screws. Refit all vacuum hoses in their original positions. Ensure that the choke earth strap (where fitted) is secured with an upper body fixing screw.
50 Adjust the choke (see Section 4).
51 Refit the carburettor to the engine.
52 Always adjust the carburettor idle speed and mixture after any work has been carried out on the carburettor, preferably with the aid of a CO meter.

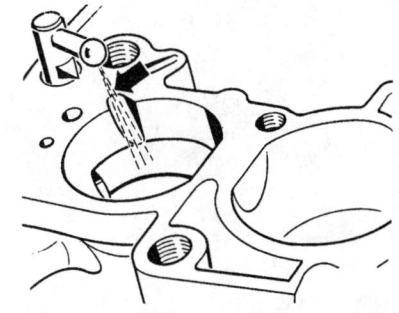

Alignment of accelerator pump injection nozzle

Chapter F5

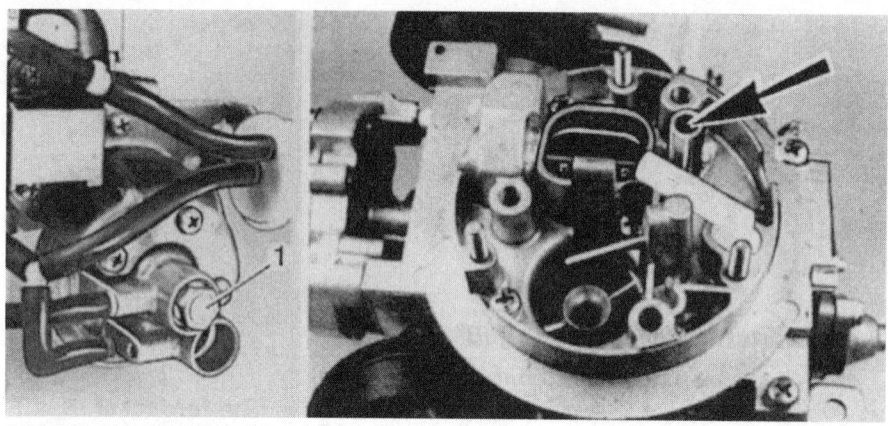

Idle adjustment screw location
1 Idle speed regulating valve
Idle (mixture) air control screw arrowed

4 Service adjustments

Adjustment pre-conditions

1 Refer to Part B for general advice on the pre-conditions for correct adjustment of this carburettor.
2 Disconnect the engine breather hose from the air filter and plug the opening in the air filter.
3 Reconnect the breather hose after all adjustments are completed. If the CO level increases more than 1 to 1.5%, change the sump oil. If the CO level increases after an oil change, suspect worn or sticking piston rings. If no CO change is noted on connecting/disconnecting the breather hose, suspect a clogged crankcase breather (PCV) system.

Idle speed and mixture (CO)

4 Run the engine at 3000 rpm for 30 seconds to clear the manifold of fuel vapours then allow the engine to idle.
5 Remove the air filter assembly and place it clear of the carburettor. The vacuum hoses must remain connected.

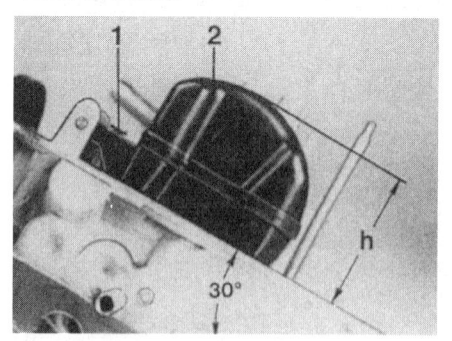

Float level checking
1 Needle valve pin
2 Float
h Float height

6 Use the idle speed regulating valve to set the specified idle speed *(see illustration)*.
7 Check the CO level. If incorrect, adjust the idle air screw to obtain the correct level. In some instances, the screw is accessed by removing a plug in the air filter. Turning the screw clockwise (inwards) will increase the CO level. Turning the screw anti-clockwise (outwards) will reduce the CO level.
8 Repeat paragraphs 6 and 7 until both adjustments are correct.
9 Clear the manifold every 30 seconds during the setting operation by running the engine at 3000 rpm for 30 seconds.
10 Increase the speed to 2000 rpm and note the CO reading. The cruise reading should be less than half the idle CO reading.
11 Refit the air filter assembly, ensuring that the vacuum hoses remain connected.

Float level

12 It is not possible to adjust the plastic float. It is possible, however, to check the level.
13 Hold the upper body at an angle of 30° with the float tag gently touching the ball of the fully-closed needle valve.
14 Measure the distance between the upper body (without its gasket) and the top of the float (see Specifications) *(see illustration)*.
15 If the level is incorrect, check the needle valve seat for correct position. Remove the float and check the float weight (see Specifications).

Accelerator pump adjustment
1 Clamping screw
2 Pump cam

16 If the float seat and weight are satisfactory, renew the float if the level is still incorrect.

Accelerator pump

17 On the Pierburg 2E2 carburettor, it is possible to adjust the volume of fuel injected by the accelerator pump.
18 Loosen the clamping screw *(see illustration)*.
19 Move the cam in direction (+) to increase the volume or in direction (-) to decrease the volume.
20 Tighten the clamping screw on completion.

Automatic choke

Fast idle (throttle actuator)

21 Note that the throttle actuator fast idle speed is not normally adjustable. The stop screw on the control arm was set in manufacture and the end sheared off. However, if the control arm becomes bent, or is otherwise tampered with, the following method is a way of resetting the fast idle speed. Since the basic idle speed is dependent on the setting of the control arm, this adjustment should not be made lightly.
22 Warm the engine to normal running temperature and leave it running.
23 Remove the vacuum hose (colour-coded brown) from the throttle actuator and record the fast idle speed. Refer to Specifications for the correct figure.
24 Adjust as necessary by carefully bending the control arm in the appropriate direction.
25 Adjust the idle speed and mixture on completion.

Fast idle (warm-up cam) - control position

26 The following operations (paragraphs 27 to 39) should not be attempted unless the settings have been maladjusted. Pierburg special tool 4.07360.02 is required for both parts of the procedure *(see illustration)*.
27 Attach a vacuum pump to the throttle actuator and operate it so that the actuator pushrod is withdrawn. The pushrod must remain in this position during the following adjustments.
28 Remove the two screws and disconnect the waxstat assembly.
29 Check that the slide is correctly located *(see illustration)*.
30 Attach the test tool with the 8.15 mm long side facing into the carburettor.

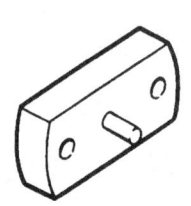

Pierburg setting tool 4.07360.02

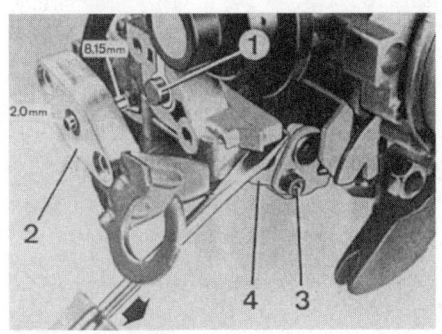

Pierburg 28/30 2E2 carburettor

Setting fast idle - warm-up cam control position

1 Slide
2 Tool 4.07360.02
3 Clamping screw
4 Warm-up cam lever

31 Slacken screw '3' in illustration above.
32 Use a screwdriver to gently push the warm-up cam '4' against the pin '5'. Hold this position and tighten screw '3'.
33 Open the throttle plate slightly then slowly close it. The warm-up cam should readopt the position taken in paragraph 32.
34 Grease the cam where indicated by the arrow *(see illustration)*.

Fast idle (warm-up cam) - warm-up position

35 Only carry out the following adjustments

Setting fast idle - warm-up position

6 Clamping screw
7 Lever
8 Lever
9 Adjustment screw

Measuring fast idle clearance

9 Adjustment screw

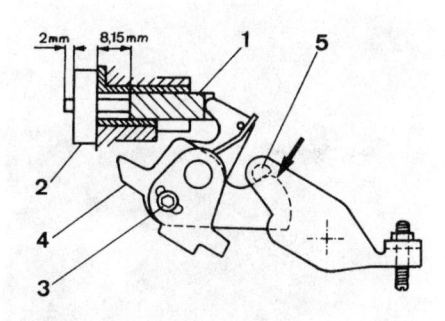

Setting fast idle - warm-up cam control position

1 Slide
2 Tool 4.07360.02
3 Clamping screw
4 Warm-up cam lever
5 Pin

(paragraphs 36 to 38) if screw (9) *(see illustration)* has been maladjusted.
36 Remove the test tool and re-attach it with the 2.0 mm long side facing into the carburettor *(see illustrations)*.
37 Use the shank of a twist drill to measure the clearance between the wall of the throttle bore and the throttle plate. Refer to Specifications for the required drill size.
38 Slacken screw '6' then compress levers '7' and '8' and adjust the clearance measured in paragraph 37 by turning the adjustment screw '9' in the appropriate direction.
39 Remove the special tool. Refit the waxstat assembly and secure with the two screws.

Choke pull-down

40 Remove the three screws and detach the bi-metal coil housing from the carburettor.
41 Fully close the choke flap using the choke control lever. The throttle plate must be closed.
42 If the flap does not close completely, set clearance 'A' *(see illustration)* to between 0.2 and 1.0 mm. The gap is adjusted by bending lever '2' in the appropriate direction.
43 Refer to Part D for a method of testing the vacuum reservoir (where fitted).
44 Remove the vacuum hose from the

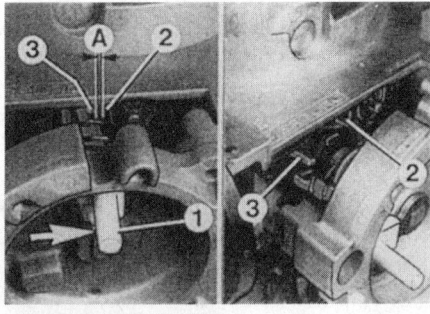

Closure of choke flap

1 Move choke control lever fully in direction of arrow
2 Diaphragm rod
3 Adjustment lever
A Clearance

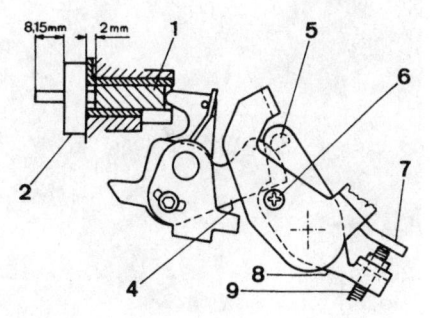

Setting fast idle - warm-up position

1 Slide
2 Tool 4.07360.02
4 Warm-up cam lever
5 Pin
6 Clamping screw
7 Lever
8 Lever
9 Adjustment screw

carburettor base to the inlet connection (supply side) of the pull-down unit and attach a vacuum pump to the connection. Remove the second hose from the outlet side and leave the connection unplugged.
45 Operate the pump and the pull-down should move to the first stage.
46 Maintaining the vacuum, plug the pull-down outlet connection and operate the pump until 225 mmHg (300 mbars) is obtained. The pull-down should now move to the second stage and hold vacuum for at least 10 seconds. If the diaphragm does not operate as described, renew the pull-down unit.
47 Detach the pull-down to reservoir vacuum hose from the connection on the pull-down unit. Do not plug the connection.
48 Operate the vacuum pump and the choke flap should open to the first stage setting. Lightly close the choke flap and use the shank of a twist drill to measure the a clearance between the lower section of the choke flap and the air intake. Refer to Specifications for the required drill size.
49 Adjust as necessary by turning the first stage pull-down adjusting screw *(see illustration)* in the appropriate direction. This

Testing choke vacuum pull-down

1 Pull-down unit
2 Outlet connection
3 First stage adjustment screw 'a'

F5•13

Chapter F5

Measuring choke pull-down clearance

Choke pull-down adjustment
1. Close choke flap by moving choke control lever fully in direction of arrow
2. Second stage adjustment screw 'a1'

Choke alignment marks

clearance should only need to be checked after the pull-down unit has been renewed, or if the setting has been disturbed.

50 Plug the pull-down outlet connection.
51 Fully operate the vacuum pump and the choke flap should open to the second stage setting. Lightly close the choke flap and use the shank of a twist drill to measure the 'a1' clearance between the lower section of the choke flap and the air intake *(see illustration)*. Refer to Specifications for the required drill size.
52 Adjust as necessary by turning the second stage pull-down adjusting screw *(see illustration)* in the appropriate direction. Where a vacuum pump is not available, a small screwdriver can also be used to push on the 'a1' adjusting screw. If this method is used, the screw should be pushed until a resistance is felt. The clearance at this point is the first stage setting. Continue pushing until the screw cannot be pushed any further. The clearance now obtained is the second stage setting.
53 Reconnect all the vacuum hoses.
54 Refit the bi-metal coil housing, ensuring that the spring locates in the slot of the choke lever. Secure loosely with the three screws.
55 Align the cut mark on the bi-metal cover with the correct mark on the choke assembly housing and tighten the three screws *(see illustration)*.
56 Refit the air filter assembly, ensuring that the vacuum hoses remain connected.

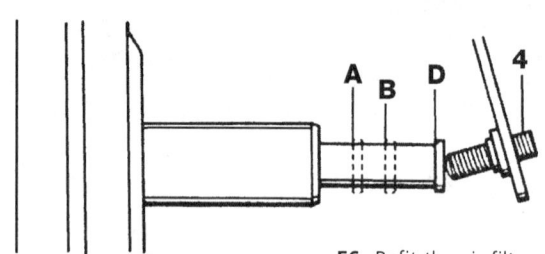

5 Component testing

Throttle plate actuator

Engine cold
1 The pushrod should be fully extended in the cold start position *(see illustration)*.
2 Start the engine and the pushrod should retract to the hot idle position.
3 However, a fast idle should be maintained according to the waxstat starter position.

Engine running (hot)
4 With the engine idling, check that the pushrod holds the engine at the specified idle speed.
5 Increase the engine speed to over 1200 rpm and the pushrod should retract.
6 Gradually lower the engine speed. As 1200 rpm is passed, the pushrod should extend.

7 Switch off the ignition. The pushrod should fully retract as the engine stalls and then fully extend to the cold start position.
8 Start the engine. The pushrod should retract to the hot idle position.
9 Disconnect the electrical plug to the switchover valve. If the pushrod retracts, the valve is operating satisfactorily.
10 If the pushrod does not retract, test the thermal time valve (TTV) and the switchover valve as described below.

Engine stopped
11 Remove the two vacuum hoses from the actuator and plug connection '2' *(see illustration)*.
12 Connect a vacuum pump to connection '1' and operate the pump to obtain 525 mmHg (750 mbars). The pushrod should be completely withdrawn (position 'A') *(see illustration left)* and the vacuum should be maintained.
13 If the engine is at operating temperature, there must also be a gap between the throttle stop screw and the pushrod.
14 Remove the plug from connection '2'. The actuator should move to position 'B' and the vacuum should be held.
15 Renew the actuator if it does not comply with the above.

Thermal time valve (TTV)
16 Cool the valve to a temperature less than 4°C.
17 Disconnect the vacuum hose to the TTV and attach a vacuum pump. Operate the pump. No reading should be obtained *(see illustration)*.

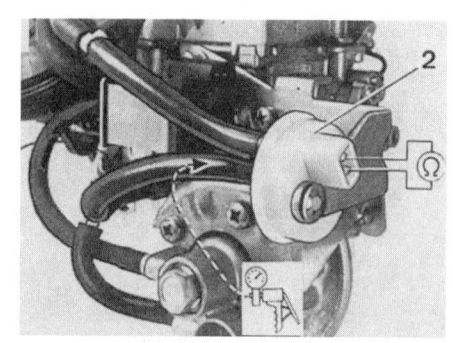

Throttle plate actuator positions

A Deceleration position (pushrod totally withdrawn)
B Idle position
D Starting position
4 Throttle stop screw (sheared off)

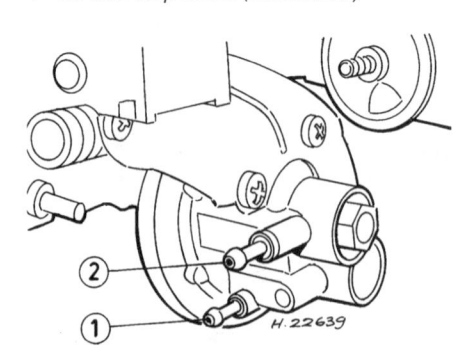

Throttle plate actuator testing
1 Connect a vacuum pump to this connection
2 Plug this connection

Thermal time valve (2) vacuum and resistance testing

F5•14

Pierburg 28/30 2E2 carburettor

18 Switch on the ignition. Wait 5 to 10 seconds and the valve should be heated to a temperature greater than 15°C.
19 Operate the vacuum pump. 300 mmHg (400 mbars) should be obtained and maintained for at least 10 seconds.
20 Check the voltage supply and earth at the electrical connection.
21 The TTV resistance should be 4.5 to 7.5 ohms at 20°C.
22 Renew the TTV if it does not comply with the above.

Electrical switchover valve

23 Check for a voltage supply. If no supply is available, check the wiring back to the ignition switch.
24 With the ignition on, connect a temporary jumper lead between the switchover valve earth terminal and a suitable engine earth. If the switch is now activated, check the wiring and the switchover valve relay (usually located in the relay box).
25 Disconnect the vacuum hoses and connect a vacuum pump to one of the connectors *(see illustration)*.
26 With the ignition on, operate the vacuum pump. No vacuum reading should be obtained.
27 Switch off the ignition and operate the vacuum pump again. Now 300 mmHg (400 mbars) should be obtained and maintained for at least 10 seconds.
28 Renew the switchover valve if it does not behave as described.

Thermal switches

29 Refer to Part D for general tests on the thermal switch, automatic choke electrical heater and the inlet manifold and throttle body heaters.

Thermal switch for inlet manifold heater

30 Below 55°C ± 10°C, a voltmeter should indicate battery voltage (switch open).
31 Above 65°C ± 10°C, the voltmeter should indicate zero volts (switch closed).
32 Renew the thermal switch if it does not function in accordance with the above.

Thermal switch for automatic choke

33 Below 33°C, a voltmeter should indicate battery voltage (switch open).
34 Above 42°C, the voltmeter should indicate zero volts (switch closed).
35 Renew the thermal switch if it does not function in accordance with the above.

Thermal valve

36 Refer to Part D for general tests on the thermal valve fitted to the choke pull-down and secondary throttle vacuum hoses (some VW variants).
37 Below 17°C, no vacuum should register (valve open).
38 Above 53°C, normal idle vacuum should register (valve closed).
39 Renew the thermal valve if it does not function in accordance with the above.

6 Fault diagnosis

Refer to Part D for diagnosis of general carburettor faults. The following faults are specific to 2E2 carburettors.

Poor choke operation/poor cold running

- [ ] Over or under-choking due to pull-down diaphragm failure, reservoir failure, relaxing of bi-metal or poor adjustment.
- [ ] Sticking choke flap.
- [ ] Failure of inlet manifold pre-heater.
- [ ] Failure of thermal time valve or electrical switchover valve.
- [ ] Incorrect routing of vacuum hoses (common error).
- [ ] Incorrect dechoke adjustment.
- [ ] Defective choke waxstat (idle speed on choke too low).
- [ ] Breakage of plastic choke operating mechanism.

Testing electrical switchover valve (1)

Throttle actuator withdrawn at idle

- [ ] Defective relay.

High idle speed

- [ ] Defective choke waxstat.
- [ ] Defective pull-down assembly.
- [ ] Defective thermal time valve or throttle actuator.

Heavy fuel consumption

- [ ] A leaking power valve diaphragm or O-ring seal.

Hesitation

- [ ] The accelerator pump diaphragm utilises a slot and spring-loaded ball into which the pump actuating lever fits. If the spring becomes weak, the delay in operation can cause a flat spot on acceleration.
- [ ] Defective suction valve, pushrod spring or diaphragm.
- [ ] Corrosion of carburettor actuating levers.

Uneven running

- [ ] Air leak due to defective rubber mounting flange.
- [ ] Clogging of idle air adjustment assembly.

Lack of power

- [ ] Failure of secondary throttle plate diaphragm.

Notes

Part F Chapter 6
Pierburg 24/28, 28/30 & 28/32 2E3 carburettor

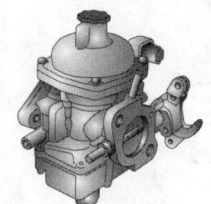

Contents

Component testing	5	Identification	2
Fault diagnosis	6	Principles of operation	1
General servicing	3	Service adjustments	4

Specifications

Manufacturer	Ford		Ford		Ford	
Model	Sierra 1800		Sierra 1800		Sierra 1800	
Year	Sep.1984 to Jun.1986		Jun.1986 to Jan.1987		1984 to Jun.1986	
Engine code	REB (OHC)		REB (OHC) 66 kW		REB (OHC) 66 kW	
Capacity (cm³)/no. of cyls	1796/4		1796/4		1796/4	
Oil temperature (°C)	80		80		80	
Transmission	Manual		Manual		Automatic	
Carb. ident. (Ford)	85HF 9510 AB		85HF 9510 KB		85HF 9510 JA	
Idle speed (rpm)	800 ± 20		800 ± 25		800 ± 25	
Fast idle speed (rpm)	1900 ± 50		1900 ± 50		1900 ± 50	
CO @ idle (% vol.)	1.25 ± 0.25		1.25 ± 0.25		1.25 ± 0.25	
Stage (venturi)	1	2	1	2	1	2
Venturi diameter	23	26	23	26	23	26
Main jet	107.5	130	107.5	135	107.5	130
Air correction jet	85	60	85	60	-	-
Idle jet	45		45		45	
Accel. pump jet	-		50		-	
Float level (mm)	27.5 ± 1.0		27.5 ± 1.0		27.5 ± 1.0	
Needle valve size (mm)	1.75		1.75		1.75	
Throttle damper	2mm ± 0.4		2mm ± 0.4		2mm ± 0.4	
Choke pull-down (mm)	3.0 ± 0.2		3.0 ± 0.2		3.0	
Bi-metal housing mark	on index		on index		on index	

Manufacturer	Ford		Ford		Ford	
Model	Sierra 1800		Sierra & Sapphire 1800		Sierra & Sapphire 1800	
Year	Jun.1986 to Jan.1987		Feb.1987 to 1988		Feb.1987 to 1988	
Engine code	REB (OHC) 66 kW		RED (OHC) 15/04		RED (OHC) 15/04	
Capacity (cm³)/no. of cyls	1796/4		1796/4		1796/4	
Oil temperature (°C)	80		80		80	
Transmission	Automatic		Manual		Automatic	
Carb. ident. (Ford)	85HF 9510 JB		85HF 9510 KC		85HF 9510 JC	
Idle speed (rpm)	800 ± 25		875 ± 25		800 ± 25	
Fast idle speed (rpm)	1900 ± 50		1900 ± 50		1900 ± 50	
CO @ idle (% vol.)	1.25 ± 0.25		1.25 ± 0.25		1.25 ± 0.25	
Stage (venturi)	1	2	1	2	1	2
Venturi diameter	23	26	23	26	23	26
Main jet	102.5/105	130	102.5	130	102.5	130
Idle jet	45		45		45	
Float level (mm)	27.5 ± 1.0		27.5 ± 1.0		27.5 ± 1.0	
Needle valve size (mm)	1.75		1.75		1.75	
Throttle damper	-		2mm ± 0.4		-	
Choke pull-down (mm)	3.7		4.0		3.7	
Bi-metal housing mark	5mm lean		5mm lean		5mm lean	

Chapter F6

Manufacturer	Ford	Ford	Ford
Model	Sierra & Sapphire 1800	Sierra & Sapphire 1800	Sierra & Sapphire 1800
Year	June 1987 to 1988	1988 to 1991	1988 to 1991
Engine code	RED (OHC) 15/05	R2A (CVH) 66kW 15/04	R2A (CVH) 66kW 15/04
Capacity (cm³)/no. of cyls	1796/4	1796/4	1796/4
Oil temperature (°C)	80	80	80
Transmission	Manual	Manual	Automatic
Carb. ident. (Ford)	87HF 9510 AA	87YF 9510 AC	87YF 9510 EC
Idle speed (rpm)	875 ± 25	875 ± 25	800 ± 25
Fast idle speed (rpm)	1900 ± 50	2000 ± 100	1900 ± 100
CO @ idle (% vol.)	1.25 ± 0.5	1.00 ± 0.25	1.00 ± 0.25
Stage (venturi)	1 2	1 2	1 2
Venturi diameter	23 26	22 23	22 23
Main jet	102.5 130	100 105	97.5 105
Idle jet	45	47.5	47.5
Float level (mm)	27.5 ± 1.0	27.5 ± 1.0	27.5 ± 1.0
Needle valve size (mm)	1.75	1.75	1.75
Throttle damper	-	1700 ± 100 rpm	1700 ± 100 rpm
Choke pull-down (mm)	4.0	2.3	2.5
Bi-metal housing mark	5mm lean	on index	on index

Manufacturer	Ford	Ford	Ford
Model	Granada & Scorpio 1.8	Granada & Scorpio 1.8	Granada & Scorpio 1.8
Year	Oct.1984 to Jun.1986	Jun.1986 to Feb.1987	Feb.1987
Engine code	REC (OHC) 66kW 15/04	REC (OHC) 66kW 15/04	REC (OHC) 66kW 15/04
Capacity (cm³)/no. of cyls	1796/4	1796/4	1796/4
Oil temperature (°C)	80	80	80
Transmission	Manual	Manual	Manual
Carb. ident. (Ford)	85HF 9510 KA	85HF 9510 KB	87HF 9510 KC
Idle speed (rpm)	875 ± 25	875 ± 25	875 ± 25
Fast idle speed (rpm)	1900 ± 50	1900 ± 50	1900 ± 50
CO @ idle (% vol.)	1.25 ± 0.25	1.25 ± 0.25	1.25 ± 0.25
Stage (venturi)	1 2	1 2	1 2
Venturi diameter	23 26	23 26	23 26
Main jet	107.5 130	107.5 135	102.5 130
Idle jet	45	45	45
Air correction jet	-	85	60
Float level (mm)	27.5 ± 1.0	27.5 ± 1.0	27.5 ± 1.0
Needle valve size (mm)	1.75	1.75	1.75
Throttle damper	2mm ± 0.4	-	2mm ± 0.4
Choke pull-down (mm)	3.0	3.7	4.0
Bi-metal housing mark	on index	on index	5mm lean

Manufacturer	Vauxhall	Vauxhall/Opel	Vauxhall
Model	Nova 1.3	Nova/Corsa 1.4	Astra/Belmont 1.3
Year	1985 to 1989	1989 to 1992	1984 to 1989
Engine code	13SB SOHC (55kW)	14NV SOHC (53kW) (15/04)	13SC SOHC (55kW)
Capacity (cm³)/no. of cyls	1297/4	1389/4	1297/4
Oil temperature (°C)	80	80	60
Transmission	-	-	MT
Carb. identification	90 107 515	90 107 560	90 107 515
Idle speed (rpm)	925 ± 25	925 ± 25	925 ± 25
Fast idle speed (rpm)	2300 ± 200	2400 ± 200	2300 ± 200
CO @ idle (% vol.)	0.75 ± 0.25	0.75 ± 0.25	1.25 ± 0.25
Stage (venturi)	1 2	1 2	1 2
Venturi diameter (K)	20 24	20 24	- -
Main jet (Gg)	97.5 112.5	95 110	97.5 112.5
Air correction jet (a)	80 100	117.5 90	80 100
Basic throttle position (mm)	- 0.08 ± 0.02	- -	- 0.08 ± 0.02
Idle jet (g)	37.5	45	37.5
Accelerator pump jet (i)	40	-	40
Float level (mm)	29 ± 1.0	29 ± 1.0	29 ± 1.0
Needle valve (mm) (P)	1.5	1.5	1.5
Float weight (grams)	5.85 ± 0.3	5.85 ± 0.3	5.85 ± 0.3
Choke fast idle gap (mm)	0.85 ± 0.05	-	-
Choke pull-down (mm) (a)	1.7	1.9 ± 0.2	1.7 ± 0.2
Choke pull-down (mm) (a1)	2.4	2.7 ± 0.2	2.4 ± 0.15
De-choke (mm)	2.5 ± 1.0	2.5 ± 1.0	2.5 ± 1.0

Pierburg 24/28, 28/30 & 28/32 2E3 carburettor

Manufacturer	Vauxhall	Vauxhall/Opel	Vauxhall/Opel
Model	Astra/Belmont 1.3	Astra/Belmont/Kadett 1.4	Astra/Belmont/Kadett 1.6
Year	1984 to 1989	1989 to 1991	1989 to 1991
Engine code	13SC SOHC (55kW)	14NV SOHC (55kW) 15/04	16SV SOHC (60kW) 15/04
Capacity (cm³)/no. of cyls	1297/4	1389/4	1598/4
Oil temperature (°C)	60	70	60
Transmission	AT	-	MT
Carb. identification	90 107 516	90 107 560	90 107 522
Idle speed (rpm)	825 ± 25	925 ± 25	925 ± 25
Fast idle speed (rpm)	2600 ± 200	2400 ± 200	2200 ± 200
CO @ idle (% vol.)	1.25 ± 0.25	1.0 ± 0.5	1.0 ± 0.5
Stage (venturi)	1 2	1 2	1 2
Venturi diameter (K)	20 24	20 24	- -
Main jet (Gg)	97.5 112.5	95 110	95 105
Air correction jet (a)	80 100	117.5 90	110 80
Basic throttle position (mm)	- -	- -	- 0.08 ± 0.02
Idle jet (g)	37.5	45	42.5
Accelerator pump jet (i)	40	40	-
Float level (mm)	29 ± 1.0	29 ± 1.0	29 ± 1.0
Needle valve (mm) (P)	1.5	1.5	1.5
Float weight (grams)	5.85 ± 0.3	5.85 ± 0.3	5.85 ± 0.3
Choke fast idle gap (mm)	-	0.95 ± 0.05	-
Choke pull-down (mm) (a)	1.7 ± 0.2	1.9 ± 0.2	1.6 ± 0.2
Choke pull-down (mm) (a1)	2.4 ± 0.15	2.7 ± 0.2	2.05 ± 0.15
De-choke (mm)	4.0 ± 1.0	2.0 ± 0.5	2.5 ± 1.0

Manufacturer	Vauxhall	Vauxhall	Vauxhall
Model	Astra/Belmont/Cavalier 1.6	Cavalier 1300	Cavalier 1300
Year	1989 to 1991	1985 to 1988	1985 to 1988
Engine code	16SV SOHC (60kW) 15/04	13S	13S
Capacity (cm³)/no. of cyls	1598/4	1297/4	1297/4
Oil temperature (°C)	60	60	60
Transmission	AT	MT	AT
Carb. identification	90 107 523	90 107 515	90 107 516
Idle speed (rpm)	925 ± 25	925 ± 25	825 ± 25
Fast idle speed (rpm)	2700 ± 200	2300 ± 200	2600 ± 200
CO @ idle (% vol.)	1.0 ± 0.5	1.25 ± 0.25	1.25 ± 0.25
Stage (venturi)	1 2	1 2	1 2
Venturi diameter (K)	20 24	20 24	20 -
Main jet (Gg)	95 105	97.5 112.5	97.5 112.5
Air correction jet (a)	110 80	80 100	80 100
Basic throttle position (mm)	- 0.08 ± 0.02	- 0.08 ± 0.02	- 0.08 ± 0.02
Idle jet (g)	42.5	37.5	37.5
Accelerator pump jet (i)	40	40	40
Float level (mm)	29 ± 1.0	29 ± 1.0	29 ± 1.0
Needle valve (mm) (P)	1.5	1.5	1.5
Float weight (grams)	5.85 ± 0.3	5.85 ± 0.3	5.85 ± 0.3
Choke fast idle gap (mm)	-	-	0.95 ± 0.05
Choke pull-down (mm) (a)	1.6 ± 0.2	1.7 ± 0.2	1.7 ± 0.2
Choke pull-down (mm) (a1)	2.05 ± 0.15	2.4 ± 0.15	2.4 ± 0.15
De-choke (mm)	4.0 ± 1.0	2.5 ± 1.0	4.0 ± 1.0

Manufacturer	Vauxhall/Opel	Vauxhall/Opel	Vauxhall/Opel
Model	Cavalier/Vectra 1.4	Cavalier/Vectra 1.6	Cavalier/Vectra 1.6
Year	1989 to 1992	1988 to 1992	1988 to 1992
Engine code	14NV SOHC (55kW) 15/04	16SV SOHC (60kW) 15/04	16SV SOHC (60kW) 15/04
Capacity (cm³)/no. of cyls	1389/4	1598/4	1598/4
Oil temperature (°C)	80	80	80
Transmission	-	MT	AT
Carb. identification	90 107 560	90 107 522	90 107 523
Idle speed (rpm)	925 ± 25	925 ± 25	825 ± 25
Fast idle speed (rpm)	2400 ± 200	2200 ± 200	2700
CO @ idle (% vol.)	1.0 ± 0.5	1.0 ± 0.5	1.0 ± 0.5
Stage (venturi)	1 2	1 2	1 2
Venturi diameter (K)	24 -	20 24	20 24
Main jet (Gg)	95 110	95 105	95 105
		92.5 (90 on)	92.5 (90 on)
Air correction jet (a)	117.5 90	110 80	110 80
Basic throttle position (mm)	- -	- 0.08 ± 0.02	- 0.08 ± 0.02

F6•3

Chapter F6

Manufacturer	Vauxhall/Opel (continued)	Vauxhall/Opel (continued)	Vauxhall/Opel (continued)
Model	Cavalier/Vectra 1.4	Cavalier/Vectra 1.6	Cavalier/Vectra 1.6
Year	1989 to 1992	1988 to 1992	1988 to 1992
Idle jet (g)	45	42.5	42.5
Accelerator pump jet (i)	-	40	40
Float level (mm)	29 ± 1.0	29 ± 1.0	29 ± 1.0
Needle valve (mm) (P)	1.5	1.5	1.5
Float weight (grams)	5.85 ± 0.3	5.85 ± 0.3	5.85 ± 0.3
Choke pull-down (mm) (a)	1.9 ± 0.2	1.6 ± 0.2	-
Choke pull-down (mm) (a1)	2.7 ± 0.2	2.05 ± 0.15	-
De-choke (mm)	2.0 ± 0.5	2.5 ± 1.0	4.0 ± 1.0

Manufacturer	Vauxhall/Opel	Vauxhall/Opel	Vauxhall
Model	Cavalier/Vectra 1.8	Cavalier/Vectra 1.8	Carlton 1.8
Year	1989 to 1992	1989 to 1992	1987 to 1990
Engine code	18SV SOHC (66kW) 15/04	18SV SOHC (66kW) 15/04	18SV SOHC (66kW)
Capacity (cm³)/no. of cyls	1796/4	1796/4	1796/4
Oil temperature (°C)	80	80	80
Transmission	MT	AT	MT
Carb. identification	90 107 570	90 107 911	90 107 504
Idle speed (rpm)	925 ± 25	825 ± 25	875 ± 25
Fast idle speed (rpm)	2100 ± 200	2100 ± 200	2100 ± 200
CO @ idle (% vol.)	1.0 ± 0.5	1.0 ± 0.5	0.75 ± 0.25
Stage (venturi)	1 2	1 2	1 2
Venturi diameter (K)	- -	- -	22 26
Main jet (Gg)	107.5 125	107 125	107.5 132.5
Air correction jet (a)	110 90	110 90	110 90
Basic throttle position (mm)	- -	- -	- 0.08 ± 0.02
Idle jet (g)	42.5	42.5	42.5
Accelerator pump jet (i)	-	-	50
Float level (mm)	29 ± 1.0	29 ± 1.0	29 ± 1.0
Needle valve (mm) (P)	1.5	1.5	1.5
Float weight (grams)	5.85 ± 0.3	5.85 ± 0.3	5.85 ± 0.3
Choke fast idle gap (mm)	0.9 ± 0.2	0.9 ± 0.2	-
Choke pull-down (mm) (a)	2.2 ± 0.2	2.2 ± 0.2	2.1 ± 0.2
Choke pull-down (mm) (a1)	3.3 ± 0.2	3.3 ± 0.2	3.3 ± 0.15
De-choke (mm)	2.5 ± 1.0	4.0 ± 1.0	2.5 ± 1.0

Manufacturer	Vauxhall	Volkswagen	Volkswagen
Model	Carlton 1.8	Polo 1.3	Polo 1.3
Year	1987 to 1990	1983 to 1985	1985 to 1987
Engine code	18SV SOHC (66kW)	HK (40kW)	MH (40kW)
Capacity (cm³)/no. of cyls	1796/4	1272/4	1272/4
Oil temperature (°C)	80	80	80
Transmission	AT	-	-
Carb. identification	90 107 505	052 129 016 B	030 129 016 C
Idle speed (rpm)	775 ± 25	800 ± 50	800 ± 50
Fast idle speed (rpm)	2100 ± 200	2000 ± 100	2000 ± 100
CO @ idle (% vol.)	0.75 ± 0.25	3.0 ± 0.5	1.0 ± 0.5
Stage (venturi)	1 2	1 2	1 2
Venturi diameter (K)	22 26	19 23	21 23
Main jet (Gg)	107.5 132.5	95 110	102.5 110
Air correction jet (a)	110 90	120 130	110 130
Basic throttle position (mm)	- 0.08 ± 0.02	- 0.05 ± 0.02	- 0.05 ± 0.02
Idle jet (g)	42.5	45	47.5
Accelerator pump jet (i)	50	35	35
Float level (mm)	29 ± 1.0	27.5 ± 1.0	27.5 ± 1.0
Needle valve (mm) (P)	1.5	2.5	2.5
Float weight (grams)	5.85 ± 0.3	5.85 ± 0.3	5.85 ± 0.3
Choke fast idle gap (mm)	-	0.95 ± 0.05	-
Choke pull-down (mm) (a)	1.9 ± 0.2	-	-
Choke pull-down (mm) (a1)	2.85 ± 0.15	2.4 ± 0.2	2.4 ± 0.2
Choke pull-down (mm) (a2)	-	-	-
De-choke (mm)	4.0 ± 1.0	2.0 ± 1.0	2.0 ± 1.0

Pierburg 24/28, 28/30 & 28/32 2E3 carburettor

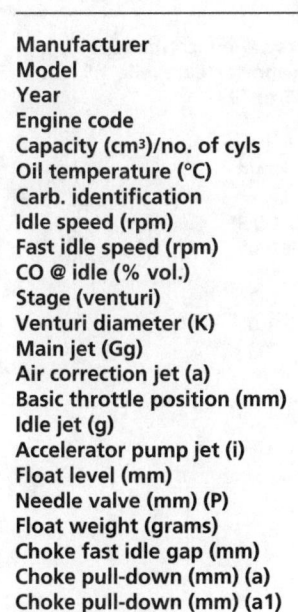

Manufacturer	Volkswagen		Volkswagen		Volkswagen	
Model	Polo 1.3		Golf/Jetta/Van 1.3		Golf/Jetta/Van 1.3	
Year	1987 to 1990		1983 to 1985		1985 to 1987	
Engine code	2G (40kW)		HK (40kW)		MH (40kW)	
Capacity (cm³)/no. of cyls	1272/4		1272/4		1272/4	
Oil temperature (°C)	80		80		80	
Carb. identification	030 129 016 F		052 129 016 B		030 129 016 C	
Idle speed (rpm)	800 ± 50		800 ± 50		800 ± 50	
Fast idle speed (rpm)	2000 ± 100		2000 ± 100		2000 ± 100	
CO @ idle (% vol.)	1.0 ± 0.5		3.0 ± 0.5		1.0 ± 0.5	
Stage (venturi)	1	2	1	2	1	2
Venturi diameter (K)	21	23	19	23	21	23
Main jet (Gg)	102.5	110	95	110	102.5	110
Air correction jet (a)	110	130	120	130	110	130
Basic throttle position (mm)	-	0.05 ± 0.02	-	0.05 ± 0.02	-	0.05 ± 0.02
Idle jet (g)	47.5		45		47.5	
Accelerator pump jet (i)	30		35		35	
Float level (mm)	27.5 ± 1.0		27.5 ± 1.0		27.5 ± 1.0	
Needle valve (mm) (P)	2.5		2.5		2.5	
Float weight (grams)	5.85 ± 0.3		5.85 ± 0.3		5.85 ± 0.3	
Choke fast idle gap (mm)	0.95 ± 0.05		-		-	
Choke pull-down (mm) (a)	1.6 ± 0.1		-		-	
Choke pull-down (mm) (a1)	2.8 ± 0.15		2.4 ± 0.2		2.4 ± 0.2	
De-choke (mm)	2.0 ± 1.0		2.0 ± 1.0		2.0 ± 1.0	

Manufacturer	Volkswagen		Volkswagen		Volkswagen	
Model	Golf/Jetta/Van 1.3		Golf/Jetta 1.3 Cat.		Transporter/Caravelle 1.9	
Year	1987 to 1991		1990 to 1991		1982 to 1985	
Engine code	2G (40kW)/NU (37kW)		2G (40kW)		DG (57kW)	
Capacity (cm³)/no. of cyls	1272/4		1272/4		1913/4	
Oil temperature (°C)	80		80		80	
Transmission	-		-		MT	
Carb. identification	030 129 016 F		030 129 016N		025 129 015	
Idle speed (rpm)	800 ± 50		800 ± 50		900 ± 50	
Fast idle speed (rpm)	2000 ± 100		2000 ± 100		2000 ± 200	
CO @ idle (% vol.)	1.0 ± 0.5		1.0 ± 0.5		1.5 ± 0.5	
Special conditions	-		CO: 0 to 1.5 at CO pipe		-	
Stage (venturi)	1	2	1	2	1	2
Venturi diameter (K)	19	23	21	23	22	26
Main jet (Gg)	95	110	102.5	110	102.5	110
Air correction jet (a)	120	130	110	130	50	45
Basic throttle position (mm)	-	0.05 ± 0.02	-		-	
Idle jet (g)	45		40		45	
Accelerator pump jet (i)	35		-		45	
Float level (mm)	27.5 ± 1.0		-		27.5 ± 1.0	
Needle valve (mm) (P)	2.5		-		2.5	
Float weight (grams)	5.85 ± 0.3		5.85 ± 0.3		5.85 ± 0.3	
Choke fast idle gap (mm)	-		-		1.3 ± 0.05	
Choke pull-down (mm) (a)	-		2.4 ± 0.2		-	
Choke pull-down (mm) (a1)	2.4 ± 0.2		4.0 ± 0.2		3.3	
De-choke (mm)	2.0 ± 1.0		-		-	

Manufacturer	Volkswagen		Volkswagen		Volkswagen	
Model	Transporter/Caravelle 1.9		Transporter/Caravelle 1.9		Transporter/Caravelle 1.9	
Year	1982 to 1985		1985 to 1987		1985 to 1987	
Engine code	DG (57kW)		DG (57kW)		DG (57kW)	
Capacity (cm³)/no. of cyls	1913/4		1913/4		1913/4	
Oil temperature (°C)	90		80		80	
Transmission	AT		-		-	
Carb. identification	025 129 015 A		025 129 015 H		025 129 015 J	
Idle speed (rpm)	900 ± 50		900 ± 50		900 ± 50	
Fast idle speed (rpm)	2000 ± 200		2000 ± 200		2000 ± 200	
CO @ idle (% vol.)	1.5 ± 0.5		1.5 ± 0.5		1.5 ± 0.5	
Stage (venturi)	1	2	1	2	1	2
Venturi diameter (K)	22	26	22	26	22	26
Main jet (Gg)	102.5	110	102.5	110	102.5	110
Air correction jet (a)	50	45	50	45	50	45
Basic throttle position (mm)	-	-	-	0.05 ± 0.02	-	0.05 ± 0.02

Chapter F6

Manufacturer	Volkswagen (continued)	Volkswagen (continued)	Volkswagen (continued)
Model	Transporter/Caravelle 1.9	Transporter/Caravelle 1.9	Transporter/Caravelle 1.9
Year	1982 to 1985	1985 to 1987	1985 to 1987
Idle jet (g)	45	45	45
Accelerator pump jet (i)	45	45	30
Float level (mm)	27.5 ± 1.0	27.5 ± 1.0	27.5 ± 1.0
Needle valve (mm) (P)	2.5	2.5	2.5
Float weight (grams)	5.85 ± 0.3	5.85 ± 0.3	5.85 ± 0.3
Choke fast idle gap (mm)	1.3 ± 0.05	1.3 ± 0.05	1.3 ± 0.05
Choke pull-down (mm) (a)	-	-	-
Choke pull-down (mm) (a1)	3.3	2.6 ± 0.2	2.6 ± 0.2
De-choke (mm)	-	3.5 ± 1.0	3.5 ± 1.0

Manufacturer	Volkswagen	
Model	LT 2.4	
Year	Oct. 1986 to 1992	
Engine code	DL (66kW)	
Capacity (cm^3)/no. of cyls	2383/6	
Oil temperature (°C)	80	
Carb. identification	073 129 015 A	
Idle speed (rpm)	750 ± 50	
Fast idle speed (rpm)	1800 ± 50	
CO @ idle (% vol.)	1.0 ± 0.5	
Stage (venturi)	1	2
Venturi diameter (K)	24	26
Main jet (Gg)	107.5	135
Air correction jet (a)	110	100
Idle jet (g)	50	
Accelerator pump jet (i)	45	
Float level (mm)	-	
Float weight (grams)	5.85 ± 0.3	
Choke pull-down (mm) (a)	3.5 ± 0.15	
Choke pull-down (mm) (a1)	7.2 ± 0.2	

1 Principles of operation

Introduction

1 The following technical description of the Pierburg 2E3 carburettor should be read in conjunction with the more detailed description of carburettor principles in Part A.

Construction

2 The Pierburg 2E3 carburettor is a downdraught progressive twin venturi instrument with a vacuum-controlled secondary throttle *(see illustration)*. The throttle shafts are made of steel, while the throttle plates, all jets and the emulsion tube are manufactured from brass. The internal fuel channels and air passages are drilled and sealed with lead plugs where necessary. The choke system is semi-automatic in operation and acts on the primary venturi alone. The major body components are cast in light alloy.

3 Most versions of the 2E3 carburettor are used in conjunction with an electrical heater fitted to the inlet manifold. The purpose of the heater is to improve atomisation of the air/fuel mixture during the warm-up period. A thermal switch is usually wired to the supply voltage so that the heater is switched off at a pre-determined temperature. Some versions also use a throttle body heater to prevent carburettor icing. Both heaters function on the positive temperature coefficient (PTC) principle. As the temperature rises, the heater resistance also rises. The choke strangler flap is controlled by a bi-metal coil which is heated by both an electrical supply and the engine coolant.

4 From 1988, the 2E3 carburettor fitted to the Ford ICVH engine uses the ESC II ECU and a power relay for finer control of the choke bi-metal coil during warm-up.

Fuel control

5 Fuel flows into the carburettor through a fine mesh filter located in the fuel inlet connection. The fuel level in the float chamber is controlled by a spring-loaded needle valve and plastic float assembly *(see illustration overleaf)*. The float level is considered critical and is set very accurately during production. The float chamber is vented internally into the upper air intake which is on the clean-air side of the air filter. Some variations use a vapour trap to prevent excess vapours and poor starting when the engine is hot. A calibrated fuel return system is provided to ensure that relatively cool fuel is supplied to the carburettor.

Idle, slow running and progression

6 Fuel is drawn from the primary main well into the base of a vertical well which dips down into the fuel. A combined idle jet, emulsion tube and air corrector is placed in the well. The fuel is mixed with air, drawn in through the calibrated air corrector and the holes in the tube, to form an emulsion. The resulting mixture is drawn through a channel to be discharged from the idle orifice under the primary throttle plate. A tapered mixture control screw is used to vary the outlet and this ensures fine control of the idle mixture *(see illustration overleaf)*.

7 A progression slot provides a further air contribution to the emulsion when the throttle is closed. As the progression slot is uncovered by the opening throttle, the vacuum draw overcomes the air bleed into the slot and a reversal occurs. Fuel is now drawn out to add extra enrichment to the idle mixture during initial acceleration.

8 The idle speed is set by an adjustable screw. The adjustable mixture screw is tamper proofed at production level in accordance with emission regulations.

Pierburg 24/28, 28/30 & 28/32 2E3 carburettor

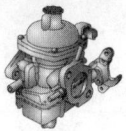

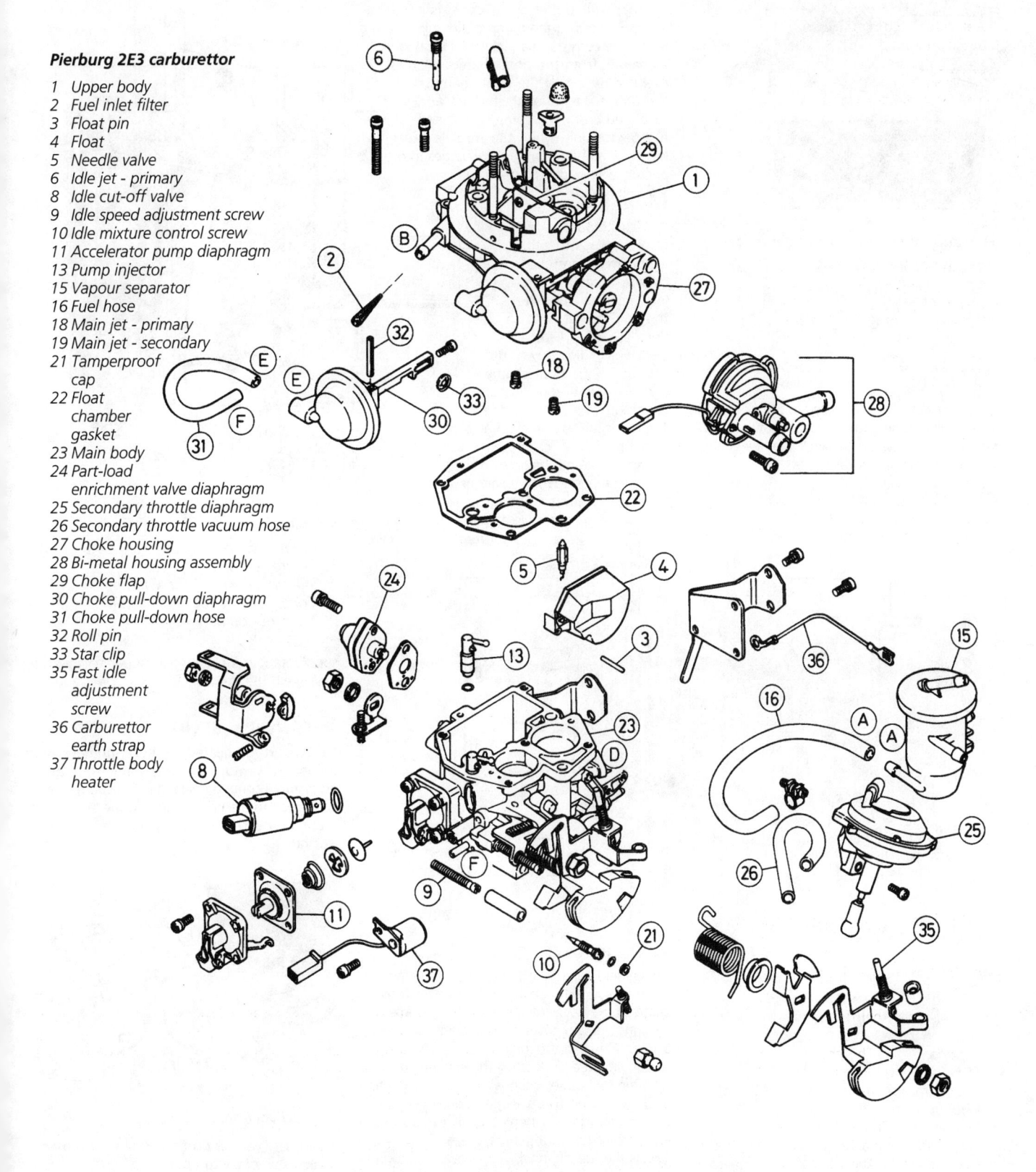

Pierburg 2E3 carburettor

1. Upper body
2. Fuel inlet filter
3. Float pin
4. Float
5. Needle valve
6. Idle jet - primary
8. Idle cut-off valve
9. Idle speed adjustment screw
10. Idle mixture control screw
11. Accelerator pump diaphragm
13. Pump injector
15. Vapour separator
16. Fuel hose
18. Main jet - primary
19. Main jet - secondary
21. Tamperproof cap
22. Float chamber gasket
23. Main body
24. Part-load enrichment valve diaphragm
25. Secondary throttle diaphragm
26. Secondary throttle vacuum hose
27. Choke housing
28. Bi-metal housing assembly
29. Choke flap
30. Choke pull-down diaphragm
31. Choke pull-down hose
32. Roll pin
33. Star clip
35. Fast idle adjustment screw
36. Carburettor earth strap
37. Throttle body heater

F6•7

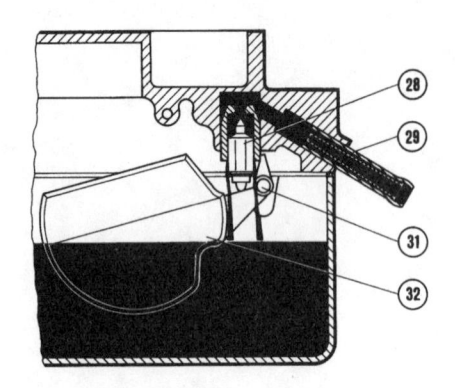

Chapter F6

Fuel supply and float arrangement

28 Float needle valve
29 Fuel supply inlet
31 Float pivot pin
32 Float

Idle cut-off valve (some variants)

9 An idle cut-off valve is used to prevent run-on when the engine is shut down. It utilises a 12-volt solenoid plunger to block the idle channel when the ignition is switched off.

Accelerator pump

10 The accelerator pump is controlled by a diaphragm and is mechanically-operated by a lever and cam attached to the primary throttle linkage. The outlet valve consists of a ball incorporated into the pump outlet injector. The inlet valve consists of an inlet seal located in a channel from the float chamber. Excess fuel is returned to the float chamber through an additional channel and calibrated bush. The pump is designed to operate only when the throttle is less than half-open and it discharges into the primary venturi *(see illustration)*.

Main circuit

11 The amount of fuel discharged into the airstream is controlled by a calibrated main jet. Fuel is drawn through the jet, into the base of a vertical well which dips down into the fuel in the float chamber. A combined emulsion tube and air correction jet is placed in the well. The fuel is mixed with air, drawn in through the calibrated air correction jet and the holes in the emulsion tubes, to form an air/fuel emulsion. The resulting mixture is discharged from the main nozzle through an auxiliary venturi into the main airstream.

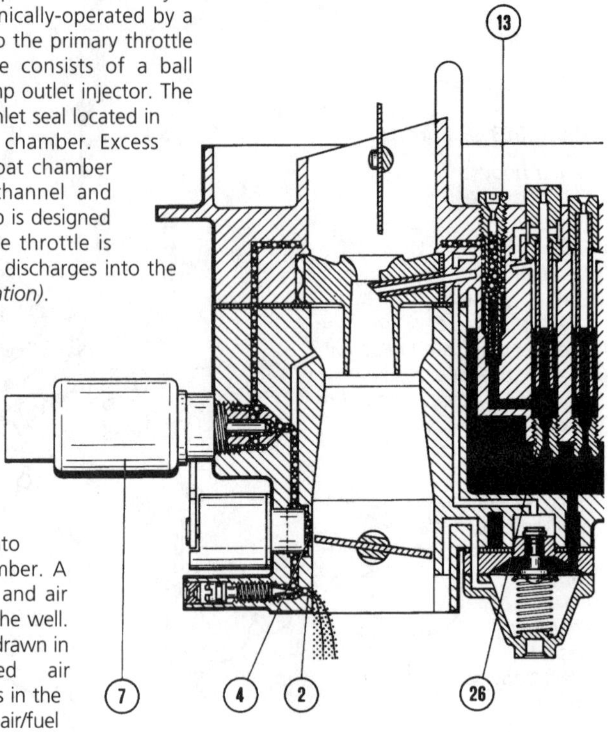

Idle circuit

2 Idle mixture orifice
4 Progression slot
7 Idle cut-off valve (where fitted)
13 Combined idle fuel and air corrector jet
26 Main jet - primary venturi

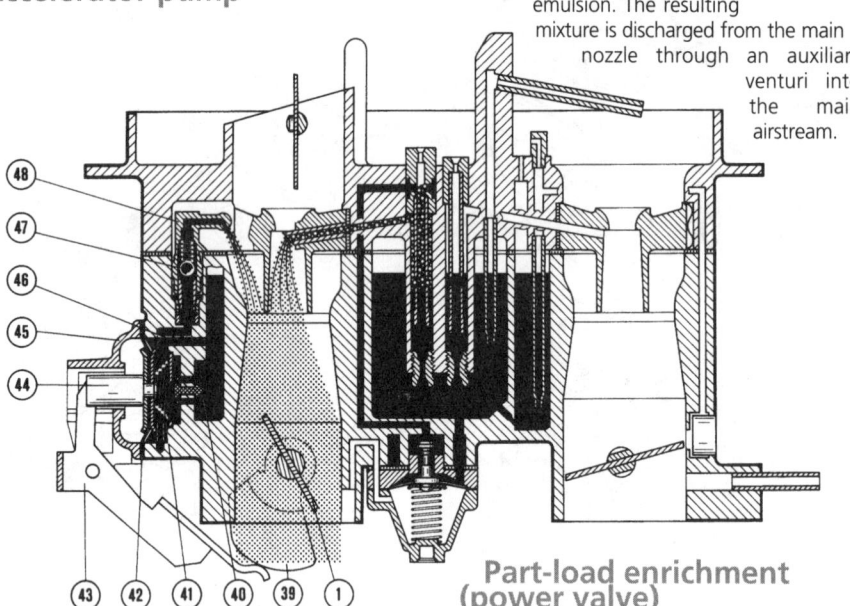

supplement the fuel in the upper part of the main well. The fuel level rises in the well and the fuel mixture is enriched.

Secondary action

13 A port is located in both primary and secondary venturis. Airways run from these ports into a common passage. A vacuum hose is connected to the passage and to the diaphragm that controls the secondary throttle plate *(see illustration)*.

Part-load enrichment (power valve)

12 Fuel flows from the float chamber into the enrichment chamber through a fuel channel. An air passage is taken from under the throttle plate to the cover of the chamber. At idle and during light-throttle operation, manifold vacuum draws the diaphragm back against spring pressure to close off the enrichment valve and the fuel outlet channel. Under acceleration and wide-open throttle operation, the vacuum in the manifold is depleted. The diaphragm returns under spring pressure and the valve opens the fuel channel. This allows fuel to flow through the channel and a calibrated bushing to

Accelerator pump circuit

1 Throttle plate - primary venturi
39 Accelerator pump cam
40 Suction valve
41 Spring
42 Diaphragm
43 Accelerator pump lever
44 Plunger
45 Pump cover
46 Return jet
47 Outlet (ball) valve
48 Pump injector

Venturi vacuum sources

A Primary venturi port
B Secondary venturi port
C Vacuum supply pipe

Pierburg 24/28, 28/30 & 28/32 2E3 carburettor

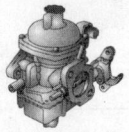

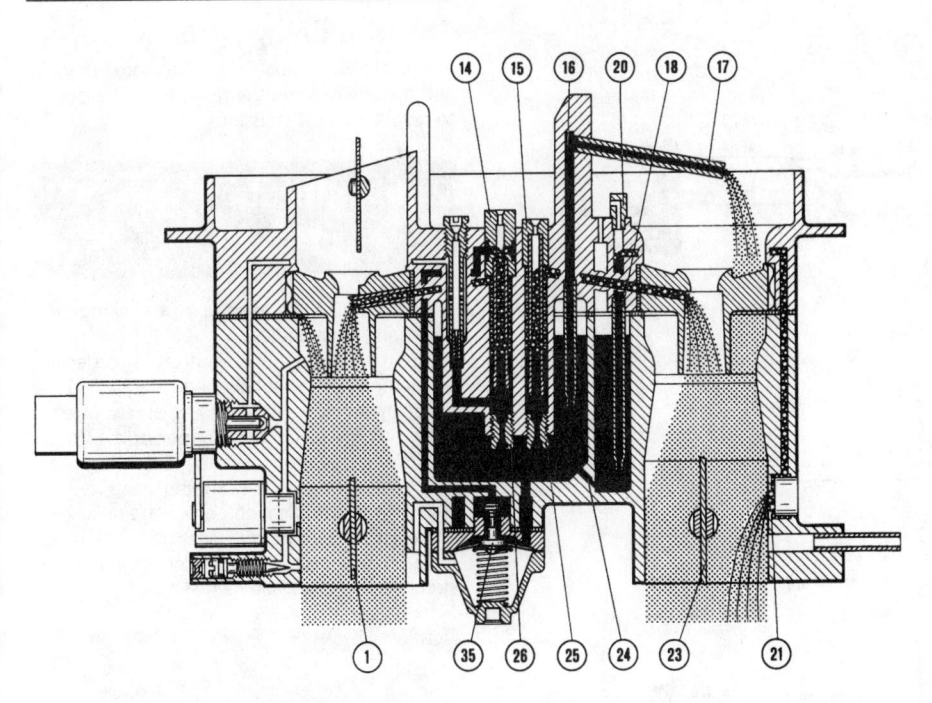

Full-load enrichment circuit

1 Throttle plate - primary venturi
14 Air corrector jet with emulsion tube - primary venturi
15 Air corrector jet with emulsion tube - secondary venturi
16 Calibrated channel for full-load enrichment - secondary venturi
17 Nozzle for full-load enrichment - secondary venturi
18 Emulsion tube for progression fuel - secondary venturi
20 Air bleed for progression fuel - secondary venturi
21 Progression slot - secondary venturi
23 Throttle plate - secondary venturi
24 Fuel drilling
25 Main jet - secondary venturi
26 Main jet - primary venturi
35 Part-load enrichment valve

14 During normal operation at low speeds, only the primary venturi is employed. When the air velocity through the primary venturi reaches a certain level, depression acts upon the port to operate the secondary diaphragm and the secondary throttle. Vacuum created in the secondary venturi will further control the rate of secondary opening.
15 The primary linkage is arranged to prevent the secondary plate from opening when the air speed may be high but the engine is cruising on a light throttle. Secondary action will not take place until the primary throttle is about half open.
16 On some variants, a thermal valve is connected to the vacuum supply hose so that the secondary throttle plate is inoperative during the engine warm-up period. The valve remains open (low vacuum) when the engine is cold and closes at a pre-determined temperature to restore full vacuum to the diaphragm.
17 Once the secondary throttle plate has opened, the action of the secondary main circuit is similar to that of the primary circuit.
18 A progression jet is used to prevent hesitation as the secondary throttle plate starts to open. Fuel is drawn from the float chamber into the base of a vertical tube which dips down into the fuel. The fuel is mixed with air drawn in through a calibrated air jet to form an emulsion. The emulsified mixture is discharged into the secondary venturi, via a progression slot, at the initial opening of the secondary throttle plate.

Full-load enrichment

19 At full-load and high engine speeds, the velocity of air creates a depression sufficient to raise fuel from the float chamber into the base of a vertical tube. The fuel then passes through a calibrated bushing to the upper section of the secondary air intake, where it is discharged into the airstream from the full-load enrichment nozzle *(see illustration)*.

Cold start system

20 The choke system is semi-automatic in operation and utilises a flap in the primary air intake. The system is primed by depressing the accelerator pedal once or twice.
21 The choke strangler flap is controlled by a combined coolant and electrically-heated bi-metal coil *(see illustration)*.
22 On Ford and VW engines, the electrical supply to the choke is made through a coolant-heated thermal switch.
23 The electrical supply initially heats the choke coil after the first start from cold. As coolant passing through the bi-metal water housing warms up, it adds to the heating action applied to the choke spring. The choke flap will thus remain open while the coolant (and engine) remain warm. When the coolant reaches a preset temperature, the thermal switch cuts out the electrical supply (Ford and VW) and the coolant flow remains the only source of choke heating.
24 The choke flap is eccentrically-mounted, so that during cranking it is partially open to prevent an over-rich fuel mixture.
25 Once the engine has fired, the choke flap must open slightly to weaken the mixture and avoid flooding during idle and light-throttle operation. This is achieved by using manifold vacuum to actuate a pull-down diaphragm. A linkage attached to the diaphragm will then pull upon the flap.
26 On early Ford OHC models, a direct manifold-to-choke vacuum connection was made via a hose. The connection is made through the carburettor base.
27 The type of pull-down fitted can make either a single movement to actuate the diaphragm or may employ a two-stage pull-down system. When the two-stage pull-down system is used, the vacuum signal is relayed through a thermal time valve (TTV). The TTV is partially open to atmosphere at cold start time. When the engine fires, the vacuum applied to the pull-down diaphragm is low and it will only partially operate to pull-down gap 'a' *(see illustrations overleaf)*.
28 After 3 to 5 seconds, the electrically-heated TTV will close the connection to atmosphere and full manifold vacuum is applied to the pull-down diaphragm. The pull-down now fully operates to open the choke flap to gap 'a1'. The two pull-down stages ensure maximum richness for the few seconds after a cold start and then a rapid opening of the choke flap to reduce over-richness.
29 The Ford ICVH engine utilises a T-piece in the hose from the carburettor base to the pull-down diaphragm. The basic method of operation, however, is the same.
30 Some versions may use a thermal valve heated by the engine coolant to accomplish the two pull-down stages. In this instance, the second pull-down will not operate until the coolant temperature rises to over 50°C.

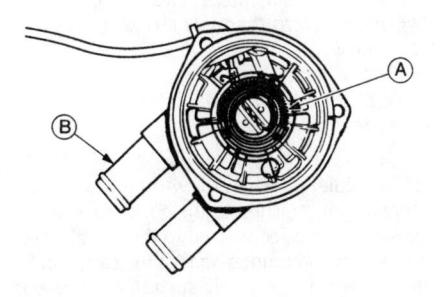

Bi-metal coil heating sources

A Electric heating coil
B Coolant water housing

Chapter F6

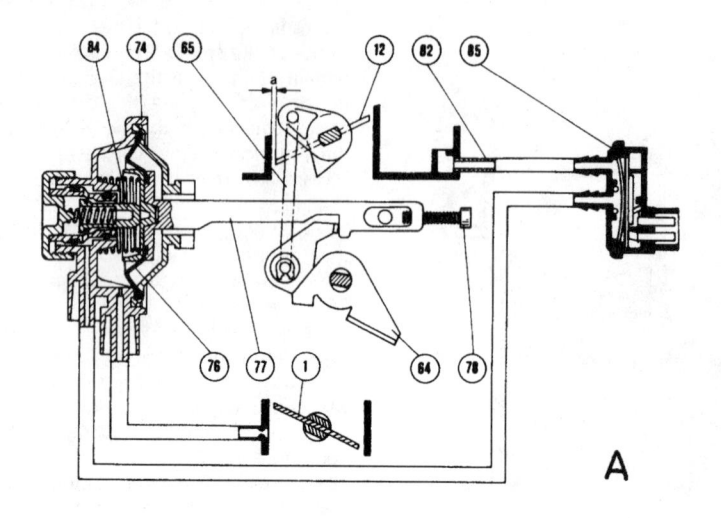

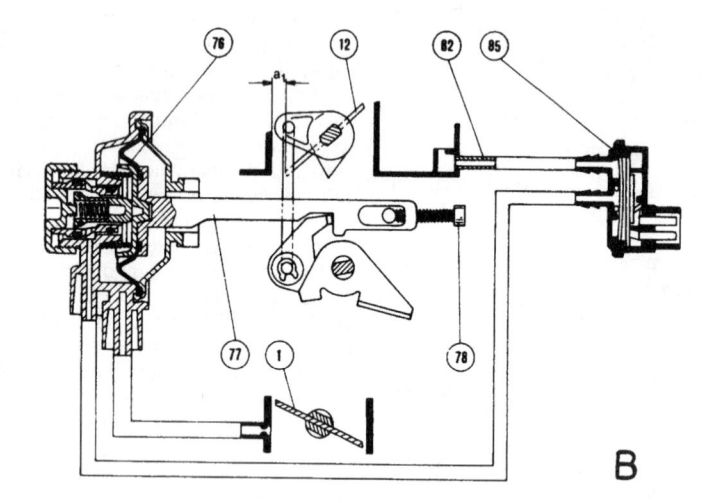

Choke pull-down operation
A Stage 1 pull-down
B Stage 2 pull-down
1 Throttle plate - primary venturi
12 Choke flap
64 Choke lever
65 Choke connecting rod
74 Pull-down assembly
76 Diaphragm
77 Diaphragm rod
78 Pull-down adjustment screw 'a1'
82 Connection to thermal time valve (TTV)
84 Control valve
85 Thermal time valve (TTV)
a Stage 1 pull-down gap
a1 Stage 2 pull-down gap

31 Fast idle is achieved with the aid of a stepped cam attached to the choke spindle. An adjustable screw, connected to the throttle lever mechanism and butting against the cam, can be used to vary the fast idle speed. This screw is fitted with a tamperproof cap. As the bi-metal coil is heated and the flap opens, the screw will rest on successively less-stepped parts of the cam. The idle speed is thus progressively reduced, until ultimately the cam is released and the idle speed returns to normal.

De-choke (wide-open kick)

32 If the throttle is opened fully when the engine is cold, the pull-down vacuum will deplete and the choke flap will tend to close. This may cause flooding and to prevent this, a wide-open kick mechanism is employed. When the throttle is opened fully, a cam on the throttle lever will turn the choke lever anti-clockwise to partially open the flap.

Choke relay and vacuum damper

33 This system is used only on the Ford ICVH engine from 1988. The ESC II ECU and a power relay achieve finer control of the choke bi-metal coil during warm-up. The ECU controls the rate at which the choke is opened. Current from the alternator is regularly switched on and off at various frequencies, according to coolant and ambient temperature.

34 The vacuum damper governs the rate of throttle closing to reduce emissions. The damper is operated by solenoid and is also controlled by the ECU.

Throttle damper

35 A throttle damper is fitted to some models, and this slows down the rate of throttle closing to reduce exhaust emissions.

2 Identification

1 Pierburg 2E is stamped upon the carburettor upper and main bodies.
2 The manufacturer's identification code may be stamped on a metallic tag attached to the cover by an upper body fixing screw or on a corner of the carburettor upper body. Where the tag is missing, refer to Part B for other means of identifying the carburettor.
3 The Ford identification code is stamped on a corner of the carburettor upper body.
4 Early versions of this carburettor may be stamped with the trade name Solex.

3 General servicing

Introduction

1 Read this Chapter in conjunction with Part B which describes some of the operations in more detail. It is assumed that the carburettor is removed for this service. However, many of the operations can be tackled with the carburettor in place. Where this is undertaken, first remove the carburettor upper body and soak the fuel out of the float chamber using a clean tissue or soft cloth.

Modifications - Ford

2 An idle cut-off valve kit (available from Ford main agents) can be fitted to the idle circuit where a running-on condition exists. An idle cut-off valve is fitted as standard to vehicles with catalytic converters.

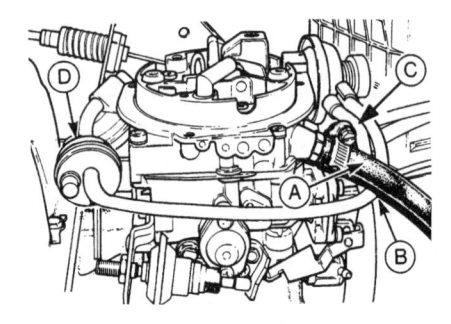

Vacuum connection to thermal time valve (TTV)
A Fuel inlet hose
B Hose to TTV
C Hose to vacuum source
D TTV

Pierburg 24/28, 28/30 & 28/32 2E3 carburettor

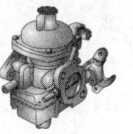

Dismantling and checking

3 Remove the carburettor from the engine (see Part B) (see illustration).
4 Check the carburettor visually for damage and wear.
5 Note the location and routing of the choke vacuum hoses and disconnect them. Remove the four screws and detach the carburettor upper body.
6 Remove the electrical earth strap (if fitted).
7 Inspect the float chamber for corrosion and calcium build-up.
8 Use a straight-edge to check for distorted flanges on all facing surfaces.
9 Tap out the float pin and remove the float, needle valve and float chamber gasket. The needle valve seat is not removable (see illustration).
10 Check that the anti-vibration ball is free in the needle valve end.
11 Check the needle valve tip for wear and ridges. Wear is more likely with the brass needle valve tip than when a viton one is used. Use a viton-tipped replacement when possible.
12 The float should be checked for damage

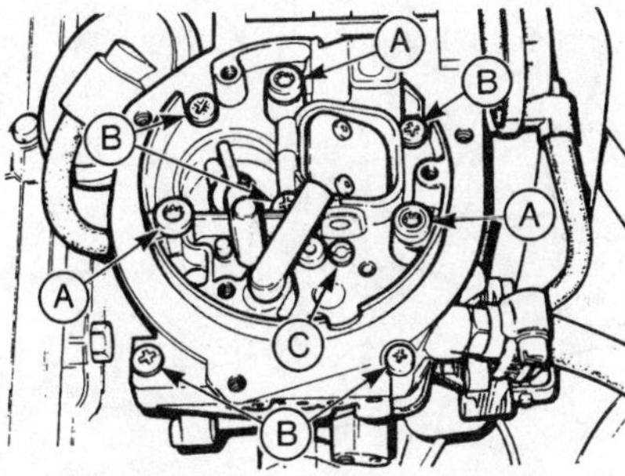

Carburettor securing screws

A Carburettor-to-manifold Torx screws
B Carburettor upper-to-main body fixing screws
C Idle jet

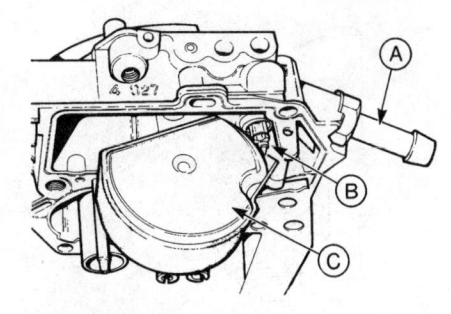

and ingress of petrol. Shaking the float will indicate the presence of fuel inside it.
13 Renew the float pin if it shows signs of wear.
14 Remove the fuel filter from its position in the fuel inlet connection. Clean the filter and renew it if necessary.
15 Remove the mixture screw and inspect the tip for damage and ridges.
16 Remove the four screws and detach the accelerator pump cover, diaphragm, spring and seal assembly. Check the diaphragm for fatigue and damage.
17 The pump injector is a push fit in the body. Carefully prise it from its location and test it by shaking it. No noise from the outlet ball would indicate that the valve is seized.
18 Remove the primary idle jet assembly, and both main jets. The primary idle jet can be removed from the carburettor without removing the upper body. It is not possible to remove any of the other jets or emulsion tubes (see illustrations).
19 Check that the channels from the float chamber into the emulsion tube wells are clear.
20 Note the jet sizes and their locations for correct installation during reassembly.
21 Check the jet calibration against that specified. It is possible that the jets may have been transposed (or the wrong size fitted) during the last overhaul.
22 Remove the two screws and detach the

Fuel supply system

A Inlet tube
B Needle valve
C Float

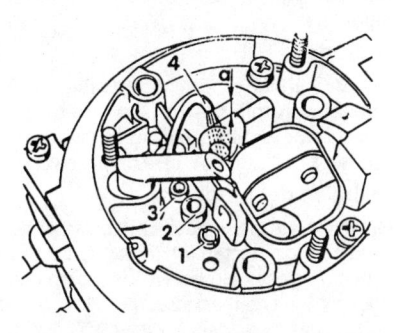

power valve housing cover, spring and diaphragm assembly. Check the diaphragm for damage and fatigue. Check the action of the power valve and the condition of the small seal. Check that the channel into the emulsion tube well is clear.
23 Remove and check the condition of the secondary throttle vacuum hose. Attach a vacuum pump to the vacuum connector and operate the pump until the diaphragm is actuated. Renew the diaphragm assembly if it does not operate fully or if vacuum is not maintained for at least 10 seconds.
24 Disconnect the secondary throttle operating rod by twisting the rod out of its socket on the throttle lever. Remove the two (or three) screws and detach the diaphragm assembly from the body.
25 Do not disturb the adjustment of the secondary throttle angle, unless absolutely necessary.
26 Inspect the choke flap, spindle and linkage for stickiness and wear.
27 Test the choke pull-down unit as described in Section 4.
28 Punch out the roll pin that secures the choke diaphragm assembly to the upper body. Remove the three screws that secure the choke housing to the upper body. Allow the housing to drop. It is unnecessary to disconnect the choke linkage. Remove the star fixing clip and detach the pull-down diaphragm assembly (see illustrations).

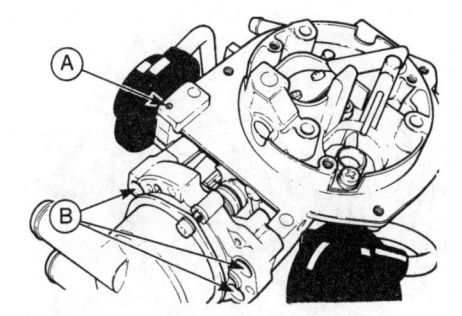

Location of upper jets in upper body

1 Idle jet - primary venturi
2 Main emulsion tube/air corrector - primary venturi
3 Main emulsion tube/air corrector - secondary venturi
4 Full-load enrichment tube
a Tube height above atomiser (VW models):
   To end April 1984 - a = 15 mm
   From May 1984 - a = 12 mm

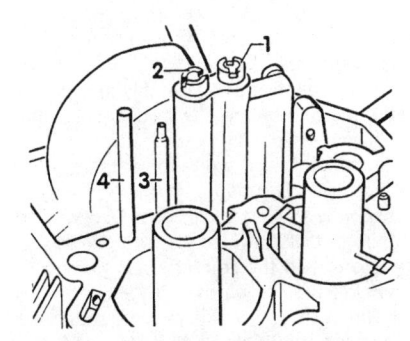

Location of lower jets in upper body

1 Main jet - primary venturi
2 Main jet - secondary venturi
3 Full-load enrichment tube
4 Secondary progression tube

Choke diaphragm assembly and lever housing

A Diaphragm assembly securing roll pin
B Choke lever housing securing screws

Star clip (arrowed) retaining diaphragm arm

F6•11

Chapter F6

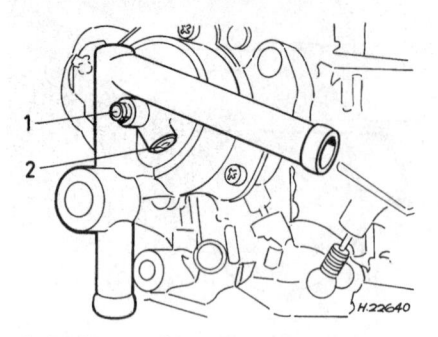

Choke bi-metal housing cover - some VW models

1 Hexagon head
2 Calibration screw
Under no circumstances must these two items be tampered with - maladjustment can only be corrected by a new choke cover

29 Certain VW models are fitted with a cover to the bi-metal housing, with a hexagon head and locknut *(see illustration)*. Under no circumstances should this nut be tampered with as it is set at the factory. Maladjustment will almost certainly mean a new choke housing cover will be required.

Preparation for reassembly

30 Inspect all vacuum hoses for condition and splits. Renew where necessary.
31 Clean the jets, carburettor body assemblies, float chamber and internal channels. An air line may be used to clear the internal channels once the carburettor is fully dismantled. Note that if high-pressure air is directed into the channels and passages with the diaphragms still in place, diaphragm damage may result. Spraying carburettor cleaner into all the channels and passages in the carburettor body will often clear them of gum and dirt.
32 During reassembly, a complete set of new gaskets should be fitted. Also renew the needle valve, the float pivot pin and all diaphragms. Inspect and renew (where necessary) the mixture screw, main jets, idle jet and the accelerator pump injector. Renew worn linkages, springs, vacuum hoses and other parts where necessary.
33 Ensure that all jets are firmly locked into their original positions (but do not over-tighten). A loose jet can cause a rich (or even lean) running condition.
34 Clean all mating surfaces and flanges of old gasket material and reassemble with new gaskets. Ensure that housings are positioned with their air and fuel routes correctly aligned.

Reassembly

35 Slide the choke diaphragm assembly into position and secure with a new star clip and roll pin. Refit the choke housing and secure with the three screws.
36 Ensure that the choke flap and linkage move smoothly and progressively.
37 Refit the secondary throttle diaphragm

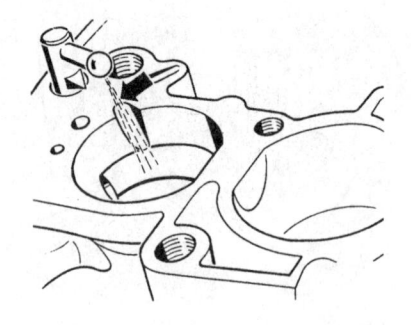

Alignment of accelerator pump injector

assembly and secure with the fixing screws. Reconnect the throttle operating rod and the vacuum hose.
38 Check that the secondary throttle plate is fully closed. The adjustment screw should not normally be used to alter the throttle plate position. However, if necessary, it can be adjusted so that the plate is open just enough to prevent its seizure in the throttle body.
39 Refit the power diaphragm, spring and cover assembly, then secure with the two screws.
40 Refit two main jets and a primary idle jet into their original positions (do not transpose the jets).
41 Align the pump injector *(see illustration)* and tap it into position after renewing the small seal on the injector body.
42 Refit the accelerator pump seal, spring, diaphragm and cover assembly, then secure with the four screws.
43 Refit the idle mixture screw after renewing the small seal. Turn the screw in gently until it just seats. From this position, unscrew it three full turns. This will provide a basic setting to allow the engine to be started.
44 Place the fuel filter in the fuel inlet tube.
45 Insert the needle valve into the seat with the ball facing outwards. Refit the float and pivot pin. Ensure that the top of the needle valve engages into the slot on the float.
46 Check the float level (see Section 4). Refit the float gasket to the upper body.
47 Refit the upper body to the main body and secure with the four screws. Ensure that the

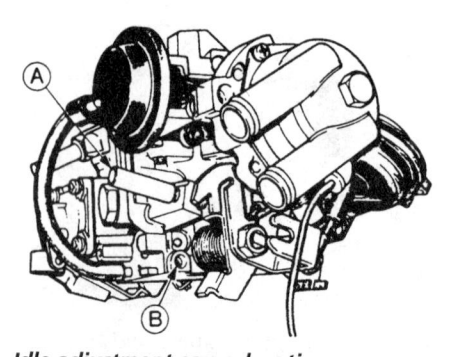

Idle adjustment screw location

A Idle speed adjustment screw
B Idle mixture control screw

choke earth strap (where fitted) is secured by one of the upper body screws.
48 Refit the choke vacuum hoses in their original positions.
49 Check that the full-load enrichment tube is directed into the centre of the second venturi. Gently bend the tube so that this is accomplished. On VW models, check the tube height as shown in the illustration on page F6•11.
50 Refit the carburettor to the engine.
51 Always adjust the carburettor idle speed and mixture after any work has been carried out on the carburettor, preferably with the aid of a CO meter.
52 Adjust the choke (see Section 4).

4 Service adjustments

Adjustment pre-conditions

1 Refer to Part B for general advice on the pre-conditions for correct adjustment of this carburettor.

VW models

2 On VW models, disconnect the engine breather hose from the air filter and plug the opening in the air filter. Reconnect the breather hose after all adjustments are completed.

Vauxhall/Opel models

3 On Vauxhall/Opel models, the breather hose may remain connected while the adjustments are being made. However, on completion, disconnect the breather hose.

All models

4 If the CO level decreases more than 1 to 1.5%, change the sump oil. If the CO level still decreases after an oil change, suspect worn or sticking piston rings. If no CO change is noted on connecting/disconnecting the breather hose, suspect a clogged crankcase breather (PCV) system.

Idle speed and mixture (CO)

5 Run the engine at 3000 rpm for 30 seconds to clear the manifold of fuel vapours, then allow the engine to idle.
6 Remove the air filter assembly and place it clear of the carburettor. The vacuum hoses must remain connected.
7 Use the idle speed screw to set the specified idle speed *(see illustration)*.
8 Check the CO level. If incorrect, remove the tamperproof plug and adjust the idle mixture screw to obtain the correct level. Turning the screw clockwise (inwards) will reduce the CO level. Turning the screw anti-clockwise (outwards) will increase the CO level. Refer to Part B for a method of setting the idle mixture without the aid of a CO meter.
9 Repeat paragraphs 7 and 8 until both adjustments are correct.
10 Clear the manifold every 30 seconds during

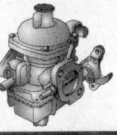

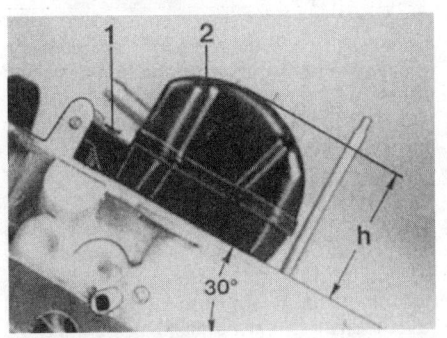

Pierburg 24/28, 28/30 & 28/32 2E3 carburettor

Float level checking
1. Needle valve pin
2. Float
h. Float height

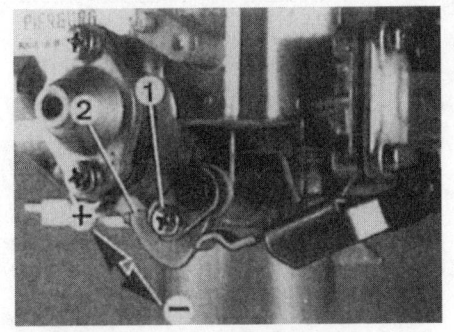

Accelerator pump adjustment
1. Clamping screw
2. Pump cam

Fast idle adjustment - engine running
3. Fast idle adjustment screw
4. Stepped cam

the setting operation by running the engine at 3000 rpm for 30 seconds.

11 Increase the speed to 2000 rpm and note the CO reading. The cruise reading should be less than half the idle CO reading.

12 Fit a new tamperproof plug to the mixture adjusting screw on completion.

13 Refit the air filter assembly, ensuring that the vacuum hoses remain connected.

Float level

14 It is not possible to adjust the plastic float. It is possible, however, to check the level.

15 Hold the upper body at an angle of 30° with the float tag gently touching the ball of the fully-closed needle valve.

16 Measure the distance between the upper body (without its gasket) and the top of the float (see Specifications) *(see illustration)*.

17 If the level is incorrect, check the needle valve seat for correct position. Remove the float and check the float weight (see Specifications). If the float seat and weight are satisfactory, renew the float if the level is still incorrect.

Accelerator pump

18 On the Pierburg 2E3 carburettor, it is possible to adjust the volume of fuel injected by the accelerator pump.

19 Loosen the clamping screw (1) *(see illustration)*. Move the cam in direction (+) to increase the volume or in direction (-) to decrease the volume.

20 Tighten the clamping screw on completion.

Automatic choke

Fast idle

21 Warm the engine to normal running temperature and adjust the idle speed and mixture before attempting choke fast idle adjustment.

22 Remove the air filter assembly and place it clear of the carburettor. The vacuum hoses must remain connected.

23 Position the fast idle adjustment screw against the second-highest step of the fast idle cam *(see illustration)*.

24 Start the engine without moving the throttle and record the fast idle speed (see Specifications).

25 Remove the tamperproof plug and adjust as necessary by turning the fast idle screw in the appropriate direction.

26 Because access to the adjustment screw is limited, stop the engine and partially open the throttle so that a small screwdriver can be used.

Choke pull-down (Ford)

27 Remove the three screws and detach the bi-metal coil housing from the carburettor.

28 Position the fast idle screw on the highest step of the fast idle cam.

29 Move the pull-down operating rod up to its stop by fully pushing on the pull-down adjusting screw or by using a vacuum pump *(see illustration)*. At the same time, use the shank of a twist drill to measure the gap between the lower section of the choke flap and the air intake *(see illustration)*. See Specifications for correct drill size.

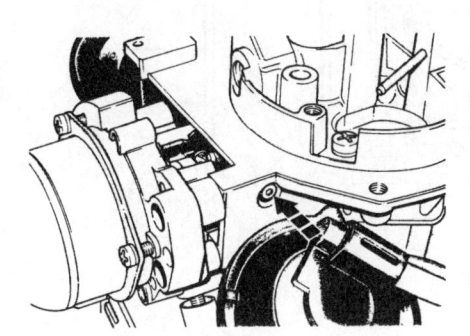

30 Adjust as necessary, using a 2.5 mm Allen key to turn the pull-down adjusting screw in the appropriate direction *(see illustration)*.

31 Refit the bi-metal coil housing and ensure that the spring locates in the slot of the choke lever. Secure loosely with the three screws.

32 Align the cut mark on the bi-metal cover with the correct mark on the choke assembly housing and tighten the three screws. Note that the choke housing has six screw holes and any three can be used *(see illustration)*.

Choke pull-down (VW and Vauxhall/Opel)

33 Remove the three screws and detach the bi-metal coil housing from the carburettor.

Push on pull-down adjusting screw (arrowed) to achieve maximum pull-down clearance

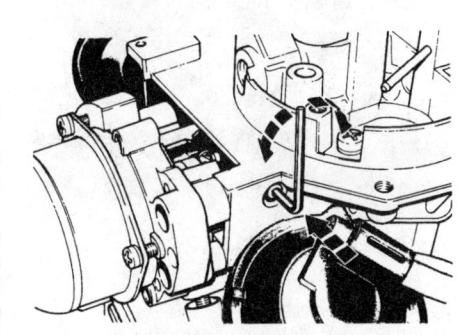

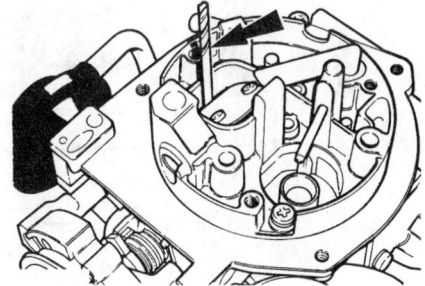

Checking choke flap clearance using a twist drill

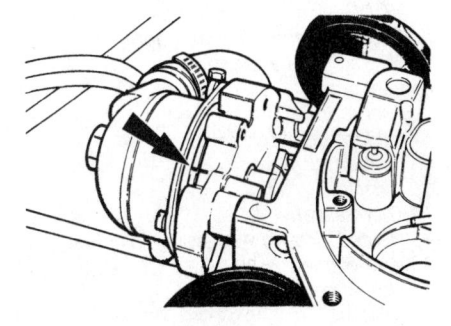

Choke pull-down adjustment

Choke alignment marks

Chapter F6

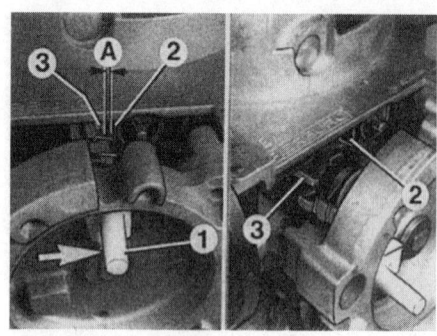

Closure of choke flap

1. Move choke control lever fully in direction of arrow
2. Diaphragm rod
3. Adjustment lever
A. Clearance = 0.2 to 1.0 mm

34 Fully close the choke flap using the choke control lever. The throttle plate must be closed.
35 If the flap does not close completely, set clearance 'A' *(see illustration)* to between 0.2 and 1.0 mm. The gap is adjusted by bending the lever '3' in the appropriate direction.
36 Remove the vacuum hose from the carburettor base to the inlet connection (supply side) of the pull-down unit and attach a vacuum pump to the connection. Remove the second hose from the outlet side and leave the connection unplugged *(see illustrations)*.
37 Operate the pump, and the pull-down should move to the first stage.
38 Maintaining the vacuum, plug the pull-down outlet connection and then operate the pump until 225 mmHg (300 mbars) is obtained. The pull-down should now move to the second stage and hold vacuum for at least 10 seconds. If the diaphragm does not operate as described, renew the pull-down unit.
39 Note that if the pull-down unit is a single-stage type, follow the procedure for testing the second stage of the two-stage unit described above.
40 Place the fast idle screw on the highest step of the fast idle cam.

Single-stage pull-down unit

41 Where a single-stage pull-down unit is fitted, remove the outlet vacuum hose and plug the pull-down connection. Move the pull-down operating rod up to its stop by operating the vacuum pump. Lightly close the choke flap and use the shank of a twist drill to measure the 'a1' gap between the lower section of the choke flap and the air intake. See Specifications for the required drill size. Adjust as necessary by turning the pull-down adjusting screw '4' in the appropriate direction *(see illustration)*.

Two-stage pull-down unit

42 Where a two-stage pull-down unit is fitted, detach the pull-down to the thermal time valve (or thermal valve) vacuum hose from the connection on the pull-down unit. Do not plug the connection. Operate the vacuum pump and the choke flap should open to the first stage setting. Lightly close the choke flap and use the shank of a twist drill to measure the a clearance between the lower section of the choke flap and the air intake. See Specifications for the required drill size.
43 Adjust as necessary by turning the first stage pull-down adjusting screw '3' in the appropriate direction. Note that the a clearance should only be checked if the pull-down unit has been renewed or the setting has been

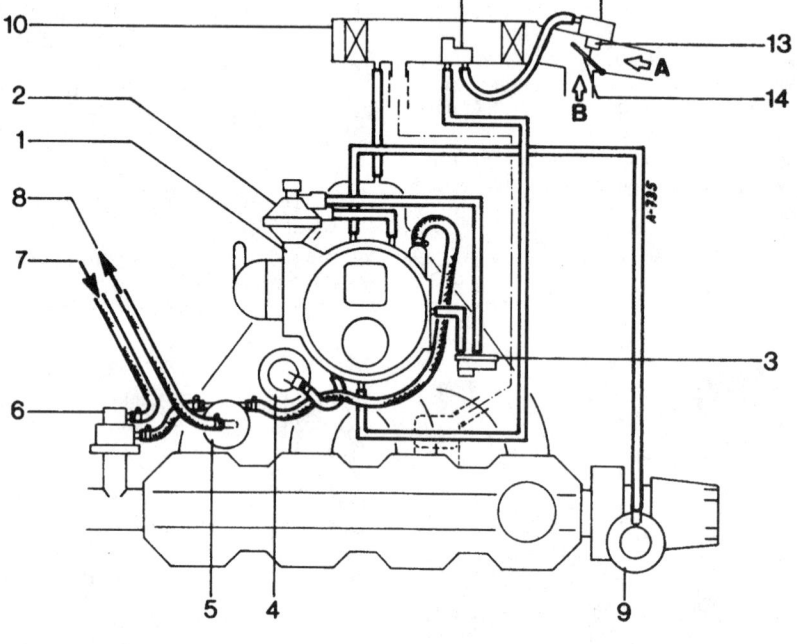

Typical vacuum hose connections - Vauxhall/Opel

1. Carburettor
2. Pull-down diaphragm
3. TTV
4. Secondary throttle diaphragm
5. Vapour separator
6. Fuel pump
7. Fuel supply
8. Fuel return
9. Ignition distributor
10. Air filter
11. Thermal valve
12. Heated air warm-up system diaphragm
13. Wax element
14. Hot air control flap
A. Cold air
B. Warm air

Testing vacuum pull-down

1. Pull-down unit
2. Outlet connection
3. First stage adjustment screw 'a'

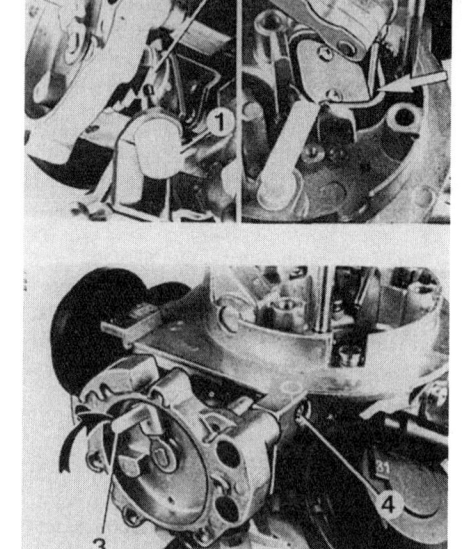

Choke pull-down adjustment

1. Fast idle adjustment screw
2. Stepped cam
3. Close choke flap by moving choke control lever fully in direction of arrow
4. Second stage adjustment screw 'a1'

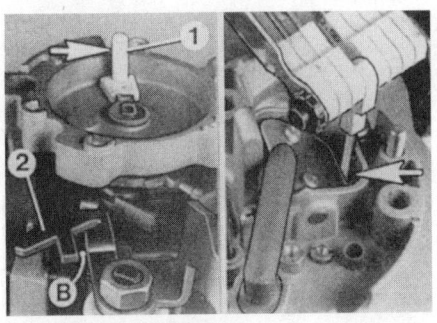

Pierburg 24/28, 28/30 & 28/32 2E3 carburettor

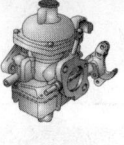

De-choke adjustment

1 Close choke flap by moving choke control lever fully in direction of arrow
2 Dechoke lever
B Adjustment tag

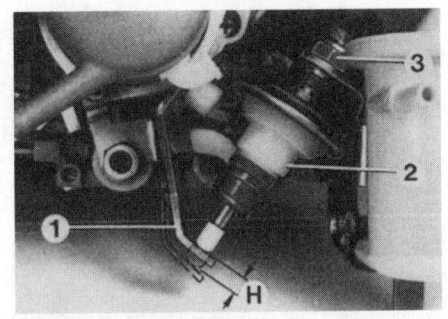

Throttle damper adjustment

1 Lever
2 Damper
3 Locknut
H Lift = 3.0 ± 0.5 mm

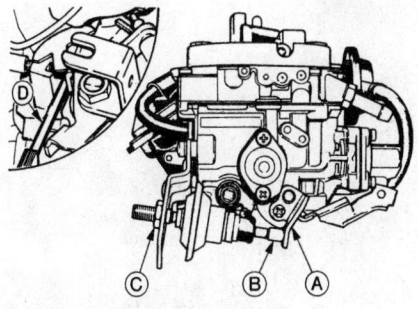

Throttle damper adjustment

A Actuating lever
B Damper plunger
C Damper locknut
Inset shows 2 mm feeler gauge (D) in place

disturbed. Plug the pull-down outlet connection. Fully operate the vacuum pump and the choke flap should open to the second stage setting. Lightly close the choke flap and use the shank of a twist drill to measure the 'a1' clearance between the lower section of the choke flap and the air intake. Refer to Specifications for the required drill size.

44 Adjust as necessary by turning the second stage pull-down adjusting screw '4' in the appropriate direction. Where a vacuum pump is not available, a small screwdriver can also be used to fully push on the a1 adjusting screw. In this instance, the screw should be pushed until a resistance is felt. The clearance obtained at this point is the first stage setting. Continue pushing until the screw cannot be pushed any further. The clearance now obtained is the second stage setting.

De-choke adjustment

45 Fully close the choke flap and hold it in this position. The operation is simplified with the aid of a rubber band, arranged between the choke control lever and the carburettor body.
46 Fully operate the throttle and the choke flap should be forced open to leave a small clearance.
47 Use the shank of a twist drill to measure the gap between the lower section of the choke flap and the air intake. Refer to Specifications for the required drill size.
48 Adjust as necessary by bending the tag 'B' (see illustration) in the appropriate direction.
49 Reconnect all the vacuum hoses.
50 Refit the bi-metal coil housing, ensuring that the spring locates in the slot of the choke lever. Secure loosely with the three screws.
51 Align the cut mark on the bi-metal cover with the correct mark on the choke assembly housing and tighten the three screws.
52 Refit the air filter assembly, ensuring that the vacuum hoses remain connected.

Throttle damper (automatic transmission models)

53 Warm the engine to normal running temperature and ensure that the idle speed and mixture are correctly adjusted.

54 Slacken the damper locknut and wind the damper up until a gap of 0.05 mm exists between the dashpot rod and the throttle lever (see illustration).
55 Wind the damper down 2.5 turns and tighten the locknut in this position to complete.

Throttle damper (Ford OHC engine)

56 Stop the engine and slacken the damper locknut (see illustration).
57 Position a 2 mm feeler gauge between the idle speed screw and throttle lever.
58 Adjust the damper so that the plunger just touches the operating lever without compressing the plunger. Tighten the locknut in this position.

Vacuum damper (Ford ICVH engine)

59 Put the ECU into service-adjust mode. The service connector is located by the battery. Allow the engine to idle and use a jump lead to connect the service connector to earth for at least ten seconds (see illustration).
60 The vacuum damper will be activated and the engine speed will rise to 1700 ± 100 rpm.
61 If the speed does not rise, first check the vacuum hose and diaphragm for leaks.
62 Locate the damper solenoid (on the offside inner wing) and check for a voltage supply when the ignition is switched on.
63 Check the solenoid earth which is made through terminal 12 on the ECU. While the solenoid is activated, the reading on the solenoid earth connection will be 1 volt. When not activated, the reading will be nominal battery voltage.
64 Adjust the engine speed as necessary by turning the adjustment screw in the appropriate direction (see illustration).
65 Turn off the service adjuster by ensuring that the jump lead is no longer connected to earth and then by simply switching off the ignition.

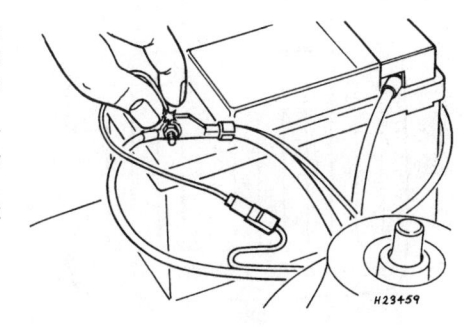

5 Component testing

Vacuum components

1 After removing the accelerator pump injector, attach the hose of a vacuum pump to the injector body (opposite end to injector nozzle). Operate the pump until 300 mm Hg is registered. Renew the injector assembly if the vacuum is not maintained for 10 seconds (see illustration).

Earth service connector for at least 10 seconds

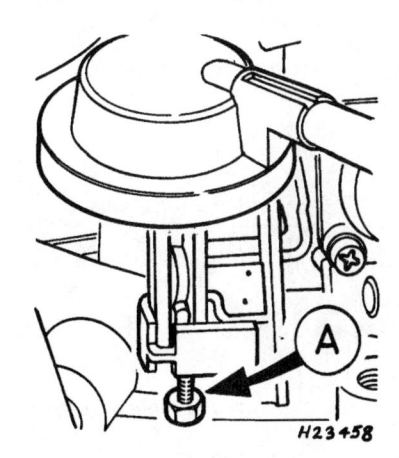

Vacuum damper adjustment (A)

F6•15

Chapter F6

Testing accelerator pump injector assembly with a vacuum pump

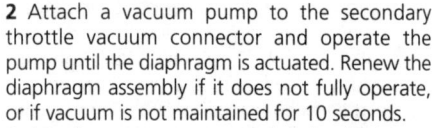

Vacuum gauge connected to choke vacuum source connector

Thermal time valve testing
3 TTV
4 Electrical connector plug

2 Attach a vacuum pump to the secondary throttle vacuum connector and operate the pump until the diaphragm is actuated. Renew the diaphragm assembly if it does not fully operate, or if vacuum is not maintained for 10 seconds.

3 Attach a vacuum pump to a choke diaphragm connector (seal the second connector with a finger if there is more than one connector) and operate the pump until the diaphragm is actuated. Renew the diaphragm if it does not fully operate, or if vacuum is not maintained for 10 seconds (see illustration).

4 Start the engine and attach a vacuum gauge to the choke vacuum source connector, then to the secondary throttle vacuum source connector on the carburettor body. If manifold vacuum is not obtained, check for a blockage at the appropriate connector.

Thermal time valve (VW, Vauxhall/Opel and Ford OHC)

5 With the engine cold, disconnect the vacuum hose to the TTV and attach a vacuum pump. Operate the pump and it should not be possible to obtain a reading (see illustration).

6 Keep operating the pump and start the engine. Within 5 to 10 seconds, 300 mmHg (400 mbars) should be obtained and held for at least 10 seconds.

7 If the TTV does not function as above, check the voltage supply and earth at the electrical connection.

8 The TTV resistance should be 4.5 to 7.5 ohms at 20°C.

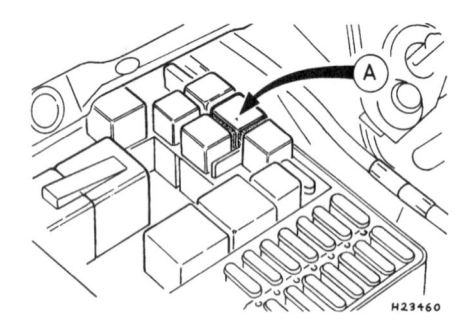

9 If the electrical supply is satisfactory, renew the TTV if it does not function correctly.

Thermal switch

10 Refer to Part D for general tests on the thermal switch, automatic choke electrical heater, and the inlet manifold and throttle body heaters.

11 Below 55 ± 10°C, a voltmeter should indicate battery voltage (switch open).

12 Above 65 ± 10°C, the voltmeter should indicate zero volts (switch closed).

13 Renew the thermal switch if it does not function in accordance with the above.

Thermal valve (VW)

14 Refer to Part D for general tests on the thermal valve fitted to the choke pull-down and secondary throttle vacuum hoses (some models).

15 Below 17°C, no vacuum should register (switch open).

16 Above 53°C, normal idle vacuum should register (switch closed).

17 Renew the thermal valve if it does not function in accordance with the above.

Choke relay (Ford)

18 Allow the engine to cool completely.

19 Remove the air filter and operate the throttle once or twice to set the choke flap. Check that the flap blocks the carburettor air intake.

20 Start the engine and check that the cold idle speed is within limits.

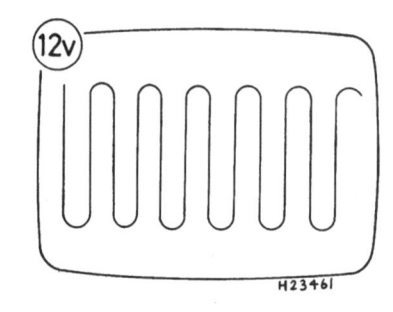

Choke relay location (A)

Choke relay oscilloscope trace

21 Check that the choke pull-down operates satisfactorily.

22 As the engine warms up, check that the choke flap gradually opens until it is fully open.

23 If the choke flap operation is unsatisfactory, check the choke pull-down adjustment and look for a sticking, worn or broken linkage, or split vacuum hoses.

24 It is possible to test the choke pulsing by putting the ECU into service-adjust mode. The service connector is located by the battery. Allow the engine to idle and use a jump lead to connect the service connector to earth for at least 10 seconds. The vacuum damper will be activated and the engine speed will rise to 1700 rpm.

25 Switch on the ignition and place a finger on the choke relay. Regular pulsing should be felt (see illustration).

26 Attach a voltmeter to the choke electrical connection. With the engine running, the instrument should alternate between 6 to 8 volts and almost zero. An oscilloscope with a low-voltage facility is recommended for this test. A trace similar to that shown (see illustration) should be obtained.

27 If voltage is low or zero, attach the voltmeter between the alternator output supply to the choke and earth. If there is still no voltage, repair or renew the alternator (see illustration).

28 If voltage is present at the alternator but not at the choke, first check for a constant voltage supply to relay pin 30. Check for continuity between the relay pin (87b) and the automatic choke. Check for a voltage supply (with the ignition on) to relay pin 85. Finally, check for continuity between relay earth pin 86 and ECU terminal 11. If all connections are satisfactory, renew the relay.

29 Turn off the service adjuster by ensuring that the jump lead is no longer connected to earth and then by simply switching off the ignition.

30 A faulty air temperature or coolant temperature sensor will also affect choke operation.

Air temperature sensor

31 Connect a voltmeter across the terminals at the air temperature sensor in the air filter

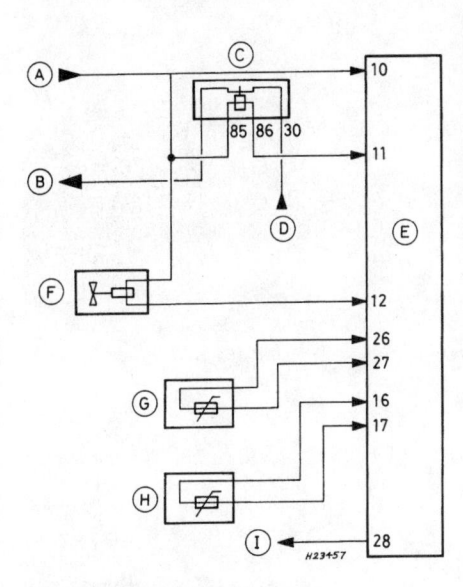

Pierburg 24/28, 28/30 & 28/32 2E3 carburettor

Measuring air temperature sensor voltage

Measuring coolant temperature sensor voltage (engine warm)

Choke relay wiring diagram

- A From ignition switch
- B To choke housing
- C Choke relay
- D From alternator
- E ECU
- F Vacuum damper solenoid
- G Coolant temperature sensor
- H Air temperature sensor
- I To service connector

assembly. The voltage will vary from about 3.5 volts (cold air) to 1 volt (hot air) *(see illustration)*.

32 Check for a nominal battery voltage supply to pin 10 of the ECU. The pins on the ECU are impossible to probe with the ECU connected and it may be necessary to push a sharp pin through the wire.

Coolant temperature sensor

33 Connect a voltmeter across the terminals at the coolant temperature sensor in the inlet manifold. The voltage when the engine is cold will be about 3 volts. Start the engine and the voltage should slowly reduce to between 0.5 and 0.8 volts when the engine is hot *(see illustration)*.

ECU multi-plug

34 The ECU is bolted to the offside inner wing. Ensure that the ignition is switched off, then remove the ECU multi-plug by unscrewing the central bolt. Check the multi-plug connecting pins for corrosion and ensure that they make good contact.

6 Fault diagnosis

Refer to Part D for diagnosis of general carburettor faults. The following faults are specific to 2E3 carburettors.

Poor choke operation/poor cold running

☐ Over-choking due to pull-down diaphragm failure, relaxing of bi-metal coil or poor adjustment.
☐ Sticking choke flap.
☐ Failure of inlet manifold pre-heater or throttle body heater.
☐ Failure of thermal time valve or coolant-heated thermal switch.

Heavy fuel consumption

☐ Leaking power valve diaphragm or O-ring seal.

Hesitation

☐ The accelerator pump diaphragm utilises a slot and spring-loaded ball into which the pump actuating lever fits. If the spring becomes weak, the delay in operation can cause a flat spot on acceleration.

Uneven running

☐ Air leak due to defective rubber mounting flange.

Lack of power

☐ Failure of secondary throttle plate diaphragm.

Notes

Part F Chapter 7
Pierburg-Solex 35 PDSI carburettor

Contents

Component testing 5
Fault diagnosis 6
General servicing 3
Identification 2
Principles of operation 1
Service adjustments 4

Specifications

Manufacturer	Opel	Vauxhall/Opel	Vauxhall/Opel	Vauxhall
Model	Kadett 1.3	Astra/Kadett 1.2	Astra/Kadett 1.2	Astra 1.3
Year	1979 to 1987	1980 to 1984	1980 to 1984	1984 to 1989
Engine code	13N	12N	12S	13N SOHC (44kW)
Capacity (cm³)/no. of cyls	1297/4	1196/4	1196/4	1297/4
Oil temperature (°C)	60	60	60	60
Carb. identification	9 276 954 A	9 276 930/949 A	9 276 931/951 A	9 276 954 A
Idle speed (rpm)	875 ± 25	875 ± 25	875 ± 25	925 ± 25
Fast idle speed (rpm)	3600 ± 50	3600 ± 50	3600 ± 50	3600 ± 50
CO @ idle (% vol.)	1.5 ± 0.5	1.75 ± 0.75	1.75 ± 0.25	1.25 ± 0.25
Venturi diameter (K)	26	26	26	26
Idle jet (g)	50	50	50	50
Main jet (Gg)	122.5	125	125	122.5
Air correction jet (a)	80	80	80	80
Accelerator pump jet (i)	50	50	50	50
Float level (mm)	17.5 ± 1.0	17.5 ± 1.0	17.5 ± 1.0	17.5 ± 1.0
Needle valve (mm) (P)	1.75	1.75	1.75	1.75
Float weight (grams)	7.0 ± 0.5	7.0 ± 0.5	7.0 ± 0.5	7.0 ± 0.5
Choke fast idle gap (mm)	0.65 ± 0.05	0.7 ± 0.05	0.7 ± 0.05	0.65 ± 0.05
Choke pull-down (mm)	3.2 ± 0.2	-	-	3.2 ± 0.2

Chapter F7

1 Principles of operation

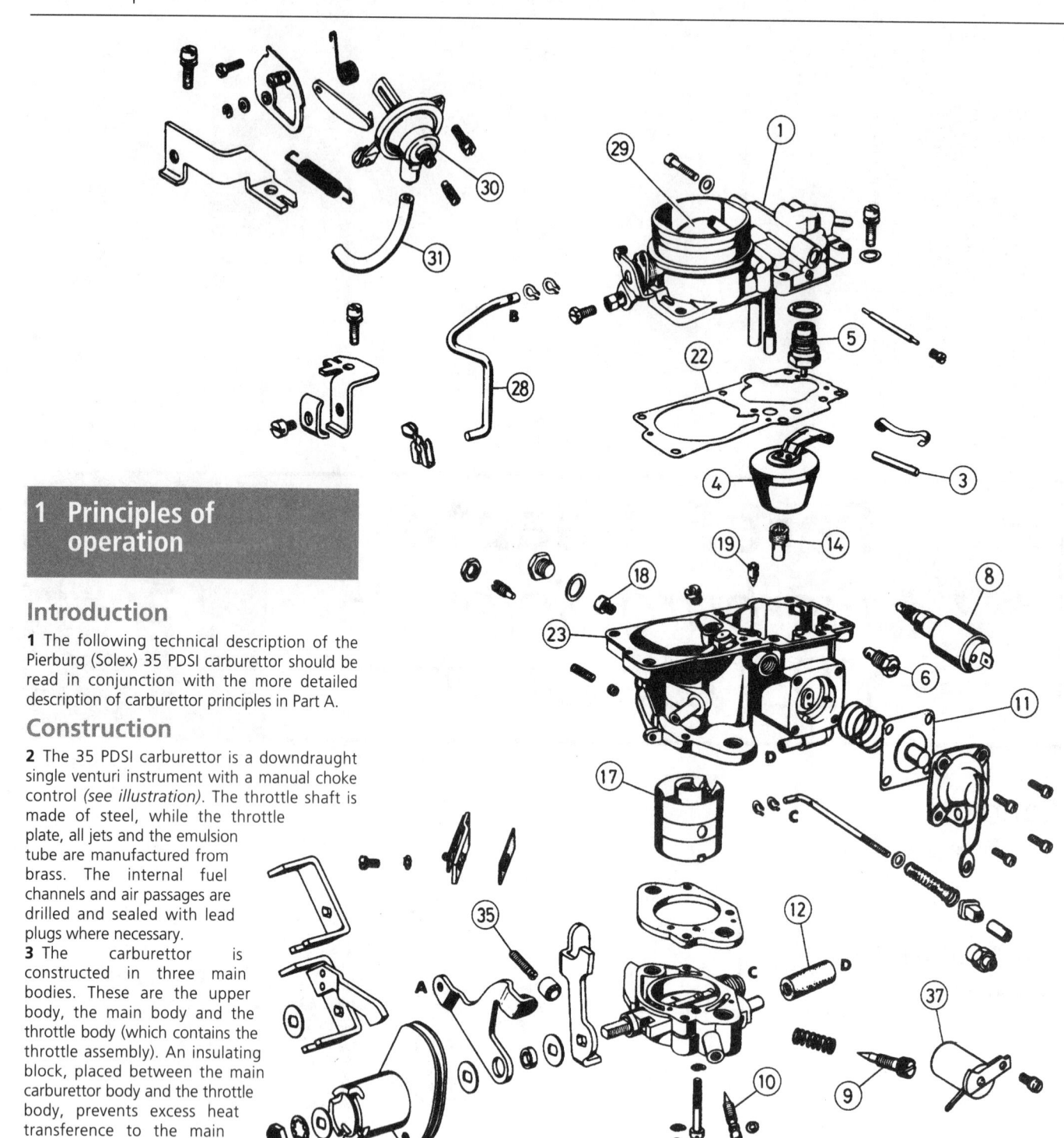

Introduction

1 The following technical description of the Pierburg (Solex) 35 PDSI carburettor should be read in conjunction with the more detailed description of carburettor principles in Part A.

Construction

2 The 35 PDSI carburettor is a downdraught single venturi instrument with a manual choke control *(see illustration)*. The throttle shaft is made of steel, while the throttle plate, all jets and the emulsion tube are manufactured from brass. The internal fuel channels and air passages are drilled and sealed with lead plugs where necessary.

3 The carburettor is constructed in three main bodies. These are the upper body, the main body and the throttle body (which contains the throttle assembly). An insulating block, placed between the main carburettor body and the throttle body, prevents excess heat transference to the main body.

Pierburg - Solex PDSI carburettor

1 Upper body
3 Float pin
4 Float
5 Needle valve
6 Idle jet
8 Idle cut-off valve (where fitted)
9 Bypass idle speed screw
10 Idle mixture control screw
11 Accelerator pump diaphragm
12 Bypass mixture hose
14 Part-load enrichment valve
17 Auxiliary venturi
18 Main jet
19 Full-load enrichment valve
21 Tamperproof cap
22 Float chamber gasket
23 Main body
28 Choke link rod (mechanical pull-down)
29 Choke flap
30 Choke pull-down diaphragm (vacuum pull-down)
31 Choke vacuum pull-down hose
35 Fast idle adjustment screw
37 Throttle body heater (where fitted)

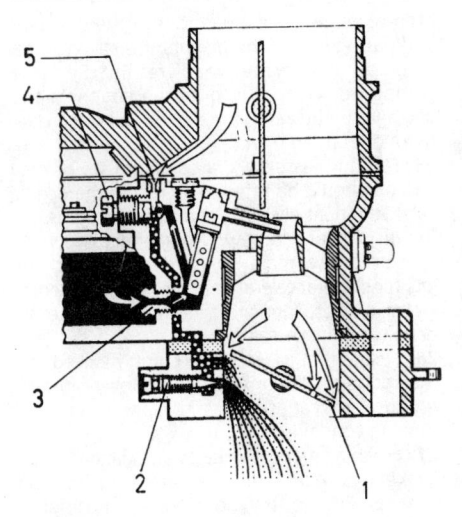

Pierburg-Solex 35 PDSI carburettor

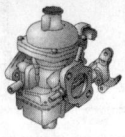

Idle circuit
1 Throttle plate
2 Idle mixture control screw
3 Main jet
4 Idle fuel jet
5 Idle air corrector jet

4 An electrical heater may also be fitted to the carburettor body, close to the throttle area. The purpose of this heater is to improve atomisation of the air/fuel mixture and prevent carburettor icing during warm-up. The heater functions on the positive temperature coefficient (PTC) principle. As the temperature rises, the heater resistance also rises.

Fuel control
5 Fuel flows into the carburettor through an inlet connection. The fuel level in the float chamber is controlled by a needle valve and plastic float assembly.

Idle, slow running and progression
6 Fuel, sourced from the main well, passes into the idle channel through a metered idle jet. Here it is mixed with a small amount of air from a calibrated air bleed. The resulting emulsion is drawn through a channel to be discharged from the idle orifice under the primary throttle plate. A tapered mixture screw is used to vary the outlet and this ensures fine control of the idle mixture. A number of progression holes provide extra enrichment as they are uncovered by the opening throttle during initial acceleration (see illustration).
7 The idle speed is set by an adjustable air regulating screw. The adjustable mixture screw is tamper proofed at production level, in accordance with emission regulations.

Idle cut-off valve
8 An idle cut-off valve is used on some models to prevent run-on when the engine is shut down. When fitted, the cut-off valve and idle jet are combined as one unit. A 12-volt solenoid plunger is used to block the idle jet when the ignition is switched off.

Idle bypass circuit
9 The idle bypass circuit provides a means of more accurately controlling idle emissions than a conventional idle mixture circuit. The throttle plate is locked in a specified position and sealed with a tamperproof cap. Eighty percent of the fuel required for idle is provided by the normal idle circuit. The remainder of the idle mixture is controlled through the idle bypass circuit (see illustration).
10 Fuel, sourced from the float chamber, is drawn through a stand-pipe into the roof of the float chamber. Here it is mixed with air introduced from the main air intake. The emulsion is drawn through a passage and short hose interconnection into the throttle section, where it is discharged from the bypass orifice under the throttle plate. The emulsion is controlled by a regulating screw which is also used to adjust the idle speed.

Accelerator pump
11 The PDSI accelerator pump is controlled by a diaphragm and is mechanically operated by a rod attached to the throttle linkage. During acceleration, fuel is pumped through a ball valve, into a pump injector where it is discharged into the venturi.

Main circuit
12 The amount of fuel discharged into the airstream is controlled by a calibrated main jet placed in the float chamber. Fuel is drawn through the main jet into the base of a well arranged at an angle. The well dips down into the fuel in the float chamber. An emulsion tube is placed in the well, capped by a calibrated air corrector jet. The fuel is mixed with air, drawn in through the air corrector and through the holes in the emulsion tube. The resulting emulsified mixture is discharged from the main nozzle through an auxiliary venturi (see illustration).

Part-load enrichment
13 An air passage is taken from under the throttle plate to the part-load enrichment chamber. At idle and during light-throttle operation, manifold vacuum in the passage pulls the enrichment plunger back against spring pressure. This seats the part-load enrichment valve to close off a fuel outlet channel. During acceleration and wide-open throttle operation, the vacuum in the manifold is depleted. The diaphragm returns under spring pressure and pushes on the valve to open the channel. Fuel then flows through a calibrated bush in the channel to supplement the fuel in the main well. The fuel level rises in the well and the fuel mixture is enriched.

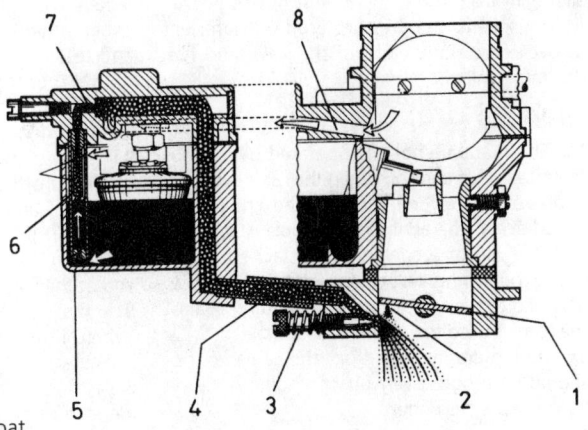

Full-load enrichment
14 At full-load and high engine speeds, the velocity of air creates a depression sufficient to raise fuel from the float chamber into a channel. The pressure of fuel overcomes a cone-shaped weight (0.28 grammes) and passes through a calibrated bushing to the upper section of the air intake where it is discharged into the

Bypass mixture control circuit
1 Throttle plate
2 Bypass mixture outlet
3 Bypass idle speed screw
4 Connecting hose
5 Bypass fuel jet
6 Stand-pipe
7 Bypass mixture jet
8 Bypass air passage

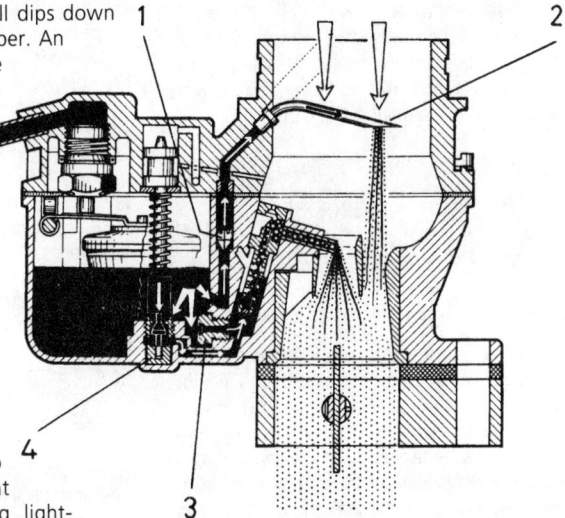

Main, partial and full-load enrichment circuits
1 Full-load enrichment valve
2 Full-load enrichment nozzle
3 Main jet
4 Part-load enrichment valve (open)

Chapter F7

airstream from the full-load enrichment nozzle. At low speeds, the pressure drop is insufficient to overcome the weight of the valve and fuel discharge will not take place.

Manual choke

15 The manual choke is operated by a dash-mounted cable control. When the cable is pulled, it operates a lever that pulls the choke flap closed across the air intake. Fast idle is achieved with the aid of a curved cam attached to the choke operating lever. An adjustable screw, attached to the throttle lever and butting against the cam, is used to vary the fast idle speed.
16 During engine warm-up, the cable control should be progressively pushed home until the choke flap is fully open.

Choke pull-down

17 Once the engine has fired, the choke flap must open slightly to weaken the mixture and avoid flooding. This is achieved by two different methods, depending on the version of the PDSI fitted. On the first type, an increase in airflow through the air intake partially opens the choke flap against the action of a spring. A stop ensures that the choke is only opened a small amount. On the second type, manifold vacuum is used to actuate a diaphragm. A linkage attached to the diaphragm will then pull upon the choke flap.

2 Identification

1 Earlier versions of this carburettor have Solex stamped upon the main body, whereas later versions may be stamped with the trade name Pierburg.
2 The manufacturer identification code is stamped on a metallic tag attached to the carburettor cover by an upper body fixing screw.
3 Where the tag is missing, refer to Part B for other means of identifying the carburettor.

3 General servicing

Introduction

1 Read this Chapter in conjunction with Part B which describes some of the operations in more detail. It is assumed that the carburettor is removed for this service. However, many of the operations can be tackled with the carburettor in place. Where this is undertaken, first remove the upper body assembly and soak the fuel out of the float chamber using a clean tissue or soft cloth.

Dismantling and checking

2 Remove the carburettor from the engine (see Part B).
3 Check the carburettor visually for damage and wear.

4 Remove the idle cut-off valve assembly (where fitted). Clean it with carburettor cleaner and test the plunger operation by connecting the valve to the battery or other voltage supply (or use the valve supply wire in the engine compartment). Touch the valve body to earth with the ignition on. Repeat this several times and ensure that the plunger tip advances and retracts cleanly. Renew the valve if the action is faulty or if cleaning does not improve its operation. Inspect the idle jet screwed into the end of the valve.
5 Remove the idle jet from the main body (where fitted separately on models without an idle cut-off valve).
6 Disconnect the choke vacuum hose or linkage (depending on pull-down type) then remove the six screws and detach the carburettor upper body.
7 Inspect the float chamber for corrosion and calcium build-up.
8 Remove the leaf spring, then tap out the float pin and remove the float, needle valve and float chamber gasket.
9 Check the needle valve for wear and ridges.
10 The float should be checked for damage and ingress of petrol.
11 Renew the float pin if it shows signs of wear.
12 Use a straight-edge to check for distorted flanges on all facing surfaces.
13 Unscrew the idle mixture and bypass screws, then inspect their tips for damage or ridges.
14 Remove the four screws and detach the accelerator pump cover, diaphragm and spring. Check the diaphragm for fatigue and damage.
15 Unscrew the air corrector jet. It is not possible to remove the emulsion tube.
16 Remove the plug in the float chamber and unscrew the main jet. Check that the channel from the main jet into the main emulsion tube well is clear.
17 Remove and check the enrichment valve for signs of wear, damage or stickiness. Check that the channel into the emulsion tube well is clear.
18 Check the action of the enrichment plunger. Refit the enrichment weight.
19 Remove the two screws and separate the carburettor main body and throttle body assemblies. The throttle body can be renewed separately if the spindles or throttle bores are worn. Use a straight-edge to check for distorted flanges on the facing surfaces.
20 Do not disturb the adjustment of the throttle angle unless absolutely necessary.
21 Inspect the choke flap, spindle and linkage for stickiness and wear.
22 Attach a vacuum pump to the choke diaphragm connector (where fitted) and operate the pump until the diaphragm is actuated. Renew the diaphragm if it does not operate fully or if the vacuum is not maintained for 10 seconds.

Preparation for reassembly

23 Clean the jets, carburettor body assemblies, float chamber and internal channels. An air line may be used to clear the internal channels once the carburettor is fully dismantled. Note that if high-pressure air is directed into the channels and passages with the diaphragms still in place, diaphragm damage may result. Spraying carburettor cleaner into all the channels and passages in the carburettor body will often clear them of gum and dirt.
24 During reassembly, a complete set of new gaskets should be fitted. Also renew the needle valve, the float pivot pin and all diaphragms.
25 Inspect and renew (where necessary) the mixture screw, main jet, air corrector and idle jets, and the accelerator pump injector. Renew worn linkages, springs, vacuum hoses and other parts where necessary.
26 Ensure that all the jets are firmly locked into their original positions (but do not over-tighten). A loose jet can cause a rich (or even lean) running condition.
27 Clean all mating surfaces and flanges of old gasket material and reassemble with new gaskets. Ensure that housings are positioned with their air and fuel routes correctly aligned.

Reassembly

28 Assemble the main and throttle bodies with a new gasket block, then secure with the two screws.
29 Where the primary throttle position has been disturbed and a throttle setting gauge is available, use it to set the throttle angle. Otherwise, temporarily adjust the throttle plate so that it is open just enough to prevent its seizure in the throttle body. An adjustment method with the engine running is detailed in Section 4.
30 Screw the enrichment valve into the float chamber. Refit the enrichment weight.
31 Refit the air corrector and main jets into their original positions. Refit the plug to the float chamber with a new seal.
32 Refit the accelerator pump spring, diaphragm and cover assembly, then secure with the four screws.
33 Refit the idle mixture screw after renewing the seal. Turn the screw in gently until it just seats. From this position, unscrew it three full turns. This will provide a basic setting to allow the engine to be started.
34 Refit the bypass regulating screw. Obtain a basic setting in the same way as for the mixture screw above.
35 Screw the needle valve into the upper body and refit the float gasket. Refit the float, pivot pin and leaf spring.
36 Check the float level, see Section 4.
37 Refit the upper body to the main body and secure with the six screws. Reconnect the choke vacuum hose or choke link (depending on pull-down type).
38 Refit the idle cut-off valve assembly (or separate idle jet) and lock firmly into position.
39 Ensure that the choke flap and linkage move smoothly and progressively.
40 Adjust the choke with reference to Section 4.
41 Refit the carburettor to the engine.
42 Always adjust the carburettor idle speed and mixture after any work has been carried out on the carburettor, preferably with the aid of a CO meter.

Pierburg-Solex 35 PDSI carburettor

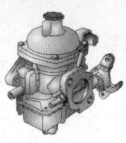

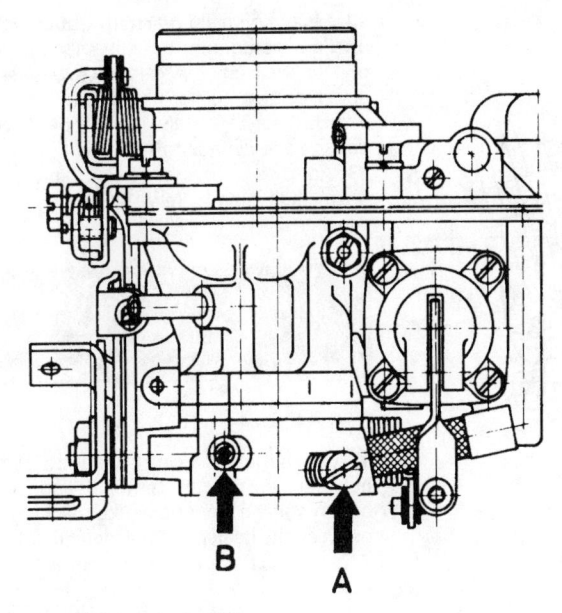

Idle adjustment screw location
A Bypass idle speed screw
B Idle mixture control screw

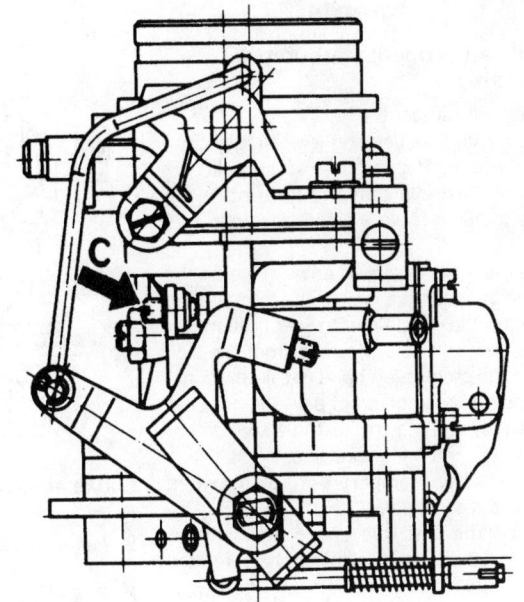

Setting basic throttle position
C Throttle stop screw

4 Service adjustments

Adjustment pre-conditions

1 Refer to Part B for general advice on the pre-conditions for correct adjustment of this carburettor.
2 Locate the crankcase breather hose fitted to the air cleaner. This hose should remain connected throughout the following adjustments. When all adjustments are complete, disconnect the breather hose. If the CO level decreases more than 1 to 1.5%, change the engine oil and check the breather system for blockages. If the CO level still decreases after an oil change, suspect worn or sticking piston rings.

Idle adjustment

3 Run the engine at 3000 rpm for 30 seconds to clear the manifold of fuel vapours, then allow the engine to idle.
4 Use the idle bypass regulating screw to set the specified idle speed (see illustration).
5 Check the CO level. If incorrect, remove the tamperproof plug and adjust the idle mixture screw to obtain the correct level. Turning the screw clockwise (inwards) will reduce the CO level. Turning the screw anti-clockwise (outwards) will increase the CO level.
6 Repeat paragraphs 4 and 5 until both adjustments are correct. Adjusting the idle bypass screw will also affect the CO level.
7 Fit a new tamperproof plug to the mixture control screw on completion.

Basic throttle position

8 If the idle speed and CO cannot be set correctly, it is possible that the basic throttle position is incorrect. One setting method is to remove the carburettor and use a Pierburg gauge to accurately set the throttle position. Another method is to use a very low-reading vacuum gauge connected to the vacuum advance connector. The correct angle is set when the gauge registers 8 ± 4 mmHg (10 ± 5 mbars).
9 However, the following method can also be used to set the throttle plate and will result in an accurate and stable idle speed and CO level.
10 Allow the engine to idle then screw in the bypass regulating screw until it is fully seated. The speed should drop to between 600 and 650 rpm.
11 Adjust the throttle stop screw if necessary until 600 to 650 rpm is obtained. Note that the fast idle adjustment screw may need to be unscrewed at this point if it is likely to hold the throttle open (see illustration).
12 Unscrew the bypass screw until the specified idle speed is once again attained.
13 Reset the CO to the correct level.
14 If the CO needs a large adjustment at this stage, repeat paragraphs 10 to 13. Once the proper level of CO is reached at the specified idle speed, the carburettor is properly adjusted.
15 Reset the fast idle screw so that it just touches the fast idle cam with the choke flap fully open.

Float level

16 Hold the upper body in a vertical position with the float tag gently touching the pin of the needle valve.
17 Measure the distance between the upper body (with the gasket in position) and the bottom of the float.
18 Adjust as necessary by bending the inner float tag.

Accelerator pump

19 On the PDSI carburettor, it is possible to adjust the volume of fuel injected by the accelerator pump.
20 Turn the brass nut clockwise to increase the volume, or anti-clockwise to decrease the volume (see illustration).

Accelerator pump adjustment
1 Turn brass nut to adjust pump volume

F7•5

Chapter F7

Choke adjustments

Fast idle adjustment (carburettor removed)

21 Invert the carburettor.
22 Pull the choke operating lever to fully close the choke flap. The fast idle screw will butt against the fast idle cam and force open the throttle plate to leave a small clearance *(see illustration)*.
23 Use the shank of a twist drill to measure the clearance between the wall of the throttle bore and the throttle plate. Refer to Specifications for the required drill size. Measure from the side opposite the progression holes *(see illustration)*.
24 Remove the tamperproof plug and adjust as necessary by turning the fast idle adjustment screw in the appropriate direction.
25 Fit a new tamperproof plug when adjustment is complete.
26 Check the fast idle speed against that specified once the carburettor has been refitted to the engine.

Fast idle adjustment (engine running)

27 Run the engine to normal operating temperature, then switch off.
28 Fully close the choke flap using the choke operating lever. The lever must be against the choke stop *(see illustration)*.
29 Start the engine and open the choke flap as far as possible. Refer to Specifications for the fast idle speed.
30 Adjust as necessary by turning the adjustment screw in the appropriate direction.

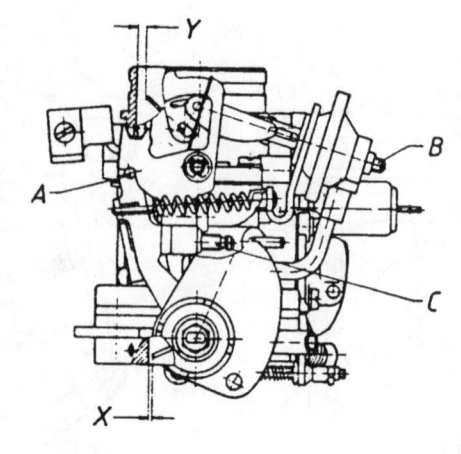

Choke adjustments
A Choke stop
B Pull-down adjustment screw
C Fast idle adjustment screw
X Fast idle clearance
Y Pull-down clearance

Choke vacuum pull-down (some versions)

31 Remove the vacuum hose and attach a vacuum pump to the choke pull-down connector. Operate the pump until 450 mmHg (600 mbars) is obtained. If the diaphragm does not operate fully or if the vacuum is not maintained for at least 10 seconds, renew the pull-down unit.
32 Maintaining the vacuum obtained in the previous paragraph, use the shank of a twist drill to measure the clearance between the upper section of the choke flap and the air intake. Refer to Specifications for the required drill size *(see illustration)*.
33 Adjust as necessary by turning the pull-down adjusting screw in the appropriate direction.

5 Component testing

Throttle body heater

1 Turn the ignition on. Connect a voltmeter between the heater terminal and earth. If battery voltage is not obtained, check the wiring between the heater and the ignition switch.
2 Disconnect the electrical connector to the heater.
3 Connect a test lamp between the positive battery terminal and the connector terminal leading to the heater. If the lamp does not light, renew the heater.

6 Fault diagnosis

Refer to Part D for diagnosis of general carburettor faults.

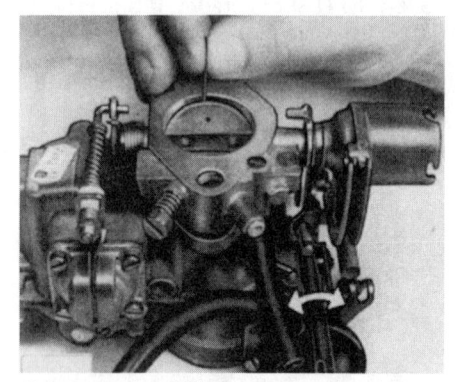

Using a twist drill to measure fast idle clearance

Close choke flap and run engine to check fast idle speed

Using a twist drill to measure pull-down clearance with vacuum applied

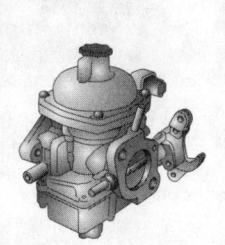

Part F Chapter 8
Pierburg-Solex 31 PIC-7 carburettor

F8

Contents

Component testing 5
Fault diagnosis 6
General servicing 3
Identification 2
Principles of operation 1
Service adjustments 4

Specifications

Manufacturer	Volkswagen	Volkswagen	Volkswagen
Model	Polo 1.05	Polo 1.1	Polo 1.1 Formel-E
Year	1981 to 1985	1981 to 1984	1982 to 1984
Engine code	GL (29kW)	HB (37kW)	HB8 (37kW)
Capacity (cm^3)/no. of cyls	1043/4	1093/4	1093/4
Oil temperature (°C)	80	80	80
Carb. identification	052 129 017	052 129 017 A	052 129 017 D
Idle speed (rpm)	950 ± 50	950 ± 25	950 ± 50
Fast idle speed (rpm)	2400 ± 100	2400 ± 100	2500 ± 100
CO @ idle (% vol.)	1.0 ± 0.5	1.0 ± 0.5	1.0 ± 0.5
Venturi diameter (K)	23	25.5	23
Idle jet (g)	40	42.5	40
Main jet (Gg)	117.5	132.5	115
Air correction jet (a)	125	105	120
Accelerator pump jet (i)	45	45	45
Needle valve (mm) (P)	1.5	1.5	1.5
Float weight (grams)	10.5 ± 0.5	10.5 ± 0.5	10.5 ± 0.5
Basic throttle position (mm)	0.28 ± 0.03	0.18 ± 0.03	0.32 ± 0.03
Choke fast idle gap (mm)	0.95 ± 0.05	0.9 ± 0.05	0.9 ± 0.05
Choke pull-down (mm) (a)	1.8 ± 0.2	2.0 ± 0.2	-
Choke pull-down (mm) (a1)	2.5 ± 0.2	2.5 ± 0.2	2.2 ± 0.2

Manufacturer	Volkswagen	Volkswagen	Volkswagen
Model	Golf 1.05	Golf & Van 1.1	Golf/Jetta 1.1 Formel-E
Year	1984 to 1985	1981 to 1983	1981 to 1983
Engine code	GN (33kW)	GG (37kW)	GG8 (37kW)
Capacity (cm^3)/no. of cyls	1043/4	1093/4	1093/4
Oil temperature (°C)	80	80	80
Carb. identification	052 129 017	036 129 017	036 129 017 B
Idle speed (rpm)	950 ± 50	950 ± 50	950 ± 50
Fast idle speed (rpm)	2600 ± 100	2400 ± 100	2400 ± 100
CO @ idle (% vol.)	1.0 ± 0.5	1.0 ± 0.5	1.0 ± 0.5
Venturi diameter (K)	23	25.5	23
Idle jet (g)	40	42.5	40
Main jet (Gg)	117.5	132.5	115
Air correction jet (a)	125	105	120
Accelerator pump jet (i)	45	45	45
Needle valve (mm) (P)	1.5	1.5	1.5
Float weight (grams)	10.5 ± 0.5	10.5 ± 0.5	10.5 ± 0.5
Basic throttle position (mm)	0.28 ± 0.03	0.18 ± 0.03	0.32 ± 0.03
Choke fast idle gap (mm)	0.95 ± 0.05	0.9 ± 0.05	0.9 ± 0.05
Choke pull-down (mm) (a)	-	-	-
Choke pull-down (mm) (a1)	1.8 ± 0.2	2.0 ± 0.2	2.2 ± 0.2

Chapter F8

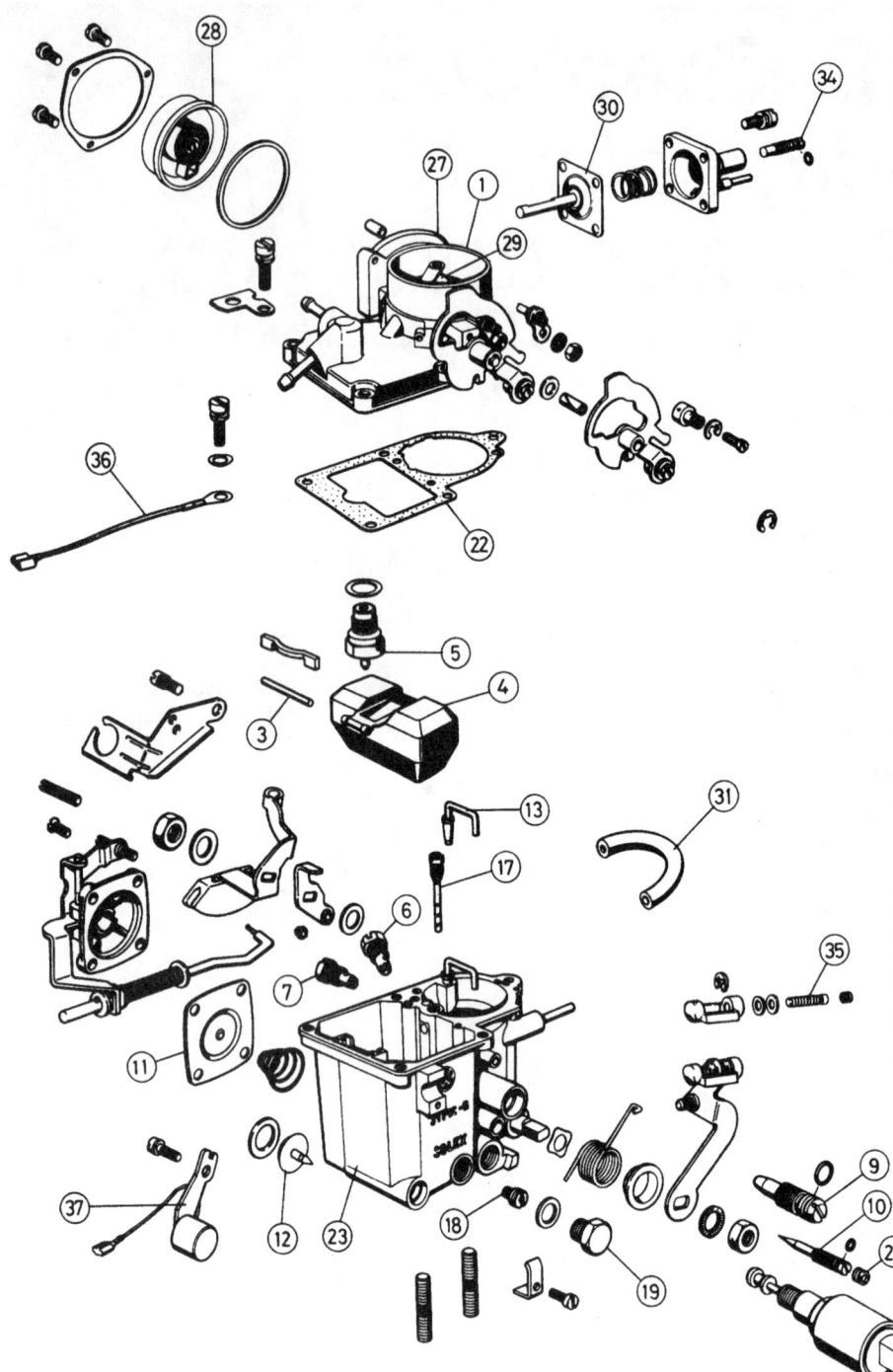

Pierburg - Solex PIC-7 carburettor

1. Upper body
3. Float pin
4. Float
5. Needle valve
6. Idle jet
7. Bypass jet
8. Idle cut-off valve
9. Bypass idle speed screw
10. Idle mixture control screw
11. Accelerator pump diaphragm
12. Accelerator pump valve
13. Pump injector
17. Combined air corrector and emulsion tube
18. Main jet
19. Main jet plug
21. Tamperproof cap
22. Float chamber gasket
23. Main body
27. Choke housing
28. Bi-metal housing assembly
29. Choke flap
30. Choke pull-down diaphragm
31. Choke pull-down hose
34. Pull-down adjustment screw
35. Fast idle adjustment screw
36. Carburettor earth strap
37. Throttle body heater

1 Principles of operation

1 The following technical description of the Pierburg (Solex) 31 PIC-7 carburettor should be read in conjunction with the more detailed description of carburettor principles in Part A.

Construction

2 The 31 PIC-7 carburettor is a downdraught single venturi instrument with a manually-controlled thermo-choke *(see illustration)*. The throttle shaft is made of steel, while the throttle plate, all jets and the emulsion tube are manufactured from brass. The internal fuel channels and air passages are drilled and sealed with lead plugs where necessary *(see illustration)*.

3 An electrical heater is fitted to the carburettor body, close to the throttle area. The purpose of the heater is to improve atomisation of the air/fuel mixture and to prevent carburettor icing during warm-up. A thermal switch is wired to the supply voltage so that the heater is switched off at a pre-determined temperature.

4 Because the carburettor is mounted on a flexible flange, an earth strap, connected to the body by an upper body fixing screw, provides a ground path for the electrical components fitted to the carburettor body.

Fuel control

5 Fuel flows into the carburettor through an inlet connection. The fuel level in the float chamber is controlled by a needle valve and plastic float assembly. The float chamber is vented internally to the upper air intake which is on the clean-air side of the air filter. A calibrated fuel return system is provided to ensure that relatively cool fuel is supplied to the carburettor.

Idle, slow running and progression

6 Fuel, sourced from the main well, passes into the idle channel through a metered idle jet. Here it is mixed with a small amount of air from a calibrated air bleed. The resulting emulsion is drawn through a channel, into a chamber where it is mixed with the bypass emulsion. The total idle mixture is then discharged from the main idle orifice under the primary throttle plate. A tapered mixture screw is used to vary the channel to the chamber and this ensures fine control of the idle mixture.

7 A number of progression holes provide a further air contribution to the emulsion (upstream of the chamber) while the throttle is closed. As the progression holes are uncovered by the opening throttle, the vacuum draw overcomes the air bleed into the holes and a reversal occurs. Fuel is now drawn out to add extra enrichment to the idle mixture during initial acceleration.

8 The adjustable mixture screw is tamper

Pierburg-Solex 31 PIC-7 carburettor

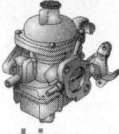

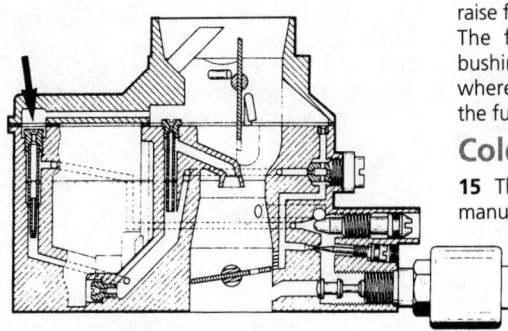

Internal fuel channels and air passages

proofed at production level, in accordance with emission regulations.

Idle bypass circuit

9 The idle bypass circuit provides a means of more accurately controlling idle emissions than a conventional idle mixture circuit. The throttle plate is locked in a specified position and sealed with a tamperproof cap. Eighty percent of the fuel required for idle is provided by the normal idle circuit. The remainder of the idle mixture is controlled through the idle bypass circuit.

10 Fuel sourced from the main well is drawn through a channel into the roof of the float chamber. Here it is mixed with air introduced from the main air intake. The resulting mixture is drawn through a bypass jet and passage, past the regulating screw and into a chamber, where it is mixed with the idle emulsion. The total idle mixture is then discharged from the main idle orifice under the primary throttle plate. The emulsion is controlled by a regulating screw which is also used to adjust the idle speed.

Idle cut-off valve

11 An idle cut-off valve is used to prevent run-on when the engine is shut down. It utilises a 12-volt solenoid plunger to block the idle mixture outlet when the ignition is switched off.

Accelerator pump

12 The 31 PIC-7 accelerator pump is controlled by a diaphragm and is mechanically operated by a rod attached to the throttle linkage. During acceleration, fuel is pumped through a ball valve, into a pump injector where it is discharged into the venturi.

Main circuit

13 The amount of fuel discharged into the airstream is controlled by a calibrated main jet placed in the float chamber. Fuel is drawn through the main jet into the base of a well, arranged at an angle. The well dips down into the fuel in the float chamber. An emulsion tube is placed in the well, capped by a calibrated air corrector jet. The fuel is mixed with air, drawn in through the air corrector and through the holes in the emulsion tube. The resulting emulsified mixture is discharged into the airstream from the main nozzle.

Full-load enrichment

14 At full-load and high engine speeds, the velocity of air creates a depression sufficient to raise fuel from the float chamber into a channel. The fuel then passes through a calibrated bushing to the upper section of the air intake, where it is discharged into the airstream from the full-load enrichment nozzle.

Cold start system

15 The 31 PIC-7 cold start system is basically a manually-controlled thermo-choke. The choke is operated by a dash-mounted cable control. When the cable is pulled, it actuates a lever that releases the choke mechanism. The choke flap is controlled by a bi-metal spring and will take position across the air intake depending on ambient temperature. Fast idle is achieved with the aid of a curved cam attached to the choke operating lever. An adjustable screw, attached to the throttle lever and butting against the cam, is used to vary the fast idle speed.

16 During engine warm-up, the cable control should be progressively pushed home until the choke flap is fully open. However, if the cable is not pushed home, any increase in ambient temperature at the choke body will act upon the bi-metal to open the choke flap.

Choke pull-down

17 Once the engine has fired, the choke flap must open slightly to weaken the mixture and avoid flooding during idle and light-throttle operation. This is achieved by using manifold vacuum to actuate a pull-down diaphragm. A linkage attached to the diaphragm will then pull upon the flap.

2 Identification

1 Solex 31 PIC(T)-7 is stamped upon the carburettor main body. Later versions of this carburettor may be stamped with the trade name Pierburg.
2 The manufacturer identification code is stamped on a metallic tag attached to the cover by an upper body fixing screw.
3 Where the tag is missing, refer to Part B for other means of identifying the carburettor.

3 General servicing

Introduction

1 Read this Chapter in conjunction with Part B, which describes some of the operations in more detail. It is assumed that the carburettor is removed for this service. However, many of the operations can be tackled with the carburettor in place. Where this is undertaken, first remove the upper body assembly, and soak the fuel out of the float chamber using a clean tissue or soft cloth.

Dismantling and checking

2 Remove the carburettor from the engine (see Part B). The PIC-7 carburettor is bolted to a flexible mounting flange. Unscrew the four fixing nuts from underneath the inlet manifold. Withdraw the carburettor, complete with the mounting flange and studs, from the top of the inlet manifold.
3 Unscrew the two fixing nuts and detach the carburettor from the mounting flange. Inspect the mounting flange for splits and wear. Renew if necessary.
4 Check the carburettor visually for damage and wear.
5 Remove the idle cut-off valve assembly, after slackening the nut with a 17 mm open-ended spanner. Clean the valve with carburettor cleaner, then test the plunger operation by connecting the valve to the battery or other voltage supply (or use the valve supply wire in the engine compartment). Touch the valve body to earth with the ignition on. Repeat this several times and ensure that the plunger tip advances and retracts cleanly. Renew the valve if the action is faulty or if cleaning does not improve its operation.
6 Disconnect the choke vacuum hose then remove the five screws and detach the carburettor upper body. The carburettor earth wire is connected to one of the fixing screws and will be removed with the screw.
7 Inspect the float chamber for corrosion and calcium build-up.
8 Remove the float chamber gasket.
9 Use a straight-edge to check for distorted flanges on all facing surfaces.
10 Remove the needle valve assembly (or needle and seat) from the upper body.
11 Check the needle valve for wear and ridges.
12 Remove the plastic retainer, float pin and float assembly from the main body.
13 Check the float for damage and ingress of petrol.
14 Renew the float pin if it shows signs of wear.
15 Unscrew the idle mixture and bypass screws, then inspect their tips for damage or ridges.
16 Remove the four screws and detach the accelerator pump cover, diaphragm and spring. Check the diaphragm for fatigue and damage. Note that the pump injector is not removable.
17 Remove the brass retainer and carefully push out the pump poppet valve from inside the float chamber.
18 Remove the idle jet from the main body. It is just possible to unscrew this jet with the carburettor installed on the engine and the upper body in position.
19 Remove the auxiliary idle jet for the bypass emulsion. This may be installed on the outside of the body (adjacent to the idle jet or in a channel in the top of the main body). Where the auxiliary jet is installed in the body, there will either be a false (undrilled) auxiliary jet fitted adjacent to the idle jet or the channel will be blanked off. Where an idle jet and auxiliary jet (drilled or undrilled) are both installed, take care that the jets are not transposed.

Chapter F8

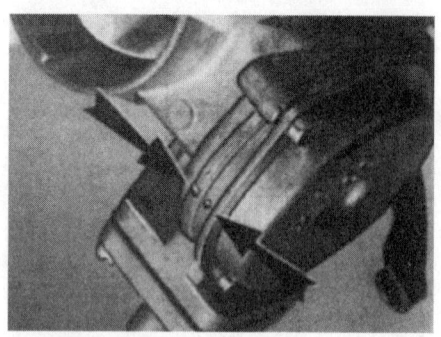

3.35 Choke alignment marks

20 Unscrew the combined air corrector jet and emulsion tube.
21 Remove the plug in the float chamber and unscrew the main jet. Check that the channel from the main jet into the main emulsion tube well is clear.
22 Do not disturb the adjustment of the throttle angle. It is set during manufacture and the end of the throttle stop screw sheared off to make the angle non-adjustable.
23 Inspect the choke flap, spindle and linkage for stickiness and wear.
24 Attach a vacuum pump to the choke diaphragm connector and operate the pump until the diaphragm is actuated. Renew the diaphragm if it does not operate fully or if the vacuum is not maintained for 10 seconds.
25 Remove the three screws and detach the choke bi-metal cover and spring assembly.
26 Remove the four screws and detach the choke pull-down cover, spring and diaphragm from the housing. Check the diaphragm for fatigue.

Preparation for reassembly

27 Clean the jets, carburettor body assemblies, float chamber and internal channels. An air line may be used to clear the internal channels once the carburettor is fully dismantled. Note that if high-pressure air is directed into the channels and passages with the diaphragms still in place, diaphragm damage may result. Spraying carburettor cleaner into all the channels and passages in the carburettor body will often clear them of gum and dirt.
28 During reassembly, a complete set of new gaskets should be fitted. Also renew the needle valve, float pivot pin and all diaphragms.
29 Inspect and renew (where necessary) the mixture screw, main jet, air corrector/ emulsion tube, idle and auxiliary jets, and the accelerator pump injector. Renew worn linkages, springs, vacuum hoses and other parts where necessary.
30 Ensure that all the jets are firmly locked into their original positions (but do not over-tighten). A loose jet can cause a rich (or even lean) running condition.
31 Clean all mating surfaces and flanges of old gasket material, then reassemble with new gaskets.
32 Ensure that housings are positioned with their air and fuel routes correctly aligned.

Reassembly

33 Refit the choke diaphragm and spindle assembly to the choke housing. Ensure that the slot in the spindle faces outwards and that the choke flap operating lever is engaged in the slot. Refit the spring and cover and secure with the four screws.
34 Refit the bi-metal coil housing with a new gasket, ensuring that the spring locates in the slot of the choke lever. Loosely secure the retaining ring with the three screws.
35 Align the cut mark on the bi-metal cover with the correct mark on the choke assembly housing and tighten the three screws *(see illustration)*.
36 Refit the air corrector and main jets into their original positions. Refit the plug to the float chamber with a new seal.
37 Refit the idle jet and seal and the auxiliary bypass jet (do not transpose the jets). Take particular care not to inadvertently transpose the auxiliary jet and the air corrector/emulsion tube. These two assemblies are similar in appearance, and have a similar thread.
38 Locate the poppet valve and retainer in the accelerator pump housing. Refit the spring, diaphragm and cover assembly, then secure with the four screws.
39 Refit the idle mixture screw after renewing the seal. Turn the screw in gently until it just seats. From this position, unscrew it three full turns. This will provide a basic setting to allow the engine to be started.
40 Refit the bypass regulating screw after renewing the seal. Obtain a basic setting in the same way as for the mixture screw above.
41 Screw the needle valve assembly (or needle and seat) into the upper body, complete with a new seal. Locate the float, pivot pin and plastic retaining piece into the main body and refit the float gasket. The float level is not adjustable.
42 Pull back the fast idle arm, refit the upper body to the main body and secure with the five screws. Ensure that the earth strap is secured by one of the fixing screws and reconnect the vacuum hose.

4.4 Idle adjustment screw location
1 Bypass idle speed screw
2 Idle mixture control screw

43 Refit the idle cut-off valve assembly and lock it firmly into position.
45 Ensure that the choke flap and linkage move smoothly and progressively.
46 Adjust the choke (see Section 4).
47 Assemble the mounting flange to the base of the carburettor and secure with the two nuts and washers.
48 Refit the carburettor to the engine and secure with the four nuts and washers underneath the inlet manifold.
49 Always adjust the carburettor idle speed and mixture after any work has been carried out on the carburettor, preferably with the aid of a CO meter.

4 Service adjustments

Adjustment pre-conditions

1 Refer to Part B for general advice on the pre-conditions for correct adjustment of this carburettor.
2 Locate the crankcase breather hose fitted to the air cleaner. Disconnect this hose and plug the opening in the air filter. When all adjustments are complete, reconnect the breather hose. If the CO level increases by more than 1 to 1.5%, change the engine oil and check the breather system for blockages. If the CO level still increases after an oil change, suspect worn or sticking piston rings.

Idle speed and mixture (CO)

3 Run the engine at 3000 rpm for 30 seconds to clear the manifold of fuel vapours, then allow the engine to idle.
4 Use the idle bypass regulating screw to set the specified idle speed *(see illustration)*.
5 Check the CO level. If incorrect, remove the tamperproof plug and adjust the idle mixture screw to obtain the correct level. Turning the screw clockwise (inwards) will reduce the CO level. Turning the screw anti-clockwise (outwards) will increase the CO level.
6 Repeat paragraphs 4 and 5 until both adjustments are correct. Adjusting the idle bypass screw will also affect the CO level.
7 Fit a new tamperproof plug to the mixture control screw on completion.

Float level

8 The float level is not adjustable. If the level appears to be incorrect, remove the float and check the float weight (see Specifications). If the weight is satisfactory, renew the float.

Accelerator pump

9 On the PIC-7 carburettor, it is possible to adjust the volume of fuel injected by the accelerator pump.
10 The adjusting screw can take various forms, depending on carburettor type. Turn the adjusting screw in direction (+) to increase the

Pierburg-Solex 31 PIC-7 carburettor

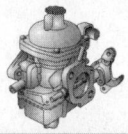

Accelerator pump adjustment - early type
a Turn brass nut to adjust pump output

Accelerator pump adjustment - later type
a Turn screw to adjust pump output

Using a twist drill to measure fast idle clearance
11 Choke operating lever
12 Fast idle adjustment screw

fuel volume or in direction (-) to decrease the volume *(see illustrations)*.

Choke adjustments

Fast idle adjustment (carburettor removed)

11 Invert the carburettor.
12 Pull the choke operating lever to fully close the choke flap. The fast idle screw will butt against the fast idle cam and force open the throttle plate to leave a small clearance.
13 Use the shank of a twist drill to measure the clearance between the wall of the throttle bore and the throttle plate. Refer to Specifications for the required size. Measure from the side opposite the progression holes *(see illustration)*.
14 Remove the tamperproof plug and adjust as necessary by turning the fast idle adjustment screw in the appropriate direction *(see illustration)*.
15 Fit a new tamperproof plug on completion.
16 Check the fast idle speed against the specified figure once the carburettor has been refitted to the engine.

Fast idle adjustment (engine running)

17 Run the engine to normal operating temperature then switch it off.
18 Fully close the choke flap using the choke operating lever. Push the lever back until the point of the adjustment screw is aligned with the step on the fast idle cam.

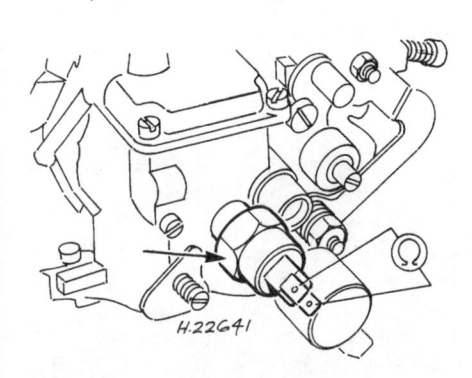

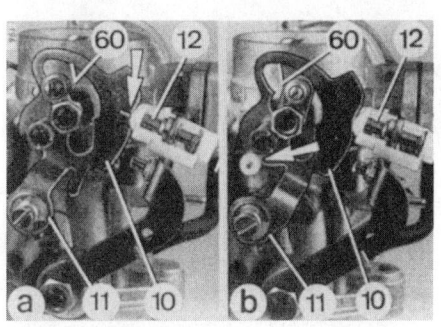

4.14 Fast idle speed adjustment - both types shown
10 Cam
11 Choke operating lever
12 Fast idle adjustment screw
60 Curved cam face

19 Start the engine and record the fast idle speed. Refer to Specifications for the correct value.
20 Adjust as necessary by turning the adjustment screw in the appropriate direction.

Choke vacuum pull-down

21 Close the choke flap using the choke operating lever (or the choke operating arm) as described in paragraph 18.
22 Remove the vacuum hose and attach a

Testing throttle body heater
24 Throttle body heater
25 Electrical connector - connect a test lamp where arrowed

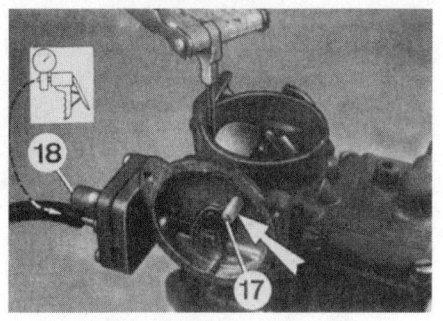

Location of thermal switch (arrowed)

4.22 Choke pull-down adjustment
17 Choke operating arm
18 Pull-down adjustment screw

vacuum pump to the choke pull-down connector. Operate the pump until the diaphragm is actuated. Renew the diaphragm if it does not operate fully or if the vacuum is not maintained for at least 10 seconds *(see illustration)*.
23 Maintaining the vacuum obtained in paragraph 22, use the shank of a twist drill to measure the clearance between the upper section of the choke flap and the air intake. Refer to Specifications for the required drill size.
24 Adjust as necessary by turning the pull-down adjusting screw in the appropriate direction.

5 Component testing

Thermal switch tests

1 Refer to Part D for general tests on the thermal switch and throttle body heater *(see illustrations)*.
2 Below 40 ± 10°C, a voltmeter should indicate battery voltage (switch open).
3 Above that temperature, the voltmeter should indicate zero volts (switch closed).
4 Renew the thermal switch if it does not function in accordance with the above.

Chapter F8

Removing the throttle body heater

5 Remove the screw and detach the fixing plate and spring. Be careful that the spring does not fly out and become lost. Remove the heater from its location on the carburettor body.

6 Fault diagnosis

Refer to Part D for diagnosis of general carburettor faults. The following faults are specific to the 31 PIC-7 carburettor.

Poor idle/low-speed hesitation

- [ ] The idle jet is rather small and very prone to clogging with dirt.
- [ ] Idle and auxiliary bypass jets transposed.
- [ ] Air leak at mounting flange.
- [ ] Blocked accelerator pump injector.

Lack of power

- [ ] Blocked full-load enrichment tube (the outlet is a fine hole on the underside of the tube).

Poor cold running

- [ ] Carburettor earth wire missing/faulty.
- [ ] Throttle body heater faulty.
- [ ] Faulty choke bi-metal coil or pull-down.

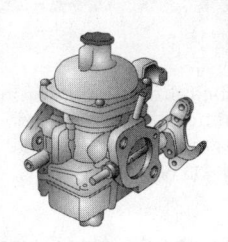

Part G Chapter 1
Solex 32 BIS carburettor

G1

Contents

Fault diagnosis	5	Principles of operation	1
General servicing	3	Service adjustments	4
Identification	2		

Specifications

Manufacturer	Renault	Renault	Renault
Model	5 & Extra 1.1 (B/C/S/F401)	5 & Extra 1.4 (B/C/F402)	9 & 11 1.1 (L421/C371)
Year	1985 to 1992	1985 to 1991	1982 to 1986
Engine code	C1EG750	C1JA768 or C1JE768	C1EF715
Capacity (cm³)/no. of cyls	1108/4	1397/4	1108/4
Oil temperature (°C)	80	80	80
Carb. ident. (Solex)	32 BIS 13282	32 BIS 13314	32 BIS 13145
Carb. ident. (vehicle)	836	849	797
Idle speed (rpm)	625 ± 50 (Extra: 700 ± 50)	625 ± 25	650 ± 50
CO @ idle (% vol.)	1.0 ± 0.5	1.0 ± 0.5	1.0 ± 0.5
Venturi diameter (K)	23	24	23
Idle jet (g)	42	40	39
Main jet (Gg)	110	112	110
Air correction jet (a)	145	155	150
Accelerator pump jet (i)	40	40	45
Needle valve (mm) (P)	1.3	1.6	1.6
Choke fast idle gap (mm)	0.70	0.75	0.65
Fast idle position (OP)	20°	20°30'	11°15
Vent valve (mm)	3 ± 0.5	3 ± 0.5	3 ± 0.5

Manufacturer	Renault	Renault
Model	9 & 11 1.4 (L422, B/C/372)	19 & Chamade 1.2 (B/C/L530)
Year	1982 to 1985	1990 to 1991
Engine code	C1JF715	C1G730
Capacity (cm³)/no. of cyls	1397/4	1237/4
Oil temperature (°C)	80	80
Carb. ident. (Solex)	32 BIS 13274	32 BIS
Carb. ident. (vehicle)	829	936
Idle speed (rpm)	625 ± 25	700 ± 50
CO @ idle (% vol.)	1.0 ± 0.5	1.5 ± 0.5
Venturi diameter (K)	24	24
Idle jet (g)	43	42
Main jet (Gg)	117	120
Air correction jet (a)	155	125
Accelerator pump jet (i)	40	40
Needle valve (mm) (P)	1.8	1.3
Choke fast idle gap (mm)	0.75	0.70
Fast idle position (OP)	20°30	20°
Choke pull-down (mm) (OVAD)	3.2	-
Vent valve (mm)	3 ± 0.5	3 ± 0.5

G1•1

Chapter G1

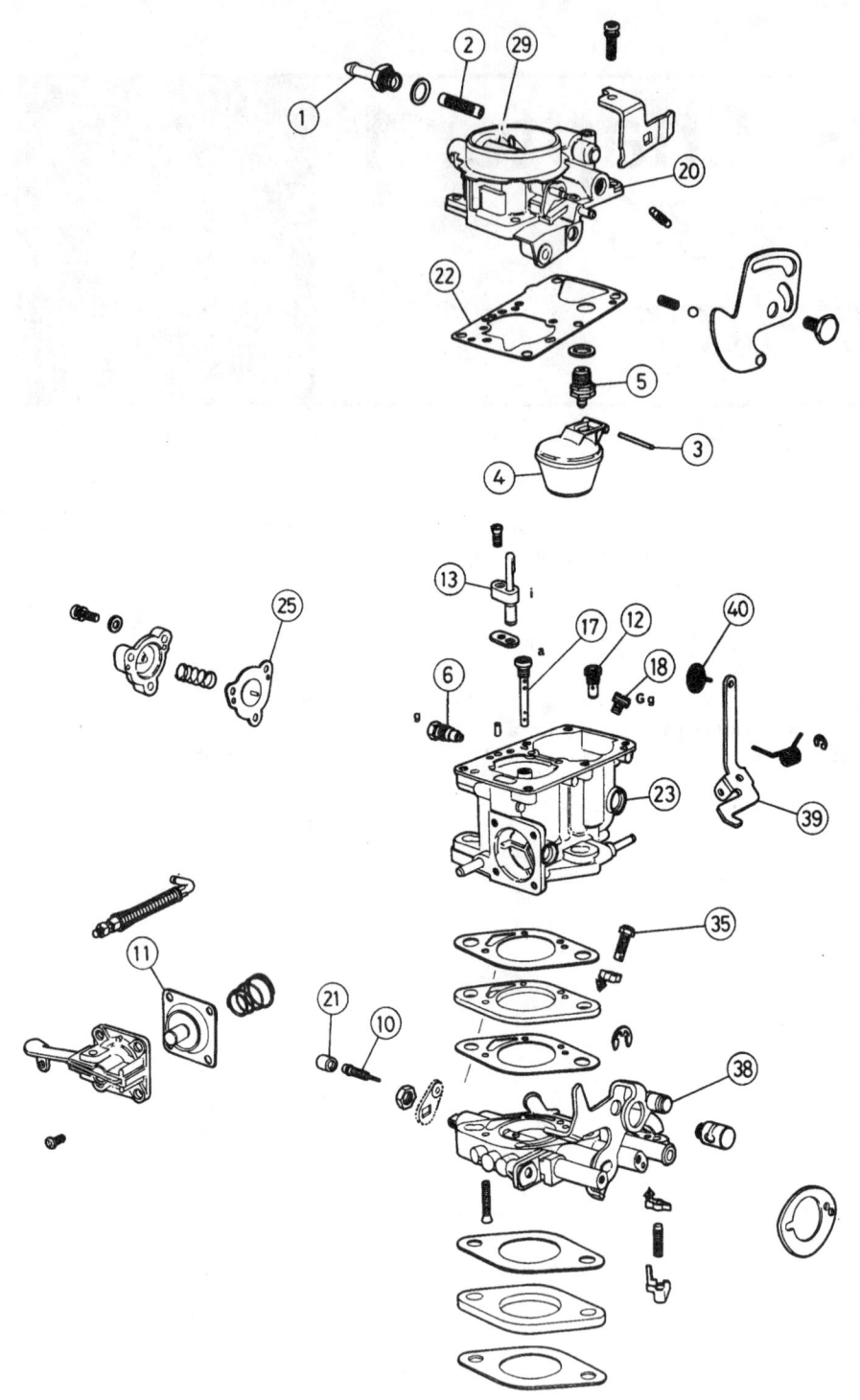

Solex BIS carburettor

1. Fuel inlet connection
2. Fuel filter
3. Float pin
4. Float
5. Needle valve
6. Idle jet
10. Idle mixture control screw
11. Accelerator pump diaphragm
12. Accelerator pump valve
13. Pump injector
17. Combined air corrector and emulsion tube
18. Main jet
20. Upper body
21. Tamperproof cap
22. Float chamber gasket
23. Main body
25. Power valve diaphragm
29. Choke flap
35. Fast idle adjustment screw
38. Throttle body
39. Vent valve mechanism
40. Vent valve

1 Principles of operation

Introduction
1 The following technical description of the Solex 32 BIS carburettor should be read in conjunction with the more detailed description of carburettor principles in Part A.

Construction
2 The Solex BIS carburettor is a downdraught single venturi instrument with a manual choke control *(see illustration)*. The throttle shaft is made of steel, while the throttle valve, all jets and the emulsion tube are manufactured from brass. The internal fuel channels and air passages are drilled and sealed with lead plugs where necessary *(see illustration)*.

3 The carburettor is constructed in three main bodies. These are the upper body, main body and throttle body (which contains the throttle assemblies). An insulating block placed between the main carburettor body and the throttle body, prevents excess heat transference to the main body.

4 The throttle body contains a heating flange through which hot engine coolant is piped. The purpose of the flange is to improve atomisation of the air/fuel mixture and to prevent carburettor icing during warm-up.

Fuel control
5 Fuel flows into the carburettor through a fine mesh filter. The fuel level in the float chamber is controlled by a needle valve and plastic float assembly. An anti-vibration ball is incorporated into the needle valve design. The float chamber uses a dual venting arrangement. Venting is to atmosphere at idle or with the engine shut down. At engine speeds above idle, a lever attached to the throttle closes the atmospheric vent. This allows the float chamber to vent into the upper air intake which is on the clean-air side of the air filter.

Idle, slow running and progression
6 Although early models of the BIS carburettor utilised an idle bypass control, the applications covered in this manual use a conventional idle system.

7 Fuel, sourced from the main well, passes into the idle channel through a metered idle jet. Here it is mixed with a small amount of air from a calibrated air bleed and the resulting emulsion is drawn through a channel to be discharged from the idle orifice under the primary throttle plate. A tapered mixture screw is used to vary the outlet and this ensures fine control of the idle mixture. A progression slot provides extra enrichment as it is uncovered by the opening throttle during initial acceleration.

8 The idle speed is set by an adjustable screw. The adjustable mixture screw is tamper proofed at production level, in accordance with emission regulations.

Solex 32 BIS carburettor

1 Brass accelerator pump inlet valve
2 Part-load enrichment valve
3 Spring
4 Vacuum channel
a Air corrector jet
F Float
Gg Main jet
g Idle fuel jet
i Accelerator pump injector
K Venturi
M Accelerator pump diaphragm
M1 Part-load enrichment diaphragm
P Needle valve
s Emulsion tube
U1 Idle air jet

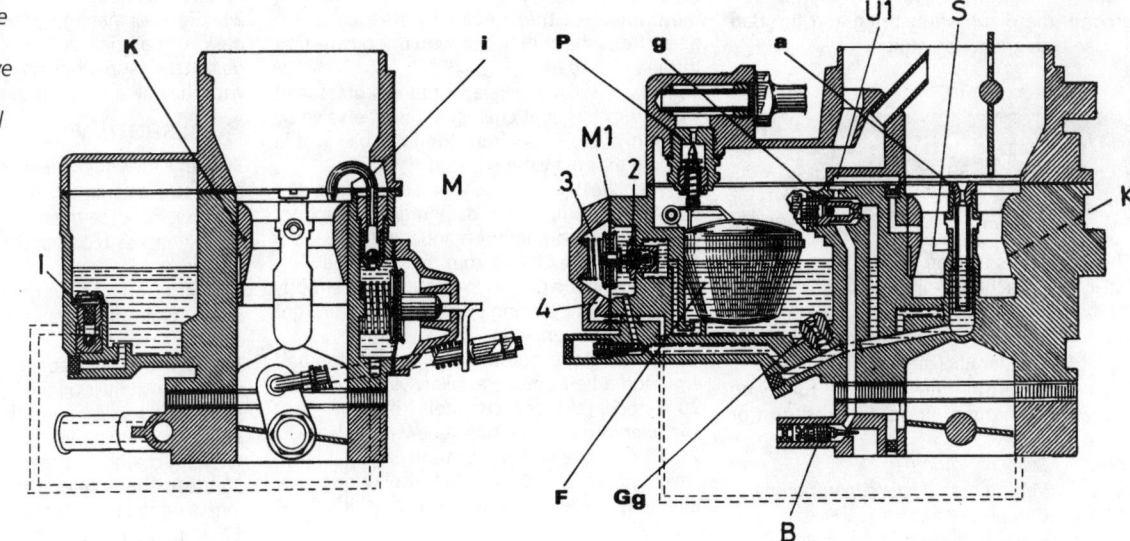

Internal fuel channels and air passages

Accelerator pump

9 The BIS accelerator pump is controlled by a diaphragm and is mechanically operated by a lever attached to the throttle linkage. During acceleration, fuel is pumped through a ball valve located in the pump injector where it is discharged into the primary venturi. The brass inlet valve, located in the float chamber, also allows excess fuel to return to the chamber.

Main circuit

10 Fuel is drawn through a calibrated main jet into the base of the auxiliary venturi. An emulsion tube is placed in the auxiliary venturi, capped with an air corrector jet. The fuel is mixed with air, drawn in through the air corrector and through the holes in the emulsion tube. The resulting emulsified mixture is discharged into the main airstream. This is accomplished through four discharge orifices placed at 90° intervals in the upper reaches of the auxiliary venturi.

Part-load enrichment (power valve)

11 Fuel flows from the float chamber into the enrichment chamber, through a fuel channel and a brass inlet valve. An air passage is taken from under the throttle plate to the cover of the chamber.
12 At idle and during light-throttle operation, manifold vacuum draws the diaphragm back against spring pressure. The diaphragm pintle is withdrawn from the valve and the spring-loaded ball seats to close off the inlet channel.
13 Under acceleration and wide-open throttle operation, the vacuum in the manifold is depleted. The diaphragm returns under spring pressure and the power diaphragm pintle pushes the ball to open the inlet valve. Fuel then flows through the valve into the enrichment chamber. From here it passes through a calibrated jet into a fuel channel leading to the primary main well. The fuel level rises in the well and the fuel mixture is enriched.

Manual choke operation

14 The manual choke is operated by a dash-mounted cable control. When the cable is pulled, it operates a lever that pulls the choke flap closed across the air intake. Fast idle is achieved with the aid of a curved cam attached to the choke operating lever. An adjustable screw, attached to the throttle lever and butting against the cam, is used to vary the fast idle speed.
15 During engine warm-up, the cable control should be progressively pushed home until the choke flap is fully open.

Choke pull-down

16 Once the engine has fired, the choke flap must open slightly to weaken the mixture and avoid flooding. This is achieved by two different methods, depending on the version of the BIS fitted.
17 On the first type, an increase in airflow through the air intake partially opens the choke flap against the action of a spring. A stop ensures that the choke is only opened a small amount.
18 On the second type, manifold vacuum is used to actuate a diaphragm *(see illustration)*. A linkage attached to the diaphragm will then pull upon the choke flap. A vacuum take-off is drilled into the base of the carburettor and a second vacuum take-off is mounted on the carburettor side of the throttle plate. Both take-off points relay the vacuum signal into a common passage and thence to the vacuum diaphragm, depending on throttle position. Once the engine fires, a vacuum signal from take-off passage number one (continuous vacuum) will pull the choke flap slightly open against a mechanical stop. As the throttle plate is opened through approximately 25°, the flap slips off its stop. This means that the range of choke flap movement is increased. However, movement of the flap is now finely balanced by vacuum signal against the diaphragm return spring. As the throttle plate opens to uncover the second vacuum take-off (regulated vacuum), this vacuum will join with the initial

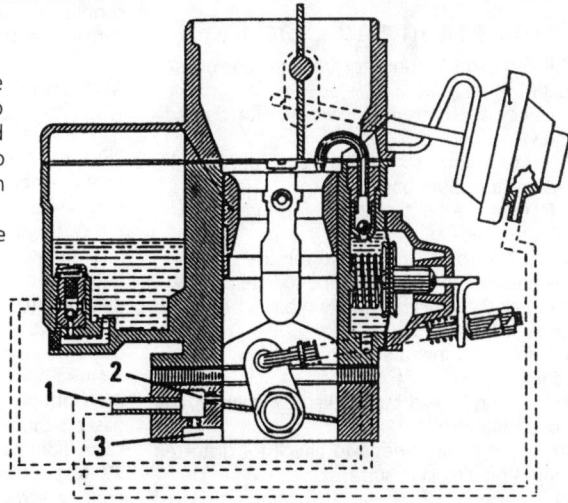

Vacuum-operated choke pull-down
1 Vacuum connector
2 Regulated vacuum signal
3 Continuous vacuum signal

Chapter G1

vacuum pull to provide a stronger vacuum signal. This stronger vacuum signal will overcome the diaphragm spring and the flap will open by a greater amount.

2 Identification

1 The Solex identification code is stamped on a metallic tag attached to the cover by an upper body fixing screw. This tag quotes the Solex part number and the vehicle manufacturer part number. It also identifies the carburettor type.
2 Later carburettors may have the following information stamped upon the carburettor body:
  13282   Solex part number
  Ren 836 Vehicle manufacturer part number
  32 BIS Carburettor type
3 Where the tag is missing, refer to Part B for other means of identifying the carburettor.

3 General servicing

Introduction

1 Read this Chapter in conjunction with Part B, which describes some of the operations in more detail. It is assumed that the carburettor is removed for this service. However, many of the operations can be tackled with the carburettor in place. Where this is undertaken, first remove the carburettor upper body and soak the fuel out of the float chamber using a clean tissue or soft cloth.

Dismantling and checking

2 Remove the carburettor from the engine (see Part B).
3 Check the carburettor visually for damage and wear.
4 Remove the six screws and detach the carburettor upper body.
5 Inspect the float chamber for corrosion and calcium build-up.
6 Tap out the float pin and remove the float, needle valve and float chamber gasket.
7 Check that the anti-vibration ball is free in the valve end.
8 Check the needle valve tip for wear and ridges.
9 The float should be checked for damage and ingress of petrol.
10 Use a straight-edge to check for distorted flanges on all facing surfaces.
11 Renew the float pin if it shows signs of wear.
12 Unscrew the inlet tube and inspect the fuel filter. Clean the filter housing of debris and dirt and renew the filter if necessary.
13 Remove the mixture screw and inspect the tip for damage and ridges.
14 Unscrew the fixing screw and remove the accelerator pump injector from its location in the body. Test the injector by shaking it. No noise from the outlet ball would indicate that the valve is seized.
15 Unscrew the accelerator pump's brass inlet valve from the float chamber. Test the valve by shaking it. No noise from the inlet ball would indicate that the valve is seized.
16 Remove the four screws and detach the accelerator pump cover, diaphragm and spring. Check the diaphragm for fatigue and damage.
17 Remove the idle jet from the main body.
18 Unscrew the plug in the float chamber body to expose an opening. Remove the main jet through this opening.
19 Remove the combined air corrector and emulsion tube from the auxiliary venturi.
20 Check that the channel from the float chamber into the emulsion tube well is clear.
21 Check the jet calibration against that specified. It is possible that the wrong size jets may have been fitted during the last overhaul.
22 Remove the three screws and detach the power valve housing cover, spring and diaphragm from the body. Check the diaphragm for damage. The brass outlet valve is cast into the body and is not removable. The ball in the outlet valve should seal the outlet. Depress and release the ball with a small screwdriver and it should move smoothly in and out. Check that the channel into the emulsion tube well is clear.
23 Remove the two screws and separate the carburettor main body and throttle body assemblies. The throttle body can be renewed separately if the spindles or throttle bores are worn. Use a straight-edge to check for distorted flanges on the facing surfaces.
24 Attach a vacuum pump to the pull-down diaphragm (where fitted) and operate the pump to obtain 300 mmHg (400 mbars). The diaphragm should operate fully and the vacuum should be maintained for at least 30 seconds. Renew the diaphragm assembly if it fails these tests. Check the vacuum hose for leaks and splits and renew if necessary.

Preparation for reassembly

25 Clean the jets, carburettor body assemblies, float chamber and internal channels. An air line may be used to clear the internal channels once the carburettor is fully dismantled. Note that if high-pressure air is directed into the channels and passages with the diaphragms still in place, diaphragm damage may result. Spraying carburettor cleaner into all the channels and passages in the carburettor body will often clear them of gum and dirt.
26 During reassembly, a complete set of new gaskets should be fitted. Also renew the needle valve, float pin and all diaphragms.
27 Inspect and renew (where necessary) the mixture screw, main jet, idle jet, air corrector jet/emulsion tube and the accelerator pump inlet valve and injector. Renew worn linkages, screws, springs, vacuum hoses and other parts where necessary.
28 Ensure that all the jets are firmly locked into their original positions (but do not over-tighten). A loose jet can cause a rich (or even lean) running condition.
29 Clean all mating surfaces and flanges of old gasket material and reassemble with new gaskets. Ensure that housings are positioned with their air and fuel routes correctly aligned.

Reassembly

30 Refit the choke diaphragm assembly (where used) to the carburettor upper body.
31 Assemble the main and throttle bodies with a new gasket block and secure with the two screws.
32 Refit the power diaphragm, spring and cover assembly, then secure with the three screws.
33 Refit the emulsion tube/air corrector and main jet into their original positions.
34 Refit the idle jet into the main body.
35 Refit the accelerator pump inlet valve into the float chamber, after renewing the seal.
36 Refit the accelerator pump injector, after renewing the small seal or gasket.
37 Refit the pump spring, diaphragm and cover assembly, then secure with the four screws.
38 Refit the idle mixture screw after renewing the seal. Turn the screw in gently until it just seats. From this position, unscrew it three full turns. This will provide a basic setting to allow the engine to be started.
39 Clean or renew the fuel filter and refit the inlet tube.
40 Place a new float chamber gasket in position on the upper body.
41 Renew the needle valve assembly using a new sealing washer. Ensure that it is firmly locked into position (but do not over-tighten).
42 Refit the float and secure with the float pin.
43 The float level is not adjustable on the BIS carburettor. Refer to Section 4.
44 Refit the upper body to the main body and secure with the six screws.
45 Reconnect the choke pull-down hose (where fitted).
46 Ensure that the choke flap and linkage move smoothly and progressively.
47 Adjust the choke fast idle and pull-down. Refer to Section 4.
48 Refit the carburettor to the engine.
49 Always adjust the carburettor idle speed and mixture after any work has been carried out on the carburettor, preferably with the aid of a CO meter.

4 Service adjustments

Adjustment pre-conditions

1 Refer to Part B for general advice on the pre-conditions for correct adjustment of this carburettor.

Idle speed and mixture (CO)

2 Run the engine at 3000 rpm for 30 seconds to clear the manifold of fuel vapours, then allow the engine to idle.

Solex 32 BIS carburettor

3 Use the idle speed screw to set the specified idle speed *(see illustration)*.
4 Check the CO level. If incorrect, remove the tamperproof plug and adjust the idle mixture screw to obtain the correct level. Refer to Part B for a method of setting the idle mixture without the aid of a CO meter. Turning the screw clockwise (inwards) will reduce the CO level. Turning the screw anti-clockwise (outwards) will increase the CO level.
5 Repeat paragraphs 3 and 4 until both adjustments are correct.
6 Clear the manifold every 30 seconds during the setting operation by running the engine at 3000 rpm for 30 seconds.
7 Increase the speed to 2000 rpm and note the CO reading. The cruise reading should be less than half the idle CO reading.
8 Fit a new tamperproof plug to the mixture control screw on completion.

Float level

9 The float level is not normally adjustable on the BIS carburettor and no adjustment data is available. However, it is possible to alter the level by varying the thickness of the needle valve sealing washer, the standard thickness being 1.0 mm.

Accelerator pump travel

10 Invert the carburettor and insert the shank of a 3.0 mm diameter twist drill between the wall of the throttle bore and the throttle plate.
11 The accelerator pump lever should now be at the end of its travel.
12 If adjustment is required, loosen the adjustment locknut and turn the adjustment nut *(see illustration)* in the appropriate direction.
13 Tighten the locknut on completion.

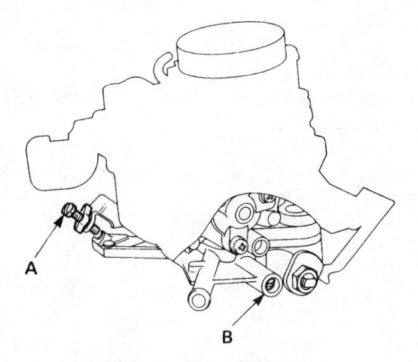

Idle adjustment screw location
A Idle speed adjustment screw
B Idle mixture control screw

Choke adjustments

Fast idle

14 The carburettor must be removed from the engine in order to make the following fast idle adjustment. Refer to Part B for a method of setting the fast idle speed without removing the carburettor.
15 Invert the carburettor and pull the choke operating lever to fully close the choke flap. The fast idle screw will butt against the fast idle cam and force open the throttle plate to leave a small clearance.
16 Use the shank of a twist drill to measure the clearance between the wall of the throttle bore and the throttle plate. Refer to Specifications for the required drill size. Measure from the side opposite the progression holes *(see illustration)*.
17 Remove the tamperproof plug and adjust as necessary by turning the fast idle adjustment screw in the appropriate direction.
18 Fit a new tamperproof plug on completion.
19 Note that the fast idle throttle angle may also be set by means of a Solex or Pierburg throttle angle gauge. Refer to Specifications for the appropriate throttle angle.

Choke pull-down (vacuum pull-down carburettor)

20 Pull the choke operating lever to fully close the choke flap.
21 Use a vacuum pump to pull the diaphragm operating rod up to its stop (or push the mechanism with a small screwdriver). At the same time, use the shank of a twist drill to measure the gap between the lower section of the choke flap and the air intake. Refer to Specifications for the required drill size.
22 Remove the plug in the diaphragm cover and adjust as necessary by turning the adjustment screw in the appropriate direction.
23 Renew the plug when adjustment is complete.

Float chamber vent valve

24 Ensure that the choke flap is fully open, the throttle plate is fully closed and the throttle lever is back against its idle stop.
25 Measure the clearance (X) between the float chamber cover and the valve *(see illustration)*. Refer to Specifications for the clearance.
26 Adjust as necessary by carefully bending the control arm in the appropriate direction.

5 Fault diagnosis

Refer to Part D for diagnosis of general carburettor faults.

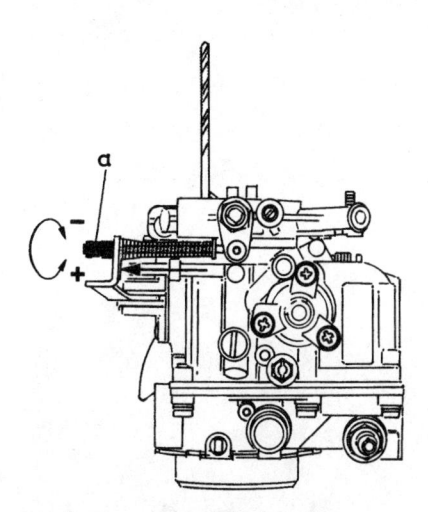

Accelerator pump adjustment
a Turn brass nut to adjust pump output

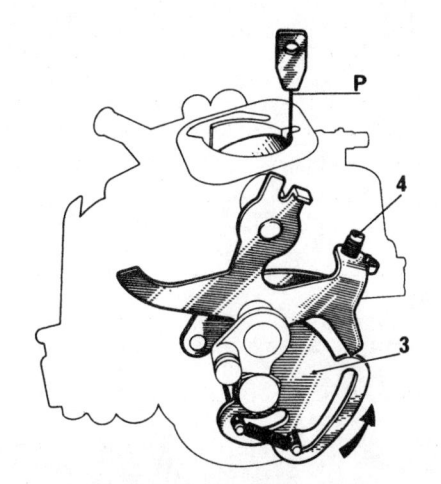

Using a twist drill (P) to measure fast idle clearance
3 Choke operating lever
4 Fast idle adjustment screw

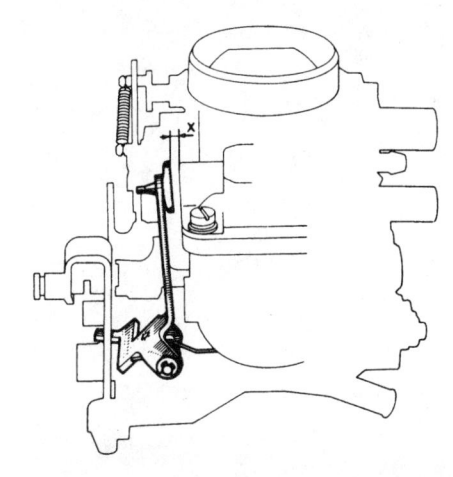

Checking vent valve clearance
X Clearance (refer to Specifications)

Notes

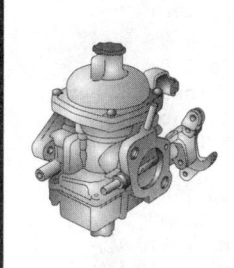

Part G Chapter 2
Solex 35 & 38 EEIT carburettor

Contents

Fault diagnosis	5	Principles of operation	1
General servicing	3	Service adjustments	4
Identification	2		

Specifications

Manufacturer	Ford	Ford	Ford	Ford
Model	Cortina 2300	Cortina 2300 auto.	Cortina 2300	Cortina 2300 auto.
Year	Apr.1979 to Jun.1981	Apr.1979 to Jun.1981	Jun.1981 to 1982	Jun.1981 to 1982
Engine code	YYR (OHV)	YYR (OHV)	YYR (OHV)	YYR (OHV)
Capacity (cm^3)/no. of cyls	2294/V6	2294/V6	2294/V6	2294/V6
Oil temperature (°C)	80	80	80	80
Transmission	Manual	Automatic	Manual	Automatic
Carb. ident. (Ford)	80TF 9510 AJA	80TF 9510 AFA	82TF 9510 VA	82TF 9510 RA
	80TF 9510 AJB	80TF 9510 AFB	82TF 9510 AHA	82TF 9510 AJA
Idle speed (rpm)	800 ± 50	800 ± 50	800 ± 20	800 ± 20
Fast idle speed (rpm)	2900 ± 100	2900 ± 100	2900 ± 100	2900 ± 100
CO @ idle (% vol.)	1.5 ± 0.5	1.5 ± 0.5	1.5 ± 0.25	1.5 ± 0.25
Venturi diameter	26 (x2)	26 (x2)	26 (x2)	26 (x2)
Idle jet	47.5 (x2)	47.5 (x2)	47.5 (x2)	47.5 (x2)
Main jet	137.5 (x2)	137.5 (x2)	137.5 (x2)	137.5 (x2)
Air correction jet	200 (x2)	200 (x2)	185 (x2)	190 (x2)
Accel. pump jet	40 (x2)	45 (x2)	40 (x2)	45 (x2)
Float level 1 (mm)	14.5 ± 0.5	14.5 ± 0.5	11.0 ± 0.5	11.0 ± 0.5
Needle valve size (mm)	2.0	2.0	2.5	2.5
Choke modulator gap (mm)	1.9 ± 0.1	1.9 ± 0.1	1.8 ± 0.1	1.8 ± 0.1
Choke pull-down (mm)	3.1 ± 0.2	3.1 ± 0.2	3.2 ± 0.2	3.2 ± 0.2
Choke phasing (mm)	0.3 to 0.6	0.3 to 0.6	0.3 to 0.6	0.3 to 0.6

Chapter G2

Manufacturer	Ford	Ford	Ford	Ford
Model	Sierra 2300	Sierra 2300 auto.	Granada 2300	Granada 2300 auto.
Year	1982 to 1984	1982 to 1984	1978 to 1979	1978 to 1979
Engine code	YYT (OHV)	YYT (OHV)	YYH (OHV)	YYH (OHV)
Capacity (cm³)/no. of cyls	2294/V6	2294/V6	2294/V6	2294/V6
Oil temperature (°C)	80	80	80	80
Transmission	Manual	Automatic	Manual	Automatic
Carb. ident. (Ford)	82TF 9510 AHA	82TF 9510 AJA	78TF 9510 CA / 79TF 9510 DA	78TF 9510 FA / 79TF 9510 EA
Idle speed (rpm)	800 ± 20	800 ± 20	800 ± 50	800 ± 50
Fast idle speed (rpm)	3000 ± 100	3000 ± 100	2900 ± 100	2900 ± 100
CO @ idle (% vol.)	1.5 ± 0.25	1.5 ± 0.25	1.5 ± 0.5	1.5 ± 0.5
Venturi diameter	26 (x2)	26 (x2)	25 (x2)	25 (x2)
Idle jet	47.5 (x2)	47.5 (x2)	42.5 (x2)	42.5 (x2)
Main jet	137.5 (x2)	137.5 (x2)	130 (x2)	130 (x2)
Air correction jet	200 (x2)	200 (x2)	200 (x2)	200 (x2)
Accel. pump jet	-	-	40 (x2)	45 (x2)
Float level 1 (mm)	11.0 ± 0.5	11.0 ± 0.5	11.0 (black float)	11.0 (black float)
Float level 2 (mm)	-	-		14.5 (white float) / 14.5 (white float)
Needle valve size (mm)	2.0	2.0	-	-
Choke modulator gap (mm)	1.8 ± 0.1	1.8 ± 0.1	1.9 ± 0.1	1.9 ± 0.1
Choke pull-down (mm)	3.2 ± 0.2	3.2 ± 0.2	3.1 ± 0.2	3.1 ± 0.2
Choke phasing (mm)	0.3 to 0.6	0.3 to 0.6	0.3 to 0.6	0.3 to 0.6
Manufacturer	Ford	Ford	Ford	Ford
Model	Granada 2300	Granada 2300 auto.	Granada 2300	Granada 2300 auto.
Year	1980 to 1981	1980 to 1981	1982 to 1985	1982 to 1985
Engine code	YYH (OHV)	YYH (OHV)	YYP (OHV)	YYP (OHV)
Capacity (cm³)/no. of cyls	2294/V6	2294/V6	2294/V6	2294/V6
Oil temperature (°C)	80	80	80	80
Transmission	Manual	Automatic	Manual	Automatic
Carb. ident. (Ford)	80TF 9510 AJA / 80TF 9510 AJB	80TF 9510 AFA / 80TF 9510 AFB	82TF 9510 ABA / 82TF 9510 AHA	82TF 9510 ACA / 82TF 9510 AJA
Idle speed (rpm)	800 ± 50	800 ± 50	800 ± 50	800 ± 50
Fast idle speed (rpm)	2900 ± 100	2900 ± 100	3000 ± 100	3000 ± 100
CO @ idle (% vol.)	1.5 ± 0.5	1.5 ± 0.5	1.5 ± 0.5	1.5 ± 0.5
Venturi diameter	26 (x2)	26 (x2)	26 (x2)	26 (x2)
Idle jet	47.5 (x2)	47.5 (x2)	47.5 (x2)	47.5 (x2)
Main jet	137.5 (x2)	137.5 (x2)	137.5 (x2)	137.5 (x2)
Air correction jet	200 (x2)	200 (x2)	185 (x2)	190 (x2)
Accel. pump jet	40 (x2)	45 (x2)	40 (x2)	45 (x2)
Float level 1 (mm)	14.5 ± 0.5	14.5 ± 0.5	11.0 ± 0.5	11.0 ± 0.5
Needle valve size (mm)	2.0	2.0	2.5	2.5
Choke modulator gap (mm)	1.9 ± 0.1	1.9 ± 0.1	1.8 ± 0.1	1.8 ± 0.1
Choke pull-down (mm)	3.5 ± 0.2	3.3 ± 0.2	3.2 ± 0.2	3.2 ± 0.2
Choke phasing (mm)	0.3 to 0.6	0.3 to 0.6	0.3 to 0.6	0.3 to 0.6
Manufacturer	Ford	Ford	Ford	Ford
Model	Granada 2800	Granada 2800 auto.	Granada 2800	Granada 2800 auto
Year	1978 to 1979	1978 to 1979	1980 to 1981	1980 to 1981
Engine code	PYA (OHV)	PYA (OHV)	PYA (OHV)	PYA (OHV)
Capacity (cm³)/no. of cyls	2792/V6	2792/V6	2792/V6	2792/V6
Oil temperature (°C)	80	80	80	80
Transmission	Manual	Automatic	Manual	Automatic
Carb. ident. (Ford)	78TF 9510 EA / 79TF 9510 GA	78TF 9510 BA / 79TF 9510 HA	80TF 9510 AMA / 80TF 9510 AMB	80TF 9510 ASA / 80TF 9510 ASB
Idle speed (rpm)	800 ± 50	800 ± 50	800 ± 50	800 ± 50
Fast idle speed (rpm)	2900 ± 100	2900 ± 100	2900 ± 100	2900 ± 100
CO @ idle (% vol.)	1.5 ± 0.5	1.5 ± 0.5	1.5 ± 0.5	1.5 ± 0.5
Venturi diameter	28 (x2)	28 (x2)	28 (x2)	28 (x2)
Idle jet	45 (x2)	45 (x2)	50 (x2)	50 (x2)
Main jet	147.5 (x2)	145 (x2)	150 (x2)	150 (x2)
Air correction jet	210 (x2)	200 (x2)	200 (x2)	200 (x2)
Accel. pump jet	50 (x2)	50 (x2)	50 (x2)	50 (x2)
Float level 1 (mm)	14.5 ± 0.5	14.5 ± 0.5	13.0 ± 0.5	13.0 ± 0.5
Needle valve size (mm)	2.0	2.0	2.5	2.5
Choke modulator gap (mm)	2.1 ± 0.1	2.1 ± 0.1	1.9 ± 0.1	1.9 ± 0.1
Choke pull-down (mm)	4.0 ± 0.2	4.0 ± 0.2	4.2 ± 0.2	4.5 ± 0.2
Choke phasing (mm)	0.3 to 0.6	0.3 to 0.6	0.3 to 0.6	0.3 to 0.6

Solex 35 & 38 EEIT carburettor

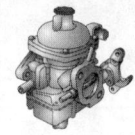

Manufacturer	Ford	Ford
Model	Granada 2800	Granada 2800 auto
Year	1982 to 1985	1982 to 1985
Engine code	PYA (OHV)	PYA (OHV)
Capacity (cm³)/no. of cyls	2792/V6	2792/V6
Oil temperature (°C)	80	80
Transmission	Manual	Automatic
Carb. ident. (Ford)	82 TF 9510 AEA	82 TF 9510 AFA
	82 TF 9510 AKA	82 TF 9510 ALA
Idle speed (rpm)	800 ± 50	800 ± 50
Fast idle speed (rpm)	3000 ± 100	3000 ± 100
CO @ idle (% vol.)	1.5 ± 0.5	1.5 ± 0.5
Venturi diameter	28 (x2)	28 (x2)
Idle jet	50 (x2)	50 (x2)
Main jet	150 (x2)	150 (x2)
Air correction jet	200 (x2)	200 (x2)
Accel. pump jet	50 (x2)	50 (x2)
Float level 1 (mm)	11.0 ± 0.5	11.0 ± 0.5
Needle valve size (mm)	2.5	2.5
Choke modulator gap (mm)	1.8 ± 0.1	1.8 ± 0.1
Choke pull-down (mm)	4.5 ± 0.2	4.2 ± 0.2
Choke phasing (mm)	0.3 to 0.6	0.3 to 0.6

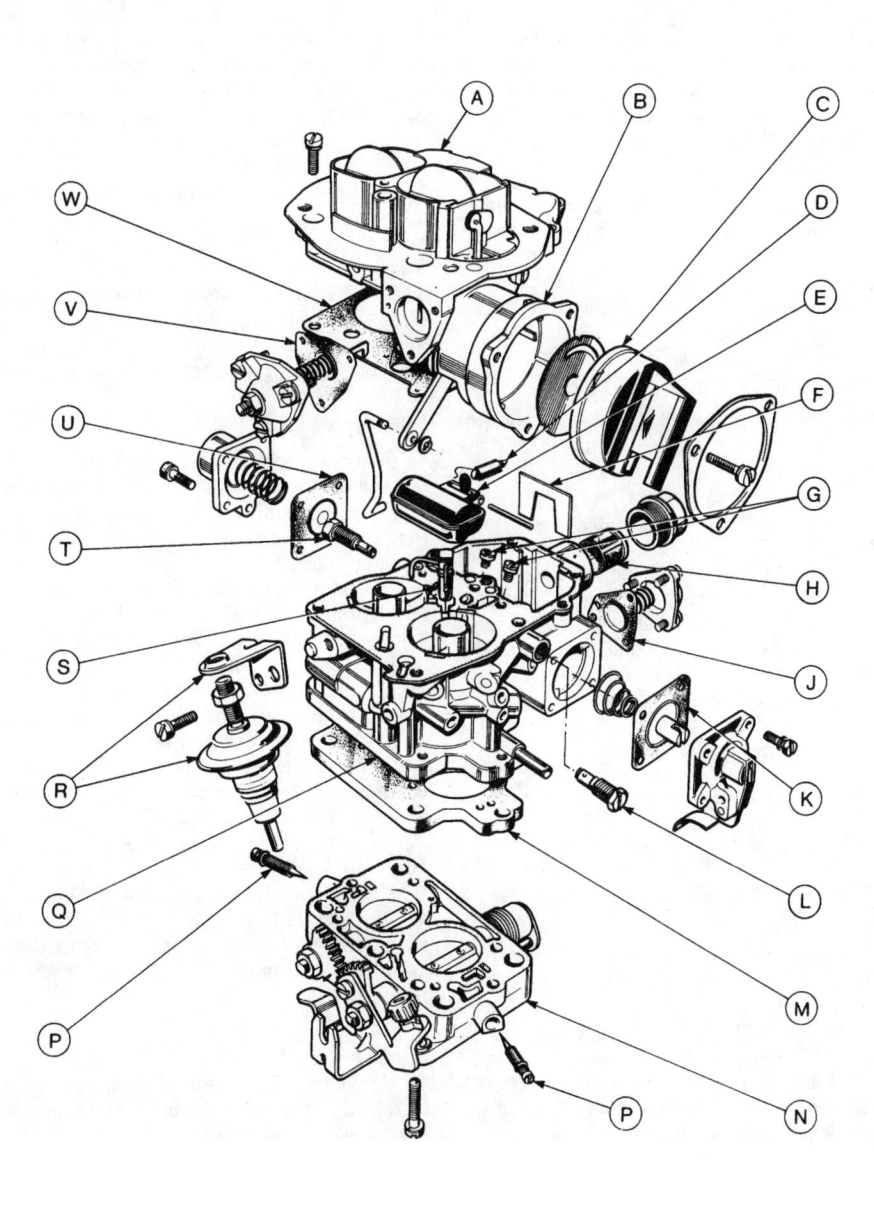

1 Principles of operation

Introduction

1 The following technical description of the Solex EEIT carburettor should be read in conjunction with the more detailed description of carburettor principles in Part A.

Construction

2 The Solex EEIT carburettor is a synchronised twin venturi downdraught instrument suitable for V6 engines *(see illustration)*. Each barrel has separate fuel and air circuits, supplied from a

Solex EEIT carburettor - 82 type

A Upper body
B Automatic choke housing
C Choke bi-metal assembly
D Needle valve
E Float
F Plastic retaining piece
G Main jets
H Fuel filter
J Power valve diaphragm
K Accelerator pump diaphragm
L Idle jet
M Gasket block
N Throttle body assembly
P Mixture screws
Q Main body assembly
R Throttle damper and bracket
S Accelerator pump injector
T Idle jet
U Anti-stall diaphragm
V Pull-down diaphragm
W Top cover-to-main body gasket

Chapter G2

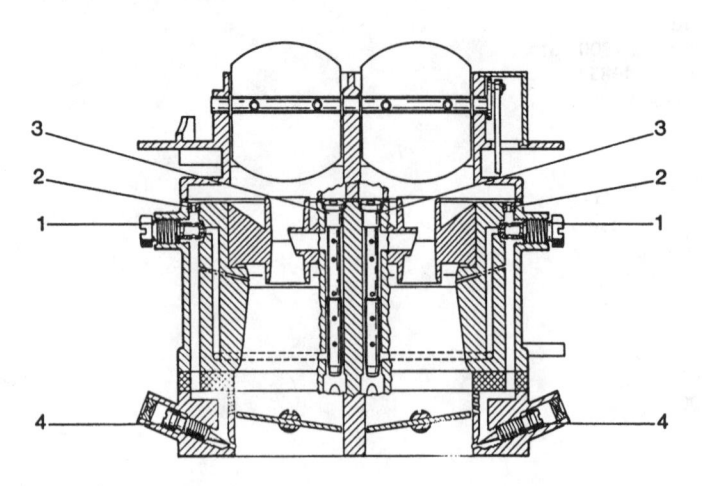

Basic idle system
1. Idle jets
2. Idle air bleeds
3. Air correction jets with emulsion tube
4. Mixture control screws

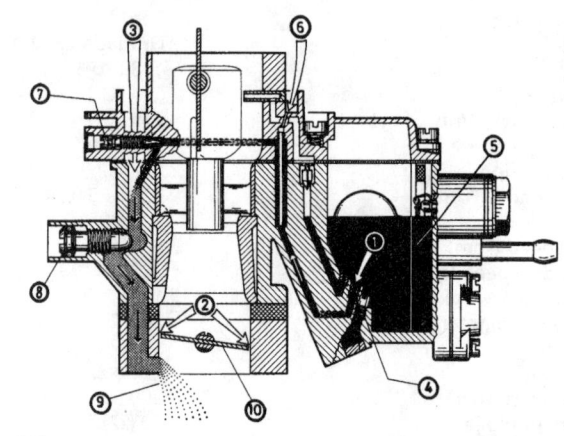

Bypass idle system
1. Bypass fuel supply
2. Main air supply
3. Bypass air supply
4. Main jet
5. Float chamber
6. Bypass air bleed
7. Bypass mixture screw
8. Bypass air screw
9. Bypass fuel mixture
10. Throttle plate

common float chamber, and provides the fuel **requirements for three cylinders.**

3 The carburettor is constructed in three main bodies. These are the upper body, main body and throttle body, which contains the throttle assemblies. Each throttle valve is controlled by a toothed segment, geared to open the valves synchronously in opposite directions. The valves are closed by a return spring acting upon one of the toothed segments. An insulating block, placed between the main carburettor body and the throttle body, prevents excess heat transference to the main body.

4 The EEIT carburettor has been subjected to a number of modifications to the basic design, mainly involving different methods of achieving idle CO adjustment and choke control. The three basic types and the periods when they were fitted are as follows:

Standard 77   Fitted prior to June 1979
80 type   Fitted between June 1979 and August 1981
82 type   Fitted after August 1981

Standard 77 type

5 The Standard 77 type allowed separate adjustment of the basic idle mixture and the bypass mixture. This was achieved by two throttle body-mounted mixture screws to vary the basic idle mixture and a single cover-mounted mixture screw, used in conjunction with an air bleed screw, to vary the bypass idle mixture. The throttle plate was tamper proofed and locked in position, although adjustment was still possible. The choke control was coolant-heated.

80 type

6 In the 80 type, the earlier basic idle adjusters were replaced with non-adjustable fixed idle bushings. The bypass idle mixture was varied by a single auxiliary mixture screw, in conjunction with an air bleed screw. There were two alternative locations for the auxiliary screw; it was either body-mounted near the air bleed screw or mounted in the upper body. It was not possible to adjust the throttle plate because this was set in production and the end of the adjusting screw was then sheared off. The choke control was electrically-heated.

82 type

7 The bypass system of the 82 type is sealed and totally non-adjustable. Two mixture screws (one for each barrel) are used to vary the basic idle mixture. Idle speed (and the throttle plate) are fully adjustable and the choke control is electrically-heated.

Fuel control

8 Fuel flows horizontally into the carburettor through a fine mesh filter. The fuel level in the float chamber is controlled by a needle valve and plastic float assembly. The needle seat is pressed into the float chamber and is not replaceable. An anti-vibration ball is incorporated into the needle valve design. A hairpin clip, attached to the needle valve seat and to the float arm, prevents the needle from sticking in the seat as the fuel level drops. The float chamber is vented internally into the venturi. A calibrated fuel return system is provided to ensure that relatively cool fuel is supplied to the carburettor.

Idle and slow running

9 Two idle systems are provided to improve emission control, these being the basic idle system and the idle bypass system.

Basic idle system

10 Fuel, sourced from the main wells, will pass into the idle channels through metered idle jets, one for each barrel. Here the fuel is mixed with a small amount of air from a calibrated air bleed. The emulsion formed is drawn through two channels to the throttle body, where it is discharged from the idle orifices under the throttle plates (see illustration).

11 Up to June 1979 (Standard 77), a tapered mixture control screw (in each barrel) was used to vary the outlets and this ensured fine control of the idle mixture. The throttle plate was tamper proofed and locked in position, although adjustment was still possible.

12 In the 80 type carburettor, the basic idle adjusters were replaced with non-adjustable fixed idle bushings. It was no longer possible to adjust the throttle plate.

13 The 82 type carburettor uses two mixture screws (one per barrel) to vary the basic idle mixture. The idle speed (and the throttle plate position) are fully adjustable by an idle speed screw.

Idle bypass circuit

14 A supplementary air passage is drilled from under the throttle valve, through the carburettor body to atmosphere. The majority of air required for idle passes through this bypass passage. Fuel, sourced from the float chamber, will pass through a metered idle jet into the auxiliary idle channel. Here the fuel is mixed with a small amount of air from a calibrated air bleed to form an emulsion (see illustration).

15 Up to August 1981 (Standard 77 and 80 types), the fuel/air mixture is regulated by a tapered mixture control screw before being drawn into the supplementary air passage where it is further controlled by an idle bypass air screw. This screw controls idle speed and the throttle plate is locked into a set position.

16 From August 1981 (82 type), the bypass system was sealed and totally non-adjustable.

17 The adjustable mixture, idle speed and air bleed screws are tamper proofed at production level, in accordance with the emission regulations.

Progression

18 A number of progression drillings in each barrel are uncovered by the opening throttles as the engine is accelerated.

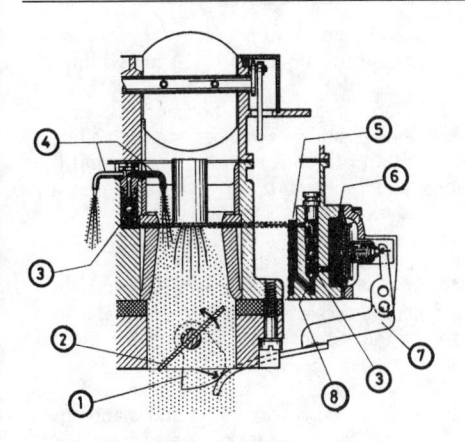

Solex 35 & 38 EEIT carburettor

Main circuit

20 The amount of fuel discharged into the airstream is controlled by calibrated main jets, one for each barrel. Fuel is drawn from the float chamber, through the main jets, into the base of two vertical wells which dip down into the fuel. Two emulsion tubes, one for each barrel, are placed in the wells. The fuel is mixed with air drawn in through calibrated air correction jets and the holes in the emulsion tubes. The resulting emulsified mixture is discharged from the main nozzles through two auxiliary venturis. An additional air jet is mounted over each emulsion well to prevent a syphoning effect when the engine is stopped (see illustration).

Power enrichment and economy circuit

21 Fuel flows into the inner chamber from the float chamber through a brass outlet valve. An air passage is taken from under the throttle plate to the cover of the power diaphragm chamber. At idle and during light-throttle operation, manifold vacuum in the passage draws the diaphragm back against spring pressure. The diaphragm pintle is withdrawn from the outlet valve and a spring-loaded ball seats to close off the channel.

22 During acceleration and wide-open throttle operation, the vacuum in the manifold collapses. The diaphragm returns under spring pressure and the power diaphragm pintle pushes the ball to open the fuel channel. Fuel then flows through the valve into the two power jets, to supplement the fuel in the main well. The fuel level rises in each well and the fuel mixture is enriched.

23 At full-load and high engine speed, even more fuel is required. The velocity of air creates a depression sufficient to raise fuel from the float chamber into two channels. The fuel then passes through calibrated bushings to the upper section of the air intakes, where it is discharged into the airstream from the full-load enrichment tubes (see illustration).

Cold start system

24 The EEIT carburettor uses a semi-automatic choke starting system (see illustration). A bi-metal spring is used to control two strangler choke flaps on a common spindle which shut off the air intakes. Heating of the spring may be by engine coolant (up to June 1979) or by an electrical 12-volt supply (from June 1979) (see illustration). The system is primed by depressing the accelerator pedal once or twice.

25 The choke flaps are eccentrically mounted so that during cranking, they are partially opened to prevent an over-rich fuel mixture.

26 Once the engine has fired, the choke flaps must open slightly to weaken the mixture and avoid flooding during idle and light-throttle operation. This is achieved by using manifold

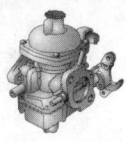

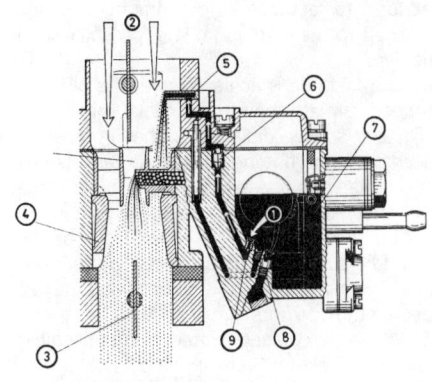

Accelerator pump system

1 Pump actuating cam
2 Throttle plate
3 Outlet valve
4 Pump injectors
5 Float chamber
6 Diaphragms
7 Pump lever
8 Inlet valve

Accelerator pumps

19 The EEIT carburettor uses two accelerator pumps. Both are diaphragm-controlled. One is operated by a lever and cam attached to the throttle linkage and the other by manifold vacuum. Both pumps are actuated in the conventional manner and discharge through the same twin-nozzle pump injector. The vacuum-actuated pump operates on load and doubles as an anti-stall device. During idle or low-speed running, the manifold vacuum will be high. As a stall situation develops, the vacuum will deplete and the pump is actuated (see illustration).

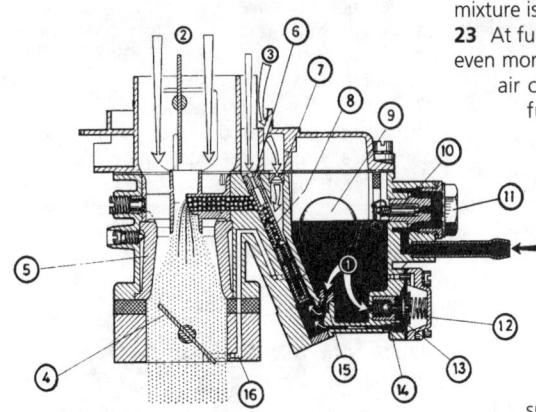

Main circuit and power circuit

1 Fuel supplies to main/power circuits
2 Main air supply
3 Air supply to anti-syphon valve
4 Throttle plate
5 Venturi
6 Air corrector
7 Anti-syphon air bleed
8 Emulsion tube
9 Float
10 Needle valve
11 Fuel inlet
12 Power diaphragm
13 Power valve
14 Power jet
15 Main jet
16 Vacuum passage for power valve

Full-load enrichment

1 Fuel supplies to enrichment tubes and bypass idle circuits
2 Main air supply
3 Throttle plate
4 Venturi
5 Full-load enrichment tube
6 Valve
7 Float chamber
8 Main jet
9 Enrichment jet

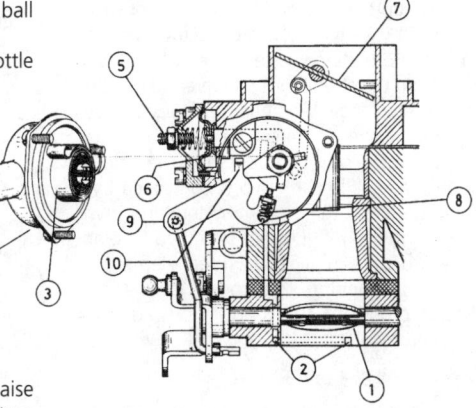

Automatic choke

1 Throttle plate
2 Vacuum passage to diaphragm
3 Bi-metal spring
4 Bi-metal housing
5 Pull-down adjusting screw
6 Pull-down diaphragm
7 Choke flap
8 Fast idle screw
9 Choke lever
10 Wide-open kick adjustment tag

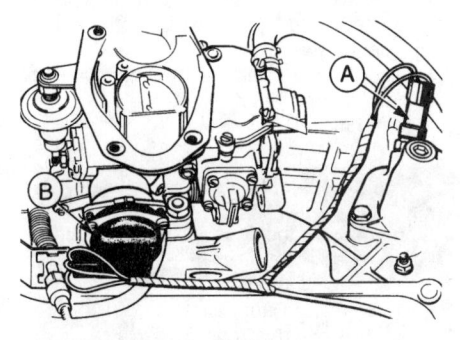

Electric automatic choke

A Thermo-switch   B Electric choke housing

Chapter G2

vacuum to actuate a diaphragm. Linkage attached to the diaphragm will then pull upon the flaps.

27 The fast idle is achieved with the aid of a stepped cam attached to the choke spindle. An adjustable screw, connected to the throttle lever mechanism and butting against the cam, can be used to vary the fast idle speed. As the bi-metal coil is heated and the flap opens, the screw will rest on successively less-stepped parts of the cam. Idle speed is thus progressively reduced until ultimately, the cam is released and the idle speed returns to normal.

28 Where a coolant-heated bi-metal coil is used, the choke will remain almost closed until the coolant becomes hot enough to heat the bi-metal coil. This may initially cause rich operation for the first few minutes after a cold start.

29 Where an electrically-heated choke is used, the choke will open fairly quickly and this may cause engine hesitation during warm-up. Should the engine be inadvertently left with the ignition switched on, the choke will operate to the fully-open position, causing poor starting with a cold engine.

30 For a tighter control of the choke flaps during the warm-up period, the EEIT carburettor (from June 1979) uses two separate electrical heating elements. Both elements take their (7 to 9-volt) supply from the alternator and therefore function only while the engine is running *(see illustration)*.

31 Element one is a direct feed and begins to heat the coil slowly immediately the engine starts running. Element two is controlled by a thermo-switch in the coolant system and it will not function until a predetermined coolant temperature is reached. Either element is capable of opening the choke individually, although proper control is only exercised when both operate jointly.

Throttle dashpot

32 The throttle dashpot allows the throttle plate to close slowly to introduce normal idle vacuum in a controlled manner.

2 Identification

1 A metal tag giving the Ford identification code is attached to one of the carburettor upper body fixing screws.
2 Solex or Pierburg stamped upon the cover is the only identification mark used by the carburettor manufacturer.

3 General servicing

Introduction

1 Read this Chapter in conjunction with Part B, which describes some of the operations in more

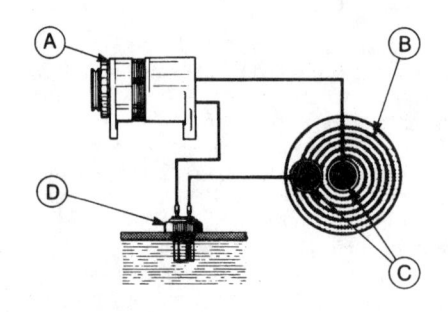

Electric automatic choke wiring circuit

A Alternator
B Bi-metal coil
C Heating elements
D Thermo-switch

detail. It is assumed that the carburettor is removed for this service. However, many of the operations can be tackled with the carburettor in place. Where this is undertaken, first soak the fuel out of the float chamber using a clean tissue or soft cloth, after removing the upper body assembly.

Dismantling and checking

2 Remove the carburettor from the engine (see Part B).
3 Make visual checks for damage and wear.
4 Remove the seven screws, disconnect the choke link rod and detach the carburettor upper body.
5 Use a straight-edge to check for distorted flanges on all facing surfaces.
6 Inspect the float chamber for corrosion and calcium build-up.
7 Remove the plastic float retaining piece, tap out the float pin, then remove the float, needle valve and float chamber gasket. The needle seat is pressed into the float chamber and is not replaceable *(see illustration)*.
8 Check that the anti-vibration ball is free in the valve end.
9 Check the needle valve tip for wear and ridges. This is more likely with the brass needle valve tip than when a viton one is used. Use a viton-tipped replacement when possible.
10 The float should be checked for damage and for ingress of petrol. Shaking the float will

indicate any ingress of petrol.
11 Renew the float pin if it shows signs of wear.
12 Remove the hexagon bolt and inspect the fuel filter. Clean the chamber and the fuel inlet and return of debris and dirt. Ensure that the inlet and fuel return connections are tightly pushed into the upper body.
13 Remove the mixture screws and inspect their tips for damage and ridges.
14 Remove the four screws and detach the mechanical accelerator pump cover, diaphragm and spring. Check the diaphragm for fatigue and damage.
15 Remove the four screws and detach the anti-stall device cover, spring and diaphragm. Check the diaphragm for fatigue and damage.
16 The pump injector is a push fit in the body. Carefully prise it from its location using two thin screwdrivers, then test it by shaking. No noise from the outlet ball would indicate that the valve is seized *(see illustration)*.
17 Remove the two idle jets from the carburettor body.
18 Remove the main jets and check that the channels into the emulsion tube wells are clear. The emulsion tubes and air correctors are not removable. Carefully remove the small auxiliary idle fuel jet (located between the two main jets in the float chamber).
19 Remove the three screws and detach the power valve cover, spring and diaphragm from the body. Check the diaphragm for fatigue and damage.
20 The power valve brass outlet valve is cast into the body and is not removable. The ball in the outlet valve should seal the outlet. Depress and release the ball with a small screwdriver. It should smoothly move in and out.
21 Very carefully remove the two small power jets and check that the channels into the emulsion tube wells are clear.
22 Remove the six screws and separate the carburettor main body and throttle body assemblies. The throttle body can be renewed separately if the spindles or throttle bores are worn. Inspect the toothed segments and renew them if they are sticky in action or worn.

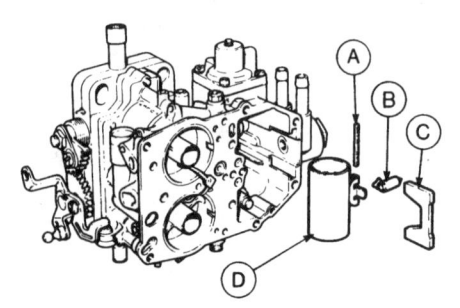

Needle valve and float components

A Float pin
B Needle valve
C Plastic retaining piece
D Float

Removing accelerator pump injector - and showing jet locations

A Accelerator pump injector
B Idle jets
C Main jets
D Auxiliary idle fuel jet

Solex 35 & 38 EEIT carburettor

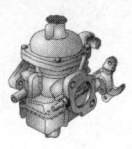

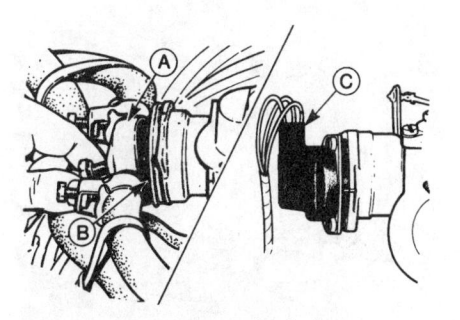

Disconnecting automatic choke

A Choke outer housing
B Housing O-ring seal
C Electric choke loom connection

23 Remove the plastic dust cover from the choke linkage and the heat shield from the inside of the choke housing. Inspect the choke spindle, mechanism and levers for stickiness and wear.
24 Complete removal of the choke housing is normally unnecessary. However, it can be accomplished after removal of the two screws and the nut retaining the choke operating mechanism *(see illustration)*.
25 Remove the three screws and detach the cover, spring and diaphragm from the choke housing. Check the diaphragm for fatigue and damage *(see illustration)*.

Preparation for reassembly

26 Clean the carburettor body, the jets and internal channels, then clean any sediment from the float chamber. An air line may be used to clear the internal channels once the carburettor is fully dismantled. Spraying carburettor cleaner into all the channels and passages in the carburettor body will often clear them of gum and dirt.
27 Note that if an air line is used with the diaphragms in place and air is directed into the diaphragm passages, diaphragm damage may result.
28 During reassembly, a complete set of new gaskets should be fitted. Also renew the needle valve, float pin and all diaphragms.
29 Inspect and renew (where necessary) the mixture screws, main jets, idle jets and pump injector. Renew worn linkages, springs and other parts where necessary.
30 Ensure that all jets are firmly locked into their original positions (but do not overtighten). A loose jet can cause a rich (or even lean) running condition.
31 Clean all mating surfaces and flanges of old gasket material. Ensure that housings are assembled with their air and fuel routes correctly aligned.

Reassembly

32 Refit the choke diaphragm, spring and cover to the choke housing assembly, then secure with the three screws.
33 Refit the choke housing to the carburettor body (if removed) and secure with the two screws.

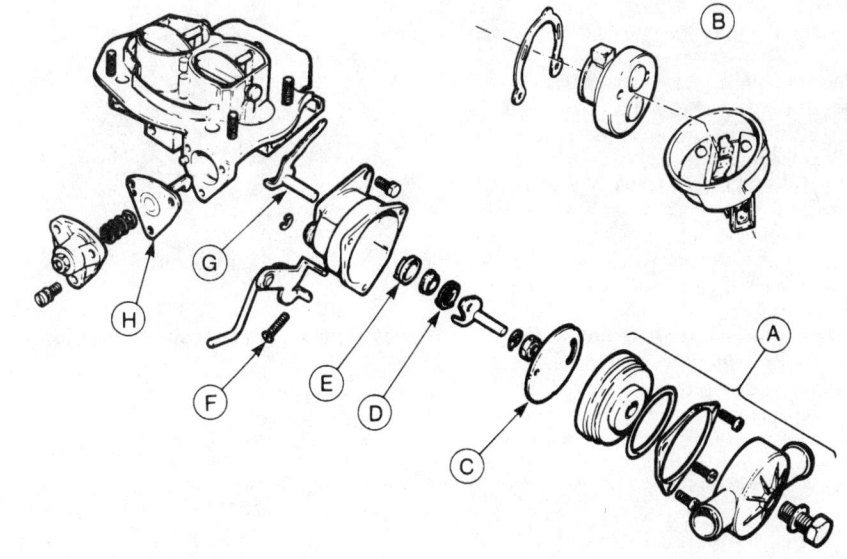

Automatic choke assembly

A Bi-metal coil assembly (coolant-heated choke)
B Bi-metal Coil assembly (electric choke)
C Internal heat shield
D Cam retaining spring
E Fast idle cam
F Fast idle adjusting screw
G Upper choke link
H Pull-down diaphragm

34 Assemble the main body and throttle bodies with a new gasket block and secure with six screws. Tighten the screws progressively and evenly to avoid distortion of the assemblies.
35 Synchronise the throttles, see Section 4.
36 Refit the two small power jets. Refit the power diaphragm, spring and cover assembly, then secure with the three screws.
37 Refit the main jets and auxiliary idle fuel jet into the float chamber.
38 Refit the two idle jets.
39 Refit the anti-stall diaphragm, spring and cover assembly, then secure with the four screws.
40 Refit the mechanical pump spring, diaphragm and cover assembly, then secure with the four screws.
41 Push the pump injector into the body, renewing the small seal on the injector body. Fill the float chamber partially with petrol and operate the mechanical accelerator pump. The injected fuel should strike the throttle plates at the clearance from the inner air intake walls given below *(see illustration)*. If not, adjust as necessary by carefully bending the injector tubes:

2.3 engine (MT)   3 to 6 mm
2.3 engine (AT)   1 to 3 mm
2.8 engine   1 to 3 mm

42 Refit the idle mixture screws and carefully turn them in until they just seat. Unscrew three turns each (five turns for the Standard 77 type). This will provide a basic setting so that the engine can be started.
43 Clean or renew the fuel filter and refit the hexagon bolt.
44 Renew the needle valve. Insert the needle valve into the valve body with the seat facing inwards. Ensure that the hairpin clip (where fitted) is correctly connected to the needle valve and to the float tag.
45 Refit the float, float pivot pin and the plastic float retaining piece.
46 Adjust the float level. Refer to Section 4 for details on adjustment.
47 Place a new float chamber gasket on the carburettor body.
48 Refit the upper body assembly and secure with the seven screws.
49 Refit the choke link rod to the choke arm.
50 Refit the carburettor to the engine.
51 Always adjust the carburettor idle speed and mixture after any work has been carried out on the carburettor, preferably with the aid of a CO meter.
52 Ensure that the choke flap and linkage moves smoothly and progressively. See Section 4 for details on choke adjustment. Firmly place the plastic dust cover in position over the choke linkage. If this becomes displaced in service, it could jam the choke linkage.

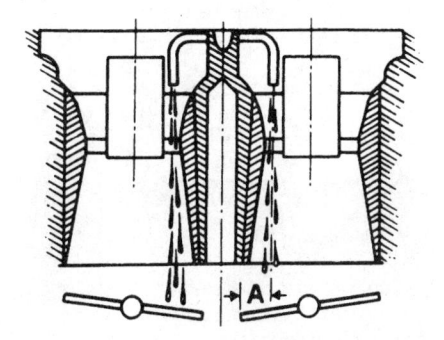

Accelerator pump stroke fuel pattern

For dimension A, see text

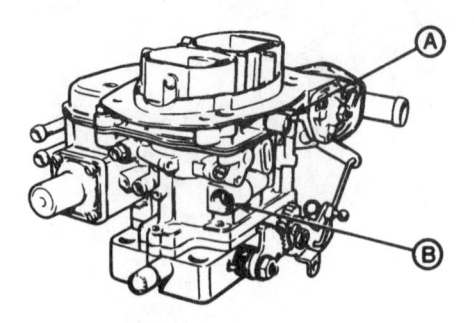

Chapter G2

Bypass idle adjustment screw location - Standard 77 type
A *Bypass mixture screw*
B *Bypass idle speed screw*

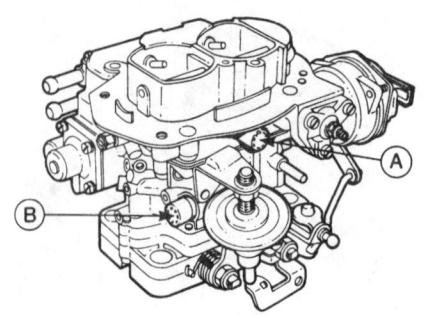

Bypass idle adjustment screw location - 80 type
A *Bypass mixture screw*
B *Bypass idle speed screw*

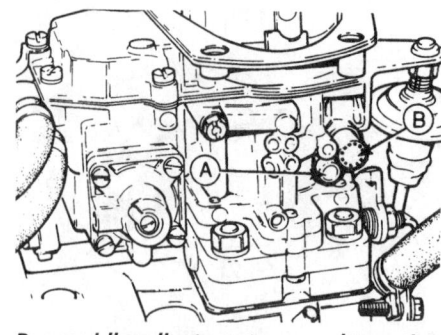

Bypass idle adjustment screw alternative location - 80 type
A *Bypass mixture screw*
B *Bypass idle speed screw*

4 Service adjustments

Adjustment preconditions

1 Refer to Part B for general advice on preconditions to correct adjustment of this carburettor.

Bypass idle adjustment: Standard 77 and 80 type

2 Run the engine at 3000 rpm for 30 seconds to clear the manifold of fuel vapours, then allow the engine to idle.
3 Check the idle speed and compare with the specified value. If incorrect, remove the tamperproof plug and use the air bypass screw to set the correct idle rpm. Note that adjustment of the idle speed will affect the CO level *(see illustrations)*.
4 Check the CO level against the specified value. If incorrect, remove the tamperproof cap and adjust the auxiliary idle mixture screw to achieve the correct level. Turning the screws clockwise (inwards) will reduce the CO level. Turning the screws anti-clockwise (outwards) will increase the CO level.

5 Repeat paragraphs 3 and 4 until the CO and idle speed are correct.
6 If the results are unsatisfactory, make the basic idle adjustment (Standard 77 only).
7 Increase the speed to 2000 rpm and note the CO reading. The cruise reading should be less than half the idle CO reading.
8 Fit new tamperproof caps/plugs to the mixture adjusting screws.

Basic idle adjustment: Standard 77

9 Turn in the air bypass screw until it is fully seated.
10 Remove the tamperproof caps from the two basic idle mixture screws and carefully turn in the idle mixture screws until they just seat. Unscrew each screw five full turns *(see illustration)*.
11 Start the engine, remove the tamperproof cap from the throttle stop screw and adjust the screw until 600 ± 20 rpm is obtained.
12 Adjust both mixture screws by equal increments until 2.5 to 3 % CO is obtained.
13 Unscrew the air bypass screw to achieve 800 ± 20 rpm.
14 Adjust the auxiliary idle mixture screw to achieve the correct CO level. If the CO needs a large adjustment at this stage, repeat paragraphs 9 to 13. Once the correct CO is reached at the correct idle speed, the carburettor is properly adjusted.
15 Fit new tamperproof caps to the adjusting screws.

Idle adjustment: 82 type

16 Run the engine at 3000 rpm for 30 seconds to clear the manifold of fuel vapours, then allow the engine to idle.
17 Use the idle speed screw to set the specified idle speed *(see illustration)*.
18 Check the CO level and compare with the specified value. If incorrect, remove the tamperproof plug and adjust to the correct level.
19 Repeat paragraphs 17 and 18 until both adjustments are correct.
20 Clear the manifold every 30 seconds during the setting operation by running the engine at 3000 rpm for 30 seconds.
21 Fit a new tamperproof plug to the mixture adjusting screw.

Throttle plate synchronisation

22 Inspect the toothed segments for wear, which occurs where the segment teeth mesh together. Renew the segments if there is play between the teeth *(see illustration)*.

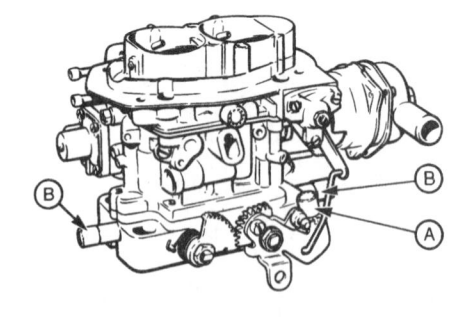

Carburettor basic idle adjustment screw location - Standard 77 type
A *Basic idle speed screw*
B *Basic idle mixture screws*

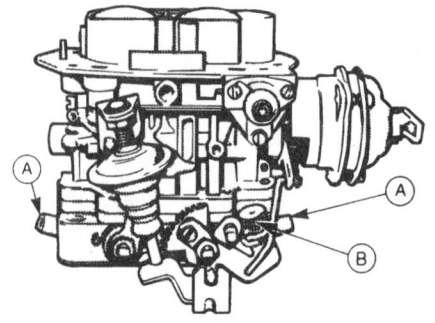

Carburettor basic idle adjustment screw location - 82 type
A *Basic idle speed screw*
B *Basic idle mixture screws*

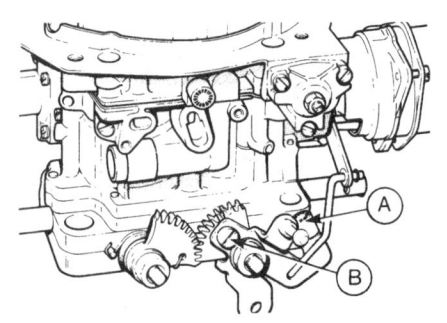

Throttle plate synchronisation adjustment
A *Basic idle adjustment*
B *Throttle plate synchronisation screw*

Solex 35 & 38 EEIT carburettor

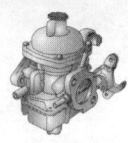

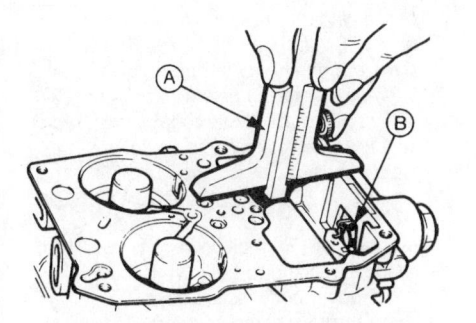

Checking float level adjustment
A Depth gauge
B Float level adjusting tag

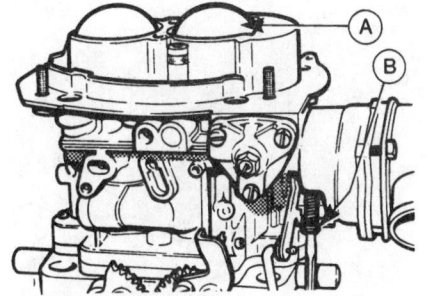

Fast idle adjustment
A Choke plates fully open
B Fast idle adjustment screw

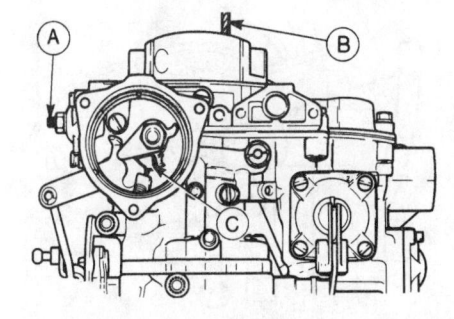

Carburettor set for choke flap pull-down adjustment
A Diaphragm adjustment screw
B Twist drill
C Choke mechanism set on high cam

23 Remove the tamperproof cap from the throttle stop screw and turn the screw out until it is clear of the throttle stop.
24 Block open the choke flaps so that the fast idle screw is released.
25 Slacken the synchronisation adjusting screw.
26 Open the throttle and allow both throttle plates to snap shut.
27 Tap the plates to ensure that they are both fully closed and lock up the synchronisation screw. Check for binding in the throttle bores and re-adjust as necessary.
28 Partially open the throttles using the throttle stop screw, until the first progression hole (in both barrels) is just uncovered. The position of each throttle plate relative to each progression hole should be exactly the same. This position is more important than the fully-closed position. Re-adjust as necessary.

Float level

29 Fill the float chamber with petrol until the float fully closes the needle valve. Use a depth gauge to measure the distance between the carburettor body face (without the gasket) and the top of the float. Adjust as necessary by bending the float tag *(see illustration)*.

Automatic choke

30 Warm the engine to normal running temperature before making any of the choke adjustments.

Fast idle

31 Adjust the idle speed and mixture, as described above.
32 Remove the air filter assembly and place it clear of the carburettor with the vacuum hoses still connected.
33 Partially open the throttle and fully close the choke flaps. Release the throttle and the choke flaps. The fast idle adjustment screw should remain against the highest step of the fast idle cam *(see illustration)*.
34 Start the engine without moving the throttle and record the fast idle speed. Refer to Specifications for the correct value.
35 Adjust as necessary by turning the fast idle screw in the appropriate direction. Because access to the adjustment screw is limited, stop the engine and partially open the throttle. A half-turn of the screw will alter the speed by approximately 100 rpm.
36 Refit the air filter assembly, ensuring that the vacuum hoses remain connected.

Choke vacuum pull-down

37 Remove the three screws and detach the bi-metal coil housing from the carburettor.
38 Remove the internal heat shield.

39 Partially open the throttle and fully close the choke flaps. Release the throttle and the choke flaps. The fast idle adjustment screw should remain against the highest step of the fast idle cam.
40 Start the engine without moving the throttle.
41 Carefully close the choke flaps until a resistance is felt.
42 Use the shank of a twist drill to measure the gap between the lower part of the choke flaps and the air intake (see Specifications for the required drill size).
43 Adjust as necessary by turning the diaphragm adjusting screw *(see illustration)* in the appropriate direction
44 Adjust the choke phasing, as described below.

Choke phasing

45 Refer to paragraphs 37 to 41.
46 Hold the choke flaps in this position. This can be accomplished using the drill mentioned in paragraph 42 above.
47 Partially open the throttle and the fast idle cam will fall into its natural position. The fast idle screw will locate on the second-highest step of the cam to leave a small operating clearance 'x' *(see illustration)*. See Specifications.
48 Adjust as necessary by bending the phasing adjustment tag.
49 Refit the internal heat shield.
50 Refit the bi-metal coil housing and ensure that the spring locates in the slot of the choke lever. Secure loosely with the three screws.
51 Align the cut mark on the bi-metal cover with the correct mark on the choke assembly housing, and tighten the three screws *(see illustration)*.

Choke modulator spring gap

52 This adjustment is only necessary if the choke operation is still unsatisfactory after the fast idle, choke pull-down and choke phasing have been adjusted.
53 Remove the seven screws, disconnect the choke link rod and detach the carburettor upper body.
54 Use the shank of a twist drill to measure the

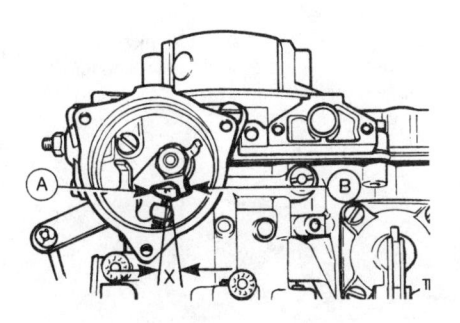

Choke phasing adjustment
X Operating clearance (see Specifications)
A Fast idle cam
B Phasing adjustment tag

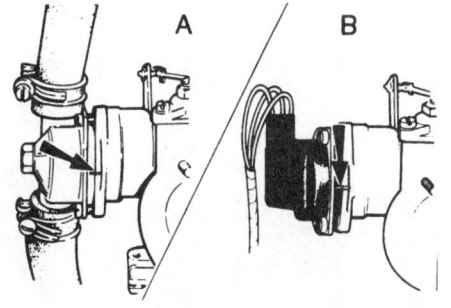

Choke housing alignment marks
A Coolant-heated choke system
B Electric choke system

Chapter G2

Choke modulator spring adjustment
A Choke lever
B Modulator spring

Throttle damper adjustment
A Plunger B Throttle lever
C Feeler gauge (0.05 mm)

gap between the choke lever and the modulator spring. Refer to Specifications for the correct drill size *(see illustration)*.
55 Adjust as necessary by bending the modulator spring.
56 Refit the carburettor upper body.

Wide-open kick
57 Fully close the choke flaps and fully open the throttle valves.
58 Measure the gap between the lower part of the choke flaps and the air intake. This should be 10 ± 1 mm.
59 Adjust as necessary by bending the tag on the choke lever.

Throttle damper (where fitted)
60 Warm the engine to normal running temperature and adjust the idle speed and mixture before attempting throttle damper adjustment.
61 Slacken the locknut and turn the damper until a clearance of 0.05 mm exists between the plunger and the throttle lever *(see illustration)*.
62 Make a reference mark on the casing and screw the damper down towards the throttle lever exactly 3 turns (2.3 engines) or 2 turns (2.8 engines). Tighten the locknut on completion.
63 Ensure that the idle screw contacts the throttle stop. Blip the throttle a few times, check that the damper does not bind or stick and that it returns the throttle slowly to its correct idle speed.

5 Fault diagnosis

Refer to Part D for general diagnosis of carburettor faults. The following faults are specific to Solex EEIT carburettors.

Diaphragm failure
☐ The power valve, anti-stall device and accelerator pump are all internally linked. A failure of one diaphragm will therefore affect all three circuits

Poor choke operation
☐ Failure of the 7 to 9-volt supply output from the alternator to the automatic choke (the choke will take much longer to open fully):
Check the alternator output supply to the choke with a voltmeter. The reading should be 7 to 9 volts with the engine running. If there is no alternator output, repair the alternator or take a new wire from the coil + terminal to the choke control. The 7-volt supply at the coil will work quite satisfactorily

Hesitation or lack of power
☐ Blockage of the small power jets or fuel channels leading to the main fuel wells
☐ Loose upper body fixing screws
☐ Worn throttle segments can cause fluffy pick-up
☐ Displaced fuel return restrictor:
Pulling on the fuel return pipe connector in the upper body can cause it to loosen. The restrictor plate can become displaced and fuel will return to the tank unrestricted. Where this happens, the flow into the float chamber is reduced and high-speed power loss is the result. Remove the return connector and refit the restrictor plate into its correct position. Knurl the return connector and refit, ensuring that it is tightly locked into position (see illustration)

Poor idle and/or stalling
☐ One or both idle jets blocked:
*A common fault, which often causes the engine idle speed to vary over several hundred rpm. This is because the anti-stall diaphragm is actuated as the engine tries to stall. The extra fuel from the pump injector makes the engine pick up briefly and as the engine again tries to stall, the whole cycle repeats.
It is very difficult to clear the dirt, which often becomes trapped in the jet body. In a few miles the problem will recur. When repeated idle jet blockage occurs, renew the idle jet assembly. Place a finger over the idle bypass air supply. The correct response is for the engine to stall. Should the engine speed pick up, the idle adjustment is likely to be incorrect. Under no circumstances should the air bleed be sealed off, as sometimes happens when work is carried out by an unqualified person*

Idle speed too high
☐ Maladjusted or sticking throttle damper. This could also result in a clonking noise from the rear axle as the gears change from being driven to driving

Removing restrictor plate and fuel return connector from location in upper body

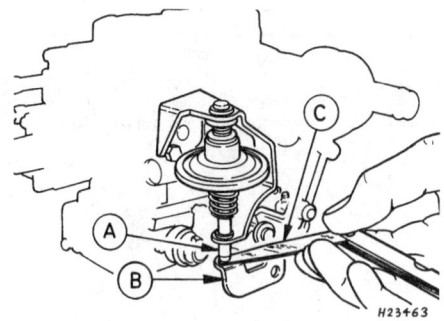

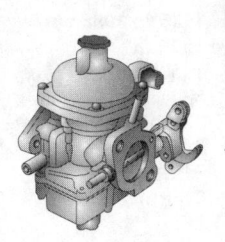

Part G Chapter 3
Solex 32, 34 & 35 PBISA carburettor

G3

Contents

Fault diagnosis	5	Principles of operation	1
General servicing	3	Service adjustments	4
Identification	2		

Specifications

Manufacturer	Citroën	Citroën	Citroën	Citroën
Model	AX 10	AX 11	AX 14	BX 14
Year	1987 to 1992	1987 to 1992	1988 to 1992	1988 to 1992
Engine code	C1A (TU9)	H1A (TU1)	K1G	K1G (TU3A)
Capacity (cm³)/no. of cyls	954/4	1124/4	1360/4	1360/4
Oil temperature (°C)	90	90	90	90
Carb. ident. (Solex)	32 PBISA 16 13442	32 PBISA 16	34 PBISA 17 13643	34 PBISA 17 13643
Carb. ident. (vehicle)	412	411	481	481
Idle speed (rpm)	750 ± 50	750 ± 50	750 ± 50	750 ± 50
CO @ idle (% vol.)	0.8 to 1.2	0.8 to 1.2	0.8 to 1.2	0.8 to 1.2
Venturi diameter (K)	25	25	26	26
Idle jet (g)	46 or 47	46	44 ± 2	44 ± 2
Main jet (Gg)	127	127.5	132 ± 5	132 ± 5
Air correction jet (a)	155	175	155 ± 10	155 ± 10
Emulsion tube (s)	31	EM	EC	EC
Accelerator pump jet (i)	40	40	40	40
Float level (mm)	38	38	38	38
Needle valve (mm) (P)	1.6	1.6	1.6	1.6
Choke fast idle gap (mm)	0.8	0.5	0.6 ± 0.05	0.6
Fast idle position (OP)	19°40	-	18°	18°
Choke pull-down (mm) (OVAD)	2.8	-	-	3.5

Manufacturer	Citroën	Citroën	Citroën	Citroën
Model	LNA 11E, 11RE	Visa (954 cc)	Visa 11 L, Super E	Visa 11 L, Super E
Year	1982 to 1986	1985 to 1987	1981 to 1983	1981 to 1983
Engine code	XW7 (1095F)	108C (XV8)	109/5E/5F (XW7)	109/5E/5F (XW7)
Capacity (cm³)/no. of cyls	1124/4	954/4	1124/4	1124/4
Oil temperature (°C)	80	80	80	80
Transmission	-	-	MT	AT
Carb. ident. (Solex)	32 PBISA 12 13168	32 PBISA 12 13378	32 PBISA 12 13168	32 PBISA 12 13168
Carb. ident. (vehicle)	CIT 341	370	CIT 341	CIT 341
Idle speed (rpm)	725 ± 25	725 ± 25	750 ± 50	700 ± 50
CO @ idle (% vol.)	0.8 to 1.2	0.8 to 1.2	1.5 ± 0.5	0.8 to 1.0
Venturi diameter (K)	24	25	24	24
Idle jet (g)	44	46	44	44
Main jet (Gg)	120	122	120	120
Air correction jet (a)	170	155	170	170
Accelerator pump jet (i)	35	35	35	35
Float level (mm)	38	38	38	38
Needle valve (mm) (P)	1.6	1.6	1.6	1.6
Choke fast idle gap (mm)	0.75	0.8	0.75	0.75
Fast idle position (OP)	21°	-	-	-
Fast idle position (OPR)	14°05'	-	14°05'	14°05'

Chapter G3

Manufacturer	Citroën	Citroën	Citroën	Citroën
Model	Visa 11E, 11RE & Convertible	Visa Super X	Visa 14 TRS	C15E 1360 Super Van
Year	1983 to 1987	1981 to 1982	1984 to 1986	1986 to 1988
Engine code	109/5F (XW7)	129/5 (XZ5X)	150D (XY7)	150D (XY7)
Capacity (cm³)/no. of cyls	1124/4	1219/4	1360/4	1360/4
Oil temperature (°C)	80	80	80	80
Carb. ident. (Solex)	32 PBISA 12 13377	32 PBISA 11 13052	34 PBISA 12 13589	32 PBISA 12 13589
Carb. ident. (vehicle)	341	240	350	350
Idle speed (rpm)	700 ± 50	925 ± 25	725 ± 25	725 ± 25
CO @ idle (% vol.)	0.8 to 1.2	1.5 ± 0.5	2.0 ± 0.5	0.8 to 1.2
Venturi diameter (K)	24	25	26	26
Idle jet (g)	44	42	45	45
Main jet (Gg)	120	127.5	130	130 ± 5
Air correction jet (a)	170	160	160	160
Emulsion tube (s)	-	-	EC	EC
Accelerator pump jet (i)	35	40	40	40
Float level (mm)	38	38	38	38
Needle valve (mm) (P)	1.6	1.5	1.6	1.6
Choke fast idle gap (mm)	0.75	0.90	0.75	0.75
Fast idle position (OPR)	14°05'	-	20°40'	20°40'
Choke pull-down (mm) (OVAD)	-	-	3.5	-

Manufacturer	Citroën	Citroën	Citroën	Citroën
Model	C15E 1360 Super Van	C25E 1.8	C25E 1800	C25E 2.0
Year	1988 to 1992	1987 to 1988	1989 to 1991	1987 to 1992
Engine code	K1G	XM7T (169)	170C (XN1TA)	XN1T (170B)
Capacity (cm³)/no. of cyls	1360/4	1796/4	1971/4	1971/4
Oil temperature (°C)	90	90	90	90
Carb. ident. (Solex)	34 PBISA 17 13643	34 PBISA 16 13434	34 PBISA 16	34 PBISA 16 13434
Carb. ident. (vehicle)	481	A315	425	A315
Idle speed (rpm)	750 ± 50	800 ± 50	825 ± 25	825 ± 25
CO @ idle (% vol.)	0.8 to 1.2	1.5 ± 0.5	1.5 ± 1.0	1.5 ± 1.0
Venturi diameter (K)	26	25	25	25
Idle jet (g)	44 ± 2	44 or 46	45	44 or 46
Main jet (Gg)	132 ± 5	130	127.5	130
Air correction jet (a)	155 ± 10	160 or 170	155	160 or 170
Emulsion tube (s)	EC	01	-	01
Accelerator pump jet (i)	40	50	50	50
Float level (mm)	38	38	38	38
Needle valve (mm) (P)	1.6	1.6	1.6	1.6
Idle position (PRN)	-	9°	9°	9°
Choke fast idle gap (mm)	0.6	0.90	-	0.90
Fast idle position (OP)	18°	21°45'	20°	21°45'
Choke pull-down (mm) (OVAD)	3.5	-	-	-

Manufacturer	Fiat	Fiat	Fiat	Fiat
Model	Ducato 1.8	Ducato 2.0	Ducato 2.0	Ducato 2.0 Maxi
Year	1982 to 1988	1982 to 1986	1986 to 1992	1986 to 1992
Engine code	XM7T (169B) OHV	XN1T (170B) OHV	XN1T (170B) OHV	XN1TA (170C) OHV
Capacity (cm³)/no. of cyls	1796/4	1971/4	1971/4	1971/4
Oil temperature (°C)	90	90	90	90
Carb. ident. (Solex)	34 PBISA 16 13434	34 PBISA 16 13434	34 PBISA 16 13434	34 PBISA 16
Carb. ident. (vehicle)	PEU A315	PEU A315	PEU A315	PSA 425
Idle speed (rpm)	850 ± 50	900	825 ± 25	925 ± 25
CO @ idle (% vol.)	3.0 max	3.0 max	1.5 ± 0.5	1.75 ± 0.25
Venturi diameter (K)	25	25	25	25
Idle jet (g)	44 or 46	44 or 46	44 or 46	45
Main jet (Gg)	130	130 ± 5	130 ± 5	127.5
Air correction jet (a)	160 or 170	160 or 170	160 or 170	155
Emulsion tube (s)	01	01	01	-
Accelerator pump jet (i)	50	50	50	50
Float level (mm)	38	38	38	38
Needle valve (mm) (P)	1.6	1.6	1.6	1.6
Idle position (PRN)	9°	9°	9°	9°
Choke fast idle gap (mm)	0.90	0.90	0.90	0.90
Fast idle position (OP)	21°45'	21°45'	21°45'	20°

Solex 32, 34 & 35 PBISA carburettor

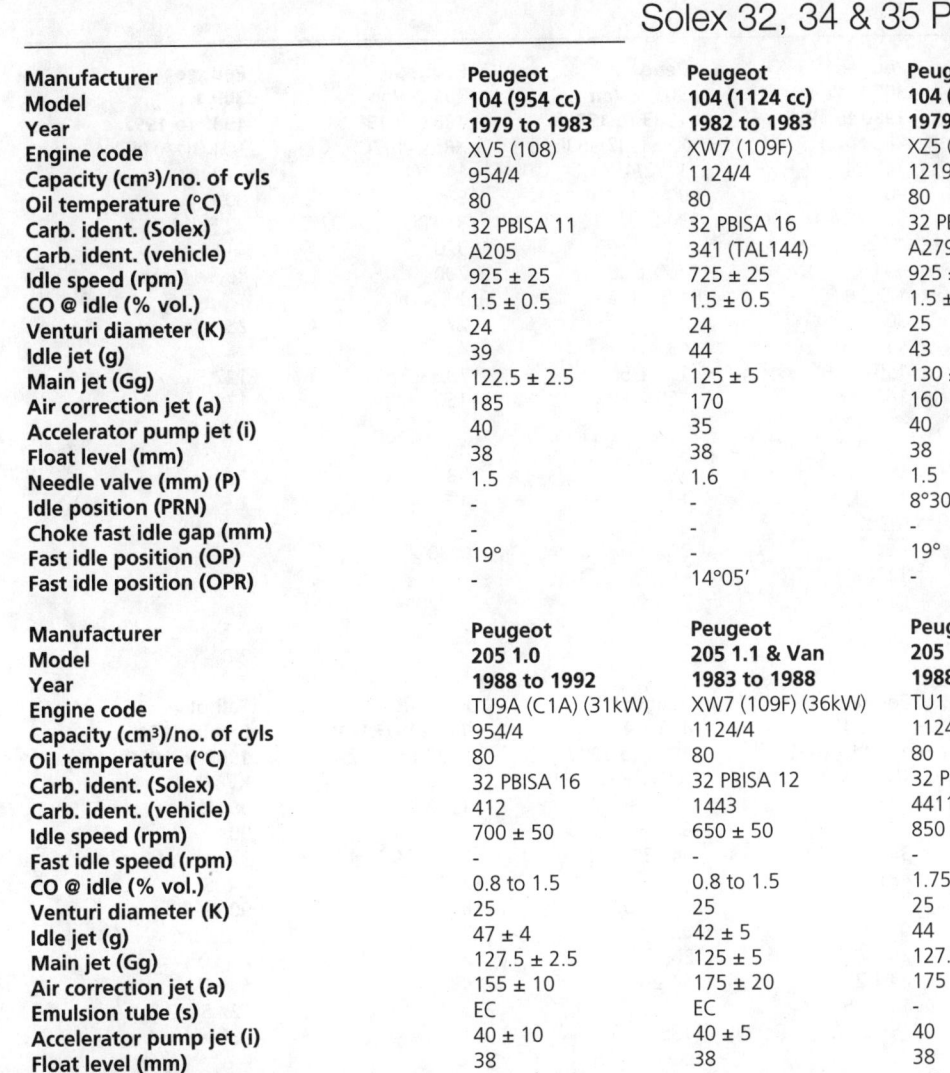

Manufacturer	Peugeot	Peugeot	Peugeot	Peugeot
Model	104 (954 cc)	104 (1124 cc)	104 (1219 cc)	205 1.0
Year	1979 to 1983	1982 to 1983	1979 to 1983	1983 to 1988
Engine code	XV5 (108)	XW7 (109F)	XZ5 (129)	XV8 (108C) (31kW)
Capacity (cm³)/no. of cyls	954/4	1124/4	1219/4	954/4
Oil temperature (°C)	80	80	80	80
Carb. ident. (Solex)	32 PBISA 11	32 PBISA 16	32 PBISA 11 13011	32 PBISA 12 13378
Carb. ident. (vehicle)	A205	341 (TAL144)	A279	370
Idle speed (rpm)	925 ± 25	725 ± 25	925 ± 25	650 ± 50
CO @ idle (% vol.)	1.5 ± 0.5	1.5 ± 0.5	1.5 ± 0.5	0.8 to 1.5
Venturi diameter (K)	24	24	25	25
Idle jet (g)	39	44	43	46
Main jet (Gg)	122.5 ± 2.5	125 ± 5	130 ± 2.5	122.5 ± 5
Air correction jet (a)	185	170	160	155
Accelerator pump jet (i)	40	35	40	35
Float level (mm)	38	38	38	38
Needle valve (mm) (P)	1.5	1.6	1.5	1.6
Idle position (PRN)	-	-	8°30'	-
Choke fast idle gap (mm)	-	-	-	0.8
Fast idle position (OP)	19°	-	19°	21°
Fast idle position (OPR)	-	14°05'	-	-

Manufacturer	Peugeot	Peugeot	Peugeot	Peugeot
Model	205 1.0	205 1.1 & Van	205 1.1 & Van	205 1.4 GR
Year	1988 to 1992	1983 to 1988	1988 to 1992	1983 to 1987
Engine code	TU9A (C1A) (31kW)	XW7 (109F) (36kW)	TU1 (H1A) (40kW)	XY7 (150D)
Capacity (cm³)/no. of cyls	954/4	1124/4	1124/4	1360/4
Oil temperature (°C)	80	80	80	80
Carb. ident. (Solex)	32 PBISA 16	32 PBISA 12	32 PBISA 16	34 PBISA 12 13376
Carb. ident. (vehicle)	412	1443	4411	144
Idle speed (rpm)	700 ± 50	650 ± 50	850 ± 50	650 ± 50
Fast idle speed (rpm)	-	-	-	1400 ± 100
CO @ idle (% vol.)	0.8 to 1.5	0.8 to 1.5	1.75 ± 0.25	1.5 ± 0.5
Venturi diameter (K)	25	25	25	25
Idle jet (g)	47 ± 4	42 ± 5	44	42
Main jet (Gg)	127.5 ± 2.5	125 ± 5	127.5	130 ± 5
Air correction jet (a)	155 ± 10	175 ± 20	175	175
Emulsion tube (s)	EC	EC	-	EC
Accelerator pump jet (i)	40 ± 10	40 ± 5	40	35
Float level (mm)	38	38	38	38
Needle valve (mm) (P)	1.6	1.6	1.6	1.6
Fast idle position (OP)	-	19°	-	20°40'
Choke pull-down (mm) (OVAD)	-	2.8	-	3.5

Manufacturer	Peugeot	Peugeot	Peugeot	Peugeot
Model	205 1.4 XR, GR, CJ	305 & Van	305 GL	305 & Van
Year	1988 to 1992	1978 to 1983	1983 to 1986	1978 to 1980
Engine code	TU3A (K1G) (51kW)	XL5 (118)	XL5 (118) (47kW)	XR5 (142) (53kW)
Capacity (cm³)/no. of cyls	1360/4	1290/4	1290/4	1472/4
Oil temperature (°C)	80	90	90	90
Carb. ident. (Solex)	34 PBISA 17	34 PBISA 14 13193	34 PBISA 14 13309	35 PBISA 9 12839
Carb. ident. (vehicle)	481	354	254	202
Idle speed (rpm)	800 ± 50	900	900 ± 50	900
CO @ idle (% vol.)	0.8 to 1.5	1.5 ± 0.5	1.5 ± 0.5	1.5 ± 0.5
Venturi diameter (K)	26	26	26	30
Idle jet (g)	44 ± 2	43	43	45
Main jet (Gg)	132	132.5 ± 2.5	132.5 ± 0.5	155 ± 5
Air correction jet (a)	155	160	160	160
Accelerator pump jet (i)	40	40	40	40
Float level (mm)	38	38	38	38
Needle valve (mm) (P)	1.6	1.5	1.5	1.5
Idle position (ORF)	-	0°50'	0°50'	0°30'
Fast idle position (OP)	18°	-	-	-
Fast idle position (OPR)	-	12°30'	12°30	12°

Chapter G3

Manufacturer	Peugeot	Peugeot	Peugeot	Peugeot
Model	305 & Van	305 & Van	305 & Van	309 1.1
Year	1980 to 1983	1983 to 1988	1983 to 1987	1989 to 1992
Engine code	XR5 (142) (53kW)	XR5 (142) (53kW)	XR5A (142C)	TU1 (H1A) (40kW)
Capacity (cm³)/no. of cyls	1472/4	1472/4	1472/4	1124/4
Oil temperature (°C)	90	90	90	80
Carb. ident. (Solex)	35 PBISA 14 13008	34 PBISA 16	34 PBISA 16 13292	32 PBISA 161
Carb. ident. (vehicle)	A283	320	320	4111
Idle speed (rpm)	900	700 ± 50	700	850 ± 50
CO @ idle (% vol.)	1.5 ± 0.5	1.5 ± 0.5	1.5 ± 0.5	1.5 ± 0.5
Venturi diameter (K)	30	27	27	25
Idle jet (g)	45	43	43	46
Main jet (Gg)	150 ± 2.5	132 ± 5	132 ± 5	127.5
Air correction jet (a)	160	150	150	175
Emulsion tube (s)	-	-	-	EM
Accelerator pump jet (i)	40	40	40	40
Float level (mm)	38	38	38	38
Needle valve (mm) (P)	1.5	1.5	1.5	1.6
Idle position (ORF)	0°30'	-	-	-
Idle position (PRN)	-	9°30'	9°30'	-
Fast idle position (OPR)	12°	-	-	-
Fast idle position (OP)	-	20°20'	20°20'	-
Choke fast idle gap (mm)	-	-	-	0.5
Choke pull-down (mm) (OVAD)	-	-	-	2.8

Manufacturer	Peugeot	Peugeot	Renault	Talbot
Model	309 1.4	405 1.4	14 1218 (R1210)	Samba (954 cc)
Year	1989 to 1992	1988 to 1992	1977 to 1982	1983 to 1986
Engine code	TU3A (K1G) (51kW)	TU3A (K1G) (51kW)	129C710	XV8
Capacity (cm³)/no. of cyls	1360/4	1360/4	1218/4	954/4
Oil temperature (°C)	80	80	80	90
Carb. ident. (Solex)	34 PBISA 17	34 PBISA 17	32 PBISA 11 12817	32 PBISA 11
Carb. ident. (vehicle)	481	481	714	A205
Idle speed (rpm)	750 ± 50	750 ± 50	800 ± 25	900 ± 50
CO @ idle (% vol.)	0.8 to 1.5	0.8 to 1.5	2.25 ± 0.25	1.5 ± 0.5
Venturi diameter (K)	26	26	25	24
Idle jet (g)	44 ± 2	44 ± 2	43	40 ± 5
Main jet (Gg)	132 ± 5	132 ± 5	127.5	122.5 ± 2.5
Air correction jet (a)	155 ± 10	155 ± 10	170	185 ± 10
Emulsion tube (s)	EC	EC	9	-
Accelerator pump jet (i)	40	40	40	40 ± 5
Float level (mm)	38	38	38	20 ± 2
Needle valve (mm) (P)	1.6	1.6	1.5	1.5
Idle position (PRN)	-	-	8°20'	-
Fast idle position (OP)	0.6 (mm)	0.6 (mm)	19°50'	20°40'
Choke fast idle gap (mm)	-	-	-	1.0
Choke pull-down (mm) (OVAD)	3.5	3.5	-	-

Manufacturer	Talbot	Talbot	Talbot	Talbot
Model	Samba (1124 cc)	Express 1.8	Express, Sportsman 1.8	Express, Sportsman 1.8
Year	1982 to 1986	1982 to 1985	1985 to 1991	1985 to 1991
Engine code	5A1 (XW7)	XM7T (169)	XM7T (169B) (49kW)	XN1T (170B) (58kW)
Capacity (cm³)/no. of cyls	1124/4	1796/4	1796/4	1971/4
Oil temperature (°C)	90	90	80	90
Carb. ident. (Solex)	32 PBISA 13137	34 PBISA 16 13434	34 PBISA 16 13434	34 PBISA 16 13434
Carb. ident. (vehicle)	144	A315	A315	PEU A315
Idle speed (rpm)	700 ± 50	825 ± 25	825 ± 25	825 ± 25
CO @ idle (% vol.)	1.5 ± 0.5	1.5 ± 0.5	1.5 ± 0.5	1.5 ± 0.5
Venturi diameter (K)	25	25	25	25
Idle jet (g)	42 ± 5	46	46	44 or 46
Main jet (Gg)	125 ± 5	130	130 ± 5	130 ± 5
Air correction jet (a)	180 ± 15	170	170	160 or 170
Accelerator pump jet (i)	35 ± 5	50	50	50
Float level (mm)	20 ± 2	38	38	38
Needle valve (mm) (P)	1.6	1.6	1.6	1.6
Idle position (PRN)	-	9°	9°	9°
Choke fast idle gap (mm)	1.0	0.90	0.90	0.90
Fast idle position (OP)	-	21°45'	21°45'	21°45'

Solex 32, 34 & 35 PBISA carburettor

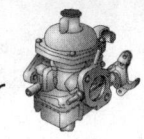

	Talbot	Talbot
Manufacturer		
Model	Express 2.0	Express, Triaxle 2.0
Year	1982 to 1985	1985 to 1992
Engine code	XN1T (170A)	XN1TA (170C) (72kW)
Capacity (cm³)/no. of cyls	1971/4	1971/4
Oil temperature (°C)	90	90
Carb. ident. (Solex)	34 PBISA 16 13434	34 PBISA 16
Carb. ident. (vehicle)	PEU A315	PEU A425
Idle speed (rpm)	825 ± 25	925 ± 25
CO @ idle (% vol.)	1.5 ± 0.5	1.75 ± 0.25
Venturi diameter (K)	25	25
Idle jet (g)	44 or 46	45
Main jet (Gg)	130 ± 5	127.5
Air correction jet (a)	160 or 170	155
Accelerator pump jet (i)	50	50
Float level (mm)	38	38
Needle valve (mm) (P)	1.6	1.6
Idle position (PRN)	9°	9°
Choke fast idle gap (mm)	0.90	-
Fast idle position (OP)	21°45'	20°

1 Principles of operation

Introduction

1 The following technical description of the Solex PBISA carburettor should be read in conjunction with the more detailed description of carburettor principles in Part A.

Construction

2 The Solex PBISA carburettor is a downdraught single venturi instrument with a manual choke control *(see illustration)*. The throttle shaft is made of steel, while the throttle plate, all jets and the emulsion tube are manufactured from brass. The internal fuel channels and air passages are

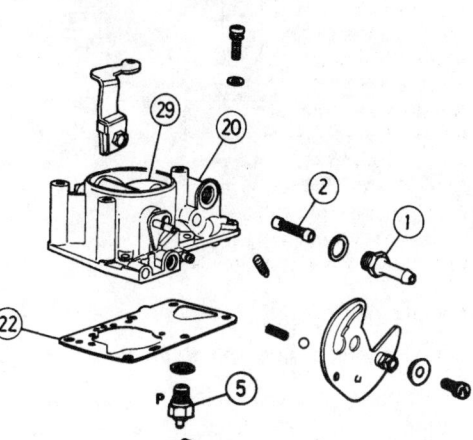

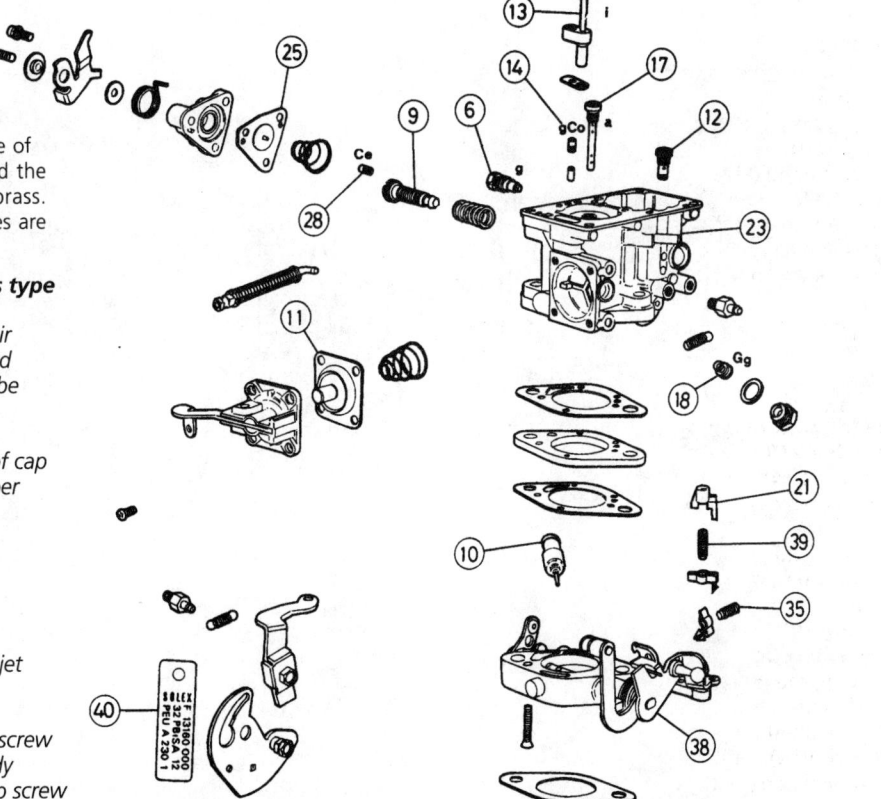

Solex PBISA carburettor - idle bypass type

1 Fuel inlet connection
2 Fuel filter
3 Float pin
4 Float
5 Needle valve
6 Idle jet
9 Bypass idle speed screw
10 Idle mixture control screw
11 Accelerator pump diaphragm
12 Accelerator pump valve
13 Pump injector
14 Bypass enrichment jet
17 Combined air corrector and emulsion tube
18 Main jet
20 Upper body
21 Tamperproof cap
22 Float chamber gasket
23 Main body
25 Part-load enrichment diaphragm
28 Part-load enrichment jet
29 Choke flap
35 Fast idle adjustment screw
38 Throttle body
39 Throttle stop screw
40 Identification tag

G3•5

Chapter G3

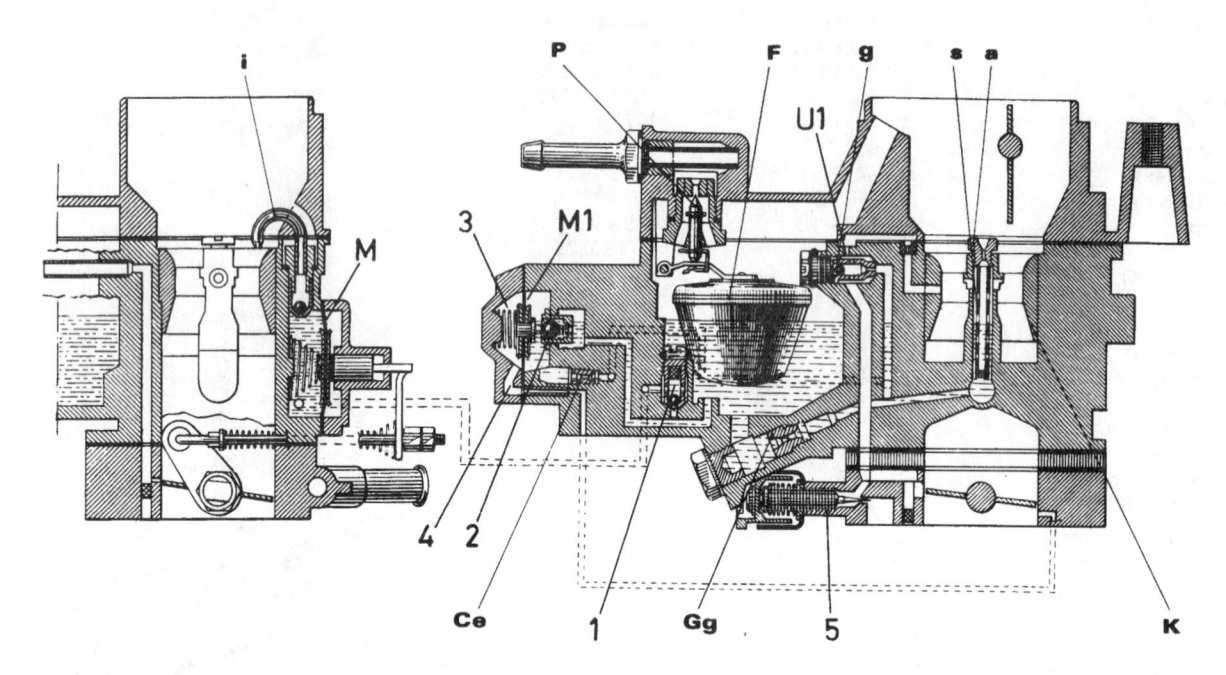

Internal fuel channels and air passages - PBISA without idle bypass

1. Accelerator pump brass inlet valve
2. Part-load enrichment valve
3. Spring
4. Vacuum channel
5. Idle mixture control screw
- a Air corrector jet
- Ce Fuel jet - part-load enrichment
- F Float
- g Idle fuel jet
- Gg Main jet
- i Accelerator pump injector
- K Venturi
- M Accelerator pump diaphragm
- M1 Part-load enrichment diaphragm
- P Needle valve
- s Emulsion tube
- U1 Idle air bleed

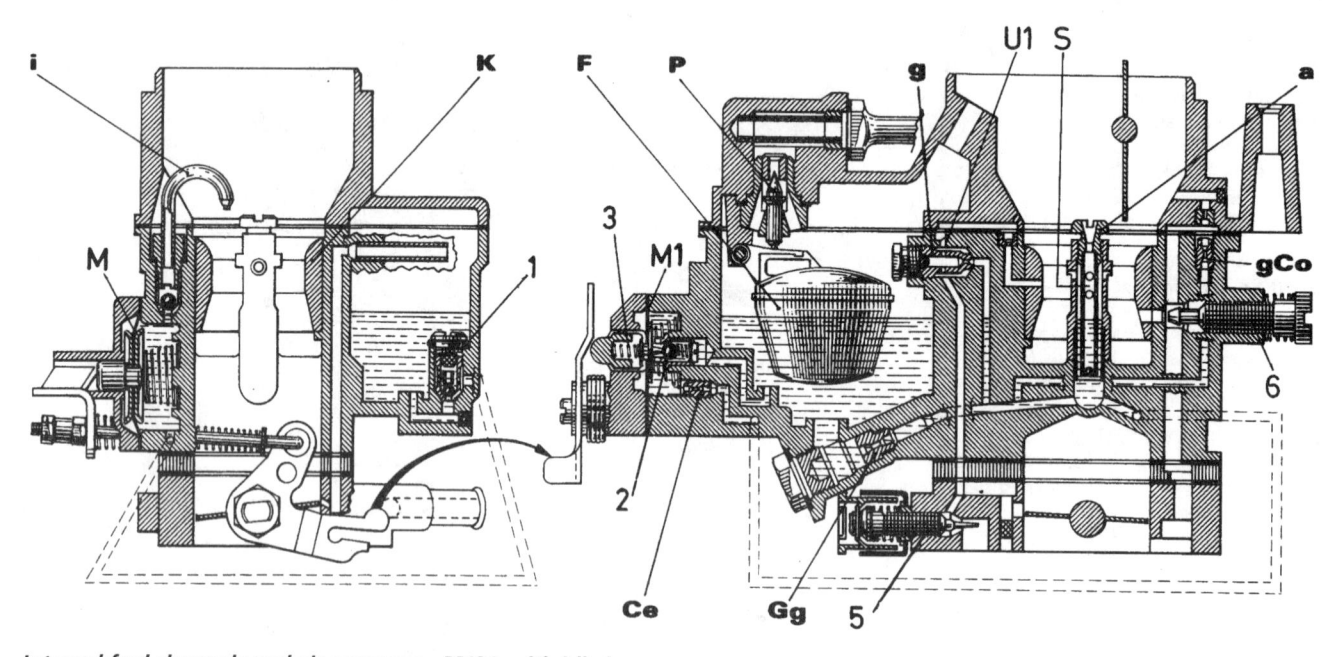

Internal fuel channels and air passages - PBISA with idle bypass

1. Brass accelerator pump inlet valve
2. Part-load enrichment valve
3. Spring
5. Idle mixture control screw
6. Bypass idle speed screw
- a Air corrector jet
- Ce Fuel jet - part-load enrichment
- F Float
- g Idle fuel jet
- gCo Bypass fuel jet
- Gg Main jet
- i Accelerator pump injector
- K Venturi
- M Accelerator pump diaphragm
- M1 Part-load enrichment diaphragm
- P Needle valve
- S Emulsion tube
- U1 Idle air bleed

Solex 32, 34 & 35 PBISA carburettor

drilled and sealed with lead plugs where necessary *(see illustrations)*.

3 The carburettor is constructed in three main bodies. These are the upper body, main body and throttle body (which contains the throttle assembly). An insulating block, placed between the main carburettor body and the throttle body, prevents excess heat transference to the main body.

4 The throttle body contains a heating flange through which hot engine coolant is piped. The purpose of the flange is to improve atomisation of the air/fuel mixture and to prevent carburettor icing during warm-up.

Fuel control

5 Fuel flows into the carburettor through a fine mesh filter. The fuel level in the float chamber is controlled by a needle valve and plastic float assembly. An anti-vibration ball is incorporated into the needle valve design. The float chamber is vented internally into the carburettor throat which is on the clean-air side of the air filter.

Idle, slow running and progression

6 Fuel, sourced from the main well, passes into the idle channel through a metered idle jet. Here it is mixed with a small amount of air from a calibrated air bleed. The resulting emulsion is drawn through a channel to be discharged from the idle orifice under the primary throttle plate. A tapered mixture screw is used to vary the outlet and this ensures fine control of the idle mixture.

7 A progression slot provides extra enrichment as it is uncovered by the opening throttle during initial acceleration.

8 The idle speed is set by an adjustable screw. The adjustable mixture screw is tamper proofed at production level, in accordance with emission regulations.

Idle bypass circuit (some variations)

9 The idle bypass circuit provides a means of more accurately controlling idle emissions than a conventional idle mixture circuit. The throttle plate is locked in a specified position and sealed with a tamperproof cap. Eighty percent of the fuel required for idle is provided by the normal idle circuit. The remainder of the idle mixture is controlled through the idle bypass circuit.

10 Fuel, sourced from the main well, is drawn into the bypass passage. Air is sourced from the upper reaches of the main venturi. An air and fuel emulsion is drawn through the bypass passage and discharged from the bypass orifice under the throttle plate. The emulsion is controlled by a regulating screw which is also used to adjust the idle speed.

Accelerator pump

11 The PBISA accelerator pump is controlled by a diaphragm and is mechanically operated by a lever and rod attached to the throttle linkage. During acceleration, fuel is pumped through a ball valve located in the pump injector and is discharged into the primary venturi. The brass inlet valve located in the float chamber also returns excess fuel to the chamber.

Main circuit

12 Fuel is drawn through a calibrated main jet into the base of the auxiliary venturi. An emulsion tube is placed in the auxiliary venturi, capped with an air corrector jet. The fuel is mixed with air drawn in through the air corrector and through the holes in the emulsion tube. The resulting emulsified mixture is discharged into the main airstream. This is accomplished through four orifices placed at 90° intervals in the upper reaches of the auxiliary venturi.

Part-load enrichment (power valve) - some variations

13 Fuel flows from the float chamber into the enrichment chamber, through a fuel channel and a brass inlet valve. An air passage is taken from under the throttle plate to the cover of the chamber. At idle and during light-throttle operation, manifold vacuum draws the diaphragm back against spring pressure. The diaphragm pintle is withdrawn from the valve and the spring-loaded ball seats to close off the inlet channel.

14 Under acceleration and wide-open throttle operation, the vacuum in the manifold is depleted. The diaphragm returns under spring pressure and the power diaphragm pintle pushes the ball to open the inlet valve. Fuel then flows through the valve into the enrichment chamber. From here it passes through a calibrated jet into a fuel channel leading to the primary main well. The fuel level rises in the well and the fuel mixture is enriched.

Full-load enrichment (some variations)

15 At full-load and high engine speeds, the velocity of air creates a depression sufficient to raise fuel from the float chamber into a channel. The fuel then passes through a calibrated bushing to the upper section of the air intake. Here it is mixed with a small amount of air from a calibrated air bleed and the emulsified mixture is then discharged into the airstream from the full-load enrichment nozzle.

Manual choke operation

16 The manual choke is operated by a dash-mounted cable control. When the cable is pulled, it operates a lever that pulls the choke flap closed across the air intake. Fast idle is achieved with the aid of a curved cam attached to the choke operating lever. This cam actuates another lever to which is fixed an adjustable screw. The screw butts against the throttle lever and is used to vary the fast idle speed.

17 During engine warm-up, the cable control should be progressively pushed home until the choke flap is fully open.

Choke pull-down

18 Once the engine has fired, the choke flap must open slightly to weaken the mixture and avoid flooding. This is achieved by two different methods, depending on the version of the PBISA carburettor fitted. On the first type, an increase in airflow through the air intake partially opens the choke flap against the action of a spring. A stop ensures that the choke is only opened a small amount. On the second type, manifold vacuum is used to actuate a diaphragm. A linkage attached to the diaphragm will then pull upon the choke flap.

2 Identification

1 The Solex identification code is stamped on a metallic tag attached to the carburettor cover by an upper body fixing screw. This tag quotes the Solex part number and the vehicle manufacturer part number. It also identifies the carburettor type.

2 Later carburettors may have this information stamped upon the carburettor body:
  13168   Solex part number
  Cit 341   Vehicle manufacturer part number
  32 PBISA Carburettor type

3 Where the tag is missing, refer to Part B for other ways of identifying the carburettor.

3 General servicing

Introduction

1 Read this Chapter in conjunction with Part B, which describes some of the operations in more detail. It is assumed that the carburettor is removed for this service. However, many of the operations can be tackled with the carburettor in place. Where this is undertaken, first remove the carburettor upper body and soak the fuel out of the float chamber using a clean tissue or soft cloth.

Dismantling and checking

2 Remove the carburettor from the engine (see Part B).

3 Check the carburettor visually for damage and wear.

4 Disconnect the choke pull-down hose (where fitted).

5 Disconnect the choke spring (some variations), then remove the six screws and detach the carburettor upper body.

6 Inspect the float chamber for corrosion and calcium build-up.

7 Tap out the float pin and remove the float, needle valve and float chamber gasket.

8 Check that the anti-vibration ball is free in the valve end.

9 Check the needle valve tip for wear and ridges.

10 The float should be checked for damage and ingress of petrol.

Chapter G3

11 Renew the float pin if shows signs of wear.
12 Use a straight-edge to check for distorted flanges on all facing surfaces.
13 Unscrew the fuel inlet tube and inspect the fuel filter. Clean the filter housing of debris and dirt and renew the filter if necessary.
14 Remove the mixture screw and idle bypass screw (where fitted), and inspect the tips for damage or ridges.
15 If the accelerator pump injector is a push fit in the body, carefully prise it from its location.
16 If the accelerator pump injector is retained by a fixing screw, unscrew the fixing screw and carefully prise it from its location. If the injector is tight, the bottom of the injector is visible from inside the pump housing. It can be gently tapped with a suitable drift until the injector becomes free.
17 Test the accelerator pump injector by shaking it. No noise from the outlet ball would indicate that the valve is seized.
18 Unscrew the accelerator pump's brass inlet valve from the float chamber and test it by shaking. No noise would indicate that the valve is seized.
19 Remove the four screws and detach the accelerator pump cover, diaphragm and spring. Check the diaphragm for fatigue and damage.
20 Remove the idle jet from the main body.
21 Remove the main jet from the float chamber. It may be necessary to remove a plug in the float chamber body to expose an opening. Unscrew and withdraw the main jet through this opening. Check that the channel from the float chamber into the emulsion tube well is clear.
22 Remove the combined air corrector and emulsion tube from the auxiliary venturi.
23 Check the jet calibration against that specified. It is possible that the wrong size jets may have been fitted during the last overhaul.
24 Remove the three screws and detach the power valve housing cover, spring and diaphragm from the body (where fitted). Check the diaphragm for damage.
25 Unscrew the brass power valve from the body. The ball in the valve should seal the outlet. Depress and release the ball with a small screwdriver and it should move smoothly in and out.
26 Unscrew and remove the small power jet from inside the power valve housing. Check that the channel into the emulsion tube well is clear.
27 Remove the two screws and separate the carburettor main body and throttle body assemblies. The throttle body can be renewed separately if the spindles or throttle bores are worn. Use a straight-edge to check for distorted flanges on the facing surfaces. Do not disturb the adjustment of the throttle angle, unless absolutely necessary.
28 Inspect the choke spindle, mechanism and levers for stickiness and wear. Note that on some variations, the disconnected choke lever on the main body now has a wider range of movement. Be careful that the small ball bearing, located behind the choke lever, is not lost if the lever is moved to its full extent.
29 Attach a vacuum pump to the pull-down diaphragm (where fitted) and operate the pump to obtain 300 mmHg (400 mbars). The diaphragm should operate fully and the vacuum should be maintained for at least 30 seconds. Renew the diaphragm assembly if it fails these tests. Check the vacuum hose for leaks and splits and renew if necessary.

Preparation for reassembly

30 Clean the jets, carburettor body assemblies, float chamber and internal channels. An air line may be used to clear the internal channels once the carburettor is fully dismantled. Note that if high-pressure air is directed into the channels and passages with the diaphragms still in place, diaphragm damage may result. Spraying carburettor cleaner into all the channels and passages in the carburettor body will often clear them of gum and dirt.
31 During reassembly, a complete set of new gaskets should be fitted. Also renew the needle valve, the float pin and all diaphragms.
32 Inspect and renew (where necessary) the mixture screw, main jet, air corrector/ emulsion tube, idle jet and the accelerator pump inlet valve and injector. Renew worn linkages, screws, springs and other parts where necessary.
33 Ensure that all the jets are firmly locked into their original positions (but do not over-tighten). A loose jet can cause a rich (or even lean) running condition.
34 Clean all mating surfaces and flanges of old gasket material and reassemble with new gaskets. Ensure that housings are positioned with their air and fuel routes correctly aligned.

Reassembly

35 Refit the choke diaphragm assembly (where used) to the carburettor upper body.
36 Assemble the main and throttle bodies with a new gasket block and secure with the two screws.
37 Where the primary throttle position has been disturbed and a throttle setting gauge is available, use it to set the throttle angle. Otherwise, temporarily adjust the throttle plate so that it is open just enough to prevent its seizure in the throttle body. An adjustment method with the engine running is detailed in Section 4.
38 Refit the power jet and valve assembly (where used) into their original positions.
39 Refit the power diaphragm, spring and cover assembly (where used) and secure with the three screws.
40 Refit the emulsion tube/air corrector and main jet into their original positions. Refit the plug to the float chamber with a new seal.
41 Refit the idle jet into the main body and lock it firmly into position.
42 Refit the accelerator pump spring, diaphragm and cover assembly, then secure with the four screws.
43 Refit the accelerator pump inlet valve into the float chamber, after renewing the small seal on the valve body.
44 Refit the accelerator pump injector, after renewing the small seal (or gasket) on the injector body.
45 Refit the idle mixture screw. Turn the screw in gently until it just seats. From this position, unscrew it three full turns. This will provide a basic setting to allow the engine to be started.
46 Refit the idle bypass screw (where fitted). Obtain a basic setting in the same way as described for the mixture screw above.
47 Clean or renew the fuel filter then refit the fuel inlet tube (with a new sealing washer).
48 Renew the float chamber gasket and locate in position on the upper body.
49 Renew the needle valve assembly, using a new sealing washer. Ensure that it is firmly locked into position (but do not over-tighten).
50 Refit the float and secure with the float pin.
51 Adjust the float level with reference to Section 4.
52 Refit the upper body to the main body and secure with the six screws.
53 Reconnect the choke spring (where fitted - mechanical pull-down).
54 Reconnect the choke pull-down hose (where fitted - vacuum pull-down).
55 Ensure that the choke flap and linkage move smoothly and progressively.
56 Adjust the choke fast idle and pull-down, see Section 4.
57 Refit the carburettor to the engine.
58 Always adjust the carburettor idle speed and mixture after any work has been carried out on the carburettor, preferably with the aid of a CO meter.

4 Service adjustments

Adjustment pre-conditions

1 Refer to Part B for general advice on the pre-conditions for correct adjustment of this carburettor.

Idle speed and mixture (CO)

Standard idle system

2 Run the engine at 3000 rpm for 30 seconds to clear the manifold of fuel vapours, then allow the engine to idle.
3 Use the idle speed screw to set the specified idle speed (see illustration).
4 Check the CO level. If incorrect, remove the tamperproof plug and adjust the idle mixture screw to obtain the correct level. Turning the screw clockwise (inwards) will reduce the CO level. Turning the screw anti-clockwise (outwards) will increase the CO level. Refer to Part B for a method of setting the idle mixture without the aid of a CO meter.
5 Repeat paragraphs 3 and 4 until both adjustments are correct.
6 Clear the manifold every 30 seconds during the setting operation by running the engine at 3000 rpm for 30 seconds.

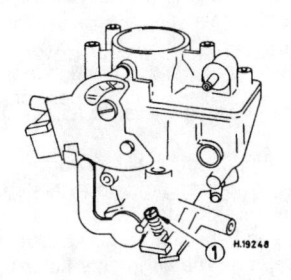

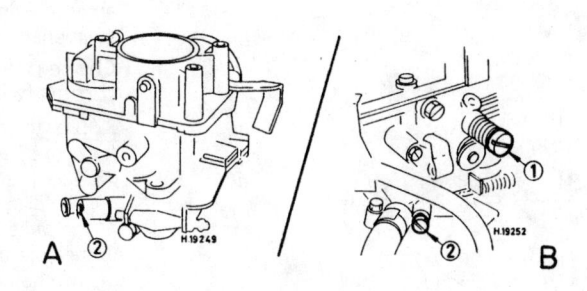

Solex 32, 34 & 35 PBISA carburettor

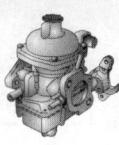

Idle adjustment screw location

A Without idle bypass
B With idle bypass

1 Idle speed adjustment screw
2 Idle mixture control screw

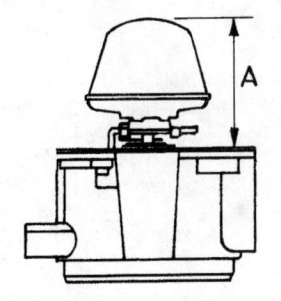

Float level adjustment

A Float level

7 Increase the speed to 2000 rpm and note the CO reading. The cruise reading should be less than half the idle CO reading.
8 Fit a new tamperproof plug to the mixture control screw on completion.

Bypass idle system

9 Run the engine at 3000 rpm for 30 seconds to clear the manifold of fuel vapours, then allow the engine to idle.
10 Use the idle bypass regulating screw to set the correct idle speed (see Specifications).
11 Check the CO level. If incorrect, remove the tamperproof plug and adjust the idle mixture screw to obtain the correct level. Turning the screw clockwise (inwards) will reduce the CO level. Turning the screw anti-clockwise (outwards) will increase the CO level. Refer to Part B for a method of setting the idle mixture without the aid of a CO meter.
12 Repeat paragraphs 10 and 11 until both adjustments are correct.

13 Fit a new tamperproof plug to the mixture control screw on completion.

Basic throttle position

14 If the idle speed and CO cannot be set correctly, it is possible that the basic throttle position is incorrect. The manufacturer's recommended method is to remove the carburettor and use a Renault, Solex or Pierburg throttle setting gauge to accurately set the throttle position.
15 However, an alternative method can be used to set the throttle plate. Note that this is not the manufacturer's recommended method but will nevertheless result in an accurate and stable idle speed and CO level.
16 Allow the engine to idle.
17 Screw in the bypass regulating screw until it is fully seated. The idle speed should drop to two-thirds of the idle speed figure. For example, if the idle speed is specified as 900 rpm, the speed should drop to 600 rpm.

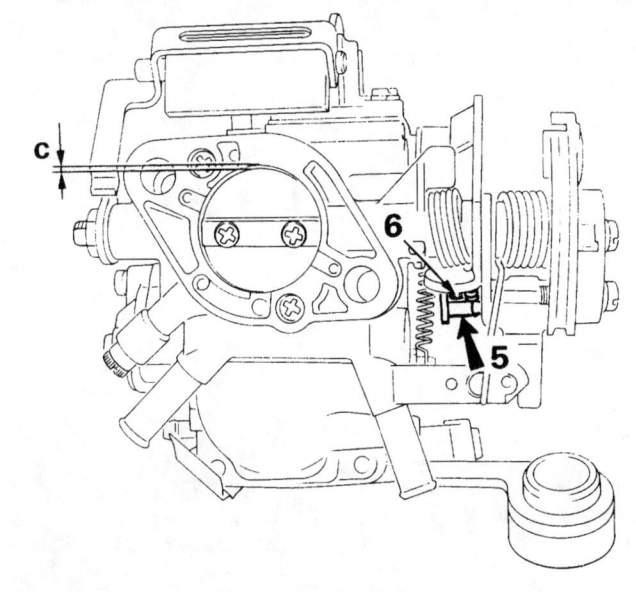

18 Remove the tamperproof plug and adjust the throttle stop screw until 600 rpm is obtained.
19 Unscrew the bypass screw until 900 rpm is once again attained.
20 Reset the CO to the correct level.
21 If the CO needs a large adjustment at this stage, repeat paragraphs 16 to 20. Once the proper CO level is reached at the specified idle speed, the carburettor is properly adjusted.
22 Note that the rpm figures used in the above example are based on a hypothetical idle speed of 900 rpm. Substitute the correct figures for the carburettor being adjusted (see Specifications).
23 Fit new tamperproof plugs to the mixture control and throttle stop screws on completion.

Float level

24 Invert the upper body so that the float faces upwards.
25 Measure the distance between the upper body (with its gasket) and the upper face of the plastic float. Refer to Specifications for the correct float level (see illustration).
26 Adjust as necessary by bending the float pivot arm. Otherwise, renew the float.

Choke adjustments

Fast idle

27 The carburettor must be removed from the engine in order to make the following fast idle adjustment. Refer to Part B for a method of setting the fast idle speed without removing the carburettor.
28 Invert the carburettor and pull the choke operating lever to fully close the choke flap. The fast idle screw will butt against the fast idle cam and force open the throttle plate to leave a small clearance.
29 Use the shank of a twist drill to measure the clearance between the wall of the throttle bore and the throttle plate. Refer to Specifications for the required drill size. Measure from the side opposite the progression slot.
30 Adjust as necessary by turning the fast idle adjustment screw (6) (see illustration) in the appropriate direction.
31 Alternatively, the fast idle throttle angle may be set by means of a Solex or Pierburg throttle

Fast idle adjustment

5 Choke operating lever
6 Fast idle adjustment screw
c Fast idle clearance - refer to Specifications

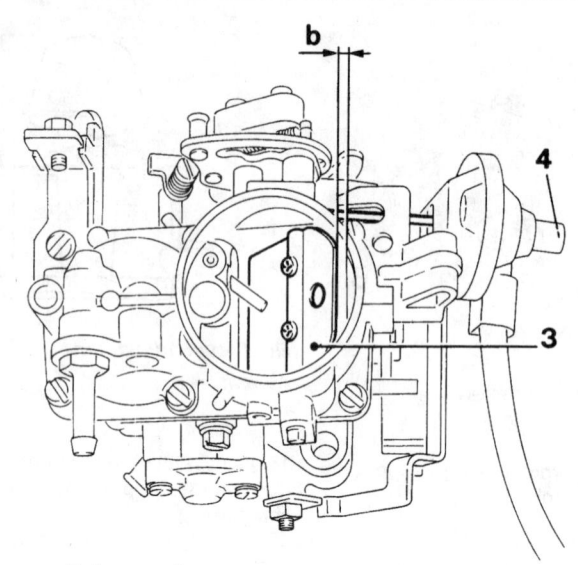

Chapter G3

Choke vacuum pull-down adjustment
3 Choke flap
4 Adjustment screw
b Pull-down clearance - refer to Specifications

angle gauge. Refer to Specifications for the appropriate throttle angle.

Choke pull-down (vacuum pull-down carburettor)

32 Pull the choke operating lever to fully close the choke flap.

33 Use a vacuum pump or small screwdriver to pull the diaphragm operating rod up to its stop. At the same time, use the shank of a twist drill to measure the gap between the upper section of the choke flap and the air intake. Refer to Specifications for the required drill size.

34 Remove the plug in the diaphragm cover and adjust as necessary by turning the adjustment screw (4) *(see illustration)* in the appropriate direction. Renew the plug when adjustment is complete.

5 Fault diagnosis

Refer to Part D for diagnosis of general carburettor faults.

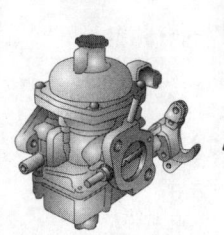

Part G Chapter 4
Solex 32 & 35 SEIA carburettor

G4

Contents

Fault diagnosis 5
General servicing 3
Identification 2
Principles of operation 1
Service adjustments 4

Specifications

Manufacturer	Renault	Renault	Renault	Renault
Model	18 1.4 (R1340/1350)	Fuego 1.4 (R1360)	Trafic P1000/P1200 rwd	Trafic P1000/P1200 rwd
Year	1978 to 1984	1980 to 1984	1981 to 1986	1981 to 1986
Engine code	847A720	847A720	841J705	841J705
Capacity (cm³)/no. of cyls	1397/4	1397/4	1647/4	1647/4
Oil temperature (°C)	80	80	80	80
Carb. ident. (Solex)	32 SEIA 13126	32 SEIA 13126	35 SEIA	35 SEIA
Carb. ident. (vehicle)	795	795	738	822
Idle speed (rpm)	775 ± 25	775 ± 25	750 ± 25	750 ± 25
CO @ idle (% vol.)	2.25 ± 0.25	2.5 ± 0.5	2.5 ± 0.5	2.5 ± 0.5
Venturi diameter (K)	24	24	26	26
Idle jet (g)	45	45	45	45
Main jet (Gg)	127.5	127.5	135	130
Air correction jet (a)	160	160	205	205
Emulsion tube (s)	X1	X1	NU	NU
Accelerator pump jet (i)	35	35	40	40
Float level (mm)	11.7	11.7	11.7 ± 1	11.7
Needle valve (mm) (P)	1.5	1.5	1.7	1.7
Idle position (PRN)	9°15'	9°15'	9°15'	9°15'
Choke fast idle gap (mm)	0.8	0.8	0.85	0.9
Fast idle position (OP)	21°	21°	-	-
Choke pull-down (mm) (OVAD)	-	-	4.5	-
Vent valve (mm)	3.5 ± 0.5	3.5 ± 0.5	3.5 ± 0.5	3.5 ± 0.5
Manufacturer	Renault	Renault	Renault	Renault
Model	Trafic P1400 rwd	Trafic P1400 rwd	Trafic P1400 rwd	Trafic P1400 rwd
Year	1984 to 1985	1984 to 1985	1984 to 1985	1986 to 1989
Engine code	829E720	829E720	829E720	J5R726
Capacity (cm³)/no. of cyls	1995/4	1995/4	1995/4	1995/4
Oil temperature (°C)	80	80	80	80
Carb. ident. (Solex)	35 SEIA	35 SEIA	35 SEIA 13187	35 SEIA
Carb. ident. (vehicle)	778	780	811	780
Idle speed (rpm)	800 ± 25	700 ± 50	800 ± 25	700 ± 50
CO @ idle (% vol.)	2.5 ± 0.5	2.5 ± 0.5	2.5 ± 0.5	1.5 ± 0.5
Venturi diameter (K)	27	27	27	27
Idle jet (g)	48	48	48	48
Main jet (Gg)	135	135	135	135
Air correction jet (a)	155	155	155	155
Emulsion tube (s)	-	X14	-	X14
Accelerator pump jet (i)	45	45	45	45
Float level (mm)	11.7 ± 1	11.7	11.7	11.7
Needle valve (mm) (P)	1.7	1.7	1.7	1.7
Idle position (PRN)	9°45'	-	-	-
Choke fast idle gap (mm)	1.00	1.20	1.10	1.20
Choke pull-down (mm) (OVAD)	3.5	4.0	-	4
Vent valve (mm)	3.5 ± 0.5	3.5 ± 0.5	3.5 ± 0.5	3.5 ± 0.5

Chapter G4

Manufacturer	Renault	Renault	Renault	Renault
Model T1000/T1200fwd	Trafic P1400 rwd	Trafic P1400 rwd	Trafic T1000/T1200 fwd	Trafic
Year	1986 to 1989	1989 to 1992	1981 to 1986	1981 to 1986
Engine code	J5R726	J5RA726 or C726	A1MP707	A1MQ708
Capacity (cm³)/no. of cyls	1995/4	1995/4	1647/4	1647/4
Oil temperature (°C)	80	80	80	80
Transmission	-	-	MT	AT
Carb. ident. (Solex)	35 SEIA	35 SEIA	35 SEIA 13202	35 SEIA
Carb. ident. (vehicle)	888/911	888/911	808	813
Idle speed (rpm)	800 ± 50	800 ± 50	750 ± 25	650 ± 25
CO @ idle (% vol.)	1.5 ± 0.5	1.5 ± 0.5	2.5 ± 0.5	1.5 ± 0.5
Venturi diameter (K)	26	26	26	26
Idle jet (g)	45	45	45	44
Main jet (Gg)	135	135	130	130
Air correction jet (a)	135	135	205	205
Emulsion tube (s)	-	X14	NU	NU
Accelerator pump jet (i)	45	45	40	40
Float level (mm)	11.7	11.7 ± 1	11.7	11.7
Needle valve (mm) (P)	1.7	1.7	1.7	1.7
Idle position (PRN)	-	9°15'	9°15'	-
Choke fast idle gap (mm)	1.15	1.15	0.8	0.95
Fast idle position (OP)	-	22°40	20°15	-
Choke pull-down (mm) (OVAD)	4.7	4.7	5.0	-
Vent valve (mm)	3.4 ± 0.5	3.4	3.5 ± 0.5	3.5 ± 0.5

Manufacturer	Renault	Renault	Renault	Renault
Model	Trafic T1000 fwd	Trafic T1100 fwd	Trafic T1300	Trafic T1300
Year	1986 to 1989	1989 to 1992	1986 to 1989	1986 to 1989
Engine code	FIN720	FIN720	J5R716	J5R716
Capacity (cm³)/no. of cyls	1721/4	1721/4	1995/4	1995/4
Oil temperature (°C)	80	80	80	80
Carb. ident. (Solex)	35 SEIA	35 SEIA	35 SEIA	35 SEIA
Carb. ident. (vehicle)	870	978	888	911
Idle speed (rpm)	700 ± 25	700 ± 25	800 ± 50	800 ± 50
CO @ idle (% vol.)	1.5 ± 0.5	1.5 ± 0.5	1.5 ± 0.5	1.5 ± 0.5
Venturi diameter (K)	26	26	26	26
Idle jet (g)	45	45	45	45
Main jet (Gg)	127.5	127.5	135	135
Air correction jet (a)	160	145	135	135
Emulsion tube (s)	-	-	-	X14
Accelerator pump jet (i)	40	40	45	45
Float level (mm)	11.7	11.7	11.7	11.7
Needle valve (mm) (P)	1.7	1.7	1.7	1.7
Choke fast idle gap (mm)	0.9	0.9	1.15	1.15
Choke pull-down (mm) (OVAD)	4.0	4.0	4.7	4.7
Vent valve (mm)	3.4	3.4	3.4	3.4

Manufacturer	Renault	Renault	Renault	Renault
Model	Trafic T1400	Master P35 rwd	Master P35 rwd	Master P35 rwd
Year	1989 to 1992	1981 to 1985	1986 to 1989	1986 to 1989
Engine code	J5RA716	829A730	J5R728	J5R728
Capacity (cm³)/no. of cyls	1995/4	1995/4	1995/4	1995/4
Oil temperature (°C)	80	80	80	80
Carb. ident. (Solex)	35 SEIA	35 SEIA 13136	35 SEIA	35 SEIA
Carb. ident. (vehicle)	888/911	712	824	901
Idle speed (rpm)	800 ± 50	800 ± 25	800 ± 25	800 ± 50
CO @ idle (% vol.)	1.5 ± 0.5	2.0 ± 1.0	1.5 ± 0.5	1.5 ± 0.5
Venturi diameter (K)	26	26	26	26
Idle jet (g)	45	44	40	45
Main jet (Gg)	135	132.5	130 or 132.5	135
Air correction jet (a)	-	140	140	135
Emulsion tube (s)	-	X15	X15	-
Accelerator pump jet (i)	45	45	45	45
Float level (mm)	11.7	11.7 ± 1	11.7	11.7
Needle valve (mm) (P)	1.7	1.7	1.7	1.7
Basic throttle position (PF)	-	9°15'	-	-
Choke fast idle gap (mm)	1.15	1.10	1.25	1.15
Fast idle position (OP)	-	22°40	-	-
Choke pull-down (mm) (OVAD)	4.7	-	4.5	4.7
Vent valve (mm)	3.4	3.5 ± 0.5	3.5 ± 0.5	3.4

Solex 32 & 35 SEIA carburettor

Manufacturer	Renault	Renault	Renault	Renault
Model	Master P35 rwd	Master P35 rwd	Master P35 rwd	Master T35 fwd
Year	1989 to 1991	1989 to 1991	1989 to 1991	1981 to 1985
Engine code	J5R718 or 728	J5R718 or 728	J5R718 or 728	829731
Capacity (cm³)/no. of cyls	1995/4	1995/4	1995/4	1995/4
Oil temperature (°C)	80	80	80	80
Carb. ident. (Solex)	35 SEIA 13136	35 SEIA	35 SEIA	35 SEIA 12962
Carb. ident. (vehicle)	712	824	901	711
Idle speed (rpm)	800 ± 25	800 ± 25	800 ± 50	800 ± 25
CO @ idle (% vol.)	2.0 ± 1.0	2.0 ± 1.0	1.5 ± 0.5	1.5 ± 0.5
Venturi diameter (K)	26	26	26	26
Idle jet (g)	44	40	45	44
Main jet (Gg)	135	130	135	135
Air correction jet (a)	140	140	135	140
Emulsion tube (s)	-	X15	-	-
Accelerator pump jet (i)	45	45	45	45
Float level (mm)	11.7 ± 1	11.7	11.7	11.7 ± 1
Needle valve (mm) (P)	1.7	1.7	1.7	1.7
Choke fast idle gap (mm)	0.85	1.25	1.15	1.1
Choke pull-down (mm) (OVAD)	-	4.5	4.7	-
Vent valve (mm)	3.5 ± 0.5	3.5 ± 0.5	3.4	-

Manufacturer	Renault	Renault	Renault	Renault
Model	Master T35 fwd	Master T35 fwd	Master T35 fwd	Master T35 fwd
Year	1981 to 1985	1986 to 1989	1986 to 1989	1986 to 1989
Engine code	829731	J5R718	J5R718	J5R718
Capacity (cm³)/no. of cyls	1995/4	1995/4	1995/4	1995/4
Oil temperature (°C)	80	80	80	80
Carb. ident. (Solex)	35 SEIA	35 SEIA 12962	35 SEIA	35 SEIA
Carb. ident. (vehicle)	823	711	823	901A
Idle speed (rpm)	800 ± 25	800 ± 25	800 ± 25	800 ± 25
CO @ idle (% vol.)	1.5 ± 0.5	2.0 ± 1.0	2.0 ± 1.0	1.5 ± 0.5
Venturi diameter (K)	26	26	26	26
Idle jet (g)	40	44	40	45
Main jet (Gg)	132.5	135	132.5	135
Air correction jet (a)	140	140	140	135
Emulsion tube (s)	X14	X14	X14	-
Accelerator pump jet (i)	45	45	45	45
Float level (mm)	11.7	11.7 ± 1	11.7	11.7
Needle valve (mm) (P)	1.7	1.7	1.7	1.7
Basic throttle position (PF)	-	9°15'	-	-
Choke fast idle gap (mm)	1.25	1.10	1.25	1.15
Fast idle position (OP)	22°40	-	-	-
Choke pull-down (mm) (OVAD)	4.5	-	4.5	4.7
Vent valve (mm)	3.5 ± 0.5	-	3.5 ± 0.5	3.4

Manufacturer	Renault	Renault	Renault
Model	Master T35 fwd	Master T35 fwd	Master T35 fwd
Year	1989 to 1992	1989 to 1992	1989 to 1992
Engine code	J5R718 or 728	J5R718 or 728	J5R718 or 728
Capacity (cm³)/no. of cyls	1995/4	1995/4	1995/4
Oil temperature (°C)	80	80	80
Carb. ident. (Solex)	35 SEIA 12962	35 SEIA	35 SEIA
Carb. ident. (vehicle)	711	823	901A
Idle speed (rpm)	800 ± 25	800 ± 25	800 ± 25
CO @ idle (% vol.)	2.0 ± 1.0	2.0 ± 1.0	1.5 ± 0.5
Venturi diameter (K)	26	26	26
Idle jet (g)	44	40	45
Main jet (Gg)	135	132.5	135
Air correction jet (a)	140	140	135
Emulsion tube (s)	X14	X14	X15
Accelerator pump jet (i)	45	45	45
Float level (mm)	11.7 ± 1	11.7	11.7 ± 1
Needle valve (mm) (P)	1.7	1.7	1.7
Idle position (PRN)	9°15'	-	-
Choke fast idle gap (mm)	1.1	1.25	1.15
Fast idle position (OP)	22°40	-	22°40
Choke pull-down (mm) (OVAD)	-	4.5	4.7
Vent valve (mm)	-	3.5 ± 0.5	3.4

Chapter G4

Manufacturer	Volvo	Volvo
Model	340, 343 & 345 1.4	340, 343 & 345 1.4
Year	1982 to 1983	1983 to 1987
Engine code	B14 3E	B14 3E
Capacity (cm^3)/no. of cyls	1397/4	1397/4
Oil temperature (°C)	80	80
Carb. ident. (Solex)	32 SEIA 13132	32 SEIA 13201/13256
Carb. ident. (vehicle)	796	814/828
Idle speed (rpm)	900 ± 50 Manual	900 ± 50 Manual
	800 ± 50 Auto	800 ± 50 Auto
CO @ idle (% vol.)	2.0 +10.5	2.5 ± 0.5
Venturi diameter (K)	24	24
Idle jet (g)	45 ± 3	43 ± 3
Main jet (Gg)	128 ± 2.5	122.5 ± 2.5
Air correction jet (a)	155 ± 5	165 ± 5
Emulsion tube (s)	X16	X17
Accelerator pump jet (i)	35	35
Float level (mm)	22.7	22.7
Needle valve (mm) (P)	1.5	1.5
Choke fast idle gap (mm)	0.8	0.8
Fast idle position (OP)	-	-
Choke pull-down (mm) (OVAD)	4.5 ± 0.5	4.5 ± 0.5
Vent valve (mm)	3.5 ± 0.5	3.5 ± 0.5

1 Principles of operation

Introduction

1 The following technical description of the Solex SEIA carburettor should be read in conjunction with the more detailed description of carburettor principles in Part A.

Construction

2 The Solex SEIA carburettor is a down-draught single venturi instrument with a manual choke control *(see illustration)*. The throttle shaft is made of steel, while the throttle plate, all jets and the emulsion tube are manufactured from brass. The internal fuel channels and air passages are drilled and sealed with lead plugs where necessary *(see illustration)*.

3 The carburettor is constructed in three main bodies. These are the upper body, main body and throttle body (which contains the throttle assembly). An insulating block, placed between the main carburettor body and the throttle body, prevents excess heat transference to the main body.

4 The throttle body contains a heating flange through which hot engine coolant is piped. The purpose of the flange is to improve atomisation of the air/fuel mixture and to prevent carburettor icing during warm-up.

Fuel control

5 Fuel flows into the carburettor through a fine mesh filter. The fuel level in the float chamber is controlled by a needle valve and plastic float assembly. An anti-vibration ball is incorporated into the needle valve design.

6 The float chamber uses a dual-venting arrangement. Venting is to atmosphere at idle or with the engine shut down but at engine speeds higher than idle, a lever attached to the throttle closes the atmospheric vent. This allows the float chamber to vent into the upper air intake which is on the clean-air side of the air filter.

Idle, slow running and progression

7 Fuel, sourced from the main well, passes into the idle channel through a metered idle jet. Here it is mixed with a small amount of air from a calibrated air bleed. The resulting emulsion is drawn through a channel to be discharged from the idle orifice under the primary throttle plate. A tapered mixture screw is used to vary the outlet and this ensures fine control of the idle mixture.

8 A progression slot provides extra enrichment as it is uncovered by the opening throttle during initial acceleration.

9 The idle speed is set by an adjustable screw. The adjustable mixture screw is tamper proofed at production level, in accordance with emission regulations.

Idle cut-off valve (some variations)

10 An idle cut-off valve is used to prevent run-on when the engine is shut down. It utilises a 12-volt solenoid plunger to block the idle jet when the ignition is switched off.

Idle bypass circuit (some variations)

11 The idle bypass circuit provides a means of more accurately controlling idle emissions than a conventional idle mixture circuit. The throttle plate is locked in a specified position and sealed with a tamperproof cap. Eighty per cent of the fuel required for idle is provided by the normal idle circuit. The remainder of the idle mixture is controlled through the idle bypass circuit.

12 Fuel, sourced from the main well, is drawn into the bypass passage. Air is sourced from the upper reaches of the main venturi. The air and fuel emulsion is drawn through the bypass passage and discharged from the bypass orifice under the throttle plate. The emulsion is controlled by a regulating screw which is also used to adjust the idle speed.

Accelerator pump

13 The SEIA accelerator pump is controlled by a diaphragm and is mechanically operated by a lever and cam attached to the throttle linkage. During acceleration, fuel is pumped through a ball valve located in the pump injector and is then discharged into the primary venturi. The brass inlet valve located in the float chamber also returns excess fuel to the chamber.

Main circuit

14 The amount of fuel discharged into the airstream is controlled by a calibrated main jet. Fuel is drawn through the main jet into the base of a well which is arranged at an angle of 45°. The well dips down into the fuel in the float chamber. An emulsion tube is placed in the well, capped by a calibrated air corrector jet. The emulsion tube/air corrector assembly is force-fitted into the main well and is not removable. The fuel is mixed with air, drawn in through the air corrector and through the holes in the emulsion tube, and the resulting emulsified mixture is discharged from the main nozzle through an auxiliary venturi.

Part-load enrichment (power valve)

15 Fuel flows from the float chamber into the enrichment chamber, through a fuel channel and a brass inlet valve. An air passage is taken

Solex 32 & 35 SEIA carburettor

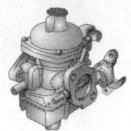

from under the throttle plate to the cover of the chamber. At idle, and during light-throttle operation, manifold vacuum draws the diaphragm back against spring pressure. The diaphragm pintle is withdrawn from the valve and the spring-loaded ball seats to close off the inlet channel.

16 Under acceleration and wide-open throttle operation, the vacuum in the manifold is depleted. The diaphragm returns under spring pressure and the power diaphragm pintle pushes the ball to open the inlet valve. Fuel then flows through the valve into the enrichment chamber. From here it passes through a calibrated jet into a fuel channel leading to the primary main well. The fuel level rises in the well and the fuel mixture is enriched.

Full-load enrichment (some variations)

17 At full-load and high engine speeds, the velocity of air creates a depression sufficient to raise fuel from the float chamber into a channel. The fuel then passes through a calibrated bushing to the upper section of the air intake. Here it is mixed with a small amount of air from a calibrated air bleed and the emulsified mixture is then discharged into the airstream from the full-load enrichment nozzle.

Manual choke operation

18 The manual choke is operated by a dash-mounted cable control. When the cable is pulled, it operates a lever that pulls the choke flap closed across the air intake. Fast idle is achieved with the aid of a curved cam attached to the choke operating lever. An adjustable screw, attached to the throttle lever and butting against the cam, is used to vary the fast idle speed.

Solex SEIA carburettor - idle bypass version

1. Fuel inlet connection
2. Fuel filter
3. Float pin
4. Float
5. Needle valve
6. Idle jet
7. Idle jet - when idle cut-off valve fitted
8. Idle cut-off valve
9. Bypass idle speed screw
10. Idle mixture control screw
11. Accelerator pump diaphragm
12. Accelerator pump valve
13. Pump injector
14. Bypass enrichment jet
17. Air corrector jet
18. Main jet
20. Upper body
21. Tamperproof cap
22. Float chamber gasket
23. Main body
24. Insulator block
25. Part-load enrichment diaphragm
28. Part-load enrichment jet
29. Choke flap
35. Fast idle adjustment screw
38. Throttle body
39. Throttle stop screw
40. Vent valve

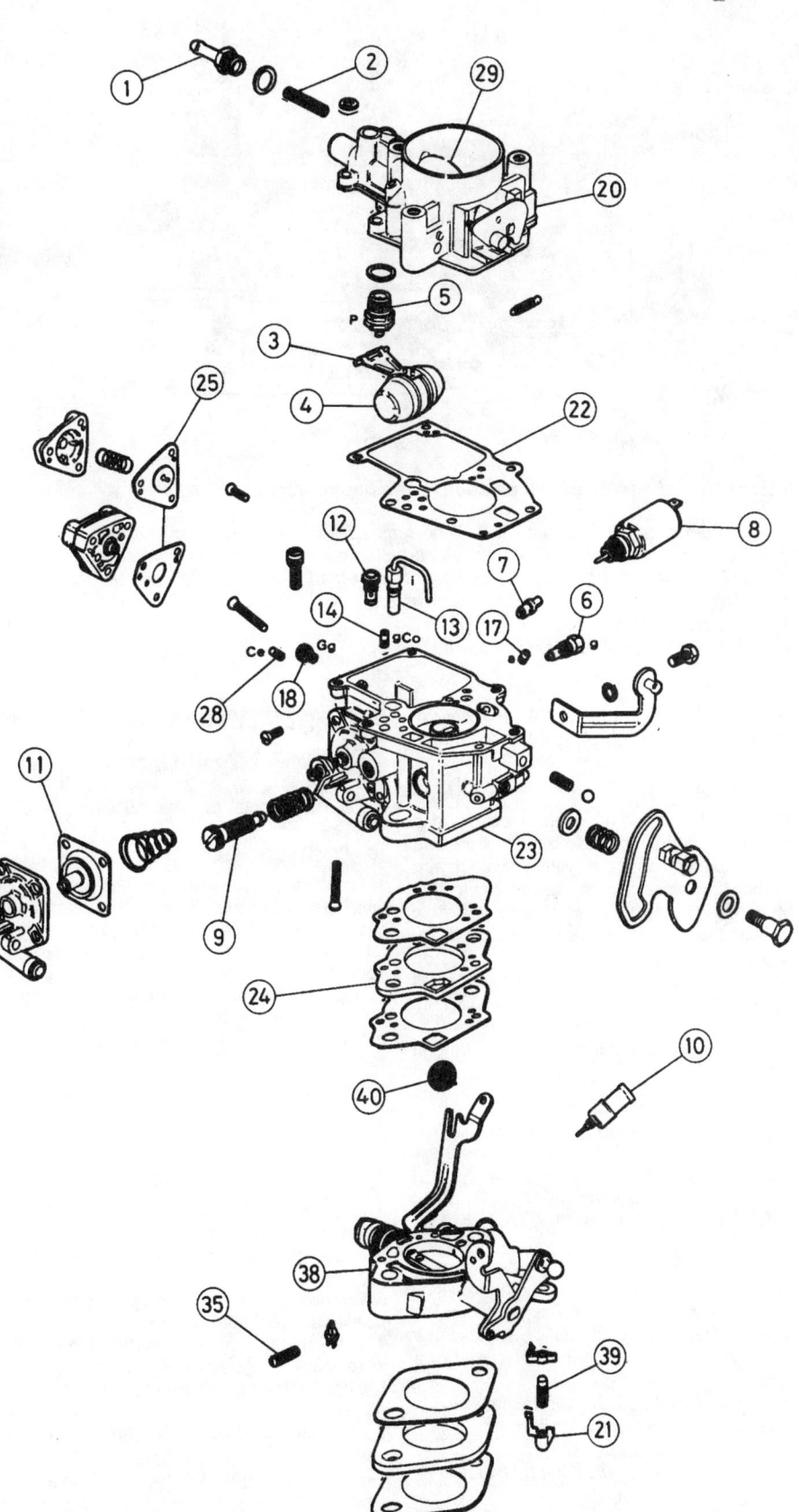

Chapter G4

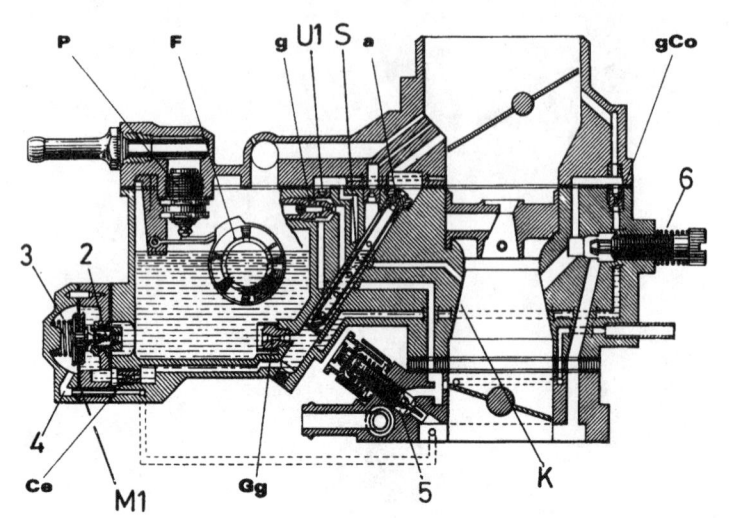

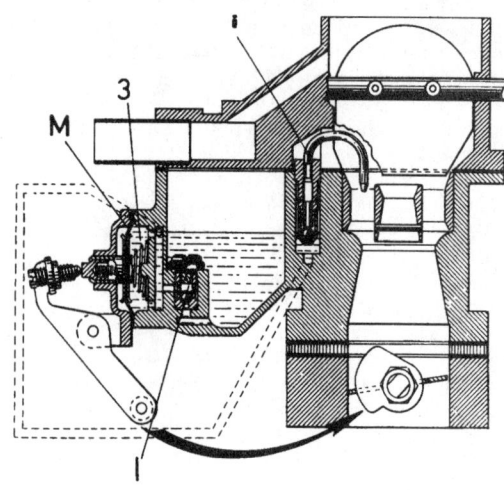

Internal fuel channels and air passages - idle bypass version

1 Accelerator pump brass inlet valve
2 Part-load enrichment valve
3 Spring
4 Vacuum channel
5 Idle mixture control screw
6 Bypass idle speed screw
a Air corrector jet
Ce Fuel jet - part-load enrichment
F Float
g Idle fuel jet
gCo Bypass fuel jet
Gg Main jet
i Accelerator pump injector
K Venturi
M Accelerator pump diaphragm
M1 Part-load enrichment diaphragm
P Needle valve
S Emulsion tube
U1 Idle air bleed

19 During engine warm-up, the cable control should be progressively pushed home until the choke flap is fully open.

Choke pull-down

20 Once the engine has fired, the choke flap must open slightly to weaken the mixture and avoid flooding. This is achieved by two different methods, depending on the version of the SEIA fitted. On the first type, an increase in airflow through the air intake partially opens the choke flap against the action of a spring. A stop ensures that the choke is only opened a small amount. On the second type, manifold vacuum is used to actuate a diaphragm. A linkage attached to the diaphragm will then pull upon the choke flap.

2 Identification

1 The Solex identification code is stamped on a metallic tag attached to the carburettor cover by an upper body fixing screw. This tag quotes the Solex part number and the vehicle manufacturer part number. It also identifies the carburettor type.
2 Later carburettors may have this information stamped upon the carburettor body:
   13126 Solex part number
   795 Vehicle manufacturer part number
   32 SEIA Carburettor type
3 Where the tag is missing, refer to Part B for other ways of identifying the carburettor.

3 General servicing

Introduction

1 Read this Chapter in conjunction with Part B which describes some of the operations in more detail. It is assumed that the carburettor is removed for this service. However, many of the operations can be tackled with the carburettor in place. Where this is undertaken, first remove the carburettor upper body and soak the fuel out of the float chamber using a clean tissue or soft cloth.

Dismantling and checking

2 Remove the carburettor from the engine (see Part B).
3 Check the carburettor visually for damage and wear.
4 Remove the five screws and detach the carburettor upper body.
5 Inspect the float chamber for corrosion and calcium build-up.
6 Tap out the float pin and remove the float, needle valve and float chamber gasket.
7 Check that the anti-vibration ball is free in the valve end.
8 Check the needle valve tip for wear and ridges.
9 The float should be checked for damage and ingress of petrol.
10 Renew the float pin if it shows signs of wear.
11 Use a straight-edge to check for distorted flanges on all facing surfaces.
12 Unscrew the fuel inlet tube and inspect the fuel filter. Clean the filter housing of debris and dirt, then renew the filter if necessary.
13 Remove the mixture screw and idle bypass screw (where fitted) and inspect the tips for damage or ridges.
14 The accelerator pump injector is a push fit in the body. Carefully prise it from its location and test it by shaking. No noise from the outlet ball would indicate that the valve is seized.
15 Unscrew the accelerator pump's brass inlet valve from the float chamber and test it by shaking. No noise would indicate that the valve is seized.
16 Remove the four screws and detach the accelerator pump cover, diaphragm and spring. Check the diaphragm for fatigue and damage.
17 Unscrew the idle jet from the main body.
18 Remove the three screws and detach the power valve housing cover, spring and diaphragm from the body. Check the diaphragm for damage.
19 Unscrew the brass power valve from the body. The ball in the valve should seal the outlet. Depress and release the ball with a small screwdriver and it should move smoothly in and out.
20 Unscrew and remove the small power jet from inside the power valve housing. Check that the channel into the emulsion tube well is clear.
21 Remove the main jet through the power valve location hole.
22 Check that the main channel from the float chamber into the emulsion tube well is clear.
23 Check the jet calibration against that specified. It is possible that the wrong size jets may have been fitted during the last overhaul. The combined air corrector and emulsion tube are not removable.

Solex 32 & 35 SEIA carburettor

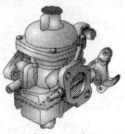

24 Remove the two screws and separate the carburettor main body and throttle body assemblies. The throttle body can be renewed separately if the spindles or throttle bores are worn. Use a straight-edge to check for distorted flanges on the facing surfaces. Do not disturb the adjustment of the basic throttle angle unless absolutely necessary.
25 Inspect the choke pull-down spindle, mechanism and levers for stickiness and wear.
26 Remove the screws and detach the choke pull-down cover, spring and diaphragm from the housing (where fitted). Check the diaphragm for fatigue.

Preparation for reassembly

27 Clean the jets, carburettor body assemblies, float chamber and internal channels. An air line may be used to clear the internal channels once the carburettor is fully dismantled. Note that if high-pressure air is directed into the channels and passages with the diaphragms still in place, diaphragm damage may result. Spraying carburettor cleaner into all the channels and passages in the carburettor body will often clear them of gum and dirt.
28 During reassembly, a complete set of new gaskets should be fitted. Also renew the needle valve, float pin and all diaphragms.
29 Inspect and renew (where necessary) the mixture screw, main jet, idle jet and the accelerator pump inlet valve and injector. Renew worn linkages, screws, springs, and other parts where necessary.
30 Ensure that all jets are firmly locked into their original positions (but do not over-tighten). A loose jet can cause a rich (or even lean) running condition.
31 Clean all mating surfaces and flanges of old gasket material and reassemble with new gaskets.
32 Ensure that housings are positioned with their air and fuel routes correctly aligned.

Reassembly

33 Refit the choke pull-down diaphragm and spindle assembly (where used) to the choke housing. Refit the spring and cover, then secure with the screws.
34 Assemble the main and throttle bodies with a new gasket block and secure with the two screws.
35 Where the basic throttle position has been disturbed and a throttle setting gauge is available, use it to set the throttle angle. Otherwise, temporarily adjust the throttle plate so that it is open just enough to prevent its seizure in the throttle body. An adjustment method with the engine running is detailed in Section 4.
36 Screw the main jet into its original position.
37 Refit the idle jet into the main body and lock it firmly into position.
38 Refit the power jet and valve assembly into their original positions.
39 Refit the power diaphragm, spring and cover assembly, then secure with the three screws.
40 Refit the accelerator pump spring, diaphragm and cover assembly, then secure with the four screws.
41 Screw the accelerator pump inlet valve into the float chamber after renewing the small seal on the valve body.
42 Refit the accelerator pump injector after renewing the small seal on the injector body.
43 Refit the idle mixture screw. Turn the screw in gently until it just seats. From this position, unscrew it three full turns. This will provide a basic setting to allow the engine to be started.
44 Refit the idle bypass screw (where used). Obtain a basic setting in the same way as described for the mixture screw above.
45 Clean or renew the fuel filter and refit the fuel inlet tube.
46 Fit the new needle valve assembly using a new sealing washer. Ensure that it is firmly locked into position (but do not over-tighten). Refit the float and secure with the float pin.
47 Adjust the float level with reference to Section 4.
48 Locate a new float chamber gasket in position on the upper body.
49 Refit the upper body to the main body and secure with the five screws.
50 Inspect the choke pull-down spindle, linkage and operating mechanism for stickiness and wear.
51 Ensure that the choke flap and linkage move smoothly and progressively.
52 Adjust the choke fast idle and pull-down with reference to Section 4.
53 Refit the carburettor to the engine.
54 Always adjust the carburettor idle speed and mixture after any work has been carried out on the carburettor, preferably with the aid of a CO meter.

4 Service adjustments

Adjustment pre-conditions

1 Refer to Part B for general advice on the pre-conditions for correct adjustment of this carburettor.

Idle speed and mixture (CO)

Standard idle system

2 Run the engine at 3000 rpm for 30 seconds to clear the manifold of fuel vapours, then allow the engine to idle.
3 Use the idle speed screw to set the specified idle speed.
4 Check the CO level. If not as specified, remove the tamperproof plug and adjust the idle mixture screw to obtain the correct level. Turning the screw clockwise (inwards) will reduce the CO level. Turning the screw anti-clockwise (outwards) will increase the CO level. Refer to Part B for a method of setting the idle mixture without the aid of a CO meter.
5 Repeat paragraphs 3 and 4 until both adjustments are correct.
6 Clear the manifold every 30 seconds during the setting operation by running the engine at 3000 rpm for 30 seconds.
7 Increase the speed to 2000 rpm and note the CO reading. The cruise reading should be less than half the idle CO reading.
8 Fit a new tamperproof plug to the mixture screw on completion.

Bypass idle system

9 Run the engine at 3000 rpm for 30 seconds to clear the manifold of fuel vapours, then allow the engine to idle.
10 Use the idle bypass screw to set the specified idle speed *(see illustration)*.
11 Check the CO level. If incorrect, remove the tamperproof plug and adjust the idle mixture screw to obtain the correct level. Turning the screw clockwise (inwards) will reduce the CO level. Turning the screw anti-clockwise (outwards) will increase the CO level.
12 Repeat paragraphs 10 and 11 until both adjustments are correct.
13 Fit a new tamperproof plug to the mixture screw on completion.

Basic throttle position

14 If the idle speed and CO cannot be set correctly, it is possible that the basic throttle position is incorrect. The manufacturer's recommended method is to remove the carburettor and use a Renault, Solex or Pierburg throttle setting gauge to accurately set the throttle position.
15 However, an alternative method can be used to set the throttle plate. Please note that this is not the manufacturer's recommended method but will nevertheless result in an accurate and stable idle speed and CO level.
16 With the engine idling, screw in the idle bypass screw until it is fully seated. The idle speed should drop to approximately two-thirds of the specified idle speed figure. For example, if the idle speed is specified as 900 rpm, the speed should drop to 600 rpm.
17 Adjust the throttle stop screw until 600 rpm is obtained.
18 Unscrew the bypass screw until 900 rpm is once again attained.
19 Reset the CO to the correct level.
20 If the CO needs a large adjustment at this stage, repeat paragraphs 16 to 19. Once the proper level of CO is obtained at the specified idle speed, the carburettor is properly adjusted.
21 Note that the rpm figures used in the above example are based on a hypothetical idle speed of 900 rpm. Substitute the correct figures for the carburettor being adjusted (see Specifications).

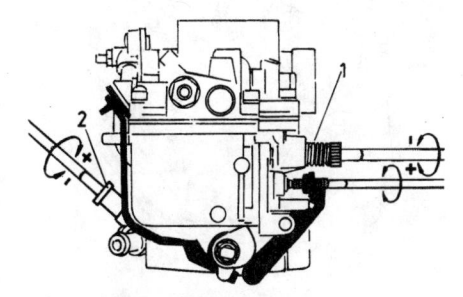

Idle adjustment screw location
1 Bypass idle speed screw
2 Idle mixture control screw

Chapter G4

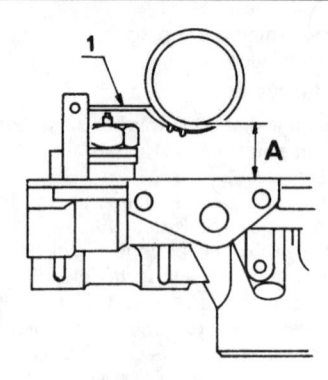

Float level adjustment
A Float level
1 Float pivot arm

Float level

22 Invert the carburettor upper body so that the float faces upwards and the needle valve is depressed.
23 Measure the distance between the upper body (without its gasket) and the lower face of the plastic float. Refer to Specifications for the correct float level *(see illustration)*.
24 Adjust as necessary by bending the float pivot arm. Otherwise, renew the float.

Accelerator pump travel

25 Invert the carburettor and bring the roller on the accelerator pump lever just into contact with the pump cam *(see illustration)*.
26 In this position, turn in the adjustment screw until it contacts the pump plunger then turn the screw in a further half-to-one turn.

Choke adjustments

Fast idle

27 The carburettor must be removed from the

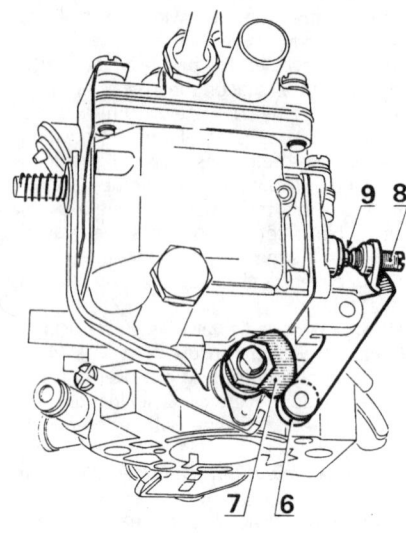

Accelerator pump travel
6 Pump roller   8 Adjustment screw
7 Pump cam   9 Pump plunger

engine in order to make the following fast idle adjustment. Refer to Part B for a method of setting the fast idle speed without removing the carburettor.
28 Invert the carburettor then pull the choke operating lever to fully close the choke flap *(see illustration)*. The fast idle screw will butt against the fast idle cam and force open the throttle plate to leave a small clearance.
29 Use the shank of a twist drill to measure the clearance between the wall of the throttle bore and the throttle plate. Refer to Specifications for the required drill size. The clearance may be measured from either side of the throttle plate, since the gap on each side should be approximately equal. If not, the throttle plate may be centralised after loosening the throttle plate screws. Retighten the screws on completion.
30 Adjust the gap as necessary by turning the fast idle adjustment screw in the appropriate direction.
31 Alternatively, the fast idle throttle angle may be set by means of a Solex or Pierburg throttle angle gauge. Refer to Specifications for the appropriate throttle angle.

Choke pull-down (vacuum pull-down carburettor)

32 Pull the choke operating lever to fully close the choke flap.
33 Use a small screwdriver to pull the diaphragm operating rod up to its stop. At the same time, use the shank of a twist drill to measure the gap between the upper section of the choke flap and the air intake. Refer to Specifications for the required drill size *(see illustration)*.
34 Remove the plug in the diaphragm cover and adjust as necessary by turning the adjustment screw in the appropriate direction. Renew the plug when adjustment is complete.

Vent valve

35 Measure the clearance X between the float chamber cover and the valve *(see illustration)*.
36 Adjust as necessary by bending the control arm in the appropriate direction.

5 Fault diagnosis

Refer to Part D for diagnosis of general carburettor faults.

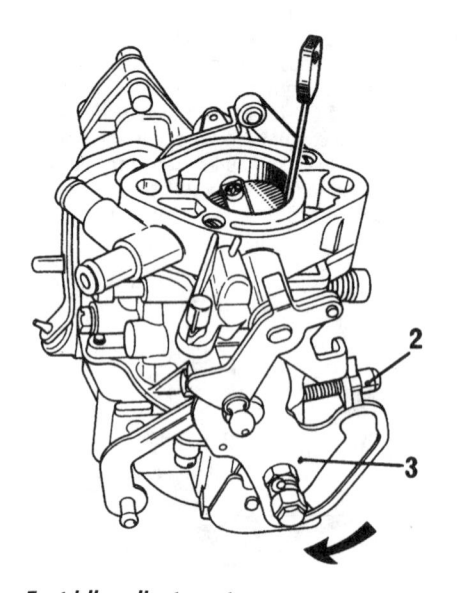

Fast idle adjustment
2 Fast idle adjustment screw
3 Choke operating lever

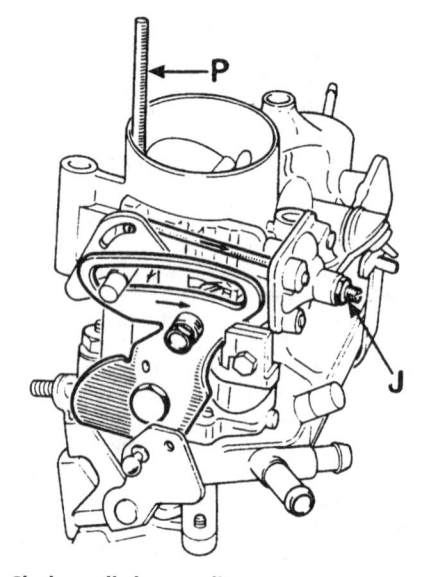

Choke pull-down adjustment
J Pull-down adjustment screw
P Twist drill

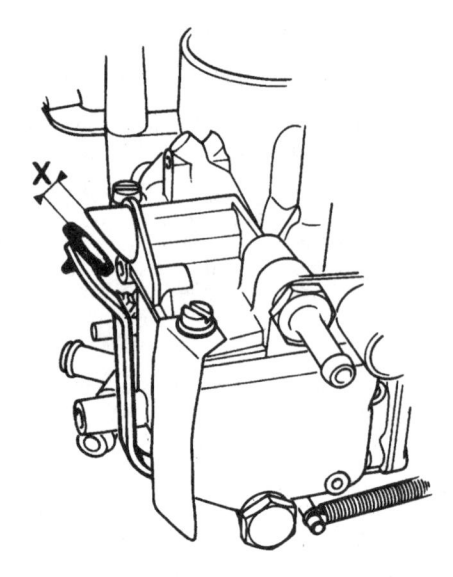

Vent valve adjustment
X Vent valve clearance

G4•8

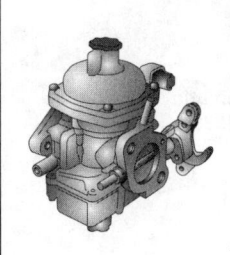

Part G Chapter 5
Solex 32/34 & 34/34 Z1 carburettor

G5

Contents

Component testing	5	Identification	2
Fault diagnosis	6	Principles of operation	1
General servicing	3	Service adjustments	4

Specifications

Manufacturer	Citroën		Citroën		Citroën	
Model	BX 16		BX 16		BX 16	
Year	1983 to 1984		1984 to 1988		1988 to 1991	
Engine code	171B (XU5S)		171C (XU5S)		B2C (XU52C)	
Capacity (cm³)/no. of cyls	1580/4		1580/4		1580/4	
Oil temperature (°C)	80		80		80	
Carb. ident. (Solex)	32/34 Z1 13279		32/34 Z1 13543		32/34 Z1 13928	
Carb. ident. (vehicle)	CIT319		385/7		464	
Idle speed (rpm)	650 + 50		650 ± 50		800 ± 50	
CO @ idle (% vol.)	0.8 to 1.5		1.5 ± 0.5		0.8 to 1.5	
Stage (venturi)	**1**	**2**	**1**	**2**	**1**	**2**
Venturi diameter (K)	24	26	24	26	-	
Idle jet (g)	42	-	41	-	-	
Main jet (Gg)	140 ± 5	120 ± 5	140	120	112.5	125
Air correction jet (a)	200	155	190	155	-	
Emulsion tube (s)	23	18	-	-	-	
Accelerator pump jet (i)	40	35	40	35	-	
Idle position (PRN)	11°	9°	11°	9°	11°	9°
Float level (mm)	33 ± 1		33 ± 1		33 ± 1	
Needle valve (mm) (P)	1.8		1.8		-	
Choke fast idle gap (mm)	0.45 (20°C)		0.45 (20°C)		0.45 (20°C)	
Fast idle position (OP)	-		17°		-	
Choke pull-down (mm) (OVAD)	6.0 ± 0.5 (20°C)		6 ± 0.5 (20°C)		6 ± 0.5 (20°C)	

Chapter G5

Manufacturer	Citroën		Citroën		Citroën	
Model	BX 19 GT		BX 19 TRS		BX 19 4x4	
Year	1984 to 1986		1986 to 1990		1990 to 1992	
Engine code	159A (XU9S)		D2A (159A) XU92C		D2E (XU92C)	
Capacity (cm³)/no. of cyls	1905/4		1905/4		1905/4	
Oil temperature (°C)	80		80		80	
Carb. ident. (Solex)	34/34 Z1 13485		34/34 Z1 13494		34/34 Z1	
Carb. ident. (vehicle)	PEU381		427		PSA501	
Idle speed (rpm)	650 + 100		675 ± 25		750 ± 50	
Fast idle speed (rpm)	3250		-		1900	
CO @ idle (% vol.)	1.5 ± 0.5		1.5 ± 0.5		0.8 to 1.5	
Stage (venturi)	1	2	1	2	1	2
Venturi diameter (K)	25	27	25	27	26	27
Idle jet (g)	42 ± 10	90	44 ± 3	90 ± 10	45 ± 3	90 ± 10
Main jet (Gg)	115 ± 5	122.5 ± 5	117 ± 5	115 ± 5	115 ± 5	125 ± 5
Air correction jet (a)	145 ± 20	160 ± 20	145 ± 20	160 ± 20	125 ± 20	140 ± 30
Emulsion tube (s)	27	ZC	18	ZC	-	
Accelerator pump jet (i)	40 ± 20	55 ± 20	40	55 ± 20	40	40
Idle position (PRN)	11°	9°	11°	9°	11°	9°
Float level (mm)	33 ± 1		33 ± 1		33 ± 1	
Needle valve (mm) (P)	1.8		1.8		1.8	
Fast idle position (OP)	0.45 (20°C)		-		-	
Fast idle position (OPF)	-		15°30 (20°C)		-	
Choke pull-down (mm) (OVAD)	6 ± 0.5 (20°C)		6 ± 0.5 (20°C)		3.8	
Manufacturer	Citroën		Peugeot		Peugeot	
Model	XM 2.0		305 GT		305 Automatic	
Year	1989 to 1992		1983 to 1988		1983 to 1988	
Engine code	R2A (XU102C) 15/04		XU5S (171C) (66kW)		XU5S (171C) (66kW)	
Capacity (cm³)/no. of cyls	1998/4		1580/4		1580/4	
Oil temperature (°C)	80		80		80	
Transmission	-		MT		AT	
Carb. ident. (Solex)	34/34 Z1		32/34 Z1 13425		32/34 Z1 13425	
Carb. ident. (vehicle)	448		385/6		385/6	
Idle speed (rpm)	750 ± 50		700 ± 50		850 ± 50	
CO @ idle (% vol.)	0.8 to 1.5		1.5 ± 0.5		1.5 ± 0.5	
Stage (venturi)	1	2	1	2	1	2
Venturi diameter (K)	26	27	24	26	24	26
Idle jet (g)	47	90	42	-	42	-
Main jet (Gg)	118 ± 5	120 ± 5	140	120	140	120
Air correction jet (a)	155	160	190	155	190	155
Emulsion tube (s)	32	ZC	-			
Accelerator pump jet (i)	45	40	40	35	40	35
Idle position (PRN)	11°	9°	11°	9°	11°	9°
Float level (mm)	33 ± 1		33 ± 1		33 ± 1	
Needle valve (mm) (P)	1.8		1.8		1.8	
Fast idle position (OP)	-		17°		17°	
Choke pull-down (mm) (OVAD)	-		6.0 ± 0.5 (20°C)		6.0 ± 0.5 (20°C)	
Manufacturer	Peugeot		Peugeot		Peugeot	
Model	305 (1905 cc)		305 (1905 cc)		309 1.6	
Year	1984 to 1987		1987 to 1988		1988 to 1989	
Engine code	XU9S (159A)		XU92C (D2A)		XU52C (B2A) (68kW)	
Capacity (cm³)/no. of cyls	1905/4		1905/4		1580/4	
Oil temperature (°C)	80		80		80	
Carb. ident. (Solex)	34/34 Z1 13485		34/34 Z1		34/34 Z1	
Carb. ident. (vehicle)	381		427/428		473/485	
Idle speed (rpm)	675 ± 75		675 ± 75		800 ± 50	
Fast idle speed (rpm)	-		3250		2300	
CO @ idle (% vol.)	1.5 ± 0.5		1.5 ± 0.5		0.8 to 1.5	
Stage (venturi)	1	2	1	2	1	2
Venturi diameter (K)	25	27	25	27	25	27
Idle jet (g)	42 ± 10	90	44 ± 3	-	46 ± 3	50 ± 10
Main jet (Gg)	115	122.5	117.5 ± 5	115 ± 5	112 ± 5	130 ± 5
Air correction jet (a)	145 ± 20	160 ± 20	145 ± 20	160 ± 20	145 ± 20	160 ± 20
Emulsion tube (s)	27	ZC	18	ZC	18	ZC
Accelerator pump jet (i)	40 ± 20	55 ± 20	40	55	40	35
Idle position (PRN)	-	11°	9°	11°	9°	
Float level (mm)	33 ± 1		33 ± 1		33 ± 1	
Needle valve (mm) (P)	1.8		1.8		1.8	
Choke fast idle gap (mm)	0.45 (20°C)		-		-	
Fast idle position (OP)	-		-		15°30'	
Choke pull-down (mm) (OVAD)	6.0 ± 0.5 (20°C)		5.5 ± 0.5		6 ± 0.5 (20°C)	

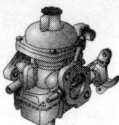

Solex 32/34 & 34/34 Z1 carburettor

Manufacturer	Peugeot		Peugeot		Peugeot	
Model	309 1.6		405 1.6		405 1.9 & 4x4	
Year	1989 to 1992		1988 to 1992		1988 to 1992	
Engine code	XU52C (B2B) (68kW)		XU52C (B2A) (68kW)		XU92C (D2D) (81kW)	
Capacity (cm³)/no. of cyls	1580/4		1580/4		1905/4	
Oil temperature (°C)	80		80		80	
Carb. ident. (Solex)	34/34 Z1		34/34 Z1		34/34 Z1	
Carb. ident. (vehicle)	473/485		446/460		447/462/493	
Idle speed (rpm)	800 ± 50		750 ± 100		750 ± 100	
Fast idle speed (rpm)	2300		2300		2200	
CO @ idle (% vol.)	0.8 to 1.5		0.8 to 1.5		0.8 to 1.5	
Stage (venturi)	1	2	1	2	1	2
Venturi diameter (K)	25	27	25	27	26	27
Idle jet (g)	44 ± 3	70 ± 10	45 ± 3	50 ± 10	44 ± 3	90 ± 10
Main jet (Gg)	112 ± 5	112 ± 5	112.5	132.5	117 ± 5	120 ± 5
Air correction jet (a)	145 ± 20	140 ± 20	145 ± 20	140 ± 20	150 ± 20	140 ± 20
Emulsion tube (s)	18	ZC	18	ZC	BZ	ZC
Accelerator pump jet (i)	40	35	35	40	40	40
Idle position (PRN)	11°	9°	11°	9°	11°	9°
Float level (mm)	33 ± 1		33 ± 1		33 ± 1	
Needle valve (mm) (P)	1.8		1.8		1.8	
Choke pull-down (mm) (OVAD)	6 ± 0.5 (20°C)		6.0 (20°C)		6.0 (20°C)	
Manufacturer	Peugeot		Peugeot		Peugeot	
Model	405 1.9 & 4x4		405 1.9		405 1.9 Auto	
Year	1988 to 1992		1990 to 1992		1990 to 1992	
Engine code	XU92C (D2D) (81kW)		XU92C (D2H) (80kW)		XU92C (D2H) (80kW)	
Capacity (cm³)/no. of cyls	1905/4		1905/4		1905/4	
Oil temperature (°C)	80		80		80	
Transmission	AT		MT		AT	
Carb. ident. (Solex)	34/34 Z1		34/34 Z1		34/34 Z1	
Carb. ident. (vehicle)	455/463		547/548		549	
Idle speed (rpm)	750 ± 100		750 ± 100		750 ± 50	
Fast idle speed (rpm)	2400		2200		2200	
CO @ idle (% vol.)	0.8 to 1.5		0.8 to 1.5		0.8 to 1.5	
Stage (venturi)	1	2	1	2	1	2
Venturi diameter (K)	26	27	26	27	26	27
Idle jet (g)	44 ± 3	90 ± 10	45	110	44	110
Main jet (Gg)	120 ± 5	120 ± 5	115	122	115	122
Air correction jet (a)	150 ± 20	140 ± 20	140	160	140	160
Emulsion tube (s)	BZ	ZC	BZ	ZC	3Z	ZC
Accelerator pump jet (i)	40	40	45	40	45	40
Idle position (PRN)	11°	9°	11°	9°	11°	9°
Float level (mm)	33 ± 1		33 ± 1		33 ± 1	
Needle valve (mm) (P)	1.8		1.8		1.8	
Choke pull-down (mm) (OVAD)	6.0 (20°C)		5.7		5.7	
Manufacturer	Peugeot		Peugeot		Peugeot	
Model	505 2.0		505 2.0		605 2.0	
Year	1985 to 1992		1985 to 1992		1990 to 1992	
Engine code	XN1A (106E) (72kW)		XN1A (106E) (72kW)		XU102C (R2A) (84kW)	
Capacity (cm³)/no. of cyls	1971/4		1971/4		1998/4	
Oil temperature (°C)	90		90		80	
Transmission	MT		AT		-	
Carb. ident. (Solex)	34/34 Z1 13490		34/34 Z1 13523		34/34 Z1	
Carb. ident. (vehicle)	394/3		396/3		448/480	
Idle speed (rpm)	900 ± 50		900 ± 50		750 ± 100	
Fast idle speed (rpm)	-		-		1900	
CO @ idle (% vol.)	1.5 ± 0.5		1.5 ± 0.5		0.8 to 1.5	
Stage (venturi)	1	2	1	2	1	2
Venturi diameter (K)	25	27	25	27	26	27
Idle jet (g)	41	-	41	-	47	90
Main jet (Gg)	117	130	117	130	120	120
Air correction jet (a)	140	130	140	130	155	160
Emulsion tube (s)	-		-		3Z	ZC
Accelerator pump jet (i)	40	55	40	55	45	40
Idle position (PRN)	11°	9°	11°	9°	11°	9°
Choke pull-down (mm) (OVAD)	2.0	5.0	2.0	5.0	3.8	
Float level (mm)	33 ± 1		33 ± 1		33 ± 1	
Needle valve (mm) (P)	1.8		1.8		1.8	
Fast idle position (OPF)	15°50'		15°50'		-	

Chapter G5

Solex Z1 carburettor

1. Upper body
2. Fuel inlet filter
3. Float pin
4. Float
5. Needle valve
6. Idle jet (primary)
7. Float chamber vent valve
10. Idle mixture control screw
11. Accelerator pump diaphragm
13. Pump injector
15. O-ring
16. Emulsion tube and air corrector - primary venturi
17. Emulsion tube and air corrector - secondary venturi
18. Main jet - primary venturi
19. Main jet - secondary venturi
21. Tamperproof cap
22. Float chamber gasket
23. Main body
24. Throttle body heater flange - coolant water type
27. Choke housing
28. Thermostatic capsule
29. Choke coolant housing
30. Choke pull-down diaphragm

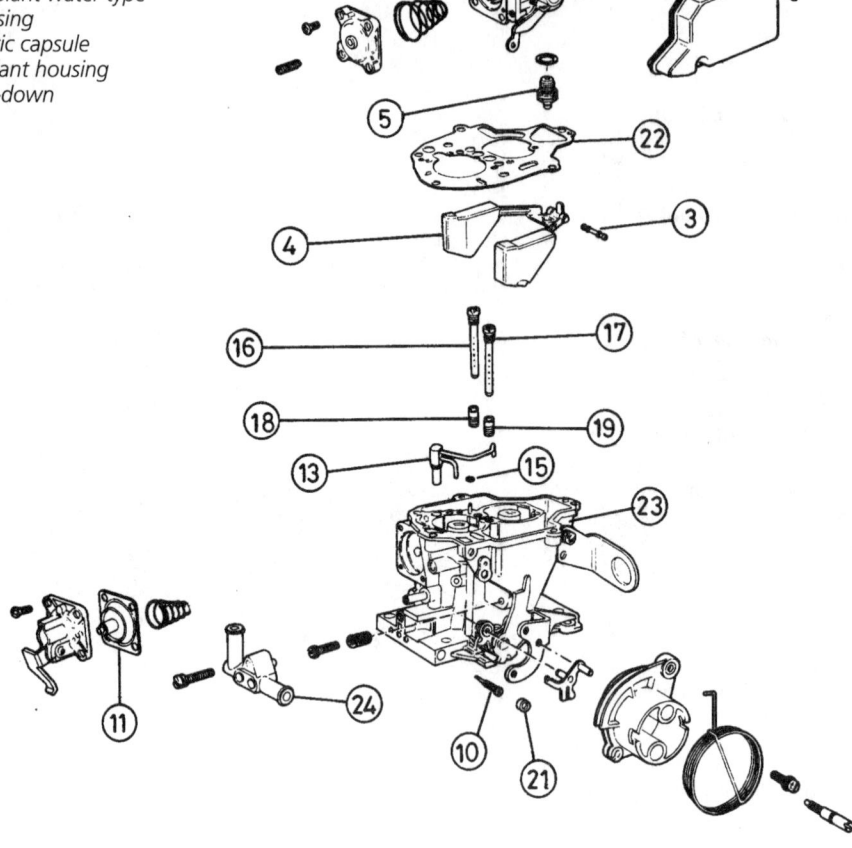

1 Principles of operation

Introduction

1 The following technical description of the Solex Z1 carburettor should be read in conjunction with the more detailed description of carburettor principles in Part A.
2 The Z1 carburettor is sometimes referred to as a CISAC carburettor.

Construction

3 The Solex Z1 carburettor is a downdraught progressive twin venturi instrument (see illustration). The venturis are arranged so that the secondary throttle plate will not start to open until the primary throttle valve is about two-thirds open. The choke system is automatic in operation, controlled by a thermostatic capsule which is heated by the engine coolant.
4 The throttle shafts are made of steel, while the throttle plates and all the emulsion tubes and jets are manufactured from brass. The internal fuel channels and air passages are drilled and sealed with lead plugs where necessary.
5 On some variations, a heating flange is bolted to the carburettor base through which hot engine coolant is piped. The purpose of the flange is to improve atomisation of the air/fuel mixture during the warm-up period. Some versions use a throttle body heater to prevent carburettor icing. The heater is normally operational with the ignition on and functions on the PTC (positive temperature coefficient) principle. As the temperature rises, the heater resistance also rises.

Fuel control

6 Fuel flows into the carburettor through a fine mesh filter. The fuel level in the float chamber is controlled by a needle valve and plastic float assembly. An anti-vibration ball is incorporated into the needle valve design (see illustration).
7 The float chamber utilises a dual-venting arrangement, operated by an electrical vent valve. Venting is to atmosphere with the engine shut down but once the ignition is switched on, the valve closes off the atmospheric vent. This allows the float chamber to vent into the upper air intake which is on the clean-air side of the air filter.
8 A calibrated fuel return system is provided on some variations to ensure that relatively cool fuel is supplied to the carburettor.

Idle, slow running and progression

9 Fuel, sourced from the main well, passes into the idle channel through a metered idle jet. Here it is mixed with a small amount of air from a calibrated air bleed and the resulting emulsion is drawn through a channel to be discharged from the idle orifice under the primary throttle plate. A tapered mixture screw is used to vary the outlet and this ensures fine control of the idle mixture.
10 A progression slot provides enrichment as it is uncovered by the opening throttle during initial acceleration.
11 The idle speed is set by an adjustable screw. The adjustable mixture screw is tamper proofed at production level, in accordance with emission regulations.

Idle cut-off valve (some variations)

12 An idle cut-off valve is used to prevent run-on when the engine is shut down. It utilises a 12-volt solenoid plunger to block the idle jet when the ignition is switched off.

Accelerator pump

13 The Solex Z1 accelerator pump is controlled

Solex 32/34 & 34/34 Z1 carburettor

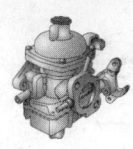

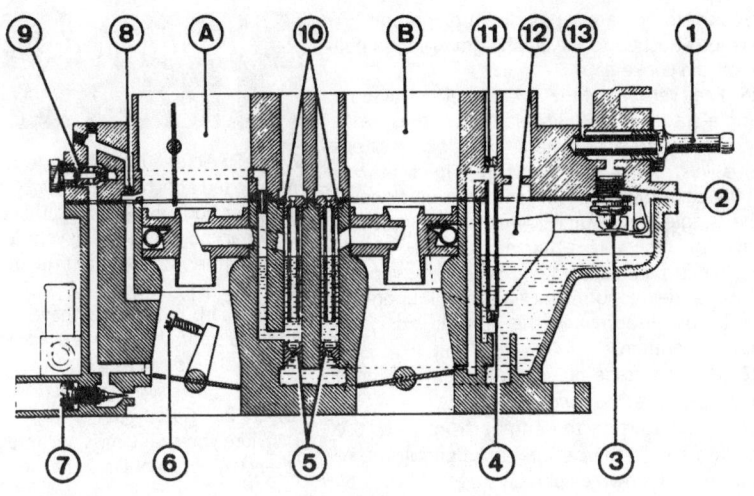

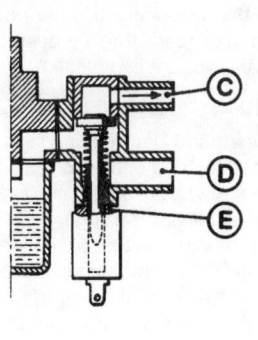

Main and idle circuits

1. Fuel inlet connection
2. Float needle valve
3. Inner float tag
4. Progression fuel jet - secondary venturi
5. Main jets - primary and secondary venturi
6. Throttle stop screw
7. Idle mixture control screw
8. Idle air jet
9. Idle fuel jet
10. Combined air corrector jet with emulsion tube - primary and secondary venturis
11. Progression air jet - secondary venturi
12. Float
13. Fuel filter
A. Primary venturi
B. Secondary venturi
C. Float chamber vent - air filter
D. Float chamber vent - atmosphere
E. Electrical vent valve

by a diaphragm and is mechanically operated by a lever and cam attached to the primary throttle linkage. During acceleration, fuel is pumped through a ball valve located in the pump injector, where it is discharged into both primary and secondary venturis. The inlet ball valve is located in a channel from the float chamber. Excess fuel/air mixture is returned to the float chamber through a separate fuel channel *(see illustration)*.

Main circuit

14 The amount of fuel discharged into the airstream is controlled by a calibrated main jet. Fuel is drawn through the main jet, into the base of a vertical well which dips down into the fuel in the float chamber. An emulsion tube is placed in the well. The fuel is mixed with air, drawn in through the air corrector and through the holes in the emulsion tube. The resulting emulsified mixture is discharged from the main orifice through an auxiliary venturi.

Part-load enrichment (power valve)

15 Fuel flows from the float chamber into the enrichment chamber, through a fuel channel and a brass inlet valve. An air passage is taken from under the throttle plate to the cover of the chamber. At idle and during light-throttle operation, manifold vacuum draws the diaphragm back against spring pressure. The diaphragm pintle is withdrawn from the valve and the spring-loaded ball seats to close off the inlet channel.

16 Under acceleration and wide-open throttle operation, the vacuum in the manifold is depleted. The diaphragm returns under spring pressure and the power diaphragm pintle pushes the ball to open the inlet valve. Fuel then flows through the valve into the enrichment chamber. From here, it passes through a calibrated jet into a fuel channel leading to the primary main well. The fuel level rises in the well and the fuel mixture is enriched.

Secondary action

17 Once the primary throttle valve is about two-thirds open, the secondary throttle plate will begin to open. At full-throttle, the linkage is arranged so that both throttle plates will be fully open.

18 A progression circuit is used to prevent hesitation as the secondary throttle plate starts to open. An emulsified mixture is discharged into the secondary venturi, via a progression drilling, at the initial opening of the secondary throttle plate.

19 Once the secondary throttle plate has

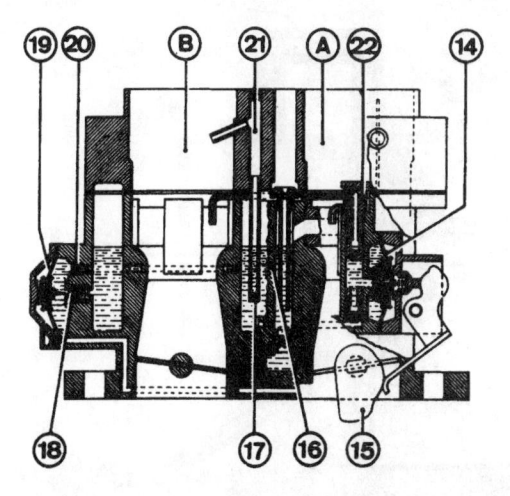

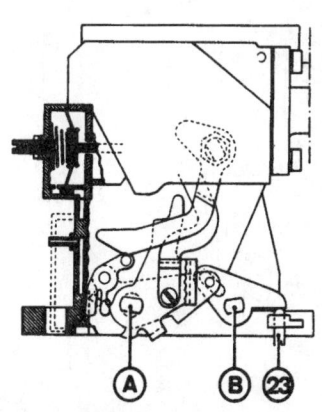

Accelerator pump, part and full-load enrichment circuits

14. Accelerator pump diaphragm
15. Accelerator pump cam
16. Fuel channel to main well - part-load enrichment
17. Fuel supply tube - full-load enrichment
18. Inlet ball valve - part-load enrichment
19. Diaphragm
20. Calibrated part-load enrichment jet
21. Full-load enrichment tube
22. Accelerator pump injectors
23. Throttle stop screw - secondary throttle plate
A. Primary venturi
B. Secondary venturi

G5•5

Chapter G5

opened, the action of the secondary main circuit is similar to the primary circuit.

20 When the choke is operating, a tag on the lever locks the secondary throttle operating linkage and secondary throttle operation on choke is thus avoided.

Full-load enrichment

21 At full-load and high engine speeds, the velocity of air creates a depression sufficient to raise fuel from the float chamber into a channel. The fuel then passes through a calibrated bushing to the upper section of the air intake. Here it is mixed with a small amount of air from a calibrated air bleed and the emulsified mixture is discharged into the airstream from the full-load enrichment nozzle.

Choke operation

22 The Z1 carburettor uses an automatic choke starting system. A thermostatic capsule is used to control a strangler choke flap arranged in the primary air intake. Heating of the capsule is by coolant from the engine cooling system.

23 Fast idle is achieved when a lever (with an adjustable screw) butts against the capsule and pushes upon the throttle valve mechanism. As the capsule is heated and the lever is released, the idle speed will progressively return to normal.

Choke pull-down

24 Once the engine has fired, the choke flap must open slightly to weaken the mixture and avoid flooding during idle and light-throttle operation. This is achieved by using manifold vacuum to actuate a pull-down diaphragm. A linkage attached to the diaphragm will then pull upon the choke flap.

25 Early versions of the Z1 carburettor utilised a single-stage pull-down unit, whereas later versions used a two-stage pull-down system (see illustration). Carburettors with the two-stage pull-down system (and later versions of the single-stage pull-down unit) employ a vacuum reservoir attached to the choke mechanism. As vacuum empties the reservoir, a stronger depression is formed to pull upon the choke diaphragm and this further aids pull-down operation.

26 The two-stage pull-down system functions as follows (see illustration).

27 When starting the engine from cold, the choke flap fills the carburettor upper air intake and the pull-down diaphragms are held back by spring pressure. Once the engine has started, vacuum will pull diaphragm M1 against stop rod P to move the choke flap control rod and complete the pull-down first stage.

28 As the engine continues to run, vacuum increases and passes through restriction C to empty reservoir K. In turn, diaphragm M2 is moved against the position of adjusting screw R. Diaphragm M1 will follow the movement of M2 to move the choke flap control rod and complete the pull-down second stage.

29 Vehicles with automatic transmission may employ an additional vacuum signal. This relays vacuum from the carburettor base, via a delay valve and restrictor, to further aid the emptying of the reservoir K.

2 Identification

1 The Solex identification code is stamped on a metallic tag attached to the carburettor cover by an upper body fixing screw. This tag quotes the Solex part number and the vehicle manufacturer part number. It also identifies the carburettor type.

2 Later carburettors may have this information stamped upon the carburettor body:
   F13 379   Solex part number
   CIT 391   Vehicle manufacturer part number
   32-34 Z1 Carburettor type

3 Where the tag is missing, refer to Part B for other ways of identifying the carburettor.

3 General servicing

Introduction

1 Read this Chapter in conjunction with Part B, which describes some of the operations in more detail. It is assumed that the carburettor is removed for this service. However, many of the operations can be tackled with the carburettor in place. Where this is undertaken, first remove the carburettor upper body and soak the fuel out of the float chamber using a clean tissue or soft cloth.

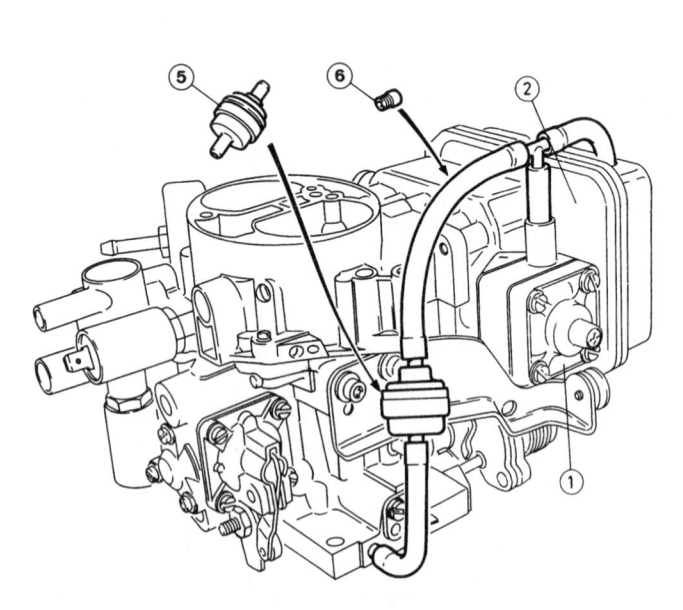

Choke two-stage pull-down components
1 Pull-down assembly
2 Reservoir (some variations)
5 Delay valve
6 Restrictor

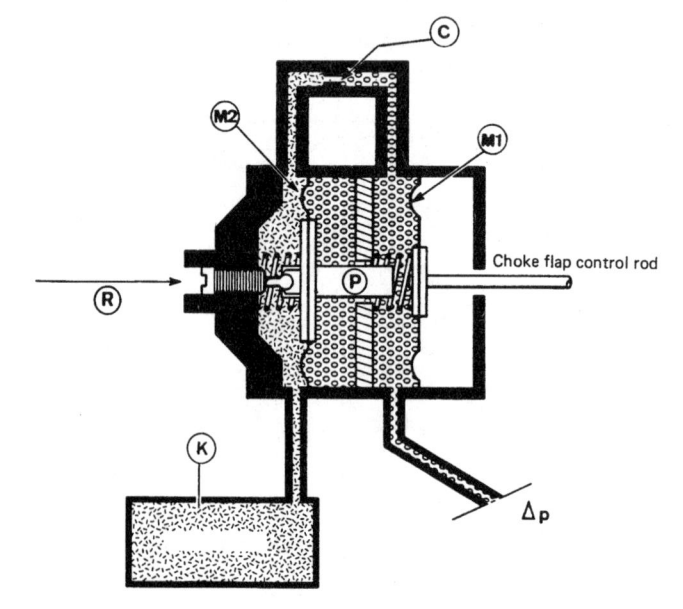

Choke two-stage pull-down operation
C Restrictor
K Reservoir
M1 Stage 1 diaphragm
M2 Stage 2 diaphragm
P Stop rod
p1 Inlet manifold vacuum
p2 Carburettor vacuum
R Adjustment screw

Solex 32/34 & 34/34 Z1 carburettor

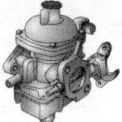

Dismantling and checking

2 Remove the carburettor from the engine (see Part B).
3 Check the carburettor visually for damage and wear.
4 Remove the idle cut-off valve assembly (where fitted) and clean it with carburettor cleaner. Test the plunger operation by connecting the valve to the battery or other voltage supply (or use the valve supply wire in the engine compartment). Touch the valve body to earth with the ignition on. Repeat this several times and ensure that the plunger tip advances and retracts cleanly. Renew the valve if the action is faulty or if cleaning does not improve its operation.
5 Detach the throttle spring then remove the two screws and take off the throttle drum.
6 Remove the pin and spring assembly that holds the fast idle lever to the throttle lever. Note the arrangement of the throttle and fast idle levers for ease of reassembly later.
7 Remove the five screws and detach the carburettor upper body. Remove and inspect the O-ring.
8 Inspect the float chamber for corrosion and calcium build-up.
9 Tap out the float pin and remove the float, needle valve and float chamber gasket.
10 Use a straight-edge to check for distorted flanges on all facing surfaces.
11 Check that the anti-vibration ball is free in the valve end.
12 Check the needle valve tip for wear and ridges.
13 The float should be checked for damage and ingress of petrol.
14 Renew the float pin if it shows signs of wear.
15 Unscrew the fuel inlet tube and inspect the fuel filter. Clean the filter housing of debris and dirt and renew the filter if necessary.
16 Remove the mixture screw and inspect the tip for damage or ridges.
17 The accelerator pump injector is a push fit in the body. Carefully prise it from its location and test it by shaking. No noise from the outlet ball would indicate that the valve is seized.
18 Remove the four screws and detach the accelerator pump cover, diaphragm and spring. Check the diaphragm for fatigue and damage.
19 Remove the idle jet from the upper body.
20 Unscrew the primary and secondary combined air corrector and emulsion tubes.
21 Use a long thin screwdriver to unscrew the main jets which are located at the bottom of the emulsion tube wells. Invert the carburettor over a cupped hand to catch the jets as they fall out of the wells. Note that the primary main jet is located on the power valve side of the carburettor and the secondary main jet is located on the choke side of the carburettor.
22 Note the size and location of all the jets, for correct installation during reassembly.
23 Check the jet calibration against that specified. It is possible that the jets may have been transposed (or the wrong size fitted) during the last overhaul.
24 Check that the channels from the float chamber into the emulsion tube wells are clear.
25 Remove the three screws and detach the power valve housing cover, spring and diaphragm from the body. Check the diaphragm for fatigue and damage.
26 The brass outlet (power) valve is cast into the body and is not removable. The ball in the outlet valve should seal the outlet. Depress and release the ball with a small screwdriver. It should move smoothly in and out.
27 Unscrew and remove the small power jet from inside the power valve housing. Check that the channel into the emulsion tube well is clear.
28 Do not disturb the adjustment of the secondary throttle angle, unless absolutely necessary.
29 Remove the fixing screw and remove either the electrical throttle body heater or the heating flange.
30 Remove the four screws and detach the choke pull-down cover, spring and diaphragm from the housing. Check the diaphragm for fatigue.
31 Remove the two screws and detach the choke mechanism reservoir (or plain cover if fitted). Inspect the O-ring for damage.

Preparation for reassembly

32 Clean the jets, carburettor body assemblies, float chamber and internal channels. An air line may be used to clear the internal channels once the carburettor is fully dismantled. Note that if high-pressure air is directed into the channels and passages with the diaphragms still in place, diaphragm damage may result. Spraying carburettor cleaner into all the channels and passages in the carburettor body will often clear them of gum and dirt.
33 During reassembly, a complete set of new gaskets should be fitted. Also renew the needle valve, the float pin and all diaphragms.
34 Inspect and renew (where necessary) the mixture screw, main jet, air corrector /emulsion tubes, idle jet and the accelerator pump injector. Renew worn linkages, screws, springs, and other parts where necessary.
35 Ensure that all the jets are firmly locked into their original positions (but do not over-tighten). A loose jet can cause a rich (or even lean) running condition.
36 Clean all mating surfaces and flanges of old gasket material and reassemble with new gaskets.
37 Ensure that housings are positioned with their air and fuel routes correctly aligned.

Reassembly

38 Refit the choke diaphragm and spindle assembly to the choke housing. Refit the spring and cover and secure with the four screws.
39 Check that the secondary throttle plate is fully closed. The adjustment screw should not normally be used to alter the throttle plate position. Where a throttle setting gauge is available, use it to set the throttle angle. The correct angle is 9°. In the absence of a setting gauge, the screw can be adjusted so that the throttle plate is open just enough to prevent its seizure in the throttle body.
40 Refit the coolant heating flange (where used) and secure with the screw.
41 Refit the electrical throttle body heater (where used). Take care that if the throttle body heater is of the type shown (see illustration), the component parts are fitted correctly. An incorrectly-assembled heating resistance may result in a short circuit to earth. Later versions of the Z1 utilise a unitary-construction heater.
42 Refit the power jet into its original position.
43 Refit the power diaphragm, spring and cover assembly, then secure with the three screws.
44 Refit the main jets and emulsion tube/air correctors into their original positions (do not transpose the jets).
45 Refit the idle jet into the upper body and lock it firmly into position.
46 Refit the accelerator pump spring, diaphragm and cover assembly, then secure with the four screws.
47 Carefully refit the accelerator pump injector

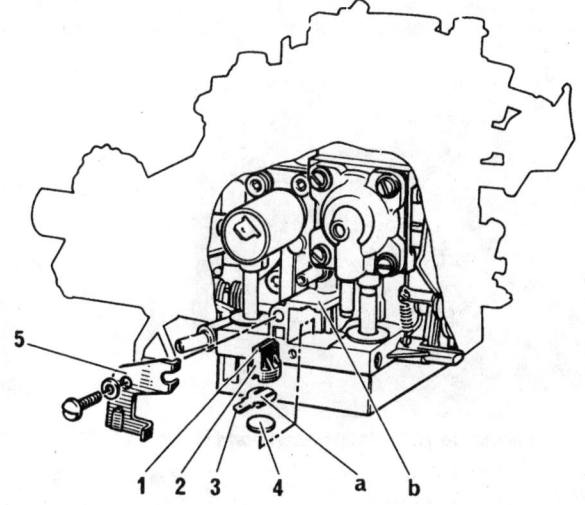

1 Positioning pin
2 Spacer
3 Connecting terminal
4 Resistance
5 Securing lug
a Tab (a) must be on same side as resistance (4)
b Carburettor

Installation of throttle body heater

Chapter G5

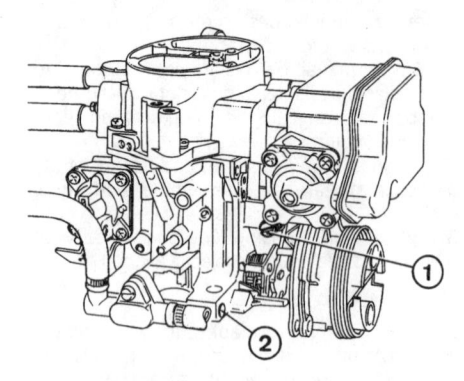

Idle adjustment screw location
1. Idle speed adjustment screw
2. Idle mixture control screw

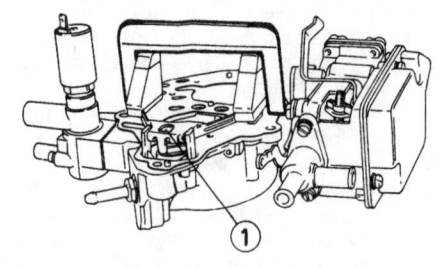

Float level adjustment
1. Inner float tag

after renewing the small seal on the injector body.

48 Refit the idle mixture screw after renewing the small seal. Turn the screw in gently until it just seats. From this position, unscrew it two full turns. This will provide a basic setting to allow the engine to be started.
49 Clean or renew the fuel filter and refit the fuel inlet tube with a new sealing washer.
50 Locate a new float chamber gasket in position on the upper body.
51 Fit the new needle valve assembly using a new sealing washer. Ensure that it is firmly locked into position (but do not over-tighten). Refit the float and secure with the float pin.
52 Adjust the float level with reference to Section 4.
53 Renew the upper body O-ring, then refit the upper body to the main body and secure with the five screws. Reconnect the fast idle lever to the throttle lever and secure with the pin and spring. Attach the throttle drum and secure with the two screws. Refit the throttle spring to the drum and check that the tension is sufficient to actuate the throttle successfully.
54 Refit the idle cut-off valve (where used).
55 Ensure that the choke flap and linkage move smoothly and progressively and inspect the operating mechanism for stickiness and wear.
56 Renew the choke mechanism O-ring, then refit the reservoir (or plain cover) to the choke mechanism and secure with the two screws.
57 Adjust the choke fast idle and pull-down with reference to Section 4.
58 Refit the carburettor to the engine.
59 Always adjust the carburettor idle speed and mixture after any work has been carried out on the carburettor, preferably with the aid of a CO meter.

4 Service adjustments

Adjustment pre-conditions

1 Refer to Part B for general advice on the pre-conditions for correct adjustment of this carburettor.

Idle speed and mixture (CO)

2 Run the engine at 3000 rpm for 30 seconds to clear the manifold of fuel vapours, then allow the engine to idle.
3 Use the idle speed screw to set the specified idle speed (see illustration).
4 Check the CO level. If incorrect, remove the tamperproof plug and adjust the idle mixture screw to obtain the correct level. Turning the screw clockwise (inwards) will reduce the CO level. Turning the screw anti-clockwise (outwards) will increase the CO level. Refer to Part B for a method of setting the idle mixture without the aid of a CO meter.
5 Repeat paragraphs 3 and 4 until both adjustments are correct.
6 Clear the manifold every 30 seconds during the setting operation by running the engine at 3000 rpm for 30 seconds.
7 Increase the speed to 2000 rpm and note the CO reading. The cruise reading should be less than half the idle CO reading.
8 Fit a new tamperproof plug to the mixture control screw on completion.

Float level

9 Invert the carburettor upper body so that the float faces upwards and the needle valve is depressed.
10 Measure the distance between the upper body (with its gasket) and the upper face of the plastic float. Refer to Specifications for the correct float level.
11 Adjust as necessary by bending the inner float tag (see illustration).
12 The upper faces of the float should not differ in height by more than 1 mm. Adjust by bending the float arms if necessary.

Automatic choke

13 Allow the temperature of the thermostatic capsule to stabilise for a minimum of 30 minutes at an ambient temperature of 20°C. All Z1 carburettor choke adjustments should be undertaken at this temperature. At the time of writing, adjustment specifications were not available for all the Z1 carburettors covered by this Chapter.

Single-stage pull-down unit

14 Remove the two screws and detach the choke mechanism reservoir (or plain cover if fitted).
15 Measure dimension 'a' (see illustration). The correct measurement at 20°C is 27.6 mm.
16 If adjustment is necessary, insert a screwdriver into aperture 'd' (see illustration). Adjust by turning screw '5' (see illustration) in the appropriate direction.

Choke thermostatic capsule dimension (a)
- a Refer to text
- 3 Roller
- 4 Adjustment screw for fast idle clearance

Adjustment aperture for dimension (a)
- d Insert screwdriver here and adjust screw (5)

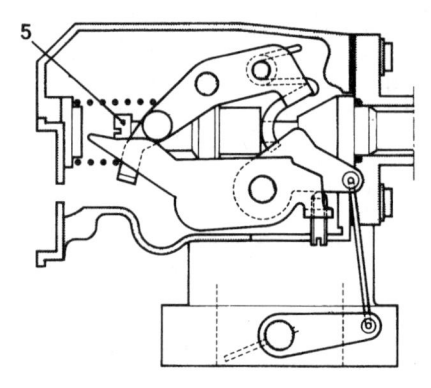

Adjustment screw for dimension (a)
- 5 Adjust dimension (a) by turning screw in appropriate direction

Solex 32/34 & 34/34 Z1 carburettor

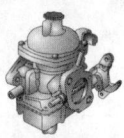

Fast idle clearance
b Measure fast idle clearance with a twist drill
6 Secondary throttle stop screw - do not adjust; for information only

Measuring choke pull-down clearance
1 Push diaphragm operating rod in direction of arrow
2 Locknut (where used)
3 Pull-down adjustment screw

Measurement of choke pull-down or dechoke clearance
a Clearance - use drill of correct diameter

Measurement of dechoke clearance
4 Bend adjustment fork lugs in appropriate direction

17 To carry out the following fast idle adjustment, the carburettor must be removed from the engine. Refer to Part B for a method of setting the fast idle speed without removing the carburettor.
18 Use the shank of a twist drill to measure the gap 'b' *(see illustration)* between the wall of the throttle bore and the throttle plate. The correct clearance at 20°C is 0.45 mm.
19 Adjust as necessary by turning the fast idle adjustment screw '4' in the appropriate direction.
20 Use thin-nose pliers to push the diaphragm operating rod up to its stop. At the same time, use the shank of a twist drill to measure the pull-down gap between the upper section of the choke flap and the air intake. Refer to Specifications for the required drill size. Where data is not available, adjust to 6.0 mm at 20°C *(see illustrations)*.
21 Remove the plug in the diaphragm cover (loosen the locknut, where applicable) and adjust as necessary by turning the adjustment screw in the appropriate direction. Tighten the locknut and renew the plug when adjustment is complete.
22 Open the throttle so that the primary throttle plate is fully open. At the same time, use the shank of a twist drill to measure the gap between the upper section of the choke flap and the air intake. The correct clearance at 20°C is 8 mm.

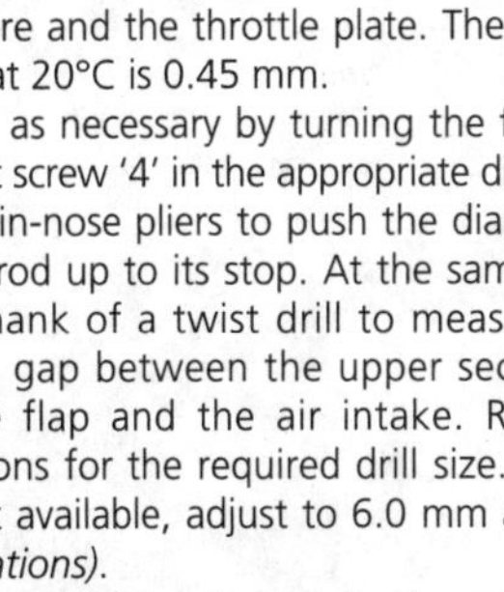

23 Adjust as necessary by bending the fork lugs *(see illustration)* in the appropriate direction. Opening the fork lugs will increase the clearance and closing the fork lugs will decrease the clearance.
24 Renew the O-ring, then refit the reservoir (or plain cover) to the choke mechanism and secure with the two screws.
25 Note that it is also possible to check and adjust the choke with the engine running, using a special tool Citroën part number OUT 10 4066-T or Peugeot part number 0143 ZZ *(see illustration)*.

Two-stage pull-down unit

26 Carry out paragraphs 14 to 18 above.
27 Use thin-nose pliers to push the diaphragm operating rod until a resistance is felt. At the same time, use the shank of a twist drill to measure the pull-down gap between the upper section of the choke flap and the air intake. Note that stage one is not adjustable and no data was available at the time of writing. Make a note of the stage one gap and compare with that for stage two.
28 Use the thin-nose pliers to push the diaphragm operating rod fully up to its stop. At the same time, use the shank of a twist drill to measure the pull-down gap between the upper section of the choke flap and the air intake. Refer to Specifications for the required drill size.
29 Remove the plug in the diaphragm cover and adjust stage two, as necessary, by turning the adjustment screw in the appropriate direction. Renew the plug after adjustment is completed.

5 Component testing

Throttle body heater

1 With the ignition on, connect a voltmeter between the heater terminal and earth. If battery voltage is not obtained, check the wiring between the heater and ignition switch.
2 Disconnect the electrical connector to the heater and connect a test lamp between the positive battery terminal and the connector terminal leading to the heater. If the lamp does not light, renew the heater. Take care, if the throttle body heater is of the type shown *(see illustration)*, that the component parts are fitted as shown. An incorrectly-assembled heating resistance may result in a short circuit to earth. Later versions of the Z1 utilise a unitary-construction heater.

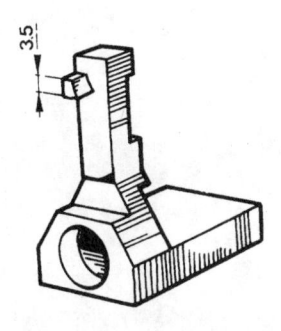

Citroën/Peugeot special tool for engine-running choke adjustments

Using a test lamp to test throttle body heater

Chapter G5

Float chamber vent valve

3 With the ignition on, connect a voltmeter between the valve terminal and earth. If battery voltage is not obtained, check the wiring between the valve and ignition switch.
4 Test the plunger operation by connecting the valve to a voltage supply. Using a torch, look into the valve through the lower connection spigot.
5 Dismantle and clean the valve if it does not actuate. Renew the valve if it is faulty or if cleaning does not improve its operation.

6 Fault diagnosis

Refer to Part D for diagnosis of general carburettor faults. The following faults are specific to the Solex Z1 carburettor.

Poor choke operation/poor cold starting

- [ ] Failure of choke thermostatic capsule.
- [ ] Poor O-ring seal between the choke reservoir and the body (where fitted).
- [ ] Defective pull-down vacuum hose (where fitted).
- [ ] Defective choke pull-down.
- [ ] Also refer to Cold starting and warm-up problems in Part D.

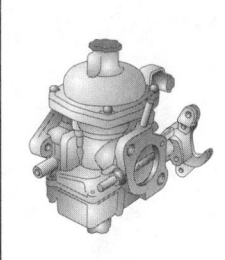

Part G Chapter 6
Solex 28/34 Z10 carburettor

Contents

Component testing	5	Identification	2
Fault diagnosis	6	Principles of operation	1
General servicing	3	Service adjustments	4

Specifications

Manufacturer	Renault		Renault		Renault	
Model	5 1.7 (B/C40G)		9 & 11 1.7 (L42N, B/C37N)		9 & 11 1.7 (L42N, B/C37N)	
Year	1987 to 1990		1986 to 1989		1986 to 1989	
Engine code	F2NH740		F2NE708		F2NE708	
Capacity (cm³)/no. of cyls	1721/4		1721/4		1721/4	
Oil temperature (°C)	80		80		80	
Carb. ident. (Solex)	28/34 Z10		28/34 Z10 13535		28/34 Z10	
Carb. ident. (vehicle)	932		920		943	
Idle speed (rpm)	800 ± 50		700 ± 50		800 ± 50	
CO @ idle (% vol.)	1.5 ± 0.5		1.5 ± 0.5		1.5 ± 0.5	
Stage (venturi)	1	2	1	2	1	2
Venturi diameter (K)	20	27	20	27	20	27
Idle jet (g)	46	50	47		46	50
Main jet (Gg)	97.5	145	102	145	97.5	145
Air correction jet (a)	200	190	210	190	200	190
Accelerator pump jet (i)	40	35	40	35	40	35
Basic throttle position (PF)	-		0°30'	-	0°30'	-
Float level (mm)	33.5		33.5		33.5	
Needle valve (mm) (P)	1.8		1.8		1.8	
Choke fast idle gap (mm)	0.95		1.00		1.00	
Fast idle position (OP)	24°30'		25°30'		25°30'	
Choke pull-down (mm) (OVAD)	2.2		-		2.2	
Vent valve (mm)	2.0		1.3		1.3	

G6•1

Chapter G6

Manufacturer	Renault	Renault	Volvo
Model	21 & Savanna 1.7	21 & Savanna 1.7 (B/L/K481)	340 1.7 & Catalyst
Year	1986 to 1988	1986 to 1992	1986 to 1991
Engine code	F2NC710	F2NB712	B172K
Capacity (cm³)/no. of cyls	1721/4	1721/4	1721/4
Oil temperature (°C)	80	80	(Hot)
Carb. ident. (Solex)	28/34 Z10 13748	28/34 Z10 13767	28/34 CISAC Z10 13346/13463
Carb. ident. (vehicle)	889	970	857/894
Idle speed (rpm)	700 ± 50	700 ± 25	650 ± 25
CO @ idle (% vol.)	1.5 ± 0.5	1.0 ± 0.5	2.25 ± 0.75
Stage (venturi)	1 / 2	1 / 2	1 / 2
Venturi diameter (K)	20 / 27	20 / 26	20 / 26
Idle jet (g)	45 / 50	47 / 45	40 / 40
Main jet (Gg)	100 / 145	97.5 / 122.5	95 / 120
Air correction jet (a)	210 / 190	200 / 145	185 / 145
Accelerator pump jet (i)	40 / 35	40 / 35	- / 46
Basic throttle position (PF)	- / 0°30'	- / -	- / 0°30'
Idle position (PRN)	-	-	8°30' / -
Float level (mm)	33 ± 0.5	33 ± 0.5	33.8
Needle valve (mm) (P)	1.8	1.8	1.8
Choke fast idle gap (mm)	1.0 ± 0.1	0.95	-
Fast idle position (OP)	25°30	24°30	26° ± 30'
Choke pull-down (mm) (OVAD)	2.2 ± 0.1	-	3.5
Vent valve (mm)	2.0 ± 1.0	1.3	3.0

Manufacturer	Volvo	Volvo
Model	440, 460 1.7	440, 460 1.7 Catalyst
Year	1989 to 1990	1989 to 1991
Engine code	B18KP111	B18KPD111
Capacity (cm³)/no. of cyls	1721/4	1721/4
Oil temperature (°C)	80	80
Carb. ident. (Solex)	28/34 CISAC Z10 13459/13746	28/34 CISAC Z10 14003
Carb. ident. (vehicle)	900	900
Idle speed (rpm)	825 ± 75	825 ± 75
CO @ idle (% vol.)	1.75 ± 0.75	1.75 ± 0.75
Stage (venturi)	1 / 2	1 / 2
Venturi diameter (K)	20 / 27	20 / 27
Idle jet (g)	46 / 50	46 / 50
Main jet (Gg)	100 / 140 ± 2.5	100 / 140 ± 2.5
Air correction jet (a)	175 ± 5 / 155 ± 5	175 ± 5 / 155 ± 5
Emulsion tube (s)	Z / EZ	Z / EZ
Accelerator pump jet (i)	35 / 35	35 / 35
Basic throttle position (PF)	- / 0°30'	- / 0°30'
Fast idle position (OP)	-	26° ± 30'
Float level (mm)	33.8	33.8
Needle valve (mm) (P)	1.8	1.8
Vent valve (mm)	4.0	4.0

1 Principles of operation

Introduction

1 The following technical description of the Solex 28/34 Z10 carburettor should be read in conjunction with the more detailed description of carburettor principles in Chapter 1.

2 The Z10 carburettor is sometimes referred to as a CISAC carburettor.

Construction

3 The Solex Z10 carburettor is a downdraught progressive twin venturi instrument (see illustration). The venturis are arranged so that the secondary throttle valve will not start to open until the primary throttle valve is about two-thirds open. The choke control is manual in operation.

4 The throttle shafts are made of steel, while the throttle plates and all the emulsion tubes and jets are manufactured from brass. The internal fuel channels and air passages are drilled and sealed with lead plugs where necessary.

5 On some variations, a heating flange is bolted to the carburettor base through which hot engine coolant is piped. The purpose of the flange is to improve atomisation of the air/fuel mixture during the warm-up period. Some versions use a throttle body heater to prevent carburettor icing. The heater is normally operational with the ignition on and functions on the PTC (positive temperature coefficient) principle. As the temperature rises, the heater resistance also rises.

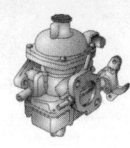

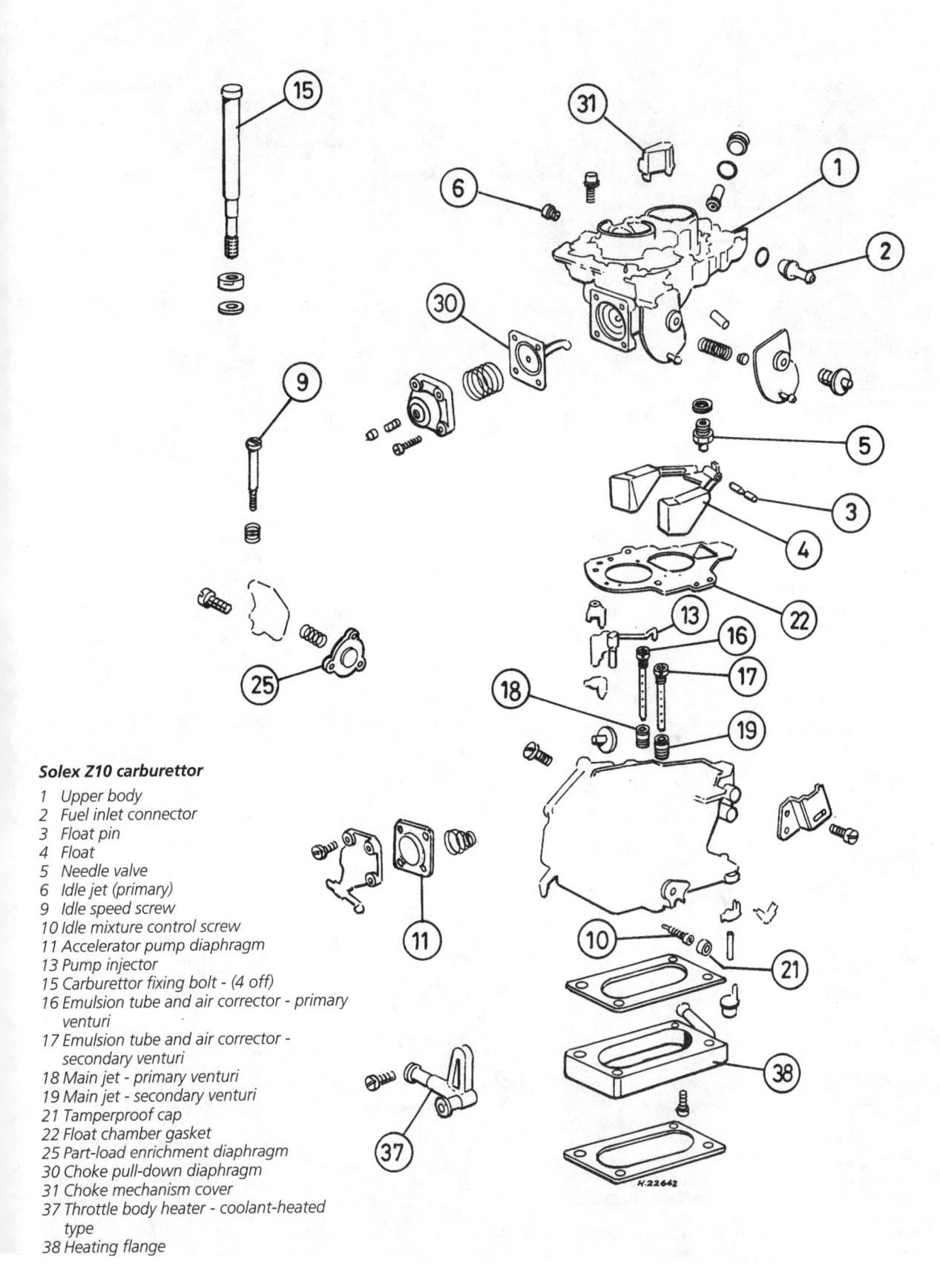

Solex 28/34 Z10 carburettor

Solex Z10 carburettor

1. Upper body
2. Fuel inlet connector
3. Float pin
4. Float
5. Needle valve
6. Idle jet (primary)
9. Idle speed screw
10. Idle mixture control screw
11. Accelerator pump diaphragm
13. Pump injector
15. Carburettor fixing bolt - (4 off)
16. Emulsion tube and air corrector - primary venturi
17. Emulsion tube and air corrector - secondary venturi
18. Main jet - primary venturi
19. Main jet - secondary venturi
21. Tamperproof cap
22. Float chamber gasket
25. Part-load enrichment diaphragm
30. Choke pull-down diaphragm
31. Choke mechanism cover
37. Throttle body heater - coolant-heated type
38. Heating flange

Chapter G6

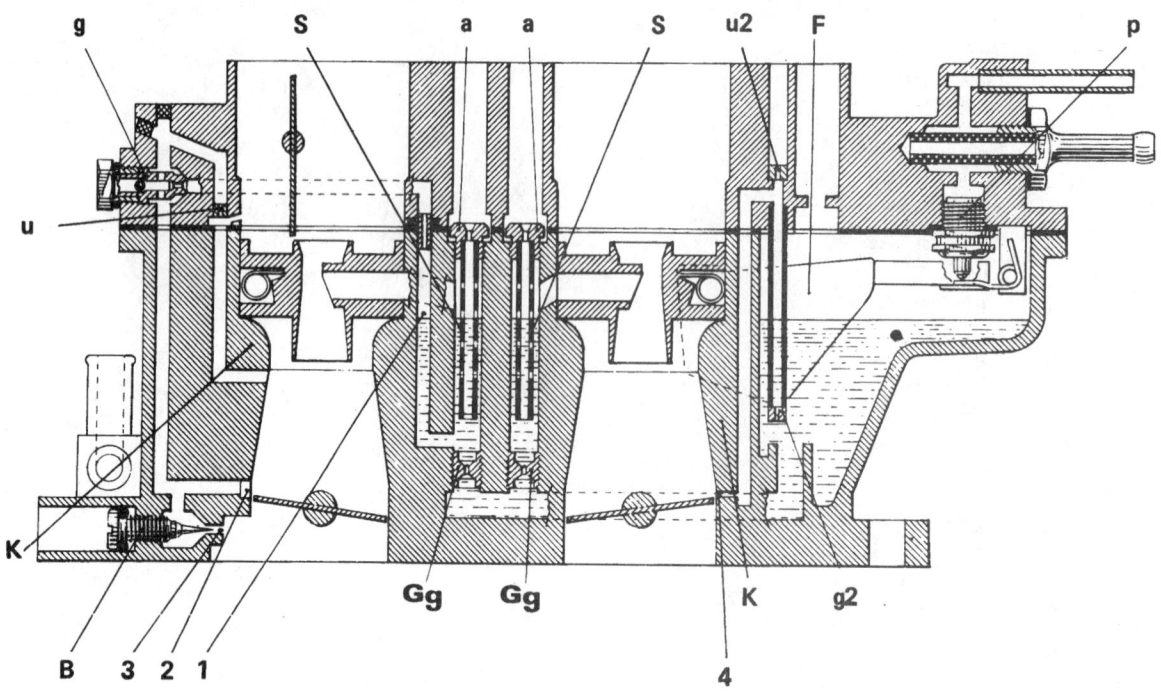

Idle and main circuits

1. Idle fuel channel
2. Progression slot - primary venturi
3. Idle mixture outlet
4. Progression slot - secondary venturi
- a Air corrector jet - primary and secondary venturis
- B Idle mixture control screw
- F Float
- g Idle fuel jet
- g2 Fuel jet - secondary progression
- Gg Main jets - primary and secondary venturis
- K Venturi - primary and secondary
- P Needle valve
- S Emulsion tube - primary and secondary
- u Idle air corrector jet
- u2 Air corrector jet - secondary progression

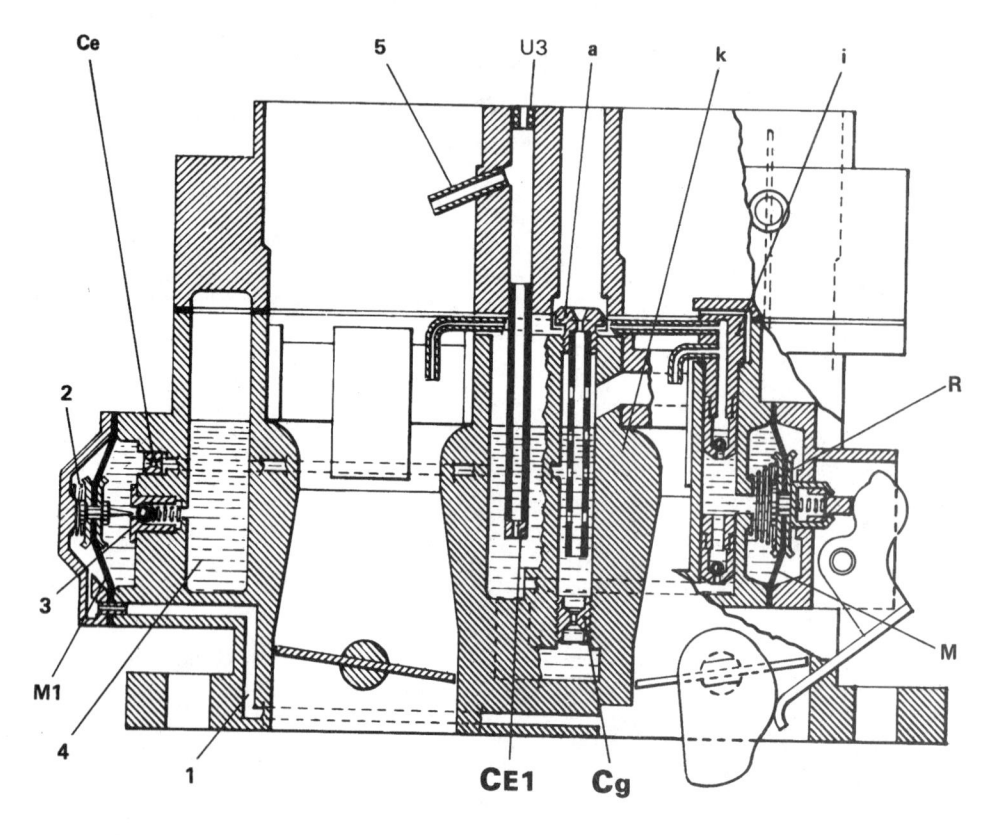

Accelerator pump and enrichment circuits

1. Vacuum passage
2. Spring
3. Part-load enrichment valve
4. Float chamber
5. Full-load enrichment nozzle
- a Combined air corrector jet with emulsion tube - primary venturi
- Ce Part-load enrichment fuel jet
- CE1 Full-load enrichment fuel jet
- Cg Main jet - primary venturi
- i Accelerator pump injector
- k Primary venturi
- M Accelerator pump diaphragm
- M1 Part-load enrichment diaphragm
- R Spring
- U3 Full-load enrichment air jet

Solex 28/34 Z10 carburettor

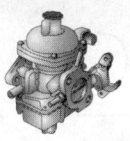

Fuel control

6 Fuel flows into the carburettor through a fine mesh filter. The fuel level in the float chamber is controlled by a needle valve and plastic float assembly. An anti-vibration ball is incorporated into the needle valve design. A hairpin clip, attached to the needle valve seat and to the float arm, prevents the needle from sticking in the seat as the fuel level drops.

7 The float chamber uses a dual-venting arrangement. Venting is to atmosphere at idle or with the engine shut down. At engine speeds higher than idle, a lever attached to the throttle closes the atmospheric vent and this allows the float chamber to vent into the upper air intake which is on the clean-air side of the air filter.

Idle, slow running and progression

8 Fuel, sourced from the main well, passes into the idle channel through a metered idle jet. Here it is mixed with a small amount of air from a calibrated air bleed. The resulting emulsion is drawn through a channel to be discharged from the idle orifice under the primary throttle plate. A tapered mixture screw is used to vary the outlet and this ensures fine control of the idle mixture (see illustration).

9 A progression slot provides extra enrichment as it is uncovered by the opening throttle during initial acceleration.

10 The idle speed is set by an adjustable screw. The adjustable mixture screw is tamper proofed at production level, in accordance with emission regulations.

Idle cut-off valve (some variations)

11 An idle cut-off valve is used to prevent run-on when the engine is shut down. It utilises a 12-volt solenoid plunger to block the idle channel when the ignition is switched off.

Accelerator pump

12 The Solex Z10 accelerator pump is controlled by a diaphragm and is mechanically operated by a lever and cam attached to the primary throttle linkage. During acceleration, fuel is pumped through a ball valve located in the pump injector and is discharged into the primary or secondary venturi (or both venturis, depending on carburettor variation). The inlet ball valve is located in a channel from the float chamber. Excess fuel/air mixture is returned to the float chamber through a separate fuel channel (see illustration).

Main circuit

13 The amount of fuel discharged into the airstream is controlled by a calibrated main jet. Fuel is drawn through the main jet into the base of a vertical well which dips down into the fuel in the float chamber. An emulsion tube is placed in the well. The fuel is mixed with air drawn in through the air corrector and through the holes in the emulsion tube. The resulting emulsified mixture is discharged from the main orifice through an auxiliary venturi.

Part-load enrichment (power valve)

14 Fuel flows from the float chamber into the enrichment chamber, through a fuel channel and a brass inlet valve. An air passage is taken from under the throttle plate to the cover of the chamber. At idle and during light-throttle operation, manifold vacuum draws the diaphragm back against spring pressure. The diaphragm pintle is withdrawn from the valve and the spring-loaded ball seats to close off the inlet channel.

15 Under acceleration and wide-open throttle operation, the vacuum in the manifold is depleted. The diaphragm returns under spring pressure and the power diaphragm pintle pushes the ball to open the inlet valve. Fuel then flows through the valve into the enrichment chamber. From here, it passes through a calibrated jet into a fuel channel leading to the primary main well. The fuel level rises in the well and the fuel mixture is enriched.

Secondary action

16 Once the primary throttle plate is about two-thirds open, the secondary throttle plate will start to open. At full-throttle, the linkage is arranged so that both throttle plates will be fully open.

17 A progression circuit is used to prevent hesitation as the secondary throttle plate starts to open. An emulsified mixture is discharged into the secondary venturi, via a progression drilling, at the initial opening of the secondary throttle plate.

18 Once the secondary throttle plate has opened, the action of the secondary main circuit is similar to the primary circuit.

19 When the choke is in operation (with the choke control pulled out more than halfway), a tag on the lever locks the secondary throttle operating linkage. Secondary throttle operation on half- to full-choke is thus avoided.

Full-load enrichment

20 At full-load and high engine speeds, the velocity of air creates a depression sufficient to raise fuel from the float chamber into a channel. The fuel then passes through a calibrated bushing to the upper section of the secondary air intake. Here it is mixed with a small amount of air from a calibrated air bleed and the emulsified mixture is then discharged into the airstream from the full-load enrichment nozzle.

Manual choke operation

21 The manual choke is operated by a dash-mounted cable control. When the cable is pulled, it operates a lever that pulls the choke flap closed across the primary air intake. Fast idle is achieved with the aid of a curved cam attached to the choke operating lever. An adjustable screw, attached to the throttle lever and butting against the cam, is used to vary the fast idle speed.

22 During engine warm-up, the cable control should be progressively pushed home until the choke flap is fully open.

Choke pull-down

23 Once the engine has fired, the choke flap must open slightly to weaken the mixture and avoid flooding. This is achieved by using manifold vacuum to actuate a diaphragm. A linkage attached to the diaphragm then pulls upon the choke flap.

Anti-stall device

24 This device is normally only fitted to vehicles equipped with power steering. Turning the steering wheel to full lock on these models places such a load upon the engine that the idle speed will drop and the engine may stall.

25 With the anti-stall system, turning the power steering beyond a given amount of lock opens a hydraulic switch. In turn, a vacuum passage is opened to operate the anti-stall device which pulls upon the throttle lever to give a faster idle speed. In this way, a stall is prevented. Once the steering wheel is straightened, the hydraulic switch closes and the idle speed returns to normal.

2 Identification

1 The Solex identification code is stamped on a metallic tag attached to the carburettor cover by an upper body fixing screw. This tag quotes the Solex part number and the vehicle manufacturer part number. It also identifies the carburettor type.

2 Later carburettors may have this information stamped upon the carburettor body:

F13406   Solex part number
REN 883   Vehicle manufacturer part number
28-34 Z10   Carburettor type

3 Where the tag is missing, refer to Chapter 2 for other ways of identifying the carburettor.

3 General servicing

Introduction

1 Read this Chapter in conjunction with Chapter 2, which describes some of the operations in more detail. It is assumed that the carburettor is removed for this service. However, many of the operations can be tackled with the carburettor in place. Where this is undertaken, first remove the carburettor upper body and soak the fuel out of the float chamber using a clean tissue or soft cloth.

Dismantling and checking

2 Remove the carburettor from the engine (see Chapter 2).

3 Check the carburettor visually for damage and wear.

4 Remove the idle cut-off valve assembly (where fitted) and clean it with carburettor

Chapter G6

cleaner. Test the plunger operation by connecting the valve to the battery or other voltage supply (or use the valve supply wire in the engine compartment). Touch the valve body to earth with the ignition on. Repeat this several times and ensure that the plunger tip advances and retracts cleanly. Renew the valve if the action is faulty or if cleaning does not improve its operation.

5 Remove the five screws and detach the carburettor upper body.
6 Inspect the float chamber for corrosion and calcium build-up.
7 Tap out the float pin and remove the float, needle valve, hairpin clip and float chamber gasket.
8 Check that the anti-vibration ball is free in the valve end.
9 Check the needle valve tip for wear and ridges.
10 The float should be checked for damage and ingress of petrol.
11 Renew the float pin if it shows signs of wear.
12 Use a straight-edge to check for distorted flanges on all facing surfaces.
13 Unscrew the hexagon plug and inspect the fuel filter. Unscrew the fuel inlet tube and clean the filter housing and inlet channel of debris and dirt. Renew the filter if necessary.
14 Remove the mixture screw and inspect the tip for damage or ridges.
15 The accelerator pump injector is a push fit in the body. Carefully prise it from its location and test it by shaking. No noise from the outlet ball would indicate that the valve is seized.
16 Unscrew the retaining nut and remove the throttle lever and vent valve assembly. The accelerator pump retaining screws will now be more readily accessible.
17 Remove the four screws and detach the accelerator pump cover, diaphragm and spring. Check the diaphragm for fatigue and damage.
18 Remove the idle jet from the upper body.
19 Unscrew the primary and secondary combined air corrector and emulsion tubes.
20 Use a long thin screwdriver to unscrew the main jets. They are located at the bottom of the emulsion tube wells. Invert the carburettor over a cupped hand to catch the jets as they fall out of the wells. The primary main jet is located on the power valve side of the carburettor and the secondary main jet is located on the choke side of the carburettor.
21 Note the sizes and locations of all the jets for correct installation during reassembly.
22 Check the jet calibration against that specified. It is possible that the jets may have been transposed (or the wrong size fitted) during the last overhaul.
23 Check that the channels from the float chamber into the emulsion tube wells are clear.
24 Remove the three screws and detach the power valve housing cover, spring and diaphragm from the body. Check the diaphragm for fatigue and damage.
25 The brass outlet (power) valve is cast into the body and is not removable. The ball in the outlet valve should seal the outlet. Depress and release the ball with a small screwdriver and it should move smoothly in and out.
26 Remove the fixing screw and remove either the electrical heating resistance or the heating flange.
27 Remove the fixing screw and separate the lower carburettor flange (where fitted). This flange may be either plastic or aluminium in construction. Note the position before removal to facilitate easy reassembly. Use a straight-edge to check for distorted flanges on the facing surfaces. Inspect the flexible joint for wear and distortion and renew the joint if the locating stud is broken or if wear is apparent. Check that the breather connection is clear of dirt and carbon. Do not disturb the adjustment of the secondary throttle angle unless absolutely necessary.
28 Remove the four screws and detach the choke pull-down cover, spring and diaphragm from the housing. Push the plastic operating lever downwards to release the diaphragm rod and check the diaphragm for fatigue. Remove the plastic linkage shield from the choke mechanism.

Preparation for reassembly

29 Clean the jets, carburettor body assemblies, float chamber and internal channels. An air line may be used to clear the internal channels once the carburettor is fully dismantled. Note that if high-pressure air is directed into the channels and passages with the diaphragms still in place, diaphragm damage may result. Spraying carburettor cleaner into all the channels and passages in the carburettor body will often clear them of gum and dirt.
30 During reassembly, a complete set of new gaskets should be fitted. Also renew the needle valve, the float pin and all diaphragms.
31 Inspect and renew (where necessary) the mixture screw, main jet, air corrector/ emulsion tubes, idle jet and the accelerator pump injector. Renew worn linkages, screws, springs, and other parts where necessary.
32 Ensure that all the jets are firmly locked into their original positions (but do not over-tighten). A loose jet can cause a rich (or even lean) running condition.
33 Clean all mating surfaces and flanges of old gasket material and reassemble with new gaskets.
34 Ensure that housings are positioned with their air and fuel routes correctly aligned.

Reassembly

35 Refit the choke diaphragm and rod assembly to the choke housing. Lock the end of the diaphragm spindle into the plastic operating lever. Refit the spring and cover and secure with the four screws.
36 Check that the secondary throttle plate is fully closed. The adjustment screw should not normally be used to alter the throttle plate position. Where a throttle setting gauge is available, use it to set the throttle angle. The correct angle is 0°30'. In the absence of a setting gauge, the screw can be adjusted so that the throttle plate is open just enough to prevent its seizure in the throttle body.
37 Refit the lower carburettor flange and flexible joint, then secure with the fixing screw.
38 Refit the coolant heating flange (when used) and secure with the fixing screw.
39 Refit the electrical heating resistance (when used). Take care, if the throttle body heater is of the type shown *(see illustration)*, that the component parts are fitted correctly. An incorrectly-assembled heating resistance may result in a short circuit to earth. Later versions of the Z10 carburettor utilise a unitary-construction heater.
40 Refit the power diaphragm, spring and cover assembly, then secure with the three screws. Ensure that the idle speed pushrod and spring are correctly assembled and move freely in the housing cover.

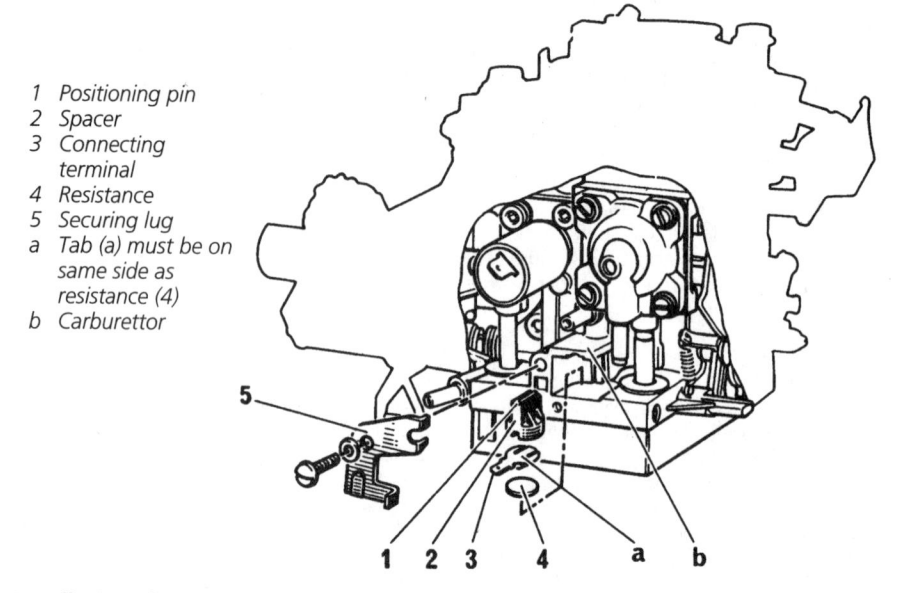

1 Positioning pin
2 Spacer
3 Connecting terminal
4 Resistance
5 Securing lug
a Tab (a) must be on same side as resistance (4)
b Carburettor

Installation of throttle body heater

Solex 28/34 Z10 carburettor

41 Refit the main jets and emulsion tube/air correctors into their original positions (do not transpose the jets).
42 Refit the idle jet into the upper body, complete with a new seal, then lock it firmly into position.
43 Refit the accelerator pump spring, diaphragm and cover assembly, then secure with the four screws.
44 Slide the collar, spring and vent valve assembly over the primary throttle spindle. Refit the throttle lever and secure with the hexagon nut.
45 Carefully refit the accelerator pump injector after renewing the small seal on the injector body.
46 Refit the idle mixture screw. Turn the screw in gently until it just seats. From this position, unscrew it three full turns. This will provide a basic setting to allow the engine to be started.
47 Clean or renew the fuel filter and refit the hexagon plug with a new sealing washer. Refit the fuel inlet tube with a new sealing washer.
48 Locate a new float chamber gasket in position on the upper body.
49 Fit the new needle valve assembly, using a new sealing washer. Ensure that it is firmly locked into position (but do not over-tighten). Refit the float and secure with the float pin.
50 Adjust the float level with reference to Section 4.
51 Refit the upper body to the main body and secure with the five screws.
52 Refit the idle cut-off valve (where used).
53 Ensure that the choke flap and linkage move smoothly and progressively and inspect the operating mechanism for stickiness and wear.
54 Refit the choke mechanism shield.
55 Adjust the choke fast idle and pull-down, and the vent valve, with reference to Section 4.
56 Refit the carburettor to the engine.
57 Always adjust the carburettor idle speed and mixture after any work has been carried out on the carburettor, preferably with the aid of a CO meter.

4 Service adjustments

Adjustment pre-conditions

1 Refer to Chapter 2 for general advice on the pre-conditions for correct adjustment of this carburettor.

Idle speed and mixture (CO)

2 Run the engine at 3000 rpm for 30 seconds to clear the manifold of fuel vapours, then allow the engine to idle.
3 Use the idle speed screw to set the specified idle speed (see illustration).
4 Check the CO level. If incorrect, remove the tamperproof plug and adjust the idle mixture screw to obtain the correct level. Turning the screw clockwise (inwards) will reduce the CO level. Turning the screw anti-clockwise (outwards) will increase the CO level. Refer to Chapter 2 for a method of setting the idle mixture without the aid of a CO meter.
5 Repeat paragraphs 3 and 4 until both adjustments are correct.
6 Clear the manifold every 30 seconds during the setting operation by running the engine at 3000 rpm for 30 seconds.
7 Increase the speed to 2000 rpm and note the CO reading. The cruise reading should be less than half the idle CO reading.
8 Fit a new tamperproof plug to the mixture control screw on completion.

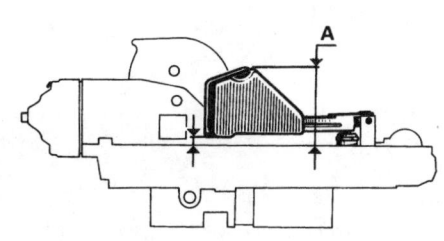

Float level

9 Invert the carburettor upper body so that the float faces upwards and the needle valve is depressed.
10 Measure the distance between the upper body (with its gasket) and the upper face of the plastic float. Refer to Specifications for the correct float level (see illustration).
11 Adjust as necessary by bending the inner float tag.
12 The upper faces of the float should not differ in height by more than 1 mm. Adjust by bending the float arms if necessary.

Choke adjustments

Fast idle

13 The carburettor must be removed from the engine in order to make the following fast idle adjustment. Refer to Chapter 2 for a method of setting the fast idle speed without removing the carburettor.
14 Invert the carburettor and pull the choke operating lever to fully close the choke flap. The fast idle screw will butt against the fast idle cam and force open the throttle plate to leave a small clearance (see illustration).
15 Use the shank of a twist drill to measure the clearance between the wall of the throttle bore and the throttle plate. Refer to Specifications for the required drill size. Measure from the side opposite the progression holes.
16 Adjust as necessary by turning the fast idle adjustment screw (48) in the appropriate direction.
17 Note that the fast idle throttle angle may also be set by means of a Solex or Pierburg throttle angle gauge. Refer to Specifications for the appropriate throttle angle.

Vacuum pull-down

18 Pull the choke operating lever to fully close the choke flap.
19 Measure the clearance x between the

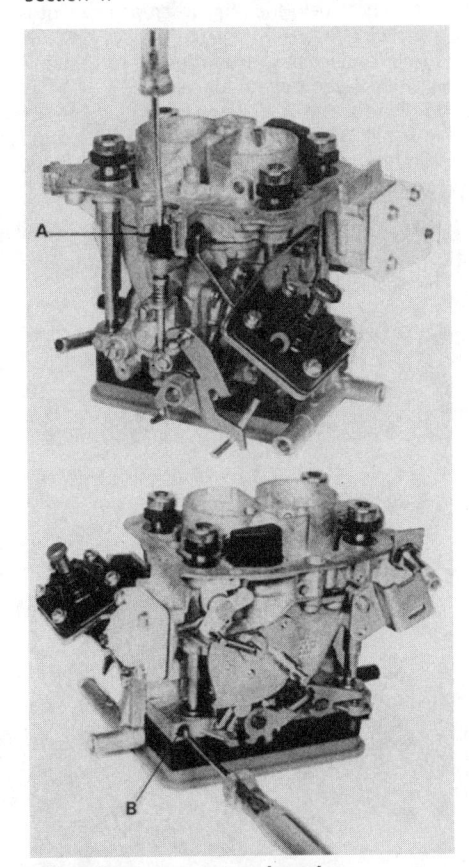

Idle adjustment screw location
A Idle speed adjustment screw
B Idle mixture control screw

Float level adjustment
A Float level

Fast idle adjustment
Arrow shows fast idle clearance
48 Fast idle adjustment screw
49 Carburettor base securing screw

Chapter G6

Choke clearance and pull-down adjustment

10 Pull-down clearance
11 Lever
12 Diaphragm operating rod
46 Pull-down adjustment screw
47 Clearance adjustment screw
x Choke clearance = 0.95 ± 0.05 mm

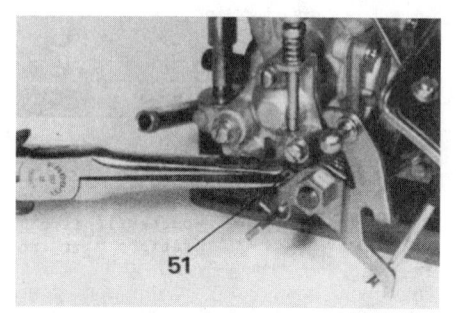

Vent valve adjustment

51 Use pliers to twist lever

adjustment screw and the plastic lever *(see illustration)*.
20 Adjust as necessary by turning the adjustment screw in the appropriate direction.
21 Use a small screwdriver to push the diaphragm operating rod up to its stop. At the same time, use the shank of a twist drill to measure the gap between the lower section of the choke flap and the air intake. Refer to Specifications for the required drill size.

22 Remove the plug in the diaphragm cover and adjust as necessary by turning the adjustment screw in the appropriate direction. Renew the plug when adjustment is complete.

Vent valve

23 Measure the clearance between the float chamber cover and the valve.
24 Adjust as necessary by bending the control arm in the appropriate direction *(see illustration)*.

5 Component testing

Anti-stall device (vehicles with power steering)

1 Warm the engine to normal operating temperature and check that the idle speed and mixture are correctly adjusted. Ensure that the front wheels are in the straight-ahead position and that the steering wheel is not turned during the following tests.

2 Remove the air filter assembly and place it to one side. Ensure that all the hoses remain connected.
3 Disconnect the vacuum pipe from the anti-stall device. The connection is colour-coded blue *(see illustration)*.
4 Connect a vacuum pump to the device, and allow the engine to idle. Operate the vacuum pump until 600 mmHg (800 mbars) is registered. The idle speed should have risen to 1050 ± 50 rpm.
5 Remove the plug (where fitted) in the diaphragm cover and adjust as necessary by turning the adjustment screw in the appropriate direction *(see illustration)*. Renew the plug when adjustment is complete.
6 Disconnect the vacuum pump and reconnect the vacuum hose to the anti-stall device.

Alternative method

7 Disconnect the vacuum pipe from the anti-stall device. The connection is colour-coded blue.
8 Disconnect a pipe from a vacuum connection on the carburettor. Connect a vacuum pipe between this connection and the one on the anti-stall device and allow the engine to idle. The idle speed should have risen to 1050 ± 50 rpm.
9 Remove the plug (where fitted) in the diaphragm cover and adjust as necessary by turning the adjustment screw in the appropriate direction. Renew the plug when adjustment is complete.
10 Reconnect the vacuum hoses to the anti-stall device and carburettor.
11 Note that it is also possible to actuate the anti-stall device by disconnecting the wiring from the vacuum switch valve and joining the two connectors together.

Throttle body heater

12 Refer to Chapter 4 for a method of testing the electrical throttle body heater.

6 Fault diagnosis

Refer to Chapter 4 for diagnosis of general carburettor faults.

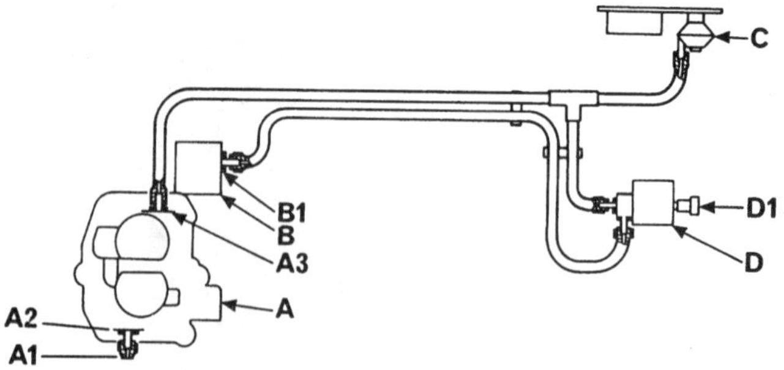

Vacuum connection diagram - anti-stall device

A   Carburettor
A1 Plug on connector pipe - black
A2 Locating ring on carburettor - red
A3 Locating ring on carburettor - black
B   Anti-stall device
B1 Locating ring on device - dark blue
C   Ignition control unit
D   Vacuum switch valve
D1 Filter

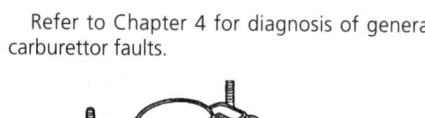

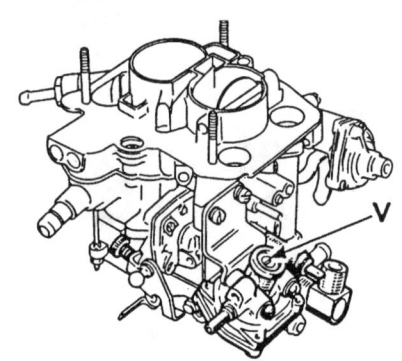

Anti-stall device

V Adjustment screw

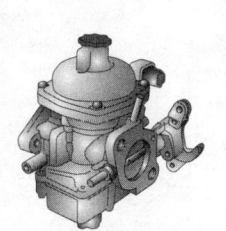

Part G Chapter 7
Solex 34/34 Z11 carburettor

G7

Contents

Component testing	5	Identification	2
Fault diagnosis	6	Principles of operation	1
General servicing	3	Service adjustments	4

Specifications

Manufacturer	Volvo	Volvo	Volvo
Model	360 2.0	240 2.3	240 2.3
Year	1985 to 1989	1987 to 1990	1987 to 1990
Engine code	B200K	B230K	B230K
Capacity (cm³)/no. of cyls	1990/4	2316/4	2316/4
Oil temperature (°C)	(Hot)	(Hot)	(Hot)
Transmission	-	MT	AT
Carb. ident. (Solex)	34/34 CISAC Z11 13401	-	-
Carb. ident. (vehicle)	1378207	-	-
Idle speed (rpm)	900 ± 50	900	900
CO @ idle (% vol.)	1.5 (+1 -0.5)	1.75 ± 0.75	1.0 ± 0.5
Stage (venturi)	1　　2	1　　2	1　　2
Venturi diameter (K)	15　　27	-	-
Idle jet (g)	41　　60	46	46
Main jet (Gg)	120　115	125　142	125　142
Air correction jet (a)	145　130	160　130	160　130
Emulsion tube (s)	ZN	ZC	-
Accelerator pump jet (i)	60	-	-
Float level (mm)	33.8	33 ± 1	33 ± 1
Needle valve (mm) (P)	2.1	-	-
Choke fast idle gap (mm)	2.7	2.5	1.5
Choke pull-down (mm) (OVAD)	2.7	2.7	2.7
Vent valve (mm)	0.5	0.5	0.5

Manufacturer	Volvo	Volvo	Volvo
Model	240 2.3 Catalyst	240 2.3 Catalyst	740 2.0
Year	1989 to 1990	1989 to 1990	1987 to 1988
Engine code	B230K	B230K	B200K
Capacity (cm³)/no. of cyls	2316/4	2316/4	1986/4
Oil temperature (°C)	(Hot)	(Hot)	(Hot)
Transmission	MT	AT	-
Carb. ident. (Solex)	-	133320	-
Carb. ident. (vehicle)	-	1326406	-
Idle speed (rpm)	800	900	900
CO @ idle (% vol.)	1.0 ± 0.5	1.0 ± 0.5	1.75 ± 0.75
Stage (venturi)	1　　2	1　　2	1　　2
Main jet (Gg)	125　142	125　142	120　135
Air correction jet (a)	160　130	160　130	145　130
Float level (mm)	33 ± 1	33 ± 1	33 ± 1
Idle jet (g)	46	46	41
Choke fast idle gap (mm)	2.5	1.5	1.0
Choke pull-down (mm) (OVAD)	2.7	2.7	2.7
Vent valve (mm)	0.5	0.5	0.5

Chapter G7

1 Principles of operation

Introduction

1 The following technical description of the Solex 34/34 Z11 carburettor should be read in conjunction with the more detailed description of carburettor principles in Part A. The Z11 carburettor is sometimes referred to as a CISAC carburettor.

Construction

2 The Solex Z11 carburettor is a downdraught progressive twin venturi instrument with either a mechanically-operated or vacuum-controlled secondary throttle (see illustration). Early versions of the carburettor tended to control the secondary throttle by a mechanical linkage, whereas later versions use a vacuum-controlled device. The choke control is manual in operation and operates on the primary venturi alone.

3 The throttle shafts are made of steel, while the throttle plates and all the emulsion tubes and jets are manufactured from brass. The internal fuel channels and air passages are drilled and sealed with lead plugs where necessary.

4 An electrical heater is fitted to the carburettor main body to improve atomisation of the air/fuel mixture and to prevent carburettor icing during warm-up. The heater is normally operational with the ignition on and functions on the PTC (positive temperature coefficient) principle. As the temperature rises, the heater resistance also rises.

Fuel control

5 Fuel flows into the carburettor through a fine mesh filter. The fuel level in the float chamber is controlled by a needle valve and plastic float assembly. An anti-vibration ball is incorporated into the needle valve design.

6 The float chamber uses a dual-venting arrangement. Venting is to atmosphere at idle or with the engine shut down. At engine speeds higher than idle, a lever attached to the throttle closes the atmospheric vent and this allows the float chamber to vent into the upper air intake which is on the clean-air side of the air filter.

7 A calibrated fuel return system is provided on some variations to ensure that relatively cool fuel is supplied to the carburettor.

Idle, slow running and progression

8 Fuel, sourced from the main well, passes into the idle channel through a metered idle jet.

Solex Z11 carburettor

1 Upper body
2 Fuel inlet connector
3 Float pin
4 Float
5 Needle valve
6 Idle jet (primary)
9 Bypass idle speed screw
10 Idle mixture control screw
11 Accelerator pump diaphragm
13 Pump injector
14 Fuel filter
16 Emulsion tube and air corrector - primary venturi
17 Emulsion tube and air corrector - secondary venturi
18 Main jet - primary venturi
19 Main jet - secondary venturi
21 Tamperproof cap
22 Float chamber gasket
23 Main body
25 Part-load enrichment diaphragm
26 Part-load enrichment jet
27 Secondary throttle diaphragm (where fitted)
29 Choke flap
30 Choke pull-down diaphragm
37 Throttle body heater
38 Float chamber vent valve

Solex 34/34 Z11 carburettor

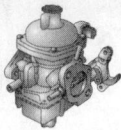

Here it is mixed with a small amount of air from a calibrated air bleed and the resulting emulsion is drawn through a channel, to be discharged from the idle orifice under the primary throttle plate. A tapered mixture screw is used to vary the outlet and this ensures fine control of the idle mixture *(see illustration)*.

9 A progression slot provides extra enrichment as it is uncovered by the opening throttle during initial acceleration.

10 The adjustable mixture screw is tamper proofed at production level, in accordance with emission regulations.

Idle cut-off valve (some variants)

11 An idle cut-off valve is used to prevent run-on when the engine is shut down. It utilises a 12-volt solenoid plunger to block the idle channel when the ignition is switched off.

Idle bypass circuit

12 The idle bypass circuit provides a means of more accurately controlling idle emissions than a conventional idle mixture circuit. The throttle plate is locked in a specified position and is sealed with a tamperproof cap. Eighty percent of the fuel required for idle is provided by the normal idle circuit. The remainder of the idle mixture is controlled through the idle bypass circuit.

13 Fuel, sourced from the main well, is drawn into the bypass passage. Air is sourced from the upper reaches of the main venturi. The air and fuel emulsion is drawn through the bypass passage and discharged from the bypass orifice under the throttle plate. The emulsion is controlled by a regulating screw which is also used to adjust the idle speed.

Accelerator pump

14 The Solex Z11 accelerator pump is controlled by a diaphragm and is mechanically operated by a lever and cam attached to the primary throttle linkage. During acceleration, fuel is pumped through a ball valve located in the pump injector and is discharged into both primary and secondary venturis. The inlet ball valve is located in a channel from the float chamber. Excess fuel/air mixture is returned to the float chamber through a separate fuel channel *(see illustration)*.

Main circuit

15 The amount of fuel discharged into the airstream is controlled by a calibrated main jet. Fuel is drawn through the main jet into the base of a vertical well which dips down into the fuel in the float chamber. An emulsion tube is placed in the well. The fuel is mixed with air, drawn in through the air corrector and through the holes in the emulsion tube. The resulting emulsified mixture is discharged from the main orifice through an auxiliary venturi.

Part-load enrichment (power valve)

16 Fuel flows from the float chamber into the enrichment chamber, through a fuel channel

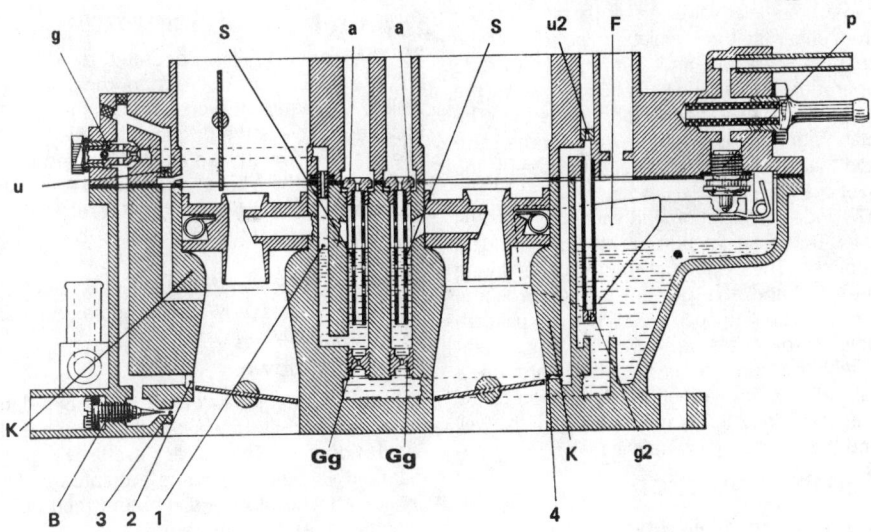

Idle and main circuits

1 Idle fuel channel
2 Progression slot - primary venturi
3 Idle mixture outlet
4 Progression slot - secondary venturi
a Air corrector jet - primary and secondary venturis
B Idle mixture control screw
F Float
g Idle fuel jet
g2 Fuel jet - secondary progression
Gg Main jets - primary and secondary venturis
K Venturi - primary and secondary
p Needle valve
S Emulsion tube - primary and secondary
u Idle air corrector jet
u2 Air corrector jet - secondary progression

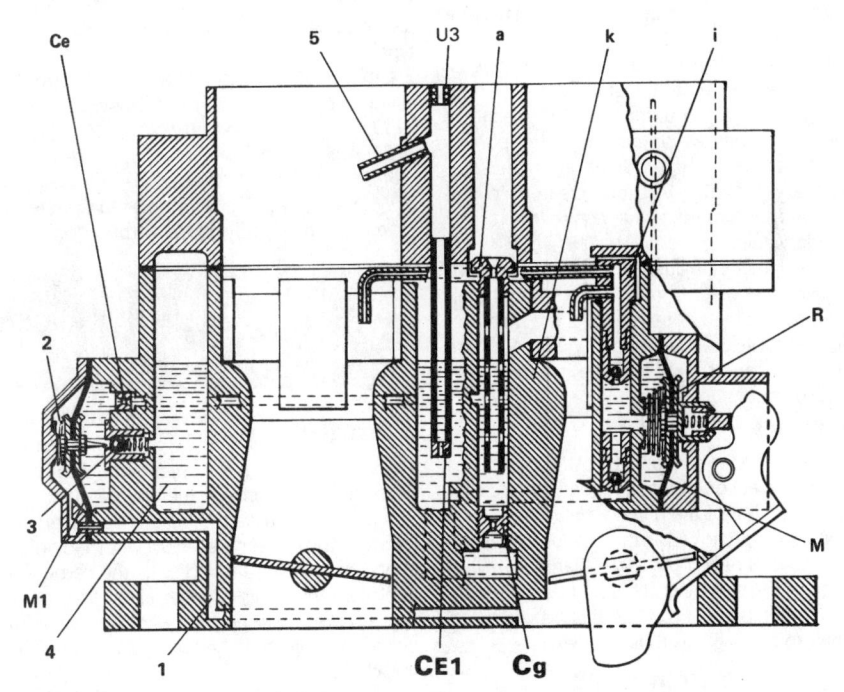

Accelerator pump and enrichment circuits

1 Vacuum passage
2 Spring
3 Part-load enrichment valve
4 Float chamber
5 Full-load enrichment nozzle
a Combined air corrector jet with emulsion tube - primary venturi
Ce Part-load enrichment fuel jet
CE1 Full-load enrichment fuel jet
Cg Main jet - primary venturi
i Accelerator pump injector
k Primary venturi
M Accelerator pump diaphragm
M1 Part-load enrichment diaphragm
R Spring
U3 Full-load enrichment air jet

Chapter G7

and a brass inlet valve. An air passage is taken from under the throttle plate to the cover of the chamber. At idle and during light-throttle operation, manifold vacuum draws the diaphragm back against spring pressure. The diaphragm pintle is withdrawn from the valve and the spring-loaded ball seats to close off the inlet channel.

17 Under acceleration and wide-open throttle operation, the vacuum in the manifold is depleted. The diaphragm returns under spring pressure and the power diaphragm pintle pushes the ball to open the inlet valve. Fuel then flows through the valve into the enrichment chamber. From here, it passes through a calibrated jet into a fuel channel leading to the primary main well. The fuel level rises in the well and the fuel mixture is enriched.

Secondary action

Manually-controlled type

18 Once the primary throttle plate is about two-thirds open, the secondary throttle plate will start to open. At full-throttle, the linkage is arranged so that both throttle plates will be fully open.

Vacuum-controlled type

19 A port is located in both the primary and secondary venturis. Airways run from the port in each venturi into a common vacuum hose leading to the diaphragm that operates the secondary throttle plate.
20 During normal operation at low speeds, only the primary venturi is employed. When air velocity through the primary venturi reaches a certain level, depression acts upon the port to operate the secondary diaphragm and the secondary throttle. Vacuum created in the secondary venturi will further control the rate of secondary opening.
21 The primary linkage is arranged to prevent the secondary plate from opening when the air speed may be high but the engine is cruising on a light throttle. Secondary action will not take place until the primary throttle is about two-thirds open.

Both types

22 Once the secondary throttle plate has opened, the action of the secondary main circuit is similar to that of the primary circuit.
23 When the choke is in operation (with the choke control pulled out more than halfway), a tag on the lever locks the secondary throttle operating linkage. Secondary throttle operation on half to full-choke is thus avoided.

Full-load enrichment

24 At full-load and high engine speeds, the velocity of air creates a depression sufficient to raise fuel from the float chamber into a channel. The fuel then passes through a calibrated bushing to the upper section of the secondary air intake. Here it is mixed with a small amount of air from a calibrated air bleed and the emulsified mixture is then discharged into the airstream from the full-load enrichment nozzle.

Manual choke operation

25 The manual choke is operated by a dash-mounted cable control. When the cable is pulled, it operates a lever that pulls the choke flap closed across the primary air intake. Fast idle is achieved with the aid of a curved cam attached to the choke operating lever. An adjustable screw, attached to the throttle lever and butting against the cam, is used to vary the fast idle speed.
26 During engine warm-up, the cable control should be progressively pushed home until the choke flap is fully open.

Choke pull-down

27 Once the engine has fired, the choke flap must open slightly to weaken the mixture and avoid flooding. This is achieved by using manifold vacuum to actuate a diaphragm. A linkage attached to the diaphragm then pulls upon the choke flap.

2 Identification

1 The Solex identification code is stamped on a metallic tag attached to the carburettor cover by an upper body fixing screw. This tag quotes the Solex part number and the vehicle manufacturer part number. It also identifies the carburettor type.
2 Later carburettors may have this information stamped upon the carburettor body:
 133320   Solex part number
 1326408 Vehicle manufacturer part number
 34-34 Z11 Carburettor type
3 Where the tag is missing, refer to Chapter for other ways of identifying the carburettor.

3 General servicing

Introduction

1 Read this Chapter in conjunction with Part B, which describes some of the operations in more detail. It is assumed that the carburettor is removed for this service. However, many of the operations can be tackled with the carburettor in place. Where this is undertaken, first remove the carburettor upper body and soak the fuel out of the float chamber using a clean tissue or soft cloth.

Dismantling and checking

2 Remove the carburettor from the engine (see Part B).
3 Check the carburettor visually for damage and wear.
4 Remove the idle cut-off valve assembly (where fitted) and clean it with carburettor cleaner. Test the plunger operation by connecting the valve to the battery, or other voltage supply (or use the valve supply wire in the engine compartment). Touch the valve body to earth with the ignition on. Repeat this several times and ensure that the plunger tip advances and retracts cleanly. Renew the valve if the action is faulty or if cleaning does not improve its operation.
5 Remove the five screws, disengage the vent valve and detach the carburettor upper body.
6 Inspect the float chamber for corrosion and calcium build-up.
7 Tap out the float pin and remove the float, needle valve and float chamber gasket.
8 Use a straight-edge to check for distorted flanges on all facing surfaces.
9 Check that the anti-vibration ball is free in the needle valve end.
10 Check the needle valve tip for wear and ridges.
11 The float should be checked for damage and ingress of petrol.
12 Renew the float pin if it shows signs of wear.
13 Unscrew the fuel inlet tube and inspect the fuel filter. Clean the filter housing of debris and dirt and renew the filter if necessary.
14 Remove the idle mixture and bypass screws, then inspect the tips for damage or ridges.
15 The accelerator pump injector is a push fit in the body. Carefully prise it from its location and test it by shaking. No noise from the outlet ball would indicate that the valve is seized.
16 Remove the four screws and detach the accelerator pump cover, diaphragm and spring. Check the diaphragm for fatigue and damage.
17 Remove the idle jet from the upper body.
18 Unscrew the primary and secondary combined air correctors and emulsion tubes.
19 Use a long thin screwdriver to unscrew the main jets which are located at the bottom of the emulsion tube wells. Invert the carburettor over a cupped hand to catch the jets as they fall out of the wells. The primary main jet is located on the power valve side of the carburettor and the secondary main jet is located on the choke side of the carburettor.
20 Note the sizes and locations of all the jets, for correct installation during reassembly.
21 Check the jet calibration against that specified. It is possible that the jets may have been transposed (or the wrong size fitted) during the last overhaul.
22 Check that the channels from the float chamber into the emulsion tube wells are clear.
23 Remove the three screws and detach the power valve housing cover, spring and diaphragm from the body. Check the diaphragm for fatigue and damage.
24 The brass outlet (power) valve is cast into the body and is not removable. The ball in the outlet valve should seal the outlet. Depress and release the ball with a small screwdriver and it should move smoothly in and out.
25 Unscrew and remove the small power jet from inside the power valve housing. Check that the channel into the emulsion tube well is clear.
26 Disconnect the vacuum hose from the secondary throttle diaphragm (where fitted).

Solex 34/34 Z11 carburettor

Attach a vacuum pump to the connection and operate the pump to obtain 300 mm (400 mbars). Renew the secondary diaphragm assembly if this reading is not obtained, or if vacuum is not maintained for at least 30 seconds.

27 Check the three vacuum hoses for fatigue and wear.

28 Do not disturb the adjustment of the primary or secondary throttle angles, unless absolutely necessary.

29 Remove the four screws and detach the choke pull-down cover, spring and diaphragm from the housing. Check the diaphragm for fatigue and wear. Remove the plastic linkage shield from the choke mechanism.

Preparation for reassembly

30 Clean the jets, carburettor body assemblies, float chamber and internal channels. An air line may be used to clear the internal channels once the carburettor is fully dismantled. Note that if high-pressure air is directed into the channels and passages with the diaphragms still in place, diaphragm damage may result. Spraying carburettor cleaner into all the channels and passages in the carburettor body will often clear them of gum and dirt.

31 During reassembly, a complete set of new gaskets should be fitted. Also renew the needle valve, the float pin and all diaphragms.

32 Inspect and renew (where necessary) the mixture screw, main jet, air corrector/ emulsion tubes, idle jet and the accelerator pump injector. Renew worn linkages, screws, springs and other parts where necessary.

33 Ensure that all the jets are firmly locked into their original positions (but do not over-tighten). A loose jet can cause a rich (or even lean) running condition.

34 Clean all mating surfaces and flanges of old gasket material and reassemble with new gaskets.

35 Ensure that housings are positioned with their air and fuel routes correctly aligned.

Reassembly

36 Refit the choke diaphragm and spindle assembly to the choke housing. Refit the spring and cover, then secure with the four screws.

37 Check that the secondary throttle plate is fully closed. The adjustment screw should not normally be used to alter the throttle plate position. However, if necessary, it can be adjusted so that the plate is open just enough to prevent its seizure in the throttle body.

38 Where the primary throttle plate position has been disturbed, it should be adjusted so that the plate is open just enough to prevent its seizure in the throttle body. An adjustment method with the engine running is detailed in Section 4. Adjustment data for use with a throttle angle tool on this carburettor is not available.

39 Refit the power jet into its original position.

40 Refit the power diaphragm, spring and cover assembly, then secure with the three screws.

41 Refit the main jets and emulsion tubes/air correctors into their original positions (do not transpose the jets).

42 Refit the idle jet into the upper body (with a new seal) and lock it firmly into position.

43 Refit the accelerator pump spring, diaphragm and cover assembly, then secure with the four screws.

44 Carefully refit the accelerator pump injector, after renewing the small seal on the injector body.

45 Refit the idle mixture screw. Turn the screw in gently until it just seats. From this position, unscrew it four full turns. This will provide a basic setting to allow the engine to be started.

46 Refit the idle bypass screw. Obtain a basic setting in the same way as described for the mixture screw above but unscrew it by five full turns.

47 Clean or renew the fuel filter and refit the fuel inlet tube with a new sealing washer.

48 Locate a new float chamber gasket in position on the upper body.

49 Fit the new needle valve assembly, using a new sealing washer. Ensure that it is firmly locked into position (but do not over-tighten). Refit the float and secure with the float pin.

50 Adjust the float level with reference to Section 4.

51 Refit the upper body to the main body and secure with the five screws. Re-engage the vent valve mechanism.

52 Refit the idle cut-off valve.

53 Ensure that the choke flap moves smoothly and progressively, then inspect the operating mechanism for stickiness and wear.

54 Refit the choke mechanism shield.

55 Adjust the choke fast idle and pull-down with reference to Section 4.

56 Refit the carburettor to the engine.

57 Always adjust the carburettor idle speed and mixture after any work has been carried out on the carburettor, preferably with the aid of a CO meter.

4 Service adjustments

Adjustment pre-conditions

1 Refer to Part B for general advice on the pre-conditions for correct adjustment of this carburettor.

Idle speed and mixture (CO)

2 Run the engine at 3000 rpm for 30 seconds to clear the manifold of fuel vapours, then allow the engine to idle.

3 Use the idle bypass screw to set the specified idle speed (see illustration).

4 Check the CO level. If incorrect, remove the tamperproof plug and adjust the idle mixture screw to obtain the correct level. Turning the screw clockwise (inwards) will reduce the CO level. Turning the screw anti-clockwise (outwards) will increase the CO level. Refer to Part B for a method of setting the idle mixture without the aid of a CO meter.

5 Repeat paragraphs 3 and 4 until both adjustments are correct.

6 Clear the manifold every 30 seconds during the setting operation by running the engine at 3000 rpm for 30 seconds.

7 Fit a new tamperproof plug to the mixture control screw on completion.

Basic throttle position

8 If the idle speed and CO cannot be set correctly, it is possible that the basic throttle position is incorrect. The manufacturer's recommended method is to remove the carburettor and use a Renault, Solex or Pierburg throttle setting gauge to accurately set the throttle position. Unfortunately, adjustment data is not available for this carburettor.

9 However, there is an alternative method that can be used to set the throttle plate. Please note that this is not the manufacturer's recommended method but will nevertheless result in an accurate and stable idle speed and CO level.

10 With the engine idling, screw in the idle bypass screw until it is fully seated. The idle speed should drop to approximately two-thirds of the specified idle speed figure. For example, if the idle speed is specified as 900 rpm, the speed should drop to 600 rpm.

11 Adjust the throttle stop screw until 600 rpm is obtained.

12 Unscrew the bypass screw until 900 rpm is once again attained.

13 Reset the CO to the correct level.

14 If the CO needs a large adjustment at this stage, repeat paragraphs 10 to 13. Once the proper level of CO is obtained at the specified idle speed, the carburettor is properly adjusted.

15 Note that the rpm figures used in the above example are based on a hypothetical idle speed of 900 rpm. Substitute the correct figures for the carburettor being adjusted (see Specifications).

Float level

16 Invert the carburettor upper body so that the float faces upwards and the needle valve is depressed.

17 Measure the distance between the upper body (with its gasket) and the upper face of the

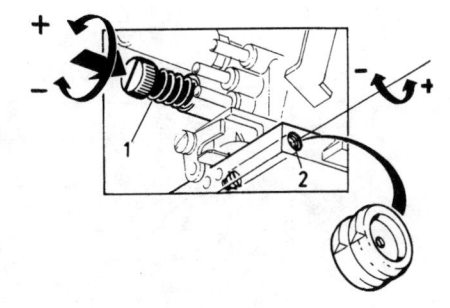

Idle adjustment screw location

1 Bypass idle speed screw
2 Idle mixture screw

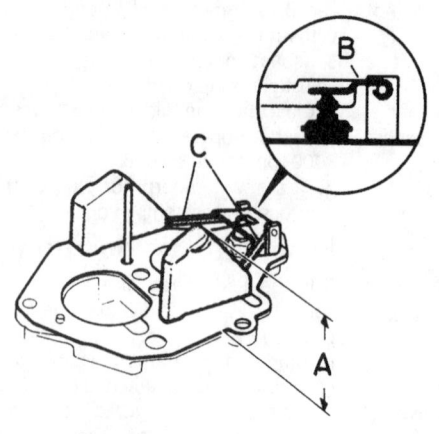

Chapter G7

Float level adjustment
A Float level   B Inner float tag   C Float arms

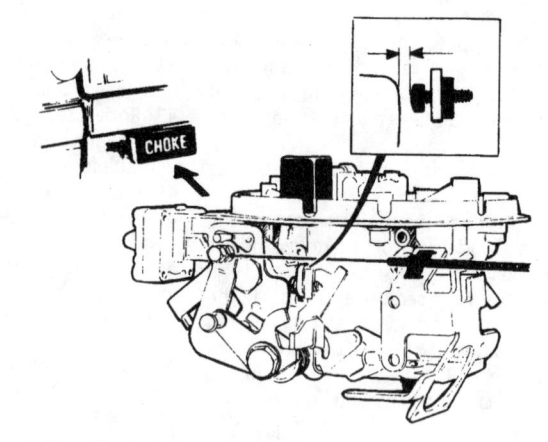

Fast idle adjustment
Arrows show fast idle clearance

plastic float (refer to Specifications for the correct float level) *(see illustration)*.
18 Adjust as necessary by bending the inner float tag.
19 The upper faces of the float should not differ in height by more than 1.0 mm. Adjust by bending the float arms (C) if necessary.

Choke adjustments

Fast idle

20 Push the choke control all the way in so that the choke flap is fully open.
21 Use the shank of a twist drill to measure the clearance between the fast idle cam and the fast idle screw *(see illustration)*. Refer to Specifications for the required drill size.
22 Adjust as necessary by turning the fast idle adjustment screw in the appropriate direction.

Vacuum pull-down

23 Pull the choke operating lever to fully close the choke flap.
24 Use a small screwdriver to push the diaphragm operating rod up to its stop. At the same time, use the shank of a twist drill to measure the gap between the lower section of the choke flap and the air intake. Refer to Specifications for the required drill size *(see illustration)*.
25 Remove the plug in the diaphragm cover and adjust as necessary by turning the adjustment screw in the appropriate direction. Renew the plug when adjustment is complete.

Vent valve

26 Ensure that the throttle is fully closed.
27 Adjust the vent valve to obtain a maximum clearance of 0.5 mm *(see illustration)*.
28 It should now be possible to blow through the vent valve but at the slightest movement of the throttle, it should no longer be possible to do so.

5 Component testing

Throttle body heater

1 Refer to Part D for a method of testing the electrical throttle body heater.

6 Fault diagnosis

Refer to Part D for diagnosis of general carburettor faults.

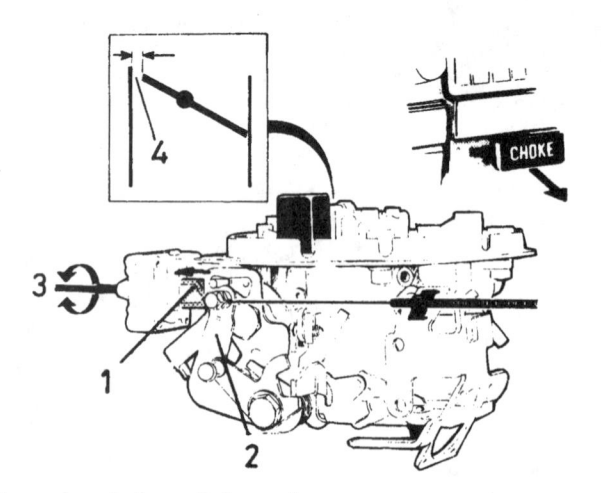

Measuring choke pull-down clearance
1 Diaphragm operating rod
2 Choke operating lever
3 Clearance adjustment point
4 Pull-down clearance

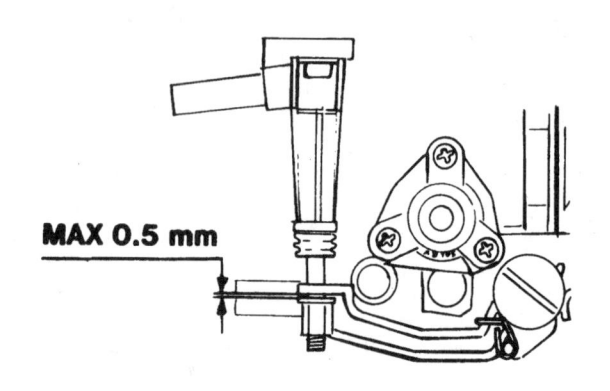

Vent valve adjustment

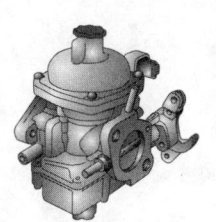

Part H Chapter 1
Weber 28/36, 32 & 32/36 DARA carburettor

Contents

Fault diagnosis 5
General servicing 3
Identification 2
Principles of operation 1
Service adjustments 4

Specifications

Manufacturer	Renault	Renault	Renault
Model	18 1.6 (R1342)	18 2.0 (R1343, 1353)	18 2.0 (R1343, 1353)
Year	1983 to 1986	1982 to 1986	1982 to 1986
Engine code	A6ML725	849L716 (J6R)	849L716 (J6R)
Capacity (cm³)/no. of cyls	1647/4	1995/4	1995/4
Oil temperature (°C)	80	80	80
Transmission	–	MT	MT
Carb. identification	32 DARA 38	32 DARA 42/100	32 DARA 42/101
Idle speed (rpm)	800 ± 50	800 ± 50	800 ± 50
CO @ idle (% vol.)	1.5 ± 0.5	1.5 ± 0.5	1.5 ± 0.5

Stage (venturi)	1	2	1	2	1	2
Venturi diameter	24	26	26	26	26	26
Idle jet	47	45	52	45	52	45
Main jet	132	150	132	132	135	130
Air correction jet	180	145	160	145	155	155
Emulsion tube	F53	F6	F58	F6	F58	F56
Accel. pump jet	60		60		60	
Float level (mm)	7		7		7	
Float stroke (mm)	8		8		8	
Needle valve size (mm)	2.00		2.25		2.25	
Choke fast idle gap (mm)	1.4 (max)		1.3 (max)		1.3 (max)	
Choke pull-down (mm)	7.5		10		10	
De-choke (mm)	10		9		9	
Defuming/vent valve (mm)	0.5		–		–	

Chapter H1

Manufacturer	Renault	Renault	Renault
Model	18 2.0 Auto (R1343)	Fuego 1.6 (R1362)	Fuego 1.6 (R1362)
Year	1984 to 1986	1982 to 1986	1982 to 1986
Engine code	J6RK711	A6ML725	A6ML725
Capacity (cm³)/no. of cyls	1995/4	1647/4	1647/4
Oil temperature (°C)	80	80	80
Transmission	AT	MT	AT
Carb. identification	32 DARA 41	32 DARA 38	32 DARA 39
Idle speed (rpm)	900 ± 50	800 ± 50	650 ± 25
CO @ idle (% vol.)	1.0 ± 0.5	1.5 ± 0.5	1.5 ± 0.5
Special conditions	AT in Drive	—	—
Stage (venturi)	1 / 2	1 / 2	1 / 2
Venturi diameter	26 / 26	24 / 26	24 / 26
Idle jet	52 / 42/105	47 / 45	47 / 45
Main jet	135 / 140	132 / 150	132 / 150
Air correction jet	155 / 140	180 / 145	180 / 145
Emulsion tube	F58 / F6	F53 / F6	F53 / F6
Accel. pump jet	60	60	60
Float level (mm)	7	7	7
Float stroke (mm)	8	8	8
Needle valve size (mm)	2.25	2.00	2.00
Choke fast idle gap (mm)	1.4 (max)	1.4 (max)	1.4 (max)
Choke pull-down (mm)	10	7.5	7.5
De-choke (mm)	9	10	10

Manufacturer	Renault	Renault	Renault
Model	Fuego 2.0 (R1363)	Fuego 2.0 (R1363)	20 2.0 (R1277)
Year	1980 to 1984	1980 to 1984	1981 to 1984
Engine code	829J710 or J6RK711	829J710 or J6RK711	829G702
Capacity (cm³)/no. of cyls	1995/4	1995/4	1995/4
Oil temperature (°C)	80	80	80
Transmission	MT	AT	MT
Carb. identification	32 DARA 40	32 DARA 41	32 DARA 42/102
Idle speed (rpm)	800 ± 50	900 ± 50	800 ± 50
CO @ idle (% vol.)	1.0 ± 0.5	1.0 ± 0.5	1.5 ± 0.5
Special conditions	—	AT in Neutral	—
Stage (venturi)	1 / 2	1 / 2	1 / 2
Venturi diameter	26 / 26	26 / 26	26 / 26
Idle jet	55 / 45	52 / 42/105	52 / 45
Main jet	132 / 140	135 / 140	135 / 130
Air correction jet	155 / 140	155 / 140	155 / 155
Emulsion tube	F58 / F6	F58 / F6	F58 / F6
Accel. pump jet	60	60	60
Float level (mm)	7	7	7
Float stroke (mm)	8	8	8
Needle valve size (mm)	2.25	2.25	2.25
Choke fast idle gap (mm)	1.3 (max)	1.4 (max)	1.3 (max)
Choke pull-down (mm)	10	10	10
De-choke (mm)	9	9	9

Manufacturer	Renault	Renault	Renault
Model	20 2.0 (R1277)	20 2.2 (R1279)	20 2.2 (R1279)
Year	1981 to 1984	1980 to 1984	1980 to 1984
Engine code	829H703	851A700	851B701
Capacity (cm³)/no. of cyls	1995/4	2165/4	2165/4
Oil temperature (°C)	80	80	80
Transmission	AT	MT	AT
Carb. identification	32 DARA 43/104	32/36 DARA 6/100/101	32/36 DARA 7
Idle speed (rpm)	675 ± 25	800 ± 50	675 ± 25
CO @ idle (% vol.)	1.5 ± 0.5	1.5 ± 0.5	1.5 ± 0.5
Stage (venturi)	1 / 2	1 / 2	1 / 2
Venturi diameter	26 / 26	26 / 28	26 / 28
Idle jet	57 / 42	62 / 42	60 / 42
Main jet	135 / 135	127 / 145	130 / 160
Air correction jet	155 / 140	155 / 155	160 / 170

Weber 28/36, 32 & 32/36 DARA carburettor

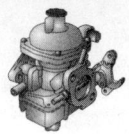

Manufacturer	Renault (continued)		Renault (continued)		Renault (continued)	
Model	20 2.0 (R1277)		20 2.2 (R1279)		20 2.2 (R1279)	
Year	1981 to 1984		1980 to 1984		1980 to 1984	
Stage (venturi)	1	2	1	2	1	2
Emulsion tube	F58	F6	F58	F6	F58	F6
Accel. pump jet	60		60		60	
Float level (mm)	7		7 ± 0.25		7 ± 0.25	
Float stroke (mm)	8		–		–	
Needle valve size (mm)	2.25		2.25		2.25	
Choke fast idle gap (mm)	1.3 (max)		1 ± 0.05 (2nd. step)		1.05 ± 0.05 (2nd. step)	
Choke pull-down (mm)	10		10 ± 0.50		10 ± 0.50	
De-choke (mm)	9		9 ± 1.0		10 ± 1.0	

Manufacturer	Renault		Renault		Renault	
Model	25 2.0 (B297)		25 2.0 (B297)		25 2.0 GTS (B297)	
Year	1984 to 1989		1984 to 1989		1990 to 1991	
Engine code	J6R N 706		J6R V 707		J6R D 734	
Capacity (cm³)/no. of cyls	1995/4		1995/4		1995/4	
Oil temperature (°C)	80		80		80	
Transmission	MT		AT		–	
Carb. identification	28/36 DARA 0		28/36 DARA 1		28/36 DARA 8/8C	
			28/36 DARA 4/100			
Idle speed (rpm)	700 ± 50		800 ± 50		700 ± 50	
CO @ idle (% vol.)	1.5 ± 0.5		1.5 ± 0.5		1.5 ± 0.5	
Special conditions	–		AT in Drive		–	
Stage (venturi)	1	2	1	2	1	2
Venturi diameter	22	29	22	29	22	29
Idle jet	42	42	40	50	42	42
Main jet	112	155	112	155	112	155
Air correction jet	200	100	200	100	180	100
Emulsion tube	F99	F56	F99	F56	F99	F7
Accel. pump jet	50		50		60	
Engine code	J6R N 706		J6R V 707		J6R D 734	
Float level (mm)	7		7		7	
Float stroke (mm)	8		8		8	
Needle valve size (mm)	2.25		2.25		2.25	
Choke fast idle gap (mm)	0.8 ± 0.05		0.8 ± 0.05		0.8 (2nd. notch)	
Choke pull-down (mm)	7.5		7.5		5.5 ± 0.5	
De-choke (mm)	5.5		6.5		6 ± 0.5	

Manufacturer	Renault		Renault	
Model	Espace (J112)		Espace (J112)	
Year	1985 to 1988		1988 to 1991	
Engine code	J6RC234		J6RD734	
Capacity (cm³)/no. of cyls	1995/4		1995/4	
Oil temperature (°C)	80		80	
Carb. identification	32 DARA 40/103		28/36 DARA 0	
Idle speed (rpm)	800 ± 50		700 ± 50	
CO @ idle (% vol.)	1.5 ± 0.5		1.5 ± 0.5	
Stage (venturi)	1	2	1	2
Venturi diameter	26	26	22	29
Idle jet	55	45	42	42
Main jet 132	140	112	155	
Air correction jet	160	140	200	100
Emulsion tube	F58	F6	F99	F56
Accel. pump jet	60		50	
Float level (mm)	7		7	
Float stroke (mm)	8		8	
Needle valve size (mm)	2.25		2.25	
Choke fast idle gap (mm)	1.3 (max)		0.8 (2nd. notch)	
Choke pull-down (mm)	10		7.5 ± 0.5	
De-choke (mm)	9		–	

H1•3

Chapter H1

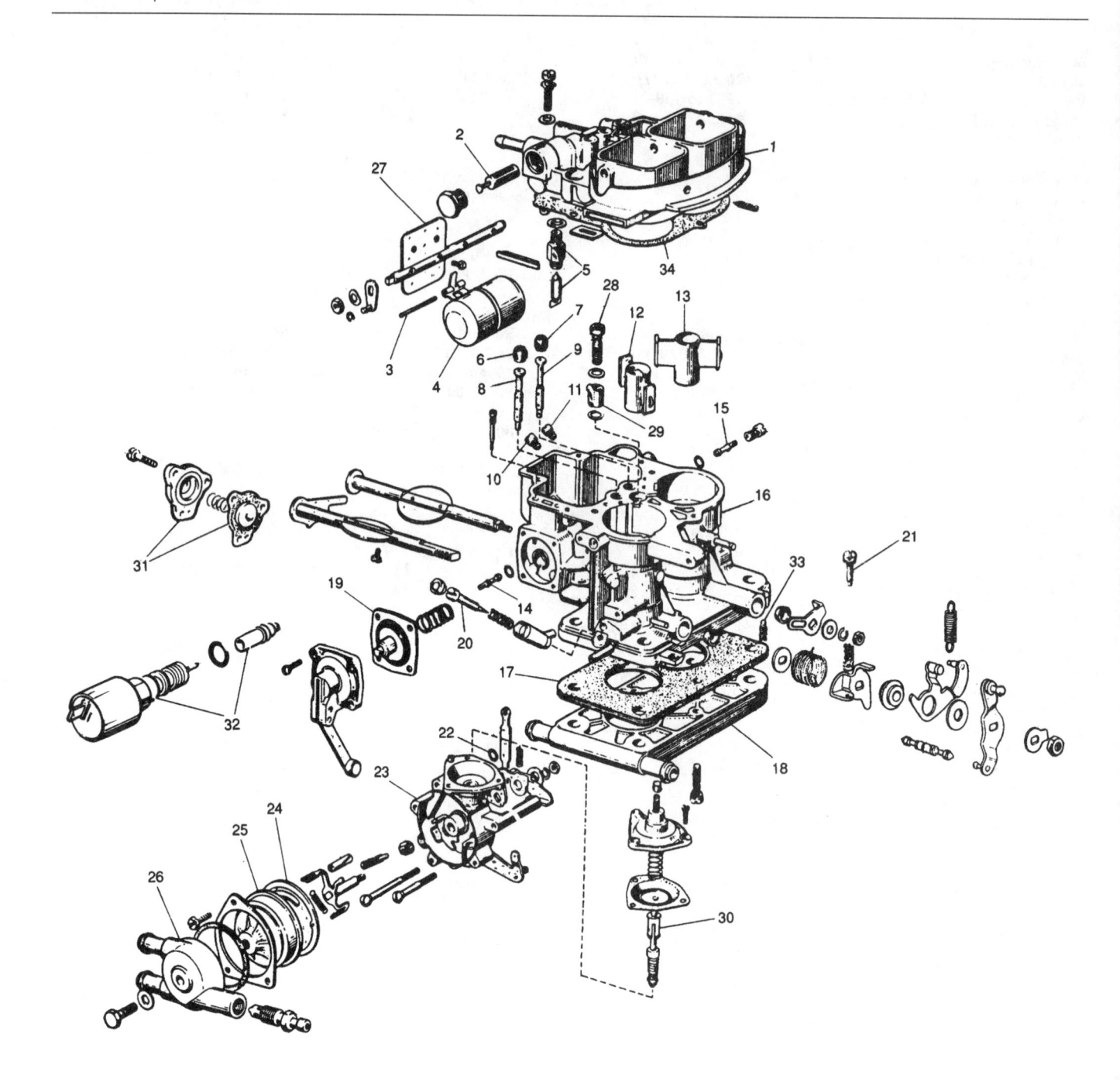

Weber DARA carburettor

1. Upper body
2. Fuel inlet filter
3. Float pin
4. Float
5. Needle valve assembly
6. Air corrector (primary)
7. Air corrector (secondary)
8. Emulsion tube (primary)
9. Emulsion tube (secondary)
10. Main jet (primary)
11. Main jet (secondary)
12. Auxiliary venturi (primary)
13. Auxiliary venturi (secondary)
14. Idle jet (primary)
15. Idle jet (secondary)
16. Main body
17. Insulating block
18. Heating flange
19. Accelerator pump diaphragm
20. Idle mixture control screw
21. Idle speed adjustment screw
22. Choke seal
23. Choke housing
24. Heat shield
25. Bi-metal housing
26. Choke water jacket
27. Choke flap (2)
28. Pump discharge valve
29. Pump injector
30. Choke diaphragm
31. Power valve assembly (where fitted)
32. Idle cut-off valve and primary idle jet (where fitted)
33. Secondary throttle valve adjustment screw
34. Float chamber gasket

Weber 28/36, 32 & 32/36 DARA carburettor

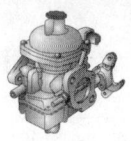

1 Principles of operation

Introduction

1 The following technical description of the Weber DARA carburettor should be read in conjunction with the more detailed description of carburettor principles in Part A.

Construction

2 The Weber DARA carburettor is a downdraught, progressive twin venturi instrument *(see illustration)*. It is available in throttle sizes of 28/32, 32/32 and 32/36 mm. The venturis are arranged so that the secondary throttle valve will not begin to open until the primary throttle valve is two-thirds-open. The choke system is semi-automatic in operation and is controlled by a bi-metal coil heated by the engine coolant. The throttle shafts are made of steel. The throttle valves of brass, as are the emulsion tubes and jets, with the exception of the accelerator pump injector which is die-cast. The internal fuel channels and air passages are drilled and sealed with lead plugs where necessary. A heating flange is bolted to the carburettor base and hot engine coolant is piped through it, the purpose being to improve atomisation of the air/fuel mixture.

3 There are a number of variations to the basic design and these are mentioned at the appropriate point in the text.

Fuel control

4 Fuel flows into the carburettor through a fine mesh filter. The fuel level in the float chamber is controlled by a needle valve and brass float assembly. An anti-vibration ball is incorporated into the needle valve design. A plastic or hairpin clip, attached to the needle valve seat and to the float arm, prevents the needle from sticking in the seat as the fuel level drops *(see illustration)*.

5 The float chamber is either vented internally to the clean-air side of the air filter or uses a dual venting arrangement. Where dual venting is used, venting is to atmosphere at idle or with the engine shut down. At engine speeds above idle, a lever attached to the throttle opens a valve to the upper air intake and venting is then to the clean-air side of the air filter. On the Weber DARA carburettor, this valve is known as a defuming valve.

Idle, slow running and progression

6 Fuel, sourced from the main well, passes into the primary idle channel through a metered idle jet. Here it is mixed with a small amount of air from a calibrated air bleed. The resulting emulsion is drawn through a channel, to be discharged from the idle orifice under the primary throttle plate. A tapered mixture screw is used to vary the outlet and this ensures fine control of the idle mixture. A number of progression drillings provide enrichment as they are uncovered by the opening throttle during initial acceleration *(see illustrations)*.

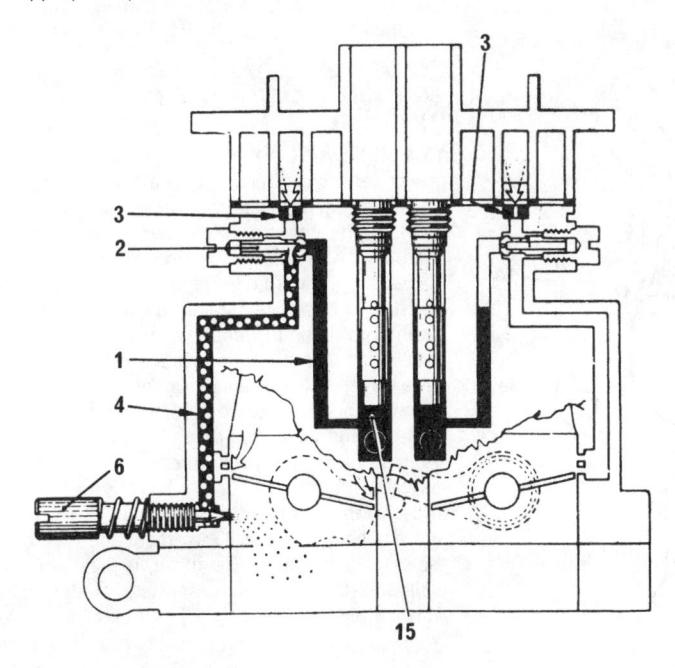

Inlet and main circuits

1 Fuel filter
2 Float
3 Needle valve assembly
4 Float arm
5 Main jet
6 Main well
7 Emulsion tube
8 Air corrector
9 Auxiliary venturi
10 Main venturi
11 Main fuel outlet
12 Float chamber vent
13 Float chamber vent
14 Float pin

Primary idle circuit

1 Idle fuel channel
2 Idle jet
3 Air bleed
4 Idle fuel/air channel
6 Idle mixture control screw
15 Main well

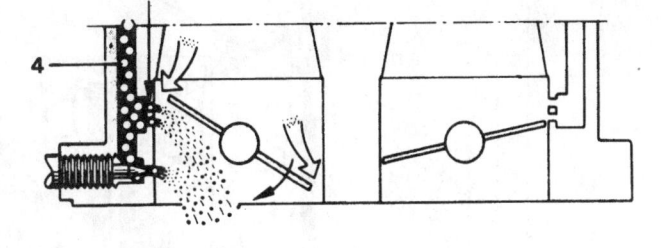

Primary progression circuit

4 Idle fuel/air channel
16 Progression outlet

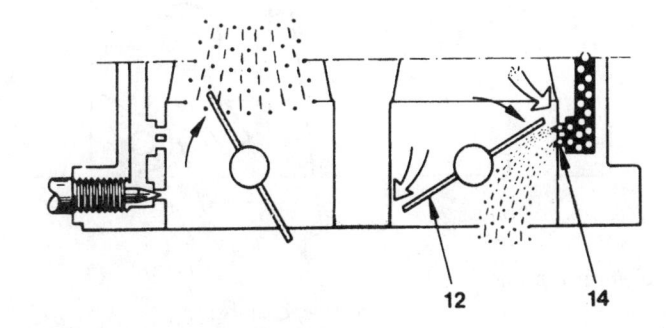

Secondary progression circuit

12 Secondary throttle plate
14 Progression outlet

H1•5

Chapter H1

Idle bypass circuit

A Bypass regulating screw
B Basic idle mixture control screw
J Idle fuel/air channel (secondary)
K Progression channel (secondary)

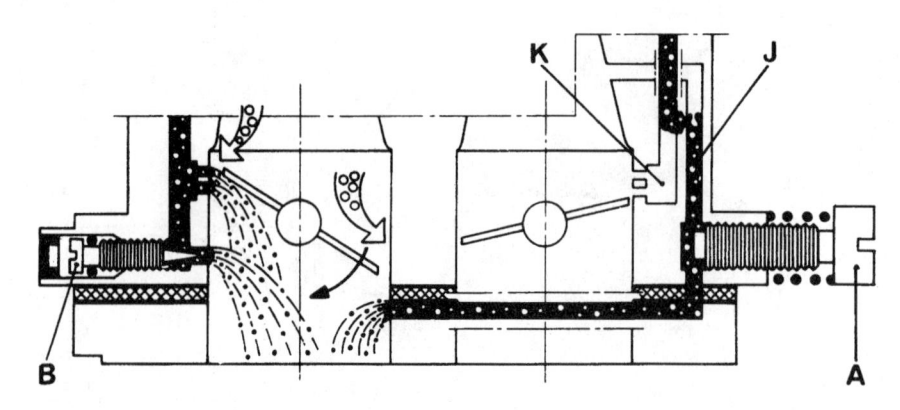

7 The idle speed is set by an adjustable screw. The adjustable mixture screw is tamper proofed during production, in accordance with emission regulations.

Idle cut-off valve (some models)

8 An idle cut-off valve is used to prevent run-on when the engine is shut down. It utilises a 12-volt solenoid plunger to block the idle jet when the ignition is switched off.

Idle bypass circuit (some models)

9 The idle bypass circuit provides a means of more accurately controlling idle emissions than a conventional idle mixture circuit. The throttle plate is locked in a set position and is sealed with a tamperproof cap. Eighty percent of the fuel required for idle is provided by the normal idle circuit. The remainder of the idle mixture is controlled through the idle bypass circuit (see illustration).

10 A fuel channel links the secondary idle fuel circuit with the bypass passage. An air and fuel emulsion is drawn through the passage to be discharged from the bypass orifice under the primary throttle plate. The emulsion is controlled by a regulating screw which is also used to adjust the idle speed.

Accelerator pump

11 The Weber DARA accelerator pump is controlled by a diaphragm and is mechanically operated by a lever and cam attached to the primary throttle linkage. During acceleration, fuel is pumped through a discharge valve and ball into the pump injector where it is discharged into the primary venturi. The inlet valve consists of a ball valve located in a channel from the float chamber. Excess fuel and air is returned to the float chamber through a separate fuel channel (see illustration).

Main circuit

12 The amount of fuel discharged into the airstream is controlled by a calibrated main jet. Fuel is drawn through the main jet into the base of a vertical well which dips down into the fuel in the float chamber. An emulsion tube is placed in the well. The fuel is mixed with air, drawn in through the air corrector and through the holes in the emulsion tube. The resulting emulsified mixture is discharged from the main orifice through an auxiliary venturi.

Power enrichment and economy circuit (some models)

13 Fuel flows from the float chamber into the power valve chamber through a fuel channel. An air passage is taken from under the throttle plate to the cover of the power diaphragm chamber. At idle, and during light-throttle operation, manifold vacuum draws the diaphragm back against spring pressure. The diaphragm pintle is withdrawn from the brass outlet valve and the spring-loaded ball seats to close off the outlet channel. Under acceleration and wide-open throttle operation, the vacuum in the manifold is depleted. The diaphragm returns under spring pressure and the power diaphragm pintle pushes the ball to open the outlet valve. Fuel then flows through the valve and a calibrated jet to supplement the fuel in the primary main well. The fuel level rises in the well and the fuel mixture is enriched (see illustration).

Secondary action

14 Once the primary throttle valve is about two-thirds-open, the secondary throttle plate will begin to open. At full-throttle, the linkage is arranged so that both throttle plates will be fully open.

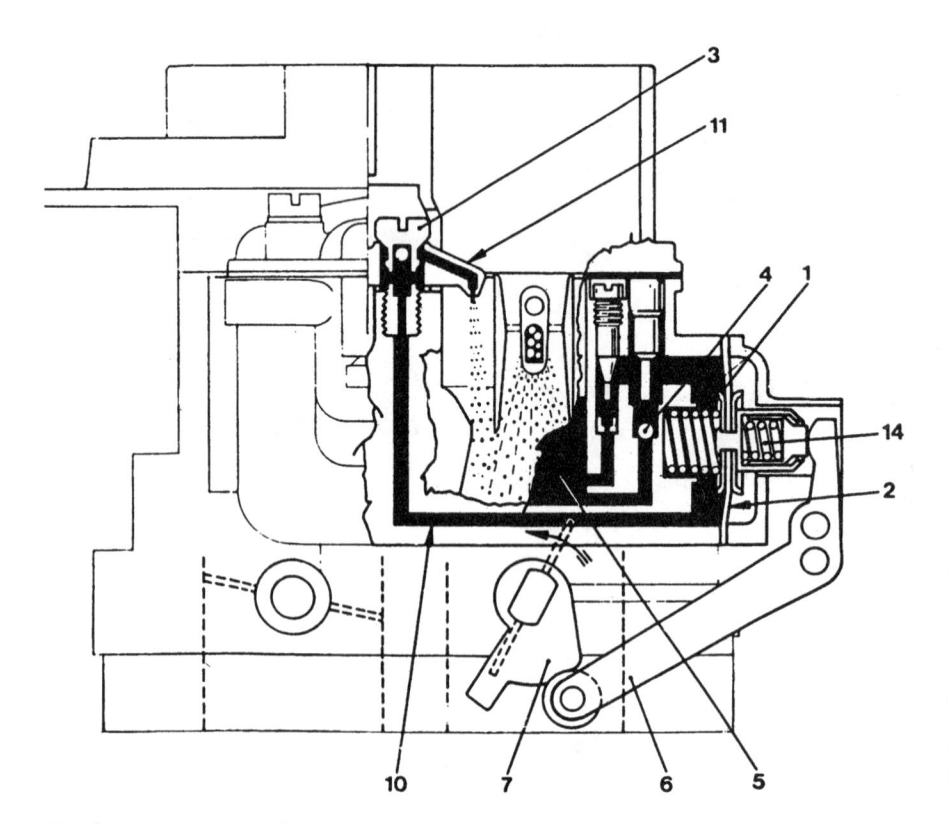

Accelerator pump circuit

1 Spring
2 Diaphragm
3 Pump discharge valve
4 Inlet ball
5 Float chamber
6 Pump actuating lever
7 Pump cam
10 Fuel outlet channel
11 Pump injector
14 Spring

Weber 28/36, 32 & 32/36 DARA carburettor

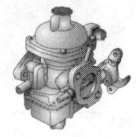

15 A progression jet is used to prevent hesitation as the secondary throttle plate begins to open. This jet is similar in construction and action to the primary idle jet and is often referred to as the secondary idle jet. An emulsified mixture is discharged into the secondary venturi via a progression drilling at the initial opening of the secondary throttle plate.

16 Once the secondary throttle plate has opened, then the action of the secondary main circuit is similar to the primary circuit.

17 At full-load and high engine speeds, even more fuel is required. The velocity of air creates a depression sufficient to raise fuel from the float chamber into a channel. The fuel then passes through a calibrated bushing to the upper section of the secondary air intake. Here it is mixed with a small amount of air from a calibrated air bleed. The emulsified mixture is then discharged into the airstream from a full-load enrichment outlet placed in the barrel.

Choke operation

18 The Weber DARA carburettor uses a semi-automatic choke starting system *(see illustration)*. A bi-metal spring is used to control a strangler choke flap via an air intake. Heating of the spring is by coolant from the engine cooling system. The system is primed by slowly depressing the accelerator pedal once or twice.

19 Once the engine has fired, the choke flap must open slightly to weaken the mixture and avoid flooding during idle and light-throttle operation. This is achieved by using manifold vacuum to actuate a diaphragm. A linkage attached to the diaphragm will then pull upon the choke flap.

20 Fast idle is achieved with the aid of a stepped cam attached to the choke spindle. An adjustable screw, connected to the throttle lever mechanism and butting against the cam, can be used to vary the fast idle speed. As the bi-metal coil is heated and the plate opens, then the screw will rest on successively less-stepped parts of the cam. The idle speed is thus progressively reduced, until ultimately the cam is released and the idle speed returns to normal.

Wide-open kick (dechoke)

21 If the throttle is fully opened during cold acceleration, the pull-down vacuum will be depleted and the choke flap will tend to close. This may cause flooding and to prevent this, a wide-open kick mechanism is employed. When the throttle is fully opened, a cam on the throttle lever will turn the choke lever anti-clockwise to partially open the choke flap.

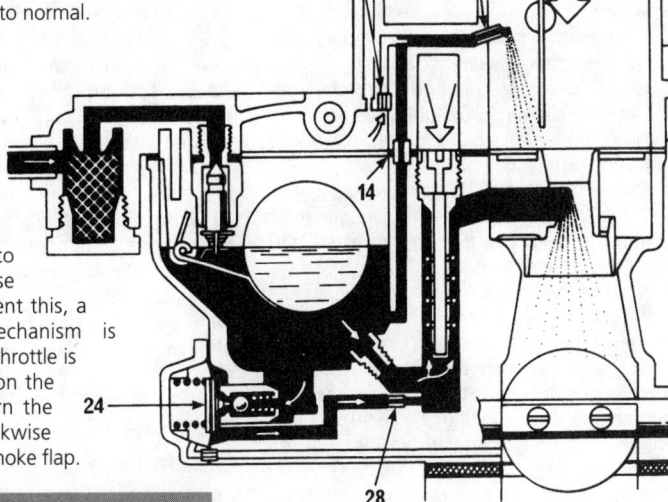

2 Identification

The Weber identification code is stamped on the carburettor base flange.

3 General servicing

Introduction

1 Read this Chapter in conjunction with Part B, which describes some of the operations in more detail. It is assumed that the carburettor is removed for this service. However, many of the operations can be tackled with the carburettor in place. Where this is undertaken, first soak the fuel out of the float chamber using a clean tissue or soft cloth after removing the upper body assembly.

Dismantling and checking

2 Remove the carburettor from the engine (see Part B).

3 Check visually for damage and wear. Where an idle cut-off valve is used, it is secured with a 2 mm socket-head grub screw. Slacken this screw before removing the idle cut-off valve. If the valve is loose in the body, a new carburettor will be required.

4 Use a small screwdriver to prise off the securing circlip and detach the upper end of the choke operating link from the choke spindle arm.

5 Loosen the three screws and pull the choke housing away from the main body. Remove the five screws and detach the carburettor upper body.

6 Use a straight-edge to check for distorted flanges on all facing surfaces.

7 Inspect the float chamber for corrosion and calcium build-up.

Power and full-load enrichment circuits

14 Full-load calibrated bush
15 Full-load air bleed
16 Full-load outlet
24 Power valve diaphragm
28 Calibrated jet

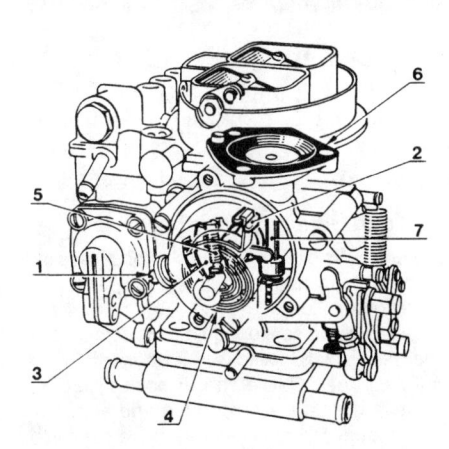

8 Tap out the float pin and remove the float, needle valve, clip and needle valve seat. Recover the float chamber gasket.

9 Check that the anti-vibration ball is free in the valve end.

10 Check the needle valve tip for wear and ridges. This is more likely with the brass needle valve tip than when a viton one is used. Use a viton-tipped replacement when possible.

11 The float should be checked for damage and ingress of petrol.

12 Renew the float pin if it shows signs of wear.

13 Remove the hexagon bolt and inspect the fuel filter. Clean any debris and dirt from the filter chamber.

14 Remove the mixture screw and idle bypass screw (where fitted) and inspect the tips for damage or ridges.

15 Remove the four screws and detach the accelerator pump housing, diaphragm and spring. Check the diaphragm for fatigue and damage.

16 Unscrew the pump discharge valve from the body and remove the valve and the pump injector. Shake the discharge valve. No noise from the outlet ball indicates that the valve is seized. Check that the lead pellet that seals the valve is present. If loose or missing, the pump action will be impaired.

17 Remove the two idle jet assemblies from the carburettor body. The idle jets are pushed into a holder and may be separated (by pulling) for cleaning or renewal. Where an idle cut-off valve is used, the primary idle jet will be pushed into the end of the valve. It may be separated (by pulling) for cleaning or renewal. Some

Semi-automatic choke

1 Fast idle adjustment screw
2 Lever tang
3 Cam lever
4 Bi-metal coil
5 Spring
6 Diaphragm
7 Diaphragm rod

Chapter H1

applications may not have a secondary idle jet. Note that the idle jet assemblies can be removed from the carburettor body without removing the upper body.

18 Unscrew the primary and secondary main jets, air correctors and emulsion tubes.

19 Check that the channels from the float chamber into the emulsion tube wells are clear.

20 Note the jet sizes and locations for correct installation during assembly.

21 Check the jet calibration against that specified. It is possible that the jets may have been transposed (or the wrong size fitted) during the last overhaul.

22 Remove the primary and secondary auxiliary venturis where necessary. A Weber extractor tool is available for this purpose if required. Check that the primary and secondary auxiliary venturis are not loose in the main body as this is a source of uneven running. If a venturi is loose, knurl the mating flanges with a file to ensure a tight fit.

23 Remove the three screws and detach the power valve housing cover, spring and diaphragm from the body (where fitted). Check the diaphragm for damage. The brass outlet valve is cast into the body and is not removable. The ball in the outlet valve should seal the outlet. Depress and release the ball with a small screwdriver and it should move smoothly in and out. Check that the channel into the emulsion tube well is clear. A blank cover may be fitted in some instances where a power valve is not used.

24 Note the position of the heating flange (if fitted) relative to the lower carburettor flange and make alignment marks if necessary. Remove the screw and separate the heating flange from the lower carburettor flange. Use a straight-edge to check for distorted flanges on the facing surfaces.

25 Do not disturb the adjustment of the primary and secondary throttle angles, unless absolutely necessary.

26 Inspect the choke spindle, mechanism and levers for stickiness and wear.

27 Remove the three fixing screws that secure the bi-metal coil housing to the choke assembly housing. Note the position of the alignment marks and remove the coil housing from the carburettor body. Remove the internal heat shield.

28 Remove the three screws, then twist and disconnect the fast idle link rod (ball and socket) and detach the choke housing.

29 Remove the three screws and detach the choke diaphragm cover, spring and diaphragm from the housing. Check the diaphragm for fatigue. Also check the collars and spring fitted to the diaphragm rod for stickiness and damage.

Preparation for reassembly

30 Clean the jets, carburettor body assemblies, float chamber and internal channels. An air line may be used to clear the internal channels once the carburettor is fully dismantled. Note that if high-pressure air is directed into the channels and passages with the diaphragms still in place, diaphragm damage may result. Spraying carburettor cleaner into all the channels and passages in the carburettor body will often clear them of gum and dirt.

31 During reassembly, a complete set of new gaskets should be fitted. Also renew the needle valve, float pin and all diaphragms.

32 Inspect and renew (where necessary) the mixture screw, main jets, idle jets, air corrector jets and accelerator pump injector. Renew worn screws, linkages, springs and other parts where necessary.

33 Ensure that all jets are firmly locked into their original positions (but do not over-tighten). A loose jet can cause a rich (or even lean) running condition.

34 Clean all mating surfaces and flanges of old gasket material and reassemble with new gaskets. Ensure that housings are positioned with their air and fuel routes correctly aligned.

Reassembly

35 Refit the choke diaphragm and spindle assembly to the choke housing. Ensure that both plastic sleeves on the diaphragm spindle are pushed into position and are fully located. Refit the spring and cover, then secure with the three screws.

36 Renew the vacuum O-ring seal, engage the choke fast idle rod ball and socket and refit the choke housing to the carburettor float cover. Loosely secure with the three screws.

37 Check that the secondary throttle plate is fully closed. The adjustment screw should not normally be used to alter the throttle plate position. However, if necessary, it can be adjusted so that the plate is open just enough to prevent its seizure in the throttle body.

38 On idle bypass type carburettors, where the primary throttle position has been disturbed and a throttle setting gauge is available, use it to set the throttle angle. If a setting gauge is not available, temporarily adjust the throttle plate so that it is open just enough to prevent its seizure in the throttle body. An adjustment method with the engine running is detailed in Section 4.

39 Assemble the heating flange (where fitted) to the main body with a new gasket block and secure with the screw.

40 Refit the power diaphragm, spring and cover assembly (where fitted) and secure with the three screws.

41 Refit the emulsion tubes, air correctors and main jets into their original positions (do not transpose the jets).

42 Assemble the idle jet to the idle cut-off valve (where fitted). Refit the assembly using a new seal. Tighten the retaining socket-head grub screw.

43 Push the idle jet(s) into their holders and refit to the carburettor body with new seals (do not transpose the jets).

44 Assemble the pump discharge valve and pump injector into the body, complete with new sealing washers. Ensure that the nozzle points into the primary venturi.

45 Refit the accelerator pump spring, diaphragm and cover assembly, then secure with the four screws.

46 Refit the idle bypass screw (where fitted). Turn the screw in gently until it just seats. From this position unscrew it three full turns. This will provide a basic setting to enable the engine to be started.

47 Refit the idle mixture screw. Use the same method described in the previous paragraph to obtain a basic setting.

48 Clean or renew the fuel filter and secure with the hexagon bolt.

49 Fit a new float gasket to the upper body. Renew the needle valve assembly. Screw the valve seat into the upper body using a new sealing washer and ensure that it is firmly locked into position (do not over-tighten). Transfer the hairpin or plastic clip from the old needle valve to the ball end of the new one. Place the clip and valve assembly onto the inner float tag. Lower the float and needle valve assembly into the seat and secure with the float pin.

50 Adjust the float level. Refer to Section 4 for details on float adjustment.

51 Refit the upper body. Ensure that the lower choke link passes through the aperture in the upper body as the two assemblies are pressed together. Secure with the five screws. Fully tighten the three choke housing securing screws.

52 Reconnect the choke link lever to the choke spindle arm and secure with the circlip.

53 Ensure that the choke flaps and linkage move smoothly and progressively.

54 Adjust the defuming valve (where fitted), choke fast idle and vacuum pull-down. Refer to Section 4 for details on all adjustments.

55 Refit the carburettor to the engine.

56 Always adjust the carburettor idle speed and mixture after any work has been carried out on the carburettor, preferably with the aid of a CO meter.

4 Service adjustments

Adjustment preconditions

1 Refer to Part B for general advice on the preconditions to correct adjustment of this carburettor.

Idle speed and mixture (CO)

Standard idle system (where used)

2 Run the engine at 3000 rpm for 30 seconds to clear the manifold of fuel vapours, then allow the engine to idle.

3 Use the idle speed adjustment screw to set the specified idle speed (see illustration).

4 Check the CO level. If it is not as specified, remove the tamperproof plug and adjust the idle mixture control screw to achieve the correct level. Turning the screw clockwise (inwards) will reduce the CO level. Turning the screw anti-clockwise (outwards) will increase the CO level.

5 Repeat paragraphs 3 and 4 until both adjustments are correct.

6 Clear the manifold every 30 seconds during

Weber 28/36, 32 & 32/36 DARA carburettor

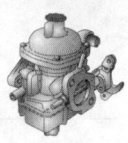

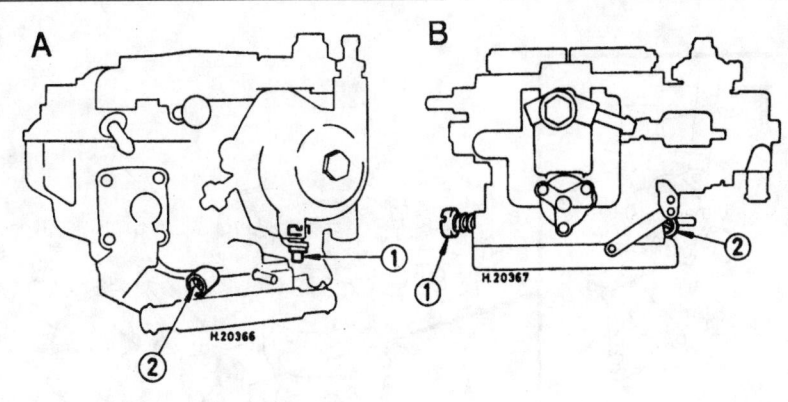

Idle speed and mixture screw location

A Idle speed and mixture adjustment (standard idle)
1 Idle speed adjustment screw
2 Idle mixture control screw

B Idle speed and mixture adjustment (idle by-pass)
1 Idle speed air regulating screw
2 Idle mixture control screw

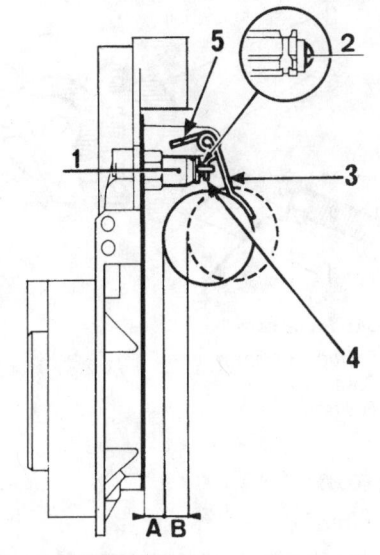

Float level measurement

A Float level
B Float stroke
1 Needle valve assembly
2 Needle valve ball
3 Float arm
4 Inner float tag
5 Outer float tag

the setting operation by running the engine at 3000 rpm for 30 seconds.

7 Increase the speed to 2000 rpm and note the CO reading. The cruise reading should be less than half the idle CO reading.

8 Fit a new tamperproof plug to the mixture adjustment screw.

Idle bypass system (where used)

9 Run the engine at 3000 rpm for 30 seconds to clear the manifold of fuel vapours, then allow the engine to idle.

10 Use the idle bypass regulating screw to set the specified idle speed.

11 Check the CO level. If it is not as specified, remove the tamperproof plug and adjust the idle mixture control screw to the correct level. Turning the screw clockwise (inwards) will reduce the CO level. Turning the screw anti-clockwise (outwards) will increase the CO level.

12 Repeat paragraphs 10 and 11 until both adjustments are correct.

Setting the primary throttle plate

13 If it is not possible to set the idle speed and CO correctly, it is possible that the basic throttle position is incorrect. The manufacturer's recommended method is to remove the carburettor and use a Renault, Solex or Pierburg throttle setting gauge to set the throttle position in mm or degrees.

14 However, an alternative method can be used to set the throttle plate. Please note that this is not the manufacturer's recommended method but nevertheless will result in an accurate and stable idle speed and CO level.

15 Allow the engine to idle.

16 Screw in the air bypass regulating screw until it is fully seated. The idle speed should drop to two-thirds of the specified idle speed figure. In this example, a hypothetical specified idle speed of 900 rpm will be used so the speed should drop to 600 rpm. Substitute the correct figures for the particular vehicle being worked on.

17 Adjust the throttle valve adjustment screw until 600 rpm is attained.

18 Unscrew the bypass screw until 900 rpm is once again reached.

19 Reset the CO to the correct level.

20 If the CO needs a large adjustment at this stage, repeat paragraphs 15 to 19. Once the proper CO is reached at the correct idle speed, the carburettor is properly adjusted.

Float level/stroke

21 Hold the upper body in a vertical position, with the float tag gently touching the ball of the fully-closed needle valve.

22 Measure the distance between the upper body (without the gasket) and the top of the float (see illustration).

23 Adjust as necessary by bending the inner float tag.

24 Place the upper body in a horizontal position and allow the float to hang down.

25 Measure the distance between the upper body (complete with gasket) and the top of the float.

26 Subtract the measurement in paragraph 22 from the measurement in paragraph 25. This figure is the float stroke.

27 Adjust as necessary by bending the outer float tag.

Defuming valve (float chamber vent)

28 Invert the carburettor and push the defuming valve operating rod fully downwards (towards the upper body). The throttle plate will be forced open to leave a small clearance.

29 Use the shank of a twist drill to measure the clearance between the throttle plate and the wall of the throttle bore (see illustration). Refer to Specifications for the required drill size.

30 Adjust as necessary by turning the adjustment screw in the appropriate direction.

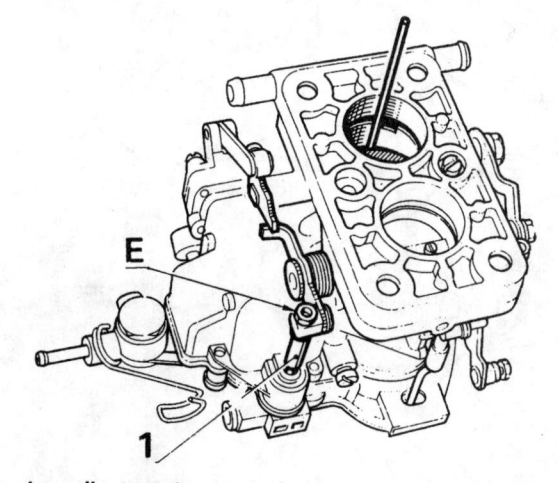

Defuming valve adjustment

E Adjustment nut
1 Defuming valve control lever

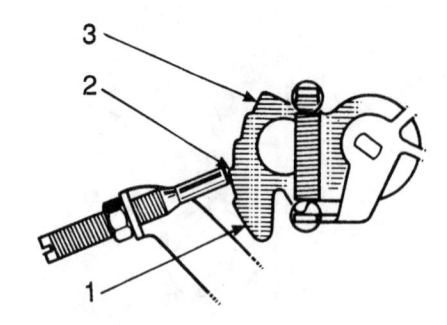

Chapter H1

Choke lever cam

1 Position 1 (maximum)
2 Position 2
3 Position 3

Automatic choke

Fast idle

31 The carburettor must be removed from the engine in order to make the fast idle adjustment (see Part B).
32 Invert the carburettor.
33 Partially open the throttle and fully close the choke flaps. The adjustment screw will butt against the fast idle cam and force open the throttle plate to leave a small clearance. Refer to Specifications for the position of the screw on the cam *(see illustration)* which could be in positions 1 (max), 2 or 3. Use position 2 if no position is specified.
34 Use the shank of a twist drill to measure the clearance between the wall of the throttle bore and the throttle plate. Refer to Specifications for the required drill size and measure the clearance from the progression holes.
35 Adjust as necessary by turning the adjustment screw in the appropriate direction *(see illustration)*.

Vacuum pull-down

36 Remove the three screws and detach the bi-metal coil housing from the carburettor.

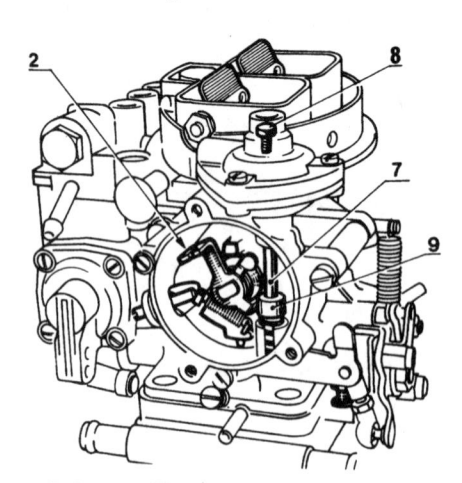

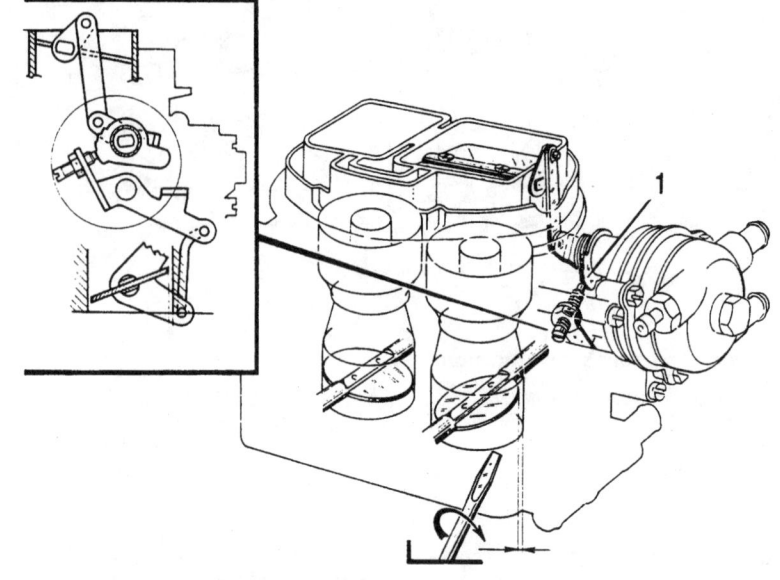

Fast idle adjustment screw location (1)

37 Remove the internal plastic heat shield.
38 Partially open the throttle and fully close the choke flaps.
39 Release the throttle and fit an elastic band to the choke operating lever so that the choke flaps remain in the fully on position.
40 Use a small screwdriver to push open the diaphragm up to its stop. At the same time, use the shank of a twist drill to measure the gap between the lower section of the choke flap and the air intake. Refer to Specifications for the required drill size.
41 Remove the plug and adjust as necessary by turning the diaphragm adjustment screw in the

Pull-down adjustment

2 Choke lever tang   8 Adjustment screw
7 Diaphragm rod   9 Sleeve

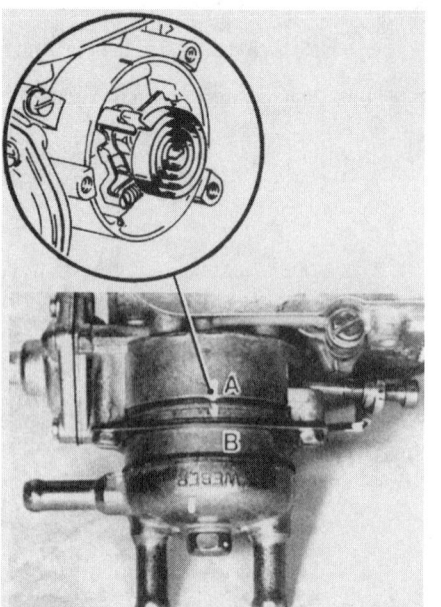

Choke alignment marks (A & B)

appropriate direction *(see illustration)*. Renew the plug when the adjustment is completed.
42 Remove the elastic band.
43 Refit the internal heat shield and ensure that the peg in the housing locates into the hole in the shield.
44 Refit the bi-metal coil housing and ensure that the spring locates in the slot of the choke lever tang. Secure loosely with the three screws. Align the cut mark on the bi-metal cover with the correct mark on the choke assembly housing and tighten the three screws *(see illustration)*.

5 Fault diagnosis

Refer to Part D for diagnosis of general carburettor faults. The following faults are specific to Weber DARA carburettors.

Poor choke operation

☐ Non-operation of choke pull-down diaphragm, due to diaphragm fatigue.

Hesitation or lack of power

☐ Loose auxiliary venturi(s).
☐ Failure of accelerator pump discharge valve, resulting in poor pump injection.
☐ Accelerator pump diaphragm shaft worn - the delay in operation can cause a flat spot on acceleration.

Poor idle and/or stalling

☐ Carburettor base flange distorted as a result of over-tightening the carburettor mounting bolts.
☐ Distortion at the flanges of the main body and heater flange sections - this will cause air leaks, leading to general poor running.

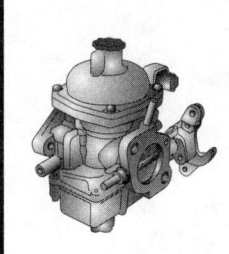

Part H Chapter 2
Weber 32 DFT carburettor

H2

Contents

Fault diagnosis 5
General servicing 3
Identification 2
Principles of operation 1
Service adjustments 4

Specifications

Manufacturer	Ford	Ford	Ford
Model	Fiesta 1300	Fiesta XR2	Fiesta XR2
Year	**1978 to 1982**	**1981 to 1983**	**1983 to 1986**
Engine code	J3E (OHV)	L3E (OHV)	LUB (CVH)
Capacity (cm³)/no. of cyls	1298/4	1598/4	1597/4
Oil temperature (°C)	80	80	80
Transmission	Manual	Manual	Manual
Carb. ident. (Ford)	781F 9510 AB	V821F 9510 AA	81SF 9510 AB
Carb. ident. (Weber/Solex)	32 DFT	32/34 DFT 6	32/34 DFT 4B
Idle speed (rpm)	775 ± 25	800 ± 25	800 ± 25
Fast idle speed (rpm)	2800 ± 100	2700 ± 100	2700 ± 100
CO @ idle (% vol.)	1.5 ± 0.25	1.5 ± 0.25	1.25 ± 0.25
Special conditions	Fan on	-	-

Stage (venturi)	1	2	1	2	1	2
Venturi diameter	22	22	24	25	24	25
Idle jet	50	55	50	60	50	60
Main jet	107	105	115	120	115	125
Air correction jet	230	165	160	150	160	150
Emulsion tube	F22	F30	F30	F30	F30	F30
Accel. pump jet	40		-		-	
Float level (mm)	36 ± 0.3		36 ± 0.3		35 ± 0.5	
Float stroke (mm)	8 ± 0.25		8 ± 0.25		8 ± 0.25	
Needle valve size (mm)	1.5		-		1.75	
Throttle valve gap (mm)	0.5 to 0.55		-		-	
Choke pull-down (mm)	5.5 ± 0.5		6.0 ± 0.5		5.5 ± 0.3	
Choke phasing (mm)	2.5 ± 0.5		2.0 ± 0.5		2.0 ± 0.5	
Bi-metal housing mark	2.0 mm lean		on index		on index	

Chapter H2

Manufacturer	Ford
Model	Escort XR3
Year	1980 to 1982
Engine code	LUA (CVH)
Capacity (cm³)/no. of cyls	1597/4
Oil temperature (°C)	80
Transmission	Manual
Carb. ident. (Ford)	81SF 9510 AA/AB
Carb. ident. (Weber/Solex)	32/34 DFT 4/4B
Idle speed (rpm)	800 ± 50
Fast idle speed (rpm)	2700 ± 100
CO @ idle (% vol.)	1.5 ± 0.5
Special conditions	Fan on

Stage (venturi)	1	2
Venturi diameter	24	25
Idle jet	50	60
Main jet	115	120
Air correction jet	160	150
Emulsion tube	F30	F30
Accel. pump jet	50	

Float level (mm)	36 ± 0.3
Float stroke (mm)	8 ± 0.25
Needle valve size (mm)	1.75
Choke pull-down (mm)	6.0 ± 0.5
Choke phasing (mm)	2.0 ± 0.5
Bi-metal housing mark	2.0 mm lean

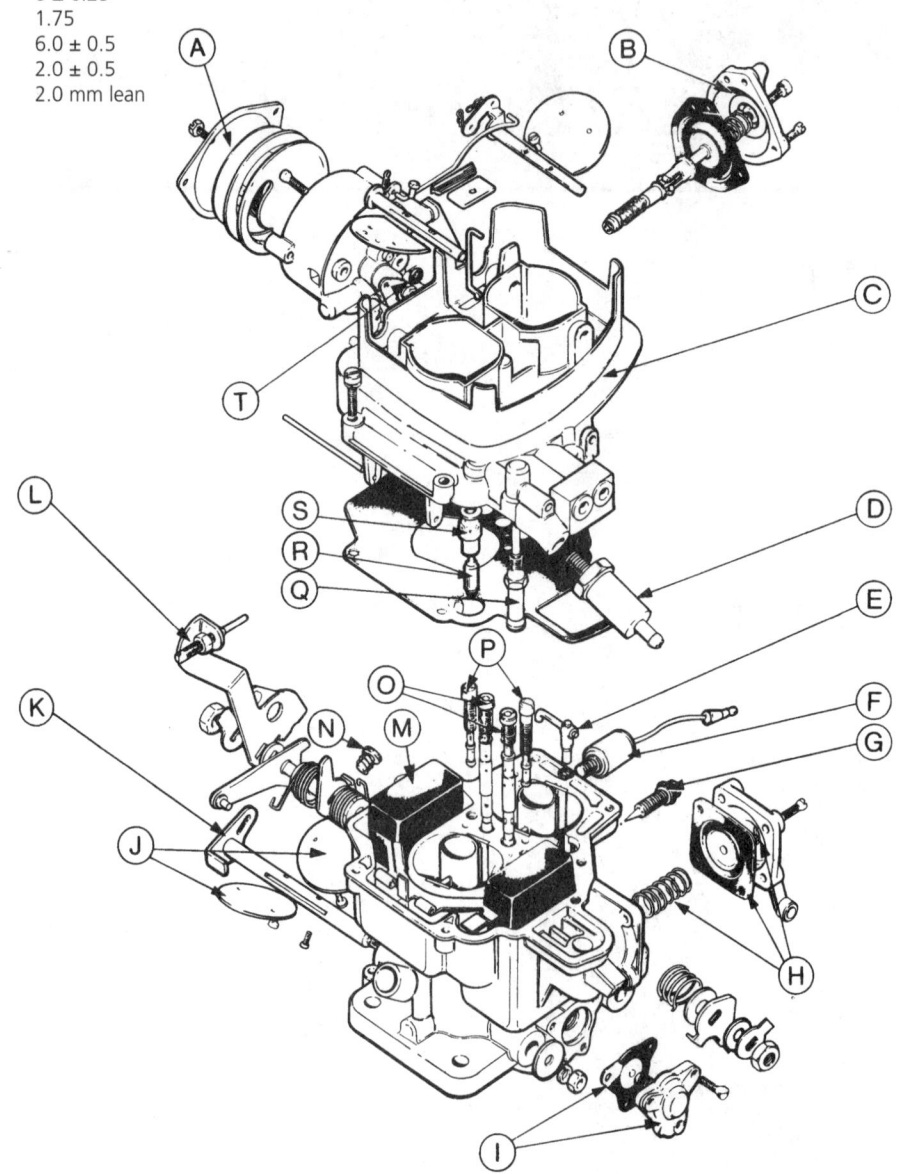

Weber DFT carburettor

- A Electric choke housing
- B Choke pull-down diaphragm assembly
- C Upper body assembly
- D Fuel filter
- E Accelerator pump injector
- F Idle cut-off valve
- G Mixture screw
- H Accelerator pump assembly
- I Power valve diaphragm assembly
- J Throttle plates
- K Secondary throttle spindle
- L Fast idle adjuster
- M Float
- N Idle speed screw
- O Combined emulsion tube, air correction and main jets
- P Idle jets
- Q Fuel return connection
- R Needle valve
- S Needle valve seat
- T Rubber seal

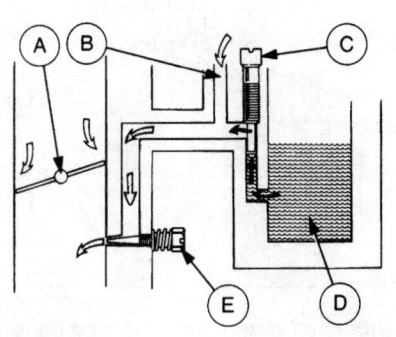

Weber 32 DFT carburettor

Idle system

A Throttle plate
B Air bleed
C Idle jet
D Float chamber
E Mixture screw

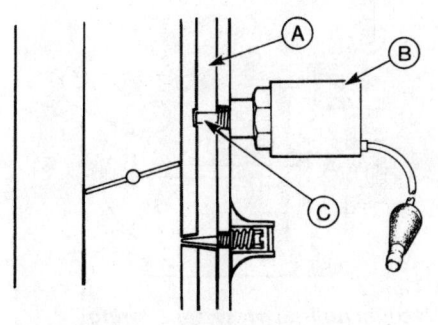

Idle cut-off valve system

A Idle gallery
B Idle cut-off valve
C Idle cut-off valve plunger blocking idle channel

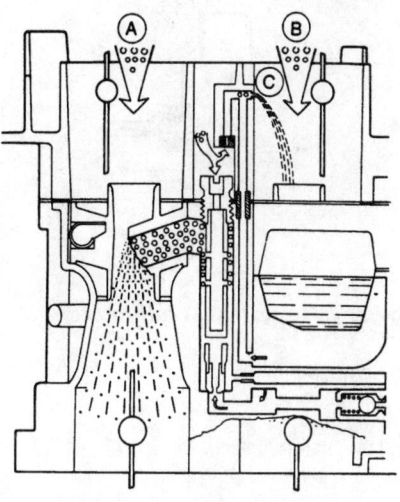

Main circuit, power and full-load enrichment

A Primary airflow
B Secondary airflow
C Full-load enrichment

1 Principles of operation

Introduction

1 The following technical description of the Weber DFT carburettor should be read in conjunction with the more detailed description of carburettor principles in Part A.

Construction

2 The Weber 32 DFT carburettor is a downdraught progressive twin venturi instrument *(see illustration)*. The venturis are arranged so that the secondary throttle valve will not begin to open until the primary throttle valve is two-thirds open. An idle cut-off valve is fitted to the idle circuit and the choke control is semi-automatic in operation. The choke strangler flaps are controlled by an electrically-heated bi-metal coil. Throttle and choke shafts are made of steel and run in teflon (PTFE) bushes. The throttle valves are of brass and the choke valves made from steel. All emulsion tubes and jets are made of brass, with the exception of the accelerator pump discharge tube which is die-cast. Internal fuel channels and air passages are drilled and sealed with lead plugs where necessary.

Fuel control

3 Fuel flows into the carburettor through a fine mesh filter. The fuel level in the float chamber is controlled by a needle valve and plastic float assembly. An anti-vibration ball is incorporated into the needle valve design. A plastic or hairpin clip, attached to the needle valve seat and to the float arm, prevents the needle from sticking in the seat as the fuel level drops. The float chamber is vented internally to the clean-air side of the air filter. A calibrated fuel return system is provided to ensure that relatively cool fuel is supplied to the carburettor.

Idle, slow running and progression

4 Fuel, sourced from the float chamber, passes into the primary idle well through a metered idle jet. Here it is mixed with a small amount of air from a calibrated air bleed. The emulsion formed is drawn through a channel to the throttle body, where it is discharged from the idle orifice under the primary throttle plate. A tapered mixture screw is used to vary the outlet and this ensures fine control of the idle mixture. A number of progression drillings provide enrichment as they are uncovered by the opening throttle during initial acceleration *(see illustration)*.

5 The idle speed is set by an adjustable screw. The adjustable mixture screw is tamper proofed at production level, in accordance with emission regulations.

Idle cut-off valve

6 An idle cut-off valve is used to prevent run-on when the engine is switched off. It utilises a 12-volt solenoid plunger to block the idle fuel channel when the ignition is switched off *(see illustration)*.

Accelerator pump

7 The accelerator pump is controlled by a diaphragm and is mechanically operated by a

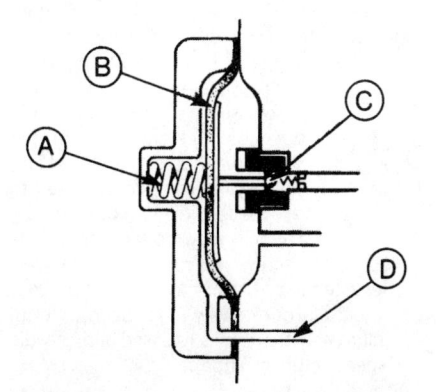

Power valve system during light-throttle operation

A Return spring (compressed)
B Diaphragm (pulled back)
C Power valve (closed)
D High manifold vacuum

cam and lever attached to the primary throttle linkage. The outlet valve consists of a ball incorporated into the pump outlet injector. The inlet valve consists of a ball valve located in a channel from the float chamber. Excess fuel is returned to the float chamber through an additional channel and calibrated bush.

Main circuit

8 The amount of fuel discharged into the airstream is controlled by a calibrated main jet. The main jet and air corrector are pushed into opposite ends of an emulsion tube and the assembly is placed into a vertical well which dips down into the fuel. Fuel is drawn from the float chamber, through the main jet, into the well, to be mixed with air drawn in through the air corrector and the holes in the emulsion tube. The resulting emulsified mixture is discharged from the main nozzle through an auxiliary venturi *(see illustration)*.

Power enrichment and economy circuit

9 Fuel flows from the float chamber into the power valve chamber through a fuel channel. An air passage is taken from under the throttle plate to the cover of the power diaphragm chamber. At idle, and during light-throttle operation, manifold vacuum in the passage draws the diaphragm back against spring pressure. The diaphragm pintle is withdrawn from the brass outlet valve and the spring-loaded ball seats to close off the channel *(see illustration)*.

10 Under acceleration and wide-open throttle operation, the vacuum in the manifold is depleted. The diaphragm returns under spring pressure and the power diaphragm pintle pushes the ball to open the outlet valve. Fuel then flows through the valve and a calibrated jet to supplement the fuel in the primary main well.

H2•3

Chapter H2

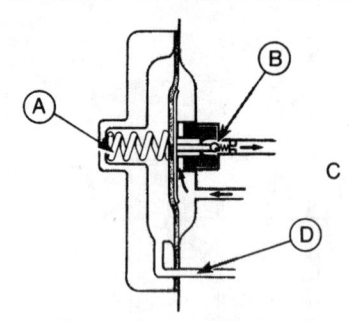

Power valve system at full-throttle

A Return spring (extended)
B Power valve (open)
C Fuel flow
D Low manifold vacuum

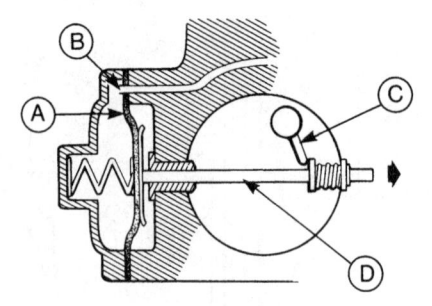

Vacuum pull-down system during starting or acceleration

A Diaphragm
B Vacuum supply (high)
C Choke linkage
D Pushrod

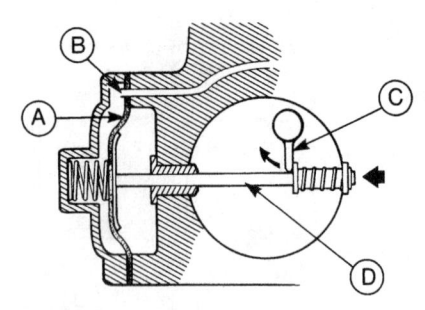

Vacuum pull-down system during light-throttle operation

A Diaphragm
B Vacuum supply (high)
C Choke linkage
D Pushrod

The fuel level rises in the well and the fuel mixture is enriched *(see illustration)*.

Secondary action

11 Once the primary throttle valve is about two-thirds open, the secondary throttle valve will begin to open. At full-throttle, the linkage is arranged so that both throttle plates are fully open. Once the secondary throttle plate has opened, the action of the secondary main circuit is similar to the primary circuit.

12 A separate jet is used to prevent hesitation as the secondary throttle plate commences to open. This is often referred to as the secondary idle jet, although it is in reality a progression jet. The action of the secondary idle circuit is similar to the primary circuit. An emulsified mixture is discharged into the secondary venturi, via a progression drilling, at the initial opening of the secondary throttle plate.

13 At full-load and high engine speed, even more fuel is required. The velocity of air creates a depression sufficient to raise fuel from the float chamber into a channel. The fuel then passes through a calibrated bushing to the upper section of the secondary air intake. Here it is mixed with a small amount of air from a calibrated air bleed and the emulsified mixture is then discharged into the airstream from the full-load enrichment outlet.

Cold start system

14 The DFT carburettor uses a semi-automatic choke starting system. A bi-metal spring is used to control two strangler choke flaps on a common spindle to shut off both air intakes. Heating of the coil spring is by an electric heating element, with the electrical supply taken from the alternator. This ensures that the choke will only be opened with the engine running. For starting the engine from cold, the choke flaps and fast idle are set by depressing the accelerator pedal once or twice.

15 Once the engine has fired, the choke flaps must open slightly to weaken the mixture and avoid flooding during idle and light-throttle operation. This is achieved by using manifold vacuum to actuate a pull-down diaphragm. Linkage attached to the diaphragm will then pull upon the flaps *(see illustrations)*.

16 Fast idle is achieved with the aid of a stepped cam attached to the choke spindle. An adjustable screw, connected to the throttle lever mechanism and butting against the cam, can be used to vary the fast idle speed. As the bi-metal coil is heated and the flaps open, the screw will rest on successively less-stepped parts of the cam. Idle speed is thus progressively reduced, until ultimately the cam is released and the idle speed returns to normal.

Wide-open kick

17 If the throttle is fully opened during acceleration when the engine is cold, the pull-down vacuum will deplete and the choke flaps tend to close. This may cause flooding and to prevent this, a wide-open kick mechanism is employed. When the throttle is fully opened, a cam on the throttle lever will turn the choke lever anti-clockwise to partially open the choke flaps *(see illustration)*.

2 Identification

The Weber identification code is stamped on the carburettor base flange.

A metal tag, giving the Ford identification code, is attached to one of the upper body fixing screws.

3 General servicing

Introduction

1 Read this Chapter in conjunction with Part B which describes some of the operations in more detail. It is assumed that the carburettor is removed for this service. However, many of the operations can be tackled with the carburettor in place. Where this is undertaken, first soak the fuel out of the float chamber using a clean tissue or soft cloth, after removing the upper body assembly.

Dismantling and checking

2 Remove the carburettor from the engine (see Part B).

3 Make visual checks for damage and wear.

4 Remove the six screws, hold the choke fast idle lever clear of the choke housing and detach the carburettor upper body.

5 Use a straight-edge to check for distorted flanges on all facing surfaces.

6 Inspect the float chamber for corrosion and calcium build-up.

7 Tap out the float pin and remove the float,

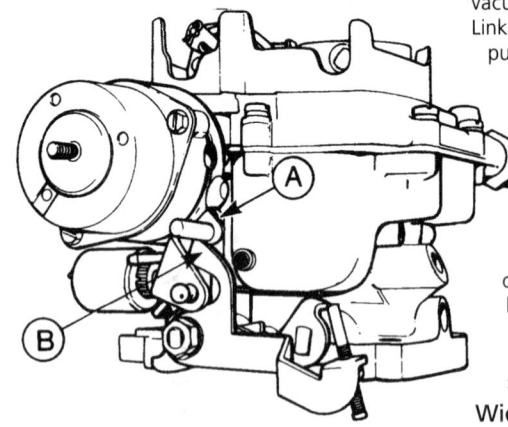

Wide-open kick system (throttle fully open)

A Choke lever turned anti-clockwise and partially opening choke plate
B Cam section on throttle lever

Weber 32 DFT carburettor

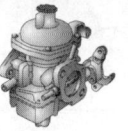

needle valve and clip. Remove the float chamber gasket and needle valve seat *(see illustration)*.
8 Check that the anti-vibration ball is free in the valve end.
9 Check the needle valve tip for wear and ridges. This is more likely with the brass needle valve tip than when a viton one is used. Use a viton-tipped replacement when possible.
10 The float should be checked for damage and ingress of petrol. Shaking the float will indicate the presence of fuel.
11 Renew the float pin if it shows signs of wear.
12 Unscrew the fuel filter housing assembly and renew the filter if clogged. Clean the housing of debris and dirt. Unscrew the fuel return connection and check that the fine drilling is clear.
13 Remove the mixture screw and inspect the tip for damage and ridges.
14 Remove the four screws and remove the accelerator pump cover, diaphragm and spring. Check the diaphragm for fatigue and damage.
15 The pump injector is a push fit in the body. Carefully prise it from its location and test it by shaking. No noise from the outlet ball indicates that the valve is seized.
16 Remove the primary and secondary idle jet assemblies, then the main jets, air correctors and emulsion tubes *(see illustration)*.
17 Check that the channel from the float chamber into the emulsion tube well is clear.
18 The idle jets are pushed into a holder. They can be separated, by pulling, for cleaning or renewal. Likewise, the main jets and air correctors are pushed into the opposite ends of the emulsion tubes and may also be separated, by pulling, for cleaning or renewal. Note that the idle jet and the main jet assemblies can be removed from the carburettor body without removing the upper body.
19 Note the jet sizes and locations, for correct installation during reassembly. The primary main and idle jets are located on the accelerator pump side of the carburettor, while the secondary main and idle jets are located on the choke side of the carburettor.
20 Check the jet calibration against that specified. It is possible that the jets may have been transposed (or the wrong size fitted) during the last overhaul.
21 Remove the primary and secondary auxiliary venturis, where necessary. A Weber extractor tool is available for this purpose.
22 Check that the primary and secondary auxiliary venturis are not loose, since this can cause uneven running. If a venturi is loose, knurl the mating flanges with a file to ensure a tight fit.
23 Remove the three screws and remove the power valve cover, spring and diaphragm from the body. Check the diaphragm for fatigue and damage.
24 The brass outlet valve is cast into the body and is not removable. The ball in the outlet valve should seal the outlet. Depress and release the ball with a small screwdriver and it should move smoothly in and out. Check that the

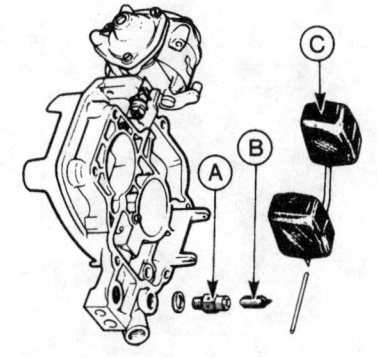

Float assembly

A Needle valve seat
B Needle valve
C Float

channel into the primary emulsion tube well is clear.
25 Inspect the choke spindle, mechanism and levers for stickiness and wear.
26 Remove the three screws, twist and disconnect the lower choke link rod and detach the choke housing. Check the mechanism for stickiness and wear. A broken or defective mechanism is a common reason for poor choke operation with this carburettor.
27 Remove the three screws and remove the choke pull-down cover, spring and diaphragm from the housing *(see illustration)*. Check the diaphragm for fatigue and damage.

Preparation for reassembly

28 Clean the jets and internal channels, the carburettor body assemblies and the float chamber. An air line may be used to clear the internal channels once the carburettor is fully dismantled. Note that if an air line is used with

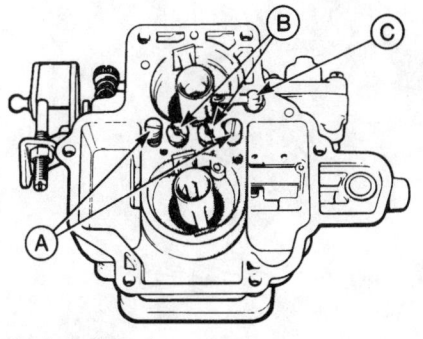

Jet locations

A Idle jets
B Combined main and air correction jets
C Accelerator pump injector

the diaphragms in place and air is directed into the diaphragm passages, diaphragm damage may result.
29 Spraying carburettor cleaner into all the channels and passages in the carburettor body will often clear them of gum and dirt.
30 During reassembly, a complete set of new gaskets should be fitted. Also renew the needle valve and float pin, and all diaphragms.
31 Inspect and renew (where necessary) the mixture screw, main jets, idle jets, air corrector jets and accelerator pump injector assembly. Renew worn linkages and springs where necessary.
32 Ensure that all jets are firmly locked into their original positions (but do not overtighten). A loose jet can cause a rich (or even lean) running condition.
33 Clean all mating surfaces and flanges of old gasket material and reassemble with new gaskets.

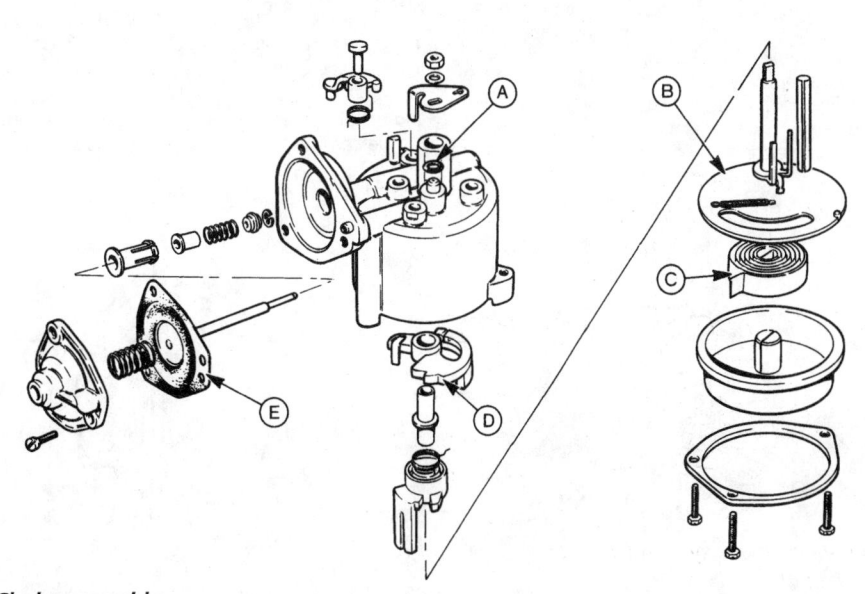

Choke assembly

A Housing O-ring seal
B Plastic heat shield
C Bi-metal coil
D Fast idle cam
E Pull-down diaphragm

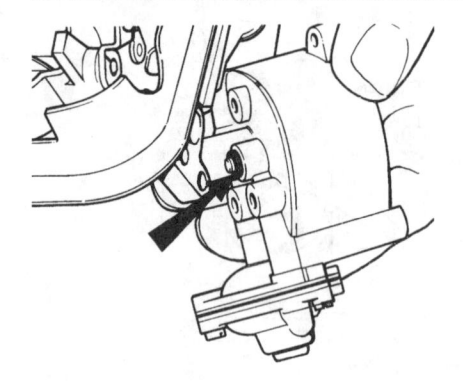

Chapter H2

Installing choke housing
O-ring seal arrowed

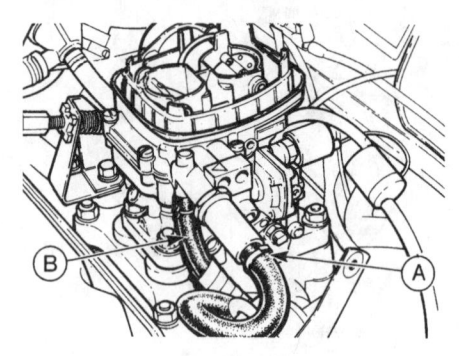

Fuel hose connections
A Fuel supply   B Fuel return

4 Service adjustments

Adjustment preconditions

1 Refer to Part B for general advice on preconditions to correct adjustment of this carburettor.

Idle speed and mixture (CO)

2 Run the engine at 3000 rpm for 30 seconds to clear the manifold of fuel vapours, then allow the engine to idle.
3 Use the idle speed screw to set the specified idle speed *(see illustration)*.
4 Check the CO level. If not as specified, remove the tamperproof plug and adjust to the correct level.
5 Repeat paragraphs 3 and 4 until both adjustments are correct.
6 Clear the manifold every 30 seconds during the setting operation by running the engine at 3000 rpm for 30 seconds.
7 Fit a new tamperproof plug to the mixture adjusting screw.
8 The manufacturer states that variations of ± 0.25% CO and ± 25 rpm are acceptable during idle.

Float level/stroke

9 Hold the upper body in a vertical position with the float tag gently touching the ball of the fully-closed needle valve.
10 Measure the distance between the upper body (with the gasket in place) and the base of the float *(see illustration)*.
11 Adjust as necessary by bending the inner float tag.
12 Place the upper body in a horizontal position and allow the float to drop.
13 Measure the distance between the upper body (with the gasket in place) and the base of the float.
14 Subtract the measurement in paragraph 10 from the measurement in paragraph 13. This figure is the float operating stroke.
15 Adjust as necessary by bending the outer float tag.

Automatic choke

Fast idle

16 Warm the engine to normal running temperature and adjust the idle speed and mixture before attempting choke fast idle adjustment.
17 Remove the air filter assembly and place it clear of the carburettor with the vacuum hoses still connected.
18 Partially open the throttle and fully close the choke flaps *(see illustration)*. Release the throttle and the choke flaps. The fast idle adjustment screw should remain against the highest step of the fast idle cam.
19 Start the engine without moving the throttle and record the fast idle speed.

34 Ensure that housings are assembled with their air and fuel routes correctly aligned.

Reassembly

35 Refit the choke diaphragm and spindle assembly to the choke housing. Ensure that both plastic sleeves on the diaphragm spindle are pushed into position and fully located. Refit the spring and cover, then secure with the three screws.
36 Renew the vacuum O-ring seal, engage the choke link rod into the choke lever arm, then refit the choke housing to the carburettor float cover and secure with the three screws *(see illustration)*.
37 Check that the secondary throttle plate is fully closed. The adjustment screw should not normally be used to alter the throttle plate position. However, if necessary, it can be adjusted so that the plate is open just enough to prevent the plate seizing in the throttle body.
38 Refit the power diaphragm, spring and cover assembly, then secure with the three screws.
39 Ensure that the air correctors and main jets are pushed fully into the emulsion tubes. Refit the assemblies into their original positions in the carburettor body (do not transpose the jets).
40 Ensure that the idle jets are pushed fully into the holders. Refit into their original positions in the carburettor body (do not transpose the jets).
41 Refit the pump injector into the main body (renew the small seal on the injector body).
42 Refit the accelerator pump spring, diaphragm and cover assembly, then secure with the four screws.
43 Refit the idle mixture screw. Turn the screw in carefully until it just seats, then unscrew it three full turns. This will provide a basic setting to allow the engine to be started.
44 Refit the fuel filter housing assembly and the fuel return connection *(see illustration)*.
45 Renew the needle valve assembly. Screw the valve seat into the float chamber with a new sealing washer and ensure that it is firmly locked into position.
46 Fit a new float chamber gasket. Insert the needle valve into the valve seat with the ball facing outwards, then refit the float and pin, ensuring that the plastic clip is correctly connected to the float and to the float needle.
47 Adjust the float level. Refer to Section 4 for details on float adjustment.
48 Pull back the choke fast idle arm, then refit the carburettor upper body and secure with the six screws.
49 Refit the idle cut-off valve.
50 Ensure that the choke flap and linkage move smoothly and progressively.
51 Refit the carburettor to the engine.
52 Always adjust the carburettor idle speed and mixture after any work has been carried out on the carburettor, preferably with the aid of a CO meter.
53 Adjust the choke, (see Section 4).

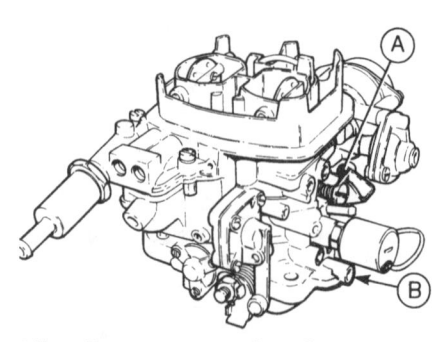

Idle adjustment screw location
A Idle speed screw
B Idle mixture (CO) screw

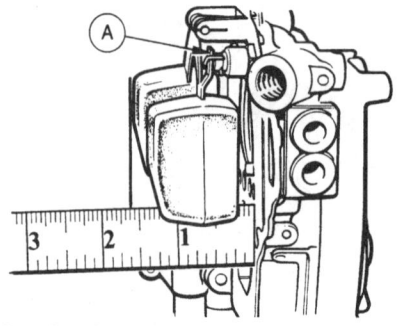

Float level adjustment
A Adjusting tag

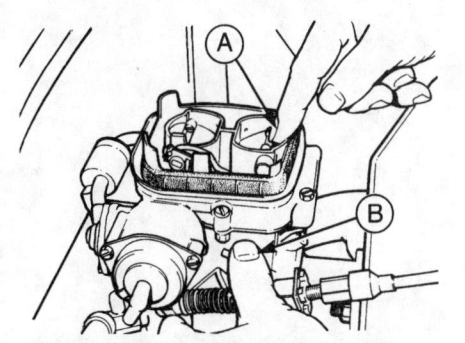

Weber 32 DFT carburettor

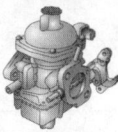

Linkage positioned to check fast idle
A Choke flap held closed
B Throttle held partially open

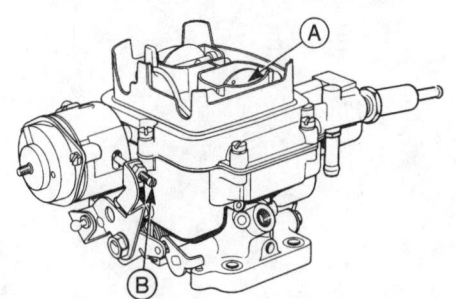

Fast idle adjustment
A Choke plates open
B Fast idle adjustment screw

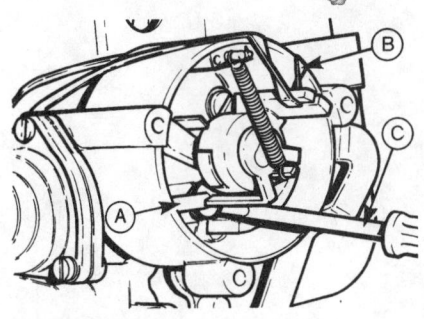

Vacuum pull-down check
A Diaphragm operating rod
B Elastic band   C Screwdriver

20 Adjust to the specified speed by turning the fast idle screw in the appropriate direction (see illustration).
21 Refit the air filter assembly, ensuring that the vacuum hoses remain connected.

Choke vacuum pull-down

22 Remove the three screws and detach the bi-metal coil housing from the carburettor.
23 Remove the internal plastic heat shield.
24 Partially open the throttle and fully close the choke flaps.
25 Release the throttle and fit an elastic band to the choke operating lever so that the choke flaps remain in the fully-on position (see illustration).
26 Use a small screwdriver to push open the diaphragm up to its stop, then use the shank of a twist drill to measure the gap between the lower section of the choke flap and the air intake. Refer to Specifications for the required drill size.
27 Remove the tamperproof plug and adjust as necessary by turning the diaphragm adjusting screw (see illustration) in the appropriate direction. Fit a new plug after adjustment is completed and remove the elastic band.
28 Adjust the choke phasing, as described below.

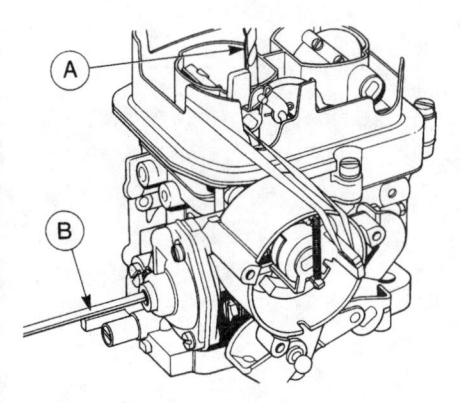

Choke phasing

29 Partially open the throttle and position the fast idle screw so that it is located tight against the second-highest step of the cam (see illustration).
30 Use the shank of a twist drill to measure the gap between the lower section of the choke flap and the air intake. Refer to Specifications for the required drill size.
31 Adjust as necessary by bending the phasing adjustment tag (see illustration).
32 Refit the internal heat shield and ensure that the peg in the shield locates into the hole in the housing.
33 Refit the bi-metal coil housing, ensure that the spring locates in the slot of the choke lever, then secure loosely with the three screws.
34 Align the cut mark on the bi-metal cover with the correct mark on the choke assembly housing and tighten the three screws (see illustration).

5 Fault diagnosis

Refer to Part D for general diagnosis of carburettor faults. The following faults are specific to the Weber 32 DFT carburettor.

Poor choke operation

☐ Failure of the voltage supply from the alternator to the automatic choke. The choke will take much longer to open fully: *Check the alternator supply to the choke with a voltmeter - expect a reading of 6 to 8 volts with the engine running*
☐ Broken choke mechanism - the mechanism is plastic and prone to breaking

Idle speed too high

☐ Broken choke mechanism can jam against fast idle cam.

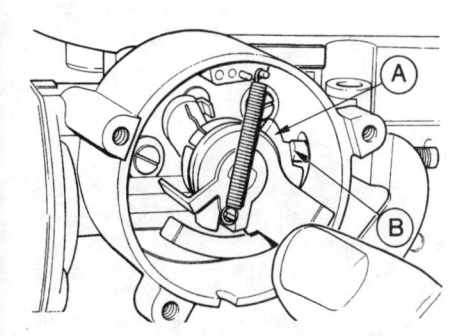

Vacuum pull-down adjustment
A Twist drill   B Screwdriver

Choke mechanism set at phase point
A Fast idle cam
B Fast idle adjustment screw

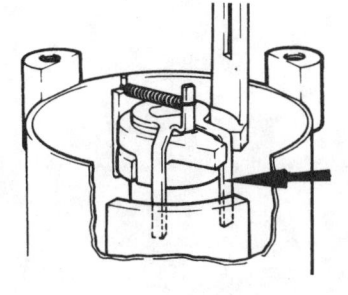

Choke phasing adjustment tag (arrowed)

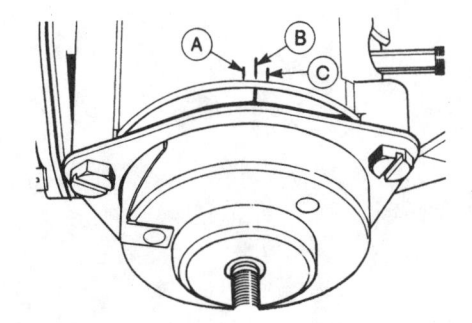

Choke housing alignment marks
A Rich position   C Lean position
B Index mark

Notes

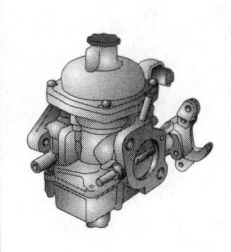

Part H Chapter 3
Weber 28/30 & 30/34 DFTH carburettor

Contents

Component testing - 30/34 DFTH carburettor 5
Fault diagnosis 6
General servicing 3
Identification 2
Principles of operation 1
Service adjustments 4

Specifications

28/30 DFTH carburettor

Manufacturer	Ford		Ford		Ford	
Model	Sierra 1600 E-max		Sierra & Sapphire 1600		Sierra & Sapphire 1600	
Year	1983		1984 to 1988		1988 to 1991	
Engine code	LSD (OHC)		LSE (OHC) 55kW 15/04		LSE (OHC) 55kW 15/04	
Capacity (cm³)/no. of cyls	1597/4		1597/4		1597/4	
Oil temperature (°C)	80		80		80	
Transmission	Manual		Manual		Manual	
Carb. ident. (Ford)	84HF 9510 CA		84HF 9510 DA		84HF 9510 DB	
Carb. ident. (Weber/Solex)	28/30 DFTH 1A		28/30 DFTH 1A1		-	
Idle speed (rpm)	800 ± 25		800 ± 50		800 ± 25	
Fast idle speed (rpm)	1700 ± 100		1700 ± 100		1700 ± 100	
CO @ idle (% vol.)	1.0 ± 0.25		1.0 ± 0.25		1.0 ± 0.25	
Stage (venturi)	1	2	1	2	1	2
Venturi diameter	21	23	21	23	21	23
Idle jet	50	40	50	40	50	40
Main jet	97	110	97	110	97	110
Air correction jet	185	190	185	190	185	190
Emulsion tube	F59	F22	F59	F22	F59	F22
Accel. pump jet	40		40		40	
Float level (mm)	6.0 ± 0.5		6.0 ± 0.5		6.0 ± 0.5	
Float stroke (mm)	1.5		2.0		2.0	
Choke pull-down (mm)	6.25 ± 0.25		6.0 ± 0.25		6.0 ± 0.25	

H3•1

Chapter H3

28/30 DFTH carburettor (continued)

Manufacturer	Ford
Model	Sierra & Sapphire 1600
Year	1987 to 1991
Engine code	LSE (OHC) 15/05
Capacity (cm³)/no. of cyls	1597/4
Oil temperature (°C)	80
Transmission	Manual
Carb. ident. (Ford)	88HF 9510 AA
Idle speed (rpm)	875 ± 50
Fast idle speed (rpm)	1700 ± 100
CO @ idle (% vol.)	0.75 ± 0.25

Stage (venturi)	1	2
Venturi diameter	21	23
Idle jet	50	70
Main jet	95	115
Air correction jet	195	170
Emulsion tube	F59	F22
Float level (mm)	6.5 ± 0.5	
Choke pull-down (mm)	6.0 ± 0.5	

30/34 DFTH carburettor

Manufacturer	Ford	Ford	Ford
Model	Sierra & Sapphire 2000	Sierra & Sapphire 2000	Sierra & Sapphire 2000
Year	1985 to 1989	1985 to 1989	1985 to 1989
Engine code	NES (OHC) 77kW	NES (OHC) 77kW	NES (OHC) 77kW
Capacity (cm³)/no. of cyls	1993/4	1993/4	1993/4
Oil temperature (°C)	80	80	80
Transmission	Manual	Automatic	Manual
Carb. ident. (Ford)	85HF 9510 CA	85HF 9510 DA	85HF 9510 CB
Carb. ident. (Weber/Solex)	30/34 DFTH 3A/3A-02	30/34 DFTH 4A/4A-02	-
Idle speed (rpm)	800 ± 50	800 ± 50	875 ± 50
CO @ idle (% vol.)	1.0 ± 0.25	1.0 ± 0.25	1.0 ± 0.25

Stage (venturi)	1	2	1	2	1	2
Venturi diameter	25	27	25	27	25	27
Idle jet	45	45	45	45	42	45
Main jet	112	135	110	135	110	130
Air correction jet	165	150	160	150	160	160
Emulsion tube	F22	F22	F22	F22	F22	F22
Accel. pump jet	45		45		-	
Float level 1 (mm)	8.0 ± 0.5		8.0 ± 0.5		8.0 ± 0.5	
Needle valve size (mm)	2.25		2.25		2.25	
Choke pull-down (mm)	9.0		8.0		8.0	
Bi-metal housing mark	on index		on index		on index	

Manufacturer	Ford	Ford	Ford
Model	Sierra & Sapphire 2000	Granada 2000	Granada 2000
Year	1985 to 1989	1985 to 1989	1985 to 1989
Engine code	NES (OHC) 77kW	NEL (OHC)	NEL (OHC)
Capacity (cm³)/no. of cyls	1993/4	1993/4	1993/4
Oil temperature (°C)	80	80	80
Transmission	Automatic	Manual	Automatic
Carb. ident. (Ford)	85HF 9510 DB	85HF 9510 CA	85HF 9510 DA
Carb. ident. (Weber/Solex)	-	30/34 DFTH 3A/3A-02	30/34 DFTH 4A/4A-02
Idle speed (rpm)	875 ± 50	800 ± 50	800 ± 50
CO @ idle (% vol.)	1.0 ± 0.25	1.0 ± 0.25	1.0 ± 0.25

Stage (venturi)	1	2	1	2	1	2
Venturi diameter	25	27	25	27	27	27
Idle jet	42	45	45	45	45	45
Main jet	110	130	112	135	110	135
Air correction jet	170	160	165	150	160	150
Emulsion tube	F22	F22	22	F22	F22	F22
Accel. pump jet	-		45		45	
Float level (mm)	8.0 ± 0.5		8.0 ± 0.5		8.0 ± 0.5	
Needle valve size (mm)	2.25		2.25		2.25	
Choke pull-down (mm)	8.0		9.0		8.0	
Bi-metal housing mark	on index		-		-	

Weber 28/30 & 30/34 DFTH carburettor

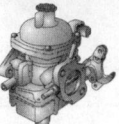

1 Principles of operation

Introduction

1 The following technical description of the Weber DFTH carburettor should be read in conjunction with the more detailed description of carburettor principles in Part A.

Construction

2 The Weber DFTH carburettor is a downdraught twin venturi instrument with a vacuum-controlled secondary throttle *(see illustrations)*.

3 On 28/30 DFTH carburettors from April 1988, an idle cut-off valve is fitted to the idle circuit and the choke control is semi-automatic in operation. The choke strangler flap is controlled by a coolant-heated bi-metal coil.

4 On 30/34 DFTH carburettors, the choke control is fully automatic in operation and the single choke strangler flap is controlled by an electrically-heated bi-metal coil. Control of the idle speed is electronic and adjustment has been made obsolete.

5 On both carburettor types, throttle and choke shafts and the choke flap are made of steel, while the throttle valves are of brass. All emulsion tubes and jets are made of brass, with the exception of the accelerator pump discharge injector which is die-cast. The internal fuel channels and air passages are drilled and sealed with lead plugs where necessary.

Fuel control

6 Fuel flows into the carburettor through a fine mesh filter. The fuel level in the float chamber is controlled by a needle valve and plastic float assembly. An anti-vibration ball is incorporated into the needle valve design.

7 A clip, attached to the needle valve seat and to the float arm, prevents the needle from sticking in the seat as the fuel level drops. The float chamber is vented internally to the clean-air side of the air filter.

Idle, slow running and progression

8 Fuel, sourced from the float chamber, passes into the primary idle well through a metered idle jet. Here it is mixed with a small amount of air from a calibrated air bleed. The emulsion formed is drawn through a channel to the throttle body where it is discharged from the idle orifice under the primary throttle plate. A tapered mixture screw is used to vary the outlet and this ensures fine control of the idle mixture.

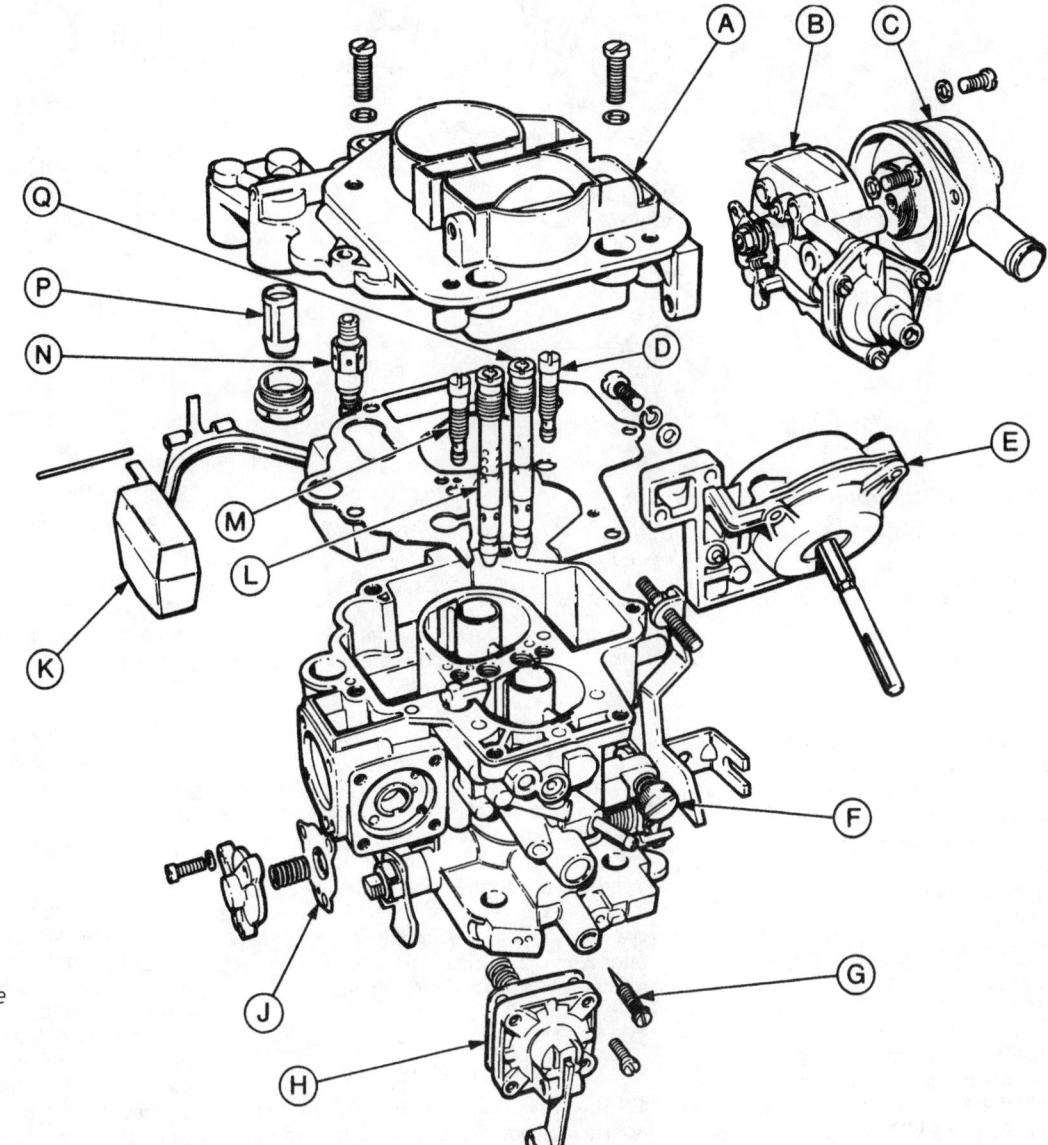

Weber 28/30 DFTH carburettor

- A Upper body assembly
- B Choke housing
- C Choke bi-metal assembly
- D Secondary idle jet
- E Secondary throttle vacuum unit
- F Idle speed screw
- G Idle mixture screw
- H Accelerator pump diaphragm
- J Power valve diaphragm
- K Float
- L Primary emulsion tube assembly
- M Primary idle jet
- N Needle valve
- P Fuel inlet filter
- Q Secondary emulsion tube assembly

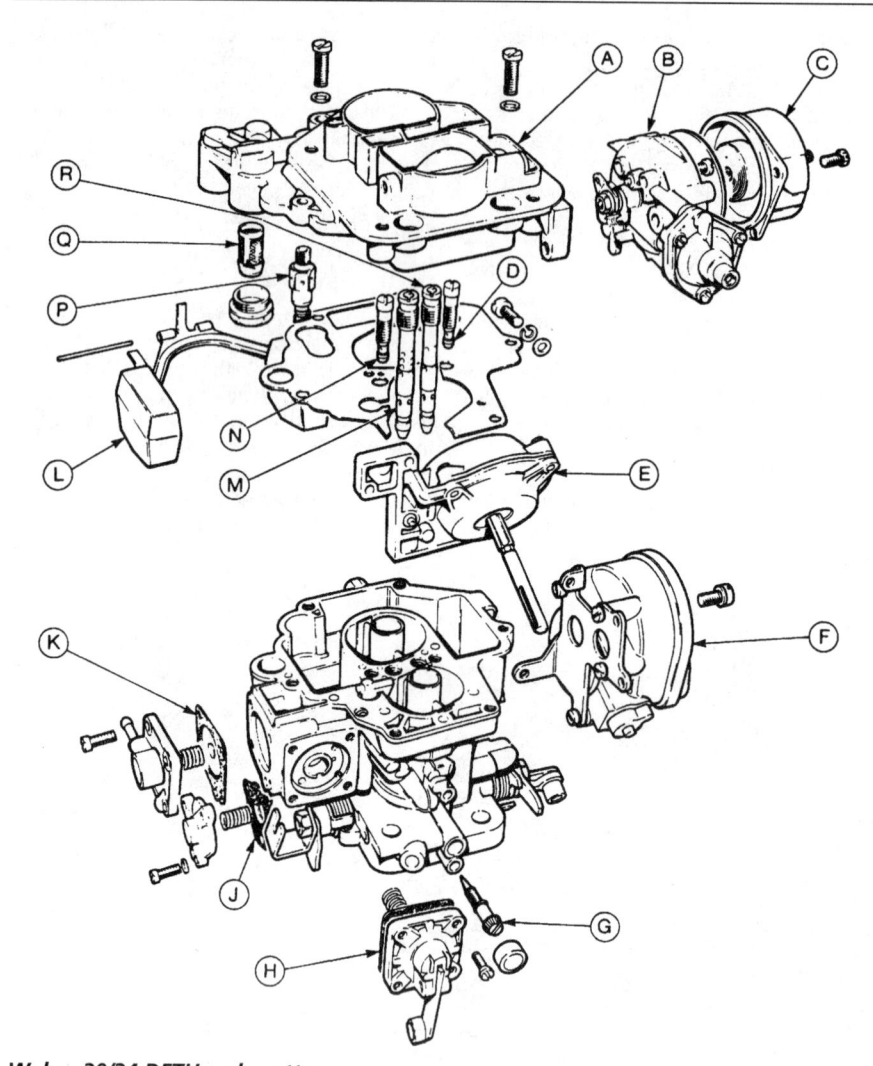

Chapter H3

Weber 30/34 DFTH carburettor

- A Upper body assembly
- B Choke housing
- C Choke bi-metal assembly
- D Secondary idle jet
- E Secondary throttle vacuum unit
- F Stepper motor
- G Idle mixture screw
- H Accelerator pump diaphragm
- J Power valve diaphragm
- K Low vacuum enrichment (LOVE) diaphragm
- L Float
- M Primary emulsion tube assembly
- N Primary idle jet
- P Needle valve
- Q Fuel inlet filter
- R Secondary emulsion tube assembly

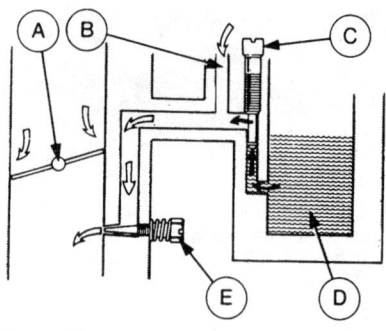

Idle system

- A Throttle plate
- B Air bleed
- C Idle jet
- D Float chamber
- E Mixture screw

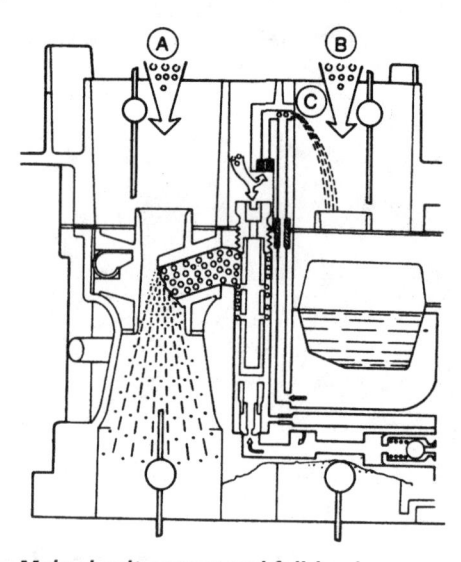

Main circuit, power and full-load enrichment

- A Primary airflow
- B Secondary airflow
- C Full-load enrichment

A progression slot, partially covered by the closed throttle at idle, provides enrichment as it is uncovered by the opening throttle during initial acceleration *(see illustration)*.

9 The idle speed is set by an adjustable screw. The adjustable mixture screw is tamper proofed at production level, in accordance with emission regulations.

Idle cut-off valve - 28/30 DFTH carburettor

10 An idle cut-off valve was only fitted to the 28/30 DFTH carburettor after April 1988. It is used to prevent run-on after engine shutdown and utilises a 12-volt solenoid plunger to block the idle fuel channel when the ignition is switched off.

Accelerator pump

11 The accelerator pump is controlled by a diaphragm and is mechanically operated by a lever and cam actuated by the primary throttle linkage. The outlet valve consists of a ball incorporated into the pump outlet injector. The inlet valve consists of a ball valve located in a channel from the float chamber. Excess fuel is returned to the float chamber through an additional channel and calibrated bush.

Anti-stall device - 30/34 DFTH carburettor

12 The Low Vacuum Enrichment device (sometimes known as a LOVE unit) fitted to the 30/34 DFTH carburettor, is used to overcome stalling due to a lean mixture. The LOVE unit is basically a vacuum-controlled accelerator pump. It is diaphragm-operated and functions in the conventional manner, discharging through the same pump injector as the mechanical pump. During idle or low-speed running, the manifold vacuum will be high. As a stall situation develops, the vacuum will deplete and the pump injector is actuated.

Main circuit

13 The amount of fuel discharged into the airstream is controlled by a calibrated main jet. The main jet and air corrector are pushed into opposite ends of an emulsion tube and the assembly is placed into a vertical well which dips down into the fuel. Fuel is drawn from the float chamber, through the main jet, into the well, to be mixed with air drawn in through the air corrector and the holes in the emulsion tube. The resulting emulsified mixture is discharged from the main nozzle through an auxiliary venturi *(see illustration)*.

H3•4

Weber 28/30 & 30/34 DFTH carburettor

Power enrichment and economy circuit

14 Fuel flows from the float chamber into the power valve chamber through a fuel channel. An air passage is taken from under the throttle plate to the cover of the power diaphragm chamber. At idle and during light-throttle operation, manifold vacuum in the passage draws the diaphragm back against spring pressure. The diaphragm pintle is withdrawn from the brass outlet valve and the spring-loaded ball seats to close off the channel *(see illustration)*.

15 Under acceleration and wide-open throttle operation, the vacuum in the manifold is depleted. The diaphragm returns under spring pressure and the power diaphragm pintle pushes the ball to open the outlet valve. Fuel then flows through the valve and a calibrated jet to supplement the fuel in the primary main well. The fuel level rises in the well and the fuel mixture is enriched *(see illustration)*.

Power valve system during light-throttle operation
A Return spring (compressed)
B Diaphragm (pulled back)
C Power valve (closed)
D High manifold vacuum

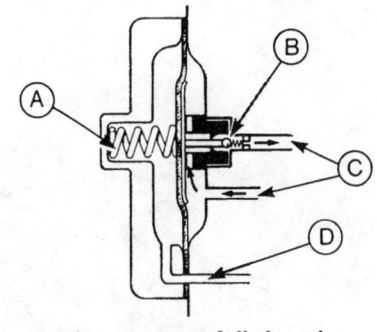

Power valve system at full-throttle
A Return spring (extended)
B Power valve (open)
C Fuel flow
D Low manifold vacuum

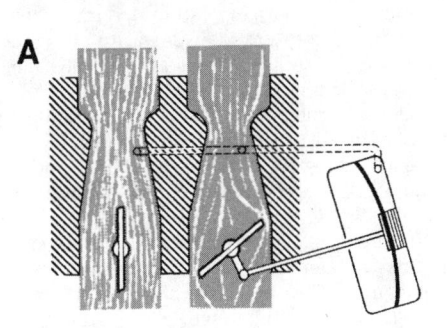

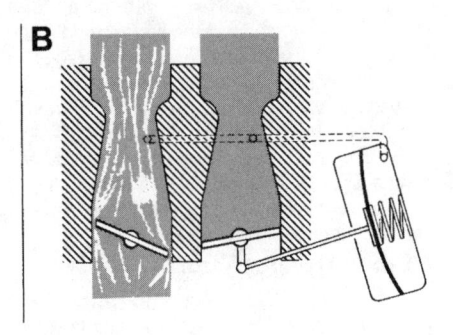

Secondary action

16 A port is located in both primary and secondary venturis. Airways run from these ports into a common passage leading to the diaphragm that operates the secondary throttle plate *(see illustration)*.

17 During normal operation at low speeds, the engine uses only the primary venturi. When air velocity through the primary venturi reaches a certain level, depression acts upon the port to operate the secondary diaphragm and the secondary throttle. Vacuum created in the secondary venturi will further control the rate of secondary opening.

18 The primary linkage is arranged to prevent the secondary plate from opening when air speed high but the engine is cruising on a light throttle. Secondary action will not take place until the primary throttle is about two-thirds open.

19 On 30/34 DFTH carburettors, secondary throttle operation is prevented during warm-up on automatic transmission-equipped vehicles. This is accomplished by use of a ported vacuum switch (PVS) in the cooling system. During warm-up, the PVS remains open to bleed off the vacuum created in the primary venturi port and airway. Once a predetermined coolant temperature is reached, the PVS closes and normal operation of the secondary throttle is restored.

20 Once the secondary throttle plate has opened, the action of the secondary main circuit is similar to that of the primary circuit.

21 A progression jet is used to prevent hesitation as the secondary throttle plate commences to open. This jet is similar in construction and action to the primary idle jet and is often referred to as the secondary idle jet. An emulsified mixture is discharged into the secondary venturi via two progression drillings, at the initial opening of the secondary throttle plate.

22 At full-load and high engine speed, even more fuel is required. The velocity of air creates a depression sufficient to raise fuel from the float chamber into a channel. The fuel then passes through a calibrated bushing to the upper section of the secondary air intake. Here it is mixed with a small amount of air from a calibrated air bleed and the emulsified mixture is then discharged into the airstream from the full-load enrichment outlet.

Secondary action
A High air speed in primary venturi, secondary throttle plate open
B Low air speed in primary venturi, secondary throttle plate closed

Cold start system

28/30 DFTH carburettor

23 The 28/30 DFTH carburettor uses a semi-automatic choke starting system. A bi-metal spring is used to control a strangler choke flap which shuts off the primary air intake. Heating of the coil spring is by engine coolant. For starting the engine from cold, the choke flap and fast idle are set by depressing the accelerator pedal once or twice.

24 Once the engine has fired, the choke flap must open slightly to weaken the mixture and avoid flooding during idle and light-throttle operation. This is achieved by using manifold vacuum to actuate a diaphragm. Linkage attached to the diaphragm will then pull upon the choke flap *(see illustrations)*.

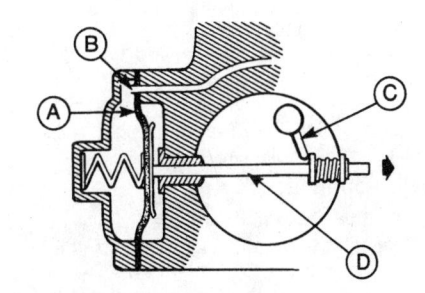

Vacuum pull-down system during starting or acceleration
A Diaphragm
B Vacuum supply (low)
C Choke linkage (unrestricted)
D Pushrod

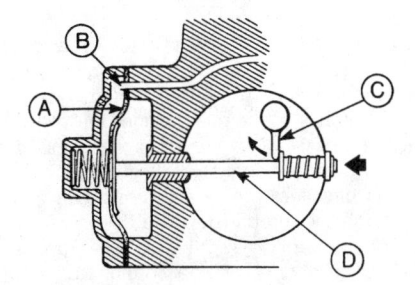

Vacuum pull-down system during light-throttle operation
A Diaphragm
B Vacuum supply (high)
C Choke linkage
D Pushrod

Chapter H3

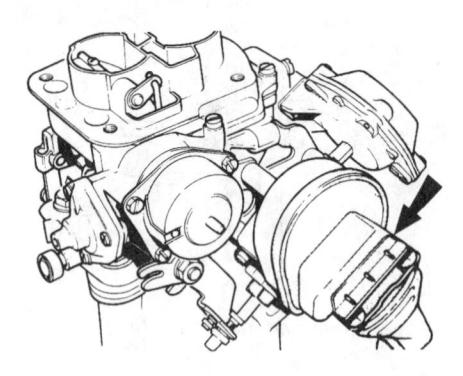

Carburettor stepper motor (arrowed)

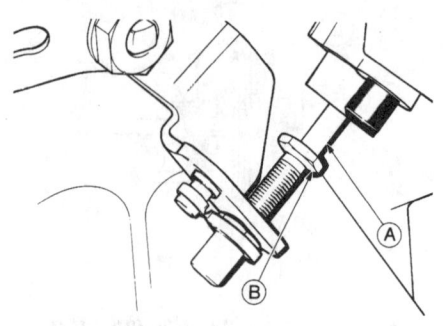

Idle switch contacts
A Stepper motor plunger
B Adjustment screw

Wide-open kick
A Choke lever turned anti-clockwise and partially opening choke plate
B Cam section in throttle lever

25 The fast idle is achieved with the aid of a stepped cam attached to the choke spindle and connected to the throttle lever by a linkage. An adjustable screw, butting against the cam, can be used to vary the fast idle speed. As the bi-metal coil is heated and the flap opens, then the screw will rest on successively less-stepped parts of the cam. Idle speed is thus progressively reduced, until ultimately the cam is released and the idle speed returns to normal.

30/34 DFTH carburettor

26 The 30/34 DFTH carburettor uses a fully automatic choke starting system, complete with stepper motor control of the idle speed (see illustration). A bi-metal spring is used to control a strangler choke flap located in the primary air intake. Heating of the coil spring is via an electrical supply from the alternator.

27 The stepper motor plunger acts directly upon the primary throttle lever (see illustration) and is controlled by the ESC II Engine Management Module. This is an Electronic Control Unit (or ECU). Throttle position and idle speed are automatically set for idle, fast idle and deceleration, and for changes in electrical load. The coolant sensor resistance changes in response to variations in engine coolant temperature and this results in a varying voltage signal to the ECU. The ECU reacts to this changing voltage signal and is able to vary the idle speed to suit different engine operating temperatures.

28 The stepper motor is a four-phase unit mounted on the carburettor. It drives a cam mechanism through a reduction drive system and operates on the spring-loaded throttle stop. The motor windings are sequentially pulsed in pairs, to achieve rotation of the motor spindle in either direction. The motor earth connection is through the throttle stop and this enables the stepper motor to sense when the engine is idling or decelerating, according to engine speed.

29 During deceleration the throttle is completely closed, cutting off the fuel to aid economy and reduce emissions. Throughout the warm-up period, the plunger will extend to prevent the engine stalling. During idle at normal operating temperature, the motor will maintain a constant idle speed. An electrical load caused by use of headlights or heater fan, etc., will be sensed by the drop in engine speed and the stepper motor will compensate by raising the idle speed to its former level. When the load is removed, the idle speed will tend to rise and the motor will lower the engine speed so that the status quo is restored.

30 At engine speeds below 2000 rpm (except under deceleration), the stepper motor will enter a self-clean mode. The plunger will "jitter" until idle is established. This establishes intermittent contact between the plunger and throttle adjuster and is meant to keep the contact surfaces clean.

31 Once the engine ignition is switched off, the ECU will first retract the stepper motor plunger to prevent run-on and then fully extend it to ventilate the inlet manifold.

32 Two relays, a key power relay and a power-hold relay, are used to control the voltage to the stepper motor. The relays are switched on by the ignition key but the power-hold relay is switched off by the ECU after it has completed the anti-run-on and manifold ventilation cycles.

33 The ECU also controls the ignition system and a number of other electrical functions. However, anything other than carburettor control is beyond the terms of reference of this Manual.

34 Once the engine has fired, the choke flap must open slightly to weaken the mixture and avoid flooding during idle and light-throttle operation. This is achieved by using manifold vacuum to actuate a pull-down diaphragm. Linkage attached to the diaphragm will then pull upon the choke flap.

Wide-open kick

35 If the throttle is opened fully during acceleration when the engine is cold, the pull-down vacuum will deplete and the choke flap will tend to close. This may cause flooding and to prevent this, a wide-open kick mechanism is employed. When the throttle is opened fully, a cam on the throttle lever will turn the choke lever anti-clockwise to partially open the choke flap (see illustration).

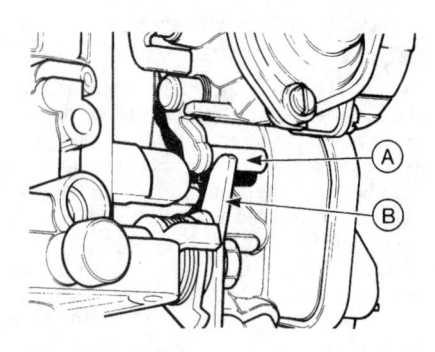

2 Identification

The Weber identification code is stamped on the carburettor base flange.

A metal tag, giving the Ford identification code, is attached to one of the upper body fixing screws.

3 General servicing

Introduction

1 Read this Chapter in conjunction with Part B, which describes some of the operations in more detail. It is assumed that the carburettor is removed for this service. However, many of the operations can be tackled with the carburettor in place. Where this is undertaken, first soak the fuel out of the float chamber using a clean tissue or soft cloth, after removing the upper body assembly.

Dismantling and checking

2 On 30/34 DFTH carburettors, depress the locking clip and disconnect the multi-plug from the stepper motor. Do not pull on the multi-plug wires.

3 Remove the carburettor from the engine (see Part B).

4 Make visual checks for damage and wear.

5 On 28/30 DFTH carburettors, remove the six screws, hold the choke fast idle lever clear of the choke housing and detach the carburettor upper body.

6 On 30/34 DFTH carburettors, remove the six screws and detach the carburettor upper body.

7 Use a straight-edge to check for distorted flanges on all facing surfaces.

8 Inspect the float chamber for corrosion and calcium build-up.

9 Tap out the float pin, then remove the float,

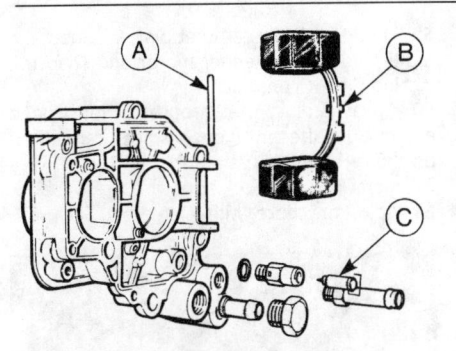

Weber 28/30 & 30/34 DFTH carburettor

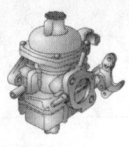

Upper body and float components
A Float retaining pin
B Float
C Needle valve

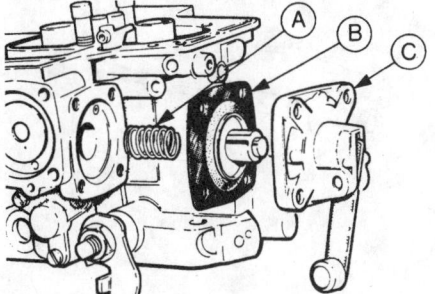

Accelerator pump assembly
A Spring
B Diaphragm
C Pump cover

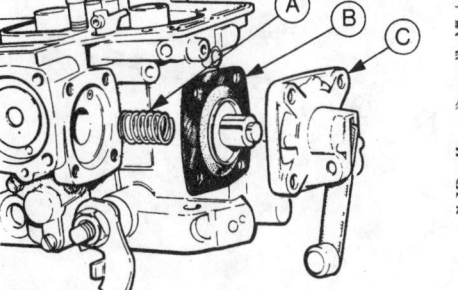

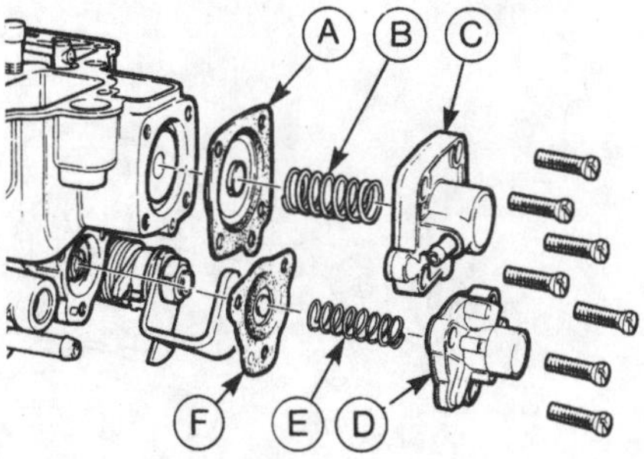

Power valve and low vacuum enrichment (LOVE) diaphragms
A Low vacuum diaphragm
B Diaphragm return spring
C Cover
D Cover
E Diaphragm return spring
F Power valve diaphragm

needle valve and hairpin clip, float chamber gasket and needle valve seat *(see illustration)*.
10 Check that the anti-vibration ball is free in the valve end.
11 Check the needle valve tip for wear and ridges. This is more likely with the brass needle valve tip than when a viton one is used. Use a viton-tipped replacement when possible.
12 The float should be checked for damage and ingress of petrol. Shaking the float will indicate the presence of fuel.
13 Renew the float pin if it shows signs of wear.
14 Unscrew the fuel filter housing assembly. The fuel filter housing is located upon a stub joined to the main body by a narrow neck. Take care that this neck is not sheared if excess force is required to shift the filter retaining nut. Renew the fuel filter if clogged and clean the housing of debris and dirt.
15 Remove the mixture screw and inspect the tip for damage and ridges.
16 Remove the four screws and remove the accelerator pump cover, diaphragm and spring. Check the diaphragm for fatigue and damage *(see illustration)*.
17 On 30/34 DFTH carburettors, remove the four screws and remove the anti-stall device housing, spring and diaphragm. Check the diaphragm for fatigue and damage *(see illustration)*.
18 The pump injector is a push fit in the main carburettor body. Carefully prise it from its location and test it by shaking. No noise from the outlet ball indicates that the valve is seized.
19 Remove the primary and secondary idle jet assemblies, the main jets, air correctors and emulsion tubes.
20 Check that the channel from the float chamber into the emulsion tube well is clear.
21 The idle jets are pushed into a holder and can be separated, by pulling, for cleaning or renewal. Likewise, the main jets and air correctors are pushed into the opposite ends of the emulsion tubes and may also be separated, by pulling, for cleaning or renewal. The idle jet and the main jet assemblies can be removed from the carburettor body without removing the upper body.
22 Note the jet sizes and locations for correct installation during reassembly. The primary main and idle jet are located on the accelerator pump side of the carburettor, while the secondary main and idle jet are located on the choke side of the carburettor.
23 Check the jet calibration against that specified. It is possible that the jets may have been transposed (or the wrong size fitted) during the last overhaul.
24 Remove the primary and secondary auxiliary venturis, where necessary. Weber provide an extractor tool for removing these items. Check that the primary and secondary auxiliary venturis are not loose in the main body, as this can cause uneven running. If a venturi is loose, knurl the mating flanges with a file to ensure a tight fit.

25 Remove the three screws, then remove the power valve cover, spring and diaphragm from the body. Check the diaphragm for fatigue and porosity *(see illustration)*.
26 The brass outlet valve is cast into the body and is not removable. The ball in the outlet valve should seal the outlet. Depress and release the ball with a small screwdriver and it should move smoothly in and out. Check that the channel into the primary emulsion tube well is clear.
27 Disconnect the secondary throttle operating rod *(see illustration)*. Pull the lower section of the rod downwards and twist it out of its socket. Remove the four screws and remove the secondary throttle vacuum unit cover, spring and diaphragm from the housing. Check the diaphragm for fatigue and renew as necessary *(see illustration)*.
28 On 30/34 DFTH carburettors, remove the four screws, and detach the carburettor stepper motor.
29 Inspect the choke spindle, mechanism and levers for stickiness and wear *(see illustration overleaf)*.
30 Remove the three screws, twist and disconnect the lower choke link rod and detach the choke housing. Check the mechanism for stickiness and wear.
31 Remove the three screws and remove the

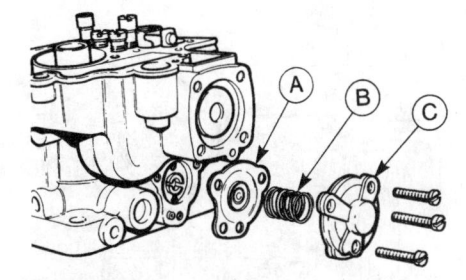

Power valve assembly
A Diaphragm
B Diaphragm return spring
C Cover

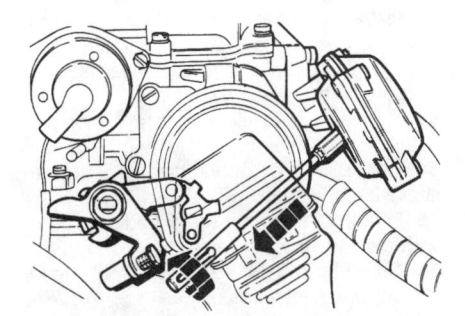

Disconnecting link rod from secondary venturi vacuum unit

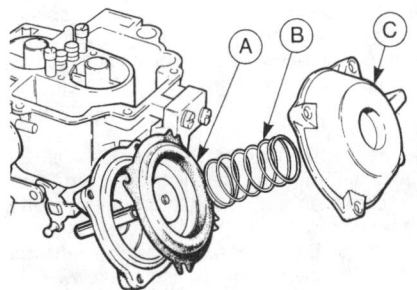

Secondary throttle vacuum unit
A Diaphragm
B Spring
C Diaphragm cover

Chapter H3

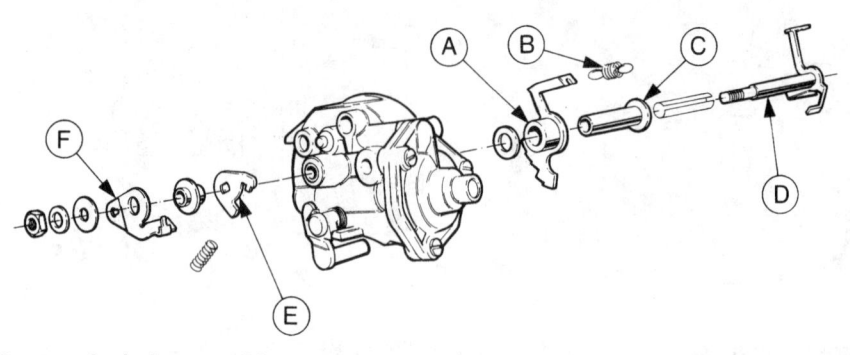

Automatic choke assembly

A Choke upper operating link
B Fast idle cam return spring
C Spindle sleeve
D Connecting rod and lever assembly
E Pull-down link
F Actuating lever

choke pull-down cover, spring and diaphragm from the housing. Check the diaphragm for fatigue and damage.

Preparation for reassembly

32 Clean the jets and internal channels, the carburettor body assemblies and the float chamber. An air line may be used to clear the internal channels once the carburettor is fully dismantled. If an air line is used with the diaphragms in place and air is directed into the diaphragm passages, diaphragm damage may result.
33 Spraying carburettor cleaner into all the channels and passages in the carburettor body will often clear them of gum and dirt.
34 During reassembly, a complete set of new gaskets should be fitted. Also renew the needle valve and float pin, and all diaphragms.
35 Inspect and renew (where necessary) the mixture screw, main jets, idle jets, air corrector jets and pump injector assembly. Renew worn linkages and springs where necessary.
36 Ensure that all jets are firmly locked into their original positions (but do not overtighten). A loose jet can cause a rich (or even lean) running condition.
37 Clean all mating surfaces and flanges of old gasket material and reassemble with new gaskets.
38 Ensure that housings are assembled with their air and fuel routes correctly aligned.

Reassembly

39 Refit the choke diaphragm and spindle assembly to the choke housing. Ensure that both plastic sleeves on the diaphragm spindle are pushed into position and fully located. Refit the spring and cover, then secure with the three screws.
40 Renew the vacuum O-ring seal and fit the choke link rod into the choke lever arm. Refit the choke housing to the carburettor upper body and secure with the three screws.
41 On 30/34 DFTH carburettors, refit the carburettor stepper motor and secure with the four screws.
42 Check that the secondary throttle plate is fully closed. The adjustment screw should not normally be used to alter the throttle plate position. However, if necessary, it can be adjusted so that the plate is open just enough to prevent the plate from seizing in the throttle body.
43 Refit the secondary throttle diaphragm, spring and cover assembly and secure with the four screws. Reconnect the secondary throttle operating rod.
44 Refit the power diaphragm, spring and cover assembly, and secure with the three screws.
45 Ensure that the air corrector and main jets are pushed fully into the emulsion tubes. Refit the assemblies into their original positions (do not transpose the jets).
46 Ensure that the idle jets are pushed fully into their holders and that they are refitted into their original positions (do not transpose the jets).
47 Refit the pump injector, after renewing the small seal on the injector body.
48 On 30/34 DFTH carburettors, refit the anti-stall device diaphragm, spring and cover assembly, then secure with the four screws.
49 Refit the accelerator pump spring, diaphragm and cover assembly, then secure with the four screws.
50 Refit the idle mixture screw. Carefully turn the screw in until it just seats, then unscrew it three full turns. This will provide a basic setting to allow the engine to be started.
51 Refit the fuel filter housing assembly.
52 Renew the needle valve assembly. Screw the valve seat into the upper body, using a new sealing washer, and ensure that it is firmly locked into position. Insert the needle valve into the seat with the ball facing outwards, then fit a new float chamber gasket, float and pin. Ensure that the plastic clip is correctly connected to the float and to the needle valve.
53 Adjust the float level. Refer to Section 4 for details on adjustment.
54 On 28/30 DFTH carburettors, pull back the choke fast idle arm.
55 Refit the carburettor upper body and secure with the six screws.
56 On 28/30 DFTH carburettors, refit the idle cut-off valve (where fitted).
57 Ensure that the choke flap and linkage move smoothly and progressively.
58 Refit the carburettor to the engine.
59 On 30/34 DFTH carburettors, reconnect the multi-plug to the stepper motor and snap the locking clip into position.
60 Always adjust the carburettor idle speed and mixture after any work has been carried out on the carburettor, preferably with the aid of a CO meter.
61 Adjust the choke, with reference to Section 4.

4 Service adjustments

Adjustment preconditions

1 Refer to Part B for general advice on preconditions to correct adjustment of the carburettor.

Idle speed and mixture (CO) - 28/30 DFTH carburettor

2 The air filter can be removed and placed to one side (or loosely assembled in position) with the vacuum hose still connected.
3 Run the engine at 3000 rpm for 30 seconds to clear the manifold of fuel vapours, then allow the engine to idle.
4 Use the idle speed screw to set the specified idle speed *(see illustration)*.
5 Check the CO level and compare with the specified value. If incorrect, remove the tamperproof plug and adjust to the correct level. Turning the screw clockwise (inwards) will reduce the CO level. Turning the screw anti-clockwise (outwards) will increase the CO level.
6 Repeat paragraphs 4 and 5 until both adjustments are correct.
7 Clear the manifold every 30 seconds during the setting operation by running the engine at 3000 rpm for 30 seconds.
8 Fit a new tamperproof plug to the mixture adjusting screw.
9 Refit the air filter, ensuring that the vacuum hoses remain connected.

Idle mixture (CO) - 30/34 DFTH carburettor

10 Run the engine at 3000 rpm for 30 seconds to clear the manifold of fuel vapours, then allow the engine to idle.

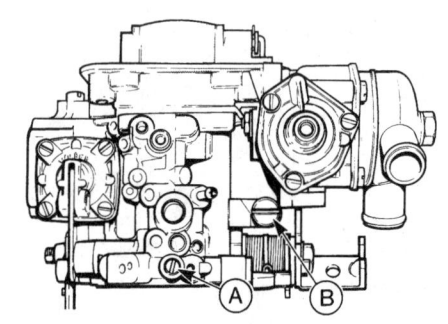

Idle adjustment screw location

A Idle mixture screw   B Idle speed screw

Weber 28/30 & 30/34 DFTH carburettor

Idle mixture screw location (arrowed)

11 Check the CO level and compare with the specified value. If incorrect, remove the tamperproof plug and adjust to the correct level *(see illustration)*. Turning the screw clockwise (inwards) will reduce the CO level. Turning the screw anti-clockwise (outwards) will increase the CO level.
12 Clear the manifold every 30 seconds during the setting operation by running the engine at 3000 rpm for 30 seconds.
13 Fit a new tamperproof plug to the mixture adjusting screw.

Idle speed - 30/34 DFTH carburettor

14 Warm the engine to normal running temperature and adjust the idle mixture.
15 If the stepper motor or carburettor have been renewed, it may be necessary to adjust the idle screw to its datum position. This is achieved by slackening the locknut and adjusting the screw to give the screw head-to-throttle lever height shown *(see illustration)*.
16 Remove the air filter and place it to one side (or loosely assemble in position) with the vacuum hoses still connected.
17 Check that all electrical loads are switched off.
18 Disconnect the idle-adjust lead if it is connected. This is a yellow lead near the coil. If the wire is connected to earth, the idle speed will be raised by 75 rpm.
19 Accelerate the engine to a speed of more than 2500 rpm two or three times, then place a 1.0 mm feeler blade between the stepper motor plunger and the adjusting screw and allow the engine to idle *(see illustration)*.

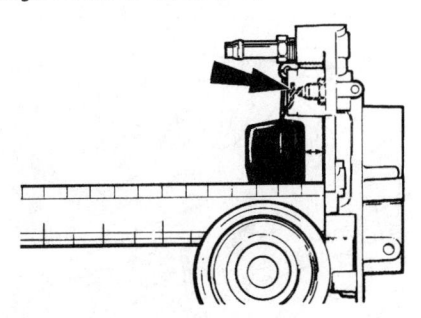

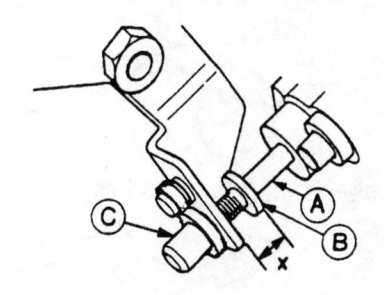

Stepper motor basic adjustment
A Plunger C Tamperproof cap
B Adjustment screw x = 7.5 ± 1.0 mm

20 If the idle speed is not 875 ± 25 rpm, remove the tamperproof cap, slacken the locknut and adjust the screw to achieve the correct figure.
21 Repeat paragraph 19, then remove the feeler blade and the idle speed should fall to 800 ± 50 rpm.
22 If the idle speed varies or other faults are present, carry out the stepper motor checks in Section 5.
23 Fit a new tamperproof plug to the adjusting screw then refit the air filter, ensuring that the vacuum hoses remain connected.
24 Reconnect the idle-adjust lead, if disconnected.

Float level

25 Hold the carburettor upper body in a vertical position with the float tag gently touching the ball of the fully-closed needle valve.
26 Measure the distance between the upper body (with the gasket in place) and the base of the float *(see illustration)*.
27 Adjust as necessary by bending the inner float tag.

Automatic choke

Fast idle - 28/30 DFTH carburettor

28 Warm the engine to normal running temperature and adjust the idle speed and mixture before attempting choke fast idle adjustment.
29 Remove the air filter assembly and place it clear of the carburettor, with the vacuum hose still connected.

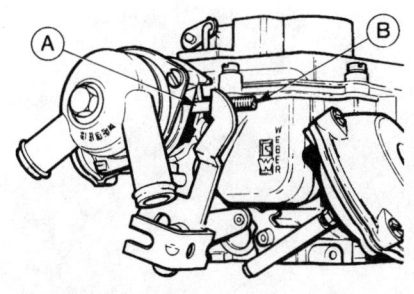

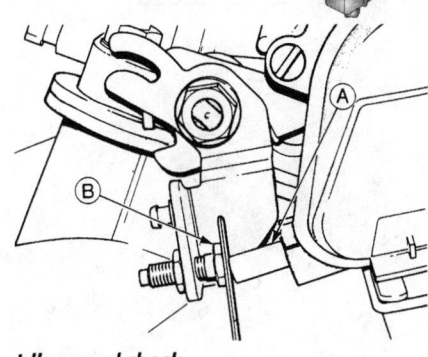

Idle speed check
A Plunger B Adjustment screw
1.0 mm feeler blade inserted between stepper motor plunger and adjustment screw

30 Partially open the throttle and fully close the choke flap. Slowly open the plate until the fast idle adjustment screw can be placed against the third-highest step of the fast idle cam. Release the throttle so that the fast idle adjustment screw remains against the third-highest step but with the choke flap open *(see illustration)*.
31 Start the engine without moving the throttle and record the fast idle speed. Refer to Specifications for the correct value.
32 Adjust as necessary by turning the fast idle screw in the appropriate direction.
33 Refit the air filter assembly, ensuring that the vacuum hose remains connected.

Choke vacuum pull-down

34 Remove the three screws and detach the bi-metal coil housing from the carburettor.
35 Remove the internal plastic heat shield.
36 Partially open the throttle and fully close the choke flap.
37 Release the throttle and fit an elastic band to the choke operating lever so that the choke flap remains in the fully-closed position.
38 Use a small screwdriver to push open the diaphragm to its stop *(see illustration)* then use the shank of a twist drill to measure the gap between the lower section of the choke flap

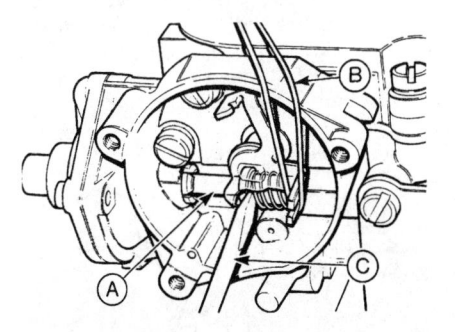

Float level adjustment
Adjustment tag arrowed

Fast idle adjustment
A Screw on middle/ third cam
B Fast idle screw

Setting choke operating lever for pull-down check
A Diaphragm operating rod
B Elastic band
C Screwdriver

Hold choke lever in position and push diaphragm open

H3•9

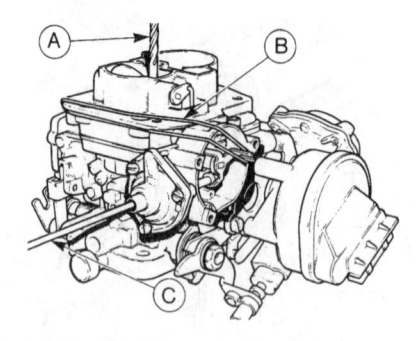

Chapter H3

Vacuum pull-down adjustment
A Twist drill   C Screwdriver
B Elastic band

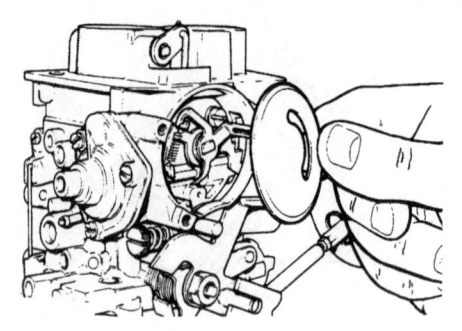

Refitting internal heat shield

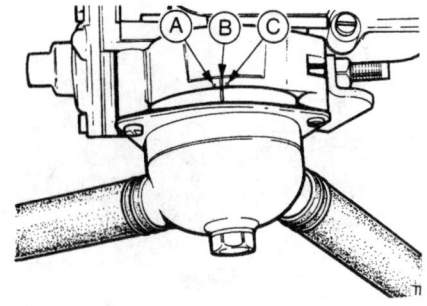

Choke housing alignment marks
A Rich position   C Lean position
B Index mark

and the air intake. Refer to Specifications for the required drill size.

39 Remove the tamperproof plug and adjust as necessary by turning the diaphragm adjusting screw *(see illustration)* in the appropriate direction. Renew the plug after adjustment is complete and remove the elastic band.

40 Refit the internal heat shield and ensure that the hole in the shield locates into the peg in the housing *(see illustration)*.

41 Refit the bi-metal coil housing. Ensure that the spring locates in the slot of the choke lever and secure loosely with the three screws.

42 Align the cut mark on the bi-metal cover with the correct mark on the choke assembly housing and tighten the three screws *(see illustration)*.

5 Component testing - 30/34 DFTH carburettor

Automatic choke

Engine cold

1 Allow the engine to cool completely, then remove the air filter and check that the choke flap blocks the carburettor air intake *(see illustration)*.

2 Start the engine and check that the cold idle speed is about 1500 rpm. There is no official figure, as the fast idle is set by the stepper motor according to temperature.

3 Check that the choke pull-down operates satisfactorily. As the engine warms up, check that the choke flap gradually opens until it is fully open. The fast idle speed should progressively decrease.

4 If the choke flap operation is unsatisfactory, check the choke pull-down adjustment and look for sticking, worn or broken linkage.

5 Attach a voltmeter to the choke electrical connection and expect a reading of 6 to 8 volts with the engine running *(see illustration)*.

6 If the voltage is low or zero, attach the voltmeter to the choke output connection on the alternator. If there is still no voltage, repair or renew the alternator.

7 If voltage is present at the alternator but not at the choke, check the wiring from the alternator to the choke for a break or bad connection.

Engine warm

8 Switch the ignition on and then off. As the ignition is switched off, the stepper motor plunger should first retract fully and then after four seconds, extend to ventilate the inlet manifold *(see illustration)*.

9 Start the engine and check that the idle speed is within the specified limits. If not, refer to Section 4 for details on stepper motor idle adjustment.

10 Note the idle speed, then blip the throttle and check that the plunger completely retracts and then extends to return the throttle to its previous idle speed.

11 Switch on the headlight main beam and switch the heater fan to maximum. The engine should maintain its idle speed.

12 If stepper motor operation is unsatisfactory in the above tests, or if it does not respond to idle adjustment and jitters, stalls, idles irregularly or cycles between 800 and 1500 rpm, use emery paper to clean the contact surfaces between the plunger and the throttle adjustment plate. The stepper motor earth connection is made through these two components and a good contact is essential.

13 If stepper motor operation is still unsatisfactory and you are sure there is no mechanical or ignition fault and that the valve clearances are correct, carry out the following tests:

ECU checks

14 Note the following when carrying out checks on the ECU *(see illustration)*:

a) Ford advise the use of a Break Out Box for these tests (Ford part number 29 001 and test lead part number 29 002) *(see illustration)*. However, these items will not be available to many of those reading this Manual and the following tests can be made without them. An oscilloscope with a low-voltage facility will be useful but a good quality multimeter with an impedance of 10 000 ohms can also be used quite satisfactorily.

b) The ECU controls a number of electrical functions but we are confined, by the terms

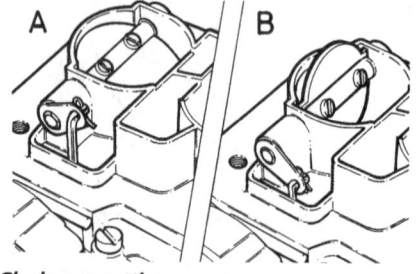

Choke operation
A Choke plate closed (choke on, engine cold)
B Choke plate open (choke off, engine hot)

Checking for voltage at choke (engine running)

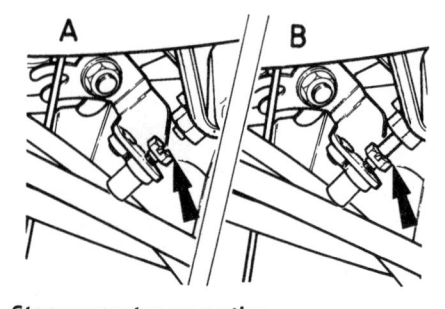

Stepper motor operation
A Plunger fully retracted
B Plunger fully extended

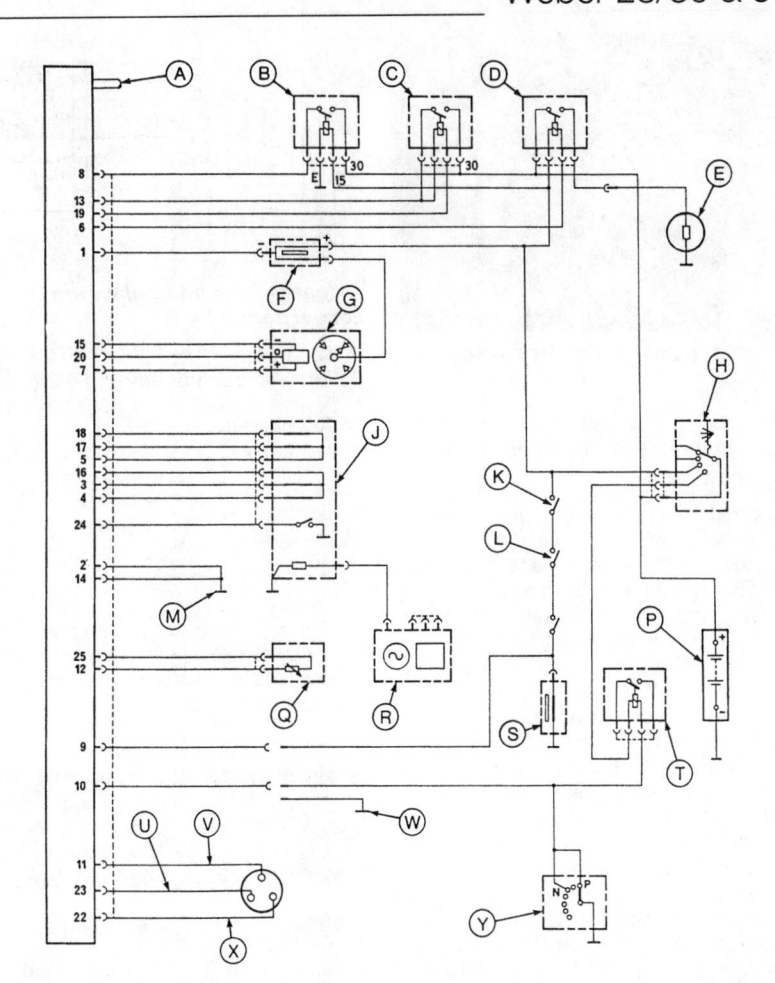

Weber 28/30 & 30/34 DFTH carburettor

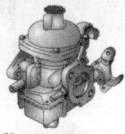

ECU (ESC II module) wiring diagram

- A Vacuum connection
- B Key power relay
- C Power-hold relay
- D Intake heater relay
- E Intake heater assembly
- F Ignition coil
- G Distributor
- H Ignition switch
- J Carburettor stepper motor
- K Air conditioning switch (where fitted)
- L De-icing switch
- M Pressure switch (in earth line)
- P Battery
- Q Engine coolant temperature sensor
- R Alternator
- S Air conditioning clutch (where fitted)
- T Starter relay (automatic transmission only)
- U Octane adjust lead (blue)
- V Octane adjust lead (red)
- W Earth connection (manual transmission only)
- X Idle adjust lead (yellow)
- Y Automatic transmission switch

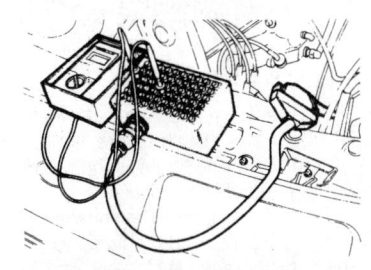

Ford Break Out Box, showing lead connected to ECU and multimeter

of reference of this Manual, to a check on the carburettor functions alone.
c) Switch the ignition on for all voltage tests and off for all resistance tests.
d) Avoid component damage by switching the ignition off when making or breaking electrical connections (particularly at the ECU multi-plug).

15 The ECU is connected to the nearside wing. Cut the retaining cable tie and peel back the waterproof cover on the ECU multi-plug.
16 Disconnect the multi-plug and remove the three small screws. Turn the plug over so that the connector is facing upwards and remove the oblong seal from around the connector.
17 Pull the multi-plug apart and slide the casing away so that the back of the plug and the wire connections are exposed. Push the multi-plug into the ECU and use a voltmeter to probe the terminal connections at the back of the multi-plug. Use thin test probes to avoid pin damage. The pin numbers are marked on the side of the plug that is now exposed.

Key power relay

18 Connect the (+) lead of the multi-meter to ECU terminal 8 and the (-) lead to terminal 2. Check for a battery voltage reading with the ignition on (see illustration).
19 Repeat paragraph 18 but with the (+) lead connected to terminal 8 and the (-) lead connected to terminal 14. Once again, battery voltage should be obtained with the ignition on.
20 Probing the voltage supply and earth connections in this way is a test of the complete circuit. If a voltage is not available, test the key power relay and check the wiring and earth connections. The key power relay is located under the dash on the passenger side, near the heater. The relay number is M2.

Coolant temperature sensor

21 Now test the coolant temperature sensor by connecting the (+) lead of the multi-meter to ECU terminal 12 and the (-) lead to terminal 25. When the engine is cold, the voltage will be about 4 volts. Start the engine and the voltage should slowly reduce to about 1.0 volt when the engine is hot (see illustration).
22 If the results are unsatisfactory, retest at the coolant temperature sensor (CTS) which is located in the inlet manifold (see illustration). If the CTS has become open or short-circuited, the ECU will operate in fail-safe mode and substitute a resistance that will allow the stepper motor to operate as if the engine was warm. Although the choke flap will operate

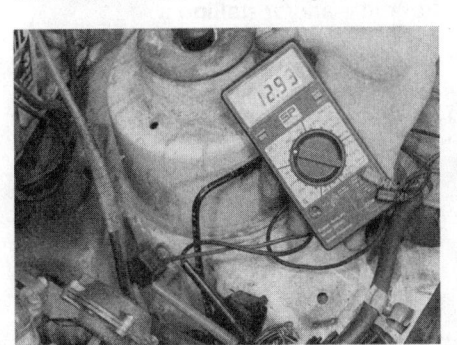

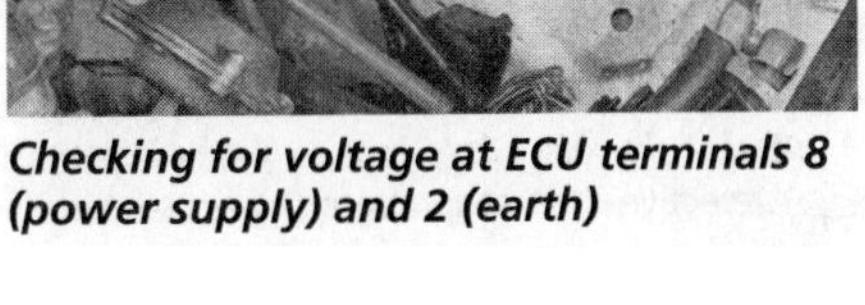

Checking for voltage at ECU terminals 8 (power supply) and 2 (earth)

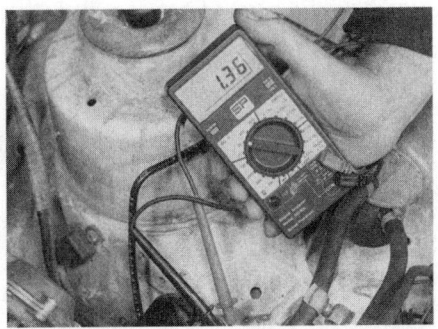

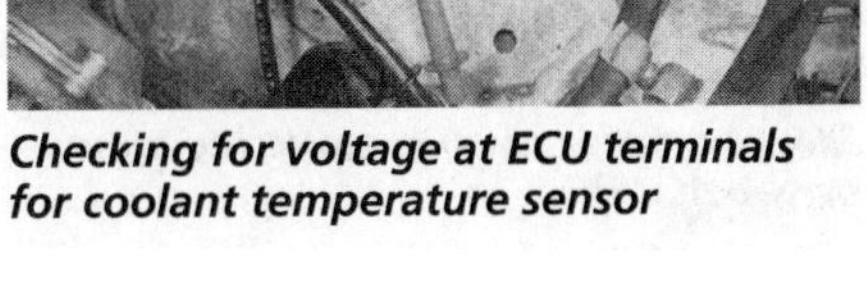

Checking for voltage at ECU terminals for coolant temperature sensor

H3•11

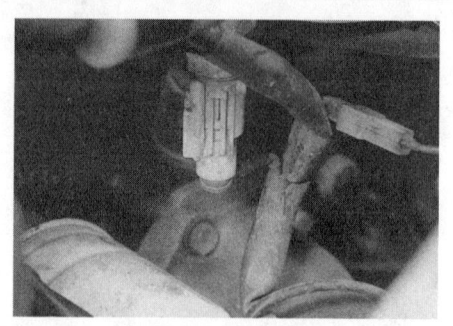

Chapter H3

Location of coolant temperature sensor

Location of power-hold relay (arrowed) in fusebox

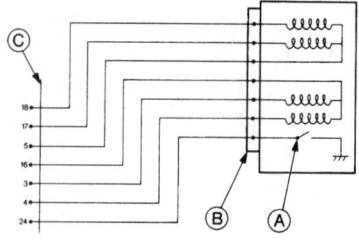

Stepper motor internal wiring connections

A Idle switch
B Multi-plug connection
C ESC II module (ECU)

normally, the fast idle speed will be reduced and stalling may occur during warm-up.

23 A supply voltage of 5 volts indicates that the CTS is open-circuit.

24 Measure the CTS resistance at the temperatures in the following table:

Temperature (°C)	Resistance (kilohms)
0	90 to 100
20	35 to 40
40	15 to 18
60	7 to 8
100	1.9 to 2.2

Power-hold relay

25 Connect the (+) lead of the multi-meter to terminal 13 of the ECU and the (-) lead to terminal 19. With the ignition on, nominal battery voltage should be indicated.

26 Switch off the ignition. The voltage should hold for 4 to 5 seconds and then drop to zero.

27 If the results are unsatisfactory, check the power-hold relay, the wiring to the relay and the ECU connections 13 and 19. The relay is located in the fusebox and is labelled D *(see illustration)*.

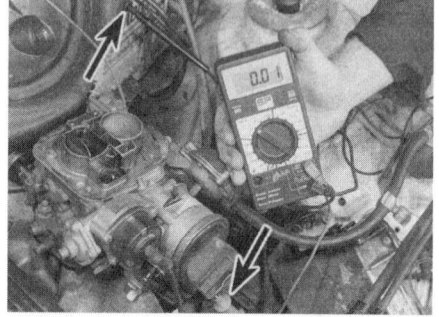

Stepper motor earth

28 Connect the (+) lead of the multi-meter to ECU terminal 24 and the (-) lead to terminal 2 or 14. With the engine idling and the switch closed, the voltage should be no more than 0.02 volts. Open the throttle and the voltage will rise to between 4.0 and 4.5 volts.

29 Probe terminals 18, 17, 5, 16, 3 and 4 in turn with the positive lead, with the negative lead in terminals 2 or 14. The voltages obtained will vary between 1.0 and 5.0 volts as the stepper motor operates *(see illustration)*.

30 The tests in paragraphs 28 and 29 can be carried out at the stepper motor but the terminals are not marked. The earth terminal is furthest away from the nearside wing *(see illustrations)*.

31 If all signals into and out of the ECU are present but the stepper motor does not act satisfactorily, the stepper motor must be faulty.

32 On the other hand, if the signals tested for in paragraphs 18 to 27 above are present but those tested for in paragraphs 28 and 29 are not available, then, if the wiring is fault-free, suspect the ECU.

33 If the results of all tests are satisfactory, reconnect the ECU multi-plug and retest as in paragraphs 1 to 13 above. If all the faults have now gone, a bad connection may have been the cause. If the problem is still present, test the ECU by substituting a known-good unit.

34 Dynamic testing of voltages is by far the best way of diagnosing faults. For the record, the stepper motor resistances measured at the ECU multi-plug terminals (with the multi-plug disconnected) are as follows:

ECU terminal

+ve	-ve	Resistance (ohms)
16	2	Open-circuit
5	2	Open-circuit
16	3	2 to 6
16	4	2 to 6
5	17	2 to 6
5	18	2 to 6

35 After testing is completed, reassemble the multi-plug. Pull the waterproof cover over the plug and secure with a new cable tie. A poor seal to the plug could allow water to affect the connection.

6 Fault diagnosis

28/30 DFTH carburettor

Refer to Part D for general diagnosis of carburettor faults. The following faults are specific to the Weber 28/30 DFTH carburettor.

Poor choke operation

☐ Failure of voltage supply from the alternator to the automatic choke. The choke will take much longer to open fully:
Check the alternator supply to the choke with a voltmeter - expect a reading of 6 to 8 volts with the engine running

30/34 DFTH carburettor

Refer to Part D for general diagnosis of carburettor faults. The following faults are specific to the Weber 30/34 DFTH carburettor.

Poor idle and/or stalling

☐ Poor contact between stepper motor plunger and throttle stop
☐ Broken stepper motor drivebelt or belt skidding due to worn, missing or broken teeth:
Remove the retaining bracket and lift the cover to inspect the belt (see illustration). The belt is not available as a spare part and a replacement stepper motor will need to be obtained

Poor cold starting

☐ Defective stepper motor
☐ Defective relay
☐ Defective coolant temperature sensor

Checking voltage at stepper motor earth connection (engine running, throttle closed)

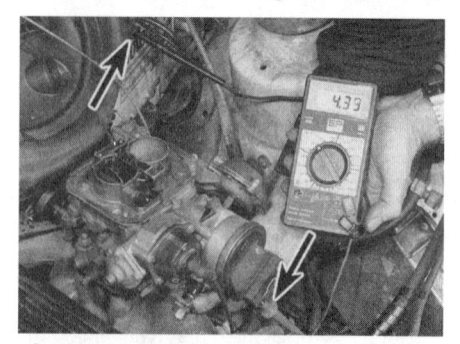

Checking voltage at stepper motor earth connection (engine running, throttle open)

Stepper motor cover removed to expose drivebelt

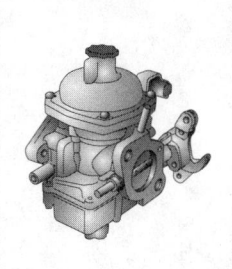

Part H Chapter 4
Weber 28/30 DFTM carburettor

H4

Contents

Component testing 5	Identification 2
Fault diagnosis 6	Principles of operation 1
General servicing 3	Service adjustments 4

Specifications

Manufacturer	Ford		Ford		Ford	
Model	Fiesta 1400		Fiesta 1.4		Fiesta 1.4 auto	
Year	**1986 to 1989**		**1989 to 1991**		**1989 to 1991**	
Engine code	FUA/FUB (CVH)		FUF (CVH) 15/04		FUF (CVH)	
Capacity (cm³)/no. of cyls	1392/4		1392/4		1392/4	
Oil temperature (°C)	80		80		80	
Transmission	Manual		Manual		Automatic	
Carb. ident. (Ford)	86SF 9510 FA		-		89SF 9510 DA/DB/DC	
Carb. ident. (Weber/Solex)	28/30 DFTM 1A		-		-	
Idle speed (rpm)	800 ± 50		800 ± 50		850 ± 50	
Fast idle speed (rpm)	2700 ± 100		2800 ± 100		2800 ± 100	
CO @ idle (% vol.)	1.5 ± 0.25		1.5 ± 0.25		1.5 ± 0.25	
Stage (venturi)	1	2	1	2	1	2
Venturi diameter	21	23	-	-	-	-
Idle jet	42	60	-	-	-	-
Main jet	102	125	100	125	100	125
Air correction jet	200	165	-	-	-	-
Emulsion tube	F22	F60	-	-	-	-
Accel. pump jet	40		-		-	
Float level (mm)	8.0 ± 0.5		-		8.0 ± 0.5	
Needle valve size (mm)	1.5		-		-	
Throttle kicker	1300 rpm		-		1300 rpm	
Choke pull-down (mm)	2.7 to 3.2		-		2.7 to 3.2	

H4•1

Chapter H4

Manufacturer	Ford
Model	Escort & Orion 1.4
Year	1986 to 1990
Engine code	FUA (CVH)
Capacity (cm³)/no. of cyls	1392/4
Oil temperature (°C)	80
Transmission	Manual
Carb. ident. (Ford)	86SF 9510 FA/FB
Carb. ident. (Weber/Solex)	28/30 DFTM 1A
Idle speed (rpm)	800 ± 50
Fast idle speed (rpm)	2700 ± 100
CO @ idle (% vol.)	1.5 ± 2.5

Stage (venturi)	1	2
Venturi diameter	21	23
Idle jet	42	60
Main jet	102	125
Air correction jet	200	165
Emulsion tube	F22	F60

Accel. pump jet	40
Float level (mm)	8.0 ± 0.5
Needle valve size (mm)	1.5
Throttle kicker	1300 ± 50 rpm
Choke pull-down (mm)	2.7 to 3.2

Weber DFTM carburettor

A Manual choke assembly
B Choke vacuum pull-down unit
C Secondary idle jet
D Secondary throttle vacuum unit
E Idle speed screw
F Idle mixture screw
G Accelerator pump assembly
H Throttle kicker
J Power valve diaphragm
K Float
L Primary emulsion tube
M Primary idle jet
N Needle valve
P Fuel inlet valve
Q Secondary emulsion tube

Weber 28/30 DFTM carburettor

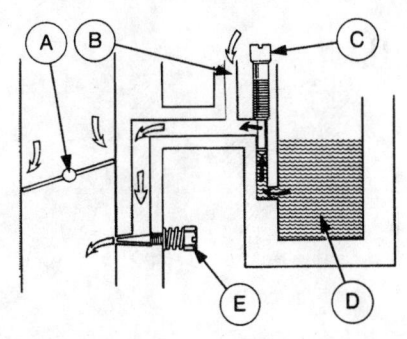

Idle system
A Throttle plate
B Air bleed
C Idle jet
D Float chamber
E Mixture screw

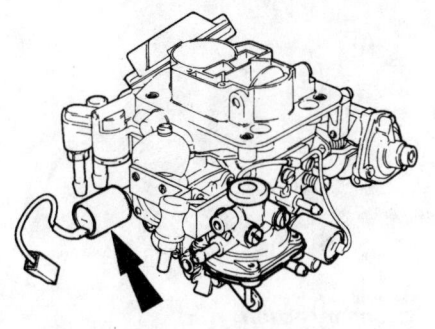

Carburettor back-bleed solenoid (arrowed)

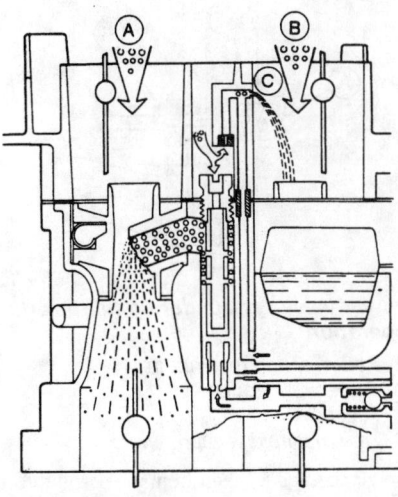

Main circuit, power and full-load enrichment
A Primary airflow
B Secondary airflow
C Full-load enrichment

1 Principles of operation

Introduction

1 The following technical description of the Weber DFTM carburettor should be read in conjunction with the more detailed description of carburettor principles in Part A.

Construction

2 The Weber 28/30 DFTM carburettor is a downdraught twin venturi instrument with a vacuum-controlled secondary throttle *(see illustration)*. The choke system is manually controlled and operates on the primary venturi alone.

3 An idle cut-off valve is fitted to the idle circuit and a vacuum-controlled throttle kicker is used as a throttle damper. Throttle and choke shafts and the choke flap are made of steel. The throttle valves are made of brass, as are all the emulsion tubes and jets, with the exception of the accelerator pump discharge injector which is die-cast. The internal fuel channels and air passages are drilled and sealed with lead plugs where necessary.

Fuel control

4 Fuel flows into the carburettor through a fine mesh filter. The fuel level in the float chamber is controlled by a needle valve and plastic float assembly and an anti-vibration ball is incorporated into the needle valve design. A plastic or hairpin clip, attached to the needle valve and to the float arm, prevents the needle valve from sticking in the seat as the fuel level drops. The float chamber is vented internally to the clean-air side of the air filter.

Idle, slow running and progression

5 Fuel, sourced from the main well, will pass into the primary idle well through a metered idle jet. Here it is mixed with a small amount of air from a calibrated air bleed. The emulsion formed is drawn through a channel to the throttle body where it is discharged from the idle orifice under the primary throttle plate. A tapered mixture control screw is used to vary the outlet and this ensures fine control of the idle mixture. A progression slot provides enrichment as it is uncovered by the opening throttle during initial acceleration *(see illustration)*.

6 Idle speed is set by an adjustable screw. This screw is tamper proofed at production level, in accordance with emission regulations.

Idle cut-off valve

7 An idle cut-off valve is used to prevent Dieseling or running-on when the engine is switched off. It utilises a 12-volt solenoid plunger to block the idle channel when the ignition is switched off.

Accelerator pump

8 The accelerator pump is controlled by a diaphragm and is mechanically operated by a lever and cam attached to the primary throttle linkage. The outlet valve consists of a ball incorporated into the pump outlet injector. The inlet valve consists of a ball valve located in a channel from the float chamber. Excess fuel is returned to the float chamber through an additional channel and calibrated bush.

Back-bleed solenoid (some models)

9 The amount of fuel required during acceleration when the engine is cold is considerably more than when it is hot. To avoid cold hesitation, the volume of fuel injected into the venturi by the accelerator pump for all operating conditions is calculated from the cold-running performance. The back-bleed system was introduced to control pump injection during hot operation, while maintaining cold operating performance.

10 The back-bleed solenoid *(see illustration)* is energised by a voltage feed supplied via a temperature-sensing switch. During cold engine operation, the switch contacts are open-circuit. The solenoid therefore has no effect on accelerator pump operation and full pump action is implemented.

11 Once the engine has reached operating temperature, the temperature switch contacts will open to introduce the voltage feed to the back-bleed solenoid. The solenoid is energised to open a channel between the pump and the float chamber. During hot operation, only a percentage of the pump capacity is injected into the venturi. The remainder is returned to the float chamber via the back-bleed channel.

Main circuit

12 The amount of fuel discharged into the air stream is controlled by a calibrated main jet. The main jet and air corrector are pushed into opposite ends of an emulsion tube and the assembly is placed into a vertical well which dips down into the fuel. Fuel is drawn from the float chamber, through the main jet, into the well, to be mixed with air drawn in through the air corrector and the holes in the emulsion tube. The resulting emulsified mixture is discharged from the main nozzle through an auxiliary venturi *(see illustration)*.

Power enrichment and economy circuit

13 Fuel flows from the float chamber into the power valve chamber through a fuel channel.

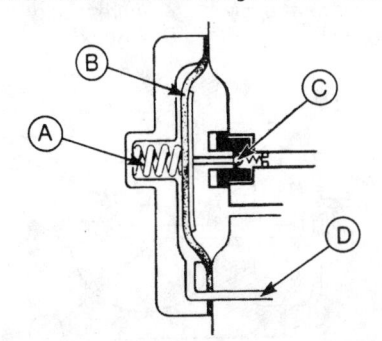

Power valve system during light-throttle operation
A Return spring (compressed)
B Diaphragm (pulled back)
C Power valve (closed)
D High manifold vacuum

H4•3

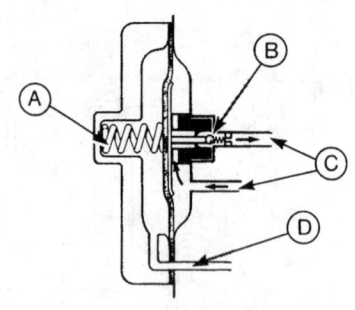

Chapter H4

Power valve system during full-throttle operation

A Return spring (extended)
B Power valve (open)
C Fuel flow
D Low manifold vacuum

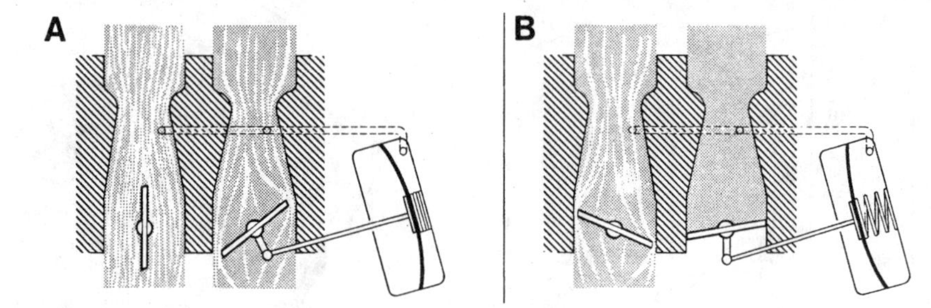

Secondary action

A High air speed in primary venturi, secondary throttle plate open
B Low air speed in primary venturi, secondary throttle plate closed

An air passage is taken from under the throttle plate to the cover of the power diaphragm chamber. At idle and during light-throttle operation, manifold vacuum draws the diaphragm back against spring pressure. The diaphragm pintle is withdrawn from the brass outlet valve and the spring-loaded ball seats to close off the outlet channel *(see illustration)*.

14 Under acceleration and wide-open throttle operation, the vacuum in the manifold is depleted. The diaphragm returns under spring pressure and the power diaphragm pintle pushes the ball to open the outlet valve. Fuel then flows through the valve and a calibrated jet to supplement the fuel in the primary main well. The fuel level rises in the well and the fuel mixture is enriched *(see illustration)*.

Secondary action

15 A port is located in both primary and secondary venturis. Airways run from these ports into a common passage leading to the diaphragm that operates the secondary throttle plate *(see illustration)*.

16 During normal operation at low speeds, the engine uses only the primary venturi. When air velocity through the primary venturi reaches a certain level, depression acts upon the port to operate the secondary diaphragm and the secondary throttle. Vacuum created in the secondary venturi will further control the rate of secondary opening.

17 The primary linkage is arranged to prevent the secondary plate from opening when air speed is high but the engine is cruising on a light throttle. Secondary action will not take place until the primary throttle is about two-thirds open.

18 Once the secondary throttle plate has opened, the action of the secondary main circuit is similar to that of the primary circuit.

19 A progression jet is used to prevent hesitation as the secondary throttle plate begins to open. This jet is similar in construction and action to the primary idle jet and is often referred to as the secondary idle jet. An emulsified mixture is discharged into the secondary venturi, via two progression drillings, at the initial opening of the secondary throttle plate.

20 At full-load and high engine speed, even more fuel is required. The velocity of air creates a depression sufficient to raise fuel from the float chamber into a channel. The fuel then passes through a calibrated bushing to the upper section of the secondary air intake. Here it is mixed with a small amount of air from a calibrated air bleed and the emulsified mixture is then discharged into the airstream from the full-load enrichment orifice.

Choke operation

21 The manual choke is operated by a dash-mounted cable. When the cable is pulled, it operates a lever that pulls the choke flap closed across the air intake. Fast idle is achieved with the aid of a curved cam attached to the choke operating lever. An adjustable screw, attached to the throttle lever and butting against the cam, is used to vary the fast idle speed.

22 Once the engine has fired, the choke flap must open slightly to weaken the mixture and avoid flooding during idle and light-throttle operation. This is achieved by using manifold vacuum to actuate a pull-down diaphragm. Linkage attached to the diaphragm will then pull upon the choke flap *(see illustrations)*.

Throttle kicker (dashpot)

23 The throttle kicker slows down the throttle plate closing action to allow the introduction of normal idle vacuum in a controlled manner and to reduce emissions *(see illustrations)*.

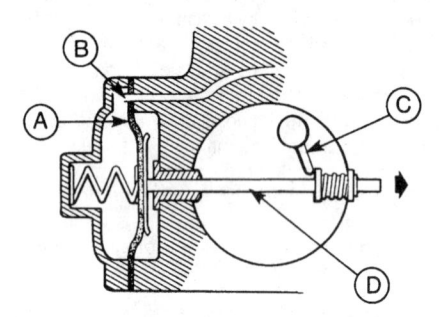

Vacuum pull-down system during starting or acceleration

A Diaphragm
B Vacuum supply (low)
C Choke linkage (unrestricted)
D Pushrod

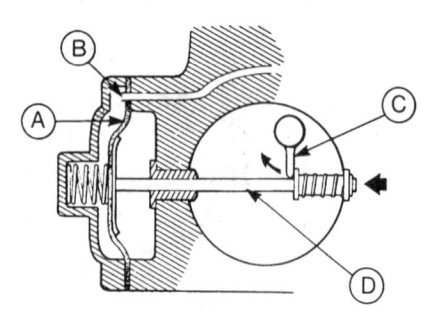

Vacuum pull-down system during light-throttle operation

A Diaphragm
B Vacuum supply (high)
C Choke linkage
D Pushrod

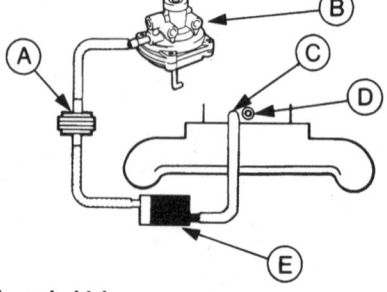

Throttle kicker system

A Vacuum sustain valve
B Throttle kicker
C Kicker port
D Mixture screw
E Fuel trap

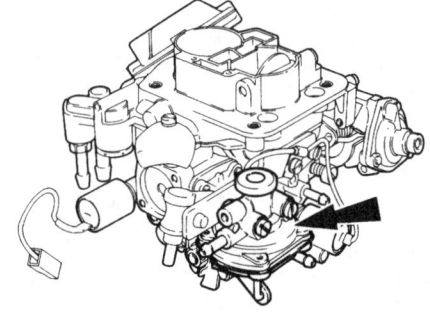

Throttle kicker assembly (arrowed)

Weber 28/30 DFTM carburettor

24 The kicker is connected to the throttle plate by a small-bore hose and is controlled by a vacuum source from the carburettor. Under normal driving conditions, the vacuum will operate the kicker through a fuel trap and sustain valve. There is no effect on throttle operation when the throttle is open.

25 During deceleration with a closed throttle, the vacuum at the kicker will hold the throttle plate partially open. As deceleration continues, the vacuum through the sustain valve will decay and the throttle plate returns fully to its stop. Because of the pulsing effect of vacuum, fuel can be drawn into the hose and will eventually reach and contaminate the diaphragm. The fuel trap is used to prevent this problem from occurring.

2 Identification

The Weber identification code is stamped on the carburettor base flange.

A metal tag giving the Ford identification code is attached to one of the upper body fixing screws.

3 General servicing

Introduction

1 Read this Chapter in conjunction with Part B, which describes some of the operations in more detail. It is assumed that the carburettor is removed for this service. However, many of the operations can be tackled with the carburettor in place. Where this is undertaken, first soak the fuel out of the float chamber using a clean tissue or soft cloth, after removing the upper body.

Dismantling and checking

2 Remove the carburettor from the engine (see Part B).
3 Make visual checks for damage and wear.
4 Remove the six screws and detach the carburettor upper body.
5 Use a straight-edge to check for distorted flanges on all facing surfaces.
6 Inspect the float chamber for corrosion and calcium build-up.
7 Tap out the float pin and remove the float, needle valve and clip, then remove the float chamber gasket and needle valve seat.
8 Check that the anti-vibration ball is free in the valve end.
9 Check the needle valve tip for wear and ridges. This is more likely with the brass needle valve tip than when a viton one is used. Use a viton-tipped replacement when possible.
10 The float should be checked for damage and ingress of petrol. Shaking the float will indicate the presence of fuel.
11 Renew the float pin if it shows signs of wear.
12 Unscrew the hexagon nut and inspect the fuel filter. Take care that this casting is not sheared if excess force is required to shift the filter retaining nut. The fuel connection and filter housing project from the cover on a narrow casting. Clean the filter housing of debris and dirt and renew the filter if necessary.
13 Remove the mixture screw and inspect the tip for damage or ridges.
14 Remove the four screws and detach the throttle kicker assembly from the body, complete with its mounting bracket. Twist and disconnect the link rod from the actuating lever. Remove a further two screws and nuts and detach the throttle kicker assembly from its mounting bracket. Remove a further four screws and remove the kicker cover, diaphragm and spring. Check the diaphragm for fatigue and damage.
15 Remove the four screws and remove the accelerator pump cover, diaphragm and spring. Check the diaphragm for fatigue and damage.
16 The pump injector is a push fit in the body. Carefully prise it from its location and test it by shaking. No noise from the outlet ball indicates that the valve is seized.
17 Unscrew the primary and secondary idle jet assemblies, main jets, air correctors and emulsion tubes. Note that the idle jet and the main jet assemblies can be removed from the carburettor body without removing the upper body *(see illustration)*.
18 Check that the channel from the float chamber into the emulsion tube well is clear.
19 The idle jets are pushed into a holder and may be separated, by pulling, for cleaning or renewal. Likewise, the main jets and air correctors are pushed into the opposite ends of the emulsion tubes and may also be separated, by pulling, for cleaning or renewal.
20 Note the jet sizes and locations for correct installation during assembly. The primary main and idle jet are located on the accelerator pump side of the carburettor, while the secondary main and idle jet are located on the choke side of the carburettor.
21 Check the jet calibration against that specified. It is possible that the jets may have been transposed (or the wrong sizes fitted) during the last overhaul.

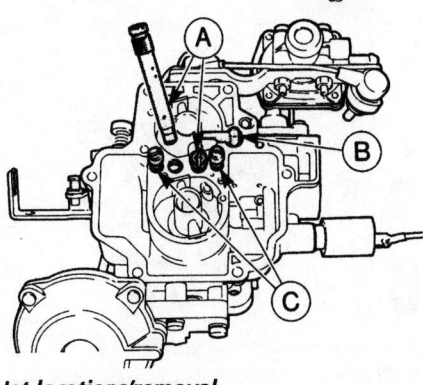

Jet locations/removal
A Emulsion tube/jet assemblies
B Accelerator pump injector
C Idle jet assemblies

22 Remove the primary and secondary auxiliary venturis where necessary. Weber provide an extractor tool for removing these items. Check that the primary and secondary auxiliary venturis are not loose in the main body, as loose venturis can cause uneven running. If a venturi is loose, knurl the mating flanges with a file to ensure a tight fit.
23 Remove the three screws and remove the power valve cover, spring and diaphragm from the body. Check the diaphragm for damage and fatigue.
24 The brass outlet valve is cast into the body and is not removable. The ball in the outlet valve should seal the outlet. Depress and release the ball with a small screwdriver and it should move smoothly in and out. Check that the channel into the emulsion tube well is clear.
25 Disconnect the secondary throttle operating rod, then pull the lower section of the rod downwards and twist it out of its socket *(see illustration)*.
26 Remove the four screws and remove the secondary throttle vacuum unit cover, spring and diaphragm from the housing. Check the diaphragm for fatigue and damage and renew as necessary *(see illustration)*.
27 Inspect the choke spindle and linkage for stickiness and wear.
28 Remove the three screws, disconnect the lower choke link rod and detach the choke housing.

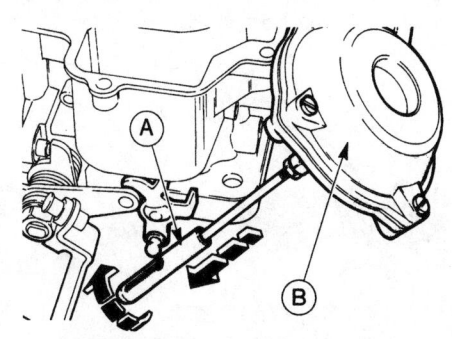

Secondary throttle vacuum unit diaphragm removal
A Operating rod   B Diaphragm cover

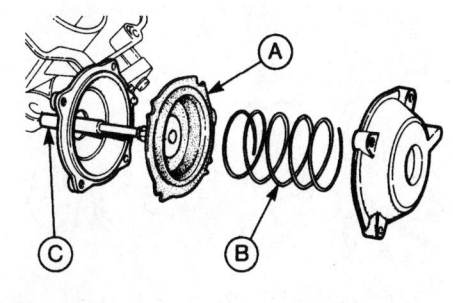

Secondary throttle vacuum unit assembly
A Diaphragm   C Operating rod
B Return spring

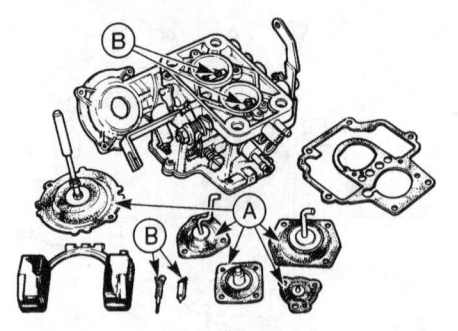

Chapter H4

Components for checking
A Check diaphragms for wear and damage
B Check for wear and damage

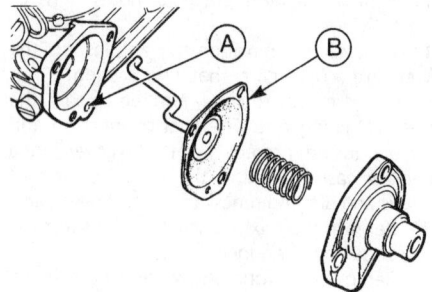

Choke pull-down assembly
A Vacuum passage
B Diaphragm

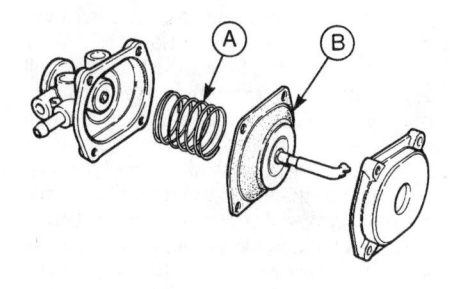

Throttle kicker assembly
A Return spring
B Diaphragm

29 Remove the three screws and detach the choke pull-down cover and spring from the housing. Pull the diaphragm rod from the plastic retaining collar, then twist and remove the diaphragm from the housing. Check the diaphragm for fatigue and damage, and renew as necessary.

Preparation for reassembly

30 Clean the jets and internal channels, the carburettor body assemblies and the float chamber. An air line may be used to clear the internal channels once the carburettor is fully dismantled. If an air line is used with the diaphragms in place and air is directed into the diaphragm channels and passages, diaphragm damage may result.
31 Spraying carburettor cleaner into all the channels and passages in the carburettor body will often clear them of gum and dirt.
32 During reassembly, a complete set of new gaskets should be fitted. Also, renew the needle valve and float pin and all diaphragms (see illustration).
33 Inspect and renew (where necessary) the mixture screw, main jets, idle jets, air corrector jets and accelerator pump injector. Renew worn linkages, springs and other parts where necessary.
34 Ensure that all jets are firmly locked into their original positions (but do not overtighten). A loose jet can cause a rich (or even lean) running condition.
35 Clean all mating surfaces and flanges of old gasket material and reassemble with new gaskets.
36 Ensure that housings are assembled with their air and fuel routes correctly aligned.

Reassembly

37 Refit the choke diaphragm, spring and cover assembly, then secure with three screws (see illustration). Push the end of diaphragm link rod through the operating lever and secure it with the plastic collar.
38 Renew the vacuum O-ring seal, then engage the choke link rod into the choke lever arm. Refit the choke housing to the carburettor upper body and secure with the three screws.
39 Check that the secondary throttle plate is fully closed. The adjustment screw should not normally be used to alter the throttle plate position. However, if necessary, it can be adjusted so that the plate is open just enough to prevent it from seizing in the throttle body.
40 Refit the secondary throttle diaphragm, spring and cover assembly, then secure with the four screws. Reconnect the secondary throttle operating rod.
41 Refit the power diaphragm, spring and cover assembly, then secure with the three screws.
42 Ensure that the air correctors and main jets are pushed fully into the emulsion tubes, then refit the assemblies into their original positions (do not transpose the jets).
43 Ensure that the idle jets are pushed fully into their holders and refit into their original positions (do not transpose the jets).
44 Refit the pump injector, after renewing the small seal on the injector body.

45 Refit the pump spring, diaphragm and cover assembly, then secure with the four screws.
46 Refit the throttle kicker spring, diaphragm and cover assembly, ensuring that the diaphragm link rod faces inwards (see illustration) and secure with the four screws. Attach the assembly to the mounting bracket, reconnect the link rod to the actuating lever and refit the assembly onto the main body.
47 Refit the idle mixture screw. Carefully turn the screw in until it just seats, then unscrew it three full turns. This will provide a basic setting to allow the engine to be started.
48 Clean or renew the fuel filter and refit the hexagon nut (see illustration).
49 Renew the needle valve assembly. Screw the valve seat into the upper body, using a new sealing washer, and ensure that it is firmly locked into position. Insert the needle valve into the valve body with the ball facing outwards, then refit the float and pivot pin (see illustration). Ensure that the clip is correctly connected to the float and to the needle valve, then fit the new float chamber gasket to the upper body.
50 Adjust the float level. Refer to Section 4 for details on adjustment.
51 Refit the upper body to the main body and secure with the six screws.
52 Refit the idle cut-off valve, using a new sealing washer.
53 Ensure that the choke flap and linkage moves smoothly and progressively.
54 Refit the carburettor to the engine.
55 Always adjust the carburettor idle speed and mixture after any work has been carried out on the carburettor, preferably with the aid of a CO meter.
56 Adjust the choke and throttle kicker. Refer to Section 4 for details on adjustment.

4 Service adjustments

Adjustment preconditions

1 Refer to Part B for general advice on preconditions to correct adjustment of this carburettor.

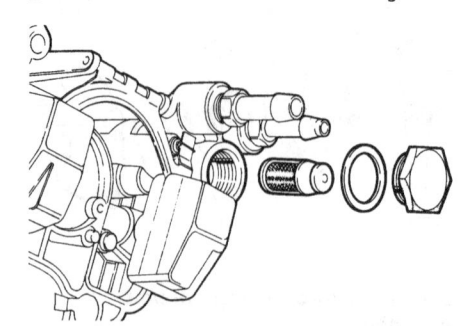

Fuel inlet filter components

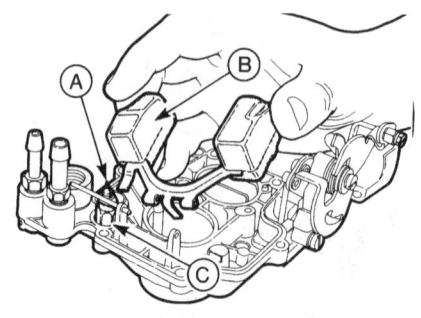

Needle valve and float assembly
A Needle valve   B Float   C Valve seat

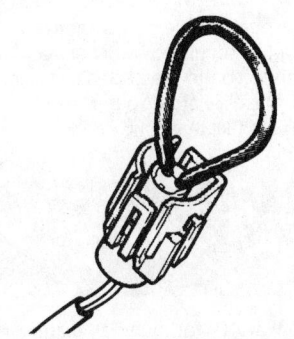

Weber 28/30 DFTM carburettor

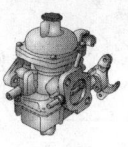

Fan temperature sensor terminals bridged with wire

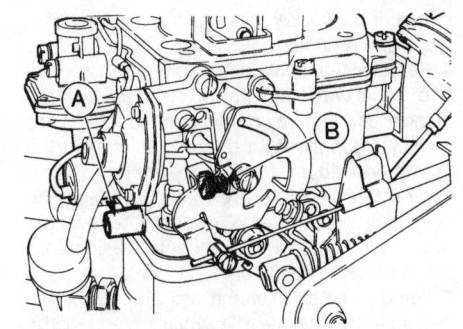

Idle adjustment screw location
A Idle mixture (CO) screw
B Idle speed screw

Fast idle

17 Pull the choke cable to fully operate the choke and at the same time, hold the choke flap as far open as possible *(see illustration)*.
18 Start the engine, record the fast idle speed and compare with the specified value.
19 Adjust as necessary by turning the fast idle screw in the appropriate direction.

Choke pull-down

20 Pull the choke cable to fully close the choke flap.
21 Use a finger to push the diaphragm operating rod up to its stop. At the same time, use the shank of a twist drill to measure the gap between the lower section of the choke flap and the air intake. Refer to Specifications for the required drill size.
22 Remove the tamperproof plug in the diaphragm cover and adjust as necessary by turning the diaphragm adjusting screw in the appropriate direction. Renew the plug after adjustment is completed.
23 Refit the air filter, ensuring that the hoses remain connected.

Throttle kicker

24 Remove the air filter assembly and place it clear of the carburettor with the vent and vacuum hoses still connected.
25 Disconnect the vacuum hose from the throttle kicker.
26 Push the linkage upward to operate the kicker and use a finger to seal the inlet connection. The diaphragm should remain in its fully-operated position until the finger is removed.
27 Plug the vacuum hose from the manifold.
28 Warm the engine to normal running temperature and adjust the idle speed and mixture.
29 Manually operate the kicker and record the engine speed. Refer to Specifications for the correct speed.
30 Remove the tamperproof plug in the diaphragm cover and adjust as necessary by turning the diaphragm adjusting screw in the appropriate direction. Renew the plug after adjustment is completed.
31 Refit the air filter, ensuring that the hoses remain connected.

2 The engine cooling fan should run continuously during the idle adjustments. Run the engine until the fan operates, then disconnect the connector plug to the fan temperature sensor and temporarily bridge the plug terminals with a piece of wire *(see illustration)*.

Idle speed and mixture (CO)

3 Run the engine at 3000 rpm for 30 seconds to clear the manifold of fuel vapours, then allow the engine to idle.
4 Remove the air filter assembly and place it clear of the carburettor with the vacuum hoses still connected.
5 Use the idle speed screw to set the specified idle speed *(see illustration)*.
6 Check the CO level and compare with the specified value. If incorrect, remove the tamperproof plug and adjust to the correct level. Turning the screw clockwise (inwards) will reduce the CO level. Turning the screw anti-clockwise (outwards) will increase the CO level.
7 Repeat paragraphs 5 and 6 until both adjustments are correct.
8 Clear the manifold every 30 seconds during the setting operation by running the engine at 3000 rpm for 30 seconds.
9 Increase the speed to 2000 rpm and note the CO reading. The cruise reading should be less than half the idle CO reading.

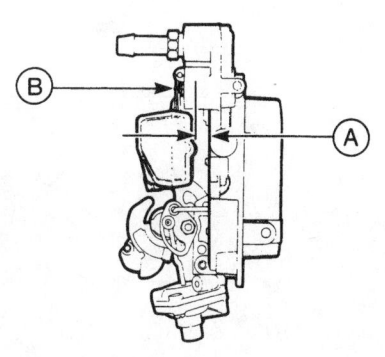

10 Fit a new tamperproof plug to the mixture adjusting screw.
11 Remove the temporary bridge wire and reconnect the fan temperature sensor plug.
12 Refit the air filter, ensuring that the vacuum hoses remain connected.

Float level

13 Hold the carburettor upper body in a vertical position with the float tag gently touching the ball of the fully-closed needle valve.
14 Measure the distance between the upper body (gasket in place) and the top of the float *(see illustration)*.
15 Adjust as necessary by bending the float tag.

Manual choke

16 Warm the engine to normal running temperature and adjust the idle speed and mixture before attempting choke fast idle or vacuum pull-down adjustment. The engine cooling fan should run continuously during the fast idle adjustment. Run the engine until the fan operates, then disconnect the connector plug to the fan temperature sensor and temporarily bridge the plug terminals with a piece of wire. Remove the air filter assembly and place it clear of the carburettor with the vent and vacuum hoses still connected.

Float level adjustment
A Float level dimension (see Specifications)
B Adjusting tag

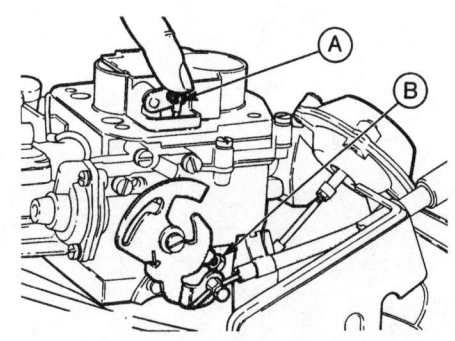

Manual choke fast idle adjustment
A Choke flap held open
B Fast idle adjustment screw

5 Component testing

Back-bleed solenoid (where fitted)

Operation

1 The back-bleed solenoid is energised by a voltage feed supplied via a temperature-sensing switch. During cold-engine operation, the switch contacts are open-circuit. Once the engine has reached

H4•7

Chapter H4

operating temperature, the temperature switch contacts will open to introduce the voltage feed to the back-bleed solenoid.

Testing

2 Test for a voltage (engine cold) at the back-bleed solenoid electrical connector. If a voltage is present with the engine cold, the temperature-sensing switch is faulty and is remaining closed at all times.

3 Test for voltage (engine hot) at the back-bleed solenoid electrical connector. If voltage is not present with the engine hot, test for a supply voltage to the temperature-sensing switch. If the supply is satisfactory, the switch is faulty and is remaining open at all times.

4 Remove the back-bleed solenoid assembly and clean with carburettor cleaner. Test the plunger operation by connecting the solenoid to a voltage supply. With the engine hot and the ignition on, touch the solenoid body to earth several times and ensure that the plunger tip advances and retracts cleanly. Renew the solenoid if the action is faulty or if cleaning does not improve its operation.

5 Remove the air filter and with the engine still hot, operate the throttle while observing the accelerator pump injector. Allow the engine to cool then repeat this test. Alternatively, cold operation can be simulated by disconnecting the electrical connection to the back-bleed solenoid. When cold, the accelerator pump should inject noticeably more fuel than when hot.

6 Fault diagnosis

Refer to Part D for general diagnosis of carburettor faults.

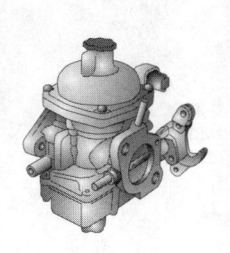

Part H Chapter 5
Weber 32/36 DGAV carburettor

H5

Contents

Fault diagnosis 5
General servicing 3
Identification 2
Principles of operation 1
Service adjustments 4

Specifications

Manufacturer	Ford	Ford	Ford
Model	Cortina 1600 (2V)	Cortina 2000	Cortina 2000 auto
Year	1981 to 1983	1981 to 1983	1981 to 1983
Engine code	LER (OHC)	NER (OHC)	NER (OHC)
Capacity (cm³)/no. of cyls	1593/4	1993/4	1993/4
Oil temperature (°C)	80	80	80
Transmission	Manual/Automatic	Manual	Automatic
Carb. ident. (Ford)	77HF 9510 GC	77HF 9510 AD	77HF 9510 BD
Carb. ident. (Weber/Solex)	32/36 DGAV 1D2	32/36 DGAV 3D3	32/36 DGAV 4D3
Idle speed (rpm)	800 ± 25	800 ± 25	800 ± 25
Fast idle speed (rpm)	2000 ± 100	2000 ± 100	2000 ± 100
CO @ idle (% vol.)	1.5 ± 0.2	1.5 ± 0.2	1.5 ± 0.2
Stage (venturi)	**1**　　**2**	**1**　　**2**	**1**　　**2**
Venturi diameter	26　　27	26　　27	26　　27
Idle jet	45　　45	45　　45	45　　45
Main jet	137　　125	135　　130	132　　140
Air correction jet	170　　120	170　　125	175　　125
Emulsion tube	F50　　F50	F66　　F66	F66　　F66
Accel. pump jet	45　　45	55　　40	55　　40
Float level 1 (mm)	41.0 ± 0.5 (brass)	41.0 ± 0.5 (brass)	41.0 ± 0.5 (brass)
Float level 2 (mm)	35.3 ± 0.5 (plastic)	35.3 ± 0.5 (plastic)	35.3 ± 0.5 (plastic)
Needle valve size (mm)	2.0	2.0	2.0
Choke gauging (mm)	5.5 ± 0.25	6.5 ± 0.25	6.5 ± 0.25
Choke pull-down (mm)	2.0 ± 0.25	1.5 ± 0.25	1.5 ± 0.25
Bi-metal housing mark	on index	on index	on index

Manufacturer	Ford	Ford	Ford
Model	Sierra 2000	Sierra 2000 auto	Capri 1600S/GT
Year	1982 to 1985	1982 to 1985	1981
Engine code	NET (OHC)	NET (OHC)	LEN (OHC)
Capacity (cm³)/no. of cyls	1993/4	1993/4	1593/4
Oil temperature (°C)	80	80	80
Transmission	Manual	Automatic	Manual/Automatic
Carb. ident. (Ford)	83HF 9510 AA	83HF 9510 BA	77HF 9510 GC
Carb. ident. (Weber/Solex)	32/36 DGAV 3G	32/36 DGAV 4G	32/36 DGAV 1D2
Idle speed (rpm)	800 ± 25	800 ± 25	800 ± 25
Fast idle speed (rpm)	2900 ± 100	2900 ± 100	2000 ± 100
CO @ idle (% vol.)	1.5 ± 0.2	1.5 ± 0.2	1.5 ± 0.2

H5•1

Chapter H5

Manufacturer	Ford (continued)	Ford (continued)	Ford (continued)
Model	Sierra 2000	Sierra 2000 auto	Capri 1600S/GT
Year	1982 to 1985	1982 to 1985	1981
Stage (venturi)	1 2	1 2	1 2
Venturi diameter	26 27	26 27	26 27
Idle jet	45 45	45 45	45 45
Main jet	130 130	130 132	137 125
Air correction jet	165 120	170 120	170 120
Emulsion tube	F66 F66	F50 F66	F50 F50
Accel. pump jet	55 40	50 40	45 45
Float level 1 (mm)	41.0 ± 0.5 (brass)	41.0 ± 0.5 (brass)	41.0 ± 0.5 (brass)
Float level 2 (mm)	35.3 ± 0.5 (plastic)	35.3 ± 0.5 (plastic)	35.3 ± 0.5 (plastic)
Needle valve size (mm)	2.0	2.0	2.0
Choke gauging (mm)	6.5 ± 0.25	6.5 ± 0.25	6.0 ± 0.25
Choke pull-down (mm)	1.5 ± 0.25	1.5 ± 0.25	2.3 ± 0.25
Bi-metal housing mark	on index	on index	on index

Manufacturer	Ford	Ford	Ford
Model	Capri 2000	Capri 2000 auto	Granada 2000
Year	1979 to 1988	1979 to 1988	1978 to 1982
Engine code	NEN (OHC)	NEN (OHC)	NEH (OHC)
Capacity (cm³)/no. of cyls	1993/4	1993/4	1993/4
Oil temperature (°C)	80	80	80
Transmission	Manual	Automatic	Manual
Carb. ident. (Ford)	77HF 9510 AD	77HF 9510 BD	77HF 9510 AD
Carb. ident. (Weber/Solex)	32/36 DGAV 3D3	32/36 DGAV 4D3	32/36 DGAV 3D3
Idle speed (rpm)	800 ± 25	800 ± 25	800 ± 25
Fast idle speed (rpm)	2000 ± 100	2000 ± 100	3000 ± 100
CO @ idle (% vol.)	1.5 ± 0.2	1.5 ± 0.2	1.5 ± 0.25
Stage (venturi)	1 2	1 2	1 2
Venturi diameter	26 27	26 27	26 27
Idle jet	45 45	45 45	45 45
Main jet	135 130	132 140	135 130
Air correction jet	170 125	175 125	170 125
Emulsion tube	F66 F66	F66 F66	F66 F66
Accel. pump jet	55 40	55 40	55 45
Float level 1 (mm)	41.0 ± 0.25	41.0 ± 0.25	41.0 ± 0.5 (brass)
Float level 2 (mm)	-	-	35.3 ± 0.5 (plastic)
Needle valve size (mm)	2.0	2.0	2.0
Choke gauging (mm)	6.5 ± 0.25	6.5 ± 0.25	6.5 ± 0.25
Choke pull-down (mm)	1.5 ± 0.25	1.5 ± 0.25	1.5 ± 0.25
Bi-metal housing mark	on index	on index	on index

Manufacturer	Ford	Ford	Ford
Model	Granada 2000 auto	Granada 2000	Granada 2000 auto
Year	1978 to 1982	1982 to 1985	1982 to 1985
Engine code	NEH (OHC)	NEP (OHC)	NEP (OHC)
Capacity (cm³)/no. of cyls	1993/4	1993/4	1993/4
Oil temperature (°C)	80	80	80
Transmission	Automatic	Manual	Automatic
Carb. ident. (Ford)	77HF 9510 BD	83HF 9510 CA	-
Carb. ident. (Weber/Solex)	32/36 DGAV 4D3	32/36 DGAV 10E	32/36 DGAV 11E
Idle speed (rpm)	800 ± 25	800 ± 50	800 ± 50
Fast idle speed (rpm)	3000 ± 100	2900 ± 100	2900 ± 100
CO @ idle (% vol.)	1.5 ± 0.25	1.5 ± 0.2	1.5 ± 0.25
Stage (venturi)	1 2	1 2	1 2
Venturi diameter	26 27	26 27	26 27
Idle jet	45 45	45 45	45 45
Main jet	132 140	130 130	130 132
Air correction jet	175 125	165 120	170 120
Emulsion tube	F66 F66	F66 F66	F50 F66
Accel. pump jet	55 40	55 40	55 45
Float level 1 (mm)	41.0 ± 0.5 (brass)	41.0 ± 0.5	41.0 ± 0.5
Float level 2 (mm)	35.3 ± 0.5 (plastic)	-	-
Needle valve size (mm)	2.0	2.0	2.0
Choke gauging (mm)	6.5 ± 0.25	6.5 ± 0.25	6.5 ± 0.25
Choke pull-down (mm)	1.5 ± 0.25	1.5 ± 0.25	1.5 ± 0.25
Bi-metal housing mark	on index	on index	on index

Weber 32/36 DGAV carburettor

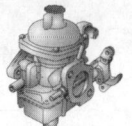

1 Principles of operation

Introduction

1 The following technical description of the Weber DGAV carburettor should be read in conjunction with the more detailed description of carburettor principles in Part A.

Construction

2 The Weber 32/36 DGAV carburettor is a downdraught progressive twin venturi instrument *(see illustration)*. The venturis are arranged so that the secondary throttle valve will not begin to open until the primary throttle valve is two-thirds open. The choke control is semi-automatic in operation and uses a bi-metal coil heated by the engine coolant. The throttle shafts are made of steel and the throttle valves of brass. All emulsion tubes and jets are manufactured from brass, with the exception of the accelerator pump injector which is die-cast. Internal fuel channels and air passages are drilled and sealed with lead plugs where necessary.

Fuel control

3 Fuel flows into the carburettor through a fine mesh filter. The fuel level in the float chamber is controlled by a needle valve and plastic float assembly (early models used a brass float) and

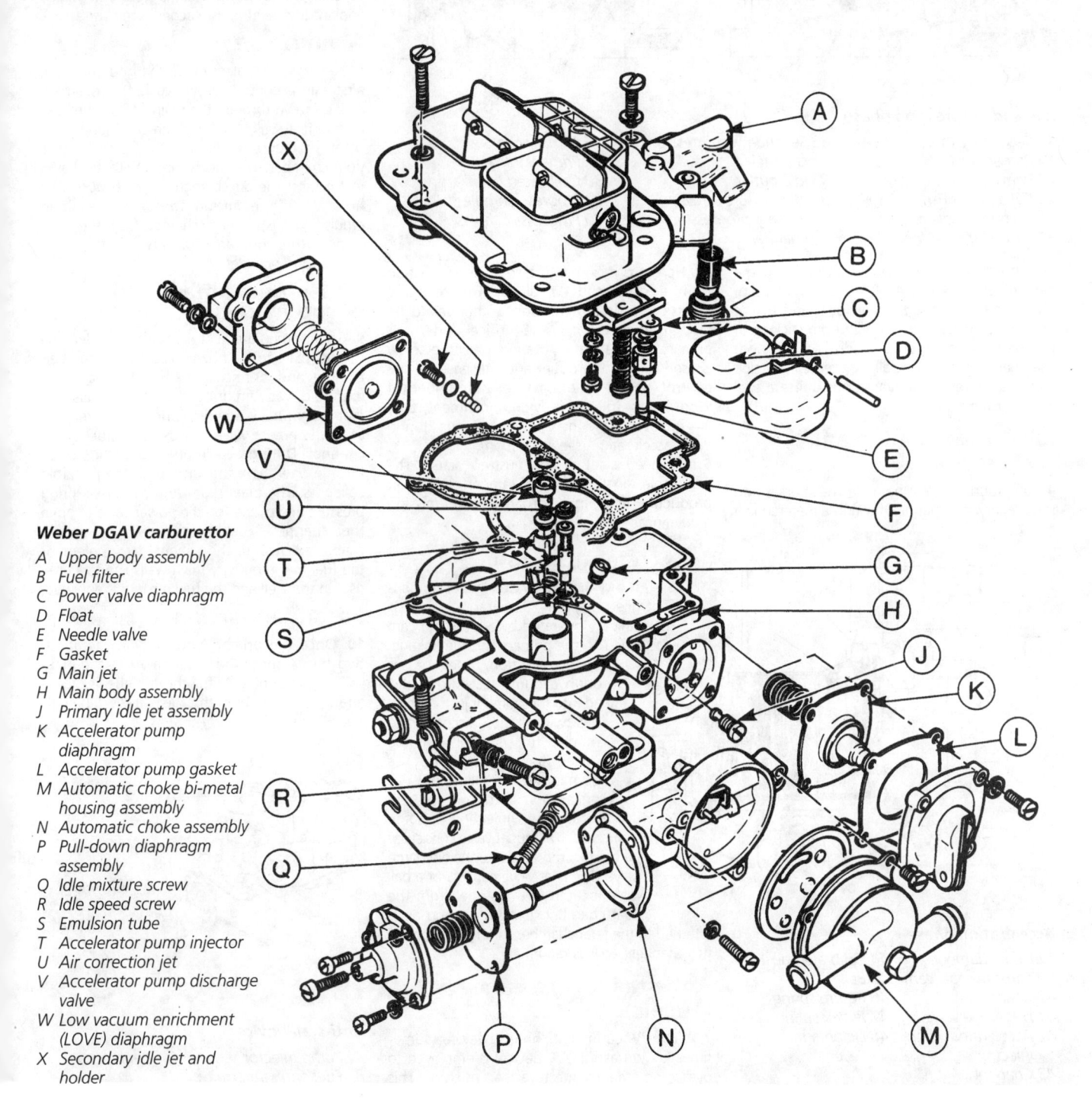

Weber DGAV carburettor
- A Upper body assembly
- B Fuel filter
- C Power valve diaphragm
- D Float
- E Needle valve
- F Gasket
- G Main jet
- H Main body assembly
- J Primary idle jet assembly
- K Accelerator pump diaphragm
- L Accelerator pump gasket
- M Automatic choke bi-metal housing assembly
- N Automatic choke assembly
- P Pull-down diaphragm assembly
- Q Idle mixture screw
- R Idle speed screw
- S Emulsion tube
- T Accelerator pump injector
- U Air correction jet
- V Accelerator pump discharge valve
- W Low vacuum enrichment (LOVE) diaphragm
- X Secondary idle jet and holder

Chapter H5

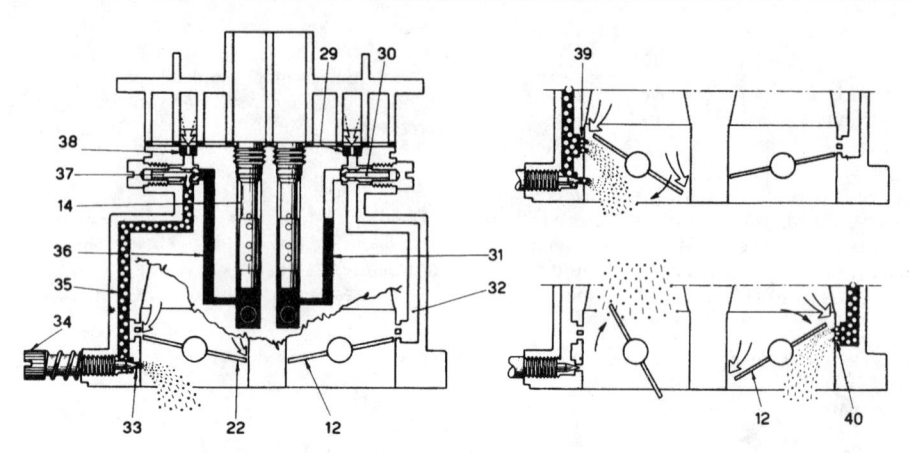

Idle and progression phase

12 Secondary throttle plate
14 Primary well
22 Primary throttle plate
29 Calibrated bush
30 Secondary idle jet
31 Secondary channel
32 Secondary progression channel
33 Idle outlet
34 Idle mixture screw
35 Primary progression channel
36 Primary channel
37 Primary idle jet
38 Calibrated bush
39 Progression holes
40 Progression holes

an anti-vibration ball is incorporated into the needle valve design. A plastic or hairpin clip, attached to the needle valve seat and to the float arm, prevents the needle from sticking in the seat as the fuel level drops. The float chamber is vented internally to the clean-air side of the air filter. Some variations utilise a fuel return system.

Idle, slow running and progression

4 Fuel, sourced from the main well, passes into the primary idle channel through a metered idle jet. Here it is mixed with a small amount of air from a calibrated air bleed. The resulting emulsion is drawn through a channel to be discharged from the idle orifice under the primary throttle plate. A tapered mixture screw is used to vary the outlet and this ensures fine control of the idle mixture. A number of progression drillings provide enrichment, they are uncovered by the opening throttle during initial acceleration (see illustration).

5 Idle speed is set by an adjustable screw. The adjustable mixture screw is tamper-proofed at production level, in accordance with emission regulations.

Accelerator pump

6 The Weber DGAV accelerator pump is controlled by a diaphragm and is mechanically operated by a lever and cam attached to the primary throttle linkage. During acceleration, fuel passes through a pump discharge valve and into the pump injector which has twin nozzles. According to model, the injector may be drilled for injection into the primary venturi (all models) or drilled for both primary and secondary injection (some models). The outlet valve consists of a ball incorporated into the discharge valve. The inlet valve consists of a ball valve located in a channel from the float chamber. Excess fuel and air is returned to the float chamber through a separate fuel channel (see illustration).

Anti-stall device (some models)

7 A Low Vacuum Enrichment device (sometimes known as a LOVE device) is employed to overcome stalling due to a lean mixture. This device is basically a vacuum-controlled accelerator pump. It is diaphragm-operated and functions in a conventional manner, discharging through the same pump injector as the mechanical pump. During idle or low-speed running, the manifold vacuum will be high. As a stall situation develops, the vacuum will deplete and the pump injector is actuated. Early devices operated at all times but in later variations, the device is controlled by a thermo-switch in the coolant system. This type will therefore only function during warm-up until a pre-determined coolant temperature is reached (see illustration).

Main circuit

8 The amount of fuel discharged into the airstream is controlled by a calibrated main jet. Fuel is drawn through the main jet into the base of a vertical well (into which an emulsion tube is fitted), which dips down into the fuel in the float chamber. The fuel is mixed with air drawn in through the air corrector and through the holes in the emulsion tube. The resulting emulsified mixture is discharged from the main orifice through an auxiliary venturi (see illustration opposite).

Power enrichment and economy circuit

9 An air passage is taken from under the throttle plate to the power diaphragm chamber. At idle and during light-throttle operation, manifold vacuum in the passage pulls the diaphragm back against spring pressure. This seats the power valve to close off a fuel outlet channel. During acceleration and wide-open throttle operation, the vacuum in the manifold collapses. The diaphragm returns under spring pressure and pushes on the power valve to open the channel. Fuel then flows through a calibrated bush in the channel to supplement the fuel in the primary main well. The fuel level rises in the well and the fuel mixture is enriched.

Secondary action

10 Once the primary throttle valve is about two-thirds open, the secondary throttle plate will begin to open. At full-throttle, the linkage is arranged so that both throttle plates will be fully open.

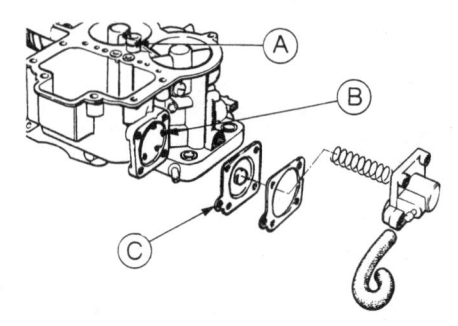

Acceleration phase

17 Float chamber
39 Throttle shaft cam
40 Channel
41 Discharge valve
42 Accelerator pump injector
43 Channel
44 Calibrated bush
45 Ball
46 Return spring
47 Buffer spring
48 Diaphragm
49 Lever

Anti-stall device

A Pump injector
B Fuel entry into unit
C Diaphragm

H5•4

Weber 32/36 DGAV carburettor

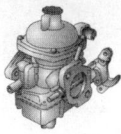

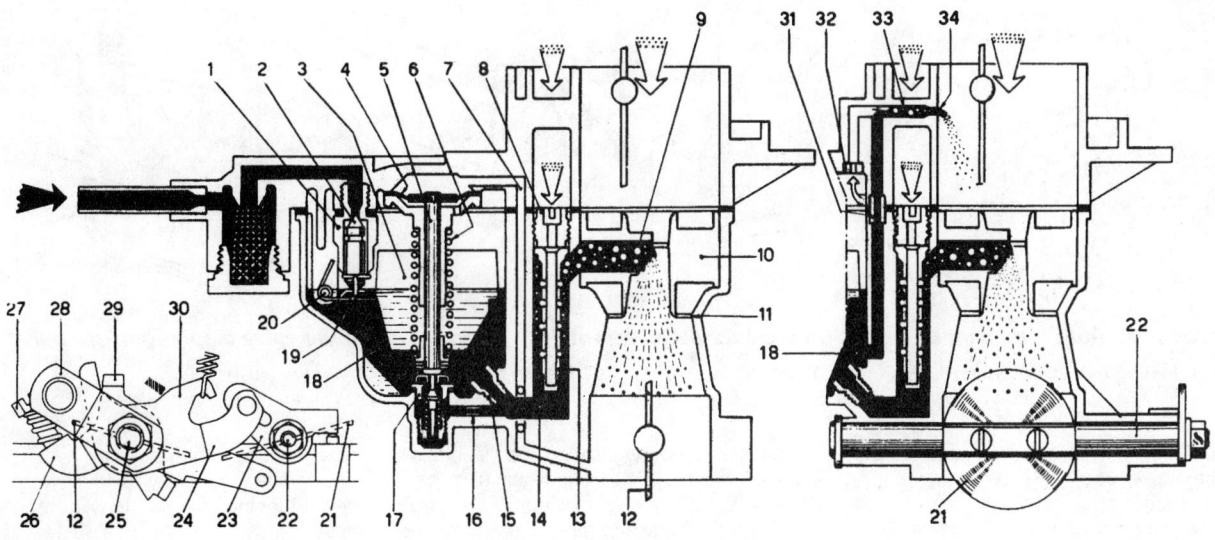

Main and power circuits

1 Needle seat	8 Air corrector	15 Main jet
2 Needle valve	9 Nozzle	16 Calibrated bush
3 Float	10 Auxiliary venturi	17 Power valve
4 Diaphragm	11 Venturi	18 Float chamber
5 Rod	12 Throttle valve	19 Spring hook
6 Spring	13 Emulsion tube	20 Float pin
7 Air passage	14 Well	21 Secondary throttle

22 Shaft	28 Lever
23 Lever	29 Lever
24 Lever	30 Lever
25 Shaft	31 Calibrated bush
26 Lever	32 Calibrated bush
27 Fast idle adjusting screw	33 Channel
	34 Full-load enrichment

11 A progression jet is used to prevent hesitation as the secondary throttle plate begins to open. This jet is similar in construction and action to the primary idle jet and is often referred to as the secondary idle jet. An emulsified mixture is discharged into the secondary venturi via two progression drillings, at the initial opening of the secondary throttle plate.
12 Once the secondary throttle plate has opened, the action of the secondary main circuit is similar to the primary.
13 At full-load and high engine speed, even more fuel is required. The velocity of air creates a depression sufficient to raise fuel from the float chamber into a channel. The fuel passes through a calibrated bushing to the upper section of the secondary air intake. It is then discharged into the airstream from the full-load enrichment nozzle.

Cold start system

14 The Weber DGAV carburettor uses a semi-automatic choke starting system. A bi-metal spring is used to control two strangler choke flaps on a common spindle to shut off the air intakes. Heating of the coil spring is by coolant from the engine cooling system. The system is primed by depressing the accelerator pedal once or twice.
15 Once the engine has fired, the choke flap must open slightly to weaken the mixture and avoid flooding during idle and light-throttle operation. This is achieved by using manifold vacuum to actuate a diaphragm. Linkage attached to the diaphragm will then pull upon the flaps.
16 Fast idle is achieved with the aid of a stepped cam attached to the choke spindle. An adjustable screw, connected to the throttle mechanism and butting against the cam, can be used to vary the fast idle speed. As the bi-metal coil is heated and the flap opens, then the screw will rest on successively less-stepped parts of the cam. Idle speed is thus progressively reduced until ultimately the cam is released and the idle speed returns to normal.

2 Identification

1 The Weber identification code is stamped on the carburettor base flange.
2 A metal tag giving the Ford identification code is attached to one of the float chamber fixing screws.
3 It should be noted that over the years, the specification for the Weber DGAV carburettor has undergone considerable changes. Since 1970, there have been over thirty different versions fitted to 1.6 and 2.0 litre Ford engines in the UK alone. For this reason, it is essential that the carburettor is properly identified before attempting a service or when obtaining spare parts.
4 At the start of this Chapter, we have compiled specifications for carburettors fitted since 1980. For earlier models, we suggest that you contact your local Weber carburettor dealer.

3 General servicing

Introduction

1 Read this Chapter in conjunction with Part B, which describes some of the operations in more detail. It is assumed that the carburettor is removed for this service. However, many of the operations can be tackled with the carburettor in place. Where this is undertaken, first soak the fuel out of the float chamber using a clean tissue or soft cloth, after removing the upper body assembly.

Dismantling and checking

2 Remove the carburettor from the engine (see Part B).
3 Make visual checks for damage and wear.
4 Use a small screwdriver to prise off the securing circlip, then detach the upper choke operating link from the choke spindle arm (see illustration).

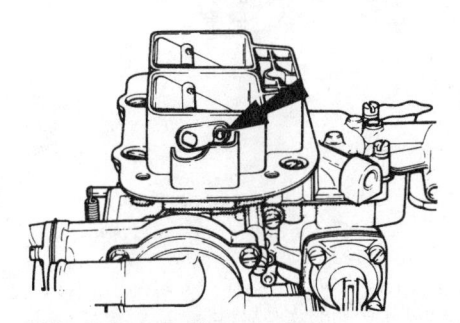

Choke link circlip (arrowed)

H5•5

Chapter H5

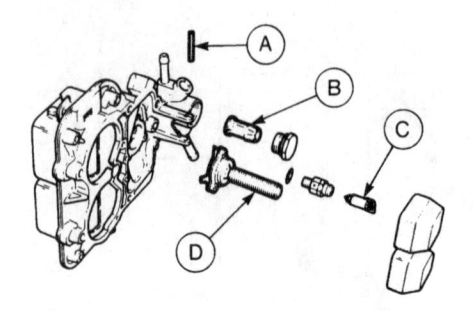

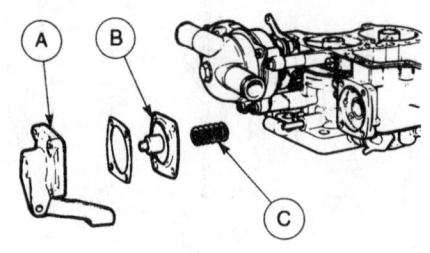

Upper body and float components
A Float retaining pin   C Needle valve
B Filter   D Power valve

Accelerator pump assembly
A Cover   C Return spring
B Diaphragm

Power valve diaphragm assembly
A Power valve
B Diaphragm bleed hole

5 Remove the six screws and detach the carburettor upper body.
6 Use a straight-edge to check for distorted flanges on all facing surfaces.
7 Inspect the float chamber for corrosion and calcium build-up.
8 Remove the float chamber gasket. Tap out the float pin and remove the float, needle valve, clip and needle valve seat (see illustration).
9 Check that the anti-vibration ball is free in the valve end.
10 Check the needle valve tip for wear and ridges. This is more likely with the brass needle valve tip than when a viton one is used. Use a viton-tipped replacement where possible.
11 The float should be checked for damage and for ingress of petrol. Shaking the float will indicate the presence of fuel.
12 Renew the float pin if it shows signs of wear.
13 Remove the hexagon bolt and inspect the fuel filter. Clean the chamber of debris and dirt.
14 Remove the mixture screw and inspect the tip for damage or ridges.
15 Remove the four screws and remove the accelerator pump housing, diaphragm and spring. Check the diaphragm for fatigue and damage (see illustration).
16 Remove the four screws and remove the anti-stall device housing, spring and diaphragm. Check the diaphragm for fatigue and damage.
17 Unscrew the accelerator pump discharge valve from the body and remove the valve and the pump injector. Shake the discharge valve. No noise from the outlet ball would indicate that the valve is seized. Check that the lead pellet that seals the valve is present. If it is loose or missing, the pump action will be impaired.
18 Remove the two idle jet assemblies from the carburettor body. The idle jets are pushed into a holder and may be separated, by pulling, for cleaning or renewal. Note that the idle jet assemblies can be removed from the carburettor body without removing the upper body.
19 Unscrew the primary and secondary main jets, air correctors and emulsion tubes.
20 Check that the channel from the float chamber into the emulsion tube well is clear.
21 Note the jet sizes and locations for correct installation during assembly.
22 Check the jet calibration against that specified. It is possible that the jets may have been transposed (or the wrong sizes fitted) during the last overhaul.
23 Remove the primary and secondary auxiliary venturis where necessary. A Weber extractor tool is available for this purpose. Check that the primary and secondary auxiliary venturis are not loose in the main body as this is a source of uneven running. If a venturi is loose, knurl the mating flanges with a file to ensure a tight fit.
24 Remove the three screws and detach the power valve diaphragm assembly from the upper body. Check the diaphragm for damage and fatigue.
25 Unscrew and remove the power valve from the float chamber floor (see illustration). Check that the pin moves freely in the valve body. Renew the valve if there is any doubt about its serviceability.
26 Inspect the choke spindle, mechanism and levers for stickiness and wear (see illustration).
27 Remove the three screws, twist and disconnect the choke lower link rod and detach the choke housing.
28 Remove the three screws and detach choke pull-down housing, spring and diaphragm from the cover. Check the diaphragm for fatigue and damage.

Preparation for reassembly

29 Clean the jets and internal channels, the carburettor body assemblies and the float chamber. An air line may be used to clear the internal channels once the carburettor is fully dismantled. If an air line is used with the diaphragms in place and air is directed into the diaphragm passages, diaphragm damage may result.
30 Spraying carburettor cleaner into all the channels and passages in the carburettor body will often clear them of gum and dirt.
31 During reassembly, a complete set of new gaskets should be fitted. Also renew the needle valve and float pin, and all diaphragms.
32 Inspect and renew (where necessary) the mixture screw, main jets, idle jets, air corrector jets and accelerator pump injector. Renew worn linkages, springs and other parts where necessary.
33 Ensure that all jets are firmly locked into their original positions (but do not overtighten). A loose jet can cause a rich (or even lean) running condition.
34 Clean all mating surfaces and flanges of old gasket material, and reassemble with a new gasket.
35 Ensure that housings are assembled with their air and fuel routes correctly aligned.

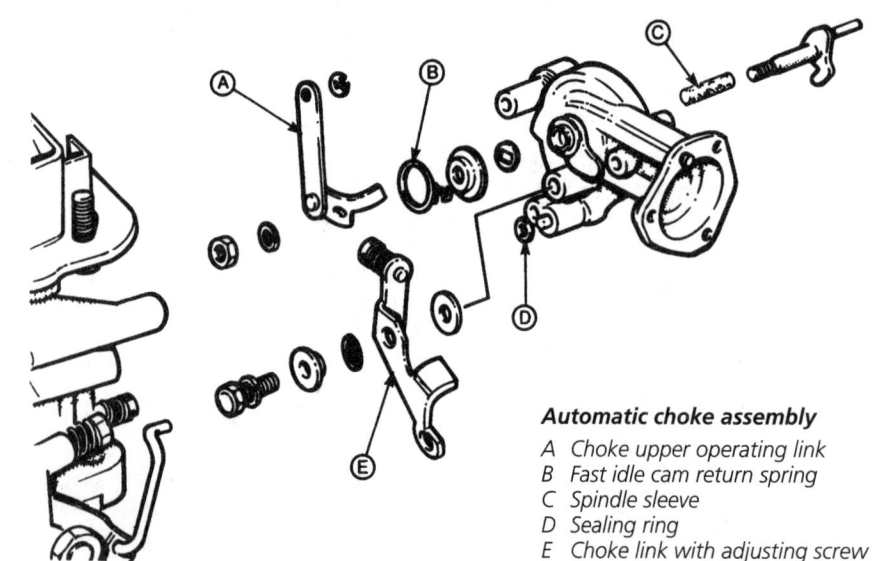

Automatic choke assembly
A Choke upper operating link
B Fast idle cam return spring
C Spindle sleeve
D Sealing ring
E Choke link with adjusting screw

Weber 32/36 DGAV carburettor

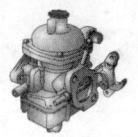

Reassembly

36 Refit the choke pull-down diaphragm, spring and housing, then secure with the three screws.
37 Renew the vacuum seal, then engage the choke link rod into the choke lever arm. Refit the choke housing and secure with the three screws.
38 Check that the secondary throttle plate is fully closed. The adjustment screw should not normally be used to alter the throttle plate position. However, if necessary, it can be adjusted so that the plate is open just enough to prevent it from seizing in the throttle body.
39 Refit the power diaphragm assembly to the upper body and loosely secure with the three screws. Compress the return spring so that the diaphragm does not kink or distort, tighten the retaining screws, then release the return spring. Refit the power valve into the float chamber using a new sealing washer.
40 Refit the emulsion tubes, air correctors and main jets into their original positions (do not transpose the jets).
41 Refit the two idle jets to the carburettor body with new seals (do not transpose the jets).
42 Assemble the pump discharge valve and pump injector into the body, complete with new sealing washers.
43 Refit the anti-stall device diaphragm, spring and cover assembly, then secure with the four screws.
44 Refit the accelerator pump spring, diaphragm and cover assembly, then secure with the four screws.
45 Refit the idle mixture screw. Carefully turn the screw in until it just seats, then unscrew it three full turns. This will provide a basic setting to allow the engine to be started.
46 Clean or renew the fuel filter and secure with the hexagon bolt.
47 Renew the needle valve assembly. Screw the valve seat into the upper body using a new sealing washer and ensure that it is firmly locked into position.
48 Insert the needle valve into the seat with the ball facing outwards. Ensure that the clip is correctly connected to the float and the needle valve, then refit the float and pin.
49 Adjust the float level. Refer to Section 4 for details on adjustment.
50 Place the new float chamber gasket on the carburettor body.

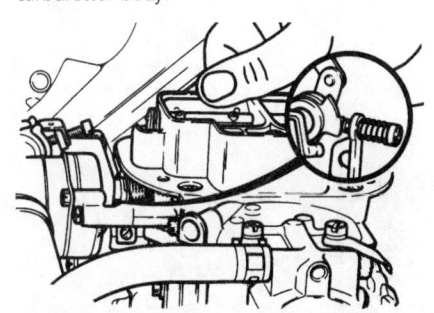

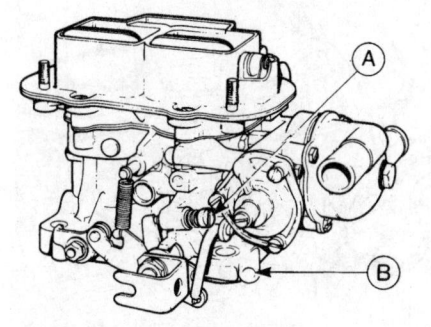

Idle adjustment screw location
A Idle speed screw
B Mixture (CO) screw

51 Pass the choke link lever through the aperture, then refit the upper body and secure with the six screws.
52 Reconnect the choke link lever to the choke spindle arm and secure with the circlip.
53 Ensure that the choke flaps and linkage move smoothly and progressively.
54 Refit the carburettor to the engine.
55 Always adjust the carburettor idle speed and mixture after any work has been carried out on the carburettor, preferably with the aid of a CO meter.
56 Adjust the choke, with reference to Section 4.

4 Service adjustments

Adjustment preconditions

1 Refer to Part B for general advice on preconditions to correct adjustment of this carburettor.

Idle speed and mixture (CO)

2 Run the engine at 3000 rpm for 30 seconds to clear the manifold of fuel vapours, then allow the engine to idle.
3 Use the idle speed screw to set the specified idle speed *(see illustration)*.
4 Check the CO level and compare with the specified value. If incorrect, remove the tamperproof plug and adjust to the correct level. Turning the screw clockwise (inwards) will reduce the CO level. Turning the screw anti-clockwise (outwards) will increase the CO level.
5 Repeat paragraphs 3 and 4 until both adjustments are correct.
6 Clear the manifold every 30 seconds during the setting operation by running the engine at 3000 rpm for 30 seconds.
7 Increase the speed to 2000 rpm and note the CO reading. The cruise reading should be less than half the idle CO reading.
8 Fit a new tamperproof plug to the mixture adjusting screw.

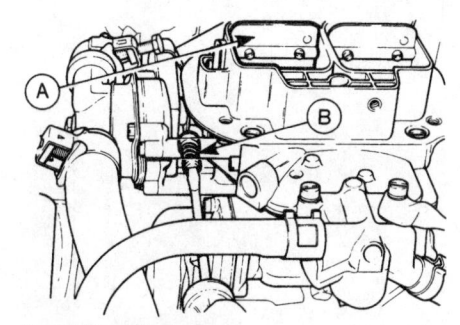

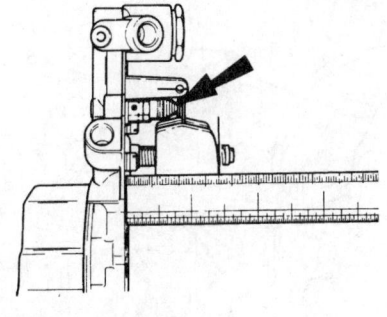

Float level adjustment
Adjusting tag arrowed

Float level/stroke

9 Hold the carburettor upper body in a vertical position with the float tag gently touching the ball of the fully-closed needle valve.
10 Measure the distance between the upper body (without the gasket) and the base of the float *(see illustration)*.
11 Adjust as necessary by bending the inner float tag.
12 Place the upper body in a horizontal position and allow the float to drop.
13 Measure the distance between the upper body (with the gasket in place) and the base of the float.
14 Subtract the measurement recorded in paragraph 10 from the measurement in paragraph 13. The resultant figure is the float operating stroke.
15 Adjust as necessary by bending the outer float tag.

Automatic choke

Fast idle

16 Warm the engine to normal running temperature and adjust the idle speed and mixture before attempting choke fast idle adjustment.
17 Remove the air filter assembly and place it clear of the carburettor with the vacuum hose still connected.
18 Partially open the throttle and fully close the choke flaps. Release the throttle and the flaps. The fast idle adjustment screw should remain against the highest step of the fast idle cam *(see illustration)*.
19 Start the engine without moving the throttle and record the fast idle speed. Refer to Specifications for the correct figure.
20 Adjust as necessary by turning the fast idle screw in the appropriate direction *(see illustration)*.

Fast idle adjustment initial setting
Adjustment screw on highest step of fast idle cam

Fast idle adjustment
A Choke flaps open
B Fast idle adjustment screw

Chapter H5

Vacuum diaphragm held fully open to check vacuum pull-down

A Elastic band
B Twist drill
C Diaphragm operating rod

21 Refit the air filter, ensuring that the vacuum hose remains connected.

Choke vacuum pull-down

22 Remove the three screws and detach the bi-metal coil housing from the carburettor.
23 Remove the internal plastic heat shield.
24 Partially open the throttle and fully close the choke flaps.
25 Release the throttle and fit an elastic band to the choke operating lever so that the choke flaps remain in the fully-on position.
26 Use a small screwdriver to push open the diaphragm up to its stop. At the same time, use the shank of a twist drill to measure the gap between the lower section of the choke flap

Vacuum pull-down adjustment

A Screwdriver
B Diaphragm housing

and the air intake. Refer to Specifications for the required drill size *(see illustration)*.
27 Remove the tamperproof plug and adjust as necessary by turning the diaphragm adjusting screw *(see illustration)* in the appropriate direction. Renew the plug after adjustment is complete and remove the elastic band.
28 Adjust the choke phasing, as described below.

Choke phasing

29 Partially open the throttle and move the choke flaps until the fast idle screw is located tight against the second-highest step of the cam.

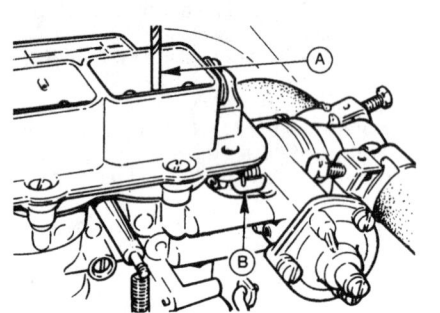

Choke phasing adjustment

A Twist drill
B Adjusting tag

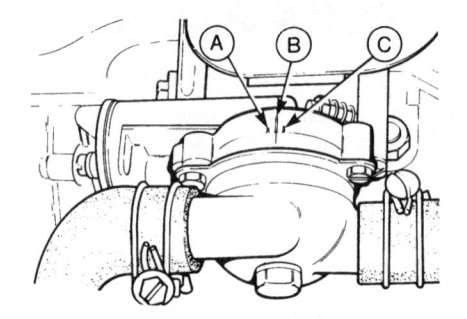

Choke housing alignment marks

A Rich position
B Index mark
C Lean position

30 Use the shank of a twist drill to measure the gap between the lower section of the choke flap and the air intake. Refer to Specifications for the required drill size.
31 Adjust as necessary by bending the phasing adjustment tag *(see illustration)*.
32 Refit the internal heat shield, ensuring that the peg in the housing locates into the hole in the shield.
33 Refit the bi-metal coil housing, ensuring that the spring locates in the slot of the choke lever, then secure loosely with the three screws.
34 Align the cut mark on the bi-metal cover with the correct mark on the choke assembly housing and tighten the three screws *(see illustration)*.

5 Fault diagnosis

Refer to Part D for general diagnosis of carburettor faults. The following faults are specific to the Weber 32/36 DGAV carburettor.

Poor choke operation

☐ Fatigue causing non-operation of choke pull-down diaphragm

Hesitation or lack of power

☐ Loose auxiliary venturi
☐ Failure of accelerator pump discharge valve, resulting in poor pump injection
☐ Failure of LOVE device diaphragm

Poor idle and/or stalling

☐ During operation at low speed and in town, the primary throttle spindle can become excessively worn:
The ultimate cure is a new carburettor but a temporary measure could be to try a slightly larger idle jet
☐ Idle jet blockage (LOVE device will constantly operate, causing fluctuating idle):
Try testing with the vacuum pump. The vacuum should hold for a few seconds before slowly returning to zero

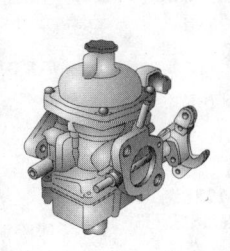

Part H Chapter 6
Weber 32 DIR carburettor

H6

Contents

Fault diagnosis 5	Principles of operation 1
General servicing 3	Service adjustments 4
Identification 2	

Specifications

Manufacturer	Alfa Romeo		Alfa Romeo		Renault	
Model	Alfasud 1.3		Alfasud 1.5		5 1.4 (R1229)	
Year	1979 to 1991		1979 to 1991		1981 to 1985	
Engine code	301.60/64		301.24		C2JP713	
Capacity (cm³)/no. of cyls	1351/4		1490/4		1397/4	
Oil temperature (°C)	90		90		80	
Transmission	-		-		MT	
Carb. identification	32 DIR 81/250		32 DIR 71/250		32 DIR 100/101	
Idle speed (rpm)	950 ± 50		950 ± 50		650 ± 50	
CO @ idle (% vol.)	3.5 max		3.5 max		1.0 ± 0.5	
Stage (venturi)	1	2	1	2	1	2
Venturi diameter	23	24	23	24	23	24
Idle jet	50	50	50	50	50	50
Main jet	122	130	122	130	117	150
Air correction jet	180	170	180	170	190	185
Emulsion tube	F68	F67	F68	F67	F20	F20
Accel. pump jet	45		50		50	
Float level (mm)	7 ± 0.25		7 ± 0.25		8	
Float stroke (mm)	-		-		8	
Needle valve size (mm)	1.75		1.75		1.75	
Choke fast idle gap (mm)	0.95 ± 0.05		0.95 ± 0.05		0.85	
Choke pull-down (mm)	5.75 ± 0.25		5.75 ± 0.25		8.0	

Manufacturer	Renault		Renault		Renault	
Model	5 1.4 Auto (R1229/1399)		5 Gordini Turbo (R122B)		5 Gordini Turbo (R122B)	
Year	1981 to 1985		1982 to 1984		1982 to 1984	
Engine code	847M712		84026		C6J750	
Capacity (cm³)/no. of cyls	1397/4		1397/4		1397/4	
Oil temperature (°C)	80		80		80	
Transmission	AT		-		-	
Carb. identification	32 DIR 90/102		32 DIR 75/101		32 DIR 107/101	
Idle speed (rpm)	600 ± 25		850 ± 50		850 ± 50	
CO @ idle (% vol.)	0.75 ± 0.25		1.25 ± 0.25		1.25 ± 0.25	
Special conditions	AT in Drive		-		-	
Stage (venturi)	1	2	1	2	1	2
Venturi diameter	23	24	26	26	23	24
Idle jet	42	50	55	50	47	
Main jet	117	150	130	145	117	135
Air correction jet	190	185	155	145	175	190
Emulsion tube	F20	F20	F50	F50	F50	F24
Accel. pump jet	50		60		60	
Float level (mm)	7		7		7	
Float stroke (mm)	8		8		8	

Chapter H6

Manufacturer	Renault (continued)	Renault (continued)	Renault (continued)
Model	5 1.4 Auto (R1229/1399)	5 Gordini Turbo (R122B)	5 Gordini Turbo (R122B)
Year	1981 to 1985	1982 to 1984	1982 to 1984
Needle valve size (mm)	1.75	1.75	1.75
Choke fast idle gap (mm)	1.1	1.0	1.0
Choke pull-down (mm)	8.0	8.0	6.0

Manufacturer	Renault		Volvo		Volvo	
Model	18 1.6 (R1341, 1351)		343, 345		343, 345	
Year	1983 to 1986		1980 to 1983		1980 to 1983	
Engine code	841M723 (A2M)		B14 1E/2E/1S/2S/3S		B14 1E/2E/1S/2S/3S	
Capacity (cm³)/no. of cyls	1647/4		1397/4		1397/4	
Oil temperature (°C)	80		-		-	
Transmission	-		MT		AT	
Carb. identification	32 DIR 98/100		32 DIR 93/100		32 DIR 93/100	
Idle speed (rpm)	650 ± 50		900 ± 50		800 ± 50	
CO @ idle (% vol.)	1.5 ± 0.5		2.0 (+1 -0.5)		2.0 (+1 -0.5)	
Stage (venturi)	**1**	**2**	**1**	**2**	**1**	**2**
Venturi diameter	23	24	24	24	24	24
Idle jet	47	40	45	50	45	50
Main jet	115	125	112	132	112	132
Air correction jet	185	140	145	165	145	165
Emulsion tube	F20	F6	F20	F6	F20	F6
Accel. pump jet	50		60		60	
Float level (mm)	7		7 ± 0.25		7 ± 0.25	
Float stroke (mm)	8		-		-	
Needle valve size (mm)	1.75		1.75		1.75	
Choke fast idle gap (mm)	0.9		0.9 ± 0.05		0.9 ± 0.05	
Choke pull-down (mm)	4.0		6 ± 0.25		6 ± 0.25	
Defuming/vent valve (mm)	0.5		-		-	

Manufacturer	Volvo		Volvo	
Model	340		340	
Year	1984 to 1991		1984 to 1991	
Engine code	B14 4E/4S		B14 4E/4S	
Capacity (cm³)/no. of cyls	1397/4		1397/4	
Transmission	MT		AT	
Carb. identification	32 DIR 104 (32 DIR 109)		32 DIR 104 (32 DIR 109)	
Idle speed (rpm)	900 ± 50		800 ± 50	
CO @ idle (% vol.)	1.5 to 3.0		1.5 to 3.0	
Stage (venturi)	**1**	**2**	**1**	**2**
Venturi diameter	23	24	23	24
Idle jet	50	50	50	50
Main jet	122 (120)	137	122 (120)	137
Air correction jet	190	190	190	190
Emulsion tube	F20	F20	F20	F20
Accel. pump jet	45		45	
Float level (mm)	7 ± 0.25		7 ± 0.25	
Needle valve size (mm)	1.75		1.75	
Choke fast idle gap (mm)	0.9 ± 0.05		0.9 ± 0.05	
Choke pull-down (mm)	6 ± 0.25		6 ± 0.25	

1 Principles of operation

Introduction

1 The following technical description of the Weber DIR carburettor should be read in conjunction with the more detailed description of carburettor principles in Part A.

Construction

2 The Weber 32 DIR carburettor is a downdraught, progressive twin venturi instrument *(see illustration)*. The venturis are arranged so that the secondary throttle valve will not begin to open until the primary throttle valve is two-thirds-open. The choke control is manual in operation. The throttle shafts are made of steel and the throttle valves of brass. All the emulsion tubes and jets are manufactured from brass, with the exception of the accelerator pump injector which is die-cast. The internal fuel channels and air passages are drilled and sealed with lead plugs where necessary. On some applications, a heating flange is bolted to the carburettor base so that hot engine coolant may be piped through it. The purpose of the flange is to improve atomisation of the air/fuel mixture.

3 There are a number of variations to the basic design and these are mentioned at the appropriate point in the following text.

Fuel control

4 Fuel flows into the carburettor through a fine mesh filter. The fuel level in the float chamber is controlled by a needle valve and brass float assembly. An anti-vibration ball is incorporated into the needle valve design. A plastic or hairpin clip, attached to the needle valve seat and to the

Weber 32 DIR carburettor

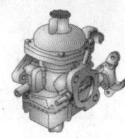

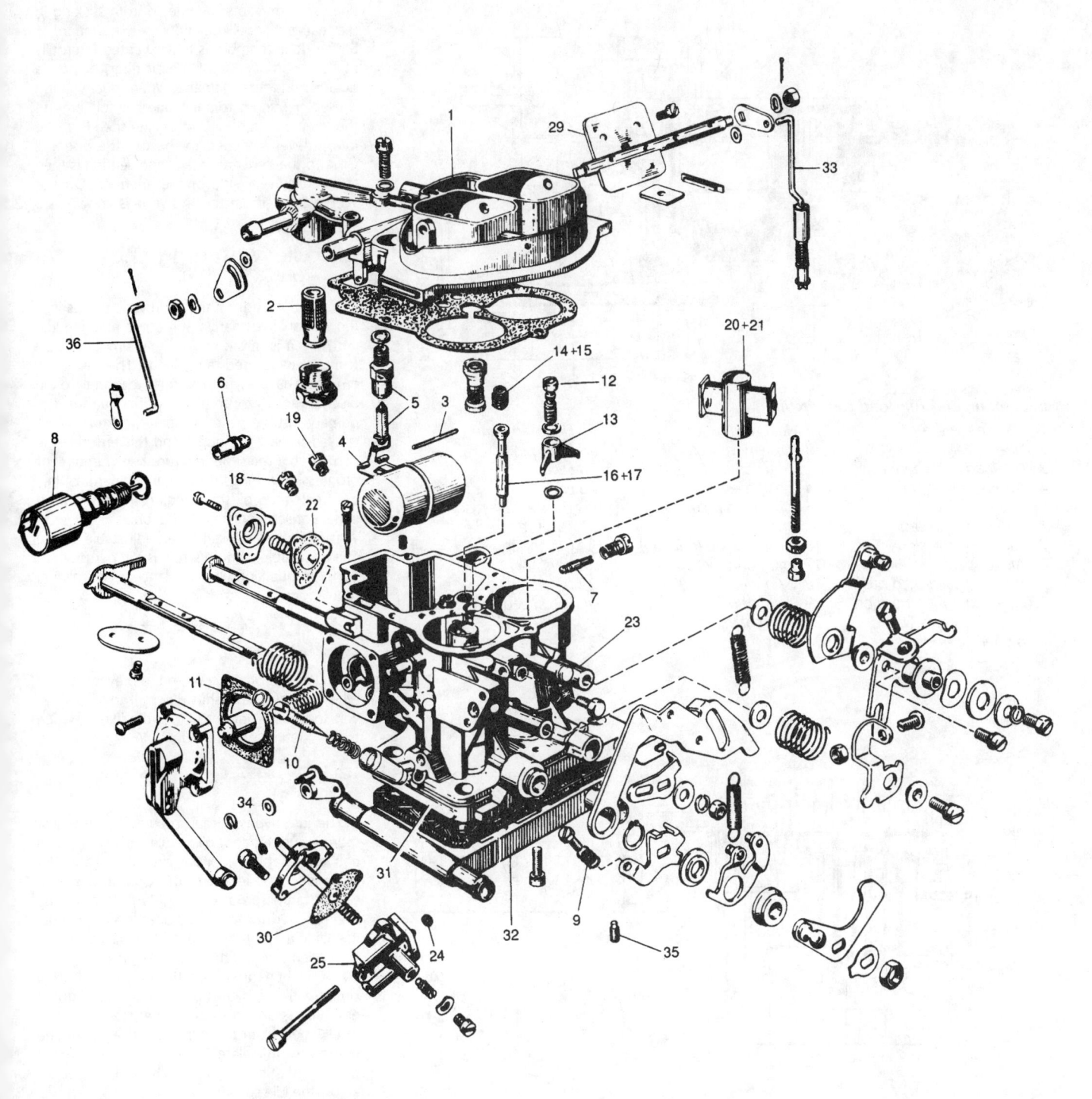

Weber DIR carburettor - standard idle model

1. Upper body
2. Fuel inlet filter
3. Float pin
4. Float
5. Needle valve assembly
6. Idle jet (primary)
7. Idle jet (secondary)
8. Idle cut-off valve (where fitted)
9. Idle speed adjustment screw
10. Idle mixture control screw
11. Accelerator pump diaphragm
13. Pump injector
14. Air corrector (primary)
15. Air corrector (secondary)
16. Emulsion tube (primary)
17. Emulsion tube (secondary)
18. Main jet (primary)
19. Main jet (secondary)
20. Auxiliary venturi (primary)
21. Auxiliary venturi (secondary)
22. Power valve diaphragm (where fitted)
23. Main body
24. Choke seal
25. Choke housing
29. Choke flap (2)
30. Choke diaphragm
31. Insulating block (where fitted)
32. Heating flange (where fitted)
33. Choke link rod
34. Circlip
35. Secondary throttle valve adjustment screw
36. Pull-down rod

H6•3

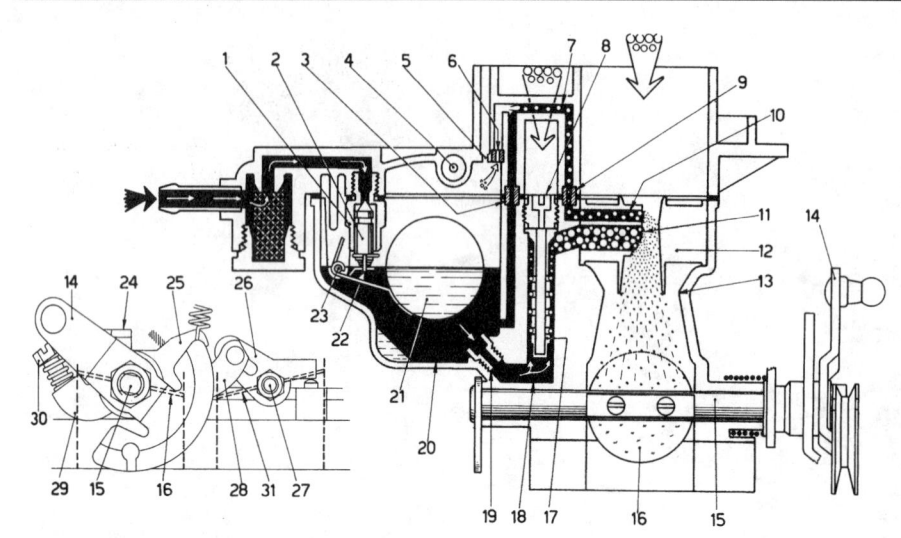

Chapter H6

Inlet, main and full-load fuel circuits

1. Needle valve seat
2. Needle valve
3. Full-load fuel channel
4. Atmospheric vent
5. Internal vent
6. Full-load air bleed
7. Full-load emulsion
8. Air corrector
9. Full-load calibrated bush
10. Full-load outlet (position of outlet varies with model)
11. Main fuel outlet
12. Auxiliary venturi
13. Main venturi
14. Throttle lever
15. Throttle spindle (primary)
16. Throttle valve (primary)
17. Emulsion tube
18. Main well
19. Main jet
20. Float chamber
21. Float
22. Float tag (inner)
23. Float pin
24. Lever
25. Lever
26. Throttle lever (secondary)
27. Throttle spindle (secondary)
28. Lever
29. Lever
30. Idle speed adjustment screw
31. Throttle valve (secondary)

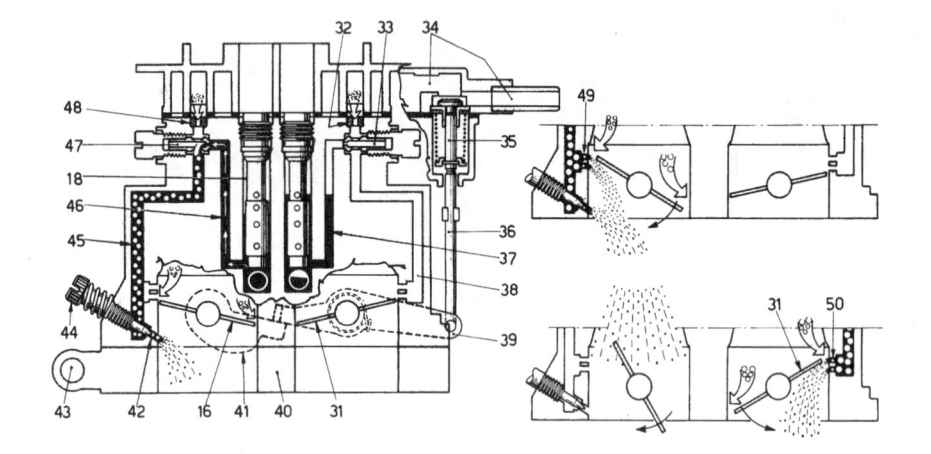

Primary and secondary idle circuits

16. Throttle valve (primary)
18. Emulsion tube (primary)
31. Throttle valve (secondary)
32. Air bleed
33. Idle jet (secondary)
34. Float chamber vents
35. Vent valve
36. Vent rod
37. Idle fuel channel (secondary)
38. Idle fuel/air channel
39. Vent lever
40. Heating flange
41. Throttle lever
42. Idle fuel/air outlet (primary)
43. Coolant passage
44. Idle mixture control screw
45. Idle fuel/air channel (primary)
46. Idle fuel channel (primary)
47. Idle jet (primary)
48. Air bleed
49. Progression drillings (primary)
50. Progression drillings (secondary)

float arm, prevents the needle from sticking in the seat as the fuel level drops *(see illustration)*.

5 The float chamber is either vented internally to the clean-air side of the air filter, or uses a dual venting arrangement. Where dual venting is used, venting is to atmosphere at idle or with the engine shut down. At engine speeds above idle, a lever attached to the throttle opens a valve to the upper air intake and venting is then to the clean-air side of the air filter. On the Weber DIR carburettor, this valve is known as a defuming valve.

Idle, slow running and progression

6 Fuel, sourced from the main well, passes into the primary idle channel through a metered idle jet. Here it is mixed with a small amount of air from a calibrated air bleed. The resulting emulsion is drawn through a channel to be discharged from the idle orifice under the primary throttle plate. A tapered mixture screw is used to vary the outlet and this ensures fine control of the idle mixture. A number of progression drillings provide enrichment as they are uncovered by the opening throttle during initial acceleration *(see illustration)*.

7 The idle speed is set by an adjustable screw. The adjustable mixture screw is tamper proofed during production, in accordance with emission regulations.

Idle cut-off valve (some models)

8 An idle cut-off valve is used to prevent run-on when the engine is shut down. It utilises a 12-volt solenoid plunger to block the idle jet when the ignition is switched off.

Idle bypass circuit (some models)

9 The idle bypass circuit provides a means of more accurately controlling idle emissions than a conventional idle mixture circuit. The throttle plate is locked in a set position and is sealed with a tamperproof cap. Eighty percent of the fuel required for idle is provided by the normal idle circuit. The remainder of the idle mixture is controlled through the idle bypass circuit.

10 A fuel channel links the primary idle fuel circuit with the bypass passage. An air and fuel emulsion is drawn through the passage and is discharged from the bypass orifice under the primary throttle plate. The emulsion is controlled by a regulating screw which is also used to adjust the idle speed.

Accelerator pump

11 The Weber DIR accelerator pump is controlled by a diaphragm and is mechanically operated by a lever and cam attached to the primary throttle linkage. During acceleration, fuel is pumped through a discharge valve and ball into the pump injector where it is discharged into the primary venturi. The inlet valve consists of a ball valve located in a channel from the float chamber. Excess fuel and air is

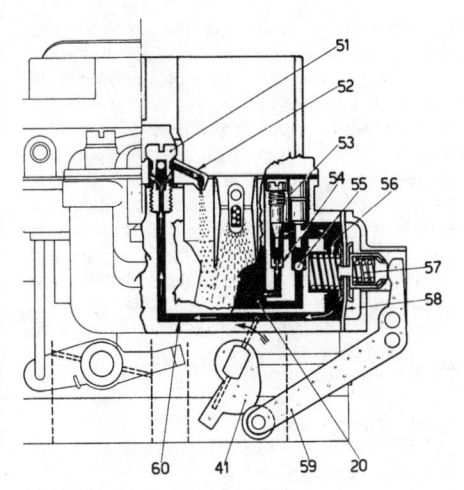

Weber 32 DIR carburettor

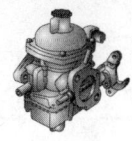

two-thirds-open, the secondary throttle plate will begin to open. At full-throttle, the linkage is arranged so that both throttle plates will be fully open.

16 On some models, a progression jet is used to prevent hesitation as the secondary throttle plate commences to open. This jet is similar in construction and action to the primary idle jet and is often referred to as the secondary idle jet. An emulsified mixture is discharged into the secondary venturi, via two progression drillings, at the initial opening of the secondary throttle plate.

17 Once the secondary throttle plate has opened, the action of the secondary main circuit is similar to the primary circuit.

18 When the choke lever is fully operated, a tag on the lever locks the secondary throttle operating linkage. Secondary throttle operation on full-choke is thus avoided. This feature is only used on some variations of the Weber DIR.

19 At full-load and high engine speeds, even more fuel is required. The velocity of air creates a depression sufficient to raise fuel from the float chamber into a channel. The fuel then passes through a calibrated bushing to the upper section of the air intake. Here it is mixed with a small amount of air from a calibrated air bleed. The emulsified mixture is then discharged into the airstream from a full-load enrichment outlet placed in the barrel. The full-load enrichment outlet may be in the upper or lower reaches of the primary barrel, secondary barrel, or both barrels, depending on application.

Choke operation

20 The manual choke is operated by a dash-mounted cable. When the cable is pulled, it operates a lever that pulls the choke flaps closed across the air intake. Fast idle is achieved with the aid of a curved cam attached to the choke operating lever. An adjustable screw, attached to the throttle lever and butting against the cam, is used to vary the fast idle speed. A number of different connecting links have been used to operate the choke linkage, depending on application *(see illustration)*.

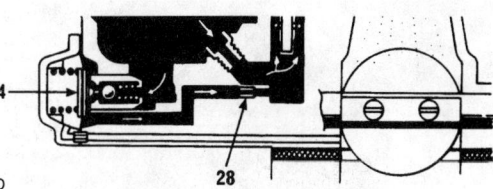

21 Once the engine has fired, the choke flap must open slightly to weaken the mixture and avoid flooding during idle and light-throttle operation. This is achieved by using manifold vacuum to actuate a diaphragm. A linkage attached to the diaphragm will then pull upon the choke flaps.

22 During engine warm-up, the cable should be progressively pushed home until the choke flap is fully open.

2 Identification

The Weber identification code is stamped on the carburettor base flange.

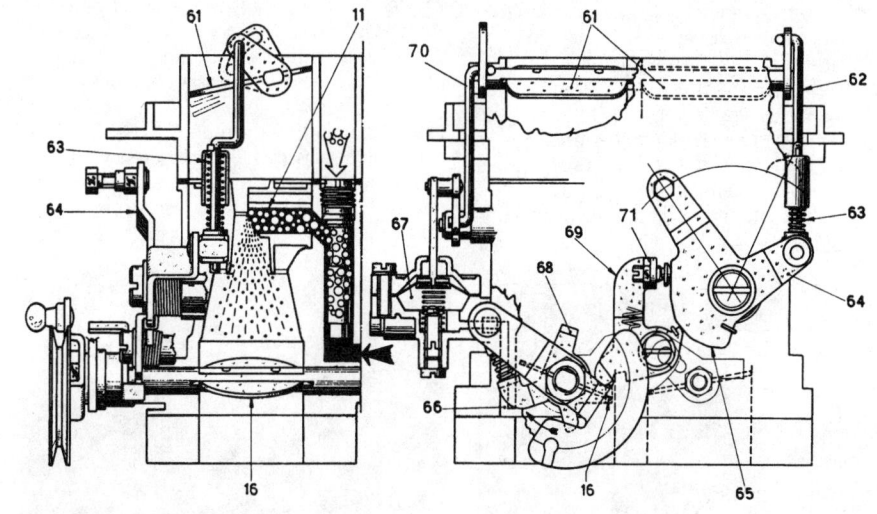

Accelerator pump circuit

20 Float chamber
41 Pump cam
51 Pump discharge valve
52 Pump injector
53 Duct plug
54 Return bleed
55 Inlet ball
56 Spring
57 Spring
58 Diaphragm
59 Pump actuating lever
60 Fuel outlet channel

returned to the float chamber through a separate fuel channel *(see illustration)*.

Main circuit

12 The amount of fuel discharged into the airstream is controlled by a calibrated main jet. Fuel is drawn through the main jet into the base of a vertical well, which dips down into the fuel in the float chamber. An emulsion tube is placed in the well. The fuel is mixed with air drawn in through the air corrector and through the holes in the emulsion tube. The resulting emulsified mixture is discharged from the main orifice through an auxiliary venturi.

Power enrichment and economy circuit (some models)

13 Fuel flows from the float chamber into the power valve chamber through a fuel channel. An air passage is taken from under the throttle plate to the cover of the power diaphragm chamber. At idle and during light-throttle operation, manifold vacuum draws the diaphragm back against spring pressure. The diaphragm pintle is withdrawn from the brass outlet valve and the spring-loaded ball seats to close off the outlet channel *(see illustration)*.

14 Under acceleration and wide-open throttle operation, the vacuum in the manifold is depleted. The diaphragm returns under spring pressure and the power diaphragm pintle pushes the ball to open the outlet valve. Fuel then flows through the valve and a calibrated jet to supplement the fuel in the primary main well. The fuel level rises in the well and the fuel mixture is enriched.

Secondary action

15 Once the primary throttle valve is about

Power enrichment circuit

24 Power valve diaphragm
28 Calibrated jet

Manual choke operation

11 Main fuel outlet
16 Throttle valve (primary)
61 Choke flaps
62 Choke link rod
63 Spring
64 Choke actuating lever
65 Cam
66 Lever
67 Diaphragm assembly
68 Lever
69 Fast idle lever
70 Pull-down rod
71 Fast idle adjustment screw

H6•5

Chapter H6

3 General servicing

Introduction

1 Read this Chapter in conjunction with Part B, which describes some of the operations in more detail. It is assumed that the carburettor is removed for this service. However, many of the operations can be tackled with the carburettor in place. Where this is undertaken, first soak the fuel out of the float chamber using a clean tissue or soft cloth, after removing the upper body assembly.
2 Because of the large number of variations to the basic design, this procedure may have to be used as a general guide. In particular, some linkage variations may not be as described.

Dismantling and checking

3 Remove the carburettor from the engine (see Part B) and check it for damage and wear.
4 Where an idle cut-off valve is fitted, it is secured with a 2 mm socket-head grub screw. Slacken this screw before removing the idle cut-off valve. If the valve is loose in the body, a new carburettor will be required.
5 Use a small screwdriver to prise the spring-loaded end of the choke operating link from the choke actuating lever *(see illustration)*.
6 Prise away the retaining clip and detach the pull-down rod from the end of the choke diaphragm assembly *(see illustration)*.
7 Remove the five screws and detach the carburettor upper body.
8 Use a straight-edge to check for distorted flanges on both facing surfaces.
9 Inspect the float chamber for corrosion and calcium build-up.
10 Tap out the float pin and remove the float, needle valve, clip and needle valve seat. Recover the float chamber gasket.
11 Check that the anti-vibration ball is free in the valve end.
12 Check the needle valve tip for wear and ridges. This is more likely with the brass needle valve tip than when a viton one is used. Use a viton-tipped replacement when possible.
13 The float should be checked for damage and ingress of petrol.
14 Renew the float pin if it shows signs of wear.
15 Remove the hexagon bolt and inspect the fuel filter. Clean any debris and dirt from the filter chamber.
16 Remove the mixture screw and Idle bypass screw (where fitted) and inspect the tips for damage or ridges.
17 Remove the four screws and detach the accelerator pump housing, diaphragm and spring. Check the diaphragm for fatigue and damage.
18 Unscrew the pump discharge valve from the body and remove the valve and the pump injector. Test the discharge valve by shaking it. No noise from the outlet ball indicates that the valve is seized. Check that the lead pellet that seals the valve is present. If loose or missing, the pump action will be impaired.
19 Slacken the grub screw (where fitted) before removing the idle jet holder. Remove the two idle jet assemblies from the carburettor body. The idle jets are pushed into a holder and may be separated (by pulling) for cleaning or renewal. Where an idle cut-off valve is fitted, the primary idle jet will be pushed into the end of the valve. It may be separated (by pulling) for cleaning or renewal. Note that the idle jet assemblies (where fitted) can be removed from the carburettor body without removing the upper body. Also note that some applications may not have a secondary idle jet.
20 Unscrew the primary and secondary main jets, air correctors and emulsion tubes.
21 Check that the channels from the float chamber into the emulsion tube wells are clear.
22 Note the jet sizes and locations for correct installation during assembly.
23 Check the jet calibration against that specified. It is possible that the jets may have been transposed (or the wrong size fitted) during the last overhaul.
24 Remove the primary and secondary auxiliary venturis where necessary. A Weber extractor tool is available for this purpose. Check that the primary and secondary auxiliary venturis are not loose in the main body as this is a source of uneven running. If a venturi is loose, knurl the mating flanges with a file to ensure a tight fit.
25 Remove the three screws and detach the power valve housing cover, spring and diaphragm (where fitted) from the body. Check the diaphragm for fatigue and damage. The brass outlet valve is cast into the body and is not removable. The ball in the outlet valve should seal the outlet. Depress and release the ball with a small screwdriver and it should move smoothly in and out. Check that the channel into the emulsion tube well is clear.
26 Note the position of the heating flange (if fitted) relative to the lower carburettor flange and make alignment marks if necessary. Remove the screw and separate the heating flange from the lower carburettor flange. Use a straight-edge to check for distorted flanges on the facing surfaces.
27 Do not disturb the adjustment of the primary and secondary throttle angles, unless absolutely necessary.
28 Inspect the choke spindle, mechanism and levers for stickiness and wear.
29 Remove the two screws and circlip, then detach the choke diaphragm housing.
30 Remove the three screws and detach the choke diaphragm cover, spring, and diaphragm from the housing. Check the diaphragm for fatigue and damage.

Preparation for reassembly

31 Clean the jets, carburettor body assemblies, float chamber and internal channels. An air line may be used to clear internal channels once the carburettor is fully dismantled. Note that if high-pressure air is directed into the channels and passages with the diaphragms still in place, diaphragm damage may result.
32 Spraying carburettor cleaner into all the channels and passages in the carburettor body will often clear them of gum and dirt.
33 During reassembly, a complete set of new gaskets should be fitted. Also renew the needle valve and float pin, and all diaphragms.
34 Inspect and renew (where necessary) the mixture screw, main jets, idle jets, air corrector jets and accelerator pump injector. Renew worn screws, linkages, springs and other parts where necessary.
35 Ensure that all jets are firmly locked into their original positions (but do not over-tighten). A loose jet can cause a rich (or even lean) running condition.
36 Clean all mating surfaces and flanges of old gasket material and reassemble with new gaskets.
37 Ensure that housings are positioned with their air and fuel routes correctly aligned.

Reassembly

38 Refit the choke pull-down diaphragm, spring and cover to the housing, then secure with the three screws.
39 Renew the vacuum seal, engage the choke lever into the choke lever arm and secure with the circlip. Secure the choke diaphragm housing with the two screws.
40 Check that the secondary throttle plate is fully closed. The adjustment screw should not normally be used to alter the throttle plate position. However, if necessary, it can be adjusted so that the plate is open just enough to prevent its seizure in the throttle body.
41 Where the primary throttle position has been disturbed and a throttle setting gauge is

Using small screwdriver to prise spring-loaded end of choke operating link from choke actuating lever

Prise away retaining clip and detach pull-down rod

Weber 32 DIR carburettor

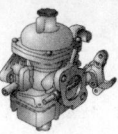

available, use it to set the throttle angle. Otherwise, temporarily adjust the throttle plate so that it is open just enough to prevent its seizure in the throttle body. An adjustment method with the engine running is detailed in Section 4.
42 Assemble the heating flange (where fitted) to the main body with a new gasket block and secure with the one screw.
43 Refit the power diaphragm, spring and cover assembly (where fitted) and secure with the three screws.
44 Refit the emulsion tubes, air correctors and main jets into their original positions (do not transpose the jets).
45 Assemble the idle jet to the idle cut-off valve (where fitted). Refit the assembly, using a new seal. Tighten the retaining socket-head grub screw.
46 Refit the idle jet(s) (where fitted) to the carburettor body, using new seals (do not transpose jets). Lock the primary idle jet holder with the socket-head grub screw (where fitted).
47 Assemble the pump discharge valve and pump injector into the body, complete with new sealing washers. Ensure that the nozzle points into the primary venturi.
48 Refit the accelerator pump spring, diaphragm and cover assembly, then secure with the four screws.
49 Refit the bypass idle screw (where fitted). Turn the screw in gently until it just seats. From this position, unscrew it three full turns. This will provide a basic setting to allow the engine to be started.
50 Refit the idle mixture screw. Use the same method described in the previous paragraph to obtain a basic setting.
51 Clean or renew the fuel filter and secure with the hexagon bolt.
52 Fit a new float gasket to the upper body. Renew the needle valve assembly. Screw the valve seat into the upper body using a new sealing washer and ensure that it is firmly locked into position (but do not over-tighten). Transfer the hairpin or plastic clip from the old needle valve to the ball end of the new one. Place the clip and valve assembly onto the inner float tag. Lower the float and needle valve assembly into the seat and secure with the float pin.
53 Adjust the float level. Refer to Section 4 for details on float adjustment.
54 Refit the upper body and secure with the five screws.
55 Reconnect the choke pull-down rod to the pull-down diaphragm assembly and secure with the retaining clip.
56 Use a small screwdriver to connect the spring-loaded end of the choke operating link to the choke operating lever.
57 Ensure that the choke flaps and linkage move smoothly and progressively.
58 Adjust the defuming valve, choke fast idle and choke vacuum pull-down. Refer to Section 4 for details on all adjustments.
59 Refit the carburettor to the engine.
60 Always adjust the carburettor idle speed and mixture after any work has been carried out on the carburettor, preferably with the aid of a CO meter.

4 Service adjustments

Adjustment preconditions

1 Refer to Part B for general advice on the preconditions to correct adjustment of this carburettor.

Idle speed and mixture (CO)

Standard idle system

2 Run the engine at 3000 rpm for 30 seconds to clear the manifold of fuel vapours, then allow the engine to idle.
3 Use the idle speed adjustment screw to set the specified idle speed *(see illustration)*.
4 Check the CO level. If it is not as specified, remove the tamperproof plug and adjust the idle mixture control screw to achieve the correct level. Turning the screw clockwise (inwards) will reduce the CO level. Turning the screw anti-clockwise (outwards) will increase the CO level.
5 Repeat paragraphs 3 and 4 until both adjustments are correct.
6 Clear the manifold every 30 seconds during the setting operation by running the engine at 3000 rpm for 30 seconds.
7 Increase the speed to 2000 rpm and note the CO reading. The cruise reading should be less than half the idle CO reading.
8 Fit a new tamperproof plug to the mixture adjustment screw.

Idle bypass system

9 Run the engine at 3000 rpm for 30 seconds to clear the manifold of fuel vapours, then allow the engine to idle.
10 Use the idle bypass regulating screw to set the specified idle speed.
11 Check the CO level. If it is not as specified, remove the tamperproof plug and adjust the idle mixture control screw to achieve the correct level. Turning the screw clockwise (inwards) will reduce the CO level. Turning the screw anti-clockwise (outwards) will increase the CO level.
12 Repeat paragraphs 10 and 11 until both adjustments are correct.

Setting the primary throttle plate

13 If it is not possible to set the idle speed and CO correctly, it is possible that the basic throttle position is incorrect. The manufacturer's recommended method is to remove the carburettor and use a Renault, Solex or Pierburg throttle setting gauge to set the throttle position in mm or degrees.
14 However, an alternative method can be used to set the throttle plate. Please note that this is not the manufacturer's recommended method but nevertheless will result in an accurate and stable idle speed and CO level. A further method is also detailed in Part B.
15 Allow the engine to idle.
16 Screw in the bypass regulating screw until it is fully seated. The idle speed should drop to two-thirds of the specified idle speed figure. In this example, a hypothetical specified idle speed of 900 rpm will be used, so the speed should drop to 600 rpm. Substitute the correct figures for the particular vehicle being worked on.
17 Adjust the throttle stop screw until 600 rpm is attained.
18 Unscrew the bypass screw until 900 rpm is once again reached.
19 Reset the CO to the correct level.
20 If the CO needs a large adjustment at this stage, repeat paragraphs 15 to 19. Once the proper CO is reached at the correct idle speed, the carburettor is properly adjusted.

Float level/stroke

21 Hold the carburettor upper body in a vertical position with the float tag gently touching the ball of the fully-closed needle valve.
22 Measure the distance between the upper body (without the gasket) and the top of the float *(see illustration overleaf)*.
23 Adjust as necessary by bending the inner float tag.
24 Place the upper body in a horizontal position and allow the float to hang down.
25 Measure the distance between the upper body (with the gasket in place) and the top of the float.
26 Subtract the measurement in paragraph 22

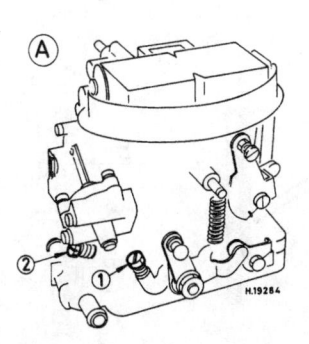

Idle speed and mixture adjustment
A Standard idle system
1 Idle speed adjustment screw
2 Idle mixture control screw
B Idle bypass system
1 Throttle plate setting screw (tamper proofed)
2 Idle mixture control screw
3 Idle speed bypass adjustment screw

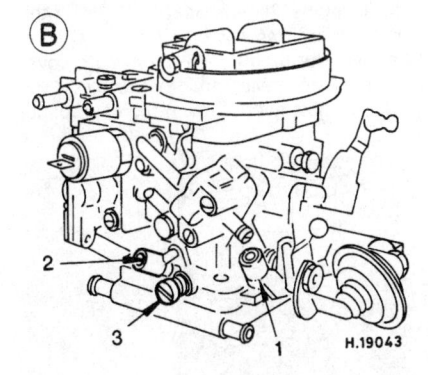

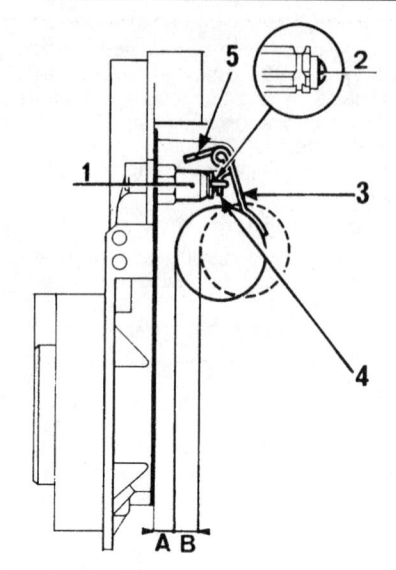

Chapter H6

Float level adjustment
A Float level
B Float stroke
1 Needle valve assembly
2 Needle valve ball
3 Float arm
4 Inner float tag
5 Outer float tag

from the measurement in paragraph 25. This figure is the float stroke.
27 Adjust as necessary by bending the outer float tag.

Defuming valve (float chamber vent)

28 Invert the carburettor and push the defuming valve operating rod fully downwards (towards the upper body). The throttle plate will be forced open to leave a small clearance.
29 Use the shank of a twist drill to measure the clearance between the throttle plate and the wall of the throttle bore. Refer to Specifications for the required drill size.
30 Adjust as necessary by turning the adjustment nut in the appropriate direction (see illustration).

Secondary barrel lock-out (where applicable)

31 Open the choke control and fully push lever (3) in the direction of the arrow (see illustration). The clearance should be 2 to 3 mm.
32 Adjust, as necessary, by releasing the

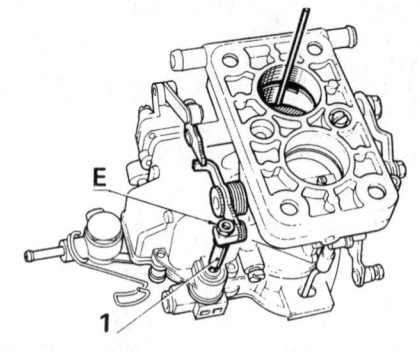

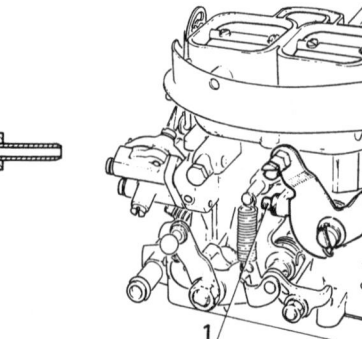

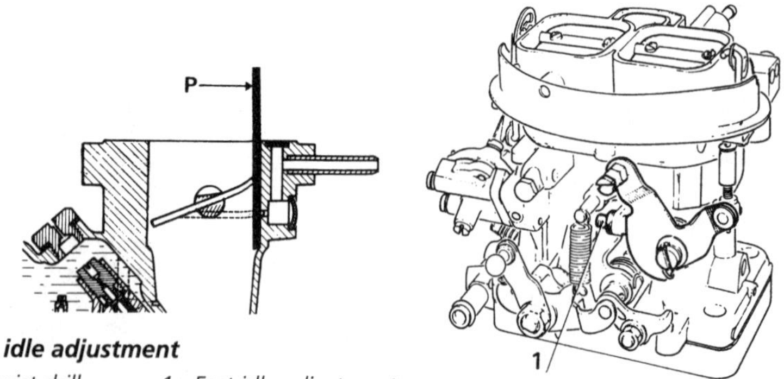

Fast idle adjustment
P Twist drill
1 Fast idle adjustment screw

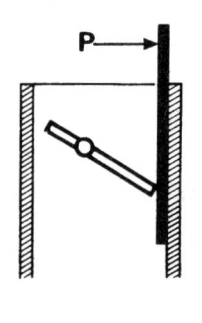

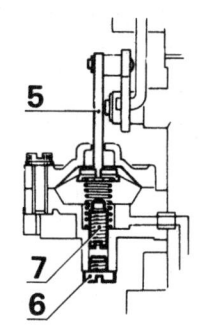

Defuming/vent valve adjustment
E Adjustment nut
1 Defuming valve control lever

retaining screws (2) and pushing lever (3) in the direction of the arrow.
33 When the clearance is correct, retighten the two screws.

Choke adjustments

Fast idle

34 The carburettor must be removed from the engine in order to make the fast idle adjustment.
35 Invert the carburettor.
36 Pull the choke operating arm to fully close the choke flap. The adjustment screw will butt against the fast idle cam and force open the throttle plate to leave a small clearance.
37 Use the shank of a twist drill to measure the clearance between the wall of the throttle bore and the throttle plate. Refer to Specifications for the required drill size and measure the clearance from the progression holes (see illustration).
38 Adjust as necessary by turning the adjustment screw in the appropriate direction.

Vacuum pull-down

39 Pull the choke operating arm to fully close the choke flap.
40 Push the diaphragm pull-down lever down fully with a small screwdriver. At the same time, use the shank of a twist drill to measure the gap between the lower section of the choke flap and the air intake. Refer to Specifications for the required drill size (see illustration).
41 Remove the plug in the diaphragm cover and adjust as necessary by turning the diaphragm adjustment screw in the appropriate

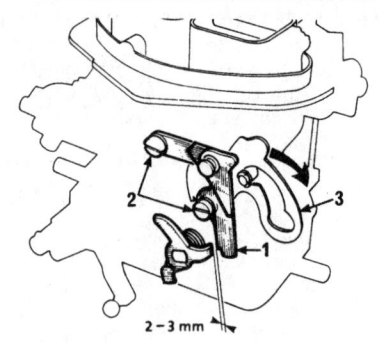

Secondary throttle lock-out adjustment
1 Secondary lock-out lever
2 Adjustment screws
3 Lever

direction. Renew the plug when the adjustment is completed.

5 Fault diagnosis

Refer to Part D for diagnosis of general carburettor faults. The following faults are specific to Weber 32 DIR carburettors.

Hesitation or lack of power
☐ Loose auxiliary venturi(s).
☐ Failure of accelerator pump discharge valve, resulting in poor pump injection.

Poor idle and/or stalling
☐ Idle jet blocked.
☐ Idle cut-off valve loose in body due to wear in locating hole - the only cure is a new carburettor body.
☐ Upper body screws loose. This seems to occur more frequently in vehicles with a large air filter assembly.
☐ During operation at low speeds and in town, the primary throttle spindle can become excessively worn. The ultimate cure is a new carburettor but a temporary measure could be to try a slightly larger idle jet.

Pull-down adjustment
P Twist drill
5 Diaphragm pull-down lever
6 Plug
7 Adjustment screw

Part H Chapter 7
Weber 30 & 30/32 DMTE carburettor

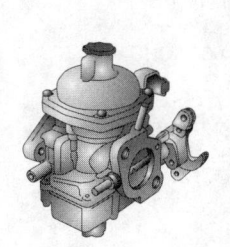

H7

Contents

Component testing 5	Identification 2
Fault diagnosis 6	Principles of operation 1
General servicing 3	Service adjustments 4

Specifications

Manufacturer	Fiat	Fiat	Fiat	
Model	Uno 60	Uno 60	Uno 70 (1300)	
Year	1985 to 1988	1985 to 1988	1985 to 1988	
Engine code	146A4.048 OHC	146A4.048 OHC	146A7.000	
Capacity (cm³)/no. of cyls	1116/4	1116/4	1301/4	
Oil temperature (°C)	100	100	100	
Transmission	MT	AT	-	
Carb. identification	30/32 DMTE 11/250	30/32 DMTE 11/250	30/32 DMTE 12/150	
Idle speed (rpm)	850 ± 50	850 ± 50	850 ± 50	
Fast idle speed (rpm)	1300	1675 ± 25	1300	
CO @ idle (% vol.)	1.0 ± 0.5	1.0 ± 0.5	1.0 ± 0.5	
Stage (venturi)	1 2	1 2i	1 2	
Venturi diameter	19 23	19 23	19 23	
Idle jet	47 70	47 70	45 70	
Main jet	90 95	90 95	90 97	
Air correction jet	195 195	195 195	220 175	
Emulsion tube	F43 F38	F43 F38	F42 F38	
Accel. pump jet	40	40	45	
Float level (mm)	7 ± 0.25	7 ± 0.25	7 ± 0.25	
Needle valve size (mm)	1.50	1.50	1.50	
Choke fast idle gap (mm)	0.95 ± 0.05	0.95 ± 0.05	0.95 ± 0.05	
Choke pull-down (mm)	4 ± 0.25	4 ± 0.25	4 ± 0.25	
Manufacturer	Fiat	Fiat	Fiat	
Model	Uno 70 (1300)	Regata 70ES	Regata 70ES	
Year	1988 to 1990	1984 to 1986	1984 to 1986	
Engine code	149A7.000 OHC	149A3.000 SOHC	149A3.000 SOHC	
Capacity (cm³)/no. of cyls	1301/4	1301/4	1301/4	
Oil temperature (°C)	100	100	100	
Transmission	-	MT	AT	
Carb. identification	30/32 DMTE 35/150	30/32 DMTE 1/250	30/32 DMTE 20/150 or 21/250	
Idle speed (rpm)	850 ± 50	850 ± 50	850 ± 50	
Fast idle speed (rpm)	1300	-	-	
CO @ idle (% vol.)	1.0 ± 0.5	1.0 ± 0.5	1.0 ± 0.5	
Stage (venturi)	1 2	1 2	1 2	
Venturi diameter	19 23	19 23	19 23	
Idle jet	45 40	47 50	45 (47) 70	
Main jet	87 90	87 95	91 100	
Air correction jet	190 160	185 165	195 220	
Emulsion tube	F30 F30	F43 F38	F47 F38	
Accel. pump jet	50	45	45	
Float level (mm)	7 ± 0.25	7 ± 0.25	7 ± 0.25	
Needle valve size (mm)	1.50	1.50	1.50	
Choke fast idle gap (mm)	1 ± 0.10	0.9 ± 0.05	0.95 ± 0.05	
Choke pull-down (mm)	3.25 ± 0.25	4 ± 0.25	4 ± 0.25	

Chapter H7

Manufacturer	Fiat	Fiat	Fiat
Model	Regata 70	Regata 70	Regata 70
Year	1986 to 1988	1986 to 1988	1988 to 1990
Engine code	149A7.000 SOHC	149A7.000 SOHC	149A7.000 SOHC
Capacity (cm³)/no. of cyls	1301/4	1301/4	1301/4
Oil temperature (°C)	100	100	100
Carb. identification	30/32 DMTE 9/250	30/32 DMTE 12/150	30/32 DMTE 36/150
Idle speed (rpm)	850 ± 50	850 ± 50	850 ± 50
CO @ idle (% vol.)	1.0 ± 0.5	1.0 ± 0.5	1.0 ± 0.5
Stage (venturi)	1 2	1 2	1 2
Venturi diameter	19 23	19 23	19 23
Idle jet	45 70	45 70	47 40
Main jet	91 100	90 97	90 90
Air correction jet	195 220	220 175	200 160
Emulsion tube	F42 F38	F42 F38	F30 F30
Accel. pump jet	45	45	50
Float level (mm)	7 ± 0.25	7 ± 0.25	7 ± 0.25
Needle valve size (mm)	1.50	1.50	1.50
Choke fast idle gap (mm)	0.95 ± 0.05	0.95 ± 0.05	0.95 ± 0.05
Choke pull-down (mm)	4 ± 0.25	4 ± 0.25	4 ± 0.25

Manufacturer	Fiat	Fiat	Fiat
Model	Strada 60 ES	Strada 60 ES City Matic	Strada 60
Year	1983 to 1985	1984	1985 to 1988
Engine code	138B1.000	-	146A4.000 or 146A4.048
Capacity (cm³)/no. of cyls	1116/4	1116/4	1116/4
Oil temperature (°C)	100	100	100
Carb. identification	30 DMTE /250	30 DMTE 7/250	30/32 DMTE 11/250
Idle speed (rpm)	850 ± 50	-	850 ± 50
CO @ idle (% vol.)	3.5 max	-	1.0 ± 0.5
Stage (venturi)	1 2	1 2	1 2
Venturi diameter	18 20	18 20	19 23
Idle jet	45 45	45 45	47 70
Main jet	82 87	82 87	90 95
Air correction jet	170 150	170 150	195 195
Emulsion tube	F27 F27	F27 F27	F43 F38
Accel. pump jet	40	40	50
Float level (mm)	7 ± 0.25	7 ± 0.25	7 ± 0.25
Needle valve size (mm)	1.50	1.50	1.50
Choke fast idle gap (mm)	0.95 ± 0.05	0.95 ± 0.05	0.95 ± 0.05
Choke pull-down (mm)	4.75 ± 0.25	4.75 ± 0.25	4 ± 0.25

Manufacturer	Fiat	Fiat	Fiat
Model	Strada 70	Strada 70 City Matic	Citivan
Year	1985 to 1988	1985 to 1988	1988 to 1991
Engine code	149A7.003	149A7.003	146 A6.000 SOHC
Capacity (cm³)/no. of cyls	1301/4	1301/4	1116/4
Oil temperature (°C)	100	100	100
Transmission	-	AT	-
Carb. identification	30/32 DMTE 9/250 / 30/32 DMTE 3/150	30/32 DMTE 20/150 or 21/250	30/32 DMTE 28/150
Idle speed (rpm)	850 ± 50	850 ± 50	800 ± 50
CO @ idle (% vol.)	1.0 ± 0.5	1.0 ± 0.5	1.0 ± 0.5
Stage (venturi)	1 2	1 2	1 2
Venturi diameter	19 23	19 23	18 20
Idle jet	45 70	45 (47) 70	45 70
Main jet	91 100	91 100	87 95
Air correction jet	195 220	195 220	210 210
Emulsion tube	F42 F38	F42 F38	F43 F38
Accel. pump jet	45	45	40
Float level (mm)	7 ± 0.25	7 ± 0.25	7 ± 0.25
Needle valve size (mm)	1.50	1.50	1.50
Choke fast idle gap (mm)	0.95 ± 0.05	0.95 ± 0.05	1 ± 0.05
Choke pull-down (mm)	4 ± 0.25	4 ± 0.25	3.75 ± 0.25

Weber 30 & 30/32 DMTE carburettor

Manufacturer	Fiat	
Model	Fiorino	
Year	1988 to 1991	
Engine code	146 A5.000 SOHC	
Capacity (cm³)/no. of cyls	1301/4	
Oil temperature (°C)	100	
Carb. identification	30/32 DMTE 27/150	
Idle speed (rpm)	800 ± 50	
CO @ idle (% vol.)	1.0 ± 0.5	
Stage (venturi)	1	2
Venturi diameter	19	23
Idle jet	45	70
Main jet	92	105
Air correction jet	205	210
Emulsion tube	F43	F38
Accel. pump jet	40	
Float level (mm)	7 ± 0.25	
Needle valve size (mm)	1.50	
Choke fast idle gap (mm)	1 ± 0.05	
Choke pull-down (mm)	4 ± 0.25	

Weber DMTE carburettor

1. Upper body
2. Float chamber gasket
3. Fuel inlet filter
4. Float pin
5. Float
6. Needle valve assembly
7. Idle jet (primary)
8. Idle jet (secondary)
9. Idle cut-off valve
10. Idle speed adjustment screw
11. Idle mixture control screw
12. Accelerator pump diaphragm
13. Throttle switch
14. Pump injector
15. Air corrector (primary)
16. Air corrector (secondary)
17. Emulsion tube (primary)
18. Emulsion tube (secondary)
19. Main jet (primary)
20. Main jet (secondary)
21. Auxiliary venturi (primary)
22. Auxiliary venturi (secondary)
24. Main body
25. Secondary throttle valve adjustment screw
26. Pull-down fulcrum lever
27. Vacuum hose
28. Choke flap
29. Choke diaphragm
30. Choke link rod
31. Circlip
33. Throttle & fast idle lever
34. Fast idle adjustment screw
35. Pump cam

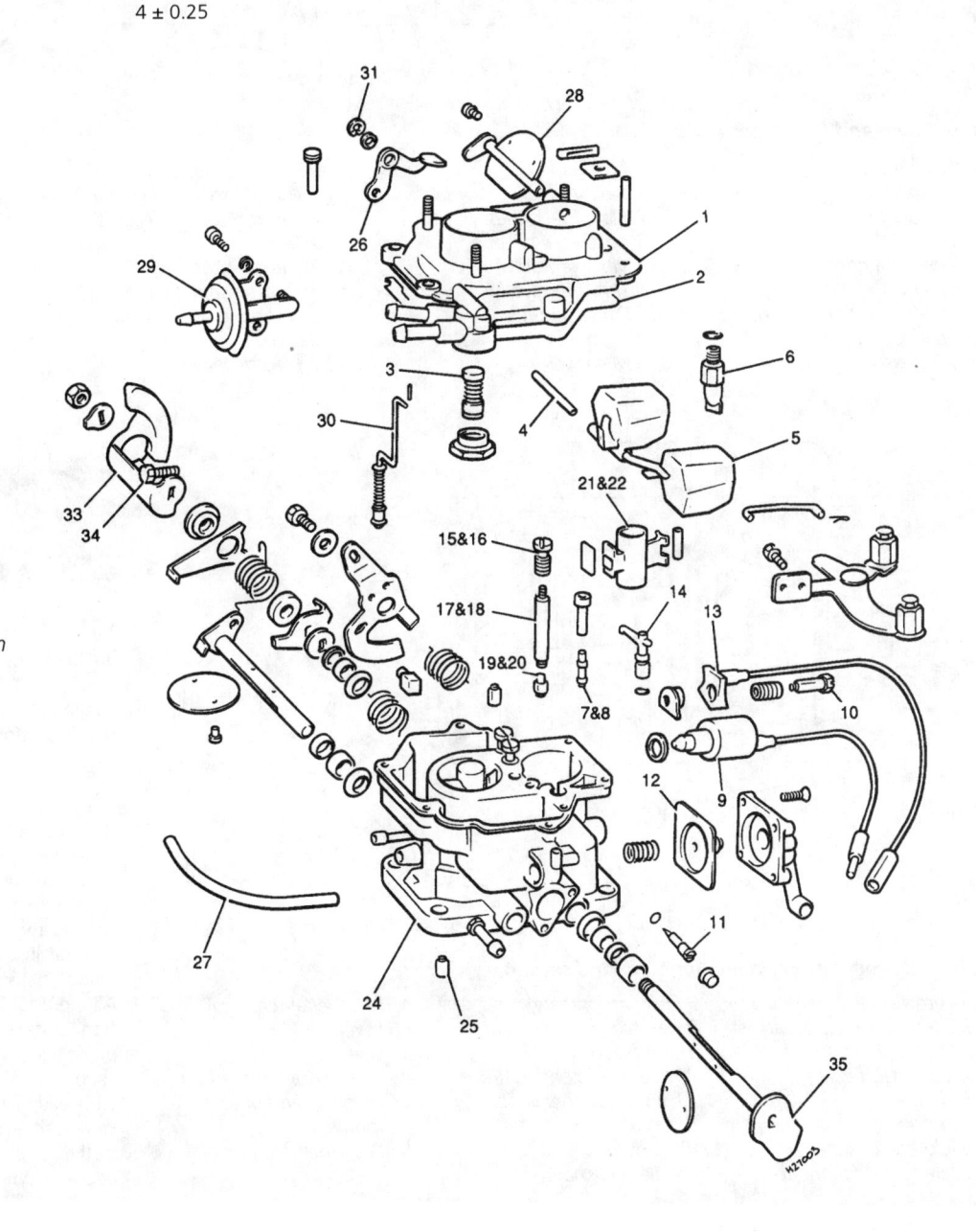

H7•3

Chapter H7

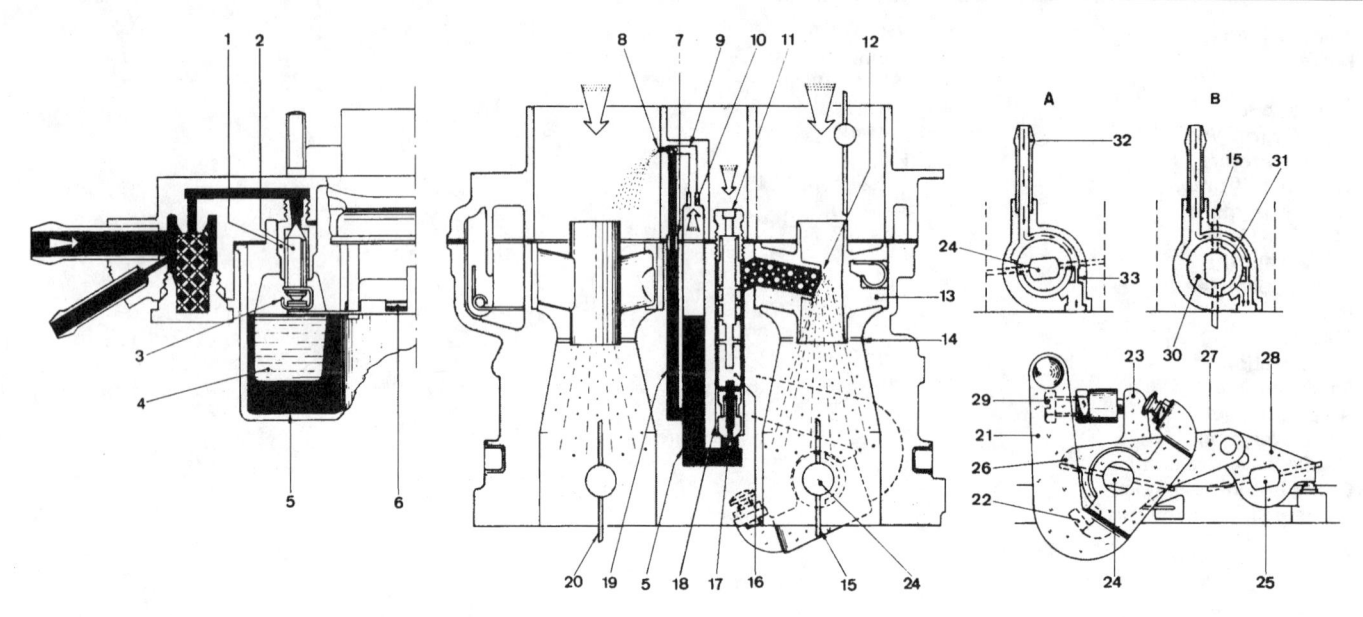

Inlet, main and full-load circuits

1 Needle valve seat
2 Needle valve
3 Needle valve clip
4 Float
5 Float chamber
6 Float pin
7 Full-load calibrated bush
8 Full-load outlet
9 Air passage
10 Air bleed
11 Air corrector
12 Main fuel outlet
13 Auxiliary venturi
14 Main venturi
15 Throttle valve (primary)
16 Emulsion tube
17 Main jet
18 Main well
19 Full-load fuel channel
20 Throttle valve (secondary)
21 Throttle control lever
22 Tab
23 Throttle stop
24 Throttle spindle (primary)
25 Throttle spindle (secondary)
26 Lug
27 Throttle lever
28 Secondary throttle lever
29 Idle speed adjustment screw
30 Rotary blanking disc
31 Groove
32 Spigot
33 Calibrated bush
A PCV device in idle position
B PCV device in open-throttle position

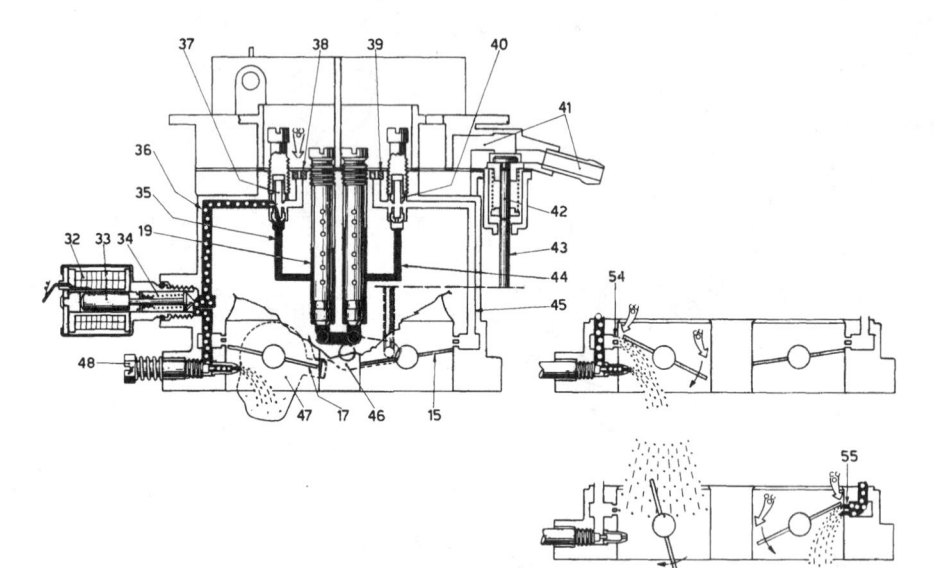

Idle and progression circuits (primary and secondary)

15 Throttle valve (secondary)
17 Throttle valve (primary)
19 Main well
32 Idle cut-off valve
33 Plunger
34 Spring
35 Idle fuel channel
36 Idle fuel/air channel
37 Idle jet (primary)
38 Air bleed
39 Air bleed
40 Idle jet (secondary)
41 Float chamber vents
42 Vent valve
43 Vent rod
44 Idle fuel channel
45 Idle fuel/air channel
46 Lever
47 Lever
48 Idle mixture control screw
54 Progression outlet (primary)
55 Progression outlet (secondary)

1 Principles of operation

Introduction

1 The following technical description of the Weber DMTE carburettor should be read in conjunction with the more detailed description of carburettor principles in Part A.

Construction

2 The Weber DMTE carburettor is a downdraught, progressive twin venturi instrument *(see illustration)*. The venturis are arranged so that the secondary throttle valve will not begin to open until the primary throttle valve is two-thirds open. The choke control is manual in operation. The throttle shafts are made of steel and the throttle valves of brass. All emulsion tubes and jets are manufactured from brass with the exception of the accelerator pump injector which is die-cast. The internal fuel channels and air passages are drilled and sealed with lead plugs where necessary. An idle cut-off valve is fitted to the idle circuit and this device is further controlled by an ECU to save fuel during deceleration.

Weber 30 & 30/32 DMTE carburettor

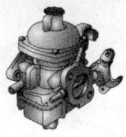

Fuel control

3 Fuel flows into the carburettor through a fine mesh filter. The fuel level in the float chamber is controlled by a needle valve and brass float assembly. An anti-vibration ball is incorporated into the needle valve design. A plastic or hairpin clip, attached to the needle valve seat and to the float arm, prevents the needle from sticking in the seat as the fuel level drops *(see illustration)*.

4 The float chamber is vented internally to the clean-air side of the air filter. A calibrated fuel return system is provided to ensure that relatively cool fuel is supplied to the carburettor.

Idle, slow running and progression

5 Fuel, sourced from the main well, passes into the primary idle channel through a metered idle jet. Here it is mixed with a small amount of air from a calibrated air bleed. The resulting emulsion is drawn through a channel to be discharged from the idle orifice under the primary throttle plate. A tapered mixture screw is used to vary the outlet and this ensures fine control of the idle mixture. A number of progression drillings provide enrichment as they are uncovered by the opening throttle during initial acceleration *(see illustration)*.

6 The idle speed is set by an adjustable screw. This screw is tamper proofed during production, in accordance with emission regulations.

Idle cut-off valve

7 An idle cut-off valve is used to prevent run-on when the engine is shut down. It utilises a 12-volt solenoid plunger to block the idle channel when the ignition is switched off.

8 The device is also controlled by an electronic fuel cut-off control unit, so that during deceleration from high engine speeds with a closed throttle, the fuel supply to the engine is cut off. This results in a fuel saving and improved emissions. Once the engine speed falls below 1800 rpm or the throttle is opened, the control unit reactivates the solenoid and normal idle fuel flow is restored.

9 Wiring of the control unit varies slightly according to model. The wiring terminals at the control unit are standard but the battery supply may be from the coil positive (+) terminal or direct from the ignition switch via a thermal switch. In the latter case, the fuel cut-off will not operate until normal operating temperature is reached. On applications with an ignition ECU, the connection from terminal 2 to the coil negative terminal (-) is made via the ignition ECU.

Positive crankcase ventilation

10 This system allows engine breather fumes to be drawn back into the engine to be re-burnt. Fumes from the engine breather outlet are conveyed by tube to a spigot on the carburettor body. A passage originating from the engine side of the throttle plate is connected to the spigot. At idle and low engine speeds, the fumes are drawn through a calibrated bush. As the throttle is opened, a disc connected to the throttle spindle rotates to open a groove. The greater volume of engine fumes produced during high-speed engine operation is thus accommodated.

Accelerator pump

11 The DMTE accelerator pump is controlled by a diaphragm and is mechanically operated by a lever and cam attached to the primary throttle linkage. The outlet valve is incorporated into the pump injector. The inlet valve consists of a ball valve located in a channel from the float chamber. Excess fuel and air is returned to the float chamber through a separate fuel channel *(see illustration)*.

Main circuit

12 The amount of fuel discharged into the airstream is controlled by a calibrated main jet. The main jet and air corrector are pushed into opposite ends of an emulsion tube and the assembly is placed into a vertical well which dips down into the fuel. Fuel from the float chamber is drawn through the main jet into the well to be mixed with air drawn in through the air corrector and through the holes in the emulsion tube. The resulting emulsified mixture is discharged from the main nozzle through an auxiliary venturi.

Secondary action

13 Once the primary throttle valve is about two-thirds-open, the secondary throttle plate

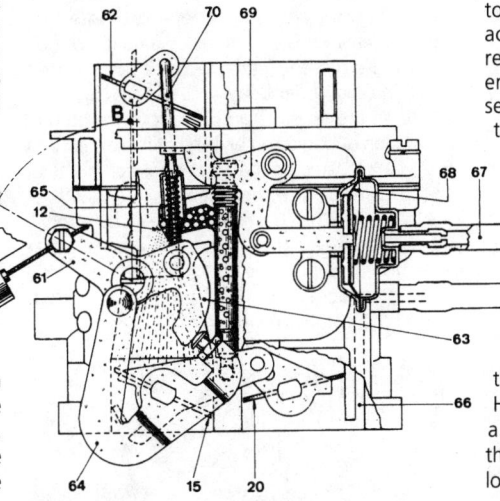

Accelerator pump circuit

5 Float chamber
52 Pump cam
53 Pump actuating lever
54 Diaphragm
55 Fuel outlet channel
56 Outlet ball
57 Pump injector nozzle
58 Spring
59 Spring
60 Inlet ball

will begin to open. At full-throttle, the linkage is arranged so that both throttle plates will be fully open.

14 A progression jet is used to prevent hesitation as the secondary throttle plate begins to open. This jet is similar in construction and action to the primary idle jet and is often referred to as the secondary idle jet. An emulsified mixture is discharged into the secondary venturi via progression drillings, at the initial opening of the secondary throttle plate. Once the secondary throttle plate has opened, the action of the secondary main circuit is similar to the primary circuit.

15 At full-load and high engine speeds, even more fuel is required. The velocity of air creates a depression sufficient to raise fuel from the float chamber into a channel. Fuel then passes through a calibrated bushing to the upper section of the secondary air intake. Here it is mixed with a small amount of air from a calibrated air bleed. The emulsified mixture is then discharged into the airstream from a full-load enrichment outlet placed in the barrel.

Manual choke operation

12 Main fuel outlet
15 Throttle valve (primary)
20 Throttle valve (secondary)
61 Choke actuating lever
62 Choke flap
63 Cam
64 Fast idle lever
65 Spring
66 Vacuum passage
67 Vacuum hose
68 Diaphragm
69 Pull-down fulcrum lever
70 Link rod

Choke operation

16 The manual choke is operated by a dash-mounted cable. When the cable is pulled, it operates a lever that pulls the choke flap closed across the primary air intake. Fast idle is achieved with the aid of a curved cam attached to the choke operating lever. An adjustable screw, attached to the throttle lever and butting against the cam, is used to vary the fast idle speed *(see illustration)*.

17 Once the engine has fired, the choke flap must open slightly to weaken the mixture and avoid flooding during idle and light-throttle operation. This is achieved by using manifold vacuum to actuate a diaphragm. A fulcrum lever, attached to the diaphragm lever, will then push upon the control link connected to the choke flap.
18 During engine warm-up, the cable should be progressively pushed home until the choke flap is fully open.

2 Identification

The Weber identification code is stamped on the carburettor base flange.

3 General servicing

Introduction

1 Read this Chapter in conjunction with Part B, which describes some of the operations in more detail. It is assumed that the carburettor is removed for this service. However, many of the operations can be tackled with the carburettor in place. Where this is undertaken, first soak the fuel out of the float chamber using a clean tissue or soft cloth, after removing the upper body assembly.

Dismantling and checking

2 Remove the carburettor from the engine (see Part B).
3 Check visually for damage and wear.
4 Use a small screwdriver to prise the spring-loaded end of the choke operating link from the choke operating lever *(see illustration)*.
5 Remove the two circlips and pull away the pull-down fulcrum lever from the upper body and the diaphragm assembly *(see illustration)*.
6 Remove the six screws and detach the carburettor upper body.
7 Use a straight-edge to check for distorted flanges on all facing surfaces.
8 Inspect the float chamber for corrosion and calcium build-up.
9 Tap out the float pin and remove the float, needle valve, clip and needle valve seat. Recover the float chamber gasket.
10 Check that the anti-vibration ball is free in the valve end.
11 Check the needle valve tip for wear and ridges. This is more likely with the brass needle valve tip than when a viton one is used. Use a viton-tipped replacement when possible.
12 The float should be checked for damage and ingress of petrol.
13 Renew the float pin if it shows signs of wear.
14 Remove the hexagon bolt and inspect the fuel filter. Clean any debris and dirt from the filter chamber.
15 Remove the mixture screw and inspect the tip for damage or ridges.
16 Remove the four screws and detach the accelerator pump housing, diaphragm and spring. Check the diaphragm for fatigue and damage.
17 The pump injector is a push fit in the body. Carefully prise it from its location and test it by shaking. No noise from the outlet ball indicates that the valve is seized.
18 Remove the primary and secondary idle jet assemblies, main jets, air correctors and emulsion tubes.
19 Check that the channel from the float chamber into the emulsion tube well is clear.
20 The idle jets are pushed into a holder and may be separated (by pulling) for cleaning or renewal. Likewise, the main jets and air correctors are pushed into the opposite ends of the emulsion tubes and may also be separated (by pulling) for cleaning or renewal. Note that the idle jet and the main jet assemblies can be removed from the carburettor body without removing the upper body.
21 Note the jet sizes and locations for correct installation during assembly. The primary main and idle jet are located on the accelerator pump side of the carburettor. The secondary main and idle jet are located on the choke side of the carburettor.
22 Check the jet calibration against that specified. It is possible that the jets may have been transposed (or the wrong size fitted) during the last overhaul.
23 Remove the primary and secondary auxiliary venturis where necessary. A Weber extractor tool is available for this purpose. Check that the primary and secondary auxiliary venturis are not loose in the main body as this is a source of uneven running. If a venturi is loose, knurl the mating flanges with a file to ensure a tight fit.
24 Inspect the choke spindle, mechanism and levers for stickiness and wear.
25 Attach a vacuum pump to the pull-down diaphragm and operate the pump to obtain 300 mm Hg. Renew the diaphragm assembly if it does not fully operate or if vacuum is not maintained for 10 seconds *(see illustration)*.
26 Remove the two screws and detach the manual choke pull-down assembly.

Preparation for reassembly

27 Clean the jets, carburettor body assemblies, float chamber and internal channels. An air line may be used to clear internal channels once the carburettor is fully dismantled. Note that if high-pressure air is directed into the channels and passages with the diaphragms still in place, diaphragm damage may result.
28 Spraying carburettor cleaner into all the channels and passages in the carburettor body will often clear them of gum and dirt.
29 During reassembly, a complete set of new gaskets should be fitted. Also renew the needle valve and float pin, and all diaphragms.
30 Inspect and renew (where necessary) the mixture screw, main jets, idle jets, air corrector jets and accelerator pump injector. Renew worn screws, linkages, springs and other parts where necessary.
31 Ensure that all jets are firmly locked into their original positions (but do not over-tighten). A loose jet can cause a rich (or even lean) running condition.
32 Clean all mating surfaces and flanges of old gasket material and reassemble with new gaskets.
33 Ensure that housings are positioned with their air and fuel routes correctly aligned.

Reassembly

34 Refit the choke pull-down diaphragm assembly and secure with the two screws.
35 Check that the secondary throttle plate is fully closed. The adjustment screw should not normally be used to alter the throttle plate position. However, if necessary, it can be

Using small screwdriver to prise spring-loaded end of choke operating link from choke operating lever

Remove circlips (1) and pull away fulcrum lever from upper body
2 Pull-down diaphragm retaining screws

Use of a vacuum pump to test pull-down diaphragm

Weber 30 & 30/32 DMTE carburettor

adjusted so that the plate is open just enough to prevent its seizure in the throttle body.

36 Ensure that the air correctors and main jets are pushed fully into the emulsion tubes. Refit the assemblies into their original positions in the carburettor body (do not transpose the jets).

37 Ensure that the idle jets are pushed fully into the holders. Refit into their original positions in the carburettor body (do not transpose the jets).

38 Refit the idle cut-off valve. Use a new seal.

39 Push the pump injector firmly into position after renewing the small seal on the injector body.

40 Refit the accelerator pump spring, diaphragm and cover assembly, then secure with the four screws.

41 Refit the idle mixture screw. Turn the screw in gently, until it just seats. From this position, unscrew it three full turns. This will provide a basic setting to allow the engine to be started.

42 Clean or renew the fuel filter and secure with the hexagon bolt.

43 Fit a new float gasket to the upper body.

44 Renew the needle valve assembly. Screw the valve seat into the upper body using a new sealing washer and ensure that it is firmly locked into position (do not over-tighten). Transfer the hairpin or plastic clip from the old needle valve to the ball end of the new one. Place the clip and valve assembly onto the inner float tag. Lower the float and needle valve assembly into the seat and secure with the float pin. Adjust the float level. Refer to Section 4 for details on float adjustment.

45 Refit the upper body and secure with the six screws.

46 Refit the pull-down fulcrum lever and two circlips to the upper body and diaphragm assembly.

47 Use a small screwdriver or pliers to refit the spring-loaded end of the choke link rod into the choke operating lever.

48 Ensure that the choke flap and linkage move smoothly and progressively.

49 Adjust the choke fast idle and the choke vacuum pull-down. Refer to Section 4 for details on all adjustments.

50 Refit the carburettor to the engine.

51 Always adjust the carburettor idle speed and mixture after any work has been carried out on the carburettor, preferably with the aid of a CO meter.

4 Service adjustments

Adjustment preconditions

1 Refer to Part B for general advice on the preconditions to correct adjustment of this carburettor.

Idle speed and mixture (CO)

2 Run the engine at 3000 rpm for 30 seconds to clear the manifold of fuel vapours, then allow the engine to idle.

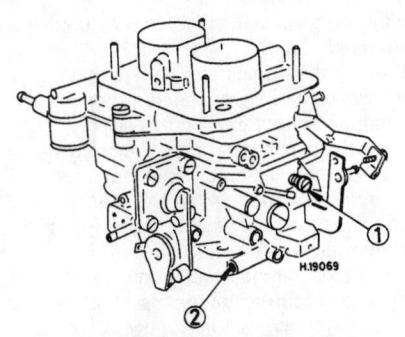

Idle speed and mixture adjustment
1 Idle speed adjustment screw
2 Idle mixture control screw

3 Use the idle speed adjustment screw to set the specified idle speed (see illustration).

4 Check the CO level. If it is not as specified, remove the tamperproof plug and adjust the idle mixture control screw to achieve the correct level. Turning the screw clockwise (inwards) will reduce the CO level. Turning the screw anti-clockwise (outwards) will increase the CO level.

5 Repeat paragraphs 3 and 4 until both adjustments are correct.

6 Clear the manifold every 30 seconds during the setting operation by running the engine at 3000 rpm for 30 seconds.

7 Increase the speed to 2000 rpm, and note the CO reading. The cruise reading should be less than half the idle CO reading.

8 Fit a new tamperproof plug to the mixture adjustment screw.

Float level/stroke

9 Hold the upper body in a vertical position with the float tag gently touching the ball of the fully-closed needle valve.

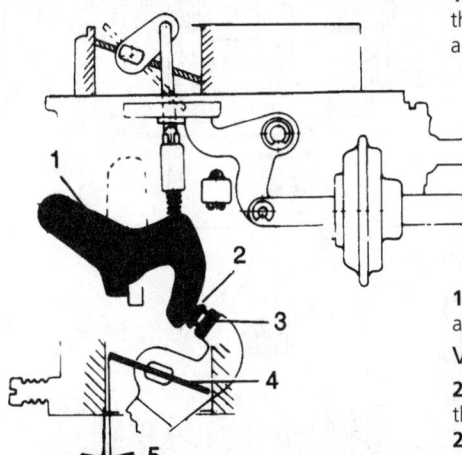

Fast idle adjustment
1 Choke actuating lever
2 Fast idle adjustment screw
3 Locknut
4 Primary throttle plate
5 Fast idle clearance

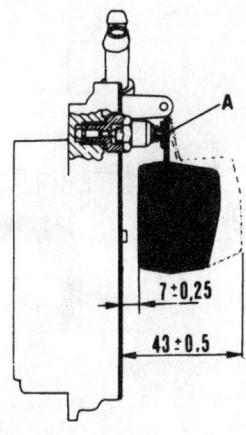

Float level adjustment
A Inner float tag

10 Measure the distance between the upper body (complete with gasket) and the top of the float (see illustration).

11 Adjust as necessary, by bending the inner float tag.

12 Place the upper body in a horizontal position and allow the float to hang down.

13 Measure the distance between the upper body (gasket in place) and the bottom of the float. The maximum stroke should be 43 ± 0.5 mm.

14 Adjust as necessary, by bending the outer float tag.

Choke adjustments

Fast idle

15 The carburettor must be removed from the engine in order to make the fast idle adjustment.

16 Invert the carburettor.

17 Pull the choke operating arm to fully close the choke flap. The adjustment screw will butt against the fast idle cam and force open the throttle plate to leave a small clearance (see illustration).

18 Use the shank of a twist drill to measure the clearance between the wall of the throttle bore and the throttle plate. Refer to Specifications for the required drill size and measure the clearance from the progression holes.

19 Adjust as necessary by turning the adjustment screw in the appropriate direction.

Vacuum pull-down

20 Pull the choke operating arm to fully close the choke flap.

21 Use a vacuum pump to pull the diaphragm operating rod up to its stop (or push the mechanism with a small screwdriver). At the same time, use the shank of a twist drill to measure the gap between the lower section of the choke flap and the air intake. Refer to Specifications for the required drill size.

22 Adjust as necessary by turning the pull-down adjustment screw (located upon the main

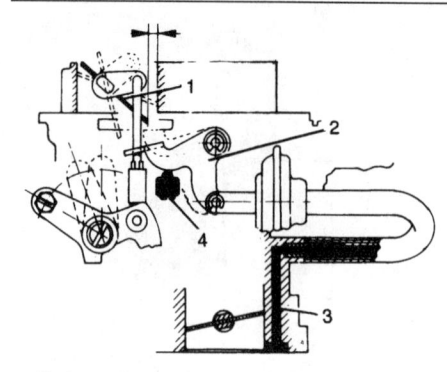

Chapter H7

Pull-down adjustment
1 Choke flap
2 Pull-down fulcrum lever
3 Vacuum passage
4 Adjustment screw

body) in the appropriate direction (see illustration).

23 Allow the engine to idle. The diaphragm lever should be fully operated. If not, attach a vacuum pump to the pull-down diaphragm and operate the pump to obtain 300 mm Hg. Renew the diaphragm assembly if it does not fully operate or if vacuum is not maintained for 10 seconds. Check the vacuum hose for fatigue and splits.

24 If the diaphragm operation is satisfactory, attach a vacuum gauge to the vacuum connection on the carburettor body. If a reading of 425 to 525 mm Hg is not obtained, check the carburettor vacuum passage for a blockage. If the carburettor is removed from the engine, check that the vacuum passage in the carburettor is clear in the following way:

25 Invert the carburettor and attach a vacuum pump to the vacuum outlet in the base. It should be possible to build a vacuum to operate the pull-down diaphragm fully.

5 Component testing

Electronic cut-off system

1 Connect a test lamp from the battery positive (+) connection to the throttle switch (see illustrations).
2 Turn the ignition on and the lamp should light and remain brightly on without flickering.
3 Start the engine and raise the speed to over 3000 rpm. The lamp should remain brightly on without flickering.
4 Decelerate the engine, closing the throttle completely. Below 3000 rpm, the lamp should switch off and then relight as the speed falls below 1600 to 1700 rpm.

Cut-off system fault diagnosis

5 If the lamp flickers or dims, check the connection to the throttle switch.
6 If the lamp does not light, check the wiring continuity and connections between the control unit, throttle switch and idle cut-off valve. Also check the control unit for a positive supply to pin number 7 and the earth at pin number 3.
7 If the lamp does not switch off, check the wiring continuity and connections between the coil and control unit pin number 2.
8 If all the connections are satisfactory yet the idle cut-off operation is unsatisfactory, suspect the ECU. Test the ECU by substitution but only after all the connections have been thoroughly checked.
9 It is possible to bypass the idle cut-off system by bridging pin numbers 6 and 7 at the control unit. All the wires can still remain connected to the control unit. Engine and fuel system operation will not be impaired by this procedure but fuel consumption may be (slightly) adversely affected.

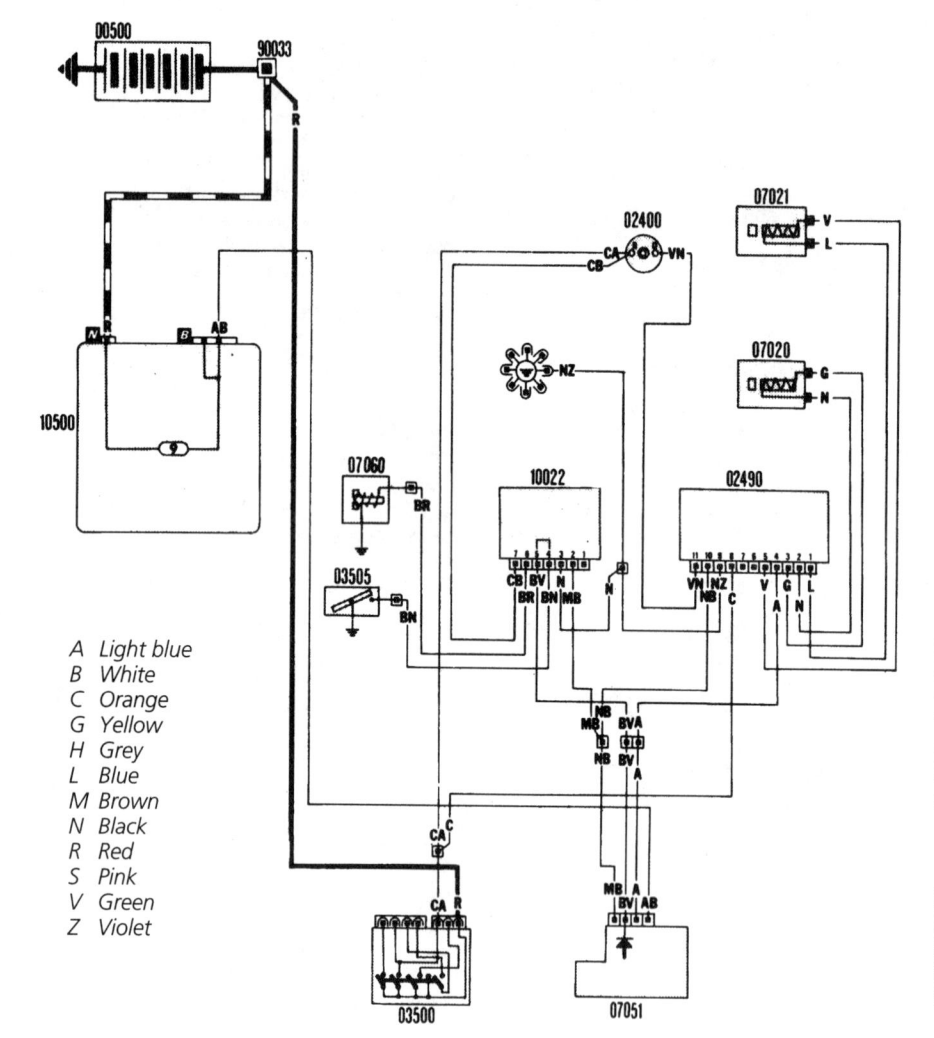

6 Fault diagnosis

Refer to Part D for diagnosis of general carburettor faults. The following faults are specific to Weber DMTE carburettors.

Poor cold starting
☐ The plastic clip into which the lower end of the choke link rod fits sometimes breaks.
☐ Failure of the choke pull-down diaphragm.

A Light blue
B White
C Orange
G Yellow
H Grey
L Blue
M Brown
N Black
R Red
S Pink
V Green
Z Violet

Supplementary wiring diagram - idle cut-off valve and associated accessories

00500 Battery
02400 Ignition coil
02490 Ignition control unit
03500 Ignition switch
03505 Throttle switch
07020 Engine speed sensor
07021 TDC sensor
07051 Economy meter
07060 Idle cut-off valve
10022 Idle cut-off valve electronic control unit
10500 Fusebox
90033 Connector block

Weber 30 & 30/32 DMTE carburettor

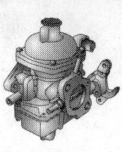

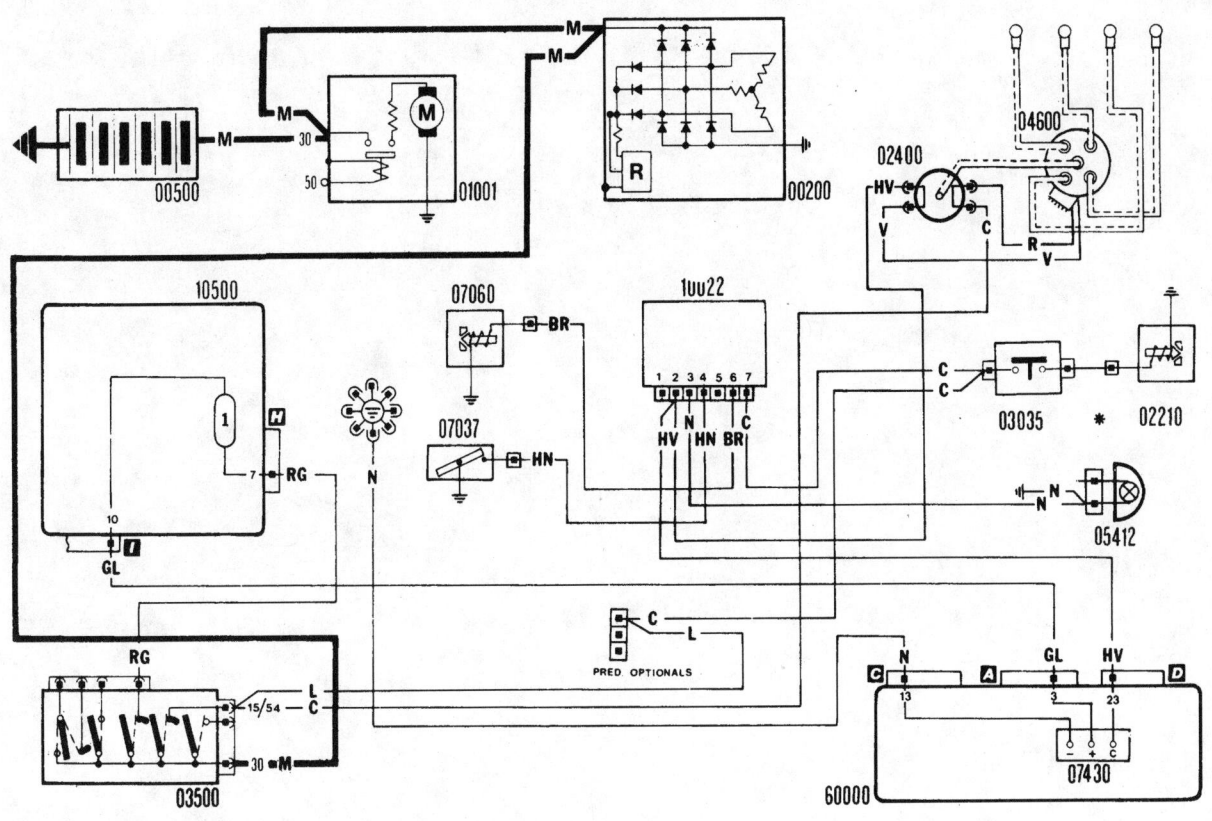

Alternative supplementary wiring diagram - idle cut-off valve and associated accessories

00200 Alternator and regulator	04600 Ignition distributor	A Light blue	M Brown
00500 Battery	05412 RH front direction indicator	B White	N Black
01001 Starter motor	07037 Throttle valve cut-off switch	C Orange	R Red
02210 Accelerator pump cut-out (some models)	07060 Idle cut-off switch	G Yellow	S Pink
02400 Ignition coil	07430 Tachometer	H Grey	V Green
03035 Thermal switch	10022 Idle cut-off switch control unit	L Blue	Z Violet
03500 Ignition switch	10500 Fusebox		
	60000 Instruments		

H7•9

Notes

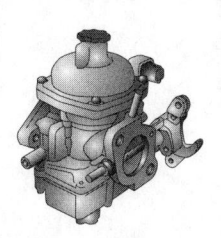

Part H Chapter 8
Weber 32/34 DMTL carburettor

H8

Contents

Fault diagnosis 5	Principles of operation 1
General servicing 3	Service adjustments 4
Identification 2	

Specifications

Manufacturer	Land Rover		Land Rover		Land Rover	
Model	90		110		90 & 110	
Year	1983 to 1986		1983 to 1986		1985 to 1990	
Engine code	OHV		OHV		OHV	
Capacity (cm^3)/no. of cyls	2286/4		2286/4		2495/4	
Oil temperature (°C)	80		80		80	
Carb. identification	32/34 DMTL 1		32/34 DMTL 1/101		32/34 DMTL 6/101	
Idle speed (rpm)	650 ± 50		650 ± 50		650 ± 50	
CO @ idle (% vol.)	1.25 ± 0.75		1.25 ± 0.75		1.25 ± 0.75	
Stage (venturi)	1	2	1	2	1	2
Venturi diameter	24	25	24	25	24	25
Idle jet	55	60	55	60	52	60
Main jet	110	115	110	115	112	112
Air correction jet	160	160	160	160	160	190
Emulsion tube	F30	F30	F30	F30	F30	F39
Accel. pump jet	40		40		40	
Float level (mm)	7 ± 0.25		7 ± 0.25		7 ± 0.25	
Needle valve size (mm)	1.75		1.75		1.75	
Choke fast idle gap (mm)	1.5 ± 0.05		1.5 ± 0.05		1.7 ± 0.05	
Choke pull-down (mm)	3.5 ± 0.25		3.5 ± 0.25		5 ± 0.25	

Chapter H8

1 Principles of operation

Introduction

1 The following technical description of the Weber DMTL carburettor should be read in conjunction with the more detailed description of carburettor principles in Part A.

Construction

2 The Weber 32/34 DMTL carburettor is a downdraught, progressive twin venturi instrument *(see illustration)*. The venturis are arranged so that the secondary throttle valve will not begin to open until the primary throttle valve is two-thirds-open. The choke control is manual in operation. The throttle shafts are made of steel and the throttle valves of brass. All the emulsion tubes and jets are manufactured from brass, with the exception of the accelerator pump injector which is die-cast. The internal fuel channels and air passages are drilled and sealed with lead plugs where necessary.

Fuel control

3 Fuel flows into the carburettor through a fine mesh filter. The fuel level in the float chamber is controlled by a needle valve and brass float assembly. An anti-vibration ball is incorporated into the needle valve design. A plastic or hairpin clip, attached to the needle valve seat and to the float arm, prevents the needle from sticking in the seat as the fuel level drops *(see illustration)*.

4 The float chamber is vented internally to the clean-air side of the air filter. A calibrated fuel return system is provided to ensure that relatively cool fuel is supplied to the carburettor.

Idle, slow running and progression

5 Fuel, sourced from the main well, passes into the primary idle channel through a metered idle jet. Here it is mixed with a small amount of air from a calibrated air bleed. The resulting emulsion is drawn through a channel to be discharged from the idle orifice under the primary throttle plate. A tapered mixture screw is used to vary the outlet and this ensures fine control of the idle mixture. A number of progression drillings provide enrichment as they are uncovered by the opening throttle during initial acceleration *(see illustration)*.

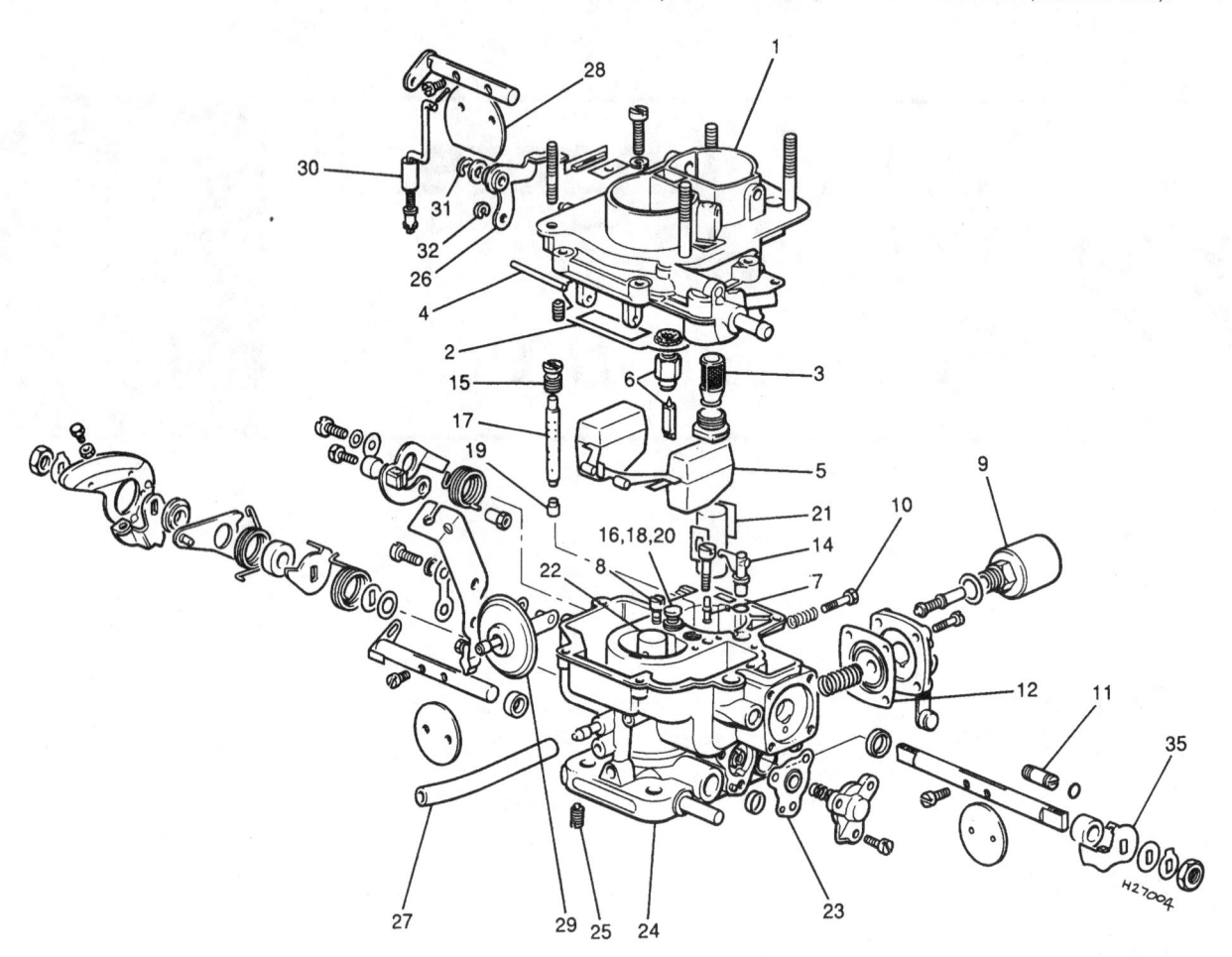

Weber DMTL carburettor

1 Upper body
2 Float chamber gasket
3 Fuel inlet filter
4 Float pin
5 Float
6 Needle valve assembly
7 Idle jet (primary)
8 Idle jet (secondary)
9 Idle cut-off valve (where fitted)
10 Idle speed adjustment screw
11 Idle mixture control screw
12 Accelerator pump diaphragm
14 Pump injector
15 Air corrector (primary)
16 Air corrector (secondary)
17 Emulsion tube (primary)
18 Emulsion tube (secondary)
19 Main jet (primary)
20 Main jet (secondary)
21 Auxiliary venturi (primary)
22 Auxiliary venturi (secondary)
23 Power valve diaphragm
24 Main body
25 Secondary throttle valve adjustment screw
26 Pull-down fulcrum lever
27 Vacuum hose
28 Choke flap
29 Choke diaphragm
30 Choke link rod
31 Circlip
32 Circlip
35 Pump cam

Weber 32/34 DMTL carburettor

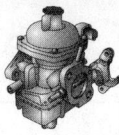

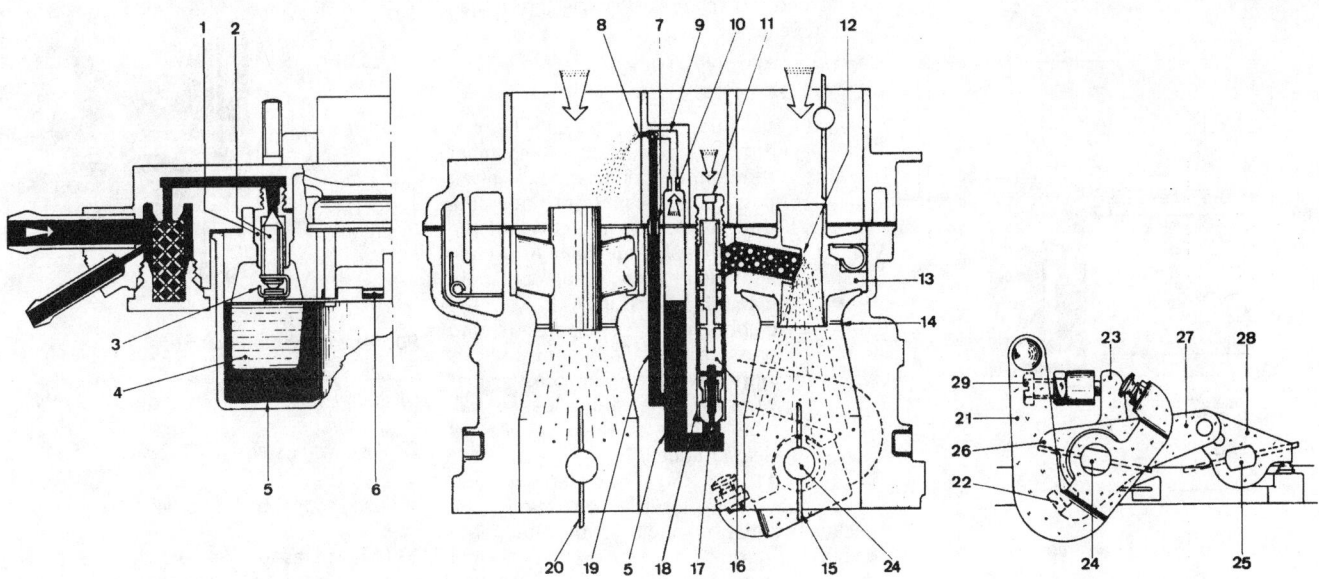

Inlet, main and full-load fuel circuits

1 Needle valve seat
2 Needle valve
3 Needle valve clip
4 Float
5 Float chamber
6 Float pin
7 Full-load calibrated bush
8 Full-load outlet
9 Air passage
10 Air bleed
11 Air corrector
12 Main fuel outlet
13 Auxiliary venturi
14 Main venturi
15 Throttle valve (primary)
16 Emulsion tube
17 Main jet
18 Main well
19 Full-load fuel channel
20 Throttle valve (secondary)
21 Throttle control lever
22 Tab
23 Throttle stop
24 Throttle spindle (primary)
25 Throttle spindle (secondary)
26 Lug
27 Throttle lever
28 Secondary throttle lever
29 Idle adjustment screw

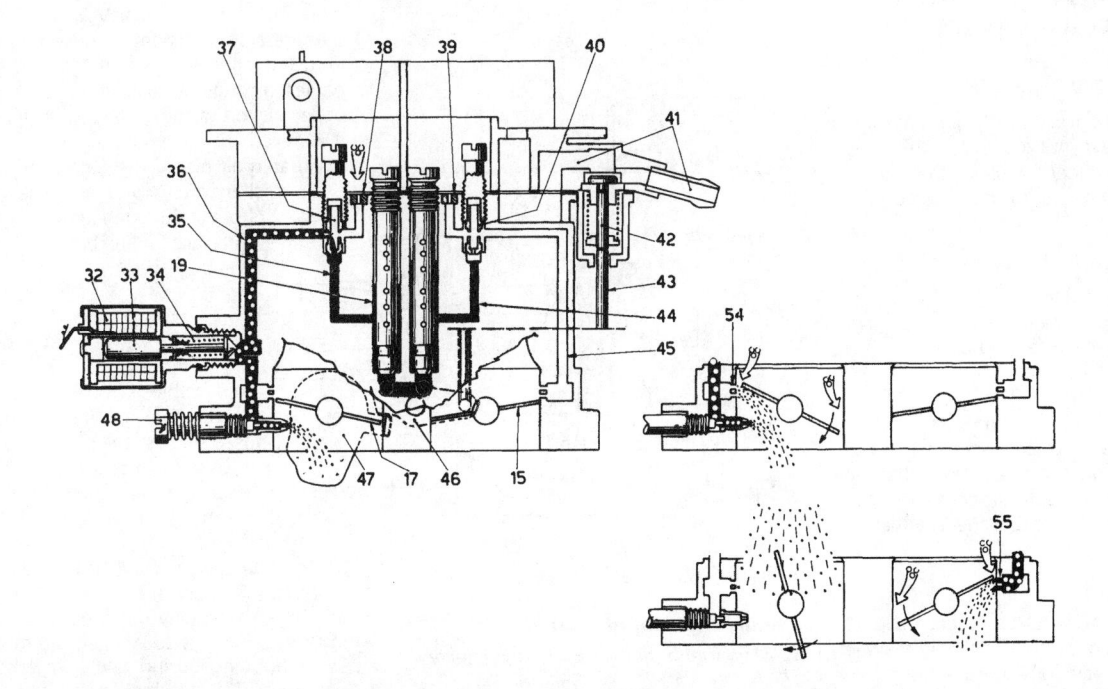

Idle and progression circuits (primary and secondary)

15 Throttle valve (secondary)
17 Throttle valve (primary)
19 Main well
32 Idle cut-off valve
33 Plunger
34 Spring
35 Idle fuel channel
36 Idle fuel/air channel
37 Idle jet (primary)
38 Air bleed
39 Air bleed
40 Idle jet (secondary)
41 Float chamber vents
42 Vent valve
43 Vent rod
44 Idle fuel channel
45 Idle fuel/air channel
46 Lever
47 Lever
48 Idle mixture control screw
54 Progression outlet (primary)
55 Progression outlet (secondary)

H8•3

Chapter H8

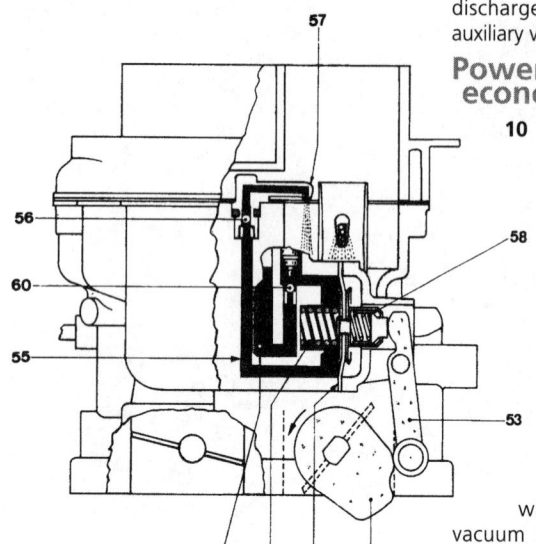

discharged from the main nozzle through an auxiliary venturi.

Power enrichment and economy circuit

10 Fuel flows from the float chamber into the power valve chamber through a fuel channel. An air passage is taken from under the throttle plate to the cover of the power diaphragm chamber. At idle and during light-throttle operation, manifold vacuum draws the diaphragm back against spring pressure. The diaphragm pintle is withdrawn from the brass outlet valve and the spring-loaded ball seats to close off the outlet channel *(see illustration)*.

11 Under acceleration and wide-open throttle operation, the vacuum in the manifold is depleted. The diaphragm returns under spring pressure and the power diaphragm pintle pushes the ball to open the outlet valve. Fuel then flows through the valve and a calibrated jet to supplement the fuel in the primary main well. The fuel level rises in the well and the fuel mixture is enriched.

Secondary action

12 Once the primary throttle valve is about two-thirds-open, the secondary throttle plate will begin to open. At full-throttle, the linkage is arranged so that both throttle plates will be fully open.

13 A progression jet is used to prevent hesitation as the secondary throttle plate commences to open. This jet is similar in construction and action to the primary idle jet and is often referred to as the secondary idle jet. An emulsified mixture is discharged into the secondary venturi, via progression drillings, at the initial opening of the secondary throttle plate. Once the secondary throttle plate has opened, the action of the secondary main circuit is similar to the primary circuit.

14 At full-load and high engine speeds, even more fuel is required. The velocity of air creates a depression sufficient to raise fuel from the float chamber into a channel. The fuel then passes through a calibrated bushing to the upper section of the secondary air intake. Here it is mixed with a small amount of air from a calibrated air bleed. The emulsified mixture is then discharged into the airstream from a full-load enrichment outlet placed in the barrel.

Choke operation

15 The manual choke is operated by a dash-mounted cable. When the cable is pulled, it operates a lever that pulls the choke flap closed across the primary air intake. Fast idle is achieved with the aid of a curved cam attached to the choke operating lever. An adjustable screw, attached to the throttle lever and butting against the cam, is used to vary the fast idle speed *(see illustration)*.

16 Once the engine has fired, the choke flap must open slightly to weaken the mixture and avoid flooding during idle and light-throttle operation. This is achieved by using manifold vacuum to actuate a diaphragm. A fulcrum lever attached to the diaphragm lever will then push upon the control link connected to the choke flap.

17 During engine warm-up, the cable should be progressively pushed home until the choke flap is fully open.

Accelerator pump circuit

5 Float chamber
52 Pump cam
53 Pump actuating lever
54 Diaphragm
55 Fuel outlet channel
56 Outlet ball
57 Pump injector nozzle
58 Spring
59 Spring
60 Inlet ball

6 The idle speed is set by an adjustable screw. The adjustable mixture screw is tamper proofed during production, in accordance with emission regulations.

Idle cut-off valve

7 An idle cut-off valve is used to prevent run-on when the engine is shut down. It utilises a 12-volt solenoid plunger to block the idle channel when the ignition is switched off.

Accelerator pump

8 The Weber DMTL accelerator pump is controlled by a diaphragm and is mechanically operated by a lever and cam attached to the primary throttle linkage. The outlet valve is incorporated into the pump injector. The inlet valve consists of a ball valve located in a channel from the float chamber. Excess fuel and air is returned to the float chamber through a separate fuel channel *(see illustration)*.

Main circuit

9 The amount of fuel discharged into the airstream is controlled by a calibrated main jet. The main jet and air corrector are pushed into opposite ends of an emulsion tube and the assembly is placed into a vertical well which dips down into the fuel. Fuel from the float chamber is drawn through the main jet into the well, to be mixed with air drawn in through the air corrector and through the holes in the emulsion tube. The resulting emulsified mixture is

Power enrichment circuit

Gg Main jet
M   Power valve diaphragm
1   Vacuum passage
2   Spring
3   Power valve ball
4   Float chamber
5   Calibrated jet

Manual choke operation

12 Main fuel outlet
15 Throttle valve (primary)
20 Throttle valve (secondary)
61 Choke actuating lever
62 Choke flap
63 Cam
64 Fast idle lever
65 Spring
66 Vacuum passage
67 Vacuum hose
68 Diaphragm
69 Pull-down fulcrum lever
70 Link rod

Weber 32/34 DMTL carburettor

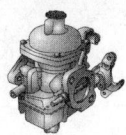

2 Identification

The Weber identification code is stamped on the carburettor base flange.

3 General servicing

Introduction

1 Read this Chapter in conjunction with Part B, which describes some of the operations in more detail. It is assumed that the carburettor is removed for this service. However, many of the operations can be tackled with the carburettor in place. Where this is undertaken, first soak the fuel out of the float chamber using a clean tissue or soft cloth, after removing the upper body assembly.

Dismantling and checking

2 Remove the carburettor from the engine (see Part B).
3 Check visually for damage and wear.
4 Use a small screwdriver to prise the spring-loaded end of the choke link rod from the choke operating lever (see illustration).
5 Remove the two circlips and pull away the pull-down fulcrum lever from the upper body and the diaphragm assembly (see illustration).
6 Remove the six screws and detach the carburettor upper body.
7 Use a straight-edge to check for distorted flanges on both facing surfaces.
8 Inspect the float chamber for corrosion and calcium build-up.
9 Tap out the float pin and remove the float, needle valve, clip and needle valve seat. Recover the float chamber gasket.
10 Check that the anti-vibration ball is free in the valve end.
11 Check the needle valve tip for wear and ridges. This is more likely with the brass needle valve tip than when a viton one is used. Use a viton-tipped replacement when possible.
12 The float should be checked for damage and ingress of petrol.
13 Renew the float pin if it shows signs of wear.
14 Remove the hexagon bolt and inspect the fuel filter. Clean any debris and dirt from the filter chamber.
15 Remove the mixture screw and inspect the tip for damage or ridges.
16 Remove the four screws and detach the accelerator pump housing, diaphragm and spring. Check the diaphragm for fatigue and damage.
17 The pump injector is a push fit in the body. Carefully prise it from its location and test it by shaking. No noise from the outlet ball indicates that the valve is seized.
18 Remove the primary and secondary idle jet assemblies, main jets, air correctors and emulsion tubes.
19 Check that the channel from the float chamber into the emulsion tube well is clear.
20 The idle jets are pushed into a holder and may be separated (by pulling) for cleaning or renewal. Likewise, the main jets and air correctors are pushed into the opposite ends of the emulsion tubes and may also be separated (by pulling) for cleaning or renewal. Note that the idle jet and the main jet assemblies can be removed from the carburettor body without removing the upper body.
21 Note the jet sizes and locations for correct installation during assembly. The primary main and idle jet are located on the accelerator pump side of the carburettor. The secondary main and idle jet are located on the choke side of the carburettor.
22 Check the jet calibration against that specified. It is possible that the jets may have been transposed (or the wrong size fitted) during the last overhaul.
23 Remove the primary and secondary auxiliary venturis where necessary. A Weber extractor tool is available for this purpose. Check that the primary and secondary auxiliary venturis are not loose in the main body as this is a source of uneven running. If a venturi is loose, knurl the mating flanges with a file to ensure a tight fit.
24 Remove the three screws and detach the power valve cover, spring and diaphragm from the body. Check the diaphragm for fatigue and damage. The brass outlet valve is cast into the body and is not removable. The ball in the outlet valve should seal the outlet. Depress and release the ball with a small screwdriver and it should move smoothly in and out. Check that the channel into the primary emulsion tube well is clear.
25 Inspect the choke spindle, mechanism and levers for stickiness and wear.
26 Attach a vacuum pump to the pull-down diaphragm and operate the pump to obtain 300 mm Hg (see illustration). Renew the diaphragm assembly if it does not fully operate or if vacuum is not maintained for 10 seconds.
27 Remove the two screws and detach the choke pull-down assembly.

Preparation for reassembly

28 Clean the jets, carburettor body assemblies, float chamber and internal channels. An air line may be used to clear internal channels once the carburettor is fully dismantled. Note that if high-pressure air is directed into the channels and passages with the diaphragms still in place, diaphragm damage may result. Spraying carburettor cleaner into all the channels and passages in the carburettor body will often clear them of gum and dirt.
29 During reassembly, a complete set of new gaskets should be fitted. Also renew the needle valve and float pin, and all diaphragms.
30 Inspect and renew (where necessary) the mixture screw, main jets, idle jets, air corrector jets and accelerator pump injector. Renew worn linkages, screws, springs and other parts where necessary.
31 Ensure that all jets are firmly locked into their original positions (but do not over-tighten). A loose jet can cause a rich (or even lean) running condition.
32 Clean all mating surfaces and flanges of old gasket material and reassemble with new gaskets.
33 Ensure that housings are positioned with their air and fuel routes correctly aligned.

Reassembly

34 Refit the choke pull-down diaphragm assembly and secure with the screws.
35 Check that the secondary throttle plate is fully closed. The adjustment screw should not normally be used to alter the throttle plate position. However, if necessary, it can be adjusted so that the plate is open just enough to prevent its seizure in the throttle body.
36 Refit the power diaphragm, spring, and cover assembly, then secure with the three screws.
37 Ensure that the air correctors and main jets are pushed fully into the emulsion tubes. Refit the assemblies into their original positions in the carburettor body (do not transpose the jets).
38 Ensure that the idle jets are pushed fully into

Using small screwdriver to prise spring-loaded end of choke operating link from choke operating lever

Remove circlips (1) and pull away fulcrum lever from upper body
2 Pull-down diaphragm retaining screws

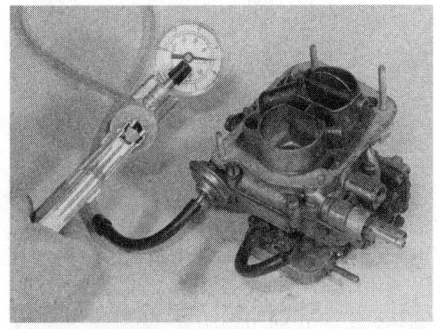

Use of vacuum pump to test pull-down diaphragm

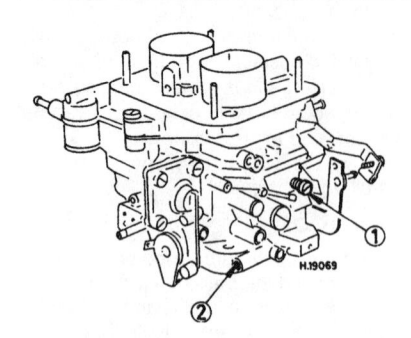

Chapter H8

Idle speed and mixture adjustment

1. Idle speed adjustment screw
2. Idle mixture control screw

the holders. Refit into their original positions in the carburettor body (do not transpose the jets).

39 Refit the idle cut-off valve, using a new seal.
40 Push the pump injector firmly into position, after renewing the small seal on the injector body.
41 Refit the accelerator pump spring, diaphragm and cover assembly, then secure with the four screws.
42 Refit the idle mixture screw. Turn the screw in gently until it just seats. From this position, unscrew it three full turns. This will provide a basic setting to allow the engine to be started.
43 Clean or renew the fuel filter and secure with the hexagon bolt.
44 Fit a new float gasket to the upper body.
45 Renew the needle valve assembly. Screw the valve seat into the upper body, using a new sealing washer, and ensure that it is firmly locked into position (but do not over-tighten). Transfer the hairpin or plastic clip from the old needle valve to the ball end of the new one. Place the clip and valve assembly onto the inner float tag. Lower the float and needle valve assembly into the seat and secure with the float pin. Refer to Section 4 for details on float adjustment.
46 Refit the upper body and secure with the six screws.
47 Refit the pull-down fulcrum lever and two circlips to the upper body and diaphragm assembly.
48 Use a small screwdriver or pliers to refit the spring-loaded end of the choke link rod into the choke operating lever.
49 Ensure that the choke flaps and linkage move smoothly and progressively.
50 Adjust the choke fast idle and the choke vacuum pull-down. Refer to Section 4 for details on all adjustments.
51 Refit the carburettor to the engine.
52 Always adjust the carburettor idle speed and mixture after any work has been carried out on the carburettor, preferably with the aid of a CO meter.

4 Service adjustments

Adjustment preconditions

1 Refer to Part B for general advice on the preconditions to correct adjustment of this carburettor.

Idle speed and mixture (CO)

2 Run the engine at 3000 rpm for 30 seconds to clear the manifold of fuel vapours, then allow the engine to idle.
3 Use the idle speed adjustment screw to set the specified idle speed (see illustration).
4 Check the CO level. If it is not as specified, remove the tamperproof plug and adjust the idle mixture control screw to achieve the correct level. Turning the screw clockwise (inwards) will reduce the CO level. Turning the screw anti-clockwise (outwards) will increase the CO level.
5 Repeat paragraphs 3 and 4 until both adjustments are correct.
6 Clear the manifold every 30 seconds during the setting operation by running the engine at 3000 rpm for 30 seconds.
7 Increase the speed to 2000 rpm and note the CO reading. The cruise reading should be less than half the idle CO reading.
8 Fit a new tamperproof plug to the mixture adjustment screw.

Float level

9 Hold the carburettor upper body in a vertical position with the float tag gently touching the ball of the fully-closed needle valve.
10 Measure the distance between the upper body (complete with gasket) and the top of the float (see illustration).
11 Adjust as necessary by bending the inner float tag.

Choke adjustments

Fast idle

12 The carburettor must be removed from the engine in order to make the fast idle adjustment.
13 Invert the carburettor.
14 Pull the choke operating arm to fully close the choke flap. The adjustment screw will butt against the fast idle cam and force open the throttle plate to leave a small clearance (see illustration).
15 Use the shank of a twist drill to measure the clearance between the wall of the throttle bore and the throttle plate. Refer to Specifications for the required drill size and measure the clearance from the progression holes.
16 Adjust as necessary by turning the adjustment screw in the appropriate direction.

Vacuum pull-down

17 Pull the choke cable to fully close the choke flap (see illustration).
18 Use a vacuum pump to pull the diaphragm operating rod up to its stop (or push the mechanism with a small screwdriver). At the same time, use the shank of a twist drill to measure the gap between the lower section of the choke flap and the air intake. Refer to Specifications for the required drill size.
19 Remove the plug in the diaphragm cover and adjust as necessary by turning the diaphragm adjustment screw in the appropriate direction. Renew the plug when adjustment is complete.

5 Fault diagnosis

Refer to Part D for diagnosis of general carburettor faults.

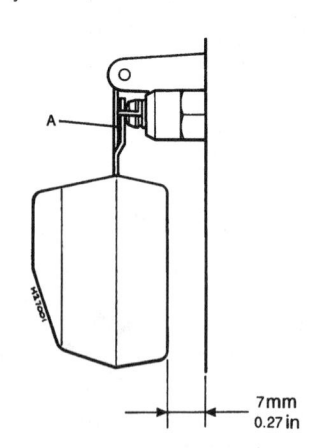

Float level adjustment
7mm
0.27 in
A Inner float tag

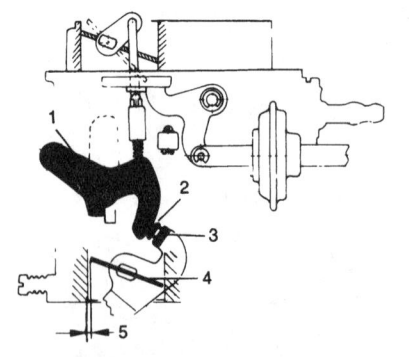

Fast idle adjustment
1 Choke actuating lever
2 Fast idle adjustment screw
3 Locknut
4 Primary throttle plate
5 Fast idle clearance

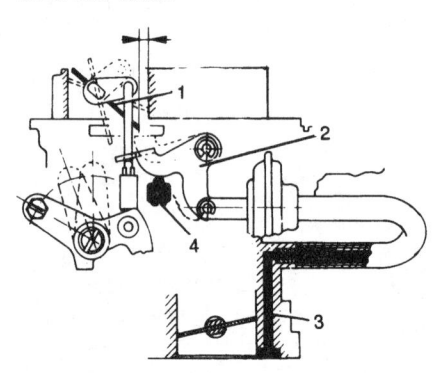

Pull-down adjustment
1 Choke flap
2 Pull-down fulcrum lever
3 Vacuum passage
4 Adjustment screw

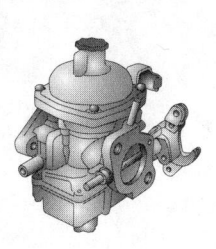

Part H Chapter 9
Weber 32 DRT carburettor

Contents

Fault diagnosis 5
General servicing 3
Identification 2
Principles of operation 1
Service adjustments 4

Specifications

Manufacturer	Renault		Renault		Renault	
Model	5 1.4 (B/C403)		5 1.4 (B/C403)		9 & 11 1.4 (L423, B/C373)	
Year	1985 to 1990		1985 to 1990		1985 to 1989	
Engine code	C2J80		C2J81		C2J7	
Capacity (cm³)/no. of cyls	1397/4		1397/4		1397/4	
Oil temperature (°C)	80		80		80	
Transmission	MT		AT		MT	
Carb. identification	32 DRT 7		32 DRT 8		32 DRT 2	
Idle speed (rpm)	700 ± 25		600 ± 25		700 ± 25	
CO @ idle (% vol.)	1.5 ± 0.5		1.5 ± 0.5		1.5 ± 0.5	
Stage (venturi)	1	2	1	2	1	2
Venturi diameter	23	24	23	24	23	24
Idle jet	52	70	52	70	52	70
Main jet	107	105	107	105	107	105
Air correction jet	220	135	220	135	220	135
Emulsion tube	F58	F56	F58	F56	F58	F56
Accel. pump jet	50		50		50	
Float level (mm)	8		8		8	
Float stroke (mm)	5		5		5	
Needle valve size (mm)	1.75		1.75		1.75	
Choke fast idle gap (mm)	0.75		0.9		0.75	
Choke pull-down (mm)	3.5		3.5		3.5	
Defuming/vent valve (mm)	0.3		0.3		0.3	

Chapter H9

Manufacturer	Renault		Renault		Renault	
Model	9 & 11 1.4 (L423, B/C373)		9 & 11 Auto 1.4 (L423, B/C373)		9 & 11 1.7 (L426, B/C376)	
Year	1985 to 1989		1985 to 1989		1984 to 1986	
Engine code	C2J7		C2JN718		F2NA700	
Capacity (cm³)/no. of cyls	1397/4		1397/4		1721/4	
Oil temperature (°C)	80		80		80	
Transmission	MT		AT		–	
Carb. identification	32 DRT 15		32 DRT 3		32 DRT 100/200	
Idle speed (rpm)	650 ± 50		650 ± 25		650 ± 25	
CO @ idle (% vol.)	1.5 ± 0.5		1.0 ± 0.5		1.5 ± 0.5	
Special conditions	–		AT in Drive		–	
Stage (venturi)	1	2	1	2	1	2
Venturi diameter	23	24	23	24	23	24
Idle jet	52	70	52	70	45	60
Main jet	110	105	107	105	105	110
Air correction jet	230	135	220	135	240	160
Emulsion tube	F58	F56	F58	F56	F58	F56
Accel. pump jet	40		50		50	
Float level (mm)	8		8		8	
Float stroke (mm)	5		5		5	
Needle valve size (mm)	1.75		1.75		1.75	
Choke fast idle gap (mm)	0.85		0.9		0.9	
Choke pull-down (mm)	3.5		3.5		8.0	
Defuming/vent valve (mm)	0.3		0.3		0.3	

Manufacturer	Renault	
Model	9 & 11 1.7 (L426, B/C376)	
Year	1984 to 1986	
Engine code	F2NA700	
Capacity (cm³)/no. of cyls	1721/4	
Oil temperature (°C)	80	
Carb. identification	32 DRT 101/201	
Idle speed (rpm)	650 ± 25	
CO @ idle (% vol.)	1.5 ± 0.5	
Stage (venturi)	1	2
Venturi diameter	23	24
Idle jet	45	60
Main jet	105	110
Air correction jet	240	160
Emulsion tube	F58	F56
Accel. pump jet	50	
Float level (mm)	8	
Float stroke (mm)	5	
Needle valve size (mm)	1.75	
Choke fast idle gap (mm)	1.00	
Choke pull-down (mm)	4	
Defuming/vent valve (mm)	0.3	

1 Principles of operation

Introduction

1 The following technical description of the Weber DRT carburettor should be read in conjunction with the more detailed description of carburettor principles in Part A.

Construction

2 The Weber DRT carburettor is a downdraught, progressive twin venturi instrument *(see illustration)*. The venturis are arranged so that the secondary throttle valve will not begin to open until the primary throttle valve is two-thirds-open. The choke control is manual in operation. The throttle shafts are made of steel and the throttle valves of brass. All the emulsion tubes and jets are manufactured from brass, with the exception of the accelerator pump injector which is die-cast. The internal fuel channels and air passages are drilled and sealed with lead plugs where necessary.

3 A heating flange is bolted to the carburettor base and hot engine coolant is piped through it. The purpose of the flange is to improve atomisation of the air/fuel mixture. The carburettor is secured to the manifold by four bolts that pass through the upper and main bodies. In conjunction with a further two screws, these bolts also fasten the upper and main body assemblies together.

Fuel control

4 Fuel flows into the carburettor through a fine mesh filter. The fuel level in the float chamber is controlled by a needle valve and brass float assembly. An anti-vibration ball is incorporated into the needle valve design. A plastic or hairpin clip, attached to the needle valve seat and to the float arm, prevents the needle from sticking in the seat as the fuel level drops.

5 The float chamber utilises a dual venting arrangement. Venting is to atmosphere at idle

Weber 32 DRT carburettor

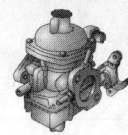

Weber DRT carburettor

1. Upper body
2. Float chamber gasket
3. Fuel inlet filter
4. Float pin
5. Float
6. Needle valve assembly
7. Idle jet (primary)
8. Idle jet (secondary)
10. Idle speed adjustment screw
11. Idle mixture control screw
12. Accelerator pump diaphragm
14. Pump injector
15. Air corrector (primary)
16. Air corrector (secondary)
17. Emulsion tube (primary)
18. Emulsion tube (secondary)
19. Main jet (primary)
20. Main jet (secondary)
21. Auxiliary venturi (primary)
22. Auxiliary venturi (secondary)
23. Power valve diaphragm (where fitted)
24. Main body
25. Secondary throttle valve adjustment screw
26. Choke housing
28. Choke flap
29. Choke diaphragm
30. Choke link rod
31. Collar
32. Defuming valve pushrod
33. Insulating block
34. Heating flange

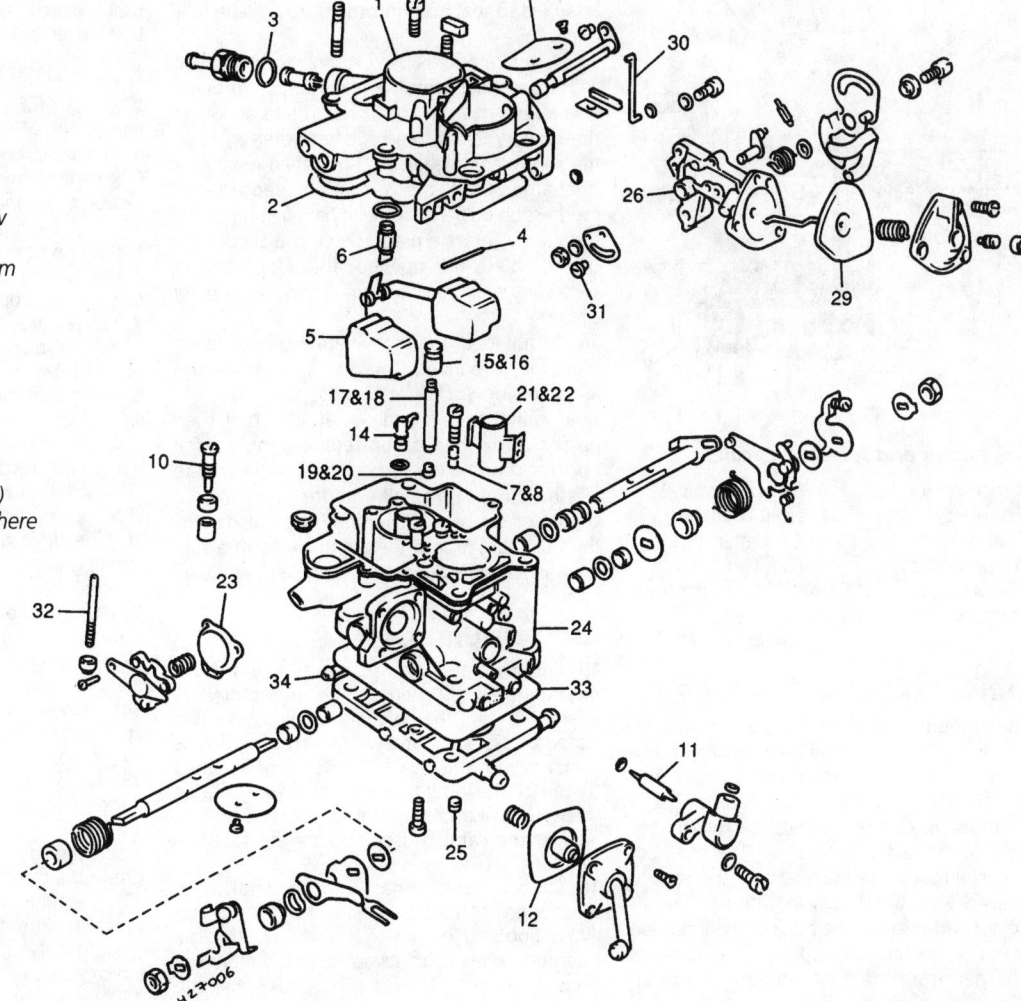

or with the engine shut down. At engine speeds above idle, a lever attached to the throttle opens a valve to the upper air intake so that the vent is to the clean-air side of the air filter. On the Weber DRT carburettor, this valve is known as a defuming valve.

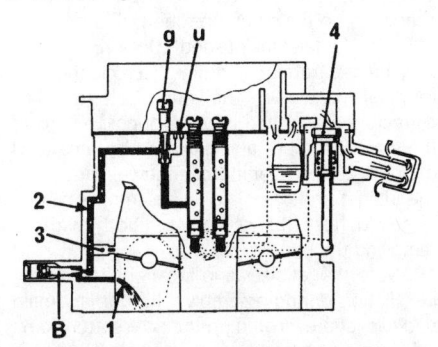

Idle, progression and defuming/vent circuits

B	Mixture screw	2	Idle fuel channel
g	Idle jet (primary)	3	Progression drilling
u	Air bleed	4	Defuming valve
1	Idle discharge		

Idle, slow running and progression

6 Fuel, sourced from the main well, passes into the primary idle channel through a metered idle jet. Here it is mixed with a small amount of air from a calibrated air bleed. The resulting emulsion is drawn through a channel to be discharged from the idle orifice under the primary throttle plate. A tapered mixture screw is used to vary the outlet and this ensures fine control of the idle mixture. A number of progression drillings provide enrichment as they are uncovered by the opening throttle during initial acceleration (see illustration).

7 The idle speed is set by an adjustable screw. The adjustable mixture screw is tamper proofed during production, in accordance with emission regulations.

Accelerator pump

8 The Weber DRT accelerator pump is controlled by a diaphragm and is mechanically operated by a lever and cam attached to the primary throttle linkage. During acceleration, fuel is pumped through a discharge valve and ball into the pump injector where it is discharged into the primary venturi. The inlet valve consists of a ball valve located in a channel from the float chamber. Excess fuel and air is returned to the float chamber through a separate fuel channel (see illustration).

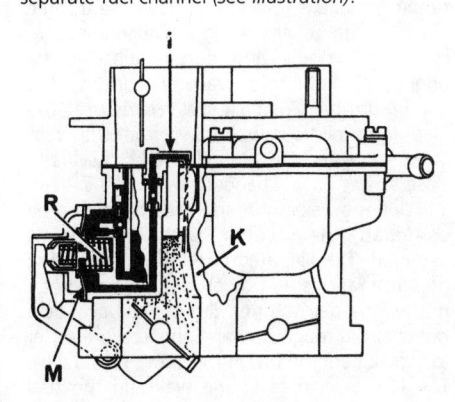

Accelerator pump circuit

| i | Pump injector nozzle | M | Diaphragm |
| K | Venturi | R | Spring |

H9•3

Chapter H9

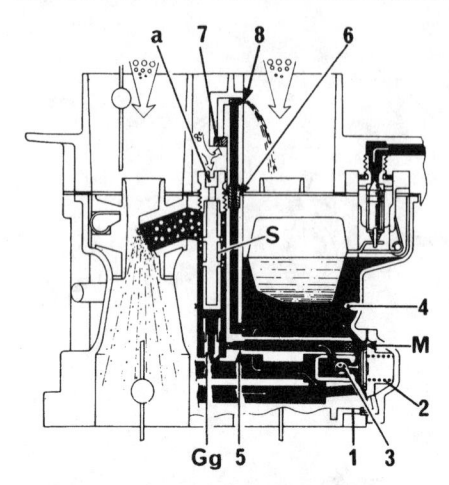

Main, power and full-load circuits

a Air corrector	3 Ball (inlet valve)
Gg Main jet	4 Float chamber
M Diaphragm	5 Calibrated bush
S Emulsion tube	6 Full-load
1 Vacuum	calibrated bush
passage	7 Air bleed
2 Spring	8 Full-load outlet

Main circuit

9 The amount of fuel discharged into the air stream is controlled by a calibrated main jet. The main jet and air corrector are pushed into opposite ends of an emulsion tube and the assembly is placed into a vertical well which dips down into the fuel. Fuel from the float chamber is drawn through the main jet into the well to be mixed with air drawn in through the air corrector and through the holes in the emulsion tube. The resulting emulsified mixture is discharged from the main nozzle through an auxiliary venturi *(see illustration)*.

Power enrichment and economy circuit (some models)

10 Fuel flows from the float chamber into the power valve chamber through a fuel channel. An air passage is taken from under the throttle plate to the cover of the power diaphragm chamber. At idle and during light-throttle operation, manifold vacuum draws the diaphragm back against spring pressure. The diaphragm pintle is withdrawn from the brass outlet valve and the spring-loaded ball seats to close off the outlet channel.

11 Under acceleration and wide-open throttle operation, the vacuum in the manifold is depleted. The diaphragm returns under spring pressure and the power diaphragm pintle pushes the ball to open the outlet valve. Fuel then flows through the valve and a calibrated jet to supplement the fuel in the primary main well. The fuel level rises in the well and the fuel mixture is enriched.

Secondary action

12 Once the primary throttle valve is about two-thirds-open, the secondary throttle plate will begin to open. At full-throttle, the linkage is arranged so that both throttle plates will be fully open.

13 A separate jet is used to prevent hesitation as the secondary throttle plate begins to open. This jet is similar in construction and action to the primary idle jet and is often referred to as the secondary idle jet. An emulsified mixture is discharged into the secondary venturi, via progression drillings, at the initial opening of the secondary throttle plate. Once the secondary throttle plate has opened, the action of the secondary main circuit is similar to the primary circuit.

14 At full-load and high engine speeds, even more fuel is required. The velocity of air creates a depression sufficient to raise fuel from the float chamber into a channel. The fuel then passes through a calibrated bushing to the upper section of the secondary air intake. Here it is mixed with a small amount of air from a calibrated air bleed. The emulsified mixture is then discharged into the airstream from a full-load enrichment outlet placed in the secondary barrel.

Choke operation

15 The manual choke is operated by a dash-mounted cable. When the cable is pulled, it operates a lever that pulls the single choke flap closed across the primary air intake. Fast idle is achieved with the aid of a curved cam attached to the choke operating lever. An adjustable screw, attached to the throttle lever and butting against the cam, is used to vary the fast idle speed.

16 Once the engine has fired, the choke flap must open slightly to weaken the mixture and avoid flooding during idle and light-throttle operation. This is achieved by using manifold vacuum to actuate a diaphragm. A linkage attached to the diaphragm will then pull upon the choke flap.

17 During engine warm-up, the cable should be progressively pushed home until the choke flap is fully open.

2 Identification

The Weber identification code is stamped on the carburettor base flange.

3 General servicing

Introduction

1 Read this Chapter in conjunction with Part B, which describes some of the operations in more detail. It is assumed that the carburettor is removed for this service. However, many of the operations can be tackled with the carburettor in place. Where this is undertaken, first soak the fuel out of the float chamber using a clean tissue or soft cloth, after removing the upper body assembly.

Dismantling and checking

2 Remove the carburettor from the engine (see Part B).
3 Check visually for damage and wear.
4 Remove the two screws and detach the carburettor upper body.
5 Use a straight-edge to check for distorted flanges on both facing surfaces.
6 Inspect the float chamber for corrosion and calcium build-up.
7 Tap out the float pin and remove the float, needle valve and clip, float chamber gasket and needle valve seat.
8 Check that the anti-vibration ball is free in the valve end.
9 Check the needle valve tip for wear and ridges. This is more likely with the brass needle valve tip than when a viton one is used. Use a viton-tipped replacement when possible.
10 The float should be checked for damage and ingress of petrol. Shaking the float will indicate the presence of fuel.
11 Renew the float pin if it shows signs of wear.
12 Unscrew the hexagon nut and inspect the fuel filter. Clean the filter housing of debris and dirt and renew the filter if necessary. In some applications, the filter is located in the inlet fuel connection.
13 Remove the mixture screw and inspect the tip for damage or ridges.
14 Remove the four screws and detach the accelerator pump cover, diaphragm and spring. Check the diaphragm for fatigue and damage.
15 The pump injector is a push fit in the body. Carefully prise it from its location and test it by shaking it. No noise from the outlet ball would indicate that the valve is seized.
16 Unscrew the primary and secondary idle jet assemblies, main jets, air correctors and emulsion tubes from their positions in the top of the main body. On some applications, the primary idle jet and holder are screwed into the outside of the carburettor body and the normal location in the top of the body is blanked off.
17 Check that the channel from the float chamber into the emulsion tube well is clear.
18 The idle jets are pushed into a holder and may be separated (by pulling) for cleaning or renewal. Likewise, the main jets and air correctors are pushed into the opposite ends of the emulsion tubes and may also be separated (by pulling) for cleaning or renewal. Note that the idle jet and the main jet assemblies can be removed from the carburettor body without removing the upper body.
19 Note the jet sizes and locations for correct installation during assembly. The primary main and idle jet are located on the accelerator pump side of the carburettor.
20 Check the jet calibration against that specified. It is possible that the jets may have been transposed (or the wrong size fitted) during the last overhaul.
21 Remove the primary and secondary auxiliary venturis where necessary. Weber provide an

Weber 32 DRT carburettor

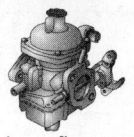

extractor tool for removing these items. Check that the primary and secondary auxiliary venturis are not loose in the main body, since loose venturis are a source of uneven running. If a venturi is loose, knurl the mating flanges with a file to ensure a tight fit.

22 Remove the three screws, slide the defuming valve pushrod downwards and detach the power valve cover, spring and diaphragm (where fitted) from the body. Although it is possible to remove this assembly in this way, access is made easier by first removing the throttle lever. Check the diaphragm for damage and fatigue. The brass outlet valve is cast into the body and is not removable. The ball in the outlet valve should seal the outlet. Depress and release the ball with a small screwdriver and it should move smoothly in and out. Check that the channel into the emulsion tube well is clear.

23 Note the position of the heating flange (where fitted) in relation to the lower carburettor flange and make alignment marks for refitting if necessary. Remove the screw and separate the heating flange from the lower carburettor flange. Use a straight-edge to check for distorted flanges on the facing surfaces.

24 Do not disturb the adjustment of the secondary throttle angle, unless absolutely necessary.

25 Inspect the choke spindle and linkage for stickiness and wear.

26 Remove the three screws, push out the lower choke link rod from the plastic retaining collar, and detach the choke housing.

27 Remove the three screws and detach the choke pull-down cover and spring from the housing. Pull the diaphragm rod from the plastic retaining collar (or remove the hairpin clip and washer) and twist and remove the diaphragm from the housing. Check the diaphragm for fatigue and renew as necessary.

Preparation for reassembly

28 Clean the jets, carburettor body assemblies, float chamber and internal channels. An air line may be used to clear internal channels once the carburettor is fully dismantled. Note that if high-pressure air is directed into the channels and passages with the diaphragms still in place, diaphragm damage may result.

29 Spraying carburettor cleaner into all the channels and passages in the carburettor body will often clear them of gum and dirt.

30 During reassembly, a complete set of new gaskets should be fitted. Also renew the needle valve and float pin, and all diaphragms.

31 Inspect and renew (where necessary) the mixture screw, main jets, idle jets, air corrector jets and accelerator pump injector. Renew worn linkages, screws, springs and other parts where necessary.

32 Ensure that all jets are firmly locked into their original positions (but do not over-tighten). A loose jet can cause a rich (or even lean) running condition.

33 Clean all mating surfaces and flanges of old gasket material and reassemble with new gaskets.

34 Ensure that housings are positioned with their air and fuel routes correctly aligned.

Reassembly

35 Refit the choke diaphragm, spring and cover assembly, then secure with the three screws. Push the end of diaphragm link rod through the operating lever and secure it with the plastic collar (or washer and hairpin clip).

36 Renew the vacuum O-ring seal, engage the choke link rod into the choke lever arm and refit the choke housing to the carburettor upper body. Secure with the three screws.

37 Check that the secondary throttle plate is fully closed. The adjustment screw should not normally be used to alter the throttle plate position. However, if necessary, it can be adjusted so that the plate is open just enough to prevent its seizure in the throttle body.

38 Assemble the heating flange to the main body with a new gasket block and secure with the one screw.

39 Refit the power diaphragm, spring and cover assembly (where used), then locate the defuming valve pushrod. Secure with the three screws. Refit the throttle lever if it was removed.

40 Ensure that the air correctors and main jets are pushed fully into the emulsion tubes. Refit the assemblies into their original positions (do not transpose the jets).

41 Ensure that the idle jets are pushed fully into their holders. Refit into their original positions (do not transpose the jets).

42 Firmly refit the pump injector after renewing the small seal on the injector body.

43 Refit the pump spring, diaphragm and cover assembly, then secure with the four screws.

44 Refit the idle mixture screw. Turn the screw in gently until it just seats. From this position, unscrew it three full turns. This will provide a basic setting to allow the engine to be started.

45 Clean or renew the fuel filter and refit the hexagon nut.

46 Fit a new float gasket to the upper body. Renew the needle valve assembly. Screw the valve seat into the upper body using a new sealing washer and ensure that it is firmly locked into position (but do not over-tighten). Transfer the hairpin or plastic clip from the old needle valve to the ball end of the new one. Place the clip and valve assembly onto the inner float tag. Lower the float and needle valve assembly into the seat and secure with the float pin.

47 Adjust the float level. Refer to Section 4 for details on adjustment.

48 Refit the upper body to the main body and secure with the two screws.

49 Ensure that the choke flap and linkage move smoothly and progressively.

50 Adjust the defuming valve, choke fast idle and vacuum pull-down. Refer to Section 4 for details on all adjustments.

51 Refit the carburettor to the engine.

52 Always adjust the carburettor idle speed and mixture after any work has been carried out on the carburettor, preferably with the aid of a CO meter.

4 Service adjustments

Adjustment preconditions

1 Refer to Part B for general advice on the preconditions to correct adjustment of this carburettor.

Idle speed and mixture (CO)

2 Run the engine at 3000 rpm for 30 seconds to clear the manifold of fuel vapours, then allow the engine to idle.

3 Remove the air filter assembly and position clear of the carburettor. If a vacuum hose is fitted, it must remain connected.

4 Use the idle speed adjustment screw to set the specified idle speed (see illustration).

5 Check the CO level. If it is not as specified, remove the tamperproof plug and adjust the idle mixture control screw to achieve the correct level. Turning the screw clockwise (inwards) will reduce the CO level. Turning the screw anti-clockwise (outwards) will increase the CO level.

6 Repeat paragraphs 4 and 5 until both adjustments are correct.

7 Clear the manifold every 30 seconds during the setting operation by running the engine at 3000 rpm for 30 seconds.

8 Increase the speed to 2000 rpm and note the CO reading. The cruise reading should be less than half the idle CO reading.

9 Fit a new tamperproof plug to the mixture adjustment screw.

10 Refit the air filter, ensuring that all vacuum hoses remain connected.

Float level/stroke

11 Hold the carburettor upper body in a vertical position with the float tag gently touching the ball of the fully-closed needle valve.

12 Measure the distance between the upper body (complete with gasket) and the top of the float (see illustration overleaf).

13 Adjust as necessary by bending the inner float tag.

14 Place the upper body in a horizontal position and allow the float to hang down.

15 Measure the distance between the upper

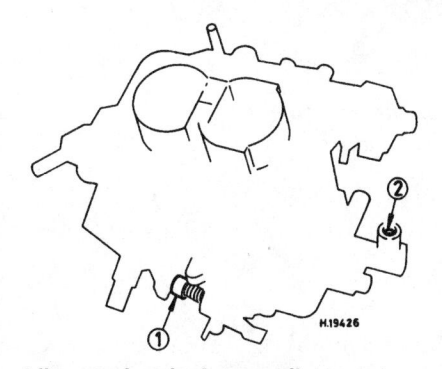

Idle speed and mixture adjustment
1 *Idle speed adjustment screw*
2 *Idle mixture control screw*

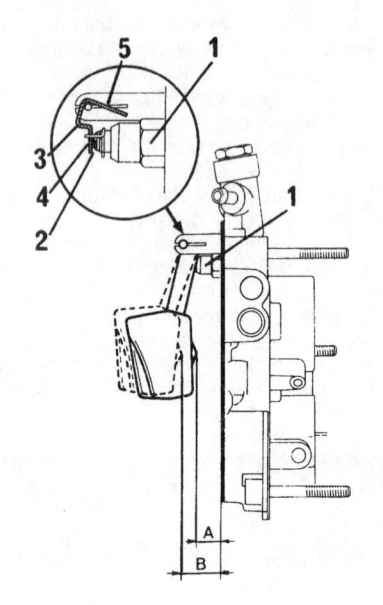

Chapter H9

Float level (A) adjustment
1 Needle valve
2 Ball
3 Float arm
4 Inner float tag
5 Outer float tag
B Float stroke

body (with the gasket in place) and the top of the float.

16 Subtract the measurement in paragraph 12 from the measurement in paragraph 15. This figure is the float stroke.

17 Adjust as necessary by bending the outer float tag.

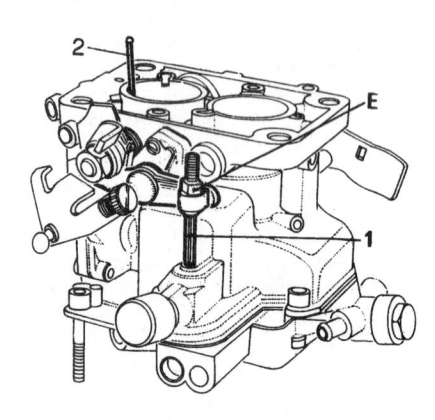

Defuming/vent valve adjustment
E Adjustment nut
1 Defuming valve operating rod
2 Twist drill

Defuming valve (float chamber vent)

18 Invert the carburettor and push the defuming valve operating rod fully downwards (towards the upper body). The throttle plate will be forced open to leave a small clearance.

19 Use the shank of a twist drill to measure the clearance between the throttle plate and the wall of the throttle bore. Refer to Specifications for the required drill size (see illustration).

20 Adjust as necessary by turning the adjustment screw in the appropriate direction.

Choke adjustments

Fast idle

21 The carburettor must be removed from the engine in order to make the fast idle adjustment.

22 Invert the carburettor.

23 Pull the choke operating arm to fully close the choke flap. The adjustment screw will butt against the fast idle cam and force open the throttle plate to leave a small clearance.

24 Use the shank of a twist drill to measure the clearance between the wall of the throttle bore and the throttle plate (see illustration). Refer to Specifications for the required drill size and measure the clearance from the progression holes.

25 Adjust as necessary by turning the adjustment screw in the appropriate direction.

Vacuum pull-down

26 Pull the choke operating arm to fully close the choke flap.

27 Use a finger to push the diaphragm operating rod up to its stop. At the same time, use the shank of a twist drill to measure the gap between the lower section of the choke flap and the air intake. Refer to Specifications for the required drill size (see illustration).

28 Remove the plug in the diaphragm cover and adjust as necessary by turning the diaphragm adjustment screw in the appropriate direction. Renew the plug after adjustment is completed.

29 Refit the air filter, ensuring that the hoses are properly connected.

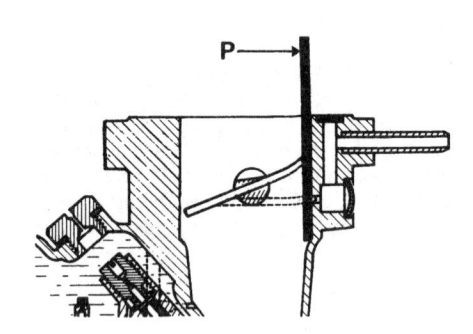

5 Fault diagnosis

Refer to Part D for diagnosis of general carburettor faults. The following faults are specific to Weber DRT carburettors.

Hesitation and poor driveability

☐ Distorted base or body flange as a result of over-tightening the carburettor mounting bolts. Distortion may occur at the flanges of the upper body, main body, or at the heater flange sections. This will cause air leaks and general poor running. Remove the gaskets and mate the two flange surfaces together. Severe or even slight distortion can now be seen. Although a gasket will take up a small amount of warping, if distortion is excessive then the carburettor is best renewed.

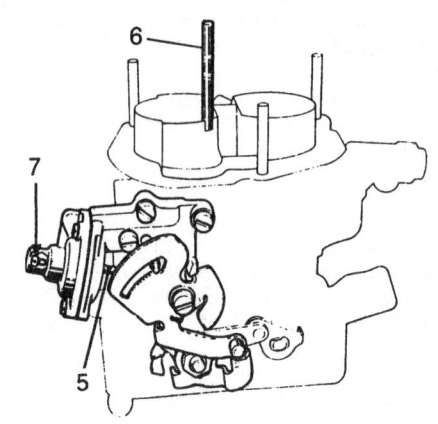

Fast idle adjustment
P Twist drill

Pull-down adjustment
5 Diaphragm operating rod
6 Twist drill
7 Adjustment screw

Part H Chapter 10
Weber 32/34 & 34 DRTC carburettor

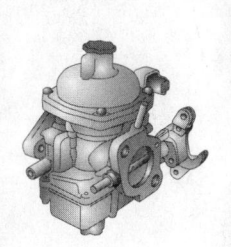

H10

Contents

Fault diagnosis 5	Principles of operation 1
General servicing 3	Service adjustments 4
Identification 2	

Specifications

Manufacturer	Citroën		Citroën		Citroën	
Model	BX16		BX16		BX16	
Year	1983 to 1984		1984 to 1988		1984 to 1988	
Engine code	171B (XU5S)		171C (XU5S)		171C (XU5S)	
Capacity (cm^3)/no. of cyls	1580/4		1580/4		1580/4	
Oil temperature (°C)	80		80		80	
Transmission	–		MT		AT	
Carb. identification	32/34 DRTC/100A		32/34 DRTC 2/100		32/34 DRTC 4/100	
Idle speed (rpm)	650 + 50		650 ± 50		650 ± 50	
CO @ idle (% vol.)	0.8 to 1.5		1.5 ± 0.5		1.5 ± 0.5	
Stage (venturi)	1	2	1	2	1	2
Venturi diameter	24	26	24	26	24	26
Idle jet	45	70	45	50	45	50
Main jet	107	115	110	112	105	112
Air correction jet	160	160	180	160	165	160
Emulsion tube	F27	F27	F27	F27	F27	F27
Accel. pump jet	55		50		50	
Float level (mm)	6.75 ± 0.25		6.75 ± 0.25		6.75 ± 0.25	
Needle valve size (mm)	1.75		1.75		1.75	
Choke pull-down (mm)	4.75		4.5		4.75	

Manufacturer	Citroën		Citroën		Peugeot	
Model	BX19		BX19		305 GT	
Year	1986 to 1990		1986 to 1990		1983 to 1988	
Engine code	D2A (159A)		D2A (159A)		XU5S (171C) (66kW)	
Capacity (cm^3)/no. of cyls	1905/4		1905/4		1580/4	
Oil temperature (°C)	80		80		80	
Transmission	MT		AT		MT	
Carb. identification	34 DRTC 12/100		34 DRTC 14/100		32/34 DRTC 4/100 or 8/100	
Idle speed (rpm)	675 ± 25		675 ± 25		700 ± 50	
CO @ idle (% vol.)	0.8 to 1.5		0.8 to 1.5		1.5 ± 0.5	
Stage (venturi)	1	2	1	2	1	2
Venturi diameter	25	27	25	27	24	26
Idle jet	52	50	47	50	45	
Main jet	110	125	110	125	105	112
Air correction jet	160	150	160	150	165	160
Emulsion tube	F45	F27	F45	F27	F27	F27
Accel. pump jet	50		50		50	
Float level (mm)	7 ± 0.25		7 ± 0.25		6.75 ± 0.25	
Needle valve size (mm)	1.75		1.75		1.75	
Choke pull-down (mm)	4.5		4.5		4.5	

Chapter H10

Manufacturer	Peugeot
Model	305 GT Automatic
Year	1983 to 1988
Engine code	XU5S (171C) (66kW)
Capacity (cm³)/no. of cyls	1580/4
Oil temperature (°C)	80
Transmission	AT
Carb. identification	32/34 DRTC 4/100 or 8/100
Idle speed (rpm)	850 ± 50
CO @ idle (% vol.)	1.5 ± 0.5

Stage (venturi)	1	2
Venturi diameter	24	26
Idle jet	45	
Main jet	105	112
Air correction jet	165	160
Emulsion tube	F27	F27
Accel. pump jet	50	
Float level (mm)	6.75 ± 0.25	
Needle valve size (mm)	1.75	
Choke pull-down (mm)	4.5	

1 Principles of operation

Introduction

1 The following technical description of the Weber DRTC carburettor should be read in conjunction with the more detailed description of carburettor principles in Part A.

Construction

2 The Weber DRTC carburettor is a downdraught, progressive twin venturi instrument *(see illustration)*. The venturis are arranged so that the secondary throttle valve will not begin to open until the primary throttle valve is two-thirds-open. The choke system is automatic in operation and is controlled by a thermostatic capsule heated by the engine coolant. The throttle shafts are made of steel. The throttle valves are made of brass, as are all the emulsion tubes and jets, with the exception of the accelerator pump injector which is die-cast. The internal fuel channels and air passages are drilled and sealed with lead plugs where necessary *(see illustration)*. The base flange contains a passage so that hot engine coolant may be piped through it. The purpose of heating the base section is to improve atomisation of the air/fuel mixture.

Fuel control

3 Fuel flows into the carburettor through a fine mesh filter. The fuel level in the float chamber is controlled by a needle valve and brass float assembly. An anti-vibration ball is incorporated into the needle valve design. A plastic or hairpin clip, attached to the needle valve seat and to the float arm, prevents the needle from sticking in the seat as the fuel level drops.

Weber DRTC carburettor

1. Upper body
2. Float chamber gasket
3. Fuel inlet filter
4. Float pin
5. Float
6. Needle valve assembly
7. Idle jet (primary)
8. Idle jet (secondary)
9. Idle cut-off valve
11. Idle mixture control screw
12. Accelerator pump diaphragm
14. Pump injector
15. Air corrector (primary)
16. Air corrector (secondary)
17. Emulsion tube (primary)
18. Emulsion tube (secondary)
19. Main jet (primary)
20. Main jet (secondary)
21. Auxiliary venturi (primary)
22. Auxiliary venturi (secondary)
23. Power valve diaphragm (where fitted)
24. Main body
25. Secondary throttle valve adjustment screw
26. Thermostatic choke assembly
28. Choke flap
29. Choke diaphragm
30. Plastic choke shield
31. Heating flange

Weber 32/34 & 34 DRTC carburettor

4 The float chamber is vented internally to the clean-air side of the air filter. A calibrated fuel return system is provided to ensure that relatively cool fuel is supplied to the carburettor.

Idle, slow running and progression

5 Fuel, sourced from the main well, passes into the primary idle channel through a metered idle jet. Here it is mixed with a small amount of air from a calibrated air bleed. The resulting emulsion is drawn through a channel to be discharged from the idle orifice under the primary throttle plate. A tapered mixture screw is used to vary the outlet and this ensures fine control of the idle mixture. A number of progression drillings provide enrichment as they are uncovered by the opening throttle during initial acceleration.

6 The idle speed is set by an adjustable screw. The adjustable mixture screw is tamper proofed during production, in accordance with emission regulations.

Idle cut-off valve

7 An idle cut-off valve is used to prevent run-on when the engine is shut down. It utilises a 12-volt solenoid plunger to block the idle channel when the ignition is switched off.

Accelerator pump

8 The Weber DRTC accelerator pump is controlled by a diaphragm and is mechanically operated by a lever and cam attached to the primary throttle linkage. The outlet valve is incorporated into the pump injector. The inlet valve consists of a ball valve located in a channel from the float chamber. Excess fuel and air is returned to the float chamber through a separate fuel channel.

Main circuit

9 The amount of fuel discharged into the airstream is controlled by a calibrated main jet. The main jet and air corrector are pushed into opposite ends of an emulsion tube and the assembly is placed into a vertical well which dips down into the fuel. Fuel from the float chamber is drawn through the main jet into the well to be mixed with air drawn in through the air corrector and through the holes in the emulsion tube. The resulting emulsified mixture is discharged from the main nozzle through an auxiliary venturi.

Power enrichment and economy circuit

10 Fuel flows from the float chamber into the power valve chamber through a fuel channel. An air passage is taken from under the throttle plate to the cover of the power diaphragm chamber. At idle and during light-throttle operation, manifold vacuum draws the diaphragm back against spring pressure. The diaphragm pintle is withdrawn from the brass outlet valve and the spring-loaded ball seats to close off the outlet channel.

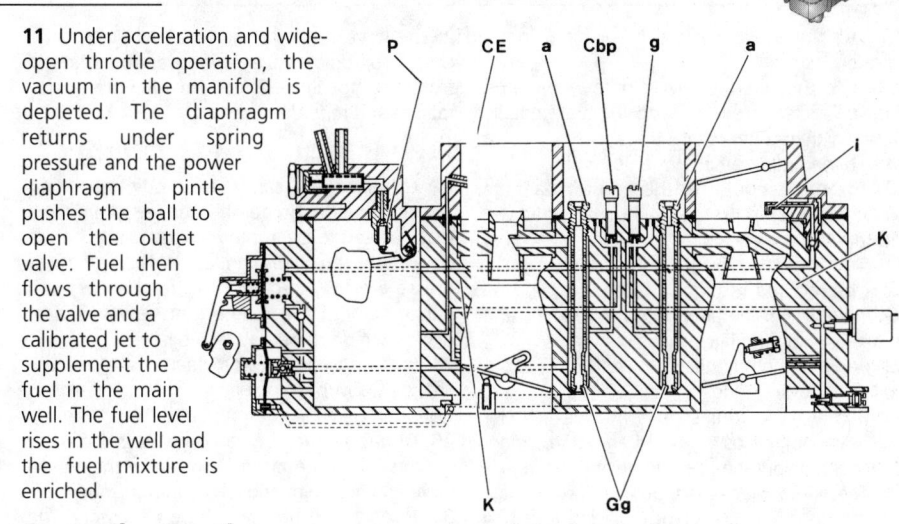

11 Under acceleration and wide-open throttle operation, the vacuum in the manifold is depleted. The diaphragm returns under spring pressure and the power diaphragm pintle pushes the ball to open the outlet valve. Fuel then flows through the valve and a calibrated jet to supplement the fuel in the main well. The fuel level rises in the well and the fuel mixture is enriched.

Secondary action

12 Once the primary throttle valve is about two-thirds open, the secondary throttle plate will begin to open. At full-throttle, the linkage is arranged so that both throttle plates will be fully open.

13 A separate jet is used to prevent hesitation as the secondary throttle plate begins to open. This jet is similar in construction and action to the primary idle jet and is often referred to as the secondary idle jet. An emulsified mixture is discharged into the secondary venturi, via progression drillings, at the initial opening of the secondary throttle plate. Once the secondary throttle plate has opened, the action of the secondary main circuit is similar to the primary circuit.

14 At full-load and high engine speeds, even more fuel is required. The velocity of air creates a depression sufficient to raise fuel from the float chamber into a channel. The fuel then passes through a calibrated bushing to the upper section of the air intake. Here it is mixed with a small amount of air from a calibrated air bleed. The emulsified mixture is then discharged into the airstream from a full-load enrichment outlet placed in the secondary barrel.

Automatic choke

15 The Weber DRTC carburettor uses an automatic choke starting system. A thermostatic capsule is used to control a strangler choke flap in the primary air intake. Heating of the capsule is by coolant from the engine cooling system.

16 Once the engine has fired, the choke flap must open slightly to weaken the mixture and avoid flooding during idle and light-throttle operation. This is achieved by using manifold vacuum to actuate a diaphragm. A linkage attached to the diaphragm will then pull upon the choke flap.

17 Fast idle is achieved when a lever with an adjustable screw butts against the capsule and pushes upon the throttle valve mechanism. As the capsule is heated and the lever released, the idle speed will progressively return to normal.

Internal fuel and air circuits

a	Air corrector	Gg	Main jet
Cbp	Idle jet (secondary)	i	Pump injector nozzle
CE	Full-load outlet	K	Venturi
g	Idle jet (primary)	P	Needle valve

2 Identification

The Weber identification code is stamped on the carburettor base flange.

3 General servicing

Introduction

1 Read this Chapter in conjunction with Part B, which describes some of the operations in more detail. It is assumed that the carburettor is removed for this service. However, many of the operations can be tackled with the carburettor in place. Where this is undertaken, first soak the fuel out of the float chamber using a clean tissue or soft cloth, after removing the upper body assembly.

Dismantling and checking

2 Remove the carburettor from the engine (see Part B).
3 Check visually for damage and wear.
4 Disconnect the choke vacuum hose, then remove the six screws and detach the carburettor upper body.
5 Use a straight-edge to check for distorted flanges on all facing surfaces.
6 Inspect the float chamber for corrosion and calcium build-up.
7 Tap out the float pin and remove the float, needle valve and clip, float chamber gasket and needle valve seat.

Chapter H10

8 Check that the anti-vibration ball is free in the valve end.

9 Check the needle valve tip for wear and ridges. This is more likely with the brass needle valve tip than when a viton one is used. Use a viton-tipped replacement when possible.

10 The float should be checked for damage and ingress of petrol. Shaking the float will indicate the presence of fuel.

11 Renew the float pin if it shows signs of wear.

12 Unscrew the hexagon nut and inspect the fuel filter. Clean the filter housing of debris and dirt and renew the filter if necessary.

13 Remove the mixture screw and inspect the tip for damage or ridges.

14 Remove the four screws and detach the accelerator pump cover, diaphragm and spring. Check the diaphragm for fatigue and damage.

15 The pump injector is a push fit in the body. Carefully prise it from its location and test it by shaking. No noise from the outlet ball indicates that the valve is seized.

16 Unscrew the primary and secondary idle jet assemblies, main jets, air correctors and emulsion tubes.

17 Check that the channel from the float chamber into the emulsion tube well is clear.

18 The idle jets are pushed into a holder and may be separated (by pulling) for cleaning or renewal. Likewise, the main jets and air correctors are pushed into the opposite ends of the emulsion tubes and may also be separated (by pulling) for cleaning or renewal. Note that the idle jet and the main jet assemblies can be removed from the carburettor body without removing the upper body.

19 Note the jet sizes and locations for correct installation during assembly. The primary main and idle jet are located on the accelerator pump side of the carburettor.

20 Check the jet calibration against that specified. It is possible that the jets may have been transposed (or the wrong size fitted) during the last overhaul.

21 Remove the primary and secondary auxiliary venturis where necessary. Weber provide an extractor tool for removing these items. Check that the primary and secondary auxiliary venturis are not loose in the main body, since this is a source of uneven running. If a venturi is loose, knurl the mating flanges with a file to ensure a tight fit.

22 Remove the three screws and detach the power valve cover, spring and diaphragm from the body. Check the diaphragm for damage and fatigue. The brass outlet valve is cast into the body and is not removable. The ball in the outlet valve should seal the outlet. Depress and release the ball with a small screwdriver and it should move smoothly in and out. Check that the channel into the emulsion tube well is clear.

23 Do not disturb the adjustment of the secondary throttle angle unless absolutely necessary.

24 Inspect the choke spindle and linkage for stickiness and wear.

25 Remove the three screws and detach the choke shield. Remove the two screws and the circlip, then detach the choke pull-down housing.

26 Remove the three screws and detach the choke pull-down cover, spring and diaphragm from the housing. Check the diaphragm for fatigue and renew as necessary.

Preparation for reassembly

27 Clean the jets, carburettor body assemblies, float chamber and internal channels. An air line may be used to clear internal channels once the carburettor is fully dismantled. Note that if high-pressure air is directed into the channels and passages with the diaphragms still in place, diaphragm damage may result.

28 Spraying carburettor cleaner into all the channels and passages in the carburettor body will often clear them of gum and dirt.

29 During reassembly, a complete set of new gaskets should be fitted. Also renew the needle valve and float pin, and all diaphragms.

30 Inspect and renew (where necessary) the mixture screw, main jets, idle jets, air corrector jets and accelerator pump injector. Renew worn linkages, screws, springs and other parts where necessary.

31 Ensure that all jets are firmly locked into their original positions (but do not over-tighten). A loose jet can cause a rich (or even lean) running condition.

32 Clean all mating surfaces and flanges of old gasket material and reassemble with new gaskets.

33 Ensure that housings are positioned with their air and fuel routes correctly aligned.

Reassembly

34 Refit the choke diaphragm, spring and cover assembly, then secure with the three screws.

35 Renew the vacuum O-ring seal and refit the choke pull-down housing to the carburettor upper body. Secure with the two screws and the circlip.

36 Check that the secondary throttle plate is fully closed. The adjustment screw should not normally be used to alter the throttle plate position. However, if necessary, it can be adjusted so that the plate is open just enough to prevent its seizure in the throttle body.

37 Refit the power diaphragm, spring and cover assembly, then secure with the three screws.

38 Ensure that the air correctors and main jets are pushed fully into the emulsion tubes. Refit the assemblies into their original positions (do not transpose the jets).

39 Ensure that the idle jets are pushed fully into their holders. Refit into their original positions (do not transpose the jets).

40 Refit the pump injector, after renewing the small seal on the injector body.

41 Refit the pump spring, diaphragm and cover assembly; secure with the four screws.

42 Refit the idle mixture control screw. Turn the screw in gently until it just seats. From this position, unscrew it three full turns. This will provide a basic setting to allow the engine to be started.

43 Clean or renew the fuel filter and refit the hexagon nut.

44 Fit a new float gasket to the upper body. Renew the needle valve assembly. Screw the valve seat into the upper body using a new sealing washer and ensure that it is firmly locked into position (but do not over-tighten). Transfer the hairpin or plastic clip from the old needle valve to the ball end of the new one. Place the clip and valve assembly onto the inner float tag. Lower the float and needle valve assembly into the seat and secure with the float pin. Adjust the float level. Refer to Section 4 for details on float adjustment.

45 Refit the upper body to the main body and secure with the six screws. Refit the choke vacuum hose. Ensure that the fast idle arm is pushed fully down. If allowed to remain high, the arm will fall into an incorrect position as the upper body is mated to the main body.

46 Refit the idle cut-off valve, using a new sealing washer.

47 Ensure that the choke flap and linkage move smoothly and progressively.

48 Adjust the automatic choke. Refer to Section 4 for details on all adjustments. Refit the plastic choke shield and secure with the three screws.

49 Refit the carburettor to the engine.

50 Always adjust the carburettor idle speed and mixture after any work has been carried out on the carburettor, preferably with the aid of a CO meter.

4 Service adjustments

Adjustment preconditions

1 Refer to Part B for general advice on the preconditions to correct adjustment of this carburettor.

Idle speed and mixture (CO)

2 Run the engine at 3000 rpm for 30 seconds to clear the manifold of fuel vapours, then allow the engine to idle.

3 Remove the air filter assembly and place it clear of the carburettor, with the vacuum hoses (where fitted) still connected.

4 Use the idle speed adjustment screw to set the specified idle speed *(see illustration)*.

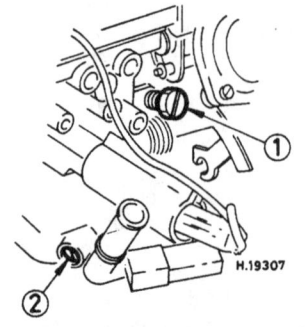

Idle speed and mixture adjustment
1 Idle speed adjustment screw
2 Idle mixture control screw

Weber 32/34 & 34 DRTC carburettor

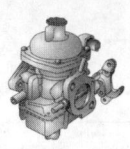

Float level adjustment
a Measurement

Float level adjustment
1 Inner float tag   2 Float leg

Thermostat adjustment
3 Thermostat lever
4 Roller on end of fast idle arm
b Distance between roller and end of lever

5 Check the CO level. If it is not as specified, remove the tamperproof plug and adjust the idle mixture control screw to achieve the correct level. Turning the screw clockwise (inwards) will reduce the CO level. Turning the screw anti-clockwise (outwards) will increase the CO level.
6 Repeat paragraphs 4 and 5 until both adjustments are correct.
7 Clear the manifold every 30 seconds during the setting operation by running the engine at 3000 rpm for 30 seconds.
8 Increase the speed to 2000 rpm and note the CO reading. The cruise reading should be less than half the idle CO reading.
9 Fit a new tamperproof plug to the mixture control screw.
10 Refit the air filter, ensuring that all the vacuum hoses are properly connected.

Float level

11 Hold the carburettor upper body in a vertical position with the float tag gently touching the ball of the fully-closed needle valve.
12 Measure the distance between the upper body (complete with gasket) and the top of the float *(see illustration)*.
13 Adjust as necessary by bending the inner float tag *(see illustration)*.
14 The height of each float must not vary by more than 1.0 mm.
15 Adjust as necessary by bending each float leg.

Automatic choke

Thermostat setting

16 Allow the temperature of the thermostatic capsule to stabilise for a minimum of 30 minutes.
17 Measure the distance between the roller and the end of the lever *(see illustration)*. Compare the reading obtained with that shown in the table below, according to the carburettor fitted and the temperature of the thermostatic capsule.
18 The table below lists temperatures in steps of 5°C. To calculate the correct dimension for any temperature between these five-degree steps (say 18°C), refer to the following example:

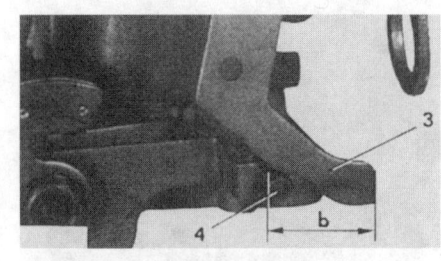

15°C = 24.7 mm or 21.5 mm
18°C = (15 + 3)°C
18°C = 24.7 + 3x ((25.6 - 24.7) /5) =
   24.7 + 0.54 = 25.24 mm
OR 18°C = 21.5 + 3x ((22.7 - 21.5) /5) =
   21.5 + 0.72 = 22.22 mm

19 Adjust as necessary by turning the adjustment screw *(see illustration)* in the appropriate direction.

Fast idle

20 The carburettor must first be removed from the engine in order to make the fast idle adjustment.
21 Invert the carburettor.
22 Use the shank of a twist drill to measure the clearance between the throttle plate and the wall of the throttle bore *(see illustration)*. Compare the reading obtained with that shown in the table below, according to the carburettor fitted and the temperature of the thermostatic capsule.
23 The table below lists temperatures in steps of 5°C. To calculate the correct dimension for any temperature between these five-degree steps (say 18°C), refer to the example in paragraph 18, substituting the values for dimension (c).
24 Adjust as necessary by turning the adjustment screw *(see illustration)* in the appropriate direction.

Thermostat adjustment
5 Adjustment screw

Fast idle adjustment
c Clearance

Fast idle adjustment
6 Fast idle adjustment screw   7 Thermostat

H10•5

Chapter H10

Thermostat opening

1 Circlip
2 Control spring
3 Circlip
4 Screws retaining pull-down housing

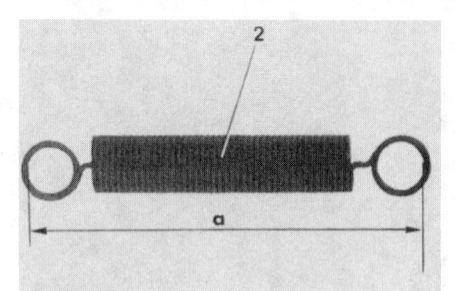

Checking control spring (2)

a Dimension = 40.5 ± 0.2 mm

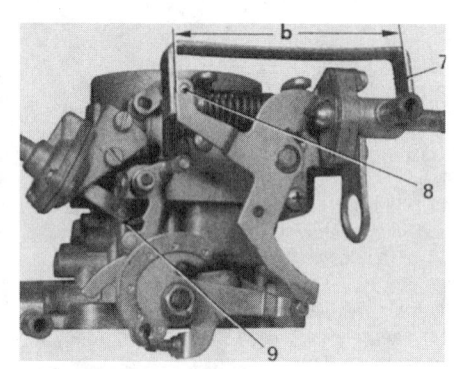

Checking choke flap opening (b)

Thermostat adjustment

7 Lever   8 Screw

Pull-down adjustment

b Dimension = 103 mm approx.
7 Clamp
8 Lever
9 Screw

Pull-down clearance (d)

Pull-down adjustment

10 Adjustment screw

Thermostat opening

25 Remove the two circlips and detach the choke control spring *(see illustration)*. Measure dimension (a) *(see illustration)* which should equal 40.5 ± 0.2 mm. If not, renew the control spring.
26 Refit the control spring and secure with the two circlips.
27 Check the choke flap opening (b) *(see illustration)* according to the temperature of the thermostatic capsule shown below.

Temperature (°C)	Dimension b (mm)
Less than 20	0
25	0 (point of opening)
30	1.50
35	5.00
40	7.25
45	10.00

28 Adjust as necessary by slackening the screw (8) *(see illustration)* and moving the lever in the appropriate direction.
29 Recheck the opening dimension at two or more temperatures. If the dimensions obtained are incorrect, even after adjustment, renew the thermostatic capsule.

Vacuum pull-down

30 Construct a clamp with a 103 mm internal dimension. Place it over the thermostatic housing coolant spigot and the choke lever as shown *(see illustration)*. The thermostat is now placed in the cold starting position.
31 Fully push the choke diaphragm operating lever up to its stop. At the same time, use the shank of a twist drill to measure the gap between the lower section of the choke flap and the air intake. Refer to Specifications for the required drill size *(see illustration)*.
32 Remove the plug and adjust as necessary by turning the diaphragm adjustment screw in the appropriate direction. Renew the plug after adjustment is completed *(see illustration)*.

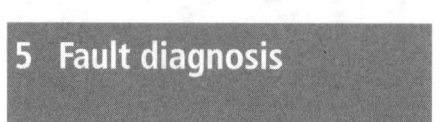

5 Fault diagnosis

Refer to Part D for diagnosis of general carburettor faults. The following faults are specific to Weber DRTC carburettors.

Hesitation and poor driveability

☐ Distorted base or body flange as a result of over-tightening the carburettor mounting bolts. Distortion may occur at the flanges of the upper body, main body, or at the heater flange sections. This will cause air leaks and general poor running. Remove the gaskets and mate the two flange surfaces together. Severe or even slight distortion can now be seen. A gasket will take up a small amount of warping but if the distortion is excessive, the carburettor is best renewed.

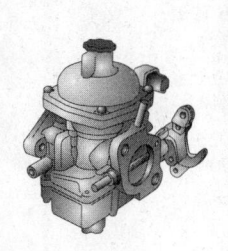

Part H Chapter 11
Weber 32 & 35 IBSH carburettor

Contents

Fault diagnosis 5
General servicing 3
Identification 2
Principles of operation 1
Service adjustments 4

Specifications

Manufacturer	Citroën	Citroën	Peugeot
Model	**AX10**	**Visa GT**	**205 1.0**
Year	**1987 to 1991**	**1983 to 1986**	**1988 to 1991**
Engine code	C1A (TU9)	150B (XY8)	TU9A (C1A) (33kW)
Capacity (cm^3)/no. of cyls	954/4	1360/4	954/4
Oil temperature (°C)	90	80	80
Carb. identification	32 IBSH 16/100	35 IBSH 20/100A1 and 35 IBSH 21/100A1	32 IBSH 16
Idle speed (rpm)	750 ± 50	975 ± 25 ('83 on: 875 ± 25)	700 ± 50
CO @ idle (% vol.)	0.8 to 1.2	2.0 ± 0.5	0.8 to 1.5
Venturi diameter	25	26	25
Idle jet	42	47	42
Main jet	132	130	132
Air correction jet	150	170	150
Emulsion tube	F108	F104	F108
Accel. pump jet	40	45	40
Float level (mm)	8 ± 0.25	9 ± 0.25	8 ± 0.25
Needle valve size (mm)	1.50	1.50	1.50
Choke fast idle gap (mm)	0.8 ± 0.05	0.35 ± 0.05	0.8 ± 0.05
Choke pull-down (mm)	4.5 ± 0.5	3.5 ± 0.25	4.5 ± 0.5

Manufacturer	Peugeot	Peugeot	Peugeot
Model	**205 GT/XS/XT/Lacoste**	**309 1.1**	**309 1.3**
Year	**1983 to 1987**	**1986 to 1989**	**1986 to 1991**
Engine code	XY8 (150B)	E1 (1E1A) (40kW)	G1 (1G1A) (47kW)
Capacity (cm^3)/no. of cyls	1360/4	1118/4	1294/4
Oil temperature (°C)	80	80	80
Carb. identification	35 IBSH 20/100A1 and 35 IBSH 21/100A1	32 IBSH 13/100	32 IBSH 14/100
Idle speed (rpm)	875 ± 25	900 ± 50	650 ± 50
Fast idle speed (rpm)	1400 ± 100	–	–
CO @ idle (% vol.)	2.0 ± 0.5	1.5 ± 0.5	1.5 ± 0.5
Venturi diameter	26	25	25
Idle jet	47	46	45
Main jet	130	130	142
Air correction jet	170	160	170
Emulsion tube	F104	F102	F102
Accel. pump jet	45	45	45
Float level (mm)	9 ± 0.25	7 ± 0.25	7 ± 0.25
Needle valve size (mm)	1.50	1.50	1.50
Choke fast idle gap (mm)	0.35 ± 0.05	0.65 ± 0.05	0.7 ± 0.05
Choke pull-down (mm)	3.5 ± 0.25	4.0 ± 0.25	4.25 ± 0.25

Chapter H11

Manufacturer	Talbot	Talbot/Chrysler	Talbot
Model	Dodge Simca 1100 Van	Horizon 1.1	Samba 1.4
Year	1978 to 1984	1978 to 1986	1983 to 1986
Engine code	3E1	2E1	5K3 (XY8)
Capacity (cm³)/no. of cyls	1118/4	1118/4	1360/4
Oil temperature (°C)	80	80	90
Carb. identification	32 IBSH 6/100	32 IBSH 2/100	35 IBSH 20/100A1 and 35 IBSH 21/100A1
Idle speed (rpm)	850 ± 50	850 ± 50	950 ± 50
CO @ idle (% vol.)	1.0 to 1.6	2.0	2.0 ± 0.5
Venturi diameter	25	26	26
Idle jet	42	40	47
Main jet	122	140	130
Air correction jet	170	180	170
Emulsion tube	F56	F56	F104
Accel. pump jet	45	45	45
Float level (mm)	6 ± 0.25	6	9 ± 0.25
Needle valve size (mm)	1.50	1.50	1.50
Choke fast idle gap (mm)	1.05 ± 0.05	1.05 ± 0.05	0.35 ± 0.05
Choke pull-down (mm)	5.25 ± 0.25	5.5	3.5 ± 0.25

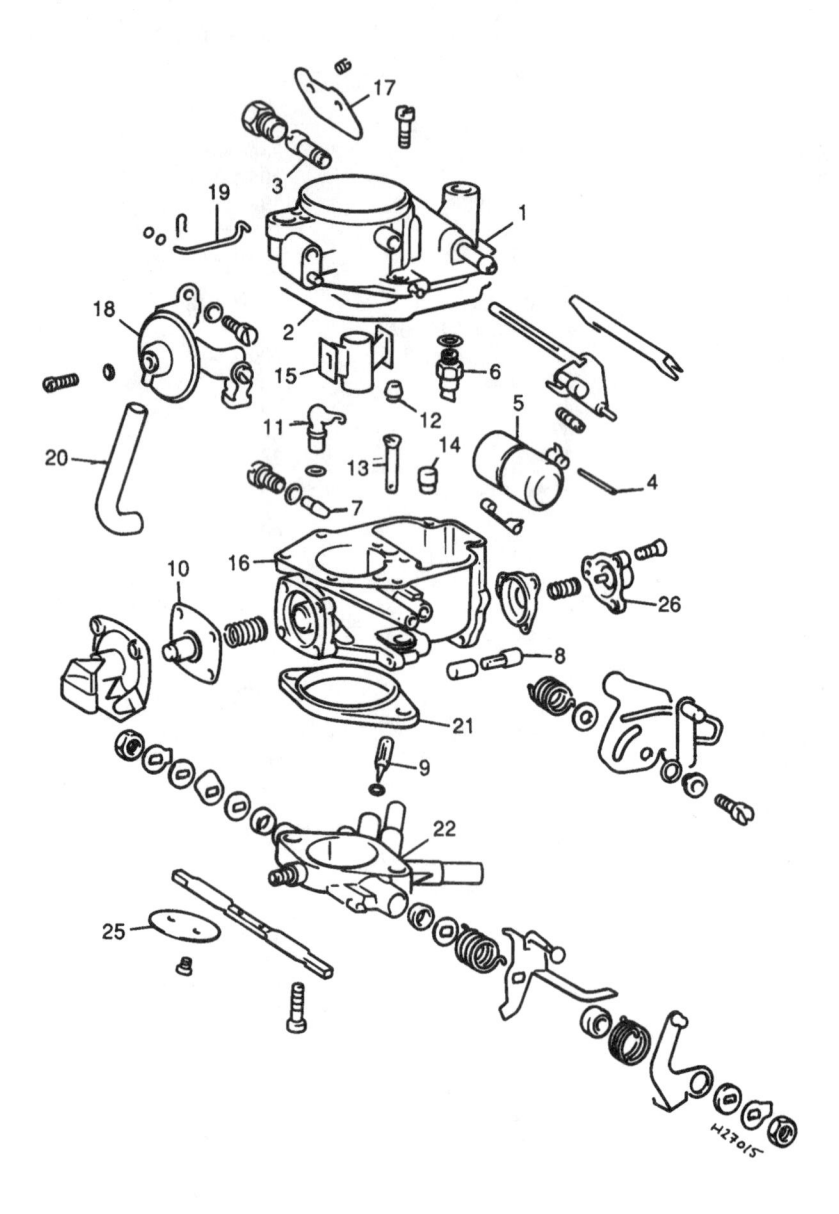

1 Principles of operation

Introduction

1 The following technical description of the Weber IBSH carburettor should be read in conjunction with the more detailed description of carburettor principles in Part A.

Construction

2 The Weber IBSH carburettor is a downdraught single venturi instrument with a manual choke control *(see illustration)*. The throttle shaft is made of steel. The throttle valve is made of brass, as are the jets and the emulsion tube. The exception is the accelerator pump injector which is die-cast. The internal fuel channels and air passages are drilled and sealed with lead plugs where necessary.

3 The carburettor is constructed in three main bodies. These are the upper body, main body and throttle body containing the throttle assemblies. An insulating block, placed between the main carburettor body and the throttle

Weber IBSH carburettor

1 Upper body
2 Float chamber gasket
3 Fuel inlet filter
4 Float pin
5 Float
6 Needle valve assembly
7 Idle jet
8 Idle speed adjustment screw
9 Idle mixture control screw
10 Accelerator pump diaphragm
11 Pump injector
12 Air corrector
13 Emulsion tube
14 Main jet
15 Auxiliary venturi
16 Main body
17 Choke flap
18 Choke diaphragm
19 Choke link rod
20 Vacuum hose
21 Insulating block
25 Throttle plate
26 Power diaphragm

Weber 32 & 35 IBSH carburettor

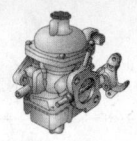

body, prevents excess heat transference to the main body.

4 The throttle body contains a heating flange through which hot engine coolant is piped. The purpose of the flange is to improve atomisation of the air/fuel mixture.

5 The Weber 35 IBSH carburettor is normally fitted in pairs in a twin carburettor application. One carburettor is designated the control carburettor and the other one the controlled carburettor. The two are joined by an adjustable linkage.

Fuel control

6 Fuel flows into the carburettor through a fine mesh filter. The fuel level in the float chamber is controlled by a needle valve and brass float assembly. An anti-vibration ball is incorporated into the needle valve design. A clip, attached to the needle valve and to the float arm, prevents the needle from sticking in the seat as the fuel level drops. The float chamber is vented internally to the clean-air side of the air filter (see illustration).

Idle, slow running and progression

7 Fuel, sourced from the main well, passes into the primary idle channel through a metered idle jet. Here it is mixed with a small amount of air from a calibrated air bleed. The resulting emulsion is drawn through a channel to be discharged from the idle orifice under the primary throttle plate. A tapered mixture screw is used to vary the outlet and this ensures fine control of the idle mixture. A number of progression drillings provide enrichment as they are uncovered by the opening throttle during initial acceleration.

8 The idle speed is set by an adjustable screw. The adjustable mixture screw is tamper proofed during production, in accordance with emission regulations.

Accelerator pump

9 The Weber IBSH accelerator pump is controlled by a diaphragm and is mechanically operated by a lever and cam attached to the primary throttle linkage. During acceleration, fuel is pumped through a discharge valve and ball into the pump injector where it is discharged into the primary venturi. The inlet valve consists of a ball valve located in a channel from the float chamber. Excess fuel is returned to the float chamber through a calibrated bush.

Main circuit

10 The amount of fuel discharged into the airstream is controlled by a calibrated main jet. Fuel is drawn through the main jet into the base of a vertical well which dips down into the fuel in the float chamber. An emulsion tube is placed in the well and is capped by a calibrated air corrector jet. The fuel is mixed with air drawn in through the air corrector and through the holes in the emulsion tube. The resulting emulsified mixture is discharged from the main nozzle through an auxiliary venturi.

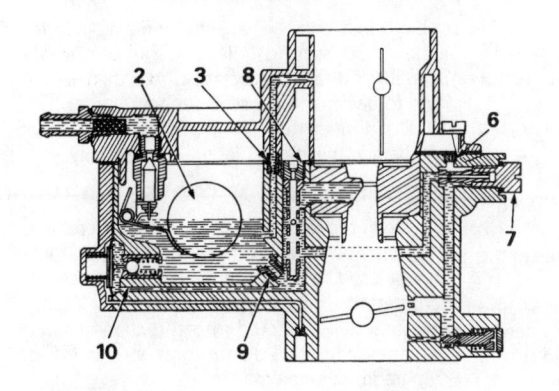

Fuel circuits
1 Needle valve
2 Float
3 Full-load calibrated bush
4 Main venturi
5 Pump injector
6 Air bleed
7 Idle jet
8 Air corrector
9 Main jet
10 Power valve

Power enrichment and economy circuit

11 Fuel flows from the float chamber into the power valve chamber through a fuel channel. An air passage is taken from under the throttle plate to the cover of the power diaphragm chamber. At idle and during light-throttle operation, manifold vacuum draws the diaphragm back against spring pressure. The diaphragm pintle is withdrawn from the brass outlet valve and the spring-loaded ball seats to close off the outlet channel.

12 Under acceleration and wide-open throttle operation, the vacuum in the manifold is depleted. The diaphragm returns under spring pressure and the power diaphragm pintle pushes the ball to open the outlet valve. Fuel then flows through the valve to supplement the fuel in the primary main well. The fuel level rises in the well and the fuel mixture is enriched.

13 At full-load and high engine speeds, even more fuel is required. The velocity of air creates a depression sufficient to raise fuel from the float chamber into a channel. The fuel then passes through a calibrated bushing to the upper section of the air intake. Here it is mixed with a small amount of air from a calibrated air bleed and the emulsified mixture is then discharged into the airstream from the full-load enrichment tube.

Choke operation

14 The manual choke is operated by a dash-mounted cable. When the cable is pulled, it operates a lever that pulls the choke flap closed across the air intake. Fast idle is achieved with the aid of a curved cam attached to the choke operating lever. An adjustable screw, attached to the throttle lever and butting against the cam, is used to vary the fast idle speed.

15 Once the engine has fired, the choke flap must open slightly to weaken the mixture and avoid flooding during idle and light-throttle operation. This is achieved by different methods on the 32 and 35 IBSH carburettors.

16 The 35 IBSH carburettor uses manifold vacuum to actuate a diaphragm (control carburettor only). A linkage attached to the diaphragm then pulls upon the choke flap.

17 One version of the 32 IBSH carburettor also utilises a diaphragm in a similar fashion to the 35 IBSH but a second version does not. Instead, an increase in airflow through the air intake partially opens the choke flap against the action of a spring. A stop ensures that the choke is only opened a small amount.

18 During engine warm-up, the cable should be progressively pushed home until the choke flap is fully open.

2 Identification

The Weber identification code is stamped on the float chamber side.

Where twin 35 IBSH carburettors are fitted, the control carburettor is stamped 35 IBSH 20/100 and the controlled carburettor is stamped 35 IBSH 21/100.

3 General servicing

Introduction

1 Read this Chapter in conjunction with Part B, which describes some of the operations in more detail. It is assumed that the carburettor is removed for this service. However, many of the operations can be tackled with the carburettor in place. Where this is undertaken, first soak the fuel out of the float chamber using a clean tissue or soft cloth, after removing the upper body assembly.

Dismantling and checking

2 Remove the carburettor from the engine (see Part B).

Chapter H11

3 Check visually for damage and wear.
4 Disconnect the choke linkage, then remove the five screws and detach the carburettor upper body.
5 Use a straight-edge to check for distorted flanges on all facing surfaces.
6 Tap out the float pin and remove the float, needle valve and plastic clip, float chamber gasket and needle valve seat.
7 Check that the anti-vibration ball is free in the valve end.
8 Check the needle valve tip for wear and ridges. This is more likely with the brass needle valve tip than when a viton one is used. Use a viton-tipped replacement when possible.
9 The float should be checked for damage and ingress of petrol.
10 Renew the float pin if it shows signs of wear.
11 Unscrew the hexagon bolt and inspect the fuel filter. Clean the filter housing of debris and dirt and renew the filter if necessary.
12 Remove the mixture screw and inspect the tip for damage and ridges.
13 Remove the four screws and detach the accelerator pump cover, diaphragm and spring. Check the diaphragm for fatigue and damage.
14 The pump injector is a push fit in the body. Carefully prise it from its location and test it by shaking. No noise from the outlet ball indicates that the valve is seized.
15 Remove the primary idle jet assembly from the upper body. The idle jet is pushed into a holder and may be separated (by pulling) for cleaning or renewal.
16 Remove the main jet, air corrector and emulsion tube. Check that the channel from the float chamber into the emulsion tube well is clear.
17 Check the jet calibration against that specified. It is possible that the wrong size jets may have been incorrectly fitted during the last overhaul.
18 Remove the auxiliary venturi from the main body where necessary. Weber provide an extractor tool for removing this component. Check that the auxiliary venturi is not loose in the main body as this is a source of uneven running. If the venturi is loose, knurl the mating flanges with a file to ensure a tight fit.
19 Remove the three screws and detach the power valve housing cover, spring and diaphragm from the body. Check the diaphragm for fatigue and damage. The brass outlet valve is cast into the body and is not removable. The ball in the outlet valve should seal the outlet. Depress and release the ball with a small screwdriver and it should move smoothly in and out. Check that the channel into the emulsion tube well is clear.
20 Remove the two screws and separate the carburettor main body and throttle body assemblies. The throttle body can be renewed separately if the spindles or throttle bores are worn.
21 Inspect the choke spindle, linkage and operating mechanism for stickiness and wear.
22 Attach a vacuum pump to the pull-down diaphragm (where fitted) and operate the pump to obtain 300 mm Hg. The diaphragm should operate fully and the vacuum be maintained for at least 30 seconds. Renew the diaphragm assembly if it fails these tests. Check the vacuum hose for leaks and perished rubber.
23 Disconnect the choke link rod and screws and detach the choke diaphragm assembly.

Preparation for reassembly

24 Clean the jets, carburettor body assemblies, float chamber and internal channels. An air line may be used to clear internal channels once the carburettor is fully dismantled. Note that if high-pressure air is directed into the channels and passages with the diaphragms still in place, diaphragm damage may result.
25 Spraying carburettor cleaner into all the channels and passages in the carburettor body will often clear them of gum and dirt.
26 During reassembly, a complete set of new gaskets should be fitted. Also renew the needle valve and float pin, and all diaphragms.
27 Inspect and renew (where necessary) the mixture screw, main jet, idle jet, air corrector jet, emulsion tube and the accelerator pump discharge valve and injector. Renew worn linkages, screws, springs, vacuum hoses and other parts where necessary.
28 Ensure that all jets are firmly locked into position (but do not over-tighten). A loose jet can cause a rich (or even lean) running condition.
29 Clean all mating surfaces and flanges of old gasket material and reassemble with new gaskets.
30 Ensure that housings are positioned with their air and fuel routes correctly aligned.

Reassembly

31 Refit the choke diaphragm assembly to the carburettor upper body and secure with the screws. Reconnect the choke link rod.
32 Assemble the main and throttle bodies with a new gasket block and secure with the two screws.
33 Refit the power diaphragm, spring and cover assembly, then secure with the three screws.
34 Refit the emulsion tube, air corrector and main jet into their original positions.
35 Refit the pump injector, after renewing the small seal on the injector body.
36 Refit the pump spring, diaphragm and cover assembly, then secure with the four screws.
37 Refit the idle mixture screw after renewing the seal. Turn the screw in gently until it just seats. From this position, unscrew it four full turns. This will provide a basic setting to allow the engine to be started.
38 Clean or renew the fuel filter and refit the hexagon bolt.
39 Renew the float chamber gasket and locate in position on the upper body. Renew the needle valve assembly. Screw the valve seat into the upper body, using a new sealing washer, and ensure that it is firmly locked into position (but do not over-tighten). Transfer the hairpin or plastic clip from the old needle valve to the ball end of the new one. Place the clip and valve assembly onto the inner float tag. Lower the float and needle valve assembly into the seat and secure with the float pin.
40 Adjust the float level. Refer to Section 4 for details on adjustment.
41 Refit the upper body to the main body and secure with the five screws. Reconnect the choke pull-down hose (where fitted).
42 Push the idle jet into its holder and refit the assembly into the upper body.
43 Ensure that the choke flap and linkage move smoothly and progressively.
44 Adjust the choke fast idle and pull-down. Refer to Section 4 for details on all adjustments.
45 Refit the carburettor to the engine.
46 Always adjust the carburettor idle speed and mixture after any work has been carried out on the carburettor, preferably with the aid of a CO meter.

4 Service adjustments

Adjustment preconditions

1 Refer to Part B for general advice on the preconditions to correct adjustment of this carburettor.

Idle speed and mixture (CO) - 32 IBSH

2 Run the engine at 3000 rpm for 30 seconds to clear the manifold of fuel vapours, then allow the engine to idle.
3 Use the idle adjustment speed screw to set the specified idle speed *(see illustration)*.

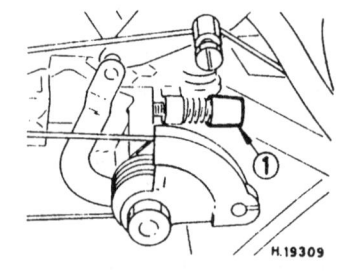

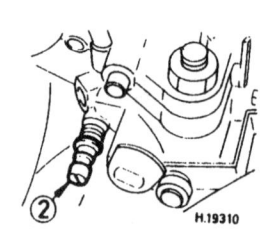

Idle speed and mixture adjustment - 32 IBSH

1 Idle speed adjustment screw   2 Idle mixture control screw

Weber 32 & 35 IBSH carburettor

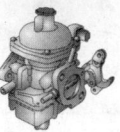

Using synchrometer to balance airflows

4 Check the CO level. If it is not as specified, remove the tamperproof plug and adjust the idle mixture control screw to achieve the correct level. Turning the screw clockwise (inwards) will reduce the CO level. Turning the screw anti-clockwise (outwards) will increase the CO level.
5 Repeat paragraphs 3 and 4 until both adjustments are correct.
6 Clear the manifold every 30 seconds during the setting operation by running the engine at 3000 rpm for 30 seconds.
7 Increase the speed to 2000 rpm and note the CO reading. The cruise reading should be less than half the idle CO reading.
8 Fit a new tamperproof plug to the mixture control screw.

Synchronising twin carburettors - 35 IBSH

9 It is important, for maximum efficiency and power, that a similar volume of airflow is drawn through each carburettor. This is achieved by synchronising the throttle valves of each carburettor so that the opening angles correspond.
10 One of two methods may be used to synchronise twin carburettors. In Method 1, a low-reading vacuum gauge is used. In Method 2, an airflow synchrometer is used.
11 Alternatively, it is possible to use a piece of tube to listen to the airflow through each carburettor. Adjustment may be made according to the subjective sound of each airflow. Acceptable results can often be achieved using this method.

Method 1

12 Disconnect the two vacuum pipes (A and B in illustration below).
13 Attach the vacuum gauge to the control carburettor connection (A).
14 Adjust the idle speed adjustment screw to obtain a minimum of 100 mm Hg (150 mbar).
15 Attach the vacuum gauge to the control carburettor connection (B).
16 Adjust the throttle synchronising adjustment screw to obtain the same setting as in paragraph 14. After adjusting the synchronisation screw, recheck that the vacuum at (A) has not altered.
17 It is probable that paragraphs 14 to 16 will need to be repeated several times before synchronisation is achieved. Blip the throttle several times and check that the vacuum measured at both (A) and (B) remains identical. If not, check for a sticking throttle mechanism.
18 Reconnect the vacuum pipes.
19 Use the idle speed adjustment screw to obtain the specified idle speed.
20 Adjust the idle mixture.

Method 2

21 Allow the engine to idle.
22 Attach a suitable airflow balancing gauge (synchrometer) to the control carburettor, and note the reading *(see illustration)*.
23 Move the synchrometer to the controlled carburettor and note the reading.
24 If the readings are not identical, adjust the synchronising adjustment screw to obtain the same setting for each carburettor.
25 It is also possible to use a twin airflow meter which can measure the airflow through both carburettors simultaneously.
26 Use the idle speed adjustment screw to obtain the correct idle speed.
27 Adjust the idle mixture.

Idle speed and mixture (CO) -35 IBSH

28 Before attempting to adjust either setting, ensure that the carburettors are properly synchronised, as described above.
29 Run the engine at 3000 rpm for 30 seconds to clear the manifold of fuel vapours, then allow the engine to idle.
30 Use the combined idle speed adjustment screw (3) *(see illustration)* to set the specified idle speed.
31 Check the CO level. If it is not as specified, remove the tamperproof plugs and adjust each idle mixture control screw by similar (small) increments until the correct level is reached. Turning the screws clockwise (inwards) will reduce the CO level. Turning the screws anti-clockwise (outwards) will increase the CO level.
32 Repeat paragraphs 30 and 31 until both adjustments are correct.
33 Clear the manifold every 30 seconds during the setting operation by running the engine at 3000 rpm for 30 seconds.
34 Increase the speed to 2000 rpm and note the CO reading. The cruise reading should be less than half the idle CO reading.
35 Fit new tamperproof plugs to the mixture control screws.

Float level

36 Hold the carburettor upper body in a vertical position with the float tag gently touching the ball of the needle valve.
37 Measure the distance between the upper body (with the gasket in place) and the top of the brass float *(see illustration)*.
38 Adjust as necessary by bending the inner float tag.

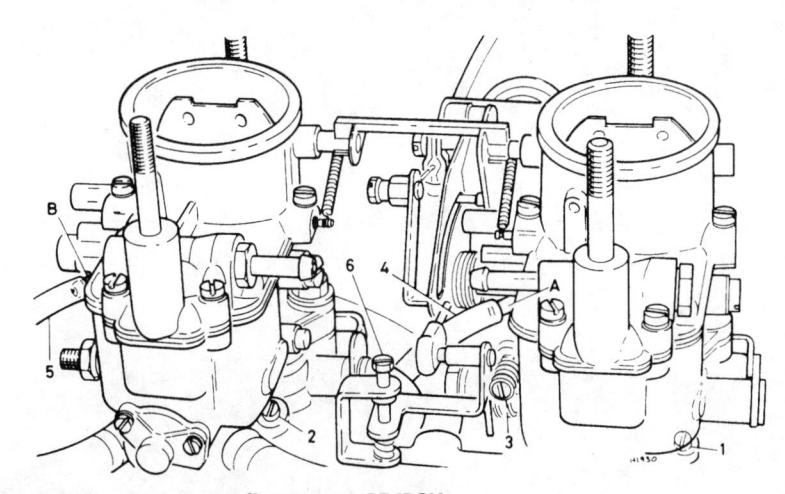

Idle speed and mixture adjustment - 35 IBSH
1 Idle mixture control screw (control carburettor)
2 Idle mixture control screw (controlled carburettor)
3 Idle speed adjustment screw
4 Vacuum hose
5 Vacuum hose
6 Throttle synchronising adjustment screw
A Vacuum connection
B Vacuum connection

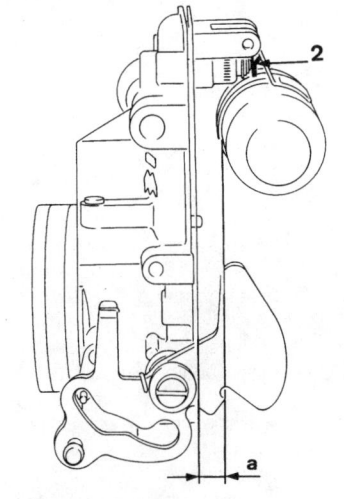

Float level adjustment
2 Float level   a Inner float tag

Chapter H11

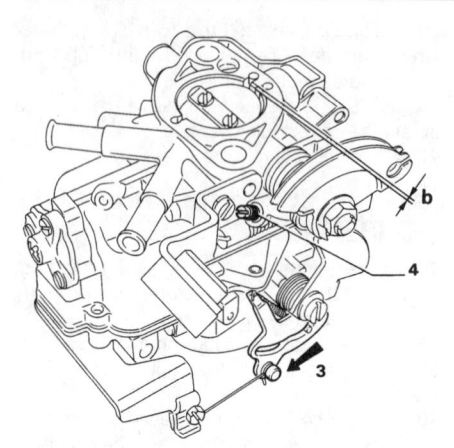

Fast idle adjustment

4 Fast idle adjustment screw
3 Fully close choke flap
b Fast idle clearance

Choke adjustments

Fast idle

39 The carburettor must be removed from the engine in order to make the fast idle adjustment.

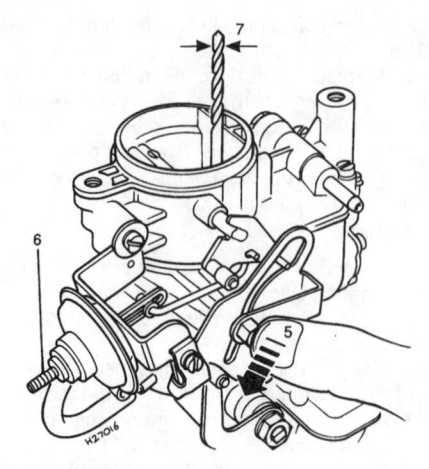

Pull-down adjustment

5 Fully close choke flap
6 Adjustment screw
7 Twist drill

40 Invert the carburettor.
41 Pull the choke operating arm to fully close the choke flap. The fast idle screw will butt against the fast idle cam and force open the throttle plate, to leave a small clearance *(see illustration)*.
42 Use the shank of a twist drill to measure the clearance between the wall of the throttle bore and the throttle plate. Refer to Specifications for the required drill size and measure the clearance from the progression holes.
43 Adjust as necessary by turning the fast idle adjustment screw in the appropriate direction.

Vacuum pull-down (where applicable)

44 Pull the choke operating arm to fully close the choke flap *(see illustration)*.
45 Use a vacuum pump to pull the diaphragm operating rod up to its stop (or push the mechanism with a small screwdriver). At the same time, use the shank of a twist drill to measure the gap between the lower section of the choke flap and the air intake. Refer to Specifications for the required drill size.
46 Remove the plug in the diaphragm cover and adjust as necessary by turning the adjustment screw in the appropriate direction. Renew the plug after adjustment is completed.

5 Fault diagnosis

Refer to Part D for diagnosis of general carburettor faults.

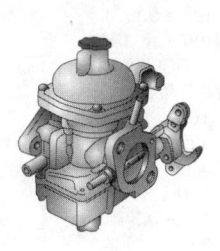

Part H Chapter 12
Weber 32 ICEV carburettor

Contents

Fault diagnosis 5
General servicing 3
Identification 2
Principles of operation 1
Service adjustments 4

Specifications

Manufacturer	Fiat	Fiat	Fiat	Fiat
Model	127 & Fiorino 1050	Panda 45 (903)	Panda 45 (903)	Uno 45 (903)
Year	1981 to 1988	1981 to 1986	1989 to 1991	1983 to 1990
Engine code	127 A.000	100 GL3.000	146 A.048 (33kW)	146 A.000 or 146 A.048
Capacity (cm^3)/no. of cyls	1049/4	903/4	903/4	903/4
Oil temperature (°C)	100	100	100	100
Carb. identification	32 ICEV 16/150 or 32 ICEV 34/150	32 ICEV 50/251	32 ICEV 61/250	32 ICEV 50/251 or 32 ICEV 60/250
Idle speed (rpm)	850 ± 50	850 ± 50	850 ± 50	850 ± 50
CO @ idle (% vol.)	3.0 max	3.0 max	1.0 ± 0.5	1.0 ± 0.5
Venturi diameter	21.5	22	22	22
Idle jet	45	47	47	47
Main jet	115	112	110	112
Air correction jet	185	170	180	170
Emulsion tube	F74	F89	F74	F89
Accel. pump jet	40	40	40	40
Float level (mm)	10.75 ± 0.25	10.75 ± 0.25	10.75 ± 0.25	10.75 ± 0.25
Float stroke (mm)	45 ± 0.5	45 ± 0.5	45 ± 0.5	45 ± 0.5
Needle valve size (mm)	1.50	1.50	1.50	1.50
Choke fast idle gap (mm)	0.8 ± 0.05	0.8	0.75	0.8 ± 0.05
Choke pull-down (mm)	4.0 ± 0.25	5.0 ± 0.25	4.5 ± 0.25	5.0 ± 0.25

Chapter H12

Manufacturer	Fiat	Fiat	Fiat	Fiat
Model	Uno 45 (903)	Uno 55 (1116)	Strada 60	Strada 65
Year	1990 to 1991	1983 to 1985	1983 to 1985	1979 to 1983
Engine code	146 A.048 OHV	138 B.000	138 B.000	138 A1.000
Capacity (cm³)/no. of cyls	903/4	1116/4	1116/4	1301/4
Oil temperature (°C)	100	100	100	100
Carb. identification	32 ICEV 61/250	32 ICEV 51/251	32 ICEV 51/251	32 ICEV 22/251
Idle speed (rpm)	775 ± 25	850 ± 50	850 ± 50	850 ± 50
CO @ idle (% vol.)	1.5 ± 0.5	3.5 max	1.5 ± 0.50	3.5 max
Venturi diameter	22	22	22	24
Idle jet	47	47	47	50
Main jet	110	115	115	122
Air correction jet	180	190	190	155
Emulsion tube	F74	F74	F74	F73
Accel. pump jet	40	40	40	50
Float level (mm)	10.75 ± 0.25	10.75 ± 0.25	10.75 ± 0.25	10.75 ± 0.25
Float stroke (mm)	45 ± 0.5	45 ± 0.5	45 ± 0.5	45 ± 0.5
Needle valve size (mm)	1.50	1.50	1.50	1.50
Choke fast idle gap (mm)	0.75	0.9 ± 0.05	0.9 ± 0.05	0.75 ± 0.05
Choke pull-down (mm)	4.50 ± 0.25	4.0 ± 0.25	4.0 ± 0.25	5.0 ± 0.25

Manufacturer	Lancia	Seat	Seat	Seat
Model	Y10 Touring	Marbella 850	Marbella 900	Ibiza 900
Year	1985 to 1988	1988 to 1991	1988 to 1991	1987 to 1991
Engine code	156 A.000	O8NCA	O9NCA	100GL7000 (146A)
Capacity (cm³)/no. of cyls	1049/4	843/4	903/4	903/4
Oil temperature (°C)	100	100	100	100
Carb. identification	32 ICEV 55/250 or 32 ICEV 55/251	32 ICEV 35/250	32 ICEV	32 ICEV 50/251
Idle speed (rpm)	850 ± 50	850 ± 50	850 ± 50	850 ± 50
CO @ idle (% vol.)	1.0 ± 0.5	1.5 ± 0.5	1.5 ± 0.5	1.5 ± 0.5
Venturi diameter	24	22	22	22
Idle jet	47	55	55	47
Main jet	122.5	110	112	107
Air correction jet	190	160	160	160
Emulsion tube	F73	F89	F89	F89
Accel. pump jet	45	40	40	40
Float level 1 (mm)	10.75 ± 0.25	10.75 ± 0.25 brass float	10.75 ± 0.25 brass float	10.75 ± 0.25
Float level 2 (mm)	–	35.85 ± 0.25 plastic float	35.85 ± 0.25 plastic float	–
Float stroke (mm)	45 ± 0.5	45 ± 0.5	45 ± 0.5	45 ± 0.5
Needle valve size (mm)	1.50	–	–	1.50
Choke fast idle gap (mm)	0.85 ± 0.05	–	–	0.8 ± 0.25
Choke pull-down (mm)	5.0 ± 0.25	–	–	5 ± 0.25

Manufacturer	Seat	Yugo
Model	Terra 900	45 (903)
Year	1988 to 1991	1983 to 1986
Engine code	O9NCA	100GL 064
Capacity (cm³)/no. of cyls	903/4	903/4
Oil temperature (°C)	100	100
Carb. identification	32 ICEV	32 ICEV 31/250
Idle speed (rpm)	850 ± 50	850 ± 50
CO @ idle (% vol.)	1.5 ± 0.5	3.0 ± 1 (85 on: 1.5 ± 0.5)
Venturi diameter	22	24
Idle jet	47	47
Main jet	112	122.5
Air correction jet	160	190
Emulsion tube	F89	F73
Accel. pump jet	40	45
Float level (mm)	10.75 ± 0.25	10.75 ± 0.25
Float stroke (mm)	45 ± 0.5	45 ± 0.5
Needle valve size (mm)	1.50	1.50
Choke fast idle gap (mm)	0.8 ± 0.25	0.85 ± 0.05
Choke pull-down (mm)	5 ± 0.25	5.0 ± 0.25

Weber 32 ICEV carburettor

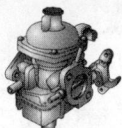

1 Principles of operation

Introduction

1 The following technical description of the Weber ICEV carburettor should be read in conjunction with the more detailed description of carburettor principles in Part A.

Construction

2 The Weber ICEV carburettor is a downdraught, single venturi instrument with either a manual or semi-automatic choke control *(see illustrations)*. The throttle shaft is made of steel. The throttle valve is made of brass, as are the jets and the emulsion tube. The exception is the accelerator pump injector which is die-cast. The internal fuel channels and air passages are drilled and sealed with lead plugs where necessary.

3 The carburettor is constructed in three main bodies. These are the upper body, main body and throttle body containing the throttle assemblies. An insulating block, placed between the main carburettor body and the throttle body, prevents excess heat transference to the main body.

4 On some applications, the throttle body contains a passage through which hot engine coolant is piped. The purpose of heating the base section is to improve atomisation of the air/fuel mixture.

Fuel control

5 Fuel flows into the carburettor through a fine mesh filter. The fuel level in the float chamber is controlled by a needle valve and plastic float assembly. An anti-vibration ball is incorporated into the needle valve design. A clip, attached to the needle valve and to the float arm, prevents the needle from sticking in the seat as the fuel level drops. The float chamber is vented internally to the clean-air side of the air filter. A

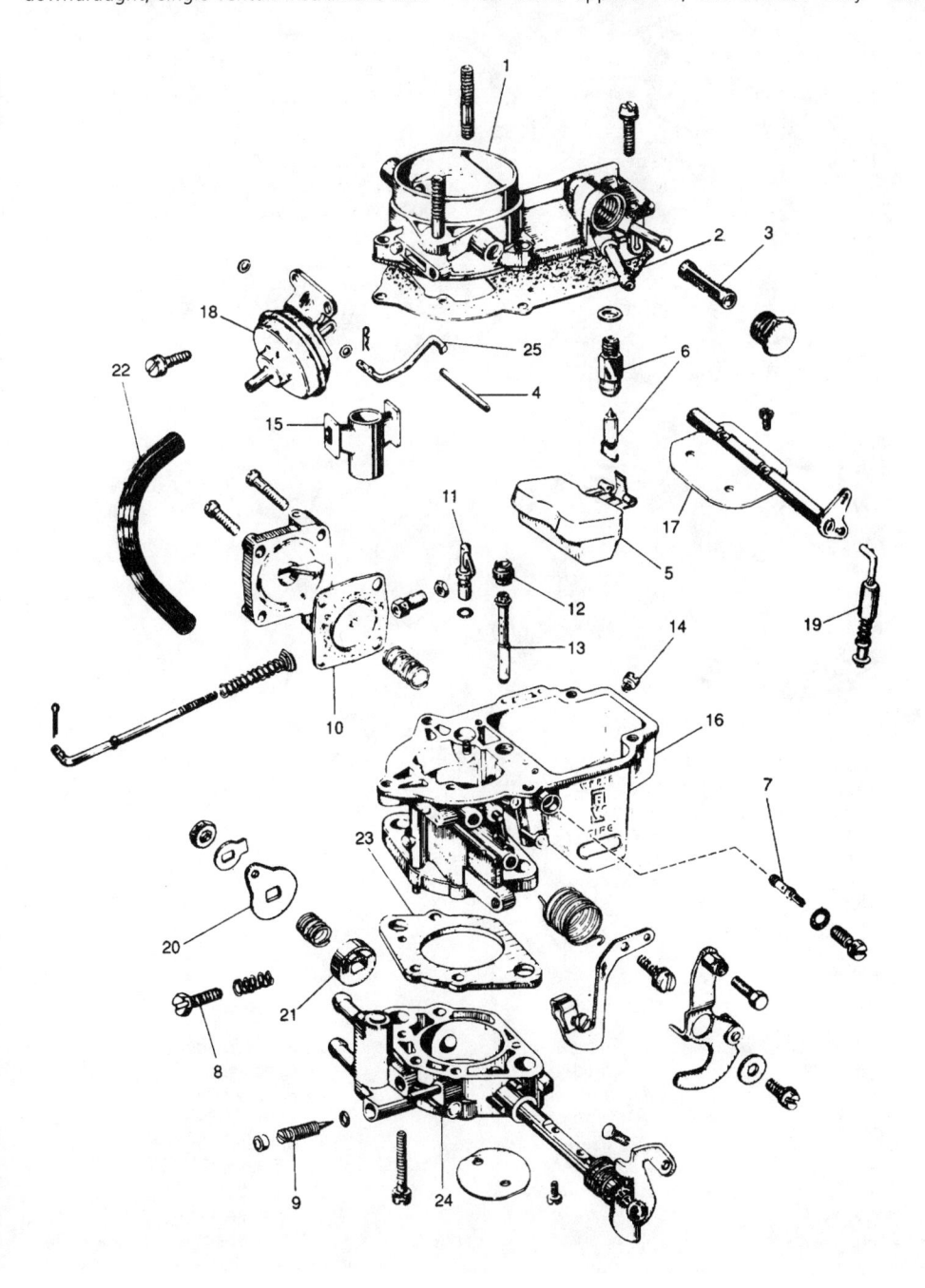

Weber ICEV carburettor - manual choke version

1. Upper body
2. Float chamber gasket
3. Fuel inlet filter
4. Float pin
5. Float
6. Needle valve assembly
7. Idle jet
8. Idle speed adjustment screw
9. Idle mixture control screw
10. Accelerator pump diaphragm
11. Pump injector
12. Air corrector
13. Emulsion tube
14. Main jet
15. Auxiliary venturi
16. Main body
17. Choke flap
18. Choke diaphragm
19. Choke link rod
20. Pump cam
21. Grooved disc
22. Vacuum hose
23. Insulating block
24. Throttle body
25. Diaphragm control rod

Chapter H12

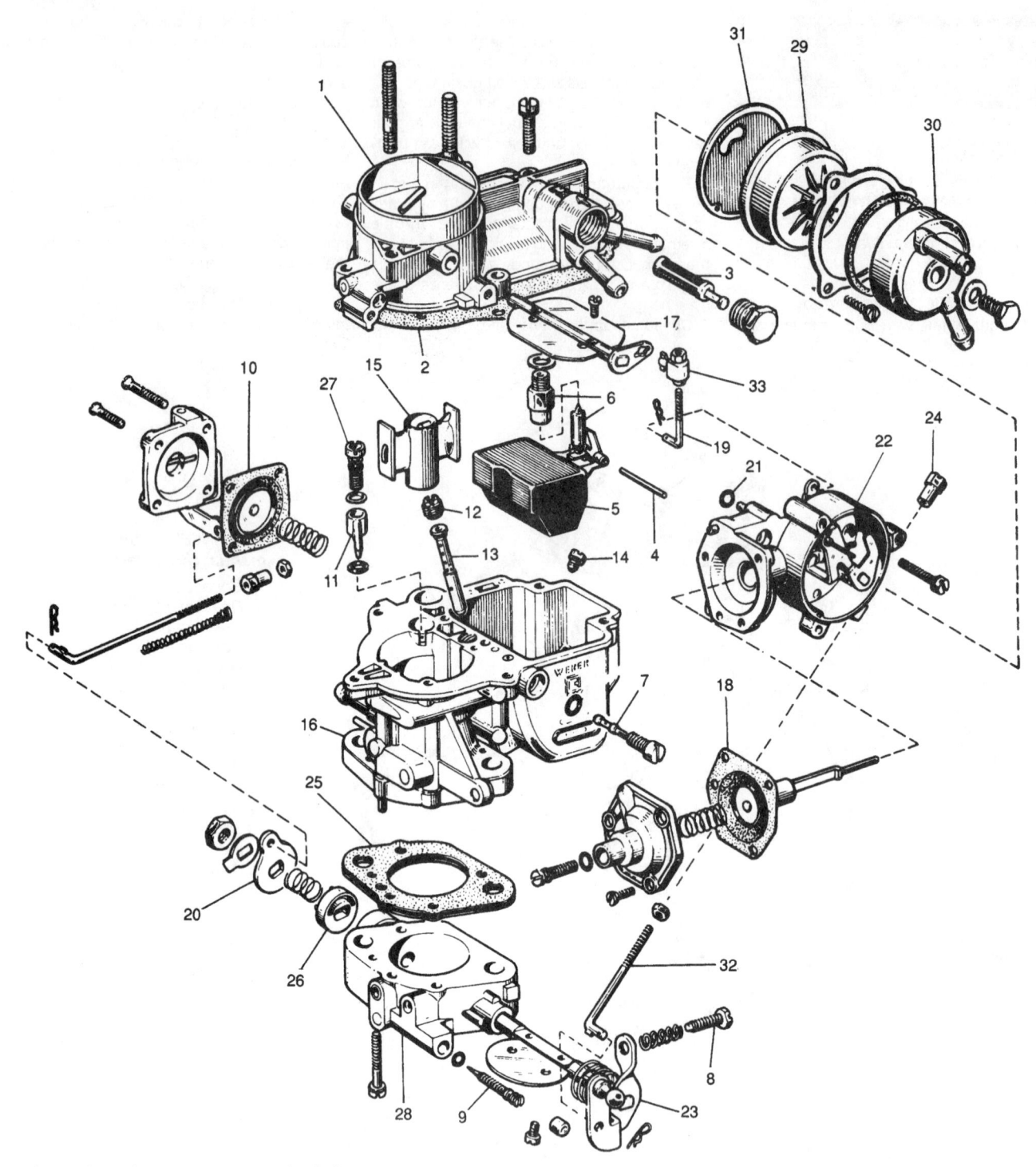

Weber ICEV carburettor - automatic choke version

1. Upper body
2. Float chamber gasket
3. Fuel inlet filter
4. Float pin
5. Float
6. Needle valve assembly
7. Idle jet
8. Idle speed adjustment screw
9. Idle mixture control screw
10. Accelerator pump diaphragm
11. Pump injector
12. Air corrector
13. Emulsion tube
14. Main jet
15. Auxiliary venturi
16. Main body
17. Choke flap
18. Choke diaphragm
19. Upper link rod
20. Pump cam
21. Vacuum O-ring seal
22. Choke housing
23. Fast idle lever
24. Fast idle adjustment screw
25. Insulating block
26. Grooved disc
27. Pump discharge valve
28. Throttle body
29. Bi-metal housing
30. Choke water jacket
31. Heat shield
32. Fast idle link rod
33. Adjustment nut

Weber 32 ICEV carburettor

calibrated fuel return system is provided to ensure that relatively cool fuel is supplied to the carburettor (see illustration).

Idle, slow running and progression

6 Fuel, sourced from the main well, passes into the primary idle channel through a metered idle jet. Here it is mixed with a small amount of air from a calibrated air bleed. The resulting emulsion is drawn through a channel to be discharged from the idle orifice under the primary throttle plate. A tapered mixture screw is used to vary the outlet and this ensures fine control of the idle mixture. A number of progression drillings provide enrichment as they are uncovered by the opening throttle during initial acceleration (see illustration).

7 The idle speed is set by an adjustable screw. In later versions of the carburettor, the adjustable mixture screw is tamper proofed during production, in accordance with emission regulations.

Positive crankcase ventilation

8 This system allows engine breather fumes to be drawn back into the engine to be re-burnt. Fumes from the engine breather outlet are conveyed by tube to a spigot on the carburettor body. A passage, originating from the engine side of the throttle plate, is connected to the spigot. At idle and low engine speeds, the fumes are drawn through a calibrated bush. As the throttle is opened, a disc connected to the throttle spindle rotates to open a groove. The greater volume of engine fumes produced during high-speed engine operation is thus accommodated.

Accelerator pump

9 The Weber ICEV accelerator pump is controlled by a diaphragm and is mechanically operated by a rod attached to the throttle linkage. During acceleration, fuel is pumped through a discharge valve and ball into the pump injector where it is discharged into the primary venturi. The inlet valve consists of a ball valve located in a channel from the float chamber. Excess fuel is returned to the float chamber through a calibrated bush (see illustration).

Main circuit

10 The amount of fuel discharged into the air stream is controlled by a calibrated main jet. Fuel is drawn through the main jet into the base of a vertical well which dips down into the fuel in the float chamber. An emulsion tube is placed in the well and is capped by a calibrated air corrector jet. The fuel is mixed with air drawn in through the air corrector and through the holes in the emulsion tube. The resulting emulsified mixture is discharged from the main nozzle through an auxiliary venturi.

Full-power enrichment

11 At full-load and high engine speeds, even more fuel is required. The velocity of air creates

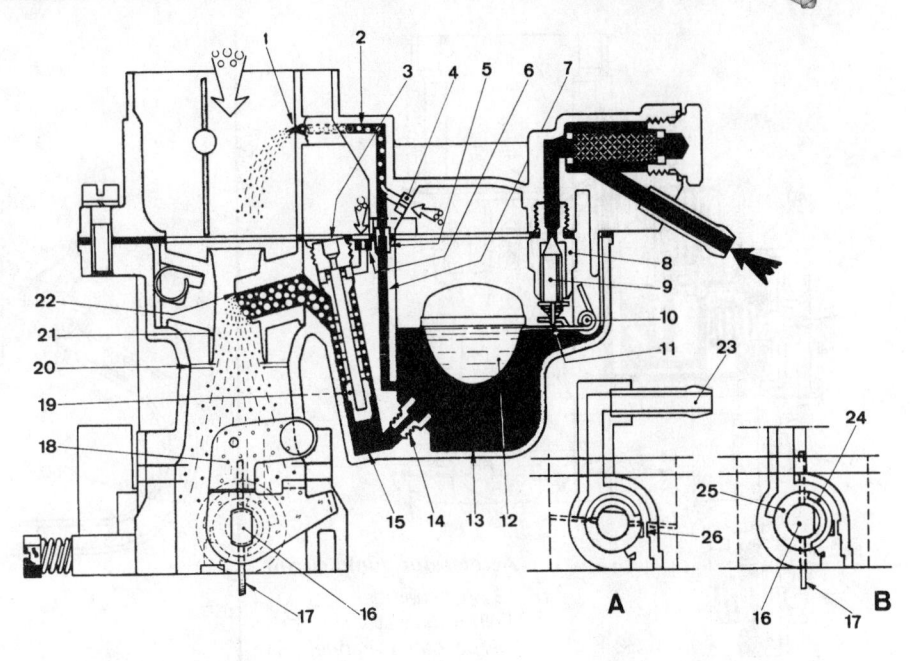

Inlet, main and full-load circuits

1. Full-load outlet
2. Full-load emulsion
3. Air corrector
4. Full-load air bleed
5. Full-load calibrated bush
6. Calibrated bush
7. Full-load fuel channel
8. Needle valve seat
9. Needle valve
10. Float pin
11. Float arm
12. Float
13. Float chamber
14. Main jet
15. Main well
16. Throttle spindle
17. Throttle valve
18. Throttle lever
19. Emulsion tube
20. Main venturi
21. Auxiliary venturi
22. Main fuel outlet
23. Spigot
24. Groove
25. Rotary blanking disc
26. Calibrated bush
A. PCV device in idle position
B. PCV device in open throttle position

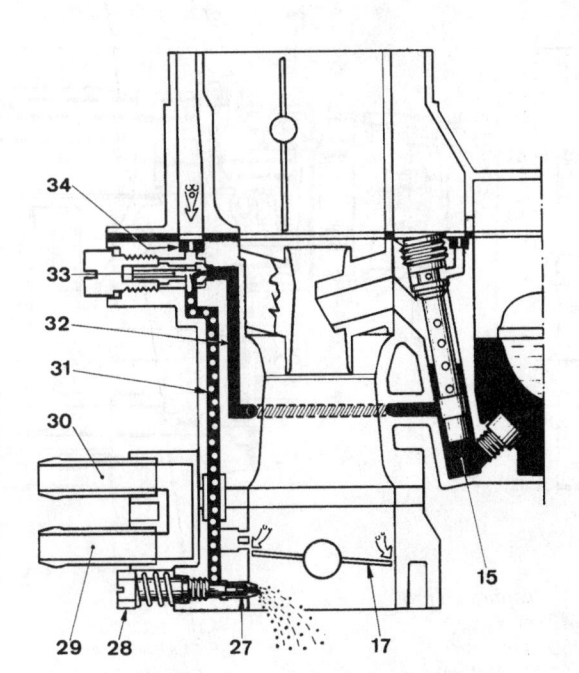

Idle and progression circuits

15. Main well
17. Throttle valve
27. Idle outlet
28. Idle mixture control screw
29. Coolant inlet (when used)
30. Coolant outlet (when used)
31. Idle fuel/air channel
32. Idle fuel channel
33. Idle jet
34. Air bleed
35. Progression outlet

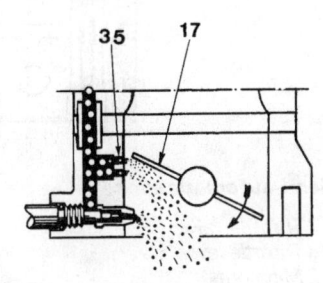

Chapter H12

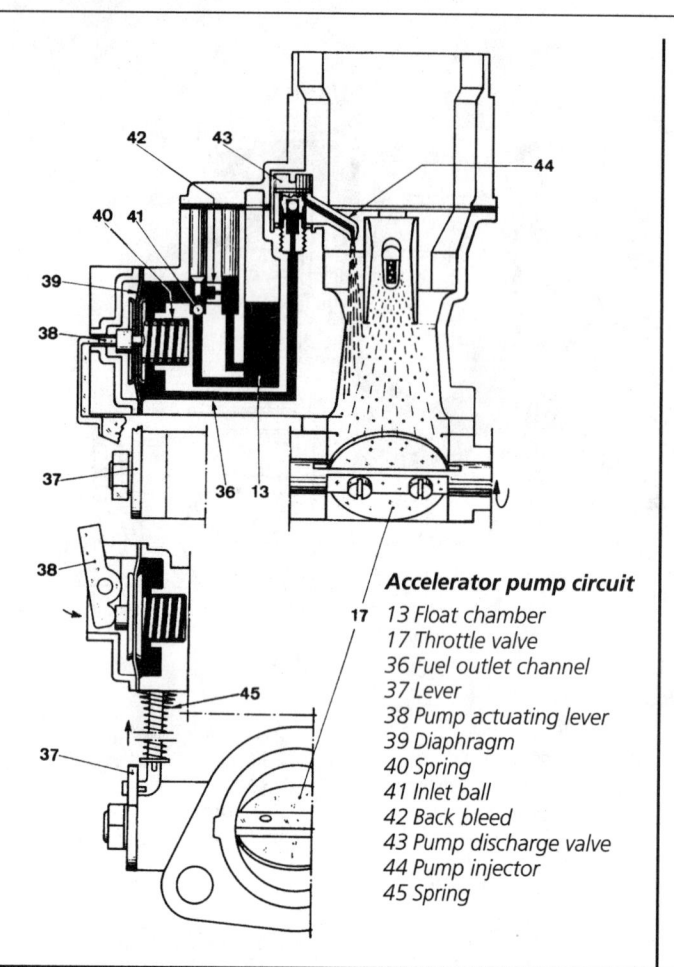

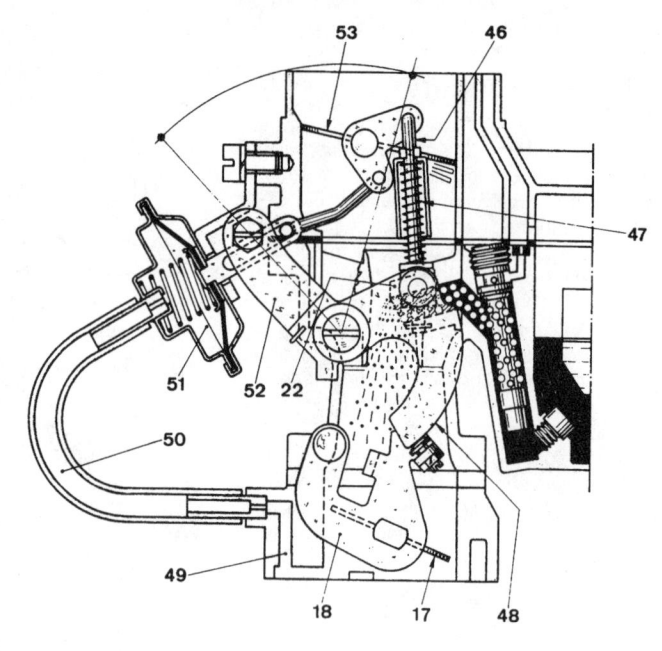

Accelerator pump circuit

- 13 Float chamber
- 17 Throttle valve
- 36 Fuel outlet channel
- 37 Lever
- 38 Pump actuating lever
- 39 Diaphragm
- 40 Spring
- 41 Inlet ball
- 42 Back bleed
- 43 Pump discharge valve
- 44 Pump injector
- 45 Spring

Manual choke

- 17 Throttle valve
- 18 Throttle lever
- 22 Nozzle
- 46 Link rod
- 47 Spring
- 48 Fast idle lever
- 49 Vacuum passage
- 50 Vacuum hose
- 51 Diaphragm
- 52 Choke actuating lever
- 53 Choke flap

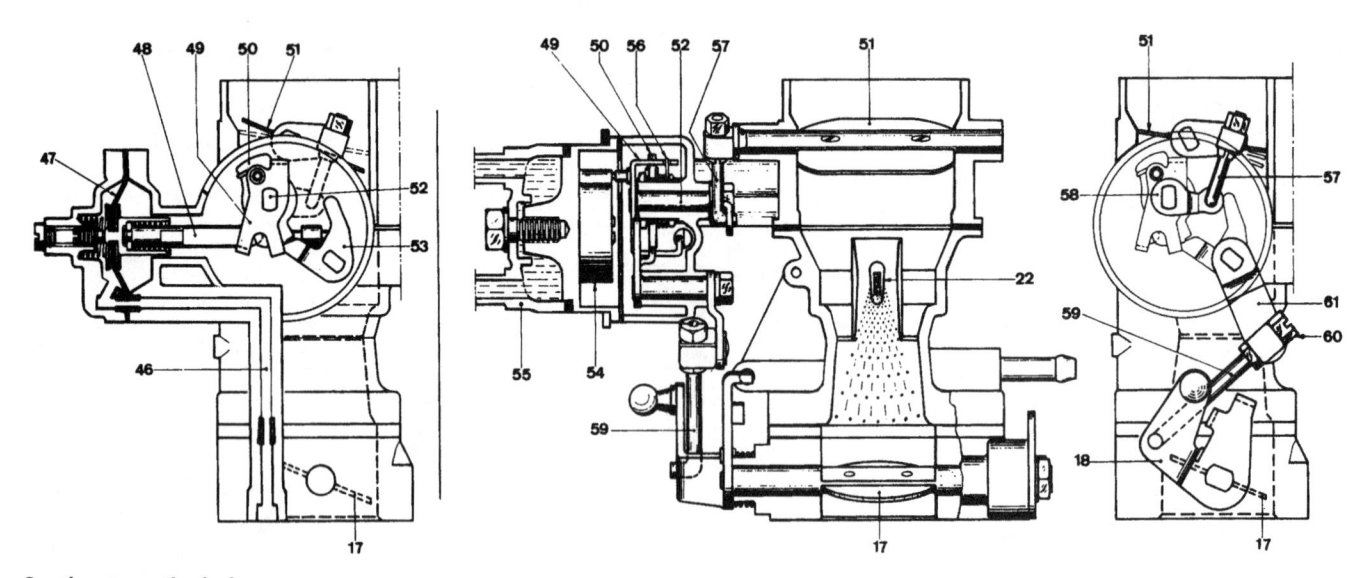

Semi-automatic choke

- 17 Throttle valve
- 18 Throttle lever
- 22 Main outlet
- 46 Vacuum passage
- 47 Diaphragm
- 48 Diaphragm rod
- 49 Lever
- 50 Cam lever
- 51 Choke flap
- 52 Spindle
- 53 lever
- 54 Bi-metal coil
- 55 Choke water jacket
- 56 Spring
- 57 Link rod
- 58 Lever
- 59 Fast idle rod
- 60 Fast idle adjustment screw
- 61 Lever

Weber 32 ICEV carburettor

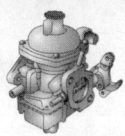

a depression sufficient to raise fuel from the float chamber into a channel. The fuel then passes through a calibrated bushing to the upper section of the air intake. Here it is mixed with a small amount of air from a calibrated air bleed and the emulsified mixture is then discharged into the air stream from the full-load enrichment tube.

Manual choke (some models)

12 The manual choke is operated by a dash-mounted cable. When the cable is pulled, it operates a lever that pulls the choke flap closed across the air intake. Fast idle is achieved with the aid of a curved cam attached to the choke operating lever. An adjustable screw, attached to the throttle lever and butting against the cam, is used to vary the fast idle speed *(see illustration)*.

13 Once the engine has fired, the choke flap must open slightly to weaken the mixture and avoid flooding. During idle and light-throttle operation, this is achieved by using manifold vacuum to actuate a diaphragm. A linkage attached to the diaphragm will then pull upon the choke flap.

14 During engine warm-up, the cable should be progressively pushed home until the choke flap is fully open.

Semi-automatic cold start system

15 A bi-metal spring is used to control a strangler choke flap in the air intake. Heating of the spring is by coolant from the engine cooling system. The system is primed by slowly depressing the accelerator pedal once or twice *(see illustration)*.

16 Once the engine has fired, the choke flap must open slightly to weaken the mixture and avoid flooding during idle and light-throttle operation. This is achieved by using manifold vacuum to actuate a diaphragm. A linkage attached to the diaphragm will then pull upon the choke flap.

17 Fast idle is achieved with the aid of a stepped cam attached to the choke spindle. An actuating lever, connected to the throttle lever by a link rod, butts against the stepped cam. As the bi-metal coil is heated and the plate opens, the actuating lever will rest on successively less-stepped parts of the cam. Idle speed is thus progressively reduced, until ultimately the cam is released and the idle speed returns to normal. An adjustable screw, connected to the link rod mechanism, can be used to vary the fast idle speed.

2 Identification

The Weber identification code is stamped on the float chamber side.

3 General servicing

Introduction

1 Read this Chapter in conjunction with Part B, which describes some of the operations in more detail. It is assumed that the carburettor is removed for this service. However, many of the operations can be tackled with the carburettor in place. Where this is undertaken, first soak the fuel out of the float chamber using a clean tissue or soft cloth, after removing the upper body assembly.

Dismantling and checking

2 Remove the two screws which secure the carburettor to the engine.
3 Remove the carburettor from the engine (see Part B).
4 Check visually for damage and wear.
5 Disconnect the choke linkage, then remove the five screws and detach the carburettor upper body.
6 Use a straight-edge to check for distorted flanges on all facing surfaces.
7 Tap out the float pin and remove the float, needle valve and plastic clip, float chamber gasket and needle valve seat.
8 Check that the anti-vibration ball is free in the valve end.
9 Check the needle valve tip for wear and ridges. This is more likely with the brass needle valve tip than when a viton one is used. Use a viton-tipped replacement when possible.
10 The float should be checked for damage and ingress of petrol.
11 Renew the float pin if it shows signs of wear.
12 Unscrew the hexagon bolt and inspect the fuel filter. Clean the filter housing of debris and dirt and renew the filter if necessary.
13 Remove the mixture screw and inspect the tip for damage and ridges.
14 Remove the four screws and detach the accelerator pump cover, diaphragm and spring. Check the diaphragm for fatigue and damage.
15 Unscrew the pump discharge valve from the body and remove the valve and the pump injector. Test the discharge valve by shaking. No noise from the outlet ball indicates that the valve is seized. Check that the lead pellet that seals the valve is present. If loose or missing, the pump action will be impaired.
16 Remove the primary idle jet assembly from the upper body. The idle jet is pushed into a holder and may be separated (by pulling) for cleaning or renewal.
17 Remove the main jet, air corrector and emulsion tube. Check that the channel from the float chamber into the emulsion tube well is clear.
18 Check the jet calibration against that specified. It is possible that the wrong size jets may have been incorrectly fitted during the last overhaul.
19 Remove the auxiliary venturi from the main body where necessary. Weber provide an extractor tool for removing this component. Check that the auxiliary venturi is not loose in the main body as this is a source of uneven running. If the venturi is loose, knurl the mating flanges with a file to ensure a tight fit.
20 Remove the two screws and separate the carburettor main body and throttle body assemblies. The throttle body can be renewed separately if the spindles or throttle bores are worn.
21 Inspect the choke spindle, linkage and operating mechanism for stickiness and wear.

Carburettors with manual choke

22 Attach a vacuum pump to the pull-down diaphragm and operate the pump to obtain 300 mm Hg. The diaphragm should operate fully and the vacuum must be maintained. Renew the diaphragm assembly if it fails these tests. Check the vacuum hose for leaks and perished rubber.

Carburettors with automatic choke

23 Remove the three fixing screws that secure the bi-metal coil housing to the choke assembly housing. Note the position of the alignment marks and remove the coil housing from the carburettor body. Remove the internal heat shield.
24 Disconnect the upper choke link rod, then remove the two screws and detach the choke housing assembly.
25 Remove the three screws and detach the choke diaphragm cover, spring and diaphragm from the housing. Check the diaphragm for fatigue.

All carburettors

26 Remove the nut, washer, accelerator pump cam and spring from the primary throttle spindle. Lift out the PCV grooved disc. Clean the carbon build-up from the disc, the recess in the body, the spigot and the passage and channel by the throttle plate.

Preparation for reassembly

27 Clean the jets, carburettor body assemblies, float chamber and internal channels. An air line may be used to clear internal channels once the carburettor is fully dismantled. Note that if high-pressure air is directed into the channels and passages with the diaphragms still in place, diaphragm damage may result.
28 Spraying carburettor cleaner into all the channels and passages in the carburettor body will often clear them of gum and dirt.
29 During reassembly, a complete set of new gaskets should be fitted. Also renew the needle valve and float pin, and all diaphragms.
30 Inspect and renew (where necessary) the mixture screw, main jet, idle jet, air corrector jet, emulsion tube and the accelerator pump discharge valve and injector. Renew worn linkages, screws, springs, vacuum hoses and other parts where necessary.
31 Ensure that all jets are firmly locked into position (but do not over-tighten). A loose jet

H12•7

Chapter H12

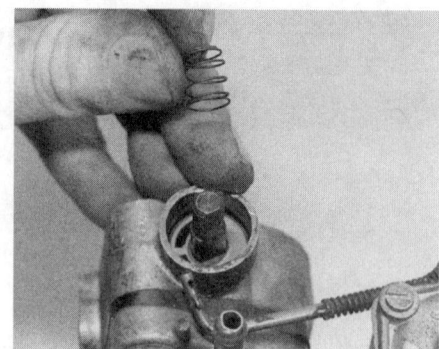

PCV valve

Refitting PCV system components
PCV spring

PCV cover (accelerator pump cam)

can cause a rich (or even lean) running condition.
32 Clean all mating surfaces and flanges of old gasket material and reassemble with new gaskets.
33 Ensure that housings are positioned with their air and fuel routes correctly aligned.

Reassembly

All carburettors

34 Refit the PCV grooved disc, spring, accelerator pump cam, washer and nut to the throttle spindle *(see illustration)*.

Carburettors with automatic choke

35 Refit the choke diaphragm and spindle to the choke housing. Refit the spring and cover, then secure with the three screws.
36 Renew the vacuum O-ring seal and refit the choke housing to the carburettor upper body. Secure with the two screws. Reconnect the upper choke link rod and ensure that the choke flap and linkage move smoothly and progressively.

All carburettors

37 Assemble the main and throttle bodies with a new gasket block, then secure with the two screws.
38 Refit the emulsion tube, air corrector and main jet into their original positions.
39 Assemble the pump discharge valve and pump injector into the body, complete with new sealing washers.
40 Refit the pump spring, diaphragm and cover assembly, then secure with the four screws.
41 Refit the idle mixture screw after renewing the seal. Turn the screw in gently until it just seats. From this position, unscrew it three full turns. This will provide a basic setting to allow the engine to be started.
42 Clean or renew the fuel filter and refit the hexagon bolt.
43 Renew the float chamber gasket and locate in position on the upper body. Renew the needle valve assembly. Screw the valve seat into the upper body, using a new sealing washer, and ensure that it is firmly locked into position (but do not over-tighten). Transfer the hairpin or plastic clip from the old needle valve to the ball

end of the new one. Place the clip and valve assembly onto the inner float tag. Lower the float and needle valve assembly into the seat and secure with the float pin.
44 Adjust the float level. Refer to Section 4 for details on adjustment.
45 Refit the upper body to the main body and secure with the five screws. Reconnect the choke pull-down hose (manual choke only).
46 Push the idle jet into its holder and refit the assembly into the upper body.
47 Ensure that the choke flap and linkage move smoothly and progressively.
48 Adjust the choke fast idle and vacuum pull-

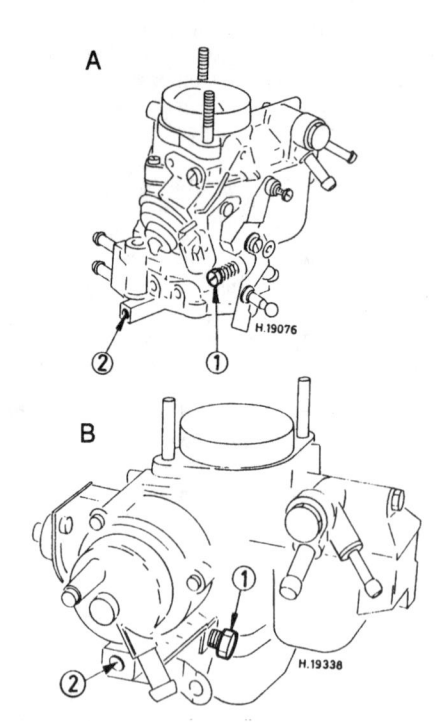

Idle speed and mixture adjustment
A Weber ICEV (manual choke)
B Weber ICEV (automatic choke)
1 Idle speed adjustment screw
2 Idle mixture control screw

down. Refer to Section 4 for details on all adjustments.
49 Refit the carburettor to the engine.
50 Always adjust the carburettor idle speed and mixture after any work has been carried out on the carburettor, preferably with the aid of a CO meter.

4 Service adjustments

Adjustment preconditions

1 Refer to Part B for general advice on the preconditions to correct adjustment of this carburettor.

Idle speed and mixture (CO)

2 Run the engine at 3000 rpm for 30 seconds to clear the manifold of fuel vapours, then allow the engine to idle.
3 Use the idle speed adjustment screw to set the specified idle speed *(see illustration)*.
4 Check the CO level. If it is not as specified, remove the tamperproof plug and adjust the idle mixture control screw to achieve the correct level. Turning the screw clockwise (inwards) will reduce the CO level. Turning the screw anti-clockwise (outwards) will increase the CO level.
5 Repeat paragraphs 3 and 4 until both adjustments are correct.
6 Clear the manifold every 30 seconds during the setting operation by running the engine at 3000 rpm for 30 seconds.
7 Increase the speed to 2000 rpm and note the CO reading. The cruise reading should be less than half the idle CO reading.
8 Fit a new tamperproof plug to the mixture control screw.

Float level/stroke

9 Hold the carburettor upper body in a vertical position with the float tag gently touching the ball of the needle valve.
10 Measure the distance between the upper body (with the gasket in place) and the top of the float (brass float). Where the float is made

H12•8

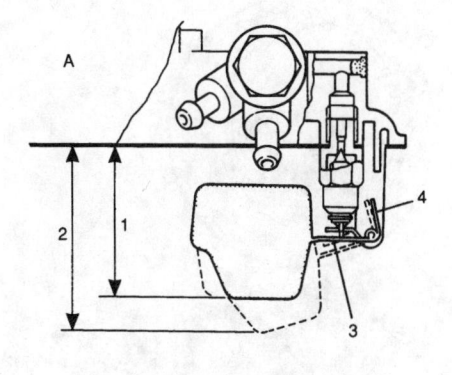

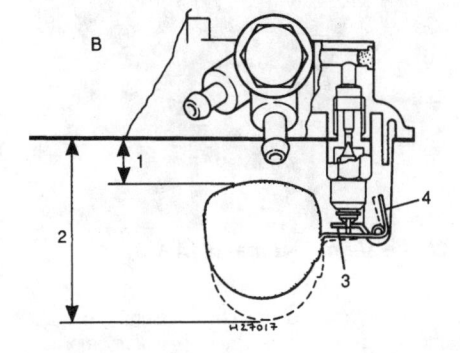

Weber 32 ICEV carburettor

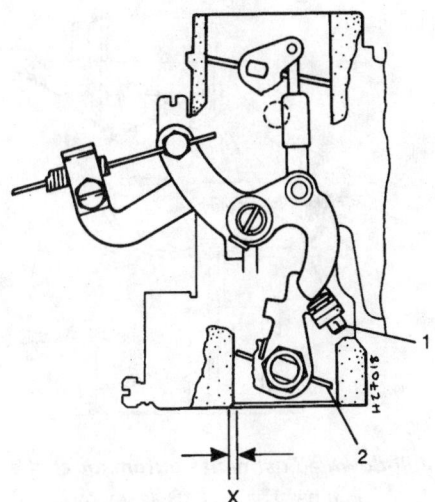

Fast idle adjustment - manual choke
1. Fast idle adjustment screw
2. Throttle valve
X. Fast idle clearance

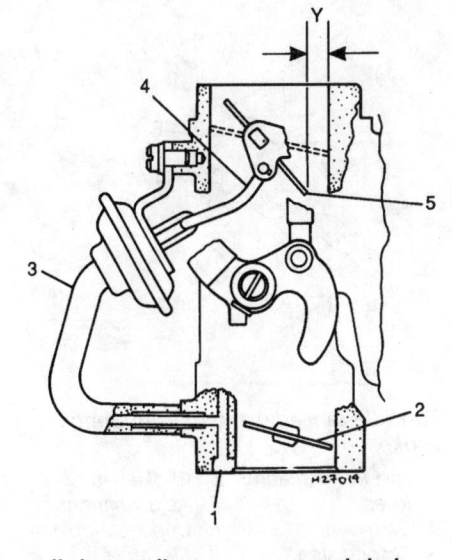

Pull-down adjustment - manual choke
1. Vacuum passage
2. Throttle valve
3. Vacuum hose
4. Diaphragm control rod
5. Choke flap
Y. Pull-down clearance

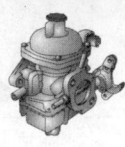

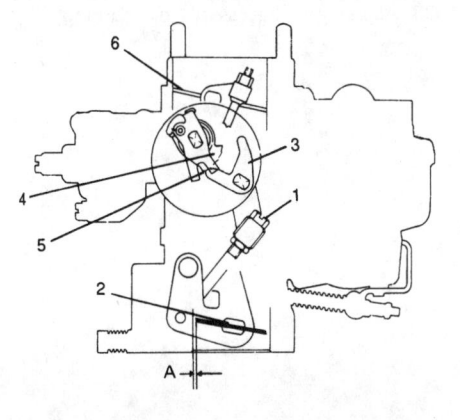

Float level adjustment
A. Plastic float level measurement
B. Brass float level measurement
1. Float level
2. Float travel
3. Inner float tag
4. Outer float tag

of plastic, measure to the bottom of the float (see illustration).
11. Adjust as necessary by bending the inner float tag.
12. Place the upper body in a horizontal position and allow the float to hang down.
13. Measure the distance between the upper body (with the gasket in place) and bottom of the float (all float types). This figure is the float stroke.
14. Adjust as necessary by bending the outer float tag.

Manual choke

Fast idle
15. The carburettor must be removed from the engine in order to make the fast idle adjustment.
16. Invert the carburettor.
17. Pull the choke operating arm to fully close the choke flap. The adjustment screw will butt against the fast idle cam and force open the throttle plate to leave a small clearance (see illustration).
18. Use the shank of a twist drill to measure the clearance between the wall of the throttle bore and the throttle plate. Refer to Specifications for the required drill size and measure the clearance from the progression holes.
19. Adjust as necessary by turning the adjustment screw in the appropriate direction.

Vacuum pull-down
20. Pull the choke operating arm to fully close the choke flap (see illustration).
21. Disconnect the vacuum hose and use a vacuum pump to pull the diaphragm operating rod up to its stop (or push the mechanism with a small screwdriver). At the same time, use the shank of a twist drill to measure the gap between the lower section of the choke flap and the air intake. Refer to Specifications for the required drill size.
22. Adjust as necessary by bending the diaphragm control rod in the appropriate direction (see illustration).

Automatic choke

Fast idle
23. The carburettor must be removed from the engine in order to make the fast idle adjustment.
24. Remove the three screws and detach the bi-metal coil housing from the carburettor.
25. Remove the internal plastic heat shield.
26. Invert the carburettor.
27. Partially open the throttle. Close the choke flap so that the fast idle actuating lever is positioned against the highest step of the fast idle cam and then release the throttle (see illustration).
28. Use the shank of a twist drill to measure the clearance between the wall of the throttle bore and the throttle plate. Refer to Specifications for

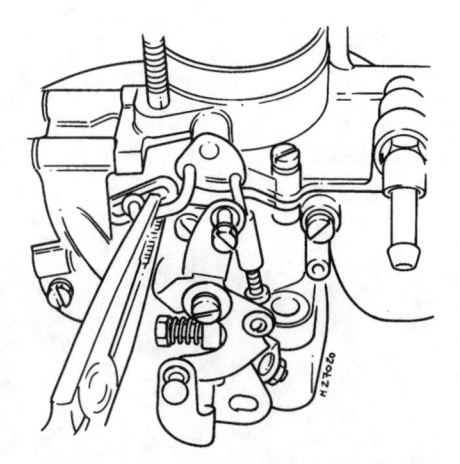

Bending control rod - manual choke

Fast idle adjustment - automatic choke
1. Fast idle adjustment screw
2. Throttle valve
3. Fast idle actuating lever
4. Cam
5. First step
6. Choke flap
A. Fast idle clearance

Chapter H12

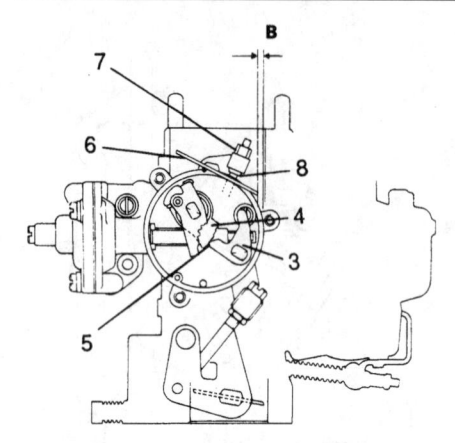

Fast idle cam adjustment - automatic choke

3 Fast idle actuating lever
4 Cam
5 Second step
6 Choke flap
7 Adjustment nut
8 Upper control link
B Clearance

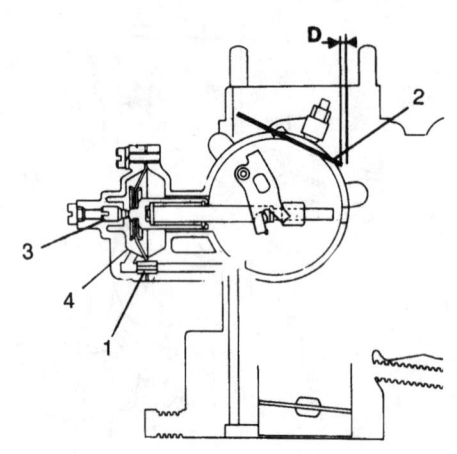

Pull-down adjustment - automatic choke

1 Vacuum passage
2 Choke flap
3 Adjustment screw
4 Diaphragm
D Pull-down clearance

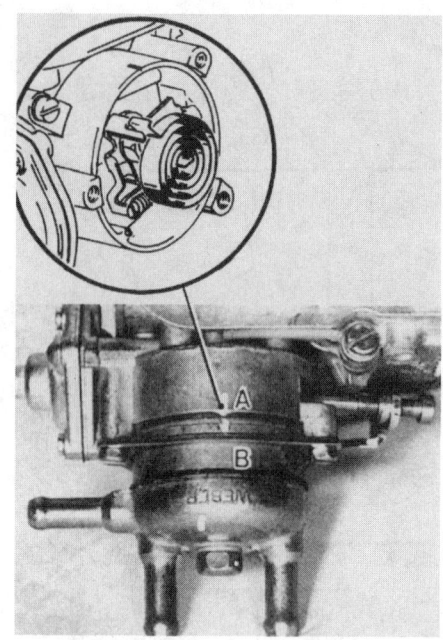

Choke alignment marks (A & B)

the required drill size and measure from the progression holes *(see illustration)*.

29 Adjust as necessary by slackening the locknut and turning the adjustment screw, on the fast idle link rod, in the appropriate direction. Retighten the locknut on completion.

Fast idle cam and vacuum pull-down

30 Partially open the throttle. Close the choke flap so that the fast idle actuating lever is positioned against the second-highest step of the fast idle cam and then release the throttle.
31 Release the throttle and fit an elastic band to the choke operating lever so that the choke flap remains in the fully on position.
32 Use the shank of a twist drill to measure the gap between the lower section of the choke flap and the air intake. The clearance should measure 3.0 to 3.5 mm *(see illustration)*.
33 Adjust as necessary by turning the adjustment nut on the upper link rod in the appropriate direction.
34 Use a small screwdriver to push open the diaphragm up to its stop, then use the shank of a twist drill to measure the gap between the lower section of the choke flap and the air intake. Refer to Specifications for the required drill size.
35 Remove the plug and adjust as necessary by turning the diaphragm adjustment screw in the appropriate direction. Renew the plug when adjustment is complete.
36 Remove the elastic band.
37 Refit the internal heat shield and ensure that the peg in the housing locates into the hole in the shield.
38 Refit the bi-metal coil housing and ensure that the spring locates in the slot of the choke lever. Secure loosely with the three screws. Align the cut mark on the bi-metal cover with the correct mark on the choke assembly housing and tighten the three screws *(see illustration)*.

5 Fault diagnosis

Refer to Part D for diagnosis of general carburettor faults. The following faults are specific to Weber ICEV carburettors.

Blockage

☐ Check the PCV passage for carbon blockage. Allow the engine to idle, then remove the PCV hose at the carburettor base and place a finger upon the spigot. A small vacuum pull should be felt.

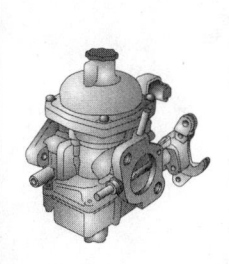

Part H Chapter 13
Weber 32 ICH carburettor

H13

Contents

Fault diagnosis	5	Principles of operation	1
General servicing	3	Service adjustments	4
Identification	2		

Specifications

Model	Fiesta 950 HC/LC
Year	1978 to 1983
Engine code	TKA (OHV)
Capacity (cm³)/no. of cyls	957/4
Oil temperature (°C)	80
Transmission	Manual
Carb. ident. (Ford)	79BF 9510 RAA
Carb. ident. (Weber/Solex)	32 ICH 4/350
Idle speed (rpm)	800 ± 50
Fast idle speed (rpm)	3200 ± 100
CO @ idle (% vol.)	1.5 ± 0.5
Venturi diameter	23
Idle jet	40
Main jet	115
Air correction jet	170
Emulsion tube	F2
Accel. pump jet	40
Float level (mm)	35 ± 0.5
Float stroke (mm)	41 ± 0.5
Needle valve size (mm)	1.5
Choke pull-down (mm)	8.5 ± 0.7

Chapter H13

1 Principles of operation

Introduction

1 The following technical description of the Weber ICH carburettor should be read in conjunction with the more detailed description of carburettor principles described in Part A.

Construction

2 The Weber 32 ICH carburettor is a downdraught single venturi instrument with a manual choke control and power valve *(see illustration)*. The throttle shaft is made of steel. The throttle valve is made of brass, as is the emulsion tube. All the jets are brass, with the exception of the accelerator pump injector which is die-cast. The internal fuel channels and air passages are drilled and sealed with lead plugs where necessary.

Fuel control

3 Fuel flows into the carburettor through a fine mesh filter. The fuel level in the float chamber is controlled by a needle valve and brass float assembly. An anti-vibration ball is incorporated into the needle valve design. A plastic or hairpin clip, attached to the needle valve seat and to the float arm, prevents the needle from sticking in the seat as the fuel level drops. The float chamber is vented externally to atmosphere.

Idle, slow running and progression

4 Fuel, sourced from the main well, passes into the idle channel through a metered idle jet. Here it is mixed with a small amount of air from a calibrated air bleed. The emulsion formed is drawn through a channel to be discharged from the idle orifice under the primary throttle plate. A tapered mixture screw is used to vary the outlet and this ensures fine control of the idle mixture. A number of progression drillings are uncovered by the opening throttle as the engine is accelerated *(see illustration)*.

5 Idle speed is set by an adjustable screw. The adjustable mixture screw is tamper-proofed at production level, in accordance with emission regulations.

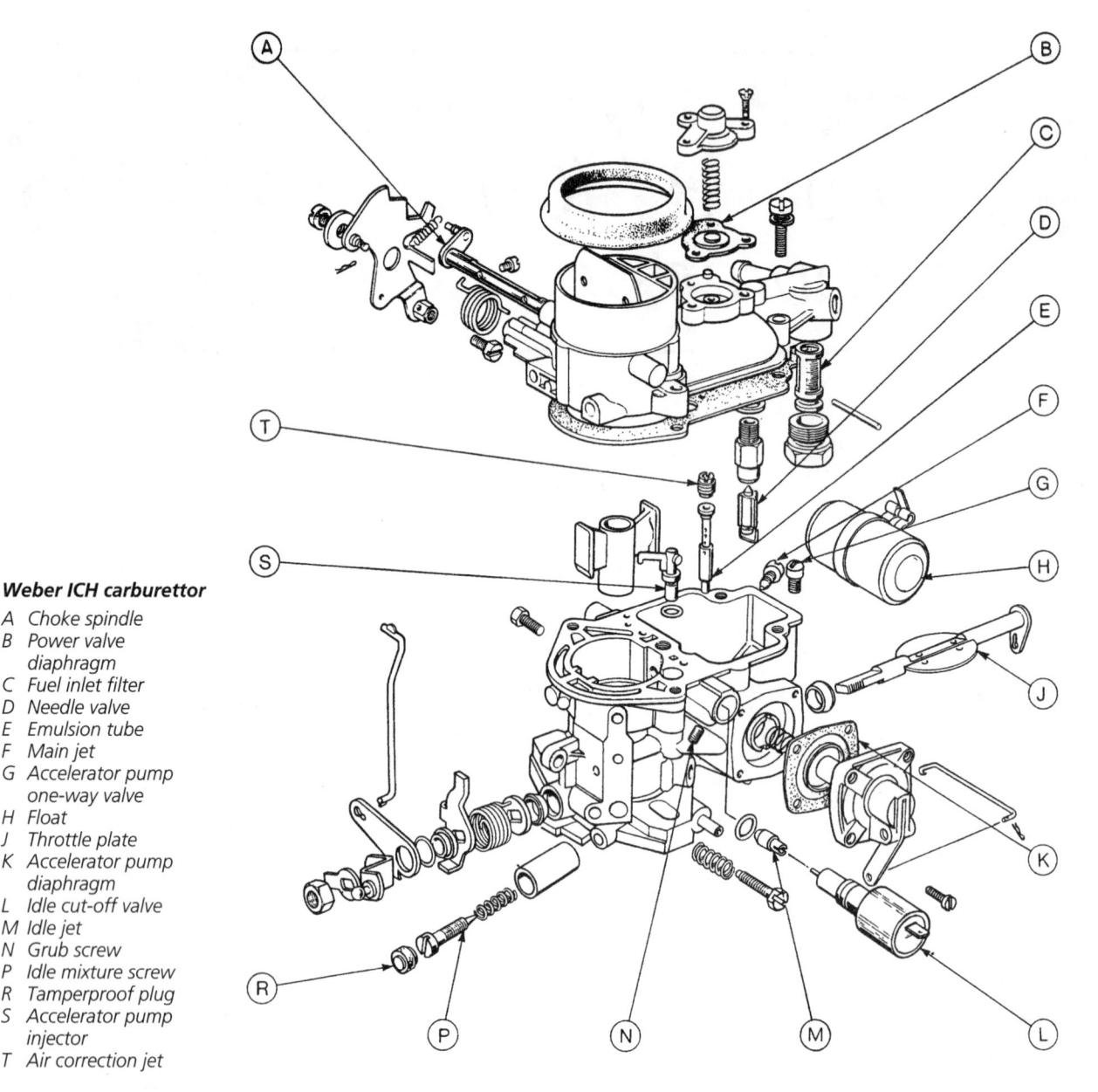

Weber ICH carburettor

- A Choke spindle
- B Power valve diaphragm
- C Fuel inlet filter
- D Needle valve
- E Emulsion tube
- F Main jet
- G Accelerator pump one-way valve
- H Float
- J Throttle plate
- K Accelerator pump diaphragm
- L Idle cut-off valve
- M Idle jet
- N Grub screw
- P Idle mixture screw
- R Tamperproof plug
- S Accelerator pump injector
- T Air correction jet

Weber 32 ICH carburettor

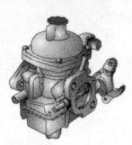

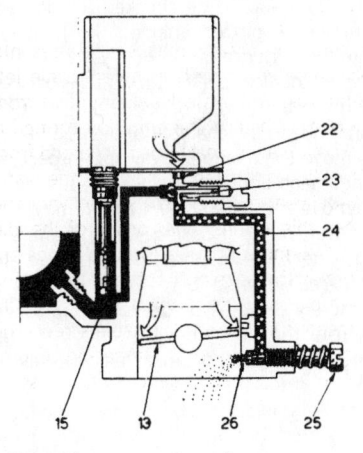

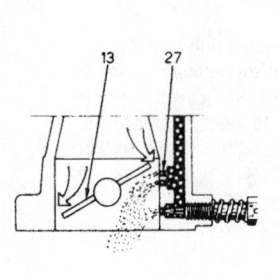

Idle and progression phase

- 13 Throttle plate
- 15 Main fuel well
- 22 Calibrated air bleed
- 23 Idle jet
- 24 Fuel channel
- 25 Mixture screw
- 26 Idle outlet
- 27 Progression holes

Acceleration phase

- 18 Float chamber
- 28 Accelerator pump injector
- 29 Delivery valve
- 30 Fuel channel
- 31 Lever
- 32 Rod
- 33 Fuel channel
- 34 Lever
- 35 Diaphragm
- 36 Spring
- 37 Spring
- 38 Inlet valve

Idle cut-off valve

6 An idle cut-off valve is used to prevent run-on when the engine is shut down. It utilises a 7-volt solenoid plunger to block the idle jet when the ignition is switched off.

Accelerator pump

7 The accelerator pump is controlled by a diaphragm and is mechanically operated by a rod attached to the throttle linkage. The outlet valve consists of a ball incorporated into the pump injector. The inlet valve consists of a brass valve located in the float chamber and this valve also returns excess fuel to the chamber (see illustration).

Main circuit

8 The amount of fuel discharged into the air stream is controlled by a calibrated main jet. Fuel is drawn through the main jet into the base of a vertical well which dips down into the fuel in the float chamber. An emulsion tube is placed in the well. The fuel is mixed with air drawn in through the air corrector and the holes in the emulsion tube. The resulting emulsified mixture is discharged from the main orifice through an auxiliary venturi.

Power enrichment and economy circuit

9 A vacuum-controlled power valve allows an air bypass of the air supply to the air corrector jet and a bushing limits the amount of air supplied to the air corrector. During idle and part-throttle operation, vacuum acts upon a diaphragm via an air passage from under the throttle plate. The diaphragm is pulled back against spring pressure to open a passage which is the bypass to the limiter bushing. The extra air causes a leaner mixture and better economy (see illustration).

10 During acceleration and wide-open throttle operation, the vacuum in the manifold and in the power valve air passage collapses. The diaphragm returns under spring pressure to close the bypass passage. With less air available at the air corrector, the fuel mixture is enriched.

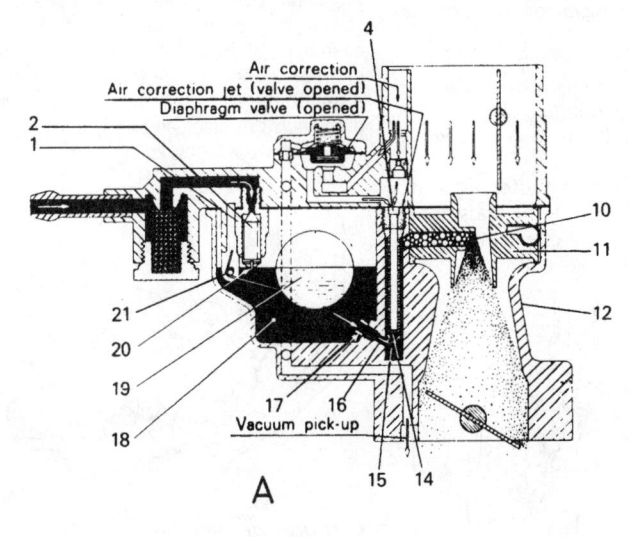

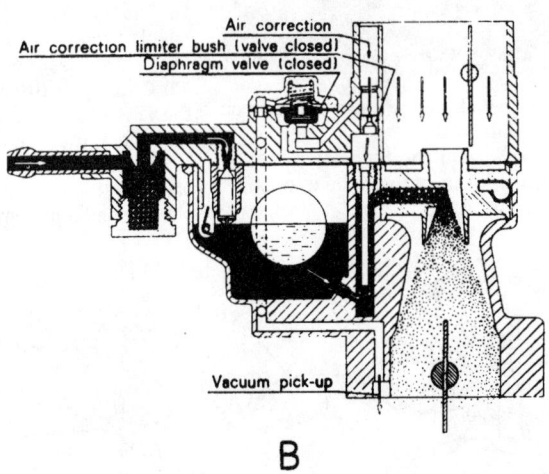

Power enrichment and economy circuit

- A Throttle light/cruise condition
- B Wide-open throttle
- 1 Needle valve seat
- 2 Needle valve
- 4 Main corrector jet
- 10 Main discharge nozzle
- 11 Auxiliary venturi
- 12 Venturi
- 14 Emulsion tube
- 15 Main fuel well
- 16 Fuel channel
- 17 Main jet
- 18 Float chamber
- 19 Float
- 20 Hairpin clip
- 21 Float pivot pin

Chapter H13

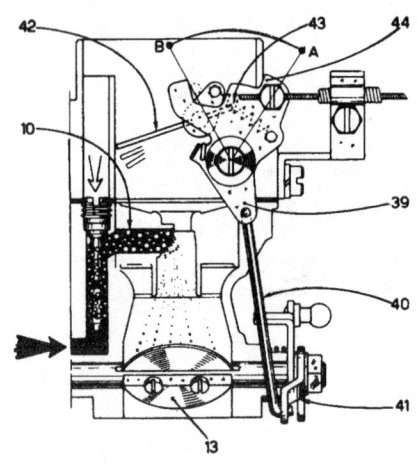

Choke operation

Lever in position A – choke on
Lever in position B – choke off

10 Main discharge nozzle	41 Lever
13 Throttle plate	42 Choke plate
39 Lever	43 Spring
40 Rod	44 Lever

Choke operation

11 The manual choke is operated by a dash-mounted cable. When the cable is pulled, it operates a lever that pulls the choke flap closed across the air intake. A linkage rod opens the throttle to give a fast idle. Once the engine has started, manifold vacuum partially opens the choke flap against the action of a spring. A stop ensures that the choke is only opened a small amount. During engine warm-up, the cable should be progressively pushed home until the choke flap is fully open *(see illustration)*.

2 Identification

The Weber identification code is stamped on the float chamber body.

A metal tag giving the Ford identification code is attached to one of the carburettor upper body fixing screws.

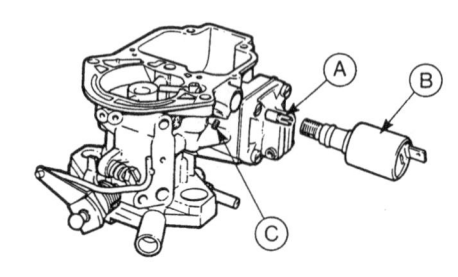

Idle cut off valve removal

A Idle jet
B Idle cut-off valve
C Securing grub screw

3 General servicing

Introduction

1 Read this Chapter in conjunction with Part B, which describes some of the operations in more detail. It is assumed that the carburettor is removed for this service. However, many of the operations can be tackled with the carburettor in place. Where this is undertaken, first soak the fuel out of the float chamber using a clean tissue or soft cloth, after removing the upper body assembly.

Dismantling and checking

2 Remove the carburettor from the engine (see Part B).
3 Make visual checks for damage and wear.
4 Use a 2 mm Allen key to unscrew the grub screw which secures the idle cut-off valve assembly to the carburettor lower body. Remove the valve and idle jet assembly *(see illustration)*.
5 Separate the idle cut-off valve and idle jet and clean with carburettor cleaner. Test the plunger operation by connecting the valve to a 6 to 7-volt supply (or use the valve supply wire in the engine compartment). With the ignition on, touch the valve body to earth several times and ensure that the plunger tip advances and retracts cleanly. Renew the valve if the action is faulty or if cleaning does not improve its operation.
6 Remove the securing clip and detach the choke link rod from the choke arm.
7 Remove the four screws and detach the carburettor upper body.
8 Use a straight-edge to check for distorted flanges on all facing surfaces.
9 Inspect the float chamber for corrosion and calcium build-up.
10 Tap out the float pin then remove the float, needle valve, clip, float chamber gasket and needle valve seat *(see illustration)*.
11 Check that the anti-vibration ball is free in the valve end.
12 Check the needle valve tip for wear and ridges. This is more likely with the brass needle valve tip than when a viton one is used. Use a viton-tipped replacement when possible.

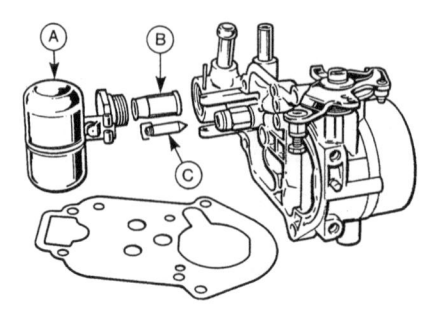

Upper body and float components

A Float
B Fuel inlet filter
C Needle valve

13 The float should be checked for damage and ingress of petrol. Shaking the float will indicate the presence of fuel.
14 Renew the float pin if it shows signs of wear.
15 Remove the hexagon bolt and inspect the fuel filter. Clean the chamber of debris and dirt.
16 Remove the mixture screw and inspect the tip for damage or ridges.
17 Remove the four screws and remove the accelerator pump housing, diaphragm and spring. Check the diaphragm for fatigue and damage *(see illustration)*.
18 Unscrew the brass accelerator pump inlet valve from the float chamber and test it by shaking. No noise indicates that the valve is seized.
19 The pump injector is a push fit in the body. Carefully prise it from its location using two small screwdrivers and test it by shaking. No noise from the outlet ball indicates that the valve is seized.
20 Remove the air corrector, emulsion tube and main jet.
21 Check that the channel into the emulsion tube well is clear.
22 Check the calibration of the jets against that specified.
23 Remove the three screws and remove the power valve housing, spring and diaphragm from the upper body. Check the diaphragm for fatigue and damage *(see illustration)*.
24 Remove the auxiliary venturi where necessary. A Weber extractor tool is available for this purpose. Check that the auxiliary venturi is not loose in the main body as this is a source of uneven running. If a venturi is loose, knurl the mating flanges with a file to ensure a tight fit.
25 Inspect the choke spindle, mechanism and levers for stickiness and wear.

Preparation for reassembly

26 Clean the jets and internal channels, the carburettor body assemblies and the float chamber. An air line may be used to clear the internal channels once the carburettor is fully dismantled. If an air line is used with the diaphragms in place and air is directed into the diaphragm passages, diaphragm damage may result.

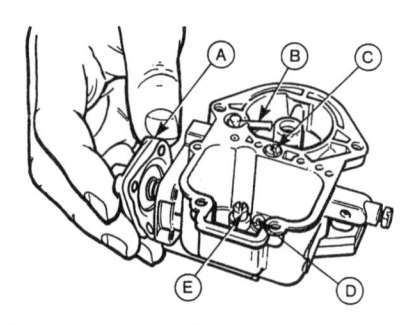

Carburettor main body

A Accelerator pump diaphragm
B Accelerator pump injector
C Air correction jet
D Main jet
E Accelerator pump one-way valve

Weber 32 ICH carburettor

27 Spraying carburettor cleaner into all the channels and passages in the carburettor body will often clear them of gum and dirt.
28 During reassembly, a complete set of new gaskets should be fitted. Also renew the needle valve and float pin, and all diaphragms.
29 Inspect and renew (where necessary) the mixture screw, main jet, idle jet, air corrector jet and pump injector. Renew worn linkages, springs and other parts where necessary.
30 Ensure that all jets are firmly locked into position (but do not overtighten). A loose jet can cause a rich (or even lean) running condition.
31 Clean all mating surfaces and flanges of old gasket material and reassemble with new gaskets.
32 Ensure that housings are assembled with their air and fuel routes correctly aligned.

Reassembly

33 Refit the power diaphragm, spring and cover assembly, then secure with the three screws.
34 Refit the main jet, emulsion tube and air corrector.
35 Refit the accelerator pump inlet valve into the float chamber and push the pump injector firmly into the body (renew the small seal on the injector body).
36 Refit the pump spring, diaphragm and cover assembly, then secure with the four screws.
37 Refit the idle mixture screw. Carefully turn the screw in until it just seats then unscrew it three full turns. This will provide a basic setting to allow the engine to be started.
38 Clean or renew the fuel filter and secure with the hexagon bolt.
39 Renew the needle valve assembly. Screw the valve seat into the upper body, using a new sealing washer, and ensure that it is firmly locked into position.
40 Place the new float chamber gasket on the upper body before refitting the float. Insert the needle valve into the valve seat (with the ball facing outwards), ensuring that the clip is correctly connected to the float and the needle valve, then refit the float and pin.
41 Adjust the float level. Refer to Section 4 for details.
42 Refit the upper body and secure with the four screws.
43 Refit the clip securing the choke link rod to the choke arm.
44 Push the idle jet into the idle cut-off valve and refit the assembly. Use a 2 mm Allen key to lock the grub screw which secures the cut-off valve to the carburettor main body *(see illustration)*.
45 Ensure that the choke flap and linkage moves smoothly and progressively.
46 Refit the carburettor to the engine.
47 Always adjust the carburettor idle speed and mixture after any work has been carried out on the carburettor, preferably with the aid of a CO meter.
48 Refer to Section 4 and adjust the choke.

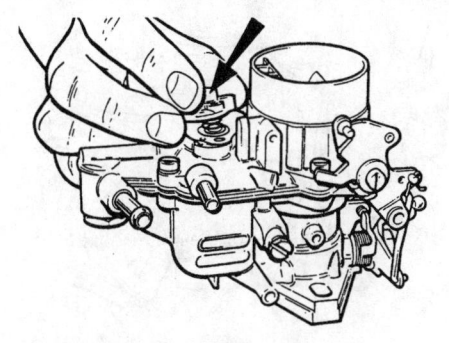

Power valve diaphragm assembly (arrowed)

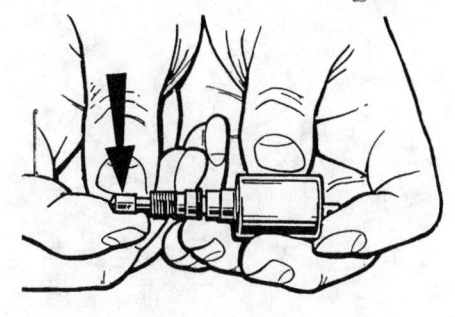

4 Service adjustments

Adjustment preconditions

1 Refer to Part B for general advice on preconditions to correct adjustment of this carburettor.

Idle speed and mixture (CO)

2 Run the engine at 3000 rpm for 30 seconds to clear the manifold of fuel vapours, then allow the engine to idle.
3 Use the idle speed screw to set the specified idle speed *(see illustration)*.
4 Check the CO level and compare with the specified value. If incorrect, remove the tamperproof plug and adjust to the correct level. Turning the screw clockwise (inwards) will reduce the CO level. Turning the screw anti-clockwise (outwards) will increase the CO level.
5 Repeat paragraphs 3 and 4 until both adjustments are correct.
6 Clear the manifold every 30 seconds during the setting operation by running the engine at 3000 rpm for 30 seconds.
7 Increase the engine speed to 2000 rpm and note the CO reading. The cruise reading should be less than half the idle CO reading.
8 Fit a new tamperproof plug to the mixture adjusting screw.

Idle jet (arrowed) fitted to idle cut-off valve

9 At idle, the manufacturer states that variations of 0.5% CO and 40 rpm are acceptable.

Float level/stroke

10 Hold the carburettor upper body in a vertical position with the float tag gently touching the ball of the needle valve.
11 Measure the distance between the upper body (with the gasket in place) and the base of the float *(see illustration)*.
12 Adjust as necessary by bending the inner float tag.
13 Place the upper body in a horizontal position and allow the float to drop.
14 Measure the distance between the upper body (with the gasket in place) and the base of the float. This figure is the float operating stroke. Adjust as necessary by bending the outer float tag.

Manual choke

Fast idle

15 Warm the engine to normal running temperature and adjust the idle speed and mixture before attempting choke fast idle adjustment.
16 Fully close the choke flap by rotating the choke cam onto its stop. This can be accomplished by pulling the dash control knob fully out and locking the choke cable in position.
17 Open the choke flap against the spring tension to its stop then start the engine and

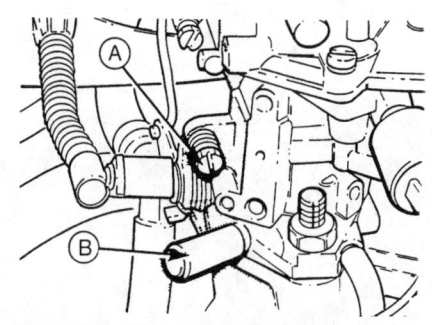

Idle adjustment screws location
A Idle speed screw B Mixture (CO) screw

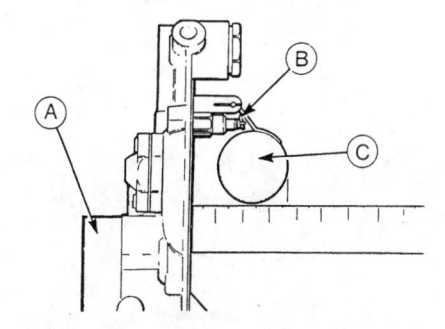

Float level adjustment
A Upper body held vertically
B Adjusting tag
C Float

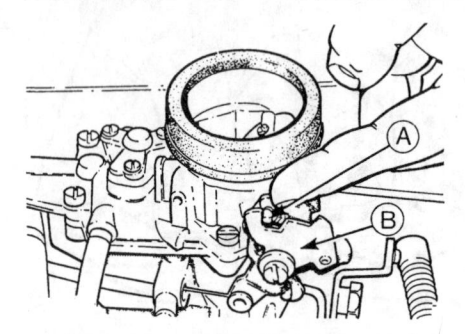

Chapter H13

Carburettor set for fast idle check
A Choke plate held as far open as possible
B Choke mechanism fully operated

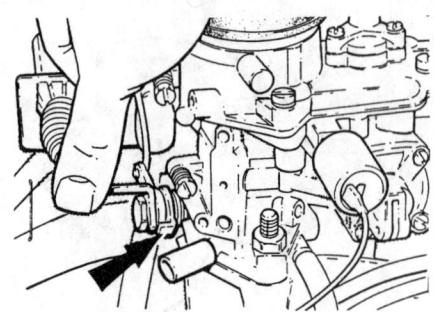

Fast idle adjusting tag (arrowed)
Throttle held open for clarity

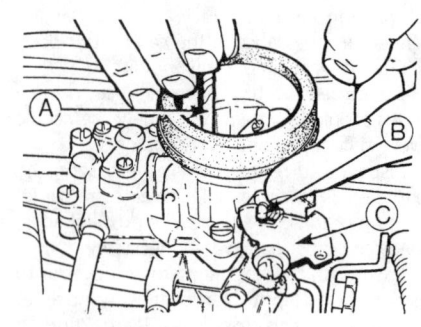

Choke pull-down adjustment
A Twist drill
B Choke flap opened against pull-down spring
C Choke linkage in fully-on position

record the fast idle speed. Refer to Specifications for the correct figure *(see illustration)*.
18 Stop the engine and adjust as necessary by bending the tag *(see illustration)*.
19 Re-check the fast idle speed following any adjustment.

Choke pull-down

20 Fully close the choke flap by rotating the choke cam onto its stop. This can be accomplished by pulling the dash control knob fully out and locking the choke cable in position.
21 Open the choke flap against the spring tension to its stop *(see illustration)*.

22 Use the shank of a twist drill to measure the gap between the lower part of the choke flap and the air intake. Refer to Specifications for the required drill size.
23 Adjust as necessary by bending the tag *(see illustration)*.

5 Fault diagnosis

Refer to Part D for diagnosis of general carburettor faults.

Choke flap pull-down adjusting tag (arrowed)

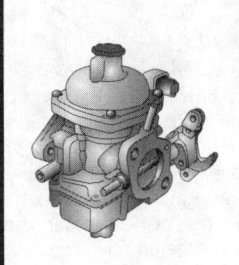

Part H Chapter 14
Weber 34 ICT carburettor

H14

Contents

Fault diagnosis 5	Principles of operation 1
General servicing 3	Service adjustments 4
Identification 2	

Specifications

Manufacturer	Bedford	Bedford	Bedford
Model	**CF 1.8**	**CF2 2.0**	**CF2 2.0**
Year	**1969 to 1984**	**1984 to 1987**	**1984 to 1987**
Engine code	SOHC	20T CIH	20T CIH
Capacity (cm³)/no. of cyls	1759/4	1979/4	1979/4
Oil temperature (°C)	80	80	80
Transmission	MT	MT	AT
Carb. identification	34 ICT 1/350	34 ICT 7/350 or 34 ICT 9/350	34 ICT 8/350
Idle speed (rpm)	800 ± 25	775 ± 25	750 ± 25
CO @ idle (% vol.)	3.5 max.	1.5 ± 1.0	1.5 ± 1.0
Venturi diameter	27	29	29
Idle jet	47	47	47
Main jet	140	150	150
Air correction jet	140	180	180
Emulsion tube	F78	F103	F103
Accel. pump jet	60	55	55
Float level (mm)	6 ± 0.5	6.25 ± 0.25	6.25 ± 0.25
Needle valve size (mm)	1.75	1.75	1.75
Choke fast idle gap (mm)	1.55	1.35 ± 0.05	1.35 ± 0.05
Choke pull-down (mm)	8.5 ± 0.5	7 ± 0.5	7 ± 0.5

Manufacturer	Bedford	Bedford
Model	**CF 2.3**	**CF 2.3**
Year	**1969 to 1984**	**1969 to 1984**
Engine code	SOHC	SOHC
Capacity (cm³)/no. of cyls	2279/4	2279/4
Oil temperature (°C)	80	80
Transmission	MT	AT
Carb. identification	34 ICT 3/350 or 351	34 ICT 4/350
Idle speed (rpm)	800 ± 25	750 ± 25 (in Drive)
CO @ idle (% vol.)	3.5 max.	3.5 max.
Venturi diameter	29	29
Idle jet	50	47
Main jet	147	147
Air correction jet	145	145
Emulsion tube	F78	F78
Accel. pump jet	55	50
Float level (mm)	6 ± 0.5	6.25
Needle valve size (mm)	1.75	1.75
Choke fast idle gap (mm)	1.55	1.5 ± 0.1
Choke pull-down (mm)	8.5 ± 0.5	8.5 ± 0.5

Chapter H14

1 Principles of operation

Introduction

1 The following technical description of the Weber ICT carburettor should be read in conjunction with the more detailed description of carburettor principles in Part A.

Construction

2 The Weber ICT carburettor is a downdraught, single venturi instrument with a manual choke control *(see illustration)*. The throttle shaft is made of steel. The throttle valve is made of brass, as are the jets and the emulsion tube. The exception is the accelerator pump injector which is die-cast. The internal fuel channels and air passages are drilled and sealed with lead plugs where necessary. A throttle damper is fitted on some models with manual transmission.

Fuel control

3 Fuel flows into the carburettor through a fine mesh filter. The fuel level in the float chamber is controlled by a needle valve and brass float assembly. An anti-vibration ball is incorporated into the needle valve design. A clip, attached to the needle valve and to the float arm, prevents the needle from sticking in the seat as the fuel level drops. The float chamber is vented externally to atmosphere. On some models, a calibrated fuel return system is provided to ensure that relatively cool fuel is supplied to the carburettor *(see illustration)*.

Idle, slow running and progression

4 Fuel, sourced from the main well, passes into the primary idle channel through a metered idle jet. Here it is mixed with a small amount of air from a calibrated air bleed. The resulting emulsion is drawn through a channel to be discharged from the idle orifice under the primary throttle plate. A tapered mixture screw is used to vary the outlet and this ensures fine control of the idle mixture. A number of progression drillings provide enrichment as they

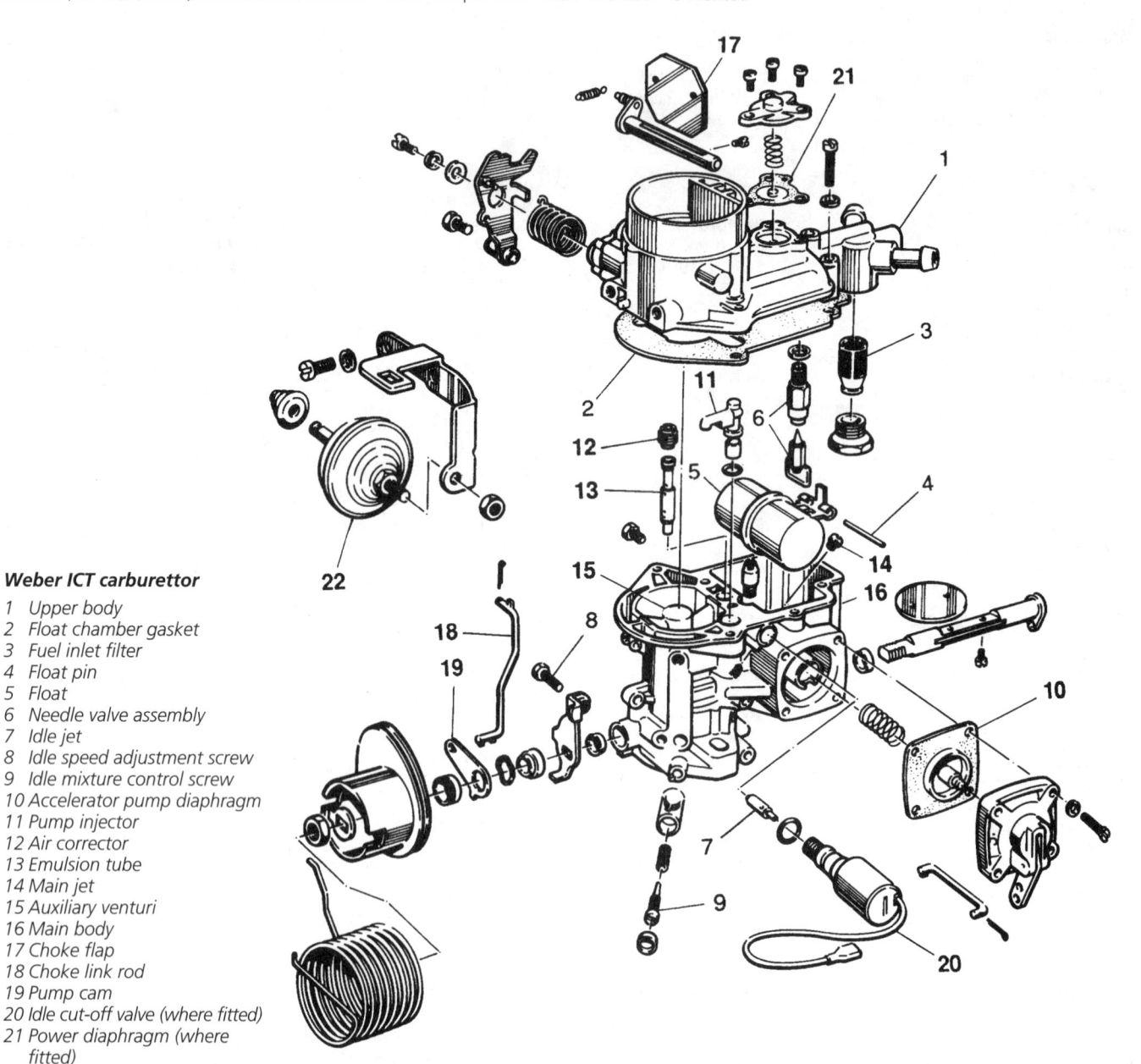

Weber ICT carburettor

1. Upper body
2. Float chamber gasket
3. Fuel inlet filter
4. Float pin
5. Float
6. Needle valve assembly
7. Idle jet
8. Idle speed adjustment screw
9. Idle mixture control screw
10. Accelerator pump diaphragm
11. Pump injector
12. Air corrector
13. Emulsion tube
14. Main jet
15. Auxiliary venturi
16. Main body
17. Choke flap
18. Choke link rod
19. Pump cam
20. Idle cut-off valve (where fitted)
21. Power diaphragm (where fitted)
22. Throttle damper (where fitted)

Weber 34 ICT carburettor

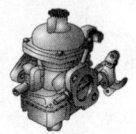

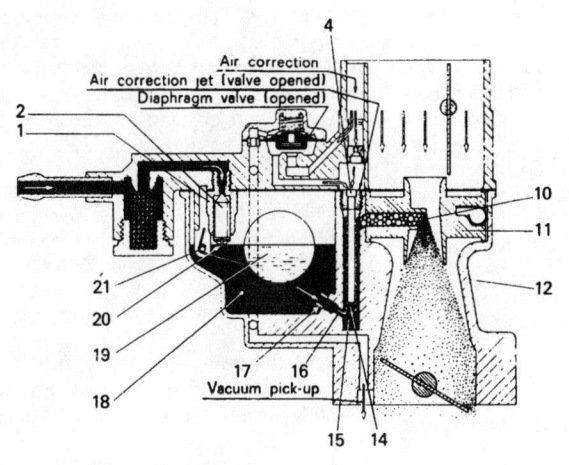

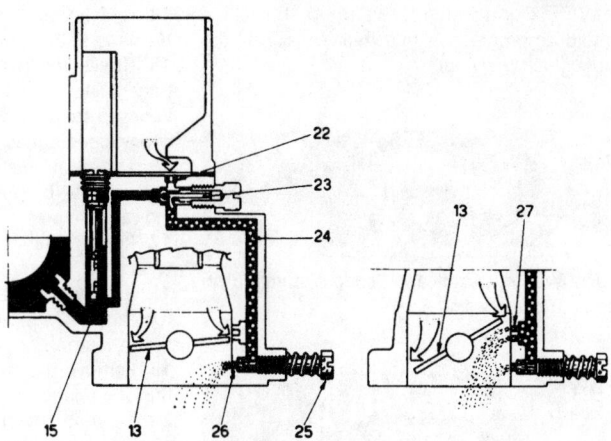

Inlet, main and power circuits

1. Needle valve seat
2. Needle valve
4. Air corrector
10. Main fuel outlet
11. Auxiliary venturi
12. Main venturi
14. Emulsion tube
15. Main well
16. Fuel passage
17. Main jet
18. Float chamber
19. Float
20. Float arm
21. Float pin

Idle and progression circuits

13. Throttle valve
15. Main well
22. Air bleed
23. Idle jet
24. Idle fuel/air channel
25. Idle mixture control screw
26. Idle outlet
27. Progression outlet

are uncovered by the opening throttle during initial acceleration *(see illustration)*.

5 The idle speed is set by an adjustable screw. The adjustable mixture screw is tamper proofed during production, in accordance with emission regulations.

Idle cut-off valve (some models)

6 An idle cut-off valve is used to prevent run-on when the engine is shut down. It utilises a 7-volt solenoid plunger to block the idle jet when the ignition is switched off.

Accelerator pump

7 The Weber 34 ICT accelerator pump is controlled by a diaphragm and is mechanically operated by a rod attached to the throttle linkage. The outlet valve consists of a ball incorporated into the pump injector. The inlet valve consists of a brass valve located in the float chamber. This valve also returns excess fuel to the chamber *(see illustration)*.

Main circuit

8 The amount of fuel discharged into the airstream is controlled by a calibrated main jet. Fuel is drawn through the main jet into the base of a vertical well which dips down into the fuel in the float chamber. An emulsion tube is placed in the well and is capped by a calibrated air corrector jet. The fuel is mixed with air drawn in through the air corrector and through the holes in the emulsion tube. The resulting emulsified mixture is discharged from the main nozzle through an auxiliary venturi.

Power enrichment and economy circuit

9 A vacuum-controlled power valve allows a bypass of the air supply to the air corrector jet. A limiter bushing limits the amount of air supplied to the air corrector. During idle and part-throttle operation, vacuum acts upon a diaphragm via an air passage from under the throttle plate. The diaphragm is pulled back against spring pressure to open a passage which is the bypass to the limiter bushing. The extra air causes a leaner mixture and better economy.

10 During acceleration and wide-open throttle operation, the vacuum in the manifold and in the power valve air passage collapses. The diaphragm returns under spring pressure to close the bypass passage. With less air available at the air corrector, the fuel mixture is enriched.

Full-power enrichment

11 At full-load and high engine speeds, even more fuel is required. The velocity of air creates a depression sufficient to raise fuel from the float chamber into a channel. The fuel then passes through a calibrated bushing to the upper section of the air intake. Here it is mixed with a small amount of air from a calibrated air bleed and the emulsified mixture is then discharged into the airstream from the full-load enrichment tube.

Choke operation

12 The manual choke is operated by a dash-mounted cable. When the cable is pulled, it operates a lever that pulls the choke flap closed across the air intake. A linkage rod opens the throttle to give a fast idle. Once the engine has started, manifold vacuum partially opens the choke flap against the action of a spring. A stop ensures that the choke is only opened a small

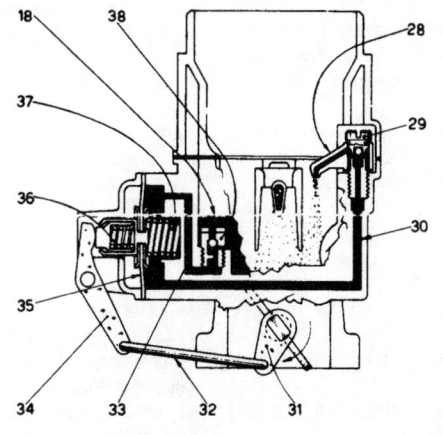

Accelerator pump circuit

18. Float chamber
28. Pump injector
29. Pump discharge valve
30. Fuel outlet channel
31. Pump cam
32. Pump link rod
33. Fuel inlet channel
34. Pump actuating lever
35. Diaphragm
36. Spring
37. Spring
38. Inlet ball

H14•3

Chapter H14

amount. During engine warm-up, the cable should be progressively pushed home until the choke flap is fully open.

2 Identification

The Weber identification code is stamped on the float chamber side.

3 General servicing

Introduction

1 Read this Chapter in conjunction with Part B, which describes some of the operations in more detail. It is assumed that the carburettor is removed for this service. However, many of the operations can be tackled with the carburettor in place. Where this is undertaken, first soak the fuel out of the float chamber using a clean tissue or soft cloth, after removing the upper body assembly.

Dismantling and checking

2 Remove the carburettor from the engine (see Part B).
3 Check visually for damage and wear.
4 Where an idle cut-off valve is fitted, use a 2 mm Allen key to remove the grub screw which secures the valve to the carburettor lower body. Remove the valve and idle jet assembly.
5 Separate the idle cut-off valve and idle jet, and clean with carburettor cleaner.
6 Test the plunger operation by connecting the valve to a 12-volt supply (or use the valve supply wire in the engine compartment). Touch the valve body to earth with the ignition on. Repeat several times and ensure that the plunger tip advances and retracts cleanly. Renew the valve if the action is faulty or if cleaning does not improve its operation.
7 Where an idle cut-off valve is not fitted, remove the primary idle jet assembly from the upper body. The idle jet is pushed into a holder and may be separated (by pulling) for cleaning or renewal.
8 Remove the securing clip or split pin and detach the choke link rod from the choke arm.
9 Detach the return spring from the throttle lever.
10 Remove the four screws and detach the carburettor upper body.
11 Use a straight-edge to check for distorted flanges on all facing surfaces.
12 Inspect the float chamber for corrosion and calcium build-up.
13 Tap out the float pin and remove the float, needle valve, clip, float chamber gasket and needle valve seat.

14 Check that the anti-vibration ball is free in the valve end.
15 Check the needle valve tip for wear and ridges. This is more likely with the brass needle valve tip than when a viton one is used. Use a viton-tipped replacement when possible.
16 The float should be checked for damage and ingress of petrol. Shaking the float will indicate the presence of fuel.
17 Renew the float pin if it shows signs of wear.
18 Remove the hexagon bolt and inspect the fuel filter. Clean any debris and dirt from the filter chamber.
19 Remove the mixture screw and inspect the tip for damage or ridges.
20 Remove the four screws and detach the accelerator pump housing, diaphragm and spring. Check the diaphragm for fatigue and damage.
21 Unscrew the brass pump inlet valve from the float chamber and test it by shaking. No noise indicates that the valve is seized.
22 The pump injector is a push fit in the body. Carefully prise it from its location and test it by shaking. No noise from the outlet ball indicates that the valve is seized.
23 Remove the air corrector, emulsion tube and main jet.
24 Check that the channel into the emulsion tube well is clear.
25 Check the calibration of the jets against that specified.
26 Remove the auxiliary venturi from the main body where necessary. Weber provide an extractor tool for removing this component. Check that the auxiliary venturi is not loose in the main body as this is a source of uneven running. If the venturi is loose, knurl the mating flanges with a file to ensure a tight fit.
27 Remove the three screws and detach the power valve housing, spring and diaphragm (where fitted) from the upper body. Check the diaphragm for fatigue and damage.
28 Inspect the choke spindle, mechanism and levers for stickiness and wear.

Preparation for reassembly

29 Clean the jets, carburettor body assemblies, float chamber and internal channels. An air line may be used to clear internal channels once the carburettor is fully dismantled. Note that if high-pressure air is directed into the channels and passages with the diaphragms still in place, diaphragm damage may result.
30 Spraying carburettor cleaner into all the channels and passages in the carburettor body will often clear them of gum and dirt.
31 During reassembly, a complete set of new gaskets should be fitted. Also renew the needle valve and float pin, and all diaphragms.
32 Inspect and renew (where necessary) the mixture screw, main jet, idle jet, air corrector jet and accelerator pump injector. Renew worn linkages, screws, springs and other parts where necessary.
33 Ensure that all jets are firmly locked into position (but do not over-tighten). A loose jet can cause a rich (or even lean) running condition.
34 Clean all mating surfaces and flanges of old gasket material and reassemble with new gaskets.
35 Ensure that housings are positioned with their air and fuel routes correctly aligned.

Reassembly

36 Refit the power diaphragm, spring and cover assembly (where fitted), then secure with three screws.
37 Refit the main jet, emulsion tube and air corrector.
38 Refit the pump inlet valve into the float chamber and push the pump injector firmly into the body. Renew the small seal on the injector body.
39 Refit the pump spring, diaphragm and cover assembly, then secure with the four screws.
40 Refit the idle mixture screw. Turn the screw in gently until it just seats. From this position, unscrew it two full turns. This will provide a basic setting to allow the engine to be started.
41 Clean or renew the fuel filter and secure with the hexagon bolt.
42 Renew the float chamber gasket and locate in position on the upper body. Renew the needle valve assembly. Screw the valve seat into the upper body, using a new sealing washer, and ensure that it is firmly locked into position (but do not over-tighten). Transfer the hairpin or plastic clip from the old needle valve to the ball end of the new one. Place the clip and valve assembly onto the inner float tag. Lower the float and needle valve assembly into the seat, and secure with the float pin.
43 Adjust the float level. Refer to Section 4 for details on adjustment.
44 Refit the upper body and secure with the four screws.
45 Refit the clip securing the choke link rod to the choke arm.
46 Push the idle jet into the idle cut-off valve (or idle jet holder, as applicable) and refit the assembly.
47 Locate the throttle lever control spring.
48 Ensure that the choke flap and linkage move smoothly and progressively.
49 Adjust the fast idle and choke pull-down. Refer to Section 4 for details on adjustment.
50 Refit the carburettor to the engine.
51 Always adjust the carburettor idle speed and mixture after any work has been carried out on the carburettor, preferably with the aid of a CO meter.

4 Service adjustments

Adjustment preconditions

1 Refer to Part B for general advice on the preconditions to correct adjustment of this carburettor.

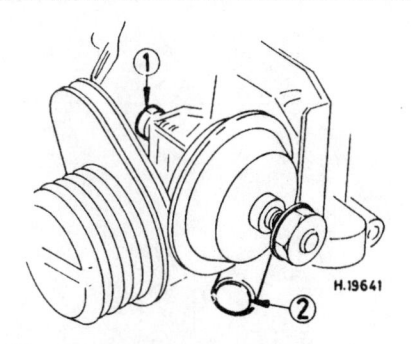

Weber 34 ICT carburettor

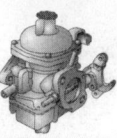

Idle speed and mixture adjustment
1 Idle speed adjustment screw
2 Idle mixture control screw

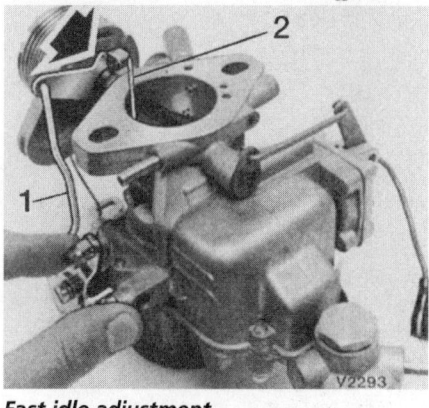

Fast idle adjustment
1 Fast idle control rod   2 Drill

Pull-down adjustment

Idle speed and mixture (CO)

2 Run the engine at 3000 rpm for 30 seconds to clear the manifold of fuel vapours, then allow the engine to idle.
3 Use the idle speed adjustment screw to set the specified idle speed *(see illustration)*.
4 Check the CO level. If it is not as specified, remove the tamperproof plug and adjust the idle mixture control screw to achieve the correct level. Turning the screw clockwise (inwards) will reduce the CO level. Turning the screw anti-clockwise (outwards) will increase the CO level.
5 Repeat paragraphs 3 and 4 until both adjustments are correct.
6 Clear the manifold every 30 seconds during the setting operation by running the engine at 3000 rpm for 30 seconds.
7 Increase the speed to 2000 rpm and note the CO reading. The cruise reading should be less than half the idle CO reading.
8 Fit a new tamperproof plug to the mixture control screw.

Float level

9 Hold the carburettor upper body in a vertical position with the float tag gently touching the ball of the needle valve.
10 Measure the distance between the upper body (with the gasket in place) and the base of the float *(see illustration)*.
11 Adjust as necessary by bending the inner float tag.

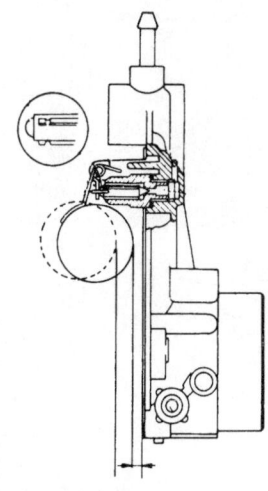

Fast idle

12 The carburettor must be removed from the engine in order to make the fast idle adjustment.
13 Invert the carburettor.
14 Pull the choke operating arm to fully close the choke flap. The fast idle lever will butt against the throttle lever and force open the throttle plate to leave a small clearance.
15 Use the shank of a twist drill to measure the clearance between the wall of the throttle bore and the throttle plate. Refer to Specifications for the required drill size and measure the clearance from the progression holes *(see illustration)*.
16 Adjust as necessary by bending the choke control rod in the appropriate direction.

Choke pull-down

17 Pull the choke operating arm to fully close the choke flap.
18 Open the choke flap against the spring tension, up to its stop.
19 Use the shank of a twist drill to measure the gap between the lower part of the choke flap and the air intake. Refer to Specifications for the required drill size *(see illustration)*.
20 Adjust as necessary by bending the adjustment tag.

Throttle damper

21 Insert the shank of a twist drill between the lower part of the choke flap and the air intake *(see illustration)*. The drill size should be as follows:

Engine type	Drill size
OHC engine	1.35 mm
CIH engine	1.15 mm

22 Adjust the damper plunger so that it just contacts the throttle lever.

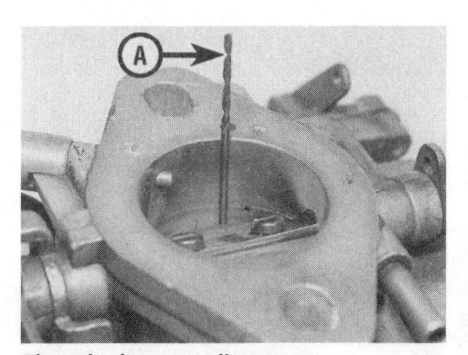

Throttle damper adjustment
A Insert twist drill between lower part of choke flap and air intake
B Adjust damper plunger so that it just contacts throttle lever

5 Fault diagnosis

Refer to Part D for diagnosis of general carburettor faults.

H14•5

Notes

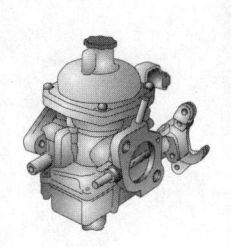

Part H Chapter 15
Weber 32 TL carburettor

H15

Contents

Component testing 5
Fault diagnosis 6
General servicing 3
Identification 2
Principles of operation 1
Service adjustments 4

Specifications

Manufacturer	Opel	Opel	Vauxhall	Vauxhall/Opel
Model	Corsa 1.2	Kadett 1.2	Nova 1.0	Nova/Corsa 1.0
Year	1987 to 1991	1983 to 1984	1983 to 1987	1988 to 1991
Engine code	E12N	12S	10S OHV (33kW)	10S OHV (33kW, 15/04)
Capacity (cm³)/no. of cyls	1196/4	1196/4	993/4	993/4
Oil temperature (°C)	80	80	80	80
Carb. identification	32 TL	32 TL 4/250	32 TL/250 to /253	32 TL 3/250
Idle speed (rpm)	925 ± 25	925 ± 25	925 ± 25	925 ± 25
Fast idle speed (rpm)	3800 ± 200	-	3800 ± 200	3800 ± 200
CO @ idle (% vol.)	1.25 ± 0.25	2 ± 0.5	1.25 ± 0.25	1.25 ± 0.25
Venturi diameter	25	25	25	25
Idle jet	50	50	47	50
Main jet	112	112	117	112
Air correction jet	75	75	75	75
Emulsion tube	F96	F96	F96	F96
Accel. pump jet	35	35	45	35
Float level (mm)	27.25 ± 0.25	27.25 ± 0.25	27.25 ± 0.25	27.25 ± 0.25
Needle valve size (mm)	1.50	1.50	1.75	1.50
Choke fast idle gap (mm)	0.7 ± 0.05	0.7 ± 0.05	0.65 ± 0.05	0.65 ± 0.05
Choke pull-down (mm)	4.3 ± 0.25	4.3 ± 0.25	4.5 ± 0.25	4.3 ± 0.25

Manufacturer	Vauxhall	Vauxhall	Vauxhall
Model	Nova 1.2	Nova 1.2	Astra 1.2
Year	1985 to 1987	1987 to 1991	1984 to 1991
Engine code	12NC (33kW)	E12GV(33kW)	12SC OHV (40kW, 15/04)
Capacity (cm³)/no. of cyls	1196/4	1196/4	1196/4
Oil temperature (°C)	80	80	80
Carb. identification	32 TL 2/250 or 251, 32 TL 5/250	32 TL	32 TL 2/250 or 251, 32 TL 5/250
Idle speed (rpm)	925 ± 25	925 ± 25	925 ± 25
Fast idle speed (rpm)	3800 ± 200	3800 ± 200	3800 ± 200
CO @ idle (% vol.)	1.25 ± 0.25	0.75 ± 0.25	1.25 ± 0.25
Venturi diameter	25	23	25
Idle jet	50	50	50
Main jet	112	102	112
Air correction jet	75	100	75
Emulsion tube	F96	F96	F96
Accel. pump jet	45	35	45
Float level (mm)	27.25 ± 0.25	27.25 ± 0.25	27.25 ± 0.25
Needle valve size (mm)	1.50	1.75	1.50
Choke fast idle gap (mm)	0.7 ± 0.05	0.8 ± 0.05	0.7 ± 0.05
Choke pull-down (mm)	4.55 ± 0.25	4.5 ± 0.25	4.5 ± 0.25

Chapter H15

1 Principles of operation

Introduction
1 The following technical description of the Weber TL carburettor should be read in conjunction with the more detailed description of carburettor principles in Part A.

Construction
2 The Weber 32 TL carburettor is a downdraught, single venturi instrument with a manual choke control and a power valve *(see illustration)*. The throttle shaft is made of steel. The throttle valve is made of brass, as are the jets and the emulsion tube. The exception is the accelerator pump injector which is die-cast. The internal fuel channels and air passages are drilled and sealed with lead plugs where necessary.

3 The carburettor is constructed in three main bodies. These are the upper body, main body and throttle body containing the throttle assemblies. An insulating block, placed between the main carburettor body and the throttle body, prevents excess heat transference to the main body.

Fuel control
4 Fuel flows into the carburettor through a fine mesh filter. The fuel level in the float chamber is controlled by a needle valve and plastic float assembly. An anti-vibration ball is incorporated into the needle valve design. A clip, attached to the needle valve and to the float arm, prevents the needle from sticking in the seat as the fuel level drops. The float chamber is vented internally to the clean-air side of the air filter *(see illustration)*.

Idle, slow running and progression
5 Fuel, sourced from the main well, passes into the upper body through a metered idle jet. Here it is mixed with a small amount of air from a calibrated air bleed. The emulsion formed is drawn through a channel to the throttle body where it is discharged from the idle orifice under the primary throttle plate. A tapered mixture control screw is used to vary the outlet and this ensures fine control of the idle mixture. A progression slot, partially covered by the closed throttle at idle, provides enrichment as it is uncovered by the opening throttle during initial acceleration. The adjustable mixture screw is tamper proofed during production, in accordance with emission regulations.

Idle bypass circuit
6 The idle bypass circuit provides a means of

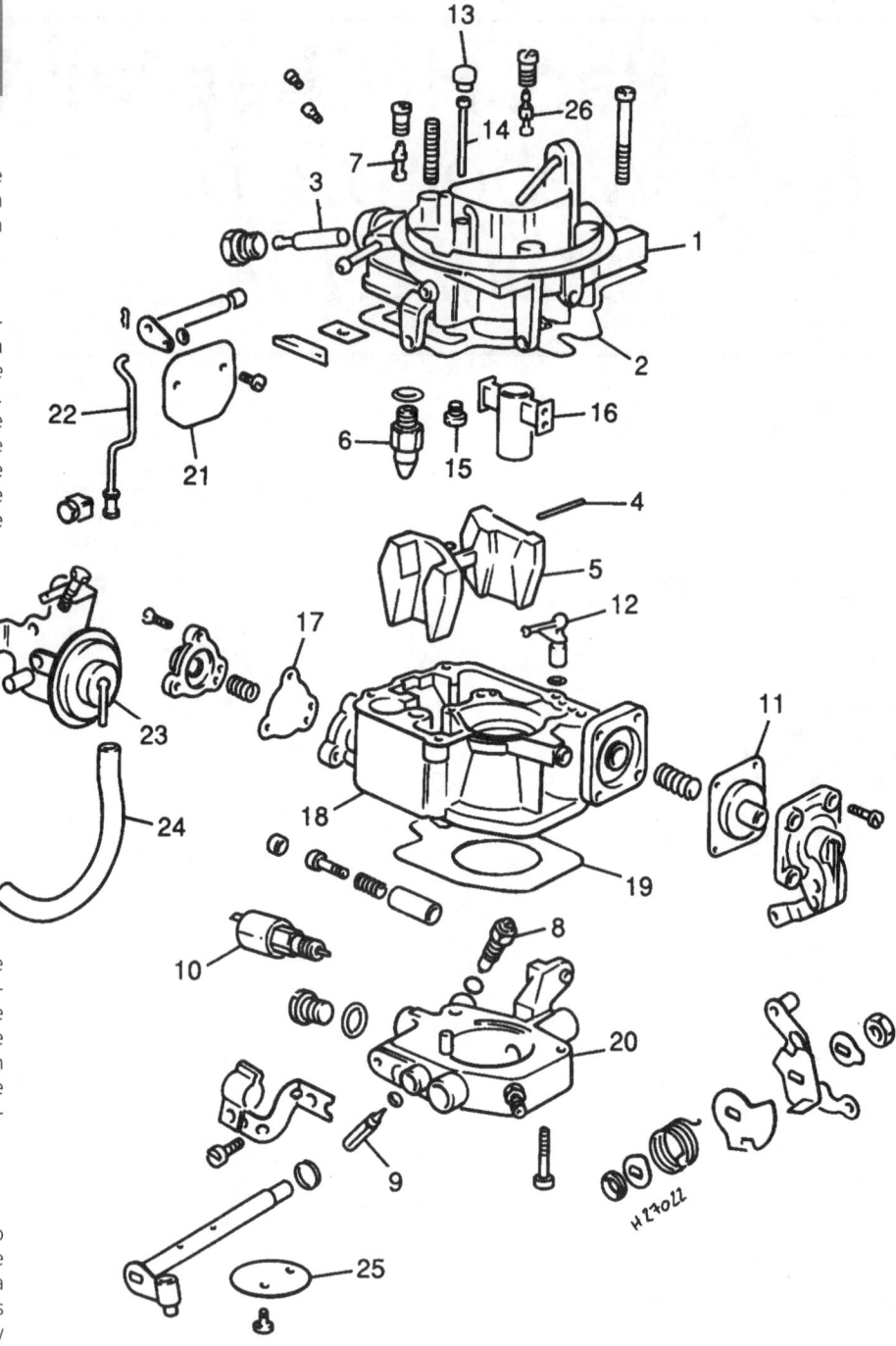

Weber TL carburettor

1 Upper body
2 Float chamber gasket
3 Fuel inlet filter
4 Float pin
5 Float
6 Needle valve assembly
7 Idle jet
8 Idle speed regulating screw
9 Idle mixture control screw
10 Idle cut-off valve (where fitted)
11 Accelerator pump diaphragm
12 Pump injector
13 Air corrector
14 Emulsion tube
15 Main jet
16 Auxiliary venturi
17 Power diaphragm
18 Main body
19 Insulator block
20 Throttle body
21 Choke flap
22 Choke link rod
23 Diaphragm
24 Vacuum hose
25 Throttle valve
26 Auxiliary fuel jet

Weber 32 TL carburettor

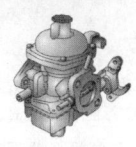

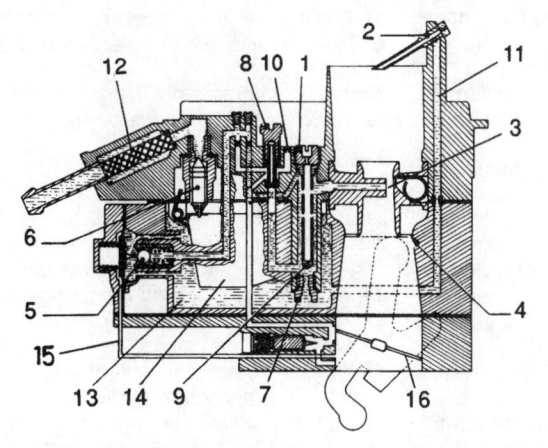

Inlet, main and full-load circuits

1. Air corrector
2. Full-load outlet
3. Main fuel outlet
4. Auxiliary venturi
5. Power valve ball
6. Needle valve assembly
7. Main jet
8. Idle jet
9. Emulsion tube
10. Air bleed
11. Full-load fuel channel
12. Fuel filter
13. Float chamber
14. Float
15. Vacuum passage
16. Throttle valve

Accelerator pump circuit

1. Float chamber
2. Fuel outlet channel
3. Pump injector
4. Pump actuating lever
5. Pump cam
6. Diaphragm
7. Spring
8. Inlet ball
9. Back bleed

more accurately controlling idle emissions than a conventional idle mixture circuit. The throttle plate is locked in a set position and sealed with a tamperproof cap. Eighty percent of the fuel required for idle is provided by the normal idle circuit. The remainder of the idle mixture is controlled through the idle bypass circuit. An auxiliary fuel jet and air bleed are also utilized.

7 A fuel channel links the primary idle fuel circuit with the bypass passage. An air-and-fuel emulsion is drawn through the passage and is discharged from the bypass orifice under the primary throttle plate. The emulsion is controlled by a regulating screw which is also used to adjust the idle speed.

Idle cut-off valve (E12GV engine)

8 An idle cut-off valve is used to prevent run-on when the engine is shut down. It utilises a 12-volt solenoid plunger to block the idle channel when the ignition is switched off.

9 The device is also controlled by a relay, so that, during engine deceleration from high engine speeds with a closed throttle, the fuel supply to the engine is cut off. This results in a fuel saving and in improved emissions. Once the engine speed falls below 1600 rpm, or the throttle is opened, the relay re-activates the solenoid and normal idle fuel flow is restored.

Hot idle temperature compensator (HITC)

10 Some variations of the Weber 32 TL carburettor utilise an HITC. This is a thermostatically-operated device that makes use of a flat bi-metal spring to open a vent into the carburettor base. The compensator remains closed under normal operating temperatures. Once the under-bonnet temperature reaches approximately 49°C, the valve will open. Additional air will then bleed into the manifold to dilute the rich fuel mixture. When the operating temperature returns to normal, the compensator valve will seat itself and the air bleed will be shut off.

Accelerator pump

11 The Weber 32 TL accelerator pump is controlled by a diaphragm and is mechanically operated by a cam and lever attached to the throttle linkage. The outlet valve is incorporated into the pump injector. The inlet valve consists of a ball valve located in a channel from the float chamber. Excess fuel is returned to the float chamber through a calibrated bush (see illustration).

Main circuit

12 The amount of fuel discharged into the airstream is controlled by a calibrated main jet. Fuel is drawn through the main jet into the base of a vertical well which dips down into the fuel in the float chamber. An emulsion tube is placed in the well and is capped by a calibrated air corrector jet. The fuel is mixed with air, drawn in through the air corrector and through the holes in the emulsion tube. The resulting emulsified mixture is discharged from the main nozzle through an auxiliary venturi.

Power enrichment and economy circuit

13 Fuel flows from the float chamber into the power valve chamber through a fuel channel. An air passage is taken from under the throttle plate to the cover of the power diaphragm chamber. At idle and during light-throttle operation, manifold vacuum draws the diaphragm back against spring pressure. The diaphragm pintle is withdrawn from the brass outlet valve and the spring-loaded ball seats to close off the outlet channel.

14 Under acceleration and wide-open throttle operation, the vacuum in the manifold is depleted. The diaphragm returns under spring pressure and the power diaphragm pintle pushes the ball to open the outlet valve. Fuel then flows through the valve and a calibrated jet to supplement the fuel in the primary main well. The fuel level rises in the well and the fuel mixture is enriched.

15 At full-load and high engine speeds, even more fuel is required. The velocity of air creates a depression sufficient to raise fuel from the float chamber into a channel. The fuel then passes through a calibrated bushing to the upper section of the air intake. Here it is mixed with a small amount of air from a calibrated air bleed and the emulsified mixture is then discharged into the airstream from the full-load enrichment tube.

Choke operation

16 The manual choke is operated by a dash-mounted cable. When the cable is pulled, it operates a lever that pulls the choke flap closed across the air intake. Fast idle is achieved with the aid of a curved cam attached to the choke operating lever. An adjustable screw, attached to the throttle lever and butting against the cam, is used to vary the fast idle speed.

17 Once the engine has fired, the choke flap must open slightly to weaken the mixture and avoid flooding. During idle and light-throttle operation, this is achieved by using manifold vacuum to actuate a diaphragm. A linkage attached to the diaphragm will then pull upon the choke flap.

18 During engine warm-up, the cable should be progressively pushed home until the choke flap is fully open.

Chapter H15

2 Identification

The Weber identification code is stamped on the base flange of the main body.

3 General servicing

Introduction

1 Read this Chapter in conjunction with Part B, which describes some of the operations in more detail. It is assumed that the carburettor is removed for this service. However, many of the operations can be tackled with the carburettor in place. Where this is undertaken, first soak the fuel out of the float chamber using a clean tissue or soft cloth, after removing the upper body assembly.

Dismantling and checking

2 Remove the two screws which secure the carburettor to the engine.
3 Remove the carburettor from the engine (see Part B).
4 Check visually for damage and wear.
5 Disconnect the choke vacuum hose, then remove the three screws and detach the carburettor upper body.
6 Use a straight-edge to check for distorted flanges on all facing surfaces.
7 Tap out the float pin and remove the float, needle valve and plastic clip, float chamber gasket and needle valve seat.
8 Check that the anti-vibration ball is free in the valve end.
9 Check the needle valve tip for wear and ridges. This is more likely with the brass needle valve tip than when a viton one is used. Use a viton-tipped replacement when possible.
10 The float should be checked for damage and ingress of petrol.
11 Renew the float pin if it appears worn.
12 Unscrew the hexagon bolt and inspect the fuel filter. Clean the filter housing of debris and dirt, and renew the filter if necessary.
13 Remove the mixture control screw and bypass regulating screw and inspect their tips for damage and ridges.
14 Remove the four screws and detach the accelerator pump cover, diaphragm and spring. Check the diaphragm for fatigue and damage.
15 The pump injector is a push fit in the body. Carefully prise it from its location and check the valve for damage.
16 Remove the primary idle jet assembly from the upper body. The idle jet is pushed into a holder and may be separated (by pulling) for cleaning or renewal. Similarly remove the auxiliary fuel jet and holder for cleaning or renewal. Note that the idle and air corrector jets can be detached from the carburettor without removing the upper body.
17 Remove the main jet, air corrector and emulsion tube. Check that the channel from the float chamber into the emulsion tube well is clear.
18 Check the jet calibration against that specified. It is possible that the wrong size jets may have been fitted during the last overhaul.
19 Remove the auxiliary venturi from the upper body where necessary. Weber provide an extractor tool for removing this component. Check that the venturi is not loose in the main body as this is a source of uneven running. If the venturi is loose, knurl the mating flanges with a file to ensure a tight fit.
20 Remove the three screws and detach the power valve housing cover, spring and diaphragm from the body. Check the diaphragm for fatigue and damage. The brass outlet valve is cast into the body and is not removable. The ball in the outlet valve should seal the outlet. Depress and release the ball with a small screwdriver. It should move smoothly in and out. Check that the emulsion tube well is clear.
21 Remove the two screws and separate the carburettor main body and throttle body assemblies. The throttle body can be renewed separately if the spindles or throttle bores are worn.
22 Do not disturb the adjustment of the throttle angle, unless absolutely necessary.
23 Inspect the choke spindle, linkage and operating mechanism for stickiness and wear.
24 Attach a vacuum pump to the pull-down diaphragm and operate the pump to obtain 300 mm Hg. The diaphragm should operate fully and the vacuum must be maintained for a minimum of 10 seconds. Renew the diaphragm assembly if it fails these tests.
25 Remove the three screws, disconnect the choke link rod and detach the choke pull-down assembly.

Preparation for reassembly

26 Clean the jets, carburettor body assemblies, float chamber and internal channels. An air line may be used to clear internal channels once the carburettor is fully dismantled. Note that if high-pressure air is directed into the channels and passages with the diaphragms still in place, diaphragm damage may result.
27 Spraying carburettor cleaner into all the channels and passages in the carburettor body will often clear them of gum and dirt.
28 During reassembly, a complete set of new gaskets should be fitted. Also renew the needle valve and float pin, and all diaphragms.
29 Inspect and renew (where necessary) the mixture screw, main jet, idle jet, air corrector jet, emulsion tube and accelerator pump injector. Renew worn linkages, screws, springs, vacuum hoses and other parts where necessary.
30 Ensure that all jets are firmly locked into position (but do not over-tighten). A loose jet can cause a rich (or even lean) running condition.
31 Clean all mating surfaces and flanges of old gasket material and reassemble with new gaskets.
32 Ensure that housings are positioned with their air and fuel routes correctly aligned.

Reassembly

33 Refit the choke pull-down assembly and secure with the three screws. Reconnect the choke link rod. Ensure that the choke flap and linkage move smoothly and progressively.
34 Assemble the main and throttle bodies with a new gasket block and secure with the two screws.
35 Temporarily adjust the throttle valve so that it is open just enough to prevent its seizure in the throttle body. The correct adjustment method with the engine running is detailed in Section 4.
36 Refit the power diaphragm, spring and cover assembly, then secure with the three screws.
37 Refit the emulsion tube, air corrector and main jet into their original positions.
38 Push the pump injector firmly into position, after renewing the small seal on the injector body.
39 Refit the pump spring, diaphragm and cover assembly, then secure with the four screws.
40 Push the idle jet into its holder and refit the assembly into the upper body. Refit the auxiliary fuel jet assembly.
41 Screw the idle cut-off valve into the throttle body assembly (where fitted).
42 Refit the idle mixture screw after renewing the seal. Turn the screw in gently until it just seats. From this position, unscrew it three full turns. This will provide a basic setting to allow the engine to be started.
43 Refit the bypass regulating screw, using the same method described in paragraph 42 to obtain a basic setting.
44 Clean or renew the fuel filter and refit the hexagon bolt.
45 Renew the float chamber gasket and locate in position on the upper body. Renew the needle valve assembly. Screw the valve seat into the upper body, using a new sealing washer, and ensure that it is firmly locked into position (but do not over-tighten). Transfer the hairpin or plastic clip from the old needle valve to the ball end of the new one. Place the clip and valve assembly onto the inner float tag. Lower the float and needle valve assembly into the seat and secure with the float pin.
46 Adjust the float level. Refer to Section 4 for details on adjustment.
47 Refit the upper body to the main body and secure with the two screws. Reconnect the choke pull-down hose.
48 Refit the carburettor to the engine.
49 Always adjust the carburettor idle speed and mixture after any work has been carried out on the carburettor, preferably with the aid of a CO meter.
50 Adjust the choke fast idle and vacuum pull-down. Refer to Section 4 for details on adjustment.

Weber 32 TL carburettor

4 Service adjustments

Adjustment preconditions

1 Refer to Part B for general advice on the preconditions to correct adjustment of this carburettor.

Idle speed and mixture (CO)

2 Run the engine at 3000 rpm for 30 seconds to clear the manifold of fuel vapours, then allow the engine to idle.
3 Use the idle bypass regulating screw to set the specified idle speed (see illustration).
4 Check the CO level. If it is not as specified, remove the tamperproof plug and adjust the idle mixture control screw to achieve the correct level. Turning the screw clockwise (inwards) will reduce the CO level. Turning the screw anti-clockwise (outwards) will increase the CO level.
5 Repeat paragraphs 3 and 4 until both adjustments are correct.
6 Clear the manifold every 30 seconds during the setting operation by running the engine at 3000 rpm for 30 seconds.
7 Increase the speed to 2000 rpm and note the CO reading. The cruise reading should be less than half the idle CO reading.
8 Fit a new tamperproof plug to the mixture adjustment screw.

Setting the primary throttle plate

9 If the throttle position has been disturbed or if the idle speed and CO cannot be set correctly, it is possible that the basic throttle angle is incorrect. Use the following method of setting the throttle position:
10 Allow the engine to idle.
11 Screw in the bypass regulating screw until it is fully seated (see illustration). The idle speed should drop to 600 ± 50 rpm. If a low-reading vacuum gauge is available, attach the gauge to the distributor vacuum advance spigot (on the carburettor). A reading of 1 to 20 mbar should be obtained.
12 Adjust the mixture control screw until 1 to 2% CO is obtained.
13 Adjust the throttle stop screw until 600 rpm (or 1 to 20 mbar) is achieved.
14 Unscrew the bypass screw until the correct idle speed of 925 ± 25 rpm is once again reached.
15 Reset the CO to the correct level. Once the proper CO is reached at the correct idle speed, the carburettor is properly adjusted.

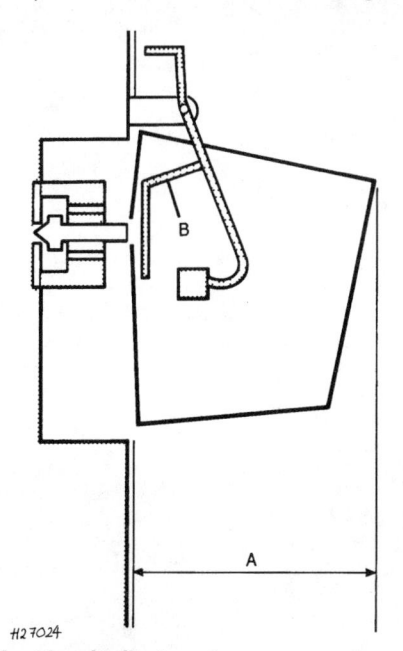

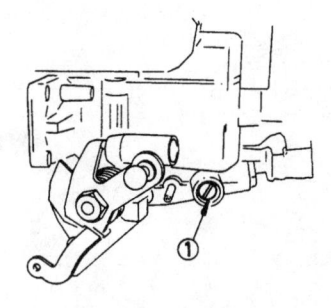

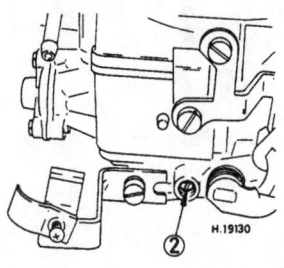

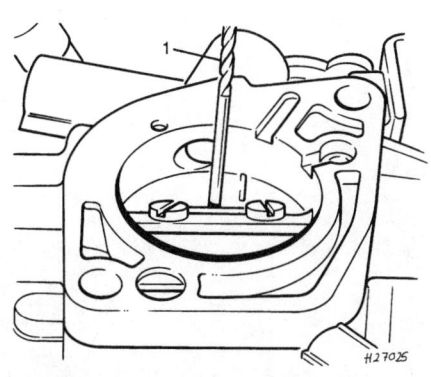

Idle speed and mixture adjustment
1 Idle bypass air regulating screw
2 Idle mixture control screw

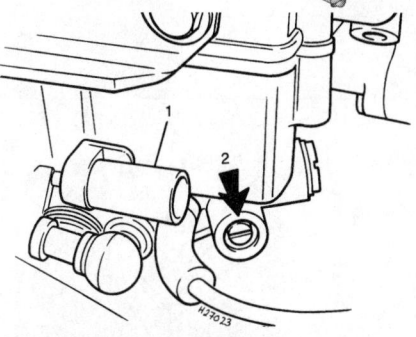

Setting primary throttle plate
1 Throttle stop screw
2 Idle bypass regulating screw

Float level

16 Hold the carburettor upper body in a vertical position with the float tag gently touching the ball of the needle valve.
17 Measure the distance between the upper body (with the gasket in place) and the base of the float (see illustration).
18 Adjust as necessary by bending the inner float tag.

Choke adjustments

Fast idle (carburettor removed from engine)

19 Invert the carburettor.
20 Pull the choke operating arm to fully close the choke flap. The adjustment screw will butt against the fast idle cam and force open the throttle plate to leave a small clearance.
21 Use the shank of a twist drill to measure the clearance between the wall of the throttle bore and the throttle plate. Refer to Specifications for the required drill size and measure the clearance from the progression holes (see illustration).
22 Adjust as necessary by turning the adjustment screw in the appropriate direction (see illustration).

Fast idle (carburettor installed)

23 Warm the engine to normal running temperature and adjust idle speed and mixture

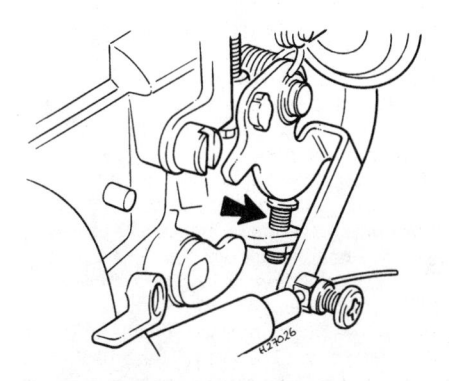

Float level adjustment
A Float level measurement
B Inner float tag

Fast idle adjustment - carburettor removed
1 Drill

Fast idle adjustment screw (arrowed)

H15•5

Chapter H15

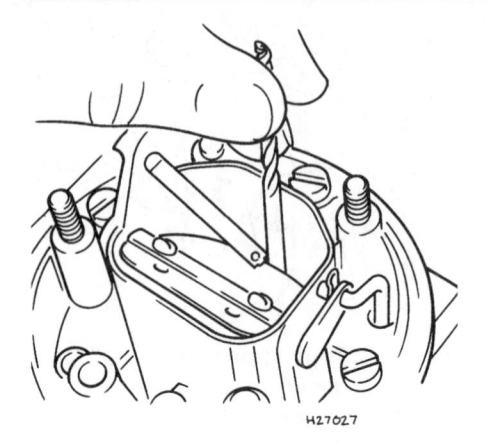

Measuring pull-down adjustment with twist drill

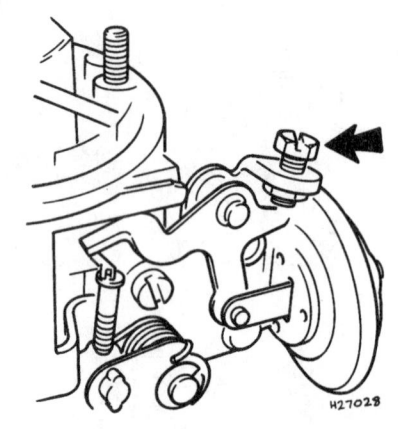

Pull-down adjustment screw (arrowed)

before attempting choke fast idle or vacuum pull-down adjustment.

24 Pull the choke cable to fully operate the choke and then hold the choke flap as fully open as possible.
25 Start the engine and record the fast idle speed.
26 Stop the engine and adjust as necessary by turning the fast idle adjustment screw in the appropriate direction.

Vacuum pull-down

27 Pull the choke operating arm to fully close the choke flap.
28 Use a vacuum pump to pull the diaphragm operating rod up to its stop (or push the mechanism with a small screwdriver). At the same time, use the shank of a twist drill to measure the gap between the lower section of the choke flap and the air intake. Refer to Specifications for the required drill size *(see illustration)*.
29 Adjust as necessary by turning the diaphragm adjustment screw in the appropriate direction *(see illustration)*.

5 Component testing

Deceleration fuel cut-off system

1 Connect a test lamp from the idle solenoid to earth (battery negative).
2 Turn the ignition on and the lamp should light and remain brightly on, without flickering.
3 Start the engine and raise the speed to approximately 2500 rpm. The lamp should remain brightly on, without flickering.
4 Disconnect the connection to the throttle valve switch and hold the wire to earth. The lamp should switch off.
5 Slowly reduce the engine speed. The lamp should remain off and the engine speed should fluctuate as the cut-off solenoid blocks the idle fuel channel. As the engine speed falls below 1600 rpm, the lamp should switch on and the engine will then run normally.
6 Remake the connection to the throttle valve switch.

Cut-off system fault diagnosis

7 If the lamp flickers or dims, check the connection to the throttle switch.
8 If the lamp does not light, check the continuity and connections between the relay, throttle switch and idle cut-off valve. Also check the relay for a positive supply.
9 If all the connections are satisfactory yet the idle cut-off operation is not as described above, suspect the relay.

Hot idle temperature compensator (HITC)

10 The HITC should remain closed below an under-bonnet temperature of about 49°C.
11 Above this temperature, the compensator will open to allow a small air bleed to bypass the throttle valve.
12 Renew the HITC if it does not behave as described above.

6 Fault diagnosis

Refer to Part D for diagnosis of general carburettor faults.

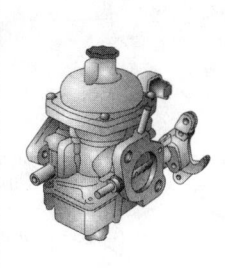

Part H Chapter 16
Weber 32 TLA carburettor

Contents

Component testing	5	Identification	2
Fault diagnosis	6	Principles of operation	1
General servicing	3	Service adjustments	4

Specifications

Manufacturer	Volkswagen	Volkswagen
Model	**Polo & Van 1.05**	**Golf/Jetta 1.05**
Year	**1985 to 1990**	**1985 to 1991**
Engine code	HZ (33kW)	HZ (37kW)
Capacity (cm^3)/no. of cyls	1043/4	1043/4
Oil temperature (°C)	80	80
Carb. identification	32 TLA 1/250 to 252	32 TLA 1/250 to 252
Idle speed (rpm)	800 ± 50	800 ± 50
Fast idle speed (rpm)	2000 ± 100	2000 ± 100
CO @ idle (% vol.)	2.0 ± 0.5	2.0 ± 0.5
Venturi diameter	22	22
Idle jet	47	47
Main jet	102	102
Air correction jet	100	100
Emulsion tube	F96	F96
Accel. pump jet	35	35
Float level (mm)	27.25 ± 0.25	27.25 ± 0.25
Needle valve size (mm)	1.75	1.75
Choke fast idle gap (mm)	0.8 ± 0.05	0.8 ± 0.05
Choke pull-down (mm)	2.5 ± 0.2	2.5 ± 0.2
De-choke (mm)	2.3 ± 0.5	2.3 ± 0.5

Chapter H16

1 Principles of operation

Introduction

1 The following technical description of the Weber TLA carburettor should be read in conjunction with the more detailed description of carburettor principles in Part A.

Construction

2 The Weber 32 TLA carburettor is a downdraught, single venturi instrument with a power valve and an idle cut-off valve fitted to the idle circuit (see illustration). The choke system is semi-automatic in operation and is controlled by a bi-metal coil heated by both engine coolant and an electrical supply. The throttle shaft is made of steel. The throttle valve is made of brass, as are the jets and the emulsion tube. The exception is the accelerator pump injector which is die-cast. The internal fuel channels and air passages are drilled and sealed with lead plugs where necessary. Early models used a conventional idle speed adjustment screw . Later models have an adjustable idle speed boost valve.

3 The carburettor is constructed in three main bodies. These are the upper body, main body and throttle body containing the throttle assemblies. An insulating block, placed between the main carburettor body and the throttle body, prevents excess heat transference to the main body.

Fuel control

4 Fuel flows into the carburettor through a fine mesh filter. The fuel level in the float chamber is controlled by a needle valve and plastic float assembly. An anti-vibration ball is incorporated into the needle valve design. A clip, attached to the needle valve and to the float arm, prevents the needle from sticking in the seat as the fuel level drops. The float chamber is vented internally to the clean-air side of the air filter. On some applications, fuel flows through a vapour separator before reaching the float chamber. The purpose of the vapour separator is to remove fuel vapours that may cause hesitation or poor running, particularly after a hot start (see illustration).

Idle, slow running and progression

5 Fuel, sourced from the main well, passes into the upper body through a metered idle jet. Here it is mixed with a small amount of air from a calibrated air bleed. The emulsion formed is drawn through a channel to the throttle body where it is discharged from the idle orifice under the primary throttle plate. A tapered mixture control screw is used to vary the outlet and this ensures fine control of the idle mixture. A progression slot, partially covered by the closed throttle at idle, provides enrichment as it is uncovered by the opening throttle during initial acceleration. In models with an idle boost system, an auxiliary fuel jet and air bleed are also utilised.

6 On models built prior to July 1985, the idle speed is set by an adjustable screw. After that date, the idle speed is regulated by an adjustable air valve. As the engine speed falls below 700 rpm, the air valve admits extra air via a two-way boost valve. The throttle plate is locked in a set position and is sealed with a tamperproof cap. The adjustable mixture screw is tamper proofed during production, in accordance with emission regulations.

Idle cut-off valve

7 An idle cut-off valve is used to prevent run-on when the engine is shut down. It utilises a 12-volt solenoid plunger to block the idle channel when the ignition is switched off.

Accelerator pump

8 The Weber 32 TLA accelerator pump is controlled by a diaphragm and is mechanically operated by a cam and lever attached to the

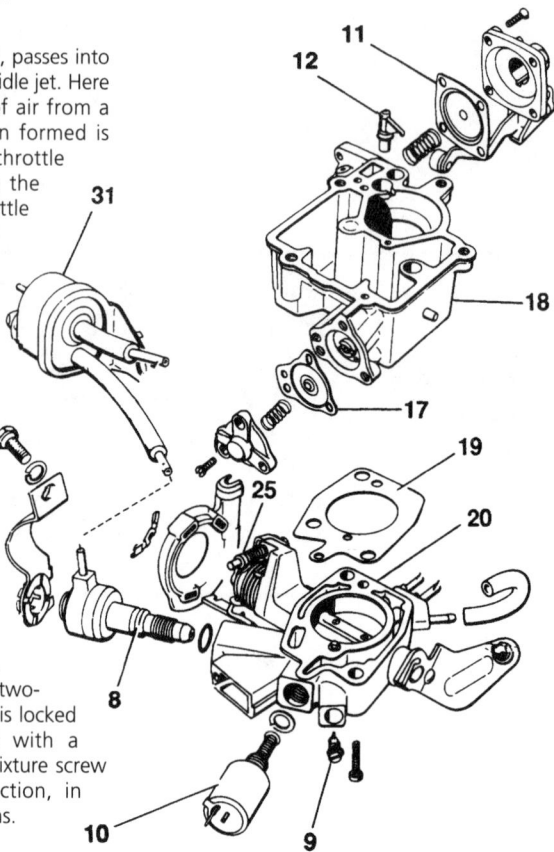

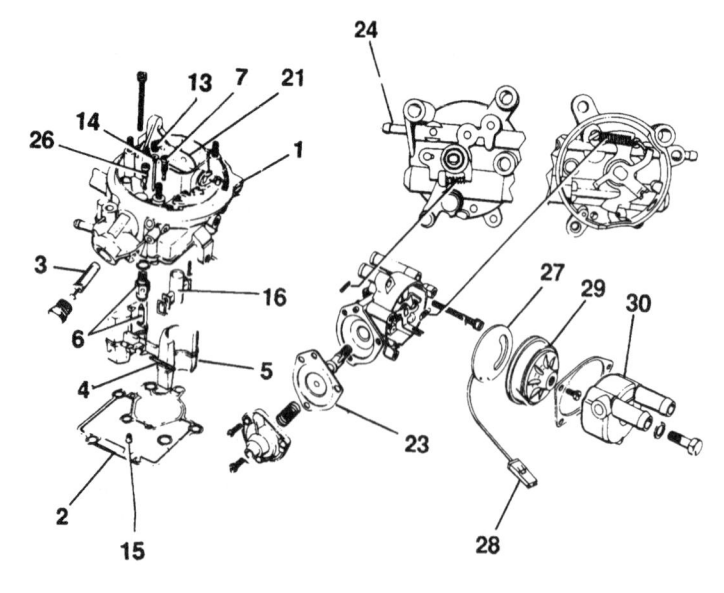

Weber TLA carburettor

1 Upper body
2 Float chamber gasket
3 Fuel inlet filter
4 Float pin
5 Float
6 Needle valve assembly
7 Idle jet
8 Idle speed air valve
9 Idle mixture control screw
10 Idle cut-off valve
11 Accelerator pump diaphragm
12 Pump injector
13 Air corrector
14 Emulsion tube
15 Main jet
16 Auxiliary venturi
17 Power diaphragm
18 Main body
19 Insulator block
20 Throttle body
21 Choke flap
23 Diaphragm
24 Vacuum connector
25 Idle stop screw
26 Auxiliary fuel jet
27 Heater plate
28 Electrical connection
29 Bi-metal coil
30 Water jacket
31 Two-way boost valve

Weber 32 TLA carburettor

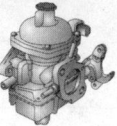

throttle linkage. The outlet valve is incorporated into the pump injector. The inlet valve consists of a ball valve located in a channel from the float chamber. Excess fuel is returned to the float chamber through a calibrated bush (see illustration).

Main circuit

9 The amount of fuel discharged into the airstream is controlled by a calibrated main jet. Fuel is drawn through the main jet into the base of a vertical well which dips down into the fuel in the float chamber. An emulsion tube is placed in the well and is capped by a calibrated air corrector jet. The fuel is mixed with air drawn in through the air corrector and through the holes in the emulsion tube. The resulting emulsified mixture is discharged from the main nozzle through an auxiliary venturi.

Power enrichment and economy circuit

10 Fuel flows from the float chamber into the power valve chamber through a fuel channel. An air passage is taken from under the throttle plate to the cover of the power diaphragm chamber. At idle and during light-throttle operation, manifold vacuum draws the diaphragm back against spring pressure. The diaphragm pintle is withdrawn from the brass outlet valve and the spring-loaded ball seats to close off the outlet channel.

11 Under acceleration and wide-open throttle operation, the vacuum in the manifold is depleted. The diaphragm returns under spring pressure and the power diaphragm pintle pushes the ball to open the outlet valve. Fuel then flows through the valve and a calibrated jet to supplement the fuel in the primary main well. The fuel level rises in the well and the fuel mixture is enriched.

12 At full-load and high engine speeds, even more fuel is required. The velocity of air creates a depression sufficient to raise fuel from the float chamber into a channel. The fuel then passes through a calibrated bushing to the upper section of the air intake. Here it is mixed with a small amount of air from a calibrated air bleed and the emulsified mixture is then discharged into the airstream from the full-load enrichment tube.

Cold start system

13 The TLA carburettor uses a semi-automatic choke starting system. A bi-metal spring is used to control a strangler choke flap in the air intake. Heating of the spring is by a combination of coolant from the engine cooling system and an electrical supply. The system is primed by depressing the accelerator pedal once or twice.

14 Once the engine has fired, the choke flap must open slightly to weaken the mixture and avoid flooding during idle and light-throttle operation. This is achieved by using manifold vacuum to actuate a diaphragm. A linkage attached to the diaphragm will then pull upon the choke flap.

15 Fast idle is achieved with the aid of a stepped cam attached to the choke spindle. An adjustable screw, connected to the throttle lever mechanism and butting against the cam, can be used to vary the fast idle speed. As the bi-metal coil is heated and the plate opens, then the screw will rest on successively less-stepped parts of the cam. Idle speed is thus progressively reduced, until ultimately the cam is released and the idle speed returns to normal.

Wide-open kick (dechoke)

16 If the throttle is fully opened during acceleration with a cold engine, the pull-down vacuum will deplete and the choke flap tend to close. This may cause flooding. To prevent this, a wide-open kick mechanism is employed. When the throttle is fully opened, a cam on the throttle lever will turn the choke lever anti-clockwise to partially open the choke flap.

2 Identification

The Weber identification code is stamped on the base flange of the main body.

3 General servicing

Introduction

1 Read this Chapter in conjunction with Part B, which describes some of the operations in more detail. It is assumed that the carburettor is removed for this service. However, many of the operations can be tackled with the carburettor in place. Where this is undertaken, first soak the fuel out of the float chamber using a clean tissue or soft cloth, after removing the upper body assembly.

Dismantling and checking

2 Remove the two screws which secure the carburettor to the engine.
3 Remove the carburettor from the engine (see Part B).
4 Check visually for damage and wear.
5 On some models, it will be necessary to remove two bolts and detach the vapour separator support frame. Disconnect the choke vacuum hose then remove the three screws. Hold the choke fast idle lever clear of the choke housing and detach the carburettor upper body.
6 Use a straight-edge to check for distorted flanges on all facing surfaces.
7 Tap out the float pin and remove the float, needle valve and plastic clip, float chamber gasket and needle valve seat.
8 Check that the anti-vibration ball is free in the valve end.
9 Check the needle valve tip for wear and

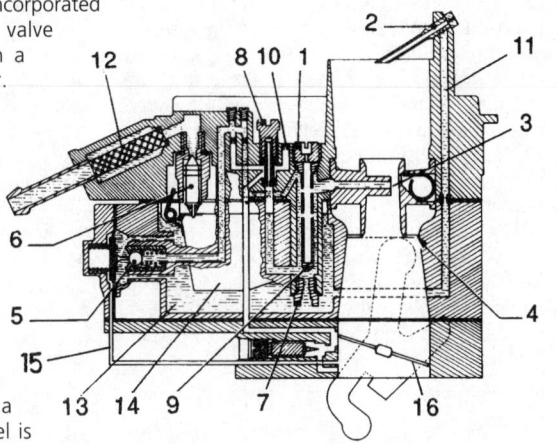

Inlet, main and full-load circuits

1 Air corrector
2 Full-load outlet
3 Main fuel outlet
4 Auxiliary venturi
5 Power valve ball
6 Needle valve assembly
7 Main jet
8 Idle jet
9 Emulsion tube
10 Air bleed
11 Full-load fuel channel
12 Fuel filter
13 Float chamber
14 Float
15 Vacuum passage
16 Throttle valve

Accelerator pump circuit

1 Float chamber
2 Fuel outlet channel
3 Pump injector
4 Pump actuating lever
5 Pump cam
6 Diaphragm
7 Spring
8 Inlet ball
9 Back bleed

Chapter H16

ridges. This is more likely with the brass needle valve tip than when a viton one is used. Use a viton-tipped replacement when possible.
10 The float should be checked for damage and ingress of petrol.
11 Renew the float pin if it appears worn.
12 Unscrew the hexagon bolt and inspect the fuel filter. Clean the filter housing of debris and dirt and renew the filter if necessary.
13 Remove the mixture screw and inspect the tip for damage and ridges.
14 Remove the idle speed air valve (models from July 1985 on).
15 Remove the four screws and detach the accelerator pump cover, diaphragm and spring. Check the diaphragm for fatigue and damage.
16 The pump injector is a push fit in the body. Carefully prise it from its location and check the valve for damage.
17 Remove the primary idle jet assembly from the upper body. The idle jet is pushed into a holder and may be separated (by pulling) for cleaning or renewal. Also remove the auxiliary fuel jet and holder (July 1985 on) for cleaning or renewal. Note that the idle jet and air corrector can be detached from the carburettor without removing the upper body.
18 Remove the main jet, air corrector and emulsion tube. Check that the channel from the float chamber into the emulsion tube well is clear.
19 Check the jet calibration against that specified. It is possible that the wrong size jets may have been fitted during the last overhaul.
20 Remove the auxiliary venturi from the upper body where necessary. Weber provide an extractor tool for removing this component. Check that the venturi is not loose in the main body as this is a source of uneven running. If the venturi is loose, knurl the mating flanges with a file to ensure a tight fit.
21 Remove the three screws and detach the power valve housing cover, spring and diaphragm from the body. Check the diaphragm for fatigue and damage. The brass outlet valve is cast into the body and is not removable. The ball in the outlet valve should seal the outlet. Depress and release the ball with a small screwdriver and it should move smoothly in and out. Check that the emulsion tube well is clear.
22 Remove the two screws and separate the carburettor main body and throttle body assemblies. The throttle body can be renewed separately if the spindles or throttle bores are worn.
23 Do not disturb the adjustment of the throttle angle unless absolutely necessary (July 1985 on).
24 Push out the plastic choke mechanism shield from under the upper body lip and remove it. Inspect the choke spindle, linkage and operating mechanism for stickiness and wear.
25 Attach a vacuum pump to the pull-down diaphragm and operate the pump to obtain 200 mm Hg. The diaphragm should operate fully and the vacuum not drop by more than 10% within a period of 30 seconds. Renew the diaphragm assembly if it fails these tests.

26 Remove the three fixing screws that secure the bi-metal coil housing to the choke assembly housing. Note the position of the alignment marks and remove the coil housing from the carburettor body. Remove the internal heat plate and electrical connection.
27 Remove the three screws, disconnect the choke link rod and detach the choke pull-down assembly.
28 Remove the three screws and detach the choke diaphragm cover, spring and diaphragm from the housing. Check the diaphragm for fatigue. Also check the plastic sleeves and spring fitted to the diaphragm rod for stickiness and damage.

Preparation for reassembly

29 Clean the jets, carburettor body assemblies, float chamber and internal channels. An air line may be used to clear internal channels once the carburettor is fully dismantled. Note that if high-pressure air is directed into the channels and passages with the diaphragms still in place, diaphragm damage may result.
30 Spraying carburettor cleaner into all the channels and passages in the carburettor body will often clear them of gum and dirt.
31 During reassembly, a complete set of new gaskets should be fitted. Also renew the needle valve and float pin, and all diaphragms.
32 Inspect and renew (where necessary) the mixture screw, main jet, idle jet, air corrector jet, emulsion tube and accelerator pump injector. Renew worn linkages, screws, springs, vacuum hoses and other parts where necessary.
33 Ensure that all jets are firmly locked into position (but do not over-tighten). A loose jet can cause a rich (or even lean) running condition.
34 Clean all mating surfaces and flanges of old gasket material and reassemble with new gaskets.
35 Ensure that housings are positioned with their air and fuel routes correctly aligned.

Reassembly

36 Refit the choke diaphragm and spindle assembly to the choke housing. Ensure that both plastic sleeves on the diaphragm spindle are pushed into position and are fully located. Refit the spring and cover, then secure with the three screws.
37 Engage the choke link rod into the choke lever arm and refit the choke housing to the carburettor upper body. Secure with the three screws.
38 Clip the choke mechanism shield into position. Ensure that the choke flap and linkage move smoothly and progressively.
39 Assemble the main and throttle bodies with a new gasket block and secure with the two screws.
40 If the throttle valve position has been disturbed (July 1985 on), then the basic angle must now be adjusted. Refer to Section 4 for details on adjustment.
41 Refit the power diaphragm, spring and cover assembly, then secure with the three screws.
42 Refit the emulsion tube, air corrector and main jet into their original positions.

43 Push the idle jet into its holder and refit the assembly into the upper body. Refit the auxiliary fuel jet assembly (July 1985 on).
44 Refit the idle cut-off valve, using a new sealing washer.
45 Refit the idle mixture screw, after renewing the seal. Turn the screw in gently until it just seats. From this position, unscrew it three full turns. This will provide a basic setting to allow the engine to be started.
46 Screw the idle speed air valve into the throttle body (July 1985 on).
47 Push the pump injector firmly into position, after renewing the small seal on the injector body.
48 Refit the pump spring, diaphragm and cover assembly, then secure with the four screws.
49 Clean or renew the fuel filter and refit the hexagon bolt.
50 Renew the float chamber gasket and locate in position on the upper body.
51 Renew the needle valve assembly. Screw the valve seat into the upper body using a new sealing washer and ensure that it is firmly locked into position (but do not over-tighten). Transfer the hairpin or plastic clip from the old needle valve to the ball end of the new one. Place the clip and valve assembly onto the inner float tag. Lower the float and needle valve assembly into the seat and secure with the float pin.
52 Adjust the float level. Refer to Section 4 for details on adjustment.
53 Refit the upper body to the main body and secure with the three screws. Reconnect the choke vacuum hose.
54 Refit the carburettor to the engine.
55 Always adjust the carburettor idle speed and mixture after any work has been carried out on the carburettor, preferably with the aid of a CO meter.
56 Adjust the choke fast idle and pull-down. Refer to Section 4 for details.

4 Service adjustments

Adjustment preconditions

1 Refer to Part B for general advice on the preconditions to correct adjustment of this carburettor. In addition, the following points must be observed:
2 The oil temperature must be at a minimum of 60°C.
3 All electrical accessories must be switched off and the radiator fan must not operate during the setting operation.
4 The engine breather hose must be disconnected at the air filter and the air filter connection plugged.

Idle speed and mixture (CO)

5 Run the engine at 3000 rpm for 30 seconds to clear the manifold of fuel vapours, then allow the engine to idle.

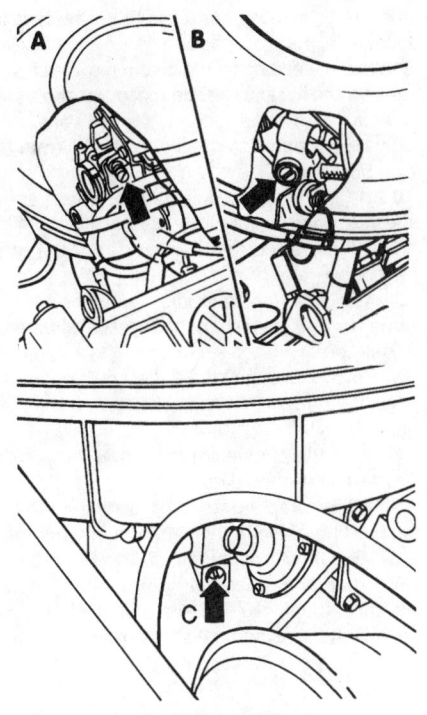

Weber 32 TLA carburettor

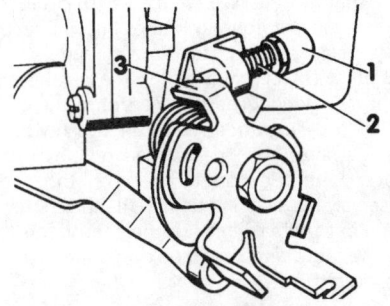

Setting throttle plate angle

1 Tamperproof cap 3 Throttle stop
2 Adjustment screw

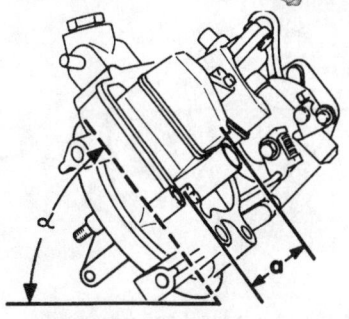

Float level adjustment

a Float level measurement 45° angle (approx.)

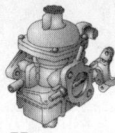

Idle speed and mixture adjustment

A Idle speed adjustment screw (pre-July 1985)
B Idle air valve screw (July 1985 on)
C Idle mixture control screw

6 Use the air valve adjustment screw to set the specified idle speed *(see illustration)*.
7 Check the CO level. If it is not as specified, remove the tamperproof plug and adjust the idle mixture control screw to achieve the correct level. Turning the screw clockwise (inwards) will reduce the CO level. Turning the screw anti-clockwise (outwards) will increase the CO level.
8 Repeat paragraphs 6 and 7 until both adjustments are correct.
9 Clear the manifold every 30 seconds during the setting operation by running the engine at 3000 rpm for 30 seconds.
10 Increase the speed to 2000 rpm and note the CO reading. The cruise reading should be less than half the idle CO reading.
11 Fit a new tamperproof plug to the mixture control screw.
12 Remove the temporary plug from the air filter connection and reconnect the engine breather hose.

Setting the throttle plate angle

13 If the throttle position has been disturbed or the idle speed and CO cannot be set correctly, it is possible that the basic throttle angle is incorrect. Use the following method of setting the throttle position:
14 Ensure that the fast idle adjustment screw is not butting against the fast idle cam.
15 Remove the tamperproof cap from the throttle stop screw *(see illustration)*.
16 Turn the stop screw outwards until a gap appears between screw and stop.
17 Adjust the throttle stop screw until it just contacts the stop.
18 Turn the stop screw inwards a further quarter-turn.
19 Fit a new tamperproof cap to the throttle stop screw.
20 Reset the idle speed and CO to the correct values by using the air valve adjustment screw and the mixture control screw, as indicated above.

Float level

21 Hold the carburettor upper body at an angle of approximately 45° with the float tag gently touching the ball of the needle valve.
22 Measure the distance between the upper body (with the gasket in place) and the base of the float *(see illustration)*.
23 Adjust as necessary by bending the inner float tag.

Automatic choke

24 Warm the engine to normal running temperature and adjust the idle speed and mixture before attempting choke fast idle or vacuum pull-down adjustment.

Fast idle

25 Remove the air filter assembly and place it clear of the carburettor. Disconnect and plug the vacuum hose.
26 Remove the three screws and detach the bi-metal coil housing from the carburettor.
27 Remove the internal heat plate.
28 Place the fast idle adjustment screw against the second-highest step of the fast idle cam *(see illustration)*.
29 Fit an elastic band to the choke operating lever and tension it so that the choke flap remains in the fully off position.
30 Start the engine without moving the throttle and record the fast idle speed.
31 Adjust as necessary by turning the adjustment screw in the appropriate direction.

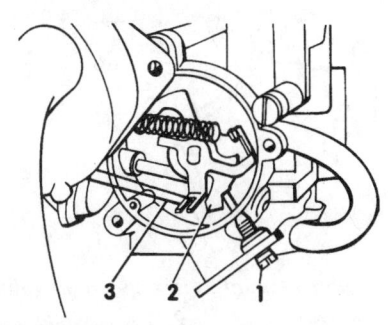

Vacuum pull-down

32 Place the fast idle adjustment screw against the highest step of the fast idle cam.
33 Fit an elastic band to the choke operating lever so that the choke flap remains in the fully on position.
34 Use a vacuum pump to pull the diaphragm operating rod up to its stop (or push the mechanism with a small screwdriver). At the same time, use the shank of a twist drill to measure the gap between the lower section of the choke flap and the air intake. Refer to Specifications for the required drill size *(see illustration)*.

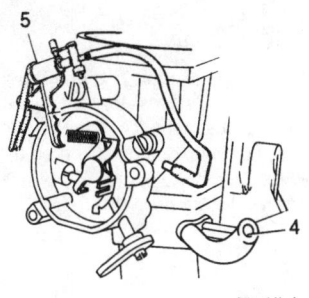

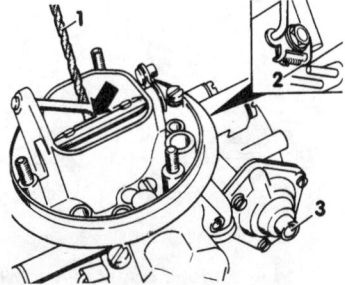

Fast idle adjustment

1 Fast idle adjustment screw
2 Fast idle cam
3 Rubber band

Pull-down adjustment

1 Twist drill
2 Measuring position
3 Adjustment screw
4 Disconnected vacuum hose
5 Vacuum pump

H16•5

Chapter H16

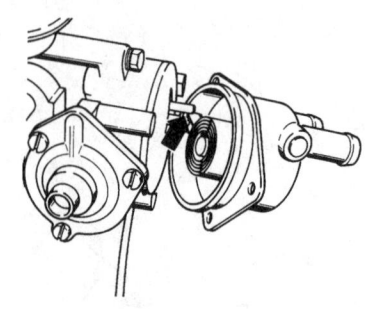

Refitting bi-metal coil housing

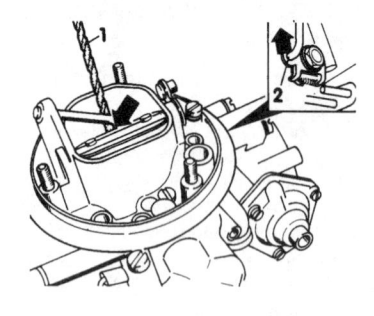

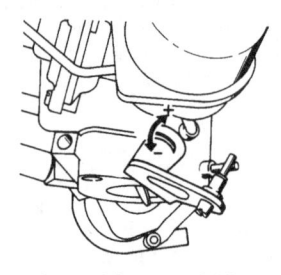

Measuring wide-open kick
1 Twist drill
2 Measuring position
+ Larger gap
− Smaller gap

37 Refit the internal heat plate and ensure that the peg in the housing locates into the hole in the shield. Reconnect the electrical supply.
38 Refit the bi-metal coil housing and ensure that the spring locates in the slot of the choke lever (see illustration). Secure loosely with the three screws. Align the cut mark on the bi-metal cover with the correct mark on the choke assembly housing and tighten the three screws.
39 Refit the air filter assembly, ensuring that the vacuum and breather hoses are properly connected.

Wide-open kick (dechoke)
40 Remove the air filter assembly.
41 Fully open the throttle and hold it in this position.
42 Press the lever (2) upwards and use the shank of a twist drill to measure the gap between the lower section of the choke flap and the air intake (see illustration). Refer to Specifications for the required drill size.
43 Adjust as necessary by bending the lever in the appropriate direction.

5 Component testing

Idle speed boost valve
1 The basic operation of the valve can be checked as follows:
2 Remove the air filter assembly and place it clear of the carburettor. Disconnect and plug the vacuum hose.
3 Use a T-piece to connect a vacuum gauge between the two-way valve and the idle speed air valve (see illustration).
4 Allow the engine to idle. The vacuum indication on the gauge should be zero.
5 Slowly close the choke flap so that the idle speed falls below 700 rpm.
6 Below 700 rpm, the idle speed will increase and vacuum should be indicated upon the gauge.
7 If vacuum is not indicated or the idle speed does not increase, proceed with testing as follows:
8 Allow the engine to idle then remove and plug the vacuum hose to the idle speed air valve.
9 Attach a vacuum pump to the valve and operate the pump to obtain 300 to 500 mm Hg (see illustration).
10 If the idle speed does not increase, renew the idle speed air valve.
11 Pull the electrical connector from the two-way boost valve.
12 Allow the engine to idle and connect a test lamp to the detached connector plug (see illustration).
13 Slowly close the choke flap so that the idle speed falls below 700 rpm. The test lamp should light.
14 Raise the engine speed to over 1100 rpm. The test lamp should go out.
15 If the lamp lights as specified and the vacuum hoses are intact, then renew the two-way valve if the operation is still unsatisfactory.
16 If the lamp does not light as specified, an electrical supply fault is indicated. The tracing of such faults is beyond the scope of this Manual.

Automatic choke electric heater
17 Turn the ignition on and use a voltmeter to check for a battery supply to the choke electrical connector. If the voltage is low or zero, check the supply back to the ignition switch if necessary.
18 Disconnect the choke heater at the electrical connector.
19 Connect a test lamp from the battery positive terminal to the heat plate connector. If the lamp does not light, renew the heat plate and earth connector.

6 Fault diagnosis

Refer to Part D for diagnosis of general carburettor faults.

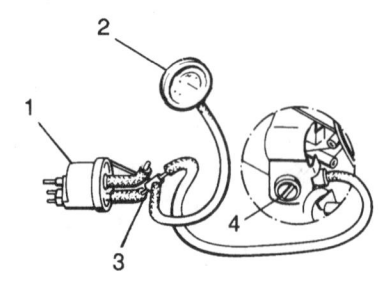

Checking idle speed boost valve with vacuum gauge
1 Two-way boost valve
2 Vacuum gauge
3 T-piece
4 Idle speed air valve

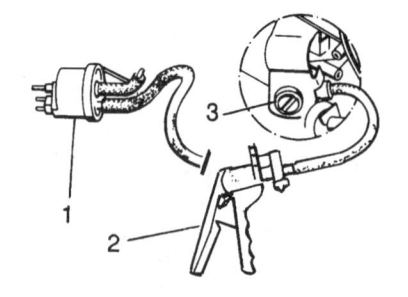

Applying vacuum to idle speed air valve
1 Two-way boost valve
2 Vacuum pump
3 Idle speed air valve

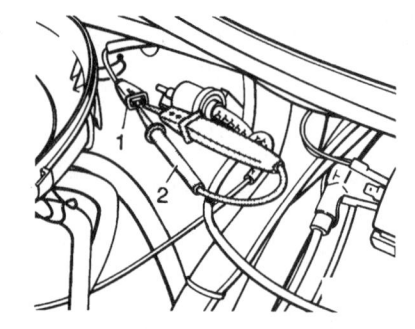

Checking electrical connector to 2-way boost valve
1 Electrical connector
2 Test lamp

35 Remove the plug in the diaphragm cover and adjust as necessary by turning the diaphragm adjustment screw in the appropriate direction. Renew the plug when adjustment is complete.
36 Remove the elastic band.

H16•6

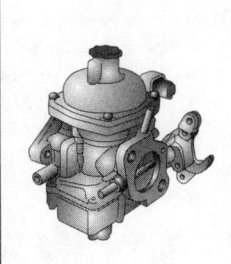

Part H Chapter 17
Weber 32/34 TLDE carburettor

H17

Contents

Component testing 5	Identification 2
Fault diagnosis 6	Principles of operation 1
General servicing 3	Service adjustments 4

Specifications

Manufacturer	Fiat	Fiat	Fiat
Model	Regata 75	Regata 85	Strada 85
Year	1985 to 1988	1985 to 1988	1985 to 1988
Engine code	138 C3.045	149 A5.000	149 A5.000
Capacity (cm³)/no. of cyls	1498/4	1498/4	1498/4
Oil temperature (°C)	100	100	100
Carb. identification	32/34 TLDE 2/150	32/34 TLDE/150	32/34 TLDE 2/150
Idle speed (rpm)	850 ± 50	850 ± 50	850 ± 50
CO @ idle (% vol.)	1.0 ± 0.5	1.0 ± 0.5	1.0 ± 0.5
Stage (venturi)	1 2	1 2	1 2
Venturi diameter	21 24	21 24	21 24
Idle jet	50 60	47 40	50 60
Main jet	112 140	110 140	112 140
Air correction jet	165 155	160 160	165 155
Emulsion tube	F74 F25	F74 F25	F74 F25
Accel. pump jet	40	40	40
Float level (mm)	30 ± 0.25	30 ± 0.25	30 ± 0.25
Needle valve size (mm)	1.75	1.75	1.75
Choke fast idle gap (mm)	0.95 ± 0.05	0.95 ± 0.05	0.95 ± 0.05
Choke pull-down (mm)	4.5 ± 0.25	4.5 ± 0.25	4.5 ± 0.25

Manufacturer	Fiat	Fiat	Fiat
Model	Tempra 1.4	Tempra 1.4 Selecta	Tempra 1.6
Year	1990 to 1991	1990 to 1991	1990 to 1991
Engine code	159A2.000 (56kW)	159A2.000 (56kW)	159A3.000 DOHC (62kW)
Capacity (cm³)/no. of cyls	1372/4	1372/4	1581/4
Oil temperature (°C)	100	100	100
Transmission	MT	AT	MT
Carb. identification	32/34 TLDE 21/151	32/34 TLDE 22/750	32/34 TLDE 23/151
Idle speed (rpm)	850 ± 50	850 ± 50	850 ± 50
Fast idle speed (rpm)	1300 ± 50	1300 ± 50	1300 ± 50
CO @ idle (% vol.)	1.0 ± 0.5	1.0 ± 0.5	1.0 ± 0.5
Stage (venturi)	1 2	1 2	1 2
Venturi diameter	21 24	21 24	21 24
Idle jet	47 40	47 40	47 40
Main jet	110 123	110 122	107 123
Air correction jet	160 160	160 160	160 160
Emulsion tube	F74 F25	F74 F25	F74 F25
Accel. pump jet	40	40	40
Float level (mm)	30 ± 1	30 ± 1	30 ± 1
Needle valve size (mm)	1.75	1.75	1.75
Choke fast idle gap (mm)	1 ± 0.05	1 ± 0.05	1 ± 0.05
Choke pull-down (mm)	3 ± 0.25	3 ± 0.25	3 ± 0.25

Chapter H17

Manufacturer	Fiat	Fiat	Fiat
Model	Tempra 1.6 Selecta	Tipo 1.4	Tipo 1.4 Selecta
Year	1990 to 1991	1988 to 1990	1988 to 1990
Engine code	159A3.000 DOHC (62kW)	160A1.000 DOHC	160A1.000 DOHC
Capacity (cm³)/no. of cyls	1581/4	1372/4	1372/4
Oil temperature (°C)	100	100	100
Transmission	AT	MT	AT
Carb. identification	32/34 TLDE 24/751	32/34 TLDE 4/150	32/34 TLDE 9/751
Idle speed (rpm)	850 ± 50	825 ± 25	850 ± 50
Fast idle speed (rpm)	1300 ± 50	1300 ± 50	1300 ± 50
CO @ idle (% vol.)	1.0 ± 0.5	1 ± 0.5	1.25 ± 0.25
Stage (venturi)	1 2	1 2	1 2
Venturi diameter	21 24	21 24	21 24
Idle jet	47 40	50 40	50 40
Main jet	107 122	110 130	110 130
Air correction jet	160 160	160 160	160 160
Emulsion tube	F74 F25	F74 F25	F74 F25
Accel. pump jet	40	40	40
Float level (mm)	30 ± 1	30 ± 0.25	30 ± 0.25
Needle valve size (mm)	1.75	1.75	1.75
Choke fast idle gap (mm)	1 ± 0.05	1 ± 0.05	1 ± 0.05
Choke pull-down (mm)	3 ± 0.25	3.75 ± 0.25	3 ± 0.25

Manufacturer	Fiat	Fiat	Fiat
Model	Tipo 1.4	Tipo 1.4 Selecta	Tipo 1.6
Year	1990 to 1991	1990 to 1991	1988 to 1990
Engine code	159A2.000 DOHC (56kW)	159A2.000 DOHC (56kW)	160A2.000 DOHC (56kW)
Capacity (cm³)/no. of cyls	1372/4	1372/4	1580/4
Oil temperature (°C)	100	100	100
Transmission	MT	AT	–
Carb. identification	32/34 TLDE 21	32/34 TLDE 22	32/34 TLDE 5/150
Idle speed (rpm)	850 ± 50	850 ± 50	825 ± 25
Fast idle speed (rpm)	1300 ± 50	1300 ± 50	1300 ± 50
CO @ idle (% vol.)	1 ± 0.5	1.0 ± 0.5	1.0 ± 0.5
Stage (venturi)	1 2	1 2	1 2
Venturi diameter	21 24	21 24	21 24
Idle jet	47 40	47 40	47 40
Main jet	110 123	110 122	110 130
Air correction jet	160 160	160 160	160 160
Emulsion tube	F74 F25	F74 F25	F74 F25
Accel. pump jet	40	40	40
Float level (mm)	30 ± 1	30 ± 1	30 ± 0.25
Needle valve size (mm)	1.75	1.75	1.75
Choke fast idle gap (mm)	1 ± 0.05	1 ± 0.05	1 ± 0.05
Choke pull-down (mm)	3 ± 0.25	3 ± 0.25	3.75 ± 0.25

Manufacturer	Fiat	Fiat
Model	Tipo 1.6	Tipo 1.6
Year	1990 to 1991	1990 to 1991
Engine code	159A3.000 DOHC (62kW)	159A3.000 DOHC (62kW)
Capacity (cm³)/no. of cyls	1581/4	1581/4
Oil temperature (°C)	100	100
Transmission	MT	AT
Carb. identification	32/34 TLDE 23	32/34 TLDE 24
Idle speed (rpm)	850 ± 50	850 ± 50
Fast idle speed (rpm)	1300 ± 50	1300 ± 50
CO @ idle (% vol.)	1.0 ± 0.5	1 ± 0.5
Stage (venturi)	1 2	1 2
Venturi diameter	21 24	21 24
Idle jet	47 40	47 40
Main jet	107 123	107 122
Air correction jet	160 160	160 160
Emulsion tube	F74 F25	F74 F25
Accel. pump jet	40	40
Float level (mm)	30 ± 1	30 ± 1
Needle valve size (mm)	1.75	1.75
Choke fast idle gap (mm)	1 ± 0.05	1 ± 0.05
Choke pull-down (mm)	3 ± 0.25	3 ± 0.25

Weber 32/34 TLDE carburettor

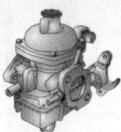

1 Principles of operation

Introduction

1 The following technical description of the Weber TLDE carburettor should be read in conjunction with the more detailed description of carburettor principles in Part A.

Construction

2 The Weber TLDE carburettor is a downdraught, progressive twin venturi instrument with a mechanically-controlled secondary throttle *(see illustration)*. The choke system is manually-controlled and operates on the primary venturi only. A vacuum-controlled device is used to control fast idle during engine warm-up. The carburettor is constructed in three main bodies. These are the upper body, main body and throttle body containing the throttle assemblies. An insulating block, placed between the main carburettor body and the throttle body, prevents excess heat transference to the main body.

3 The throttle and choke shafts and the choke flap are made of steel. The throttle valves are made of brass, as are all the emulsion tubes and jets, with the exception of the accelerator pump discharge injector which is die-cast. The internal fuel channels and air passages are drilled and sealed with lead plugs where necessary.

4 An idle cut-off valve is fitted to the idle circuit and this device is further controlled by an ECU to save fuel during deceleration.

Fuel control

5 Fuel flows into the carburettor through a fine mesh filter. The fuel level in the float chamber is controlled by a needle valve and plastic float assembly. An anti-vibration ball is incorporated into the needle valve design. A clip, attached to the needle valve and to the float arm, prevents the needle from sticking in the seat as the fuel level drops. The float chamber is vented internally to the clean-air side of the air filter. A calibrated fuel return system is provided to ensure that relatively cool fuel is supplied to the carburettor.

Idle, slow running and progression

6 Fuel, sourced from the main well, passes into the upper body through a metered idle jet. Here it is mixed with a small amount of air from a calibrated air bleed. The emulsion formed is drawn through a channel to the throttle body where it is discharged from the idle orifice under the primary throttle plate. A tapered mixture screw is used to vary the outlet and this ensures

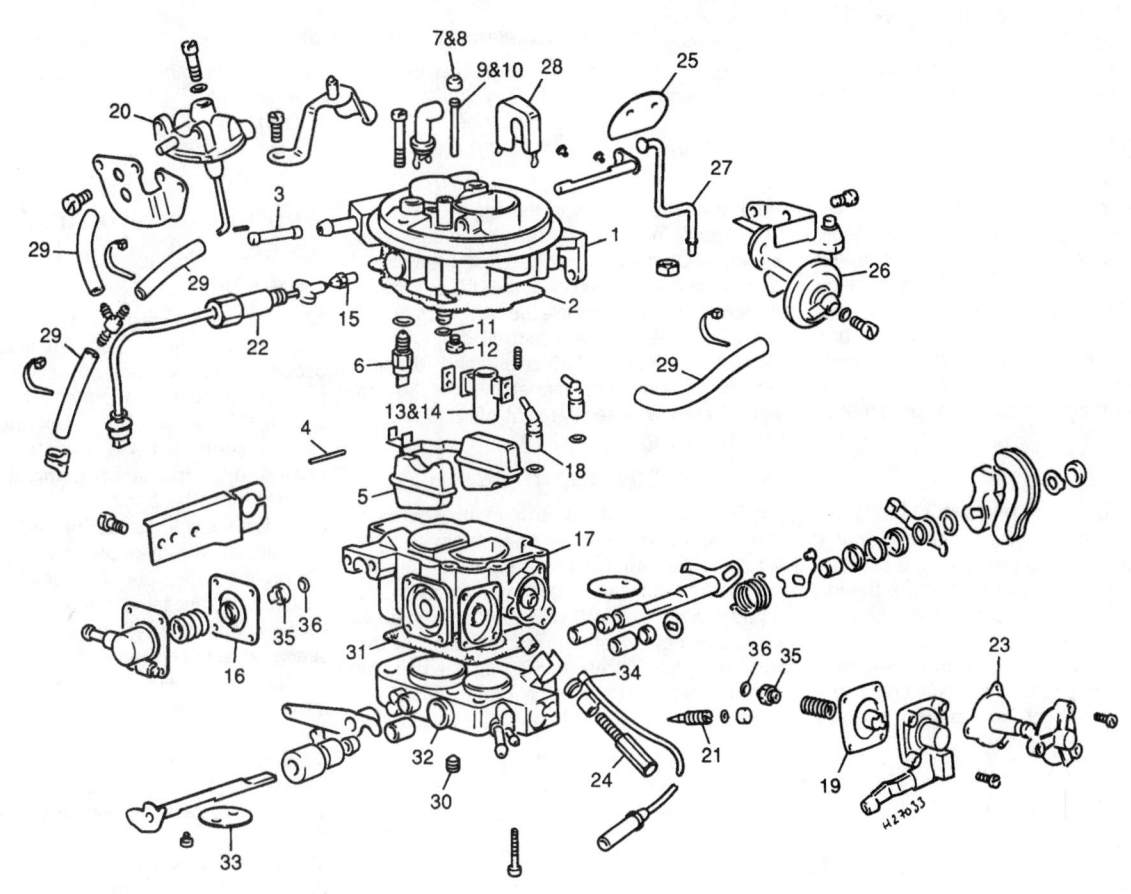

Weber TLDE carburettor

1 Upper body
2 Float chamber gasket
3 Fuel inlet filter
4 Float pin
5 Float
6 Needle valve assembly
7 Air corrector (primary)
8 Air corrector (secondary)
9 Emulsion tube (primary)
10 Emulsion tube (secondary)
11 Main jet (primary)
12 Main jet (secondary)
13 Auxiliary venturi (primary)
14 Auxiliary venturi (secondary)
15 Idle jet (primary)
16 Accelerator pump diaphragm (temperature-controlled type)
17 Main body
18 Pump injector
19 Accelerator pump diaphragm
20 Fast idle device
21 Idle mixture control screw
22 Idle cut-off valve
23 Power valve diaphragm
24 Idle speed screw
25 Choke flap
26 Choke diaphragm
27 Choke link rod
28 Choke mechanism shield
29 Vacuum hose
30 Secondary throttle valve adjustment screw
31 Insulator block
32 Throttle body
33 Throttle valve
34 Throttle switch
35 Inlet valve
36 Seal

Chapter H17

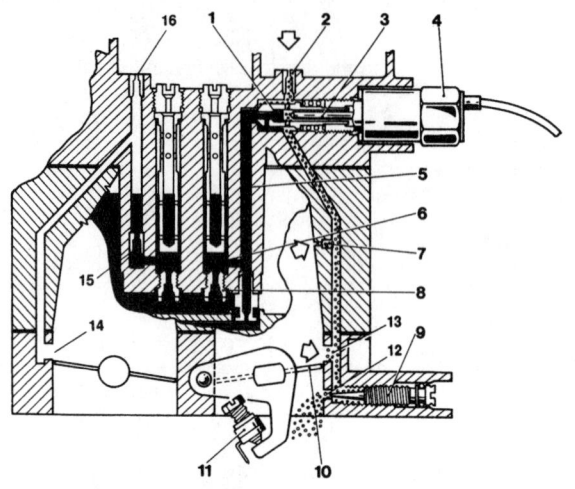

Idle and progression circuits

1. Idle jet
2. Air bleed
3. Plunger
4. Idle cut-off valve
5. Idle fuel channel
6. Main well
7. Anti-syphon hole
8. Main jet
9. Idle mixture control screw
10. Throttle valve
11. Throttle switch
12. Idle outlet
13. Primary progression outlet
14. Secondary progression outlet
15. Secondary idle jet
16. Air bleed

Accelerator pump circuit

1. Float chamber
2. Fuel outlet channel
3. Pump injector
4. Pump actuating lever
5. Pump cam
6. Diaphragm
7. Spring
8. Inlet ball
9. Back bleed

fine control of the idle mixture. A progression slot, partially covered by the closed throttle at idle, provides additional enrichment as it is uncovered by the opening throttle during initial acceleration. An anti-syphon hole connects the idle fuel channel with the primary venturi *(see illustration)*.

7 The idle speed is set by an adjustable screw. The adjustable mixture screw is tamper-proofed during production, in accordance with emission regulations.

Idle cut-off valve

8 When the ignition is switched on, a 12-volt solenoid activates the plunger to withdraw it from the idle jet. Once the ignition is switched off, the solenoid deactivates to block the idle jet. Running-on is thus prevented when the engine is shut down.

9 The device is also controlled by an electronic control unit (ECU), so that, during engine deceleration from high speeds with a closed throttle, the fuel supply to the engine is cut off. This results in a fuel saving and in improved emissions. Once the engine speed falls below 1800 rpm or the throttle is opened, the ECU reactivates the solenoid and normal idle fuel flow is restored.

10 Where the ignition is controlled by Digiplex (as is the case with 1600 cc engines), the idle cut-off function is incorporated into the Digiplex ECU. Generally, a separate cut-off ECU is used for 1400 cc engines.

Accelerator pump

11 The accelerator pump is controlled by a diaphragm and is mechanically operated by a lever and cam attached to the primary throttle linkage. The outlet valve is incorporated into the pump injector. The inlet valve consists of a brass valve assembly located in a channel from the float chamber. Excess fuel is returned to the float chamber through a calibrated bush *(see illustration)*.

Accelerator pump circuit with thermal switch

1. Pump injector
2. Outlet ball
3. Venturi depression
4. Inlet ball
5. Diaphragm
6. Spring
7. Thermal switch
8. Float chamber

Temperature-controlled accelerator pump (some models)

12 When a lean mixture is provided for normal running conditions, poor driveability often occurs during the warm-up period. This device provides a means of enriching the mixture during this period. The accelerator pump is vacuum-controlled and operates in a similar fashion to the mechanical pump above. Fuel is injected into the primary venturi through an additional injector nozzle. The vacuum supply is introduced via a thermal switch mounted into the cooling system *(see illustration)*.

13 At a coolant temperature below 25°C, the vacuum signal draws the diaphragm back against spring pressure and fuel is drawn into the pump chamber and outlet channel. As the engine speed increases, the depression in the venturi acts upon the discharge nozzle. Extra fuel is drawn past the pump outlet ball where it is discharged into the main venturi from the injector.

14 As the coolant temperature rises above 25°C, the vacuum passage is gradually closed until at 45°C it is fully closed. Less fuel is then drawn from the accelerator pump nozzle as the engine warm-up progresses. Once the engine has reached normal operating temperature, the temperature-controlled accelerator pump ceases to operate.

Main circuit

15 The amount of fuel discharged into the air stream is controlled by a calibrated main jet. Fuel is drawn through the main jet into the base of a vertical well which dips down into the fuel in the float chamber. An emulsion tube is placed in the well. The fuel is mixed with air drawn in

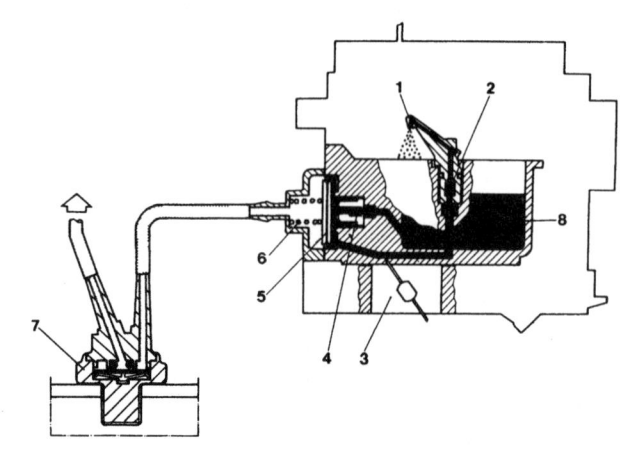

Weber 32/34 TLDE carburettor

through the air corrector and through the holes in the emulsion tube. The resulting emulsified mixture is discharged from the main nozzle through an auxiliary venturi (see illustration).

Power enrichment and economy circuit

16 Fuel flows from the float chamber into the power valve chamber through a fuel channel. An air passage is taken from under the throttle plate to the cover of the power diaphragm chamber. At idle and during light-throttle operation, manifold vacuum draws the diaphragm back against spring pressure. The diaphragm pintle is withdrawn from the brass outlet valve and the spring-loaded ball seats to close off the outlet channel.

17 Under acceleration and wide-open throttle operation, the vacuum in the manifold is depleted. The diaphragm returns under spring pressure and the power diaphragm pintle pushes the ball to open the outlet valve. Fuel then flows through the valve and a calibrated jet to supplement the fuel in the primary main well. The fuel level rises in the well and the fuel mixture is enriched.

Secondary action

18 Once the primary throttle valve is about two-thirds-open, the mechanical linkage will begin to open the secondary throttle plate. At full-throttle, the linkage is arranged so that both throttle plates will be fully open.

19 A progression jet is used to prevent hesitation as the secondary throttle plate begins to open. This jet is similar in construction and action to the primary idle jet and is often referred to as the secondary idle jet. An emulsified mixture is discharged into the secondary venturi via a progression slot at the initial opening of the secondary throttle plate.

20 Once the secondary throttle plate has opened, the action of the secondary main circuit is similar to the primary circuit.

21 At full-load and high engine speeds, even more fuel is required. The velocity of air creates a depression sufficient to raise fuel from the float chamber into a channel. The fuel then passes through a calibrated bushing to the upper section of the secondary air intake. Here it is mixed with a small amount of air from a calibrated air bleed and the emulsified mixture is then discharged into the airstream from the full-load enrichment orifice.

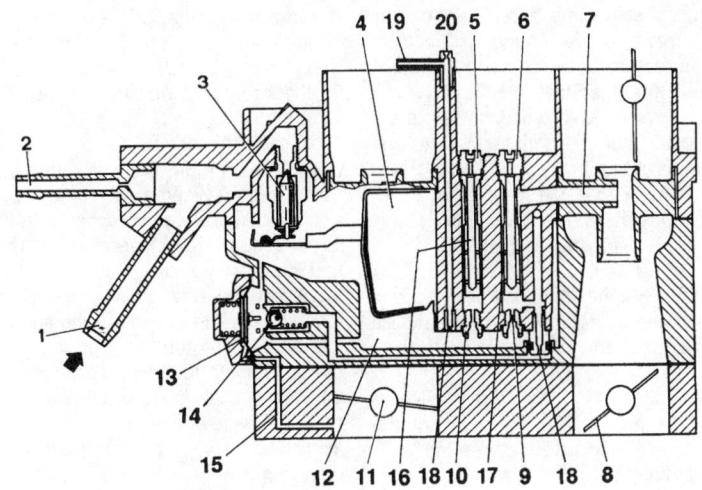

Main, power and full-load circuits

1 Fuel inlet
2 Fuel return
3 Needle valve
4 Float
5 Air corrector (secondary)
6 Air corrector (primary)
7 Auxiliary venturi
8 Throttle valve (primary)
9 Main jet (primary)
10 Main jet (secondary)
11 Throttle valve (secondary)
12 Float chamber
13 Diaphragm
14 Power valve ball
15 Vacuum passage
16 Emulsion tube (secondary)
17 Emulsion tube (primary)
18 Calibrated bush
19 Full-load outlet
20 Air bleed

Choke operation

22 The manual choke is operated by a dash-mounted cable. When the cable is pulled, it operates a lever that pulls the choke flap closed across the air intake. Fast idle is achieved with the aid of a curved cam attached to the choke operating lever. An adjustable screw, attached to the throttle lever and butting against the cam, is used to vary the fast idle speed.

23 Once the engine has fired, the choke flap must open slightly to weaken the mixture and avoid flooding during idle and light-throttle operation. This is achieved by using manifold vacuum to actuate a diaphragm. A linkage attached to the diaphragm will then pull upon the choke flap.

24 During engine warm-up, the cable should be progressively pushed home until the choke flap is fully open.

Single-stage fast idle device (some models)

25 Towards the end of the warm-up period, the engine will reach a temperature where the choke can be pushed fully home but full operating temperature is still not quite attained. During this time, the idle speed may fall to a level where stalling will occur. The single-stage fast idle device opens the throttle to maintain a fast idle (see illustration).

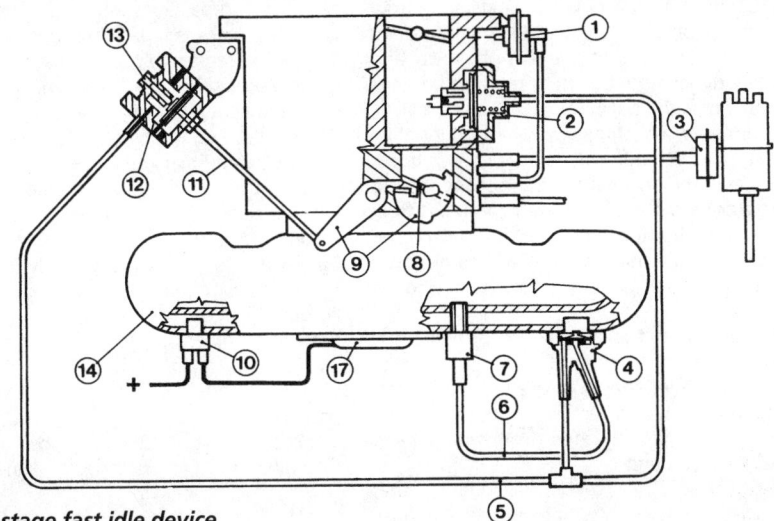

Single-stage fast idle device

1 Choke pull-down diaphragm
2 Temperature-controlled accelerator pump
3 Ignition distributor
4 Thermal switch
5 Vacuum pipe
6 Vacuum pipe
7 Manifold vacuum connection
8 Throttle valve (primary)
9 Throttle levers
10 Thermal switch (manifold heater)
11 Rod
12 Fast idle device
13 Adjustment screw
14 Inlet manifold

Chapter H17

26 A vacuum supply is introduced via a thermal switch mounted into the cooling system. At a coolant temperature below 25°C, the vacuum signal draws the fast idle diaphragm back against spring pressure. A rod connected to the diaphragm pulls upon the primary throttle lever to open the throttle plate. The extra air drawn past the plate causes the idle speed to increase.

27 As the coolant temperature rises above 25°C, the vacuum passage is gradually closed until at 45°C it is fully closed.

28 Once the engine has reached normal operating temperature, the fast idle device ceases to operate and idle speed returns to normal.

29 The thermal switch for this device is normally the same one used to control the temperature-controlled accelerator pump. A T-piece on the outlet side of the switch pipes the vacuum to each unit.

Manifold heater

30 To improve atomisation of the air/fuel mixture during the warm-up period, an inlet manifold heating device is utilised. This operates through a thermal switch so that manifold heating is discontinued once a coolant temperature of 65°C is reached.

2 Identification

The Weber identification code is stamped on the float chamber body (choke side).

3 General servicing

Introduction

1 Read this Chapter in conjunction with Part B, which describes some of the operations in more detail. It is assumed that the carburettor is removed for this service. However, many of the operations can be tackled with the carburettor in place. Where this is undertaken, first soak the fuel out of the float chamber using a clean tissue or soft cloth, after removing the upper body assembly.

Dismantling and checking

2 Remove the four screws which secure the carburettor to the engine.
3 Remove the carburettor from the engine (see Part B).
4 Check visually for damage and wear.
5 Disconnect the choke vacuum hose, then remove the two screws and detach the carburettor upper body.
6 Use a straight-edge to check for distorted flanges on all facing surfaces.
7 Inspect the float chamber for corrosion and calcium build-up.
8 Tap out the float pin and remove the float, needle valve and plastic clip, float chamber gasket and needle valve seat.
9 Check that the anti-vibration ball is free in the valve end.
10 Check the needle valve tip for wear and ridges. This is more likely with the brass needle valve tip than when a viton one is used. Use a viton-tipped replacement when possible.
11 The float should be checked for damage and ingress of petrol.
12 Renew the float pin if it appears worn.
13 Unscrew the fuel inlet tube and inspect the fuel filter. Clean the filter housing of debris and dirt and renew the filter if necessary.
14 Remove the mixture screw and inspect the tip for damage and ridges.
15 Attach a vacuum pump to the fast idle diaphragm and operate the pump to obtain 300 mm Hg. The diaphragm should fully operate and the vacuum must be maintained for a minimum of 10 seconds. Renew the diaphragm assembly if it fails these tests.
16 Remove the two screws and the circlip and detach the fast idle assembly. Remove a further four screws and detach the cover, diaphragm and spring. Check the diaphragm for fatigue and damage.
17 Remove the four screws and detach the accelerator pump cover, diaphragm, spring and inlet valve. Check the diaphragm and inlet valve for fatigue and damage.
18 Remove the four screws and detach the temperature-controlled accelerator pump cover, spring, diaphragm and inlet valve. Check the diaphragm and inlet valve for fatigue and damage. Some inlet valves are not removable.
19 The two pump injectors are a push fit in the body. Carefully prise from their locations and check the valves for damage or leakage.
20 Detach the primary idle jet and spring from the idle cut-off valve. The secondary idle jet is not removable. Note that the cut-off valve and primary idle jet assembly can be removed from the carburettor without removing the upper body.
21 Unscrew the primary and secondary main jets from the underside of the upper body. Unscrew the primary and secondary air correctors and remove the emulsion tubes from the top of the upper body. Note that the air corrector and emulsion tubes can be removed from the carburettor body without removing the upper body.
22 Check that the emulsion tube wells are clear.
23 Note the jet sizes and locations for correct installation during assembly. For reference, the primary main jet is located on the idle cut-off side of the carburettor.
24 Check the jet calibration against that specified. It is possible that the jets may have been transposed (or the wrong size fitted) during the last overhaul.
25 Remove the primary and secondary auxiliary venturis from the upper body where necessary. A Weber extractor tool is available for this purpose. Check that the primary and secondary auxiliary venturis are not loose in the main body as this is a source of uneven running. If a venturi is loose, knurl the mating flanges with a file to ensure a tight fit.
26 Remove the three screws and detach the power valve housing cover, spring and diaphragm from the body. Check the diaphragm for damage. The brass outlet valve is cast into the body and is not removable. The ball in the outlet valve should seal the outlet. Depress and release the ball with a small screwdriver and it should move smoothly in and out. Check that the channel into the emulsion tube well is clear.
27 Remove the two screws and separate the carburettor main body and throttle body assemblies. The throttle body can be renewed separately if the spindles or throttle bores are worn.
28 Pull away the plastic shield that covers the choke mechanism. Inspect the choke spindle, linkage and operating mechanism for stickiness and wear.
29 Attach a vacuum pump to the choke vacuum connector and operate the pump to obtain 300 mm Hg. Renew the diaphragm if it does not fully operate or if vacuum is not maintained for a minimum of 10 seconds.
30 Remove the three screws, pull the lower choke link rod out of the plastic retaining collar and detach the choke pull-down assembly.

Preparation for reassembly

31 Clean the jets, carburettor body assemblies, float chamber and internal channels. An air line may be used to clear internal channels once the carburettor is fully dismantled. Note that if high-pressure air is directed into the channels and passages with the diaphragms still in place, diaphragm damage may result.
32 Spraying carburettor cleaner into all the channels and passages in the carburettor body will often clear them of gum and dirt.
33 During reassembly, a complete set of new gaskets should be fitted. Also renew the needle valve and float pin, and all diaphragms.
34 Inspect and renew (where necessary) the mixture screw, main jets, idle jet, air corrector jets, emulsion tubes and accelerator pump injector. Renew worn linkages, screws, springs, vacuum hoses and other parts where necessary.
35 Ensure that all jets are firmly locked into their original positions (but do not over-tighten). A loose jet can cause a rich (or even lean) running condition.
36 Clean all mating surfaces and flanges of old gasket material and reassemble with new gaskets.
37 Ensure that housings are positioned with their air and fuel routes correctly aligned.

Reassembly

38 Refit the choke pull-down assembly and secure with the three screws. Push the end of the lower choke link rod through the plastic collar and clip it into position.
39 Assemble the main and throttle bodies with a new gasket block and secure with the two screws.

Weber 32/34 TLDE carburettor

40 Check that the secondary throttle plate is fully closed. The adjustment screw should not normally be used to alter the throttle plate position. However, if necessary, it can be adjusted so that the plate is open just enough to prevent its seizure in the throttle body.
41 Refit the power diaphragm, spring and cover assembly, then secure with the three screws. Renew the seal on the power valve jet which is adjacent to the primary main jet.
42 Refit the emulsion tubes, air correctors and main jets into their original positions (do not transpose the jets).
43 Push both pump injectors firmly into position after renewing the small seal on each injector body.
44 Renew the temperature-controlled accelerator pump inlet valve seal. Refit the inlet valve (with the seal facing inwards), then the diaphragm, spring and cover assembly, securing with the four screws.
45 Renew the accelerator pump inlet valve seal. Refit the inlet valve (with the seal facing inwards), then the spring, diaphragm and cover assembly. Secure with the four screws.
46 Refit the fast idle spring, diaphragm and cover assembly, then secure with the four screws. Reconnect the link rod to the actuating lever and secure with the circlip. Refit the assembly and secure with the two screws.
47 Refit the idle mixture screw after renewing the seal. Turn the screw in gently until it just seats. From this position, unscrew it three full turns. This will provide a basic setting to allow the engine to be started.
48 Clean or renew the fuel filter and refit the fuel inlet tube.
49 Renew the float chamber gasket and locate in position on the upper body. Renew the needle valve assembly. Screw the valve seat into the upper body, using a new sealing washer, and ensure that it is firmly locked into position (but do not over-tighten). Transfer the hairpin or plastic clip from the old needle valve to the ball end of the new one. Place the clip and valve assembly onto the inner float tag. Lower the float and needle valve assembly into the seat and secure with the float pin.
50 Adjust the float level. Refer to Section 4 for details on adjustment.
51 Refit the upper body to the main body and secure with the two screws. Reconnect the choke pull-down hose.
52 Fit the spring and idle jet to the idle cut-off valve. Do not push the jet completely into the valve. When the valve is fitted to the upper body, the idle jet will find its own position. Refit the assembly, using a new sealing washer.
53 Adjust the choke fast idle, pull-down and fast idle device. Refer to Section 4 for details on all adjustments.
54 Ensure that the choke flap and linkage move smoothly and progressively. Refit the plastic choke mechanism shield.
55 Refit the carburettor to the engine.
56 Always adjust the carburettor idle speed and mixture after any work has been carried out on the carburettor, preferably with the aid of a CO meter.

4 Service adjustments

Adjustment preconditions

1 Refer to Part B for general advice on the preconditions to correct adjustment of this carburettor.

Idle speed and mixture (CO)

2 Run the engine at 3000 rpm for 30 seconds to clear the manifold of fuel vapours, then allow the engine to idle.
3 Remove the air filter assembly and place it loosely on the carburettor. The vacuum and breather hoses must remain connected.
4 Use the idle speed adjustment screw to set the specified idle speed *(see illustration)*.
5 Check the CO level. If it is not as specified, remove the tamperproof plug and adjust the idle mixture control screw to achieve the correct level. Turning the screw clockwise (inwards) will reduce the CO level. Turning the screw anti-clockwise (outwards) will increase the CO level.
6 Repeat paragraphs 4 and 5 until both adjustments are correct.
7 Clear the manifold every 30 seconds during the setting operation by running the engine at 3000 rpm for 30 seconds.
8 Increase the speed to 2000 rpm and note the CO reading. The cruise reading should be less than half the idle CO reading.
9 Fit a new tamperproof plug to the mixture control screw.
10 Refit the air filter, ensuring that the vacuum and breather hoses are properly connected.

Float level

11 Hold the carburettor upper body in a vertical position with the float tag gently touching the ball of the fully-closed needle valve.
12 Measure the distance between the upper body (with the gasket in place) and the top of the float *(see illustration)*.
13 Adjust as necessary by bending the float tag.

Manual choke

Fast idle

14 The carburettor must be removed from the engine in order to make the fast idle adjustment.
15 Invert the carburettor.
16 Pull the choke operating arm to fully close the choke flap. The adjustment screw will butt against the fast idle cam and force open the throttle plate to leave a small clearance *(see illustration)*.
17 Use the shank of a twist drill to measure the clearance between the wall of the throttle bore and the throttle plate. Refer to Specifications for the required drill size and measure the clearance from the progression holes.
18 Adjust as necessary by turning the adjustment screw in the appropriate direction.

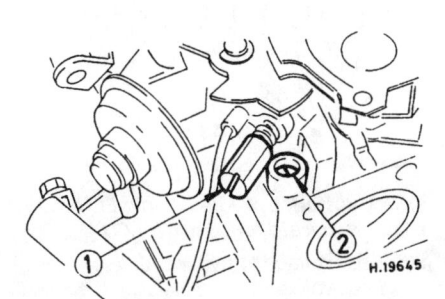

Idle speed and mixture adjustment
1 Idle speed screw
2 Idle mixture control screw

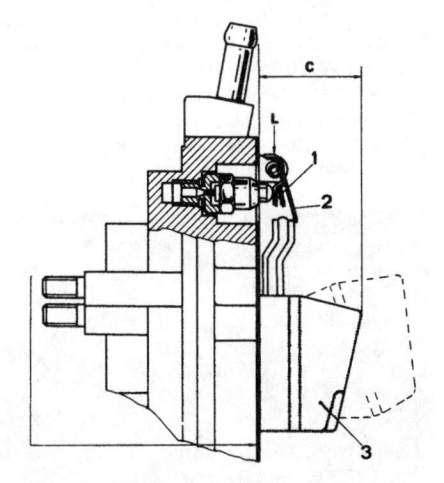

Float level measurement
1 Inner float tag
2 Float arm
3 Float
c Float level
L Outer float tag

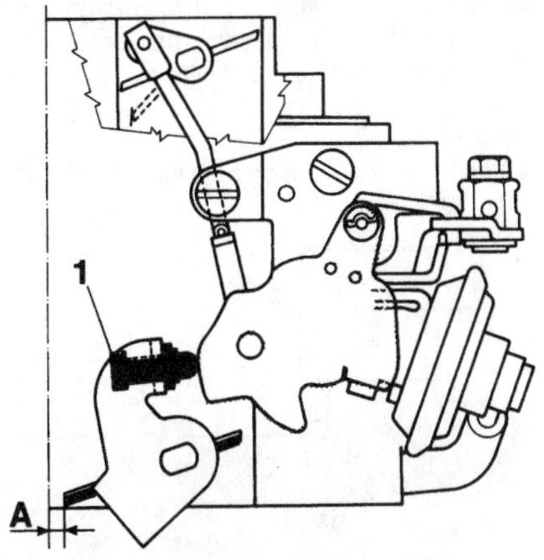

Fast idle adjustment
1 Fast idle adjustment screw
A Fast idle clearance

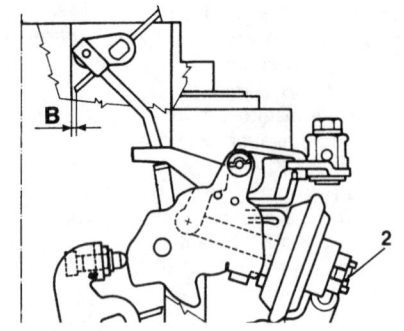

Chapter H17

Pull-down adjustment

2 Pull-down adjustment screw
B Pull-down clearance

Vacuum pull-down

19 Pull the choke operating arm to fully close the choke flap.
20 Use a vacuum pump (or a finger) to pull the diaphragm operating rod up to its stop. At the same time, use the shank of a twist drill to measure the gap between the lower section of the choke flap and the air intake. Refer to Specifications for the required drill size *(see illustration)*.
21 Remove the plug in the diaphragm cover and adjust as necessary by turning the diaphragm adjustment screw in the appropriate direction. Renew the plug when adjustment is complete.

Single-stage fast idle device

22 Check that the clearance between the throttle levers is approximately 0.5 mm. Adjust as necessary by slackening the locknut and turning the diaphragm/rod in the appropriate direction. Retighten the locknut on completion.
23 Warm the engine to normal running temperature and adjust the idle speed and mixture.
24 Allow the engine to idle then disconnect the vacuum hose from the fast idle device.
25 Connect the fast idle device to a vacuum source and record the speed, which should be 1300 ± 50 rpm.
26 Remove the plug in the diaphragm cover and adjust as necessary by turning the diaphragm adjustment screw in the appropriate direction. Renew the plug when adjustment is complete.
27 Refit all hoses into their original positions.

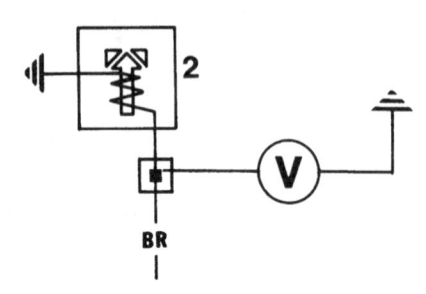

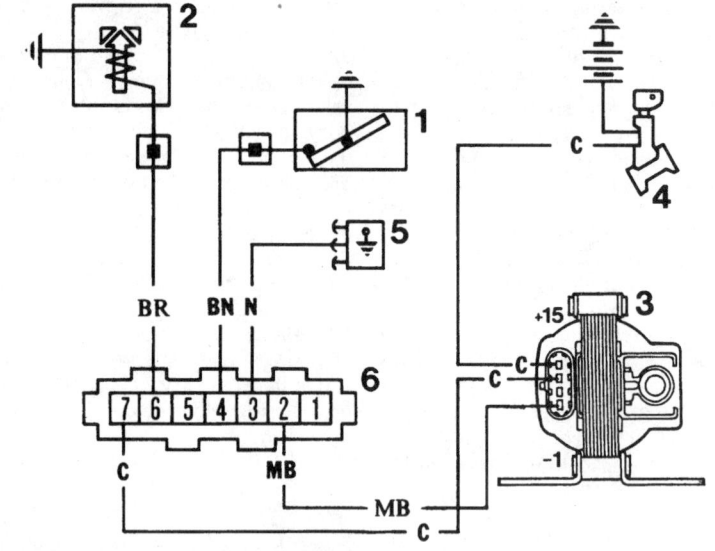

Supplementary wiring diagram - idle cut-off valve and associated accessories (separate idle cut-off ECU)

1 Throttle switch (closed)
2 Idle cut-off valve
3 Ignition coil
4 Ignition switch
5 Front left earth loom
6 Cut-off ECU
BN White/black
BR White/red
C Orange
MB Brown/white
N Black

5 Component testing

Electronic idle cut-off system

1 Connect a voltmeter from the idle cut-off valve to earth *(see illustrations)*.
2 Turn the ignition on. The voltmeter should indicate battery voltage *(see illustration)*.
3 Start the engine and raise the engine speed to over 3000 rpm. The voltmeter should still indicate battery voltage.
4 Close the throttle and decelerate the engine. Below 3000 rpm, the voltmeter should indicate zero volts and then battery voltage as the speed falls below 1600 to 1700 rpm.
5 If the voltage indicated is not as specified in the tests above, carry out the following checks according to which type of electronic control unit (ECU) is fitted. For guidance only, the separate ECU is normally fitted on 1400 cc engines and the Digiplex type on 1600 cc engines.

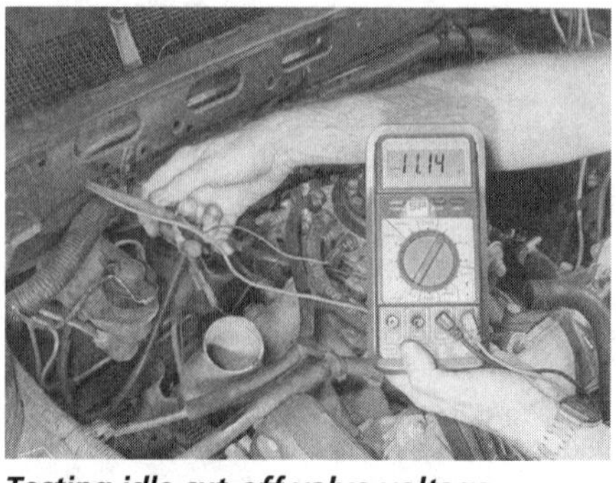

Separate cut-off ECU

6 Peel back the rubber cover from the cut-off ECU multi-plug and use the positive probe of a voltmeter (negative probe connected to earth) to probe for the following voltages at the terminals (multi-plug connected and ignition on) *(see illustration)*:
 a) Terminal 7 : Battery voltage. If the voltage is low or zero, check the wire back to the coil positive (+) terminal.
 b) Terminal 2 : Battery voltage. If the voltage is low or zero, check the wire back to the coil negative (-) terminal.
 c) Terminal 3 : 0.2 volts maximum. If the voltage is higher, check the earth connection and/or renew the earth wire.

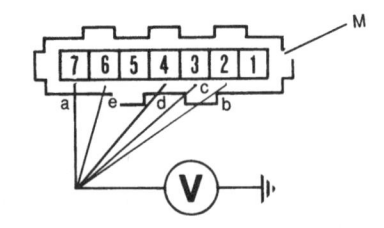

Check voltage at idle cut-off valve

2 Idle cut-off valve   BR White/Red
V Voltmeter

Testing idle cut-off valve voltage

Check voltages at idle cut-off ECU multi-plug - separate idle cut-off ECU

a Check voltage at terminal 7
b Check voltage at terminal 2
c Check voltage at terminal 3
d Check voltage at terminal 4
e Check voltage at terminal 6
M Multi-plug connection
V Voltmeter

Weber 32/34 TLDE carburettor

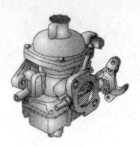

d) Terminal 4 : 0.2 volts maximum. Open the throttle and the voltage should become battery voltage. If the voltage indicated is not as specified, check the earth to the throttle switch.

e) Terminal 6 : Battery voltage. If the voltage is low or zero and the voltages at the other terminals are correct, renew the cut-off ECU.

7 If all connections are satisfactory, yet the idle cut-off operation is incorrect, suspect the ECU. Test it by substitution but only after all the connections have been thoroughly checked.

8 It is possible to bypass the idle cut-off system by bridging pin numbers 6 and 7 at the control unit. All the wires can still remain connected to the control unit. Engine and fuel system operation will not be impaired by this procedure, although fuel consumption may be (slightly) adversely affected.

Digiplex ECU

9 The Digiplex ECU is located behind the nearside headlamp. Remove the fixing screws and pull the unit from its location so that the multi-plug is more accessible *(see illustration)*.

10 Peel back the rubber cover from the Digiplex multi-plug and use the positive probe of a voltmeter (negative probe connected to earth) to probe for the following voltages at the terminals (multi-plug connected and ignition on) *(see illustration)*:

a) Terminal 5 : Battery voltage. If the voltage is low or zero, check the wire back to the coil positive (+) terminal.

b) Terminal 11 : Battery voltage. If the voltage is low or zero, check the wire back to the coil negative (-) terminal.

c) Terminal 10 : 0.2 volts maximum. If the voltage is higher, check the earth connection and/or renew the earth wire.

d) Terminal 4 : 0.2 volts maximum. Open the throttle and 3.0 volts or more should be indicated. If the voltage indicated is not as specified, check the earth to the throttle switch *(see illustration)*.

e) Terminal 6 : Battery voltage. If the voltage is low or zero and the voltages at the other terminals are correct, then the Digiplex ECU is suspect.

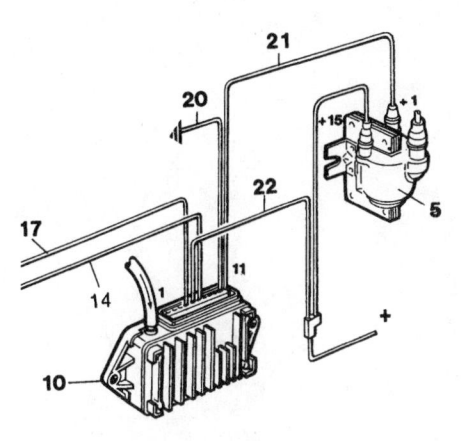

Digiplex wiring chart
5   Ignition coil
10 1600 cc engine : Digiplex ECU
14 Idle cut-off valve wire
17 Throttle switch wire
20 Earth wire
21 Rpm sensor wire
22 Voltage supply wire

11 If all connections are satisfactory yet the idle cut-off operation is incorrect, suspect the Digiplex ECU. Test the ECU by substitution but only after all the connections have been thoroughly checked.

Temperature-controlled accelerator pump

12 Disconnect the vacuum hose and attach a vacuum pump to the temperature-controlled accelerator pump. Operate the vacuum pump to obtain 300 mm Hg *(see illustration)*.

13 Release the vacuum and the injector should operate fully, injecting a small stream of fuel into the venturi. If not, check the diaphragm for damage, the pump injector for a blockage and the pump inlet and outlet balls for seizure.

Thermal switch

14 Begin with the engine cold. Remove the vacuum hose from the thermal switch outlet pipe and connect a vacuum gauge to the outlet connector.

15 At a coolant temperature below 25°C, full manifold vacuum should be obtained *(see illustration)*.

16 Run the engine and allow it to warm up.

17 As the coolant temperature rises above 25°C, the gauge vacuum reading should fall.

18 At a coolant temperature above 45°C, zero vacuum should be registered. Because vacuum will be trapped in the hose between the gauge and thermal switch, regularly remove and reconnect the gauge during the warm-up test.

19 Renew the thermal switch if its operation is unsatisfactory.

20 Refit the vacuum hose.

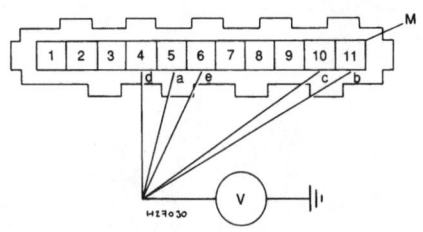

Check voltages at Digiplex ECU multi-plug
a Check voltage at terminal 5
b Check voltage at terminal 11
c Check voltage at terminal 10
d Check voltage at terminal 4
e Check voltage at terminal 6
M Multi-plug connection
V Voltmeter

6 Fault diagnosis

Refer to Part D for diagnosis of general carburettor faults.

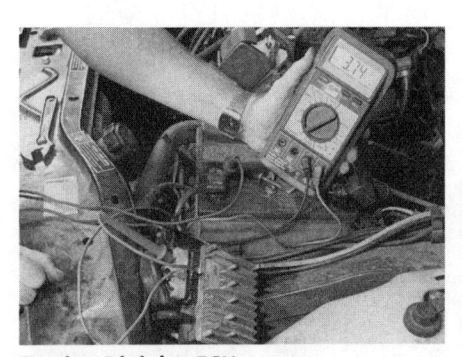

Testing Digiplex ECU
Terminal 4 : Throttle closed - 0.2 volts maximum
Terminal 4 : Throttle open - 3.74 volts (typical)

Using vacuum pump to test temperature-controlled accelerator pump

Manifold vacuum at thermal switch outlet pipe with coolant temperature below 25°C

Notes

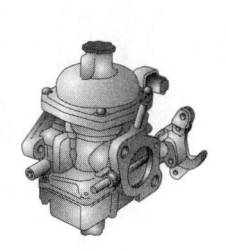

Part H Chapter 18
Weber 32/34 TLDR carburettor

Contents

Fault diagnosis 5
General servicing 3
Identification 2
Principles of operation 1
Service adjustments 4

Specifications

Manufacturer	Renault	Renault
Model	19 & Chamade 1.4 (B,C,L537)	19 & Chamade 1.4 (B,C,L537)
Year	1989 to 1991	1989 to 1991
Engine code	E6JA700	E6J7010
Capacity (cm³)/no. of cyls	1390/4	1390/4
Oil temperature (°C)	80	80
Transmission	MT	AT
Carb. identification	32 TLDR 0	32 TLDR 1
Idle speed (rpm)	750 ± 50	700 ± 50
CO @ idle (% vol.)	1.5 ± 0.5	1.5 ± 0.5

Stage (venturi)	1	2	1	2
Venturi diameter	23	24	23	24
Idle jet	50	40	52	40
Main jet	122	160	120	157
Air correction jet	175	210	175	210
Emulsion tube	F3	F56	F3	F120
Accel. pump jet	55		50	
Float level (mm)	31		31	
Needle valve size (mm)	1.75		1.75	
Choke fast idle gap (mm)	0.65		0.8	
Choke pull-down (mm)	3 ± 0.5		3 ± 0.5	
De-choke (mm)	4.5 ± 0.5		7.5 ± 0.5	

Chapter H18

1 Principles of operation

Introduction

1 The following technical description of the Weber TLDR carburettor should be read in conjunction with the more detailed description of carburettor principles in Part A.

Construction

2 The Weber TLDR carburettor is a downdraught, progressive twin venturi instrument with a vacuum controlled secondary throttle *(see illustration)*. The choke system is manually-controlled and operates on the primary venturi only.

3 The carburettor is constructed in three main bodies. These are the upper body, main body and throttle body containing the throttle assemblies. An insulating block, placed between the main carburettor body and the throttle body, prevents excess heat transference to the main body. The throttle and choke shafts and the choke flap are made of steel. The throttle valves are made of brass, as are all the emulsion tubes and jets, with the exception of the accelerator pump discharge injector which is die-cast. The internal fuel channels and air passages are drilled and sealed with lead plugs where necessary.

Fuel control

4 Fuel flows into the carburettor through a fine mesh filter. The fuel level in the float chamber is controlled by a needle valve and plastic float assembly. An anti-vibration ball is incorporated into the needle valve design. A clip, attached to the needle valve and to the float arm, prevents the needle from sticking in the seat as the fuel level drops. The float chamber is vented internally to the clean-air side of the air filter.

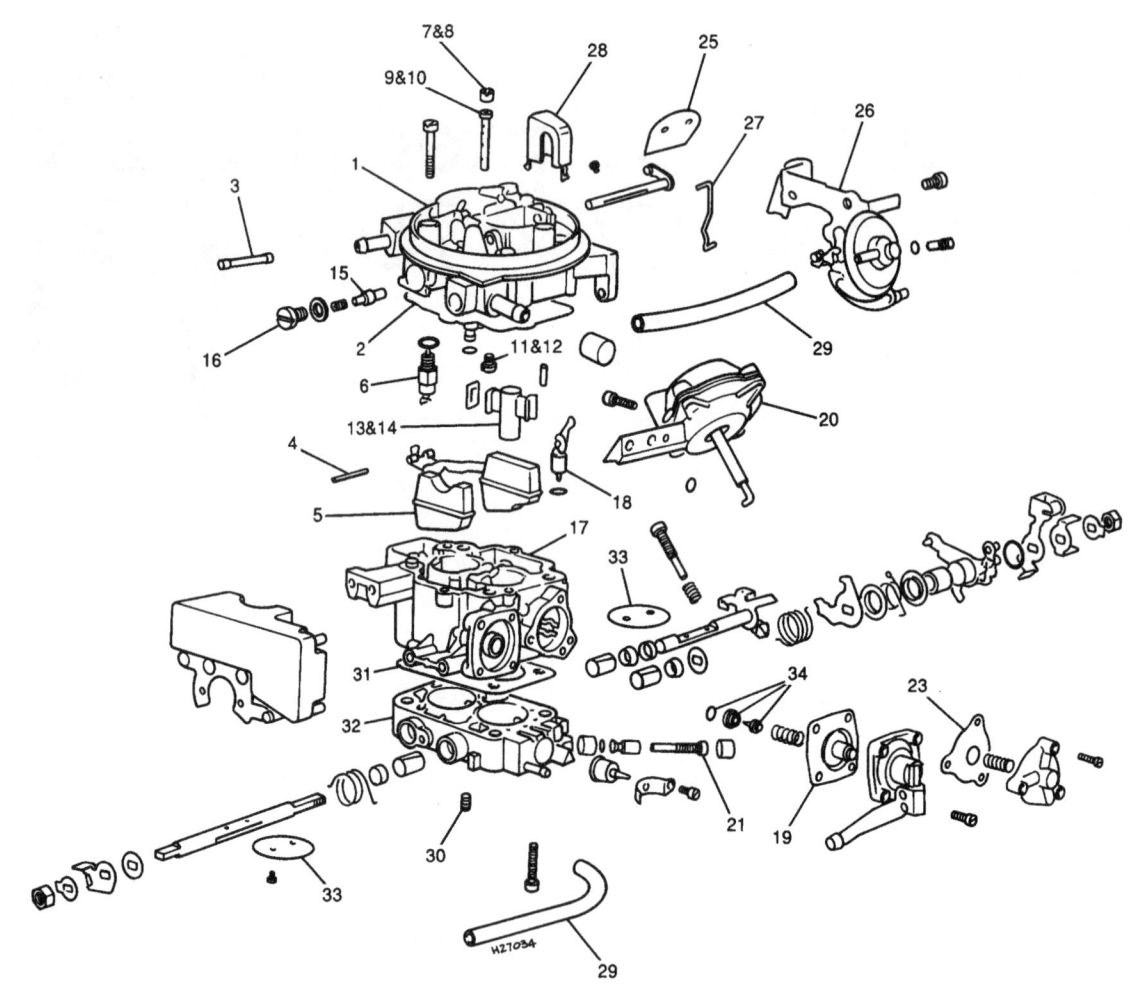

Weber TLDR carburettor

1 Upper body
2 Float chamber gasket
3 Fuel inlet filter
4 Float pin
5 Float
6 Needle valve assembly
7 Air corrector (primary)
8 Air corrector (secondary)
9 Emulsion tube (primary)
10 Emulsion tube (secondary)
11 Main jet (primary)
12 Main jet (secondary)
13 Auxiliary venturi (primary)
14 Auxiliary venturi (secondary)
15 Idle jet
16 Idle jet holder
17 Main body
18 Pump injector
19 Accelerator pump diaphragm
20 Secondary throttle diaphragm assembly
21 Idle mixture control screw
23 Power valve diaphragm
25 Choke flap
26 Choke diaphragm
27 Choke link rod
28 Choke mechanism shield
29 Vacuum hose
30 Secondary throttle valve adjustment screw
31 Insulator block
32 Throttle body
33 Throttle valve
34 Vernay valve

Weber 32/34 TLDR carburettor

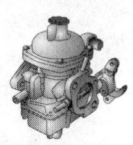

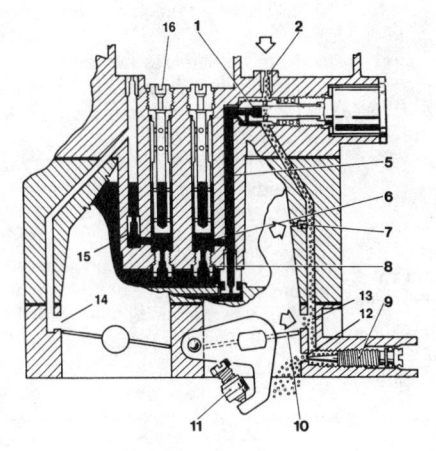

Idle and progression circuits

1. Idle jet
2. Air bleed
5. Idle fuel channel
6. Main well
7. Anti-syphon hole
8. Main jet
9. Idle mixture control screw
10. Throttle valve
11. Idle speed screw
12. Idle outlet
13. Primary progression outlet
14. Secondary progression outlet
15. Secondary idle jet
16. Air bleed

Accelerator pump circuit

1. Float chamber
2. Fuel outlet channel
3. Pump injector
4. Pump actuating lever
5. Pump cam
6. Diaphragm
7. Spring
8. Inlet ball
9. Back bleed

Idle, slow running and progression

5 Fuel, sourced from the main well, passes into the upper body through a metered idle jet. Here it is mixed with a small amount of air from a calibrated air bleed. The emulsion formed is drawn through a channel to the throttle body where it is discharged from the idle orifice under the primary throttle plate. A tapered mixture screw is used to vary the outlet and this ensures fine control of the idle mixture. A progression slot, partially covered by the closed throttle at idle, provides enrichment as it is uncovered by the opening throttle during initial acceleration. An anti-syphon hole connects the idle fuel channel with the primary venturi *(see illustration)*.

6 The idle speed is set by an adjustable screw. The adjustable mixture screw is tamper proofed during production, in accordance with emission regulations.

Accelerator pump

7 The accelerator pump is controlled by a diaphragm and is mechanically operated by a lever and cam attached to the primary throttle linkage. The outlet valve is incorporated into the pump injector. The inlet valve consists of a vernay valve located in a channel from the float chamber. Excess fuel is returned to the float chamber through a calibrated bush *(see illustration)*.

Main circuit

8 The amount of fuel discharged into the air stream is controlled by a calibrated main jet. Fuel is drawn through the main jet into the base of a vertical well which dips down into the fuel in the float chamber. An emulsion tube is placed in the well. The fuel is mixed with air drawn in through the air corrector and through the holes in the emulsion tube. The resulting emulsified mixture is discharged from the main nozzle through an auxiliary venturi *(see illustration)*.

Power enrichment and economy circuit

9 Fuel flows from the float chamber into the power valve chamber through a fuel channel. An air passage is taken from under the throttle plate to the cover of the power diaphragm chamber. At idle and during light-throttle operation, manifold vacuum draws the diaphragm back against spring pressure. The diaphragm pintle is withdrawn from the brass outlet valve and the spring-loaded ball seats to close off the outlet channel.

10 Under acceleration and wide-open throttle operation, the vacuum in the manifold is depleted. The diaphragm returns under spring pressure and the power diaphragm pintle pushes the ball to open the outlet valve. Fuel then flows through the valve and a calibrated jet to supplement the fuel in the primary main well. The fuel level rises in the well and the fuel mixture is enriched.

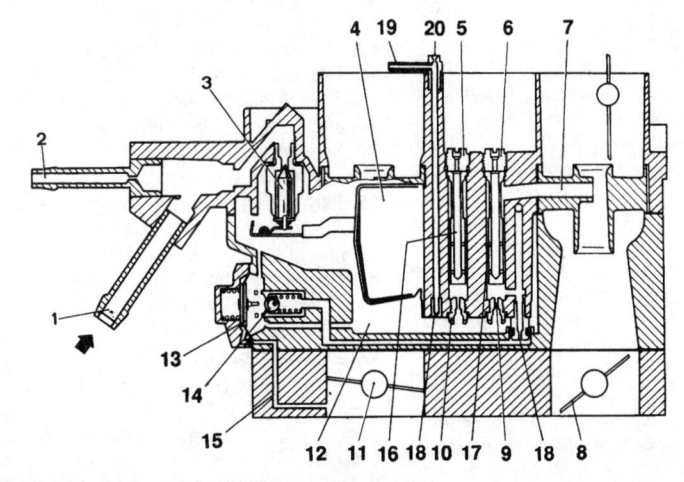

Main, power and full-load circuits

1. Fuel inlet
2. Fuel return
3. Needle valve
4. Float
5. Air corrector (secondary)
6. Air corrector (primary)
7. Auxiliary venturi
8. Throttle valve (primary)
9. Main jet (primary)
10. Main jet (secondary)
11. Throttle valve (secondary)
12. Float chamber
13. Diaphragm
14. Power valve ball
15. Vacuum passage
16. Emulsion tube (secondary)
17. Emulsion tube (primary)
18. Calibrated bush
19. Full-load outlet
20. Air bleed

H18•3

Chapter H18

Secondary action

11 A port is located in both primary and secondary venturis. Airways run from these ports into a common passage leading to the diaphragm that operates the secondary throttle plate.

12 During normal operation at low speeds, the engine uses only the primary venturi. When the air velocity through the primary venturi reaches a certain level, depression acts upon the port to operate the secondary diaphragm and the secondary throttle. Vacuum created in the secondary venturi will further control the rate of secondary opening.

13 The primary linkage is arranged to prevent the secondary plate from opening when air speed may be high but the engine is cruising on a light throttle. Secondary action will not take place until the primary throttle is about two-thirds-open.

14 A progression jet is used to prevent hesitation as the secondary throttle plate begins to open. This jet is similar in construction and action to the primary idle jet and is often referred to as the secondary idle jet. An emulsified mixture is discharged into the secondary venturi, via a progression slot, at the initial opening of the secondary throttle plate.

15 Once the secondary throttle plate has opened, the action of the secondary main circuit is similar to that of the primary circuit.

16 At full-load and high engine speeds, even more fuel is required. The velocity of air creates a depression sufficient to raise fuel from the float chamber into a channel. The fuel then passes through a calibrated bushing to the upper section of the secondary air intake. Here it is mixed with a small amount of air from a calibrated air bleed and the emulsified mixture is then discharged into the airstream from the full-load enrichment orifice.

Choke operation

17 The manual choke is operated by a dash-mounted cable. When the cable is pulled, it operates a lever that pulls the choke flap closed across the air intake. Fast idle is achieved with the aid of a curved cam attached to the choke operating lever. An adjustable screw, attached to the throttle lever and butting against the cam, is used to vary the fast idle speed.

18 Once the engine has fired, the choke flap must open slightly to weaken the mixture and avoid flooding during idle and light-throttle operation. This is achieved by using manifold vacuum to actuate a diaphragm. A linkage attached to the diaphragm will then pull upon the choke flap.

19 During engine warm-up, the cable should be progressively pushed home until the choke flap is fully open.

2 Identification

The Weber identification code is stamped on the float chamber body.

3 General servicing

Introduction

1 Read this Chapter in conjunction with Part B, which describes some of the operations in more detail. It is assumed that the carburettor is removed for this service. However, many of the operations can be tackled with the carburettor in place. Where this is undertaken, first soak the fuel out of the float chamber using a clean tissue or soft cloth, after removing the upper body assembly.

Dismantling and checking

2 Remove the four screws which secure the carburettor to the engine.

3 Remove the carburettor from the engine (see Part B).

4 Check visually for damage and wear.

5 Remove the two screws, hold the throttle open and detach the carburettor upper body.

6 Use a straight-edge to check for distorted flanges on all facing surfaces.

7 Inspect the float chamber for corrosion and calcium build-up.

8 Tap out the float pin and remove the float, needle valve and plastic clip, float chamber gasket and needle valve seat.

9 Check that the anti-vibration ball is free in the valve end.

10 Check the needle valve tip for wear and ridges. This is more likely with the brass needle valve tip than when a viton one is used. Use a viton-tipped replacement when possible.

11 The float should be checked for damage and ingress of petrol. Shaking the float will indicate the presence of fuel.

12 Renew the float pin if it appears worn.

13 Unscrew the fuel inlet tube and inspect the fuel filter. Clean the filter housing of debris and dirt and renew the filter if necessary.

14 Remove the mixture screw and inspect the tip for damage and ridges.

15 Remove the four screws and detach the accelerator pump cover, diaphragm and spring (complete with vernay valve). Check the diaphragm for fatigue and damage.

16 The pump injector is a push fit in the body. Carefully prise it from its location and check the valve for damage or leakage.

17 Remove the primary idle jet assembly from the outside of the main body. Note that the primary idle jet assembly can be removed from the carburettor without removing the upper body. The secondary idle jet is not removable.

18 Unscrew the primary and secondary main jets from the underside of the upper body. Unscrew the primary and secondary air correctors and remove the emulsion tubes from the top of the upper body. Note that the air correctors and emulsion tubes can be removed from the carburettor body without removing the upper body.

19 Check that the emulsion tube wells are clear.

20 Note the jet sizes and locations for correct installation during assembly. For reference, the primary main jet is located on the idle cut-off side of the carburettor.

21 Check the jet calibration against that specified. It is possible that the jets may have been transposed (or the wrong size fitted) during the last overhaul.

22 Remove the primary and secondary auxiliary venturis from the upper body where necessary. A Weber extractor tool is available for this purpose. Check that the primary and secondary auxiliary venturis are not loose in the main body as this is a source of uneven running. If a venturi is loose, knurl the mating flanges with a file to ensure a tight fit.

23 Remove the three screws and detach the power valve housing cover, spring and diaphragm from the body. Check the diaphragm for damage. The brass outlet valve is cast into the body and is not removable. The ball in the outlet valve should seal the outlet. Depress and release the ball with a small screwdriver and it should move smoothly in and out. Check that the channel into the emulsion tube well is clear.

24 Disconnect the secondary throttle operating rod. Pull the lower section of the rod downwards and twist it out of its socket. Remove the four screws and detach the secondary cover, spring and diaphragm from the housing. Check the diaphragm for fatigue and renew as necessary.

25 Remove the two screws and separate the carburettor main body and throttle body assemblies. The throttle body can be renewed separately if the spindles or throttle bores are worn.

26 Inspect the choke spindle and linkage for stickiness and wear. Pull away the plastic shield that covers the choke mechanism.

27 Attach a vacuum pump to the connector and operate the pump to obtain 300 mm Hg. Renew the diaphragm if it does not fully operate, or if vacuum is not maintained for a minimum of 10 seconds.

28 Remove the three screws, pull the lower choke link rod out of the plastic retaining collar and detach the choke pull-down assembly.

Preparation for reassembly

29 Clean the jets, carburettor body assemblies, float chamber and internal channels. An air line may be used to clear internal channels once the carburettor is fully dismantled. Note that if high-pressure air is directed into the channels and passages with the diaphragms or accelerator pump vernay valves still in place, damage may result.

30 Spraying carburettor cleaner into all the channels and passages in the carburettor body will often clear them of gum and dirt.

31 During reassembly, a complete set of new gaskets should be fitted. Also renew the needle valve and float pin, and all diaphragms.

32 Inspect and renew (where necessary) the

Weber 32/34 TLDR carburettor

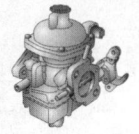

mixture screw, main jets, idle jet, air corrector jets, emulsion tubes and accelerator pump injector. Renew worn linkages, screws, springs and other parts where necessary.

33 Ensure that all jets are firmly locked into their original positions (but do not over-tighten). A loose jet can cause a rich (or even lean) running condition.

34 Clean all mating surfaces and flanges of old gasket material and reassemble with new gaskets.

35 Ensure that housings are positioned with their air and fuel routes correctly aligned.

Reassembly

36 Refit the choke pull-down assembly and secure with the three screws. Push the end of the lower choke link rod through the plastic collar and clip it into position.

37 Assemble the main and throttle bodies with a new gasket block and secure with the two screws.

38 Check that the secondary throttle plate is fully closed. The adjustment screw should not normally be used to alter the throttle plate position. However, if necessary, it can be adjusted so that the plate is open just enough to prevent its seizure in the throttle body.

39 Refit the secondary throttle diaphragm, spring and cover assembly, then secure with the four screws. Reconnect the secondary throttle operating rod.

40 Renew the seal on the power valve jet (which is adjacent to the primary main jet). Refit the power diaphragm, spring and cover assembly, then secure with the three screws.

41 Refit the emulsion tubes, air correctors and main jets into their original positions (do not transpose the jets).

42 Push the idle jet into its holder, then refit the idle jet assembly using a new sealing washer.

43 Push the pump injector firmly into position, after renewing the small seal on the injector body.

44 Refit the pump spring, diaphragm and cover assembly, then secure with the four screws. The valve on the end of the spring must face inwards and care must be taken that it is not damaged.

45 Refit the idle mixture screw after renewing the seal. Turn the screw in gently until it just seats. From this position, unscrew it three full turns. This will provide a basic setting to allow the engine to be started.

46 Clean or renew the fuel filter and refit the fuel inlet tube.

47 Refit the float gasket to the upper body.

48 Renew the needle valve assembly. Screw the valve seat into the upper body, using a new sealing washer, and ensure that it is firmly locked into position (but do not over-tighten). Transfer the hairpin or plastic clip from the old needle valve to the ball end of the new one. Place the clip and valve assembly onto the inner float tag. Lower the float and needle valve assembly into the seat and secure with the float pin.

49 Adjust the float level. Refer to Section 4 for details on adjustment.

50 Refit the upper body to the main body and secure with the two screws.

51 Ensure that the choke flap and linkage move smoothly and progressively.

52 Adjust the choke fast idle and vacuum pull-down. Refer to Section 4 for details on adjustment. Refit the plastic choke mechanism shield.

53 Refit the carburettor to the engine.

54 Always adjust the carburettor idle speed and mixture after any work has been carried out on the carburettor, preferably with the aid of a CO meter.

4 Service adjustments

Adjustment preconditions

1 Refer to Part B for general advice on the preconditions to correct adjustment of this carburettor.

Idle speed and mixture (CO)

2 Run the engine at 3000 rpm for 30 seconds to clear the manifold of fuel vapours, then allow the engine to idle.

3 Use the idle speed adjustment screw to set the specified idle speed *(see illustration)*.

4 Check the CO level. If it is not as specified, remove the tamperproof plug and adjust the idle mixture control screw to achieve the correct level. Turning the screw clockwise (inwards) will reduce the CO level. Turning the screw anti-clockwise (outwards) will increase the CO level.

5 Repeat paragraphs 3 and 4 until both adjustments are correct.

6 Clear the manifold every 30 seconds during the setting operation by running the engine at 3000 rpm for 30 seconds.

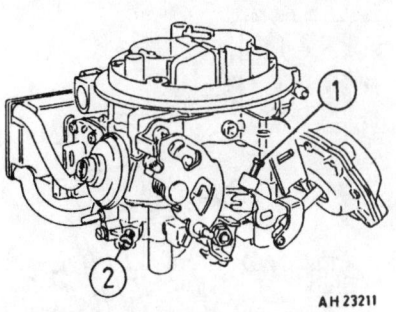

Idle speed and mixture adjustment
1 Idle speed screw
2 Idle mixture control screw

7 Increase the speed to 2000 rpm and note the CO reading. The cruise reading should be less than half the idle CO reading.

8 Fit a new tamperproof plug to the mixture control screw.

Float level

9 Hold the carburettor upper body in a vertical position with the float tag gently touching the ball of the fully-closed needle valve.

10 Measure the distance between the upper body (with the gasket in place) and the top of the float *(see illustration)*.

11 Adjust as necessary by bending the float tag.

Manual choke

Fast idle

12 The carburettor must be removed from the engine in order to make the fast idle adjustment.

13 Invert the carburettor then pull the choke operating arm to fully close the choke flap. The adjustment screw will butt against the fast idle cam and force open the throttle plate to leave a small clearance *(see illustration)*.

14 Use the shank of a twist drill to measure the

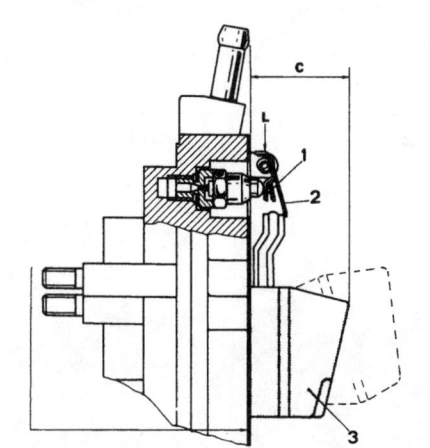

Float level measurement
1 Inner float tag   c Float level
2 Float arm   L Outer float tag
3 Float

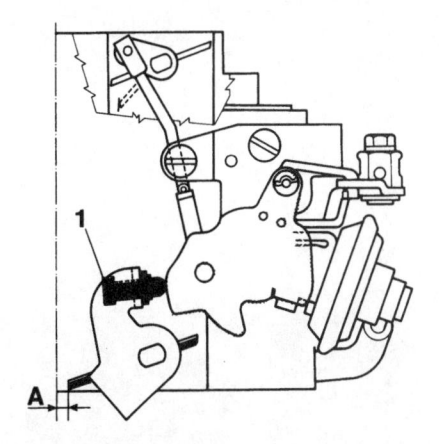

Fast idle adjustment
1 Fast idle adjustment screw
A Fast idle clearance

Chapter H18

clearance between the wall of the throttle bore and the throttle plate. Refer to Specifications for the required drill size and measure the clearance from the progression holes.

15 Adjust as necessary by turning the adjustment screw in the appropriate direction.

Vacuum pull-down

16 Pull the choke operating arm to fully close the choke flap.

17 Use a vacuum pump (or finger) to pull the diaphragm operating rod up to its stop. At the same time, use the shank of a twist drill to measure the gap between the lower section of the choke flap and the air intake. Refer to Specifications for the required drill size *(see illustration)*.

18 Remove the plug in the diaphragm cover and adjust as necessary by turning the diaphragm adjustment screw in the appropriate direction. Renew the plug when adjustment is complete.

5 Fault diagnosis

Refer to Part D for diagnosis of general carburettor faults.

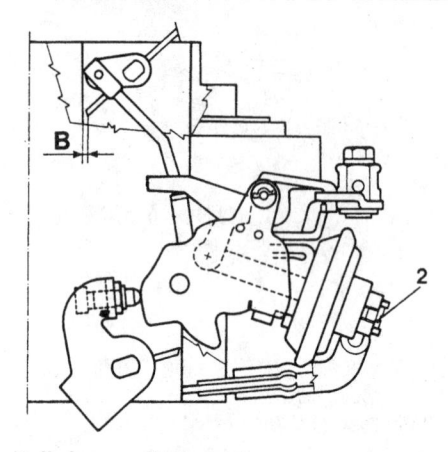

Pull-down adjustment
2 *Pull-down adjustment screw*
B *Pull-down clearance*

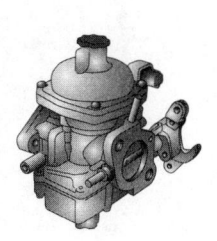

Part H Chapter 19
Weber 26/28, 28/30, 28/32 TLDM carburettor

H19

Contents

Component testing 5	Identification 2
Fault diagnosis 6	Principles of operation 1
General servicing 3	Service adjustments 4

Specifications

Manufacturer	Ford		Ford		Ford		
Model	Fiesta 1.1 & Van		Fiesta 1.1 & Van		Escort 1.1		
Year	1989 to 1991		1989 to 1991		1989 to 1990		
Engine code	GUE (HCS) 40kW 15/04		GUD (HCS) 40kW 15/05		GUC (HCS) 15/04		
Capacity (cm³)/no. of cyls	1118/4		1118/4		1118/4		
Oil temperature (°C)	80		80		80		
Transmission	Manual		Manual		Manual		
Carb. ident. (Ford)	89BF 9510 BA		89BF 9510 EA		89BF 9510 BA		
Carb. ident. (Weber/Solex)	26/28 TLDM 15A		26/28 TLDM 3B		26/28 TLDM 15A		
Idle speed (rpm)	750 ± 50		750 ± 50		750 ± 50		
Fast idle speed (rpm)	2800		2800		2800		
CO @ idle (% vol.)	1.0 ± 0.5		1.0 ± 0.25		1.0 ± 0.5		
Special conditions	Fan on		Fan on		Fan on		
Stage (venturi)	1	2	1	2	1	2	
Venturi diameter	19	20	19	20	19	20	
Idle jet	-	-	42	60	-	-	
Main jet	92	122	92	122	92	122	
Air correction jet	195	155	195	155	195	155	
Emulsion tube	F113	F75	F113	F75	F113	F75	
Accel. pump jet	-		40		-		
Float level (mm)	29 ± 1.0		29 ± 0.25		29 ± 1.0		
Needle valve size (mm)	-		1.5		-		
Throttle kicker	1550 ± 50 rpm		-		1550 ± 50 rpm		
Choke gauging (mm)	-		-		-		
Choke pull-down (mm)	1.75 ± 0.5		1.75 ± 0.25		1.75 ± 0.5		

Chapter H19

Manufacturer	Ford	Ford	Ford
Model	Escort 1.1	Escort & Orion 1.3	Escort & Orion 1.3
Year	1990 to 1991	1988 to 1990	1990 to 1991
Engine code	GUF (HCS) 40kW 15/05	JBA (HCS)	JBD 46Kw 15/04
Capacity (cm^3)/no. of cyls	1118/4	1297/4	1297/4
Oil temperature (°C)	80	80	80
Transmission	Manual	Manual	Manual
Carb. ident. (Ford)	89BF 9510 EA	89BF 9510 DA	89BF 9510 DA
Carb. ident. (Weber/Solex)	26/28 TLDM 3B	26/28 TLDM 16A	26/28 TLDM 16A
Idle speed (rpm)	750 ± 50	750 ± 50	750 ± 50
Fast idle speed (rpm)	2800	2500	2500
CO @ idle (% vol.)	1.0 ± 0.5	1.0 ± 0.5	1.0 ± 0.5
Special conditions	Fan on	Fan on	Fan on
Stage (venturi)	1 2	1 2	1 2
Venturi diameter	19 20	19 20	19 20
Idle jet	- -	42 60	- -
Main jet	92 122	90 122	90 122
Air correction jet	195 155	185 130	185 130
Emulsion tube	F113 F75	F113 F75	F113 F75
Accel. pump jet	40	-	-
Float level (mm)	29 ± 0.25	29 ± 1.0	29 ± 1.0
Needle valve size (mm)	1.5	-	-
Throttle kicker	-	1550 ± 50 rpm	1550 ± 50 rpm
Choke pull-down (mm)	1.75 ± 0.25	1.75 ± 0.5	1.75 ± 0.5

Manufacturer	Ford	Ford	Ford
Model	Escort & Orion 1.3 Cat.	Fiesta 1.4	Escort & Orion 1.4
Year	1990 to 1991	1989 to 1991	1990 to 1991
Engine code	JBE 44kW 15/05	FUG 54kW 15/05	FUH 54kW 15/05
Capacity (cm^3)/no. of cyls	1297/4	1392/4	1392/4
Oil temperature (°C)	80	80	80
Transmission	Manual	Manual	Manual
Carb. ident. (Ford)	91BF 9510 AB	91SF 9510 BA/BB	91SF 9510 BA/BB
Carb. ident. (Weber/Solex)	26/28 TLDM 20A1	28/30 TLDM 23A	28/30 TLDM 23A
Idle speed (rpm)	750 ± 50	800 ± 50	800 ± 50
Fast idle speed (rpm)	2500	3300	1900 ± 50
CO @ idle (% vol.)	1.0 ± 0.25	1.0 ± 0.25	1.0 ± 0.25
Special conditions	Fan on	Fan on	-
Stage (venturi)	1 2	1 2	1 2
Venturi diameter	19 20	20 22	20 22
Idle jet	47 60	47 60	47 60
Main jet	90 122	107 140	107 140
Air correction jet	185 130	195 170	195 170
Emulsion tube	F113 F75	F105 F75	F105 F75
Accel. pump jet	35	40	40
Float level (mm)	29 ± 0.25	31 ± 0.25	31 ± 0.25
Needle valve size (mm)	1.5	1.5	-
Throttle kicker	-	1400 rpm	-
Choke pull-down (mm)	1.75 ± 0.25	2.8 ± 0.25	3.1 ± 0.5

Manufacturer	Ford	Ford	Ford
Model	Fiesta XR2	Fiesta XR2	Fiesta 1.6S
Year	1986 to 1989	1986 to 1989	1989 to 1991
Engine code	LUB (CVH)	LUB (CVH)	LUH (CVH) 15/04
Capacity (cm^3)/no. of cyls	1597/4	1597/4	1597/4
Oil temperature (°C)	80	80	80
Transmission	Manual	Manual	Manual
Carb. ident. (Ford)	86SF 9510 AA	87SF 9510 AA/AB	89SF 9510 AA
Carb. ident. (Weber/Solex)	28/32 TLDM OA	28/32 TLDM 10A/10A1	-
Idle speed (rpm)	800 ± 50	800 ± 50	800 ± 50
Fast idle speed (rpm)	1900 ± 50	1800 ± 50	1800 ± 50
CO @ idle (% vol.)	1.5 ± 0.25	1.5 ± 0.5	1.5 ± 0.5
Stage (venturi)	1 2	1 2	1 2
Venturi diameter	21 23	21 23	21 23
Idle jet	47 60	47 60	47 60
Main jet	117 127	117 127	117 127
Air correction jet	185 125	185 125	185 125
Emulsion tube	F105 F71	F105 F71	F105 F71
Accel. pump jet	40	40	40
Float level (mm)	29 ± 0.5	31 ± 0.5	31 ± 0.5
Needle valve size (mm)	2.0	2.0	2.0
Choke pull-down (mm)	4.5 ± 0.5	4.5 ± 0.5	4.5 ± 0.5

Weber 26/28, 28/30, 28/32 TLDM carburettor

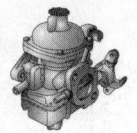

Manufacturer	Ford		Ford		Ford	
Model	Escort & Orion 1.6		Escort & Orion 1.6		Escort & Orion 1.6	
Year	1986 to 1990		1986 to 1990		1990 to 1991	
Engine code	LUC (CVH)		LUC (CVH)		LUK (CVH) 66kW 15/04	
Capacity (cm³)/no. of cyls	1596/4		1596/4		1597/4	
Oil temperature (°C)	80		80		80	
Transmission	Manual		Automatic		Manual	
Carb. ident. (Ford)	86SF 9510 AA		86SF 9510 BA		91SF 9510 CB/EB	
	89SF 9510 AA		89SF 9510 BD		-	
Carb. ident. (Weber/Solex)	28/32 TLDM OA		28/32 TLDM O1A		28/32 TLDM 26A/27A	
Idle speed (rpm)	800 ± 50		900 ± 50		800 ± 50	
Fast idle speed (rpm)	1900 ± 50		2000 ± 50		1800 ± 50	
CO @ idle (% vol.)	1.5 ± 0.25		1.5 ± 0.25		1.5 ± 0.5	
Stage (venturi)	1	2	1	2	1	2
Venturi diameter	21	23	21	23	21	23
Idle jet	47	60	47	60	47	60
Main jet	117	127	115	130	115	140
Air correction jet	185	125	185	125	180	150
Emulsion tube	F105	F71	F105	F71	F105	F57
Accel. pump jet	40		40		40	
Float level (mm)	29 ± 0.5		29 ± 0.5		31 ± 0.25	
Needle valve size (mm)	1.75		1.75		1.75	
Choke pull-down (mm)	4.5 ± 0.5		4.0 ± 0.5		4.5 ± 0.5	

Manufacturer	Ford		Ford	
Model	Escort & Orion 1.6		Escort & Orion 1.6 Cat.	
Year	1990 to 1991		1990 to 1991	
Engine code	LUK (CVH)66kW 15/04		LUJ (CVH) 65kW 15/05	
Capacity (cm³)/no. of cyls	1597/4		1597/4	
Oil temperature (°C)	80		80	
Transmission	Automatic		Manual	
Carb. ident. (Ford)	91SF 9510 GB		89SF 9510 EA	
Carb. ident. (Weber/Solex)	28/32 TLDM 28A		26/28 TLDM 22A	
Idle speed (rpm)	800 ± 50		800 ± 50	
Fast idle speed (rpm)	1800 ± 50		1800 ± 50	
CO @ idle (% vol.)	-		1.0 ± 0.25	
Stage (venturi)	1	2	1	2
Venturi diameter	-	-	21	23
Idle jet	-	-	45	60
Main jet	115	140	115	127
Air correction jet	-	-	185	125
Emulsion tube	-	-	F105	F71
Accel. pump jet	-		40	
Float level (mm)	-		29 ± 0.25	
Needle valve size (mm)	-		1.75	
Choke pull-down (mm)	-		4.5 ± 0.5	

Manufacturer	Ford		Ford		Ford	
Model	Sierra and Sapphire 2000		Sierra/Sapphire 2.0 Cat		Sierra/Sapphire 2.0 Cat	
Year	1989 to 1991		1989 to 1991		1989 to 1991	
Engine code	N8A DOHC 8V 80kW 15/04		N8A DOHC 8V 15/05		N8A DOHC 8V 15/05	
Capacity (cm³)/no. of cyls	1998/4		1998/4		1998/4	
Oil temperature (°C)	80		80		80	
Transmission	Manual/Automatic		Manual		Automatic	
Carb. ident. (Ford)	88WF 9510 AC		88WF 9510 ED		89WF 9510 AB	
Carb. ident. (Weber/Solex)	28/32 TLDM 6A		28/32 TLDM 8A3		28/32 TLDM 9A1	
	(7A Auto)					
Idle speed (rpm)	850 ± 25		850 ± 25		850 ± 25	
Fast idle speed (rpm)	1800 ± 50		1800 ± 50		1800 ± 50	
CO @ idle (% vol.)	1.0 ± 0.25		0.6 ± 0.25		0.6 ± 0.25	
Stage (venturi)	1	2	1	2	1	2
Venturi diameter	23	25	23	25	23	25
Idle jet	-	-	47	80	-	-
Main jet	115	157	112	140	112	140
Air correction jet	175	145	210	120	210	120
Emulsion tube	F114	F3	F66	F3	F66	F3
Accel. pump jet	-		40		-	
Float level (mm)	29 ± 0.5		29 ± 0.5		29 ± 0.5	
Throttle kicker	2000 ± 50 rpm		2600 ± 50 rpm		2200 ± 50 rpm	
Choke pull-down (mm)	5.0 ± 0.5		5.0 ± 0.5		5.0 ± 0.5	

Chapter H19

Manufacturer	Ford	Ford	Ford
Model	Granada 2000	Granada 2000	Granada 2000 Catalyst
Year	1989 to 1990	1989 to 1990	1989 to 1990
Engine code	N8B DOHC 8V 80kW 15/04	N8B DOHC 8V 80kW 15/04	N8B DOHC 8V 77kW 15/05
Capacity (cm³)/no. of cyls	1998/4	1998/4	1998/4
Oil temperature (°C)	80	80	80
Transmission	Manual	Automatic	Manual
Carb. ident. (Ford)	88WF 9510 AC	88WF 9510 AB	88WF 9510 ED
Carb. ident. (Weber/Solex)	28/32 TLDM 6A	28/32 TLDM 9A1	28/32 TLDM 8A3
Idle speed (rpm)	850 ± 25	875 ± 25	850 ± 25
Fast idle speed (rpm)	1800 ± 50	1800 ± 50	1800 ± 50
CO @ idle (% vol.)	1.0 ± 0.25	1.0 ± 0.25	0.6 ± 0.25
Stage (venturi)	1 2	1 2	1 2
Venturi diameter	23 25	23 25	23 25
Idle jet	- -	- -	47 80
Main jet	115 157	112 157	112 140
Air correction jet	175 145	210 145	210 120
Emulsion tube	F114 F3	F66 F3	F66 F3
Accel. pump jet	-	-	40
Float level (mm)	29 ± 0.5	29 ± 0.5	29 ± 0.5
Needle valve size (mm)	-	-	1.5
Throttle kicker	2000 ± 50 rpm	2200 ± 50 rpm	2600 ± 50 rpm
Choke pull-down (mm)	5.0 ± 0.5	5.0 ± 0.5	5.0 ± 0.5

Weber 26/28 or 28/30 TLDM carburettor

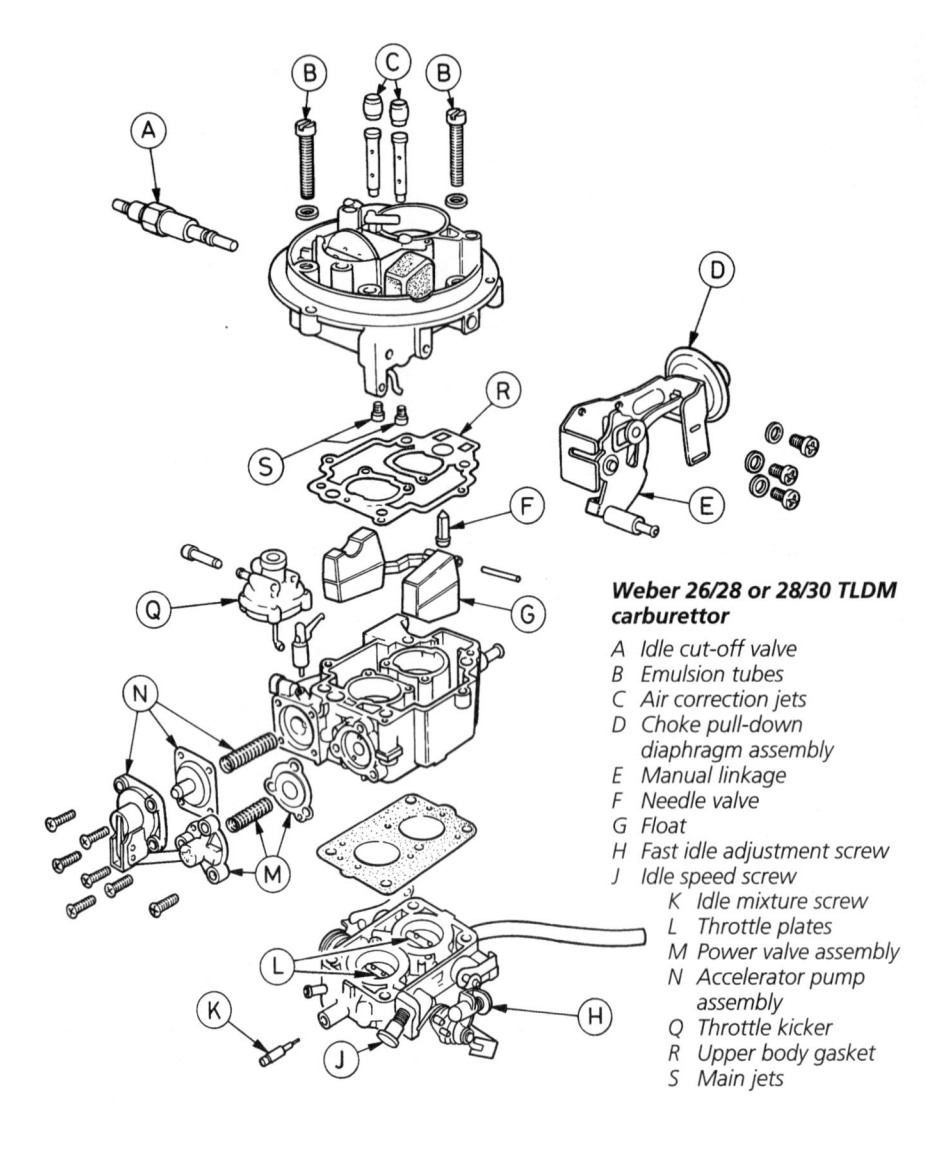

A Idle cut-off valve
B Emulsion tubes
C Air correction jets
D Choke pull-down diaphragm assembly
E Manual linkage
F Needle valve
G Float
H Fast idle adjustment screw
J Idle speed screw
K Idle mixture screw
L Throttle plates
M Power valve assembly
N Accelerator pump assembly
Q Throttle kicker
R Upper body gasket
S Main jets

1 Principles of operation

Introduction

1 The following technical description of the Weber TLDM carburettors should be read in conjunction with the more detailed description of carburettor principles in Part A.

Construction

2 The Weber TLDM carburettor series is the result of a rationalisation of the types of carburettor fitted to Ford vehicles. The requirement was for a carburettor body type that could meet fairly stringent emission regulations, yet one which would be adaptable to a wide variety of engine sizes with differing needs.

3 The Weber TLDM can appear in a number of different throttle sizes with alternative specifications. Ford refer to this carburettor either as a TLD or a TLDM.

26/28 and 28/30 TDLM

4 This variation of the Weber TLDM carburettor is a downdraught progressive twin venturi instrument with a mechanically-controlled secondary throttle. The choke system is manually controlled and operates on the primary venturi alone. An idle cut-off valve is fitted to the idle circuit and a vacuum-controlled throttle kicker is used as a throttle damper (see illustration).

28/32 TDLM (1.6 litre engine)

5 This variation of the Weber TLDM carburettor is a downdraught progressive twin venturi instrument with a vacuum-controlled secondary throttle. The choke system is semi-automatic in operation and is controlled by a bi-metal coil

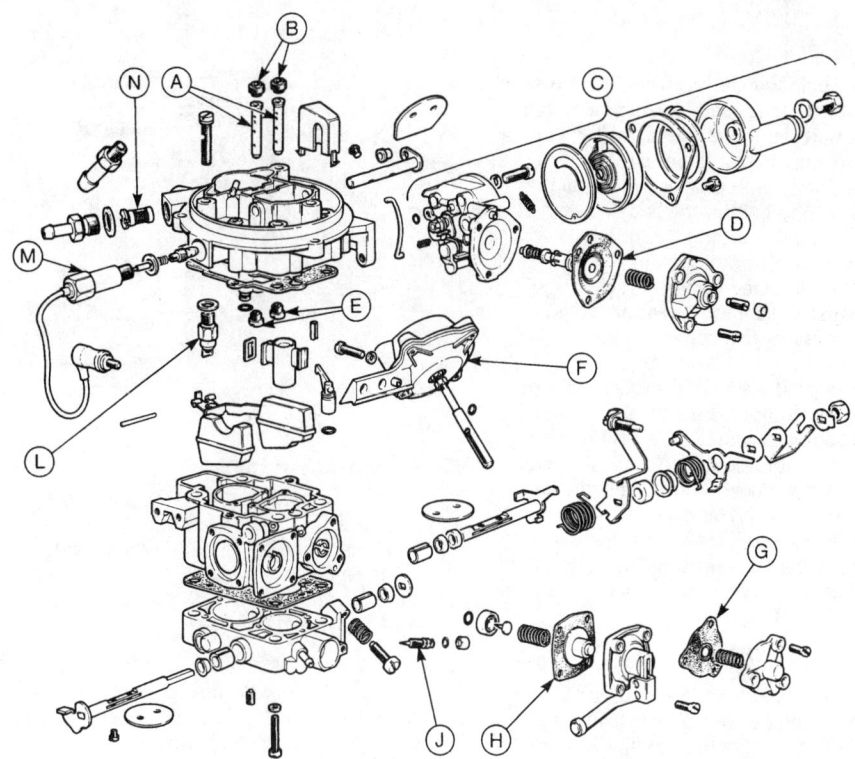

Weber 26/28, 28/30, 28/32 TLDM carburettor

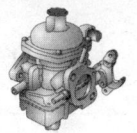

Weber 28/32 TLDM carburettor - 1.6 engine

- A Emulsion tubes
- B Air correction jets
- C Automatic choke assembly
- D Choke pull-down diaphragm assembly
- E Main jets
- F Secondary throttle diaphragm
- G Power valve diaphragm
- H Accelerator pump diaphragm
- J Idle mixture screw
- L Needle valve
- M Idle cut-off valve
- N Fuel inlet filter

heated by the engine coolant. The choke operates on the primary venturi alone. An idle cut-off valve is fitted to the idle circuit *(see illustration)*.

28/32 TDLM (2.0 litre engine)

6 This variation of the Weber TLDM carburettor is a downdraught progressive twin venturi instrument with a vacuum-controlled secondary throttle. The choke system is semi-automatic in operation and is controlled by a bi-metal coil that is electrically heated. The choke operates on the primary venturi alone. An idle cut-off valve is fitted to the idle circuit and a vacuum-controlled throttle kicker is used as a throttle damper *(see illustration)*.

All carburettors

7 The carburettor is constructed in three main bodies. These are the upper body, the main body and a throttle body containing the throttle assemblies. An insulating block, placed between the main carburettor body and the throttle body, prevents excess heat transference to the main body.

8 The throttle and choke shafts and the choke flap are made of steel. The throttle valves are made of brass, as are all emulsion tubes and jets, with the exception of the accelerator pump discharge injector which is die-cast. Internal fuel channels and air passages are drilled and sealed with lead plugs where necessary.

Fuel control

9 Fuel flows into the carburettor through a fine mesh filter. The fuel level in the float chamber is controlled by a needle valve and plastic float assembly, and an anti-vibration ball is incorporated into the needle valve design. A clip, attached to the needle valve and to the float arm, prevents the needle from sticking in the seat as the fuel level drops. The float chamber is vented internally to the clean-air side of the air filter. A calibrated fuel return system is provided on some models to ensure that relatively cool fuel is supplied to the carburettor *(see illustration)*.

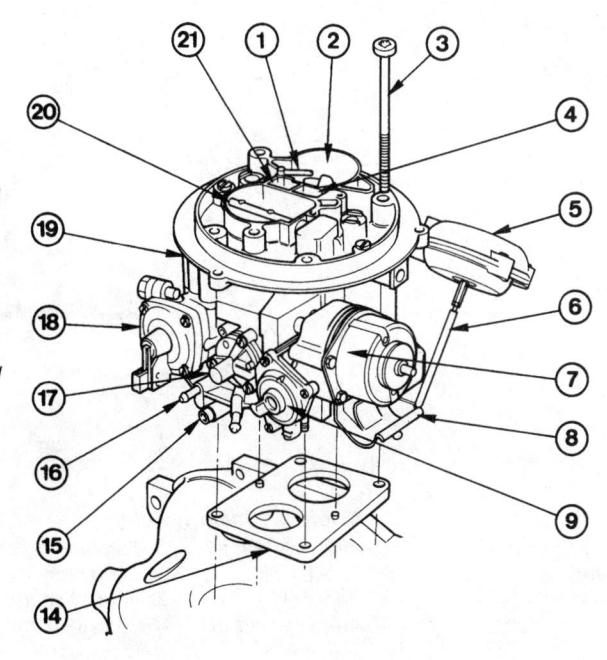

Weber 28/32 TLDM carburettor - 2.0 engine

1. Secondary high speed enrichment nozzle
2. Secondary venturi
3. Carburettor-to-manifold bolts (Torx type)
4. Secondary main metering assembly
5. Secondary throttle vacuum assembly
6. Telescopic link
7. Choke assembly
8. Water-assist base bracket
9. Choke pull-down housing
14. Carburettor-to-manifold gasket
15. Idle mixture screw
16. Vacuum port for throttle kicker
17. Power valve housing
18. Accelerator pump
19. Carburettor main body
20. Choke flap
21. Primary main metering assembly

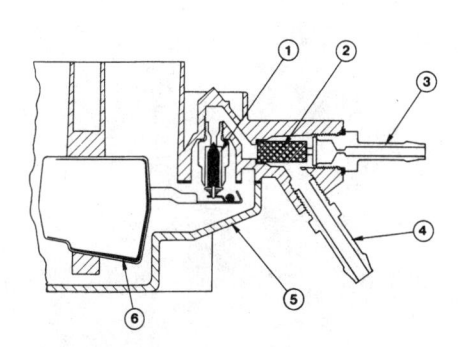

Fuel inlet system

1. Needle valve
2. Fuel filter
3. Fuel return connector with 1.1 mm restrictor
4. Fuel inlet connector
5. Carburettor main body
6. Float

Chapter H19

Idle, slow running and progression

10 Fuel, sourced from the main well, passes into the upper body through a metered idle jet. Here it is mixed with a small amount of air from a calibrated air bleed. The emulsion formed is drawn through a channel to the throttle body where it is discharged from the idle orifice under the primary throttle plate. A tapered mixture screw is used to vary the outlet and this ensures fine control of the idle mixture (see illustration).

11 A progression slot, partially covered by the closed throttle at idle, provides additional enrichment as it is uncovered by the opening throttle during initial acceleration. An anti-syphon hole connects the idle fuel channel with the primary venturi.

12 Idle speed is set by an adjustable screw. The adjustable mixture screw is tamper proofed at production level, in accordance with emission regulations.

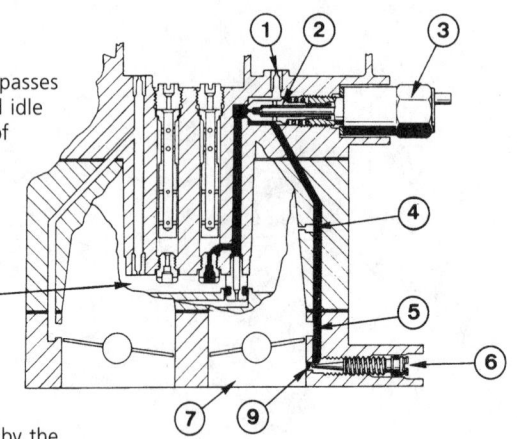

Idle cut-off valve

13 An idle cut-off valve is used to prevent run-on at engine shut down. It utilises a 12-volt solenoid plunger to block the idle jet when the ignition is switched off.

Accelerator pump

14 The accelerator pump is controlled by a diaphragm and is mechanically operated by a lever and cam attached to the primary throttle linkage. The outlet valve consists of a vernay valve incorporated into the pump injector, while the inlet valve consists of a vernay valve located in a channel from the float chamber. Excess fuel is returned to the float chamber through a calibrated bush (see illustration).

Anti-stall device -28/32 TDLM (2.0 litre engine)

15 A Low Vacuum Enrichment device (sometimes known as a LOVE device) is employed to overcome stalling due to a lean mixture. The LOVE device is basically a vacuum-controlled accelerator pump. It is diaphragm-operated, functions in a conventional manner and discharges through the same pump injector as the mechanical pump. When idling or during low-speed running, the manifold vacuum will be high. As a stall situation develops, the vacuum will deplete and the pump injector is actuated.

Main circuit

16 The amount of fuel discharged into the airstream is controlled by a calibrated main jet. Fuel is drawn through the main jet into the base of a vertical well which dips down into the fuel in the float chamber. An emulsion tube is placed in the well. The fuel is mixed with air drawn in through the air corrector and the holes in the emulsion tube. The resulting emulsified mixture is discharged from the main nozzle through an auxiliary venturi (see illustration).

Power enrichment and economy circuit

17 Fuel flows from the float chamber into the power valve chamber through a fuel channel. An air passage is taken from under the throttle plate to the cover of the power diaphragm chamber. At idle and during light-throttle operation, manifold vacuum draws the diaphragm back against spring pressure. The diaphragm pintle is withdrawn from the brass outlet valve and the spring-loaded ball seats to close off the outlet channel (see illustration).

18 Under acceleration and wide-open throttle operation, the vacuum in the manifold is depleted. The diaphragm returns under spring pressure and the power diaphragm pintle pushes the ball to open the outlet valve. Fuel then flows through the valve and a calibrated jet to supplement the fuel in the primary main well. The fuel level rises in the well and the fuel mixture is enriched.

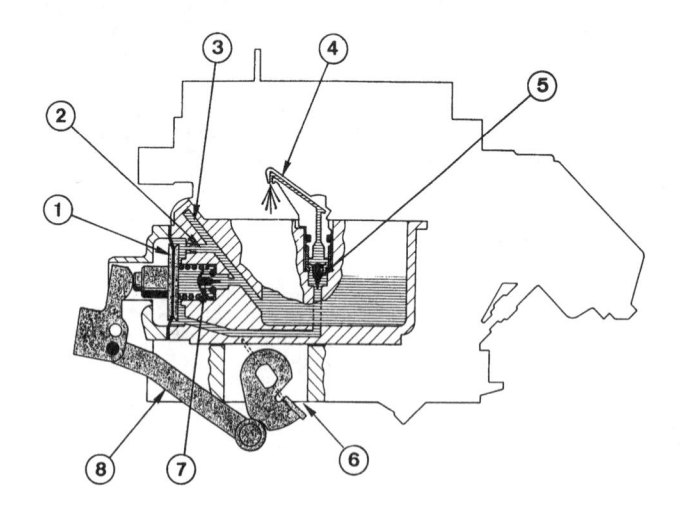

Primary idle system
1 Primary idle air bleed
2 Primary idle jet assembly
3 Idle cut-off valve
4 Anti-syphon hole
5 Progression slot
6 Idle mixture screw
7 Primary venturi
8 Main fuel well
9 Idle discharge outlet

Accelerator pump system
1 Spring-loaded diaphragm
2 Back-bleed
3 Fuel supply drilling
4 Accelerator pump injector
5 Outlet valve assembly
6 Primary venturi
7 Inlet valve assembly
8 Accelerator pump actuating lever

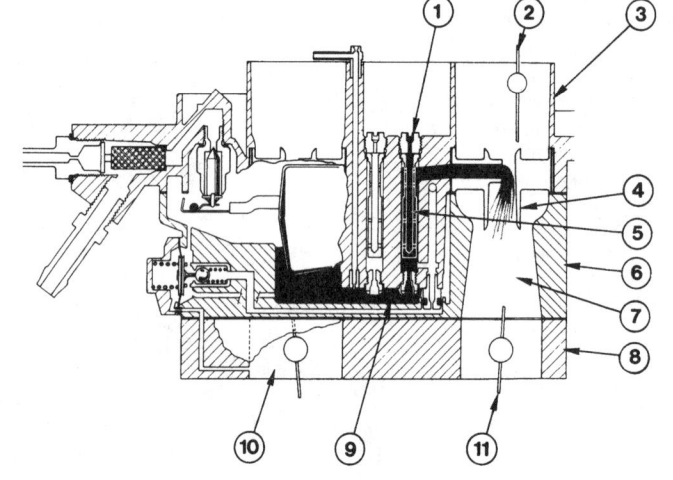

1.16 Primary main system
1 Air correction jet
2 Choke flap
3 Upper body
4 Auxiliary venturi
5 Emulsion tube
6 Main body
7 Primary venturi
8 Throttle body
9 Primary main well
10 Secondary venturi
11 Throttle plate

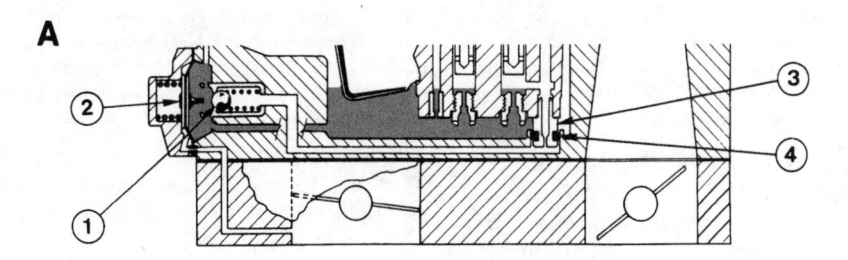

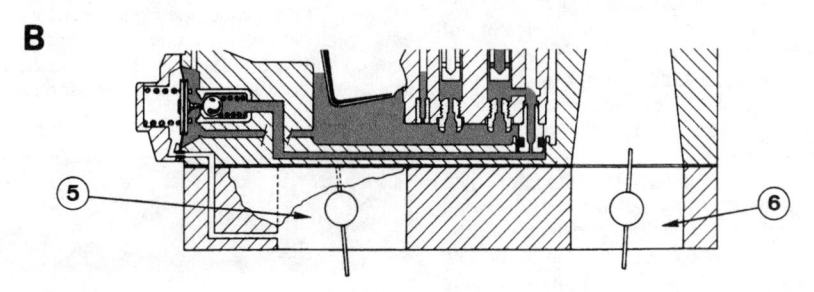

Weber 26/28, 28/30, 28/32 TLDM carburettor

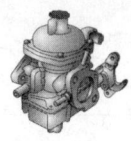

Power enrichment system
- A Power valve closed
- B Power valve open
- 1 Spring-loaded ball
- 2 Spring-loaded diaphragm
- 3 Power jet
- 4 O-ring
- 5 Secondary venturi
- 6 Primary venturi

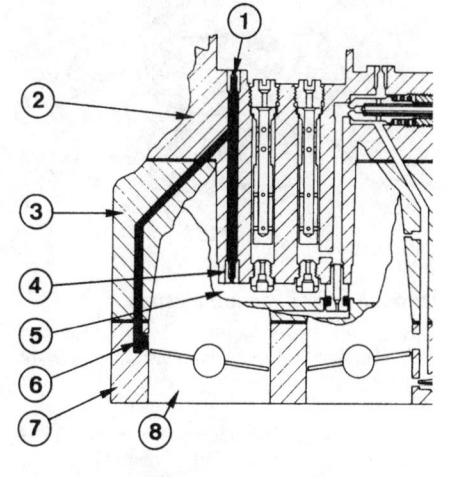

Secondary idle system
1. Secondary idle air bleed
2. Upper body
3. Main body
4. Secondary idle fuel jet
5. Main fuel well
6. Secondary progression slot
7. Throttle body
8. Secondary throttle

Secondary action

26/28 and 28/30 TDLM

19 Once the primary throttle valve is about two-thirds open, the mechanical linkage will begin to open the secondary throttle plate *(see illustration)*. At full-throttle, the linkage is arranged so that both throttle plates will be fully open.

20 A progression jet is used to prevent hesitation as the secondary throttle plate commences to open. This jet is similar in construction and action to the primary idle jet and is often referred to as the secondary idle jet. An emulsified mixture is discharged into the secondary venturi, via a progression slot, at the initial opening of the secondary throttle plate.

21 Once the secondary throttle plate has opened, the action of the secondary main circuit is similar to the primary circuit.

28/32 TDLM

22 A port is located in both the primary and secondary venturis. Airways run from these ports into a common passage leading to the diaphragm that operates the secondary throttle plate.

23 During normal operation at low speeds, the engine uses only the primary venturi. When air velocity through the primary venturi reaches a certain level, depression acts upon the port to operate the secondary diaphragm and the secondary throttle. Vacuum created in the secondary venturi will further control the rate of secondary opening *(see illustration)*.

24 The primary linkage is arranged to prevent the secondary plate from opening when air speed is high but the engine is cruising on a light throttle. Secondary action will not take place until the primary throttle is about two-thirds open.

25 Once the secondary throttle plate has opened, the action of the secondary main circuit is similar to that of the primary circuit.

26 A progression jet is used to prevent hesitation as the secondary throttle plate begins to open. This jet is similar in construction and action to the primary idle jet and is often referred to as the secondary idle jet. An emulsified mixture is discharged into the secondary venturi, via a progression slot, at the initial opening of the secondary throttle plate.

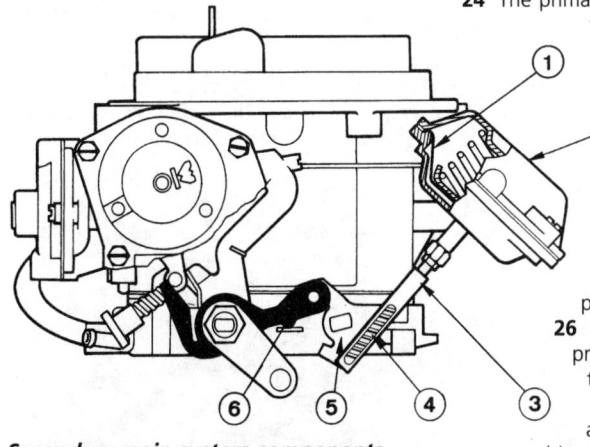

Secondary main system components
1. Diaphragm
2. Vacuum cover
3. Telescopic link
4. Telescopic spring
5. Lever
6. Spring-loaded lever assembly

27 At full-load and high engine speed, even more fuel is required. The velocity of air creates a depression sufficient to raise fuel from the float chamber into a channel. The fuel then passes through a calibrated bushing to the upper section of the secondary air intake. Here it is mixed with a small amount of air from a calibrated air bleed and the emulsified mixture is then discharged into the airstream from the full-load enrichment orifice.

Choke operation - 26/28 and 28/30 TDLM

28 The manual choke is operated by a dash-mounted cable. When the cable is pulled, it operates a lever that pulls the choke flap closed across the air intake. Fast idle is achieved with the aid of a curved cam attached to the choke operating lever. An adjustable screw, attached to the throttle lever and butting against the cam, is used to vary the fast idle speed.

29 Once the engine has fired, the choke flap must open slightly to weaken the mixture and avoid flooding during idle and light-throttle operation. This is achieved by using manifold vacuum to actuate a diaphragm and a linkage attached to the diaphragm will then pull upon the choke flap.

30 During engine warm-up, the cable should be progressively pushed home until the choke flap is fully open.

Throttle kicker (dashpot) - 26/28 TDLM, 28/30 TDLM and 28/32 TDLM (2.0 litre engine)

31 The throttle kicker slows down the throttle plate closing action to allow the introduction of normal idle vacuum in a controlled manner and to reduce emissions.

Chapter H19

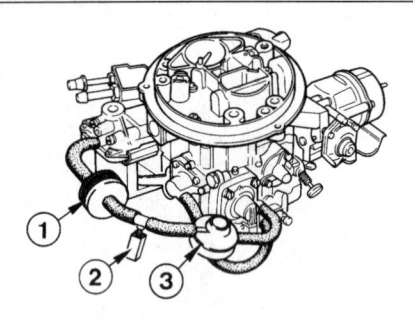

Throttle kicker vacuum system
1 Vacuum sustain valve
2 Controlled vacuum bleed with foam cover
3 Fuel trap

32 The kicker is connected to the throttle plate by a small-bore hose and is controlled by a vacuum source from the carburettor. Under normal driving conditions, the vacuum operates the kicker through a fuel trap and sustain valve. There is no effect on throttle operation while the throttle is open *(see illustration)*.

33 During deceleration with a closed throttle, the vacuum at the kicker will hold the throttle plate partially open. As deceleration continues, the vacuum through the sustain valve decays and the throttle plate will fully return to its stop.

Because of the pulsing effect of vacuum during opening and closing of the throttle, fuel can be drawn into the hose and will eventually reach and contaminate the diaphragm. A fuel trap is used to prevent such an occurrence.

Cold start system - 28/32 TDLM

34 The Weber TLDM carburettor uses a semi-automatic choke starting system. A bi-metal spring is used to control a strangler choke flap arranged in the primary air intake. Heating of the spring is by engine coolant (1.6 litre engine) or by an electrical supply from the alternator (2.0 litre engine). The system is primed by depressing the accelerator pedal once or twice *(see illustration)*.

35 Once the engine has fired, the choke flap must open slightly to weaken the mixture and avoid flooding during idle and light-throttle operation. This is achieved by using manifold vacuum to actuate a diaphragm. A linkage attached to the diaphragm will then pull upon the choke flap.

36 Fast idle is achieved with the aid of a stepped cam attached to the choke spindle. An adjustable screw, connected to the throttle lever mechanism and butting against the cam, can be used to vary the fast idle speed. As the bi-metal coil is heated and the plate opens, then the screw will rest on successively less-stepped parts of the cam. Idle speed is thus progressively reduced, until ultimately the cam is released and the idle speed returns to normal.

Wide-open kick

37 If the throttle is fully opened during acceleration when the engine is cold, the pull-down vacuum will deplete and the choke flap will tend to close. This may cause flooding and to prevent this, a wide-open kick mechanism is employed. When the throttle is fully opened, a cam on the throttle lever will turn the choke lever anti-clockwise to partially open the choke flap.

2 Identification

The Weber identification code is stamped on the choke side of the carburettor float chamber body. A metal tag giving the Ford identification code is attached to one of the upper body fixing screws.

Ford frequently refer to this carburettor as a TLD but all carburettor bodies are stamped TLDM by the manufacturer.

3 General servicing

Introduction

1 Read this Chapter in conjunction with Part B which describes some of the operations in more detail. It is assumed that the carburettor is removed for this service. However, many of the operations can be tackled with the carburettor in place. Where this is undertaken, first soak the fuel out of the float chamber using a clean tissue or soft cloth, after removing the upper body assembly.

Dismantling and checking

2 Remove the four Torx screws which secure the carburettor to the engine *(see illustration)*.

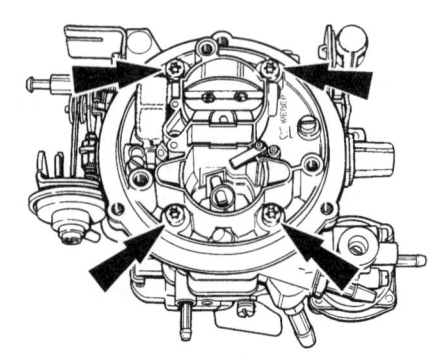

Torx type carburettor mounting screws (arrowed)

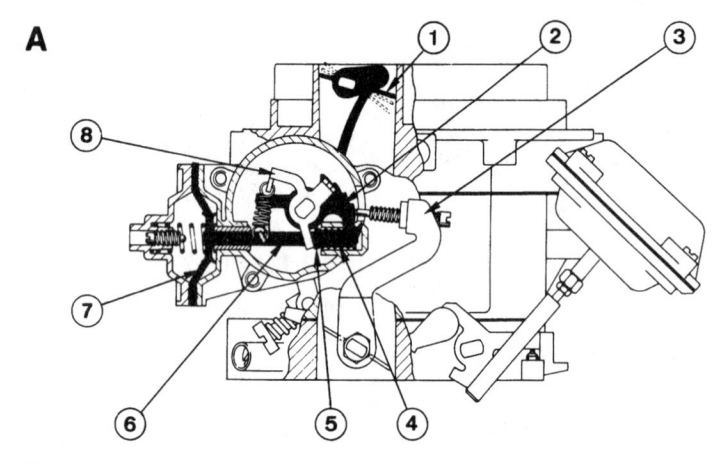

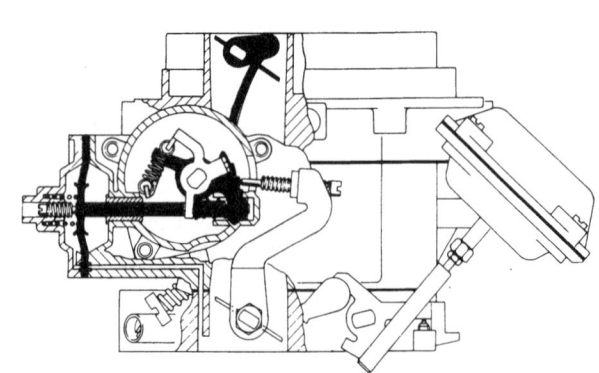

Automatic choke system

A Engine cold
B Engine warming up
1 Choke flap
2 Fast idle cam
3 Fast idle lever
4 Calibrated pull-down spring
5 Pull-down bush
6 Pull-down spindle
7 Spring-loaded diaphragm
8 Lever

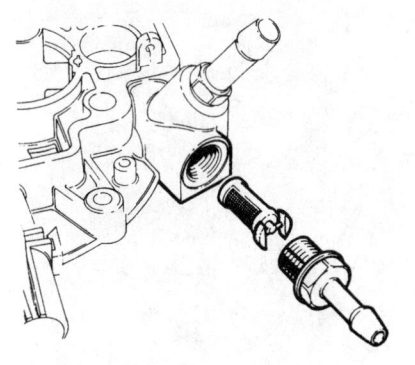

Weber 26/28, 28/30, 28/32 TLDM carburettor

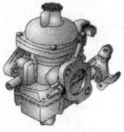

Fuel inlet filter assembly

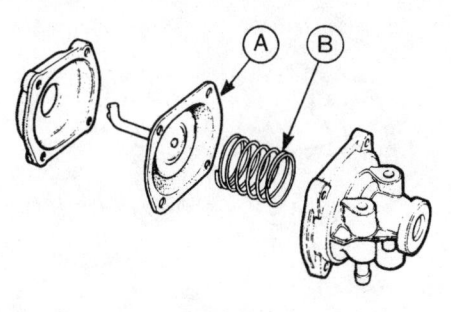

Throttle kicker assembly
A Diaphragm   B Return spring

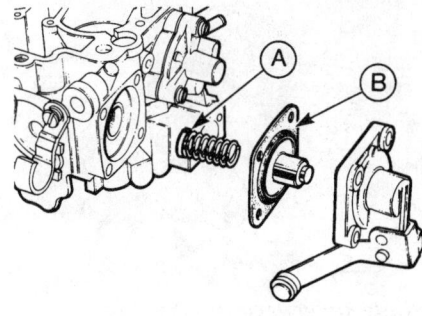

Accelerator pump assembly
A Pump valve   B Pump diaphragm

3 Remove the carburettor from the engine (see Part B).
4 Make visual checks for damage and wear.
5 On 26/28 and 28/30 TDLM carburettors, disconnect the choke vacuum hose, remove the two screws and detach the carburettor upper body.
6 On 28/32 TDLM carburettors, remove the two screws, hold the throttle open and detach the carburettor upper body.
7 Use a straight-edge to check for distorted flanges on all facing surfaces.
8 Inspect the float chamber for corrosion and calcium build-up.
9 Tap out the float pin, then remove the float, needle valve and plastic clip, float chamber gasket and needle valve seat.
10 Check that the anti-vibration ball is free in the valve end.
11 Check the needle valve tip for wear and ridges. This is more likely with the brass needle valve tip than when a viton one is used. Use a viton-tipped replacement when possible.
12 The float should be checked for damage and for ingress of petrol. Shaking the float will indicate the presence of fuel.
13 Renew the float pin if it shows signs of wear.
14 Unscrew the fuel inlet tube and inspect the fuel filter. Clean the filter housing of debris and dirt and renew the filter if necessary (see illustration).
15 Remove the mixture screw and inspect the tip for damage and ridges.

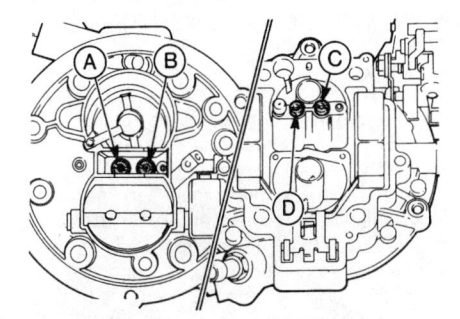

Upper body, showing jet locations
A Primary air corrector
B Secondary air corrector
C Secondary main jet
D Primary main jet

16 On 26/28 and 28/30 TDLM carburettors and on 28/32 TDLM (2.0 litre engine) carburettors, remove the two screws and detach the throttle kicker assembly. Twist and disconnect the link rod from the actuating lever. Remove a further four screws and remove the throttle kicker cover, diaphragm and spring. Check the diaphragm for fatigue and damage (see illustration).
17 Remove the four screws and remove the accelerator pump cover, diaphragm and spring (complete with vernay valve). Check the diaphragm for fatigue and damage (see illustration).
18 On 28/32 TDLM (2.0 litre engine) carburettors, remove the four screws and remove the anti-stall device cover, spring and diaphragm. Check the diaphragm for fatigue and damage. Also check the vacuum hose for splits and signs of perishing (see illustration).
19 The accelerator pump injector is a push fit in the body. Carefully prise it from its location and check the vernay valve for damage.
20 Detach the primary idle jet from the idle cut-off valve. The secondary idle jet is not removable. Note that the cut-off valve and primary idle jet assembly can be removed from the carburettor without removing the upper body.
21 Unscrew the primary and secondary main jets from the underside of the upper body. Unscrew the primary and secondary air

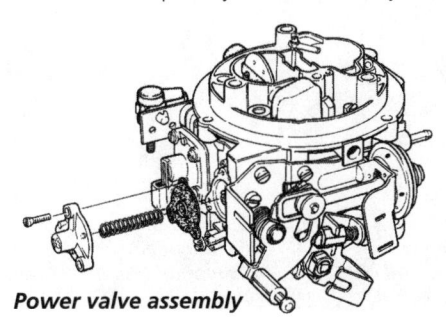

Power valve assembly

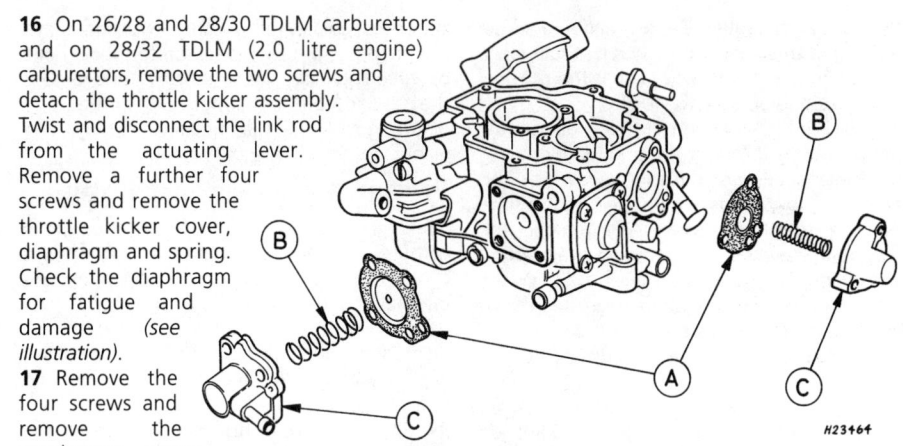

Low vacuum enrichment (LOVE) (anti-stall) device
A Diaphragm   C Diaphragm
B Return spring   cover

correctors and remove the emulsion tubes from the top of the upper body. Note that the air corrector and emulsion tubes can be removed from the carburettor body without removing the upper body (see illustration).
22 Check that the emulsion tube wells are clear.
23 Note the jet sizes and locations for correct installation during assembly. For reference, the primary main jet is located on the idle cut-off side of the carburettor.
24 Check the jet calibration against that specified. It is possible that the jets may have been transposed (or the wrong size fitted) during the last overhaul.
25 Remove the primary and secondary auxiliary venturis from the upper body where necessary. A Weber extractor tool is available for this purpose. Check that the primary and secondary auxiliary venturis are not loose in the main body as this is a source of uneven running. If a venturi is loose, knurl the mating flanges with a file to ensure a tight fit.
26 Remove the three screws and remove the power valve housing cover, spring and diaphragm from the body. Check the diaphragm for fatigue and damage (see illustration).
27 The brass outlet valve is cast into the body and is not removable. The ball in the outlet valve

H19•9

Chapter H19

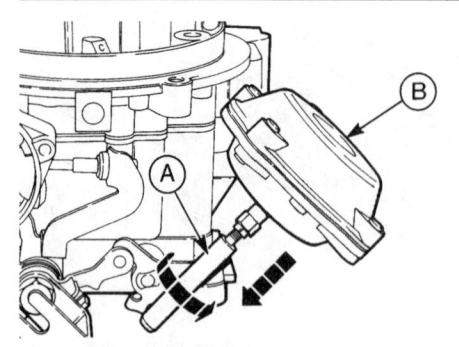

Secondary throttle vacuum assembly
A Operating link removal
B Diaphragm housing

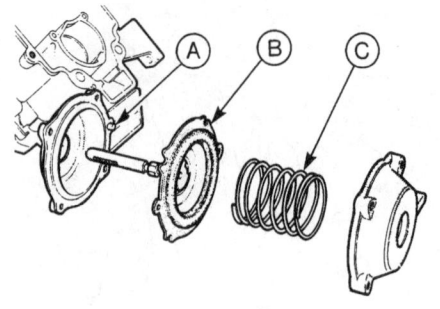

Secondary throttle diaphragm assembly
A Vacuum passage   C Return spring
B Diaphragm

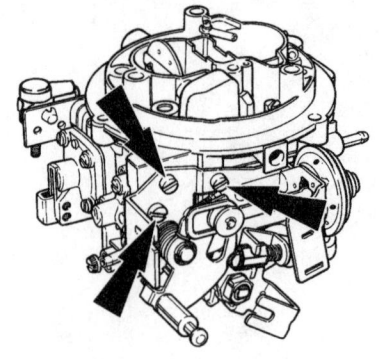

Choke assembly retaining screws (arrowed)

should seal the outlet. Depress and release the ball with a small screwdriver and it should move smoothly in and out. Check that the channel into the emulsion tube well is clear.

28 On 28/32 TDLM carburettors, disconnect the secondary throttle operating rod by pulling the lower section of the rod downwards and twisting it out of its socket (see illustration). Remove the four screws and remove the secondary throttle vacuum unit cover, spring and diaphragm from the housing. Check the diaphragm for fatigue and damage, and renew as necessary (see illustration).

29 Remove the two screws and separate the carburettor main body and throttle body assemblies. The throttle body can be renewed separately if the spindles or throttle bores are worn.

30 Inspect the choke spindle, linkage and operating mechanism for stickiness and wear.

31 On 26/28 and 28/30 TDLM carburettors, remove the three screws (see illustration), pull the lower choke link rod out of the plastic retaining collar and detach the manual choke assembly. Attach a vacuum pump to the connector and operate the pump to obtain 300 mm Hg. Renew the diaphragm if it does not operate fully or if vacuum is not maintained.

32 On 28/32 TDLM carburettors, remove the three screws, twist and disconnect the lower choke link rod and detach the choke housing (see illustration). Check the mechanism for stickiness and wear. A broken or defective mechanism is a common reason for poor choke operation. Remove the three screws and remove the choke pull-down cover, spring and diaphragm from the housing. Check the diaphragm for fatigue and damage.

Preparation for reassembly

33 Clean the jets and internal channels, the carburettor body assemblies and the float chamber. An air line may be used to clear the internal channels once the carburettor is fully dismantled. If an air line is used with the diaphragms or accelerator pump vernay valves in place and air is directed into the channels and passages, diaphragm damage may result.

34 Spraying carburettor cleaner into all the channels and passages in the carburettor body will often clear them of gum and dirt.

35 During reassembly, a complete set of new gaskets should be fitted. Also renew the needle valve and float pin, and all diaphragms.

36 Inspect and renew (where necessary) the mixture screw, main jets, idle jet, air corrector jets, emulsion tubes and accelerator pump injector. Renew worn linkages, springs, vacuum hoses and other parts where necessary.

37 Ensure that all jets are firmly locked into position (but do not overtighten). A loose jet can cause a rich (or even lean) running condition.

38 Clean all mating surfaces and flanges of old gasket material and reassemble with a new gasket.

39 Ensure that housings are assembled with their air and fuel routes correctly aligned.

Reassembly

40 On 26/28 and 28/30 TDLM carburettors, refit the manual choke assembly and secure with three screws. Push the end of the lower choke link rod through the plastic collar and clip it into position.

41 On 28/32 TDLM carburettors, refit the choke diaphragm and spindle assembly to the choke housing, ensuring that both plastic sleeves on the diaphragm spindle are pushed into position and fully located. Refit the spring and cover and secure with the three screws. Renew the vacuum O-ring seal, then engage the choke link rod into the choke lever arm. Refit the choke housing to the carburettor upper body and secure with the three screws.

42 Assemble the main and throttle bodies with a new gasket block and secure with the two screws.

43 Check that the secondary throttle plate is fully closed. The adjustment screw should not normally be used to alter the throttle plate position. However, if necessary, it can be adjusted so that the plate is open just enough to prevent it from seizing in the throttle body.

44 On 26/28 and 28/30 TDLM carburettors, refit the power diaphragm, spring and cover assembly, then secure with the three screws. Renew the seal on the power valve jet which is adjacent to the primary main jet.

45 On 28/32 TDLM carburettors, refit the secondary throttle diaphragm, spring and cover assembly, then secure with the four screws. Reconnect the secondary throttle operating rod. Renew the seal on the power valve jet (which is adjacent to the primary main jet). Refit the power diaphragm, spring and cover assembly, then secure with the three screws.

46 Refit the emulsion tubes, air correctors and main jets into their original positions (do not transpose the jets).

47 Push the accelerator pump injector firmly into position after renewing the small seal on the injector body.

48 On 28/32 TDLM (2.0 litre engine) carburettors, refit the anti-stall device

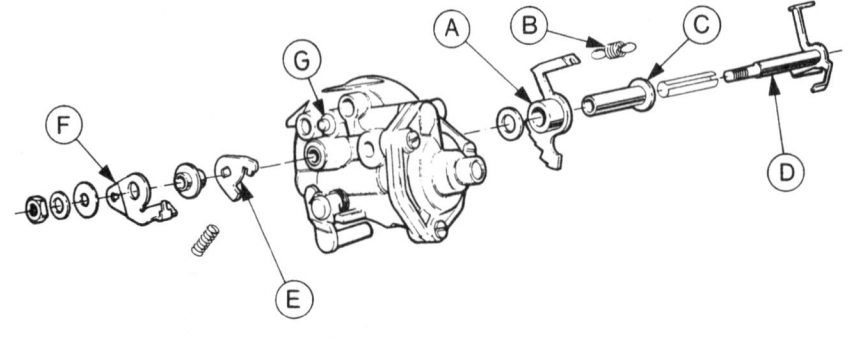

Automatic choke linkage
A Choke upper operating link
B Fast idle cam return spring
C Spindle sleeve
D Connecting rod and lever assembly
E Pull-down link
F Actuating lever
G O-ring

Weber 26/28, 28/30, 28/32 TLDM carburettor

diaphragm, spring and cover assembly, then secure with the four screws. Reconnect the vacuum hose.

49 Refit the accelerator pump spring, diaphragm and cover assembly, then secure with the four screws. The valve on the end of the spring must face inwards and care must be taken that it is not damaged.

50 On 26/28 and 28/30 TDLM carburettors and on 28/32 TDLM (2.0 litre engine) carburettors, refit the throttle kicker spring, diaphragm and cover assembly, then secure with the four screws. Ensure that the diaphragm link rod faces inwards. Reconnect the link rod to the actuating lever, then refit the assembly and secure with the two screws.

51 Refit the idle mixture screw after renewing the seal. Carefully turn the screw in until it just seats then unscrew it three full turns. This will provide a basic setting to allow the engine to be started.

52 Clean or renew the fuel filter and refit the fuel inlet tube (see illustrations).

53 Fit a new float chamber gasket to the upper body and renew the needle valve assembly. Screw the valve seat into the upper body, using a new sealing washer, and ensure that it is firmly locked into position.

54 Insert the needle valve into the valve body with the ball facing outwards, then refit the float and pivot pin. Ensure that the plastic clip is correctly connected to the float and to the needle valve.

55 Adjust the float level. Refer to Section 4 for details.

56 Refit the upper body to the main body and secure with the two screws.

57 On 26/28 and 28/30 TDLM carburettors, reconnect the choke pull-down hose.

58 Fit the idle jet to the idle cut-off valve but do not push the jet completely into the valve. When the valve is fitted to the upper body, the idle jet will find its own position. Refit the assembly using a new sealing washer.

59 Ensure that the choke flap and linkage moves smoothly and progressively.

60 Refit the carburettor to the engine.

61 Always adjust the carburettor idle speed and mixture after any work has been carried out

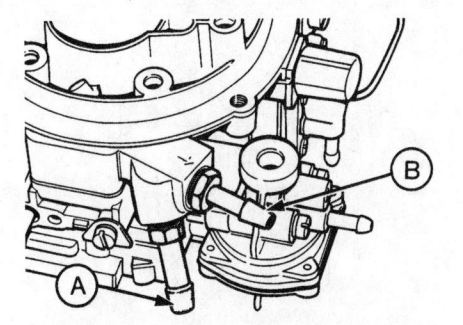

Carburettor fuel hose connections (26/28, 28/30 - 1.1 litre shown)
A Fuel inlet connection
B Fuel return connection

on the carburettor, preferably with the aid of a CO meter.

62 Adjust the choke (and throttle kicker, where applicable). Refer to Section 4 for details.

4 Service adjustments

Adjustment preconditions

1 Refer to Part B for general advice on preconditions to correct adjustment of this carburettor.

2 The engine cooling fan should run continuously during idle adjustment. Run the engine until the fan operates, then disconnect the connector plug to the fan temperature sensor and temporarily bridge the plug terminals with a piece of wire (see illustration).

Idle speed and mixture (CO)

3 Run the engine at 3000 rpm for 30 seconds to clear the manifold of fuel vapours, then allow the engine to idle.

4 Unbolt the air filter assembly and leave it positioned loosely on the carburettor with the vacuum and breather hoses still connected.

5 Use the idle speed screw to set the specified idle speed (see illustration).

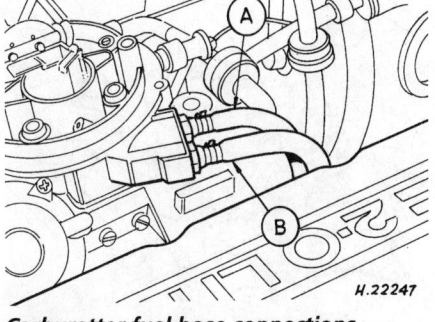

Carburettor fuel hose connections (28/32 - 2.0 litre shown)
A Fuel inlet connection
B Fuel return connection

6 Check the CO level and compare with the specified value. If incorrect, remove the tamperproof plug and adjust to the correct level. Turning the screw clockwise (inwards) will reduce the CO level. Turning the screw anti-clockwise (outwards) will increase the CO level.

7 Repeat paragraphs 5 and 6 until both adjustments are correct.

8 Clear the manifold every 30 seconds during the setting operation by running the engine at 3000 rpm for 30 seconds.

9 Increase the speed to 2000 rpm and note the CO reading. The cruise reading should be less than half the idle CO reading.

10 Fit a new tamperproof plug to the mixture adjusting screw.

11 Remove the temporary bridge wire and reconnect the fan sensor plug.

12 Refit the air filter, ensuring that the vacuum and breather hoses remain connected.

Float level

13 Hold the upper body in a vertical position with the float tag gently touching the ball of the fully-closed needle valve.

14 Measure the distance between the upper body (with the gasket in place) and the top of the float (see illustration).

15 Adjust as necessary by bending the float tag.

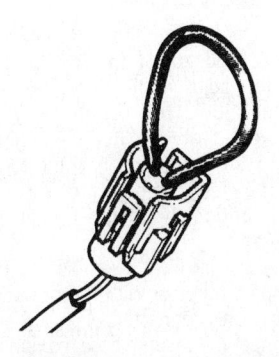

Temporary bridge wire fitted to fan temperature sensor connector plug

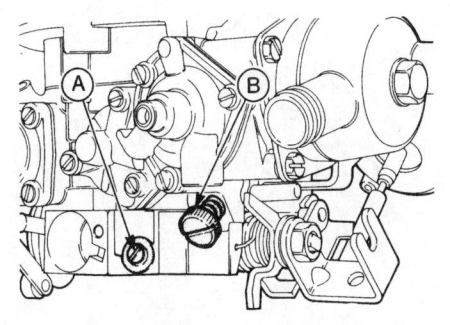

Idle adjustment screw location
A Idle mixture (CO) screw
B Idle speed screw

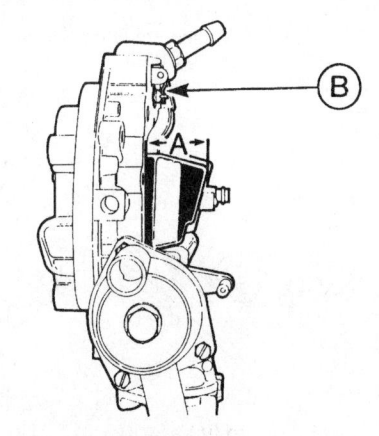

Float level adjustment
A Float level dimension (see Specifications)
B Adjusting tag

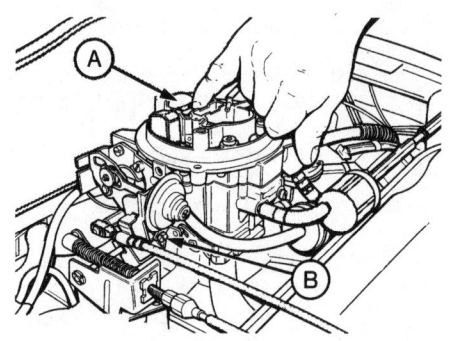

Chapter H19

Choke fast idle adjustment
A Choke flap held open
B Fast idle adjustment screw

Choke fast idle adjustment
A Fast idle cam
B Fast idle adjustment screw

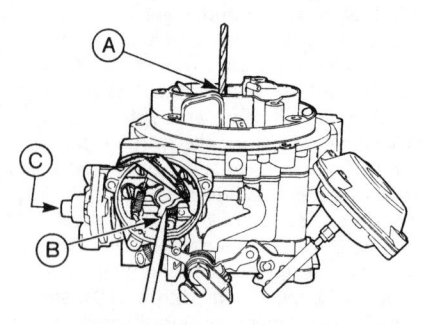

Choke plate pull-down adjustment
A Twist drill   C Adjustment
B Diaphragm held fully open   screw

Manual choke - 26/28 and 28/30 TDLM

Fast idle

16 Warm the engine to normal running temperature and adjust the idle speed and mixture before attempting fast idle adjustment.
17 The fan should run continuously during fast idle adjustment. Run the engine until the fan operates, then disconnect the connector plug to the fan temperature sensor and temporarily bridge the plug terminals with a piece of wire.
18 Remove the air filter assembly and place it clear of the carburettor with the breather and vacuum hoses still connected.
19 Pull the choke cable to fully operate the choke. At the same time, hold the choke flap as far open as possible (see illustration).
20 Start the engine and record the fast idle speed. Refer to Specifications for the correct figure.
21 Adjust as necessary by turning the fast idle screw in the appropriate direction.
22 Remove the temporary bridge wire and reconnect the fan sensor plug.
23 Refit the air filter, ensuring that the vacuum and breather hoses remain connected.

Choke pull-down

24 Pull the choke cable to fully close the choke flap.
25 Use a vacuum pump (or a finger) to pull the diaphragm operating rod up to its stop. At the same time, use the shank of a twist drill to measure the gap between the lower section of the choke flap and the air intake. Refer to Specifications for the required drill size.
26 Remove the tamperproof plug in the diaphragm cover and adjust as necessary by turning the diaphragm adjusting screw in the appropriate direction. Renew the plug after adjustment is completed.

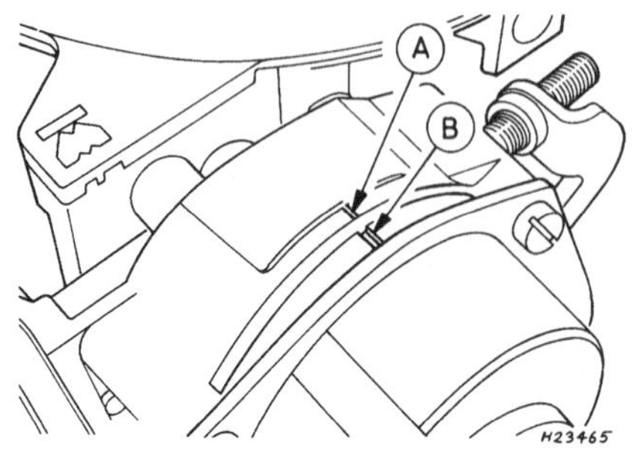

Automatic choke - 28/32 TDLM

Fast idle

27 Warm the engine to normal running temperature and adjust the idle speed and mixture before attempting choke fast idle adjustment.
28 Remove the air filter assembly and place it clear of the carburettor with the vacuum and breather hoses still connected.
29 Partially open the throttle and fully close the choke flap. Slowly open the plate until the fast idle adjustment screw can be placed against the third-highest step of the fast idle cam. Release the throttle so that the fast idle adjustment screw remains against the third-highest step but with the choke flap open (see illustration).
30 Start the engine without touching the throttle and record the fast idle speed. Refer to Specifications for the correct figure.
31 Adjust as necessary by turning the fast idle screw in the appropriate direction.

32 Refit the air filter assembly, ensuring that the vacuum and breather hoses remain connected.

Choke vacuum pull-down

33 Remove the three screws and detach the bi-metal coil housing from the carburettor.
34 Remove the internal plastic heat shield.
35 Partially open the throttle and fully close the choke flap.
36 Release the throttle and fit an elastic band to the choke operating lever so that the choke flap remains in the fully-on position.
37 Use a small screwdriver to push open the diaphragm to its stop and use the shank of a twist drill to measure the gap between the lower section of the choke flap and the air intake. Refer to Specifications for the required drill size.
38 Remove the tamperproof plug and adjust as necessary by turning the diaphragm adjusting screw (see illustration) in the appropriate direction. Renew the plug after adjustment is complete and remove the elastic band.
39 Refit the internal heat shield, ensuring that the peg in the housing locates into the hole in the shield.
40 Refit the bi-metal coil housing (ensure that the spring locates in the slot of the choke lever) and secure loosely with the three screws. Align the cut mark on the bi-metal cover with the correct mark on the choke assembly housing and tighten the three screws (see illustration).

Throttle kicker - 26/28 and 28/30 TDLM

41 Warm the engine to normal running temperature and adjust the idle speed and mixture before adjusting the throttle kicker.
42 The fan should run continuously during throttle kicker adjustment. Run the engine until the fan operates, then disconnect the connector plug to the fan temperature sensor and temporarily bridge the plug terminals with a piece of wire.
43 Remove the air filter assembly and place it clear of the carburettor with the breather and vacuum hoses still connected.
44 Disconnect the vacuum hose, complete with sustain valve and fuel trap, from the kicker (see illustration).

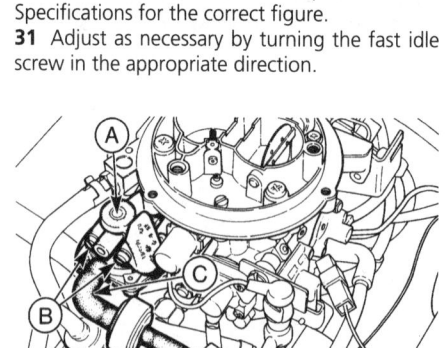

Choke housing alignment
A Punch mark
B Choke alignment mark on housing

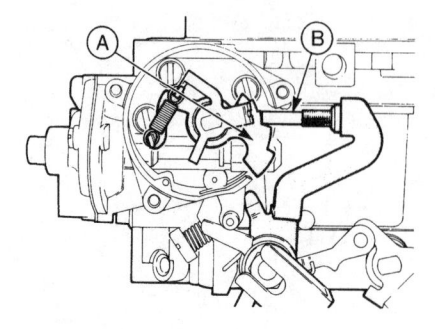

Throttle kicker adjustment
A Adjusting point   C Vacuum
B Securing screws   take-off

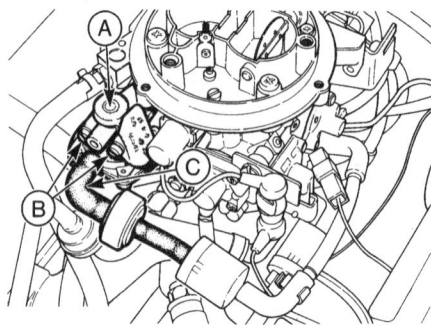

Weber 26/28, 28/30, 28/32 TLDM carburettor

45 Push the linkage upwards to operate the kicker and use a finger to seal the inlet connection. The diaphragm should maintain its fully-operated position until the finger is removed.
46 Plug the vacuum hose from the manifold.
47 Use a new length of vacuum hose (without attachments) to operate the kicker and record the engine speed. Refer to Specifications for the correct value.
48 Remove the tamperproof plug in the diaphragm cover and adjust as necessary, by turning the diaphragm adjusting screw in the appropriate direction. Renew the plug after adjustment is completed.
49 Reconnect the vacuum hose, complete with sustain valve and fuel trap, to the kicker.
50 Remove the temporary bridge wire and reconnect the fan sensor plug.
51 Refit the air filter, ensuring that the vacuum and breather hoses remain connected.

5 Component testing

Automatic choke - 28/32 TDLM (2.0 litre engine)

1 Allow the engine to cool completely.
2 Remove the air filter and check that the choke flap blocks the carburettor air intake.
3 Start the engine and check the fast idle speed. Also check that the choke pull-down operates satisfactorily.
4 As the engine warms up, check that the choke flap gradually opens until it is fully open. The fast idle speed should decrease progressively.
5 If the choke flap operation is unsatisfactory, check the choke pull-down adjustment and look for sticking, worn or broken linkage components.
6 Attach a voltmeter to the choke electrical connection. With the engine running, expect a voltage of 6 to 8 volts.
7 If voltage is low or zero, attach the voltmeter to the choke supply connection on the alternator. If there is still no voltage, repair or renew the alternator.
8 If voltage is present at the alternator but not at the choke, check the wiring from the alternator to the choke connection for a break or bad connection.

6 Fault diagnosis

Refer to Part D for diagnosis of general carburettor faults.

Notes

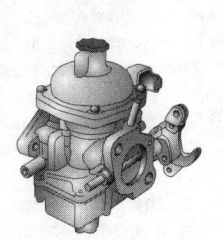

Part H Chapter 20
Weber 32 TLF carburettor

H20

Contents

Fault diagnosis	5	Principles of operation	1
General servicing	3	Service adjustments	4
Identification	2		

Specifications

Manufacturer	Fiat	Fiat	Fiat	Fiat
Model	Panda 750	Panda 1000	Panda 1000 4x4	Uno 45 (999)
Year	1986 to 1991	1986 to 1991	1986 to 1991	1985 to 1991
Engine code	156 A4.000 (Fire) OHC	156 A2.000 (Fire)	156 A3.000 (Fire)	156 A2.000 (Fire) OHC
Capacity (cm^3)/no. of cyls	770/4	999/4	999/4	999/4
Oil temperature (°C)	100	100	100	100
Carb. identification	32 TLF 11/250 or 251	32 TLF 6/250 or 251	32 TLF 8/250 or 251	32 TLF 4/250 to 252
Idle speed (rpm)	850 ± 50	850 ± 50	850 ± 50	775 ± 25
CO @ idle (% vol.)	1.0 ± 0.5	1.0 ± 0.5	1.0 ± 0.5	1.5 ± 0.5
Venturi diameter	22	22	22	22
Idle jet	47	46	46	47
Main jet	105	105	105	105
Air correction jet	170	165	165	165
Emulsion tube	F70	F70	F70	F70
Accel. pump jet	40	40	40	40
Float level (mm)	27 ± 0.5	27 ± 0.5	27 ± 0.5	27 ± 0.5
Needle valve size (mm)	1.50	1.50	1.50	1.50
Choke fast idle gap (mm)	0.7 ± 0.05	0.7 ± 0.05	0.7 ± 0.05	0.7 ± 0.05
Choke pull-down (mm)	4.5 ± 0.5	4.5 ± 0.5	4.5 ± 0.5	4.5 ± 0.25

Manufacturer	Fiat	Lancia	Lancia	Lancia
Model	Uno 60 (1108)	Y10 Fire	Y10 Fire	Y10 Fire
Year	1990 to 1991	1985 to 1988	1989	1989 to 1991
Engine code	160 A3.000 (Fire) OHC	156 A2.000 SOHC	156 A2.000 SOHC	156 A2.000 SOHC
Capacity (cm^3)/no. of cyls	1108/4	999/4	999/4	999/4
Oil temperature (°C)	100	100	100	100
Carb. identification	32 TLF 27/251	32 TLF/250	32 TLF/251	32 TLF 4/251
Idle speed (rpm)	775 ± 25	750 ± 50	750 ± 50	825 ± 25
CO @ idle (% vol.)	1.5 ± 0.5	1.5 ± 0.5	1.5 ± 0.5	1.0 ± 0.5
Venturi diameter	22	22	22	22
Idle jet	45	47	46	47
Main jet	105	105	105	105
Air correction jet	165	165	165	165
Emulsion tube	F70	170	170	F70
Accel. pump jet	40	40	40	40
Float level (mm)	27 ± 0.25	27 ± 0.25	27 ± 0.25	27 ± 0.25
Float stroke (mm)	34.2 ± 0.25	–	–	–
Needle valve size (mm)	1.50	1.50	1.50	1.50
Choke fast idle gap (mm)	0.7 ± 0.05	0.7 ± 0.05	0.7 ± 0.05	0.7 ± 0.05
Choke pull-down (mm)	4.0 ± 0.25	4.5 ± 0.5	4.0 ± 0.25	4.0 ± 0.25

Chapter H20

1 Principles of operation

Introduction

1 The following technical description of the Weber TLF carburettor should be read in conjunction with the more detailed description of carburettor principles in Part A.

Construction

2 The Weber 32 TLF carburettor is a downdraught, single venturi instrument with a manual choke control and a power valve *(see illustration)*. The throttle shaft is made of steel. The throttle valve is made of brass, as are the jets and the emulsion tube. The exception is the accelerator pump injector which is die-cast. The internal fuel channels and air passages are drilled and sealed with lead plugs where necessary.

3 The carburettor is constructed in three main bodies. These are the upper body, main body and throttle body containing the throttle assemblies. An insulating block, placed between the main carburettor body and the throttle body, prevents excess heat transference to the main body.

Fuel control

4 Fuel flows into the carburettor through a fine mesh filter. The fuel level in the float chamber is controlled by a needle valve and plastic float assembly. An anti-vibration ball is incorporated into the needle valve design. A clip, attached to the needle valve and to the float arm, prevents the needle from sticking in the seat as the fuel level drops. The float chamber is vented internally to the clean-air side of the air filter.

Idle, slow running and progression

5 Fuel sourced from the main well passes into the upper body through a metered idle jet. Here it is mixed with a small amount of air from a calibrated air bleed. The emulsion formed is drawn through a channel to the throttle body where it is discharged from the idle orifice under the primary throttle plate. A tapered mixture control screw is used to vary the outlet and this ensures fine control of the idle mixture. A progression slot, partially covered by the closed throttle at idle, provides enrichment as it is uncovered by the opening throttle during initial acceleration *(see illustration)*.

6 The idle speed is set by an adjustable screw. The adjustable mixture screw is tamper proofed during production, in accordance with emission regulations.

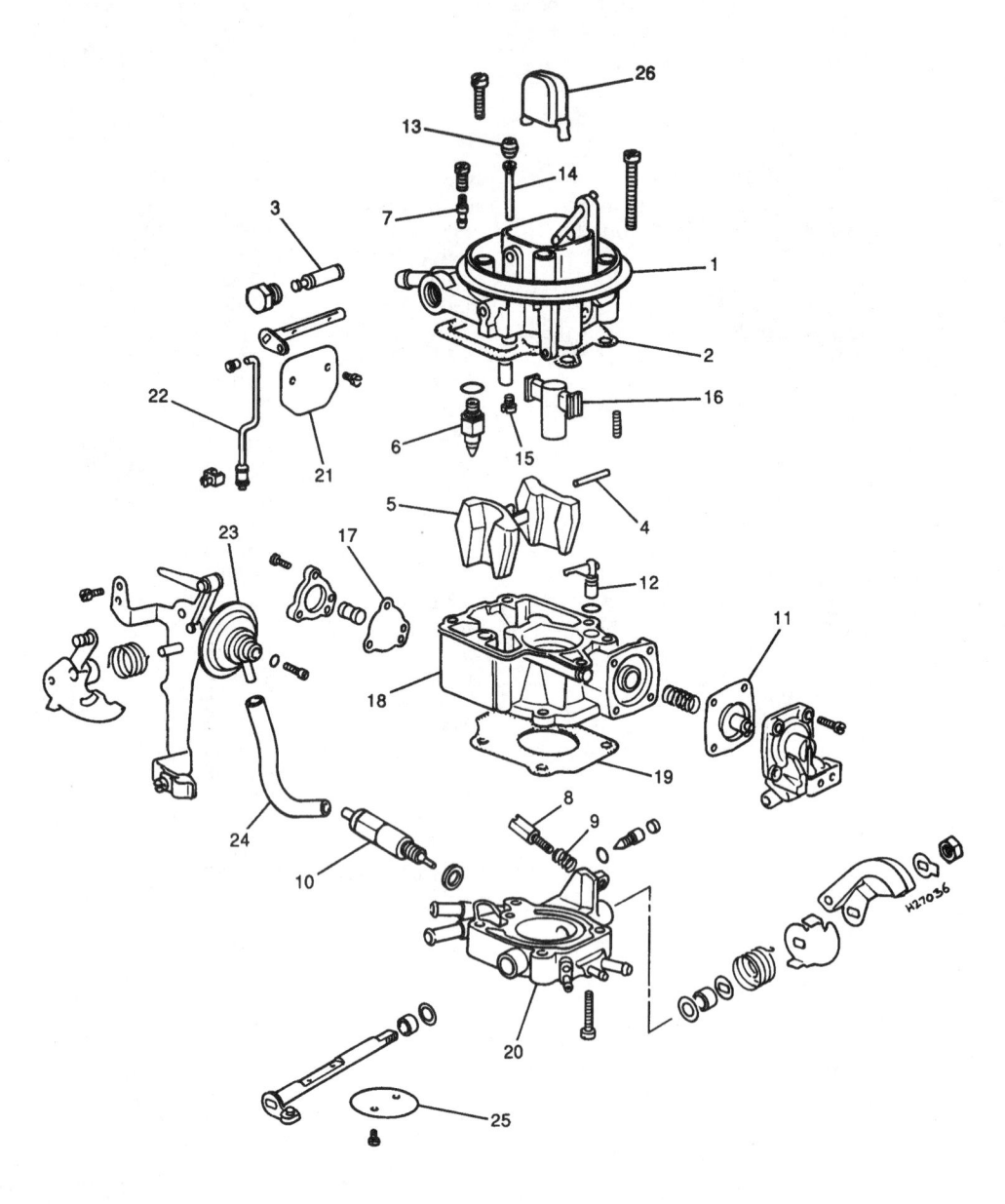

Weber TLF carburettor

1 Upper body
2 Float chamber gasket
3 Fuel inlet filter
4 Float pin
5 Float
6 Needle valve assembly
7 Idle jet
8 Idle speed adjustment screw
9 Idle mixture control screw
10 Idle cut-off valve
11 Accelerator pump diaphragm
12 Pump injector
13 Air corrector
14 Emulsion tube
15 Main jet
16 Auxiliary venturi
17 Power diaphragm
18 Main body
19 Insulator block
20 Throttle body
21 Choke flap
22 Choke link rod
23 Diaphragm
24 Vacuum hose
25 Throttle valve
26 Choke mechanism shield

Weber 32 TLF carburettor

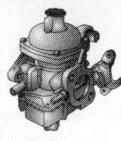

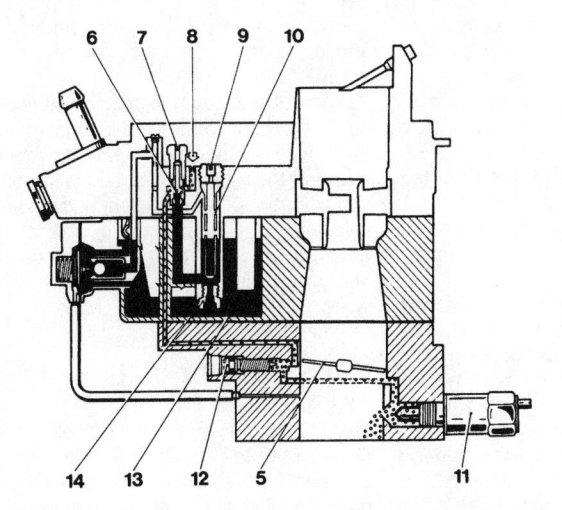

Idle circuit

5 Throttle valve
6 Idle jet
7 Idle jet holder
8 Air bleed
9 Air corrector
10 Main well
11 Idle cut-off valve
12 Idle mixture control screw
13 Float chamber
14 Main jet

Accelerator pump circuit

1 Float chamber
2 Fuel outlet channel
3 Pump injector
4 Pump actuating lever
5 Pump cam
6 Diaphragm
7 Spring
8 Inlet ball
9 Back bleed

Idle cut-off valve

7 An idle cut-off valve is used to prevent running-on when the engine is shut down. It utilises a 12-volt solenoid plunger to block the idle channel when the ignition is switched off.

Accelerator pump

8 The Weber 32 TLF accelerator pump is controlled by a diaphragm and is mechanically operated by a cam and lever attached to the throttle linkage. The outlet valve is incorporated into the pump injector. The inlet valve consists of a ball valve located in a channel from the float chamber. Excess fuel is returned to the float chamber through a calibrated bush (see illustration).

Main circuit

9 The amount of fuel discharged into the airstream is controlled by a calibrated main jet. Fuel is drawn through the main jet into the base of a vertical well which dips down into the fuel in the float chamber. An emulsion tube is placed in the well and is capped by a calibrated air corrector jet. The fuel is mixed with air drawn in through the air corrector and through the holes in the emulsion tube. The resulting emulsified mixture is discharged from the main nozzle through an auxiliary venturi (see illustration).

Power enrichment and economy circuit

10 Fuel flows from the float chamber into the power valve chamber through a fuel channel. An air passage is taken from under the throttle plate to the cover of the power diaphragm chamber. At idle and during light-throttle operation, manifold vacuum draws the diaphragm back against spring pressure. The diaphragm pintle is withdrawn from the brass outlet valve and the spring-loaded ball seats to close off the outlet channel (see illustration).

11 Under acceleration and wide-open throttle operation, the vacuum in the manifold is

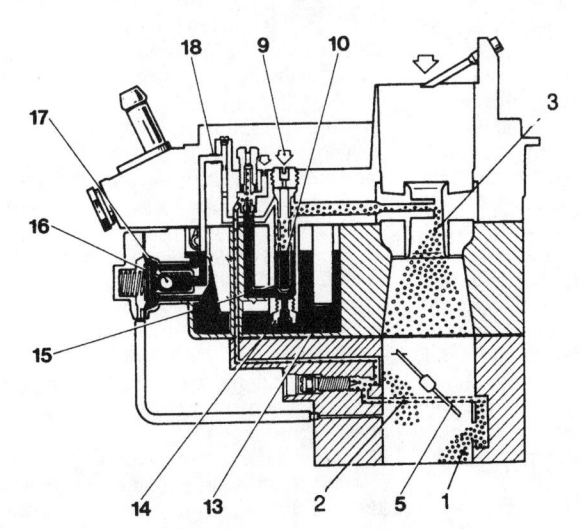

Progression and main circuits

1 Idle outlet
2 Progression outlet
3 Main outlet
5 Throttle valve
9 Air corrector
10 Main well
13 Float chamber
14 Main jet
15 Emulsion tube
16 Diaphragm
17 Power valve ball
18 Fuel channel

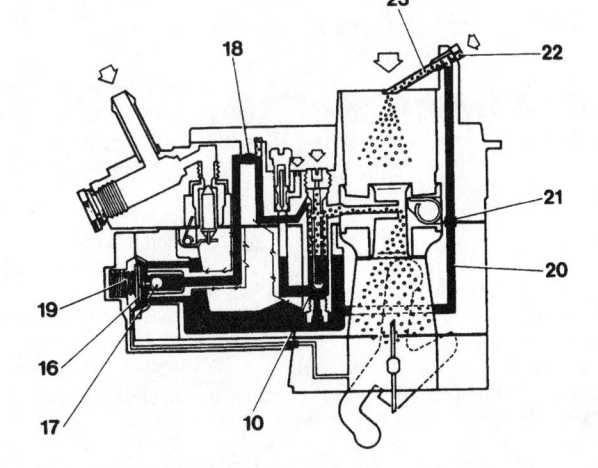

Power and full-load circuits

10 Main well
16 Diaphragm
17 Power valve ball
18 Fuel passage
19 Spring
20 Full-load fuel channel
21 Calibrated bush
22 Air bleed
23 Full-load outlet

Chapter H20

depleted. The diaphragm returns under spring pressure and the power diaphragm pintle pushes the ball to open the outlet valve. Fuel then flows through the valve and a calibrated jet to supplement the fuel in the primary main well. The fuel level rises in the well and the fuel mixture is enriched.

12 At full-load and high engine speeds, even more fuel is required. The velocity of air creates a depression sufficient to raise fuel from the float chamber into a channel. The fuel then passes through a calibrated bushing to the upper section of the air intake. Here it is mixed with a small amount of air from a calibrated air bleed and the emulsified mixture is then discharged into the airstream from the full-load enrichment tube.

Choke operation

13 The manual choke is operated by a dash-mounted cable. When the cable is pulled it operates a lever that pulls the choke flap closed across the air intake. Fast idle is achieved with the aid of a curved cam attached to the choke operating lever. An adjustable screw, attached to the throttle lever and butting against the cam, is used to vary the fast idle speed.

14 Once the engine has fired, the choke flap must open slightly to weaken the mixture and avoid flooding. During idle and light-throttle operation, this is achieved by using manifold vacuum to actuate a diaphragm. A fulcrum lever attached to the diaphragm lever will then push upon the control link connected to the choke flap.

15 During engine warm-up, the cable should be progressively pushed home until the choke flap is fully open.

2 Identification

The Weber identification code is stamped on the base flange of the main body.

3 General servicing

Introduction

1 Read this Chapter in conjunction with Part B which describes some of the operations in more detail. It is assumed that the carburettor is removed for this service. However, many of the operations can be tackled with the carburettor in place. Where this is undertaken, first soak the fuel out of the float chamber using a clean tissue or soft cloth, after removing the upper body assembly.

Dismantling and checking

2 Remove the two screws which secure the carburettor to the engine.

3 Remove the carburettor from the engine (see Part B).
4 Check visually for damage and wear.
5 Disconnect the choke vacuum hose, then remove the screws and detach the carburettor upper body.
6 Use a straight-edge to check for distorted flanges on all facing surfaces.
7 Tap out the float pin and remove the float, needle valve and plastic clip, float chamber gasket and needle valve seat.
8 Check that the anti-vibration ball is free in the valve end.
9 Check the needle valve tip for wear and ridges. This is more likely with the brass needle valve tip than when a viton one is used. Use a viton-tipped replacement when possible.
10 The float should be checked for damage and ingress of petrol.
11 Renew the float pin if it appears worn.
12 Unscrew the hexagon bolt and inspect the fuel filter. Clean the filter housing of debris and dirt and renew the filter if necessary.
13 Remove the mixture screw and inspect the tip for damage and ridges.
14 Remove the four screws and detach the accelerator pump cover, diaphragm and spring. Check the diaphragm for fatigue and damage.
15 The pump injector is a push fit in the body. Carefully prise it from its location and check the valve for damage.
16 Remove the primary idle jet assembly from the upper body. The idle jet is pushed into a holder and may be separated (by pulling) for cleaning or renewal. Note that the idle and air corrector jet can be detached from the carburettor without removing the upper body.
17 Remove the main jet, air corrector and emulsion tube. Check that the channel from the float chamber into the emulsion tube well is clear.
18 Check the jet calibration against that specified. It is possible that the wrong size jets may have been fitted during the last overhaul.
19 Remove the auxiliary venturi from the upper body where necessary. Weber provide an extractor tool for removing this component. Check that the venturi is not loose in the main body as this is a source of uneven running. If the venturi is loose, knurl the mating flanges with a file to ensure a tight fit.
20 Remove the three screws and detach the power valve housing cover, spring and diaphragm from the body. Check the diaphragm for fatigue and damage. The brass outlet valve is cast into the body and is not removable. The ball in the outlet valve should seal the outlet. Depress and release the ball with a small screwdriver and it should move smoothly in and out. Check that the emulsion tube well is clear.
21 Remove the two screws and separate the carburettor main body and throttle body assemblies. The throttle body can be renewed separately if the spindles or throttle bores are worn.
22 Push out the plastic choke mechanism shield from under the upper body lip and

remove it. Inspect the choke spindle, linkage and operating mechanism for stickiness and wear.
23 Attach a vacuum pump to the pull-down diaphragm and operate the pump to obtain 300 mm Hg. The diaphragm should operate fully and the vacuum must be maintained for a minimum of 10 seconds. Renew the diaphragm assembly if it fails these tests.
24 Pull the upper choke link rod out of the plastic retaining collar then remove the three screws and detach the choke pull-down assembly.

Preparation for reassembly

25 Clean the jets, carburettor body assemblies, float chamber and internal channels. An air line may be used to clear internal channels once the carburettor is fully dismantled. Note that if high-pressure air is directed into the channels and passages with the diaphragms still in place, diaphragm damage may result.
26 Spraying carburettor cleaner into all the channels and passages in the carburettor body will often clear them of gum and dirt.
27 During reassembly, a complete set of new gaskets should be fitted. Also renew the needle valve and float pin, and all diaphragms.
28 Inspect and renew (where necessary) the mixture screw, main jet, idle jet, air corrector jet, emulsion tube and accelerator pump injector. Renew worn linkages, screws, springs, vacuum hoses and other parts where necessary.
29 Ensure that all jets are firmly locked into position (but do not over-tighten). A loose jet can cause a rich (or even lean) running condition.
30 Clean all mating surfaces and flanges of old gasket material and reassemble with new gaskets.
31 Ensure that housings are positioned with their air and fuel routes correctly aligned.

Reassembly

32 Refit the choke pull-down assembly and secure with the three screws. Reconnect the choke link rod.
33 Clip the choke mechanism shield into position.
34 Assemble the main and throttle bodies with a new gasket block and secure with the two screws.
35 Refit the power diaphragm, spring and cover assembly, then secure with the three screws.
36 Refit the emulsion tube, air corrector and main jet into their original positions.
37 Push the pump injector firmly into position, after renewing the small seal on the injector body.
38 Refit the pump spring, diaphragm and cover assembly, then secure with the four screws.
39 Refit the idle mixture screw after renewing the seal. Turn the screw in gently until it just seats. From this position, unscrew it three full turns. This will provide a basic setting to allow the engine to be started.
40 Push the idle jet into its holder and refit the assembly into the upper body.

Weber 32 TLF carburettor

41 Refit the idle cut-off valve, using a new sealing washer.
42 Clean or renew the fuel filter and refit the hexagon bolt.
43 Renew the float chamber gasket and locate in position on the upper body. Renew the needle valve assembly. Screw the valve seat into the upper body, using a new sealing washer, and ensure that it is firmly locked into position (but do not over-tighten). Transfer the hairpin or plastic clip from the old needle valve to the ball end of the new one. Place the clip and valve assembly onto the inner float tag. Lower the float and needle valve assembly into the seat and secure with the float pin.
44 Adjust the float level. Refer to Section 4 for details on adjustment.
45 Refit the upper body to the main body and secure with the two screws. Reconnect the choke pull-down hose.
46 Ensure that the choke flap and linkage move smoothly and progressively.
47 Adjust the choke fast idle and vacuum pull-down. Refer to Section 4 for details on all adjustments.
48 Refit the carburettor to the engine.
49 Always adjust the carburettor idle speed and mixture after any work has been carried out on the carburettor, preferably with the aid of a CO meter.

4 Service adjustments

Adjustment preconditions

1 Refer to Part B for general advice on the preconditions to correct adjustment of this carburettor.

Idle speed and mixture (CO)

2 Run the engine at 3000 rpm for 30 seconds to clear the manifold of fuel vapours, then allow the engine to idle.
3 Use the idle speed adjustment screw to set the specified idle speed (see illustration).
4 Check the CO level. If it is not as specified, remove the tamperproof plug and adjust the idle mixture control screw to achieve the correct level. Turning the screw clockwise (inwards) will reduce the CO level. Turning the screw anti-clockwise (outwards) will increase the CO level.
5 Repeat paragraphs 3 and 4 until both adjustments are correct.
6 Clear the manifold every 30 seconds during the setting operation by running the engine at 3000 rpm for 30 seconds.
7 Increase the speed to 2000 rpm and note the CO reading. The cruise reading should be less than half the idle CO reading.
8 Fit a new tamperproof plug to the mixture control screw.

Float level

9 Hold the carburettor upper body in a vertical

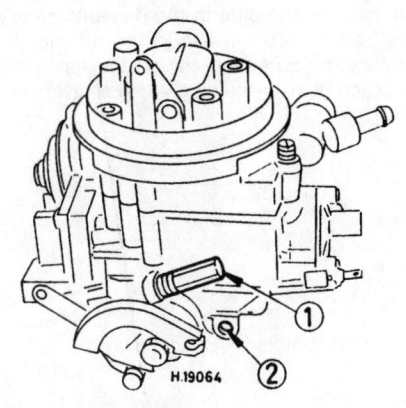

Idle speed and mixture adjustment
1 Idle speed adjustment screw
2 Idle mixture control screw

position with the float tag gently touching the ball of the needle valve.
10 Measure the distance between the upper body (with the gasket in place) and the base of the float (see illustration).
11 Adjust as necessary by bending the inner float tag.

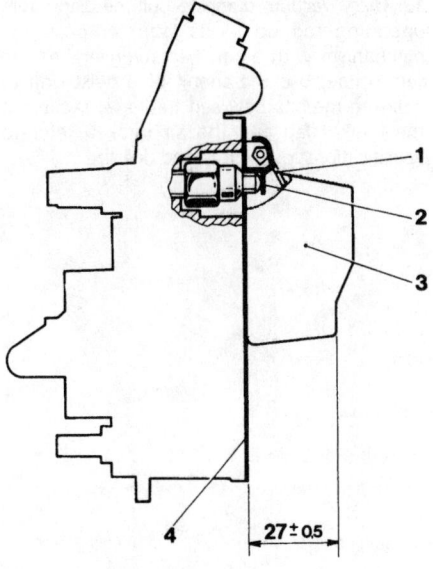

Manual choke

Fast idle

12 The carburettor must be removed from the engine in order to make the fast idle adjustment.
13 Invert the carburettor then pull the choke operating arm to fully close the choke flap. The adjustment screw will butt against the fast idle cam and force open the throttle plate to leave a small clearance (see illustration).
14 Use the shank of a twist drill to measure the clearance between the wall of the throttle bore and the throttle plate. Refer to Specifications for the required drill size and measure the clearance from the progression holes.
15 Adjust as necessary by turning the adjustment screw in the appropriate direction.

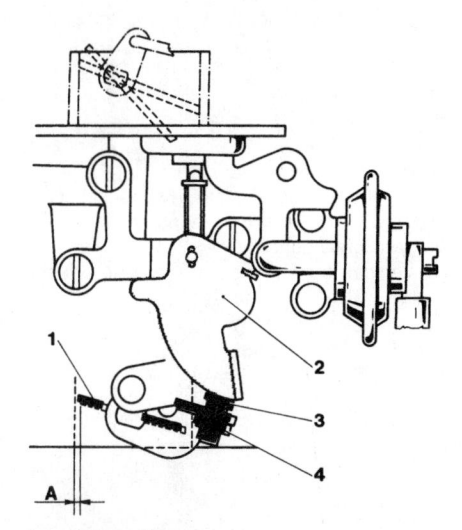

Vacuum pull-down

16 Pull the choke operating arm to fully close the choke flap (see illustration).

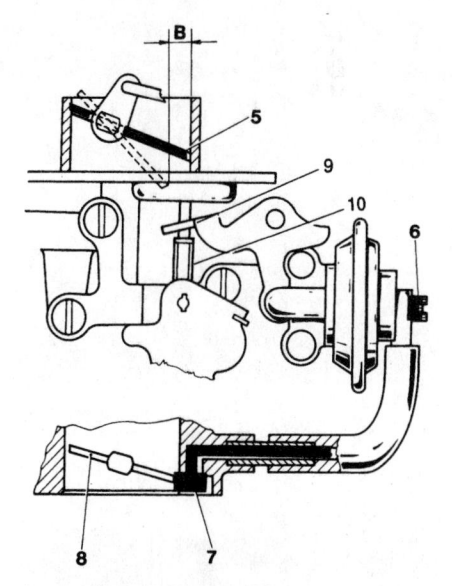

Float level adjustment
1 Outer float tag
2 Inner float tag
3 Float
4 Cover with gasket

Fast idle adjustment
1 Throttle valve
2 Choke control lever
3 Fast idle adjustment screw
4 Locknut
A Fast idle clearance

Pull-down (B) adjustment
5 Choke flap
6 Pull-down adjustment screw
7 Vacuum passage
8 Throttle valve
9 Fulcrum
10 Choke control link

Chapter H20

17 Use a vacuum pump to pull the diaphragm operating rod up to its stop (or push the mechanism with a small screwdriver). At the same time, use the shank of a twist drill to measure the gap between the lower section of the choke flap and the air intake. Refer to Specifications for the required drill size.

18 Remove the plug in the diaphragm cover and adjust as necessary by turning the diaphragm adjustment screw in the appropriate direction. Renew the plug when adjustment is complete.

5 Fault diagnosis

Refer to Part D for diagnosis of general carburettor faults.

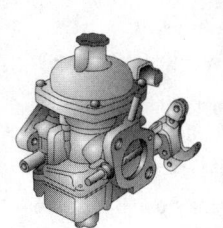

Part H Chapter 21
Weber 32 TLM carburettor

Contents

Fault diagnosis	5	Principles of operation	1
General servicing	3	Service adjustments	4
Identification	2		

Specifications

Manufacturer	Ford	Ford
Model	Fiesta 950	Fiesta 1.0 L & Van
Year	1986 to 1989	1989 to 1991
Engine code	TKB (OHV)	TLB (HCS)
Capacity (cm^3)/no. of cyls	957/4	999/4
Oil temperature (°C)	80	80
Transmission	Manual	Manual
Carb. ident. (Ford)	87BF 9510 AA	89BF 9510 AA
Carb. ident. (Weber/Solex)	32 TLM OA	32 TLM 1A
Idle speed (rpm)	800 ± 25	750 ± 50
Fast idle speed (rpm)	3300 ± 100	3400 ± 100
CO @ idle (% vol.)	1.5 ± 0.5	1.0 ± 0.5
Special conditions	-	Fan on
Venturi diameter	22	23
Idle jet	47	45
Main jet	112	110
Air correction jet	220	220
Emulsion tube	F103	F103
Accel. pump jet	45	45
Float level (mm)	26 ± 1.0	26 ± 1.0
Needle valve size (mm)	1.5	1.5
Choke pull-down (mm)	6.0 ± 0.5	6.0 ± 0.5

1 Principles of operation

Introduction

1 The following technical description of the Weber TLM carburettor should be read in conjunction with the more detailed description of carburettor principles in Part A.

Construction

2 The Weber 32 TLM carburettor is a downdraught single venturi instrument with a manual choke control and power valve (see illustration overleaf). The throttle shaft is made of steel and the throttle valve is made of brass. All jets and the emulsion tube are manufactured from brass with the exception of the accelerator pump injector, which is die-cast. The internal fuel channels and air passages are drilled and sealed with lead plugs where necessary.

3 The carburettor is constructed in three main bodies. These are the upper body, the main body and a throttle body containing the throttle assemblies. An insulating block, placed between the main carburettor body and the throttle body, prevents excess heat transference to the main body.

Fuel control

4 Fuel flows into the carburettor through a fine mesh filter. The fuel level in the float chamber is controlled by a needle valve and plastic float

Chapter H21

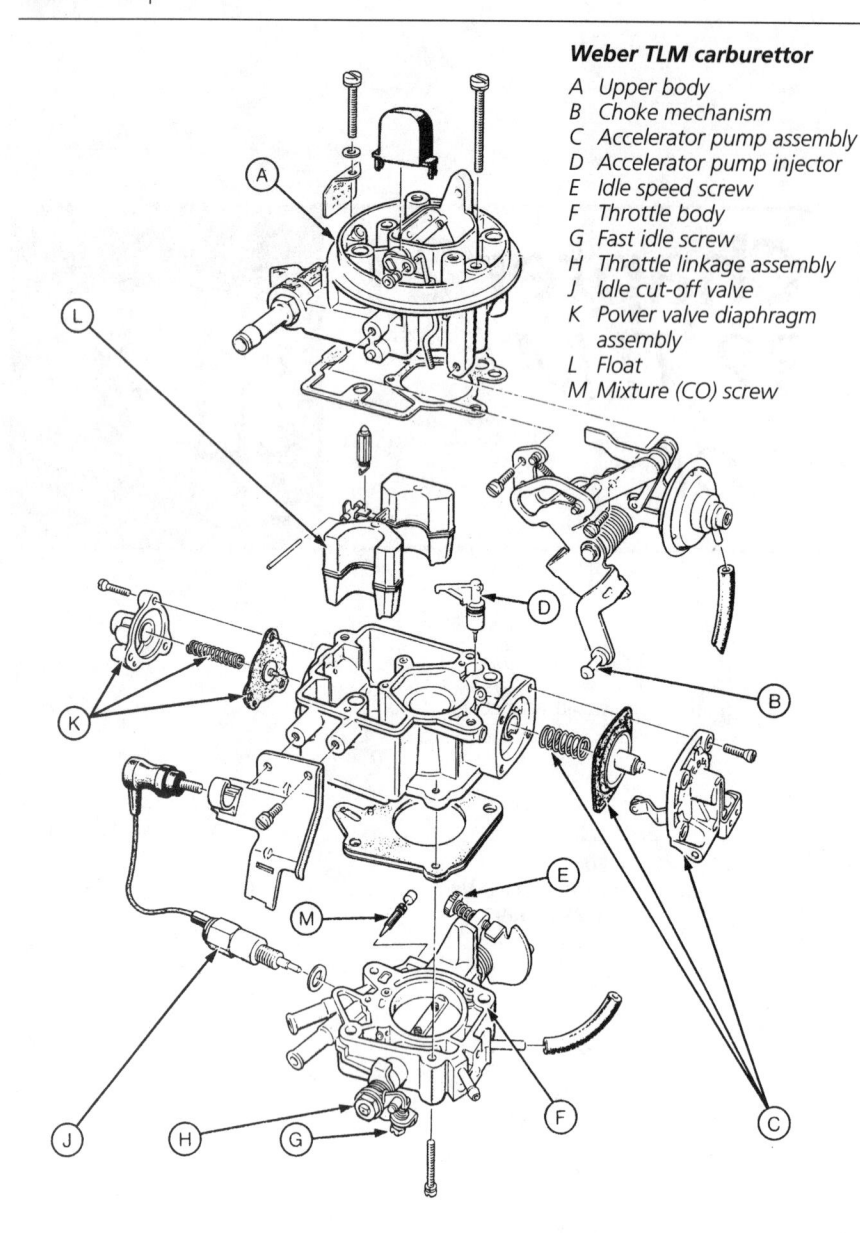

Weber TLM carburettor
A Upper body
B Choke mechanism
C Accelerator pump assembly
D Accelerator pump injector
E Idle speed screw
F Throttle body
G Fast idle screw
H Throttle linkage assembly
J Idle cut-off valve
K Power valve diaphragm assembly
L Float
M Mixture (CO) screw

Fuel inlet system
1 Needle valve
2 Fuel filter
3 Inlet connector
4 Carburettor main body
5 Float

assembly. An anti-vibration ball is incorporated into the needle valve design. A clip, attached to the needle valve and to the float arm, prevents the needle from sticking in the seat as the fuel level drops. The float chamber is vented internally to the clean-air side of the air filter (see illustration).

Idle, slow running and progression

5 Fuel sourced from the main well passes into the upper body through a metered idle jet. Here it is mixed with a small amount of air from a calibrated air bleed. The emulsion formed is drawn through a channel to the throttle body where it is discharged from the idle orifice under the primary throttle plate. A tapered mixture control screw is used to vary the outlet and this ensures fine control of the idle mixture. A progression slot, partially covered by the closed throttle at idle, provides enrichment as it is uncovered by the opening throttle during initial acceleration.

6 Idle speed is set by an adjustable screw. The adjustable mixture screw is tamper proofed at production level, in accordance with emission regulations.

Idle cut-off valve

7 An idle cut-off valve is used to prevent run-on when the engine is shut down. It utilises a 12-volt solenoid plunger to block the idle channel when the ignition is switched off.

Accelerator pump

8 The 32 TLM accelerator pump is controlled by a diaphragm and is mechanically operated by a cam and lever attached to the throttle linkage. The outlet valve consists of a valve incorporated into the pump injector, while the inlet valve consists of a ball valve located in a channel from the float chamber. Excess fuel is returned to the float chamber through a calibrated bush.

Main circuit

9 The amount of fuel discharged into the airstream is controlled by a calibrated main jet. Fuel is drawn through the main jet into the base of a vertical well which dips down into the fuel in the float chamber. An emulsion tube, capped by a calibrated air corrector jet, is placed in the well. The fuel is mixed with air drawn in through the air corrector and the holes in the emulsion tube and the resulting emulsified mixture is discharged from the main nozzle through an auxiliary venturi.

Power enrichment and economy circuit

10 Fuel flows from the float chamber into the power valve chamber through a fuel channel. An air passage is taken from under the throttle plate to the cover of the power diaphragm chamber. At idle and during light-throttle operation, manifold vacuum draws the diaphragm back against spring pressure. The diaphragm pintle is withdrawn from the brass outlet valve and the spring-loaded ball seats to close off the outlet channel.

11 Under acceleration and wide-open throttle operation, the vacuum in the manifold is depleted. The diaphragm returns under spring pressure and the power diaphragm pintle pushes the ball to open the outlet valve. Fuel then flows through the valve and a calibrated jet to supplement the fuel in the primary main well. The fuel level rises in the well and the fuel mixture is enriched.

12 At full-load and high engine speed, even more fuel is required. The velocity of air creates a depression sufficient to raise fuel from the float chamber into a channel and the fuel then passes through a calibrated bushing to the upper section of the air intake. Here it is mixed with a small amount of air from a calibrated air bleed and the emulsified mixture is then discharged into the airstream from the full-load enrichment tube.

Weber 32 TLM carburettor

Choke operation

13 The manual choke is operated by a dash-mounted cable. When the cable is pulled, it operates a lever that pulls the choke flap closed across the air intake. Fast idle is achieved with the aid of a curved cam attached to the choke operating lever. An adjustable screw, attached to the throttle lever and butting against the cam, is used to vary the fast idle speed.

14 Once the engine has fired, the choke flap must open slightly to weaken the mixture and avoid flooding. During idle and light-throttle operation, this is achieved by using manifold vacuum to actuate a diaphragm and a linkage attached to the diaphragm will then pull upon the choke flap. During engine warm-up, the cable should be progressively pushed home until the choke flap is fully open.

2 Identification

The Weber identification code is stamped on the side of the upper body.

A metallic tag giving the Ford identification code is attached to one of the carburettor upper body fixing screws.

3 General servicing

Introduction

1 Read this Chapter in conjunction with Part B which describes some of the operations in more detail. It is assumed that the carburettor is removed for this service. However, many of the operations can be tackled with the carburettor in place. Where this is undertaken, first soak the fuel out of the float chamber using a clean tissue or soft cloth, after removing the upper body assembly.

Dismantling and checking

2 Remove the two Torx screws which secure the carburettor to the engine.

3 Remove the carburettor from the engine (see Part B).
4 Make visual checks for damage and wear.
5 Disconnect the choke vacuum hose then remove the two screws and detach the carburettor upper body.
6 Use a straight-edge to check for distorted flanges on all facing surfaces.
7 Tap out the float pin, then remove the float, needle valve and plastic clip, float chamber gasket and needle valve seat.
8 Check that the anti-vibration ball is free in the valve end.
9 Check the needle valve tip for wear and ridges. This is more likely with the brass needle valve tip than when a viton one is used. Use a viton-tipped replacement when possible.
10 The float should be checked for damage and for ingress of petrol. Shaking the float will indicate the presence of fuel.
11 Renew the float pin if it shows signs of wear.
12 Unscrew the fuel inlet tube and inspect the fuel filter. Clean the filter housing of debris and dirt and renew the filter if necessary.
13 Remove the mixture screw and inspect the tip for damage and ridges.
14 Remove the four screws and remove the accelerator pump cover, diaphragm and spring. Check the diaphragm for fatigue and damage.
15 The pump injector is a push fit in the body. Carefully prise it from its location and check the vernay valve for damage.
16 Remove the primary idle jet assembly from the upper body. The idle jet is pushed into a holder and may be separated, by pulling, for cleaning or renewal (see illustration).
17 Remove the main jet, air corrector and emulsion tube (see illustration). Check that the channel from the float chamber into the emulsion tube well is clear. Note that the idle and air corrector jets can be detached from the carburettor without removing the upper body.
18 Check the jet calibration against that specified. It is possible that the wrong size jets may have been fitted during the last overhaul.
19 Remove the auxiliary venturi from the upper body, where necessary. Weber provide an extractor tool for removing this component. Check that the venturis are not loose in the main body as this is a source of uneven running.

If a venturi is loose, knurl the mating flanges with a file to ensure a tight fit.
20 Remove the three screws and remove the power valve housing cover, spring and diaphragm from the body. Check the diaphragm for fatigue and damage.
21 The brass outlet valve is cast into the body and is not removable. The ball in the outlet valve should seal the outlet. Depress and release the ball with a small screwdriver and it should move smoothly in and out. Check that the emulsion tube well is clear.
22 Remove the two screws and separate the carburettor main body and throttle body assemblies. The throttle body can be renewed separately if the spindles or throttle bores are worn.
23 Push out the plastic choke mechanism shield from under the upper body lip and remove it. Inspect the choke spindle, linkage and operating mechanism for stickiness and wear.
24 Pull the upper choke link rod out of the plastic retaining collar, remove the two screws and detach the manual choke assembly.
25 Attach a vacuum pump to the pull-down diaphragm and operate the pump to obtain 300 mm Hg. The diaphragm should operate fully and the vacuum should be maintained. Renew the diaphragm assembly if it fails these tests (see illustration).

Preparation for reassembly

26 Clean the jets and internal channels, the carburettor body assemblies and the float chamber. An air line may be used to clear the internal channels once the carburettor is fully dismantled. If an air line is used with the diaphragms in place and air is directed into the channels and passages, diaphragm damage may result.
27 Spraying carburettor cleaner into all the channels and passages in the carburettor body will often clear them of gum and dirt.
28 During reassembly, a complete set of new gaskets should be fitted. Also renew the needle valve and float pin, and all diaphragms.
29 Inspect and renew (where necessary) the mixture screw, main jet, idle jet, air corrector jet, emulsion tube and accelerator pump injector. Renew worn linkages, springs, vacuum hoses and other parts where necessary.

Jet locations
A Air corrector jet   B Idle jet

Main jet location (A)

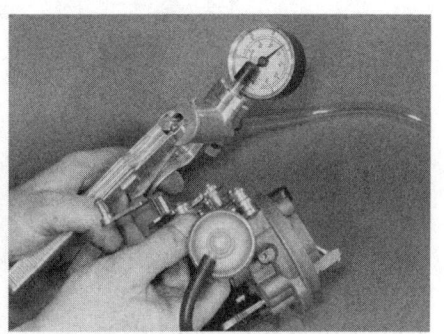

Testing pull-down diaphragm with a vacuum pump

Chapter H21

30 Ensure that all jets are firmly locked into position (but do not overtighten). A loose jet can cause a rich (or even lean) running condition.
31 Clean all mating surfaces and flanges of old gasket material and reassemble with new gaskets.
32 Ensure that housings are assembled with their air and fuel routes correctly aligned.

Reassembly

33 Refit the manual choke assembly. This a fiddly operation and best achieved as follows. Push the upper rod through the body but do not attach to the choke spindle collar yet. Secure the choke assembly with the two screws.
34 Operate the choke mechanism then insert the end of the upper rod into the plastic collar and push the rod home. Ensure that the upper rod is straight in the collar and fully home, then clip the choke mechanism shield into position. Ensure that the choke flap and linkage moves smoothly and progressively.
35 Assemble the main body and throttle body with a new gasket block, then secure with the two screws.
36 Refit the power diaphragm, spring and cover assembly, then secure with the three screws.
37 Refit the emulsion tube, air corrector and main jets into their original positions.
38 Push the pump injector firmly into position, after renewing the small seal on the injector body.
39 Refit the accelerator pump spring, diaphragm and cover assembly, then secure with the four screws.
40 Refit the idle mixture screw, after renewing the seal. Carefully turn the screw in until it just seats then unscrew it three full turns. This will provide a basic setting to allow the engine to be started.
41 Clean or renew the fuel filter and refit the fuel inlet tube.
42 Fit a new float chamber gasket to the upper body and renew the needle valve assembly. Screw the valve seat into the upper body (using a new sealing washer) and ensure that it is firmly locked into position. Insert the needle valve into the valve body with the ball facing outwards. Refit the float and pivot pin, ensuring that the plastic clip is correctly connected to the float and to the needle valve.
43 Adjust the float level. Refer to Section 4 for details on adjustment.
44 Refit the upper body to the main body and secure with the two screws. Reconnect the choke pull-down hose.
45 Push the idle jet into its holder and refit the assembly into the upper body.
46 Refit the idle cut-off valve, using a new sealing washer.
47 Ensure that the choke flap and linkage moves smoothly and progressively.
48 Refit the carburettor to the engine.
49 Always adjust the carburettor idle speed and mixture after any work has been carried out on the carburettor, preferably with the aid of a CO meter.
50 Adjust the choke with reference to Section 4.

4 Service adjustments

Adjustment preconditions

1 Refer to Part B for general advice on preconditions to correct adjustment of this carburettor.

Idle speed and mixture (CO)

2 Run the engine at 3000 rpm for 30 seconds to clear the manifold of fuel vapours, then allow the engine to idle.
3 Use the idle speed screw to set the specified idle speed (see illustration).
4 Check the CO level and compare with the specified value. If incorrect, remove the tamperproof plug and use a 3 mm Allen key to make the adjustment. Turning the screw clockwise (inwards) will reduce the CO level. Turning the screw anti-clockwise (outwards) will increase the CO level.
5 Repeat paragraphs 3 and 4 until both adjustments are correct.
6 Clear the manifold every 30 seconds during the setting operation by running the engine at 3000 rpm for 30 seconds.
7 Increase the speed to 2000 rpm and note the CO reading. The cruise reading should be less than half the idle CO reading.
8 Fit a new tamperproof plug to the mixture adjusting screw.
9 Ford state that variations of 0.5% CO and 25 rpm are acceptable at idle.

Float level

10 Hold the carburettor upper body in a vertical position with the float tag gently touching the ball of the needle valve.
11 Measure the distance between the upper body (with the gasket in place) and the base of the float (see illustration).
12 Adjust as necessary by bending the inner float tag.

Manual choke

13 Warm the engine to normal running temperature and adjust the idle speed and mixture before attempting choke fast idle or vacuum pull-down adjustment.

Fast idle

14 Pull the choke cable to fully operate the choke and at the same time, hold the choke flap as far open as possible.
15 Start the engine and record the fast idle speed. Refer to Specifications for the correct figure.
16 Stop the engine and adjust as necessary by turning the fast idle screw in the appropriate direction (see illustration).

Vacuum pull-down

17 Pull the choke cable to fully close the choke flap.
18 Use a vacuum pump to pull the diaphragm operating rod up to its stop (or push the mechanism with a small screwdriver). At the same time, use the shank of a twist drill to measure the gap between the lower section of the choke flap and the air intake. Refer to Specifications for the required drill size.
19 Remove the tamperproof plug in the diaphragm cover and adjust as necessary by turning the diaphragm adjusting screw in the appropriate direction. Renew the plug after adjustment is completed.

5 Fault diagnosis

Refer to Part D for diagnosis of general carburettor faults.

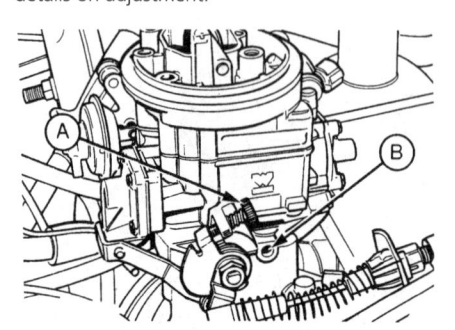

Idle adjustment screw location
A Idle speed screw
B Idle mixture (CO) screw

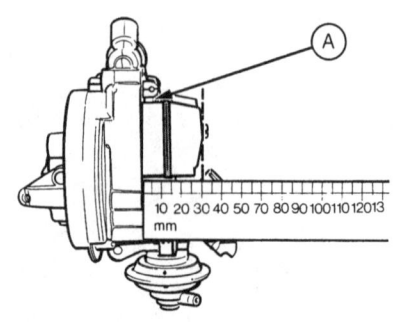

Float level adjustment
A Adjusting tag

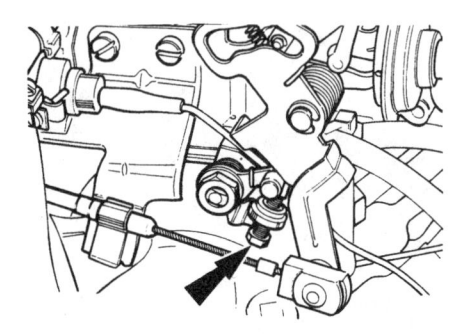

Fast idle speed check
Fast idle speed adjustment screw arrowed

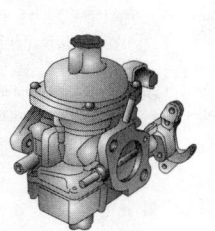

Part H Chapter 22
Weber 34 & 36 TLP carburettor

Contents

Fault diagnosis 5
General servicing 3
Identification 2
Principles of operation 1
Service adjustments 4

Specifications

Manufacturer	Citroën	Citroën	Peugeot
Model	AX14	BX16 RE	205 GR 1.4
Year	1987 to 1988	1987 to 1989	1987 to 1988
Engine code	K1A (TU3)	B1A/A	TU3 (K1A) (47kW)
Capacity (cm3)/no. of cyls	1360/4	1580/4	1360/4
Oil temperature (°C)	80	80	90
Carb. identification	34 TLP 3/100	36 TLP 1/100	34 TLP 3/100
Idle speed (rpm)	750 ± 50	700 ± 50	750 ± 50
CO @ idle (% vol.)	1.5 ± 0.5	1.5 ± 0.5	0.8 to 1.2
Venturi diameter	26	28	26
Idle jet	43	50	43
Main jet	132	142	132
Air correction jet	145	145	145
Emulsion tube	F80	F80	F80
Accel. pump jet	40	50	40
Float level (mm)	28 ± 0.25	28 ± 0.25	28 ± 0.25
Float stroke (mm)	7	7	7
Needle valve size (mm)	1.50	1.50	1.50
Choke fast idle gap (mm)	0.8	0.85 ± 0.05	0.75 ± 0.05
Choke pull-down (mm)	4.75	5 ± 0.25	5 ± 0.25

Manufacturer	Peugeot	Peugeot
Model	305 & Van (1580)	309 1.6
Year	1985 to 1991	1986 to 1989
Engine code	XU51C (B1A/A) (58kW)	XU51C (B1A/A) (58kW)
Capacity (cm3)/no. of cyls	1580/4	1580/4
Oil temperature (°C)	80	80
Transmission	–	MT
Carb. identification	36 TLP 1/100 or 200	36 TLP 1/100 or 200
Idle speed (rpm)	700 ± 50	750 ± 50
CO @ idle (% vol.)	1.5 ± 0.5	1.0 ± 0.5
Venturi diameter	28	28
Idle jet	50	50
Main jet	142	142
Air correction jet	145	145
Emulsion tube	F80	F80
Accel. pump jet	50	50
Float level (mm)	28 ± 0.25	28 ± 0.25
Float stroke (mm)	7	7
Needle valve size (mm)	1.50	1.50
Choke fast idle gap (mm)	0.85 ± 0.05	0.85 ± 0.05
Choke pull-down (mm)	5 ± 0.25	5 ± 0.25

Chapter H22

1 Principles of operation

Introduction

1 The following technical description of the Weber TLP carburettor should be read in conjunction with the more detailed description of carburettor principles in Part A.

Construction

2 The Weber TLP carburettor is a downdraught, single venturi instrument with a manual choke control and a power valve *(see illustration)*. The throttle shaft is made of steel. The throttle valve is made of brass, as are the jets and the emulsion tube. The exception is the accelerator pump injector which is die-cast. The internal fuel channels and air passages are drilled and sealed with lead plugs where necessary.

3 The carburettor is constructed in three main bodies. These are the upper body, main body and throttle body containing the throttle assemblies. An insulating block, placed between the main carburettor body and the throttle body, prevents excess heat transference to the main body.

Fuel control

4 Fuel flows into the carburettor through a fine mesh filter. The fuel level in the float chamber is controlled by a needle valve and plastic float assembly. An anti-vibration ball is incorporated into the needle valve design. A clip, attached to the needle valve and to the float arm, prevents the needle from sticking in the seat as the fuel level drops. The float chamber is vented internally to the clean-air side of the air filter *(see illustration)*.

Idle, slow running and progression

5 Fuel, sourced from the main well, passes into the upper body through a metered idle jet. Here it is mixed with a small amount of air from a calibrated air bleed. The emulsion formed is drawn through a channel to the throttle body where it is discharged from the idle orifice under the primary throttle plate. A tapered mixture control screw is used to vary the outlet and this ensures fine control of the idle mixture. A progression slot, partially covered by the closed throttle at idle, provides enrichment as it is uncovered by the opening throttle during initial acceleration.

6 The idle speed is set by an adjustable screw. The adjustable mixture screw is tamper proofed during production, in accordance with emission regulations.

Accelerator pump

7 The Weber TLP accelerator pump is controlled by a diaphragm and is mechanically operated by a cam and lever attached to the throttle linkage. The outlet valve is incorporated into the pump injector. The inlet valve consists of a ball valve located in a channel from the float chamber. Excess fuel is returned to the float chamber through a calibrated bush *(see illustration)*.

Main circuit

8 The amount of fuel discharged into the airstream is controlled by a calibrated main jet. Fuel is drawn through the main jet into the base

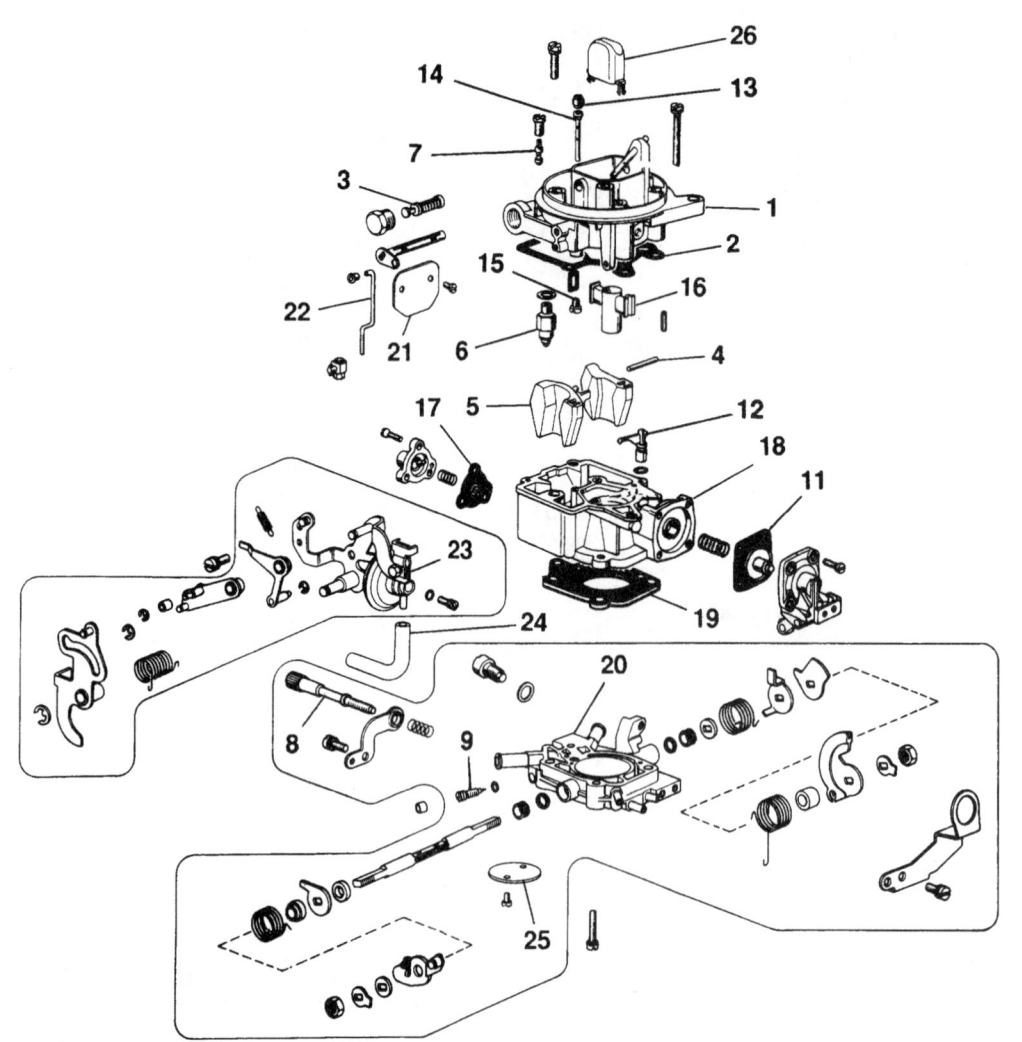

Weber TLP carburettor

1. Upper body
2. Float chamber gasket
3. Fuel inlet filter
4. Float pin
5. Float
6. Needle valve assembly
7. Idle jet
8. Idle speed adjustment screw
9. Idle mixture control screw
11. Accelerator pump diaphragm
12. Pump injector
13. Air corrector
14. Emulsion tube
15. Main jet
16. Auxiliary venturi
17. Power diaphragm
18. Main body
19. Insulator block
20. Throttle body
21. Choke flap
22. Choke link rod
23. Choke diaphragm
24. Vacuum hose
25. Throttle valve
26. Choke mechanism shield

Weber 34 & 36 TLP carburettor

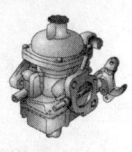

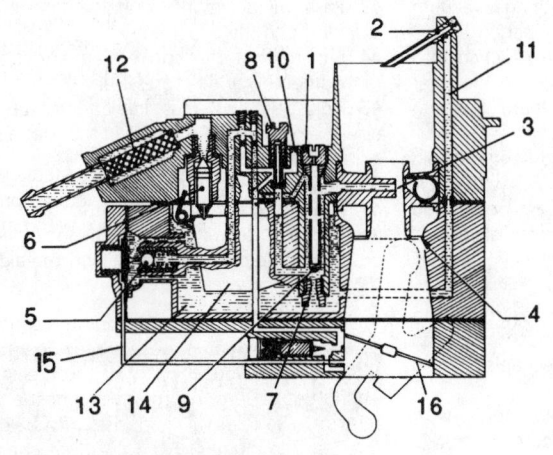

Inlet, main and full-load circuits

1. Air corrector
2. Full-load outlet
3. Main fuel outlet
4. Auxiliary venturi
5. Power valve ball
6. Needle valve assembly
7. Main jet
8. Idle jet
9. Emulsion tube
10. Air bleed
11. Full-load fuel channel
12. Fuel filter
13. Float chamber
14. Float
15. Vacuum passage
16. Throttle valve

Accelerator pump circuit

1. Float chamber
2. Fuel outlet channel
3. Pump injector
4. Pump actuating lever
5. Pump cam
6. Diaphragm
7. Spring
8. Inlet ball
9. Back-bleed

of a vertical well which dips down into the fuel in the float chamber. An emulsion tube is placed in the well and is capped by a calibrated air corrector jet. The fuel is mixed with air drawn in through the air corrector and through the holes in the emulsion tube. The resulting emulsified mixture is discharged from the main nozzle through an auxiliary venturi.

Power enrichment and economy circuit

9 Fuel flows from the float chamber into the power valve chamber through a fuel channel. An air passage is taken from under the throttle plate to the cover of the power diaphragm chamber. At idle and during light-throttle operation, manifold vacuum draws the diaphragm back against spring pressure. The diaphragm pintle is withdrawn from the brass outlet valve and the spring-loaded ball seats to close off the outlet channel.
10 Under acceleration and wide-open throttle operation, the vacuum in the manifold is depleted. The diaphragm returns under spring pressure and the power diaphragm pintle pushes the ball to open the outlet valve. Fuel then flows through the valve and a calibrated jet to supplement the fuel in the primary main well. The fuel level rises in the well and the fuel mixture is enriched.
11 At full-load and high engine speeds, even more fuel is required. The velocity of air creates a depression sufficient to raise fuel from the float chamber into a channel. The fuel then passes through a calibrated bushing to the upper section of the air intake. Here it is mixed with a small amount of air from a calibrated air bleed and the emulsified mixture is then discharged into the airstream from the full-load enrichment tube.

Choke operation

12 The manual choke is operated by a dash-mounted cable. When the cable is pulled, it operates a lever that pulls the choke flap closed across the air intake. Fast idle is achieved with the aid of a curved cam attached to the choke operating lever. An adjustable screw, attached to the throttle lever and butting against the cam, is used to vary the fast idle speed.
13 Once the engine has fired, the choke flap must open slightly to weaken the mixture and avoid flooding. During idle and light-throttle operation, this is achieved by using manifold vacuum to actuate a diaphragm. A linkage attached to the diaphragm will then pull upon the choke flap.
14 During engine warm-up, the cable should be progressively pushed home until the choke flap is fully open.

2 Identification

The Weber identification code is stamped on the base flange of the main body.

3 General servicing

Introduction

1 Read this Chapter in conjunction with Part B which describes some of the operations in more detail. It is assumed that the carburettor is removed for this service. However, many of the operations can be tackled with the carburettor in place. Where this is undertaken, first soak the fuel out of the float chamber using a clean tissue or soft cloth, after removing the upper body assembly.

Dismantling and checking

2 Remove two screws which secure the carburettor to the engine.
3 Remove the carburettor from the engine (see Part B).
4 Check visually for damage and wear.
5 Disconnect the choke vacuum hose, then remove the screws and detach the carburettor upper body.
6 Use a straight-edge to check for distorted flanges on all facing surfaces.
7 Tap out the float pin and remove the float, needle valve and plastic clip, float chamber gasket and needle valve seat.
8 Check that the anti-vibration ball is free in the valve end.
9 Check the needle valve tip for wear and ridges. This is more likely with the brass needle valve tip than when a viton one is used. Use a viton-tipped replacement when possible.
10 The float should be checked for damage and ingress of petrol.
11 Renew the float pin if it appears worn.
12 Unscrew the hexagon bolt and inspect the fuel filter. Clean the filter housing of debris and dirt and renew the filter if necessary.
13 Remove the mixture screw and inspect the tip for damage and ridges.
14 Remove the four screws and detach the accelerator pump cover, diaphragm and spring. Check the diaphragm for fatigue and damage.
15 The pump injector is a push fit in the body. Carefully prise it from its location and check valve for damage.

Chapter H22

16 Remove the primary idle jet assembly from the upper body. The idle jet is pushed into a holder and may be separated (by pulling) for cleaning or renewal. Note that the idle jet and air corrector can be detached from the carburettor without removing the upper body.
17 Remove the main jet, air corrector and emulsion tube. Check that the channel from the float chamber into the emulsion tube well is clear.
18 Check the jet calibration against that specified. It is possible that the wrong size jets may have been fitted during the last overhaul.
19 Remove the auxiliary venturi from the upper body where necessary. Weber provide an extractor tool for removing this component. Check that the venturi is not loose in the main body as this is a source of uneven running. If the venturi is loose, knurl the mating flanges with a file to ensure a tight fit.
20 Remove the three screws and detach the power valve housing cover, spring and diaphragm from the body. Check the diaphragm for fatigue and damage. The brass outlet valve is cast into the body and is not removable. The ball in the outlet valve should seal the outlet. Depress and release the ball with a small screwdriver and it should move smoothly in and out. Check that the emulsion tube well is clear.
21 Remove the two screws and separate the carburettor main body and throttle body assemblies. The throttle body can be renewed separately if the spindles or throttle bores are worn.
22 Push out the plastic choke mechanism shield from under the upper body lip and remove it. Inspect the choke spindle, linkage and operating mechanism for stickiness and wear.
23 Attach a vacuum pump to the pull-down diaphragm and operate the pump to obtain 300 mm Hg. The diaphragm should fully operate and the vacuum must be maintained for a minimum of 10 seconds. Renew the diaphragm assembly if it fails these tests.
24 Pull the upper choke link rod out of the plastic retaining collar then remove the two screws and detach the choke pull-down assembly.

Preparation for reassembly

25 Clean the jets, carburettor body assemblies, float chamber and internal channels. An air line may be used to clear internal channels once the carburettor is fully dismantled. Note that if high-pressure air is directed into the channels and passages with the diaphragms still in place, diaphragm damage may result.
26 Spraying carburettor cleaner into all the channels and passages in the carburettor body will often clear them of gum and dirt.
27 During reassembly, a complete set of new gaskets should be fitted. Also renew the needle valve and float pin, and all diaphragms.
28 Inspect and renew (where necessary) the mixture screw, main jet, idle jet, air corrector jet, emulsion tube and accelerator pump injector.

Renew worn linkages, screws, springs, vacuum hoses and other parts where necessary.
29 Ensure that all jets are firmly locked into position (but do not over-tighten). A loose jet can cause a rich (or even lean) running condition.
30 Clean all mating surfaces and flanges of old gasket material and reassemble with new gaskets. Ensure that housings are positioned with their air and fuel routes correctly aligned.

Reassembly

31 Refit the choke pull-down assembly and secure with the two screws. Reconnect the choke link and clip the choke mechanism shield into position.
32 Assemble the main and throttle bodies with a new gasket block, then secure with two screws.
33 Refit the power diaphragm, spring and cover assembly, then secure with the three screws.
34 Refit the emulsion tube, air corrector and main jet into their original positions.
35 Push the pump injector firmly into position, after renewing the small seal on the injector body.
36 Refit the pump spring, diaphragm and cover assembly, then secure with the four screws.
37 Refit the idle mixture screw after renewing the seal. Turn the screw in gently until it just seats. From this position, unscrew it three full turns. This will provide a basic setting to allow the engine to be started.
38 Clean or renew the fuel filter and refit the hexagon bolt.
39 Refit the float gasket to the upper body.
40 Renew the needle valve assembly. Screw the valve seat into the upper body, using a new sealing washer, and ensure that it is firmly locked into position (but do not over-tighten). Transfer the hairpin or plastic clip from the old needle valve to the ball end of the new one. Place the clip and valve assembly onto the inner float tag. Lower the float and needle valve assembly into the seat and secure with the float pin.
41 Adjust the float level. Refer to Section 4 for details on adjustment.
42 Refit the upper body to the main body and secure with the two screws. Reconnect the choke pull-down hose.
43 Push the idle jet into its holder and refit the assembly into the upper body.
44 Ensure that the choke flap and linkage move smoothly and progressively.
45 Adjust the choke fast idle and vacuum pull-down. Refer to Section 4 for details on adjustment.
46 Refit the carburettor to the engine.
47 Always adjust the carburettor idle speed and mixture after any work has been carried out on the carburettor, preferably with the aid of a CO meter.

4 Service adjustments

Adjustment preconditions

1 Refer to Part B for general advice on the preconditions to correct adjustment of this carburettor.

Idle speed and mixture (CO)

2 Run the engine at 3000 rpm for 30 seconds to clear the manifold of fuel vapours, then allow the engine to idle.
3 Use the idle speed adjustment screw to set the specified idle speed *(see illustration)*.
4 Check the CO level. If it is not as specified, remove the tamperproof plug and adjust the idle mixture control screw to achieve the correct level. Turning the screw clockwise (inwards) will reduce the CO level. Turning the screw anti-clockwise (outwards) will increase the CO level.
5 Repeat paragraphs 3 and 4 until both adjustments are correct.
6 Clear the manifold every 30 seconds during the setting operation by running the engine at 3000 rpm for 30 seconds.
7 Increase the speed to 2000 rpm and note the CO reading. The cruise reading should be less than half the idle CO reading.
8 Fit a new tamperproof plug to the mixture control screw.

Float level/stroke

9 Hold the carburettor upper body in a vertical position with the float tag gently touching the ball of the needle valve.

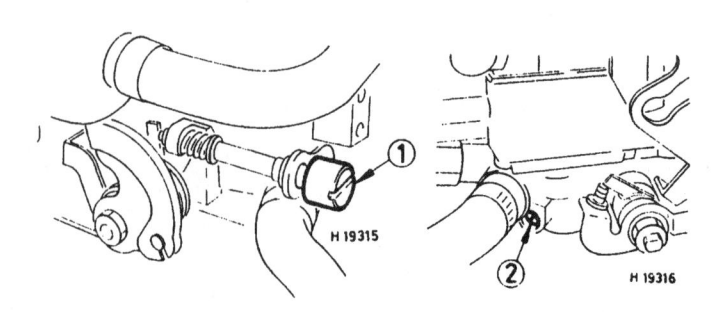

Idle speed and mixture adjustment
1 Idle speed adjustment screw *2 Idle mixture control screw*

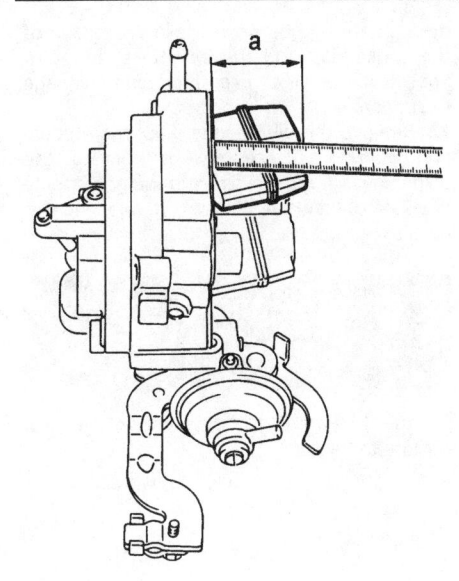

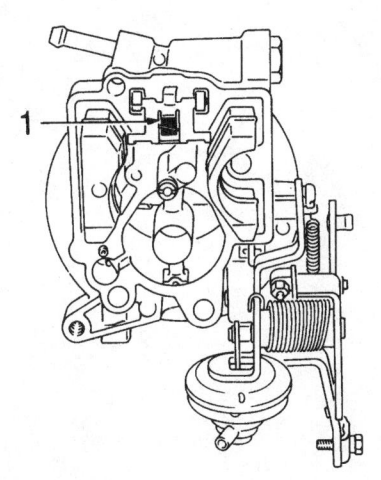

Weber 34 & 36 TLP carburettor

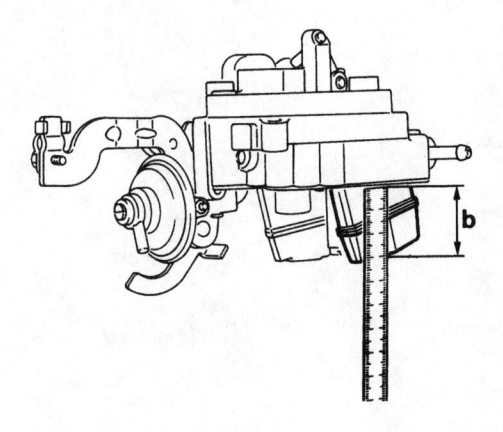

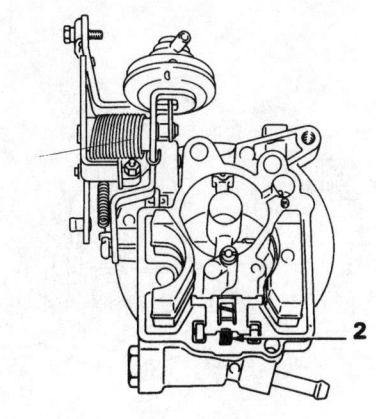

Float stroke adjustment

b Float stroke measurement   2 Outer float tag

17 Invert the carburettor then pull the choke operating arm to fully close the choke flap. The adjustment screw will butt against the fast idle cam and force open the throttle plate to leave a small clearance *(see illustration)*.
18 Use the shank of a twist drill to measure the clearance between the wall of the throttle bore and the throttle plate. Refer to Specifications for the required drill size and measure the clearance from the progression holes.
19 Adjust as necessary by turning the adjustment screw in the appropriate direction.

Vacuum pull-down

20 Pull the choke operating arm to fully close the choke flap.
21 Use a vacuum pump to pull the diaphragm operating rod up to its stop (or push the mechanism with a small screwdriver). At the same time, use the shank of a twist drill to

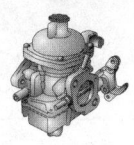

Float level adjustment

a Float level measurement
1 Inner float tag

10 Measure the distance between the upper body (with the gasket in place) and the base of the float *(see illustration)*.
11 Adjust as necessary by bending the inner float tag.
12 Place the upper body in a horizontal position and allow the float to hang down.
13 Measure the distance between the upper body (with the gasket in place) and the base of the float *(see illustration)*.
14 Subtract the measurement in paragraph 10 from the measurement in paragraph 13. This figure is the float stroke.
15 Adjust as necessary by bending the outer float tag.

Manual choke

Fast idle

16 The carburettor must be removed from the engine in order to make the fast idle adjustment.

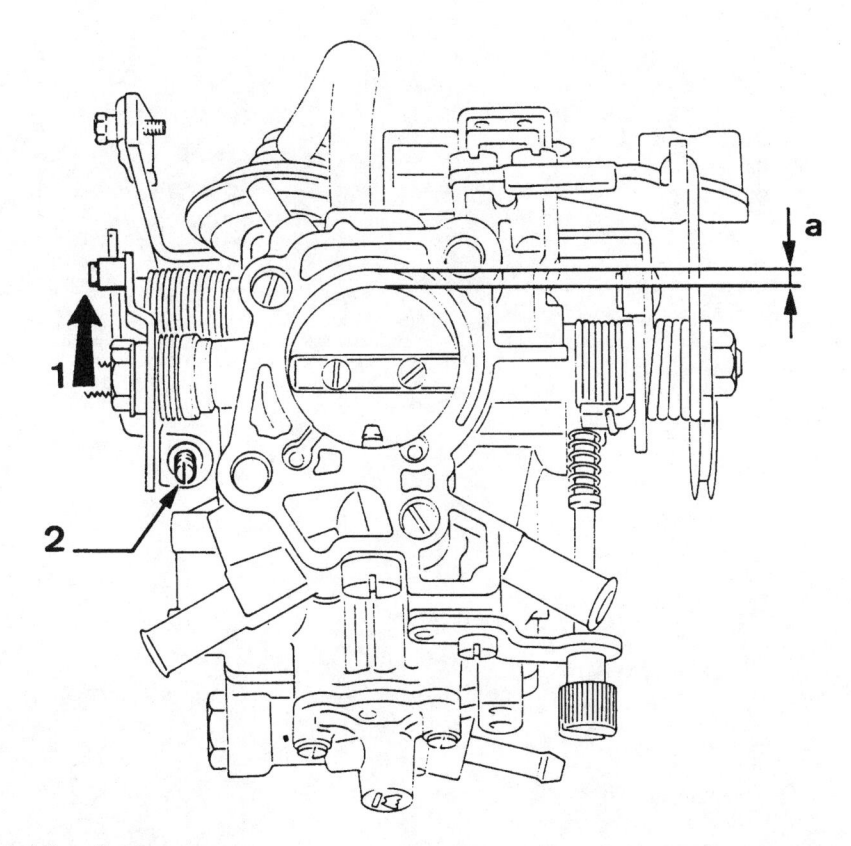

Fast idle adjustment

1 Fully operate choke lever   2 Fast idle adjustment screw   a Fast idle clearance

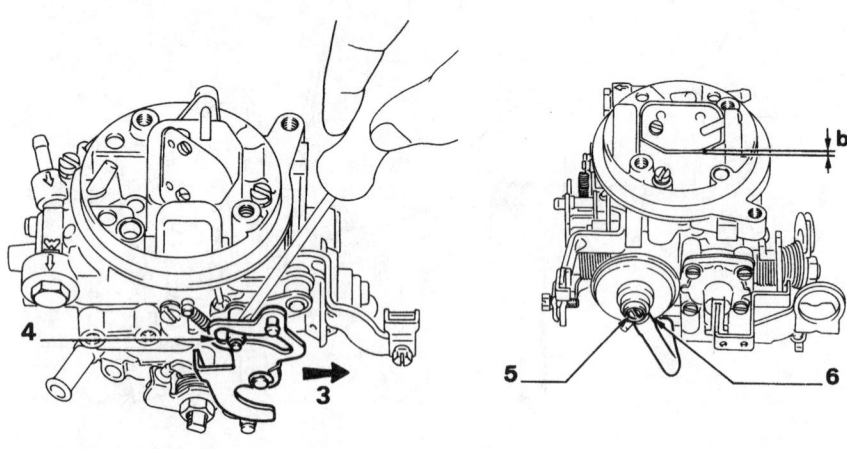

Chapter H22

measure the gap between the lower section of the choke flap and the air intake. Refer to Specifications for the required drill size *(see illustration)*.

22 Remove the plug in the diaphragm cover and adjust as necessary by turning the diaphragm adjustment screw in the appropriate direction. Renew the plug when adjustment is complete.

5 Fault diagnosis

Refer to Part D for diagnosis of general carburettor faults.

Pull-down adjustment

3 *Fully operate choke lever*
4 *Choke stop*
5 *Pull-down adjustment screw*
6 *Vacuum connection*
b *Pull-down clearance*

Reference

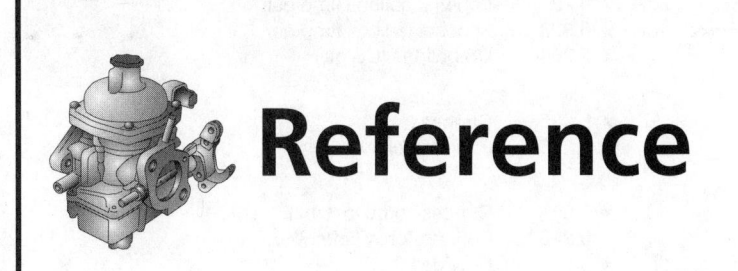

Contents

Emission regulations . . . .**REF•1**
Abbreviations . . . .**REF•1**
Conversion factors . . . .**REF•2**
Workshop practice . . . .**REF•3**
General repair procedures . . . .**REF•5**
Glossary of technical terms . . . .**REF•6**

Emission regulations

The abbreviations 15.04, 15.05 and US 83 may be used in places in this manual. They refer to EC emission regulations currently in operation in European countries. US 83 is the most stringent with regard to permitted emission levels, 15.04 and 15.05 less so.

Abbreviations

_	: Not applicable, or information not available	Nm	: Torque (unit of measure)
acw	: Anti-clockwise (rotation)	NOx	: Oxides of nitrogen
AFR	: Air/Fuel Ratio	NTC	: Negative temperature coefficient
amdt.	: Amendment	O2	: Oxygen
AT	: Automatic transmission	OP	: Fast idle position
CD	: Constant depression	OPF	: Just open to fast idle position
CO	: Carbon monoxide	OPR	: Idle to fast idle position
CO2	: Carbon dioxide	ORF	: Just open to idle position
COAS	: Choke Opening After Starting	OVAD	: Choke pull-down
CSCV	: Carburettor Speed Control Valve	PCV	: Positive Crankcase Ventilation
CTS	: Coolant Temperature Sensor	PF	: Parked throttle position (just open)
cw	: Clockwise (rotation)	PRN	: Basic idle position
ECU	: Electronic Control Unit	PTC	: Positive Temperature Coefficient
EGR	: Exhaust Gas Recirculation	PTO	: Positive Throttle Opening
HC	: Hydrocarbons	PVS	: Ported Vacuum Switch
HITC	: Hot Idle Temperature Compensator	rpm	: Revolutions per minute
ISC	: Idle Speed Control	TVS	: Thermal Vacuum Switch
LOVE	: Low Vacuum Enrichment device	TTV	: Thermo Time Valve
m/sec	: Metres per second (velocity)	UCL	: Upper Cylinder Lubricant
mm	: Millimetre	VDV	: Vacuum Delay Valve
mm Hg	: Millimetre of mercury	VV	: Variable venturi
MT	: Manual transmission	1V	: Single venturi
NIP	: Normal Idle Position	2V	: Twin venturi

Conversion factors

Length (distance)
Inches (in)	x 25.4	= Millimetres (mm)	x 0.0394	= Inches (in)
Feet (ft)	x 0.305	= Metres (m)	x 3.281	= Feet (ft)
Miles	x 1.609	= Kilometres (km)	x 0.621	= Miles

Volume (capacity)
Cubic inches (cu in; in^3)	x 16.387	= Cubic centimetres (cc; cm^3)	x 0.061	= Cubic inches (cu in; in^3)
Imperial pints (Imp pt)	x 0.568	= Litres (l)	x 1.76	= Imperial pints (Imp pt)
Imperial quarts (Imp qt)	x 1.137	= Litres (l)	x 0.88	= Imperial quarts (Imp qt)
Imperial quarts (Imp qt)	x 1.201	= US quarts (US qt)	x 0.833	= Imperial quarts (Imp qt)
US quarts (US qt)	x 0.946	= Litres (l)	x 1.057	= US quarts (US qt)
Imperial gallons (Imp gal)	x 4.546	= Litres (l)	x 0.22	= Imperial gallons (Imp gal)
Imperial gallons (Imp gal)	x 1.201	= US gallons (US gal)	x 0.833	= Imperial gallons (Imp gal)
US gallons (US gal)	x 3.785	= Litres (l)	x 0.264	= US gallons (US gal)

Mass (weight)
Ounces (oz)	x 28.35	= Grams (g)	x 0.035	= Ounces (oz)
Pounds (lb)	x 0.454	= Kilograms (kg)	x 2.205	= Pounds (lb)

Force
Ounces-force (ozf; oz)	x 0.278	= Newtons (N)	x 3.6	= Ounces-force (ozf; oz)
Pounds-force (lbf; lb)	x 4.448	= Newtons (N)	x 0.225	= Pounds-force (lbf; lb)
Newtons (N)	x 0.1	= Kilograms-force (kgf; kg)	x 9.81	= Newtons (N)

Pressure
Pounds-force per square inch (psi; lbf/in^2; lb/in^2)	x 0.070	= Kilograms-force per square centimetre (kgf/cm^2; kg/cm^2)	x 14.223	= Pounds-force per square inch (psi; lbf/in^2; lb/in^2)
Pounds-force per square inch (psi; lbf/in^2; lb/in^2)	x 0.068	= Atmospheres (atm)	x 14.696	= Pounds-force per square inch (psi; lbf/in^2; lb/in^2)
Pounds-force per square inch (psi; lbf/in^2; lb/in^2)	x 0.069	= Bars	x 14.5	= Pounds-force per square inch (psi; lbf/in^2; lb/in^2)
Pounds-force per square inch (psi; lbf/in^2; lb/in^2)	x 6.895	= Kilopascals (kPa)	x 0.145	= Pounds-force per square inch (psi; lbf/in^2; lb/in^2)
Kilopascals (kPa)	x 0.01	= Kilograms-force per square centimetre (kgf/cm^2; kg/cm^2)	x 98.1	= Kilopascals (kPa)
Millibar (mbar)	x 100	= Pascals (Pa)	x 0.01	= Millibar (mbar)
Millibar (mbar)	x 0.0145	= Pounds-force per square inch (psi; lbf/in^2; lb/in^2)	x 68.947	= Millibar (mbar)
Millibar (mbar)	x 0.75	= Millimetres of mercury (mmHg)	x 1.333	= Millibar (mbar)
Millibar (mbar)	x 0.401	= Inches of water (inH$_2$O)	x 2.491	= Millibar (mbar)
Millimetres of mercury (mmHg)	x 0.535	= Inches of water (inH$_2$O)	x 1.868	= Millimetres of mercury (mmHg)
Inches of water (inH$_2$O)	x 0.036	= Pounds-force per square inch (psi; lbf/in^2; lb/in^2)	x 27.68	= Inches of water (inH$_2$O)

Torque (moment of force)
Pounds-force inches (lbf in; lb in)	x 1.152	= Kilograms-force centimetre (kgf cm; kg cm)	x 0.868	= Pounds-force inches (lbf in; lb in)
Pounds-force inches (lbf in; lb in)	x 0.113	= Newton metres (Nm)	x 8.85	= Pounds-force inches (lbf in; lb in)
Pounds-force inches (lbf in; lb in)	x 0.083	= Pounds-force feet (lbf ft; lb ft)	x 12	= Pounds-force inches (lbf in; lb in)
Pounds-force feet (lbf ft; lb ft)	x 0.138	= Kilograms-force metres (kgf m; kg m)	x 7.233	= Pounds-force feet (lbf ft; lb ft)
Pounds-force feet (lbf ft; lb ft)	x 1.356	= Newton metres (Nm)	x 0.738	= Pounds-force feet (lbf ft; lb ft)
Newton metres (Nm)	x 0.102	= Kilograms-force metres (kgf m; kg m)	x 9.804	= Newton metres (Nm)

Power
Horsepower (hp)	x 745.7	= Watts (W)	x 0.0013	= Horsepower (hp)

Velocity (speed)
Miles per hour (miles/hr; mph)	x 1.609	= Kilometres per hour (km/hr; kph)	x 0.621	= Miles per hour (miles/hr; mph)

Fuel consumption*
Miles per gallon, Imperial (mpg)	x 0.354	= Kilometres per litre (km/l)	x 2.825	= Miles per gallon, Imperial (mpg)
Miles per gallon, US (mpg)	x 0.425	= Kilometres per litre (km/l)	x 2.352	= Miles per gallon, US (mpg)

Temperature
Degrees Fahrenheit = (°C x 1.8) + 32   Degrees Celsius (Degrees Centigrade; °C) = (°F - 32) x 0.56

*It is common practice to convert from miles per gallon (mpg) to litres/100 kilometres (l/100km), where mpg x l/100 km = 282

Safety First!

Working on your car can be dangerous. This page shows just some of the potential risks and hazards, with the aim of creating a safety-conscious attitude.

General hazards

Scalding
- Don't remove the radiator or expansion tank cap while the engine is hot.
- Engine oil, automatic transmission fluid or power steering fluid may also be dangerously hot if the engine has recently been running.

Burning
- Beware of burns from the exhaust system and from any part of the engine. Brake discs and drums can also be extremely hot immediately after use.

Crushing
- When working under or near a raised vehicle, always supplement the jack with axle stands, or use drive-on ramps. **Never venture under a car which is only supported by a jack.**
- Take care if loosening or tightening high-torque nuts when the vehicle is on stands. Initial loosening and final tightening should be done with the wheels on the ground.

Fire
- Fuel is highly flammable; fuel vapour is explosive.
- Don't let fuel spill onto a hot engine.
- Do not smoke or allow naked lights (including pilot lights) anywhere near a vehicle being worked on. Also beware of creating sparks (electrically or by use of tools).
- Fuel vapour is heavier than air, so don't work on the fuel system with the vehicle over an inspection pit.
- Another cause of fire is an electrical overload or short-circuit. Take care when repairing or modifying the vehicle wiring.
- Keep a fire extinguisher handy, of a type suitable for use on fuel and electrical fires.

Electric shock
- Ignition HT voltage can be dangerous, especially to people with heart problems or a pacemaker. Don't work on or near the ignition system with the engine running or the ignition switched on.
- Mains voltage is also dangerous. Make sure that any mains-operated equipment is correctly earthed. Mains power points should be protected by a residual current device (RCD) circuit breaker.

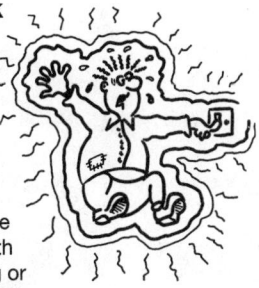

Fume or gas intoxication
- Exhaust fumes are poisonous; they often contain carbon monoxide, which is rapidly fatal if inhaled. Never run the engine in a confined space such as a garage with the doors shut.
- Fuel vapour is also poisonous, as are the vapours from some cleaning solvents and paint thinners.

Poisonous or irritant substances
- Avoid skin contact with battery acid and with any fuel, fluid or lubricant, especially antifreeze, brake hydraulic fluid and Diesel fuel. Don't syphon them by mouth. If such a substance is swallowed or gets into the eyes, seek medical advice.
- Prolonged contact with used engine oil can cause skin cancer. Wear gloves or use a barrier cream if necessary. Change out of oil-soaked clothes and do not keep oily rags in your pocket.
- Air conditioning refrigerant forms a poisonous gas if exposed to a naked flame (including a cigarette). It can also cause skin burns on contact.

Asbestos
- Asbestos dust can cause cancer if inhaled or swallowed. Asbestos may be found in gaskets and in brake and clutch linings. When dealing with such components it is safest to assume that they contain asbestos.

Special hazards

Hydrofluoric acid
- This extremely corrosive acid is formed when certain types of synthetic rubber, found in some O-rings, oil seals, fuel hoses etc, are exposed to temperatures above 400ºC. The rubber changes into a charred or sticky substance containing the acid. *Once formed, the acid remains dangerous for years. If it gets onto the skin, it may be necessary to amputate the limb concerned.*
- When dealing with a vehicle which has suffered a fire, or with components salvaged from such a vehicle, wear protective gloves and discard them after use.

The battery
- Batteries contain sulphuric acid, which attacks clothing, eyes and skin. Take care when topping-up or carrying the battery.
- The hydrogen gas given off by the battery is highly explosive. Never cause a spark or allow a naked light nearby. Be careful when connecting and disconnecting battery chargers or jump leads.

Air bags
- Air bags can cause injury if they go off accidentally. Take care when removing the steering wheel and/or facia. Special storage instructions may apply.

⚠ **Warning: Never expose the hands, face or any other part of the body to injector spray; the fuel can penetrate the skin with potentially fatal results.**

Remember...

DO
- Do use eye protection when using power tools, and when working under the vehicle.
- Do wear gloves or use barrier cream to protect your hands when necessary.
- Do get someone to check periodically that all is well when working alone on the vehicle.
- Do keep loose clothing and long hair well out of the way of moving mechanical parts.
- Do remove rings, wristwatch etc, before working on the vehicle – especially the electrical system.
- Do ensure that any lifting or jacking equipment has a safe working load rating adequate for the job.

DON'T
- Don't attempt to lift a heavy component which may be beyond your capability – get assistance.
- Don't rush to finish a job, or take unverified short cuts.
- Don't use ill-fitting tools which may slip and cause injury.
- Don't leave tools or parts lying around where someone can trip over them. Mop up oil and fuel spills at once.
- Don't allow children or pets to play in or near a vehicle being worked on.

Glossary of technical terms

When describing the components that make up a carburettor, it is unfortunate that the various carburettor manufacturers use different names to describe the various components. Translation from the Italian and German languages can also serve to confuse. During the writing of this manual, we have attempted to observe certain conventions and have standardised the description of many items. We recognise that our description may not be your description and have therefore provided a cross-reference list here as an aid to recognition. This list is fairly comprehensive, but cannot be considered exhaustive. Our own descriptions are generally listed first, and appear in bold:

acceleration :	pick-up	**inlet** :	intake
air bleed :	ventilation	**main well** :	sump
air intake :	air horn	**needle valve and seat** :	needle valve housing : needle valve body
auxiliary venturi :	secondary venturi : pre-atomiser : booster	**needle valve anti-vibration ball** :	spring-loaded ball : damper ball
bi-metal coil :	bi-metal spring	**orifice** :	outlet : nozzle : tube : spray tube : drilling
calibrated :	metered	**power valve** :	economy valve : partial load enrichment valve : econostat
channel :	passage : drilling : gallery : duct		
choke flap :	choke plate : choke valve : starter flap : strangler flap	**progression** :	transition
		progressive twin venturi :	differential twin venturi
choke :	cold starting device	**pull-down** :	anti-flood : pneumatic : COAS (see abbreviations)
damper :	kicker : dashpot		
decel valve :	deceleration valve : overrun valve	**pump injector** :	delivery valve : pump discharge tube : injection tube : pump shooter
de-choke :	de-load : de-flood : anti-flood : wide-open kick		
		running-on :	dieseling
fast idle gap :	positive throttle opening	**thermal switch** :	temperature switch : thermo-switch
filter :	cleaner : strainer	**throttle plate** :	throttle valve : throttle disc : throttle butterfly : throttle flap
float chamber :	float bowl		
float chamber vent :	de-fuming vent	**throttle spindle** :	throttle shaft
float pin :	float pivot	**throttle synchronisation** :	throttle balance
fuel channel :	channel tube		
full-load enrichment :	over-feed mixture control : supercharge circuit : econostat	**upper body** :	float cover : top cover
		vacuum :	depression : pressure drop
idle cut-off valve :	anti-run-on valve : anti-diesel1 valve : idle solenoid	**vacuum diaphragm** :	vacuum motor
		vacuum pull-down :	pneumatic pull-down : vacuum break
idle mixture screw :	volume screw	**vacuum supply** :	vacuum source : vacuum signal
idle bypass screw :	air bypass screw : constant CO screw	**venturi** :	choke : barrel : diffuser
idle jet :	slow-running jet : pilot jet		
idle speed screw :	throttle valve stop screw		